RAND McNALLY

D0825054

Motor Carriers' Road Atlas

© Davidf/Getty

Contents

The 2019 edition offers:

- Area code map
- Updated low clearance, restricted route, and weigh station info
- Updated mileage directory

Tell Rand!

Drivers know best what's happening out on the road. Let us know how we can improve the *Motor Carriers' Road Atlas* to better reflect road realities by contacting us at randmcnally.com/TellRand.

Acknowledgments The editors thank the many personnel in the state and provincial regulatory agencies who supplied the data for their states and provinces. Thanks to the Federal Highway Administration, the Federal Motor Carrier Safety Administration, and the many drivers and other individuals in the motor carrier industry who provided information and assistance during the preparation of this book. The *Motor Carriers' Road Atlas* is published for general reference and not as a substitute for independent verification by readers when circumstances warrant. While the information contained herein is believed correct when compiled, the Publisher does not guarantee its accuracy.

Cover photo: © Steve Craft/Getty

Published in U.S.A.
Printed in U.S.A.

If you have a comment, suggestion, or even a compliment, please visit us at randmcnally.com/contact or write to
Rand McNally Consumer Affairs
P.O. Box 7600
Chicago, Illinois 60680-9915

3 BU 19 18

Hazardous Materials
Tips and Facts

The U.S. Department of Transportation's (DOT) Pipeline and Hazardous Materials Safety Administration (PHMSA) and Office of Hazardous Materials Safety (OHMS) develop, issue, and revise hazardous materials (hazmat) regulations for the United States. These regulations help to control the process for transporting hazardous materials and to ensure safety.

The regulations apply equally to private and commercial carriers, including shipments for the government and military. The carrier is responsible for proper shipping papers; placarding and marking the vehicle; loading and unloading; compatibility and segregation of commodities; and blocking and bracing. If the shipper performs any of these functions, it is still up to the carrier to ensure they are done in full compliance.

The Hazardous Materials Regulations (HMR) appear in the Code of Federal Regulations (CFR), Title 49, Parts 100-185. You can view them online at the U.S. Government Publishing Office's Federal Digital System: www.gpo.gov/fdsys

Registration

Anyone who transports any of the following materials (including hazardous wastes) in interstate, intrastate, or foreign commerce must register and pay a fee by June 30 of each year or before commencing transport:

- Highway route controlled quantity of Class 7 (radioactive) material
- More than 25 kg (55 lb.) of a Division 1.1, 1.2 or 1.3 (explosive) material
- More than 1L (1.06 quarts) of a material extremely toxic by inhalation
- Bulk shipment of hazardous materials having a capacity of 13,248 L (3,500 gallons) or more for liquids or gases or more than 13.24 cubic meters (468 cubic feet) for solids
- Non-bulk shipment of hazardous materials weighing 2,268 kg (5,000 lb.) or more that requires placarding
- Any quantity of hazardous materials that requires placarding, except activities that are in direct support of farm operations.

The annual fee varies depending on U.S. Small Business Administration (**SBA**) size category (small or not-small) and not-for-profit status applicable to the carrier. A registration form with complete instructions is available at www.phmsa.dot.gov/hazmat/registration. Drivers must keep a copy of the current Certificate of Registration or a document bearing the current registration number in their vehicles at all times.

Hazmat training

All of a carrier's employees involved in any aspect of preparing hazardous materials for shipment or operating a motor vehicle must be trained. Training helps increase safety awareness and reduces hazmat accidents and incidents.

Hazmat training must include:

- General awareness and familiarization training on HMR and recognizing and identifying hazardous materials
- Function-specific training on how employees can perform their jobs while meeting the regulations
- Safety training on how employees can avoid accidents, protect themselves, and respond to an emergency
- Security awareness training on security risks associated with transport of hazardous materials and methods to enhance security
- In-depth security training on the security plan and its implementation

In addition, carriers must provide drivers with training on safe motor vehicle operation and on applicable requirements in the Motor Carrier Safety Regulations in 49 CFR Parts 390-397.

Training is required within 90 days of employment or a change in job function. Hazmat employees should receive recurrent training on the HMR at least once every three years.

Carriers must keep written records of training conducted within the last three years for current employees, and retain records of former employees for 90 days after termination.

The training record must include:

- The hazmat employee's name
- Completion date of most recent training
- Description, copy, or location of training materials
- Name and address of trainer
- Certification that employee has been trained and tested

Note that additional training requirements for drivers as specified in 49 CFR may be satisfied by compliance with current requirements for a Commercial Drivers' License (**CDL**) with a tank vehicle or hazardous materials endorsement.

Penalties

Anyone who knowingly violates the hazardous materials regulations is subject to a civil penalty of at least $250 minimum to no minimum and not more than $55,000 to $77,114 per violation, except no more than $110,000 to $179,993 if violation causes death, serious injury or sickness, or significant property damage, and no less than $495 to $463 if violation relates to training. Additional enforcement action by the DOT's Federal Motor Carrier Safety Administration (**FMCSA**) is possible. (49 CFR §107.329)

Classification of materials

The first step in the safe transportation of hazardous materials is determining whether a material falls into any of the nine Hazard Classes identified by the DOT. Use the Hazardous Materials Table (**HMT**) in 49 CFR §172.101 to determine if this is the case and, if so, to select the proper shipping name (**PSN**) and basic shipping description. If the material is listed in Appendix A and its quantity exceeds the reportable quantity, "RQ" must be added to the shipping description.

Hazardous materials fall into nine Classes:

1.) Explosives (§173.50)
2.) Flammable gases, non-flammable compressed gases, and poisonous gases (§173.115)
3.) Flammable or combustible liquid (§173.120)
4.) Other flammable materials (§173.124)
5.) Oxidizers and organic peroxides (§173.127 and §173.128)
6.) Poison, infectious substances (§173.132 and §173.134)
7.) Radioactive materials (§173.403)
8.) Corrosive materials (§173.136)
9.) Miscellaneous hazardous materials (§173.140)

Shipping papers

The shipping papers, also known as the bill of lading, are required and include important information identifying the hazardous materials being shipped. They also provide information on taking action to protect the driver's safety and the public's safety should an incident occur.

The shipping document should be prepared in accordance with regulation and include:

- The hazardous material description (e.g. flammable, flammable gas, etc.) followed by the proper shipping name, and if required, technical name
- The hazard class(es) or division(s)
- United Nations or North American ID number
- Packing group (in Roman numerals)
- Total quantity (by mass or volume)
- Number and type of packages
- Emergency contact and phone number
- Information about mitigating an incident
- Shipper's certification and signature
- Name and address of shipper (not required as per 49 CFR)

Here are some key considerations:

- Hazardous materials description is in the right order.
- Hazardous materials are listed first, have an "X" in the HM column, are in a different color, or are highlighted if the shipping paper is reproduced.
- Shipping papers are legible, printed (manually or mechanically) in English, and meet HM requirements.
- Driver can immediately reach the shipping papers while at the vehicle's controls, or leaves them on the driver's seat or in a holder in the driver's side door when away from the cab or not at the controls.
- Papers are easily recognizable and accessible to authorities and emergency response personnel.
- Emergency response information may be provided in the form of the *Emergency Response Guidebook* (**ERG**) or Material Safety Data Sheet (**MSDS**).
- Available for at least 2 years after shipment.

The shipper may use the Hazardous Waste Manifest as the shipping paper for hazardous waste shipments. Shipping paper requirements are found in 49 CFR Subpart C §§172.200-172.205. The required description of hazardous materials is found in 49 CFR §172.202.

Hazmat resources

A law enforcement agency within the U.S. Department of the Treasury, the **Bureau of Alcohol, Tobacco, Firearms and Explosives** (ATF) enforces federal laws and regulations relating to alcohol, tobacco products, firearms, explosives, and arson. Through explosives regulation and enforcement programs, the ATF works to prevent both the criminal use and accidental detonations of explosives. It uses National Response Teams and International Response Teams to investigate explosives incidents. (www.atf.gov).

The **FMCSA** develops and enforces trucking regulations, including Hazardous Materials Regulations (HMR). HMR help ensure the safe and secure transport of hazardous materials by addressing hazardous materials classification, proper packaging, employee training, hazard communication, and operational requirements. (www.fmcsa.dot.gov; (800) 832-5660)

The **National Response Center** (NRC) is the federal point of contact for reporting all oil and chemical spills anywhere in the U.S. The NRC maintains a 24-hour-per-day, 7-day-a-week, 365-day-a-year operations center. (www.nrc.uscg.mil; (800) 424-8802, (202) 267-2675)

The **Occupational Safety and Health Administration** (OSHA) strives to ensure a safe and healthful workplace by preventing work-related injuries, illnesses, and deaths. (www.osha.gov; (800) 321-6742)

The **Pipeline and Hazardous Safety Administration** (PHMSA) oversees the **Hazardous Materials Information Center** (HMIC) to help with use of the Hazardous Materials Regulations (HMR). The complete HMR, including the hazardous materials table, clarifications, and exemptions, plus links to other resources, are available at their website. (www.phmsa.dot.gov/hazmat; (800) 467-4922)

The **American Trucking Associations** (ATA) represents the interests of the trucking industry by influencing state and federal government, providing educational programs and industry research, and promoting highway and driver safety. (www.truckline.com; (703) 838-1700)

National Tank Truck Carriers, Inc. (NTTC) represents the interests of the tank truck industry before Congress and various federal agencies. Comprising approximately 180 trucking companies, its goals are to enhance safety and profitability of the industry, act as a spokesman for its members, and exchange information with major shipping organizations. (www.tanktruck.org; (703) 838-1960)

Hazmat Identifiers

HMR require the shipper to identify hazardous materials and supply the proper labels and placards. The carrier is responsible for affixing the placards and ensuring all of the proper placards are in place for the material being transported. They must also ensure that placards are immediately replaced if lost in transit.

Types of communication usually accompanying a hazardous material shipment:

- **Labels** are affixed to packages and containment devices, providing a warning about hazardous contents.
- Handwritten or stenciled **markings** appear on packages, freight containers, and transport vehicles to identify material and other information about the shipment.
- **Placards** appear on large containers and vehicles, providing warnings about hazardous contents from a distance.

Labels, markings, and placards must conform to the regulations. Elevated temperature products and marine pollutants may require specific labeling, marking, and placarding as determined by tables in 49 CFR.

Proper labeling

Packages or containment devices used in shipping hazardous materials must bear a label to provide warning about the material's hazards. The HMT identifies the proper labels for the hazardous material in column 6 of the 49 CFR §172.101 Table (see also 49 CFR §172.400). The design of each label is closely regulated and corresponds to a hazard class and division number.

Here are some general guidelines:

- The label must be visible and located near the proper shipping name.
- If multiple labels are required, they need to appear next to each other.
- Text indicating a hazard, e.g. "corrosive," is not required on labels for Classes 1, 2, 3, 4, 5, 6, and 8.
- Packages or containment devices may be labeled even when not required by the regulations, as long as the label represents a hazard of the material inside the package.

(See 49 CFR §172.400-407)

Using markings

The shipper must place markings on packages, freight containers, and vehicles containing hazardous materials.

Markings must:

- Be durable, in English, and printed on the surface of a package or a label, sign, or tag.
- Be displayed on a background of sharply contrasting color and located away from other markings such as advertising that could inhibit their effectiveness.
- Avoid the use of abbreviations unless authorized as long as the material is a hazardous material and the label represents a hazard of the material inside the package.

Non-bulk hazardous materials should be marked with the materials' proper shipping name, identification number, and the name and address of the consignor or consignee. Additional markings may be required depending on the material or container. For example, vehicles or freight containers containing lading that was fumigated or treated with a poisonous solid, liquid, or gas shall be marked FUMIGATION. Non-bulk combination packagings having an inner packaging containing liquid hazardous materials must be marked with orientation arrows. Marine pollutants as listed in Appendix B to §172.101 of the HMR also need to be marked. (49 CFR §§172.300, 173.9, 172.312, 172.322)

Placarding

Compliance

Anyone transporting hazardous materials must comply with placarding requirements. The shipper must provide the placards, while it is the carrier's responsibility to affix them to the vehicle.

Placards are similar to labels, except larger so they can convey information about a hazardous material from a distance. They are put on bulk (larger) packages and transport vehicles, and their design is regulated by the HMR.

Additional requirements:

- Vehicles, freight containers, and portable tanks containing a poisonous material that meets the Poison-Inhalation shipping description must be placarded with POISON-INHALATION HAZARD or POISON GAS placards.
- Vehicles, containers, and portable tanks that contain 454 kilograms (1,001 lb.) or more gross weight of fissile or low-specific activity uranium hexafluoride must be placarded with both RADIOACTIVE and CORROSIVE placards.
- Hazardous materials that possess secondary hazards may be placarded with subsidiary placards.
- Vehicles, containers, and portable tanks containing material that can become dangerous when wet must be placarded with DANGEROUS WHEN WET placards.
- As with labels, placards can be used even when they are not required, as long as the material is a hazardous material, the placard represents a hazard of the material inside the package, and the placarding otherwise complies with regulations.

(See 49 CFR Subpart F §§172.500-172.560 for complete requirements and exemptions.)

Known quantity

Vehicles, containers, or rail cars transporting any quantity of the following hazardous materials Classes and Divisions must be placarded:

- Explosive 1.1, 1.2, and 1.3
- Poison gas 2.3
- Dangerous when wet 4.3
- Organic peroxide 5.2
- Poison 6.1 (PG1, inhalation hazard only)
- Radioactive 7 (Required with the Radioactive Yellow III label only. See §172.203 and §§173.427-173.476)

Placards are required for the following hazardous Classes and Divisions in quantities of 454 kg (1,001 lb.) or more:

- Explosive 1.4, 1.5 (blasting agents), and 1.6
- Flammable gas 2.1
- Non-flammable gas 2.2
- Flammable 3
- Combustible liquid
- Flammable solid 4.1
- Spontaneous combustible 4.2
- Oxidizer 5.1
- Organic peroxide 5.2
- Poison 6.1 (other than inhalation)
- Corrosive 8
- Miscellaneous hazardous materials 9 (not required for U.S. domestic shipments)

Vehicles, containers, or rail cars containing two or more non-bulk shipments of hazardous materials that require different placards in this list may instead simply be placarded "Dangerous." However, when 1,000 kg (2,205 lb.) or more of one category of material is loaded at one loading facility, the placard specified in this list must be applied.

Drivers are also required to show the identification number on both sides and each end of the trailer for shipments of more than 8,820 pounds (4,000 kg) of a single commodity that is not in bulk. This is in addition to any other required labeling or placarding, and only applies if the shipment is loaded at one point and no other freight is placed in the vehicle.

Placard regulation

The DOT prohibits carriers from displaying extraneous information on placards and in placard holders, such as signs, advertisements, slogans, or other devices that could be confused with hazmat labels or placards. This includes safety slogans such as "Drive Safely." (49 CFR §172.502)

Hazardous materials placards

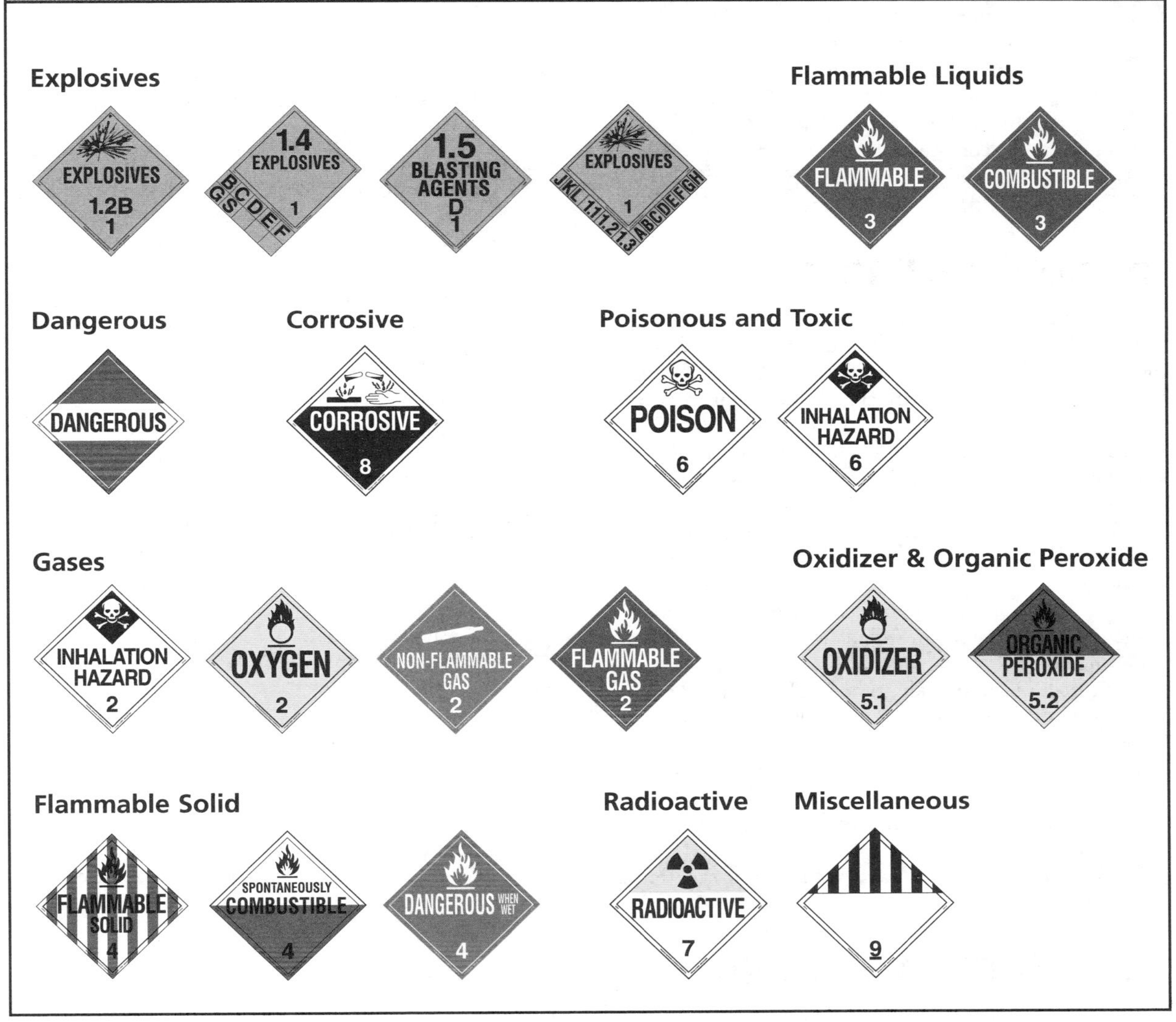

Incident Prevention and Response

There are several steps drivers can take to minimize the likelihood of a hazmat incident. We've compiled the major rules and some handy checklists that can help. By following these rules, the chances of needing the emergency phone numbers and response procedures also found in this section will hopefully remain slim.

Hazmat segregation

Hazardous materials need to be properly segregated to prevent a potentially dangerous reaction that could damage the shipment and harm people. For example, cyanides should not be stored with acids, Division 4.2 materials should not be stored with Class 8 liquids, and Division 6.1 Packing Group 1 and Hazard Zone A materials should not be stored with Class 3 material, Class 8 liquids, or Division 4.1, 4.2, 4.3, 5.1, or 5.2 material.

The table in §177.848 clearly defines which materials may or may not be stored or transported together in the same vehicle or storage facility. It also explains how certain materials must be separated during transport to avoid dangerous commingling. In general, corrosive liquids may not be loaded adjacent to flammable or oxidizing materials, unless the shipper knows that the mixture would not cause a fire or dangerous gas.

Class 1 explosives may not be loaded, stored, or transported next to each other, except as provided for in the compatibility table in §177.848. See also §177.835, which describes the special care in loading and unloading Class 1 explosives — for example, engines should be turned off, bale hooks or metal tools should not be used, and packages should not be dropped or thrown.

Loading and unloading

The regulations include specific requirements on properly loading and unloading hazardous materials. These are intended to improve safety by ensuring proper handling, preventing unnecessary movement of hazardous materials, and preventing fire.

The requirements also include special loading and unloading procedures for certain Hazard Classes, including flammable liquids, flammable solids, oxidizers, pyroforic liquids, corrosives, gases, poisonous gases, and radioactive materials. (See 49 CFR Subpart B §§177.834-177.843)

Incident response

Should a hazardous materials incident occur, follow the procedures set up by the carrier. This could include the *Emergency Response Guidebook*, the Material Safety Data Sheet, or the driver's company's procedure.

Here's some advice to help prepare for an incident:

- If involved in an accident, turn off the engine to prevent flammable materials from igniting.
- Call the emergency response phone number in the shipping document as soon as possible to ensure that emergency responders arrive at the scene quickly.
- Contact the appropriate national emergency response agency (see box) for immediate advice on handling the incident.
- Don't rush in too quickly to help. Help only if it is safe to do so; otherwise wait for emergency responders to arrive.
- Prevent others from entering the area and stay upwind of hazardous gases or fumes.
- Do not touch, taste, or smell spilled hazardous materials.
- Provide emergency responders with any information or help they need.

Reporting an incident

When a spillage of hazardous materials occurs, the driver should immediately call his or her carrier. The carrier needs to notify the National Response Center (NRC) at **(800) 424-8802 or (202) 267-2675 or www.nrc.uscg.mil** at the earliest practical moment, but at least within 12 hours, if one of the situations listed below in "Immediate notification" has occurred.

If the driver is not sure the material spilled is a reportable quantity (identified by "RQ" in the shipping papers), he or she can still contact the NRC. Note that calling other sources such as CHEMTREC® or the police does not constitute contacting NRC.

If the incident involves infectious materials, the driver may call the Centers for Disease Control **(CDC)** at **(800) 232-4636** instead of the NRC. Depending on the extent of the incident, the driver may also need to immediately contact the appropriate government agency — OSHA or ATF.

A detailed written report, DOT Form F 5800.1, must be completed within 30 days of the incident. (See 49 CFR §§171.15, 171.16, and 172.602)

Immediate notification

Immediate telephone notification to the NRC is required if:

- Someone is killed or hospitalized
- Public evacuation occurs and lasts more than one hour
- One or more transportation arteries or facilities close for one or more hours
- Radioactive or etiologic material breaks, spills, or causes a fire
- Marine pollutant release exceeds 450 L (119 gallons) liquid or 400 kg (882 lb.) solid, or continuing danger to life exists on the scene

Emergency response numbers

- CHEMTREC® (800) 262-8200
- CHEM-TEL, Inc. (888) 255-3924
- 3E Company (800) 360-3220
- Military Shipments (703) 695-4465/4696 (explosives or ammunition) or (800) 851-8061 (all other dangerous incidents)
- CANUTEC (Canada) (613) 996-6666 or (888) 226-8832
- SETIQ (Mexico) 01-800-00-214-00

What to carry in every cab

Every driver should have a copy of the ERG or some form of emergency response procedures, such as an MSDS or the company's own procedure. Copies of the ERG are available for free download at **www.phmsa.dot.gov/hazmat/outreach-training/erg.** Drivers should also carry:

- Shipping papers
- Copy of the Certificate of Registration
- Copy of training records (state mandated, so check individual state's requirements)
- Gloves
- Goggles
- Absorbent material
- Carriage by public highway information, 49 CFR Part 177 (not required, but recommended)

Stepping up security

Every day, millions of tons of hazardous materials are safely transported, but in the wrong hands they pose a significant danger.

In the wake of September 11, 2001, PHMSA has worked with hazardous materials shippers and carriers and with Federal, state, and local government agencies to enhance hazardous materials transportation security.

PHMSA has established new security requirements based on two strategies that are critical to improving security. One is developing and implementing a security plan. The other is training employees who handle and transport hazardous materials in how to recognize and react to security threats. (See 49 CFR §172.704 and 49 CFR §172.802.)

At a minimum, security plans should include:

- Personnel security measures to confirm information provided by job applicants for positions involving access to and handling of hazardous materials
- Measures to prevent unauthorized people from gaining access to hazardous materials
- Classification by job title of the official presiding over the plan, and defined duties per position or department responsible for implementing their portion of the plan as well as notifying others when portions of the plan are to be implemented.
- Measures to address security risks posed to hazardous materials en route from origin to destination

Security training should cover:

- Awareness of security risks associated with transportation of hazardous materials and methods to enhance security
- How to recognize and respond to a possible threat
- Company's security objectives, security structure, and specific security procedures
- Employee responsibilities, including actions to take in the event of a security breach

More information about enhancing hazardous materials transportation security is available online at: www.phmsa.dot.gov/hazmat.

Anti-terrorism tips for drivers

To help drivers move hazardous materials more safely and securely in the face of a terror threat (for example, if the National Threat Level is raised to Code Orange), FMCSA recommends a number of steps, including:

- Be aware if you are being followed, especially by vehicles with three or more people
- If you think you are being followed, call 911 or your dispatcher immediately
- Don't discuss cargo, destination, or trip specifics over an open channel or with people you don't know
- When leaving your facility, look for possible criminal surveillance of your truck or facility
- Be aware if someone is approaching your vehicle when you are stopped at a traffic light or in traffic
- If someone is trying to hijack you, try to keep the truck moving
- Leave your truck at a secure parking lot or truck stop whenever possible or have someone watch the vehicle
- Never leave the truck running; shut off the engine and lock up
- Avoid stopping in high crime or unsafe areas
- Use methods such as seals to prevent and identify tampering
- Check the electronic tracking system regularly and notify the dispatcher about any tampering or when it is not working
- Load and store hazardous materials only when sufficient security is around, inspecting your vehicle after all stops
- Make sure your communication devices work. Carry a backup device
- Make sure your truck has an engine kill switch, and use brake and fifth wheel locks

For more on FMCSA's commercial vehicle security programs, visit **www.fmcsa.dot.gov/regulations/hazardous-materials/hazardous-materials-security**.

Checklist for safe hazmat shipping

- ✓ Policies and procedures for transporting hazardous materials are regularly reviewed and revised to enhance security
- ✓ All hazmat employees and drivers have received initial and recurrent training
- ✓ Have determined whether material falls into any DOT Hazard Classes
- ✓ Packaging is appropriate, authorized, and properly assembled
- ✓ Packages and containers are properly marked
- ✓ Packages and containers are properly labeled
- ✓ Shipping papers are accurate and completed per hazmat regulations
- ✓ Driver has emergency response procedures
- ✓ Hazardous materials are properly loaded and unloaded
- ✓ Hazardous materials are properly segregated
- ✓ Vehicle is properly placarded and marked
- ✓ Should incident occur, it is reported immediately to carrier and NRC

Tractor/Trailer Inspection Procedure

Vehicle inspections help to catch potential problems before they occur. Conduct a walk-around inspection before you head out on the road and again during periodic rest and meal stops. The following inspection procedure for tractor/trailers was developed by the Federal Department of Transportation.

1 Left side of cab

Note general condition of left front wheel
- Condition of wheel and rim: Especially cracks, rim missing, rim bent, broken or missing studs, clamps, lugs
- Condition of tires: Properly inflated; valve stem not touching wheel, rim, or brake drum; valve cap in place; no serious cuts, bulges, tread wear, or any signs of misalignment
- Wheel bearing and hub: No leaking

Left front suspension
- Condition of springs, spring hangers, shackles
- U-bolts: No cracks, breaks, or shifting
- Condition of shock absorber

Left front brake
- Condition of brake drum and hoses
- Check air chamber mounting
- Check slack adjusters

Mirrors and brackets secure and undamaged

2 Front of cab

Condition of front axle

Condition of steering system
- No loose, worn, bent, damaged, or missing parts

Condition of windshield
- Check for damage and clean if dirty
- Check windshield wiper arms for proper spring tension
- Check wiper blades for any damage, "dead" rubber, and securement to arm

Lights and reflectors
- Cab parking, clearance, and identification lights: Clean, operating, and proper color
- Reflectors should be clean and proper color
- Right front turn signal light should be clean, operating, and proper color

3 Right side of cab

Check all items as done on left side

4 Right fuel tank area

Right fuel tank(s)
- Securely mounted, not damaged or leaking
- Fuel crossover line secure
- Tank(s) full of fuel
- Cap(s) on and secure

Condition of visible parts
- Rear of engine: Not leaking
- Transmission: Not leaking
- Drive shaft: Looks OK
- Exhaust system: Secure, not leaking, and not touching wires, fuel or air lines
- Frame and cross members: No bends, cracks, or breaks
- Air lines and electrical wiring: Secured against snagging and chafing

5 Trailer front

Air and electrical connections
- Glad hands: Properly mounted, free of damage, and not leaking
- Electrical line receptacle: Properly mounted, free of damage, plug adequately sealed, and safety catch engaged to prevent accidental disconnect
- Air and electrical lines should be properly secured against tangling, snagging, and chafing, with sufficient slack for turns

Lights and reflectors
- Front trailer clearance and identification lights: Clean, operating, and proper color
- Reflectors: Clean and proper color

6 Right rear tractor wheels area

Dual wheels
- Condition of wheels and rims: No cracks, missing or bent rims, broken or missing spacers, studs, clamps, or lugs
- Condition of tires: Properly inflated; valve stems not touching wheels, rims, or brake drum; valve caps in place; no serious cuts, bulges, tread wear, or any signs of misalignment, and no debris stuck between them
- Tires: All same type; do not mix radial and bias types on the same axle
- Tires: Evenly matched in circumference
- Wheel bearing and hub: No leaking

Tandem axles
- Repeat wheel/tire inspection as above

Suspension
- Condition of spring(s), spring hangers, shackles, and U-bolts
- Condition of torque rod arms and bushings
- Condition of shock absorber(s)
- Axle alignment

Brakes
- Condition of brake drum(s)
- Condition of hoses: Look for any chafing
- Check slack adjusters
- Check air chamber mounting
- Check springs brakes

7 Rear of tractor

Frame and cross members: Not bent, cracked, or otherwise damaged or missing

Lights and reflectors: Tail lights and turn signal lights—operating, clean, and proper color

Air and electrical lines: Properly secured to frame, not damaged or chafing

Splash guards: Present, not damaged, properly fastened, not dragging on ground or rubbing tires

8 Coupling system

Fifth wheel (lower)
- Securely mounted to frame
- No missing or damaged parts
- No visible space between upper and lower fifth wheel
- Locking jaws: Around the shank and NOT the head of kingpin
- Release lever: Properly seated and safety latch/lock engaged

Fifth wheel (upper)
- Kingpin not worn, bent, or damaged
- Sliding fifth wheel
- Mechanism not worn, bent, damaged; no parts missing
- Properly lubricated
- All locking pins present and locked in place

If air operated: No air leaks. Be sure to check that the fifth wheel is not so far forward that the tractor frame will strike landing gear during turns

Air and electric lines visible from this point:
- Should be secure from dangling, snagging, and chafing
- Should be free from damages, oil, grease

9 Right side of trailer

Front trailer support (landing gear or dollies)
- Fully raised, no missing parts, not bent or otherwise damaged
- Crank handle: Present and secured (typically on left side)
- If power operated: No air or hydraulic leaks

Spare tire(s)
- Carrier or rack: Not damaged
- Tire and/or wheel: Securely mounted in rack
- Tire and wheel condition: Adequate for a spare (proper size and properly inflated)

Lights and reflectors
- Trailer side clearance and marker lights: Clean, operating, and proper color
- Reflectors: Clean and proper color

Frame and body
- Frame and cross members: Not bent, cracked, damaged, or missing
- Body parts: Not damaged or missing
- Proper placarding

10 Right rear trailer wheels area

Dual wheels
- Condition of wheels and rims: No cracks, bent rims, broken or missing spacers, studs, clamps, or lugs
- Condition of tires: Properly inflated; valve stems not touching wheels, rims, or brake drum; valve caps in place; no serious cuts, bulges, tread wear, or any signs of misalignment, and no debris stuck between them
- Tires: All same type; do not mix radial and bias types on the same axle
- Tires: Evenly matched in circumference
- Wheel bearing and hub: No leaking

Tandem axles
- Repeat wheel and tire inspection as above
- If equipped with sliding axles: Check position and alignment; look for damaged, worn, or missing parts; all locks present, fully in place, and locked against fallout
- Flexible air lines: Not cracked, cut, crimped, or otherwise damaged; secured against tangling, dragging, and chafing

Suspension
- Condition of spring(s), spring hangers, shackles and U-bolts
- Axle alignment
- Condition of torque and rod arms, bushings

Brakes
- Condition of brake drum(s)
- Condition of hoses, lines, and valves
- Check slack adjusters
- Check air chamber mounting
- Check spring brakes (if so equipped)
- Drain moisture from air tank; close petcock

11 Rear of trailer

Lights and Reflectors
- Rear clearance and identification lights: Clean, operating, and proper color
- Reflectors: Clean and proper color
- Tail lights: Clean, operating, proper color

Cargo securement
- Cargo: Properly blocked, braced, tied, chained, etc.
- Tailboard: Up and properly secured
- End gates: Free of damage; properly secured in stake pockets
- Canvas or tarp (if required): Properly lashed down to prevent water damage, tearing, billowing, or blockage of either the mirrors or the rear lights
- Rear doors: Securely closed, latched, locked; required security seals in place
- Underride guard in place: Not cracked, bent, or broken

12 Required for double and triple trailer rigs

Check these items if you are checking a double or triple combination

Shut-off valves (at rear of trailers): In service and emergency lines
- Rear of front trailers OPEN
- Rear of last trailer CLOSED
- Converter dolly air tank drain valve CLOSED

Be sure air lines are supported and glad hands are properly connected

If spare tire is carried on converter gear (dolly): Make sure it is secured

Be sure pintle-eye of dolly is in place in pintle hook of trailer(s)

Make sure:
- Pintle hook is latched
- Safety chains are secured to trailer(s)
- Light cords are firmly in sockets on trailer(s)

This check should be repeated for each converter dolly in the rig. Remember to check each trailer if you are checking doubles or triples

13 Left rear trailer wheels area

Check all items as done on right side except for air tank draining

14 Left side of trailer

Check all items as done on right side

Also check any traffic side doors

15 Left rear tractor wheels area

Check all items as done on right side

16 Left fuel tank area

Check all items as done on right fuel tank area except for spare tire

Also check the following
- Battery (if not mounted elsewhere)
- Battery box: Securely mounted to vehicle, has secure cover
- Batteries: Secured against movement
- Battery cases: Not broken or leaking

Non-maintenance-free batteries
- Fluid in batteries at proper level
- Cell caps: Present and securely tightened
- Vents in cell caps: Free of foreign material

17 Inspect inside the cab

Get in the cab
- Make sure parking brake is on and gearshift in neutral (or "park" if automatic)
- Start engine: Listen for unusual noises

Look at the gauges
- Oil pressure: Should come up to normal seconds after engine is started
- Ammeter and/or voltmeter: Should be in normal range(s)
- Coolant temperature: Should begin gradual rise to normal operating range
- Engine oil temperature: Should begin gradual rise to normal operating range

Warning lights and buzzers: Oil, coolant charging circuit warning lights should go out right away

Inspection Steps

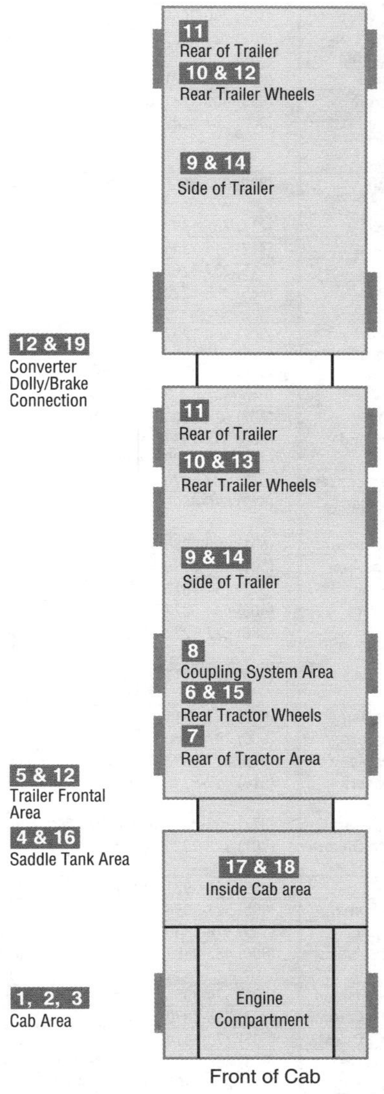

18 Controls, mirrors, windshield, and emergency equipment

Check all the following for looseness, sticking, damage, or improper setting: Steering wheels, clutch, accelerator (gas pedal), and brake controls—foot brake, trailer brake (if vehicle has one), parking brake, and retarder controls (if vehicle has them)

Check the following
- Parking and service brake stopping action
- Leaks (if vehicle has hydraulic brakes)
- Transmission controls
- Interaxle differential lock (if vehicle has one)
- Horns(s)
- Windshield wiper/washer
- Lights: Headlights, dimmer switch, turn signal, 4-way flashers; and clearance, identification, and marker light switches
- Mirror and windshield: Inspect for cracks, dirt, illegal stickers, or other line of sight obstructions

Check emergency equipment
- Safety: Spare electrical fuses (unless vehicle has circuit breakers), three red reflective triangles, and properly charged and rated fire extinguisher
- Optional: Tire chains (where required by winter conditions), tire changing equipment, list of emergency phone numbers, and accident reporting kit

19 Combination vehicle air brakes

Test
- Tractor protection valve
- Trailer emergency, parking, and service brakes

Check
- Air flow to all trailers (doubles and triples)
- Manual slack adjuster on S-Cam brakes; adjust
- Automatic slack adjusters
- Air compressor drive belt (if so equipped)
- ABS warning light
- Adequate air pressure

Fuel Tax

Fuel taxes are levied by individual states for fuel purchases and consumption within each state. IFTA governs the collection of fuel taxes. See page A7 for details regarding IFTA participation.

UNITED STATES

STATE	GENERAL			IFTA	TRIP PERMITS	
Alabama	(334) 242-9608	revenue.alabama.gov/motorfuels/	$0.1900 per gallon	(334) 242-1170	(334) 353-9135; (334) 242-2999	7-day permits issued
Alaska	(907) 269-6620	www.tax.alaska.gov/programs/programs/index.aspx?60210	$0.0800 per gallon	Non-participant	None	Not required
Arizona	(602) 255-0072; (602) 712-8473	www.azdot.gov/mvd/professional-services/FuelTaxInfo	$0.2600 per gallon	(602) 712-6775	(602) 771-2960	96-hour permits issued.
Arkansas	(501) 682-4800	www.dfa.arkansas.gov/offices/exciseTax/MotorFuelTax/Pages/Forms.aspx	$0.2250 per gallon	(501) 682-4800	(501) 682-4653	Fuel tax trip permits not issued
California	(800) 400-7115; (916) 445-6362 (outside the U.S.)	www.boe.ca.gov/info/taxoverview.htm	$0.5700 per gallon (IFTA)	(800) 400-7115	(800) 400-7115; (916) 445-6362 (outside the U.S.)	4-day permits issued. Must be obtained prior to entry
Colorado	(303) 205-8205	www.colorado.gov/pacific/tax/contact-us-25	$0.2050 per gallon	(303) 205-8205	(303) 273-1870	Issued at Ports of Entry
Connecticut	(800) 382-9463 (in CT); (860) 297-5962	www.ct.gov/drs/	$0.4170 per gallon	(860) 541-3222	(860) 541-3222	10-day permits issued for non-IFTA carriers
Delaware	(302) 760-2080	dmv.de.gov/services/TransServ/index.shtml	$0.2200 per gallon	(302) 744-2721	(302) 744-2721	72-hour permits issued by wire services
District of Columbia	(202) 727-4829	cfo.dc.gov/page/tax-rates-and-revenues-other-taxes	No IFTA membership $0.2350 per gallon	Non-participant	None	Not required
Florida	(800) 352-3671	floridarevenue.com/dor/taxes/fuel/	$0.3387 per gallon	(850) 617-3711	(800) 749-9143	10-day permits issued by wire services
Georgia	(855) 406-5221, option 4	dor.georgia.gov/motor-vehicle-services	$0.2940 per gallon ← revised quarterly	(877) 423-6711	(855) 406-5221	10-day fuel use permits issued
Hawaii	(808) 587-4242	tax.hawaii.gov/forms/a1_b3_5fuel/	$0.1700 per gallon plus county tax of $0.0880 to $0.1650 per gallon	Non-participant	None	Not required
Idaho	(800) 972-7660 ext. 7855	tax.idaho.gov/i-1119.cfm	Tax-paid gasoline that IFTA licensees purchase in Idaho and consume in another jurisdiction where a duplicate tax is assessed on gasoline may be eligible for a refund → $0.3200 per gallon	(208) 334-7806; (800) 972-7660 ext. 7806	(800) 662-7133	120-hour permits issued
Illinois	(217) 785-1397	tax.illinois.gov/motorfuel/	$0.3340 per gallon	(217) 785-1397	(217) 785-6613	96-hour permits issued
Indiana	(317) 615-7345	in.gov/dor/mcs/4106.htm	$0.4700 per gallon	(317) 615-7345	(317) 615-7345	5-day permits issued by wire services
Iowa	(515) 237-3268	www.iowadot.gov/mvd/omcs/default.htm	$0.3250 per gallon	(515) 237-3268	(515) 237-3264	72-hour permits issued
Kansas	(785) 368-8222	www.ksrevenue.org/bustaxtypesmf.html	$0.2600	(785) 368-8222	(785) 368-6501	24 and 72-hour permits Issued by Central Permits office and Ports of Entry
Kentucky	(502) 564-1257	transportation.ky.gov/Motor-Carriers/Pages/default.aspx	$0.2160 per gallon plus $0.1020 surcharge per gallon	(502) 564-1257	(502) 564-1257	10-day permits issued
Louisiana	(225) 219-7656, option 2, then option 1	revenue.louisiana.gov/Faq/QuestionsAndAnswers/3	$0.2000 per gallon	(225) 219-7656	(800) 654-1433; (225) 343-2345	Issued by wire services
Maine	(207) 624-9000 ext. 52136	www.maine.gov/sos/bmv/commercial/ftlrep.htm	$0.3120 per gallon	(207) 624-9000 ext. 52136	(207) 624-9000 ext. 52137	72-hour permits issued
Maryland	(800) 638-2937; (410) 260-7980 (Central Md.)	taxes.marylandtaxes.com/Business_Taxes/Business_Tax_Types/Motor_Fuel_Tax/default.shtml	$0.3455 per gallon	(800) 638-2937; (410) 260-7980 (Central Md.)	(800) 638-2937; (410) 260-7980 (Central Md.)	15-day permits issued
Massachusetts	(617) 887-5070	www.mass.gov/dor/all-taxes/fuels/	$0.2400 per gallon	(617) 887-6300; (887) 671-6367	(781) 431-5148	72-hour trip permits issued.
Michigan	(517) 636-4600	www.michigan.gov/taxes/0,4676,7-238-43542_43544---,00.html	$0.3900 per gallon ← revised quarterly	(517) 636-4580	(517) 636-4580	5-day permits issued by wire services
Minnesota	(651) 296-0889	www.revenue.state.mn.us/businesses/petroleum	$0.2850 per gallon	(651) 205-4141	(651) 205-4141	5-day permits issued
Mississippi	(601) 923-7150	www.dor.ms.gov/Business/Pages/Petroleum-Tax.aspx	$0.1800 per gallon	(601) 923-7150	(888) 737-0061; (601) 359-1717	Required
Missouri	(573) 751-2611	dor.mo.gov/business/fuel/	$0.1700 per gallon	(866) 831-6277 option 2	(866) 831-6277	72-hour permits issued
Montana	(406) 444-6027	www.mdt.mt.gov/business/fueltax/	$0.2925 per gallon	(406) 444-2998	(406) 444-7262	72-hour permits issued
Nebraska	(888) 622-1222; (402) 471-4435	www.dmv.nebraska.gov/mcs/ifta.html	$0.2700 per gallon	(888) 622-1222; (402) 471-4435	(402) 471-0034	72-hour permits issued. Must be obtained prior to entry
Nevada	(775) 684-4711	dmvnv.com/mchome.html	$0.2700 per gallon	(775) 684-4711	(775) 684-4711	Issued by vendors. Must be obtained prior to entry
New Hampshire	(603) 271-2311	www.nh.gov/safety/divisions/administration/roadtoll	$0.2220 per gallon	(603) 271-2302 option 1	(603) 271-2311	Issued by wire services
New Jersey	(609) 292-6500	www.state.nj.us/mvc/Commercial/index.htm	$0.4420 per gallon	(609)-633-9400	(609) 633-9400	96-hour permits issued
New Mexico	(505) 827-0392	www.mvd.newmexico.gov/fuels-tax.aspx	$0.2100 per gallon	(505) 827-0392	(505) 827-0392	Issued at Ports of Entry
New York	(518) 457-5735, option 2	www.tax.ny.gov/bus/ifta/fuel.htm	$0.3815 per gallon ← revised quarterly	(518) 457-5735	(518) 457-5735	72-hour permits issued through a service bureau
North Carolina	(877) 308-9092; (919) 707-7500	www.dornc.com/taxes/motor/ifta.html	$0.3430 per gallon ← revised semi-annually	(877) 308-9092; (919) 707-7500	(877) 308-9092; (919) 707-7500	3-day permits issued by permitting services
North Dakota	(701)-328-2725, option 3	www.dot.nd.gov/business/motor-carrier.htm	$0.2300 per gallon	(701)-328-2725 option 3	(701) 328-2621	72-hour permits issued online: www.nd.gov/ndhp/motor-carrier/e-permits
Ohio	(855) 466-3921, option 4	www.tax.ohio.gov/excise/motor_fuel.aspx	$0.2800 per gallon	(614) 466-3921	(855) 466-3921	Single trip permits issued
Oklahoma	(405) 521-3036	www.occeweb.com/TR/ifta.htm	$0.1300 per gallon	(405) 521-3036	(405) 521-2251; (405) 521-3036	120-hour permits issued
Oregon	(503) 378-5849	www.oregon.gov/ODOT/MCT/Pages/index.aspx	$0.3000 per gallon	(503) 373-1634	(503) 378-6699	Not a fuel tax state
Pennsylvania	(800) 482-4382	www.revenue.pa.gov/FormsandPublications/FormsforBusinesses/	$0.7470 per gallon	(800) 482-4382	(800) 482-4382	5-day permits issued by wire services
Rhode Island	(401) 574-8955, option 4	www.tax.ri.gov/taxforms/sales_excise/	$0.3300 per gallon	(401) 574-8955	(401) 574-8955	Issued only by permitting agents
South Carolina	(803) 896-3870	www.scdmvonline.com/	$0.1800 per gallon	(803) 896-3870	(803) 896-3870	10-day permits issued
South Dakota	(605) 773-3314	dor.sd.gov/Motor_Vehicles/Trucking_Industry/	$0.2800 per gallon	(605) 773-2104	(605) 773-4578	Required
Tennessee	(888) 468-9025; (615) 399-4267	tn.gov/revenue/topic/motor-fuel-taxes	$0.2100 per gallon	(888) 468-9025, option 3	(888) 468-9025; (615) 399-4267	7-day permits issued by wire services
Texas	(800) 252-1383; (800) 299-1700	www.comptroller.texas.gov/taxes/fuels/	$0.2000 per gallon	(800) 252-1383	(800) 299-1700	20-day permits issued
Utah	(801) 297-6800	tax.utah.gov/fuel	$0.2940 per gallon	(801) 297-6800	(801)-297-6800	96-hour permits issued
Vermont	(802) 828-2070	www.dmv.vermont.gov/commercial_trucking	$0.3100 per gallon	(802) 828-2070; (802) 828-8073	(800) 749-6058; (800) 833-3762	72-hour permits issued
Virginia	(804) 249-5130	www.dmv.virginia.gov/commercial/#taxact/	$0.2020 per gallon plus $0.0350 surcharge per gallon	(804) 249-5130	(804) 249-5130	10-day trip permits issued
Washington	(360) 664-1852	www.dol.wa.gov/vehicleregistration/fueltax.html	$0.4940 per gallon	(360) 664-1858	(360) 664-1858	3-day permits issued
West Virginia	(304) 558-3333; (800) 982-8297	ax.wv.gov/Business/MotorFuel/Pages/MotorFuelTax.aspx	$0.3570 per gallon	(304) 926-0799	(304) 926-0799	10-day permits issued
Wisconsin	(608) 266-9900	www.dot.state.wi.us/business/carriers/index.htm	$0.3290 per gallon	(608) 266-9900	(608) 266-9900	72-hours permits issued online or by wire services for single trips
Wyoming	(307) 777-4826	www.dot.state.wy.us/home/trucking_commercial_vehicles.html	$0.2400 per gallon	(307) 777-4827	(307)-777-4827	Can be issued at Ports of Entry. Good for 96 hours.

CANADA

PROVINCE	GENERAL			IFTA	TRIP PERMITS	
Alberta	(780) 427-3044	www.finance.alberta.ca/publications/tax_rebates/fuel/overview.html	$0.1835 per litre	(780) 427-3044	(800) 662-7138; (403) 342-7138	Single trip permits issued
British Columbia	(888) 388-4440	www2.gov.bc.ca/gov/content/taxes/sales-taxes/motor-fuel-carbon-tax	$0.2267 per litre	(250) 387-0635	(250) 387-9686; (877) 388-4440 (in Canada)	Single trip permits issued
Manitoba	(800) 782-0318 (in MB); (204) 945-5603	gov.mb.ca/finance/taxation/taxes/gasoline.html	$0.1400 per litre	(800) 782-0318 (in MB); (204) 945-5603	(877) 812-0009; (204) 945-3961	Single trip permits issued
New Brunswick	(800) 669-7070; (506) 453-2404	www2.gnb.ca/content/gnb/en/departments/finance/taxes/gasoline_motive_fueltax.html	$0.2150 per litre	(800) 669-7070; (506) 453-2404	(800) 669-7070	7-day permits issued
Newfoundland and Labrador	(877) 729-6376	www.servicenl.gov.nl.ca/drivers/safetycode/fuel-tax.html	$0.2150 per litre	(709) 729-1786	(709) 729-1786	Single trip permits issued
Northwest Territories	(867) 767-9244; (800) 661-0820	www.fin.gov.nt.ca/services/fuel-tax	$0.0910 per litre	Non-participant	(866) 225-3505; (867) 767-9088 ext 31181	Single trip permits issued at weigh stations and online
Nova Scotia	(902) 424-6300; (800) 565-2336	www.novascotia.ca/sns/access/business/tax-commission/fuel-tax.asp	$0.1540 per litre	(902) 424-2850	(902) 424-6300; (800) 565-2336 option 5	Single trip permits issued through permit agencies
Nunavut	(867) 975-5800; (800) 316-3324	www.gov.nu.ca/finance/information/petroleum-taxes	$0.0910 per litre	Non-participant	None	Not issued
Ontario	(866) 668-8297	www.fin.gov.on.ca/en/tax/ft/index.html	$0.1430 per litre	(866) 668-8297	(866) 668-8297	Single trip permits issued through permit agencies
Prince Edward Island	(902) 368-4070	www.princeedwardisland.ca/en/information/finance/gasoline-tax	$0.2020 per litre	(902) 569-7541	(902) 569-7541	Single trip permits issued at weigh stations
Québec	(800) 237-4382 (in QC); (418) 652-4382 (outside QC)	www.revenuquebec.ca/en/entreprises/taxes/	$0.2020 per litre	(800) 237-4382 (in QC); (418) 652-4382 (outside QC)	(800) 237-4382 (in QC); (418) 652-4382 (outside QC)	Issued through permit agencies
Saskatchewan	(800) 667-6102 ext. 7749; (306) 787-7749 (outside SK)	finance.gov.sk.ca/taxes/ft	$0.1500 per litre	(800) 667-6102 ext. 7749 (in SK); (306) 787-7749	(800) 667-7575 (in SK); (306) 775-6969	Single trip permits issued
Yukon	(867) 667-5343	www.finance.gov.yk.ca/fueltax.html	$0.0702 per litre	Non-participant	(867) 667-5345	Single trip permits issued at weigh stations

Motor Carrier Programs

Deregulation and standardization of the trucking industry

Drivers know their industry is a thicket of rules and regulations. At the same time, they often hear about deregulation. This section highlights some of the most important legislative developments of the last 25 years and explains key results — far-reaching programs that affect truckers every day.

Deregulation refers to a series of legislative actions taken in the early 1980s. Contrary to popular perception, this legislation was not meant to eliminate rules. Instead, one goal was to change how operating authority was granted, and another was to standardize weight and size limits across the country. In the early 1990s, new legislation further clarified and extended these provisions and as mandated participation in programs designed to ensure that goals would be achieved.

Operating authority

Between 1935 and 1980, motor carriers were granted operating authority by the Interstate Commerce Commission (**ICC**) on the basis of whether their business constituted a public convenience and necessity. This requirement meant that carriers holding authority for particular routes could argue that new carriers weren't necessary. The regulatory barriers to entry into the industry were high. The 1980 Motor Carrier Act, one of the first pieces of deregulation legislation, changed the requirements for operating authority to being able to meet a fit, willing, and able standard. This means that a carrier need only show ability to service a route, not whether that ability is demanded by the market. As a result, the process of gaining entry into the industry became easier.

Standardization

While motor carrier operations were being simplified, other legislation combined international weight and size limits with the restoration and completion of the interstate highway system. Two important pieces of legislation helped begin the process.

- The Federal-Aid Highway Act of 1981 marked a shift in focus in the federal highway program toward finally completing the Interstate system and then moving ahead with rehabilitating it. The "4 Rs" (resurfacing, restoration, rehabilitation, and reconstruction) were addressed in hopes of completing, preserving, and rehabilitating the Interstate system.
- The 1982 Surface Transportation Assistance Act (**STAA**) identified many concerns relating to highway infrastructure and funding. But it also established weight and size limits for trucks and longer combination vehicles (**LCV**) to help stave off premature deterioration of highways. A chart of the current weight and size provisions is found on pages A14-A15. By the early 1990s, 14 states had managed to slowly expand the use of LCVs, but this expansion was halted in 1991 by the Intermodal Surface Transportation Efficiency Act (**ISTEA**). (See page A13 for details on LCVs.)

In addition to imposing a freeze on LCVs, ISTEA contained Title IV, the Motor Carrier Act of 1991, which required state uniformity in vehicle registration and fuel tax reporting. Four key components of ISTEA Title IV were the imposition of deadlines for states to participate in the International Registration Plan, deadlines for participation in the International Fuel Tax Agreement, instructions directing the ICC to establish a new procedure for motor carriers to register operating authority with states (Single State Registration System), and finally, the ISTEA "freeze" that set limits on weight and size requirements for trucks with double or triple trailers weighing more than 80,000 pounds.

International Fuel Tax Agreement (IFTA)

The International Fuel Tax Agreement is a base state fuel tax program based on the International Registration Plan principle. IFTA was designed to simplify fuel tax administration and collection, improve fuel tax-related efficiency and workflow, and decrease cash transactions and paperwork.

IFTA jurisdictions include the 48 contiguous U.S. states and the 10 Canadian provinces. A carrier's base state issues fuel credentials, which allow travel in each member jurisdiction. IFTA advantages are numerous and include:

- IFTA significantly reduces paperwork and compliance burdens.
- Only one IFTA license is issued, a copy of which must be kept in the vehicle cab.
- Only two IFTA decals are required. They must be placed on the exterior portion of both sides of the cab.
- Possession of the IFTA license and decal permit a vehicle to operate in all member jurisdictions.
- Only one quarterly fuel tax report is required, detailing operations in all member jurisdictions.
- Because fuel tax overpayments are compared to tax liabilities between jurisdictions, IFTA reciprocity can reduce or eliminate cash transactions.
- IFTA enables only one check to or one refund from the base state.
- Audits are conducted by the base jurisdiction only.
- Fuel bonds are no longer required, unless carriers fail to file returns or when audits indicate severe problems requiring a bond.

NAFTA Trucking Pilot Program

In April 2011, the United States and Mexico announced a Pilot Program to implement the NAFTA trucking provisions for operations beyond the U.S. border commercial zones. Mexico also has implemented a similar program. The particulars of the Pilot Program include:

- A duration of no more than three years;
- There is no limit on the number of U.S. or Mexican participating carriers;
- Mexican carriers must:
  - Complete OP-1MX application;
  - Successfully pass a Pre-Authority Safety Audit (PASA); and,
  - Have appropriate insurance coverage
- Strong enforcement initiatives:
  - Stage 1: Provisional authority is issued, trucks will be checked every time they cross the border for 3 months
  - Stage 2: Number of checks will equal the average number for all border truck crossings, with trucks required to have a CVSA decal, and will undergo a Compliance Review within 18 months
  - Stage 3: Permanent authority will be issued upon conclusion of the pilot.
- Transportation of hazardous materials is not allowed in the Pilot Program;
- Mexican and U.S. trucks will be tracked for compliance with various regulations including the prohibition to transport domestic cargo (only international cargo transportation is allowed under NAFTA);
- All motor carriers participating in the Pilot must comply with all regulations impacting motor carrier operations in both countries, including limits on driving hours, fiscal and financial liability requirements, vehicle environmental standards, registration procedures, etc.

To obtain more information about cross-border truck operations into Mexico, please visit Mexico's Secretaria de Comunicaciones y Transportes (SCT): http://www.sct.gob.mx/transporte-y-medicina-preventiva/autotransporte-federal/autotransporte-transfronterizo-de-carga-internacional/

International Registration Plan (IRP)

The International Registration Plan is the result of more than 30 years of cooperative effort by all jurisdictions of the United States and Canada to create a fair vehicle registration reciprocity agreement. IRP combines benefits of its predecessors, the Uniform Proration and Reciprocity Agreement and the Multistate Reciprocity Agreement.

Crucial IRP benefits include "one plate per vehicle" and equitable distribution of license fees. By 1973, this agreement became what is known today as the International Registration Plan. Today, membership in IRP includes all 48 contiguous U.S states, the District of Columbia, and the ten Canadian provinces.

IRP incorporated in 1994 and became mandatory in 1997. States or provinces that did not participate in IRP faced forfeiture of their ability to regulate interstate trucking. IRP was adopted on time by all relevant jurisdictions. IRP has many benefits:

- Under IRP, registering a fleet of interjurisdictional vehicles is a one-stop process for motor carriers.
- Motor carriers can operate in any IRP jurisdiction displayed on the cab card (provided that proper operating authority has been obtained).
- Payment of license fees is simple: Fees are paid on the basis of total distance operated in all jurisdictions.
- Only one license plate and one cab card is issued for each apportionable fleet vehicle registered under the plan.

Unified Carrier Registration Agreement (UCRA)

In 2005, the federal highway bill known as the Safe, Accountable, Flexible, Efficient Transportation Equity Act, A Legacy for Users (SAFETEA-LU) repealed the Single State Registration System (SSRS) and replaced it with the Unified Carrier Registration Agreement (UCRA). The SSRS repeal was effective January 1, 2007.

Highlights of the UCRA:

- Like the SSRS, the UCRA is a program whereby fees are collected and distributed to states.
- The UCRA is a state-run program.
- All interstate motor carriers are required to register. If a carrier has a USDOT number, it's subject to the regulations.
- Fees are based on the total number of commercial vehicles operated, not on a per-vehicle basis. This means fees are in tiers. Entities covered by the UCRA but which do not operate commerical motor vehicles (brokers, freight forwarders, and leasing companies) are assessed at the rate of the smallest motor carrier operation tier.
- For UCRA fleet measurement purposes, a commercial vehicle is a vehicle used in interstate commerce with a gross vehicle weight or gross vehicle weight rating of at least 10,001 pounds; or, if a passenger vehicle, one that is built to carry more than 10 persons, including the driver; or any vehicle that transports hazardous materials in a quantity requiring placarding.

For UCRA registration, visit www.ucr.in.gov.

Comprehensive Safety Analysis 2010

Comprehensive Safety Analysis 2010 (CSA 2010) is an initiative by the Federal Motor Carrier Safety Administration (FMCSA) intended to improve large truck and bus safety. The FMCSA has developed a new operational model based on the CSA initiative. The new operational model involves a series of new enforcement and compliance procedures, including specific driver and carrier measurements. Based on the measurements, drivers and carriers may be subject to intervention and, in some cases, penalties.

For more information from the official U.S. DOT site, go to http://ai.fmcsa.dot.gov/sms

Mexican and Canadian Regulations

Mexican regulations

Customs and Immigration:

From the U.S. into Mexico:

U.S. carriers can provide through-trailer service into Mexico, with most shipments between Mexico and the U.S. being interchanged with a Mexican trucking firm at the border. A number of U.S. carriers either enter into joint ventures with Mexican trucking firms or establish a Mexican company to provide service. As required under the North American Free Trade Agreement, Mexico's transportation ministry, the Secretaria de Comunicaciones y Transportes (SCT), has an application form for U.S. carriers seeking operating authority into Mexico. The authority by SCT is valid to transport international cargo only in Mexico.

Additional information can be found at **www.sct.gob.mx/transporte-y-medicina-preventiva/autotransporte-federal/temas-internacionales/autotransporte-transfronterizo-mexico-estados-unidos/**.

From Mexico into the United States:

Shipments from Mexico may clear U.S. Customs at the border point, and only the normal paperwork is needed unless the shipment is moving "in-bond" for clearance somewhere other than the border crossing point. The U.S. and Mexico agreed in early 2011 to implement the NAFTA trucking provisions. On July 8, the U.S. Department of Transportation (DOT) announced a NAFTA trucking pilot program for Mexican long-haul motor carriers to operate beyond the U.S. border commercial zones. The application process for such MX carriers can be found at **cms.fmcsa.dot.gov/registration/form-op-1mx**.

- All southern border ports of entry require the submission of manifest information to U.S. Customs and Border Protection (CBP) via the Automated Commercial Environment (ACE) e-Manifest program. Use of e-Manifests is mandatory at all U.S. land ports of entry. Carriers can submit the required information through the ACE Secure Data Portal, by electronic data interchange (EDI), or by using the services of a third party. For more information, go to **www.cbp.gov/trade/automated**.

Amendments to Customs Law:

On December 9, 2013, Mexico issued a decree amending various provisions to their customs law, in order to promote transparency and simplification of procedures, promote trade openness among trade participants, and establish an effective exchange of information between authorities through electronic systems.

Here is a summary of the amendments: Importers and exporters can carry out customs clearance through an appointed legal representative, without having to use a customs broker, and can be done at any customs location. The legal representative must be registered with the Tax Administration Service (SAT), and companies must have their pedimentos validated through the SAT's customs electronic system. Filing documents digitally, will allow users to have an easier system to correct information in custom documents.

What drivers need to know about operating in Mexico:

Highways

- Of a total network of 29,000 miles of paved roads, only 8.5% are four-lane
- Curves are up to two times tighter
- Lateral clearance is 5'9", as opposed to 30' in the U.S.
- Total gvw of 97,000 lbs. is allowed, as opposed to 80,000 lbs. in the U.S.

Primary commercial corridors

- Known as ET routes
- Includes A-2 (two-lane) and A-4 (four-lane) highways
- 53' trailers are permitted on ET routes
- Overall tractor-trailer length permitted on ET routes: up to 23 m (75.5')

Permits

- A permit is required to operate an American-owned trailer more than 20 km (12.4 miles) from the border
- Permits are issued by the Secretary of the Economy and require the carrier to post a bond
- Permits are good for 30 days, during which time only one entrance and one exit is allowed
- A new bond is required for each separate trailer
- Bond fees are not refundable

Required documents:

Shipments into Mexico require the following documentation. Drivers should have copies. Originals should be mailed to the border as soon as they are ready.

- Bill of lading, written in both English and Spanish and showing final destination
- Commercial invoice, written in Spanish
- Shipper's export declaration
- Packing list
- Import permit (for about 200 items)
- NOM certification (product quality standards)
- NAFTA certificate of origin
- General certificate of origin
- Mexican manifest
- Pedimento (Mexican customs entry form)

General issues to keep in mind when transporting in Mexico:

- The trade balance between the U.S. and Mexico currently creates some import and export lane imbalances, which can make it difficult to find backhauls.
- Equipment maintenance and availability of parts may be limited.
- There are differences between the countries in licensing and training drivers; a U.S. CDL is valid in Mexico and a Mexican Licencia Federal (Mexico Federal CDL) is valid in the U.S. The licenses have reciprocity.
- Carriers must be properly insured to operate in Mexico.
- Some goods and services that drivers take for granted—for example, truck stops—are not as prevalent in Mexico.

Vehicle Inspections

Mexico's federal department of transportation, the Secretaría de Comunicaciones y Transportes (SCT), issued a regulation on June 29, 2012 establishing timetables for inspecting Commercial Motor Vehicle (CMV) equipment operating in Mexico, including U.S. based equipment. The Norma Oficial Mexicana NOM-068-SCT-2-2014 established the requirements for performing such inspections, but the timeframes for conducting the inspections had not been determined. SCT has now determined that all CMVs, including tractors and trailers, and, if applicable, dollies, must be inspected every six months and must have a decal or paperwork verifying such an inspection has been performed. SCT stated that Mexico will accept U.S. inspections conducted at the federal and state level that comply with annual CMV inspections required under 49CFR 396.17. However, again, such inspections will have to be performed every six months rather than the yearly inspection required under 49CFR §396.17.(c). In essence, carriers can comply with this Mexican vehicle inspection program by having Mexico bound vehicles inspected and showing a CVSA decal issued in the last six months.

In addition to those issues, laws and regulations on accidents are different in Mexico. The legal system allows the injured parties to waive prosecution. If this does not happen, the trucker may spend time in jail waiting for an investigation. If the trucker is found liable, he or she may have to stay in jail until the trial.

Specific questions concerning operating within Mexico should be addressed to:

Director General de Autotransporte Federal
Secretaria de Communicaciones y Transportes
Calzada de las Bombas No. 411
Colonia San Bartolo Coapa
Mexico, 04920 D.F.

Mexican and Canadian Regulations

©istockphoto

Canadian regulations

Customs and Immigration:

From the U.S. into Canada:

- At the border, you may be asked to show proof of citizenship (e.g. birth certificate or passport)
- Be prepared with all relevant customs documentation, such as the Canada Customs Manifest, bill of lading, and Canada Customs Invoice
- Some shipments may be moved "in-bond" to a government-licensed sufferance warehouse
- Information can be supplied to the Canada Border Services Agency (CBSA) in advance through the Pre-Arrival Review System (PARS) for pre-approval of cross-border shipments. However, starting November 1, 2012, highway motor carriers entering Canada must submit only e-manifests through CBSA's Advance Commercial Information (ACI) system. Motor carriers must register with CBSA and ensure they have the capabilities required to communicate with CBSA. For more information please visit CBSA's e-manifest site: **www.cbsa-asfc.gc.ca/prog/manif/menu-eng.html.**
- U.S. drivers may haul goods across the border in both directions, but may not move goods from one point in Canada to another

From Canada into the United States:

- Documentation required: Entry Manifest (or other form of merchandise release), commercial invoice and bill of lading (or other right-to-make-entry evidence).
  Goods entering the United States are subject to advance cargo information rules administered by U.S. CBP. In addition, food products are subject to prior notification requirements established by the Food and Drug Administration.
- Canadian drivers moving hazardous materials in the United States must be in possession of a valid driver card issued under the Free and Secure Trade Program (FAST card) or a Transportation Worker Indentification Credential (TWIC) issued by the U.S. Department of Homeland Security (DHS).
- All U.S./Canada land ports of entry require the submission of manifest information to U.S. CBP via the ACE e-Manifest program. Carriers can submit the required information through the ACE Secure Data Portal, by EDI, or by using the services of a third party. For more information, go to **www.cbp.gov/trade/automated**.

What drivers need to know about operating in Canada:

Language

- English is a principal language in all provinces except Québec
- While English is spoken in major Québec cities, French is the principal language and English may not be spoken in areas away from primary business centers

Operating authority

- Safety fitness and evidence of adequate liability insurance is the basis for granting permission to operate
- In some provinces, an application must be filed with the transportation department or provincial Ministry of Transport where the carrier is headquartered or wishes to operate
- Ontario requires any carrier operating in its province to register for the Commercial Vehicle Operators Registration (CVOR) program, see **www.mto.gov.on.ca/english/about/printable-forms.shtml**
- All Canadian provinces are members of the Commercial Vehicle Safety Alliance (CVSA), and may inspect commercial vehicles to CVSA standards

Rates, tariffs, and taxation

- Economic regulation has been phased out in Canada
- Carriers and shippers negotiate the rate for services provided
- All Canadian provinces are members of the International Fuel Tax Agreement (IFTA) and the International Registration Plan (IRP)

Environmental concerns

- Carriers should be certain that trucks are in full compliance with environmental regulations
- Some provinces have programs for on-road vehicle emission testing
- Canadian law allows trucks to be impounded and operators held responsible for defects affecting the environment

Questions concerning any aspect of trucking should be referred to the Ministry of Transport in the appropriate province. Specific questions concerning operating within Canada should be directed to:

Transport Canada
Questions@tc.gc.ca
(613) 990-2309 or toll free (866) 995-9737
www.tc.gc.ca

Border Security

The United States has implemented a program called Customs-Trade Partnership Against Terrorism (C-TPAT) to improve security throughout supply chains moving goods across the border. The Canadian counterpart of C-TPAT is the Partners in Protection (PIP) program. The Mexican counterpart of C-TPAT is called Nuevo Esquema de Empresas Certificada (NEEC). Information about NEEC is available at **www.certificacionneec.com.**

Canada, Mexico, and the U.S. have developed a joint program called Free and Secure Trade (FAST). Although FAST is a voluntary program, Customs is promoting it as the program that will allow for expedited clearance at ports of entry. Drivers have to apply to be accepted into the FAST program, at which time a fee is collected. The application is processed, and includes extensive background checks on the drivers. Once approved, the driver will be given a FAST card, which is valid for five years, to use at specially designated lanes. Participating in FAST requires all parts of the supply chain to be C-TPAT certified, including the carrier, driver, importer and manufacturer, with the driver holding a FAST card. For more information on C-TPAT and FAST, see **www.cbp.gov/border-security/ports-entry/cargo-security/c-tpat-customs-trade-partnership-against-terrorism.**

As mentioned before, the Transportation Security Administration (TSA) requires Mexican and Canadian drivers transporting placarded amounts of hazardous materials in the United States undergo a background check equal to that of U.S.-based drivers. TSA has designated the FAST card and the TWIC as compatible to the Hazardous Materials Endorsement background check. Canadian and Mexican drivers holding such credentials are in compliance with TSA's security threat assessment regulations

As of January 31, 2008, the United States, under the Western Hemisphere Travel Initiative (WHTI), requires all individuals entering the U.S. at land crossings to carry a passport or other secure document. Commercial drivers are subject to this requirement and should pay close attention to State Department and Department of Homeland Security announcements. The FAST card is considered a WHTI compliant travel document.

Road Construction and Conditions

Icy, snowy roads or construction traffic can turn routine shipments into costly headaches. Check the status of roads with this useful list of state and province phone numbers and websites. It's a handy quick reference before you seek out an alternate route.

511 Hotline Information

The U.S. Federal Highway Administration has begun implementing a national system of highway and road conditions/construction information for travelers. Under the new plan, travelers can dial 511 and get up-to-date information on roads and highways.

Implementation of 511 is the responsibility of state and local agencies.

For more details, visit:
www.fhwa.dot.gov/trafficinfo/511.htm

United States

Alabama
(888) 588-2848
www.dot.state.al.us
alitsweb2.dot.state.al.us/RoadConditions

Alaska
511
(907) 465-8952
511.alaska.gov
www.dot.state.ak.us

Arizona
511
(888) 411-7623
www.az511.com
www.azdot.gov

Arkansas
(800) 245-1672
(501) 569-2374
www.arkansashighways.com
www.idrivearkansas.com

California
(800) 427-7623
www.dot.ca.gov
Los Angeles area: 511
www.go511.com
San Francisco Bay area: 511
www.511.org
Sacramento area: 511
www.sacregion511.org
San Diego area: 511
(619) 669-1900
www.511sd.com

Colorado
511
(303) 639-1111
(877) 315-7623
www.cotrip.org
www.codot.gov

Connecticut
(860) 594-2000
(860) 594-2650
www.ct.gov/dot
www.i-84waterbury.com

Delaware
(800) 652-5600
(302) 760-2080
www.deldot.gov

Florida
511
www.fl511.com
www.fdot.gov

Georgia
511
(877) 694-2511
(404) 635-8000
www.511ga.org

Hawaii
(808) 587-2220
hidot.hawaii.gov

Idaho
511
(888) 432-7623
www.511.idaho.gov
www.itd.idaho.gov

Illinois
(800) 452-4368
www.gettingaroundillinois.com
www.dot.il.gov

Indiana
(800) 261-7623
(866) 849-1368
www.in.gov/dot
www.in.gov/indot/2420.htm

Iowa
511
(800) 288-1047
www.511ia.org
www.iowadot.gov

Kansas
511
(800) 585-7623
(785) 296-3585
www.kandrive.org
www.ksdot.org

Kentucky
511
(866) 737-3767
www.drive.ky.gov
transportation.ky.gov

Louisiana
511
(877) 452-3683
www.511la.org
www.dotd.la.gov

Maine
511
(207) 624-3000
(800) 675-7453
www.maine.gov/mdot

Maryland
511
(855) 466-3511
(410) 582-5650
www.md511.org
www.roads.maryland.gov

Massachusetts
511
Metro Boston:
(617) 986-5511
Central: (508) 499-5511
Western : (413) 754-5511
www.mass511.com

Michigan
(800) 381-8477
(517) 373-2090
www.michigan.gov/drive

Minnesota
511
(651) 296-3000
In MN: (800) 657-3774
www.511mn.org
www.dot.state.mn.us

Mississippi
511
(601) 359-7001
www.mdottraffic.com
www.mdot.ms.gov

Missouri
(888) 275-6636
(573) 751-2551
www.modot.org

Montana
511
(800) 226-7623
(406) 444-6200
www.mdt511.com
www.mdt.mt.gov

Nebraska
511
(800) 906-9069
(402) 471-4567
www.511.nebraska.gov
www.dot.nebraska.gov

Nevada
511
(877) 687-6237
(775) 888-7000
www.nevadadot.com
www.nvroads.com

New Hampshire
511
(603) 271-3734
www.nhtmc.com
www.nh.gov/dot

New Jersey
511
(866) 511-6538
www.511nj.org
www.state.nj.us/transportation

New Mexico
511
(800) 432-4269
(505) 827-5100
www.nmroads.com
www.dot.state.nm.us

New York
511
(888) 465-1169
www.511ny.org
www.dot.ny.gov
Thruway: (800) 847-8929
www.thruway.ny.gov

North Carolina
511
(877) 511-4662
www.ncdot.gov/travel/511
www.ncdot.gov

North Dakota
511
(855) 637-6237
www.dot.nd.gov
www.dot.nd.gov/travel-info-v2

Ohio
(614) 466-7170
www.dot.state.oh.us
www.buckeyetraffic.org
(continued in next column)
Cincinnati metro area:
511
www.ohgo.com/dashboard/cincinnati
Turnpike:
(440) 234-2030
(440) 234-2081
www.ohioturnpike.org

Oklahoma
(844) 465-4997
(405) 522-2800
okroads.org
www.okladot.state.ok.us

Oregon
511
(800) 977-6368
(888) 275-6368
www.oregon.gov/odot
www.tripcheck.com

Pennsylvania
511
(888) 783-6783
(800) 349-7623
www.511pa.com
www.penndot.gov

Puerto Rico
(800) 981-3021
(787) 977-2200
its.dtop.gov.pr/es/Default.aspx
www.dtop.gov.pr/carretera

Rhode Island
511
(888) 401-4511
(401) 222-2450
www.dot.ri.gov/travel

South Carolina
511
(877) 511-4672
(855) 467-2368
www.511sc.org
www.dot.state.sc.us

South Dakota
511
(866) 697-3511
www.sddot.com
www.safetravelusa.com/sd

Tennessee
511
(877) 244-0065
www.tn511.com
www.tn.gov/tdot

Texas
(800) 452-9292
(512) 463-8588
www.txdot.gov
www.drivetexas.org

Utah
511
(866) 511-8824
(801) 887-3700
www.udot.utah.gov
www.utahcommuterlink.com

Vermont
511
www.vtrans.vermont.gov

Virginia
511
(866) 695-1182
(800) 367-7623
www.511virginia.org
www.virginiadot.org/travel

Washington
511
(800) 695-7623
www.wsdot.wa.gov/traffic

Washington, D.C.
311
(202) 737-4404
(202) 673-6813
ddot.dc.gov

West Virginia
511
(877) 982-7623
www.wv511.org
www.transportation.wv.gov

Wisconsin
511
(866) 511-9472
www.511wi.gov

Wyoming
511
(888) 996-7623
www.wyoroad.info

Cell Phone Emergency Number

- 911 is the preferred cell phone emergency number for all 50 states and the District of Columbia.

Cell Phone and Texting Laws

Starting January 3, 2012, the Federal Motor Carriers Safety Administration (FMSCA) and the Pipeline and Hazardous Materials Safety Administration (PHMSA) joined together to create a new federal law restricting the use of hand-held mobile telephones by drivers of commercial motor vehicles (CMVs).

This rulemaking was designed to improve safety on the nation's highways by reducing the prevalence of distracted driving-related crashes, fatalities, and injuries involving drivers of CMVs. CMV drivers may only use hand-held devices if the vehicle is pulled off the road in a safe location and not being operated, or for emergencies.

The Governors Highway Safety Association (GHSA) has issued a compilation of state laws that limit and prohibit drivers' use of cell phones or texting. No state bans all cell-phone use by all drivers, but in many places broader restrictions apply to new drivers and certain others. State texting prohibitions are much more common. For more details, go to **www.ghsa.org**. It might be noted that at least half the Canadian provinces also prohibit the use of hand-held cell phones by all drivers.

Canada

Alberta
511
(877) 262-4997
(888) 799-1522
511.alberta.ca
www.ama.ab.ca

British Columbia
(800) 550-4997
www.drivebc.ca

Manitoba
511
(877) 627-6237
(204) 945-3704
www.manitoba.ca/roadinfo

New Brunswick
511
(800) 561-4063
(506) 453-3939
www.gnb.ca/roads

Newfoundland & Labrador
Avalon region: (709) 729-2382
Eastern region: (709) 466-4120
Central region: (709) 292-4300
Western region: (709) 635-4127
Labrador region: (709) 896-7840
www.roads.gov.nl.ca

Nova Scotia
511
(902) 424-3933
In Canada: (888) 780-4440
511.gov.ns.ca

Ontario
511
In ON: (800) 268-4686
In Toronto: (416) 235-4686
www.mto.gov.on.ca/english/traveller

Prince Edward Island
511
(902) 368-4770
In Canada: (855) 241-2680
www.gov.pe.ca/roadconditions

Québec
511
(888) 355-0511
www.quebec511.gouv.qc.ca/en

Saskatchewan
(888) 335-7623
Saskatoon area: (306) 933-8333
Regina area: (306) 787-7623
www.saskatchewan.ca/residents/transportation/highways/highway-hotline

Mexico

www.sct.gob.mx/carreteras (Spanish)

On-the-Road Resources

Hotel/Motel Toll-free Numbers & Websites

Don't get stranded without a place to stay. Call ahead for reservations and room availability with this list of selected hotels and motels.

Adam's Mark Hotels & Resorts
(716) 845-5100
www.adamsmark.com

Aloft Hotels
(877) 462-5638
www.alofthotels.com

America's Best Inns & Suites
(800) 237-8466
www.americasbestinns.com

America's Best Value Inn
(888) 315-2378
www.americasbestvalueinn.com

AmericInn
(800) 634-3444
www.americinn.com

Baymont Inn & Suites
(800) 337-0550
www.baymontinns.com

Best Western
(800) 780-7234
www.bestwestern.com

Budget Host
(800) 283-4678
www.budgethost.com

Clarion Hotels
(877) 424-6423
www.clarionhotel.com

Coast Hotels & Resorts
(800) 716-6199
www.coasthotels.com

Comfort Inn
(877) 424-6423
www.comfortinn.com

Comfort Suites
(877) 424-6423
www.comfortsuites.com

Courtyard by Marriott
(888) 236-2427
www.courtyard.marriot.com

Crowne Plaza Hotel & Resorts
(877) 227-6963
www.crowneplaza.com

Days Inn
(800) 225-3295
www.daysinn.com

Delta Hotels & Resorts
(888) 890-3222
www.deltahotels.com

Doubletree Hotels, Guest Suites, Resorts & Clubs
(800) 560-7753
www.doubletree3.hilton.com

Drury Hotels
(800) 378-7946
www.druryhotels.com

Econo Lodge
(877) 424-6423
www.econolodge.com

Embassy Suites Hotels
(800) 362-2779
www.embassysuites3.hilton.com

Extended Stay Hotels
(800) 804-3724
www.extstay.com

Fairfield Inn & Suites
(888) 236-2427
www.fairfield.marriott.com

Fairmont Hotels & Resorts
(800) 257-7544
www.fairmont.com

Four Points by Sheraton
(800) 368-7764
www.fourpoints.com

Four Seasons
(800) 819-5053
www.fourseasons.com

Hampton Inn
(800) 445-8667
www.hamptoninn3.hilton.com

Hilton Hotels
(800) 445-8667
www.hilton.com

Holiday Inn Hotels & Resorts
(888) 465-4329
www.holidayinn.com

Homewood Suites
(800) 445-8667
www.homewoodsuites3.hilton.com

Howard Johnson
(800) 221-5801
www.hojo.com

Hyatt Hotels & Resorts
(888) 591-1234
www.hyatt.com

InterContinental Hotels & Resorts
(888) 424-6835
www.intercontinental.com

Jameson Inns
(855) 527-4138
www.jamesoninns.com

Knights Inn
(800) 477-0629
www.knightsinn.com

La Quinta Inns & Suites
(800) 753-3757
www.lq.com

Le Méridien Hotels & Resorts
(800) 543-4300
www.lemeridienfamily.com

Loews Hotels
(800) 235-6397
www.loewshotels.com

MainStay Suites
(877) 424-6423
www.mainstaysuites.com

Marriott International
(888) 236-2427
www.marriott.com

Microtel Inns & Suites
(800) 337-0050
www.microtelinn.com

Motel 6
(800) 466-8356
www.motel6.com

Omni Hotels & Resorts
(800) 843-6664
www.omnihotels.com

Park Inn
(800) 670-7275
www.parkinn.com

Preferred Hotels & Resorts
(866) 990-9491
www.preferredhotels.com

Quality Inn & Suites
(877) 424-6423
www.qualityinn.com

Radisson Hotels & Resorts
(800) 967-9033
www.radisson.com

Ramada Worldwide
(800) 854-9517
www.ramada.com

Red Lion Hotels
(800) 733-5466
www.redlion.com

Red Roof Inn
(800) 733-7663
www.redroof.com

Renaissance Hotels
(888) 236-2427
www.renaissancehotels.com

Residence Inn by Marriott
(888) 236-2427
www.residenceinn.com

The Ritz-Carlton
(800) 542-8680
www.ritzcarlton.com

Rodeway Inn
(877) 424-6423
www.rodewayinn.com

Sheraton Hotels & Resorts
(800) 325-3535
www.sheraton.com

Sleep Inn
(877) 424-6423
www.sleepinn.com

Super 8
(800) 454-3213
www.super8.com

Travelodge Hotels
(800) 525-4055
www.travelodge.com

Westin Hotels & Resorts
(800) 937-8461
www.westin.starwoodhotels.com

Wyndham Hotels & Resorts
(877) 999-3223
www.wyndham.com

NOTE:
All toll-free reservation numbers are for the U.S. and Canada unless otherwise noted. These numbers were accurate at press time, but are subject to change.

Area Codes

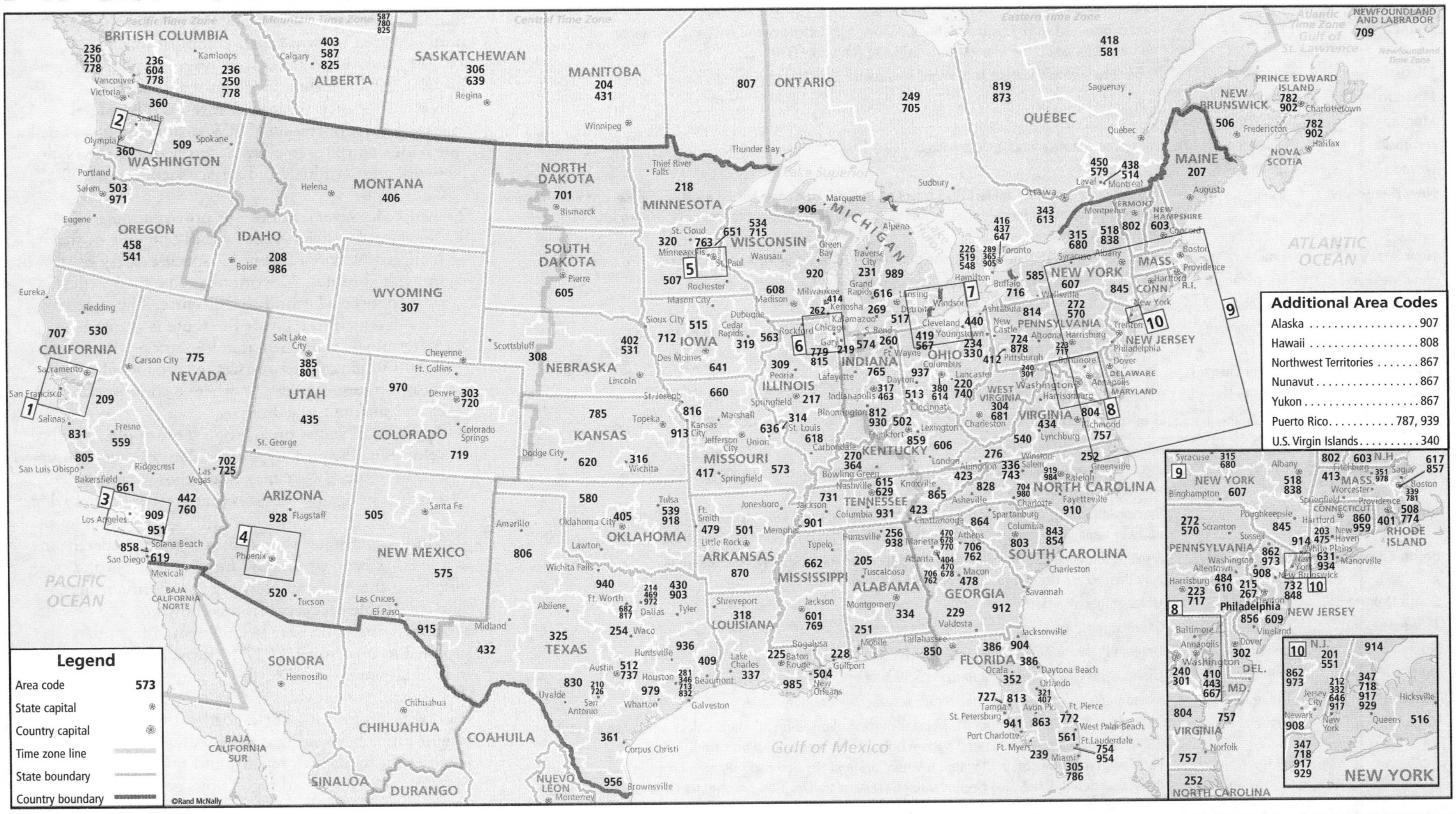

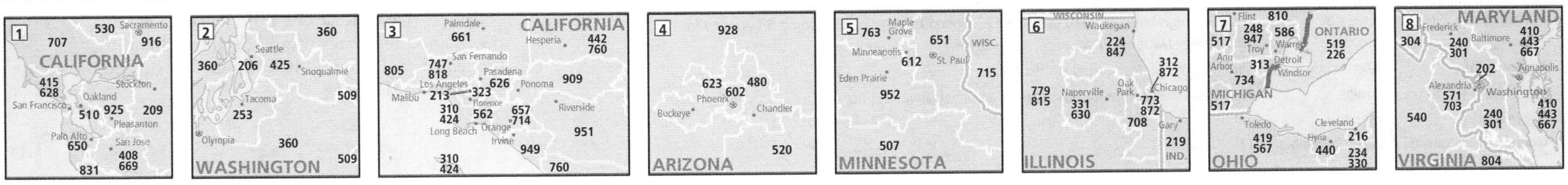

State Access Policies

STATE	DISTANCE ALLOWED IN MILES FROM NATIONAL NETWORK	COMMENTS
Alabama	1 mile	All state highways with 12' lane width or designated
Alaska	5 miles	See 17 AAC 25.014(f) for LCV exceptions
Arizona	1 mile	Up to 102" wide allowed on state designated routes connecting to National Network unless posted
Arkansas	Unlimited	Unless otherwise posted
California	1 mile	Terminal access on signed routes; 1 mi. service access on signed routes for fuel, food, lodging, and repairs
Colorado	Unlimited	Unless otherwise posted; subject to local ordinances
Connecticut	1 mile	Access beyond 1 mi. by letter of permission for 28' twin combo and 53' trailer. For information, visit www.ct.gov/dot
Delaware	1 mile	From identified designated routes; others by permit
District of Columbia	See comment	By permit only; call (202) 442-4670 or (202) 442-9467 or fax (202) 442-4867. For web-enabled permitting, visit http://ddot.dc.gov/ddot/site/default.asp
Florida	Unlimited	Unless otherwise posted
Georgia	1 mile	Unless otherwise posted
Hawaii	Unlimited	Unless otherwise posted or if under special permit
Idaho	See comment	1 mi. road access for food, fuel, repair, rest facilities, and terminals
Illinois	See comment	1 mi. access from a Class I highway unless prohibited by signage; 5 mi. from Class I, II or III highways on the state highway system at 80,000 lbs. and on locally designated routes and streets at 80,000 lbs. to points of loading and unloading and to service facilities
Indiana	Unlimited	
Iowa	See comment	To nearest truckstop for food, fuel, or lodging
Kansas	Unlimited	All U.S. and state routes
Kentucky	5 miles	On state-maintained highways, unless exiting from an interstate or parkway where 15 miles is allowed, or 1 mile on non-state maintained roads for access to a terminal or facility for food, fuel, repairs, or rest. Access beyond these distances subject to permit from the Dept. of Vehicle Regulation at (502) 564-7000. For long-term access to roads contact the Dept. of Highways at (502) 564-7183.
Louisiana	10 miles	From legally available routes, unless prohibited
Maine	Unlimited	Overdimension loads–permit required; phone Bureau of Motor Vehicles (207) 624-9000 and press 1, then ext. 52134 for permit request
Maryland	See comment	For access provisions for semi-trailers exceeding 48' in length up to but not exceeding 53' in length, stinger-steer auto/boat transporters, truck or truck-tractor semi-trailer combination designed for and transporting automobiles or boats, maxi-cube combinations, saddle-mount or full-mount combinations, and truck-tractor-semi-trailer/trailer (doubles) combinations call 410-582-5734. For additional information on size/weight visit the following website: www.roads.maryland.gov/cvo. There may be other travel restrictions in local jurisdictions and it is not possible to post them all. Drivers should remain alert for highway signage posted well in advance of the restricted route and avoid them.
Massachusetts	Unlimited	U.S. and state highways only
Michigan	5 miles	From Interstate and state trunklines; 1 mi. on other roads; up to 102" wide trailers allowed statewide
Minnesota	1 mile	Access beyond 1 mi. by written petition, followed by letter permission and publication; no free distance off the Minnesota Twin Trailer Network (TTN)
Mississippi	Unlimited	Subject to highway weight and height limitations
Missouri	1 mile	
Montana	Unlimited	
Nebraska	Unlimited	All U.S. and state routes, unless posted
Nevada	Unlimited	
New Hampshire	1 mile	On state highways. 53' trailers may travel on authorized routes. For information please visit www.nh.gov/safety/divisions/dmv/forms/documents/trailerlist.pdf. To use city or town streets and roads, prior local approval is required.
New Jersey	2 miles	From Interstates and routes designated in NJAC 16:32-1.4 as NJ Access Network
New Mexico	See comment	20 mi. for deliveries and reasonable distance for food, fuel, repairs, and rest
New York	See comment	1 mi. on all highways; petition for access beyond this distance
North Carolina	See comment	53' trailers may travel 3 miles from all primary routes unless restricted; twin trailers may travel 3 miles from designated routes unless restricted; all other access by written permission
North Dakota	See comment	10 mi. on state routes
Ohio	Unlimited	Unless otherwise posted
Oklahoma	See comment	5 mi. on state routes
Oregon	1 mile	Unless otherwise posted
Pennsylvania	1 mile	Access approval required for additional distance, for 102" wide equipment, 53' trailers, and twin 28' 6" semitrailers
Rhode Island	1 mile	Tractor-semitrailer combos and 102" width: all roads; upon leaving Designated Network, all twin trailers are required to obtain permits if distance traveled exceeds 1 mi.
South Carolina	See comment	5 mi. to terminals (SC Reg. definition) and facilities for food, fuel, rest, and repair. All other access (for twin trailers only) by petition
South Dakota	Unlimited	Unless otherwise posted
Tennessee	Unlimited	Shortest reasonable route
Texas	Unlimited	Unless otherwise posted
Utah	Unlimited	Unless otherwise posted or if under special permit
Vermont	1 mile	Reasonable access for food, fuel, repair, rest facilities, and terminals
Virginia	1 mile	53' semitrailer with maximum 41' kingpin spacing allowed on all roads unless otherwise posted; 28' 6" twin-trailers—Designated System only. Permit required beyond 1 mi.; Permission must be obtained within towns, cities and Henrico and Arlington counties. An access network has also been identified for twin-trailers. Contact Virginia Dept. of Transportation: (804) 786-2967
Washington	Unlimited	On state highways. WA 410 and WA 123 closed to vehicles exceeding 5,000 gvw in Mt. Rainier National Park
West Virginia	See comment	Within 2 mi. of designated routes
Wisconsin	15 miles	Plus highways designated by state in administrative law Trans 276
Wyoming	Unlimited	

As reported by individual states November, 2017

©DesignPics, Inc/Alamy

Access Routes

Title 49 USC, 31114 provides that the states may not deny reasonable access to vehicles of the width and length limits required by Title 49 USC, 31111 and 31113 between the National Network and terminals; facilities for food, fuel, repairs, and rest; and points of loading and unloading for household goods carriers, motor carriers of passengers, and single-unit trailers normally used in twin-trailer combinations.

The individual states were originally allowed by the DOT to establish their own reasonable access provisions for such vehicles. However, the Federal Highway Administration (**FHWA**) subsequently issued a rule requiring states to allow access between the National Network and terminals and service facilities in 1990.

This includes several important provisions:

- No state may deny access within one mile of the National Network except for specific safety reasons on individual routes. A petition may be filed with the state for access beyond this distance. The state has 90 days in which to reply or the route is granted.
- A "terminal" is defined as any location where freight originates, terminates, or is handled in the transportation process; or where a commercial motor carrier maintains facilities.
- Approval of access on any one route applies to all vehicles of the same type, regardless of ownership. Furthermore, a state may not impose blanket restrictions against vehicles that are 102 inches wide.

Individual states should be consulted to determine if access has been established for distances beyond one mile from the National Network for specific routes. The reasonable access provisions shown on the accompanying table have been prepared from data supplied in November, 2017 to Rand McNally by the individual states.

Federal law provides that states may not deny reasonable access for vehicles loaded to Interstate System weight limits between that system and terminals and facilities for food, fuel, repairs, and rest. However, the FHWA has never issued regulations governing what access is reasonable for such vehicles. Nevertheless, it considers that at least one mile on state or state-maintained highways should be allowed and that further distance should be carefully considered by state authorities.

Longer Combination Vehicles

Longer Combination Vehicles (**LCVs**) are defined as any combination of a truck tractor and two or more trailers or semitrailers which operate on the Interstate System at a gross vehicle weight (gvw) greater than 80,000 pounds.

In late 1991, Congress passed legislation which froze the grandfathered weight that LCVs may carry on the Interstate System to what was allowed in a state on June 1, 1991. The legislation also froze the length of commercial motor vehicles with two or more cargo-carrying units to whatever length of cargo-carrying units were in actual and lawful use on the National Network on June 1, 1991.

This table does not include the maximum gross weight limit for LCVs; check with each individual state. It does show the overall length limits in feet for the cargo-carrying units of double and triple trailer combinations, whether a permit is required, and the routes on which they may operate.

The data is accurate as of November, 2017; you should check with state officials in states where you will travel as these requirements are subject to change. Rand McNally cannot be responsible should the regulations change.

STATE	DOUBLE TRAILERS	TRIPLE TRAILERS	PERMIT REQUIRED	COMMENTS
Alaska	95'	120'	Required for triples only.	Information on LCV routes can be found at 17 AAC 25.014. All roads subject to spring weight restrictions are posted at the division website. Local roads are subject to municipal ordinances.
Arizona	95'	95'	Permits required for all LCVs	95' is cargo carrying length or combined trailer length. Allowed on I-15 and short sections of US routes 89, 89A, 160, 163, and state routes 98 and 389. Restricted to 20 miles south of Utah state line
Colorado	111'	115.5'	Annual permit required	Restricted to designated Interstate and state highway segments
Florida	106'	—	Required	Allowed only on Florida Turnpike
Hawaii	65'	—	No	Allowed on all National Network routes except HI-95 between H-1 and Barbers Point Harbor
Idaho	95'	95'	Required; good for 1 year from date of issuance	Allowed on Interstate and designated state highways
Indiana	106'	104.5'	Annual tandem trailer permit required	Allowed only on Indiana Toll Road, plus 15 miles access, subject to Indiana DOT approval
Iowa	100'	100'	Required	These combinations are restricted to travel within the Sioux City Commercial Zones. Combinations entering from Nebraska are limited to a cargo-carrying length of 65 feet
Kansas	109'	109'	Access permits, valid for 6 months, required for access between Kansas Turnpike and terminals located within a 10-mile radius of each toll booth except at NE end of Turnpike where 20-mile radius allowed. Special Vehicle Combination (SVC) permits are good for 1 year and are required for operation on I-70 between Colorado state line and Exit 19	Allowed only on Kansas Turnpike. SVC triples allowed only on I-70 from Colorado state line to exit 19
Massachusetts	104'	—	Required	Allowed on Massachusetts Turnpike only (I-90) from Boston to New York state line
Michigan	58'	—	Required	Allowed on Interstate and designated state highways
Mississippi	65'	—	No	Allowed on all National Network routes
Missouri	110'	109'	Annual permit required for all LCV combinations	LCV blanket permits. This permit may include combinations defined as Rocky Mountain Doubles (RMD), Turnpike Doubles (TPD), and triple-trailers currently allowed to operate on turnpikes in other states. Annual blanket permits are available for LCVs up to 120' in overall length to travel to and from locations within 20 miles of the western border of this state. 120,000 lbs. is allowed for LCVs entering from the Kansas border. 95,000 lbs. is allowed for LCVs entering from the Nebraska border and 90,000 lbs. is allowed for LCVs entering from the Oklahoma border. All other dimensions shall be legal. This permit authorizes travel over specified routes on the state highway system
Montana	93'	100'	Required for double trailer combinations if either trailer exceeds 28.5'. Annual or trip permits available; require continuous travel. Special triple vehicle annual or single loading or service trip permit required	Allowed on National Network routes except US 87 from milepost 79.3 to milepost 82.5. Doubles have length and access limits. Triples allowed only on Interstate System and granted a 2-mile access off Interstate System for loading or service. Montana allows an overall length of 105' for Cabover tractors and 110' for conventional tractors.
Nebraska	95'	95'	Annual length permit required for cargo-carrying combinations greater than 65'	Triples can only travel empty. LCVs allowed on I-80 from Wyoming state line to exit 440 (NE 50); only doubles allowed a 6-mile access to designated staging areas
Nevada	95'	95'	Required	Allowed on all National Network routes
New York	102'	—	Annual tandem trailer permits required	Allowed on tolled sections of New York Thruway system with access to specific points
North Dakota	100'	100'	Required if combination has gross vehicle weight of 80,000 lbs. or more	Allowed on all National Network routes with 10-mile access from National Network; 103' cargo carrying length for a truck-trailer and truck-trailer-trailer on National Network
Ohio	102'	95'	Required for units measured exceeding 61 ft. measured from front of first trailer or load to rear of last trailer or load. Not to exceed 68 ft.	Allowed only on Ohio Turnpike system and with access to designated terminal points located at certain exits
Oklahoma	110'	95'	Required for all combinations	Allowed on National Network and legally available routes. 5-mile access from legal routes
Oregon	68'	105'	Permit required if gross vehicle weight is 80,000 lbs. or more	Oregon Doubles allowed on all National Network routes. Triples allowed only on routes approved by Oregon DOT by permit. Access determined by Oregon DOT. No single trailer can exceed 35', and the overall length (including power unit) cannot exceed 105'
South Dakota	110'	110'	Required if combination has gross vehicle weight of 80,000 lbs. or more	Doubles with cargo-carrying length of 81.5 feet or less are allowed on all National Network routes with statewide access unless restricted by South Dakota DOT. Doubles over 81.5 feet and triples are allowed on the Interstate System and selected state routes. Access must be approved by South Dakota DOT.
Utah	95'	95'	Required	95' is "Combined Trailer Length". LCV's up to 81' combined trailer length, are allowed on all highways without authorization. LCV's longer than 81' are allowed on all interstate highways and other highways as authorized by UDOT. All National Network routes with access routes approved by Utah DOT for combinations of less than 81'. Combinations 81' and over may operate only on National Network routes: I-15, I-70 from jct. I-15 to Colorado state line, I-80, I-84 from jct. I-80 to Idaho state line, I-215 and UT 201 from I-15 to 5600 West, Salt Lake City
Washington	68'	—	Required for cargo-carrying units over 60' but not exceeding 68'	Allowed on all National Network and state routes except WA 410 and WA 123 in Mt. Rainier N.P. May be restricted by local ordinances
Wyoming	81'	—	No	Allowed on all National Network routes and unlimited access off National Network to terminals

Sources: Federal Register 23 CFR Part 658, Appendix C, and review by the FHWA in November, 2017

Length and weight freeze

In late 1991, as part of ISTEA, Congress imposed a freeze that addressed the issues of increasing vehicle size and weight and routes where LCVs could operate. The law stated that only those vehicles and routes which were in use as of June 1, 1991, could continue to be used. No expansions of routes or vehicles would be permitted, and the freeze is still in effect.

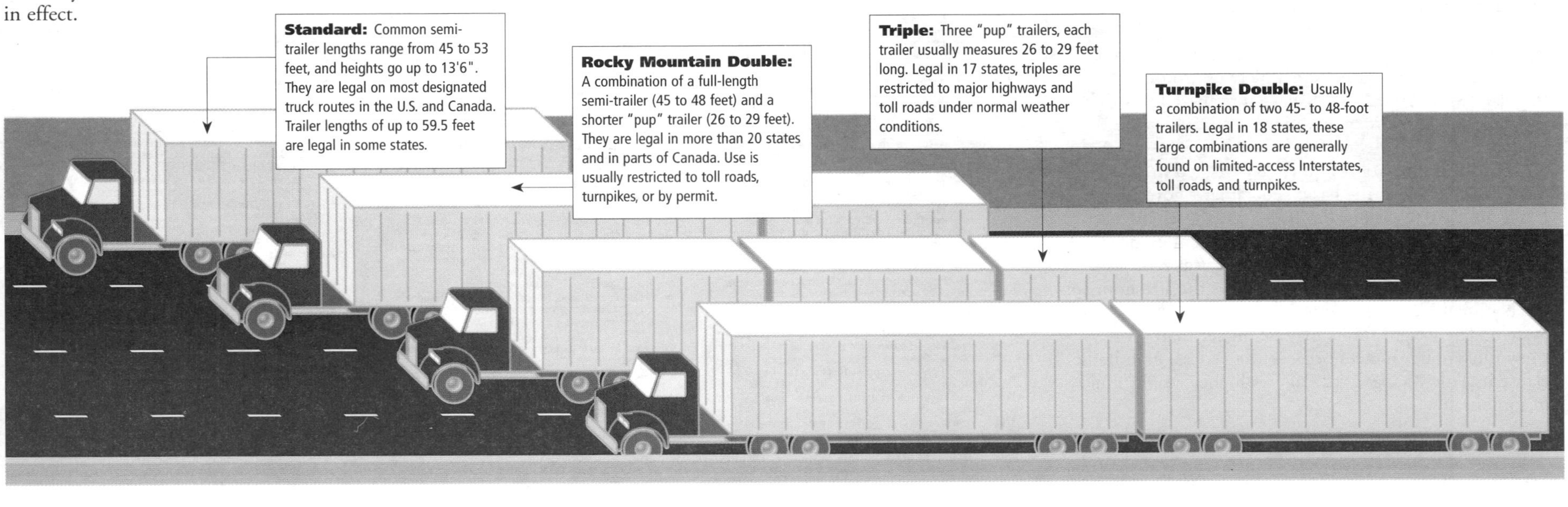

Standard: Common semi-trailer lengths range from 45 to 53 feet, and heights go up to 13'6". They are legal on most designated truck routes in the U.S. and Canada. Trailer lengths of up to 59.5 feet are legal in some states.
Rocky Mountain Double: A combination of a full-length semi-trailer (45 to 48 feet) and a shorter "pup" trailer (26 to 29 feet). They are legal in more than 20 states and in parts of Canada. Use is usually restricted to toll roads, turnpikes, or by permit.
Triple: Three "pup" trailers, each trailer usually measures 26 to 29 feet long. Legal in 17 states, triples are restricted to major highways and toll roads under normal weather conditions.
Turnpike Double: Usually a combination of two 45- to 48-foot trailers. Legal in 18 states, these large combinations are generally found on limited-access Interstates, toll roads, and turnpikes.

National Weight and Size Provisions

U.S. Interstate System/ National Network

Federal law governs (1) the weight of vehicles on the Interstate System, (2) the width of vehicles on the National Network, and (3) the minimum length of some vehicles and the maximum length of others on the National Network. The National Network consists of the Interstate System and designated Federal-aid primary highways.

Title 23 USC, 127 provides the following weight requirements for the Interstate System:

- Axle weight: 20,000 pounds
- Tandem axle weight: 34,000 pounds
- Gross vehicle weight (gvw): 80,000 pounds
- Compliance with the Federal bridge formula

Title 49 USC, 31111 and 31112 provides the following truck length requirements on National Network routes.

Semitrailers:

States shall not impose a length limit of less than 48 feet or the grandfathered length (see chart) on a semitrailer operating in a tractor-semitrailer combination. All states now allow the operation of 53-foot semitrailers on at least some highways.

Twin trailers:

All states must allow the operation of twin trailer (tractor-semitrailer-trailer) combinations where neither trailer exeeds 28 feet in length.

Overall length:

States cannot set overall length limitations on tractor-semitrailer or tractor-semitrailer-trailer combinations regardless of the length of the semitrailers or trailers.

ISTEA freeze:

ISTEA froze the cargo-carrying length of commercial motor vehicles with two or more cargo-carrying units to whatever limit was in effect in a state on June 1, 1991. See the LCV chart on page A13.

Title 49 USC, 31113 provides a maximum width limit of 102 inches on National Network routes. Regulations in Title 23 CFR have interpreted this to be the same as the approximate metric equivalent of 2.6 meters, or 102.36 inches.

The Transportation Equity Act enacted in 1998 made no changes to the basic Federal laws governing the Interstate System weight limits, National Network size limits, or the freeze on the size of long combination and other multi-cargo carrying unit commerical vehicles.

The Weight/Size Limit table shows the size limits on the National Network and weight limits on the Interstate System. The weight limits may be higher than those shown in some instances because the Federal grandfather clause in Title 23 USC, 127 allows higher weight limits in some states.

Legal weight/size limits for interstate routes

	LEGAL SIZE LIMITS FOR INTERSTATE AND DESIGNATED ROUTES					LEGAL WEIGHT LIMITS FOR INTERSTATE ROUTES AND ACCESS THERETO		
State	Width	Height	Semitrailer in Tractor-semitrailer combo	Full Trailer	Doubles*	Single Axle (lbs.)	Tandem Axle (lbs.)	Gross Vehicle Weight (lbs.)
Alabama	102" ●	13'6"	57'	28'6"	Not specified ○	20,000	34,000	80,000
Alaska	102"	15'0"	53'	53'	Not specified ○○	20,000	38,000	Not applicable
Arizona	102"	14'0"	57'6"	28'6"	Not specified ○	20,000	34,000	80,000
Arkansas	102"	13'6"	53'6"	28' ✻	Not specified ○○○	20,000	34,000	80,000
California	102"	14'0"	53' ■	Not specified	Not specified ○	20,000	34,000	80,000
Colorado	102"	14'6" ✧	57'4" ■■	57'4" ✻✻	Not specified ○	20,000	36,000	80,000
Connecticut	102" ●●	13'6"	53' ■■■	28'	Not specified ★	22,400 ~	36,000 ☆	80,000 ◗
Delaware	102"	13'6"	53'	Not specified	Not specified ★★	20,000	34,000	80,000
Dist. of Columbia	102"	13'6"	53' □	28'	Not specified ★	20,000 ~~	34,000 ~~	80,000
Florida	102"	13'6"	57' □□□	28'	Not specified ★	22,000 ~~~	44,000 ~~~	80,000 ~~~
Georgia	102"	13'6"	53'	28'	Not specified ★	20,340	34,000 ✪✪✪	80,000
Hawaii	108"	14'0"	48'	65'	65'	22,500	34,000	80,000
Idaho	102"	14'0"	53'	53'	Not specified ★★★	20,000	34,000 ☆☆	80,000 ●●●●
Illinois	102"	13'6"	53'	28'6"	Not specified ○	20,000	34,000	80,000
Indiana	102"	13'6"	53'	28'6"	Not specified ○	20,000	34,000	80,000 ◗◗
Iowa	102"	13'6"	53'	28'6" ○	Not specified ○	20,000	34,000	80,000
Kansas	102"	14'0"	59'6"	28'6"	Not specified ○	20,000	34,000	80,000
Kentucky	102"	13'6"	53'	28'	Not specified ★	20,000	34,000	80,000 ◗◗✖
Louisiana	102"	14'0"	59'6"	30'	Not specified ✪	20,000	34,000 ▭	80,000 ◗◗
Maine	102"	13'6" ◆	48' □□	48'	Not specified ○	20,000 I	34,000 ❖	80,000
Maryland	102"	13'6"	48' +	28'	Not specified ★	20,000 III	34,000 ▭▭	80,000 ✖✖
Massachusetts	102"	13'6"	53'	28'	Not specified ★	22,400	34,000	80,000
Michigan	102"	13'6"	53' ++	28'6"	Not specified ✪✪	20,000	34,000	80,000
Minnesota	102"	13'6"	53' +++	45'	Not specified ○	20,000	34,000	80,000
Mississippi	102"	13'6"	53'	30'	Not specified ✪	20,000	34,000	80,000
Missouri	102"	14'0"	53'	Not specified	Not specified IIIII	20,000	34,000	80,000
Montana	102"	14'0"	53'	28'6"	Not specified ○	20,000	34,000	80,000
Nebraska	102"	14'6"	53'	40'	65'	20,000	34,000	80,000
Nevada	102"	14'0"	53'	28'6"	70'	20,000	34,000	80,000
New Hampshire	102"	13'6"	53' □	48'	Not specified ★	20,000 II	34,000 II✚	80,000
New Jersey	102"	13'6"	53'	28'	Not specified ★	22,400	34,000	80,000
New Mexico	102"	14'0"	57'6"	28'6"	Not specified ○	21,600	34,320	86,400
New York	102"	13'6"	53' ▼	28'6"	Not specified ○	22,400	36,000	80,000
North Carolina	102"	13'6"	53'	28'	Not specified IIII	20,000	38,000	80,000 ◗
North Dakota	102"	14'0"	53'	53'	110'	20,000	34,000	80,000
Ohio	102"	13'6"	53'	28'6"	Not specified ○	20,000	34,000	80,000
Oklahoma	102"	13'6"	59'6"	29'	Not specified ★★	20,000	34,000	80,000
Oregon	102"	14'0"	53'	40'	Not specified ▽	20,000	34,000	80,000 ❖❖
Pennsylvania	102"	13'6"	53'	Not specified	Not specified ○	20,000	34,000 ✚✚	80,000
Rhode Island	102"	13'6"	53' □	53'	Not specified ○	22,400	44,000	80,000 ◗
South Carolina	102"	13'6"	53' ▼▼	28'6"	Not specified ○	20,000	35,200	80,000 ◗◗
South Dakota	102"	14'0"	53'	Not specified	81'6" ▽▽	20,000 ▬	34,000 ▬	80,000
Tennessee	102"	13'6"	50' ▼▼▼	48'	Not specified ○	20,000	34,000	80,000
Texas	102"	14'0"	59'	59'	Not specified ○	20,000	34,000	80,000
Utah	102"	14'0"	53'	48'	Not specified ◇	20,000	34,000	80,000 ◗◗◗
Vermont	102"	13'6"	53'	28'	Not specified ★	22,400	36,000	80,000 ◗
Virginia	102"	13'6"	53' □	28'6"	Not specified ○	20,000	34,000	80,000 ◗◗
Washington	102"	14'0"	53' #	53'	61' ◇◇	20,000	34,000	105,500 ◗◗
West Virginia	102"	13'6"	53' ##	28'	Not specified ★	20,000	34,000	80,000
Wisconsin	102"	13'6"	53' ▼	48'	Not specified ○	20,000	34,000	80,000
Wyoming	102"	14'0"	60'	40'	81' ◇◇◇	20,000	36,000	117,000 ✖✖✖

Compiled from data supplied by each state in November, 2017

- * "Doubles" are a tractor-semitrailer-full trailer combination
- ● 102" wide vehicles permitted on highways with lane widths of 12' or greater
- ●● Metric equivalent 102.36"
- + Semitrailers exceeding 48' in length up to a length not to exceed 53' operated in combination with a truck-tractor are allowed only on Interstate routes and Maryland State Highways that are part of the National Network. Call 410-582-5734 for access provisions. Regulations for these vehicles: kingpin setback measured as the distance from the kingpin to the front of the semi-trailer may not exceed 4'; may not have more than 41' spacing from the kingpin to the center of the rear tandem and cannot have more than 35% of that distance as overhang measured from the center of the rear tandem to the end of the semi-trailer.
- ++ Trailers over 50' require no more than 40'6" spacing, plus or minus 6", as measured from kingpin to center of reamost axle when equipped with rear tandem (2) axle
- +++ Trailers of 48'1" to 53' require no more than 43' from kingpin to center of rear axle group
- ✧ Height limit of 13'0" for all roads that are not designated routes
- ◆ Height plus 6" of load, for a total of 14'0"
- ■ All trailers over 48' up to and including 53' trailers require no more than 40' spacing from kingpin to center of rear axle
- ■■ No overall length limit for tractor-semitrailer combination with a single trailer length of 57'4" or less. 75' overall length limit applies to specialized haulers including boat and auto transporters.
- ■■■ Semitrailers greater than 48' and less than or equal to 53' require a distance of not more than 43' from kingpin to center of rearmost axle with tires in contact with roadway. Trailers of 48' or less: no kingpin axle requirements
- ✻ 28'6" for trailers with 1982 or older year model operating on 12/1/82
- ✻✻ No overall length specified for tractor and full 57'4" trailer
- ★ Overall length of trailers is not specified but trailers are limited to 28' each
- ★★ Length of doubles not specified but trailers are limited to 29' each
- ★★★ Overall length is 68' for the trailing units including space between
- IIII Length of doubles not specified but trailers are limited to 28' each; 28'6" for trailers with 1982 or older year model
- IIIII Length of doubles not specified but trailers are limited to 28' each; 28'6" for trailers with 1982 or older year model—these combinations are restricted to a 65' overall length
- ▽ (1) 75' overall on Group 1 highways; first trailer in combination not to exceed 40'. (2) No overall length limit on Group 1 highways if the measurement from the front of the first trailer to the rear of the second trailer does not exceed 60' (including distance between trailers). (3) If distance from the front of the first trailer to the rear of the second trailer exceeds 60' (up to a maximum of 68') and overall length exceeds 75', see Route Map 7 for designated routes that allow no limit in overall length
- ▽▽ Maximum length of either trailer may not exceed 45'
- ✪ Length of doubles not specified but trailers are limited to 30' each
- ✪✪ Length of doubles not specified providing each trailer does not exceed 28'6"; or the overall length is 58' for the trailing units including space between when coupled together
- ▼ Trailers of 48' to 53' require no more than 43' spacing from kingpin to center of rear axle
- ▼▼ Trailers over 50' require no more than 40'6" spacing, plus or minus 6", as measured from kingpin to center of rearmost axle
- ▼▼▼ Measured from kingpin to end of trailer or load. If trailer length exceeds 48' the distance from the kingpin to the center of the rear axle or group limited to 41'. 48' or shorter trailers: no kingpin requirements
- ◇ Overall length is 61' for the combined trailer units including space between
- ◇◇ Trailers from 61' to 68' require a permit
- ◇◇◇ Length of doubles not specified but combined length of trailers not to exceed 81'. Heavier trailer must be first unit behind the tractor if there is a weight difference exceeding 5,000 lb.
- # Trailers from 53' to 56' require a permit
- ## Trailers from 48' to 53' require no more than 37' spacing from last axle of tractor to first axle of semitrailer
- ○ Length of doubles not specified but trailers are limited to 28'6" each
- ○○ Length limited to 95' from front of first trailer to rear of second trailer
- ○○○ Tractor cannot exceed 40'. Trailers cannot exceed 28' apiece unless manufactured and in use prior to Dec. 2, 1982–these trailers may be 28'6" in length
- □ Trailers of 48' to 53' require no more than 41' spacing from kingpin to center of rear axle group
- □□ 53' trailers may operate on designated routes. Trailers of 48'1" to 53' require no more than 43' from kingpin to center of rear axle group
- □□□ Trailers of 48' to 57' require no more than 41' spacing from kingpin to center of rear axle group

- ~ Axles spaced greater than 6' apart
- ~~ If gross vehicle weight exceeds 73,000 lb.
- ~~~ Weight on tires shall not exceed maximum allowed by manufacturer
- I If gross vehicle weight exceeds 73,280 lbs., otherwise 22,000 lbs.
- II If gross vehicle weight exceeds 73,280 lbs.
- III Vehicles registered 73,000 lbs. or less, single axle weight is 22,400 lbs. Vehicles registered for more than 73,000 lbs., single axle weight is 20,000 lbs. Weight on tires shall not exceed maximum allowed by manufacturer.
- ✚ Per axle on axles not more than 8' apart; 20,000 lbs. per axle on axles more than 8' apart
- ✚✚ If gross vehicle weight and registered gross weight both exceed 73,280 lbs.
- ❖ Two consecutive sets of tandem axles may carry a gross load of 34,000 lbs. each if the overall distance between first and last axle is 36' or more
- ❖❖ Two consecutive sets of tandem axles may carry a gross load of 34,000 lbs. each if the overall distance between the first and last axle is 36' or more. An Interstate Weight Permit is available that allows 34,000 lbs. on each tandem axle if the overall length between tandems is 30' or more. Call (503) 373-0000
- ▭ Two consecutive sets of tandem axles must have 40" or more between the first and last axles of the consecutive set
- ▭▭ Two consecutive sets of tandem axles may carry a gross load of 34,000 lbs. each if the overall distance between first and last axle is 36' or more. Weight on tires shall not exceed maximum allowed by manufacturer
- ▬ Single-tired axles (other than steering tires) are limited to 500 lbs. per inch of tire width
- ◗ Must comply with Federal bridge formula and have 51' spacing from center of the first to center of the last axle
- ◗◗ Provided vehicle complies with Federal bridge gross weight formula
- ◗◗◗ Must comply with Utah bridge table B extended and have 51' from first to fifth axle
- ✖ Interstate routes only. Access route limits vary by highway class from 44,000 lbs. to 80,000 lbs.
- ✖✖ Provided vehicle complies with Federal bridge gross weight formula. Weight on tires shall not exceed maximum allowed by manufacturer
- ✖✖✖ Must have enough axles to comply with the Federal bridge formula
- ☆ If axles are less than 6' apart, 18,000 lbs. per axle in tandem axle. If axles are greater than 6' apart, 22,400 lbs. per axle in tandem axle
- ☆☆ 37,800 lbs. when gross weight does not exceed 79,000 lbs. on the interstate with exempt commodities
- ●●●● Permit needed to exceed 80,000 lbs. up to 105,500 lbs.
- ✪✪✪ If gross weight is less than 73,280 lbs. and length is less than 55', then the tandem weight is 40,680 lbs.

North American Federal Weight and Size Limits

Weight and size limits are the legal limits provided in the Federal laws of the United States and Mexico. Canada limits are the limits provided in the extraprovincial agreement adopted by each province. U.S. states and Canadian provinces have the authority to adopt weight and size limits for some highways that may vary from these limits. Be sure to check the laws for those states and provinces in which you plan to drive.

	CANADA[1]		UNITED STATES[2]		MEXICO[3]	
Weight/Mass Limits	Metric (kg)	English (lb.)	Metric (kg)	English (lb.)	Metric (kg)	English (lb.)
Steering axle:	5500	12,125	9070[4]	20,000[4]	6500	14,330
Single drive axle:	9100	20,060	9070	20,000	11,000	24,250
Single trailer axle:	9100	20,060	9070	20,000	10,000	22,045
Tandem drive axle:	17,000	37,480	15,420	34,000	19,500	43,000
Tandem trailer axle:	17,000	37,480	15,420	34,000	18,000	39,685
Tridem axle with various spreads						
8' (2.44 m)+ spread	21,000	46,295	19,050	42,000	22,500	49,605
10' (3.05 m) spread	23,000	50,705	19,730	43,500	22,500	49,605
12' (3.66 m) spread	24,000	52,910	20,410	45,000	22,500	49,605
Gross vehicle weights						
4-axle tractor—semitrailer:	31,600	69,665	29,940	66,000	35,500	78,265
5-axle tractor—semitrailer:	39,500	87,080	36,290	80,000	44,000	97,000
6-axle tractor—semitrailer with tandem at 8' (2.44 m) + tridem spread:	43,500	95,900	(39,915)[5]	(88,000)[5]	48,500	106,920
5-axle double:	39,700	87,520	(39,010)[5]	(86,000)[5]	47,500	104,720
6-axle double:	47,600	104,940	(45,360)[5]	(100,000)[5]	56,000	123,455
7-axle double:	53,500	117,945	(50,350)[5]	(111,000)[5]	60,500	133,375
8-axle double:	53,500	117,945	(54,430)[5]	(120,000)[5]	60,500	133,375
8-axle B-train double:	62,500	137,785	(56,020)[5]	(123,500)[5]	60,500	133,375

	CANADA[1]		UNITED STATES[2]		MEXICO[3]	
Size Limits	Metric (m)	English (ft.)	Metric (m)	English (ft.)	Metric (m)	English (ft.)
Width:	2.6	8.5	2.6	8.5	2.6	8.5
Height:	4.15	13.6	NS[6]	NS[6]	4.15	13.6
Length						
Semitrailer:	16.2	53.15	14.63	48.0[7]	NS	NS
Full trailer (in doubles):	NS	NS	8.53	28.0	NS	NS
B-train trailer:	NS	NS	8.53	28.0	NS	NS
Box length 8 (in B-train):	20.0	65.6	NS[9]	NS[9]	NS	NS
Tractor—semitrailer:	23.0	75.5	NS	NS	20.8	68.24
Tractor—semitrailer—full trailer:	25.0	82.0	NS	NS	28.5	93.5
Tractor & B-train double:	25.0	82.0	NS	NS	31.0	101.7

NS Not specified

1 Limits shown for Canada are from the extraprovincial agreement adopted by each province for its designated highway system. Some provinces have more permissive and some have more restrictive limits for their other highways. If a province has more permissive limits, these limits apply to the designated highways as well

2 The U.S. Federal weight limits apply only to the Interstate System, except when higher state weight limits are grandfathered. The single- and tandem-axle weights for IL, MN, and MO are lower than the Federal limits and only apply to non-Interstate and non-designated highways. For a single axle, eight states —CT, FL, GA, HI, MA, NJ, NM, and RI—and the District of Columbia have grandfathered limits higher than the Federal limit. For tandem axles, eight states—CO, CT, FL, MA, NM, NC, RI, and WY—and the District of Columbia have grandfathered limits higher than the Federal limit. For a single axle off the Interstate System, six states—LA, ME, NH, NY, SC, and VT—have a limit higher than 20,000 pounds. For tandem axles off the Interstate System, ten states—AL, AK, DE, GA, LA, ME, NH, NY, SC, and VT—have a limit higher than 34,000 pounds

3 Weight limits for Mexico apply to its "A" and "B" highway systems. Mexico also has "C" and "D" highway systems which have more restrictive limits

4 States may limit the steering axle to the manufacturer's weight rating if less than 20,000 lbs. (9070 kg)

5 These weights ( ) are illegal in the U.S. on the Interstate System. For comparative purposes, these are weights that would be allowed if the 80,000-lb. gvw limit were removed and the current Federal Bridge Formula applied to typical configurations

6 Not specified at the Federal level. The lowest value enforced by the states, however, is 13.5 feet (4.12 m)

7 This is the minimum length states must allow under Federal law. All states, however, do allow 53' (16.15 m) semitrailers to operate under at least some conditions. A permit may be required for their operation

8 "Box length" and "cargo-carrying length" both are defined as the distance from the front of the first cargo unit to the rear of the last, including the distance between units

9 If each unit is 28' (8.53 m) or less in length, the box length is not specified. If either or both units are over 28.5' (8.69 m) long, box length is controlled by the Longer Combination Vehicle (LCV) "freeze" provisions described in the text

Source: Federal Highway Administration in October, 2017

Multistate overweight/oversize permit specifications

Data is provided in pounds and feet; permitted vehicles may not exceed the weights and sizes listed in this table.

	NETC	NASTO	MULTI-STATE PERMIT AGREEMENT	WRA
Length	90'0"	90'0"	100'0"	110'0"
Width	14'0"	14'0"	14'0"	14'0"
Height	13'6"	13'6"	14'0"	14'0"
Weight (in pounds)				
Single Axle	25,000	25,000	20,000	21,500
Tandem Axles	50,000	50,000	40,000	43,000
Tridem Axles	60,000	60,000	60,000	53,000
Pounds per Inch of Tire Width	600	600		600
Gross Weight (6 axles)	120,000	120,000	120,000	160,000
(5 axles)	108,000	108,000		

Bridge Formula Table

The purpose of the Federal bridge weight formula is to protect bridges on the Interstate System by controlling the number and spacing of truck axles.

Distance in feet between the extremes of any group of 2 or more consecutive axles	Maximum load in pounds carried on any group of 2 or more consecutive axles* 2 axles	3 axles	4 axles	5 axles	6 axles	7 axles	8 axles	9 axles
4	†34,000							
5	†34,000							
6	†34,000							
7	†34,000							
8 and less	†34,000	34,000						
more than 8	38,000	42,000						
9	39,000	42,500						
10	40,000	43,500						
11		44,000						
12		45,000	50,000					
13		45,000	50,500					
14		46,500	51,500					
15		47,000	52,000					
16		48,000	52,500	58,000				
17		48,500	53,500	58,500				
18		49,500	54,000	59,000				
19		50,500	54,500	60,000				
20		51,000	55,500	60,500	66,000			
21		51,500	56,000	61,000	66,500			
22		52,500	56,500	61,500	67,000			
23		53,000	57,500	62,500	68,000			
24		54,000	58,000	63,000	68,500	74,000		
25		54,500	58,500	63,500	69,000	74,500		
26		55,500	59,500	64,000	69,500	75,000		
27		56,000	60,000	65,000	70,000	75,500		
28		57,000	60,500	65,500	71,000	76,500	82,000	
29		57,500	61,500	66,000	71,500	77,000	82,500	
30		58,500	62,000	66,500	72,000	77,500	83,000	
31		59,000	62,500	67,500	72,500	78,000	83,500	
32		60,000	63,500	68,000	73,000	78,500	84,500	90,000
33			64,000	68,500	74,000	79,000	85,000	90,500
34			64,500	69,000	74,500	80,000	85,500	91,000
35			65,500	70,000	75,000	80,500	86,000	91,500
36			‡ 66,000	70,500	75,500	81,000	86,500	92,000
37			‡ 66,500	71,000	76,000	81,500	87,000	93,000
38			‡ 67,500	71,500	77,000	82,000	87,500	93,500
39			68,000	72,500	77,500	82,500	88,500	94,000
40			68,500	73,000	78,000	83,500	89,000	94,500
41			69,500	73,500	78,500	84,000	89,500	95,000
42			70,000	74,000	79,000	84,500	90,000	95,500
43			70,500	75,000	80,000	85,000	90,500	96,000
44			71,500	75,500	80,500	85,500	91,000	96,500
45			72,000	76,000	81,000	86,000	91,500	97,500
46			72,500	76,500	81,500	87,000	92,500	98,000
47			73,500	77,500	82,000	87,500	93,000	98,500
48			74,000	78,000	83,000	88,000	93,500	99,000
49			74,500	78,500	83,500	88,500	94,000	99,500
50			75,500	79,000	84,000	89,000	94,500	100,000
51			76,000	80,000	84,500	89,500	95,000	100,500
52			76,500	80,500	85,000	90,500	95,500	101,000
53			77,500	81,000	86,000	91,000	96,500	102,000
54			78,000	81,500	86,500	91,500	97,000	102,500
55			78,500	82,500	87,000	92,000	97,500	103,000
56			79,500	83,000	87,500	92,500	98,000	103,500
57			80,000	83,500	88,000	93,000	98,500	104,000
58				84,000	89,000	94,000	99,000	104,500
59				85,000	89,500	94,500	99,500	105,000
60				85,500	90,000	95,000	100,500	105,500

Permissible Federal gross loads for vehicles in regular operation is based on weight formula

$$W = 500 \left(\frac{LN}{N-1} + 12N + 36 \right)$$

W = the maximum weight in pounds that can be carried on a group of two or more axles to the nearest 500 pounds

L = spacing in feet between the outer axles of any two or more consecutive axles

N = number of axles being considered

* The permissible loads are computed to the nearest 500 pounds

† Tandem axle by definition

‡ Exception to Bridge Formula Table and Law. See text for explanation

Weights shown in red are over the Federal gvw on the Interstate System

Source: U.S. DOT Federal Highway Administration, *Bridge Formula Weights*, October, 2017

Bridge formula definitions

The following definitions are used in conjunction with the Bridge Formula Table.

Gross Weight:
The weight of a vehicle combination without load plus the weight of any load thereon. (The Federal gross weight limit on the Interstate System and reasonable access thereto is 80,000 pounds.)

Single Axle Weight:
The total weight transmitted to the road by all wheels whose centers may be included between two parallel transverse vertical planes not more than 40 inches apart, extending across the full width of the vehicle. (The Federal single axle weight limit on the Interstate System and reasonable access thereto is 20,000 pounds.)

Tandem Axle Weight:
The total weight transmitted to the road by two or more consecutive axles whose centers may be included between parallel vertical planes spaced more than 40 inches and not more than 96 inches apart, extending across the full length of the vehicle. (The Federal tandem axle weight limit on the Interstate System and reasonable access thereto is 34,000 pounds.)

Consecutive Axle Weight:
The Federal law states that any two or more consecutive axles may not exceed the weight as computed by the formula even though the single axles, tandem axles, and gross weights are within the legal requirements.

State/Provincial Weight and Size Limits

Limits are for state and provincial highway systems. Weight and size limits may vary between the state systems and the National Network System.

UNITED STATES

STATE	STEERING AXLE	SINGLE AXLE	TANDEM AXLE	GROSS VEHICLE WEIGHT	WIDTH	HEIGHT	STRAIGHT TRUCK	SEMITRAILER
Alabama	NS	20,000 lb.	34,000 lb.	80,000 lb.	● (102" on highways with lane widths of 12' or more, 96" on highways with lane widths under 12')	13'6"	40'	57' (on highways with lane widths 12' or greater; semitrailers from 53'6" to 57' cannot exceed 41' from kingpin to center of rear axle)
Alaska	600 lb./inch	20,000 lb. (or 600 lb./inch)	38,000 lb. (or 600 lb./inch)	Determined by formula	102"	15'0" (When operating between the Fox weigh station and Prudhoe Bay on the Dalton and Elliott Highways, vehicle may have a height, including load, of 17')	45'	53'
Arizona	20,000 lb.	20,000 lb.	34,000 lb.	80,000 lb.	102"	14'0"	40'	53'
Arkansas	20,000 lb.	20,000 lb.	34,000 lb.	80,000 lb.	102"	13'6"	40'	53'6"
California	20,000 lb. (or tire mfg. rating, whichever is less)	20,000 lb.	34,000 lb.	80,000 lb.	102"	14'0"	40'	● (Unlimited; 38' maximum from kingpin to center of rear axle on single axle trailers; 40' maximum from kingpin to center of rear axle on 2 or more axle trailers)
Colorado	20,000 lb.	20,000 lb.	40,000 lb.	85,000 lb.	102"	13'0" (14'6" on state designated highways only)	45'	57'4"
Connecticut	NS	22,400 lb.	36,000 lb. (If axles are less than 6' apart, 18,000 lb. per axle; if axles are greater than 6' apart, 22,400 lb. per axle)	80,000 lb. (5-axle unit with 51' spacing between first and fifth axle)	102"	13'6"	45'	48'
Delaware	NS	22,400 lb.	40,000 lb.	80,000 lb.	102"	13'6"	40'	53'
District of Columbia	NS	20,000 lb.	34,000 lb. (34,000 lb. if GVW over 73, 000 lb.; 37,000 lb. if GVW under 73,000 lb.)	79,000 lb.	96"	13'6"	40'	48' (maximum spacing of 41' from kingpin to center at rear axle assembly)
Florida	NS	22,000 lb.	44,000 lb.	80,000 lb.	102" (96" on lanes less than 12')	13'6"	40'	● (48' (no bridge requirements); semitrailers from 48' to 57' cannot exceed 41' from kingpin to center of rear axle or rear group of axles, underride protection in rear of trailer)
Georgia	NS	20,340 lb.	37,340 lb. (Legal tandem weight on tractor semi-trailer combinations is 40,680 lb.)	80,000 lb.	102" (102" on roads with 12' or wider lane widths)	13'6"	ND	53'
Hawaii	22,500 lb.	22,500 lb.	34,000 lb.	88,000 lb.	108"	14'0"	45'	48'
Idaho	20,000 lb.	20,000 lb.	37,800 lb. (when not over 80,000 lb.)	105,500 lb.	102"	14'0"	45'	48' (53' on Interstate and many non-Interstate highways)
Illinois	20,000 lb.	20,000 lb.	34,000 lb.	80,000 lb.	102"	13'6"	42'	53' (trailers longer than 48' must not exceed 42'6" from kingpin to rear axle)
Indiana	12,000 lb.	20,000 lb.	34,000 lb.	80,000 lb. (800 lb./inch of tire, as measured between the flanges of the rim)	102"	13'6"	40'	53' (Limit of 43' from kingpin to center of rear axle on 53' trailers)
Iowa	20,000 lb.	20,000 lb.	34,000 lb.	80,000 lb. (exception for livestock and construction vehicles. See Iowa DOT Max. Gross Weight Table 2 (Non-Interstate Highways))	102"	13'6"	45'	● (53' (single), 28'6" (doubles))
Kansas	20,000 lb.	20,000 lb.	34,000 lb.	85,500 lb.	102"	14'0"	45'	59'6"
Kentucky	700 lb. (per inch of width for all tires)	20,000 lb.	34,000 lb.	80,000 lb.	102" (15 miles from all Interstate and parkway exits)	13'6"	45'	53'
Louisiana	12,000 lb.	22,000 lb.	37,000 lb.	80,000 lb. (5-axle combination)	96"	13'6"	45'	59'6"
Maine	NS	22,400 lb.	38,000 lb.	80,000 lb. (or 100,000 lb. with 6 axles)	102"	● (13'6" vehicle 14'0" load)	45'	48' (distance from center of rear axle of the tractor and center of the rear axle of the trailer must not exceed 38'; 53' semitrailers with kingpin to center of rearmost trailer axle not exceeding 43' may operate on designated routes only)
Maryland	● (tire manufacturer rating)	20,000 lb. (Vehicles registered 73,000 lb. or less, single axle weight is 22,400 lb. Vehicles registered over 73,000 lb., single axle weight is 20,000 lb. formula)	34,000 lb. (1,000 lb. tolerance allowed on US and State Routes only. No tolerance given on Interstate Highways.)	80,000 lb. (by bridge formula)	102" (Unless prohibited by posted signs. Vehicles/combinations exceeding 96" wide are prohibited from traveling on I-895.)	13'6"	40' (including overhang)	48' (Call 410-582-5734 for access provisions for semi-trailers in excess of 48'; see pages A12 & A14 for additional information.)
Massachusetts	NS	22,400 lb.	34,000 lb.	80,000 lb.	102"	13'6"	40'	53'
Michigan	700 psi	20,000 lb.	34,000 lb.	80,000 lb.	96" (102" on designated highways)	13'6"	40'	50' (53' permitted on designated routes; Semitrailers longer than 50 feet shall have a wheelbase of 37 feet to 41 feet (measured from the kingpin coupling to the center of the axles or to the center of the tandem axle assembly if equipped with 2 axles).)
Minnesota	600 lb./inch (of tire width)	20,000 lb.	34,000 lb. (w/min. spacing of 40")	80,000 lb. (Any vehicle combination with 5 or more axles with minimum spacing)	102"	13'6"	45' (including overhang)	53' (including overhang; trailers from 48' to 53' require no more than 43' from kingpin to center of rear axle group)
Mississippi	12,000 lb.	20,000 lb.	34,000 lb.	80,000 lb.	102"	13'6"	40'	53'
Missouri	22,000 lb. (or tire mfg. rating, whichever is less)	22,000 lb.	36,000 lb. (w/min. spacing of 40")	80,000 lb. (by bridge formula)	102" (when less than 10 mi. from interstate or designated highway; otherwise 96")	13'6" (when more than 10 mi. from interstate or designated highway; otherwise 14'0")	45'	53'
Montana	● (should not exceed tire mfg. rating)	20,000 lb.	34,000 lb.	80,000 lb.	102"	14'0"	55'	53'
Nebraska	NS	20,000 lb.	34,000 lb.	95,000 lb. (refer to bridge chart)	102"	14'6"	40'	53'
Nevada	600 lb./inch (of tire width)	20,000 lb.	34,000 lb.	80,000 lb.	102"	14'0"	70'	53'
New Hampshire	NS	22,400 lb.	36,000 lb.	80,000 lb.	102"	13'6"	45'	48' (53' trailers allowed on designated access highways only)
New Jersey	NS	22,400 lb.	34,000 lb.	80,000 lb.	96" (102" on designated highways)	13'6"	40'	48' (53' trailers allowed on designated access highways only)
New Mexico	NS	21,600 lb.	34,320 lb.	86,400 lb. (doubles & tractor- semi-trailer combinations)	102"	14'0"	40'	48'
New York	22,400 lb.	22,400 lb.	36,000 lb.	80,000 lb.	96" (102" on designated truck access highways and highways outside NYC with 10' or more lane widths.)	13'6"	40'	48' (53' trailers allowed on designated access highways only)
North Carolina	NS	20,000 lb.	38,000 lb.	80,000 lb. (must comply with bridge formula and have 51' outside bridge (first to last axle) to gross 80,000 lb.)	102"	13'6"	40'	53'
North Dakota	550 lb./inch (of tire width)	20,000 lb.	34,000 lb.	105,500 lb. (on state highways unless posted; 80,000 lb. on county and local roads)	102"	14'0"	50'	53'
Ohio	650 lb./inch (of tire width)	20,000 lb.	34,000 lb.	80,000 lb.	102"	13'6"	50'	53'
Oklahoma	20,000 lb.	20,000 lb.	34,000 lb.	90,000 lb. (5-axle unit)	102"	13'6"	45'	53'
Oregon	600 lb./inch (of tire width up to 20,000 lb.)	20,000 lb.	34,000 lb.	80,000 lb.	102"	14'0"	40'	53'
Pennsylvania	20,000 lb.	20,000 lb.	34,000 lb.	80,000 lb.	96" (102" on designated highways)	13'6"	40'	53'
Rhode Island	NS	22,400 lb.	44,000 lb.	80,000 lb. (5-axle unit with 51' spacing between 1st and 5th axle)	102"	13'6"	40'	53' (on Interstates and on non-Interstate routes with prior approval. Call (401) 588-3020, ext. 2034)
South Carolina	NS	22,000 lb.	39,600 lb.	80,608 lb.	102"	13'6"	40'	53'
South Dakota	600 lb./inch (of tire width)	20,000 lb. (single-tired axle is limited to 500 lb./inch of tire width)	34,000 lb.	80,000 lb. (on Interstate system. Primary highway weights governed by bridge formula and number of axles)	102"	14'0"	45'	53'
Tennessee	20,000 lb.	20,000 lb.	34,000 lb.	80,000 lb.	102"	13'6"	45'	50' (trailers measuring 48' to 50' from kingpin to rear of trailer require a distance of 41' or less from kingpin to center of rear axle group)
Texas	● (tire manufacturer rating)	20,000 lb.	34,000 lb.	80,000 lb.	102"	14'0"	45'	59'
Utah	● (tire manufacturer rating)	20,000 lb.	34,000 lb.	80,000 lb.	102"	14'0"	45'	48'
Vermont	600 lb./inch (of tire width)	22,400 lb.	36,000 lb.	80,000 lb.	102"	13'6"	46'	53' (trailers require no more than 41' from kingpin to center of rear axle group)
Virginia	650 lb./inch	20,000 lb.	34,000 lb.	80,000 lb. (with 51' of total axle spacing)	102"	13'6"	40'	53' (Trailers of 48' to 53' require no more than 41' spacing from kingpin to center of rear axle group)
Washington	● (600 lb./inch of tire width; all other tires are limited to 500lb./inch of tire width)	20,000 lb.	34,000 lb.	105,500 lb. (refer to Federal formula B)	102"	14'0"	40'	53' (trailers from 53' to 56' require a permit)
West Virginia	20,000 lb.	20,000 lb.	34,000 lb.	80,000 lb.	102"	13'6"	40'	● (53' with distance between rear tractor axle and front trailer axle not exceeding 37')
Wisconsin	13,000 lb. (Class B Highway: 12,000 lb.)	20,000 lb. (Class B Highway: 12,000 lb.)	34,000 lb. (Class B Highway: 20,400 lb.)	80,000 lb. (Class B Highway: 48,000 lb.)	102"	13'6"	45'	48'/53' (trailers require no more than 41' from kingpin to rearmost axle)
Wyoming	20,000 lb.	20,000 lb.	36,000 lb.	● (by bridge formula, table 1)	102"	14'0"	60'	● (60' in tractor-trailer combination; 48' for first trailer in doubles combination)

CANADA

PROVINCE	STEERING AXLE	SINGLE AXLE	TANDEM AXLE	TRIDEM	GVW	WIDTH	HEIGHT
Alberta	6,000 kg	9,100 kg	17,000 kg	● (21,000 kg to 24,000 kg depending on spread)	63,500 kg (A-train, 53,500 kg; B-train, 63,500 kg; C-train, 60,500 kg; Jeep logger, 56,500 kg Any other vehicle/vehicle combo, 53,500 kg)	2.6 m	4.15 m
British Columbia	6,000 kg	9,100 kg	17,000 kg	24,000 kg	63,500 kg for 8 axle unit	2.6 m	4.15 m
Manitoba							
Provincial (RTAC)	● (6,000 kg on tractors; 7,300 kg on straight trucks)	9,100 kg	17,000 kg (minimum 1.0 m to 1.85 m axle spread)	● (21,000 kg with 2.4 m to less than 3.0 m axle spread; 23,000 kg with 3.0 m to less than 3.6 m axle spread; 24,000 kg with 3.6 m to 3.7 m)	62,500 kg for 8 axle unit	2.6 m	4.15 m
A-1	● (6,000 kg on tractors; 7,300 kg on straight trucks)	9,100 kg	16,000 kg (minimum 1.0 m to 1.85 m axle spread)	● (21,000 kg with 2.4 m to less than 3.0 m axle spread; 23,000 kg with 3.0 m to 3.7 m axle spread)	56,500 kg for 8 axle unit	2.6 m	4.15 m
B-1	6,000 kg	8,200 kg	14,500 kg (minimum 1.0 m to 1.85 m axle spread)	20,000 kg	47,630 kg for 8 axle unit	2.6 m	4.15 m
New Brunswick	5,500 kg	9,100 kg	18,000 kg	● (18,000 kg to 26,000 kg depending on spread and type of vehicle)	● (GVW based on number of axles and spread)	2.6 m	4.15 m
Newfoundland and Labrador	● (5,500 kg; depends on tire width)	9,100 kg	18,000 kg	26,000 kg	49,500 kg	2.6 m	4.15 m
Northwest Territories	● (gross allowable weight rating)	9,100 kg (6,000 kg on super single axle)	17,000 kg	● (21,000 kg to 24,000 kg depending on spread)	● (39,500 kg to 63,500 kg depending on number of axles and configurations)	2.6 m (width of 2.6m-3.2m need lights and flags; width of greater than 3.2m need permit)	4.2 m
Nova Scotia	5,500 kg	9,100 kg	18,000 kg	26,000 kg	● (41,000 kg to 62,500 kg depending on number of axles and configurations)	2.6 m	4.15 m
Ontario	● (5,000 kg to 9,000 kg; depends on tire width, axle rating and vehicle configuration. SPIF tractor/trailers limited to 7700kg max)	● (9,000 kg with single tires; 10,000 kg with dual tires also depends on SPIF vs. non-SPIF, axle rating and tire size)	● (depends on spread and configuration)	● (depends on spread and configuration)	● (depends on spread and configuration)	2.6 m	4.15 m
Prince Edward Island	5,500 kg (a steering axle can be as high as 9,100 kg, but gross vehicle wt. is based on a max. steering axle wt. of 5,500 kg)	9,100 kg (an axle other than steering with single wheels has max. allowable wt. of 6,000 kg)	18,000 kg	● (21,000 kg to 26,000 kg depending on spread and configuration)	62,500 kg	2.6 m	4.15 m
Québec	5,500 kg	● (9,000 kg with single tires; 10,000 kg with dual tires)	18,000 kg	● (21,000 kg to 26,000 kg depending on spread)	● (depends on axle configuration, type of vehicle and time of year)	2.6 m	4.15 m
Saskatchewan	7,250 kg (power units are allowed 5,500 kg)	9,100 kg	17,000 kg	● (21,000 kg to 24,000 kg depending on spread and configuration)	● (depends on spread, configuration, time of year, and route)	2.6 m	4.15 m
Yukon	NS	10,000 kg	19,100 kg	24,000 kg	63,500 kg (for 7 or 8 axle B train, less for other configurations)	2.6 m	4.2 m

Notes: As reported by individual states and provinces, November, 2017

NP Not permitted
NS Not specified
ND Not designated
NL Not legal

U.S.	FULL TRAILER	TRACTOR AND SEMITRAILER	TRACTOR AND SEMI- AND FULL TRAILER	TRACTOR AND TRIPLES	OTHER/SPECIAL
AL	57' (on highways with lane widths 12' or greater)	NS	28'6" plus 28'6" plus tractor length	NP	
AK	53'	75'	95'	● (by specialized seasonal permit only on limited routes)	● (seasonal weight limits vary by district; visit dot.alaska.gov/mscve and Commercial Vehicle Enforcement to see current weight restrictions)
AZ	28'6"	65'	28'6" plus 28'6" plus tractor length	I-15 only	
AR	28'6"	● (tractor cannot exceed 40' and single trailer cannot exceed 53'6")	● (tractor cannot exceed 40'. Trailers cannot exceed 28' apiece unless manufactured and in use prior to Dec. 2 1982–these trailers may be 28'6" in length)	NP	
CA	NS	65'	● (75' if trailers not more than 28'6" each; 65' if either trailer is greater than 28'6")	NP	
CO	28'6"	● (No overall length limit for a combination with a single trailer length of 57'4" or less in length)	● (No overall length limit for a combination of units with trailers 28'6" or less in length)	● (permitted on selected Interstate routes and to access to their terminals)	
CT	NS	NS if trailer is 48' or less	NP	NP	
DE	NS	65'	NS	NP	
DC	28'	NS (if kingpin to center of rear axle assembly is 41' or less)	NP	NP	
FL	28'	68'	NS if trailers are 28' or less*	NP	● (bridge formula for axle weight limits: Distance from #1 to #5 axle (outside bridge) = 51'; 2 or more axles (internal bridge) = Federal formula. * Twin 48' trailers allowed on Florida Turnpike only)
GA	53'	100'	● (Unlimited length if each trailer is 28' or less)	NL	
HI	NS	65'	65'	NP	
ID	48' (53' on Interstate and many non-Interstate highways)	75' (unless otherwise specified)	● (68' of trailers allowed on National Network roads. 61' of trailers, or 75' overall, allowed on non-National Network roads)	● (allowed on Interstate and state-designated routes with Extra-Length permit)	NS (seasonal weight limits on non-designated routes are variable–approx. Feb to May. Information on highways under Frost Law available by calling (208) 334-8420, or 511.idaho.gov)
IL	● (53' (single), 28'6" (doubles))	● (65' overall length (bumper to bumper) and/or 55' from center of front axle to center of rear axle)	60' (overall on Class III and non-designated highways)	NP	
IN	53'	60' (no overall length if trailer is 53' or less)	NS (if each trailer is 28'6" or less, or 65' for 3-vehicle combination)	● (allowed only on Indiana Toll Road and within 15 miles of makeup/breakup lot)	
IA	● (53' (single), 28'6" (doubles))	● (no overall length if trailer is 53' or less)	28'6" each trailer	NP	● (auto transporters are allowed 65' plus overhang not exceeding 3' in front and 4' in rear)
KS	NS	no limit	28'6" each trailer	● (allowed on designated routes only)	Truck and trailer: 65'
KY	NP	65' (on non-designated highways)	● (allowed on designated routes only)	NP	
LA	30'	65'	● (allowed on designated routes only)	NP	
ME	48' (distance from center of rear axle of the tractor and center of the rear axle of the trailer must not exceed 38')	65' (48' trailer: 69'; 53' trailer: 74')	● (NP on state roads unless on designated Maine system except for reasonable access. Call DOT (207) 624-3620 for information)	NP	Seasonal weight limits apply, Feb. 1-June 1
MD	28' each	NS (except semitrailer length restricted to 48' on nondesignated routes)	● (Combination must travel on Interstate and designated Maryland state highway routes. A semitrailer or trailer being operated in this combination may not exceed 28' in length for each unit.)	NP	● (Cargo carrying power units combination restricted to 62'. This combination allowed on all highways unless prohibited by posted signs (Note width restriction for I-895). Other combinations which include 65' auto/boat transporters, 75' stingers, and 97' saddlemounts must travel Interstate and designated highways. See pages A12-A14.)
MA	33'	NS	NS (Overall length of trailers is not specified but trailers are limited to 28' each)	NP	
MI	28'6"	● (No overall length restriction as long as semitrailer length does not exceed 50')	59'	NP	Seasonal weight limits apply (frost information: (800) 787-8960)
MN	45' (including overhang)	75' (including overhang)	75' (each trailer not to exceed 28'6")	NL	Seasonal weight limits apply (State Trunk Hwys. are posted if less than 10 ton axle limit. Local roads posted if other than 5 ton axle limit)
MS	30'	NS if trailer is 53' or less	● (maximum 30' for semitrailer and 30' for full trailer in doubles combination)	NP	
MO	NS	60' (when trailer & load do not exceed 53'; 60' overall length when operated more than 10 mi. from interstate, designated, or primary hwy.)	65' (NS when trailer length does not exceed 28' & operated within 10 mi. of Interstate, designated, or primary highway; otherwise, 65' overall length)	NP	● (non-designated defined as primary system segments located more than 10 miles from Interstate and designated routes)
MT	NS	75'	● (allowed if both trailers are 28'6" or combined trailer length of 61')	● (allowed only on Interstate routes with permit)	Seasonal weight limits apply (call (406) 444-0468)
NE	40'	65' (NS if trailer is 53' or less)	65' (NS if semitrailer and full trailer is 65' or less, including any connecting devices)	● (permit required; restricted routes)	Seasonal weight limits apply
NV	NS	70'	70' (including connection devices)	● (allowed on Interstate and designated routes only)	Seasonal weight limits apply
NH	28' or less	NS if trailer is 48' or less	NS (if trailers do not exceed 28' each, allowed only on designated and Interstate routes. Not allowed on non-designated routes except on authorized reasonable access routes.)	NP	Seasonal weight limits apply (RSA 236:3-a, applies to State roads. City or town streets and roads fall under local ordinances when applicable. Please contact the local jurisdiction for seasonal limits.)
NJ	48'	NS if trailer is 48' or less	● (allowed only on Interstate and designated routes)	NP	
NM	48'	65'	● (each trailer not to exceed 28'6" or combined length of 65')	NP	
NY	48'	65'	65' (full and semitrailers in doubles not to exceed 28'6" each)	NP	Seasonal weight limits apply
NC	48'	60' (60' legal on all highways; there is no overall length limitation for a 53' trailer on designated highways)	NP (allowed on designated routes full and semitrailers in doubles not to exceed 28'6" each)	NP (allowed on designated highway. Full and semitrailers in doubles not to exceed 28'6" each.)	● (tractor and full trailer combination not to exceed 60')
ND	53'	75', 95' and 110' on designated hwys. (75' max on non-designated highways)	75', 95' and 110' on designated hwys. (75' max on non-designated highways)	75', 95' and 110' on designated hwys. (75' max on non-designated highways)	Seasonal weight limits apply (tractor and full trailer combination not to exceed 75')
OH	28'6"	NS if trailer is 53' or less	NS if trailer is 28'6" or less	NP (except on Ohio Turnpike)	
OK	29'	NS	NS	● (allowed on Interstate and divided highways with permit only)	
OR	40'	● (60' overall on all Group 1 highways with maximum 53' trailer. No overall length limit on National Network highways with a maximum 53' trailer)	● ((1) 75' overall on Group 1 hwys.; first trailer in combination not to exceed 40'. (2) No overall length limit on Group 1 hwys. if the measurement from the front of the first trailer to the rear of the second trailer does not exceed 60' (including distance between trailers). (3) If distance from the front of the first trailer to the rear of the second trailer exceeds 60' (up to a maximum of 68') and overall length exceeds 75', see Route Map 7 for designated routes that allow no limit in overall length.)	● (allowed on Interstate and state-designated routes by permit only)	● (Route Map 7 can be obtained from the Oregon Department of Transportation or at Ports of Entry)
PA	53'	NS if trailer is 28'6" or less	NS if trailer is 28'6" or less	NP	● (Truckers map can be obtained from the PA Department of Transportation or at Welcome Centers)
RI	28'6"	NS if trailer is 48'6" or less	NS if trailer is 28'6" or less	NP	
SC	53'	NS	NP	NP	
SD	NS	● (controlled by single trailer length)	● (overall length, excluding tractor, may not exceed 81'6". Neither trailer may exceed 45'.)	● (allowed on Interstate and designated highways by permit only)	Seasonal weight limits apply (call DOT at (605) 773-3704)
TN	NS	NS (but trailer may not exceed 50,' or 41' axle group from kingpin to center of rear axle)	NP (allowed if both trailers are 28'6" or less)	NP	Truck and trailer: 75'
TX	NS	NS if trailer is 59' or less	NS if trailer is 28'6" or less	NP	● (any vehicle combination that contains a truck tractor does not have a minimum legal length; any vehicle combination that does not contain a truck tractor is limited to 65' overall length)
UT	48'	NS if trailer is 53' or less	● (two trailers hooked together shall not exceed 61')	● (allowed with permit only. Permit must be obtained prior to beginning operation and takes 2 to 4 weeks)	Truck and trailer: 65'
VT	53' (distance from kingpin to the center of the rear axle group must not exceed 41')	75' (distance from center rearmost axle must not exceed 41')	NP (allowed if both trailers are 28' or less on Interstate highways only)	NP	● (truck tractor & semi-trailer combination 48' to 53' max., 75' no permit required; over 75' permit required) (no fee permit required if between 68' and 75' and operating on US-4 from the NH state line to the s. jct. of VT-100)
VA	NP	NS	NP	NP	
WA	53'	NS if trailer is 53' or less	61' (trailers from 61' to 68' require a permit)	NP	● (truck & trailer: 75', seasonal weight limits apply; postings are available at Ports of Entry)
WV	NS	70'	28' each trailer	NP	
WI	48'/53' (distance from rear-most axle must not exceed 41')	65'/75'	● (allowed only on designated routes)	NP	Truck and full trailers: 65'
WY	40'	NS	NS (but cannot exceed 81' from front of first trailer to rear of second trailer. Heavier trailer must be first if weight differences exceeds 5,000 lb.)	NP	

CAN.	STRAIGHT TRUCK	SEMITRAILER	FULL TRAILER	TWIN TRAILERS	TRACTOR AND SEMITRAILER	A-TRAIN	TRIPLES	OTHER
AB	12.5 m	16.2 m	12.5 m	20 m box length	23 m	26 m	● (LCVs (Rocky Mountain Doubles, Turnpike Doubles and Triples) allowed on designated routes by permit only)	
BC	12.5 m	16.2 m	12.5 m	● (20 m for A, B & C trains)	23 m	27.5 m	NP	● (LCVs (Rocky Mountain Doubles and Turnpike Doubles) allowed on designated routes by permit only)
MB								
	12.5 m	16.2 m box length	12.5 m	● (20 m for B & C trains (box length))	23 m	25 m	● (LCVs (Rocky Mountain Doubles, Turnpike Doubles and Triples) allowed on designated routes by permit only)	
	12.5 m	NS	12.5 m	NS	● (20 m or 23 m if combination conforms to RTAC specifications)	● (23 m or 25 m if combination conforms to RTAC specifications)	NL	● (LCVs not legal)
	12.5 m	NS	12.5 m	NS	● (20 m or 23 m if combination conforms to RTAC specifications)	● (23 m or 25 m if combination conforms to RTAC specifications)	NL	● (LCVs not legal)
NB	12.5 m	16.2 m	12.5 m	● (25 m overall length, 20 m box length)	23 m	25 m (A, B & C trains may operate at 25m overall length on all highways subject to compliance with the GVW limit of highway on which it is operating.)	NP	● (Seasonal weight limits apply; LCVs not legal)
NL	12.5 m	16.2 m	NS (18.5 m for box length of truck–tow bar–trailer configuration)	18.5 m	23 m	25 m	NP	
NT	12.5 m	16.2 m	12.5 m	20 m	25 m	26 m	NP	● (LCV Doubles up to 31 meters allowed on designated routes by permit only. On Enhanced Visibility Highways, vehicles up to 31 meters can travel without an escort. On all other highways, vehicles greater than 29 meters must be followed by an escort.)
NS	12.5 m	16.2 m	12.5 m	20 m	23 m	27.5 m (A, B & C trains)	NP	● (LCV Doubles up to 40 meters allowed on designated routes by permit only (overall length).)
ON	12.5 m	● (16.2 m if compliant with Ont. Regulation 413/05 Vehicle Configuration, 14.65 m if non-compliant)	12.5 m	20 m	23 m	● (B trains 27.5 m, A & C trains 25 m if compliant with Ont. Regulation 413/05, 23 m if non-compliant)	NS	● (LCV Doubles up to 40 meters allowed on designated routes by permit only (overall length).)
PE	12.5 m	16.2 m	12.5 m	20 m	23 m	27.5 m	NP	● (nonconforming permits required for nonconforming combinations)
QC	12.5 m	10 m–16.2 m	12.5 m–14.65 m	25 m (A train box length 18.5 m. B & C trains box length 20 m.)	23 m	25 m (A, B and C trains on designated highways only)	by permit only	● (seasonal weight limits apply)
SK	12.5 m	16.2 m	16.2 m	20 m	23 m	26 m	by permit only	● (seasonal weight limits apply)
YK	12.5 m	16.2 m	12.5 m	● (18.5 m box length for A train; 20 m box length for B & C trains)	23 m	25 m	NP	

State/Provincial Contacts

All carriers must comply with U.S. DOT Title 49 (49 CFR 100-185) in addition to hazmat regulations issued by individual states. In Canada, hazmat haulers must comply with all regulations stipulated in Canada's 1992 Transportation of Dangerous Goods Act.

Many states operate "One-Stop Shops," but the types of permits and documentation available from each differ from state to state. Contact each state to determine what is available at its One-Stop Shop.

Interstate haulers must always obtain federal operating authority (Certificate of Authority) first, then go through the SSRS. For federal operating authority, contact the FMCSA at (800) 832-5660 (www.fmcsa.dot.gov). Intrastate haulers must check with each state to determine whether state-certified operating authority is required.

The Unified Carrier Registration system has been implemented and is now being enforced. Contact information at the state level for this program is provided, when possible, on page A18. The main registration site is www.ucr.in.gov. More details are on page A7.

Vehicle Registration

UNITED STATES

STATE	PHONE	WEBSITE	FAX	IRP PHONE
Alabama	(334) 242-9006	revenue.alabama.gov/motorvehicle/index.html	(334) 242-9073	(334) 242-2999
Alaska	(907) 269-5551; (855) 269-5551 (in Alaska)	doa.alaska.gov/dmv/reg/index.htm	None	Non-participant
Arizona	(602) 255-0072; (800) 251-5866	www.azdot.gov/MVD/VehicleServices/commercial-vehicle-registration	None	(602) 712-6775
Arkansas	(501) 682-4692	www.dfa.arkansas.gov/offices/motorVehicle/Pages/default.aspx	(501) 682-4756	(501) 682-4653
California	(800) 777-0133	www.dmv.ca.gov/portal/dmv/detail/vr/commercial	None	(916) 657-7971
Colorado	(303) 205-5608	www.colorado.gov/pacific/dmv/vehicles	(303) 205-5978	(303) 205-5607
Connecticut	(800) 842-8222 (in CT, excluding Hartford); (860) 263-5700 (Hartford area and outside CT)	www.ct.gov/dmv/	None	(860) 263-5281
Delaware	(302) 744-2701	www.dmv.de.gov/	None	(302) 744-2701
District of Columbia	(202) 737-4404	dmv.dc.gov/service/vehicle-registrations-and-tags	None	(202) 729-7079
Florida	(850) 617-2000	www.flhsmv.gov/html/titlinf.html	None	(850) 617-3711
Georgia	(855) 406-5221	dor.georgia.gov/vehicle-registration	None	(855) 406-5221
Hawaii	(808) 532-7730 (in Honolulu); (808) 270-7363 (on Maui)	hidot.hawaii.gov/highways/safe-communites/motorcycle/motor-vehicle-registration/	(808) 270-7858 (Maui)	Non-participant
Idaho	(208) 334-8611	www.trucking.idaho.gov/registrations.html	(208) 334-2006	(208) 334-8611
Illinois	(800) 252-8980	cyberdriveillinois.com/departments/vehicles/cft/	None	(217) 782-4815
Indiana	(888) 692-6841	www.in.gov/bmv/2334.htm	None	(317) 615-7340
Iowa	(515) 237-3110	www.iowadot.gov/mvd/vehicleregistration/default.htm	(515) 237-3257	(515) 237-3268
Kansas	(785) 296-3621	www.ksrevenue.org/vehicle.html	(785) 296-2383	(785) 296-3621
Kentucky	(502) 564-1257	transportation.ky.gov/motor-vehicle-licensing/Pages/default.aspx	(502) 564-2950	(502) 564-1257
Louisiana	(225) 925-6146	omv.dps.state.la.us/	(225) 925-4984	(877) 905-3854
Maine	(207) 624-9000	www.maine.gov/sos/bmv/registration/	(207) 624-9013	(207) 624-9000 ext. 52135
Maryland	(410) 768-7000	www.mva.maryland.gov/vehicles/registration/	(410) 768-7163	(410) 787-2971
Massachusetts	(857) 368-8000	www.massrmv.com/	None	(857) 368-8120
Michigan	(888) 767-6424	www.michigan.gov/sos/	None	(517) 322-1097
Minnesota	(651) 297-2126	dps.mn.gov/divisions/dvs/Pages/Vehicle-Registration.aspx	(651) 215-0027	(651) 205-4141
Mississippi	(601) 923-7141	www.dor.ms.gov/TagsTitles/Pages/default.aspx	(601) 923-7134	(601) 923-7142
Missouri	(573) 526-3669	dor.mo.gov/motorv/	(573) 751-0916	(573) 751-7100
Montana	(406) 444-3661	dojmt.gov/driving/vehicle-title-and-registration/	(406) 444-0116	(406) 444-2998
Nebraska	(402) 471-3918	www.dmv.nebraska.gov/dvr/mvreg/vehreg.html	(402) 471-3920	(402) 471-4435; (888) 622-1222
Nevada	(775) 684-4830	www.dmvnv.com/nvregreq.htm	(775) 684-4992	(775) 684-4711 ext. 1
New Hampshire	(603) 227-4030	www.nh.gov/safety/divisions/dmv/registration/index.htm	(603) 271-1061	(603) 227-4110
New Jersey	(609) 292-6500; (888) 486-3339 (in NJ)	www.state.nj.us/mvc/Vehicle/index.htm	None	(609) 633-9400
New Mexico	(888) 683-4636	www.mvd.newmexico.gov/Vehicles/Vehicle-Registration/Pages/Home.aspx	None	(505) 827-0392
New York	(518) 457-6512	www.dot.ny.gov/divisions/operating/osss/truck	(518) 457-4637	(518) 473-5834
North Carolina	(919) 715-7000	www.ncdot.org/dmv/vehicle_services/	None	(919) 861-3720; (704) 392-2112
North Dakota	(701) 328-2725	www.dot.nd.gov/divisions/mv/vehicle.htm	(701) 328-1487	(701) 328-2725
Ohio	(614) 752-7800	bmv.ohio.gov/vehicle-registration.aspx	None	(614) 777-8400; (800) 477-0007
Oklahoma	(405) 521-3036	occeweb.com/tr/Trucking.htm	(405) 525-2906	(405) 521-3036
Oregon	(503) 378-6699	www.oregon.gov/ODOT/MCT/Pages/REG.aspx	(503) 378-5765	(503) 378-6643
Pennsylvania	(800) 932-4600	www.dmv.pa.gov/VEHICLE-SERVICES/Pages/Vehicle-Services.aspx	None	(800) 932-4600; (717) 412-5300
Rhode Island	(401) 462-4368	www.dmv.ri.gov/registrations/	(401) 462-5786	(401) 946-0090
South Carolina	(803) 896-5000	scdmvonline.com/	None	(803) 896-3870
South Dakota	(605) 773-3541	dor.sd.gov/Motor_Vehicles/Titling_and_Registration/Titling_Motor_Vehicles.aspx	(605) 773-2550	(605) 773-3314
Tennessee	(615) 741-3101; (888) 871-3171	www.tn.gov/revenue/topic/vehicle-registration	(615) 253-4260	(615) 399-4265; (888) 826-3151
Texas	(888) 368-4689	www.txdmv.gov/motor-carriers	(512) 465-4129	(800) 299-1700
Utah	(801) 297-7780; (800) 368-8824	dmv.utah.gov/register	None	(801) 297-6800; (888) 251-9555 (in UT)
Vermont	(888) 998-3766	dmv.vermont.gov/registrations/drivers	(802) 828-2098	(802) 828-2071
Virginia	(804) 497-7100	www.dmv.state.va.us/	None	(804) 249-5130
Washington	(360) 902-3770	dol.wa.gov/vehicleregistration/commercialvehicles.html	None	(360) 664-1858
West Virginia	(304) 558-3900	www.transportation.wv.gov/DMV/Vehicle-Services/Registrations/Pages/default.aspx	(304) 926-0797	(304) 926-0799
Wisconsin	(608) 266-9900	dot.state.wi.us/business/carriers/index.htm	(608) 267-6886	(608) 266-9900
Wyoming	(307) 777-4375	www.dot.state.wy.us/home/titles_plates_registration.html	(307) 777-4772	(307) 777-4829

CANADA

PROVINCE	PHONE	WEBSITE	FAX	IRP PHONE
Alberta	(403) 297-2920	www.transportation.alberta.ca/520.htm	(403) 297-2917	(403) 297-2920
British Columbia	(800) 663-3051	www.icbc.com/vehicle-registration/buy-vehicle/Pages/Registering-a-vehicle-in-B-C-.aspx	None	(800) 665-4336; (604) 443-4450
Manitoba	(204) 985-7000 (in Winnipeg); (800) 665-2410	mpi.mb.ca/en/Reg-and-Ins/Registration/Pages/reg-overview.aspx	(204) 954-5325	(204) 985-7775 (in Winnipeg); (866) 798-1185
New Brunswick	(888) 762-8600; (506) 684-7901	www.snb.ca/e/1000/1011e.asp	None	(506) 453-2215
Newfoundland and Labrador	(877) 636-6867	www.servicenl.gov.nl.ca/department/branches/divisions/mr.html	None	(877) 636-6867
Northwest Territories	(867) 767-9087	www.dot.gov.nt.ca/DMV/Registration	(867) 669-9094	Non-participant
Nova Scotia	(800) 898-7668; (902) 424-5851	www.novascotia.ca/sns/rmv/default.asp	(902) 424-0720	(902) 450-3933
Nunavut	(867) 975-7840	gov.nu.ca/edt/documents/motor-vehicle-office-listings	(867) 975-7870	Non-participant
Ontario	(800) 267-8097; (416) 326-1234	www.ontario.ca/driving-and-roads/register-vehicle-permit-licence-plate-and-sticker	(416) 235-4414	(416) 235-3923; (866) 587-6770 (in ON)
Prince Edward Island	(902) 368-5271	www.princeedwardisland.ca/en/topic/motor-vehicle-registration	(902) 368-5395	(902) 368-5201; (902) 368-5202
Québec	(514) 873-7620 (Montréal); (418) 643-7620 (Quebec City); (800) 361-7620 (elsewhere)	www.saaq.gouv.qc.ca/en/vehicle_registration/index.php	None	(418) 528-4343 (Quebec City); (800) 837-6030 (rest of QC)
Saskatchewan	(844) 855-2744	www.sgi.sk.ca/	(306) 347-9037	(306) 751-1250
Yukon	(800) 661-0408 ext. 5315 (in YK); (867) 667-5315	www.hpw.gov.yk.ca/mv/mvvehreg.html	(867) 393-6220	Non-participant

UNITED STATES

ST	IRP WEBSITE	IRP FAX	TRIP PERMITS PHONE	TRIP PERMITS WEBSITE	TRIP PERMITS FAX	TRIP PERMITS COMMENTS
AL	revenue.alabama.gov/motorvehicle/IRPIFTA_Efile_FAQ.cfm	(334) 242-9073	(334) 242-2999	www.alabamainteractive.org/dor_tfp/welcome.action	(334) 242-9073	7-day permit issued
AK	Non-participant	Non-participant	(907) 883-4591	doa.alaska.gov/dmv%5Creg%5Cdual.htm	None	May be obtained at the Tok weigh station
AZ	azdot.gov/mvd/MotorCarrierServices/InternationalRegistrationPlan	(602) 712-3284	(602) 771-2960	azdot.gov/mvd/MotorCarrierServices/commercial-permits	(602) 272-1887	96-hour permits issued
AR	trucking.arkansas.gov/	(501) 683-0693	(501) 682-4653	trucking.arkansas.gov/	None	72-hour permits issued
CA	www.dmv.ca.gov/portal/dmv/?1dmy&urile=wcm:path:/ dmv_content_en/dmv/vehindustry/irp/irpinfo	(916) 657-6628	(800) 777-0133	www.dmv.ca.gov/portal/dmv/?1dmy&urile=wcm:path:/ dmv_content_en/dmv/pubs/brochures/fast_facts/ffvr36	None	4-day permits issued
CO	www.colorado.gov/pacific/dmv/international-registration-plan	(303) 205-5981	(303) 205-5607	www.colorado.gov/pacific/csp/permits-and-forms	None	72-hour trip permits issued at ports of entry
CT	www.ct.gov/dmv	None	(860) 263-5281	www.ct.gov/dmv/cwp/view.asp?a=802&q=244528	None	72-hour permits issued by permit companies
DE	www.dmv.de.gov/services/TransServ/MC/IRP/index.shtml	(302) 739-6299	(302) 744-2701	www.dmv.de.gov/services/TransServ/MC/IRP/pages/irpForms.shtml	None	Issued by wire services
DC	dmv.dc.gov/node/1119611	(202) 729-7174	(202) 729-7083	dmv.dc.gov/service/trip-permits	(202) 729-7174	6-day permit issued
FL	www.hsmv.state.fl.us/dmv/faqcarriers.html	(850) 617-3931	(850) 617-3711	flhsmv.gov/html/titlinf.html	None	10-day permit issued by wire services
GA	motor.etax.dor.ga.gov/motor/MVDOnline.aspx	None	(855) 406-5221	cvisn.dor.ga.gov/	None	72-hour permits issued
HI	Non-participant	Non-participant	None	None	None	Not required
ID	www.trucking.idaho.gov/registrations.html	(208) 334-2006	(208) 334-8611	www.accessidaho.org/secure/itd/ports/trippermits.html	(208) 334-2006	
IL	cyberdriveillinois.com/departments/vehicles/cft/	(217) 524-0123	(217) 785-1800	cyberdriveillinois.com/departments/vehicles/cft/	None	
IN	www.in.gov/dor/4242.htm	(317) 615-7310	(317) 615-7340	www.in.gov/isp/2504.htm	None	72-hour permits issued
IA	iowadot.gov/mvd/omcs/default.htm	(515) 237-3225	(515) 237-3264	www.iowadot.gov/mvd/motorcarriers/osowpermits_forms.html	(515) 237-3257	72-hour permits issued
KS	www.ksrevenue.org/dmvirp.html	(785)-296-6548	(785) 296-3621	truckingks.org	None	Issued by Central Permits Office
KY	www.dmc.kytc.ky.gov/	(502) 564-2950	(502) 564-1257	transportation.ky.gov/Motor-Carriers/Pages/ International-Registration-Plan.aspx	(502) 564-2950	
LA	www.la-trucks-online.org/	(337) 993-9949	(877) 905-3854	www.la-trucks-online.org/	None	48-hour permits issued by wire service
ME	www.maine.gov/sos/bmv/commercial/irp.html	(207) 624-9086	(207) 624-9000	www.maine.gov/sos/bmv/commercial/irp.html	(207) 624-9086	72-hour permits issued
MD	www.mva.maryland.gov/Vehicle-Services/REG/IRP/default.htm	(410) 768-7163	(410) 787-2971	www.mva.maryland.gov/About-MVA/INFO/27300/27300-65T.htm	(410) 768-7163	72-hour permits issued
MA	www.massrmv.com/Registration/ InternationalRegistrationPlanIRP.aspx	None	(857) 368-8120	www.massrmv.com/rmv/irp/	None	72-hour permits issued
MI	www.michigan.gov/sos/	(517) 322-1058	(517) 322-1097	www.michigan.gov/sos/	(517) 322-1058	72-hour permits issued
MN	dps.mn.gov/divisions/dvs/pages/ dvs-content-detail.aspx?pageID=578	(651) 215-0027	(651) 205-4141	www.dps.state.mn.us/	(651) 215-0027	
MS	www.dor.ms.gov/Business/Pages/International-Registration.aspx	(601) 923-7133	(601) 359-1717	www.dor.ms.gov/Business/Pages/International-Registration.aspx	(601) 359-5928	72-hour permits issued
MO	www.modot.org/mcs/IRP/index.htm	(537) 751-0916	(573) 751-7100	www.modot.org/mcs/	(573) 751-0916	72-hour permits issued
MT	www.mdt.mt.gov/business/mcs/licenses.shtml	(406) 444-0800	(406) 444-6130	www.mdt.mt.gov/business/mcs/licenses.shtml	(406)-444-9263	72-hour permits issued
NE	www.dmv.state.ne.us/mcs/irp.html	(402) 471-4024; (402) 471-3920	(402) 471-4435; (888) 622-1222	www.clickdmv.ne.gov/	(402) 471-4024; (402) 471-3920	72-hour permits issued
NV	www.dmvnv.com/mcoverview.htm	(775) 684-4619	(775) 684-4711	dmvnv.com/mcpermits.htm	None	Issued by wire services
NH	www.nh.gov/safety/divisions/dmv/registration/irp/	(603) 271-8211	(603) 227-4110	www.nh.gov/safety/divisions/administration/roadtoll/ wire_service.html	None	3-day single trip permits issued by wire services
NJ	www.state.nj.us/mvc/Commercial/IRP.htm	(609) 633-9394	(609) 633-9400	www.state.nj.us/mvc/Commercial/IRP.htm	(609) 633-9394	Issued by wire services
NM	www.mvd.newmexico.gov/international-registration-plan-irp.aspx	(505) 476-1571	(505) 827-0392	www.mvd.newmexico.gov/port-of-entry-information.aspx	None	Issued at Ports of Entry
NY	dmv.ny.gov/motor-carriers/international-registration-plan-irp	(518) 486-6579	(518) 473-5834	dmv.ny.gov/motor-carriers/international-registration-plan-irp	(518) 486-6579	72-hour permits issued
NC	www.ncdot.gov/dmv/vehicle/irp/	(919) 733-5300	(919) 861-3720	www.ncdot.gov/dmv/vehicle/irp/	(919) 733-5300	
ND	www.dot.nd.gov/business/motor-carrier.htm	(701) 328-3500	(701) 328-2725	www.nd.gov/ndhp/motor-carrier/e-permits/trip-permit	None	72-hour permits issued
OH	www.bmv.ohio.gov/vr-irp-geninfo.aspx	(614) 771-4016	(614) 777-8400; (800) 477-0007	www.bmv.ohio.gov/vr-irp-72hr.aspx	(614) 771-4016	72-hour permits issued by wire services
OK	occeweb.com/tr/Trucking.htm	(405) 525-2906	(405) 521-3036	www.occeweb.com/tr/TempPermits.htm	(405) 525-2906	72-hour permits issued
OR	www.oregon.gov/ODOT/MCT/Pages/REG.aspx	(503) 378-5765	(503) 378-6699	www.oregon.gov/ODOT/DMV/pages/vehicle/trippermit.aspx	(503) 378-6880	10-day permit issued
PA	www.dmv.pa.gov/VEHICLE-SERVICES/Title-Registration/ Apportioned/Pages/default.aspx	(717) 783-6349	(717) 412-5300; (800) 932-4600	www.dmv.state.pa.us/centers/commercialDriversCenter.shtml	None	Issued by wire service
RI	www.ri.gov/DMV/irp	None	(401) 946-0090	www.ri.gov/DMV/irp	None	
SC	scdmvonline.com/DMVNew/ default.aspx?n=international_registration_plan	(803) 896-3871; (803) 896-2698	(803) 896-3870	scdmvonline.com/	None	Issued by wire service
SD	dor.sd.gov/Motor_Vehicles/Trucking_Industry/ International_Registration_Plan.aspx	(605) 773-8416	(605) 698-3925	dor.sd.gov/Motor_Vehicles/Trucking_Industry/ International_Registration_Plan.aspx	None	
TN	www.tn.gov/revenue/article/international-registration-plan	(615) 361-5924	(615) 399-4265; (888) 826-3151	www.tn.gov/revenue/article/international-registration-plan	(615) 361-5924	Issued by wire services; obtain permit prior to entry
TX	www.txdmv.gov/motor-carriers/commercial-fleet-registration/ apportioned-registration	(512) 465-4273	(800) 299-1700	www.txdmv.gov/motorists/register-your-vehicle/ temporary-permits	None	72- and 144-hour permits issued
UT	motorcarrier.utah.gov	(801) 297-6899	(801) 965-4892	motorcarrier.utah.gov/	None	
VT	dmv.vermont.gov/commercial_trucking/IRP	(802) 828-3577	(802) 828-2070	dmv.vermont.gov/commercial_trucking/online_permits	None	72-hour permits issued
VA	dmv.state.va.us/commercial/#mcs/programs/irp/	(804) 367-1073	(804) 249-5130	www.dmv.virginia.gov/commercial/#mcs/programs/ trip_permits/index.asp	(804) 367-1073	10-day permits issued
WA	dol.wa.gov/vehicleregistration/prorate.html	(360) 570-7829	(360) 704-6340	dol.wa.gov/vehicleregistration/commercialpermits.html	(360) 704-6350	3-day permits issued
WV	www.transportation.wv.gov/DMV/Motor-Carriers/Pages/ IRP-IFTA.aspx	(304) 926-0797	(304) 926-0799	www.transportation.wv.gov/DMV/Motor-Carriers/Pages/ Trip-Permits.aspx	(304) 926-0797	10-day permits issued
WI	www.dot.state.wi.us/business/carriers/irp.htm	(608) 267-6886	(608) 266-9900	wisconsindot.gov/Pages/dmv/com-drv-vehs/mtr-car-trkr/ trip-permits.aspx	(608) 267-6886	72-hour permits issued
WY	www.dot.state.wy.us/home/trucking_commercial_vehicles/irp.html	(307) 777-4772	(307) 777-4829	www.dot.state.wy.us/home/trucking_commercial_vehicles/ commercial_permits/trip_permits.html	(307) 777-4772	Issued at Ports of Entry.

CANADA

PR	IRP WEBSITE	IRP FAX	TRIP PERMITS PHONE	TRIP PERMITS WEBSITE	TRIP PERMITS FAX	TRIP PERMITS COMMENTS
AB	finance.alberta.ca/publications/tax_rebates/irp/overview.html	(403) 297-2917	(403) 297-2920	www.transportation.alberta.ca/561.htm	(403) 297-2917	
BC	www.th.gov.bc.ca/cvse/commercial_transport.htm	(604) 443-4451	(800) 559-9688	www.cvse.ca/permit_centre.htm	(250) 784-2426	
MB	mpi.mb.ca/en/Reg-and-Ins/Registration/Commercial/ Pages/IRP-eligible.aspx	(204) 953-4998(Win.); (866) 798-1186	(204) 985-7775 (in Winnipeg); (866) 798-1185	mpi.mb.ca/en/Reg-and-Ins/Registration/Commercial/Pages/ IRP-eligible.aspx	(866) 798-1185	
NB	www.pxw1.snb.ca/snb7001/e/2000/2006e_6.asp	(506) 453-3076	(506) 453-2215	www.pxw1.snb.ca/snb7001/e/2000/2006e_6.asp	(506) 453-3076	
NL	www.servicenl.gov.nl.ca/drivers/safetycode/	(709) 729-0102	(877) 636-6867	www.gs.gov.nl.ca/drivers/safetycode/single-trip.html	(709) 729-0102	
NT	Non-participant	Non-participant	(877) 767-9088	www.idmv.dot.gov.nt.ca/Vehicle-Services/Permits	(877) 795-4405	
NS	www.gov.ns.ca/snsmr/access/drivers/ international-registration-plan.asp	(902) 450-3971	(902) 450-3933	novascotia.ca/sns/access/drivers/international-registration-plan.asp	(902) 450-3971	30-day permits issued
NU	Non-participant	Non-participant	(867) 975-7840	www.gov.nu.ca/edt/transportation	(867) 975-7870	
ON	www.mto.gov.on.ca/english/trucks/ international-registration-plan.shtml	(416) 235-3924; (866) 587-6771(ON)	(416) 235-3923; (866) 587-6770 (in Ontario)	www.mto.gov.on.ca/english/trucks/ international-registration-plan.shtml	None	
PE	www.princeedwardisland.ca/en/topic/motor-vehicle-registration	(902) 368-6269	(902) 368-5100	www.princeedwardisland.ca/en/information/ transportation-infrastructure-and-energy/full-reciprocity-plan-frp	None	
QC	www.saaq.gouv.qc.ca/en/vehicle_registration/irp/index.php	(418) 646-5677	(514) 873-7620 (Montréal); (418) 643-7620 (Québec City); (800) 361-7620 (elsewhere)	saaq.gouv.qc.ca/en/vehicle-registration/temporary-registration/	None	
SK	www.sgi.sk.ca/businesses/irp/index.html	(306) 359-0867	(306) 775-6969 (outside SK); (800) 667-7575 (inside SK)	www.sgi.sk.ca/businesses/permits/index.html	(306) 775-6909	Issued through permit office
YK	Non-participant	Non-participant	(867) 667-8250; (800) 661-0408 ext 8250	www.hpw.gov.yk.ca/trans/maintenance/permits.html	(867) 667-3608	Single trip permits issued at weigh stations

Operating Authority

UNITED STATES

STATE	PHONE	WEBSITE	FAX	COMMENTS	UCR PHONE
Alabama	(334) 242-5176; (888) 505-9047	www.psc.alabama.gov/transportation/transportation.htm	(334) 242-2534		(888) 505-9047
Alaska	None	None	None		(907) 365-1228
Arizona	(602) 712-4388	www.azdot.gov/mvd/MotorCarrierServices/NewEntrantProgram	(602)-712-3252		Non-participant
Arkansas	(501) 569-2000	www.arkansashighways.com/intrstrate_authority_registration/ intrastate_authority_permit.aspx	(501) 569-2400		(501) 683-0947
California	(415) 703-2782; (800) 877-8867 (household goods); (916) 657-8153 (other property)	For household goods: www.cpuc.ca.gov/ For other property: dmv.ca.gov/	(415) 703-1758		(916) 657-8153
Colorado	(303) 894-2000	www.dora.state.co.us/puc/transportation	(303) 894-2065		(303) 894-2000, option 4
Connecticut	(860) 263-5700	www.ct.gov/dmv/site/default.asp	None		(860) 263-5700
Delaware	(302) 744-2701	www.dmv.de.gov/services/TransServ/index.shtml	None		(302) 744-2701, option 2
District of Columbia	(202) 671-0682	ddot.dc.gov/service/commercial-vehicles	None		Non-participant
Florida	(850) 414-4700	www.floridatruckinginfo.com/	None		Non-participant
Georgia	(404) 624-7212	www.cvisn.dor.ga.gov/gtp/faq	None		(404) 624-7247
Hawaii	(808) 586-2020	puc.hawaii.gov/filing/motor-carriers/	(808) 586-2066		Non-participant
Idaho	(208) 334-8611	trucking.idaho.gov/registrations.html	(208) 334-2006		(208) 334-8611
Illinois	(217) 782-4654	www.icc.illinois.gov/transportation/	None		(217) 782-4654
Indiana	(317) 615-7200	www.in.gov/dor/4106.htm	None		(317) 615-7350
Iowa	(515) 237-3268	iowadot.gov/mvd/omcs/	(515) 237-3225		(515) 237-3268
Kansas	(785) 271-3145	kcc.state.ks.us/trans/	(785) 271-3124		(785) 271-3145
Kentucky	(502) 564-1257	transportation.ky.gov/Motor-Carriers/Pages/default.aspx	(502) 696-3900		(502) 564-1257
Louisiana	(225) 342-4439; (888) 342-5717	www.lpsc.louisiana.gov/motor.aspx	(225) 342-2831		(225) 925-6146
Maine	(207) 624-9000 ext. 52131	www.maine.gov/sos/bmv/commercial/	(207) 622-5332		(207) 624-9000 ext. 52131
Maryland	(800) 543-4564 (in MD); (410) 582-5734	www.marylandroads.com/cvo	None	Transporters of alcoholic beverages must contact Comptroller office: (410) 260-7980	Non-participant
Massachusetts	(617) 305-3559	www.mass.gov/eea/grants-and-tech-assistance/ guidance-technical-assistance/agencies-and-divisions/dpu/ dpu-divisions/transportation-division/	(617) 478-2598		(617) 305-3559
Michigan	(517) 284-3250	www.michigan.gov/msp/0,4643,7-123-72297_59877---,00.html	(517) 284-8127		(517) 284-3250
Minnesota	(651) 215-6330	www.dot.state.mn.us/cvo/	(651) 366-3718		(651) 215-6333
Mississippi	(888) 737-0061; (601) 359-1717	mdot.ms.gov/portal/enforcement.aspx	(601) 576-1373		(888) 737-0061
Missouri	(866) 831-6277; (573) 751-7100	modot.org/mcs/	(573) 522-6708		(866) 831-6277
Montana	(406) 444-6130	www.mdt.mt.gov/business/mcs	(406) 444-0800		(406) 444-2998
Nebraska	(888) 622-1222	www.dmv.ne.gov/mcs/index.html	(402) 471-4024		(402) 471-4435
Nevada	(775) 684-4711	dmvnv.com/mchome.html	(775) 684-4619		Non-participant
New Hampshire	(603) 271-2311	www.nh.gov/safety/divisions/administration/roadtoll/index.html	(603) 271-6758		(603) 271-2311
New Jersey	(609) 984-2830 (alcoholic beverages); (609) 275-2604 (household goods); (609) 292-7081 (hazardous waste)	www.state.nj.us/transportation/freight/trucking/	None	Generally unregulated except for alcoholic beverages, household goods, hazardous waste, and solid waste	Non-participant
New Mexico	(505) 827-4519	nmprc.state.nm.us/transportation/index.html	(505) 827-4023		(505) 827-4519
New York	(518) 457-6512	www.dot.ny.gov/divisions/operating/osss/truck/ registration-licensing?nd=nysdot	None		(518) 457-6512
North Carolina	(919) 715-8683	www.nccrimecontrol.org/Index2.cfm?a=000003,000014,000740	None		(919) 819-3720
North Dakota	(701) 328-5128	nd.gov/ndhp/motor-carrier	(701) 328-0397		(701) 328-1287
Ohio	(614) 466-3392	www.puco.ohio.gov/puco/	None		(614) 466-3392
Oklahoma	(405) 521-2251	occeweb.com/tr/Trucking.htm	(405) 521-2916		(405) 521-2251
Oregon	(503) 378-6699	www.oregon.gov/ODOT/MCT/pages/reg.aspx	(503) 378-6880		Non-participant
Pennsylvania	(717) 787-1168	www.puc.state.pa.us/consumer_info/transportation/ motor_carrier/applications.aspx	None		(717) 783-5934; (717) 783-3846
Rhode Island	(401) 941-4500	www.ripuc.org/utilityinfo/motorcarriers.html	(401) 941-9161		(401) 941-4500
South Carolina	(803) 896-8282	www.scdps.gov/scstp/	(803) 896-2698		(803) 896-3870
South Dakota	(605) 773-4578	sdtruckinfo.com/	None		(605) 773-4595
Tennessee	(615) 399-4266	www.tn.gov/revenue/topic/motor-carrier	(615) 361-5924		(615) 399-4266
Texas	(888) 368-4689	www.txdmv.gov/motor-carriers	(512) 465-4129		(800) 299-1700
Utah	(801) 965-4892	www.udot.utah.gov/	(801) 965-4847		(801) 964-4588
Vermont	(802) 828-2078	dmv.vermont.gov/commercial_trucking	(802) 828-2092		Non-participant
Virginia	(804) 249-5130	www.dmv.virginia.gov/commercial/	(804) 367-1122		(804) 249-5130
Washington	(360) 664-1222	www.utc.wa.gov/regulatedIndustries/transportation/commonCarriers	(360) 586-1181		(360) 664-1222
West Virginia	(304) 340-0427	www.psc.state.wv.us/scripts/Directory/trans.cfm	None		(800) 247-8789
Wisconsin	(608) 266-9900	wisconsindot.gov/Pages/dmv/com-drv-vehs/mtr-car-trkr/mc-authority.aspx	(608) 267-6886		(608) 266-9900
Wyoming	(307) 777-4850	www.dot.state.wy.us/home/trucking_commercial_vehicles/ operating_authority.html	(307) 777-4772		Non-participant

CANADA

PROVINCE	PHONE	WEBSITE	FAX	COMMENTS	
Alberta	(403) 340-5444	www.transportation.alberta.ca	(403) 340-4806		
British Columbia	(250) 952-0577	www.th.gov.bc.ca/cvse/commercial_transport.htm	(250) 952-0578		
Manitoba	(204) 945-3890	www.gov.mb.ca/mit/mcd/index.html	(204) 948-2078		
New Brunswick	(506) 453-3939	www2.gnb.ca/content/gnb/en/departments/dti/trucking.html	(506) 453-2900		
Newfoundland & Labrador	(877) 636-6867	www.servicenl.gov.nl.ca/drivers/safetycode/	None		
Northwest Territories	(867) 767-9040	www.dot.gov.nt.ca/DMV/Commercial	None		
Nova Scotia	(902) 424-2297	novascotia.ca/tran/trucking/	(902) 424-0532		
Nunavut	(888) 975-5999	gov.nu.ca/edt/information/ overviewcontact-information-transportation	None		
Ontario	(416) 246-7166; (800) 387-7736 (in Ontario)	www.mto.gov.on.ca/english/trucks/index.shtml	(905) 704-2039		
Prince Edward Island	(902) 368-5100	www.princeedwardisland.ca/en/topic/transportation-infrastructure-and-energy	(902) 368-5395		
Québec	(514) 873 6424 (in Montréal); (888) 461-2433 (elsewhere)	www.ctq.gouv.qc.ca/en/home.html	(418) 644-8034		
Saskatchewan	(866) 933-5290 (inside SK); (306) 933-5290 (outside SK)	highways.gov.sk.ca/trucking/	(306) 933-5276		
Yukon	(867) 667-5297; (800) 661-0408 ext 5297	www.hpw.gov.yk.ca/trans/transportservices/index.html	(867) 667-5799		

UNITED STATES

ST	UCR WEBSITE	TRIP PERMITS PHONE	TRIP PERMITS WEBSITE	TRIP PERMITS FAX	TRIP PERMITS COMMENTS
AL	psc.alabama.gov/Transportation/interstatereg.htm	(334) 242-1170	www.alabamainteractive.org/dor_tfp	(334) 353-8038	7 day permit issued
AK	dot.alaska.gov/mscve/index.cfm?go=mscve.cve	(907) 883-4591	doa.alaska.gov/dmv/reg/dual.htm	None	One-time 30 day commercial pass
AZ	Non-participant	(602) 771-2960	www.azdot.gov/mvd/MotorCarrierServices/commercial-permits/single-trip-permits	(602) 272-1887	Verify at any Arizona Port of Entry
AR	www.dfa.arkansas.gov/trucking/Pages/default.aspx	(501) 569-2381	arkansashighways.com/permits_list.aspx	None	
CA	www.ucr.in.gov	(800) 400-7115	www.dot.ca.gov/hq/traffops/engineering/trucks/ops-guide/registration.htm	None	Required before entering California
CO	www.colorado.gov/pacific/dora/UCR	(303) 273-1870	www.colorado.gov/pacific/csp/permits-and-forms	(303) 273-1939	
CT	www.ct.gov/dmv/cwp/view.asp?a=810&q=245104	(860) 549-2000	ct.gov/dot/cwp/browse.asp?A=1394&BMDRN=2000&BCOB=0&C=17512	None	
DE	dmv.de.gov/services/TransServ/MC/index.shtml	(302) 744-2700	www.deldot.gov/osow/application/	(302) 739-7808	
DC	Non-participant	(202) 442-4670	tops.ddot.dc.gov/DDOTPermitSystem/DDOTPermitOnline/TruckPermit/Landing.aspx	None	Required
FL	Non-participant	None	None	None	Not required
GA	www.cvisn.dor.ga.gov/Welcome/UCR	None	www.cvisn.dor.ga.gov/	None	
HI	Non-participant	None	None	None	Not required
ID	trucking.idaho.gov/registrations.html	(208) 334-8611	www.accessidaho.org/secure/itd/tportal/ports/trippermits.html	(208) 334-2006	
IL	www.ucr.in.gov; www.icc.illinois.gov/motorcarrier/ucr.aspx	None	None	None	Not required
IN	www.ucr.in.gov	(317) 615-7200	www.in.gov/dor/mcs/	None	Required
IA	www.iowadot.gov/mvd/motorcarriers/ucr.html	(515) 237-3264	www.iowadot.gov/mvd/omcs/osowpermits_determine.html	(515) 237-3257	Required
KS	www.kcc.state.ks.us/trans/ucr.htm	None	www.ksdot.org/permit_links.asp	None	Issued by Central Permits office and Ports of Entry
KY	drive.ky.gov/motor-carriers/Pages/Commercial-Motor-Vehicle-Credentials.aspx	(502) 564-1257	transportation.ky.gov/motor-carriers/Pages/default.aspx	(502) 564-4138	
LA	www.expresslane.org/Pages/faqs.aspx/#eleven	(800) 654-1433 (225) 343-2345	perba.dotd.louisiana.gov/perba/perba.nsf	(225) 377-7108	
ME	www5.informe.org/cgi-bin/online/ucr/index.pl	(207) 624-9000 ext. 52134	www.maine.gov/sos/bmv/commercial/FuelTax.htm	(207) 624-9062	Required
MD	Non-participant	None	None	None	Not required
MA	www.mass.gov/eea/grants-and-tech-assistance/guidance-technical-assistance/agencies-and-divisions/dpu/dpu-divisions/transportation-division/unified-carrier-registration-program-ucr.html	None	None	None	Not required
MI	www.michigan.gov/msp/0,4643,7-123-72297_59877_72520---,00.html	None	None	None	Not required
MN	www.dot.state.mn.us/cvo/unifiedcarrier.html	(651) 297-2126	dps.mn.gov/divisions/dvs/Pages/dvs-content-detail.aspx?pageID=607	None	
MS	mdot.ms.gov/portal/enforcement.aspx; www.ucr.in.gov	(601) 359-7001	mdot.ms.gov/portal/home.aspx	(601) 359-7834	Not required
MO	www.modot.mo.gov/mcs/UCR/	(866) 831-6277	www.modot.org/mcs/index.htm	(573) 751-0916	
MT	www.mdt.mt.gov/business/mcs/licenses.shtml	(406) 444-7262	www.mdt.mt.gov/business/mcs/permits.shtml	(406) 444-9263	Call to verify requirements
NE	www.dmv.nebraska.gov/mcs/ucr.html	(402) 471-4435	dortruckpermits.nebraska.gov/permit/login.asp	(402) 471-4024	72 hour permit must be purchased prior to entry
NV	Non-participant	None	None	None	Not required
NH	www.nh.gov/safety/divisions/administration/roadtoll/unified_carrier.html	None	None	None	Not required
NJ	Non-participant	None	None	None	Not required
NM	www.nmprc.state.nm.us/transportation/unified-carrier-registration.html	None	None	None	Not required
NY	www.dot.ny.gov/divisions/operating/osss/truck/unified-carrier-reg	None	None	None	Not required
NC	www.ncdot.gov/dmv/vehicle/irp/	None	None	None	Not required
ND	www.nd.gov/ndhp/motor-carrier	None	None	None	Not required
OH	www.puco.ohio.gov/puco/index.cfm/puco-forms/motor-carrier-registration-forms	None	None	None	Not required
OK	www.occeweb.com/TR/UCR.htm	(405) 521-2211	www.occeweb.com/tr/TempPermits.htm	None	
OR	Non-participant	(503) 378-6699	www.oregon.gov/ODOT/MCT/	(503) 378-6880	Required
PA	www.puc.pa.gov/utility_industry/transportation/motor_carrier/ucr_information.aspx	(717) 787-5355	www.pahighways.com/truckinfo.html	None	Required
RI	www.ripuc.org/utilityinfo/motorcarriers/UCR_forms.pdf	None	None	None	Not required
SC	www.scdmvonline.com/dmvnew/default.aspx?n=unified_carrier_registration_(ucr)	None	None	None	Not required
SD	dor.sd.gov/Motor_Vehicles/Trucking_Industry/UCR.aspx	(605) 773-4578	sdtruckinfo.com/permitting.aspx	(605) 773-7144	
TN	tn.gov/revenue/article/unified-carrier-registration-intrastate-authority	None	None	None	Not required
TX	www.txdmv.gov/motor-carriers/unified-carrier-registration	(512) 465-3000	www.txdmv.gov/motorists/register-your-vehicle/temporary-permits	(512) 465-4129	
UT	www.udot.utah.gov/main/f?p=100:pg:0::::V,T:,402	(801) 965-4892	www.udot.utah.gov/public/mcs/f?p=155:1:1900671666152::NO:::	(801) 965-4847	
VT	Non-participant	None	dmv.vermont.gov/commercial_trucking/online_permits	(802) 828-3577	Required
VA	www.dmv.virginia.gov/commercial/#mcs/programs/ucra/index.asp	(804) 249-5130	None	(804) 367-1073	Required
WA	www.utc.wa.gov/regulatedIndustries/transportation/commonCarriers/Pages/unifiedCarrierRegistration.aspx	None	None	None	
WV	www.psc.state.wv.us/UnifiedCarrier/	(304) 558-3900	www.transportation.wv.gov/DMV/Motor-Carriers/Pages/Trip-Permits.aspx	None	
WI	www.dot.wisconsin.gov/business/carriers/ucr.htm	(608) 266-9900	www.dot.wisconsin.gov/business/carriers/trip-permits.htm	None	
WY	Non-participant	(307) 777-4376	www.whp.dot.state.wy.us/home/ports.html	(307) 777-4772	Issued at Port of Entry

CANADA

PR		TRIP PERMITS PHONE	TRIP PERMITS WEBSITE	TRIP PERMITS FAX	TRIP PERMITS COMMENTS
AB		(403) 342-7138	www.transportation.alberta.ca/520.htm	(403) 340-5278	Issued from Central Permits Office
BC		(800) 559-9688	www.th.gov.bc.ca/cvse/permits.html	None	
MB		(204) 945-3961	www.gov.mb.ca/mit/mcd/mcpd/index.html	(204) 945-6499	
NB		(888) 762-8600	www.pxw1.snb.ca/snb7001/e/2000/2006e_1.asp	(506) 444-4488	
NL		None	None	None	
NT		(866) 225-3505	www.dot.gov.nt.ca/Highways/Scales	None	
NS		None	None	None	
NU		None	None	None	
ON		None	None	None	
PE		None	None	None	
QC		(514) 873-6424	www.ctq.gouv.qc.ca/en/home.html	(418) 644-8034	
SK		(800) 667-7575 (inside SK); (306) 775-6969 (outside SK)	www.highways.gov.sk.ca/trucking-permits/	(306) 775-6909	Issued through permit office
YK		(867) 667-5297; (800) 661-0408 ext 5297	www.hpw.gov.yk.ca/trans/transportservices/transport_permits.html	(867) 667-5799	

State Police

UNITED STATES

STATE	PHONE	WEBSITE	EMERGENCY PHONE	EMERGENCY CELL PHONE
Alabama	(334) 242-4395 (Motor Carrier Safety)	dps.alabama.gov	911	*47
Alaska	(907) 269-5511	dps.alaska.gov	911	911
Arizona	(602) 223-2522 (Commercial Vehicle Enforcement)	azdps.gov/Services/Commercial_Vehicles/	911	911
Arkansas	(501) 618-8000	www.asp.state.ar.us	911	911
California	(800) 835-5247	www.chp.ca.gov	911	911
Colorado	(303) 239-4500	csp.state.co.us	911	911
Connecticut	(860) 685-8190	www.ct.gov/dps	911	911
Delaware	(302) 739-5900	dsp.delaware.gov/	911	911
D.C.	(202) 727-9099	mpdc.dc.gov	911	911
Florida	(850) 617-3010 (Motor Carrier Compliance)	www.flhsmv.gov/florida-highway-patrol/	911	911; *FHP
Georgia	(404) 624-7000; (404) 624-7211 (Motor Carrier Compliance)	dps.georgia.gov	911	911; *GSP
Hawaii	(808) 587-2652	dps.hawaii.gov	911	911
Idaho	(208) 884-7000; (208) 884-7220 (Commercial Vehicle Safety)	isp.idaho.gov/	911; (208) 846-7500	911; *477
Illinois	(217) 782-6267 (Commercial Motor Vehicle)	isp.state.il.us	911	911
Indiana	(317) 232-8248; (317) 615-7373 (Commercial Vehicle Enforcement)	www.in.gov/isp/	911	911
Iowa	(515) 725-6090	www.dps.state.ia.us/ISP/index.shtml	911; (800) 525-5555 (non-emergency)	911
Kansas	(785) 296-6800	www.kansashighwaypatrol.org/	911	911; *HP *KTA
Kentucky	(502) 782-1800	www.kentuckystatepolice.org	911; (800) 222-5555 (in KY)	911; (800) 222-5555 (in KY)
Louisiana	(225) 925-6006	www.lsp.org/	911	911; *577 (road emergencies)
Maine	(207) 624-7200; (207) 624-8909 (Commercial Vehicle Enforcement)	www.state.me.us/dps/msp/	911	911
Maryland	(410) 653-4200; (410) 768-7388 (Automotive Safety Enforcement Div.)	www.mdsp.org/	911	911; #77 (non-emergency)
Massachusetts	(508) 820-2300	www.mass.gov/msp	911	911
Michigan	(517) 332-2521	www.michigan.gov/msp	911	911
Minnesota	(651) 201-7000	dps.mn.gov/divisions/msp	911	911
Mississippi	(601) 987-1212	www.dps.state.ms.us	911	911; *HP
Missouri	(573) 751-3313; (573) 526-6128 (Commercial Vehicle Enforcement)	dps.mo.gov/	911	911; *55 (non-emergency)
Montana	(406) 444-3780	dojmt.gov/highwaypatrol/	911; (855) 647-3777	911
Nebraska	(402) 471-4545; (402) 471-0105 (Commercial Vehicle Enforcement)	statepatrol.nebraska.gov/	911; (800) 525-5555	911; *55
Nevada	(775) 687-5300	nhp.nv.gov/	911	911; *NHP
New Hampshire	(603) 223-4381; (603) 223-8778 (Commercial Vehicle Enforcement)	nh.gov/safety/divisions/nhsp/	911; (800) 525-5555	911; *77
New Jersey	(609) 882-2000	www.state.nj.us/lps/njsp/	911	911; #77 (aggressive drivers)
New Mexico	(505) 827-9300 (State Police); (505) 476-2457 (Motor Transportation Police)	nmsp.dps.state.nm.us	911	911
New York	(518) 436-2825; (917) 492-7100 (NYC only)	troopers.ny.gov	911; (800) 842-2233 (NY State Thruway)	911
North Carolina	(919) 733-7952; (919) 715-8683 (Motor Carrier Enforcement)	www.ncdps.gov/Our-Organization/Law-Enforcement	911	911; *47
North Dakota	(701) 328-2455; (701) 328-5128 (Motor Carrier Operations)	www.nd.gov/ndhp/	911	911
Ohio	(614) 466-4056; (877) 772-8765	statepatrol.ohio.gov	911	911; #677 (non-emergency)
Oklahoma	(405) 425-2424; (405) 521-6060 (Commercial Vehicle Enforcement)	www.dps.state.ok.us/ohp	911	911; *55
Oregon	(503) 378-3720	www.oregon.gov/OSP/	911	911
Pennsylvania	(717) 783-5599	psp.pa.gov	911; (800) 932-0586 (PA Turnpike)	911; *11 (Penn. Turnpike only)
Rhode Island	(401) 444-1000	risp.ri.gov/	911	911
South Carolina	(803) 896-7920	www.scdps.gov/schp/	911	911; *47
South Dakota	(605) 773-3105	dps.sd.gov/	911	911
Tennessee	(615) 251-5175	www.tn.gov/safety/section/thp	911	911; *THP
Texas	(512) 424-2000	www.txdps.state.tx.us	911	911; (800) 525-5555 (non-emergency road assistance)
Utah	(801) 965-4518	publicsafety.utah.gov/highwaypatrol/	911	911
Vermont	(802) 244-8781	vsp.vermont.gov	911	911
Virginia	(804) 674-2000	www.vsp.state.va.us	911	911; #77 (aggressive drivers)
Washington	(360) 596-4000	www.wsp.wa.gov	911	911
West Virginia	(304) 746-2100	www.wvsp.gov/	911	911
Wisconsin	(608) 266-3212	wisconsindot.gov/Pages/about-wisdot/who-we-are/dsp/dsp.aspx	911	911
Wyoming	(307) 777-4321	www.whp.dot.state.wy.us/home.html	911; (800) 442-9090 (in state)	911

Overweight/Oversize

UNITED STATES

STATE	PHONE	WEBSITE	FAX	COMMENTS
Alabama	(800) 499-2782	www.dot.state.al.us/maweb/oversize&overweightpermitinformation.htm	(334) 832-9084	Required
Alaska	(800) 478-7636 (inside AK); (907) 365-1200 (outside AK)	dot.alaska.gov/mscve/main.cfm?go=permits	(866) 345-2641 (inside AK); (907) 365-1221 (outside AK)	
Arizona	(602) 771-2960	www.azdot.gov/mvd/MotorCarrierServices/commercial-permits/oversize-overweight-permits	(602) 272-1887	Can be issued at Ports of Entry. Permits for use on routes other than state routes are procured from the proper local authority.
Arkansas	(501) 569-2381	www.arkansashighways.com/highway_police/oversize_overweight_permits.aspx	(501) 569-4998	
California	(916) 322-1297	www.dot.ca.gov/hq/traffops/permits/	(916) 322-4966 (single trip); (916) 445-0469 (annual permit)	For legal truck size inquiries (not permits), call (916) 654-5741.
Colorado	(800) 350-3765; (303) 757-9539	www.coloradodot.info/business/permits/truckpermits	(303) 757-9719	
Connecticut	(860) 594-2880	www.ct.gov/dot/cwp/view.asp?A=1394&Q=259546	(860) 594-2949	
Delaware	(302) 744-2700	www.deldot.gov/osow/application/login	(302) 739-7808	
District of Columbia	(202) 442-4670	ddot.dc.gov/page/permit-applications-use-public-spaces	None	All application materials must be submitted online.
Florida	(850) 410-5777	www.fdot.gov/maintenance/OWODPermits.shtm	None	Applications no longer accepted by fax or email.
Georgia	(844) 837-5500	www.dot.ga.gov/PS/Permits/OversizePermits	(575) 353-7732	
Hawaii	(808) 831-6712	hidot.hawaii.gov/highways/home/doing-business/guide-to-permits/oversized-and-overweight-vehicles-on-state-highways/	None	
Idaho	(208) 334-8420; (800) 662-7133 (in Idaho)	trucking.idaho.gov/permits.html	(208) 334-8419	
Illinois	(217) 785-1477; (800) 252-8636 (in Illinois)	truckpermits.dot.illinois.gov/	None	All permits must be ordered online.
Indiana	(317) 615-7320	www.in.gov/dor/4243.htm	None	
Iowa	(515) 237-3264	www.iowadot.gov/mvd/omcs/osowpermits.html	(515) 237-3257	
Kansas	(785) 368-6501	www.truckingks.org/	(785) 296-6558	
Kentucky	(502) 564-1257	drive.ky.gov/motor-carriers/Pages/Overweight-Over-Dimensional.aspx	(502) 564-0992	
Louisiana	(800) 654-1433; (225) 343-2345	perba.dotd.louisiana.gov/welcome.nsf	(225) 377-7108	
Maine	(207) 624-9000 ext. 52134; (800) 698-7747 (Maine Turnpike)	www.maine.gov/sos/bmv/commercial/olpermits.html	(207) 622-5332	The Maine Turnpike has its own specified size and weight limitations. For more info call (800) 698-7747.
Maryland	(800) 846-6435; (410) 582-5734	www.sha.state.md.us/index.aspx?PageId=58	(800) 945-3416	
Massachusetts	(781) 431-5148	www.massdot.state.ma.us/highway/DoingBusinessWithUs/PermitsRoadAccessPrograms/CommercialTransport.aspx	(781) 431-5014	
Michigan	(517) 241-8999	www.michigan.gov/mdot/0,1607,7-151-9625_56949-253714--,00.html	None	
Minnesota	(651) 296-6000	www.dot.state.mn.us/cvo/oversize/oversize.html	(651) 215-9677	Permit applications are not accepted by fax.
Mississippi	(888) 737-0061; (601) 359-1717	www.expresspass.ms.gov/trucking/instruct.htm	(601) 359-1602	
Missouri	(866) 831-6277; (573) 751-7100	www.modot.org/mcs/	(573) 751-7408	
Montana	(406) 444-7262	www.mdt.mt.gov/business/mcs/permits.shtml	(406) 444-0800	
Nebraska	(402) 471-0034	dortruckpermits.nebraska.gov/permit/login.asp	None	
Nevada	(800) 552-2127; (775) 888-7410	www.nevadadot.com/business/trucker/overdimensional/	(775) 888-7103	
New Hampshire	(603) 271-2691	www.nh.gov/dot/org/operations/highwaymaintenance/overhaul/index.htm	(603) 271-5990	
New Jersey	(609) 530-6089	nj.gotpermits.com/	None	
New Mexico	(505) 476-2475	www.nmmtdpolice.org/	(505) 476-2477	Permit applications are not accepted by fax.
New York	(888) 783-1685; (518) 485-2999	www.dot.ny.gov/nypermits	(518) 457-1036	
North Carolina	(888) 574-6683 (single-trip permit); (919) 733-7154 (single-trip permit); (888) 221-8166 (annual permit); (919) 733-4740 (annual permit)	connect.ncdot.gov/business/trucking/Pages/overpermits.aspx	(888) 222-8347 (single trip); (919) 662-4318 (annual)	
North Dakota	(701) 328-2621	www.nd.gov/ndhp/motor-carrier/e-permits	(701) 328-1642	
Ohio	(614) 351-2300	dot.state.oh.us/permits	(614) 728-4099	
Oklahoma	(405) 425-7012	www.swpermitsok.com/	(405) 522-9006	
Oregon	(503) 373-0000	www.oregon.gov/ODOT/MCT/Pages/OD.aspx	(503) 378-2873	Permit applications are not accepted by fax.
Pennsylvania	(717) 787-4680; (800) 331-3414 (Pennsylvania Turnpike)	www.penndot.gov/Doing-Business/Permits/HaulingInformation	(717) 787-9890	
Rhode Island	(401) 462-5747	www.ri.gov/DMV/OSOW/	(401) 462-5791	
South Carolina	(803) 737-6769; (877) 349-7190	www.scdot.org/doing/permits_OSOW.aspx	(803) 737-2199	
South Dakota	(605) 773-4578 (info)	sdtruckinfo.com/sizeandweight.aspx	None	
Tennessee	(615) 741-3821	www.tn.gov/tdot/topic/centralservices-permits	(615) 741-1159	Issued by DOT or wire services
Texas	(800) 299-1700	www.txdmv.gov/motor-carriers/oversize-overweight-permits	(512) 465-4248	
Utah	(801) 965-4892	www.udot.utah.gov/main/f?p=100:80:0:::1:T,V:4213,	(801) 965-4847	
Vermont	(802) 828-2064	dmv.vermont.gov/commercial_trucking/permitting_rules	(802) 828-5418	
Virginia	(804) 497-7135	www.dmv.virginia.gov/general/#hauling.asp	(804) 367-0063	
Washington	(360) 704-6340	www.wsdot.wa.gov/CommercialVehicle/permitting.htm	(360) 704-6391	
West Virginia	(304) 558-0384	www.transportation.wv.gov/highways/maintenance/hauling_permits/Pages/default.aspx	(304) 558-0591	All permits must be ordered online.
Wisconsin	(608) 266-7320	www.dot.state.wi.us/business/carriers/osowgeneral.htm	(608) 264-7751	
Wyoming	(307) 777-4376	www.whp.dot.state.wy.us/home/ports.html	(307) 777-4399	

CANADA

PROVINCE	PHONE	WEBSITE	FAX	COMMENTS
Alberta	(800) 662-7138 (in North America); (403) 342-7138 (in Alberta)	transportation.alberta.ca/2737.htm	(403) 340-5278	
British Columbia	(800) 559-9688	www.th.gov.bc.ca/CVSE/tps/index.htm	(250) 784-2426	
Manitoba	(204) 945-3961; (877) 812-0009	gov.mb.ca/mit/mcd/mcpd/index.html	(204) 945-6499	
New Brunswick	(506) 453-2982	www.pxw1.snb.ca/snb7001/e/2000/2006e.asp	(506) 444-4488	
Newfoundland and Labrador	(877) 636-6867	www.gs.gov.nl.ca/drivers/safetycode/spcl-perm-size.html	(709) 729-0102	
Northwest Territories	(877) 737-7786; (867) 984-3341; (867) 777-7283	www.dot.gov.nt.ca/DMV/Commercial	(877) 795-4405	Permits can be issued at weigh scales.
Nova Scotia	(902) 424-5851; (800) 898-7668 (inside Nova Scotia)	gov.ns.ca/snsmr/paal/rmv/paal280.asp	(902) 424-4633	
Nunavut	(867) 975-7840	www.gov.nu.ca/edt	(867) 975-7820	
Ontario	(416) 246-7166 ext. 6306	mto.gov.on.ca/english/trucks/oversize/	(905) 704-2545	
Prince Edward Island	(902) 437-8534	www.princeedwardisland.ca/en/topic/driving	(902) 437-8540	
Québec	(800) 361-7620	www.saaq.gouv.qc.ca/en/e_forms/special_permit/index.php	(514) 873-4302	
Saskatchewan	(800) 667-7575 (inside Saskatchewan); (306) 775-6969 (outside Saskatchewan)	highways.gov.sk.ca/special-weights/	(306) 775-6909	
Yukon	(867) 667-5297; (800) 661-0408	www.hpw.gov.yk.ca/trans/transportservices/transport_permits.html	(867) 667-5799	

Hazardous Materials

UNITED STATES

STATE	PHONE	WEBSITE	FAX
Alabama	(334) 242-4395	dps.alabama.gov/Home/ wfContent.aspx?ID=40&ID2=10&PLH1=plhHighwayPatrol-MotorCarrier	(334) 277-3285
Alaska	(907) 365-1200	dot.alaska.gov/mscve	(907) 365-1221
Arizona	(800) 251-5866	azdot.gov/mvd/forms-and-publications	None
Arkansas	(501) 569-2422	www2.adeq.state.ar.us/hazwaste/branch_programs/transport.htm	(501) 568-4921
California	(916) 843-3400	www.chp.ca.gov/Programs-Services/Programs/Commercial-Vehicle-Section	None
Colorado	(303) 273-1900; (303) 894-2000 (permits)	www.colorado.gov/pacific/csp/hazardous-materials	(303) 273-1911
Connecticut	(860) 263-5700 (DMV)	www.ct.gov/dmv/cwp/view.asp?a=2594&q=245446	None
Delaware	(302) 744-2506	dmv.de.gov/services/driver_services/drv_svcs.shtml	None
D.C.	(202) 535-2600 (DOEE)	doee.dc.gov/service/hazardous-waste	(202) 535-2881
Florida	(850) 617-3010	www.flhsmv.gov/hazmat/	None
Georgia	(404) 624-7211	dps.georgia.gov/annual-permit-transportation-hazardous-materials	(404) 624-7295
Hawaii	(855) 347-8371	hidot.hawaii.gov/highways/library/motor-vehicle-safety-office/hazardous-materials-endorsement/	None
Idaho	(208) 334-8611	trucking.idaho.gov/hazmat.html	(208) 334-2006
Illinois	(217) 785-1181	www.cyberdriveillinois.com/departments/drivers/drivers_license/CDL/hazmat.html	(217) 782-9159
Indiana	(800) 423-0765	in.gov/dhs/3161.htm	(317) 234-7234
Iowa	(515) 237-3135 (515) 290-2193	www.iowadot.gov/mvd/CDL/hazmat.htm	None
Kansas	(785) 271-3145	www.ksrevenue.org/hazmat.html	(785) 271-3124
Kentucky	(502) 564-1257	drive.ky.gov/driver-licensing/Pages/Commercial-Drivers-License-Information.aspx	(502) 564-4138
Louisiana	(225) 925-6113	www.lsp.org/esu.html#hazmat	(225) 925-4048
Maine	(207) 287-7688	www.maine.gov/dep/waste/transpinstall/hazwastetransa.html	(207) 287-7826
Maryland	(800) 950-1682 (MD only); (410) 768-7000	mva.maryland.gov/Driver-Services/Apply/CDL/Hazmat.htm	None
Massachusetts	(857) 368-8000	www.massrmv.com/LicenseandID/CDLPermitandLicense.aspx	None
Michigan	(517) 206-2312	michigan.gov/msp/0,4643,7-123-72297_59877---,00.html	(517) 284-8127
Minnesota	(651) 297-5029	dot.state.mn.us/cvo/hazmat/hazmat.html	None
Mississippi	(601) 987-1212	www.dps.state.ms.us/driver-services/new-drivers-license/commercial-operator-license-classes-a-b-c-d/	None
Missouri	(866) 831-6277	www.modot.org/mcs/safety/	(573) 522-4260
Montana	(406) 444-3300	www.mdt.mt.gov/mdt/organization/mcs.shtml	(406) 444-7681
Nebraska	(402) 471-0105	statepatrol.nebraska.gov/vnews/display.v/ART/5669d9021e10b	(402) 471-3295
Nevada	(775) 888-7000	www.nevadadot.com/Doing_Business/Trucking/Permit_Conditions_and_Restrictions.aspx	(775) 888-7115
New Hampshire	(603) 223-8780 (CVE)	www.nh.gov/safety/divisions/nhsp/fob/troopg/links.html	None
New Jersey	(609) 530-8026	www.nj.gov/transportation/freight/trucking/hazardous.shtm	None
New Mexico	(888) 683-4636	mvd.newmexico.gov/hazardous-material-endorsement.aspx	None
New York	(518) 457-6512	www.dot.ny.gov/divisions/operating/osss/truck/carrier	None
North Carolina	(919) 715-7000	www.ncdot.gov/dmv/driver/commercial/	(919) 733-7554
North Dakota	(701) 328-5128 (MCO)	www.nd.gov/ndhp/faq/56	(701) 328-0397
Ohio	(614) 466-3392 (MCRD)	www.puco.ohio.gov/puco/index.cfm/information-by-industry/motor-carrier-industry-information/#sthash.oWmxWGxC.dpbs	None
Oklahoma	(405) 521-2251	www.occeweb.com/TR/HazWaste.htm	None
Oregon	(503) 378-6336; (503) 378-3667 (MCE)	www.oregon.gov/ODOT/MCT/Pages/SAFETY.aspx	(503) 378-3567
Pennsylvania	(717) 412-5300	www.dmv.pa.gov/Driver-Services/Commercial-Driver/Hazmat-Endorsement/Pages/default.aspx	None
Rhode Island	(401) 462-5813	www.dmv.ri.gov/licenses/hazmat/index.php	(401) 462-5805
South Carolina	(803) 896-5500	www.scdps.gov/scstp/	None
South Dakota	(605) 773-6883	dps.sd.gov/licensing/driver_licensing/hazardous_materials_endorsement.aspx	(605) 773-3018
Tennessee	(615) 253-5221	www.tn.gov/safety/article/hazmat	(615) 253-2092
Texas	(512) 424-2000; (512) 424-2600	www.txdps.state.tx.us/DriverLicense/hme.htm	None
Utah	(801) 945-4892	www.udot.utah.gov/main/f?p=100:80:0:::1:T,V:4201,	(801) 965-4847
Vermont	(802) 828-0598	dmv.vermont.gov/licenses/commercial/hazmat	(802) 828-2098
Virginia	(800) 367-7623 (DOT); (804) 497-7100 (DMV)	www.virginiadot.org/info/hazmat.asp	None
Washington	(360) 902-3900	www.dol.wa.gov/driverslicense/cdlhazmat.html	None
West Virginia	(304) 340-0456	www.psc.state.wv.us/AllianceTransInfo/default.htm	(304) 340-0394
Wisconsin	(608) 264-7447	wisconsindot.gov/Pages/dmv/com-drv-vehs/cdl-how-aply/hazardousmaterials.aspx	None
Wyoming	(307) 777-4800	www.dot.state.wy.us/home/driver_license_records/license_commercial.default.html	None

CANADA

PROVINCE	PHONE	WEBSITE	FAX
Alberta	(780) 427-2731	www.transportation.alberta.ca/519.htm	None
British Columbia	(250) 952-0577	www.th.gov.bc.ca/cvse/dangerous_goods.htm	(250) 952-0578
Manitoba	(888) 463-0521	www.tc.gc.ca/eng/tdg/safety-menu.htm	None
New Brunswick	(866) 814-1477	www.tc.gc.ca/eng/tdg/safety-menu.htm	None
Newfoundland and Labrador	(866) 814-1477	www.tc.gc.ca/eng/tdg/safety-menu.htm	None
Northwest Terr.	(888) 463-0521	www.tc.gc.ca/eng/tdg/safety-menu.htm	None
Nova Scotia	(902) 424-7769	novascotia.ca/tran/trucking/dangerousgoods.asp	None
Nunavut	(888) 463-0521	www.tc.gc.ca/eng/tdg/safety-menu.htm	None
Ontario	(416) 973-1868	www.tc.gc.ca/eng/tdg/safety-menu.htm	None
Prince Edward I.	(866) 814-1477	www.tc.gc.ca/eng/tdg/safety-menu.htm	None
Québec	(514) 283-5722	www.tc.gc.ca/eng/tdg/safety-menu.htm	None
Saskatchewan	(888) 463-0521	www.tc.gc.ca/eng/tdg/safety-menu.htm	None
Yukon	(888) 463-0521	www.tc.gc.ca/eng/tdg/safety-menu.htm	None

Hazardous Waste

UNITED STATES

ST	PHONE	WEBSITE	FAX
AL	(334) 271-7730	adem.alabama.gov/programs/land/default.cnt	(334) 279-3050
AK	(907) 365-1200	dot.alaska.gov/mscve	(907) 365-1221
AZ	(800) 251-5866	azdot.gov/mvd/forms-and-publications	(602) 771-4246
AR	(501) 569-2422	www2.adeq.state.ar.us/hazwaste/branch_programs/transport.htm	(501) 568-4921
CA	(916) 324-2439	www.dtsc.ca.gov/HazardousWaste/Transporters.cfm	(916) 327-4502
CO	(303) 692-3300; (303) 692-3355 (permits)	www.colorado.gov/pacific/cdphe/hazardous-waste-transporters-guidance-and-policy	(303) 759-5355
CT	(888) 424-3366	www.ct.gov/deep/site/default.asp	(860) 424-4059
DE	(302) 739-9403	www.awm.delaware.gov/SHWMB/Pages/HazardousWaste.aspx	(302) 739-5060
DC	(202) 535-2600 (DOEE)	doee.dc.gov/service/hazardous-waste	(202) 535-2881
FL	(850) 245-8705	dep.state.fl.us/waste/categories/hwRegulation/pages/Manifest.htm	None
GA	(404) 656-2833	epd.georgia.gov/hazardous-waste-technical-guidance	None
HI	(808) 586-4226	health.hawaii.gov/shwb/hazwaste/	(808) 586-7509
ID	(208) 373-0502	www.deq.idaho.gov/waste-mgmt-remediation/hazardous-waste/	None
IL	(217) 782-3397	epa.state.il.us/land/hazardous-waste/index.html	None
IN	(317) 234-6951; (800) 451-6027	www.in.gov/idem/4995.htm#rcra	(317) 234-0428
IA	(515) 725-8337	www.iowadnr.gov/InsideDNR/RegulatoryLand/ContaminatedSites/HazWasteFees.aspx	None
KS	(785) 296-1600	www.kdheks.gov/waste/	(785) 296-8909
KY	(502) 564-6716	waste.ky.gov/HWB/Pages/default.aspx	(502) 564-4245
LA	(888) 342-5717	lpsc.louisiana.gov/regs3_motor.aspx	(225) 342-2831
ME	(207) 287-7688	www.maine.gov/dep/waste/transpinstall/hazwastetransa.html#ru	(207) 287-7826
MD	(410) 537-3400	www.mde.state.md.us/programs/Land/SolidWaste/ApplicationsFormsandInstructions/Pages/Programs/LandPrograms/Solid_Waste/forms/index.aspx	None
MA	(617) 292-5576	www.mass.gov/eea/agencies/massdep/service/approvals/bwp-hw-05.html	(617) 556-1049
MI	(517) 284-6562	www.michigan.gov/deq/0,4561,7-135-3312_7235---,00.html	None
MN	(651) 296-6300	www.pca.state.mn.us/index.php/waste/index.html	None
MS	(601) 961-5220	deq.state.ms.us/mdeq.nsf/page/ECED_HazWaste	(601) 961-5703
MO	(866) 831-6277	www.modot.org/mcs/index.htm	(573) 522-6708
MT	(406) 444-5300	deq.mt.gov/Land/HazWaste/hazTransReq	(406) 444-1374
NE	(402) 471-0105	statepatrol.nebraska.gov/vnews/display.v/ART/5669d9021e10b	(402) 471-3295
NV	(775) 888-7000	www.nevadadot.com/Doing_Business/Trucking/Permit_Conditions_and_Restrictions.aspx	(775) 888-7115
NH	(603) 271-3203	des.nh.gov/organization/divisions/waste/orcb/srcis/hwtp/index.htm	(603) 271-2181
NJ	(609) 292-7081	www.nj.gov/dep/dshw/hwr/regislic/vehrenew.htm	(609) 292-3970
NM	(505) 476-6000	www.nmenv.state.nm.us/HWB/index.htm	(505) 476-6030
NY	(518) 402-8792	www.dec.ny.gov/chemical/8483.html	(518) 402-9034
NC	(919) 707-8200	portal.ncdenr.org/web/wm/hw	None
ND	(701) 328-5166	www.ndhealth.gov/WM/	(701) 328-5200
OH	(614) 644-2924	epa.ohio.gov/dmwm/Home/Transporters.aspx	(614) 644-3146
OK	(405) 521-2915	www.occeweb.com/TR/HazWaste.htm	None
OR	(503) 229-5696; (800) 452-4011 (in Oregon)	www.deq.state.or.us/lq/hw/index.htm	(503) 229-6124
PA	(717) 787-6239	www.dep.pa.gov/Business/Land/Waste/SolidWaste/HazardousWaste/Transportation/Pages/default.aspx	None
RI	(401) 222-2797, ext. 7134	www.dem.ri.gov/programs/wastemanagement/facilities/index.php	(401) 222-3812
SC	(803) 898-0456	www.scdhec.gov/Environment/LW/HazardousWaste/	None
SD	(605) 773-3153	denr.sd.gov/des/wm/hw/hwmainpage.aspx	None
TN	(615) 532-0780	www.tennessee.gov/environment/topic/sw-hazardous-waste-management	(615) 532-0938
TX	(512) 239-6413	www.tceq.texas.gov/permitting/waste_permits/ihw_permits/ihw.html	(512) 239-6410
UT	(801) 536-0200	www.hazardouswaste.utah.gov/	(801) 536-0222
VT	(802) 828-1138	dec.vermont.gov/about-dec/a-z/waste-topics	None
VA	(804) 698-4000	www.deq.state.va.us/Programs/LandProtectionRevitalization/SolidHazardousWasteRegulatoryPrograms/HazardousWaste.aspx	None
WA	(360) 407-6700	ecy.wa.gov/programs/hwtr/hw_manifests/index.html	(360) 407-6715
WV	(304) 340-0456	www.psc.state.wv.us/AllianceTransInfo/default.htm	(304) 340-0394
WI	(262) 884-2342	dnr.wi.gov/topic/waste/hazardous.html	None
WY	(307) 777-7937	deq.wyoming.gov/shwd/	(307) 635-1784

CANADA

PR	PHONE	WEBSITE	FAX
AB	(780) 427-2731	www.transportation.alberta.ca/519.htm	None
BC	(604) 666-2955; (250) 356-5044 (HW Prog.)	www2.gov.bc.ca/gov/content/environment/waste-management/hazardous-waste/transporting-hazardous-waste	(250) 356-0299
MB	(888) 463-0521; (204) 945-7086 (HW Prog.)	www.gov.mb.ca/conservation/eal/haz-waste/index.html	(204) 945-5229
NB	(866) 814-1477	www.tc.gc.ca/eng/tdg/safety-menu.htm	None
NL	(866) 814-1477	www.tc.gc.ca/eng/tdg/safety-menu.htm	None
NT	(888) 463-0521	www.tc.gc.ca/eng/tdg/safety-menu.htm	None
NS	(866) 814-1477	www.tc.gc.ca/eng/tdg/safety-menu.htm	None
NU	(888) 463-0521	www.tc.gc.ca/eng/tdg/safety-menu.htm	None
ON	(416) 973-1868	www.tc.gc.ca/eng/tdg/safety-menu.htm	None
PE	(866) 814-1477	www.tc.gc.ca/eng/tdg/safety-menu.htm	None
QC	(514) 283-5722	www.tc.gc.ca/eng/tdg/safety-menu.htm	None
SK	(888) 463-0521	www.tc.gc.ca/eng/tdg/safety-menu.htm	None
YK	(888) 463-0521; (800) 661-0408 (Env. YK)	environmentyukon.gov.yk.ca/	(867) 393-6213

Radioactive Materials

UNITED STATES

STATE	PHONE	WEBSITE	FAX
Alabama	(334) 206-5391; (800) 582-1866 (in Alabama)	www.adph.org/radiation/index.asp?ID=1872	(334) 206-5387
Alaska	(907) 465-5105	dec.state.ak.us/air/am/rad/radhome.htm	(907) 465-5129
Arizona	(800) 251-5866	azdot.gov/mvd/forms-and-publications	None
Arkansas	(501) 661-2301	www.healthy.arkansas.gov/programsServices/hsLicensingRegulation/RadiationControl/Pages/default.aspx	(501) 280-4407
California	(916) 843-3400	www.chp.ca.gov/Programs-Services/Programs/Commercial-Vehicle-Section	(916) 322-3154
Colorado	(303) 273-1913; (303) 877-9757 (emergency)	www.colorado.gov/pacific/csp/nuclear-materials-transportation	(303) 273-1911
Connecticut	(860) 424-3029	www.ct.gov/deep/cwp/view.asp?a=2713&q=324824&deepNav_GID=1639	None
Delaware	(302) 744-4546	dhss.delaware.gov/dhss/dph/hsp/orc.html	(302) 739-3839
District of Columbia	(800) 321-6742; (800) 424-8802 (emer., USCG NRC)	www.osha.gov/SLTC/trucking_industry/transportinghazardousmaterials.html	None
Florida	(850) 245-4545	www.floridahealth.gov/environmental-health/radiation-control/radmat/index.html	(850) 921-6364
Georgia	(404) 362-2675	epd.georgia.gov/air/radioactive-materials-program	(404) 363-7100
Hawaii	(808) 586-4700	health.hawaii.gov/irhb/radiation/	(808) 586-5838
Idaho	(208) 884-7220	www.isp.idaho.gov/cvs/index.html	(208) 884-7192
Illinois	(217) 782-2700	www.illinois.gov/iema/nrs/Pages/default.aspx	None
Indiana	(317) 464-7394	www.in.gov/dhs/3889.htm	(317) 234-7234
Iowa	(515) 281-0419	idph.iowa.gov/Portals/1/userfiles/124/Transportation_Radioactive_Materials_IDPH_Rad_Health.pdf	(515) 281-4529
Kansas	(785) 296-1560	www.kdheks.gov/radiation/indexRadMat.html	(785) 296-0984
Kentucky	(502) 564-3700 (business hrs.); (800) 255-2587 (emergency)	chfs.ky.gov/dph/radiation.htm	(502) 564-1492
Louisiana	(225) 219-3041	www.deq.louisiana.gov/portal/PROGRAMS/Radiation.aspx	(225) 219-3154
Maine	(207) 287-5676; (207) 287-4770	www.maine.gov/dhhs/mecdc/environmental-health/rad/	(207) 287-3059
Maryland	(410) 537-3300; (800) 633-6101 ext. 3300 (in-state)	mde.maryland.gov/PROGRAMS/AIR/Pages/index.aspx	(410) 537-3198
Massachusetts	(617) 242-3035	www.mass.gov/eohhs/gov/departments/dph/programs/environmental-health/exposure-topics/radiation/	(617) 242-3457
Michigan	(517) 284-5087	www.michigan.gov/deq/0,4561,7-135-3306_63145---,00.html	(517) 373-4797
Minnesota	(651) 201-4400	www.health.state.mn.us/divs/eh/radiation/	(651) 201-4606
Mississippi	(601) 987-6893	msdh.ms.gov/msdhsite/_static/30,0,102.html	(601) 987-6887
Missouri	(573) 751-3907	dnr.mo.gov/env/hwp/rad/index.html	None
Montana	(406) 444-0496	deq.mt.gov/Land/hazwaste	(406) 444-1374
Nebraska	(402) 471-2079; (888) 242-1100	dhhs.ne.gov/publichealth/Pages/puh_enh_rad_index.aspx	(402) 471-0169
Nevada	(775) 687-7550; (775) 684-4622 (permits)	dpbh.nv.gov/Reg/Radiation_Control_Programs/	(775) 687-7552
New Hampshire	(603) 271-4588	www.dhhs.nh.gov/dphs/radiological/index.htm	(603) 225-2325
New Jersey	(609) 984-5636	www.nj.gov/dep/rpp/	(609) 633-2210
New Mexico	(505) 476-8600; (505) 827-9329 (emergency)	www.env.nm.gov/nmrcb/ram.html	(505) 476-8654
New York	(518) 402-9625	www.dec.ny.gov/chemical/296.html	(518) 402-9627
North Carolina	(919) 814-2250	www.ncradiation.net/rms/rms.htm	None
North Dakota	(701) 328-5188	www.ndhealth.gov/AQ/RAD/materials.htm	(701) 328-5185
Ohio	(800) 686-7826	www.puco.ohio.gov/puco/index.cfm/be-informed/consumer-topics/radioactive-shipments-and-security	(614) 752-8351
Oklahoma	(405) 702-5100	www.deq.state.ok.us/lpdnew/radindex.html	(405) 702-5101
Oregon	(503) 373-0982	www.oregon.gov/ODOT/MCT/pages/index.aspx	(503) 378-8815
Pennsylvania	(717) 787-2480	www.dep.pa.gov/Business/RadiationProtection/RadiationControl/Radioactive-Material-In-Solid-Waste-Monitoring/Pages/Transporting-Radioactive-Solid-Waste.aspx	(717) 783-8965
Rhode Island	(401) 222-5960	www.health.ri.gov/regulations/?parm=Radiation	None
South Carolina	(803) 898-0422	www.scdhec.net/environment/lwm/	(803) 898-0391
South Dakota	(605) 773-3153	www.state.sd.us/eforms/secure/eforms/E2149V2-RadioactiveMaterialsandRadiationMachineRegistrationForm.pdf	(605) 773-6035
Tennessee	(615) 532-0364	tn.gov/environment/topic/permit-radiological-health	None
Texas	(512) 239-6466	www.tceq.texas.gov/permitting/radmat	(512) 239-6464
Utah	(801) 536-4250 (business hrs.); (801) 536-4123 (non-business hrs.)	www.radiationcontrol.utah.gov/	(801) 533-4097
Vermont	(802) 828-1138 (business hrs.); (800) 641-5005 (24 hrs.)	www.anr.state.vt.us/dec/wastediv/index.htm	None
Virginia	(804) 897-6500	www.vdh.virginia.gov/radiological-health/radiological-health/transportation-of-radioactive-materials/	(804) 897-6576
Washington	(360) 236-3224	www.doh.wa.gov/CommunityandEnvironment/Radiation	(360) 236-2255
West Virginia	(304) 558-2981	www.wvdhhr.org/rtia/radiological_health.asp	(304) 558-0524
Wisconsin	(608) 267-4789; (715) 799-4937 (Menominee Indian Tribe lands only)	www.dhs.wisconsin.gov/radiation/radioactivematerials/index.htm	(608) 267-3695; (715) 799-6153 (Menominee Indian Tribe lands only)
Wyoming	(307) 777-7937	deq.wyoming.gov/shwd/	(307) 635-1784

CANADA

PROVINCE	PHONE	WEBSITE	FAX
ALL PROVINCES & TERRITORIES	(613) 992-4624 (TC); (613) 995-5894 (CNSC)	www.tc.gc.ca/eng/tdg/safety-menu.htm (Transport Canada); www.cnsc-ccsn.gc.ca/eng/ (Canadian Nuclear Safety Comission)	(613) 993-5925 (TC); (613) 995-5086 (CNSC)

Hazardous Spill Reporting

UNITED STATES

STATE	PHONE
Alabama	(800) 843-0699
Alaska	(907) 269-3063 (central); (907) 451-2121 (north); (907) 465-5340 (southeast); (800) 478-9300 (non-business hours); (907) 269-0667 (International)
Arizona	(602) 771-2330; (800) 234-5677
Arkansas	(800) 322-4012 (emergency); (800) 327-8411 (non-emergency)
California	(800) 852-7550; (916) 845-8911
Colorado	(877) 518-5608
Connecticut	(866) 337-7745; (860) 424-3338 (emergency)
Delaware	(800) 662-8802
District of Columbia	(202) 727-6161; (202) 671-3308
Florida	(800) 320-0519; (850) 245-2010 (business hours)
Georgia	(800) 241-4113 (emergency); (770) 387-4900 (non-emergency)
Hawaii	(800) 586-4249; (808) 247-2191 (non-business hours)
Idaho	(800) 632-8000 (in state); (208) 846-7610
Illinois	(800) 782-7860 (in state); (217) 782-7860
Indiana	(888) 233-7745; (800) 451-6027 (non-emergency)
Iowa	(515) 725-8694
Kansas	(785) 291-3333
Kentucky	(800) 928-2380; (502) 564-2380
Louisiana	(877) 925-6595; (225) 925-6595
Maine	(800) 452-4664 (hazmat); (800) 482-0777 (oil)
Maryland	(866) 633-4686
Massachusetts	(888) 304-1133
Michigan	(800) 292-4706; (800) 662-9278 (non-emergency)
Minnesota	(800) 422-0798; (651) 649-5451
Mississippi	(800) 222-6362
Missouri	(573) 634-2436
Montana	(406) 324-4777
Nebraska	(402) 471-7421; (877) 297-2368 (non-business hours)
Nevada	(888) 331-6337 (in state); (775) 687-9485 (out of state)
New Hampshire	(603) 271-3899 (business hours); (603) 223-4381 (non-business hours)
New Jersey	(877) 927-6337 option 2
New Mexico	(505) 827-9329; (505) 476-6000 (non-emergency)
New York	(800) 457-7362; (518) 457-7362
North Carolina	(800) 858-0368
North Dakota	(800) 472-2121
Ohio	(800) 282-9378
Oklahoma	(800) 522-0206
Oregon	(800) 452-0311
Pennsylvania	(800) 541-2050
Rhode Island	(401) 222-1360 (business hours); (401) 222-3070 (non-business hours)
South Carolina	(888) 481-0125
South Dakota	(605) 773-3296 (business hours); (605) 773-3231 (non-business hours)
Tennessee	(615) 741-0001
Texas	(800) 832-8224
Utah	(801) 536-4123
Vermont	(802) 828-1138 (business hours); (800) 641-5005
Virginia	(800) 468-8892
Washington	(800) 258-5990
West Virginia	(800) 642-3074
Wisconsin	(800) 943-0003
Wyoming	(307) 777-7781

CANADA

PROVINCE	PHONE
Alberta	(800) 222-6514 (in province); (780) 422-4505
British Columbia	(800) 663-3456
Manitoba	(204) 944-4888
New Brunswick	(800) 565-1633 (in province); (902) 426-6030
Newfoundland and Labrador	(800) 563-9089 (in province); (709) 772-2083 (in St. John's)
Northwest Territories	(867) 920-8130
Nova Scotia	(800) 565-1633 (in province); (902) 426-6030
Nunavut	(867) 920-8130
Ontario	(800) 268-6060 (in province); (416) 325-3000
Prince Edward Island	(800) 565-1633 (in province); (902) 426-6030
Québec	(866) 283-2333 (in province); (514) 283-2333
Saskatchewan	(800) 667-7525
Yukon	(867) 667-7244

†	place or route does not appear on the map		
‡	route not labeled on map		
EB	eastbound route	NB	northbound route
SB	southbound route	WB	westbound route

Low clearance locations

Structures with a legal or less-than-legal clearance on the U.S., the Trans-Canada, state, provincial, and other major routes used by motor carriers are listed here. Generally, county and local roads with any low clearance locations are not included in the listings. Information on vertical obstructions such as overpasses, trusses, and tunnels was provided to Rand McNally by the individual state and provincial highway departments from their bridge inventory files. Each structure is listed by route and location. Its vertical clearance, provided by the state or province, is given, as well as its grid location on the appropriate map.

Heights listed are believed to be accurate, but they may not take into consideration any discrepancies caused by curvatures in the roadway or changes resulting from ongoing roadway and/or structure maintenance. Heights listed are not to be relied on as indicating the actual safe clearance available, nor are the lists of low clearance locations to be taken as being all-inclusive. Neither the sources nor Rand McNally can warrant the height of listed clearances, and the driver of the vehicle is ultimately responsible for determining that adequate clearance exists before proceeding along any route.

Structures of less-than-legal clearance on routes restricted to trucks are NOT listed in the low clearance locations.

Permanent weigh stations

Locations of permanent weigh stations were supplied by state, provincial, and other official agencies. Each permanent weigh station is keyed to, and the location shown on, the appropriate state, provincial, and city map. The list of permanent weigh stations in this directory indicates the direction in which scales operate (when available); the map may not have an arrow for each direction at each location, due to space limitations. If the state or province also uses portable scales, that fact is noted. Almost every state, all provinces, the Northwest Territories, and Yukon have portable scales.

States may conduct motor carrier inspections at weigh station locations. The directory provides information about weigh station locations where motor carrier inspections are performed.

States and provinces may use weigh station locations as ports of entry for the issuance of permits; weigh stations that are also ports of entry are identified in the listings.

Restricted routes

Routes that restrict use by motor carriers for any of a number of reasons are listed. These routes are selected from information provided to Rand McNally by the individual states and provinces. Selected routes are restricted due to state or local laws banning truck travel, low-weight bridges, or tunnel limitations, or are unsafe for year-round truck travel due to extreme weather conditions. When planning a trip, companies and drivers should be aware that if a route is listed as a restricted route, it is not repeated in the list of low clearance locations even though it may have one or more structures of less than legal clearance.

ALABAMA

See state and city maps **pages 4-5**

★ located on city map

LOW CLEARANCE LOCATIONS

Statutory height: 13'6"
Structures with 13'6" or less clearance

Route	Location	Height	Map Key
AL 10	Greenville	10'0"	L-7
US 11	York	13'4"	J-2
AL 53	Ardmore–west, east of jct. I-65	11'6"	A-6
US 82	Gordo	13'6"	G-3
US 90/98	Mobile–Bankhead Tunnel	12'0"	★ S-8
AL 111	Wetumpka–at Coosa River Bridge	12'6"	I-8
Swan Bridge Rd.	Cleveland–1 mi. west at Locust Fork River Bridge	13'0"	D-7

PERMANENT WEIGH/INSPECTION STATIONS

■ also serves as Port of Entry
All scale locations are also vehicle inspection sites

Route	Location	Map Key
■ I-20 WB	New Hopewell–milepost 209	F-11

Alabama also uses portable scales

RESTRICTED ROUTES

Routes that restrict use by motor carriers

Route	Location
I-10	Mobile–Wallace Tunnel (restricted for Hazmat)
AL 22	AL 191 to †Chilton Co. Hwy. 15
AL 26	Hurtsboro to US 431
†AL 37	AL 84 to Fort Rucker
AL 77	I-59 to US 411 (Rainbow City)
AL 81	I-85 exit 38 to Notasulga
AL 105	Ozark to AL 10
AL 106	US 31 to US 29
AL 111	Wetumpka, over Coosa River
AL 179	US 278 to AL 168
US 231	Oneonta to US 11
AL 235	US 231 to Laniers
Natchez Trace Pkwy.	Mississippi state line to Tennessee state line

ALASKA

See state and city maps **page 6**

LOW CLEARANCE LOCATIONS

Structures with 15'0" or less clearance

Route	Location	Height	Map Key
Calhoun Av.	Juneau	13'3"	H-2
†Dyea Rd.	Skagway	11'2"	H-11
†Old Sterling Hwy.	Anchor Point	13'2"	H-7

PERMANENT WEIGH STATIONS

■ also serves as Port of Entry for Vehicle Registration only

Route	Location	Map Key
AK 1 EB, WB (Glenn Hwy.)	Anchorage–approx. 11 mi. northeast, milepost 10.6	G-7
AK 1 NB (Seward Hwy.)	Anchorage–approx. 10 mi. south, at Potters Marsh, milepost 115.5	G-7
AK 1 EB, WB (Sterling Hwy.)	Sterling–approx. 14 mi. east, milepost 82.5	G-7
■ AK 2 NB, SB (Alaska Hwy.)	Tok–approx. 5 mi. east, milepost 1308.6	F-9
AK 2 NB, SB (Richardson Hwy.)	Fairbanks–milepost 357.8	E-8
AK 2 NB, SB (Elliot Hwy.) & AK 6 (Steese Hwy.)	Fairbanks–approx. 10 mi. north, Elliot Hwy. milepost 0/Steese Hwy. milepost 11.5	D-8
AK 3 NB, SB (George Parks Hwy.)	Fairbanks–approx. 10 mi. southwest, milepost 356	E-8

Alaska also uses portable scales

RESTRICTED ROUTES

Routes that restrict use by motor carriers

Route	Location
None reported	

† place or route does not appear on the map
‡ route not labeled on map
EB eastbound route NB northbound route
SB southbound route WB westbound route

ARIZONA

See state and city maps **pages 8-9**
◆ located on Grand Canyon National Park map **page 7**
◗ located on Yuma map **page 7**

LOW CLEARANCE LOCATIONS

Statutory height: 13'6"
Structures with 13'6" or less clearance

Route	Location	Height	Map Key
AZ 84 EB	Casa Grande–mile point 177.66	13'3"	K-8
US 191	Morenci–tunnel at mile point 169.90	12'6"	K-13
AZ 288	4 mi. north of jct. AZ 188 at Salt River–mile point 262.44	12'3"	I-10

PERMANENT WEIGH/INSPECTION STATIONS

■ also serves as Port of Entry
All scale locations are also vehicle inspection sites

Route	Location	Map Key
■ I-8 EB, WB	Yuma–3 mi. east of California state line	L-2, ◗ L-6
■ I-8 Bus. EB, WB	Yuma–3 mi. east of California state line	L-2, ◗ L-6
■ I-10 EB	Ehrenburg–1 mi. east of California state line	I-2
■ I-10 EB, WB	San Simon–7 mi. west of New Mexico state line	M-14
■ I-15 NB, SB	†Black Rock–0.75 mi. north of Exit 27	A-4, ◆ A-4
■ I-19 NB, SB	Nogales–at US-Mexico border	O-10
■ I-40 WB	Sanders–20 mi. west of New Mexico state line	E-13
■ I-40 EB, WB	Topock–3.8 mi. east of California state line	G-3
■ US 60	Springerville–25 mi. west of New Mexico state line	H-13
■ US 70	Duncan/Franklin–4 mi. west of New Mexico state line	L-14
■ AZ 72	Parker–1 mi. east of California state line	H-3
■ AZ 85	Lukeville–just north of Mexico border	N-6
■ US 89	Page–5 mi. south of Utah state line	A-9, ◆ A-10
■ US 89 Alt.	Fredonia–5 mi. south of Utah state line	A-7, ◆ A-7
■ US 93 SB	Kingman–3 mi. northwest	E-3
■ US 95 NB, SB	San Luis–just north of Mexico border	L-2
■ US 160	Teec Nos Pos–6 mi. west of New Mexico state line	A-14
■ US 191	Douglas–at jct. AZ 80	O-13
■ AZ 286	Sasabe–just north of Mexico border	O-9
■ Towner Av.	Naco–just north of Mexico border	O-12

Arizona also uses portable scales

RESTRICTED ROUTES

Routes that restrict use by motor carriers

Route	Location
AZ 64	Grand Canyon to jct. US 89
AZ 67	Jacob Lake to North Rim
AZ 88	AZ 188 to US 60
AZ 89	Prescott to jct. US 93
AZ 89A	AZ 89 to I-17
AZ 99	AZ 87 to AZ 260
US 191	Morenci to Alpine
AZ 261	AZ 260 to AZ 273
AZ 266	Bonita to US 191
AZ 273	AZ 260 to AZ 261
AZ 288	Young to AZ 88
AZ 289	I-19 to Arivaca
AZ 366	Turkey Flat to US 191
AZ 473	Hawley Lake to AZ 260

ARKANSAS

See state and city maps **pages 10-11**
★ located on city map
◆ located on Memphis map **page 94**

LOW CLEARANCE LOCATIONS

Statutory height: 13'6"
Structures with 13'6" or less clearance

Route	Location	Height	Map Key
AR 7	Camden–north, 0.8 mi. northwest of US 79	12'8"	K-6
AR 42	Turrell–0.01 mi. east of AR 77	11'6"	E-13
AR 69	Trumann–0.82 mi. east of AR 463	9'6"	D-12
†AR 69 Spur	Trumann–south of AR 69	12'7"	D-12
AR 75	Parkin	12'0"	F-12
AR 134	Garland City–jct. US 82	13'6"	L-3
‡AR 282	Mountainburg–approx. 4.5 mi. southwest	12'1"	D-2
AR 296	Mandeville–approx. 0.5 mi. southwest	10'11"	L-2
AR 331	Pottsville–0.11 mi. south of US 64	11'6"	F-5
AR 365	North Little Rock–0.4 mi. west of US 70	12'6"	G-7

PERMANENT WEIGH STATIONS

■ also serves as Port of Entry

Route	Location	Map Key
■ I-30 EB, WB	†Guernsey–4 mi. southwest of Hope	K-3
■ I-40 EB, WB	Alma–4.5 mi. west	★ H-20, E-2
I-40 WB	†Riverside–just west of Tennessee state line	◆ K-1, F-14
■ I-40 EB	West Memphis–11.5 mi. west	F-13
I-49 NB, SB	Springdale	★ E-19, B-2
I-55 SB	Blytheville–south of Missouri state line	C-14
I-55 NB	†Bridgeport–east of West Memphis	◆ K-1, F-14
■ I-55 SB	Marion–south of US 64	F-13
US 71 NB, SB	Ashdown	K-2

Arkansas also uses portable scales

RESTRICTED ROUTES

Routes that restrict use by motor carriers

Route	Location
AR 1	US 62 to Missouri state line
†AR 8	North jct US 65 to south jct US 65
AR 13	US 165 to US 79
AR 17	AR 38 to US 64
†AR 17	AR 153 to Ethel
AR 20	Lambrook to south of AR 44
AR 33	AR 17 to AR 37
AR 33	AR 38 to US 64
†AR 35	Halley to †Dewey
AR 36	Georgetown to West Point
AR 37	Grubbs to Tuckerman
AR 37	AR 14 to AR 18
AR 37	AR 17 to AR 14
AR 39	AR 1 to US 49
AR 42	AR 37 to Hickory Ridge
AR 42	AR 75 to I-55
AR 46	US 270 to I-530
AR 50	Crawfordsville to Clarkedale
AR 53	I-30 to AR 51
AR 56	Evening Shade to Poughkeepsie
AR 58	AR 115 to Poughkeepsie
AR 58	AR 354 to Williford
†AR 58E	US 62 to Williford
AR 69	AR 163 to I-555
AR 74	AR 23 to AR 21
†AR 74	AR 123 to †Bass
AR 78	US 70 to AR 306
AR 86	US 70 to US 63
AR 87	Bradford to Denmark
AR 87	Elizabeth to Missouri state line
AR 106	AR 69 to AR 69 Bus.
AR 107	AR 16 to AR 110
AR 107	AR 124 to AR 25
AR 110	AR 25 to AR 124
AR 110	AR 107 to Heber Springs
AR 113	AR 10 to Wye
AR 121	US 79 to AR 1 (west of La Grange)
AR 121	AR 78 to AR 261
AR 121	AR 261 to AR 1
AR 124	Jerusalem to AR 95
AR 124	Springfield to US 65
AR 124	AR 25 to AR 36
AR 124	AR 95 to AR 9
AR 124	AR 110 to AR 157
AR 133	AR 160 to Lacey
AR 134	US 71 to AR 196
AR 139	Pollard to Missouri state line
AR 139	AR 90 to US 62
AR 141	Hooker to Knob
AR 144	Lake Village to AR 257
AR 145	AR 37 to AR 14
AR 145	AR 37 to AR 42
AR 151	AR 148 to AR 18
AR 156	Moffit to AR 170
AR 157	US 167 to AR 14
AR 160	US 165 to US 65
AR 163	US 64 to AR 1
AR 171	AR 36 to AR 25
AR 175	US 62 to Wirth
†AR 182	AR 51 to Gurdon
AR 195	AR 355 to AR 73
AR 200	Rosston to Morris
†AR 212	Glendale to Star City
AR 214	Fisher to Whitehall
AR 214	AR 163 to AR 463
AR 218	I-40 to AR 147
AR 228	Light to Sedgwick
AR 228	I-555 to AR 91
AR 229	Leola to Traskwood
AR 230	AR 91 to Old US 67
†AR 234	†AR 317 to †Paraloma
AR 241	AR 302 to AR 17
AR 243	Marvell to AR 121
AR 251	Missouri state line to AR 115
AR 259	AR 306 to AR 284
AR 261	US 70 to AR 121
AR 261	AR 121 to AR 259
AR 267	AR 31 to US 67 Bus.
AR 267 Spur	AR 31 to AR 267
AR 289	US 62 to AR 9
†AR 290	†AR 128 to AR 171
AR 291	Tull to AR 46
†AR 293	US 82 to AR 144
AR 293	AR 114 to AR 54
†AR 298	AR 9 to AR 5
AR 302	Clarendon to US 70
AR 304	US 67 to Delaplaine
AR 306	US 49 to Colt
AR 309	AR 109 to AR 10
AR 318	AR 5 to AR 367
AR 318	AR 20 to AR 316
†AR 324	AR 9 to †Lake Sylvia campground
AR 328	Success to US 67
AR 328	AR 251 to Maynard
AR 351	US 49 to AR 358
AR 356	AR 92 to AR 225
AR 358	US 49 to AR 141
†AR 360	Gin City to Canfield
†AR 373	AR 14 to AR 214
†AR 386	Wrightsville to †Asher Rd.
AR 395	Byron to Salem

† place or route does not appear on the map
‡ route not labeled on map
EB eastbound route NB northbound route
SB southbound route WB westbound route

CALIFORNIA

See state and city maps **pages 12-15**
◆ located on Los Angeles maps **pages 18-19**
● located on Sacramento map **page 16**
◗ located on San Diego & Vicinity map **page 17**
✧ located on San Francisco Bay Area map **page 13**

LOW CLEARANCE LOCATIONS

Statutory height: 14'0"
Structures with 14'0" or less clearance

Route	Location	Height	Map Key
I-5 NB	San Diego–Pershing Dr. off ramp	13'10"	◗ L-10
CA 33 NB, SB	Ventura–Matilija Tunnels	13'4"	SI-9
CA 110 NB	Los Angeles–College St. overpass	13'6"	◆ J-2
CA 110 NB	Los Angeles–Hill St. overpass	13'5"	◆ J-2
†CA 151 EB, WB	Summit City–Coram overpass	13'9"	NE-5
CA 238 SB	Fremont–2.2 mi. north of I-680	14'0"	✧ NI-18

PERMANENT WEIGH/INSPECTION STATIONS

■ also serves as Port of Entry
All scale locations are also vehicle inspection sites

Route	Location	Map Key
CA 4 WB	Murphys	NL-9
I-5 NB	Castaic	SI-10
I-5 NB, SB	Cottonwood	NF-6
I-5 SB	†Grapevine	SH-9
■ I-5 SB	Mt. Shasta–south	NC-5
I-5 NB, SB	†San Onofre–5.25 mi. south of San Clemente	SL-13
I-5 NB, SB	Santa Nella Village–north of jct. CA 33	SB-5
■ CA 7 NB	Calexico–east of E. Carr Rd.	SM-18
■ I-8 WB	Winterhaven–6 mi. west	SM-19
I-10 EB, WB	Banning–east of CA 243	SJ-14
■ I-10 WB	Blythe–west	SK-19
I-15 NB	Cajon Junction	◆ A-17, SI-13
I-15 SB	Mountain Pass–east	SF-17
I-15 NB, SB	Rainbow	SL-14
US 50 WB	Camino	NJ-9
CA 58 EB	Keene	SG-10
CA 58 WB	Mojave–7 mi. west of CA 14	SG-11
CA 70 WB	Keddie–at jct. CA 89	NG-8
I-80 EB, WB	Antelope–12.5 mi. northeast of downtown Sacramento	● F-5, NJ-17
I-80 EB, WB	Cordelia–southwest of Fairfield	NL-6
■ I-80 WB	Truckee–east of CA 89	NI-10
CA 91 EB, WB	Anaheim–Peralta Hills area	◆ H-13, SJ-12
CA 99 NB	Chowchilla–north	SA-6
US 101 NB, SB	Gilroy	SB-4
US 101 SB	†Little River–8.5 mi. north of Arcata	ND-2
US 101 NB	San Rafael–3.5 mi. north of jct. I-580	✧ NC-11, NL-5
US 101 SB	San Rafael–4.5 mi. north of jct. I-580	✧ NC-11, NL-5
US 101 NB, SB	Thousand Oaks–6 mi. north of jct. CA 23	SJ-9
US 101 SB	Willits–6 mi. south	NH-3
CA 108 WB	†Lyons Dam–northeast of Long Barn	NL-10
CA 188 NB	Tecate	SN-15
CA 299 WB	Blue Lake	ND-2
CA 299 EB	Whiskeytown	NE-5
I-580 EB, WB	Livermore	NM-6
I-680 NB	Fremont	✧ NJ-19, NM-6
I-680 NB, SB	Walnut Creek	✧ ND-17, NL-6
I-880 NB, SB	Fremont–north of CA 262	✧ NJ-18, NN-6
■ Enrico Fermi Dr. NB	†Otay Mesa–east of CA 905	◗ M-6

California also uses portable scales

RESTRICTED ROUTES

Routes with special restrictions refer to: www.dot.ca.gov/hq/traffops/engineering/trucks
[for designated STAA routes, see maps]

Other routes that restrict use by motor carriers

Route	Location
CA 1	Los Angeles International Airport–Sepulveda Tunnel (Combustibles or flammables only)
CA 1	Pacifica–Tom Lantos Tunnels (Explosives, flammables or combustibles only)
CA 1	CA 27 to CA 23 (No through trucks with 4 or more axles)
CA 1	CA 246 to †Central Av. (No trucks over 3 tons)
CA 2	I-210 to Big Pines Hwy.
CA 20	CA 29 to CA 53 (Hazmat only)
CA 24	Oakland–Caldecott Tunnel (Explosives, flammables, or poisonous gas only)
CA 75	Coronado–Coronado Bay Bridge (Corrosives, explosives or flammables only)
CA 80	San Francisco-Oakland Bay Bridge (Explosives or flammables only)
CA 83	Upland–Base Line Rd. to CA 30 (No trucks over 5 tons)
CA 84	Rio Vista, on the Cache Slough Ferry (No tractor-trailers)
CA 84	CA 238 to I-680 (Hazmat only)
CA 85	US 101 to I-280 (No trucks over 4.5 tons)
CA 108	Tuolumne/Mono County line to west of US 395 (no trucks with a KPRA over 38 feet)
CA 110	Pasadena–US 101 to †Glenarm St. (No trucks over 3 tons)
CA 152	Watsonville–†Carlton Rd. to Gilroy, †Watsonville Rd. (No vehicles over 45 ft.)
CA 154	CA 246 to US 101 (Hazmat only)
CA 170	at NB US 101 on-ramp (Turning movement restriction)
CA 173	CA 138 to CA 189
CA 175	US 101 to CA 29 (No vehicles over 39 ft.)
CA 183 SB	CA 156 to CA 1 (No trucks over 7 tons, detour available)
CA 220	North of Rio Vista, on the J-Mac Ferry (No tractor-trailers)
CA 246	Lompoc to CA 1 (No trucks over 3 tons)
CA 260	Alameda–†Central Av. to I-880 (Hazmat only)
I-580	San Leandro–Foothill Blvd. to Oakland, †Grand Av. (No trucks over 4.5 tons)

COLORADO

See state and city maps **pages 21-22**
★ located on city map
◆ located on Denver & Vicinity map **page 22**
◗ located on Ft. Collins map **page 22**

LOW CLEARANCE LOCATIONS

Maximum height permitted in Eisenhower & Johnson tunnels: 13'11" on I-70, at milepost 213.65.

Overheight and hazardous loads detour over Highway 6 Loveland Pass, weather permitting. Check with weigh stations for other detours if Loveland Pass closed due to snow.

Statutory height: 13'0" on nondesignated highways; 14'6" on selected designated highways.
Structures with 14'6" or less clearance

Route	Location	Min. Height	Max. Height	Map Key
US 6	Eagle–0.67 mi. east at Eagle River, milepost 150.24	14'4"	14'4"	F-9
CO 14	Poudre Park–tunnel 4.7 mi. west, milepost 107.25	14'5"	14'5"	B-12
US 50 Bus. EB (Santa Fe Av.)	Pueblo–just south of I-25/US 85/87 at Arkansas River	13'6"	13'6"	★ J-2
I-70 EB	Idaho Springs–milepost 238.689	14'0"	no max.	E-12
I-70/US40/US 287	†Deer Trail–4.92 mi. west at milepost 346.25	14'3"	14'3"	F-16
CO 95 NB (Sheridan Blvd.)	Denver–at I-70, milepost 9.013	14'1"	17'4"	◆ I-6
CO 95 SB (Sheridan Blvd.)	Denver–at I-70, milepost 9.013	14'1"	16'11"	◆ I-6
CO 144	Fort Morgan–at I-76 overpass, milepost 0.01	13'3"	13'3"	D-16
CO 265	Commerce City–0.5 mi. north of Race St.	11'4"	11'5"	◆ H-7
US 550/CO 789	Ouray–tunnel 1.17 mi. south at milepost 90.86	13'9"	13'9"	K-7

PERMANENT WEIGH/INSPECTION STATIONS

■ also serves as Port of Entry
All scale locations are also vehicle inspection sites

Route	Location	Map Key
■ I-25 NB, SB	Timnath–1.6 mi. south of CO 14	◗ C-10, C-13
■ I-25/US 85/87 NB, SB	Monument–0.5 mi. north of CO 105	G-14
■ I-25/US 85/87 NB	Trinidad–2 mi. south (joint port with New Mexico)	M-14
■ US 50/287 EB, WB	Lamar–0.5 mi. west of CO 196	J-19
■ I-70 EB, WB	Limon–0.25 mi. west of CO 71	G-16
■ I-70 EB, WB	Loma–4 mi. west of Fruita (joint port with Utah)	G-4
■ I-70/US 6/40 EB, WB	Lawson–1.5 mi. east	E-12
■ I-76 EB, WB	Ft. Morgan–6 mi. west of jct. US 34 & US 6	D-16
■ US 85 NB, SB	Platteville–0.5 mi. south of CO 66	D-14
■ US 160/491 NB, SB	Cortez–2 mi. south	M-5

Colorado also uses portable scales

RESTRICTED ROUTES

Restrictions vary. Call 303-757-9539 for detailed information.

For other truck restrictions in Colorado, refer to: www.codot.gov/business/permits/truckpermits/restrictions.html

Other routes that restrict use by motor carriers

Route	Location
CO 10	US 50 to CO 71
CO 12	US 160 to I-25
CO 14	CO 125 to US 287
CO 15	Capulin to US 160
CO 17	New Mexico state line to US 285
US 34	Grand Lake to US 36
US 36	US 34 to Estes Park
US 50	Sargents to Maysville
CO 55	US 6 to US 138
CO 65	CO 92 to I-70
CO 67	Cripple Creek to US 24
CO 71	US 350 to CO 10
CO 78	CO 165 to Pueblo County Road 212
CO 82	Aspen to Twin Lakes (max. truck length 35')
CO 92	US 50 to CO 133
CO 96	Sugar City to Arlington
CO 105	CO 103 to end of road
CO 119	CO 72 to CO 7
CO 131	Oak Creek to US 40
CO 133	Bowie to CO 82
CO 138	Stirling to CO 113
CO 149	US 160 to US 50
US 160	east of Las Animas County line to Pritchett
CO 165	CO 96 to CO 78
CO 279	CO 119 to Central City
CO 325	CO 13 to River Falls State Park
CO 330	CO 65 to Collbran
US 550	Hermosa to Ouray

† place or route does not appear on the map
‡ route not labeled on map
EB eastbound route NB northbound route
SB southbound route WB westbound route

CONNECTICUT

See state and city maps page 23
★ located on city map

LOW CLEARANCE LOCATIONS

Statutory height: 13'6"
Structures with 13'6" or less clearance

Route	Location	Height	Map Key
US 1	Branford–northeast of CT 142	13'1"	★ J-10
US 1	Darien–0.1 mi. southwest of CT 124	11'3"	H-4
US 1	Madison–2.1 mi. west of CT 79	12'8"	G-9
US 1	Milford–Milford Pkwy. Overpass	11'6"	★ J-7
US 1	Stamford–0.6 mi. west of I-95	13'1"	D-3
US 6	Bristol–0.4 mi. west of CT 69	13'6"	D-7
CT 10	Farmington–US 6 overpass	13'6"	C-8
CT 10	Hamden–0.4 mi. west of CT 15	13'6"	★ H-10
CT 12	Lisbon–I-395 overpass	13'4"	D-13
CT 53	Bethel–1.3 mi. south of CT 302	11'4"	F-4
CT 53	Norwalk–CT 15 overpass	11'4"	H-4
CT 57	Westport–CT 15 overpass	12'7"	H-5
†CT 71	Wallingford	10'0"	E-8
CT 72	Plymouth–0.2 mi. west of Hartford County line	13'3"	D-7
CT 81	Clinton–0.1 mi. north of US 1	11'5"	G-10
CT 104	Stamford–CT 15 overpass	11'10"	H-3
CT 106	New Canaan–0.4 mi. north of CT 15	11'1"	H-4
CT 106	New Canaan–CT 15 overpass	12'11"	H-4
CT 110	Stratford–0.2 mi. north of I-95	11'1"	★ I-7
CT 113	Stratford–RR north of I-95	13'0"	★ J-6
CT 115	Seymour–0.2 mi. east of CT 8	12'3"	F-6
CT 130	Bridgeport–I-95 overpass	12'10"	★ J-6
CT 133	Brookfield–0.2 mi. east of US 7/202	12'1"	E-4
CT 135	Fairfield–0.1 mi. south of I-95	10'7"	★ J-5
CT 136	Westport–0.1 mi. south of I-95	10'11"	H-4
CT 137	Stamford–CT 15 overpass	11'9"	H-4
CT 138	Lisbon–southwest, 1 mi. west of CT 12	12'7"	D-13
CT 146	Branford–RR north of Branford River	9'6"	★ J-11
CT 146	Branford–south of US 1	10'0"	★ NJ-11
CT 146	Guilford–1.25 mi. southwest	11'8"	G-9
CT 146	Leetes Island	13'6"	G-8
CT 159	Windsor–0.1 mi. northeast of CT 305	12'9"	B-9
CT 243	New Haven–CT 15 overpass	12'6"	★ H-9
CT 275	Eagleville–0.2 mi. west of CT 32	12'0"	B-11
CT 322 WB	Milldale–CT 10 overpass	12'7"	G-8
CT 533	Vernon–0.06 south of I-84	12'7"	B-10
CT 598	Hartford–Library Building	12'0"	★ I-13
†CT 598	Hartford–Main St. overpass	13'3"	★ H-13
CT 598	Hartford–Prospect St. overpass	10'11"	★ I-13
CT 649	Groton–2.25 mi. east of CT 349	10'6"	★ F-2
CT 847	Waterbury	12'10"	★ B-2

PERMANENT WEIGH STATIONS

Route	Location	Map Key
I-84 EB	Danbury–Exit 2	F-3
I-84 WB	Union–3.4 mi. south of Massachusetts state line	A-12
I-91 NB	Middletown–1.4 mi. north of Exit 18	E-8
I-95 NB	Greenwich–0.9 mi. south of Exit 3	I-3
I-95 NB	Waterford–1.1 mi. west of CT 85	★ F-1, F-12
I-95 SB	Waterford–1.3 mi. west of CT 85	★ F-1, F-12

Connecticut also uses portable scales

RESTRICTED ROUTES

Routes that restrict use by motor carriers

Route	Location
CT 15	New York state line to I-91
CT 42	CT 63 to CT 10
CT 42	CT 67 to CT 8
CT 49	CT 216 to CT 138
CT 82	CT 149 to CT 151
CT 89	CT 195 to Mt. Hope
CT 97	CT 14 to US 6
CT 109	US 202 to CT 61
CT 136	CT 57 to CT 59
CT 145	CT 80 to CT 148
CT 150	CT 22 to I-91
CT 189	CT 539 to Massachusetts state line
CT 198	Chaplin to US 6
CT 216	CT 49 to Clark Falls
CT 796 (Milford Pkwy.)	US 1 to CT 15

DELAWARE

See state and city maps page 24
★ located on city map

LOW CLEARANCE LOCATIONS

Statutory height: 13'6"
Structures with 13'6" or less clearance

Route	Location	Height	Map Key
DE 52 (Pennsylvania Av.)	Wilmington–0.75 mi. west of jct. I-95	13'5"	★ C-8
DE 100 (Montchanin Rd.)	Winterthur	12'0"	★ B-8
†Local road 336D	Stanton–1 mi. south	9'10"	★ C-7
†14th St.	Wilmington–at †N. Scott St.	13'1"	★ C-8
‡18th St.	Wilmington–just south of ‡Augustine Cut-off	12'6"	★ B-9
Barley Mill Rd.	Ashland–covered bridge at Red Clay Creek	11'3"	★ B-7
†Beech St.	Wilmington–at †N. Coleman St.	12'6"	★ C-8
†Casho Mill Rd.	Newark–between DE 2 and DE 273	8'7"	★ D-5
†Central Av.	Laurel	12'5"	L-2
†Foxhill Ln.	Wooddale–between DE 48 (Lancaster Pike) & Barley Mill Rd., west of Centerville Rd. at Red Clay Creek Bridge	13'0"	★ B-7
†French St.	Wilmington–just south of †E. Front St.	13'2"	★ C-9
†Gilpin Av.	Wilmington–just south of †N. Dupont St.	12'7"	★ C-8
†James St.	Newport–0.1 mi. south of jct. DE 4	12'10"	★ C-8
†Lovering Av.	Wilmington–at †Augustine Cut Off	12'6"	★ C-8
†Lovers Ln.	Kirkwood–0.75 mi. north, west of DE 71	12'8"	D-2
North Chapel St.	Newark	12'0"	★ D-6
†Old Ogletown Rd.	DE 273 to †Augusta Dr.	10'0"	★ D-6
†Rising Sun Ln.	Wilmington–between DE 52 (Pennsylvania Av.) & DE 141	12'3"	★ B-8
Smith Bridge Rd.	Wilmington–at Brandywine Creek	11'0"	★ A-8
†Telegraph Rd.	Stanton–0.5 mi. west	10'8"	★ C-7

PERMANENT WEIGH/INSPECTION STATIONS

■ also serves as Port of Entry
All scale locations are also vehicle inspection sites

Route	Location	Map Key
■ US 13 NB	Smyrna–5 mi. north	F-2
US 301 NB	Middletown–just east of Maryland state line	E-1

Delaware also uses portable scales

RESTRICTED ROUTES

Routes that restrict use by motor carriers

Route	Location
DE 2/4 (Christina Pkwy.)	DE 2 Bus. to S. College Av.
DE 6	DE 1 to DE 9
US 13	Laurel, over Broad Creek
US 13 (E. 4th St.)	Wilmington, DE 9 to N. Church St.
US 13 Bus. (S. Walnut St.)	Wilmington, A St. to E. 4th St.
DE 17	DE 26 to Roxana
DE 82	DE 52 to Pennsylvania state line

DISTRICT OF COLUMBIA

See district map page 111
◆ located on Central Washington, D.C. map

LOW CLEARANCE LOCATIONS

Statutory height: 13'6"
Structures with 13'6" or less clearance

Route	Location	Height	Map Key
NORTHEAST			
Florida Av.	1 block south of US 50 (New York Av.)	13'6"	F-7
L St.	east of 1st St., under Washington Terminal Yards	13'6"	F-7
M St.	east of 1st St., under Washington Terminal Yards	13'6"	F-7
NORTHWEST			
Connecticut Av.	Q St. underpass, near jct. of Connecticut Av. and New Hampshire Av.	13'6"	F-6
Massachusetts Av.	underpass at Thomas Circle–jct. of 14th St., M St. & Vermont Av.	12'6"	F-6
†Potomac River Fwy.	US 50 (Theodore Roosevelt Memorial Bridge) overpass–between 23rd St. and the Rock Creek & Potomac Pkwy.	13'0"	◆ L-3
SOUTHEAST			
South Capitol St.	south of Virginia Av.	13'1"	◆ N-9
SOUTHWEST			
2nd St.	underpass at Virginia Av.	13'6"	G-7
3rd St.	underpass at Virginia Av.	13'5"	G-7
7th St.	underpass at Virginia Av.	13'6"	G-7

PERMANENT WEIGH/INSPECTION STATIONS

Scale location is also a vehicle inspection site

Route	Location	Map Key
I-295 SB	Washington D.C.–near Maryland state line	H-6

The District of Columbia also uses portable scales

RESTRICTED ROUTES

All National Park Service roads are restricted routes.

Other routes that restrict use by motor carriers

Route	Location
US 50	US 1 to Virginia state line
I-66	Theodore Roosevelt Memorial Bridge to US 50
9th St. NE	over New York Av.
17th St. NW/SW	H St. to Independence Av. SW
27th St. NW	over Broad Branch
31st St. NW	over C&O Canal
Kenilworth Ter. NE	over Watts Branch

† place or route does not appear on the map
‡ route not labeled on map
EB eastbound route NB northbound route
SB southbound route WB westbound route

FLORIDA

See state and city maps pages 26-27
★ located on city map
◗ located on city map page 24
◆ located on city map page 25

LOW CLEARANCE LOCATIONS

Statutory height: 13'6"
Structures with 13'6" or less clearance

Route	Location	Height	Map Key
FL 600	Lakeland	13'6"	◆ J-2
†6th St.	Miami Beach–FL 907/Alton Rd.	11'10"	◆ L-9
†Bloxham St.	Tallahassee–FL 61 overpass	12'6"	◗ M-8
†College St.	Jacksonville–I-95 overpass	12'8"	★ H-2
†Gadsden St.	Tallahassee–US 27 overpass	13'0"	◗ M-8
†Washington St.	Lake City–US 41 overpass	12'6"	C-7

PERMANENT WEIGH/INSPECTION STATIONS

All scale locations are also vehicle inspection sites

Route	Location	Map Key
US 1 NB, SB	Bunnell	E-10
US 1 NB, SB	Boulougne–2.5 mi. south of Georgia state line	A-8
US 1 NB, SB	Plantation Key	S-12
I-4 EB, WB	Seffner	◆ B-5, J-7
I-10 EB, WB	Ellaville	B-5
I-10 EB, WB	Pensacola–3 mi. east of Alabama state line	R-2
I-10 EB, WB	Sneads–west of exit 158	R-8
US 17 NB, SB	East Palatka	E-9
US 17 NB, SB	Yulee–south of jct. I-95, 3 mi. south of Georgia state line	B-9
US 19 NB, SB	Old Town	E-6
US 27/129	Branford- just west of east jct with US 129	D-6
FL 60 EB, WB	†Hopewell–at FL 39	◆ C-6, J-8
I-75 NB, SB	Port Charlotte–5.1 mi. south of jct. US 17	M-8
I-75 NB, SB	White Springs	C-6
I-75 NB, SB	Wildwood–9 mi. north of FL 44	G-8
US 90 EB, WB	Pensacola–west of US 90 Alt.	◗ I-7, R-2
I-95 NB, SB	Flagler Beach	E-10
I-95 NB	Hobe Sound	M-13
I-95 SB	Palm City–milepost 113	L-12
I-95 NB, SB	Yulee–south of jct. US 17	A-9
FL 121 NB, SB	Macclenny	C-8
US 441 NB, SB	Lake City–north	C-7

Florida also uses portable scales

RESTRICTED ROUTES

Routes that restrict use by motor carriers

Route	Location
FL 105/A1A	American Beach to FL 105
US 221	US 27 to Ash St through Perry
US 441	FL 100A to US 41 through Lake City
FL 922/Broad Cswy.	US 1 to Bay Harbor Islands

GEORGIA

See state and city maps pages 28-30
◆ located on Atlanta & Vicinity map page 30

LOW CLEARANCE LOCATIONS

If load exceeds 13'6" height, an oversize permit is required. The permit will include the route of travel which will route around any low clearances.

Statutory height: 13'6"

Route	Location	Height	Map Key
GA 2	Ringgold	11'7"	B-2
GA 12	Warrenton	13'6"	G-9
US 23/29/78	Druid Hills	10'0"	◆ E-5
GA 44	Union Point	13'6"	F-8
GA 92	Fairburn, SE of US 29	10'0"	F-4

PERMANENT WEIGH STATIONS

Route	Location	Map Key
I-16 EB, WB	Blitchton, mile point 144	J-12
I-20 WB	Bremen–3.8 mi. east of US 27, mile point 15	E-2
I-20 EB	Grovetown, mile point 187.5	F-10
I-20 WB	Grovetown, mile point 187.8	F-10
I-20 EB	Lithia Springs, mile point 43	E-4
I-75 NB, SB	Forsyth–1.2 mi. north of exit, mile point 190	H-5
I-75 NB, SB	Ringgold–0.5 mi. south of exit, mile point 343	B-3
I-75 NB, SB	Valdosta–1.6 mi. north of exit, mile point 23	O-7
US 84 WB	Ludowici–south	L-11
I-85 NB, SB	La Grange, mile point 22.5	H-3
I-85 NB	Lavonia–2.3 mi. south of GA 17, mile point 171	C-8
I-85 SB	Lavonia–3.5 mi. south, mile point 169	C-8
I-95 NB, SB	Darien–6.1 mi. north of exit, mile point 54	M-12
I-95 SB	Port Wentworth–mile point 111	J-13

Georgia also uses portable scales

RESTRICTED ROUTES

All Interstate, U.S., and State highways within the I-285 loop in Atlanta

All through routes in the town of Newnan are prohibited.

Other routes that restrict use by motor carriers

Route	Location
GA 45	GA 41 to GA 234
GA 136	GA 9 to US 19
GA 216	Milford to GA 37

HAWAII

See state and city maps page 30
★ located on city map

LOW CLEARANCE LOCATION

Statutory height: 14'0"
Structure with 14'0" or less clearance

Route	Location	Height	Map Key
HI 63	Honolulu–1.5 mi. west of I-H3	13'0"	M-5

PERMANENT WEIGH/INSPECTION STATIONS

Route	Location	Map Key
O`AHU		
HI 64 (Sand Island Access Rd.)	Honolulu	★ G-7

Port-of-Entry Locations
Portable scales may be used at POE locations

Route	Location	Map Key
HAWAI`I		
HI 19	Hilo–milepost 0	M-10
HI 270	†Kawaihae–milepost 3.4	L-8
KAUA`I		
†HI 51	Līhue–milepost 0	I-2
MAUI		
HI 32	Kahului–milepost 2.8	I-8
O`AHU		
HI 64 (Sand Island Access Rd.)	Honolulu–milepost 0	★ G-7

Hawaii also uses portable scales

RESTRICTED ROUTES

Routes that restrict use by motor carriers

Route	Location
None reported	

IDAHO

See state and city maps page 31
★ located on city map

LOW CLEARANCE LOCATIONS

Statutory height; 14'0"
Structures with 14'0" or less clearance

Route	Location	Height	Map Key
US 20/26 Bus. SB	Idaho Falls–milepost 333.48	13'8"	★ B-9
US 20/26 Bus. NB	Idaho Falls–milepost 333.49	14'0"	★ B-9
US 30	Pocatello–milepost 334.14	13'7"	L-7
US 95 Bus.	Craigmont	14'0"	F-2

PERMANENT WEIGH STATIONS

■ also serves as Port of Entry

Route	Location	Map Key
■ US 2/95 NB, SB	Bonners Ferry–north at milepost 510.6	B-2
■ US 12/95	Lewiston–milepost 309.79	F-1
■ US 12/95	Lewiston Hill–north, milepost 317.9	F-1
■ I-15 NB, SB	Inkom–14 mi. southeast of Pocatello, milepost 59.01	L-7
■ I-15 NB, SB	†Sage Junction–6 mi. south of Hamer at ID 33, milepost 141.86	J-7
US 20 SB	Ashton–4.5 miles southwest	J-8
■ ID 55	Horseshoe Bend–milepost 65.38	J-2
■ I-84 EB, WB	Boise–southeast at milepost 67	K-2
■ I-84 EB, WB	†Cotterel–approx. 7 mi. south of jct. I-86, milepost 229.02	M-6
■ I-90 EB, WB	Haugan, MT–15 mi. east of Idaho state line (joint port with Montana)	D-3
■ I-90 EB	Huetter–3.5 mi. west of US 95, milepost 8.15	★ E-9, D-1
■ US 93 NB, SB	Hollister–milepost 26.16	M-4
■ US 95	Marsing–milepost 26.26	K-1

Idaho also uses portable scales

RESTRICTED ROUTES

Routes that restrict use by motor carriers

Route	Location
ID 11	US 12 to Headquarters
ID 14	ID 13 to Elk City
ID 21	Idaho City to Stanley
ID 29	Leadore to Montana state line
ID 57	US 2 to Nordman
ID 71	Cambridge to Oregon state line
ID 97	I-90 to ID 3

† place or route does not appear on the map
‡ route not labeled on map
EB eastbound route NB northbound route
SB southbound route WB westbound route

ILLINOIS

See state and city maps **pages 32-33**
★ located on city map
◆ located on Chicago & Vicinity map **pages 34-35**
● located on St. Louis & Vicinity map **page 57**

LOW CLEARANCE LOCATIONS

Chicago Low Clearance/Courtesy Routing Information
Chicago Communications Center
Department of Streets and Sanitation, Bureau EW and C
Room 702, City Hall, Chicago, IL 60602
(312) 744-6460 or -6461 (24-hour telephone)

Statutory height: 13'6"
*posted heights are listed for Chicago locations
Structures with 13'6" or less clearance

Route	Location	Height	Map Key
IL 1 NB, SB	Crete–4.78 mi. north of jct. IL 394	13'6"	E-13
US 6 WB	Joliet–.06 mi. east of IL 53	13'3"	◆ N-4
IL 7/53 NB	Crest Hill–0.76 mi. north of IL 53 south jct.	13'6"	◆ M-4
US 14 EB (Peterson Av.)	Chicago–0.75 mi. east of Western Av.	*12'6"	◆ G-9
US 14 WB (Peterson Av.)	Chicago–0.75 mi. east of Western Av.	*12'6"	◆ G-9
IL 14	McLeansboro–just west of IL 142	13'6"	Q-11
IL 19 EB, WB (Irving Park Rd.)	Chicago–at US 41 (Lake Shore Dr.) overpass	*12'6"	◆ G-9
IL 19 EB (Irving Park Rd.)	Chicago–between IL 50 and I-90/94	*13'6"	◆ G-8
IL 19 WB (Irving Park Rd.)	Chicago–between IL 50 and I-90/94	*13'6"	◆ G-8
US 24 Bus.	Washington–2.43 mi. east of IL 8	13'0"	G-8
IL 25 SB (Broadway)	Aurora–0.3 mi. south of New York St.	13'0"	◆ J-2
IL 25 NB, SB	Montgomery–0.5 mi. south of US 30	12'11"	K-2
US 36 EB, WB	Chrisman–just west of US 150	13'6"	J-13
US 45/52 EB, WB	Kankakee–0.1 mi. east of IL 115	12'8"	F-12
US 45/150 NB, SB (Springfield Av.)	Champaign–0.1 mi. east of Neil St.	12'6"	★ M-2
IL 50 (Cicero Av.)	Chicago–0.4 mi. north of I-90	*13'2"	◆ G-8
IL 50 NB, SB (Cicero Av.)	Chicago–just south of I-90	*13'0"	◆ G-8
US 51 Bus. SB	Decatur–0.1 mi. north of US 36	13'5"	★ O-2
IL 53 NB (N. Scott St.)	Joliet–0.49 mi. north of US 30	13'6"	◆ N-4
IL 64 EB, WB (North Av.)	Chicago–just east of I-90/94	*12'10"	◆ H-9
IL 78	Jacksonville–3.65 mi. north of US 67	13'6"	K-6
IL 78	Laura–1.26 mi. north of US 150	13'3"	F-7
IL 82 NB, SB	Geneseo–0.5 mi. north of US 6	9'10"	E-6
IL 90/91	Princeville–4.1 mi. east of IL 90	13'6"	F-7
IL 94	Golden–3.5 mi. north of US 24	13'6"	I-4
IL 94	Stronghurst–1.5 mi. south of IL 116	13'1"	G-4
IL 104	†Rees Station–northwest of Franklin	13'4"	K-6
IL 167 EB, WB	Wataga–just east of US 34	13'4"	F-6
IL 180	Williamsfield–1.31 mi. north of US 150	13'3"	F-7

PERMANENT WEIGH STATIONS

Route	Location	Map Key
US 12 SB	Richmond–1 mi. north of IL 173	A-11
US 14 NB, SB	Harvard–3 mi. north	A-10
US 24/52 EB, WB	Sheldon–1.5 mi. east at Indiana state line	G-13
US 30 EB, WB	Chicago Heights–at Torrence Av.	◆ N-10, D-13
US 30 EB, WB	Compton–west of I-39/US 51 at jct. IL 251	C-9
US 36/54 EB, WB	Pittsfield–west city limits	K-4
US 41 SB	†Rosecrans–0.25 mi. north of IL 173	A-12
US 41 NB	Wadsworth–2.2 mi. south of IL 173	A-12
I-55 NB, SB	Bolingbrook–west of IL 53, milepost 265.5	◆ K-4, D-12
I-55 NB	Litchfield–3 mi. north of IL 16, milepost 56.5	M-8
I-55 SB	Williamsville–2 mi. south, milepost 107	J-8
I-55/70 WB	Maryville–1.0 mi. west of IL 159, milepost 14	● G-9, †N-7
I-57 NB, SB	Marion–7 mi. south of IL 13, milepost 47	R-9
I-57 NB, SB	Peotone–approx. 3 mi. north, milepost 330	E-13
I-64 EB	O'Fallon–1 mi. west of jct. US 50 and IL 158, Exit 19A-B, milepost 18	● I-10, O-7
I-70 EB	Brownstown–8.8 mi. east of US 51, milepost 71	M-10
I-70 WB	Marshall–5 mi. east of IL 1, milepost 151	L-13
I-70 WB	Northeast of Marshall-4.95 miles west of Indiana state line	L-13
I-74 EB, WB	Carlock–2.5 mi. southeast, milepost 122	H-9
I-74/280 EB	Moline–1.5 mi. east of US 150, milepost 5.5	★ T-4, D-5
I-74/280 WB	Moline–3.5 mi. east of US 150, milepost 7.5	★ T-5, D-5
I-80 EB, WB	East Moline–2 mi. south of Iowa state line, milepost 2	★ R-6, D-6
I-80 EB	Mokena–1.5 mi. west of US 45, milepost 143	◆ M-7, †D-12
I-80 WB	Mokena–1.5 mi. east of US 45, milepost 147	◆ M-7, †D-12
IL 83 NB, SB	Villa Park–at St. Charles Rd.	◆ H-6, †C-12

Illinois also uses wheel load weighers and semiportable scales

RESTRICTED ROUTES

All Boulevards in Chicago are restricted routes.

Other routes that restrict use by motor carriers

Route	Location
IL 8/29/116	Peoria, over Illinois River to East Peoria
IL 9	Niota, over Mississippi River to Iowa state line
US 12/20/45	Cermak Rd. (Westchester) to Joliet Rd. (Countryside)
US 41	Chicago, from Jeffery Av. to US 12/20
US 41 NB	Gurnee–US 41 ramp to IL 132 EB (max. length is 50')
IL 64 (North Av.)	Elmhurst, from IL 83 to I-290
IL 113	I-55 to Braidwood
Green Bay Rd.	Evanston–McCormick Blvd. to Highwood
Lake Shore Dr.	Chicago, from Sheridan Rd. to Marquette Dr.
Sheridan Rd.	Chicago–US 14 to Highland Park
Washington Blvd.	US 12/20 (Bellwood) to 1st Av. (Maywood)
Washington Blvd.	IL 43 (Forest Park)

INDIANA

See state and city maps **pages 35-37**
★ located on city map

LOW CLEARANCE LOCATIONS

Statutory height: 13'6"
Structures with 13'6" or less clearance

Route	Location	Height	Map Key
IN 17	Plymouth–1.7 mi south of US 30	10'11"	C-8
US 150	Ferguson Hill–1.94 mi. north of US 40	12'10"	★ L-1
US 231	St. John–0.23 mi. south of jct. US 41	13'6"	B-4
IN 450 EB	Williams–8.3 mi. west of IN 158	12'11"	O-7
IN 450 WB	Williams–8.3 mi. west of IN 158	13'2"	O-7

PERMANENT WEIGH/INSPECTION STATIONS

■ also serves as Port of Entry
All scale locations are also vehicle inspection sites

Route	Location	Map Key
■ I-65 SB	Lowell–0.5 mi. north of IN 2	C-4
I-69 SB	Warren–0.25 mi. north of IN 124	F-11
■ I-70 WB	Richmond–1.03 mi. west of US 35	J-13
■ I-70 EB	Terre Haute–just east of the Illinois state line	L-4
■ I-74 WB	West Harrison–at Ohio state line	M-14
I-94 EB	northeast of Chesterton–5.7 mi. west of jct. US 421	A-6
■ I-94 WB	northeast of Chesterton–5.7 mi. west of jct. US 421	A-6

Indiana also uses portable scales

RESTRICTED ROUTES

Routes that restrict use by motor carriers

Route	Location
IN 46	Bowling Green, over Eel River
IN 62	IN 250 to Dillsboro
IN 550	Loogootee to Lacy

IOWA

See state and city maps **pages 38-39**
★ located on city map
◆ located on Quad Cities map **page 33**

LOW CLEARANCE LOCATIONS

Statutory height: 13'6"
Structures with 13'6" or less clearance

Route	Location	Actual Height	Posted Height	Map Key
IA 14	Corydon–north	13'6"	13'3"	L-10
US 61 Bus. NB (Brady St.)	Davenport–0.1 mi. north of 4th St.	12'0"	11'8"	◆ S-2
US 61 Bus. SB (Harrison St.)	Davenport–0.3 mi. north of US 61/67 (River Dr.)	12'1"	11'8"	◆ S-2
US 75	Hull–1.4 miles north of jct. US 18	13'9"	13'6"	B-2
IA 163 WB (E. University Av.)	Des Moines–0.09 mi. west of E 21st St.	13'9"	13'6"	★ B-20
IA 415 NB (2nd Av.)	Des Moines–0.9 mi. south of I-35/80	13'8"	13'5"	★ B-19
IA 415 SB (2nd Av.)	Des Moines–0.9 mi. south of I-35/80	13'8"	13'5"	★ B-19

PERMANENT WEIGH/INSPECTION STATIONS

Scales serve all directions unless located on an Interstate route. Direction(s) served on Interstate routes are noted in the listings.

All scale locations are also vehicle inspection sites

Route	Location	Map Key
I-29 NB	Percival–1.5 mi. north of IA 2	L-3
I-29 SB	Salix–1.5 mi. south of exit 134	F-2
I-35 SB	Ames–3 mi. north of IA 210 & exit 102	H-10
I-35 SB	Northwood–south of exit 214	B-10
I-35 NB	Osceola–south of exit 33	K-9
US 71 SB	Early–north of jct. US 20	F-5
I-80 WB	Mitchelville–east at milepost 151	I-11
I-80 EB	Van Meter–at milepost 115	I-9
I-80 WB	Walnut	I-5
US 218 NB	Mt. Pleasant–south of jct. with IA 16	L-16
I-380 NB, SB	Brandon	F-14

Iowa also uses portable scales

RESTRICTED ROUTES

Routes that restrict use by motor carriers

Route	Location
IA 9	Fort Madison, over Mississippi River to Illinois state line
IA 175	I-29 to Nebraska state line

† place or route does not appear on the map
‡ route not labeled on map
EB eastbound route NB northbound route
SB southbound route WB westbound route

KANSAS

See state and city maps **pages 40-41**
◆ located on Kansas City map on **page 58**

LOW CLEARANCE LOCATIONS

Statutory height: 14'0"
Structures with 14'0" or less clearance

Route	Location	Height	Map Key
KS 31	Kincaid–0.5 mi. east	14'0"	G-18
KS 32	Wyandotte–under WB Turner Diagonal Fwy.	13'9"	◆ I-2
US 40/59	Lawrence–1 mi. south of jct. I-70	14'0"	◆ L-20
US 59	Garnett–1.0 mi. south	14'0"	G-18
KS 147	Cedar Bluff Reservoir Spillway	14'0"	E-7
KS 147	Ogallah–under EB I-70	13'9"	D-7
KS 147	Ogallah–under WB I-70	14'0"	D-7

MOTOR CARRIER INSPECTION STATIONS

▲ also serves as weigh station

Route	Location	Map Key
▲ I-35 NB, SB	Olathe–5 mi. south	E-18
▲ I-35 NB	South Haven	J-13
US 54 EB	Liberal–5 mi. east at mile marker 11.5	J-4
▲ I-70 EB	Kanorado–near Colorado state line	C-1
▲ I-70 EB, WB	Wabaunsee–2 mi. east of KS 99	D-15
▲ US 81 SB	Belleville–1 mi. south of US 36	B-12

Kansas also uses portable scales

RESTRICTED ROUTES

Routes that restrict use by motor carriers

Route	Location
KS 23	2.28 mi south of US 54 (Entrance) in Meade
US 36	Smith Center to KS 181
US 166	Chetopa to Melrose
US 183	US 54 to Coldwater

KENTUCKY

See state and city maps **pages 42-43**
★ located on city map

LOW CLEARANCE LOCATIONS

Statutory height: 13'6" on designated highways; 12'6" on other routes.
Structures with 13'6" or less clearance

Route	Location	Height	Map Key
KY 7	Colson–3 mi. east	12'10"	K-18
KY 8 (4th St.)	Newport & Covington–Licking River bridge	13'6"	★ B-19
KY 9	Newport–south of 12th St.	13'4"	★ B-20
KY 17 (Greenup St.)	Covington–near 17th St.	13'0"	★ B-19
KY 17 (Scott St.)	Covington–17th St.	11'6"	★ B-19
US 25 (Dixie Hwy.)	Erlanger–0.1 mi. northeast of KY 236 jct.	13'6"	★ C-18
KY 26	Woodbine–3 mi. southwest	12'0"	M-14
US 27 (Broadway)	Lexington–0.1 mi. southeast of KY 4, northern intersection	13'2"	★ B-15
US 27 (Monmouth St.)	Newport–south of 11th St.	13'6"	★ B-20
US 31W (22nd St.)	Louisville–0.25 mi. south at Woodland	12'3"	★ B-6
KY 40	Paintsville–0.75 mi. east of US 23/460	13'5"	I-18
US 45	Paducah–Irvin S. Cobb Bridge	13'0"	★ F-6
†US 45 Bus.	Fulton	13'6"	G-3
KY 57	2.3 mi. west of KY 627	13'4"	H-13
US 60	east of Paducah at Tennessee River	12'11"	E-4
US 60 Alt. (3rd St.)	Louisville–at Eastern Pkwy.	11'8"	★ C-7
US 60 Alt. (3rd St.)	Louisville–0.2 mi. south of Eastern Pkwy.	11'8"	★ C-7
KY 74	Middlesboro	13'2"	N-15
KY 77	Nada–2.1 mi. east of KY 11	12'0"	I-15
KY 91	Princeton–4 mi. east of US 62	13'2"	L-2
KY 94	Fulton–north, 0.1 mi. west of KY 307	11'6"	G-3
KY 139 & KY 293	Princeton–0.1 mi. west of KY 91	12'1"	L-1
US 150 (E. Broadway St.)	Louisville–0.4 mi. east of US 31	13'5"	★ B-7
KY 177	Butler–1.1 mi. west of US 27	9'9"	E-13
KY 244	Raceland–0.3 mi. north of US 23	12'10"	F-18
KY 254	Madisonville–0.2 mi. south of †KY 892	13'0"	K-3
KY 277	Central City–0.1 mi. south of KY 304	12'8"	K-4
†KY 282	Kentucky Dam Village State Resort Park	13'2"	E-4
KY 307	Fulton–0.3 mi. north of Tennessee state line	9'10"	G-3
KY 307	Fulton–1.1 mi. north of Fulton County line	12'6"	G-3
KY 408	Fancy Farm–6.1 mi. west of US 45	11'7"	G-4
KY 632	Coleman–2.6 mi west of KY 194	12'0"	J-20
KY 1031	Central City–0.1 mi. south of KY 70	11'4"	K-4
KY 1120 (W. 12th St.)	Covington–I-71/75 overpass, 0.3 mi. north of Jefferson ramp	13'5"	★ B-18
KY 1571	Ravenna	11'2"	I-14

PERMANENT WEIGH/INSPECTION STATIONS

■ also serves as Port of Entry
All scale locations are also vehicle inspection sites

Route	Location	Map Key
US 23/460	Prestonsburg–north of KY 3	I-18
■ I-24 EB, WB	Eddyville–west of milepost 36	L-1
■ US 41 SB	Henderson–north of milepost 21	I-3
US 51 NB	Fulton–just north of Tennessee state line	G-3
I-64 WB	Morehead–east of milepost 148	G-16
I-64 EB	Shelbyville–east of milepost 38.5	H-10
I-65 SB	Elizabethtown–south of milepost 90	J-8
■ I-65 NB	Franklin–southeast of milepost 4	M-6
I-71 SB	Walton–south of milepost 76	E-12
I-75 NB	Georgetown–north of milepost 130	G-12
I-75 SB	London–5 mi. south at milepost 33	L-14
I-75 NB	London–5 mi. south at milepost 33.5	L-14
I-75 SB	Walton–south of milepost 168.8	E-12

list continued in next column

Kentucky also uses portable scales

RESTRICTED ROUTES

Routes that restrict use by motor carriers

Route	Location
A Hwys.	Vehicles on the A Class Highway System are restricted to 44,000 lbs.
AA Hwys.	Vehicles on the AA Highway System are restricted to 62,000 lbs.
KY 1	KY 3 to US 60
KY 1	KY 7 to US 23
KY 2	I-64 to US 23
KY 3	KY 645 to I-64
KY 11	US 421 to KY 30
KY 11	KY 92 to US 421
KY 30	US 25 to US 421
KY 30	US 421 to KY 11
KY 30	KY 11 to KY 52
US 31E	KY 61 to Blue Grass Pkwy.
US 62	US 27 to US 68
KY 63	KY 839 to US 31E Bus.
KY 80	US 421 to Avawam
KY 80	US 460 to Virginia state line
KY 80	KY 58 to US 45
KY 90	US 27 to US 25W
KY 109	US 68 to US 62
KY 181	US 62 to KY 81
KY 181	KY 178 to US 62
KY 467	US 127 to I 75
US 460	Shelbiana to Virginia state line
US 460	US 27 to US 68 Bus.
US 460	US 68 to I-64
US 467	US 127 to I-75
National Park Rd.	Mammoth Cave National Park restricted for all truck traffic

LOUISIANA

See state and city maps **page 44**
★ located on city map
◆ located on Vicksburg map **page 56**

LOW CLEARANCE LOCATIONS

Statutory height: 13'6"
*clearance is greater than 13'6" at centerline
Structures with 13'6" or less clearance

Route	Location	Height	Map Key
†LA 1 Bus.	Natchitoches	13'3"	D-3
LA 8	Burr Ferry–Sabine River bridge (curb)	*12'3"	F-2
LA 15	Alto–Boeuf River bridge (curb)	*13'2"	C-6
US 90 (Broad Av.)	New Orleans–0.2 mi. south of I-610	13'4"	★ D-13
†US 165 Bus.	Pineville	11'10"	E-4
US 171 NB	Leesville	*13'6"	E-3
LA 538	Mooringsport–4.75 mi. southeast	*13'3"	B-1
†LA 729	Lafayette–just west of US 90, near Lafayette Regional Airport	*12'4"	★ H-14

PERMANENT WEIGH/INSPECTION STATIONS

■ also serves as Port of Entry
All scale locations are also vehicle inspection sites

Route	Location	Map Key
I-10 EB, WB	Breaux Bridge–2 mi. west of Breaux Bridge interchange	H-5
I-10 EB, WB	Laplace–1 mi. west of US 51	H-8
I-10 WB	1 mi. east of Mississippi state line (joint operation with MS)	H-10
■ I-10 EB, WB	Toomey	H-2
■ I-12 EB, WB	Hammond–approx. 1 mi. west of I-55	G-8
■ LA 12 EB, WB	Starks–west of LA 109	G-2
■ I-20 EB, WB	Delta–1 mi. west of Mississippi River	◆ K-1, C-7
■ I-20 EB, WB	Greenwood–2 mi. east of Texas state line	B-1
■ I-55 NB, SB	Kentwood	F-8
I-59 NB, SB	Nicholson, MS–1 mi. north of Mississippi state line (joint operation with MS)	H-10
US 61 EB, WB	Laplace–2 mi. east of US 51	H-8
US 71/165 SB	Pineville	E-4

Louisiana also uses portable scales

RESTRICTED ROUTES

Selected routes are restricted to either 30,000 lb., 50,000 lb., or 70,000 lb. vehicles.

Other routes that restrict use by motor carriers

Route	Location
LA 4	LA 147 to LA 34
LA 8	LA 124 to †Leland
LA 10	Palmetto to LA 77
LA 10	US 51 to Wilmer
LA 10	LA 19 to LA 67
LA 10	LA 463 to LA 112
US 11	I-10 to †North Shore
LA 14	US 167 to LA 82
LA 14	LA 101 to LA 99
LA 38	LA 432 to I-55
LA 70	US 90 to Pierre Part
LA 82	†Oak Grove to Pecan Island
US 90	US 190 to Mississippi state line
LA 92	US 167 to Milton
LA 104	LA 13 to Point Blue

† place or route does not appear on the map
‡ route not labeled on map
EB eastbound route NB northbound route
SB southbound route WB westbound route

MAINE

See state and city maps **page 45**

LOW CLEARANCE LOCATIONS

Statutory height: 13'6"
Structures with 13'6" or less clearance

Route	Location	Min. Height	Max. Height	Map Key
ME 9	Saco–mile marker 39.3	12'1"	12'6"	I-2
ME 24	Richmond–mile marker 34.9	11'2"	11'9"	G-4

PERMANENT WEIGH/INSPECTION STATIONS

Semiportable scales used
Inspections are also done at other randomly selected locations
All scale locations are also vehicle inspection sites

Route	Location	Map Key
US 1 NB	Caribou–south	B-14
US 1 NB, SB	Ellsworth–2 mi. west	F-7
US 1 SB	Houlton–near Littleton-Houlton town line	C-14
US 1 NB, SB	Kittery–approx. 3 mi. north of New Hampshire state line	J-2
US 1 SB	Presque Isle	B-14
US 1/ME 6 NB, SB	Topsfield–just south of ME 6 on US 1	C-9
US 2 EB	Rumford–west	F-2
ME 4 WB	Wilton–just north of ME 156	E-3
ME 9 WB	at Hancock-Washington County line	D-8
I-95 SB	Houlton–at U.S. Border Port of Entry	C-14
I-95 NB, SB	Kittery–approx. 3 mi. north of New Hampshire state line	J-2
I-95 NB, SB	Old Town	D-6
US 201 NB	Hinckley	E-4
US 201 NB, SB	Jackman–south of Canadian border	B-3
US 202/ME 9 NB, SB	Unity	E-5

Maine also uses portable scales

RESTRICTED ROUTES

Routes that restrict use by motor carriers

Route	Location
US 1	Kittery, over the Piscataqua River
ME 3	Bar Harbor to ME 233
ME 24	Bailey Island to Orrs Island
ME 104 (Water St.)	US 201 to ME 3
ME 153	North Parsonfield, New Hampshire state line to New Hampshire state line
ME 180	ME 179 to ME 181

MARYLAND

See state and city maps **pages 46-47**
★ located on city map
◆ located on Washington D.C. map **page 111**

LOW CLEARANCE LOCATIONS

In addition to the low clearances listed below, there are many more low clearances in local jurisdictions, but due to their volume, it is not possible to post them in this chart.

To check for clearances on State and U.S. routes, by county, visit the following website:
www.sha.maryland.gov/index.aspx?pageid=160

Drivers should remain alert for highway signage, which is posted well in advance of low clearances, and avoid them.

Statutory height: 13'6"
Structures with 13'6" or less clearance

Route	Location	Min. Height	Max. Height	Map Key
MD 7B	Perryville	13'6"	13'6"	B-16
MD 7C	North East	11'2"	12'0"	B-16
MD 36	Frostburg	11'8"	15'0"	A-3
MD 51	near West Virginia border	12'0"	13'9"	B-5
MD 75	Monrovia	12'6"	12'6"	C-11
MD 117	Boyds	12'6"	12'6"	D-10
MD 117	Boyds–1.5 mi. northwest	13'0"	13'0"	D-10
MD 222	Port Deposit–northwest of MD 276	13'6"	13'6"	B-16
MD 303	Cordova–northeast at MD 309	12'6"	12'6"	F-16
†MD 831A	Homewood–bypasses jct. of US 40 and MD 36	10'9"	15'1"	★ D-3

PERMANENT WEIGH/INSPECTION STATIONS

All scale locations are also vehicle inspection sites

Route	Location	Map Key
US 1 NB, SB	Darlington–approx. 2 mi. south of Susquehanna Dam crossing	A-15
US 13 NB, SB	Delmar–just south of Delaware state line	H-18
US 40 EB, WB	Thomas J. Hatem Memorial Bridge	B-16
US 50 EB,WB	William Preston Lane Jr. Memorial Bridge	E-14
I-68 EB	Midlothian–west, midway between exits 29 and 33	A-3
I-70/US 40 EB	New Market–1.5 mi. east of MD 75	C-11
I-70/US 40 WB	West Friendship–west of MD 32 (Exit 80)	C-12
I-83/SB	Parkton–south of exit 36	A-13
I-95 NB, SB	Tydings Memorial Bridge–toll plaza	B-16
I-270 NB, SB	Hyattstown–at Frederick and Montgomery County line, milepost 22	D-10
US 301 SB	Cecilton–at jct. with MD 299	C-17
US 301 NB, SB	Upper Marlboro–north of MD 4	F-13

Vehicle Inspection Area

Route	Location	Map Key
US 50 EB	Vienna–east	H-17
I-95 NB	Baltimore–at Caton Avenue	★ J-5, D-13
I-95 SB	Beltsville–south at jct. I-495 (Capital Beltway)	◆ D-8

Maryland also uses portable scales

RESTRICTED ROUTES

I-895 (Harbor Tunnel Thruway)
Baltimore Harbor Tunnel restricts or prohibits hazardous materials and has width and doubles restrictions. Northbound I-895 vehicles that intend to exit at the one exit prior to the tunnel may request in writing an exemption to the I-895 restrictions. For specific information, contact: Baltimore-Harbor Tunnel Thruway, P.O. Box 3432, Baltimore, MD 21225, Telephone: (410) 537-1200.

For other truck restrictions in Maryland, refer to: www.sha.maryland.gov/index.aspx?pageid=160

Other routes that restrict use by motor carriers

Route	Location
US 13 Bus.	Pocomoke City, over Pocomoke River
MD 17	Middletown to Shawan Rd./Tufton Av.
MD 25	MD 137 to MD 88
US 40	Near Piney Grove, over Sideling Hill Creek
US 40 Alt.	MD 546 to MD 36
MD 43	I-695 to I-95
MD 45	MD 439 to I-83/MD 45
MD 56	I-70 to MD 68
MD 68	†Breathedsville to US 40 Alt.
MD 75	Monrovia–Baldwin Rd. to MD 80
MD 76	US 15 to MD 77
MD 77	MD 64 to US 15
MD 109	I-270 to MD 355
MD 128	Glyndon to †Dover
MD 190	I-495 to Washington, D.C. district line
MD 144	near Frederick, westbound over Monocacy River
MD 222	US 1 to Port Deposit
MD 261	Chesapeake Beach, over Fishing Creek
MD 295 (Baltimore-Washington Pkwy.)	US 50 to MD 175
MD 315	MD 313 to MD 306
MD 355	I-495 to MD 188
MD 355	MD 80 to MD 121
MD 424	MD 3 to MD 2
MD 450	MD 3 to I-97
MD 638	US 40 Alt. to MD 36
I-695 (Inner Loop ramp)	eastbound off ramp to US 40 EB (No vehicle over 8' in width)
MD 702	Middle River, beyond MD 150 southeast
MD 717	MD 4 to MD 725
Clara Barton Pkwy.	I-495 to Washington, D.C. district line
Suitland Pkwy.	Washington, D.C. district line to MD 4

MASSACHUSETTS

See state and city maps **pages 48-49**
★ located on city map

LOW CLEARANCE LOCATIONS

Statutory height: 13'6"
Structures with 13'6" or less clearance

Route	Location	Height	Map Key
US 1	Newburyport–at MA 1A (High St.) overpass	13'6"	B-15
US 1	Westwood	13'5"	★ N-5
MA 1A (Dodge St.)	Beverly–at jct. MA 128	12'6"	C-15
MA 2 (Commonwealth Av.)	Boston–express underpass at jct. MA 2A	12'6"	★ K-7
MA 3 NB	Boston–0.4 mi. south of jct. MA 28	10'8"	★ K-7
MA 3 SB	Cambridge–0.1 mi. south of Longfellow Bridge	11'11"	★ K-7
MA 3 (Memorial Dr.)	Cambridge–express underpass at jct. MA 2A	9'0"	★ K-7
US 3/MA 2 (Memorial Dr.)	Cambridge–0.4 mi. south of River St.	12'1"	★ K-7
US 5/MA 10	Greenfield–0.2 mi. south of MA 2A, Main St.	12'4"	C-5
US 6 WB (Right lane only)	West Barnstable–0.7 mi. southwest at MA 149 overpass	13'3"	J-18
MA 6A (Main St.)	Barnstable–approx. 1 mi. west	12'11"	J-18
MA 9 (Huntington Av.)	Boston–MA 2A (Massachusetts Av.) overpass	13'0"	★ L-7
MA 9 (Main St.)	Northampton–just east of US 5	11'0"	E-5
MA 12 (Webster St./Hope Av.)	Worcester–1 mi. northwest of I-290	12'2"	★ C-18
MA 19 (Maple St.)	Warren–just south of MA 67	12'6"	F-8
MA 27 (Crescent St.)	Brockton–just east of MA 28	12'0"	G-14
MA 27 (School St.)	Brockton–just east of MA 28	10'0"	G-14
MA 28 SB (McGrath Hwy.)	Somerville–0.4 mi. south of I-93	13'5"	★ K-7
MA 30 (Main St.)	Westborough–south of MA 9	12'6"	F-11
MA 35 (High St.)	Danvers–at MA 128 overpass	13'4"	C-15
MA 41	Great Barrington–just north of US 7	12'6"	F-1
MA 62 (Main St.)	Concord	12'0"	D-12
MA 62/70 (Main St.)	Clinton	11'0"	E-11
MA 68 (Gardner St.)	Baldwinville–just east of US 202	13'6"	C-8
MA 85 (River St.)	Cordaville–0.8 mi. south of I-90	11'0"	F-11
I-93/US 1/MA 3	Boston–at Boston St. overpass	13'6"	★ L-7
MA 101 (Parker St.)	Gardner–0.75 mi. west of MA 68	12'6"	C-9
MA 107 (Broadway)	Revere–0.2 mi. south of Beach St.	13'6"	★ J-8
MA 116 (Cabot St.)	Holyoke	12'0"	★ K-11
MA 117 (Lancaster St.)	Leominster–0.3 mi. east of MA 12	12'6"	D-10
MA 122A	Holden	13'3"	E-10
MA 123	Attleboro	11'6"	H-13
MA 123 (Center St.)	Brockton–just east of MA 28	11'6"	G-14
MA 127 (Summer St.)	Manchester	13'5"	C-16
MA 129A (Eastern Av.)	Swampscott–1.2 mi. south of MA 107	13'0"	★ I-9
MA 152 (S. Main St.)	Attleboro–0.2 mi. south of MA 123	12'4"	H-13
US 202 (Elm St.)	Westfield–north of Westfield River	13'6"	G-5

† place or route does not appear on the map
‡ route not labeled on map
EB eastbound route NB northbound route
SB southbound route WB westbound route

PERMANENT WEIGH STATIONS

Route	Location	Map Key
None reported		

Massachusetts only uses portable scales

RESTRICTED ROUTES

Boston and Springfield Areas/Routing Information
Traffic on Designated (National Network) and Interstate routes has restricted travel hours in this area.
For information:
Permits Engineer, Commercial Motor Vehicles Center, Massachusetts Highway Department
525 Maple St. (MA Rte. 85), Marlborough, MA 01752, Telephone: (508) 624-0819.

Other routes that restrict use by motor carriers

Route	Location
MA 1A	Rowley to Newbury
MA 2	MA 60 to US 3
MA 2A	MA 140 to Town Farm Rd.
MA 4	MA 225 to I-95
US 5	MA 10 to Vermont state line
US 6	Fairhaven, over Acushnet River
US 7	Stockbridge south to MA 183
MA 8	North Adams, over Hoosic River
MA 8	US 20 to Becket Center
MA 8A	North Adams, over Phillips Creek
MA 12	MA 101 to MA 2A
MA 12	MA 122 south to Webster St.
US 20	MA 60 to Rose Hill Way
MA 38	I-95 to MA 62
MA 57	Sandisfield to MA 8
MA 57	West Granville to Granville
MA 62	Middleton, over Ipswich River
MA 62	MA 2 to Cambridge Turnpike
MA 66	Westhampton, over Sodom Brook
MA 97	US 1 to MA 35
MA 110	Lawrence to I-495
MA 112	Huntington to MA 66
MA 114	MA 35 to MA 1A
MA 122	Linwood to Rhode Island state line
MA 124	Harwich to Pleasant Lake
MA 125	Haverhill, over Merrimack River
MA 131 (Main St.)	Southbridge, over the Quinebaug River
MA 138	North Dighton to Taunton
MA 140	North Grafton to US 20
MA 145	Saratoga St. to Pleasant St.
MA 148	US 20 to MA 9
MA 152	Thacher St. to Riverside Av.
MA 183	Great Barrington, over Housatonic River
MA 183	Stockbridge, over Larrywaug Brook
US 202	US 20 to MA 57

MICHIGAN

See state and city maps **pages 50-51**
★ located on city map
◆ located on Detroit & Vicinity map **page 52**

LOW CLEARANCE LOCATIONS

Statutory height: 13'6"
Structures with 13'6" or less clearance:

Route	Location	Height	Map Key
MI 10 NB	Detroit–Holden Av. walkover	13'6"	◆ J-7
MI 11	Grand Rapids–west of MI 37	13'6"	★ C-3
MI 35	Gladstone–RR west of US 41	13'6"	F-2
US 24 Bus. (Cesar E. Chavez Av.)	Pontiac–just southeast of north jct. with US 24	13'3"	◆ F-4

PERMANENT WEIGH STATIONS

■ also serves as Port of Entry
All scale locations are also vehicle inspection sites

Route	Location	Map Key
US 2 EB, WB & US 41 NB, SB	Powers	G-1
US 12 EB, WB & MI 50 NB, SB	†Cambridge Jct.–south of Brooklyn	S-10
US 24 NB/SB	Erie	S-11
I-69 NB	Coldwater–6 mi. north of Indiana state line	T-8
I-75 NB, SB	Mackinac Bridge	F-8
■ I-75 NB, SB	Monroe–7.5 mi. north of Ohio state line	T-12
I-75 SB	Pontiac–1 mi. northwest of Baldwin Rd.	◆ E-4, Q-12
I-94 EB, WB	Grass Lake–7.9 mi. west of MI 52	R-10
■ I-94 EB, WB	New Buffalo–1.5 mi. north of Indiana state line	T-3
I-96 EB, WB	Fowlerville–7.8 mi. northwest of MI 59	Q-10
I-96 EB, WB	Ionia–1.2 mi. east of MI 66	P-7

Michigan also uses portable scales

RESTRICTED ROUTES

Routes that restrict use by motor carriers

Route	Location
US 2/141	US 141 to Wisconsin state line
MI 119	US 31 to Cross Village
MI 311	Burlington to I-94
Detroit-Windsor Tunnel	East Jefferson Av. to Canadian border

MINNESOTA

See state and city maps **pages 53-55**

LOW CLEARANCE LOCATIONS

Statutory height: 13'6"
Structures with 13'6" or less clearance

Route	Location	Height	Map Key
US 14	Eyota–2.1 mi. west of MN 42	13'6"	R-11
MN 23	Duluth–1.4 mi. north of †MN 39	13'6"	J-11
MN 70	Rock Creek–1.3 mi. east of I-35	13'1"	M-10
MN 93	LeSueur–0.8 mi. east of US 169	12'6"	Q-8
MN 95	Stillwater–just south of MN 96	13'4"	O-10

PERMANENT WEIGH/INSPECTION STATIONS

All scale locations are also vehicle inspection sites

Route	Location	Map Key
US 2 & MN 33 all directions	Saginaw	J-11
US 2 & US 59 all directions	Erskine	G-3
US 10/169 NB, SB	Anoka–5 mi. west	O-9
I-35 NB, SB	Hollandale–mile marker 17	S-9
I-90 EB	Ridgeway–at milepost 261	S-13
I-90 EB	Worthington–east	T-4
I-94 EB	Dilworth–at jct. US 75	I-2
I-94 WB	at Wisconsin state line	O-11

Minnesota also uses portable scales

RESTRICTED ROUTES

Restrictions vary. Call (651) 297-3935 for detailed information.

Other routes that restrict use by motor carriers

Route	Location
I-35E	St. Paul–MN 5 to I-94 (9,000 lb. max)
I-94	Minneapolis–I-394 to I-35W, at Lowry Hill tunnel (Hazmat only)

MISSISSIPPI

See state and city maps **page 56**
★ located on city map

LOW CLEARANCE LOCATIONS

Statutory height: 13'6"
Structures with 13'6" or less clearance

Route	Location	Height	Map Key
US 11	Hattiesburg–at jct. with US 49	13'1"	★ F-1
US 11 (Teresa St.)	Laurel–under RR overpass	13'4"	J-8

PERMANENT WEIGH/INSPECTION STATIONS

■ also serves as Port of Entry
All scale locations are also vehicle inspection sites

Route	Location	Map Key
■ I-10 WB	1 mi. east of Louisiana state line	M-7
■ I-10 EB	10 mi. east of Louisiana state line	M-7
■ I-10 EB, WB	Orange Grove–2 mi. west of Alabama state line	M-10
■ I-20 EB	Bovina–8 mi. east of Louisiana state line	★ J-2, H-5
■ I-20 WB	Bovina–10 mi. east of Louisiana state line	H-5
■ I-20/59 EB, WB	Kewanee–2 mi. west of Alabama state line	H-9
■ I-22/US 78 EB, WB	Fulton–14 mi. west of Alabama state line	C-9
■ MS 24/33	Centreville–at jct. MS 33/MS 24	K-4
■ MS 35 NB, SB	Sandy Hook–1 mi. north of Louisiana state line	K-7
■ US 45 Bypass NB, SB	Corinth–2 mi. south of Tennessee state line	A-9
■ US 49 EB, WB	Lula–north, 2.5 mi. east of Arkansas state line	C-5
■ I-55 NB, SB	†Nesbit–7 mi. south of Tennessee state line	A-6
■ I-55 NB	Osyka–approx. 2.0 mi. north of Louisiana state line	K-5
■ I-59 NB, SB	Nicholson–1 mi. north of Louisiana state line	M-7
■ US 61 NB,SB	Woodville–1 mi. north of Louisiana state line	K-3
■ US 72 EB, WB	Iuka–2.5 mi. west of Alabama state line	B-10
■ US 78 NB, SB	Olive Branch–3 mi. south of Tennessee state line	A-7
■ US 80 EB, WB	Kewanee–1 mi. west of Alabama state line	H-9
■ US 82 EB	Greenville–southwest, 0.5 mi. east of Arkansas state line	F-4
■ US 98 EB, WB	Lucedale–east, 6 mi. west of Alabama state line	L-9

Mississippi also uses portable scales

RESTRICTED ROUTES

Routes that restrict use by motor carriers
Vehicles on the Low Weight State Highway System are restricted to 57,650 lbs.

Other restricted routes

Route	Location
MS 1	US 61 to MS 438
MS 3	south jct. US 49W to north jct. US 49W
MS 4	I-55 to I-22/US 78
MS 4	MS 7 to MS 2
MS 4	US 61 to Strayhorn
MS 7	US 49W to US 82
MS 12	Tchula–3.1 mi. east of US 49E
MS 12	MS 1 to US 61
MS 13	US 80 to MS 25
MS 13	MS 18 to I-20
MS 14	MS 1 to Rolling Fork
MS 15	I-10 to MS 26

list continued on next page

†	place or route does not appear on the map		
‡	route not labeled on map		
EB	eastbound route	NB	northbound route
SB	southbound route	WB	westbound route

Route	Location
MS 16	MS 1 to Holly Bluff
MS 17	MS 12 to US 82
MS 18	Carlisle to Utica
MS 21	MS 19 to US 45
MS 22	Edwards–over I-20 interchange
MS 25	Dennis to Tishomingo
MS 27	MS 18 to Vicksburg
MS 29	New Augusta to Wiggins
MS 30	near Etta, 3.1 mi. west of Union County line
MS 32	US 49W to US 49E
MS 32	MS 1 to US 61
MS 32	MS 7 to MS 330
MS 35	US 82 to MS 7
MS 35	MS 8 to south jct. MS 32
MS 35	north jct. MS 32 to MS 315
MS 39	MS 16 to MS 21
MS 42	Richton to MS 63
MS 43	Canton–5.3 mi. north of Natchez Trace Parkway
MS 43	MS 26 to MS 13
US 51	Pope to MS 32
MS 172	US 72 to MS 25
MS 184	Prentiss to MS 35
MS 305	MS 4 to Olive Branch
MS 309	MS 4 to Tennessee state line
MS 310	I-55 to Harmontown
MS 315	MS 7 to US 278
MS 315	MS 328 to MS 7
MS 334	MS 9 to Toccopola
MS 336	US 278 to MS 15
MS 341	MS 9 to MS 32
MS 341	MS 32 to Webster County line
MS 407	MS 12 to McCool
MS 442	US 278 to US 49E
MS 481	US 20 to MS 35
MS 481	MS 13 to MS 43
MS 493	Meridian to MS 16
MS 501	MS 18 to Forest
MS 503	Decatur to MS 528
MS 547	US 61 to MS 28
MS 550	MS 28 to US 51
MS 567	US 98 to MS 24
†MS 571	MS 584 to Louisiana state line
Natchez Trace Pkwy.	US 51 to Alabama state line
Natchez Trace Pkwy.	US 61 to I-20

MISSOURI

See state and city maps **pages 58-59**
★ located on city map
◆ located on St. Louis & Vicinity map **page 57**
● located on Springfield map **page 57**

LOW CLEARANCE LOCATIONS

Statutory height: 14'0"
Structures with 14'0" or less clearance

Route	Location	Height	Map Key
MO 5 SB	Marceline–2.4 mi. south of US 36	13'11"	D-12
MO 5	Syracuse–0.1 mi. north of US 50	13'9"	G-12
MO 10	Excelsior Springs–approx. 0.5 mi. west of jct. County Rd. H	13'7"	E-9
MO 11	Brookfield	14'0"	D-12
MO 12 EB	Independence–0.4 mi. west of Sterling Av.	13'10"	★ I-5
MO 12 WB	Independence–0.4 mi. west of Sterling Av.	13'4"	★ I-5
MO 13	Higginsville–under KCS railroad	13'10"	F-11
MO 13	Polo–0.3 mi. south of MO 116	13'8"	D-10
MO 13	Springfield–0.2 mi. south of Chestnut Expwy.	13'11"	● A-3
MO 14	Marionville–under railroad	12'8"	K-11
MO 19	Cuba–0.7 mi. south of I-44	13'9"	H-15
MO 21	Arnold–Meramec River	14'0"	G-18
US 24	Independence–east of Arlington Av.	14'0"	◆ I-5
US 24	Kansas City–1.2 mi. west of I-435	12'3"	★ I-4
MO 28	Dixon–0.2 mi. south of †County Rd. C	13'9"	I-14
MO 30	Affton–under BNSF railroad	13'9"	◆ J-5
MO 32	Bolivar–east of MO 13	13'11"	J-11
MO 47	Union–RR north of US 50	14'0"	G-16
US 50	Sedalia–under UP railroad	14'0"	G-12
MO 59	Anderson	13'11"	L-9
US 63 Bus. SB	Moberly–1.5 mi. south of US 24	13'10"	E-13
US 69	Claycomo–at pedestrian overpass	13'8"	★ G-5
I-70 EB	Kansas City–10th St. to I-70E	13'8"	★ I-4
MO 94	West Alton–0.1 mi. west of US 67	12'8"	◆ E-6
MO 96	Carthage–east of I-49	13'9"	K-9
MO 174	Republic	14'0"	K-11
I-229	St. Joseph–NB exit to Charles St.	13'4"	★ C-4
MO 367 SB	St. Louis–under I-70	14'0"	G-6

PERMANENT WEIGH/INSPECTION STATIONS

Driver/vehicle inspections are performed at all permanent weigh stations and at portable unit sites

Route	Location	Map Key
I-29 NB	Platte City–mile marker 24	E-8
I-29 NB, SB	Watson–mile marker 121	B-7
I-35 NB, SB	Eagleville–mile marker 110	B-10
I-35 NB	Kearney–mile marker 22	★ E-6, E-9
US 36 EB	St. Joseph–approx. 5 mi. east	D-9
I-44 EB, WB	Joplin–east of exit 1, west of jct. MO 43, mile marker 2	K-9
I-44 EB, WB	St. Clair–west of jct. MO 30, mile marker 238	H-16
I-49 NB, SB	Harrisonville–north of jct. MO 7	G-9
I-55 SB	Bloomsdale–mile marker 160.2	H-18
I-55 NB	Steele–mile marker 10	N-19
I-57 SB	Charleston–west of Mississippi River Bridge	K-20
US 60/63 EB, WB	Willow Springs–2 mi. west of Willow Springs, mile marker 204	K-14
I-70 EB, WB	Foristell–east of exit 203	F-16
I-70 EB, WB	Mayview–mile marker 43.5	F-10
I-155 WB	Caruthersville–mile marker 8	M-19

Missouri also uses portable scales

RESTRICTED ROUTES

Routes that restrict use by motor carriers

Route	Location
MO 11	Baring to †County C
MO 13	MO 116 to Kingston
MO 18	Merwin to Clinton
MO 23	Concordia to Knob Noster
US 24	Keytesville, over Mussel Fork
US 24	I-435 to Winner Rd
MO 32	MO 21 to Banner
MO 32	County H to Long Lane
MO 37	Maple Grove–†County C to †County N
MO 39	MO 32 to Cedar Springs
MO 46	MO 113 to Maryville
MO 46	County F to Grant City
MO 47	Cadet to MO 425
US 61	†Old Appleton to Uniontown
MO 72	MO 21 to MO 37
MO 76	Bradleyville to MO 5
MO 77	Wyatt to MO 80
MO 94	Steedman to Marthasville
MO 96	Carthage–MO 571 to MO 37
MO 97	Lockwood to MO 32
MO 97	I-44 to Yonkerville
MO 102	east of East Prairie, MO 80 to County A
MO 111	Craig to Nishnabotna
MO 112	Seligman to MO 76
MO 116	I-29 to County Y
MO 116	County E to US 169
MO 124	Harrisburg to US 63
MO 129	County M to County AA
MO 137	Raymondville to Willow Springs
MO 139	Meadville to Humphreys
MO 142	Doniphan to Oxly
MO 142	Lanton to Thayer
MO 143	MO 34 to MO 49
MO 151	Woodlawn to Leonard
MO 153	White Oak to Risco
MO 158	US 67 to MO 14
US 159	Fortescue to MO 111
MO 161	I-70 to New Hartford
MO 179	Marion to County T
MO 245	Bona to MO 32
MO 245	US 160 to Dadeville

MONTANA

See state and city maps **pages 60-61**
★ located on city map

LOW CLEARANCE LOCATIONS

Statutory height: 14'0"
Structures with 14'0" or less clearance

Route	Location	Height	Map Key
MT 7	Wibaux–milepost 79.9	13'6"	F-20
MT 25	Wolf Point–milepost 53	13'10"	C-17
MT 42	Glasgow–milepost 76.0	12'3"	C-16
MT 55	Whitehall–milepost 13.1	14'0"	I-7
MT 65	West Glacier–milepost 1	13'6"	★ M-1
US 87	Black Eagle–milepost 3.8	13'10"	★ M-16
I-94 Bus.	Miles City–milepost 3.1	11'5"	G-17
US 191	Big Timber–milepost 0.8	14'0"	I-10
US 191	Malta–just south of US 2 at milepost 157.6	13'6"	C-14

PERMANENT WEIGH STATIONS

■ also serves as Port of Entry

Route	Location	Map Key
US 2 EB, WB	Culbertson	C-19
US 2 EB	Kalispell	★ N-1, C-4
US 2 & US 87 all directions	Havre–at the junction	B-11
US 12 all directions	Harlowtown	G-11
I-15 NB	Great Falls	E-8
I-15 SB	Helena–mile marker 201	F-7
■ I-15 NB, SB	Lima	K-6
I-15 SB	Shelby–mile marker 367	B-7
I-15/I-90 EB, WB	Butte–approx. 5 mi. west	★ M-13, H-6
MT 83 & MT 200 all directions	†Clearwater Jct.–at the jct.	F-5
MT 84 & US 191 NB, SB	Bozeman Hot Springs	I-8
US 87/89 EB	Armington	E-9
I-90 EB, WB	Billings–approx. 10 mi. west	I-13
I-90 EB, WB	Crow Agency	I-15
■ I-90 EB, WB	Haugan–mile marker 15, east of Idaho state line (joint POE with Idaho)	E-2
I-94 EB, WB	Forsyth	H-16
■ I-94 EB, WB	Wibaux	F-20
US 212 all directions	Broadus	I-18

Montana also uses portable scales

RESTRICTED ROUTES

Routes that restrict use by motor carriers

Route	Location
MT 17	US-Canada border to US 89
MT 38	US 93 (Grantsdale) to MT 1 (Porters Corners)

† place or route does not appear on the map
‡ route not labeled on map
EB eastbound route NB northbound route
SB southbound route WB westbound route

NEBRASKA

See state and city maps pages 62-63
★ located on city map

LOW CLEARANCE LOCATIONS

Statutory height: 14'6"
Structures with 14'6" or less clearance

Route	Location	Height	Map Key
NE 2	Alliance	13'3"	G-3
US 6	Lincoln–2 mi. west	13'11"	K-17
NE 41	Kimball–0.2 mi. north of US 30	13'6"	J-1
US 75 SB	Omaha–at US 275 (curb)	13'6"	★ C-19
US 275	at jct. US 6 and NE 31	14'2"	★ C-15
Lincoln Av.	York–at 14 St. and at 15 St.	13'9"	K-15

PERMANENT WEIGH/INSPECTION STATIONS

All scale locations are also vehicle inspection sites

Route	Location	Map Key
NE 2 EB, WB	Nebraska City–3 mi. west	K-19
US 6 EB, WB	Waverly–1.5 mi. northeast	K-18
US 20 & US 275 EB, WB	†Stafford–jct. 5 mi. southeast of Inman	F-13
US 30 NB, SB	North Platte–3 mi. east	J-8
US 77 NB, SB	Fremont–8 mi. north	I-18
I-80 EB, WB	North Platte–east of exit 179	J-8
I-80 EB, WB	Waverly–mile marker 415	K-18
US 81 NB, SB	Hebron–south	M-15
US 136 EB, WB	Hebron–1 mi. south	M-15

Nebraska also uses portable scales

RESTRICTED ROUTES

Routes that restrict use by motor carriers

Route	Location
NE 2/71	US 20 to South Dakota state line
NE 8	US 77 to Barneston
NE 9	South jct. NE 16 to Pender
NE 12	US 83 to US 183
†NE 16B Spur	US 83 to †Kennedy
NE 18	Stockville to US 283
NE 61	US 34 to US 6
NE 66A Spur	NE 2 to Douglas
NE 68	NE 2 to NE L82A
NE 96	US 183 to NE 91
NE 250	NE 2 to US 20

NEVADA

See state and city maps page 64
★ located on city map
◆ located on Lake Tahoe Region map page 16
● located on Reno map page 65

LOW CLEARANCE LOCATIONS

Statutory height: 14'0"
Structures with 14'0" or less clearance

Route	Location	Height	Map Key
US 50 EB	Cave Rock tunnel (Lake Tahoe)	12'4"	G-2, ◆ G-9
US 50 WB	Cave Rock tunnel (Lake Tahoe)	13'7"	G-2, ◆ G-9
NV 229 EB, WB	Halleck–at I-80E exit 321	13'6"	C-8
NV 579 (Bonanza Rd.)	Las Vegas–Bonanza underpass	13'10"	★ K-3
NV 667 (Kietzke Ln.)	Reno–0.1 mi. southwest of Victorian Av.	13'8"	● H-2
Tropicana Av.	Las Vegas–0.7 mi. west of I-15	14'0"	★ M-2

PERMANENT WEIGH/INSPECTION STATIONS

Route	Location	Map Key
I-15 NB	Las Vegas–south of exit 27	M-8
I-15 SB	Las Vegas–south of exit 64	L-9
I-80 EB, WB	†Osino–9 mi. north of exit 301	C-8

Vehicle Inspection Area

Route	Location	Map Key
I-80 WB	10 mi. east of Reno	F-2
I-80 EB	7 mi. west of Reno	F-1
I-80 EB	6 mi. west of Wadsworth	F-2

RESTRICTED ROUTES

Routes that restrict use by motor carriers

Route	Location
NV 207	US 50 to NV 206
NV 226	US 95 to California state line
NV 228	NV 227 to Jiggs

NEW HAMPSHIRE

See state and city maps page 65

LOW CLEARANCE LOCATIONS

Statutory height: 13'6"
Structures with 13'6" or less clearance

Route	Location	Height	Map Key
US 1 Bypass	Portsmouth	11'10"	L-10
US 3	Plymouth	11'9"	I-7
NH 85	Exeter	11'0"	L-9
NH 110A	Milan	13'0"	E-8
NH 119	Hinsdale–7.3 mi. north, Connecticut River bridge	11'10"	M-4
NH 175	Woodstock–over Pemigewasset River	12'5"	H-7

PERMANENT WEIGH/INSPECTION STATIONS

All scale locations are also vehicle inspection sites

Route	Location	Map Key
I-89 NB, SB	Lebanon–west of exit 18	I-5
I-93 NB, SB	Windham–between exit 3 and exit 4	M-8
NH 101 EB, WB	Epping–east of NH 125	L-9

New Hampshire also uses portable scales

RESTRICTED ROUTES

Routes that restrict use by motor carriers

Route	Location
US 1	Portsmouth, over the Piscataqua River
‡NH 1B	NH 1A to New Castle
NH 27	NH 101 to Hampton
NH 103B	Mount Sunapee to Sunapee
NH 109	Melvin Village to NH 25
NH 109	Moultonboro to Center Sandwich
NH 113A	NH 113 (North Sandwich) to NH 113 (Tamworth)
NH 123A	NH 123 to NH 10
NH 142	US 3 to †Scott
NH 171	NH 109 to Tuftonboro

NEW JERSEY

See state and city maps pages 66-67
★ located on New York City map page 72
◆ located on Philadelphia & Vicinity map page 90

LOW CLEARANCE LOCATIONS

Statutory height: 13'6"
Structures with 13'6" or less clearance

Route	Location	Height	Map Key
NJ 4	Englewood–†Jones Rd. overpass, mile marker 9.62	13'1"	★ D-10
US 30	Camden–†Baird Blvd. overpass, mile marker 2.49	13'2"	◆ E-5
NJ 53	Denville–mile marker 4.2	12'10"	E-10
NJ 73	Berlin–just north of US 30	13'3"	M-7
NJ 77	Bridgeton–north of NJ 49	13'3"	P-6
I-80 WB	Knowlton-Decatur St. overpass, mile marker 4.2	13'6"	D-6
NJ 94	Hainesburg–Scranton Branch overpass, mile marker 2.20	13'6"	D-7
NJ 124 (Madison Av.)	Madison–under RR tracks	12'9"	F-11
US 130	Brooklawn (south of Gloucester City)–mile marker 25.61	13'0"	◆ G-5
NJ 439	Elizabeth–mile marker 1.93	10'7"	★ I-6
NJ 495	Union City–Hudson Av. overpass, mile marker 1.85	13'6"	★ G-9

PERMANENT WEIGH STATIONS

■ also serves as Port of Entry

Route	Location	Map Key
■ I-78 EB,WB	Bloomsbury–mile marker 6	F-6
■ I-80 EB	1 mi. east of Pennsylvania state line	D-6
I-287 NB	Bound Brook–north, between NJ 18 & NJ 527, mile marker 9.0	G-10
I-295 NB	Carneys Point–mile marker 3.6	N-4

New Jersey also uses portable scales

RESTRICTED ROUTES

Routes that restrict use by motor carriers

Route	Location
US 1/9 (Pulaski Skwy.)	I-95 to Jersey City
US 9W	Palisades Interstate Pkwy. to New York state line
NJ 29	Frenchtown to NJ 129
NJ 52	Somers Point to Ocean City
NJ 179	NJ 29 to Pennsylvania state line
US 206	Lawrenceville to Princeton
Garden State Pkwy.	New York state line to NJ 18
Holland Tunnel	I-78 to New York state line
Lincoln Tunnel	Weehawken to New York state line
Palisades Interstate Pkwy.	New York state line to I-95

† place or route does not appear on the map
‡ route not labeled on map
EB eastbound route NB northbound route
SB southbound route WB westbound route

NEW MEXICO

See state and city maps page 68
★ located on city map

LOW CLEARANCE LOCATIONS

Statutory height: 14'0"
Structures with 14'0" or less clearance

Route	Location	Height	Map Key
†NM 118	Gallup–12.7 mi. east of Arizona state line at I-40	14'0"	D-1
†NM 118	Mentmore–8.4 mi. east of Arizona state line at I-40	13'6"	D-1
†NM 124	Grants–1.2 mi. east of NM 117/124 at I-40	13'6"	E-3
NM 152	Kingston–1.2 mi. east	12'8"	I-3
NM 152	Kingston–3.2 mi. east	12'8"	I-3
NM 161	Watrous–at I-25 overpass, exit 364	13'11"	D-7
NM 313	Algodones–just west of NM 474	13'11"	D-5
NM 423	Albuquerque–0.8 mi. west of 2nd St.	13'11"	★ K-8
NM 423 WB	Albuquerque–jct. Rio Grande Blvd.	13'11"	★ K-8
†NM 567	Pilar–6.1 mi. north of jct. NM 68 at Rio Grande	12'10"	C-6

PERMANENT WEIGH/INSPECTION STATIONS

■ also serves as Port of Entry
All scale locations are also vehicle inspection sites

Route	Location	Map Key
■ I-10 WB	Anthony–mile marker 160	J-5
■ I-10/US 70 EB	Lordsburg–23 mi. east of Arizona state line, mile marker 23	J-1
■ I-25/US 85 SB	Raton–0.3 mi. south of Colorado state line (joint POE with Colorado), mile marker 460	B-8
■ I-40 EB	Gallup–15 mi. east of Arizona state line, mile marker 12	D-1
■ I-40 EB, WB	San Jon–east of village limits and 20 mi. west of Texas state line, mile marker 357	E-9
■ US 54 WB	Nara Visa–5 mi. southwest of Texas state line, mile marker 350	D-10
■ US 54 NB	Orogrande–at mile marker 41	J-5
■ US 56 & US 64/87 WB	Clayton–south of city limits, 9 mi. northwest of Texas state line, mile marker 430	B-10
■ US 60/70/84 WB	Texico–1.5 mi. west of Texas state line, mile marker 397	F-10
■ US 62/180 WB	Carlsbad–6 mi. southwest, mile marker 26	J-8
■ US 62/180 WB	Hobbs–1.5 mi. west of Texas state line, mile marker 107	I-10

New Mexico also uses portable scales

RESTRICTED ROUTES

Routes that restrict use by motor carriers

Route	Location
NM 1	US 380 to †San Marcial
NM 3	I-25 to US 54
NM 4	US 550 to NM 126
NM 9	Hachita to NM 11
NM 12	US 180 to Reserve
NM 13	US 82 to US 285
NM 21	US 64 to US 56
NM 27	NM 152 to NM 26
NM 35	NM 15 to NM 152
NM 36	NM 603 to NM 53
NM 37	NM 48 to US 380
NM 48	US 70 to NM 37
NM 52	US 60 to I-25, via NM 142
NM 55	US 54 to US 60
NM 58	US 64 to I-25
NM 59	NM 163 to NM 52
NM 61	US 180 to NM 152
US 64	US 84 to US 285
NM 75	NM 68 to NM 518
NM 81	NM 9 to Mexican border
US 82	NM 244 to US 54 (6% grade for 16 mi.)
NM 93	Bellview to I-40
NM 94	NM 105 to NM 266
NM 95	US 64 to NM 595
NM 102	NM 402 to NM 39
NM 104	Trujillo to NM 129
NM 107	Magdalena to I-25
NM 112	US 64/84 to NM 96
NM 119	Anton Chico to Dilia
NM 120	I-25 to US 56
NM 126	US 550 to NM 4
NM 129	NM 104 to I-40/US 54
NM 130	US 82 to Cloudcroft
NM 137	US 285 to †El Paso Gap
NM 156	US 84 to NM 252
NM 159	US 180 to NM 59
NM 161	I-25 to NM 518
NM 163	NM 59 to NM 52
NM 165	I-25 to NM 14
NM 185	NM 26 to Radium Springs
NM 187	Williamsburg to north of Derry
NM 246	US 380 to US 70/285
NM 247	US 54 to US 285
NM 266	San Ignacio to NM 94
NM 278	I-40 to NM 209
NM 304	US 60 to Veguita
NM 314	NM 2 to Isleta
NM 325	US 64 to NM 456
NM 344	NM 472 to NM 14
NM 368	Arabela to US 70/380
NM 370	NM 456 to Clayton
NM 386	Antar Chico to US 84
NM 390	NM 187 to Salem
NM 392	NM 469 to I-40
NM 400	McGaffey to I-40
NM 419	NM 104 to NM 39
NM 420	NM 102 to NM 402
NM 434	NM 518 to US 64
NM 453	US 56 to US 64
NM 456	NM 76 to NM 406
NM 549	Akela to I-10
NM 551	NM 456 to Colorado state line
NM 554	NM 111 to El Rito
NM 603	NM 36 to US 60

list continued in next column

NEW YORK

See state and city maps pages 69-72
★ located on city map
◆ located on New York City maps pages 72-73

LOW CLEARANCE LOCATIONS

Statutory height: 14'0"
Structures with 13'11" or less maximum posted clearance

Route	Location	Height	Map Key
US 1	Pelham Manor–under Hutchinson River Pkwy.	12'7"	◆ D-13
NY 3	Fulton–east of NY 481	12'11"	NH-11
US 4	Northumberland–over the Hudson River	12'10"	NI-19
NY 5	Albany–just north of I-90	12'6"	★ NF-3
NY 5	Farnham–0.25 mi. south	12'6"	NK-3
NY 5	Syracuse–0.1 mi. east of Erie Blvd.	11'6"	★ SI-3
NY 5	Woodlawn–1 mi. north of NY 179	12'11"	★ NG-9
US 6	Peekskill–under the Bear Mountain State Pkwy.	12'9"	SC-6
US 6/209	Port Jervis–under Front St.	12'8"	SC-3
NY 7	Binghamton–0.1 mi. north of US 11	11'4"	★ SB-11
NY 7	Cobleskill	12'9"	NK-17
NY 7	Rotterdam–1.7 mi. northwest of NY 146	12'9"	★ ND-2
US 9	Poughkeepsie–under US 44/NY 55	12'0"	SA-6
US 9	Underwood–at I-87 overpass, exit 30	12'9"	NE-19
‡NY 9A	Ossining–0.2 mi. north of NY 133	11'3"	SD-6
‡NY 9A	Ossining–1.4 mi. north of NY 133	10'6"	SD-6
‡NY 9A/100	Briarcliffe Manor–1.5 mi. north of jct. ‡NY 117	10'10"	SD-6
NY 9J	†Stuyvesant–1.6 mi. north	12'9"	NL-19
NY 9L	Lake George–0.3 mi. northeast of US 9	12'7"	NH-19
NY 9N	Westport–1.0 mi. west	10'9"	ND-20
NY 9N/22	Port Henry–5 mi. north	12'7"	NE-20
US 9W	West Camp–1.1 mi. north	12'0"	NM-18
US 11 (Front St.)	Binghamton–south of I-81	11'11"	★ SB-11
US 11	Binghamton–0.3 mi. east of NY 7	11'0"	★ SB-11
US 11	Evans Mills–0.8 mi. south of NY 342	12'9"	NE-13
US 11	Syracuse–south of I-90	12'9"	★ SI-3
NY 12E	Watertown	12'8"	NE-12
NY 14A	Watkins Glen–northwest of NY 14	12'10"	NL-10
NY 17	Harriman–0.9 mi. west of I-87	12'11"	SC-5
NY 19	Brockport	11'10"	NI-6
NY 19	Silver Springs–just north of NY 19A	12'6"	NK-6
US 20	Alden–0.45 mi. west of Exchange St.	12'8"	NJ-9
US 20	Duanesburg–0.7 mi. northwest of NY 7	12'8"	NJ-18
US 20 Alt.	East Aurora	12'10"	NJ-4
US 20 Alt.	Warsaw–0.3 mi. east of NY 19	12'6"	NJ-6
NY 22	Petersburgh–at NY 2 overpass	12'2"	NJ-20
NY 25	Mineola–0.17 mi. northeast of Mineola Blvd.	12'11"	◆ G-17
NY 25	Mineola–at Northern State Pkwy. overpass	12'5"	◆ G-17
NY 25	Smithtown–0.5 mi. west	12'8"	★ SH-11
NY 25	Smithtown–1 mi. west	12'8"	★ SH-11
NY 26	Endicott–0.2 mi. north of NY 17C	12'6"	★ SB-9
NY 27 EB	Amityville–under NY 110	12'10"	★ SJ-8
NY 27	Brooklyn–0.9 mi. southeast of I-278	12'10"	◆ K-10
NY 27	Brooklyn–0.5 mi. west of Pennsylvania Av.	12'4"	◆ J-12
NY 27	Freeport–Meadowbrook State Pkwy. overpass	12'3"	◆ J-19
NY 27	Lynbrook–1.5 mi. west	12'6"	◆ J-16
NY 27A	West Islip	12'9"	★ SJ-10
NY 30	Duanesburg–1.5 mi. south of US 20	12'10"	NJ-18
NY 31 (College Av.)	Niagara Falls–0.5 mi. west of NY 61	12'7"	★ NB-6
NY 31	Rochester–0.9 mi. north of NY 33	12'7"	★ SF-3
‡NY 31F	Macedon–0.9 mi. north of NY 31	12'9"	NI-8
NY 32	Albany–0.7 mi. south of I-90	10'8"	★ NF-4
NY 32	Albany–south of I-787	12'10"	★ NG-4
NY 33	Rochester–east of I-390	12'0"	★ SG-2
NY 34/96	Spencer–north	12'9"	NM-11
NY 36	Dansville–at I-390 overpass	12'11"	NK-7
NY 37	Watertown–0.5 mi. north of US 11	12'6"	NE-12
‡NY 38/96	Owego	12'7"	NM-11
NY 42	Lexington–Schoharie Creek bridge	11'3"	NL-17
NY 55	Billings–1.3 mi. west at Taconic State Pkwy. overpass	12'9"	SA-6
US 62	Gowanda	12'10"	NL-3
US 62	Lackawanna–2.9 mi. north of NY 179	12'4"	★ NG-9
NY 78	Depew–north of US 20	12'9"	NJ-4
NY 85	New Scotland–0.6 mi east of NY 85A	12'9"	★ NG-2
NY 85	Slingerlands–0.7 mi. southwest of NY 140	11'2"	★ NG-3
NY 85A	Voorheesville–0.2 mi. west of NY 155	11'3"	★ NG-2
I-87	Bronx–2.3 mi. south of I-95	12'9"	◆ F-11
I-95	Bronx–I-87	12'7"	◆ F-11
I-95	Bronx–0.7 mi. east of I-87	12'10"	◆ F-11
NY 96	Owego–0.3 mi north of NY 17C	12'10"	NM-11
NY 96A	Ovid–3.7 mi. south of NY 336	12'11"	NK-10

list continued on following page

NEW YORK–NORTH CAROLINA
Low Clearance Locations • Permanent Weigh Stations • Restricted Routes

† place or route does not appear on the map
‡ route not labeled on map
EB eastbound route NB northbound route
SB southbound route WB westbound route

New York Low Clearances continued

Route	Location	Height	Map Key
NY 104	Niagara Falls–0.1 mi. north of NY 182	11'0"	★ NB-6
NY 106	Hicksville–1.5 mi. south of I-495	12'10"	◆ G-19
NY 107	Hicksville–south of NY 106	12'9"	◆ G-19
NY 107	North Massapequa–north at Southern State Pkwy.	12'5"	◆ H-20
NY 110	East Farmingdale–just north of NY 24	12'11"	★ SI-8
NY 110	Huntington Station–1.3 mi. north of NY 25	12'10"	★ SH-8
NY 110	Melville–at Northern State Pkwy. overpass	12'4"	★ SI-8
NY 112	Medford–0.4 mil south of I-495	12'9"	SF-10
NY 114	East Hampton–0.8 mi. west of NY 27	11'9"	SE-13
NY 115	Poughkeepsie–1.1 mi. northeast	10'9"	SA-6
NY 119	Elmsford–under NY 100A	12'10"	★ SI-5
NY 120	Rye–under I-95	10'7"	◆ A-16
NY 130	Cheektowaga–east of Dick Rd.	12'11"	★ NE-10
NY 134	†Kitchawan–at Taconic State Pkwy. overpass	12'3"	SD-6
‡NY 141	†Hawthorne–under Taconic State Pkwy.	13'11"	SD-6
NY 143	Ravena–under I-87	12'0"	NK-19
‡NY 164	Towners	11'0"	SB-7
NY 203	Niverville–2.5 mi northeast of US 9	12'9"	NL-19
NY 207	Campbell Hall–0.1 mi. south of NY 416	9'6"	SB-4
NY 208	Washingtonville–2.5 mi. north	9'2"	SB-5
NY 237	Holley–south of NY 31	11'11"	NH-6
NY 249	Farnham–0.25 mi. east of NY 5	12'5"	NK-3
NY 266	Tonawanda–0.5 mi. north of NY 325	12'11"	★ ND-8
I-278	Brooklyn–under east end of the Brooklyn Bridge	12'2"	◆ I-10
‡NY 293	West Point–at US 9W overpass	13'9"	SC-6
NY 311	Towners–0.3 mi. north of NY 164	10'9"	SB-7
‡NY 329	Watkins Glen–southwest	11'5"	NL-10
‡NY 334	Fonda–0.6 mi. northwest of NY 5	12'0"	NI-17
NY 335	Elsmere–0.1 mi. south of NY 443	12'6"	★ NG-3
NY 337	Rotterdam–southwest of I-890	12'6"	★ ND-1
NY 354	Buffalo–0.72 mi. west of US 62	12'9"	★ NF-9
NY 354	Buffalo–1.0 mi. west of US 62	11'11"	★ NF-9
NY 354	Buffalo–1.46 mi. west of US 62	11'6"	★ NF-9
NY 362	Bliss–0.4 mi. north of jct. NY 39	12'5"	NK-5
NY 370	Liverpool–1.3 mi. northwest of I-81	10'9"	★ SI-2
NY 370	Syracuse–0.5 mi. northwest of US 11	12'3"	★ SI-2
NY 372	Greenwich	11'0"	NI-20
NY 384	Buffalo–at jct. NY 198	12'3"	★ NE-8
NY 384	Niagara Falls–0.6 mi. east of NY 61	12'4"	★ NB-7
NY 385	Coxsackie–0.8 mi west of US 9W	12'3"	NL-19
NY 386	Scottsville	12'7"	NI-7
NY 440	Staten Island–under †Walker St.	12'11"	◆ K-7
NY 443	Delmar–2.4 mi. southwest	12'6"	NK-18
I-495	Locust Grove–at NY 135 overpass	12'9"	◆ F-20
NY 495	New York City–Lincoln Tunnel	13'0"	◆ C-1
NY 495	New York City–east end of Lincoln Tunnel access	13'11"	◆ C-2
NY 495	New York City–Queens Midtown Tunnel	12'1"	◆ E-4
Brooklyn-Battery Tunnel	New York City	12'1"	◆ I-10
Brooklyn-Queens Expwy. NB	New York City–at Astoria Blvd. overpass	12'4"	◆ G-12
F.D. Roosevelt Dr.	New York City–0.5 mi. south of R.F.K. Bridge	12'6"	◆ F-11
F.D. Roosevelt Dr.	New York City–0.25 mi. south of Williamsburg Bridge	12'8"	◆ H-4
F.D. Roosevelt Dr.	New York City–at Williamsburg Bridge	10'6"	◆ H-4
F.D. Roosevelt Dr.	New York City–just north of NY 25	12'1"	◆ C-5
F.D. Roosevelt Dr.	New York City–0.2 mi. northeast of NY 25	13'8"	◆ C-5
F.D. Roosevelt Dr.	New York City–0.9 mi. northeast of NY 25	12'2"	◆ C-5
F.D. Roosevelt Dr.	New York City–1.3 mi. northeast of NY 25	11'10"	◆ C-5
F.D. Roosevelt Dr.	New York City–at †Battery Pl. overpass	12'7"	◆ I-1
F.D. Roosevelt Dr. ramp SB	New York City–at 60th St. overpass	12'1"	◆ C-5
F.D. Roosevelt Dr. access road	New York City–at 78th St., 0.9 mi. northeast of NY 25	12'0"	◆ C-5
Harlem River Dr.	New York City–0.75 mi. south of I-95	13'9"	◆ E-11
Harlem River Dr.	New York City–at Third Av. overpass	13'8"	◆ F-11
Harlem River Dr.	New York City–at 145th St. overpass	13'7"	◆ E-11
Holland Tunnel	New York City–under Hudson River	12'6"	◆ H-9

PERMANENT WEIGH / INSPECTION STATIONS

Inspections are done randomly at rest areas

Route	Location	Map Key
None reported		

New York uses portable scales

RESTRICTED ROUTES

All Parkways are restricted routes in New York.

New York City:
53' trailers are prohibited except on I-295, I-495 and I-695 when travelling to/from Long Island

Other routes that restrict use by motor carriers

Route	Location
US 9W	New Jersey state line to Nyack
NY 17A	Florida to US 6
NY 17C (Chemung St.)	in Waverly, over the Cayuta Creek
NY 37B	Massena–over Willow St.
NY 54	NY 14A to NY 14
US 62 (Rainbow Bridge)	NY 384 to Canadian border
US 62	in Lackawanna, from NY 179 to I-190
NY 80	I-90 to NY 5
NY 89	US 20 to Ithaca
NY 94	New Jersey state line to NY 17
NY 98	Albion–over Erie Canal
NY 100A	NY 100 to NY 119
NY 117	Mount Pleasant, Taconic State Pkwy. to Pleasantville
NY 120A	Port Chester to Hutchinson River Pkwy.
NY 213	Olive Bridge–3 mi. southeast to †Atwood
NY 218 SB	south jct. US 9W to north jct. US 9W
NY 266	NY 265 to 1.5 mi. north of I-190
NY 284	New Jersey state line to US 6
NY 352	I-86 to NY 414
NY 414	Wedgewood to NY 14
NY 415	I-86 to Corning
I-495	New York City line to NY 25 (exit 73) has operating limitations during morning and evening peak traffic periods
Holland Tunnel	New York City to New Jersey
Lincoln Tunnel	New York City to New Jersey
Queensboro Bridge	New York City
R. Moses Causeway	Ocean Pkwy. to NY 27A
Yonkers Av.	NY 9A to Cross Country Pkwy.

NORTH CAROLINA

See state and city maps **pages 74-75**
★ located on city map **page 76**

LOW CLEARANCE LOCATIONS

Statutory height: 13'6"
Structures with 13'6" or less clearance

Route	Location	Height	Map Key
NC 5	Pinehurst–0.06 mi. south of NC 2	13'0"	G-9
US 15/70/501 Bus. (Roxboro St.)	Durham–0.25 mi. north of NC 147	11'4"	★ F-10
US 15/501 Bypass SB	Chapel Hill–2.8 mi. northeast of NC 86, US 15/501 Bus. overpass	12'11"	D-10
NC 55 (Alston Av.)	Durham–0.2 mi. north of NC 147	13'2"	★ G-10
NC 215	Beach Gap–Blue Ridge Pkwy. underpass	12'6"	M-4
US 220 Bus.	Stoneville–0.7 mi. south of NC 770	13'3"	B-8
NC 581	Bailey–just south of US 264 Alt.	8'6"	E-13

PERMANENT WEIGH / INSPECTION STATIONS

All scale locations are also vehicle inspection sites

Route	Location	Map Key
I-26 EB, WB	Hendersonville–north of US 64	F-1, L-6
I-40 EB, WB	Asheville–5 mi. west of I-26	L-5
I-40 EB, WB	Statesville–10 mi. west of I-77	E-5
I-40/I-85 NB, SB	Hillsborough–6 mi. west	D-10
I-77 NB, SB	Mt. Airy–3 mi. south of Virginia state line	B-6
I-85 NB, SB	Charlotte–1 mi. east of NC 273	★ G-2, F-5
I-95 NB, SB	Halifax County–13 mi. north of US 64	C-14
I-95 NB, SB	Lumberton–5 mi. north, mile marker 25	H-11

North Carolina also uses portable scales

RESTRICTED ROUTES

For other truck restrictions in North Carolina, refer to:
https://connect.ncdot.gov/business/trucking/Pages/Truck-Network-and-Restrictions.aspx

Other routes that restrict use by motor carriers

Route	Location
NC 10	Casar to NC 27
US 13 Bus.	Bethel, southern jct. with US 13 to northern jct. with US 13
US 13 Bus.	Windsor, southern jct. with US 13 to northern jct. with US 13
US 17 Bus.	Elizabeth City, jct. with Elizabeth St. to jct. with Hughes Blvd.
US 17 Bus.	Hertford, southern jct. with US 17 to northern jct. with US 17
US 19	US 74 to Dellwood
US 19E	NC 194 (Ingalls) to NC 194 (Cranberry)
US 19W	US 19 to Tennessee state line
US 23 Bus.	Dillsboro to NC 107
NC 42	Old Sparta to US 64 Alt.
NC 42	Powellsville to Colerain
NC 47	Denton to Shiptontown Rd.
NC 47	Linwood to NC 8
NC 50/210	NC 210 to Surf City
NC 61	I-40/85 to NC 62
NC 62	US 421 to NC 61
US 64	I-26 interchange to US 74 Alt.
US 64	US 23/441 to US 178
US 70	Raleigh over Capital Blvd.
NC 73	Concord to Mt. Pleasant
US 74 Alt.	Asheville, I-40 interchange to Bat Cave
US 74 Bus.	NC 120 to US 74
US 74/76	Wilmington, jct. with Military Cutoff Rd. to Wrightsville Beach
NC 80	Micaville to US 70
NC 99	Gaylord to US 264
NC 115	NC 901 to Taylor Springs Rd.
NC 151	US 23 to Blue Ridge Pkwy.
US 158	Elizabeth City to Camden
US 176	US 25 to NC 108
US 178	South Carolina state line to Rosman
NC 182	Fallston to NC 274
NC 191	NC 2 to Henderson County line
NC 197	Barnardsville to Pensacola
NC 197	north of Relief to NC 226
NC 209	Crabtree to NC 63
NC 210	Ivanhoe to Wildcat Rd.
NC 215	Balsam Grove to Explorer Rd.
US 221	Linville to Blowing Rock
US 221	NC 16 to NC 113
US 221 Alt.	South Carolina state line to US 74
NC 226	NC 197 to Tennessee state line
NC 242	NC 410 to Columbus County line
US 276	Woodrow to South Carolina state line
NC 306	NC 33 to NC 92 (via ferry)
US 421	Toll ferry to Carolina Beach
US 441	US 19 to Tennessee state line
NC 581	NC 97 to US 64
NC 770	NC 700 to Virginia state line
NC 903	Ayden to Winterville
NC 903	NC 411 to US 421
NC 904	Tabor City to NC 905
Blue Ridge Pkwy.	US 441 to Virginia state line

† place or route does not appear on the map
‡ route not labeled on map
EB eastbound route NB northbound route
SB southbound route WB westbound route

NORTH DAKOTA

See state and city maps page 77
★ located on city map

LOW CLEARANCE LOCATIONS

Statutory height: 14'0"
Structures with 14'0" or less clearance

Route	Location	Height	Map Key
US 2 Bus. (Demers Av.)	Grand Forks–at Red River bridge	13'2"	★ A-9
ND 8	Stanley–0.9 mi. north of US 2	13'7"	E-4
ND 14	Towner–0.4 mi. north of US 2	13'2"	E-7
ND 22	Dickinson–1.2 mi. south of I-94	13'5"	H-4
US 81 Bus. NB (Main Av.)	Fargo	13'7"	H B-6
US 81 Bus. NB (10th St.)	Fargo–0.5 mi. north of Main Av.	13'2"	★ B-6
US 81 Bus. SB (University Dr.)	Fargo–0.5 mi. north of Main Av.	13'10"	★ B-6
US 83 Bus. SB (7th St.)	Bismarck–0.1 mi. south of Main Av.	13'5"	★ B-3
US 83 Bus. NB (9th St.)	Bismarck–0.1 mi. south of Main Av.	13'8"	★ B-3
I-94/US 10/52	Casselton–0.5 mi. west of ND 18	13'7"	H-12

PERMANENT WEIGH/INSPECTION STATIONS

■ also serves as Port of Entry
All scale locations are also vehicle inspection sites

Route	Location	Map Key
■ ND 5 WB & I-29 NB, SB	Joliette	D-12
US 12 & US 85 all directions	Bowman	J-3
I-29 NB, SB	Mooreton–north of jct. with ND 13	I-13
I-94 EB	Beach–0.5 mi. east of Montana state line	H-2
■ I-94 WB	Fargo–10 mi. west of Minnesota state line	H-13

North Dakota also uses portable scales and weigh-in-motion scales

RESTRICTED ROUTES

Route that restricts use by motor carriers

Route	Location
None reported	

OHIO

See state and city maps pages 78-81
★ located on city map

LOW CLEARANCE LOCATIONS

Statutory height 13'6"
Structures with 13'6" or less clearance

Route	Location	Height	Map Key
OH 14	Salem–northwest of US 45	13'6"	NI-18
OH 18	Hicksville–0.5 mi. northwest of jct. OH 2 and OH 49	12'6"	NG-1
OH 19	Republic–0.6 mi. south of jct. OH 162	10'11"	NH-9
US 20	Cleveland–jct. with E. 120th St.	13'6"	★ SK-18
US 33 WB	Columbus–at Marconi Blvd.	13'3"	★ SH-18
OH 37	Delaware–1 mi. west of US 23	12'7"	NM-8
US 42	Delaware–1.2 mi. northeast of US 36	13'4"	NM-9
US 42	Mansfield–0.2 mi. east of OH 430	12'0"	NJ-11
OH 48	Covington–0.1 mi. north of US 36	12'9"	NN-3
US 62 (Rich St.)	Columbus–0.1 mi. west of Scioto River	12'7"	★ SI-18
US 62	Columbus–0.4 mi. southwest of I-71	13'5"	SC-8
OH 66	Defiance–0.5 mi. south of jct. OH 15/18	12'5"	NG-3
OH 100	Tiffin–0.3 mi. north of OH 18	11'0"	NH-8
OH 103	Willard–1.4 mi. north of US 224	13'2"	NH-10
OH 111	Defiance–0.7 mi. south of OH 424	11'9"	NG-3
OH 149	Bellaire–just west of OH 7	13'6"	SA-19
OH 175 (Richmond Rd.)	Solon–0.6 mi. north of jct. OH 43 (Aurora Rd.)	13'0"	★ SM-20
OH 212	Bolivar–0.3 mi. west	12'6"	NJ-16
OH 245	West Liberty–0.8 mi. west of US 68	12'9"	NM-5
OH 303	Hudson–0.2 mi. west of OH 91	13'6"	NG-16
US 322 (Mayfield Rd.)	Cleveland–0.3 mi. east of US 20 (Euclid Av.)	12'6"	★ SL-18
OH 335	Omega–approx. 2.7 mi. east	12'2"	SG-9
OH 350	Cuba–east of US 68	13'5"	SE-5
OH 508	DeGraff–0.3 mi. south of OH 235	12'4"	NM-5
OH 521	Delaware–1.4 mi. northeast of US 36	12'5"	NM-9
OH 558	East Fairfield–1.5 mi. west of OH 517	13'0"	NI-20
OH 611	Lorain–2.1 mi. east of OH 58	13'0"	NF-13
OH 618	Belpre–0.25 mi. north of OH 32	13'6"	SF-16
OH 666	Zanesville–0.8 mi. north	10'7"	SB-14
OH 762	Orient–1.0 mi. east of US 62	13'3"	SB-8

PERMANENT WEIGH STATIONS

Route	Location	Map Key
OH 18/57 EB, WB	Medina–northwest	NH-14
US 30 EB	Van Wert–8 mi. northwest, mile marker 6	NI-1
I-70 WB	Cambridge–mile marker 173	SA-16
I-70 EB	New Paris–1 mi. east of Indiana state line	SB-1
I-71 NB	Wilmington–north, near US 68	SD-5
I-74 EB	Harrison–west of exit 3	SF-1
I-75 NB	Bowling Green–2 mi. south of US 6	NG-6
I-75 SB	Findlay–north of US 224	NH-6
I-76 WB	Wadsworth–1 mi. west of OH 57	NH-14
I-80 WB	Hubbard–2.5 mi. west of OH 7	★ NB-14, NG-20
I-90 WB	Conneaut–east of OH 7	NC-20

Ohio also uses portable scales

RESTRICTED ROUTES

Routes that restrict use by motor carriers

Route	Location
OH 26	OH 800 to OH 7
US 27	Kentucky state line to US 52
OH 37	OH 93 to OH 555
OH 39	Salineville–OH 644 to OH 164
US 50/Columbia Pkwy.	downtown Cincinnati–I-471 to OH 125
OH 79	OH 586 to Nellie
I-90 EB	Cleveland, I-490 to I-77
OH 93	Kentucky state line to US 52
OH 96	OH 13 to OH 96
OH 146	Cumberland to OH 672
OH 163	Port Clinton to OH 2
OH 208	OH 666 to Adamsville
OH 264	US 50 to Bridgetown
OH 265	OH 285 to OH 761
OH 350	OH 123 to US 22
OH 505	OH 756 to US 52
OH 666	Zanesville to Dresden
OH 724	Carlisle to OH 145
OH 770	OH 73 to OH 247
OH 822	Steubenville, OH 7 to West Virginia state line (Market Street Bridge)
Newell Bridge (over US 30)	US 30 to West Virginia state line

OKLAHOMA

See state and city maps pages 82-83

LOW CLEARANCE LOCATIONS

Statutory height: 13'6"
Structures with 13' 6" or less clearance

Route	Location	Height	Map Key
US 75 Alt.	Beggs–0.9 mi. north of OK 16	13'6"	E-16
OK 78	Durant–north of OK 70E	13'1"	K-16

PERMANENT WEIGH STATIONS

Route	Location	Map Key
OK 3 & US 56/64 & US 287/385 EB, WB	Boise City	C-2
I-35 NB	Marietta	K-14
I-35 SB	Braman–1 mi. south of Kansas state line	B-13
I-35 NB, SB	Davis–southwest at mile point 53, 3 mi. south of OK 7	I-14
I-35 NB, SB	Tonkawa–1.5 miles north of US 60	C-13
I-40 EB, WB	El Reno–mile point 129, 3.5 mi. east of US 81	F-12
I-40 WB	Erick–3.5 mi. east of Texas state line	G-7
US 69/75 NB, SB	Colbert	K-15
US 271 NB, SB	Hugo–7 mi. south	J-18

Oklahoma also uses portable scales

RESTRICTED ROUTES

Routes that restrict use by motor carriers

Route	Location
OK 10	Bowring to Copan
OK 10	OK 10C to OK 137
OK 11	OK 20 to US 75
OK 28	OK 82 to OK 20
OK 32	OK 89 to OK 76
OK 48	US 62 to Bristow
OK 55	Retrop to Sentinal
US 58A	Canton–OK 51 to OK 58
US 59	OK 10 to Kansas state line
US 62	US 69 Bus. to OK 9A
OK 63	†Big Cedar to Arkansas state line
US 66 Bus.	US 66 to Wellston
OK 71	OK 9 to OK 2
US 75A	Mounds to Kiefer
US 77	OK 74 to OK 39
OK 78	Yuba to Texas state line
OK 82	Bengal to Red Oak
OK 82	Vian to OK 100
OK 99	Kansas state line to OK 10
OK 100	Paradise Hill to OK 82
OK 101	OK 64B to Arkansas state line
OK 123	US 60 to US 75
OK 251A	Okay to OK 80
US 271	Antlers to Clayton
US 277	OK 5A to Randlett
US 281	Geary–over Canadian River

† place or route does not appear on the map
‡ route not labeled on map
EB eastbound route NB northbound route
SB southbound route WB westbound route

OREGON

See state and city maps **pages 84-85**
★ located on city map

LOW CLEARANCE LOCATIONS

Statutory height: 14'0"
Structures with 14' 0" or less clearance

Route	Location	Height	Map Key
None reported			

PERMANENT WEIGH STATIONS

Route	Location	Map Key
I-5 NB	Ashland–2 mi. north, mile point 18.08	M-4
I-5 SB	Ashland–2 mi. north, mile point 18.24	M-4
I-5 NB	Myrtle Creek–3 mi. north, mile point 111.07	J-3
I-5 SB	Myrtle Creek–3 mi. north, mile point 111.78	J-3
I-5 NB	Woodburn–2.5 mi. north, mile point 274.18	D-4
I-5 SB	Woodburn–2.5 mi. north, mile point 274.18	D-4
OR 6 WB	Tillamook–2 mi. east, mile point 2.40	C-2
OR 7 NB	Baker City–2.75 mi. south of jct. US 30, mile point 48.4	E-15
OR 18 EB	†Valley Junction–mile point 25.5	E-3
OR 19 SB	Arlington–mile point 5.3	C-10
US 20 WB	Bend–11 mi. east, mile point 11.6	H-8
US 20 EB	Blodgett–mile point 41	F-3
US 20 WB	Blodgett–mile point 41.5	F-3
US 20 WB	†Foster–6 mi. east, mile point 32.29	G-5
US 20 EB	Philomath–1 mi. east, mile point 51.64	F-3
US 20/26 EB	Nyssa–mile point 266.41	H-17
US 20/26 EB	Vale–1.5 mi. east, mile point 248.80	H-16
US 20/OR 126 EB	Sisters–east of the junction, mile point 0.15	G-7
US 20/395 WB	Burns–1 mi. east, mile point 134.17	I-12
OR 22 EB	Eola–4 mi. west of Salem, mile point 21.53	★ F-18, E-4
OR 22 WB	Gates–1 mi. west, mile point 32.06	F-5
US 26 EB, WB	Brightwood–12 mi. east of Sandy, mile point 36.51	D-6
US 26 EB	North Plains–2 mi. northwest, mile point 54.03	C-4
US 26 EB, WB	Prineville–1 mi. east, mile point 21.17	G-8
US 26/395 EB, WB	John Day–1 mi. west, mile point 160.97	G-12
US 30 EB	Alston–mile point 52.5	B-4
US 30 EB	Deer Island–mile point 33.2	B-4
US 30 WB	Scappoose–mile point 16.50	B-4
OR 31 NB	Silver Lake–mile point 47.3	J-8
OR 36 EB	Cheshire–1 mi. west, mile point 46.15	G-3
OR 42 EB	†Brockway–2 mi. west of Winston, mile point 71.20	J-3
OR 42 NB	†Coaledo–5 mi. north of Coquille, mile point 5.50	J-1
OR 42 WB	Myrtle Point–east city limits, mile point 21.87	J-1
OR 58 WB	Lowell–4 mi. east of Lowell Junction, mile point 17.17	H-4
OR 62 NB, SB	Eagle Point–mile point 12	L-4
I-82 SB/US 730 EB, WB	Umatilla–at the junction, US 730, mile point 183.98	B-12
OR 82 WB	Minam–mile point 40.56	C-15
I-84/US 30 EB	Cascade Locks–mile point 44.93	C-6
I-84/US 30 WB	†Emigrant Hill–18 mi. east of Pendleton, mile point 226.95	C-13
I-84/US 30 WB	†Farewell Bend–25 mi. northwest of Ontario, mile point 353.31	G-16
I-84/US 30 EB	LaGrande–2 mi. northwest, at mile point 258.52	D-14
I-84/US 30 EB	†Olds Ferry–21 mi. northwest of Ontario, mile point 354.38	G-16
I-84/US 30 WB	†Wyeth–10 mi. east of Cascade Locks, mile point 54.30	C-7
US 95 NB, SB	Burns Junction–at jct. OR 78, mile point 68	K-15
US 97 NB	Bend–mile point 145.5	H-7
US 97 NB	†Juniper Butte–13.5 mi. south of Madras, mile point 106.9	F-8
US 97 SB	†Juniper Butte–15 mi. south of Madras, mile point 108.2	F-8
US 97 SB	Klamath Falls–1 mi. north, mile point 271.41	M-6
US 97 NB	Klamath Falls–1 mi. north, mile point 271.73	M-6
OR 99 NB	Ashland–2 mi. north, mile point 16.91	M-4
OR 99E NB	Hubbard–1 mi. north, mile point 27.83	D-4
OR 99E SB	Hubbard–1 mi. north, mile point 28.18	D-4
OR 99W NB	Adair Village–mile point 72.4	F-3
OR 99W SB	Dayton–north of Dayton Junction, mile point 29.10	D-4
US 101 NB	Bandon–2 mi. south, mile point 276.11	J-1
US 101 SB	Brookings—mile point 353.18	M-1
US 101 NB	Brookings—south city limits, mile point 361.17	M-1
US 101 SB	Hauser–6 mi. north of Coos Bay Bridge, mile point 227.89	I-1
US 101 NB	Tillamook–mile point 74.52	D-2
US 101	Waldport–mile point 157.40	F-2
US 101/US 26 NB	Seaside–7 mi. north, mile point 14.39	B-2
OR 126 EB	Noti–0.5 mi. east, mile point 43.00	H-3
OR 126 WB	Walterville–10 mi. east of Springfield, mile point 12.95	H-4
OR 138 WB	Glide–1 mi. west, mile point 15.14	J-3
OR 140 WB	†Lake Creek–20 mi. east of Medford, mile point 14.5	L-5
OR 140 EB	White City–mile point 2.7	L-4
US 199 SB	Selma–mile point 20.65	M-2
US 199 NB	Wilderville–8 mi. south of Grants Pass, mile point 8.7	L-3
OR 204 EB	Elgin–mile point 35.60	C-14
OR 212/224 WB	†Rock Creek–2.9 mi. east of I-205, mile point 7.94	★ M-20, D-5
OR 229 SB	Toledo–mile point 29.8	F-2
OR 226 WB	Scio–mile point 12.0	F-4
OR 241 WB	Coos Bay–east of US 101, mile point 2.4	J-1
US 395 NB	Lakeview–north of OR 140, mile point 137.28	M-10
US 395 NB	Pilot Rock–west city limits, mile point 16.12	C-13
US 730 EB, WB	†Cold Springs–at jct. OR 37, mile point 193.28	B-12

Oregon also uses portable scales

RESTRICTED ROUTES

Routes that restrict use by motor carriers

Route	Location
OR 3	Local Road near Flora to Washington state line
OR 19	South of Fossil (MP 72.09) to US 26
US 20	Sweet Home to OR 126 (Santiam Junction)
OR 22	US 101 (Hebo) to OR 18 (Valley Junction)
OR 27	US 20 to US 26 (Prineville)
US 30	I-84 (Huntington) to US 95 Spur (Weiser)
OR 36	Mapleton to Blachly
OR 37	US 730 to US 30 (Pendleton)
OR 43	Lake Oswego to I-5/I-405 (Portland)
OR 43	West Linn to Oregon City
OR 46	Cave Junction to Oregon Caves
OR 47	US 30 (Clatskanie) to US 26 (Banks)
OR 47	OR 240 (Yamhill) to OR 99W (McMinnville)
OR 53	US 101 (Nehalem) to US 26
OR 62	OR 230 (Union Creek) to Fort Klamath
OR 66	I-5 (Ashland) to US 97 (Klamath Falls)
OR 74	Heppner to US 395 (†Nye)
US 101	Yachats to north of Florence (MP 185.17)
US 101	OR 6 (Tillamook) to OR 18 (Otis Junction)
OR 140	US 395 (Lakeview) to Nevada state line
US 197	OR 216 to south of Maupin (MP 54.20)
OR 202	Olney to Jewell
OR 207	US 26 (Mitchell) to OR 74 (Heppner)
OR 214	OR 22 to Silverton
OR 216	US 197 (Tygh Valley) to US 97
OR 218	US 97 (Shaniko) to Fossil
OR 219	OR 240 to OR 210
OR 229	Kernville to Siletz
OR 234	I-5 to OR 62
OR 242	OR 126 (†Belknap Springs) to OR 126 (Sisters)
US 395	Pilot Rock to Mt. Vernon
OR 402	OR 19 (Kimberly) to US 395 (Long Creek)

PENNSYLVANIA

See state and city maps **pages 86-89**
★ located on city map
◆ located on city map **page 90**

LOW CLEARANCE LOCATIONS

Statutory height: 13'6"
Structures with 13'6" or less clearance

Route	Location	Height	Map Key
US 6	Mill Village	12'7"	WE-4
US 6/19	Cambridge Springs	13'6"	WE-4
PA 8	Butler–south of PA 356	13'5"	WK-4
PA 8 (Washington Blvd.)	Pittsburgh–0.2 mi. north of PA 380	13'0"	◆ K-7
US 13 (Highland Av.)	Chester–0.1 north of W 4th St.	12'9"	EQ-11
US 13	Glenolden at South Av.	12'6"	◆ F-2
US 13	Philadelphia–southwest of PA 611	13'2"	◆ D-4
US 13 NB (Chester Pike)	Ridley Park–0.35 mi. east of Fairview Rd.	13'1"	◆ G-1
US 13	Torresdale–north of †Rhawn St.	13'4"	◆ C-7
US 19	Fairview–south	13'6"	WH-3
PA 29	Mont Clare	13'6"	EO-11
US 30 WB	Chambersburg–0.35 mi. east of US 11	13'2"	WP-14
US 30	Stoystown	13'0"	WO-8
PA 32	Yardley–north of I-295	13'6"	EN-13
PA 36	Altoona–at 10th Av.	13'2"	★ WA-13
PA 36 (24th St.)	Altoona–at N. Branch Av.	13'1"	★ WB-13
US 40 (W. Chestnut St.)	Washington–under RR tracks	13'4"	WO-2
PA 45	Spruce Creek–south of the Little Juniata River	8'2"	WL-12
PA 51 (Carson St.)	Pittsburgh–northwest of PA 51/US 19	13'5"	◆ K-5
PA 53	Portage	13'6"	WN-10
PA 53	Wilmore	13'0"	WN-9
PA 58	Jamestown	8'0"	WG-2
PA 59	Ormsby–1.5 mi. west of PA 646	13'3"	WE-10
PA 60	Crafton	13'6"	◆ K-5
US 62	Mercer–1.5 mi. northeast of US 19	11'7"	WI-3
US 62	President–over Allegheny River	13'3"	WG-6
PA 73	north of Flourtown at Bethlehem Pike	13'5"	◆ A-3
PA 73	Tacony–Cottman Av.	13'3"	◆ C-6
PA 98 (Avonia Rd.)	Fairview–under RR tracks	13'4"	WD-3
PA 114	Mount Allen	13'3"	EO-4
PA 168	West Pittsburg	12'3"	WJ-2
PA 183	Cressona–1 mi. west of PA 61	11'8"	EL-7
PA 188	Waynesburg	13'4"	WP-3
PA 214	Seven Valleys	11'1"	EQ-5
PA 217	Blairsville–0.4 mi. south of US 22/119	13'2"	WM-7
US 219 Bus.	Meyersdale	13'6"	WQ-8
US 220 Bus.	Tyrone	12'6"	WL-11
PA 241	Elizabethtown	13'6"	EO-6
PA 259	Bolivar	11'0"	WN-7
PA 259	Bolivar–RR north	11'0"	WN-7
PA 259	Heshbon–over Blacklick Creek	13'4"	WM-8
PA 263	Center Bridge	12'0"	EM-13
PA 267	Meshoppen	13'5"	EG-8
I-279/US 22/30	Pittsburgh–Fort Pitt Tunnel	13'6"	◆ K-5
PA 288	Wampum	13'4"	WK-2
US 322	Downingtown–0.25 mi. south of US 30 Bus.	12'0"	EP-10
PA 324	Marticville–0.8 mi. east of Pequea Creek	12'0"	EQ-7
PA 339	Mahanoy City–just north of PA 54	11'5"	EK-8
PA 340	Bird in Hand–0.9 mi. east of PA 896	13'6"	EP-7
PA 352	Frazer–0.25 mi. south of US 30	10'0"	EP-10
PA 372	Atglen–1.2 mi. west of PA 41	10'5"	EP-8
I-376/US 22/30	Pittsburgh–Squirrel Hill Tunnel	13'6"	◆ K-7

list continued on next page

† place or route does not appear on the map
‡ route not labeled on map
EB eastbound route NB northbound route
SB southbound route WB westbound route

Route	Location	Height	Map Key
PA 405	Milton–south of PA 642	13'6"	EJ-4
PA 420	Prospect Park–0.4 mi. north of US 13	12'6"	◆ G-2
PA 438	La Plume–under RR tracks	11'10"	EG-9
PA 441	Middletown–0.5 mi. south of PA 230	12'0"	EO-5
PA 488	Wurtemburg–over Slippery Rock Creek	11'2"	WK-3
PA 532	Holland–north of PA 213	9'6"	EO-13
PA 532	Newtown–1.4 mi. south of PA 332	13'1"	EO-13
PA 568	Gibraltar–just south of PA 724	13'3"	EN-9
PA 611	Easton–0.1 mi. south of PA 248	12'3"	EL-12
PA 611	Portland	13'6"	EJ-12
PA 616	Railroad–0.4 mi. north of PA 851	10'0"	EQ-5
PA 616	Seitzland	10'0"	EQ-5
PA 641	Carlisle–just west of US 11	12'10"	EO-3
PA 641	Mechanicsburg	13'6"	★ ET-1
PA 690	Moscow–just east of PA 435	12'2"	EH-10
PA 764	Cross Keys	13'4"	★ WB-13
PA 849	Duncannon–just west of Juniata River	13'6"	EN-4
PA 885	Pittsburgh–just south of I-376	11'6"	◆ K-6
PA 980	†Venice	10'10"	WN-2

PERMANENT WEIGH/INSPECTION STATIONS

All scale locations are also vehicle inspection sites

Route	Location	Map Key
I-80 EB, WB	Clarion, mile marker 56	WI-6

Pennsylvania also uses portable scales

RESTRICTED ROUTES

Selected routes are restricted to various configurations. Please refer to STAA Pub. 411 on the PennDOT website: penndot.gov

Other routes that restrict use by motor carriers

Route	Location
PA 32	Erwinna to Point Pleasant
PA 44	US 6 to PA 144
PA 58	Eau Claire to PA 268
US 62	Tionesta–over Allegheny River
PA 82	Birdsboro to Elverson
PA 93	PA 424 (Hazleton) to US 209
PA 103	Allenport to Ryde
PA 130	I-376 southeast to Turtle Creek
PA 130	PA 981 (Pleasant Unity) to PA 381
PA 144	PA 879 (Moshannon) to US 6 (Galeton)
PA 151	US 30 to PA 18
PA 168	PA 18 to north of New Galilee
PA 191	PA 512 (Bangor) to Stroudsburg
US 209 Bus.	US 209 to PA 33
PA 231	PA 18 to PA 844
PA 241	PA 441 to Elizabethtown
PA 244	PA 44 to PA 449
PA 258	PA 208 to PA 18
PA 259	US 30 to Bolivar
PA 267	Lawton to Birchardville
PA 281	West Virginia state line to US 40
PA 284	PA 287 to US 15
PA 307	US 11 (Scranton) to Dunmore east of Lake Scranton
PA 329	Northampton–over Lehigh River
PA 372	PA 41 to PA 10
PA 381	Jones Mills to Rector
PA 381	West Virginia state line to US 40
PA 388	US 422 to PA 108
PA 408	Hydetown to PA 428
PA 415	Harveys Lake–over Harveys Lake inlet
PA 437	PA 309 (Mountain Top) to White Haven
PA 462	Stonybrook to Hallam
PA 534	Albrightsville–over Swamp Run
PA 551	US 422 to PA 208 (Pulaski)
PA 555	Weedville to Driftwood
PA 756	PA 403 (Johnstown) to US 219 (Geistown)
PA 848	I-81 to PA 547
PA 850	McCullochs Mills–over Willow Run
PA 858	Rushville to Middletown Center
PA 895	Pine Grove–over Swatara Creek
PA 973	PA 44 to Salladasburg

RHODE ISLAND

See state and city maps **page 91**
★ located on city map

LOW CLEARANCE LOCATIONS

Statutory height: 13'6"
Structures with 13'6" or less clearance

Route	Location	Height	Map Key
†Church St.	Valley Falls	12'8"	★ J-9
†High St.	Central Falls–approx. 0.75 mi. south of RI 123 and 0.1 mi. east of RI 114 (Broad St.)	11'3"	★ J-9
†High St.	Central Falls–approx. 1.5 mi. south of RI 123 and 0.25 mi. east of RI 114 (Broad St.)	12'0"	★ J-9
†Lincoln Av.	Warwick–0.3 mi. south of RI 37, between I-95 and US 1 (Boston Post Rd.)	10'0"	★ N-8
†East Main St.	West Warwick–approx. 0.25 mi. west of RI 33	13'6"	★ N-7
†Main St.	Woonsocket	12'0"	A-6

PERMANENT WEIGH/INSPECTION STATIONS

All scale locations are also vehicle inspection sites

Route	Location	Map Key
US 6 EB, WB	North Scituate	D-5
RI 24 NB	Tiverton	F-8
I-95 NB, SB	Wyoming–north of Exit 4	G-4
RI 146 NB	1.6 mi. south of Massachusetts state line	A-5
RI 146 SB	†North Smithfield–south of RI 104	B-5
I-295 NB, SB	east of RI 146	★ I-8, B-6

Rhode Island also uses semiportable and portable scales

RESTRICTED ROUTES

Routes that restrict use by motor carriers

Route	Location
US 1	South Kingstown–1 mi. south of RI 108
US 1	Westerly–0.3 mi. north of US 1A
US 1A	US 1 to RI 102
US 1A	South Kingstown–over Saugatucket River
RI 2	I-295 to RI 113
RI 3	Nooseneck to I-95
RI 5	Cranston–0.1 mi. south of RI 12
RI 5	North Smithfield–0.7 mi. east of RI 102
US 6A	RI 116 to Springbrook Rd.
RI 7	I-95 to Charles St.
RI 12	Cranston–just east of I-95
RI 37	I-95 to RI 2
US 44	I-95 to Canal St.
RI 91	RI 78 to McGowan Corners
RI 98	RI 96 to Massachusetts state line
RI 102	Burrillville–over Branch River
RI 107	Harrisville–east of RI 98
RI 112	RI 91 to Carolina
RI 114	Diamond Hill to RI 120
RI 114	Pawtucket–north of I-95
RI 123	RI 246 to RI 126
RI 126	I-95 to US 1
RI 152	RI 1A to US 44

SOUTH CAROLINA

See state and city maps **page 92**
★ located on city map
◆ located on Charlotte city map **page 76**

LOW CLEARANCE LOCATIONS

Statutory height: 13'6"
Structures with 13'6" or less clearance

Route	Location	Height	Map Key
SC 10	Mccormick–north of jct. with SC 28	10'6"	E-4
US 25 Bus.	Edgefield–just south of Mims St.	13'0"	E-5
SC 177	Marlboro–south of North Carolina state line	13'6"	B-10
SC 200	Winnsboro–0.1 mi. east of US 321 Bus.	13'5"	C-7
SC 421	Aiken–0.2 mi south of US 1/78	12'6"	F-6
SC 823	Mount Carmel–at Little River	12'7"	D-4

PERMANENT WEIGH/INSPECTION STATIONS

All scale locations are also vehicle inspection sites

Route	Location	Map Key
I-20 EB	Aiken County–mile marker 35	E-6
I-20 WB	Lexington–mile marker 53	E-7
I-26 WB	Columbia–17 mi. west	D-7
I-26 EB, WB	Harleyville–5 mi. east of I-95, mile marker 174E	G-9
I-26 EB	Newberry–7 mi. east	D-6
I-77 SB	Rock Hill–mile marker 85	A-8
I-77 NB	Rock Hill–1 mi. south of North Carolina state line	◆ J-3, A-8
I-85 NB	Fair Play–9 mi. north of Georgia state line	C-3
I-95 NB	Dorchester County–near mile marker 74	G-8

South Carolina also uses portable scales

RESTRICTED ROUTES

Routes that restrict use by motor carriers

Route	Location
SC 3	US 301 to Estill
SC 4	Springfield to SC 332
US 15	St. George to US 178, over Indian Field Swamp
SC 20	Golden Grove to I-185
US 21	east of Frogmore, over Harbor River
US 21 Bus.	Beaufort–over Beaufort River
SC 40	northwest of Sharon, over Bullock Creek
SC 133	SC 183 to SC 11, over Crow Creek
SC 165	US 17 to Meggett
US 221	SC 127 to Laurens, over Burnt Mill Creek
SC 332	Norway to SC 4, over Willow Swamp
US 401	I-20 to US 52, over Jeffries Creek
SC 412	SC 187 to Starr
SC 901	SC 97 to Richburg, over Rocky Creek

† place or route does not appear on the map
‡ route not labeled on map
EB eastbound route NB northbound route
SB southbound route WB westbound route

SOUTH DAKOTA

See state and city maps **page 93**
★ located on city map
◆ located on Black Hills Region map

LOW CLEARANCE LOCATIONS

Statutory height: 14'0"
Structures with 14'0" or less clearance

Route	Location	Height	Map Key
US 14	Pierre–Pierre St. northeast of Sioux Av.	11'1"	★ I-7
US 16 Alt.	Keystone–tunnel 6.5 mi. southeast at mile marker 50.49	12'1"	◆ J-3
US 16 Alt.	Keystone–tunnel 4 mi. southeast at mile marker 53.00	11'11"	◆ J-3
US 16 Alt.	Keystone–4 mi. southeast, mile marker 53.02	12'6"	◆ J-3
US 16 Alt.	Keystone–tunnel 3.3 mi. southeast at mile marker 53.65	12'6"	◆ J-3
US 16 Alt.	Keystone–2.8 mi. southeast at mile marker 54.09	9'7"	◆ J-3
SD 87	†Sylvan Lake–tunnel 6 mi. southeast in Custer State Park at mile marker 66.85	12'0"	◆ J-3
SD 87	†Sylvan Lake–tunnel 2 mi. southeast in Custer State Park at mile marker 72.00	11'9"	◆ J-3
SD 87	†Sylvan Lake–tunnel 1 mi. northwest of SD 89 at mile marker 74.65	10'4"	◆ J-3
SD 271	Java–1.1 mi. northeast of SD 130 at mile marker 167.65	12'1"	B-8

PERMANENT WEIGH/INSPECTION STATIONS

■ also serves at Port of Entry
All scale locations are also vehicle inspection sites

Route	Location	Map Key
US 12 EB, WB	Milbank	B-13
US 12/SD 73 all directions	Lemmon–southeast corner of the jct.	A-5
US 14/83 all directions	Blunt–4 mi. west at the jct.	D-8
US 18/183 all directions	Winner–west of town, just east of the jct.	F-8
■ I-29 NB	Jefferson–mile marker 13	H-13
■ I-29 SB	Sisseton–mile marker 235	A-12
SD 79 all directions	Rapid City–1 mi. south	★ J-5,◆ I-3, E-3
US 81 & SD 46 all directions	Midway	G-12
I-90 EB, WB	Mitchell–1 mi. west at exit 330	F-11
■ I-90 WB	Sioux Falls–east, mile marker 412 at Minnesota state line	F-13
■ I-90 EB	Tilford–mile marker 39	◆ H-3, D-3
US 281 NB,SB	Frederick–north, near North Dakota state line	A-10
US 281	Wolsey–4 mi. north at jct. US 14	D-10

South Dakota also uses portable scales

RESTRICTED ROUTES

Routes that restrict use by motor carriers

Route	Location
US 16 Alt.	SD 36 to Keystone
SD 87	US 385 to US 16
SD 240	Wall to I-90, exit 131
SD 244	US 16 to US 16A (Keystone)

TENNESSEE

See state and city maps **pages 94-95**
★ located on city map

LOW CLEARANCE LOCATIONS

Statutory height: 13'6"
Structures with 13'6" or less clearance

Route	Location	Height	Map Key
US 11/41/64/72	Chattanooga–just west of TN 17	13'1"	★ N-11
US 11/41/64/72	Chattanooga–east of Browns Ferry Rd.	11'9"	★ N-11
TN Secondary 17	TN Secondary 58 to US 11/41/64/72, mile marker 2.05	12'9"	★ N-11
US 25W/TN9	Clinton–north of TN 61	13'5"	C-19
US 31/TN 6 (8th Av. S.)	Nashville–0.2 mi. north of I-40, mile marker 8.24	12'7"	★ K-8
TN Secondary 33 (Maryville Pike)	Knoxville–0.8 mi. southwest of US 441, mile marker 4.76	10'2"	★ K-13
TN Secondary 33 (Maryville Pike)	Mt. Olive–0.3 mi. north, mile marker 3.00	12'8"	★ K-13
†TN Secondary 39	Riceville	13'5"	F-17
US 41/76/TN 8	Chattanooga–Bachman Tubes (tunnel), mile marker 5.04	11'9"	★ N-12
TN Secondary 47	White Bluff–2 mi. south of US 70, mile marker 8.57	11'0"	C-10
TN Secondary 58	Chattanooga–1 mi. south of I-24, mile marker 3.24	10'8"	★ M-12
US 61/TN 14 SB	Memphis–south of jct. I-55 mile marker 7.13	13'5"	★ G-1
US 64/TN 40	Cleveland–0.9 mi. east of US 11, mile marker 0.93	11'0"	G-17
TN Secondary 87	Henning–0.5 mi. east of TN Secondary 209, mile marker 20.79	8'2"	E-3
TN Secondary 131	Ball Camp to TN 62, mile marker 5.93	10'7"	D-19
TN Secondary 241	Center–6.9 mi. north, Natchez Trace Pkwy. overpass, mile marker 1.20	11'7"	F-9
TN Secondary 246	Columbia–north of jct. US 31, mile marker 0.79	10'10"	E-10
TN Secondary 252	Clovercroft–1.7 mi. southeast, mile marker 3.59	10'4"	D-11
TN Secondary 252	Clovercroft–mile marker 5.26	10'5"	D-11

PERMANENT WEIGH/INSPECTION STATIONS

All scale locations are also vehicle inspection sites

Route	Location	Map Key
I-24 EB, WB	Manchester–mile marker 115	F-13
I-40 EB, WB	Brownsville–mile marker 50	E-4
I-40/75 all directions	Farragut–mile marker 372	D-19
I-65 NB	Ardmore–5 mi. north of Alabama state line	G-11
I-65 NB, SB	approx. 2 mi. south of Kentucky state line	A-12
I-81 SB	Mohawk–southwest at mile marker 21	K-16

Tennessee also uses portable scales

RESTRICTED ROUTES

Routes that restrict use by motor carriers

Route	Location
US 64	Parksville to TN 68
TN Secondary 69	Saltillo to TN Secondary 202
TN 92	Dandridge to Chestnut Hill
TN Secondary 125	Middleton to TN Secondary 57
US 127	TN 28 to †Fairmount
TN Secondary 127	Hillsboro to Viola
TN Secondary 128	Clifton to TN 13
US 129	†Chilhowee to North Carolina state line
TN 151	Red Boiling Springs to North Springs
TN Secondary 247	TN Secondary 246 to I-65 overpass
TN Secondary 272	Lewisburg to TN Secondary 129
US 441	I-75 to Norris
Natchez Trace Pkwy.	TN 100 to Alabama state line

TEXAS

See state and city maps **pages 96-101**
★ located on city map
◆ located on Dallas/Fort Worth & Vicinity map **page 97**
✧ located on Houston & Vicinity map **page 96**
◗ located on Texarkana map **page 11**

LOW CLEARANCE LOCATIONS

Statutory height: 14'0"
Structures with 14'0" or less clearance

Route	Location	Height	Map Key
‡FM 1	Magasco–1 mi. north	13'9"	EH-12
TX 6	Alvin–jct. TX 35	14'0"	✧ I-6
‡TX 6 Bus.	Marlin–1.0 mi. north of jct. TX 7	13'9"	EH-7
I-10 WB	Houston–at jct. I-45	14'0"	✧ D-5
I-10	Houston–eastbound ramp to northbound I-69/US 59	14'0"	✧ D-5
†I-10 Bus.	Sierra Blanca–at jct. I-10	13'0"	WM-4
I-10/45	Houston–between I-10/I-45 south jct. & I-10/I-45 north jct.	14'0"	✧ D-5
TX 11 EB	Commerce–at TX 244	13'10"	ED-8
FM 12 EB	San Marcos–at jct. I-35	13'11"	EK-5
North Loop 12	Dallas–1.5 mi. east of US 75	14'0"	◆ F-11
TX 16	San Saba–1 mi. north of jct. US 190	13'6"	EI-3
†I-20 Bus.	Loraine–at jct. I-20	13'6"	WJ-12
†I-20 Bus. EB	Merkel–at east jct. I-20	13'4"	WJ-13
†I-20 Bus. WB	Merkel–at west jct. I-20	13'6"	WJ-13
†I-20 Bus.	Roscoe–at west jct. I-20	14'0"	WJ-13
†I-20 Bus. WB	Trent–east jct. I-20	13'6"	WJ-13
†I-20 Bus.	Westbrook–at west jct. I-20	13'6"	WJ-12
TX 21	Crockett–0.2 mi. west of US 287	13'6"	EH-10
I-30 EB	Arlington–at Fielder Rd.	13'6"	◆ G-6
I-30	Fort Worth–at jct. TX 183	14'0"	◆ H-3
I-30	Fort Worth–at jct. TX 183 WB to SB and NB to WB	13'6"	◆ H-3
I-30	Fort Worth–1 mi. east of TX 183 at jct. †Ridgmar/Ridglea	14'0"	◆ H-3
I-30 EB	Fort Worth–at jct. Green Oak Rd.	13'7"	◆ H-3
†I-30 Frontage Rd.	Texarkana–between †FM 559 and †FM 1397	14'0"	EC-12
TX 31 WB	Tyler–0.13 mi. east of US 69	13'9"	EF-10
TX 34 NB	Kaufman–at jct. US 175	14'0"	EE-8
I-35 Lowerdeck	Austin–0.3 mi north of FM 969 at Manor Rd.	13'6"	★ WE-6
I-35 Lowerdeck	Austin–at jct. †32nd St., 1 mi. south of Loop 111	13'6"	★ WE-6
I-35 Lowerdeck	Austin–at †38½ St.	13'6"	★ WE-6
I-35 SB	Austin–at Cesar Chavez/1st St.	14'0"	★ WE-5
I-35 NB	Salado–at jct. †Stagecoach Rd.	14'0"	EI-6
I-35E	Dallas–southbound ramp to southbound TX Loop 354	14'0"	◆ E-9
I-35W NB	Fort Worth–ramp to westbound I-820	14'0"	◆ F-4
†I-35W Bus. SB	Alvarado–at jct. I-35W	14'0"	EF-6
TX 36	Milano–south of US 79	13'11"	EJ-7
TX 36	Rosenberg–0.5 mi. north of US 90 Alt.	13'11"	EL-9
TX 36	Sealy–at jct. US 90	13'9"	EL-8
†FM 36	Caddo Mills–at jct. I-30	13'11"	ED-8
†I-37 Frontage Rd., NB	north of Calallen–NB to SB turnaround	12'0"	EP-5
†I-37 Frontage Rd., SB	Edroy–south of ‡TX 234	13'4"	EP-5
I-45	Houston–1 mi. south of I-10	14'0"	✧ D-5
I-45 NB	Huntsville–at south jct. TX 75	14'0"	EJ-9
I-45	Texas City–northbound ramp to westbound TX 6	13'11"	EL-11
†TX 46 Bus.	New Braunfels–1.7 mi. northwest of I-35	11'8"	EL-5
TX 49	Jefferson–0.5 mi. east of FM 134	13'7"	EE-11
TX 49	Lassater–north of jct. †FM 1969	13'11"	EE-11
†TX 50 Spur	Burleson–at jct. I-35W	14'0"	EF-6
TX 56	Whitesboro–at jct. US 377	13'5"	EC-7
‡FM 56	Kopperl–1.8 mi. southeast of TX 174	13'7"	EG-6
‡FM 60	Deanville–2.5 mi. southeast of TX 21	13'0"	EJ-7
US 60/287	Amarillo–south of I-40 Bus. Loop	14'0"	★ WB-2
TX 63	Burkeville–10 mi. northeast at Sabine River bridge	12'3"	EI-13
US 67 EB	Texarkana–0.53 mi. southwest of US 82	13'4"	◗ M-19
US 67/90	Alpine–3.7 mi. west of TX 118	13'7"	WO-7
US 69	Bells–0.25 mi. north of TX 56	13'11"	EC-8
I-69/US 59	Houston–westbound ramp to southbound West Loop I-610	14'0"	✧ E-4
I-69/US 59	Humble–U-turns at the San Jacinto River	13'6"	✧ A-6
†US 69 Bus./TX 103 WB	Lufkin–0.13 mi. west of †US 59 Bus.	13'8"	EH-11
†US 69 Bus./TX 103 EB	Lufkin–0.13 mi. west of †US 59 Bus.	14'0"	EH-11

list continued on following page

TEXAS
Low Clearance Locations • Permanent Weigh Stations • Restricted Routes

† place or route does not appear on the map
‡ route not labeled on map
EB eastbound route NB northbound route
SB southbound route WB westbound route

Route	Location	Height	Map Key
†TX 71 Bus.	Columbus–0.25 mi. north of US 90	13'8"	EL-8
US 75	Sherman–at TX 56 northbound US 75 U-turn to southbound US 75	14'0"	EC-7
TX 75	Conroe–2 mi. north at jct. †FM 2854	13'10"	EJ-10
US 77	Schulenburg–between US 90 & †TX 222 Spur	13'8"	EL-7
TX 78	Dallas–ramp to southbound I-635	14'0"	◆ F-12
US 80	Terrell–east of †FM 429	13'9"	EE-8
US 82	Ringgold–0.75 mi. west of US 81	13'6"	EC-5
†TX 82 Loop	San Marcos–eastbound ramp to northbound I-35	13'6"	EK-5
US 84	Snyder–at jct. ‡FM 1673	14'0"	WJ-12
‡US 84 Bus.	Snyder–1 mi. south at North jct. US 84	13'11"	WJ-12
US 87 NB	Canyon–at westbound ramp to US 60	13'7"	WD-10
US 87 NB, SB	Dalhart–0.2 mi. south of US 385	13'7"	WB-9
US 87 Bus.	Lubbock–0.5 mi. south of US 82	14'0"	★ WE-3
TX 87 SB	Orange–at jct. I-10	14'0"	EK-13
US 90	Harwood–0.25 mi. east of I-10	13'7"	EL-6
US 90	Weimar–railroad bridge 2 mi. west of I-10	14'0"	EL-7
US 90 Alt.	Houston–1.25 mi. west of jct. with I-45	14'0"	✧ E-5
US 90 Alt.	Rosenberg–at jct. TX 36	13'11"	EL-9
TX 94	Lufkin–0.13 mi. west of †TX 266 Spur	13'7"	EH-11
TX 114	Justin–south at jct. †FM 156	13'10"	◆ D-4
TX 114 Bus.	Roanoke–2.5 mi. east of I-35W	13'9"	◆ D-5
TX 114 Bus.	Roanoke–3 mi. east of I-35W at US 377 overpass	13'9"	◆ D-5
TX 117 Spur	San Antonio–at jct. with I-410	13'10"	★ ET-11
TX 121 WB	Ft. Worth–east of jct. I-35W at Sylvania Av.	13'6"	◆ G-4
FM 126	Merkel–west at jct. I-20	13'6"	WJ-13
TX 135 NB	Kilgore–1 mi. south of TX 31	13'10"	EE-10
FM 145	Farwell–0.2 mi. east of US 70/84	11'5"	WF-8
TX 146	Texas City–southbound ramp to southbound I-45	13'7"	EL-11
‡FM 166	Caldwell–0.33 mi. east of TX 36	11'8"	EJ-7
FM 171	Wichita Falls–east of US 287 Bus.	14'0"	★ WN-2
US 175 SB	Dallas–0.25 mi. south of I-45	13'6"	◆ G-11
TX 180 EB	Fort Worth–northbound ramp to I-820	13'10"	◆ H-5
US 181	Portland–at †FM 2986 southbound turnaround	13'6"	EP-6
TX 183	Fort Worth–1.0 mi. west of I-35W	13'6"	◆ G-4
TX 183 SB	Fort Worth–eastbound ramp to I-30	13'10"	◆ H-3
TX 183 NB	Fort Worth–westbound ramp to I-30	13'6"	◆ H-3
TX 183 EB	Fort Worth–northbound ramp to I-820	14'0"	◆ G-5
TX 183 EB	Irving–northbound ramp to TX 12 Loop	14'0"	◆ F-9
TX 199	Fort Worth–at jct. with I-30	13'1"	◆ H-4
TX 203	Wellington–8 mi. east	13'3"	WE-13
TX 206	Coleman–0.2 mi. north of TX 153	13'2"	EG-2
TX 207	Panhandle–0.5 mi. north of US 60	13'11"	WD-11
TX 225	Houston–eastbound ramp to northbound I-610	14'0"	✧ E-6
†TX 225 Frontage Rd.	LaPorte–westbound ramp to southbound TX 146	14'0"	✧ E-9
US 259	Daingerfield–between south jct. TX 11 and north jct. TX 11	13'7"	ED-11
TX 261 Spur	Houston–at North Loop I-610	14'0"	✧ D-5
TX 279	Amarillo–1 mi. west of US 60/87/287	13'11"	★ WB-2
US 281	Brazos–Brazos River bridge, 2.5 mi. north of I-20	14'0"	EE-4
US 281	Brazos–4.5 miles north of I-20	13'11"	EE-4
US 281 SB	San Antonio–at I-410	14'0"	★ ET-10
US 287	Wichita Falls–0.75 mi. east of †FM 369 at jct. †Huntington Rd.	13'8"	EC-4
US 287 NB	Wichita Falls–1.5 mi east of jct. †FM 369	13'11"	EC-4
US 287 NB	Wichita Falls–at jct. TX 11 Spur	13'10"	★ WN-2
‡US 287 Bus.	Wichita Falls–0.3 mi. west of TX 240	13'9"	★ WO-3
†US 290 Frontage Rd.	Austin–EB on ramp from †Industrial Oaks Blvd.	13'6"	★ WF-4
†TX 323	Overton–1.25 mi. south of TX 135	13'9"	EF-10
TX 323 Loop SB	Tyler–0.2 mi. south of west jct. TX 31	13'9"	★ EA-8
TX 325 Spur EB	Wichita Falls–at jct. I-44/US 287	13'5"	★ WN-2
TX 341 Spur SB	White Settlement–north of I-30	13'9"	◆ H-3
TX 349	Midland–at jct. I-20 Bus.	14'0"	★ WH-5
TX 359	Mathis–1.5 mi. south of I-37	14'0"	EO-5
TX 366 Spur Frontage Rd. (Woodall Rodgers Frwy.)	Dallas–between US 75 & I-35E	13'7"	◆ B-2
TX 368 Spur	San Antonio–0.13 mi. north of jct. with I-35	14'0"	★ EN-12
†FM 369	Wichita Falls–at jct. with US 287	14'0"	EC-4
TX 371 Spur	San Antonio–1.0 mi. south of jct. with US 90	13'9"	★ ET-9
‡FM 390	Gay Hill–1 mi. west of TX 36	10'6"	EK-8
I-410 (N Loop WB)	San Antonio–at I-10 W Loop	14'0"	★ ER-9
I-410 (NE Loop EB)	San Antonio–at †Starcrest Dr. exit	13'6"	★ ER-11
†TX 465 Spur	Fort Worth–northbound ramp to westbound TX-183	14'0"	◆ I-3
FM 487	Jarrell–at I-35 overpass	13'10"	EI-5
†FM 597	Abernathy–powerlines at jct. with †TX 369 Spur	14'0"	WG-10
FM 608	Roscoe–at jct. I-20 Bus.	14'0"	WJ-13
‡FM 644	Loraine–at jct. I-20	13'6"	WJ-13
FM 670	Westbrook–at jct. I-20	14'0"	WJ-12
FM 707	Tye–on shoulders under I-20	13'11"	EF-1
†FM 817	Belton–0.75 mi. south of I-35	13'6"	EI-6
†FM 817	Belton–0.5 mi. north of ‡FM 93	14'0"	EI-6
‡FM 818	west of Big Spring–at I-20 overpass	13'11"	WK-11
‡FM 818	†Lomax–3 mi. north at I-20 overpass	13'6"	WK-11
I-820 (East Loop)	Fort Worth–jct. TX 180	14'0"	◆ H-5
†I-820 (East Loop) Frontage Rd.	Fort Worth–0.25 mi. south of TX 180	14'0"	◆ H-5
‡FM 820	Big Spring–east at I-20 overpass	13'6"	WJ-11
‡FM 821	Big Spring–east at I-20 overpass	13'0"	WJ-11
FM 922	Valley View–at jct. I-35/US 77	14'0"	ED-6
FM 1085	Trent–at jct. I-20	13'6"	WJ-13
†FM 1229	Colorado City–west at jct. I-20 (exit 213)	13'8"	WJ-12
†FM 1513	New London–at jct. TX 42	13'9"	EF-10
FM 1541	Amarillo–at jct. I-27 (Washington St.)	14'0"	★ WC-2
†FM 1565	Greenville–10.4 mi. southwest at I-30 overpass	13'5"	ED-8
†FM 1570	Greenville–3.2 mi. southwest at I-30 overpass	13'5"	ED-8
FM 1572	Spofford–3.75 mi. west of US 90	13'4"	WQ-13
†FM 1686	Victoria–at jct. US 59	14'0"	EN-7
†FM 1899	Colorado City–east at jct. with I-120	13'6"	WJ-12
†FM 1997	Marshall–0.13 mi. north of US 80	10'8"	EE-11
†FM 2114 WB	West–at jct. I-35	13'6"	EG-6
†FM 2417 NB	North of Waco at jct. with I-35	14'0"	EH-6
†FM 2642	Royse City–east at jct. I-30	13'5"	EE-8
FM 2790 (Somerset Rd.)	San Antonio–at jct. I-410	13'10"	★ ET-9
†FM 2836	Colorado City–west at jct. I-20	13'6"	WJ-12
†FM 3524	Aubrey–0.13 mi. south of jct. with US 377	13'6"	ED-6
†FM 3525	Colorado City–at jct. I-20	14'0"	WJ-12

PERMANENT WEIGH/INSPECTION STATIONS

All scale locations are also vehicle inspection sites

Route	Location	Map Key
I-2/US 83 EB, WB	Donna–east of McAllen	★ WS-11, ET-5
TX 6 EB	Hallsburg	EH-7
TX 6 SB	Hearne–5.5 mi. south	EI-7
I-10 EB	Brookshire–1 mi. east of Brazos River	EL-9
I-10 EB	El Paso–5 mi. south of New Mexico state line	WK-1
I-10 EB, WB	Kingsbury–4 mi. east at mile marker 621	EL-5
I-10 WB	Sealy–1 mi. west of Brazos River	EL-8
I-10 EB	Van Horn–1 mi. west	WM-4
I-10 WB	Van Horn–3 mi. east	WM-4
I-10 WB	Vinton–1 mi. south of New Mexico state line	WK-1
I-10 EB, WB	Winnie–at mile marker 833	EK-12
I-20 EB, WB	Odessa–9 mi. west	WK-9
I-20 EB, WB	Terrell–east at mile marker 512	EE-8
I-20 EB, WB	Tyler–west at mile marker 546	EF-10
I-20 EB, WB	Weatherford–10 mi. east	EE-5
I-30 EB, WB	Mt. Pleasant–west at mile marker 158	ED-10
I-35 NB, SB	Devine–south of TX 173 at mile marker 119	EM-3
I-35 SB	San Marcos–1.3 mi. north	EL-5
I-35 NB	San Marcos–2.5 mi. north	EL-5
I-35 NB, SB	Temple–southwest at mile marker 292	EI-6
TX 35 NB	Gregory	EP-6
TX 36 EB	Cross Plains	EG-2
I-37 NB, SB	Three Rivers–north	EO-4
I-40 EB, WB	Shamrock–east at mile marker 164	WD-13
I-45 SB	Centerville–0.7 mi. north	EH-9
I-45 NB, SB	Dallas–mile marker 272	◆ I-12, EE-7
US 59 SB	Diboll	EH-11
US 59 SB	Edna–4 mi. south	EM-7
US 59	Fannin	EN-6
US 59 NB	Hungerford	EL-9
US 59 NB	Inez	EN-7
US 59	Queen City–north	ED-12
US 60 EB, WB	Hereford–3 mi. east	WE-9
US 60	Pampa–8 mi. east at TX 152	WC-12
I-69C/US 281 NB, SB	Falfurrias–south	EQ-5
US 75 SB	Denison–3.6 mi. north	EC-7
US 77 NB	Refugio–2 mi. south	EO-6
US 77 NB, SB	Riviera–0.5 mi. south	EQ-5
US 84	Snyder–at mile marker 410	WJ-12
US 87 SB	Big Spring–2 mi. north	WJ-11
US 87 SB	San Angelo–14 mi. northwest	WL-12
US 87/287 NB, SB	Dumas	WC-10
TX 176	†Frankel City–2 mi. south at jct. FM 181	WJ-8
US 181	Karnes City–south of jct. TX 123	EN-5
US 181	Skidmore–north	EO-5
Loop 250	Midland–0.25 mi. north of I-20	★ WH-5,WK-10
US 287 NB, SB	Childress–1 mi. north	WF-13
US 287 SB	Henrietta	EC-4
US 287 NB, SB	Iowa Park–5 mi. west	EC-3
US 287 Bus.	Kennedale–at mile marker 479	◆ I-5, EE-6
TX 349 NB, SB	Midland–17 mi. south at jct. FM 1787	WK-10
Loop 375 WB	El Paso–4 mi. north of I-10	WK-2
US 385 NB	Odessa–1 mi. north of TX 338 Loop	★ WG-2, WK-9

Texas uses additional portable scales throughout the state

RESTRICTED ROUTES

For other truck restrictions in Texas, refer to: www.txdot.gov/government/processes-procedures/load-zoning.html

Routes that restrict use by motor carriers

Route	Location
TX 23	US 83 to Oklahoma state line
US 67	Winfield to I-30
US 84 Bus.	northwest jct. US 84 to southeast jct. 84
TX 188	FM 136 to TX 35L
TX 198	Mabank to Malakoff
TX 214	Friona to Adrian
TX 222	FM 1720 to US 380
TX 276	TX 34 to East Tawakoni
TX 521	Brazoria–southbound ramp to TX 332

† place or route does not appear on the map
‡ route not labeled on map
EB eastbound route NB northbound route
SB southbound route WB westbound route

UTAH

See state and city maps **pages 102-103**
★ located on city map

LOW CLEARANCE LOCATIONS

Statutory height: 14'0"
Structures with 14'0" or less clearance

Route	Location	Height	Map Key
UT 9	within Zion National Park	11'4"	M-6
UT 140	Bluffdale–1.3 mi. west of I-15	12'6"	★ K-19

PERMANENT WEIGH STATIONS

■ also serves as Port of Entry (Note: Commercial Vehicle inspections can be completed at all Utah ports)
▲ also serves as vehicle inspection site

Route	Location	Map Key
■ US 6 EB, WB	Price–9 mi. north near Helper	G-10
▲ ■ I-15 NB, SB	superport near St. George–2 mi. north of Ariz. state line (joint operation)	N-4
■ I-15/84 NB, SB	Brigham City–3 mi. south at milepost 358	C-8
■ US 40 EB, WB	Heber City–4 mi. southeast	E-9
■ I-80 EB, WB	Wendover–3 mi. east of Nevada state line	D-4
▲ ■ I-80/US 189 WB	Echo–15 mi. west of Wyoming state line at milepost 181	C-9
■ US 89 NB, SB	Kanab–2 mi. north	N-7
■ US 491 EB, WB	Monticello–1 mi. east of US 191	L-13

Utah also uses portable scales and has mobile Port of Entry statewide

RESTRICTED ROUTES

Routes that restrict use by motor carriers

Route	Location
UT 9	UT 17 to US 89
UT 12	US 89 to UT 24
UT 14	UT 130 to US 89
UT 29	UT 10 to US 89
UT 31	US 89 to UT 10
UT 35	UT 32 to UT 87
UT 39	UT 16 to UT 166
UT 57	UT 10 to UT 29
UT 62	US 89 to UT 24
UT 63	UT 12 to Bryce Canyon National Park
UT 65	I-84 to I-80
UT 67 (Legacy Pkwy.)	I-215 to I-15
UT 87	US 40 to UT 35
UT 92	UT 74 to US 189
UT 95	UT 24 to US 191
UT 121	Lapoint to US 40 (Vernal)
UT 128	US 191 to I-70
UT 148	UT 143 to UT 14
UT 150	UT 32 to Wyoming state line
UT 153	UT 160 to US 89
UT 190	Brighton to UT 224
UT 224	UT 190 to Park City
UT 261	US 163 to UT 95
UT 262	US 191 to Aneth

VERMONT

See state and city maps **page 104**

LOW CLEARANCE LOCATIONS

Statutory height: 13'6"
Structure with 13'6" or less clearance

Route	Location	Height	Map Key
VT 7A	Bennington–0.2 mi. north of VT 67A	12'0"	L-2
VT 12A	Roxbury–4.1 mi. south of VT 12	13'6"	F-4
VT 12A	Roxbury–10 mi. south of VT 12	13'0"	F-4
VT 14	Royalton–0.7 mi. south of VT 107	12'1"	G-5
VT 102	Bloomfield–0.1 mi. south of VT 105	12'6"	C-8
‡VT 105A	Stevens Mills–0.2 mi. north of VT 105	12'5"	A-5
VT 114	Morgan–1 mi. north of VT 111	13'5"	B-7
VT 122 Alt.	Lyndon–over Miller Run	11'9"	D-7
‡VT 123	Westminster–0.1 mi. east of US 5	12'5"	L-5

PERMANENT WEIGH/INSPECTION STATIONS

All locations are also vehicle inspection sites

Route	Location	Map Key
US 4 EB, WB	Fair Haven–at jct. VT 4A	I-2
I-89 NB	Colchester–2 mi. north of VT 127	D-2
I-91 NB	Guilford–0.25 mi. north of Massachusetts state line	M-5
I-91 SB	Putney–0.62 mi. south of US 5	L-5
VT 279 EB	Bennington–0.3 mi. east of New York state line	M-2

Vermont also uses portable scales

RESTRICTED ROUTES

Routes that restrict use by motor carriers

Route	Location
VT 2B	US 2 to Library Rd.
VT 12	Hartland to Hartland Four Corners
VT 12A	Roxbury to East Granville
VT 15A	VT 12 to VT 15
VT 17	†South Starksboro to VT 100
VT 65	VT 12 to Brookfield
VT 105A	Canadian border to E. Richford Slide Rd.
VT 108	VT 100 to VT 15
VT 114	VT 105 to Norton
VT 122 Alt.	College Rd. to Gilman Rd.

VIRGINIA

See state and city maps **pages 105-107**
✧ located on city map **page 105**
◆ located on Washington, D.C. map **page 111**

LOW CLEARANCE LOCATIONS

Statutory height: 13'6"
Structures with 13'6" or less clearance

Route	Location	Height	Map Key
US 1	Lorton–0.2 mi. east of I-95	13'4"	E-14
VA 5	Richmond–0.8 mi. south of US 60	13'2"	✧ C-8
VA 7	Alexandria–0.6 mi. west of US 1	12'11"	◆ H-6
US 11	Staunton, SB between Commerce Rd. and Richmond Av.	10'0"	G-9
‡US 11 Bus.	Lexington–north of jct. US 60	10'6"	I-8
US 13	Chesapeake Bay Bridge Tunnel–7 mi. north of US 60	13'5"	✧ K-8
US 13	Townsend–1 mi. south	13'5"	K-19
US 23 Bus.	Appalachia, south of VA 68	13'5"	C-3
VA 24 WB	Vinton–east at Blue Ridge Pkwy. overpass	13'3"	K-6
US 29 Bus.	Charlottesville–0.1 mi. north of Bus. US 250	13'6"	✧ B-2
VA 31	Scotland–at James River ferry, both banks	12'6"	✧ G-1, ✧ H-1
VA 39	Goshen–0.1 mi. south of VA 42	11'10"	H-7
I-64 WB	Norfolk–Hampton Roads Bridge Tunnel	13'6"	✧ K-6
‡VA 240	Crozet	11'9"	H-10
US 250	Yancey Mills–7.3 mi. east of jct. I-64	13'5"	H-10
US 250 Bus.	Charlottesville–0.6 mi. east of Bus. US 29	10'11"	✧ B-3
VA 254	Staunton–east of Byp. US 11	13'4"	G-9
VA 311 NB	Crows–3.5 mi. north	13'2"	I-5
VA 311 SB	Crows–3.5 mi. north	11'0"	I-5

PERMANENT WEIGH/INSPECTION STATIONS

All scale locations are also vehicle inspection sites

Route	Location	Map Key
US 11 NB, SB	Hollins–2.25 mi. south of †US 220 Alt., just southwest of Cloverdale	K-6
US 11 NB, SB	Middletown–2.8 mi. south of VA 277 and Stephens City	D-11
US 13 NB, SB	New Church–1.25 mi. south of Maryland state line	H-20
US 13/58/460 EB, WB	Suffolk–1.32 mi. west of Chesapeake city limits	✧ N-4, M-17
US 29 SB	Madison Heights	J-9
US 50 EB, WB	Aldie–0.2 mi. west of US 15	D-13
I-64 EB, WB	Sandston (Richmond)–1 mi. east of I-295	✧ C-10, J-14
I-77 NB, SB	Bland–1 mi. south, 4.2 mi. north of †VA 717	K-2
I-81 NB, SB	Stephens City & VA 277–2.5 mi. south at mile marker 304	D-11
I-81 NB, SB	Troutville–1.4 mi. south of US 220	J-6
I-85 NB, SB	Alberta–4.7 mi. south of VA 46 at mile marker 22	M-12
I-95 NB, SB	Carson–1.39 mi. south of VA 35 at mile marker 39	L-14
I-95 NB, SB	Dumfries–1.1 mi. north of VA 234 at mile marker 154	F-14
US 301 NB, SB	Dahlgren–1 mi. southwest of Maryland state line	F-15

Virginia also uses portable scales

RESTRICTED ROUTES

Routes that restrict use by motor carriers

Route	Location
US 1 SB	VA 40 to Dinwiddie
VA 3	Fredericksburg–over Rappahannock River
VA 5	US 60 to VA 895
VA 6	US 29 to VA 151 (65-ft. restricted route)
VA 6/151	VA 151 W. interchange to VA 151 E. interchange (65-ft. restricted route)
VA 13	Powhatan–over Sallee Creek
US 15	US 29 to Maryland State Line (65-ft. restricted route)
US 15 Bus.	Warrenton–US 15 to US 211
US 15/29 Bus.	southwest jct. US 15 to northeast jct. US 15 in Remington
VA 16	US 11 to US 19 Bus.
VA 16	VA 606 to Sugar Grove
US 17	I-66 to VA 50
US 17 Bus.	US 15 Bus. to US 211
VA 22	US 250 to VA 231 (65-ft. restricted route)
US 23	Weber City–over North Fork Holston River
US 29	US 50 west jct. to US 50 east jct.
US 29 Bus.	Hurt to VA 43
VA 31	Scotland–over James River
VA 39	Goshen–over Mill Creek
VA 40	Endicott to Ferrum
VA 43	Bedford to Blue Ridge Pkwy.
US 50	West Falls Church–VA 237 to Fairfax I-66 ramps
US 52	Bastian–VA 648 to VA 614
US 52 SB	Blue Ridge Parkway to Cana, VA Secondary 691
US 52	Rocky Gap–I-77 to VA 613
US 58	US 221 to VA 8 (65-ft. restricted route)
VA 58	Damascus to Grayson County line
US 58	Hiltons to I-81
US 58	US 11 to US 21
US 58 Bus./VA 35	Courtland to US 58
US 60	Amherst to Bueno Vista (65-ft. restricted route)
US 60	I-295 to VA 33 (65-ft. restricted route)
VA 65	Clinchport to VA 72
I-66	I-495 to District of Columbia border

list continued on following page

† place or route does not appear on the map
‡ route not labeled on map
EB eastbound route NB northbound route
SB southbound route WB westbound route

Route	Location
VA 72	VA 83 to †Longfork
VA 91	Glade Spring to VA 107
VA 91	Tennessee state line to US 19 Bus.
VA 92	Clover to US 360
VA 110	VA 27 to I-395
VA 122	VA 40 to VA 697
VA 125	VA 10 to VA 337
VA 143	VA 5 to VA 132
VA 151	US 250 to VA 6 (65-ft. restricted route)
VA 155	Charles City to US 60
VA 161	Richmond–over James River
VA 189	US 258 to VA 272
US 211 Bus.	Warrenton–US 211 to US 15 Bus.
VA 231	Gordonsville to VA 22 (65-ft. restricted route)
US 250/340	VA 254 to east jct. US 340
US 301	Jarratt to VA 40
US 301 NB	I-95 exit 12 to I-95 exit 17
US 301 SB	VA 614 to VA 609
US 501	Lynchburg to Big Island (65-ft. restricted route)
US 501/VA 130	Glasgow–VA 130 S. interchange to VA 130 N. interchange (65-ft. restricted route)
Blue Ridge Pkwy.	Skyline Drive (Front Royal) to I-64 to North Carolina state line
Colonial Pkwy.	Jamestown to US 17
G. Washington Memorial Pkwy.	I-95/495 to VA 235
Skyline Dr.	I-64 to US 340

WASHINGTON

See state and city maps pages 108-109
◆ located on city maps page 110

LOW CLEARANCE LOCATIONS

Statutory height: 14'0"
Structures with 14'0" or less clearance

Route	Location	Min. Height	Max. Height	Map Key
US 2	Skykomish–tunnel 2.7 mi. northwest, milepost 45.98	13'10"	15'4"	F-9
US 2/395 SB (†Browne St.)	Spokane–0.2 mi. north of I-90, US 2 milepost 287.18	13'11"	14'0"	◆ C-2
US 2/395 NB (Division St.)	Spokane–0.2 mi. north of I-90, US 2 milepost 287.18	13'2"	13'9"	◆ C-2
I-5 NB	Vader–ramp northbound on I-5 to westbound on WA 506	13'7"	14'6"	J-6
US 12	Naches–tunnel, milepost 165.21	13'2"	14'3"	J-10
WA 14 EB	five tunnels between Cook and Underwood, mileposts 58.08, 58.45, 58.92, 59.61, and 60.23	12'3"	13'11"	M-9
WA 14 EB	Lyle–two tunnels approx. 1 mi. east, mileposts 76.77 and 76.86	12'10"	13'3"	M-10
US 97 Alt.	Chelan–Knapps Hill Tunnel	13'1"	13'2"	E-12
WA 99 SB (Alaskan Way Viaduct)	Seattle–3.8 mi. north of jct. WA 509, milepost 29.84	14'0"	14'4"	◆ E-8
WA 99 NB SB	Seattle–pedestrian overpass, 0.4 mi. south of N. 41 St., milepost 35.09	13'2"	16'0"	◆ D-7
WA 99 SB	Seattle–at Columbia St. entrance ramp southbound	13'9"	14'0"	◆ D-7
WA 123	tunnel 2.8 mi. south of jct. WA 410, mp 13.57	13'0"	14'5"	I-9
WA 125 NB	Walla Walla–north of Oregon state line, milepost 5.93	13'10"	13'10"	K-17
US 395 SB (Lewis St.)	Pasco–westbound on Lewis St. to southbound on US 395	13'10"	14'10"	K-15
WA 410	Enumclaw–over White River	14'0"	14'0"	H-8
WA 506 WB	Vader–ramp westbound on WA 506 to northbound I-5	13'7"	14'6"	J-6
WA 513 SB	Seattle–0.6 mi. north of WA 520 at Univ. of Washington, milepost 0.61	12'1"	14'11"	◆ D-8
WA 536	Mt Vernon–jct. with I-5, milepost 5.37	13'10"	16'0"	C-7

PERMANENT WEIGH STATIONS

■ also serves as Port of Entry
▲ also serves as vehicle inspection station

Route	Location	Map Key
US 2 SB	Chattaroy–milepost 303	E-19
US 2 WB	Peshastin–southeast at milepost 105	F-11
US 2 EB, WB	Reardan–milepost 262	F-18
US 2 EB, WB	Sultan–milepost 21	E-8
▲■ I-5 SB	Bow–milepost 235	C-7
I-5 SB	Everett–milepost 188	E-7
I-5 NB	Fort Lewis–southwest of DuPont at milepost 117	H-6
I-5 SB	Lexington (Kelso)–milepost 44	K-6
I-5 NB	Stanwood/Bryant–milepost 214.5	D-7
I-5 NB, SB	Tacoma–north at milepost 140.5	◆ L-8, G-7
▲■ I-5 NB	Vancouver–north at milepost 15	M-6
WA 6 WB	Raymond–milepost 3	I-4
WA 7 NB, SB	Elk Plains–southeast of Spanaway at milepost 44	H-7
WA 9 SB	Lake Stevens–south of Arlington at milepost 17	D-8
US 12 EB, WB	Morton–milepost 100	J-7
US 12 EB	Naches–6 mi. east of WA 410	I-11
US 12 EB, WB	Satsop–east of Montesano at milepost 13	H-4
US 12 WB	Walla Walla–milepost 342	K-17
■ US 12 & US 730 all directions	Wallula–milepost 308	K-15
WA 14 EB, WB	Home Valley–milepost 50	M-8
WA 14 EB, WB	Plymouth–milepost 180	L-14
WA 16 NB	Gig Harbor–milepost 10	G-6
WA 18 & I-90 NB, SB, WB	North Bend–west at milepost 26	F-8
WA 20 WB	Anacortes–at milepost 54	C-6
WA 20 EB, WB	Sedro-Woolley–milepost 69	C-7
WA 24 EB, WB	†Vernita–at Columbia River, milepost 43	I-14
WA 28 EB	Rock Island–milepost 9	G-13
WA 28 WB	Rock Island–milepost 13	G-13
I-82 EB	Grandview–milepost 76	K-13
■ I-82 WB	Plymouth–at milepost 131	L-14
I-90 EB, WB	Cle Elum–milepost 80	H-10
■ I-90 WB	Spokane–east at milepost 299	F-19
I-90 EB, WB	†Tokio–northeast of Ritzville at milepost 231	H-17
US 97 NB, SB	Brewster–milepost 265	D-13
US 97 NB, SB	Goldendale–milepost 13	L-11
US 97 NB, SB	Tonasket–milepost 315	B-14
US 97 NB, SB	Toppenish–5 mi. south of jct. WA 22, WA 220 & US 97 at milepost 57	J-12
US 101 NB, SB	†Artic–south of Aberdeen at milepost 77	H-3
US 101 NB, SB	Forks–milepost 191	E-2
US 101 SB	Hoquiam–milepost 91	H-3
US 101 EB	Port Angeles–west at milepost 237	D-4
US 101 WB	Port Angeles–east at milepost 255	D-4
US 101 EB	Raymond–milepost 57	I-4
WA 167 WB	Puyallup–milepost 5	◆ M-8, H-7
US 395 SB	Deer Park–milepost 182	E-19
US 395 EB, WB	Kettle Falls–milepost 239	B-17
US 395 NB, SB	Pasco–milepost 33	K-15
WA 410 EB	Buckley–west at milepost 18	H-8
WA 503 WB	Woodland–northeast at milepost 49	L-6

list continued in next column

Washington also uses portable scales

RESTRICTED ROUTES

Routes that restrict use by motor carriers

Route	Location
WA 20	Newhalem to Mazama (closed in winter)
WA 99	Seattle at Columbia St.
WA 99 SB	downtown Seattle–milepost 29.84
WA 123	US 12 to WA 410 (no commercial trucks allowed within Mt. Rainier National Park)
WA 125	US 12 to WA 124
WA 129	Anatone to Oregon state line
WA 165	Carbonado to Mt. Rainier National Park (no commercial trucks allowed within Mt. Rainier National Park)
WA 241	WA 22 to I-82
WA 303	Bremerton to Silverdale
WA 410	north entrance of Mt. Rainier National Park to US 12 (no commercial trucks allowed within Mt. Rainier National Park)
WA 503	Amboy to Yale
WA 505	I-5 to WA 504
WA 507	I-5 to Bucoda
WA 548	Blaine to †Alderson Rd.
WA 706	WA 7 to WA 123

WEST VIRGINIA

See state and city maps page 112
★ located on city map

LOW CLEARANCE LOCATIONS

Statutory height: 13'6" on designated highways; 12'6" on other routes
Structures with 13'6" or less clearance

Route	Location	Height	Map Key
WV 2 SB	Wheeling–at I-70	13'6"	★ D-2
WV 2 Spur	Follansbee–at Market St. bridge	10'0"	C-6
WV 6	Montgomery–over Kanawha River	13'6"	J-4
WV 10	Huntington–Hal Greer Blvd. underpass	12'6"	★ A-5
US 11/WV 9 NB	Martinsburg	13'0"	B-10
WV 14	Slate–northwest	13'5"	G-4
WV 16	Welch	12'11"	M-3
WV 17	Logan–0.02 mi. north of WV 10	9'0"	K-2
WV 28 Alt.	Ridgeley	11'11"	A-8
WV 41	Layland–over New River	9'0"	K-5
WV 63	Caldwell-0.23 mi. south of US 60	9'9"	L-7
‡WV 100 NB	†Maidsville–north of Star City	12'9"	E-8
WV 112	Hardy	11'6"	M-5
WV 112	Oakvale	10'5"	M-5
WV 112	west of Oakvale, 0.44 miles east of I-77	11'9"	M-5
WV 161	Bishop–northeast of WV 16	13'1"	M-3
US 250	Philippi–south of US 119 at Tygart Valley River bridge	10'3"	G-8
‡WV 251	Wheeling–over the Ohio River	8'0"	★ D-1
WV 527	Huntington–north of I-64	12'0"	★ B-4

PERMANENT WEIGH STATIONS

Route	Location	Map Key
I-64 EB, WB	Hurricane–east at milepost 38	I-2
I-68 WB	Morgantown–east of exit 10	E-8
I-70 EB	Wheeling–milepost 3	★ E-2, D-6
I 77 NB	Camp Creek–north of exit 14	M-5
I-77 NB, SB	Mineralwells	G-4
I-79 NB, SB	Fairmont	F-7

West Virginia also uses portable scales

† place or route does not appear on the map
‡ route not labeled on map
EB eastbound route NB northbound route
SB southbound route WB westbound route

RESTRICTED ROUTES

Routes that restrict use by motor carriers

Route	Location
WV 2 Spur	Follansbee–over Market St. Bridge
WV 4	Gassaway to I-79
WV 5	Creston to Grantsville
WV 7	Core to US 19
WV 9	WV 29 to Great Cacapon
WV 16	Five Forks to Smithville
WV 18	West Union to Blandville
WV 20	Folsom to US 19
WV 23	Ashley to Sedalia
WV 26	WV 7 to Valley Point
WV 28	†Grace to Springfield
US 33/119	Stumptown to Normantown
WV 39/55	Richwood to WV 150
US 40	near Bethlehem-over Wheeling Creek
WV 41	Clifftop to US 60
WV 41	WV 61 to Layland
WV 47	Cisco to Macfarlan
US 50	I-79 to Bridgeport
US 50	WV 93 to US 220
US 50	Gormania to Mount Storm
US 50	2 mi. east of Macomber over Cheat River
WV 66	Cass to Green Bank
WV 72	Tucker County line to Macomber
WV 74	Mountain to WV 18
WV 87	WV 2 to Evans
WV 92	Aggregates to Elkins
WV 95	US 50 to WV 14
WV 114	I-64 to Meadowbrook
WV 214	Ruthdale to Davis Creek
US 219	WV 15 to Huttonsville
US 220	Franklin to Upper Tract
US 220	Landes to Petersburg
US 220	Moorefield to Purgitsville
US 250	Moundsville to WV 88
WV 251	in Wheeling, over the Ohio River
WV 331	Mt. Alto to Cottageville
WV 612	Scarbro to I-77

WISCONSIN

See state and city maps **pages 114-115**
◆ located on city maps **page 113**

LOW CLEARANCE LOCATIONS

Statutory height: 13'6"
Structures with 13'6" or less clearance

Route	Location	Height	Map Key
WI 32 NB (S. 1st St.)	Milwaukee–0.3 mi. north of jct. WI 15/59 (National Av.)	13'3"	◆ M-3
WI 32 SB (S. 1st St.)	Milwaukee–0.3 mi. north of jct. WI 15/59 (National Av.)	13'2"	◆ M-3
WI 32 (Kinnickinnic Av.)	Milwaukee–1 mi. south of jct. WI 15/59 (National Av.)	12'9"	◆ F-6
WI 32 (Kinnickinnic Av.)	Milwaukee–1.2 mi. south of jct. WI 15/59 (National Av.)	12'9"	◆ F-6
WI 32 NB, SB	South Milwaukee–2.6 mi. north of jct. WI 100	12'0"	◆ H-7
WI 64 EB, WB	Houlton–St. Croix River bridge, 0.7 mi. west of WI 35 at Minnesota state line	13'2"	H-1

PERMANENT WEIGH STATIONS

Route	Location	Map Key
US 2/53 NB, SB	Superior–6 mi. southeast of city limits, 1.5 mi. northwest of jct. US 2 and US 53	B-3
WI 11	Dickeyville–south, 3 mi. east of Iowa state line	P-7
I-39/US 51 NB, SB	Coloma–1.5 mi. north	K-9
I-39/90 EB	Madison–southeast, 3.8 mi. east of jct. US 12/18, mile point 145.5	O-10
I-39/90 NB	Beloit–at mile point 180	◆ L-6, P-10
I-41/94/US 41 NB	Kenosha–0.25 mi. north, mile point 349.8	◆ N-8, P-13
I-41/94/US 41 SB	Racine County–0.25 mi. south of ‡County Rd. G, mile point 327.3	O-13
I-41/US 41 NB	Wrightstown–at Brown-Outagamie County line	J-12
US 41/141 NB, SB	Abrams–3 mi. south of jct. US 41 and US 141	I-13, C-11
I-43 SB	Newton–0.5 mi. south, mile point 141	K-13
I-90 EB	West Salem–2 mi. west, mile point 10.6	L-5
I-94 EB	Hudson–3.5 mi. east of jct. US 12, mile point 8	H-2
I-94 WB	Menomonie–1.5 mi. east, mile point 48.3	H-4

Wisconsin also uses portable scales

RESTRICTED ROUTES

Routes that restrict use by motor carriers

Route	Location
WI 67	Oconomowoc–over Bark River
WI 88	WI 37 to Gilmanton
WI 113	WI 188 to WI 78, over Lake Wisconsin
WI 121	Northfield to Alma Center
WI 131	La Farge to Ontario

WYOMING

See state and city maps **page 116**
★ located on city map

LOW CLEARANCE LOCATIONS

XR: Off-system road that goes under the Interstate System.
Off-system underpass roads are listed with the Interstate route name and milepost at the off-system road location.
Statutory height: 14'0"
Structures with 14'0" or less clearance

Route	Location	Height	Map Key
US 20	Shoshoni–north at Wind River Canyon Tunnels	14'0"	I-5
XR I-25	at milepost 98.57	13'5"	K-9
XR I-25	at milepost 131.59	13'8"	J-8
XR I-25	at milepost 244.96	13'7"	I-7
XR I-25	†Barber interchange–at milepost 154.24	13'7"	J-8
XR I-25	†Powder River interchange–at milepost 246	14'0"	I-7
XR I-80	at milepost 196.16	14'0"	L-5
XR I-80	†Bar Hat interchange–at milepost 23.12	13'10"	M-1
XR I-80	†Bar X interchange–at milepost 152.46	14'0"	L-4
XR I-80	†Coal interchange–at milepost 21.75	13'10"	M-1
XR I-80	†Daley interchange–at milepost 201.16	13'6"	L-5
XR I-80	†Egbert interchange–at milepost 391.39	13'11"	M-10
XR I-80	†French interchange–at milepost 28.71	13'7"	M-1
XR I-80	†GL Rd. interchange–at milepost 156.03	13'9"	L-4
XR I-80	†Hadsell interchange–at milepost 206.18	13'8"	L-6
XR I-80	†Peterson interchange–at milepost 238.16	13'10"	L-6
XR I-80	†Union interchange–at milepost 33.18	13'7"	M-1
XR I-90	†Coal Divide Rd. interchange–at milepost 178.92	14'0"	G-9
XR I-90	†Inyan Kara interchange–at milepost 172.09	13'7"	G-9
WY 96	Douglas–at I-25	12'11"	J-8
WY 255 (N. Center St.)	Casper–south of I-25	13'0"	★ A-9, J-7

PERMANENT WEIGH/INSPECTION STATIONS

■ also serves as Port of Entry
All scale locations are also vehicle inspection sites

Route	Location	Map Key
■ US 14/16/20 & WY 120 EB, WB	Cody	G-3
■ US 14/16/WY 59 all directions	Gillette–1 mi. west of jct. I-90	G-8
■ US 20 & US 85 all directions	Lusk	J-10
■ I-25 NB	Cheyenne–5 mi. north of Colorado state line	★ E-8, M-9
■ US 26 all directions	Alpine–1 mi. east of Idaho state line	I-1
■ US 26 EB, WB	Torrington–2 mi. west of east jct. with US 85	K-10
■ US 30 all directions	Kemmerer–2 mi. west	L-1
■ I-80 WB	Cheyenne–10 mi. east	M-9
■ I-80 EB	Evanston–southwest, 0.5 mi. east of Utah state line	M-1
■ I-80/US 30/287 WB	Rawlins–mile marker 209.5	L-6
■ I-80 & US 287 all directions	Laramie	★ E-6 M-8
■ US 85 NB, SB	Cheyenne–at jct. †Terry Rd.	M-9
■ I-90 & WY 338 EB, WB	Sheridan–mile marker 16	F-6
■ I-90/US 14 WB	Sundance–18 mi. west of South Dakota state line	G-10
■ US 191 all directions	Rock Springs–approx. 2 mi. north of jct. I-80	L-3
■ WY 254 all directions	Casper–1 mi. west of jct. Byp. US 20/26 & I-25/US 87	★ A-9 J-7
■ US 287 & WY 789 NB, SB	Lander	J-4
■ US 310 NB, SB	Frannie–3 mi. south of Montana state line	F-4

Wyoming also uses portable scales

RESTRICTED ROUTES

Routes that restrict use by motor carriers

Route	Location
US routes, all except US 191	in Yellowstone National Park
US 14 Alt.	US 310 to US 14
WY 22	Idaho state line to US 26/89/191
US 89/287	Moran to Yellowstone National Park boundary
WY 96	west of Douglas–I-25 to WY 91
WY 130	WY 230 (west of Ryan Park) to WY 230 (west of Laramie)
US 212	Yellowstone National Park boundary to Montana state line
WY 238	Auburn to Afton
WY 410	west of Robertson, over Blacks Fork
WY 412	US 189 to I-80
WY 430	Colorado state line to I-80 Bus.

CANADA

ALBERTA

See province and city maps pages 118-119
◆ located on Canada map page 117

LOW CLEARANCE LOCATIONS

Statutory height: 4.15 m
Structures with 4.15 m or less clearance

Route	Location	Height	Map Key
Hwy. 813 NB	Athasbasca–at jct. Hwy. 55	4.0 m	C-17

PERMANENT WEIGH/INSPECTION STATIONS

■ also serves as Port of Entry
Weigh Scale Sites which are also vehicle inspection sites

Route	Location	Map Key
■ Hwy. 1 EB	†Jumping Pound–14 km west of Hwy. 22	I-15
Hwy. 1 EB	Strathmore–20 km west	I-16
■ Hwy. 1 EB, WB	Dunmore–41 km west of Saskatchewan border	J-19
Hwy. 2 NB	†Balzac–8 km south of Airdrie	H-16
Hwy. 2 SB	Leduc–3 km south	E-16
Hwy. 2 EB, WB	Slave Lake–3 km east	B-15
■ Hwy. 2/43 EB, WB	Demmitt–1 km east of British Columbia border	C-10
■ Hwy. 3 EB, WB	†Burmis–42 km east of British Columbia border	K-16
■ Hwy. 4 NB, SB	Coutts–1 km north of U.S. border and I-15	L-18
Hwy. 9 NB, SB	Morrin–20 km north of Drumheller	H-17
Hwy. 16 EB	†Ardrossan–30 km east of Edmonton	E-17
■ Hwy. 16 WB	Vermilion–jct. Hwy. 41, 73 km west of Saskatchewan border	E-19
■ Hwy. 16 EB	†Yellowhead–20 km southwest of Hinton	F-12
Hwy. 35 EB, WB	Grimshaw–8 km north	A-12
Hwy. 43 EB, WB	Whitecourt–5 km northwest	D-14
Hwy. 49 EB	Bay Tree–at British Columbia border	B-10
Hwy. 63 NB, SB	Radway–just north of jct. Hwy. 28	D-17

Permanent Weigh Scale Sites
Semi-portable, permanent, or portable scales may be used at these sites

Route	Location	Map Key
Hwy. 1 WB	Cheadle–10 km west of Strathmore	I-17
Hwy. 1 WB	Cochrane–just west of Hwy. 22	I-16
Hwy. 2 NB	Claresholm–north end of town	J-17
Hwy. 2 SB	DeWinton–2 km north	I-16
Hwy. 2 EB, WB	Grande Prairie–10 km north	C-12
Hwy. 2 NB, SB	Rycroft–north, 77 km north of Grande Prairie	B-12
Hwy. 2A NB, SB	Red Deer	G-16
Hwy. 9 EB, WB	Hanna–3 km east	H-18
Hwy. 11 EB, WB	Rocky Mountain House–10 km east	G-15
Hwy. 13 EB, WB	Macklin, SK–4 km east of Alberta/Saskatchewan border	F-20
Hwy. 12 EB, WB	Castor–2 km east	G-18
Hwy. 14 EB, WB	Wainwright–4 km east	F-19
Hwy. 16 WB	†Acheson–15 km west of Edmonton	E-16
Hwy. 16 WB	Edson–3 km west of Hwy. 32	E-14
Hwy. 18 EB, WB	Clyde–10 km east of Westlock	D-16
Hwy. 22 NB, SB	Drayton Valley–in town	E-15
Hwy. 27 EB,WB	Trochu–east of Torrington	H-17
Hwy. 28 EB, WB	†Hoselaw–17 km southwest of Bonnyville	D-19
Hwy. 35 NB, SB	High Level–4 km south	◆ E-4
Hwy. 45 EB, WB	Two Hills–4 km east	E-18
Hwy. 88 NB, SB	Red Earth–5 km south	A-14

Alberta also uses portable scales

RESTRICTED ROUTES

For other truck restrictions in Alberta, refer to:
511.alberta.ca and www.transportation.alberta.ca/content/doctype260/Production/roadbans.pdf

Other routes that restrict use by motor carriers

Route	Location
Hwy. 6	Pincher to U.S. border (through Waterton Lakes Nat'l Pk.)
†Hwy. 10X	†Wayne to Rosedale
Hwy. 40	Hwy. 1A to †Waiparous
Hwy. 41	Elk Point to Hwy. 45
Hwy. 93	Hwy. 1 to Jasper (through Banff and Jasper Nat'l Pks.)
†Hwy. 511	Hwy. 2 to †Hwy. 509
Hwy. 734	southwest of Sundre, over the Red Deer River
†Hwy. 743	north of Peace River, over the Whitemud River
†Hwy. 766	south of Hwy. 54, over the Raven River
Hwy. 791	Hwy. 72 to Hwy. 575
‡Hwy. 814	†Beaumont to Hwy. 816
‡Hwy. 824	east of Edmonton, over Hwy. 16
Hwy. 848	Dorothy–over the Red Deer River
Hwy. 875	Hays to Rolling Hills
Hwy. 886	Buffalo–over the Red Deer River

BRITISH COLUMBIA

See province and city maps pages 118-119
★ located on city map
◆ located on Canada map page 117

LOW CLEARANCE LOCATIONS

Statutory height: 4.15 m
Structures with 4.15 m or less clearance

Route	Location	Height	Map Key
None on the primary highway system			

PERMANENT WEIGH STATIONS

■ also serves as Port of Entry

Route	Location	Map Key
VANCOUVER ISLAND		
Hwy. 1 SB	Duncan–4.8 km north at Hwy. 18	L-7
Hwy. 1 NB	Duncan–8 km north	L-7
Hwy. 19	Parksville–6.4 km south	L-6
MAINLAND		
■ Hwy. 1	Golden–west side	★ M-12, I-13
Hwy. 1 WB	Hope–11.2 km west	K-9
■ Hwy. 1 EB	Hope–12 km west	L-9
Hwy. 1 EB, WB	Kamloops–1 km east of jct. Hwy. 5 (Coquihalla Hwy.)	J-10
■ Hwy. 3	Sparwood–east	K-15
■ Hwy. 3 & Hwy. 95	Yahk–west side of town at the jct.	L-14
■ Hwy. 3A & Hwy. 97	Kaleden–at the jct., 16 km south of Penticton	K-11
Hwy. 7	Hope–1.6 km west of jct. Hwy. 1	K-9
■ †Hwy. 15 (Pacific Hwy.)	White Rock–0.48 km north of U.S. border	L-7
■ Hwy. 16	Tête Jaune Cache–at jct. Hwy. 5	F-11
Hwy. 16 & Hwy. 27	Vanderhoof–at the jct.	D-7
Hwy. 16 & Hwy. 37	Terrace–at the jct.	C-3
Hwy. 91 SB	Delta–south end of Alex Fraser Bridge	★ N-2
Hwy. 97	Dawson Creek–1.6 km north of jct. Hwy. 2	B-10
■ Hwy. 97 (Alaska Hwy.)	Fort Nelson–south side	◆ E-3
Hwy. 97	Fort St. John–0.8 km south of jct. Hwy. 29 (Alaska Hwy.)	A-10
Hwy. 97	Quesnel–north side	F-8
Hwy. 97	Redrock/Prince George–3.2 km south of jct. Hwy. 16	E-8
Hwy. 97	Vernon–2.4 km south of jct. Hwy. 97A	J-11
Hwy. 99 SB	Richmond–at north end of George Massey Tunnel	★ N-2, L-7

British Columbia also uses portable scales

RESTRICTED ROUTES

In addition to seasonal restrictions, refer to CVSE T1011 Form–"Highways with Restrictive Load Limits", at:
www.th.gov.bc.ca/cvse/whatsnew.html#tabs-2

For Traveller Information System in British Columbia, visit the DriveBC website at: www.drivebc.ca/

Other routes that restrict use by motor carriers

Route	Location
None reported	

MANITOBA

See province and city maps page 121
★ located on city map

LOW CLEARANCE LOCATIONS

Statutory height: 4.15 m
Structures with 4.15 m or less clearance

Route	Location	Height	Map Key
‡Hwy. 1A	Brandon–west at Kemnay overpass	3.7 m	L-14
Hwy. 200	Emerson	3.9 m	M-17
†Hwy. 301	Falcon Lake–at Hwy. 1 overpass	3.9 m	L-19

PERMANENT WEIGH/INSPECTION STATIONS

All scale locations are also vehicle inspection sites

Route	Location	Map Key
Hwy. 1 EB, WB	Headingley–5 km west of jct. Hwy. 1/Hwy. 100/Hwy. 101; west of Winnipeg, (204) 889-3836	L-17
Hwy. 1 EB, WB	West Hawk Lake at Ontario border, (204) 349-2206	L-19
Hwy. 2	Carroll–6.4 km east at jct. Hwy. 10	L-13
Hwy. 7 NB, SB	†Rosser–4 km north of jct. Hwy. 101, (204) 633-2167	★ A-18, K-17
Hwy. 10 NB, SB	The Pas–19 km north at jct. Hwy. 287, (204) 627-8294	E-12
Hwy. 52	Tourond–east of jct. with Hwy. 59	L-17
Hwy. 75 NB, SB	Emerson–1 km north of U.S. border, (204) 373-2779	M-17

Manitoba also uses portable scales

† place or route does not appear on the map
‡ route not labeled on map
EB eastbound route NB northbound route
SB southbound route WB westbound route

RESTRICTED ROUTES

Routes that restrict use by motor carriers

Route	Location
Hwy. 3A	Clearwater to Hwy. 3
Hwy. 10	Hwy. 45 to Hwy. 5A
Hwy.12	Anola to Hwy. 213
Hwy. 20	Dauphin to Ochre River
Hwy. 44	Hwy. 9 to Hwy. 59
†Hwy. 204	Selkirk, over Red River
Hwy. 247/334	Sanford, over La Salle River
Hwy. 250	Daly–over Assiniboine River
Hwy. 257	Hwy. 83 to Trans-Canada 1
Hwy. 328	south of Skownan, over Waterhen River
Hwy. 344	Wawanesa, over Souris River
†Hwy. 346	north of Margaret, over Souris River
Hwy. 452	Napinka, over Souris River
Hwy. 530	Treesbank, over Souris River
†Hwy. 542	south of Kirkella, over Boshill Creek
Hwy. 583	Roblin, over Shell River

NEW BRUNSWICK

See province and city maps pages 126-127
★ located on city map

LOW CLEARANCE LOCATIONS

Statutory height: 4.15 m
Structures with 4.15 m or less clearance

Route	Location	Centre Height	Side Height	Map Key
Hwy. 3	Lawrence Station	4.0 m	4.0 m	I-3
Hwy. 8	†Newcastle–south, just north of jct. Hwy. 420	4.1 m	4.1 m	F-6
‡Hwy. 100	Rothesay	4.1 m	4.1 m	I-5
Hwy. 102	Fredericton–at Waterloo Row overpass	3.5 m	3.5 m	★ M-13
Hwy. 106	Moncton	3.3 m	3.3 m	H-7
Hwy. 109	Plaster Rock	4.1 m	4.1 m	F-3
Hwy. 118	north of Chelmsford	4.1 m	4.1 m	F-6
Hwy. 121	Hampton	4.1 m	4.1 m	I-6
Hwy. 134	Bouctouche–at Little Bouctouche River	4.9 m	4.1 m	G-8
Hwy. 134	St. Louis-de-Kent–north at Kouchibouguacis River	5.0 m	3.7 m	F-7
Hwy. 134	Shediac–north at Shediac River	4.0 m	4.0 m	G-8

PERMANENT WEIGH STATIONS

All scale locations are also vehicle inspection sites

Route	Location	Map Key
Hwy. 1 EB, WB	St. Stephen–3 km east at Oak Bay	J-3
Hwy. 2 WB	†Deerwood	H-4
Hwy. 2 EB	Edmundston–2.5 km west at St. Jacques	D-2
Hwy. 2 WB	Edmundston–25 km east at Siegas	E-2
Hwy. 2 EB, WB	Fredericton–32 km west at Longs Creek	H-4
Hwy. 2 EB, WB	Moncton–25 km west at Salisbury	H-7
Hwy. 11 EB, WB	Bouctouche–8 km west	G-8
Hwy. 17 EB, WB	Campbellton–12.8 km west at Tide Head	C-4

Port-of-Entry locations may have scales

Route	Location	Map Key
Hwy. 1/3	St. Stephen	J-3
Hwy. 2	Edmundston	D-2
Hwy. 4	St. Croix	I-3
Hwy. 17	†St. Leonard	E-2
Hwy. 95	Woodstock–13 km west at Maine/New Brunswick border	G-2
Hwy. 110	Centerville	G-3
Hwy. 122	Fosterville	H-2
Hwy. 205	Clair	E-1
Hwy. 540	Lakeville–west	G-3
‡Local Rd.	Forest City–south of Fosterville	H-2

New Brunswick also uses portable scales

RESTRICTED ROUTES

Routes that restrict use by motor carriers

Route	Location
Hwy. 111	Hanford Brook to Hammondvale
Hwy. 134	Charlo to Benjamin River
†Hwy. 315	Bathurst–over Tetagouche River

NEWFOUNDLAND and LABRADOR

See province and city maps page 127
★ located on city map

LOW CLEARANCE LOCATIONS

Statutory height: 5.0 m
Structures with 5.0 m or less clearance

Route	Location	Height	Map Key
Hwy. 1 EB	Corner Brook–†Hwy. 450A (Lewin Pkwy.) overpass	5.0 m	D-16
Hwy. 1 EB	Corner Brook–Hwy. 450 (Ring Rd.) overpass	4.9 m	D-16
Hwy. 1 WB	Corner Brook–Hwy. 450 (Ring Rd.) overpass	5.0 m	D-16
Hwy. 1 EB	Glovertown–at Hwy. 310	4.6 m	D-19
Hwy. 1 WB	Glovertown–at Hwy. 310	4.5 m	D-19
Hwy. 1 EB	Grand Falls-Windsor–†Grand Falls Industrial overpass	5.0 m	D-18
Hwy. 1 EB	Grand Falls-Windsor–at †Union St.	5.0 m	D-18
Hwy. 1 WB	†Salmonier–at †Hwy. 90	4.9 m	F-20
Hwy. 2 EB	Mt. Pearl–at †Ruth Av. overpass	5.0 m	F-20
Hwy. 2 WB	Mt. Pearl–at †Ruth Av. overpass	4.8 m	F-20
Hwy. 60 EB, WB	St. John's–Hwy. 1 overpass (Donovan's Overpass) west of city boundary	5.0 m	F-20
Hwy. 220 EB, WB	Marystown	4.8 m	F-18

PERMANENT WEIGH STATIONS

■ also serves as Port of Entry
All scale locations are also vehicle inspection sites

Route	Location	Map Key
NEWFOUNDLAND		
■ Hwy. 1 EB, WB	Channel-Port aux Basques–northwest	E-16
■ Hwy. 1 WB	†Foxtrap–south, west of St. John's	F-20
Hwy. 1 EB, WB	Goobies–east	E-19
Hwy. 1 WB	Grand Falls-Windsor	D-18
Hwy. 1 EB, WB	†Pynns Brook–north of Pasadena	D-17
LABRADOR	None	

Newfoundland and Labrador also uses portable scales

Port-of-Entry Locations

Route	Location	Map Key
Hwy. 100	Argentia	F-19
Hwy. 340	Lewisporte	D-18
†Hwy. 408	Channel-Port aux Basques	E-16
Hwy. 500	Labrador City	B-19

RESTRICTED ROUTES

Routes that restrict use by motor carriers

Route	Location
Hwy. 91	Hwy. 100 to Hwy. 92
Hwy. 210	Hwy. 220 to Hwy. 212
Hwy. 310	Trans-Canada 1 to Eastport

NORTHWEST TERRITORIES

See Canada map page 117

LOW CLEARANCE LOCATIONS

Statutory height: 4.2 m
Structures with 4.2 or less clearance

Route	Location	Height	Map Key
None on the primary highway system			

PERMANENT WEIGH/INSPECTION STATIONS

■ also serves of Port of Entry
All scale locations are also vehicle inspection sites

Route	Location	Map Key
■ Hwy. 1 (Mackenzie Hwy.) & Hwy. 2	Enterprise–at the junction	D-4
Hwy. 1	Fort Simpson at KM 460	D-4
Hwy. 5	Hay River at KM 1	D-4
■ Hwy. 8 (Dempster Hwy.)	Inuvik–between the airport and town	B-3

Northwest Territories also uses portable scales

RESTRICTED ROUTES

Routes that restrict use by motor carriers

Route	Location
None reported	

NOVA SCOTIA

See province and city maps pages 126-127
★ located on city map

LOW CLEARANCE LOCATIONS

Primary highway system statutory height: 4.11 m
Structures with 4.11 m or less clearance

Route	Location	Height	Map Key
Hwy. Trunk 2	Fall River–Hwy. 102 overpass	4.1 m	K-9
Hwy. Trunk 3	Tusket–over Tusket River	4.2 m	M-5
Hwy. 102	Halifax–at jct. with Hwy. 103	4.2 m	★ M-18
Route 215	Shubenacadie	4.1 m	J-10
Route 311	Truro–at Bible Hill Subway	3.9 m	J-10

PERMANENT WEIGH STATIONS

■ also serves as Port of Entry and vehicle inspection site

Route	Location	Map Key
Hwy. 102 SB	Enfield–north of Halifax Int'l Airport	J-10
Hwy. 102 NB	†Kelly Lake–just south of Halifax Int'l Airport	K-10
Hwy. 104 EB, WB	†Aulds Cove–north of Mulgrave at Canso Causeway	I-13
■ Hwy. 104 EB	†Fort Lawrence–1.2 km east of New Brunswick border	H-8
Hwy. 104 WB	†Fort Lawrence–1.2 km east of New Brunswick border	H-8

Nova Scotia also uses portable scales

RESTRICTED ROUTES

Routes that restricts use by motor carriers

Route	Location
Hwy. 4	Thompson Station to Glenholme
MacDonald Bridge	North St., Halifax to Dartmouth

NUNAVUT

See Canada map **page 117**

LOW CLEARANCE LOCATIONS

Route	Location	Height	Map Key
None reported (Intercity travel is by air)			

PERMANENT WEIGH STATIONS

Route	Location	Map Key
Nunavut has no permanent scale facilities		

RESTRICTED ROUTES

Routes that restrict use by motor carriers

Route	Location
None reported	

ONTARIO

See province and city maps **pages 122-123**
★ located on city map
◗ located on Detroit & Vicinity map **page 52**
● located on Buffalo city map **page 70**
◆ located on Canada map **page 117**

LOW CLEARANCE LOCATIONS

Statutory height: 4.15 m
Structures with 4.15 m or less clearance

Route	Location	Height	Map Key
Hwy. 8 EB	Dundas	4.0 m	★ J-18
Hwy. 400 NB	Barrie–at Sunnidale Rd.	4.1 m	H-10
QEW–outside lane only	Fort Erie–at Bowen Rd.	3.8 m	● NE-2

PERMANENT WEIGH/INSPECTION STATIONS

■ also serves as Port of Entry
Vehicle Inspection Stations (include scales)

Route	Location	Map Key
Hwy. 7	Perth–approx. 5 km west at †Glen Tay	F-16
Hwy. 10	Brampton–north at Victoria	I-9
Hwy. 11 NB, SB	Callander–south	C-10, N-20
Hwy. 11	Cochrane–at †Third Av.	L-20
Hwy. 11 SB	Gravenhurst–0.8 km south	F-10
Hwy. 11	Hearst–at †Vandetta Rd.	K-18
Hwy. 11	New Liskeard–8 km north	M-20
Hwy. 11/17	Red Rock–north, 8 km east of jct. 11/17	L-16
Hwy. 11/17	Thunder Bay–6.5 km west	L-15
Hwy. 17	approx. 30 km west of Kenora, at †Rush Bay Rd.	◆ H-7
Hwy. 17	North Bay–at west end of bypass	C-10, N-20
Hwy. 17	Sault St. Marie–approx. 9 km north at †Heyden	B-1, N-18
Hwy. 17	Spragge–approx. 0.75 km east at jct. Hwy. 108	C-4, N-19
■ Hwy. 17	Vermilion Bay–at jct. with †Hwy. 105	K-13
Hwy. 102	Thunder Bay–north, approx. 5 km northwest of town	★ M-11, L-15
Hwy. 400 NB	King City–west, 0.5 km north of ‡King Rd.	I-10
Hwy. 400 NB, SB	Parry Sound	F-9
Hwy. 401 WB	Bowmanville–approx. 2 km east of town	I-11
Hwy. 401 EB	Ganonoque–mile marker 649	H-16
■ Hwy 401 WB	Lancaster–southwest of Québec border	E-19
Hwy. 401 EB, WB	London–west of ‡Putnam Rd. interchange 208	K-7
Hwy. 401 EB, WB	Milton–east of †James Snow Pkwy.	J-9
Hwy. 401 EB	Whitby–west, 2.25 km west of Hwy. 12	I-11
■ Hwy. 401 EB	Windsor–south, 4.6 km east of interchange 21	◗ L-9, M-4
■ Hwy. 402 EB	Sarnia–approx. 5 km east of †Mandaumin Rd.	K-5
Hwy. 407 EB, WB	Oakville–0.6 km west of †Bronte Rd.	J-9
Hwy. 416 SB	Kemptville	F-17
■ Hwy. 417 WB	Casselman–east, 1.6 km west of Hwy. 138	E-18
Hwy. 527	5.5 km north of jct. Hwy. 17	L-15
Queen Elizabeth Way EB, WB	Oakville–east of †Third Line	J-10
Queen Elizabeth Way WB	†Vineland–2 km west of ‡Victoria Av.	K-10

Ontario also uses portable scales

RESTRICTED ROUTES

Routes that restrict use by motor carriers

Route	Location
Hwy. 420	†Niagara Pkwy. to U.S. border
Windsor Tunnel	Windsor to U.S. border

PRINCE EDWARD ISLAND

See province and city maps **pages 126-127**

LOW CLEARANCE LOCATIONS

Statutory height: 4.15 m
Structures with 4.15 m or less clearance

Route	Location	Height	Map Key
None on primary highway system			

PERMANENT WEIGH/INSPECTION STATIONS

■ also serves as Port of Entry
All scale locations are also vehicle inspection sites

Route	Location	Map Key
■ Hwy. 1 EB, WB	Borden-Carleton–east	G-9

Prince Edward Island also uses portable scales

RESTRICTED ROUTES

Routes that restrict use by motor carriers

Route	Location
‡Hwy. 9	Hwy. 1 to Hwy. 2
Hwy. 12	Hwy. 2 to Alberton
Hwy. 12	Portage to Miscouche
†Hwy. 137	Hwy. 2 to Hwy. 12
†Hwy. 202	†Hwy. 201 to Hwy. 4

QUÉBEC

See province and city maps **pages 124-125**
★ located on city map

LOW CLEARANCE LOCATIONS

Clearance information is available from the Ministère des Transports, Division de la Circulation:
Call (418) 644-6320; fax (418) 646-6195.
The publication "Hauteurs libres sous les ponts et viaducs due Québec," is available for $24.95 + 7% tax + $4.00 for shipping and handling (in Canadian dollars) from Les Publications du Québec.
Call (418) 643-5150 or (800) 463-2100.

Statutory height: 4.15 m

Route	Location	Height	Map Key
Hwy. 112 EB	Montréal–just west of Autoroute 10	3.65 m	★ E-13
Hwy. 112	Montréal–east of ‡Wellington St.	4.1 m	★ E-13
Hwy. 116/229 EB	†Mont-St-Hilaire–east of Riviere Richelieu	3.9 m	M-15
Hwy. 116/229 WB	†Mont-St-Hilaire–east of Riviere Richelieu	4.0 m	M-15
Hwy. 117	Montréal–just north of Boul. Henri-Bourassa	3.95 m	★ D-11
Hwy. 138	†Le Marigot–over the Batiscan River	4.1 m	K-10
Hwy. 138	†Champlain–over the Champlain River	4.0 m	K-10
Hwy. 138	Montréal–west of †Rue Notre-Dame	4.1 m	★ B-14
Hwy. 138	†Neuville–west	4.1 m	I-18
Hwy. 143	Sherbrooke–south of Hwy. 216	4.1 m	★ N-2
Hwy. 159	St-Stanislas–over Batiscan River	4.1 m	J-17
Hwy. 175	Quebec City–over St. Lawrence River	4.1 m	★ C-5
Hwy. 223	St-Jean-sur-Richelieu–under Autoroute 35	3.9 m	M-15
Hwy. 223	St-Jean-sur-Richelieu–north of †Rue St-Charles	4.1 m	M-15
Hwy. 223	St-Jean-sur-Richelieu–south of †Rue St-Charles	4.0 m	M-15
Hwy. 226	†La Visitation-de-Yamaska	4.0 m	K-16
Hwy. 335 EB, WB	Montréal–Canadian National R.R.	4.1 m	★ D-12

PERMANENT WEIGH/INSPECTION STATIONS

■ also serves as Port of Entry
Permanent Weigh Station Scale Sites

Route	Location	Map Key
Autoroute 10 WB	†Brossard	M-15
Autoroute 10/55 EB, NB	†Deauville	M-17
†Autoroute 13 SB	†Laval	L-14
Autoroute 15 NB	Lacolle	N-15
Autoroute 20 EB	†Beloeil–east of †Ste-Julie	L-15
Autoroute 20 WB	†Boucherville	L-15
Autoroute 20 EB	†Les Cèdres–west of jct. Autoroute 30, east of Ontario border	M-14
Autoroute 20 EB	L'Islet-sur-Mer	J-13
Autoroute 20 WB	St-Nicholas	J-19
Autoroute 25 SB	Laval	★ B-12, L-14
Autoroute 40 EB, WB	†St-Augustin-de-Desmaures–west of Ste-Foy	I-18
Autoroute 40 EB	†Trois-Rivières Ouest–west of Trois-Rivières	★ C-1, K-16
Autoroute 40 EB	Vaudreuil-Dorion–4 mi. west of Autoroute 30, near interchange 26	M-13
Autoroute 50 EB	†Lochaber–near Hwy. 315	L-6
Autoroute 55 NB	St-Célestin–at jct. Hwy. 155	K-17
Autoroute 55 SB	†St-Étienne-des-Grès–north of interchange 196	J-16
Autoroute 73 SB	Charlesbourg	★ A-4, I-19
Autoroute 73 NB	†St-Étienne-de-Lauzon–south of Charny	J-19
Hwy. 101 EB,WB	Rouyn-Noranda–at jct. with Hwy. 117	G-1
Hwy. 108 WB	†Ascot	M-18
Hwy. 117 NB, SB	Louvicourt	G-3
Hwy. 132 EB, WB	New Richmond–east of jct. †Hwy. 299	G-18
Hwy. 132 EB, WB	Trois-Pistoles	H-14
Hwy. 138 EB	Baie-St-Paul	I-12
Hwy. 138 EB	Pointe-Lebel–west of Baie-Comeau	F-15
Hwy. 148 EB	†Litchfield–west of Gatineau	L-4
Hwy. 148 WB	†Lochaber–east of Gatineau	L-6
Hwy. 169 SB	Chambord	G-10
Hwy. 175 NB	Saguenay	★ C-20, G-12
Hwy. 175 NB	†Stoneham	J-11

list continued on following page

QUÉBEC–YUKON
Low Clearance Locations • Permanent Weigh Stations • Restricted Routes

† place or route does not appear on the map
‡ route not labeled on map
EB eastbound route NB northbound route
SB southbound route WB westbound route

Québec Permanent Weigh Stations continued
Weigh Station Scale Sites which are also vehicle inspection sites
Portable scales may be used at these sites

Route	Location	Map Key
Autoroute 15 NB	†Laval–at jct. ‡Autoroute 640	L-14
Autoroute 20 WB	Ste-Luce	G-15
Autoroute 30 NB, SB	Verchères	L-15
Autoroute 55 SB	Drummondville	L-16
Autoroute 55 SB	†St-Wenceslas	K-17
Hwy. 101 NB	Ville-Marie	I-1
Hwy. 108 WB	Bury	M-18
Hwy. 111 SB	Amos–south of Hwy. 386	F-2
Hwy. 112 WB	Black Lake	K-19
Hwy. 132 EB	Ste-Anne-des-Monts	F-17
Hwy. 138 NB, SB	Baie Ste-Catherine	H-13
Hwy. 138 NB, SB	†Boischatel	I-19
Hwy. 138 SB	Forestville	G-14
Hwy. 138 SB	Grandes–Bergeronnes	G-13
Hwy. 155 NB, SB	Grande-Anse–south of La Tuque	J-9
Hwy. 169 NB	St-Bruno–south of Alma	G-11
Hwy. 173 NB	St-Théophile	L-20
■ Hwy. 289 NB	Pohénégamook	I-14
Hwy. 389 SB	Baie Comeau	E-15
Hwy. 393 SB	La Sarre	F-1
Autoroute 610 WB	†Fleurimont–just east of Sherbrooke, at jct. Hwy. 112	M-18

Québec also uses portable scales

RESTRICTED ROUTES

Routes that restrict use by motor carriers

Route	Location
Hwy. 107	Hwy. 105 to Trans-Canada 117
Hwy. 112	Autoroute 410 to Hwy. 143
Hwy. 112	Hwy. 20 to Hwy. 134
Hwy. 112	Hwy. 116 to Autoroute 30
Hwy. 112	St-Lambert to Hwy. 10
Hwy. 112	Waterloo to Hwy. 10
Hwy. 116	Hwy. 223 to Hwy. 133
Hwy. 117	Ste-Adèle to St-Jérôme
Hwy. 132	Autoroute 20 to Hwy. 232
Hwy. 132	Autoroute 20 to Cacouna
Hwy. 132	Gaspé to north jct. Hwy. 197
Hwy. 132	Hwy. 171 to Hwy. 175
Hwy. 132	Kamouraska to Autoroute 20
Hwy. 132	Rivière-Ouelle to Hwy. 287
Hwy. 132	U.S. border to †Cazaville
Hwy. 132	Varennes to Pierreville
Hwy. 133	Autoroute 35 to Autoroute 10
Hwy. 133	Hwy. 116 to Autoroute 20
Hwy. 138	Autoroute 40 to Autoroute 55
Hwy. 138	Hwy. 343 to Hwy. 131
Hwy. 138	Hwy. 358 to Hwy. 367
Hwy. 138	Lanoraie-d'Autray to Hwy. 158
Hwy. 141	Hwy. 112 to Autoroute 10
Hwy. 141	Hwy. 251 to U.S. Border
Hwy. 143	Hwy. 112 to Autoroute 610
Hwy. 153	Hwy. 350 to Hwy. 40
Hwy. 153	†Grand-Mère to Hwy. 359
Hwy. 157	Shawinigan to Autoroute 40
Hwy. 170	Saguenay to La Baie
Hwy. 202	Hwy. 227 to Hwy. 133
Hwy. 207	Autoroute 30 to Hwy. 132
Hwy. 208	Hwy. 141 to Hwy. 143
Hwy. 209	Hwy. 221 to Hwy. 132
Hwy. 209	U.S. border to Hwy. 201
Hwy. 214	Hwy. 253 to East Angus
Hwy. 218	Lyster to Hwy. 271
Hwy. 219	U.S. border to Hwy. 202
Hwy. 221	U.S. border to Hwy. 202
Hwy. 223	U.S. border to Hwy. 202
Hwy. 223	Autoroute 35 to Hwy. 112
Hwy. 223	Hwy. 112 to Autoroute 30
Hwy. 225	Noyan to Sabrevois
Hwy. 229	Autoroute 30 to Ste-Julie-de-Vercheres
Hwy. 230	La Pocatiere to St-Philippe-de-Neri
Hwy. 230	St-Pascal to St-Alexandre-de-Kamouraska
Hwy. 239	Hwy. 133 to Massueville
Hwy. 247	†Fitch Bay to Hwy. 112
Hwy. 251	Hwy. 141 to St-Herménégilde
Hwy. 263	Disraeli to Hwy. 108
Hwy. 303	Hwy. 301 to Hwy. 148
Hwy. 307	Hwy. 366 to Hwy. 309
Hwy. 311	Mont-St-Michel to Trans-Canada 117
Hwy. 311	Hwy. 309 to Lac du Cerf
Hwy. 335	Hwy. 125 to Hwy. 158
Hwy. 337	Autoroute 640 to Autoroute 25
Hwy. 337	Hwy. 335 to Hwy. 125
Hwy. 337	Hwy. 341 to Hwy. 343
Hwy. 337	Hwy. 343 to Hwy. 131
Hwy. 337	Rawdon to Hwy. 343
Hwy. 338	Hwy. 201 to Autoroute 20
Hwy. 341	Hwy. 125 to Hwy. 337
Hwy. 342	Hwy. 201 to Autoroute 480
Hwy. 343	Hwy. 344 to Hwy. 158
Hwy. 344	Grenville to †Carillon
Hwy. 344	Autoroute 40 to Hwy. 148
Hwy. 344	†Rosemère to Autoroute 25
Hwy. 344	†St-Paul-l'Ermite to Hwy. 341
Hwy. 347	Hwy. 131 to St-Damien
Hwy. 348	Hwy. 349 to Hwy. 350
Hwy. 362	Hwy. 138 (Baie-St-Paul) to Hwy. 138 (La Malbaie)
Hwy. 391	Angliers to Hwy. 101
Hwy. 391	Hwy. 101 (Rollet) to Trans-Canada 117
Hwy. 395	Trans-Canada 117 to Hwy. 109
Hwy. 395	Hwy. 109 to Hwy. 397
Québec Bridge	Hwy. 132 to Hwy. 175
Victoria Bridge	†Wellington St. to Autoroute 20

SASKATCHEWAN

See province and city maps **pages 120-121**
★ located on city map

LOW CLEARANCE LOCATIONS

Statutory height: 4.15 m
Structures with 4.15 m or less clearance

Route	Location	Min. Height	Max. Height	Map Key
†Access Rd.	Nipawin–northwest at Old Nipawin Bridge	3.45 m	4.09 m	E-9
Hwy. 11	Regina	4.1 m	4.1 m	★ C-1

PERMANENT WEIGH/INSPECTION STATIONS

■ also serves as Port of Entry
Port of Entry scales do NOT issue permits; telephone the Permit Office for permit upon (or before) entry into Saskatchewan. If a truck pulls into a scale without a permit number, the driver can be charged.
All scale locations are also vehicle inspection sites

Route	Location	Map Key
■ Hwy. 1 EB, WB	Moosomin–14 km east	K-11
■ Hwy. 1 EB, WB	Swift Current–12 km west	K-4
Hwy. 6 all directions	Melfort–1 km south	F-8
■ Hwy. 7 EB, WB	Kindersley–11 km west	H-3
■ Hwy. 10 NB, SB	Yorkton–3 km south	I-10
Hwy. 11 NB, SB	Regina–2 km northwest	K-8
■ Hwy. 16 EB, WB	Marshall–2 km west	E-2
Hwy. 16 EB, WB	Saskatoon–14 km east	G-6
Hwy. 16 EB, WB	Saskatoon–17 km west	G-5
■ Hwy. 39 NB, SB	Estevan–5 km north	M-10

Saskatchewan also uses portable scales

RESTRICTED ROUTES

Routes that restrict use by motor carriers

Weight restricted to 34,500 kg maximum gross vehicle weight on the following routes:

Route	Location
Hwy. 2	Hwy. 25 to †Red Deer Hill
Hwy. 240	Hwy. 55 to Prince Albert National Park

Weight restricted to 8,000 kg maximum gross vehicle weight on the following routes:

Route	Location
Hwy. 8	Hwy. 49 to Swan Plain
Hwy. 15	Hwy. 9 to Trans-Canada 16
Hwy. 30	south of Eston to Brock
Hwy. 35	Hwy. 33 to Hwy. 48
Hwy. 31	Plenty to Hwy. 4
Hwy. 42	Hwy. 45 to Hwy. 373
Hwy. 44	Cutbank to Hwy. 11
Hwy. 44	Eyre to Hwy. 21
Hwy. 56	Indian Head to Lebret
Hwy. 80	Trans-Canada 16 to Hwy. 8
Hwy. 219	Hwy. 44 to Secondary 764
Hwy. 302	east of Prince Albert to Hwy. 682
Hwy. 306	Hwy. 6 to Riceton
Hwy. 308	Hwy. 8 to Welwyn
Hwy. 310	Secondary Hwy. 743 to Trans-Canada 16
Hwy. 332	Hazlet to Hwy. 32
Hwy. 334	Hwy. 13 to Hwy. 339
Hwy. 339	Hwy. 334 to Hwy. 39
Hwy. 342	Hwy. 4 to Hwy. 44
Hwy. 371	Alberta border to Hwy. 21

YUKON

See Canada map **page 117**

LOW CLEARANCE LOCATIONS

Statutory height: 4.2 m
Structures with 4.2 m or less clearance

Route	Location	Height	Map Key
None on the primary highway system			

PERMANENT WEIGH/INSPECTION STATIONS

■ also serves as Port of Entry
All scale locations are also vehicle inspection sites

Route	Location	Map Key
■ Alaska Hwy. 1 NB, SB	Watson Lake–in town at km 976	D-3
■ Alaska Hwy. 1 NB, SB	Whitehorse–in town at km 1420	C-2

Yukon also uses portable scales

RESTRICTED ROUTES

Routes that restrict use by motor carriers

Route	Location
None reported	

Contents & Legend

State, Provincial, and City Maps & Indexes

CONTENTS

Quick Map References

State & Province Maps

United States

Canada

Selected City Maps

This list contains only 70 of more than 350 detailed city maps in the Road Atlas. To find more city maps, consult the state/province map list above and turn to the pages indicated.

On June 5, 1984, FHWA published the final network of designated highways in all states and the District of Columbia. This list of designated routes, plus the Interstate System, makes up the **National Network** on which commercial vehicles, with dimensions authorized in Title 49 USC, 31111 and 31113, may operate. Changes in the Network have been published in subsequent issues of the *Federal Register*.

In 1988, the FHWA surveyed the individual states and published the "FHWA Survey of Routes Available to STAA Vehicles" (those subject to length and width requirements in Title 49 USC, 31111 and 31113). In this edition of the *Motor Carriers' Road Atlas*, all routes included in the "FHWA Survey of Routes," any updates of National Network routes through November 2017 for all states and the District of Columbia, and additional state-designated routes have been highlighted in orange on the individual state and urban area maps.

Routes shown represent the most accurate description of those available to vehicles subject to Federal width and minimum length requirements as of November, 2017 but neither the FHWA nor the publisher of this work can guarantee the information provided. Motor carriers should check with the various states in which they operate regarding any deletions or additions to the routes shown on the maps as available to vehicles subject to the Federal size requirements before traveling on them.

Note: Federal weight limits apply only on the Interstate System; state weight limits apply on all other highways, including the non-Interstate segments of the National Network.

MAP LEGEND

Weigh station
Designated route for vehicles with STAA-authorized dimensions

Roads and related symbols

Limited-access, multilane highway—free; toll
New road (under construction as of press time)
Other multilane highway
Principal highway
Other through highway
Other road (conditions vary — local inquiry suggested)
Unpaved road (conditions vary — local inquiry suggested)
Ramp; one way route
Car ferry (with toll unless otherwise indicated on map)
Tunnel; mountain pass
Railroad; Intracoastal Waterway
Interstate highway; Interstate highway business route
U.S. highway; U.S. highway business route
Trans-Canada highway; Autoroute
Mexican highway or Central American highway
State/provincial highway; secondary state/provincial, or county highway
TOLL Service area; toll booth or fee booth
Interchanges and exit numbers
For most states, the mileage between interchanges may be determined by subtracting one number from the other.
Highway distances (segments of one mile or less not shown):
Cumulative miles (red): the distance between arrows
Cumulative kilometers (blue): the distance between arrows
Intermediate miles (black): the distance between intersections & places

Comparative distance
1 mile = 1.609 kilometers 1 kilometer = 0.621 mile

Cities & towns size of type on map indicates relative population

National capital; state or provincial capital
County seat or independent city
City, town, or recognized place—incorporated; unincorporated
Urbanized area
Separate cities within metropolitan area

Parks, recreation areas, & other points of interest

National park
Other national park system location
National forest, national grassland, or city park; wilderness area
State/provincial park system location; state/provincial forest
State/provincial park system location—with campsites; without campsites
Campsite; wayside or roadside park
Point of interest, historic site or monument
Airport
Building
Foot trail
Golf course or country club; ski area
Hospital or medical center
Military or governmental installation; military airport
Native American tribal lands
Ranger station
Rest area—with toilets; without toilets
Tourist information center; port of entry

Physical features

Mountain peak; highest point in state/province
Lake; intermittent lake; dry lake
River; intermittent river
Dam; swamp or mangrove swamp
Desert; glacier
Continental divide

Other symbols

Area shown in greater detail on inset map
52 Inset map page indicator (if not on same page)
COOK County or parish boundary and name
State or provincial boundary
National boundary
Time zone boundary
Latitude; longitude

Map abbreviations

Listed below are some of the commonly used abbreviations on our maps. For a complete list of abbreviations that appear on the maps, go to **www.randmcnally.com/ABBR.**

Bfld.	Battlefield	N.P.	National Park
Cr.	Creek	N.R.A.	National Recreation Area
I.	Island	N.W.R.	National Wildlife Refuge
Int'l	International	S.H.S.	State Historic Site
L.	Lake	S.N.A.	State Natural Area
N.H.P.	National Historic Park	S.P.	State Park
N.H.S.	National Historic Site	S.R.A.	State Recreation Area
N.M.	National Monument	W.M.A.	Wildlife Management Area

Population figures used in this atlas are from the latest available census or are Census Bureau or Rand McNally estimates.

United States

Capital: Washington, G-17
Land area: 3,531,905 sq. mi.

Index of cities Pg. 129

Selected National Park Service locations

- Acadia National Park C-20
- Arches National Park G-6
- Badlands National Park E-9
- Big Bend National Park L-8
- Biscayne National Park M-18
- Bryce Canyon National Park G-5
- Canyonlands National Park G-6
- Capitol Reef National Park G-5
- Carlsbad Caverns National Park J-7
- Channel Islands National Park H-1
- Congaree National Park I-17
- Crater Lake National Park D-2
- Cuyahoga Valley National Park F-16
- Death Valley National Park G-3
- Denali National Park L-4
- Dry Tortugas National Park M-17
- Everglades National Park M-17
- Glacier Bay National Park M-6
- Glen Canyon Nat'l Recreation Area G-5
- Grand Canyon National Park H-4
- Grand Teton National Park E-6
- Great Sand Dunes Nat'l Park & Pres. H-7
- Great Smoky Mountains Nat'l Park H-15
- Guadalupe Mountains Nat'l Park J-7

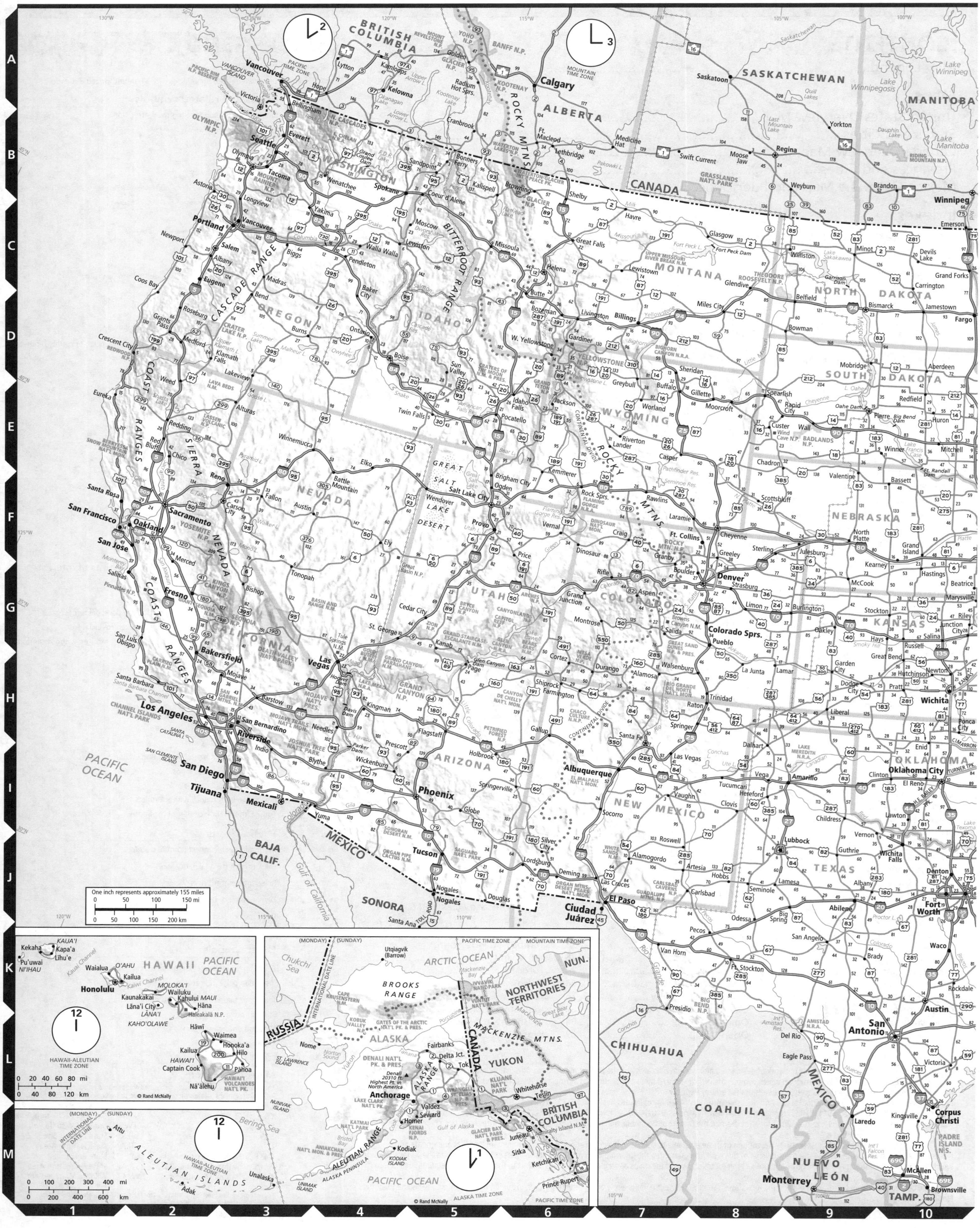

Population: 308,745,538
Largest city: New York, 8,175,133, E-18

Map legend Pg. 1

Selected National Park Service locations

- Haleakalā National Park L-2
- Hawai'i Volcanoes National Park L-2
- Hot Springs National Park I-12
- Isle Royale National Park C-13
- Kings Canyon National Park G-2
- Lake Mead Nat'l Recreation Area H-4
- Lassen Volcanic National Park E-2
- Mammoth Cave National Park H-14
- Mesa Verde National Park H-6
- Mount Rainier National Park B-3
- North Cascades National Park B-4
- Olympic National Park B-3
- Petrified Forest National Park I-5
- Redwood National Park D-1
- Rocky Mountain National Park F-7
- Sequoia National Park G-2
- Shenandoah National Park G-17
- Theodore Roosevelt National Park . . . D-8
- Voyageurs National Park C-12
- Waterton-Glacier Int'l Peace Park B-5
- Wind Cave National Park E-8
- Yellowstone National Park D-6
- Yosemite National Park F-2
- Zion National Park G-5

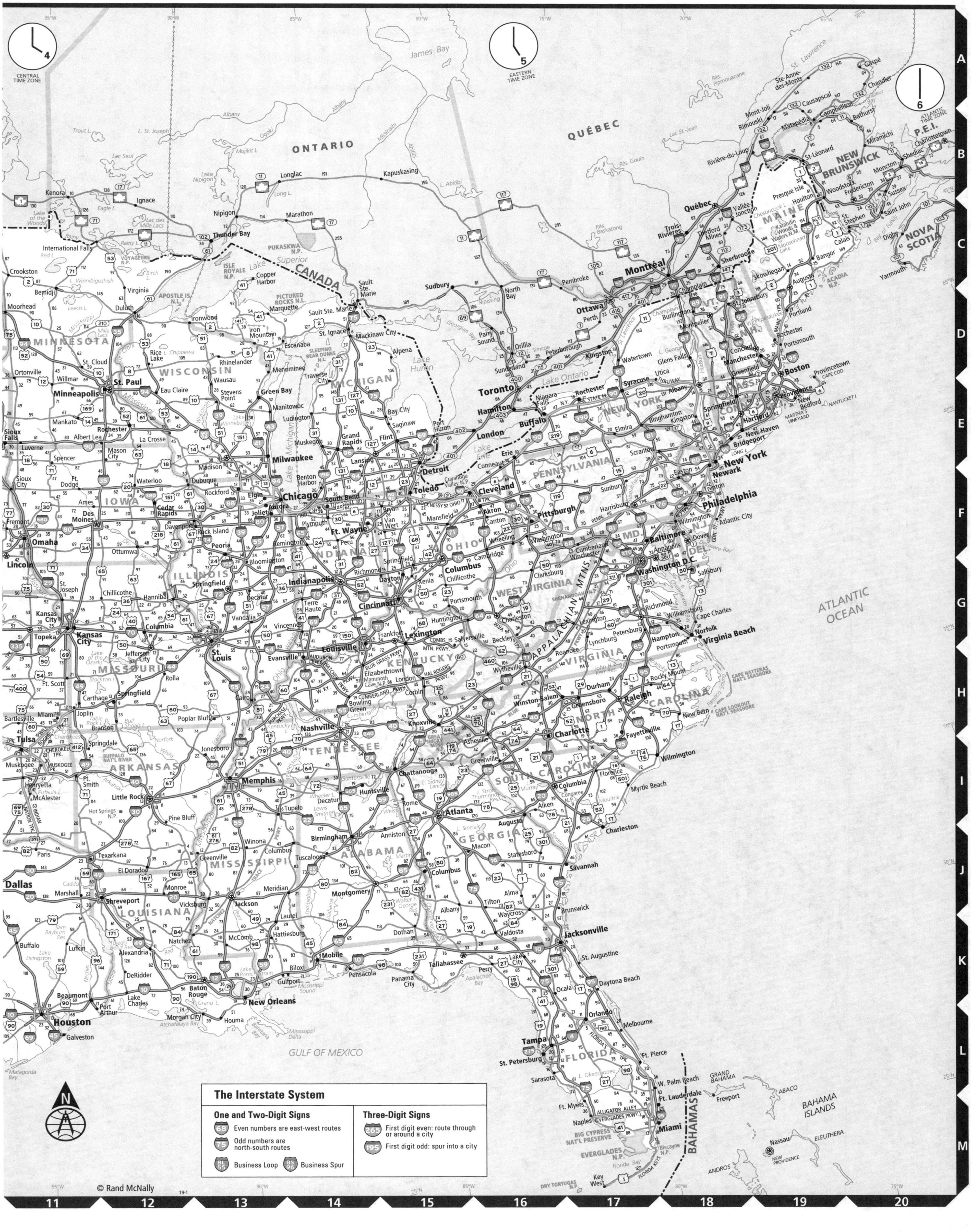

Alabama

Nickname: The Heart of Dixie
Capital: Montgomery, J-8
Land area: 50,645 sq. mi. (rank: 28th)
Population: 4,779,736 (rank: 23rd)
Largest city: Birmingham, 212,237, F-7

Index of cities Pg. 129 | Map legend Pg. 1

Route planning & on-the-road resources

Low clearances, weigh stations, & restricted routes: Page A26

Weigh station location

Designated route for vehicles with STAA-authorized dimensions

Road Conditions & Construction
(888) 588-2848; www.dot.state.al.us, alitsweb2.dot.state.al.us/RoadConditions

Toll Road Information
No tolls on state or federal highways

Determining Distances
(segments of one mile or less not shown)
Cumulative miles (red): the distance between red arrows
Intermediate miles (black): the distance between intersections & places

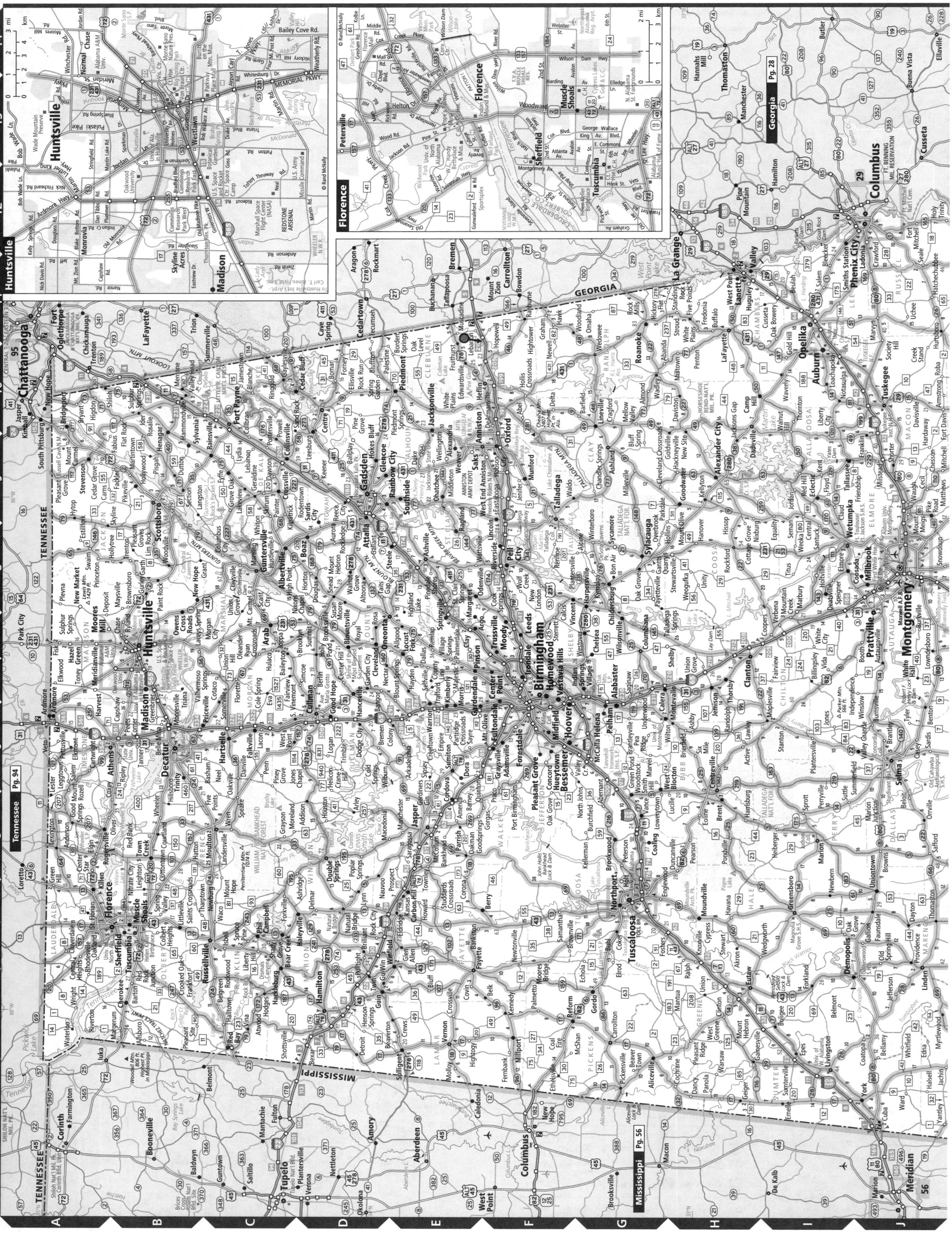

Mileage between cities	Andalusia	Anniston	Atlanta, GA	Auburn	Birmingham	Chattanooga, TN	Decatur	Dothan	Eufaula	Florence	Gadsden	Huntsville	Jasper	Meridian, MS	Mobile	Montgomery	Pensacola, FL	Phenix City	Selma	Troy	Tuscaloosa
ATLANTA, GA	252	90		109	147	117	196	207	156	244	120	188	184	289	329	161	324	109	211	195	201
BIRMINGHAM	181	64	147	110		146	83	196	175	118	62	102	39	146	258	90	253	140	87	140	58
CHATTANOOGA, TN	323	119	117	222	146		126	320	268	172	89	102	184	291	399	232	394	222	228	282	203
DOTHAN	80	215	207	121	196	320	276		52	311	226	295	233	253	196	106	150	100	150	56	210
HUNTSVILLE	280	104	188	212	102	102	25	295	274	72	75		96	243	357	189	352	242	186	239	155
MOBILE	124	285	329	223	258	399	338	196	250	326	315	357	294	135		167	57	254	161	172	204
MONTGOMERY	91	118	161	56	90	232	170	106	85	206	148	189	127	153	167		163	87	50	50	104
TUSCALOOSA	194	118	201	159	58	203	136	210	189	128	118	155	60	94	204	104	242	190	75	153	

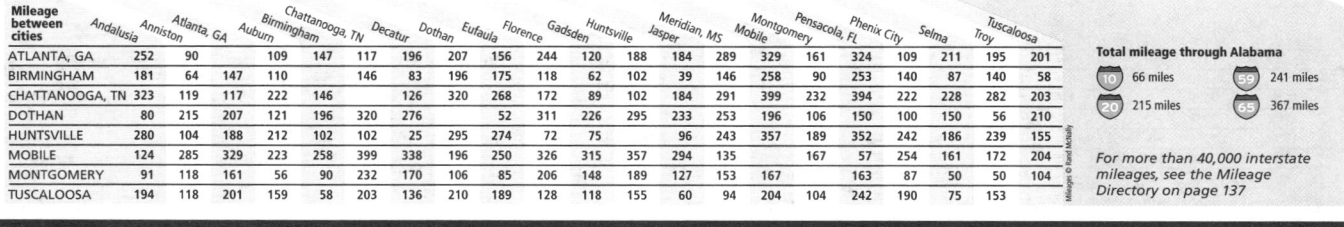

Mileages © Rand McNally

Total mileage through Alabama

- I-10: 66 miles
- I-20: 215 miles
- I-59: 241 miles
- I-65: 367 miles

For more than 40,000 interstate mileages, see the Mileage Directory on page 137

Alaska

Nickname: The Last Frontier
Capital: Juneau, H-12
Land area: 570,641 sq. mi. (rank: 1st)
Population: 710,231 (rank: 47th)
Largest city: Anchorage, 291,826, G-7

Index of cities Pg. 129 | Map legend Pg. 1

Mileage between cities	Anchorage	Fairbanks	Glennallen	Haines	Homer	Kenai	Seward	Tok	Valdez
ANCHORAGE		358	179	760	221	157	126	317	297
FAIRBANKS	358		248	646	579	514	484	204	362
HAINES	760	646	581		980	916	885	443	694
HOMER	221	579	399	980		86	169	538	518
KENAI	157	514	335	916	86		105	473	454
SEWARD	126	484	304	885	169	105		442	423
TOK	317	204	138	443	538	473	442		252
VALDEZ	297	362	118	694	518	454	423	252	

Total mileage through Alaska

(1) 408 miles (3) 325 miles
(2) 202 miles

For more than 40,000 interstate mileages, see the Mileage Directory on page 137

Route planning & on-the-road resources

Low clearances, weigh stations, & restricted routes: Page A26

Weigh station location

Designated route for vehicles with STAA-authorized dimensions

Road Conditions & Construction
511, (907) 465-8952
www.511.alaska.gov, www.dot.state.ak.us

Toll Tunnel Information
No tolls on state or federal highways

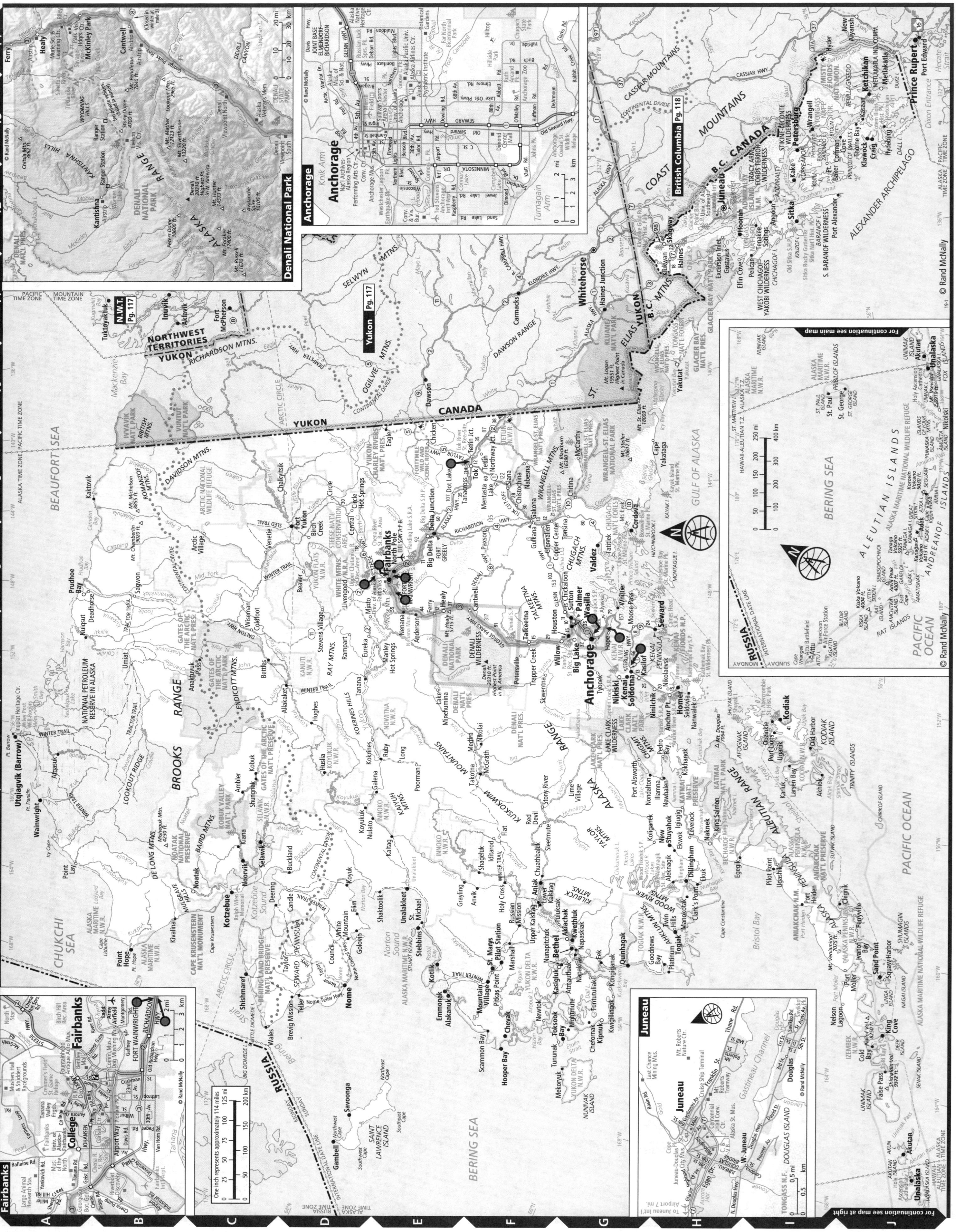

Folklorica dancers

Sights to see

- Arizona Historical Society Sanguinetti House Museum, Yuma L-6
- Arizona Museum of Natural History, Mesa J-7
- Arizona Science Center, Phoenix M-3
- Arizona State Capitol, Phoenix M-1
- Heard Museum, Phoenix L-2
- Painted Desert Inn Museum, Petrified Forest N.P. L-10
- Phoenix Art Museum, Phoenix L-2
- Taliesin West, Scottsdale H-7
- Tusayan Ruin and Museum, Grand Canyon N.P. D-9
- Yavapai Point Overlook, Grand Canyon N.P. B-1
- Yuma Territorial Prison State Historic Park, Yuma L-6

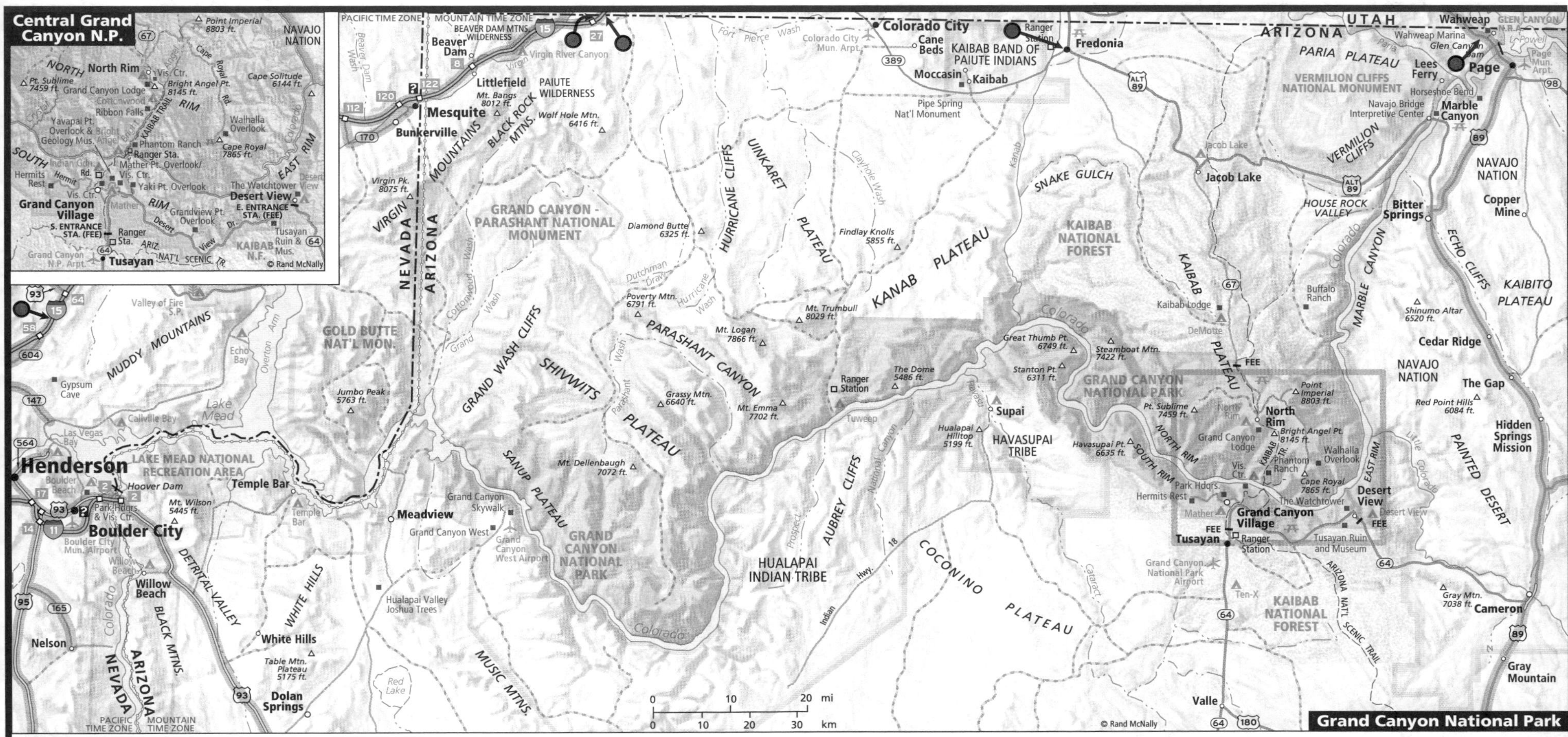

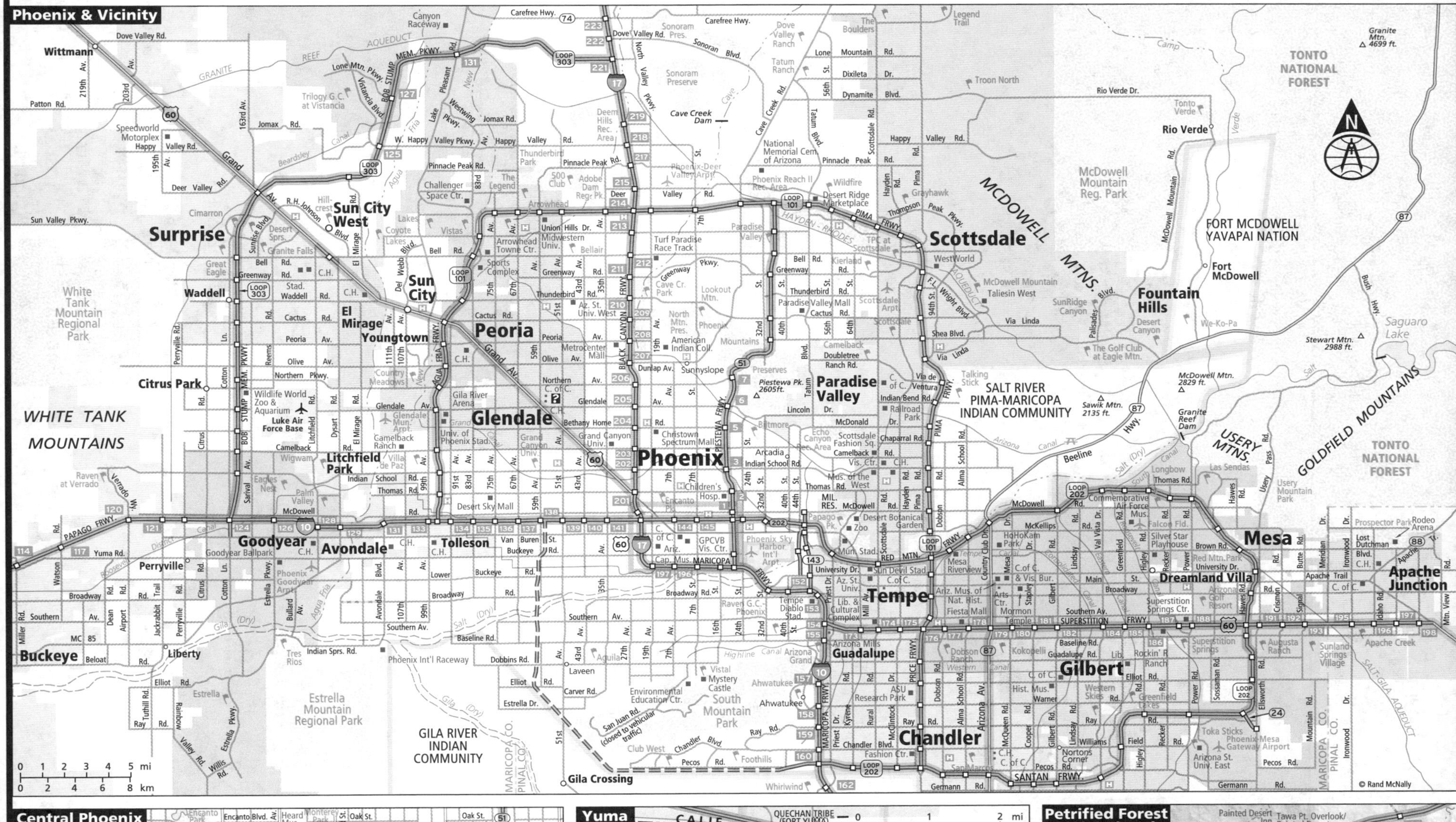

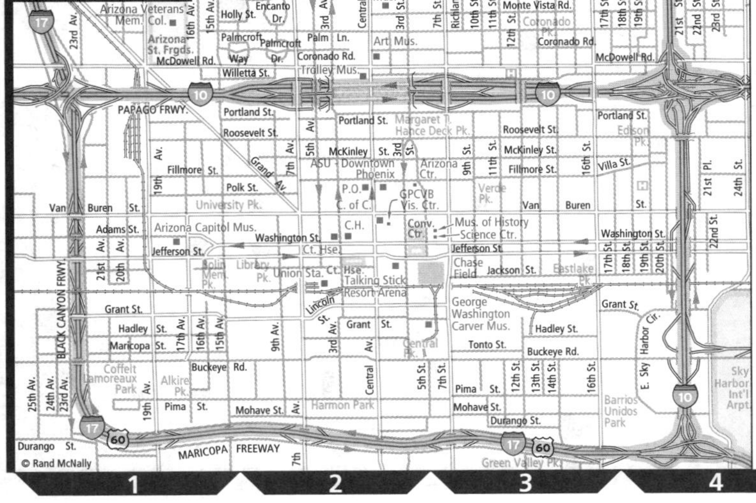

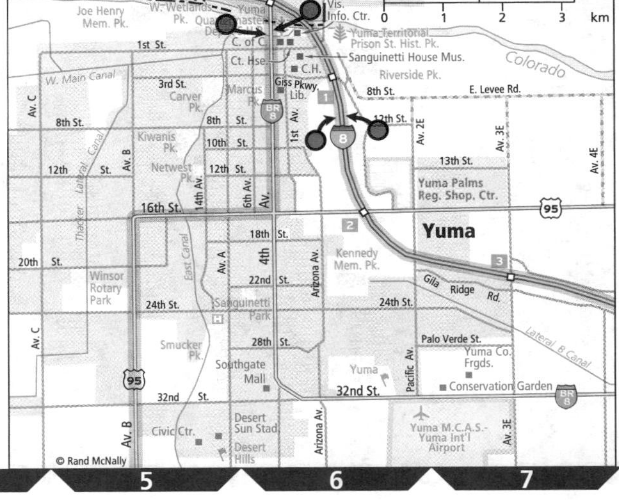

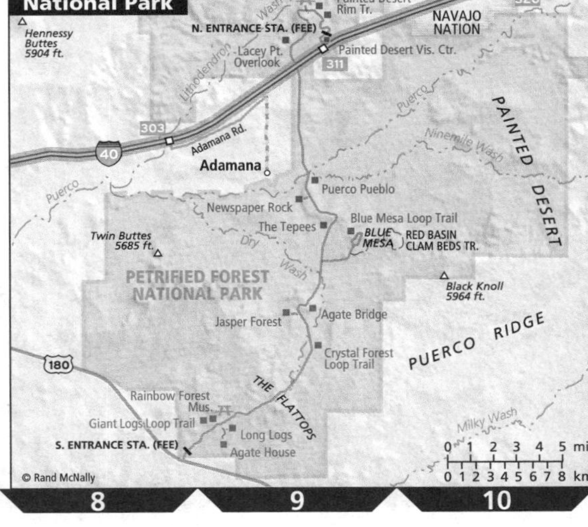

Arizona

Nickname: The Grand Canyon State
Capital: Phoenix, J-7
Land area: 113,594 sq. mi. (rank: 6th)
Population: 6,392,017 (rank: 16th)
Largest city: Phoenix, 1,445,632, J-7

Index of cities Pg. 129 | Map legend Pg. 1

Route planning & on-the-road resources

Low clearances, weigh stations, & restricted routes: Page A27

Weigh station location

Designated route for vehicles with STAA-authorized dimensions

Road Conditions & Construction
511, (888) 411-7623; www.az511.com, www.azdot.gov

Toll Road Information
No tolls on state or federal highways

Determining Distances
(segments of one mile or less not shown)
Cumulative miles (red): the distance between red arrows
Intermediate miles (black): the distance between intersections & places

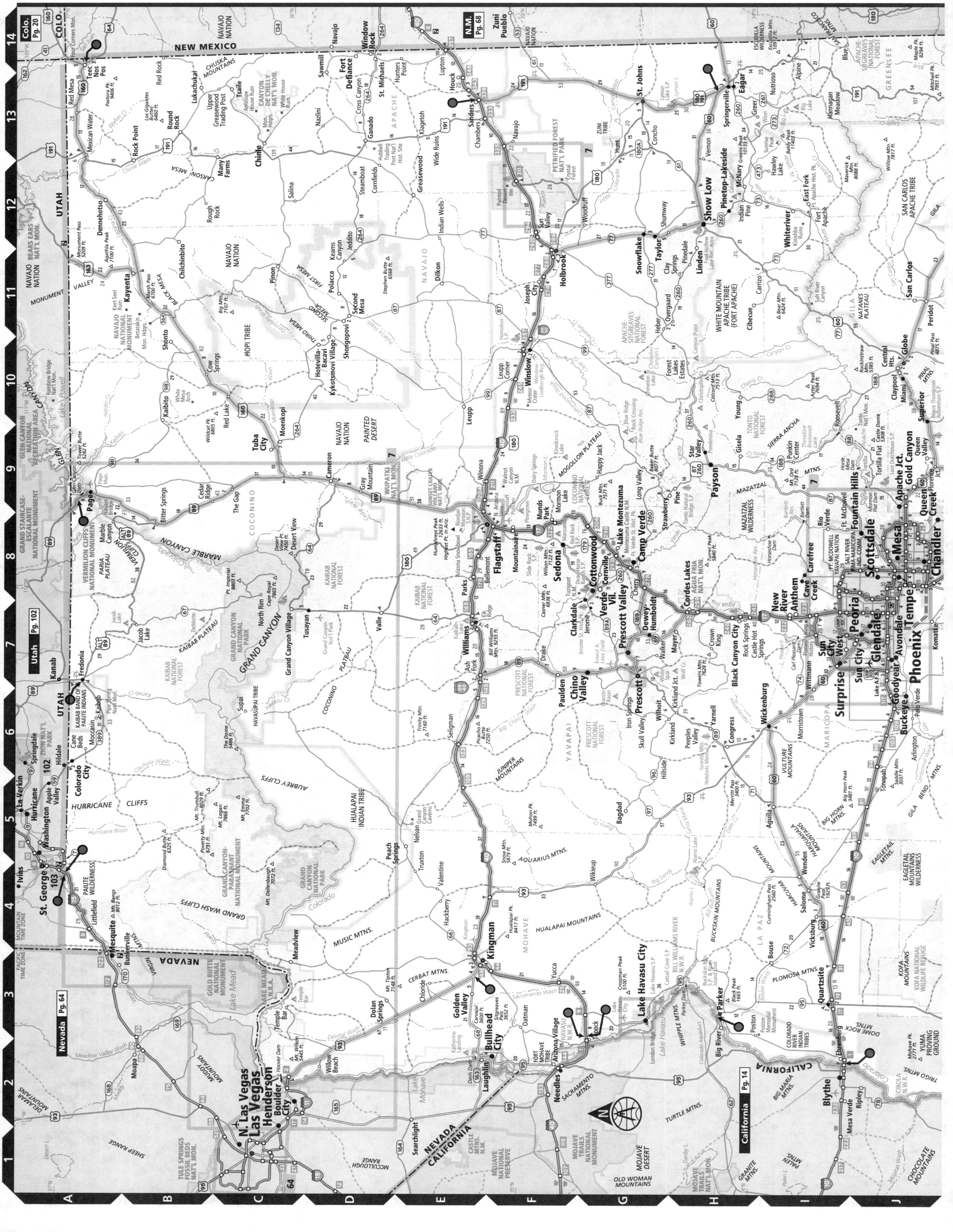

Mileage between cities	Blythe, CA	Casa Grande	Eagar	Flagstaff	Gallup, NM	Grand Canyon	Holbrook	Kingman	Lake Havasu City	Las Vegas, NV	Lordsburg, NM	Nogales	Page	Phoenix	Prescott	Shiprock, NM	Tucson	Yuma
CASA GRANDE	198		229	190	375	270	281	293	249	402	222	131	326	51	148	467	66	183
FLAGSTAFF	286	190	185		185	79	91	146	204	317	411	320	136	140	93	276	255	320
HOLBROOK	377	281	94	91	94	167		237	295	409	502	411	216	230	184	186	346	411
KINGMAN	155	293	331	146	331	171	237		58	172	514	424	282	242	148	422	358	366
PHOENIX	147	51	233	140	324	219	230	242	198	351	272	181	275		97	416	116	181
PRESCOTT	244	148	278	93	278	126	184	148	206	320	369	278	229	97		370	213	278
TUCSON	263	66	265	255	440	334	346	358	314	466	156	66	391	116	213	531		236
YUMA	267	183	412	320	505	399	411	366	154	445	392	301	456	181	278	596	236	

Total mileage through Arizona

- I-8: 178 miles
- I-17: 146 miles
- I-10: 392 miles
- I-40: 359 miles

For more than 40,000 interstate mileages, see the Mileage Directory on page 137

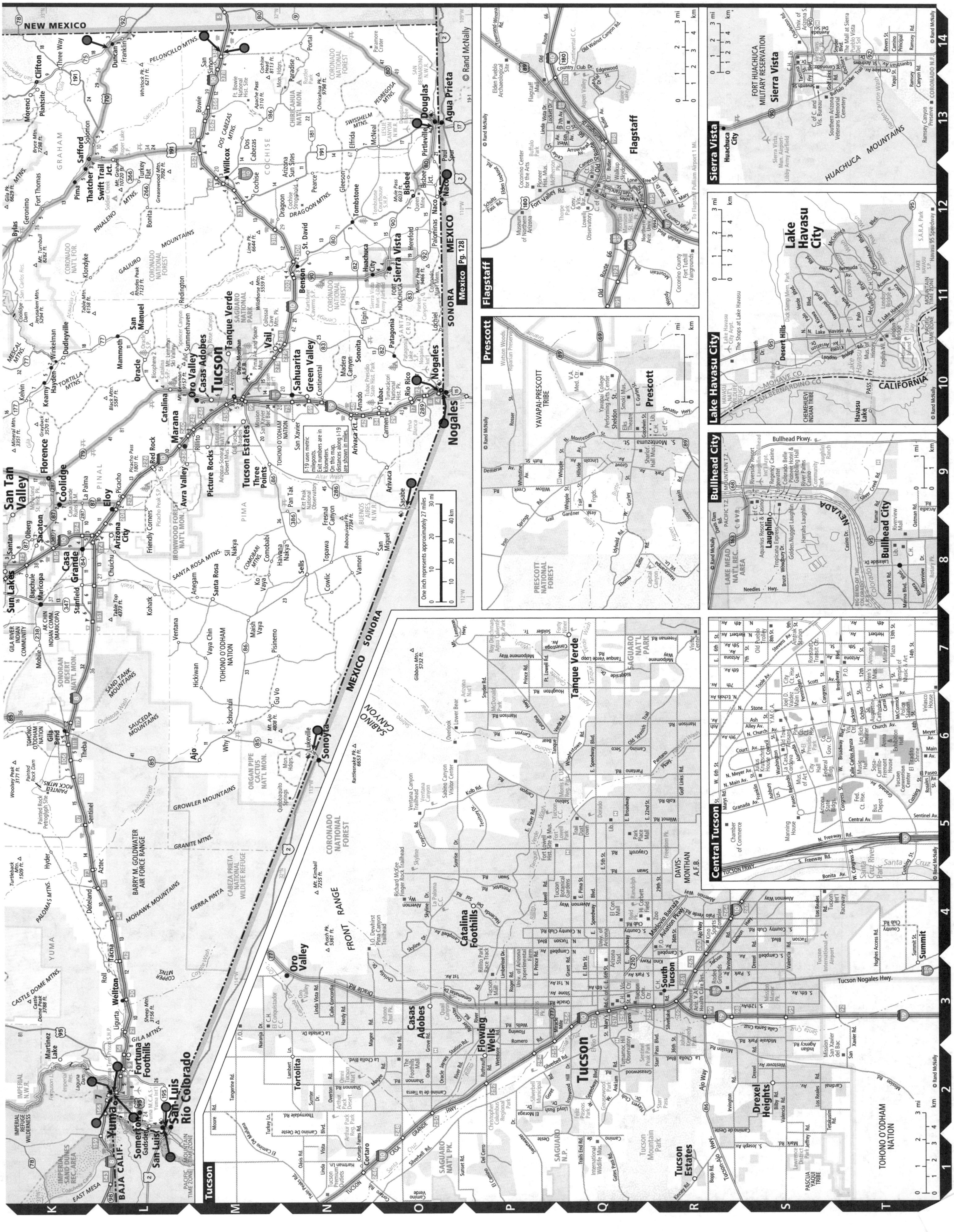

Arkansas

Nickname: The Natural State
Capital: Little Rock, G-7
Land area: 52,035 sq. mi. (rank: 27th)
Population: 2,915,918 (rank: 32nd)
Largest city: Little Rock, 193,524, G-7

Index of cities Pg. 129 | Map legend Pg. 1

Route planning & on-the-road resources

Low clearances, weigh stations, & restricted routes: Page A27

Weigh station location

Designated route for vehicles with STAA-authorized dimensions

Road Conditions & Construction
(800) 245-1672, (501) 569-2374, (501) 569-2000
www.arkansashighways.com, www.idrivearkansas.com

Toll Road Information
No tolls on state or federal highways

Determining Distances
(segments of one mile or less not shown)
Cumulative miles (red): the distance between red arrows
Intermediate miles (black): the distance between intersections & places

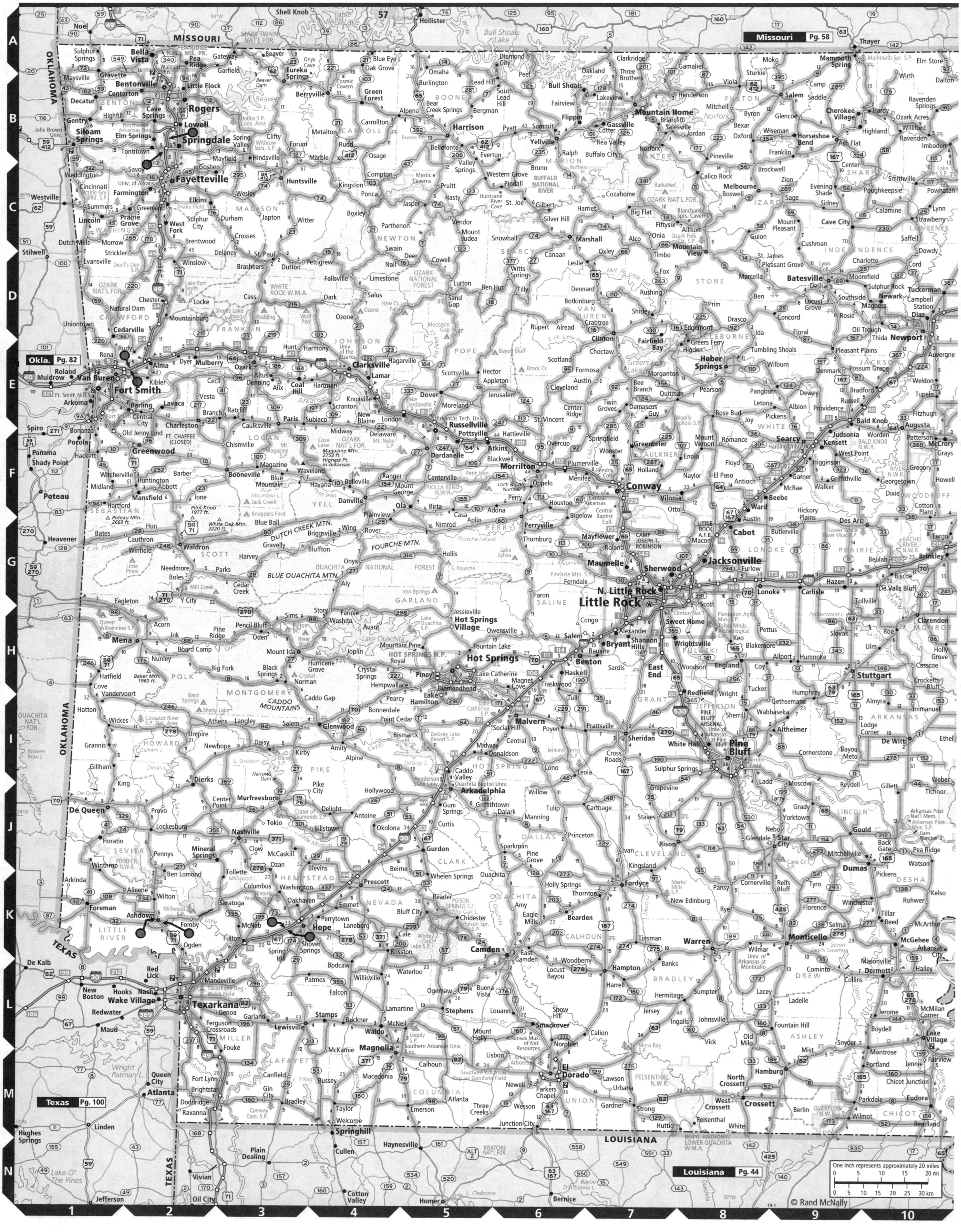

Mileage between cities	Batesville	De Queen	El Dorado	Fayetteville	Fort Smith	Greenville, MS	Harrison	Hot Springs	Jonesboro	Little Rock	Monticello	Pine Bluff	Rogers	Russellville	Texarkana	West Memphis
EL DORADO	210	141		305	227	109	255	122	249	118	67	91	325	192	89	243
FAYETTEVILLE	252	184	305		61	335	77	185	291	188	280	232	24	116	238	310
FORT SMITH	224	130	227	61		307	145	131	263	160	251	203	81	88	184	282
HARRISON	118	268	255	77	145	285		185	176	138	230	181	77	87	274	260
JONESBORO	68	274	249	291	263	221	176	185		133	223	175	253	177	274	66
LITTLE ROCK	94	143	118	188	160	147	138	54	133		92	44	208	74	142	127
TEXARKANA	235	55	89	238	184	198	274	111	274	142	152	152	258	210		268
WEST MEMPHIS	113	268	243	310	282	157	260	179	66	127	184	144	330	196	268	

Mileages © Rand McNally

Total mileage through Arkansas

- I-30: 143 miles
- I-40: 284 miles
- I-55: 72 miles
- US 65: 309 miles

For more than 40,000 interstate mileages, see the Mileage Directory on page 137

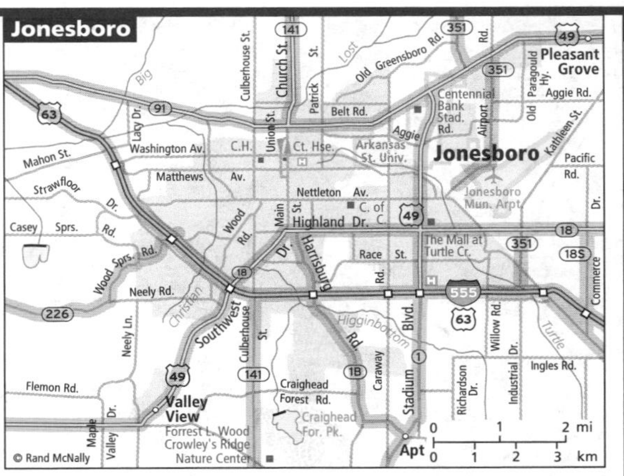

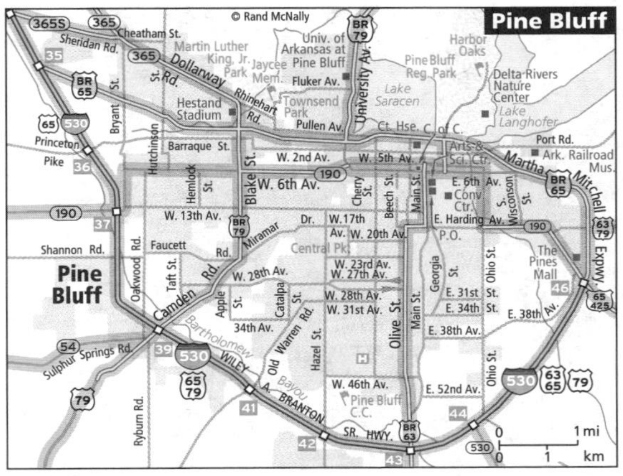

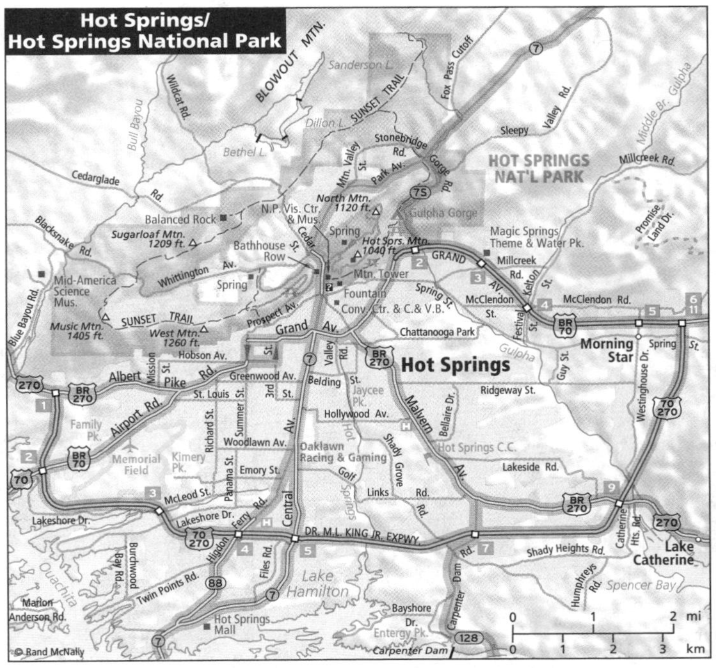

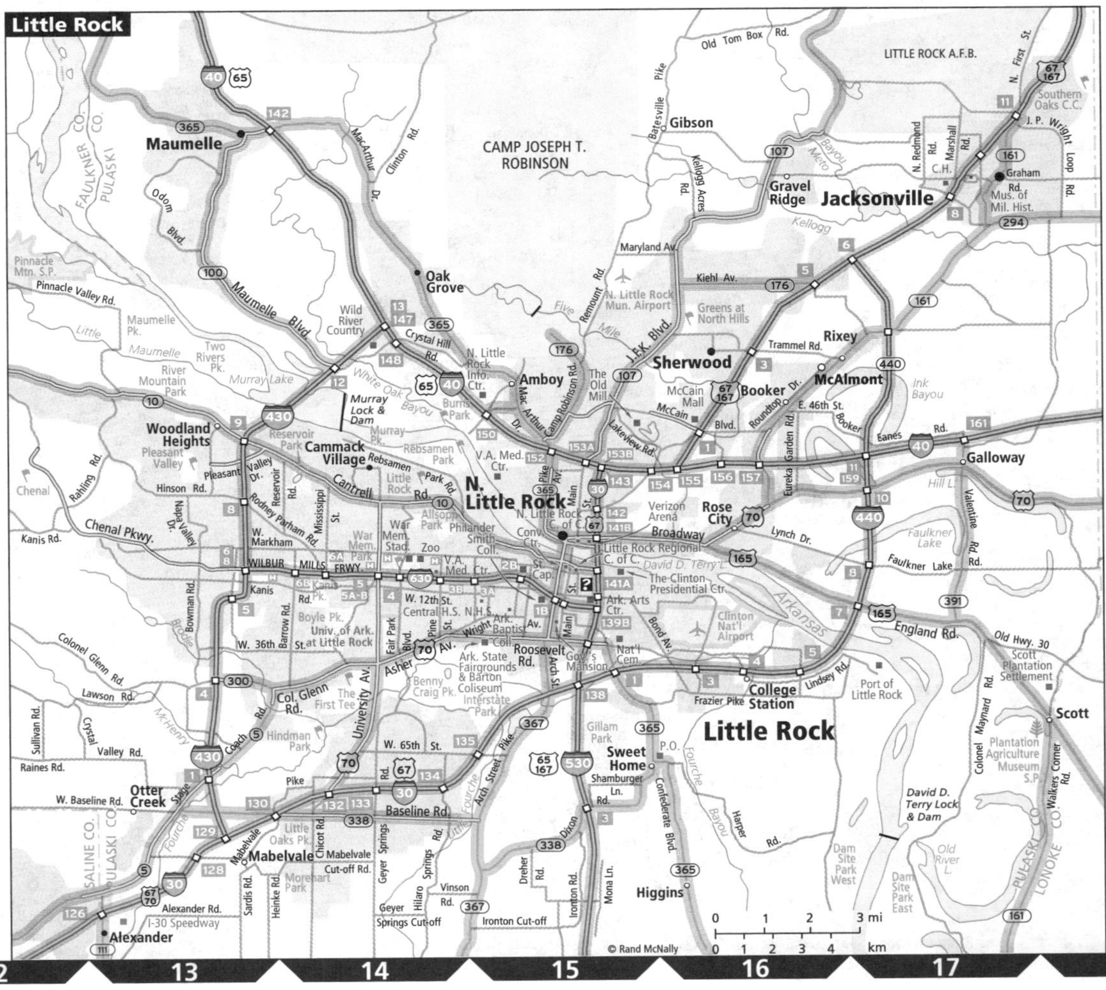

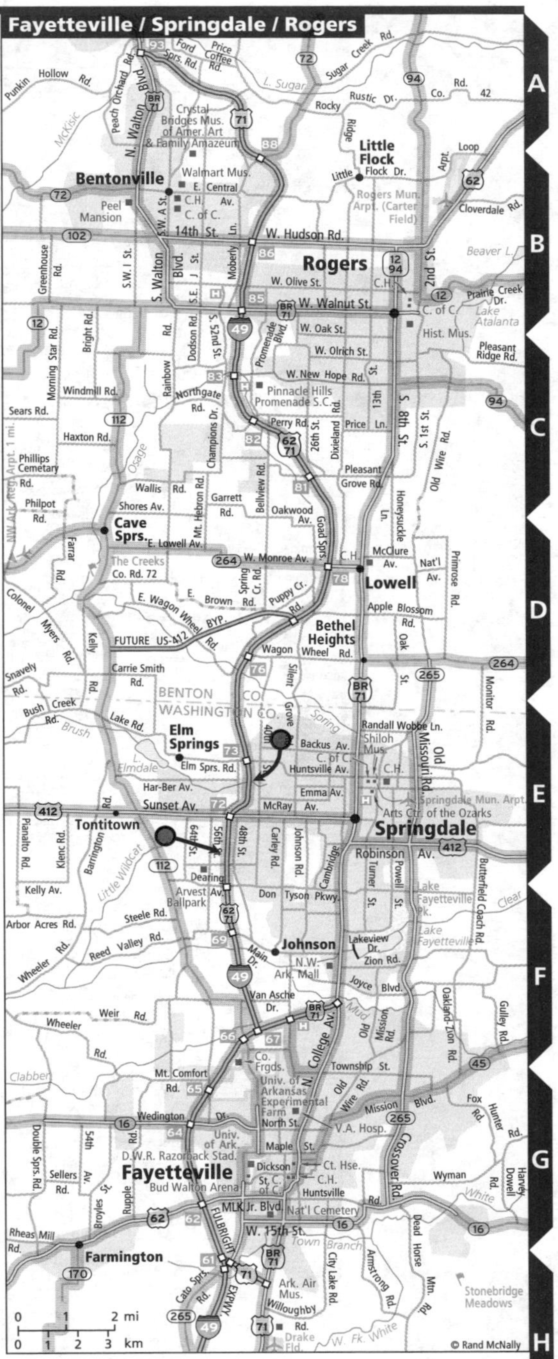

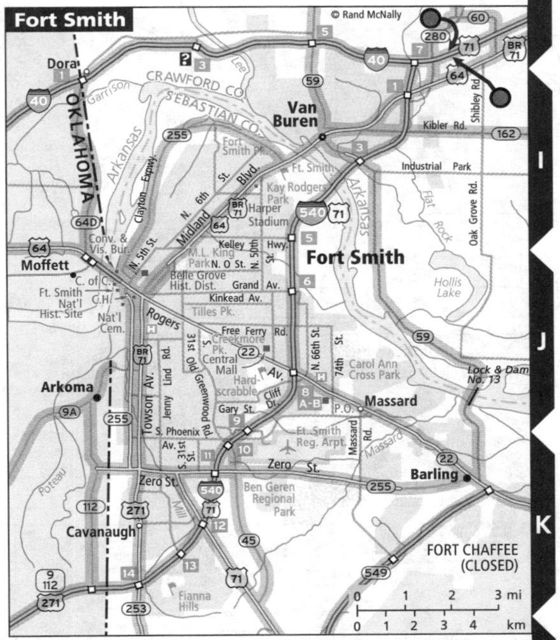

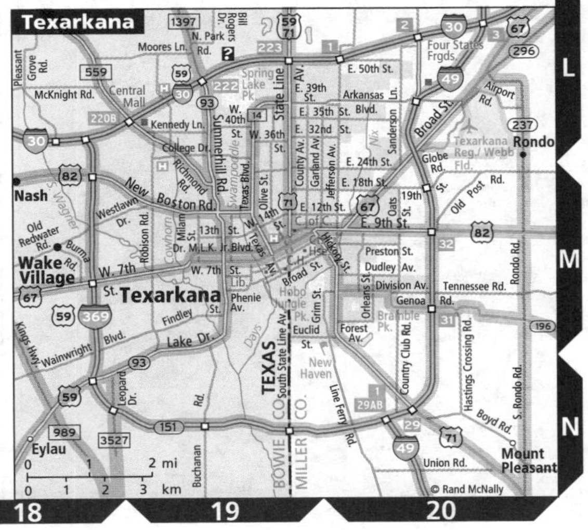

Nickname: The Golden State
Capital: Sacramento, NK-7
Land area: 155,799 sq. mi. (rank: 3rd)
Population: 37,253,956 (rank: 1st)
Largest city: Los Angeles, 3,792,621, SJ-11

Index of cities Pg. 129 | Map legend Pg. 1

Route planning & on-the-road resources

Low clearances, weigh stations, & restricted routes: Page A28

Weigh station location

Designated route for vehicles with STAA-authorized dimensions

Road Conditions & Construction
(800) 427-7623; www.dot.ca.gov
Sacramento region: 511; www.sacregion511.org
San Francisco Bay area: 511; www.511.org

Toll Bridge Information *(both use FasTrak)*
Golden Gate Bridge (San Francisco Bay area): (415) 921-5858; www.goldengate.org
Bay Area Toll Authority (all other San Francisco Bay area bridges): (415) 778-6700; bata.mtc.ca.gov

Determining Distances
(segments of one mile or less not shown)
Cumulative miles (red): the distance between red arrows
Intermediate miles (black): the distance between intersections & places

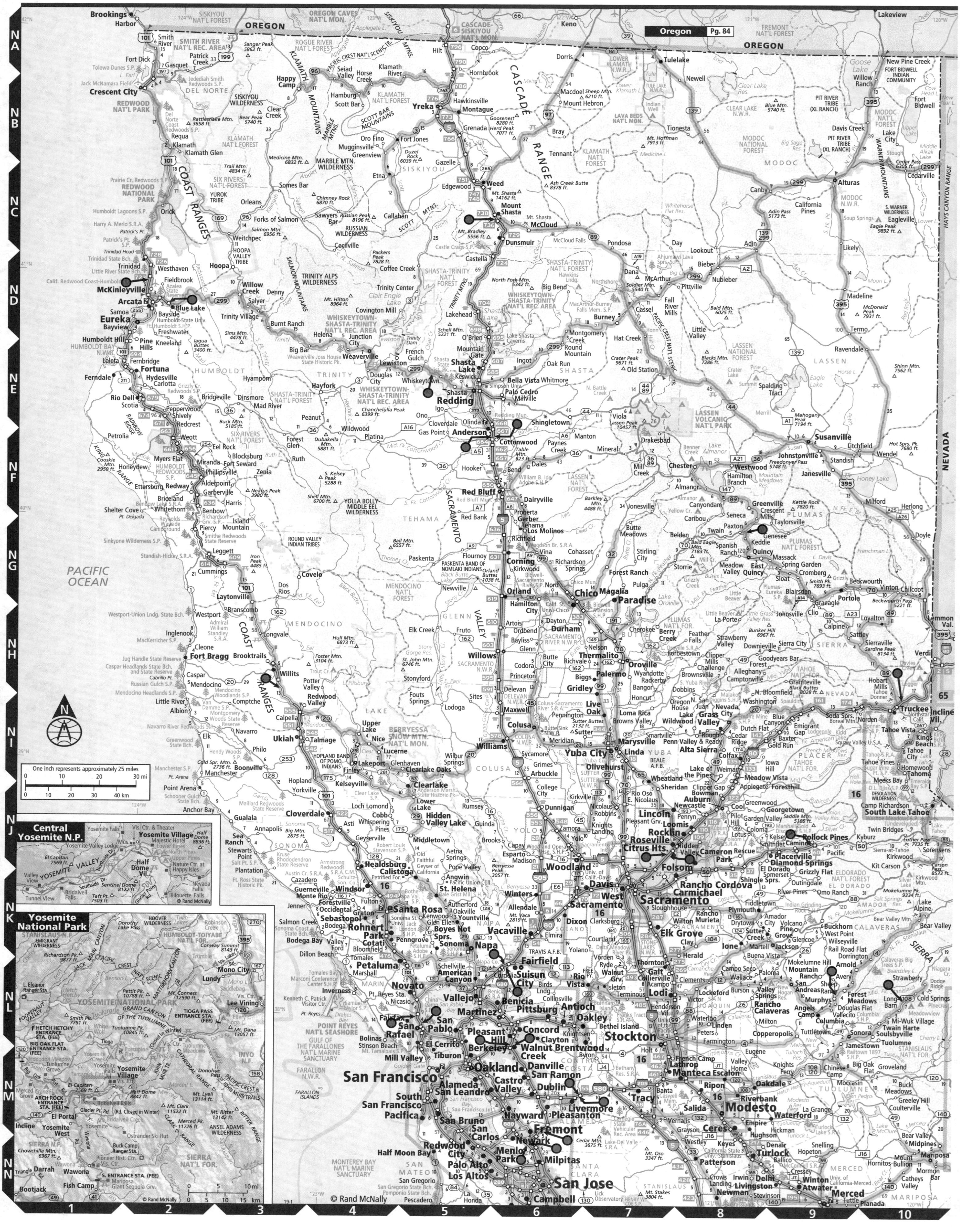

Mileage between cities	Alturas	Bishop	Crescent City	Eureka	Oakland	Oroville	Redding	Sacramento	San Francisco	San Jose	Santa Rosa	South Lake Tahoe	Stockton	Susanville	Ukiah	Vallejo	Yosemite NP	Yreka
BISHOP	383		800	566	396	360	420	318	404	432	420	194	365	287	460	376	428	456
EUREKA	291	566	81		274	241	146	292	281	315	220	441	349	280	160	269	476	244
REDDING	145	420	208	146	208	95		164	216	244	232	277	209	134	190	188	357	98
SACRAMENTO	305	318	604	292	79	71	164		87	115	103	154	47	217	149	59	191	261
SAN FRANCISCO	357	404	656	281	8	150	216	87		45	63	240	82	303	123	30	210	312
SAN JOSE	385	432	684	315	41	178	244	115	45		96	268	74	330	156	64	202	340
S. LAKE TAHOE	239	194	656	440	232	196	277	154	240	268	256		202	143	296	212	347	313
VALLEJO	329	376	628	269	22	122	188	59	30	64	50	212	76	275	110		213	284

Total mileage through California

5: 797 miles
101: 791 miles
80: 199 miles

For more than 40,000 interstate mileages, see the Mileage Directory on page 137

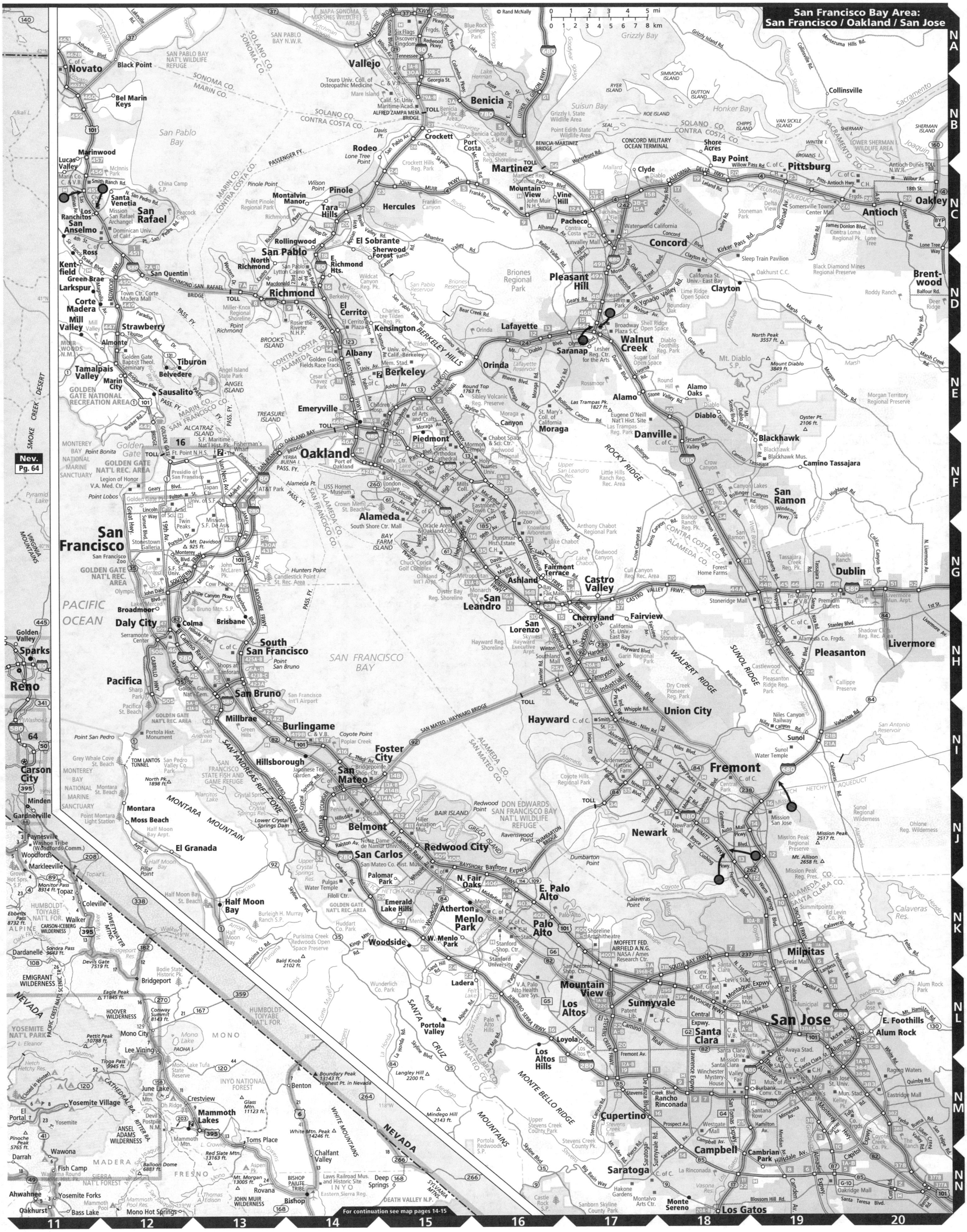

Nickname: The Golden State
Capital: Sacramento, NK-7
Land area: 155,799 sq. mi. (rank: 3rd)
Population: 37,253,956 (rank: 1st)
Largest city: Los Angeles, 3,792,621, SJ-11

Index of cities Pg. 129 | Map legend Pg. 1

Route planning & on-the-road resources

Low clearances, weigh stations, & restricted routes: Page A28

Weigh station location

Designated route for vehicles with STAA-authorized dimensions

Road Conditions & Construction
(800) 427-7623; www.dot.ca.gov
Los Angeles metro area: 511; www.go511.com
San Diego area: 511, (619) 669-1900; www.511sd.com

Toll Road Information
The Toll Roads of Orange Co. (*FasTrak*): (949) 727-4800; www.thetollroads.com
South Bay Expwy. (San Diego Co.) (*FasTrak*): (619) 661-7070; www.southbayexpressway.com

Determining Distances
(segments of one mile or less not shown)
Cumulative miles (red): the distance between red arrows
Intermediate miles (black): the distance between intersections & places

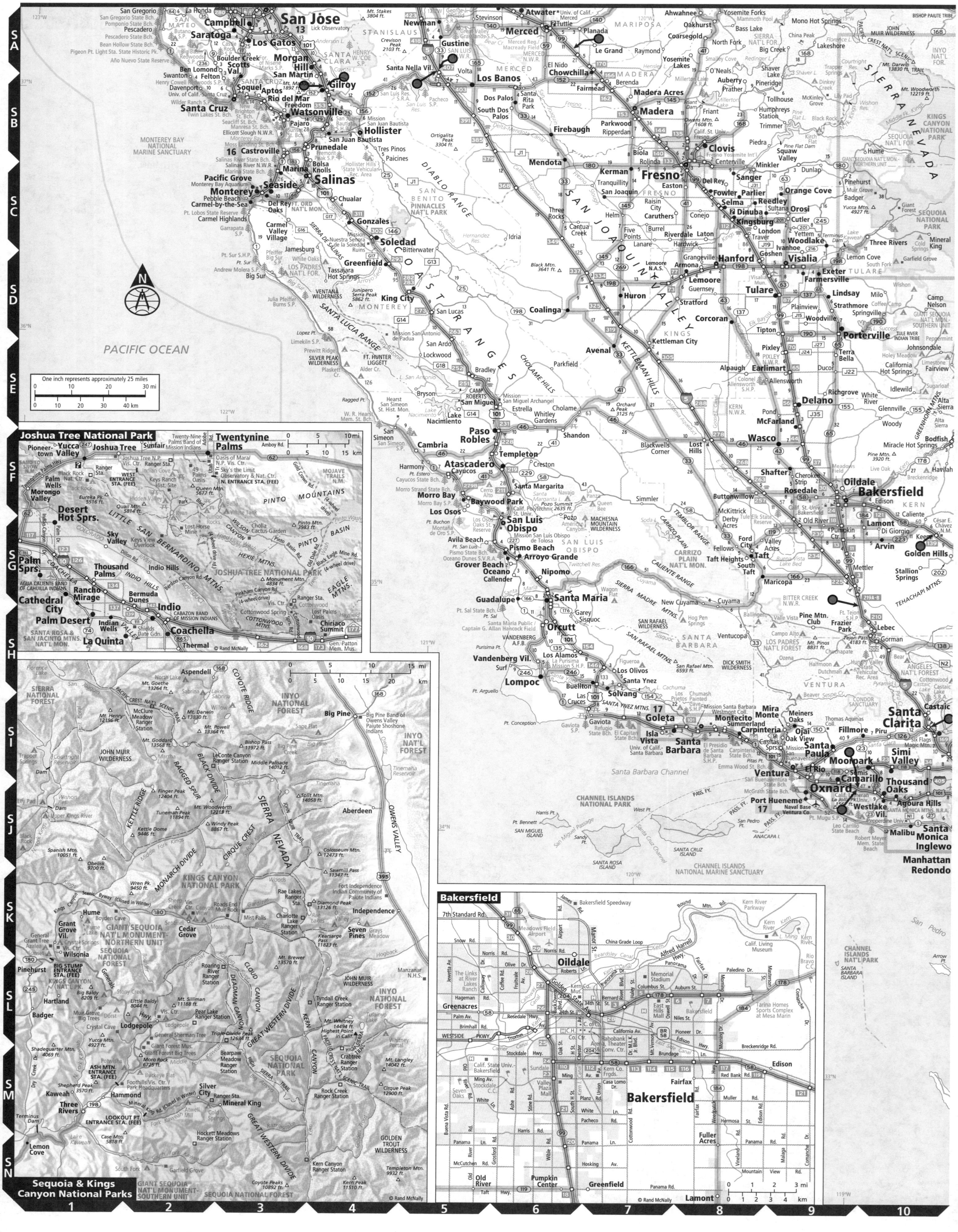

Mileage between cities	Bakersfield	Barstow	Blythe	El Centro	Fresno	Las Vegas, NV	Los Angeles	Monterey	Needles	Palm Springs	Riverside	Sacramento	San Bernardino	San Diego	San Francisco	San Luis Obispo	Santa Barbara	Sequoia NP
BAKERSFIELD		129	334	323	110	287	112	231	274	218	165	275	167	233	283	136	149	123
FRESNO	110	239	440	429		396	219	150	384	324	271	165	272	339	184	138	254	77
LOS ANGELES	112	115	223	212	219	271		329	258	107	54	383	60	120	381	200	94	232
MONTEREY	231	360	551	540	150	518	329		505	435	382	185	383	450	116	152	258	226
PALM SPRINGS	218	123	137	108	324	279	107	435	206		52	489	54	139	487	307	201	338
RIVERSIDE	165	78	168	157	271	234	54	382	222	52		436	9	97	434	254	148	285
SAN DIEGO	233	175	255	115	339	331	120	450	318	139	97	504	106		502	320	214	353
SANTA BARBARA	149	203	317	306	254	359	94	258	346	201	148	399	150	214	336	106		268

Mileages © Rand McNally

Total mileage through California

5	797 miles	15	287 miles
10	243 miles	40	155 miles

For more than 40,000 interstate mileages, see the Mileage Directory on page 137

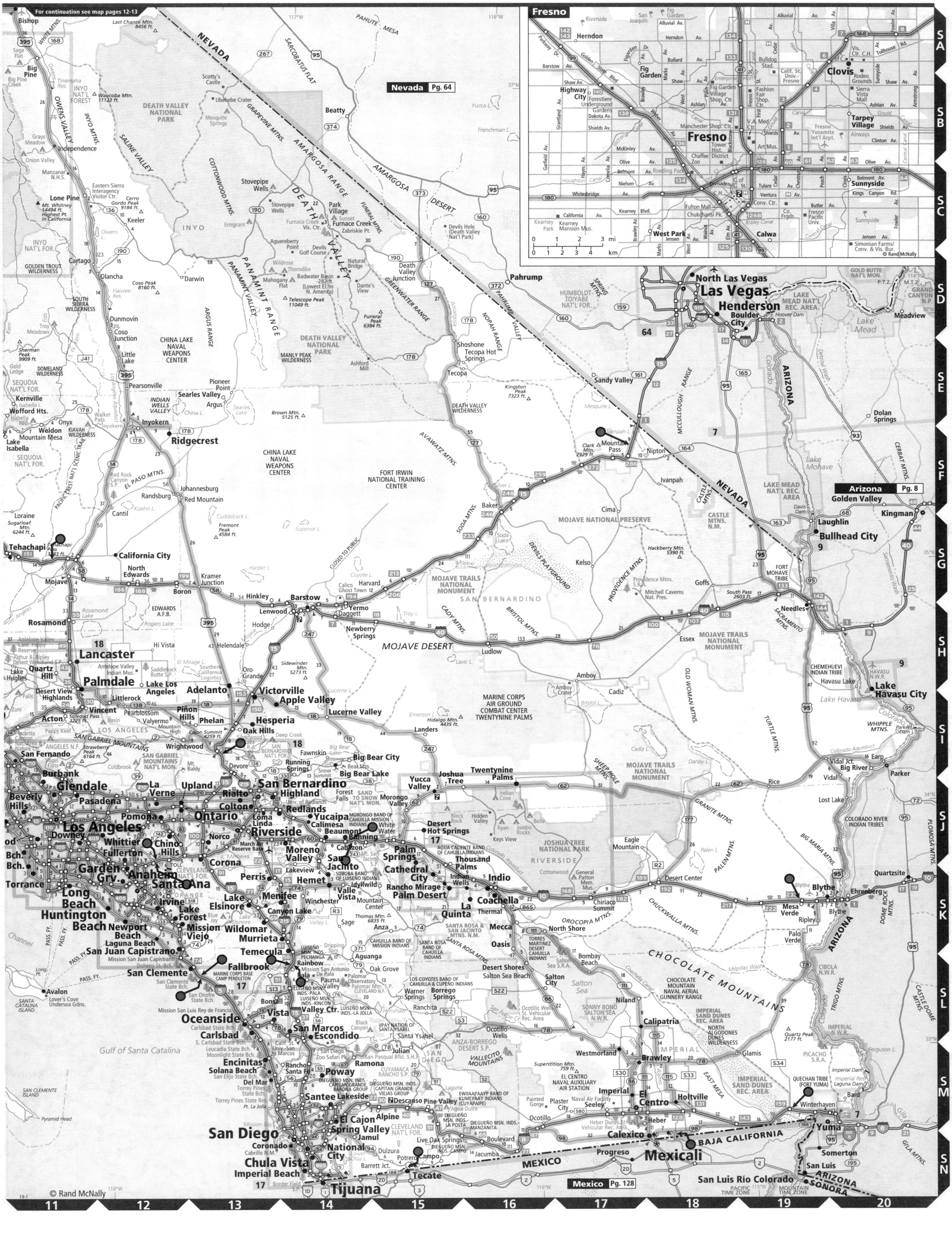

Sights to see

- California State Capitol, Sacramento I-6
- California State Railroad Museum, Sacramento H-6
- Chinatown, San Francisco C-8
- Coit Memorial Tower, San Francisco B-8
- Crocker Art Museum, Sacramento I-5
- Fisherman's Wharf, San Francisco A-7
- Ghirardelli Square, San Francisco B-7
- Golden Gate Bridge, San Francisco A-2
- Monterey Bay Aquarium, Monterey M-1
- Pier 39, San Francisco A-8
- San Francisco Cable Car Museum, San Francisco C-8
- Squaw Valley U.S.A., Olympic Valley F-8

San Francisco Fort Mason Center

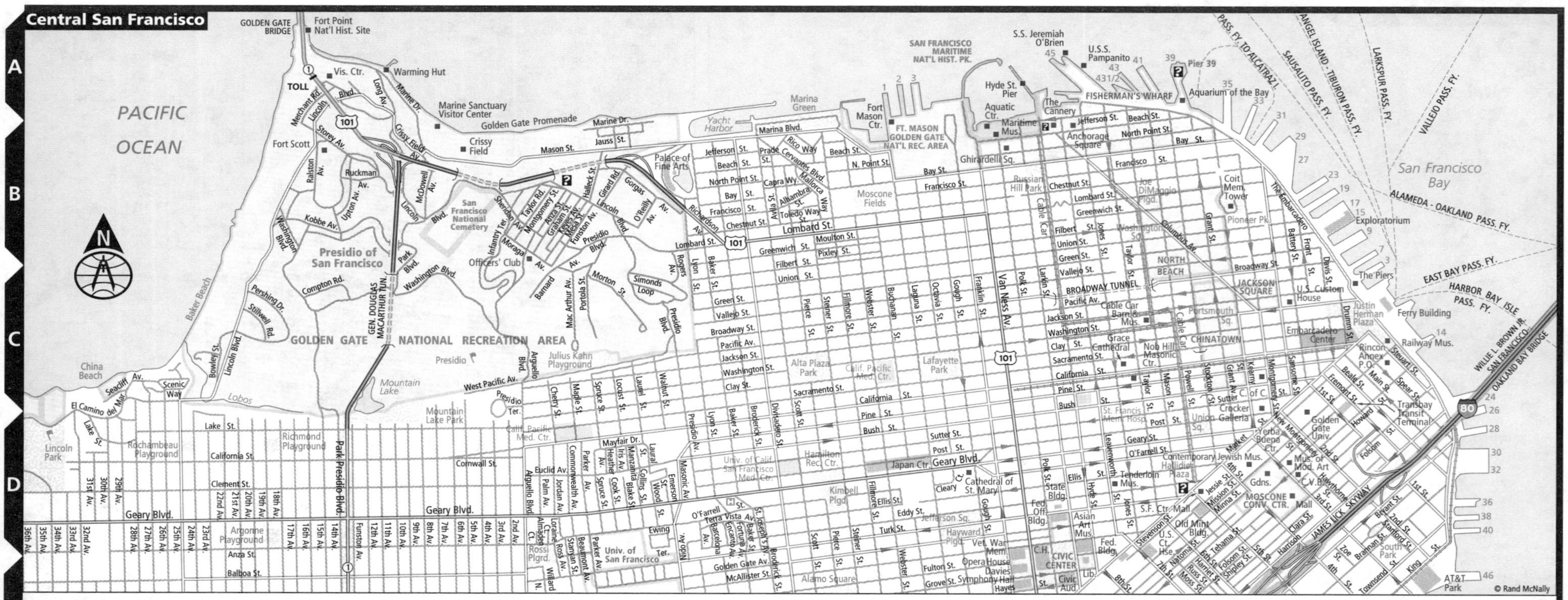

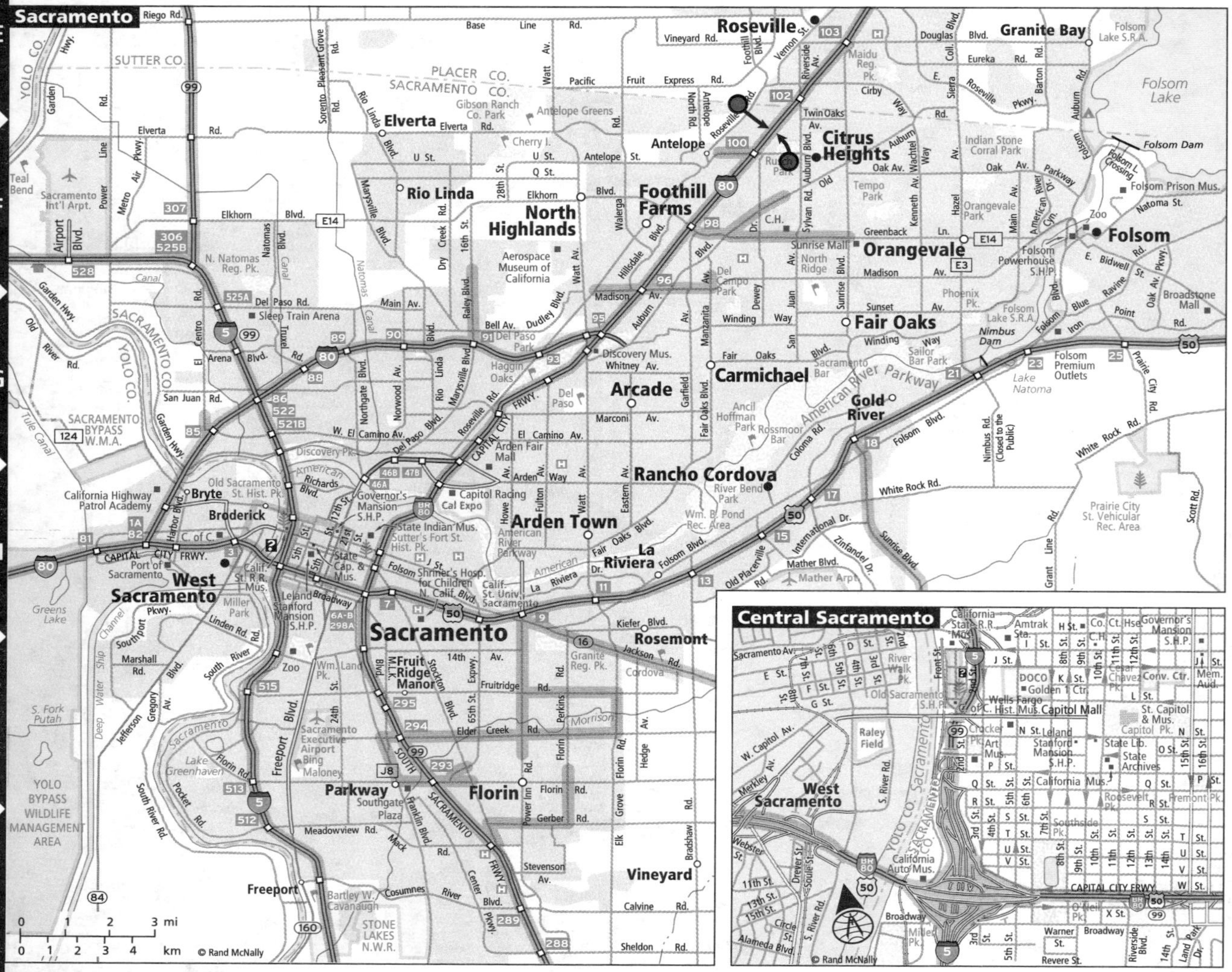

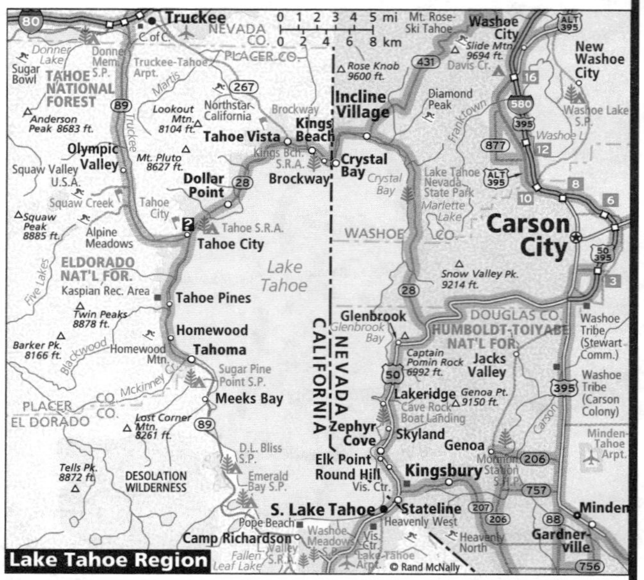

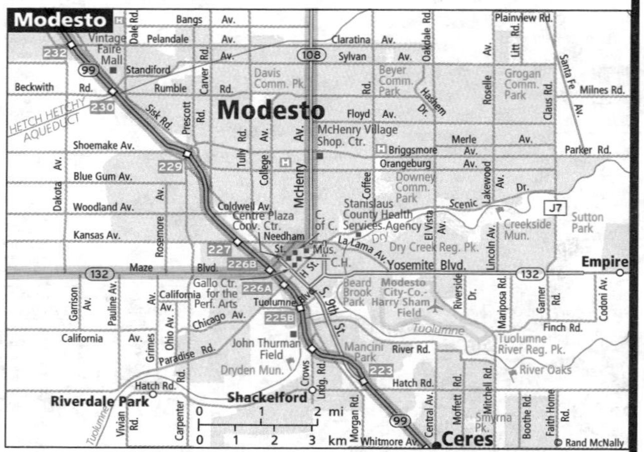

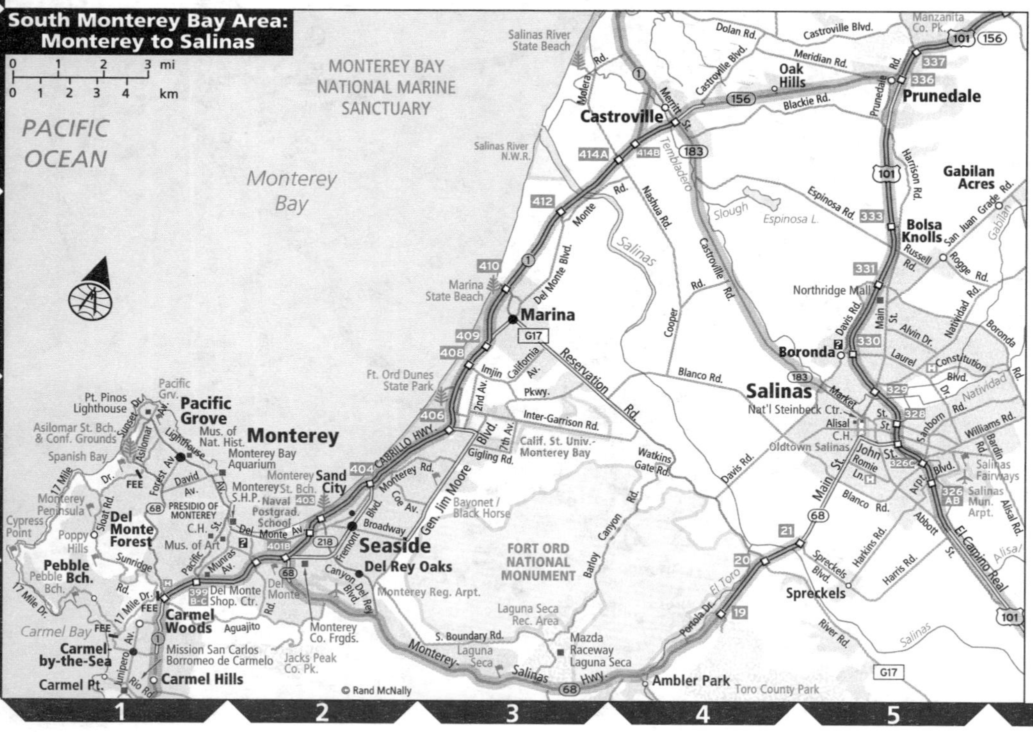

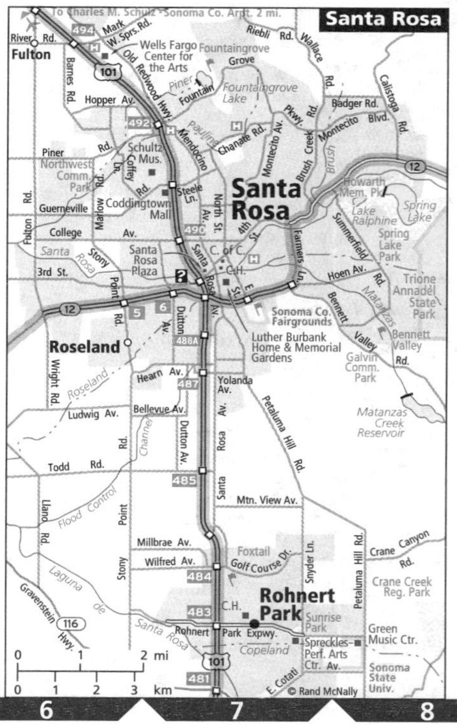

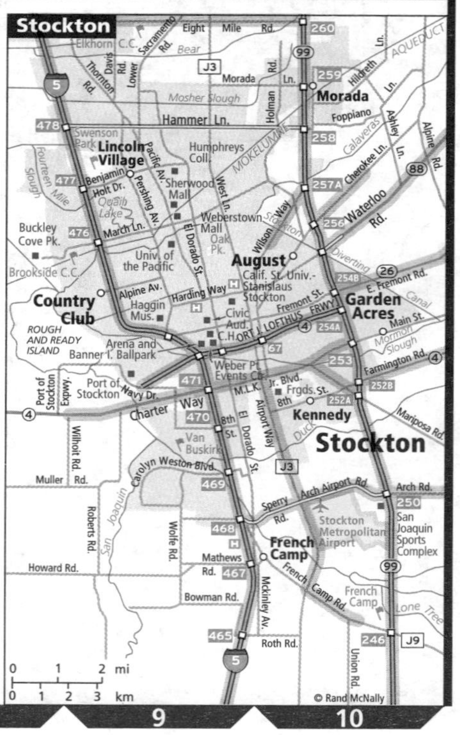

Sights to see

- Balboa Park, San Diego . . . K-10
- Birch Aquarium at Scripps Institute, San Diego . . . G-1
- Cabrillo National Monument, San Diego . . . K-1
- Gaslamp Quarter Historic District, San Diego . . . M-9
- Legoland California, Carlsbad . . . J-8
- The Living Desert Zoo and Gardens, Palm Desert . . . G-10
- Museum of Contemporary Art, San Diego . . . L-8
- Palm Springs Art Museum, Palm Springs . . . E-7
- San Diego Air & Space Museum, San Diego . . . K-9
- San Diego Zoo, San Diego . . . J-3
- SeaWorld, San Diego . . . I-1
- Stearns Wharf, Santa Barbara . . . B-5

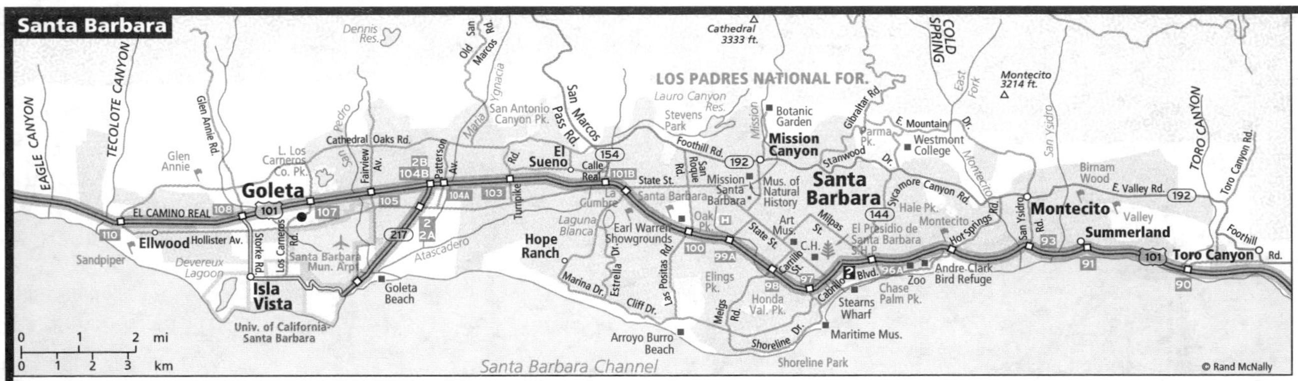

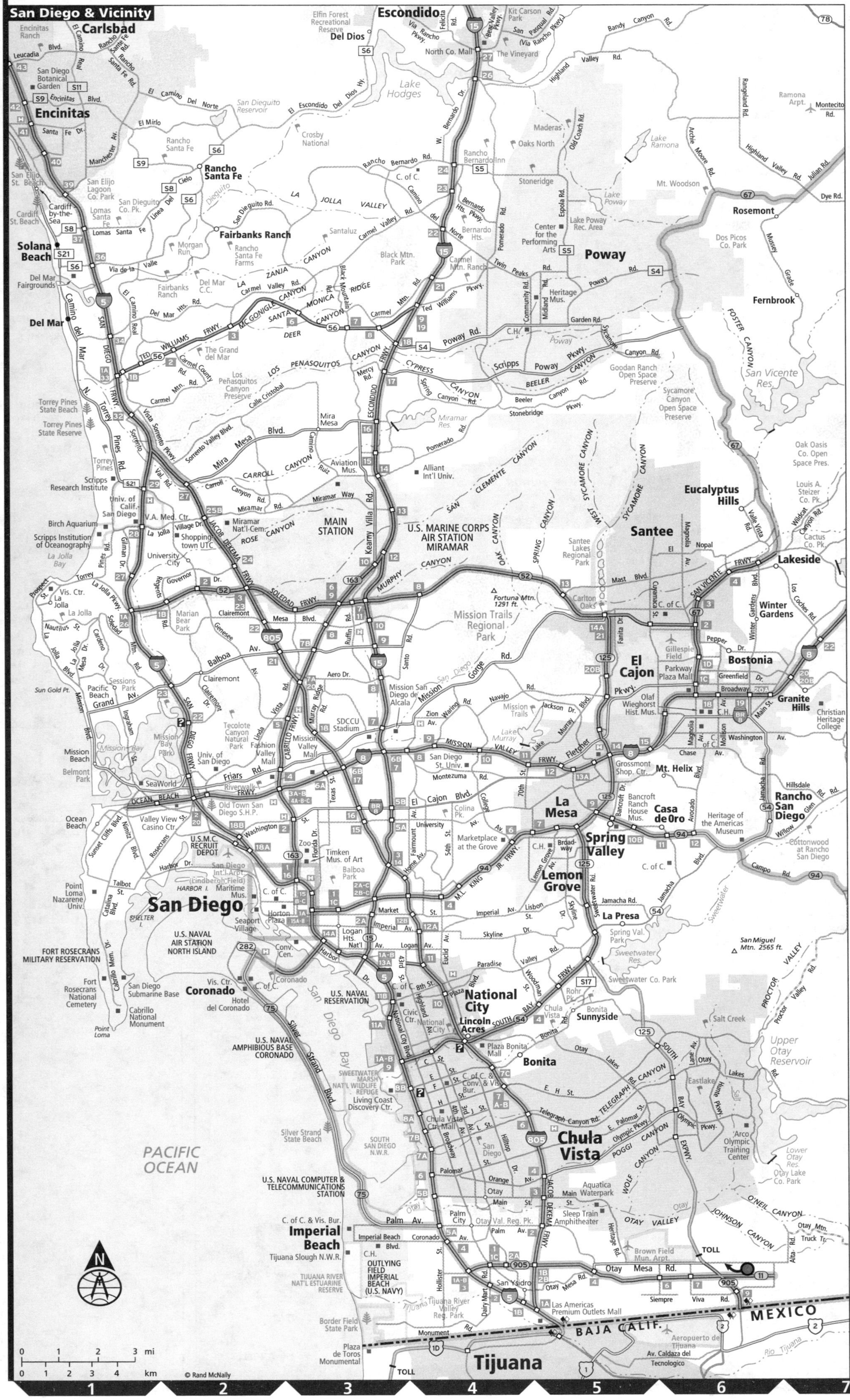

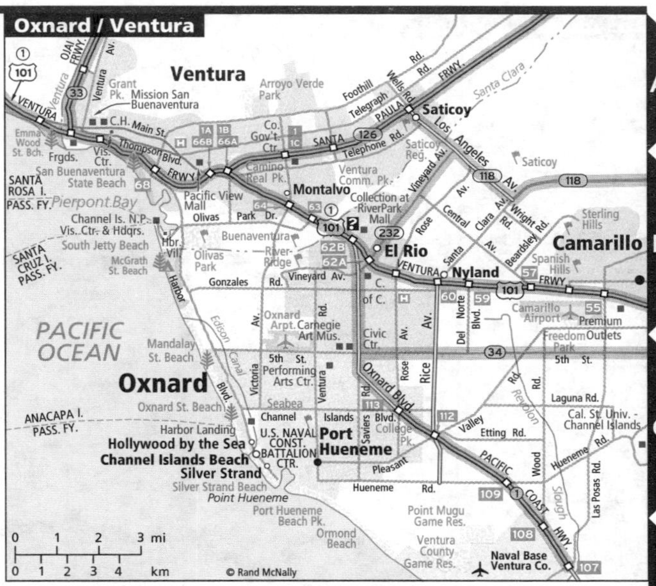

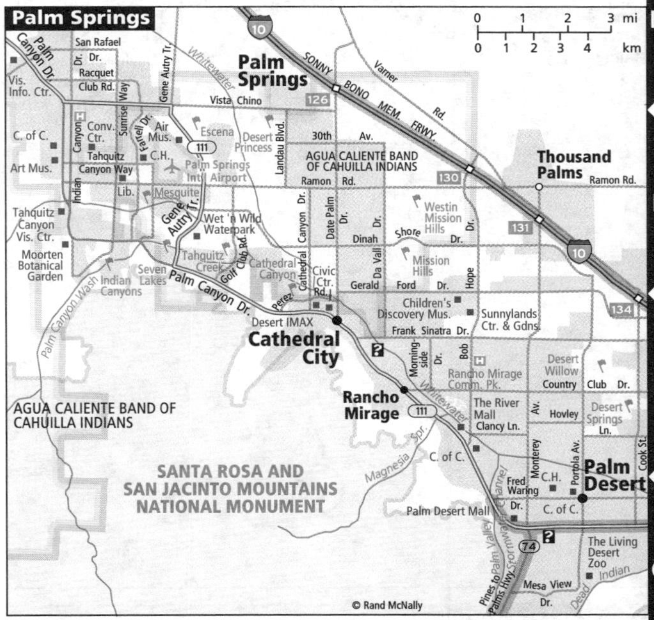

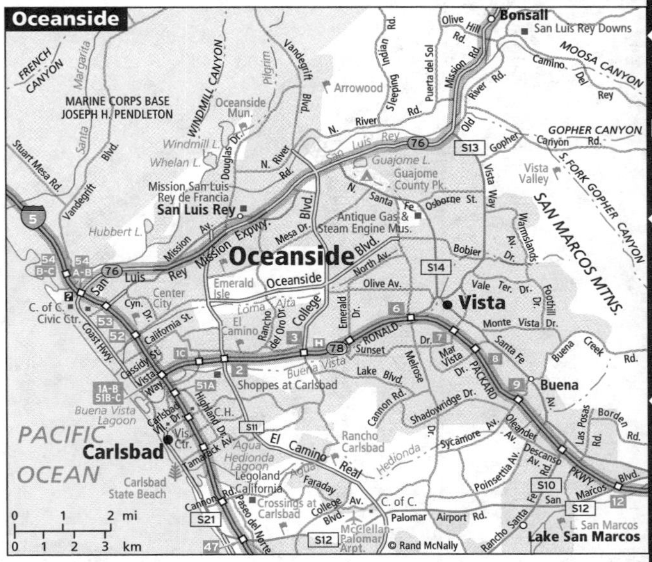

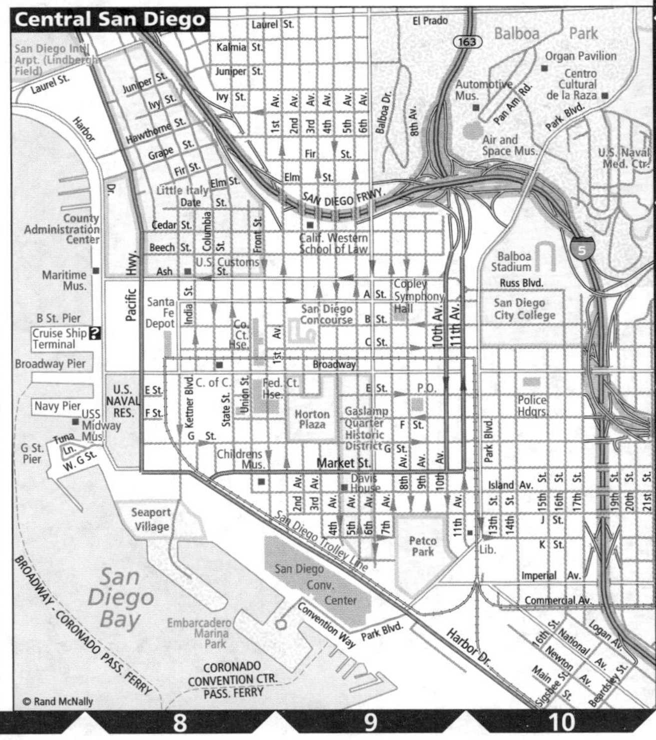

Walt Disney Concert Hall

Sights to see

- Aquarium of the Pacific, Long Beach J-8
- Disneyland, Anaheim I-11
- Dodger Stadium................................... E-7
- El Pueblo de Los Angeles K-2
- Getty Center...................................... E-4
- Hollywood Bowl.................................... D-6
- Huntington Library, San Marino D-8
- Japanese American National Museum K-3
- Knott's Berry Farm, Buena Park H-10
- Los Angeles County Art Museum..................... E-5
- Los Angeles Maritime Museum J-7
- Los Angeles Zoo and Botanical Gardens............. D-6

Huntington Beach Pier, Huntington Beach

Sights to see

- Mission San Juan Capistrano, San Juan Capistrano . . M-14
- Old Pasadena, Pasadena D-8
- Oldest Winery in California, Rancho Cucamonga . . . D-14
- The Queen Mary, Long Beach J-8
- Richard M. Nixon Library & Birthplace, Yorba Linda H-12
- Santa Monica Pier, Santa Monica. F-4
- Universal City D-5
- Venice Boardwalk F-4
- Walt Disney Concert Hall K-1
- Warner Bros. Studio, Burbank D-6
- Will Rogers State Historic Park, Pacific Palisades E-4

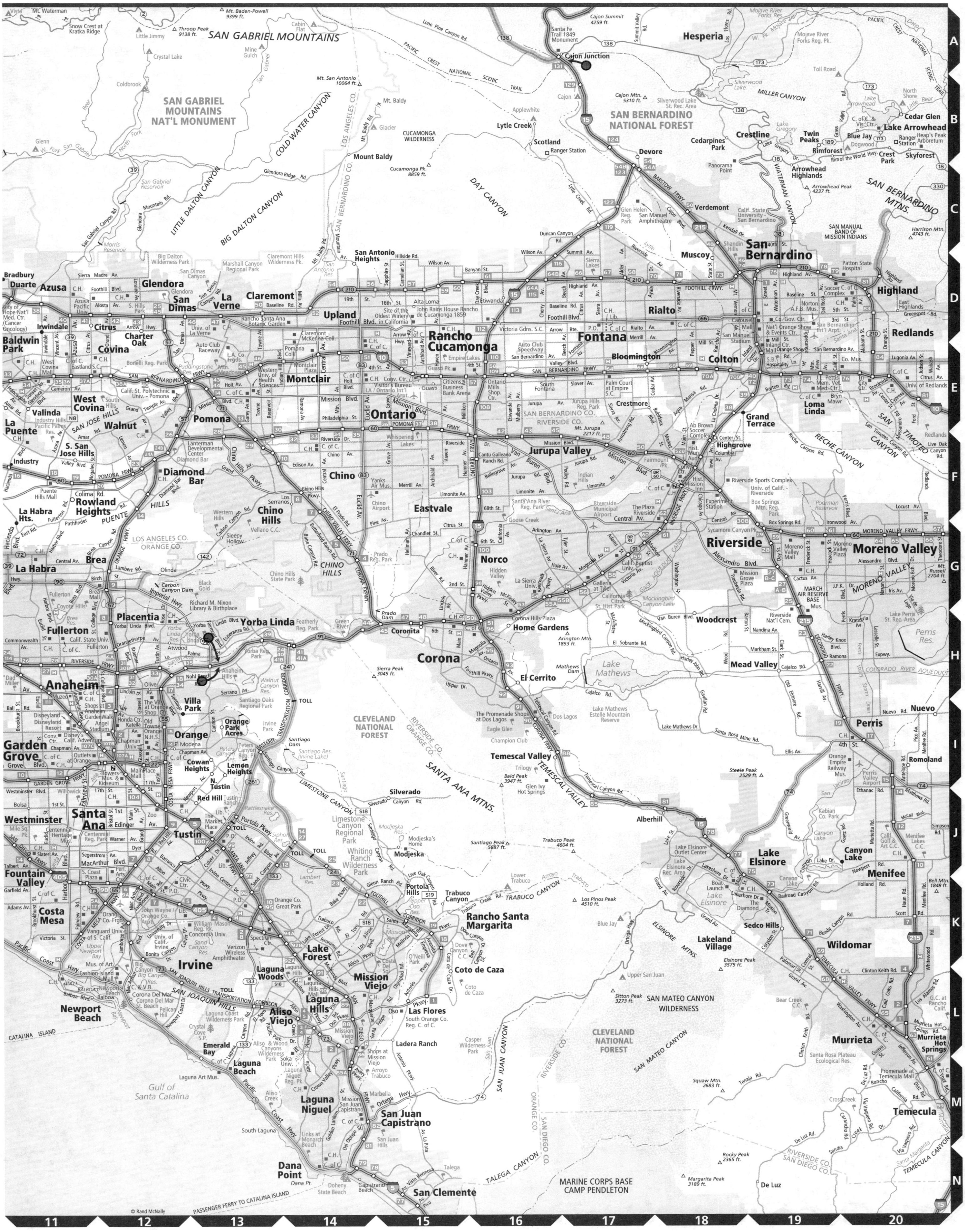

Colorado

Nickname: The Centennial State
Capital: Denver, E-13
Land area: 103,642 sq. mi. (rank: 8th)
Population: 5,029,196 (rank: 22nd)
Largest city: Denver, 600,158, E-13

Index of cities Pg. 129 | Map legend Pg. 1

Route planning & on-the-road resources

Low clearances, weigh stations, & restricted routes: Page A28

Weigh station location

Designated route for vehicles with STAA-authorized dimensions

Road Conditions & Construction
511, (303) 639-1111, (877) 315-7623; www.cotrip.org, www.codot.gov

Toll Road Information
E-470 (Denver metro) ***(ExpressToll)***:
(888) 946-3470, (303) 537-3470; www.expresstoll.com
Northwest Parkway (Denver metro) ***(GoPass)***:
(303) 533-1200; www.northwestparkway.org

Determining Distances
(segments of one mile or less not shown)
Cumulative miles (red): the distance between red arrows
Intermediate miles (black): the distance between intersections & places

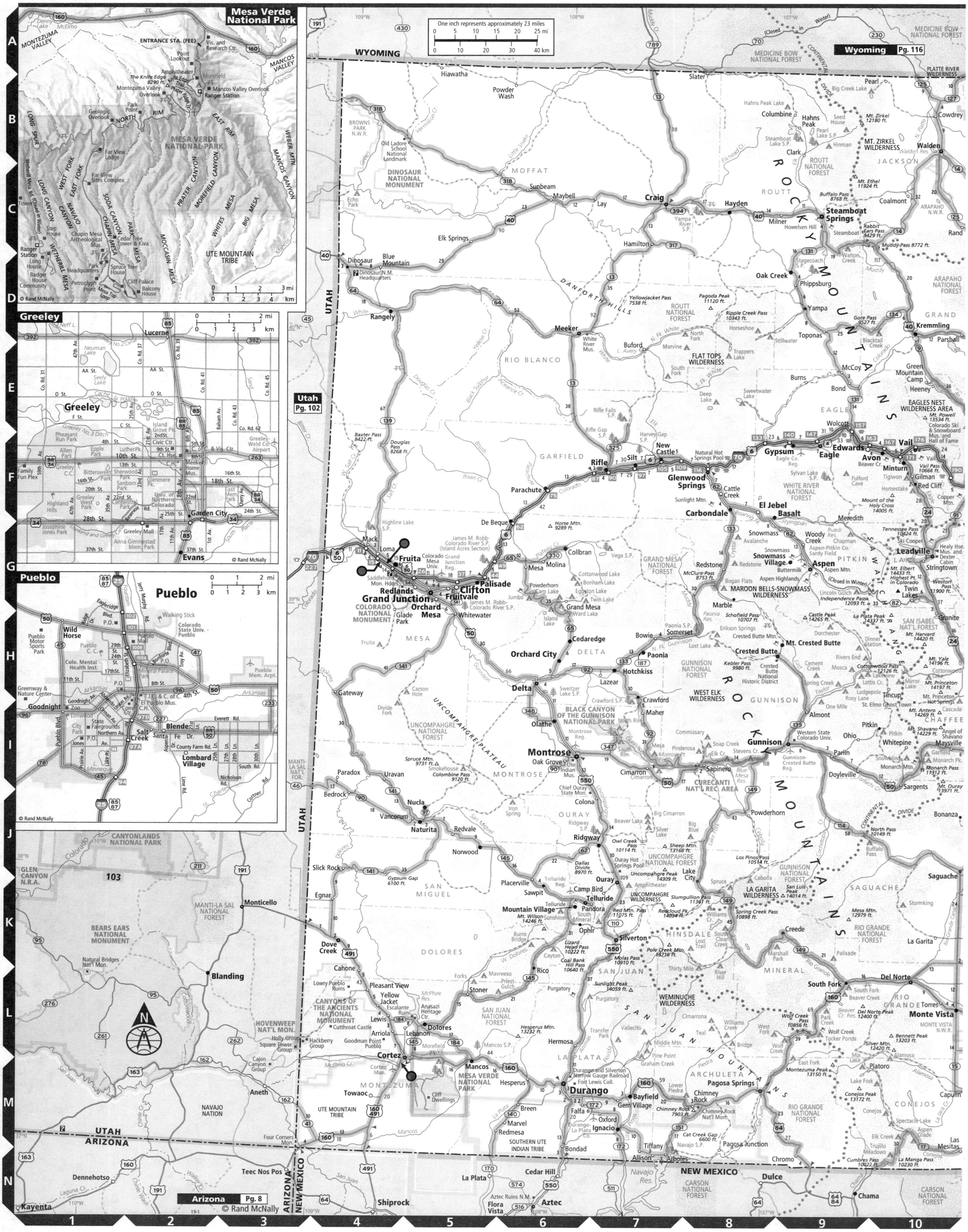

Mileage between cities	Alamosa	Aspen	Boulder	Burlington	Colorado Springs	Craig	Denver	Durango	Estes Park	Fort Collins	Glenwood Springs	Grand Junction	Gunnison	Lamar	Leadville	Pueblo	Sterling	Trinidad
BURLINGTON	311	362	186		154	363	167	460	222	220	321	410	324	108	265	189	142	275
COLORADO SPRINGS	165	265	102	154		265	74	313	139	138	224	313	171	161	127	42	198	128
DENVER	238	196	27	167	74	197		387	64	66	155	244	216	209	99	116	130	202
DURANGO	149	352	416	460	313	376	387		452	452	312	231	224	351	253	271	511	258
FORT COLLINS	303	257	54	220	138	258	66	452	42		216	305	278	262	160	181	102	267
GRAND JCT.	247	130	266	410	313	154	244	231	303	305	89		126	452	176	355	369	441
LEADVILLE	135	128	121	265	127	165	99	253	158	160	87	176	117	307		154	224	212
PUEBLO	122	307	145	189	42	308	116	271	181	181	266	355	159	119	154		240	86

Total mileage through Colorado

- 25: 300 miles
- 70: 451 miles
- 76: 185 miles
- 50: 467 miles

For more than 40,000 interstate mileages, see the Mileage Directory on page 137

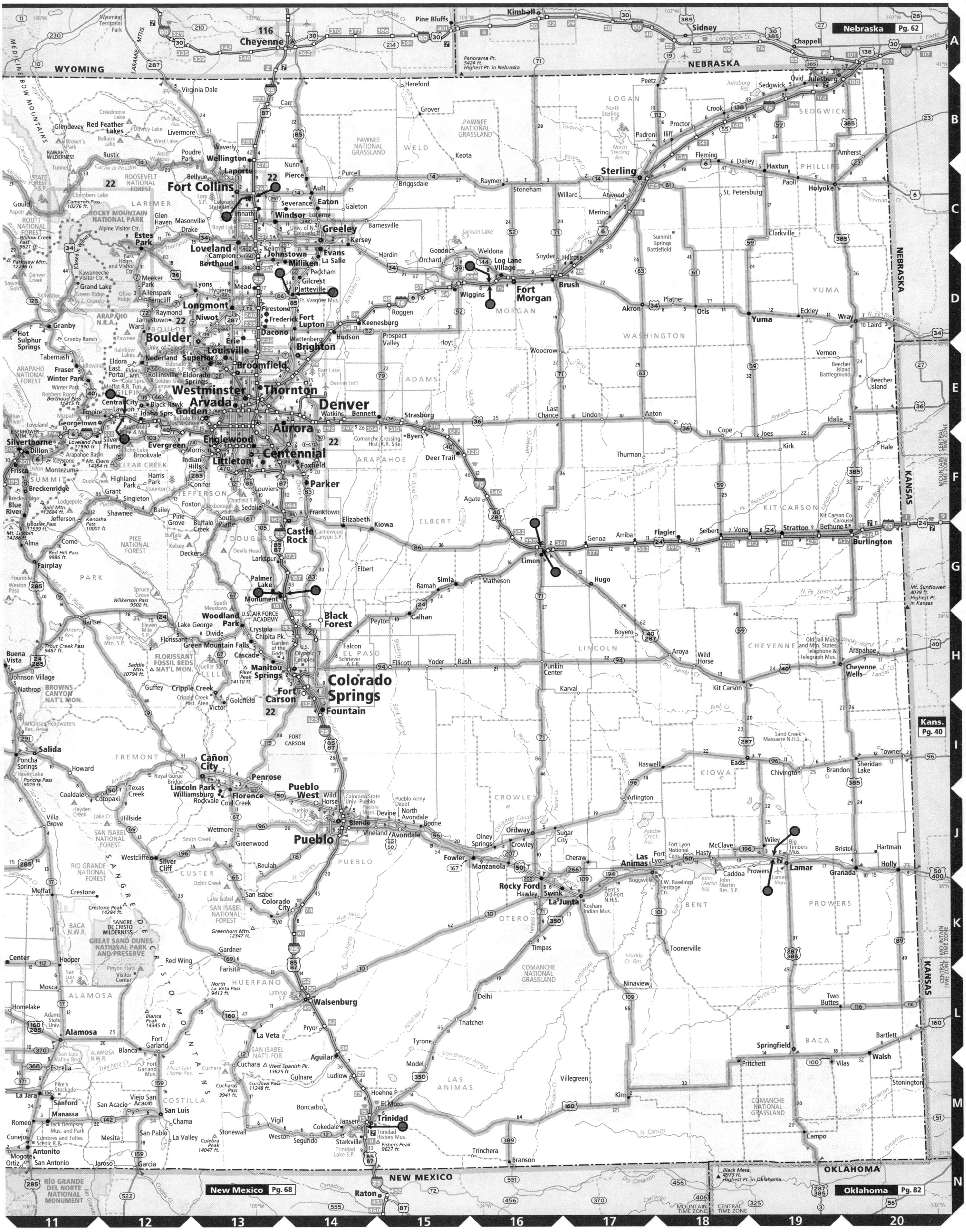

Sights to see

- Black American West Mus. & Heritage Ctr., Denver L-3
- Cave of the Winds, Colorado Springs G-1
- Colorado History Museum, Denver M-2
- Colorado State Capitol, Denver M-2
- Denver Art Museum, Denver M-2
- Denver Museum of Nature & Science, Denver I-7
- Garden of the Gods, Colorado Springs G-1
- National Center for Atmospheric Research, Boulder . . . D-4
- Old Town National Historic District, Fort Collins B-9
- ProRodeo Hall of Fame, Colorado Springs F-2
- United States Mint, Denver M-2
- World Figure Skating Hall of Fame, Colorado Springs . . I-2

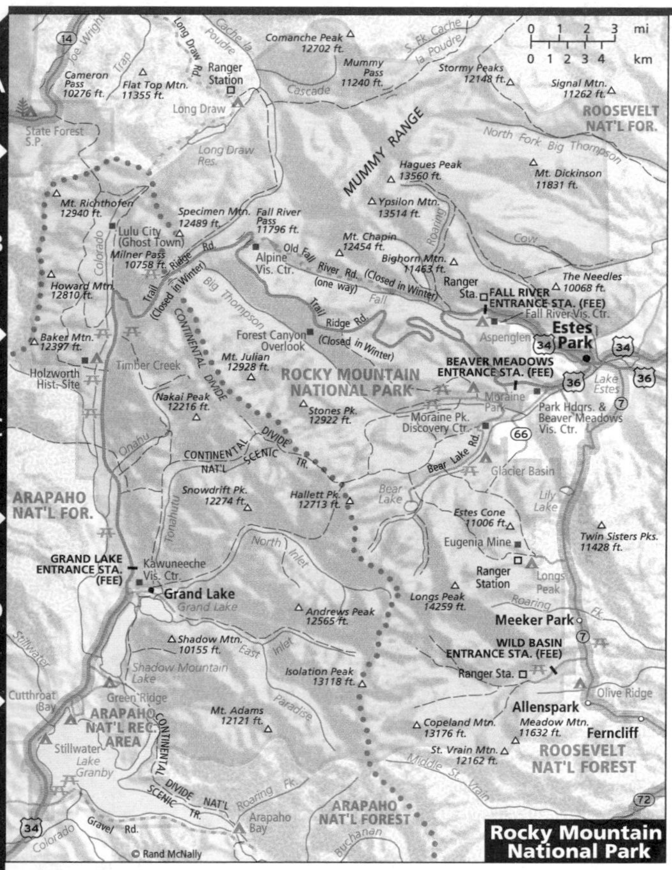

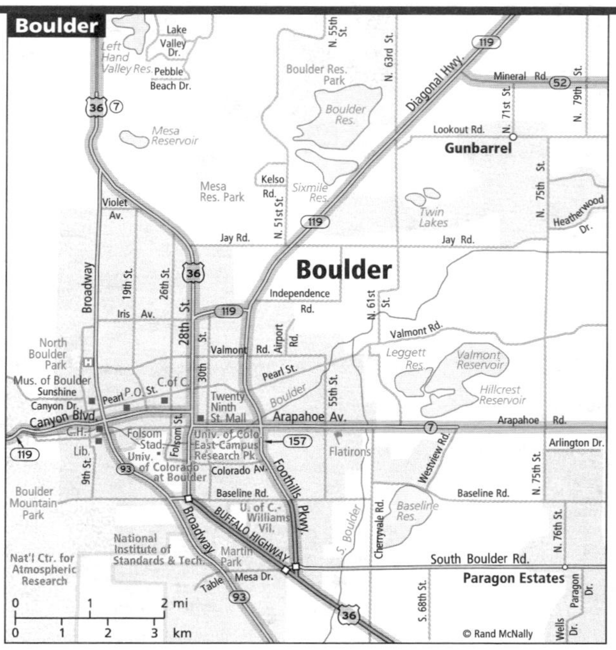

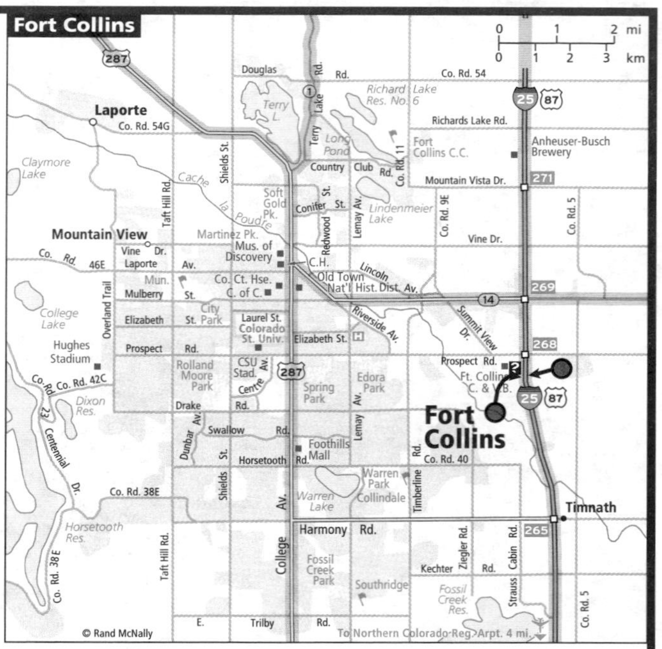

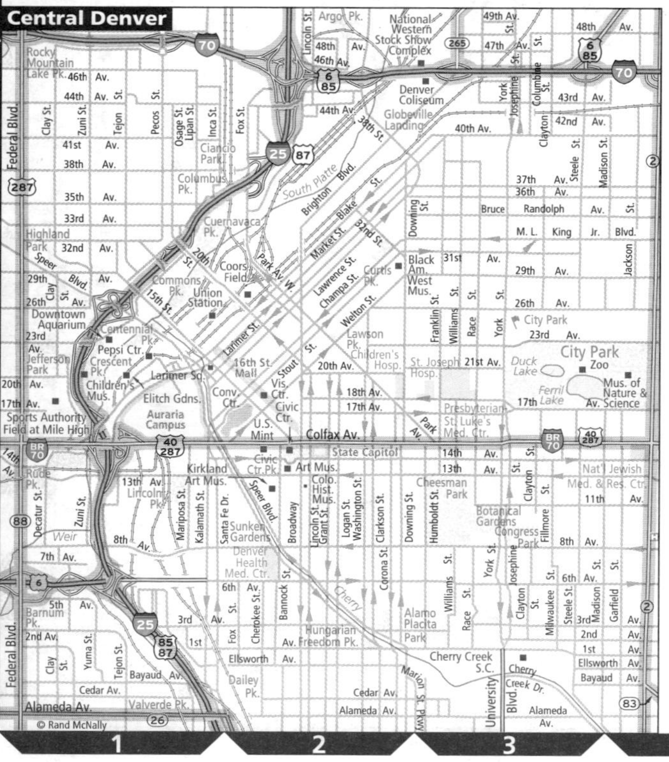

Route planning & on-the-road resources

Low clearances, weigh stations, & restricted routes: **Page A29**

Weigh station location

Designated route for vehicles with STAA-authorized dimensions

Road Conditions & Construction
(860) 594-2000, (860) 594-2650
www.ct.gov/dot, www.i-84waterbury.com
www.cttravelsmart.org

Toll Road Information
No tolls on state or federal highways

Mileage between cities	Bridgeport	Hartford	New Haven	New London	New York, NY	Putnam	Torrington	Waterbury
BRIDGEPORT		57	19	64	55	110	51	30
DANBURY	57	57	64	95	66	104	47	27
HARTFORD	57		29	55	112	47	51	30
NEW HAVEN	19	39		46	73	92	57	37
NEW LONDON	62	55	46		119	55	88	68
PUTNAM	108	47	90	53	163		73	78
TORRINGTON	51	51	57	88	105	73		20
WATERBURY	30	30	37	68	85	78	20	

Mileages © Rand McNally

Total mileage through Connecticut

84: 98 miles
95: 112 miles
91: 58 miles
395: 55 miles

For more than 40,000 interstate mileages, see the Mileage Directory on page 137

Connecticut

Nickname: The Constitution State
Capital: Hartford, C-9
Land area: 4,842 sq. mi. (rank: 48th)
Population: 3,574,097 (rank: 29th)
Largest city: Bridgeport, 144,229, H-5

Index of cities Pg. 129
Map legend Pg. 1

Delaware/Florida cities

Nickname: The First State
Capital: Dover, G-2
Land area: 1,949 sq. mi. (rank: 49th)
Population: 897,934 (rank: 45th)
Largest city: Wilmington, 70,851, C-2

Index of cities Pg. 129 | Map legend Pg. 1

Mileage between cities	Dover	Georgetown	Lewes	Milford	Newark	Salisbury, MD	Selbyville	Wilmington
DOVER		64	69	50	48	56	84	49
GEORGETOWN	64		16	17	85	27	20	86
LEWES	69	16		22	90	43	31	90
MILFORD	50	17	22		70	106	36	71
NEWARK	48	85	90	70		105	104	16
SALISBURY, MD	56	27	43	106	105		25	106
SELBYVILLE	84	20	31	36	104	25		105
WILMINGTON	49	86	90	71	16	106	105	

Total mileage through Delaware
95 23 miles
1 104 miles
13 108 miles

For more than 40,000 interstate mileages, see the Mileage Directory on page 137

Route planning & on-the-road resources

Low clearances, weigh stations, & restricted routes: Page A29

Weigh station location
Designated route for vehicles with STAA-authorized dimensions

Road Conditions & Construction
(800) 652-5600, (302) 760-2080; www.deldot.gov

Toll Road Information *(all use E-ZPass)*
Delaware Dept. of Transportation: (888) 397-2773, (302) 678-7000; www.ezpassde.com
Del. River & Bay Authority (Del. Mem. Br. & Lewes/ Cape May Ferry): (302) 571-6300; www.drba.net

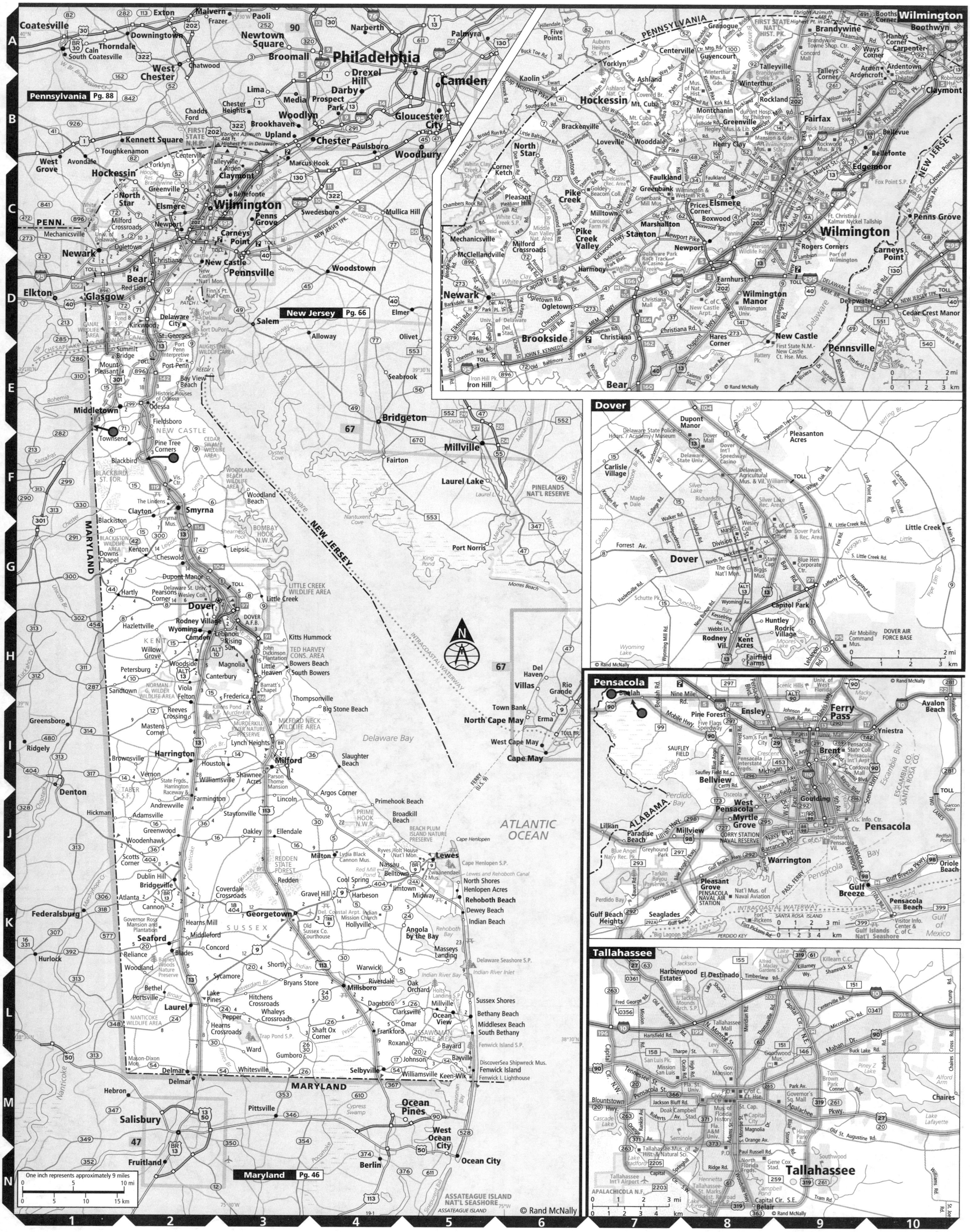

The beach at St. Petersburg/Clearwater

Sights to see

- Art Deco National Historic District, Miami Beach. L-9
- Busch Gardens, Tampa B-4
- Hugh Taylor Birch State Park, Fort Lauderdale. H-9
- Marie Selby Botanical Gardens, Sarasota H-3
- Miami Seaquarium, Miami M-9
- Norton Museum of Art, Palm Beach B-10
- Ringling Center for the Cultural Arts, Sarasota G-3
- Salvador Dali Museum, St. Petersburg. D-2
- St. Petersburg Museum of History, St. Petersburg D-2
- Thomas A. Edison & Henry Ford Winter Estates, Fort Myers M-2
- Vizcaya Museum and Gardens, Miami. M-8

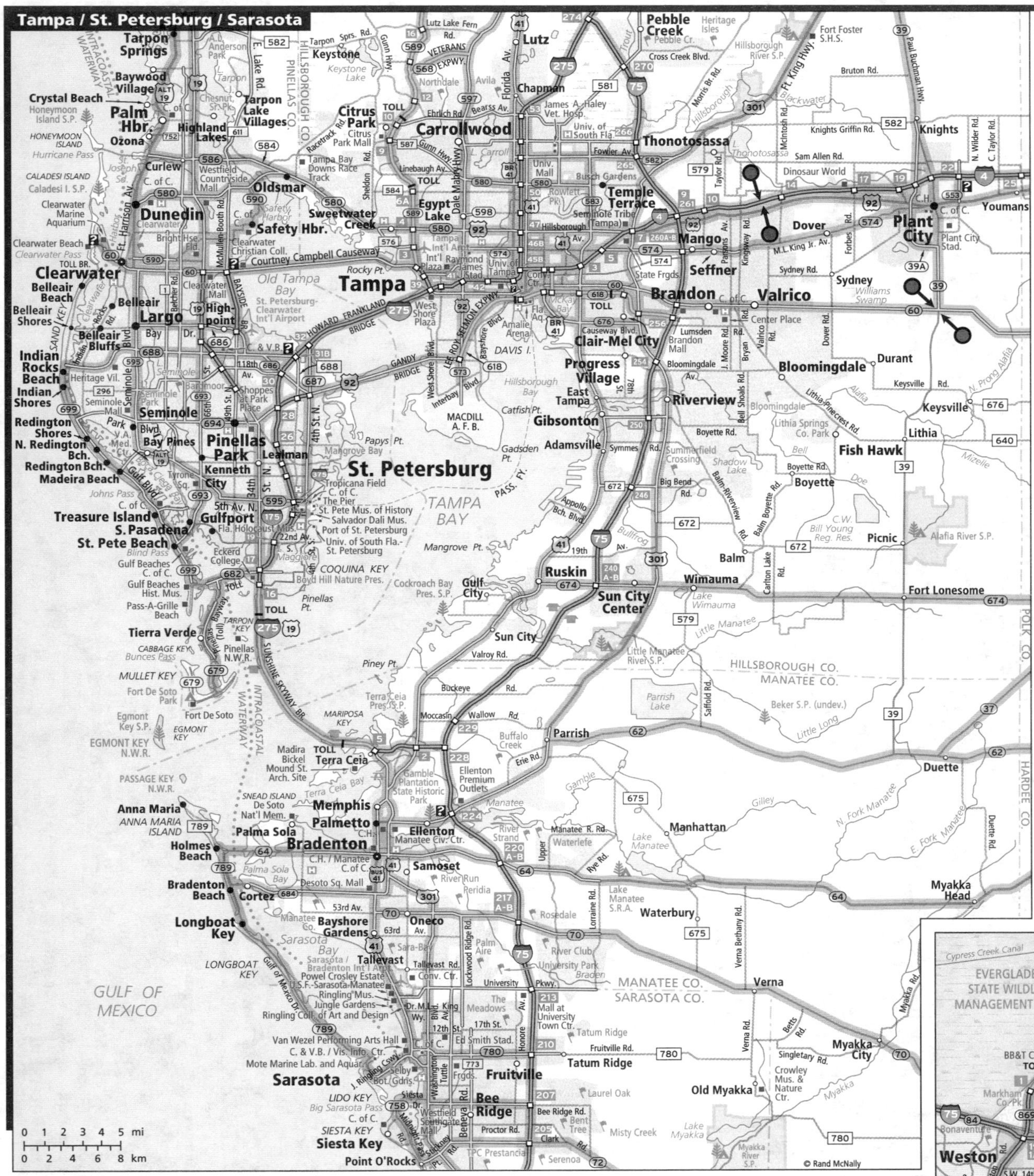

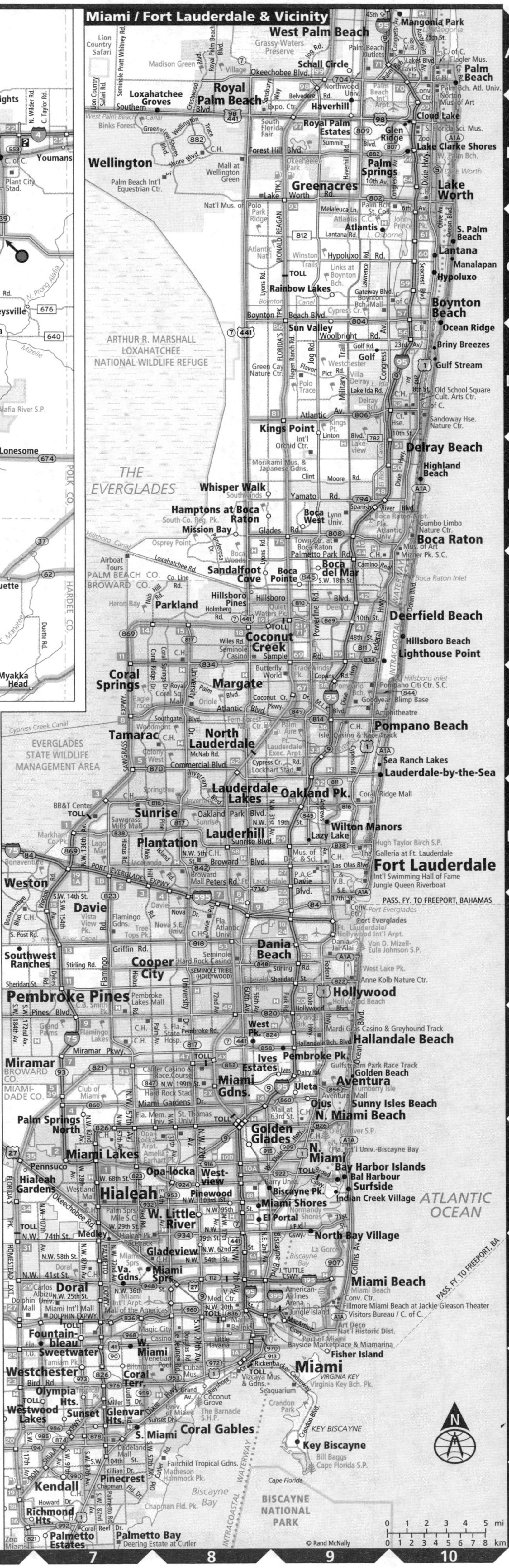

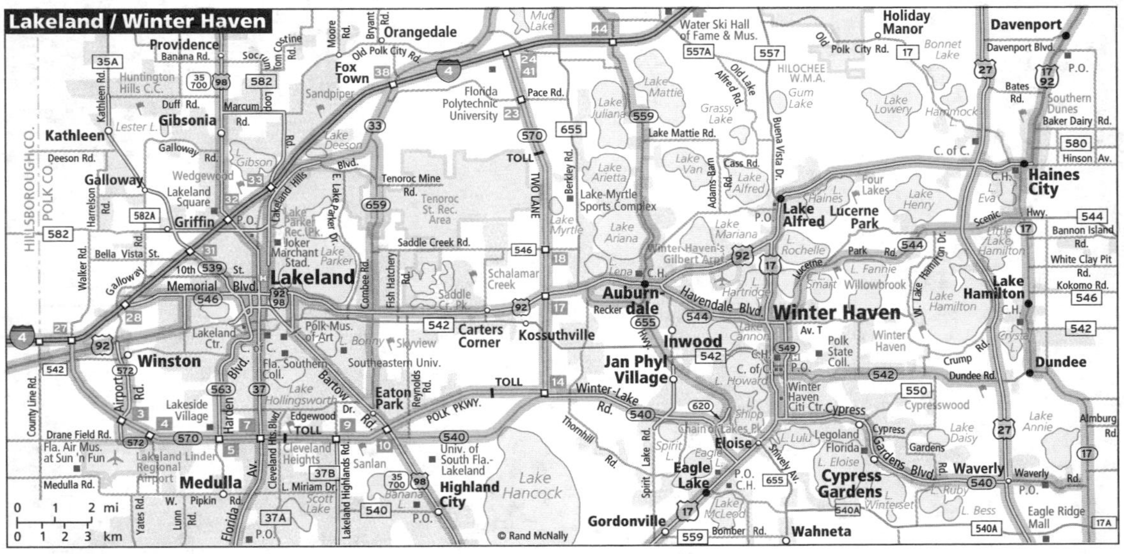

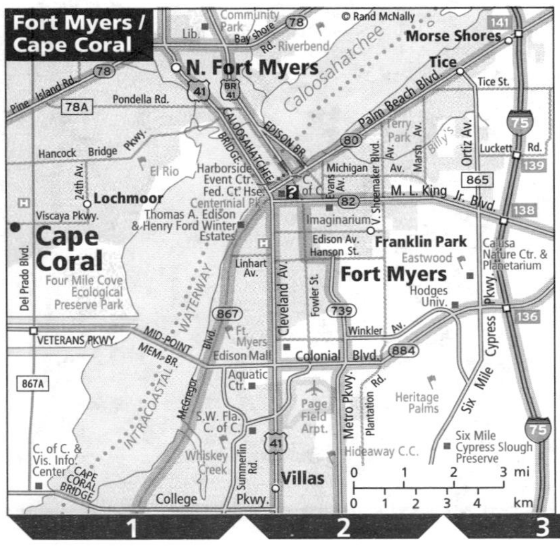

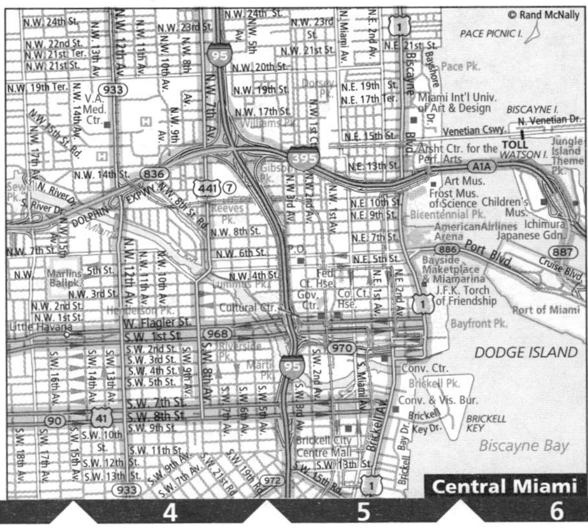

Nickname: The Sunshine State
Capital: Tallahassee, B-2
Land area: 53,625 sq. mi. (rank: 26th)
Population: 18,801,310 (rank: 4th)
Largest city: Jacksonville, 821,784, C-9

Index of cities Pg. 129 | Map legend Pg. 1

Route planning & on-the-road resources

Low clearances, weigh stations, & restricted routes: Page A30

Weigh station location

Designated route for vehicles with STAA-authorized dimensions

Road Conditions & Construction
511
www.fl511.com
www.fdot.gov

Toll Road Information *(all use SunPass unless otherwise noted)*
Florida's Turnpike Enterprise: (800) 749-7453; floridasturnpike.com
Central Florida Expressway Authority (Greater Orlando) *(also E-Pass)*: (407) 823-7277, (407) 823-7277; www.cfxway.com
Miami-Dade Expwy. Auth.: (855) 277-0848, (305) 637-3277; www.mdxway.com
Osceola Co. Expressway Auth. *(E-Pass only)*: (407) 742-0552; www.osceolaxway.com
Tampa-Hillsborough Co. Expwy. Auth.: (813) 272-6740; www.tampa-xway.com

Toll Bridge Info. *(all use SunPass)*
Escambia Co. (Bob Sikes Br.): (850) 916-5421 myescambia.com/pensacola-beach
Santa Rosa Bay Br. Auth.: (800) 749-7453 www.garconpointbridge.com
Town of Bay Hbr. Islands (Broad Causeway): www.bayharborislands-fl.gov

Mileage between cities	Atlanta, GA	Daytona Beach	Fort Lauderdale	Fort Myers	Fort Pierce	Gainesville	Jacksonville	Key West	Lakeland	Melbourne	Miami	Orlando	Panama City	Pensacola	St. Augustine	St. Petersburg	Sarasota	Tallahassee	Tampa	Titusville	West Palm Beach
FORT MYERS	579	225	139		127	254	312	275	114	173	152	171	497	591	274	117	80	397	130	211	124
JACKSONVILLE	346	92	328	312	230	72		512	196	179	351	141	264	358	38	222	253	164	199	136	286
MIAMI	661	264	26	152	123	336	351	164	223	178		234	579	673	313	262	225	479	255	221	68
ORLANDO	440	54	213	171	125	114	141	396	55	73	234		357	451	103	107	132	257	84	43	171
PENSACOLA	324	447	652	591	561	342	358	821	461	512	673	451	102		395	458	521	196	467	492	610
TALLAHASSEE	272	253	458	397	368	148	164	627	267	319	479	257	96	196	201	257	328		273	298	417
TAMPA	456	138	242	130	154	130	199	403	34	128	255	84	373	467	187	23	60	273		124	203
WEST PALM BEACH	599	199	45	124	58	273	286	231	171	112	68	171	516	610	248	227	192	417	203	155	

Total mileage through Florida

4: 132 miles	75: 471 miles
10: 362 miles	95: 382 miles

For more than 40,000 interstate mileages, see the Mileage Directory on page 137

Georgia

Nickname: The Peach State
Capital: Atlanta, E-4
Land area: 57,513 sq. mi. (rank: 21st)
Population: 9,687,653 (rank: 9th)
Largest city: Atlanta, 420,003, E-4

Index of cities Pg. 130 | Map legend Pg. 1

Route planning & on-the-road resources

Low clearances, weigh stations, & restricted routes: Page A30

Weigh station location

Designated route for vehicles with STAA-authorized dimensions

Road Conditions & Construction
511, (877) 694-2511, (404) 635-8000; www.511ga.org

Toll Road Information
No tolls on state or federal highways

Determining Distances
(segments of one mile or less not shown)
Cumulative miles (red): the distance between red arrows
Intermediate miles (black): the distance between intersections & places

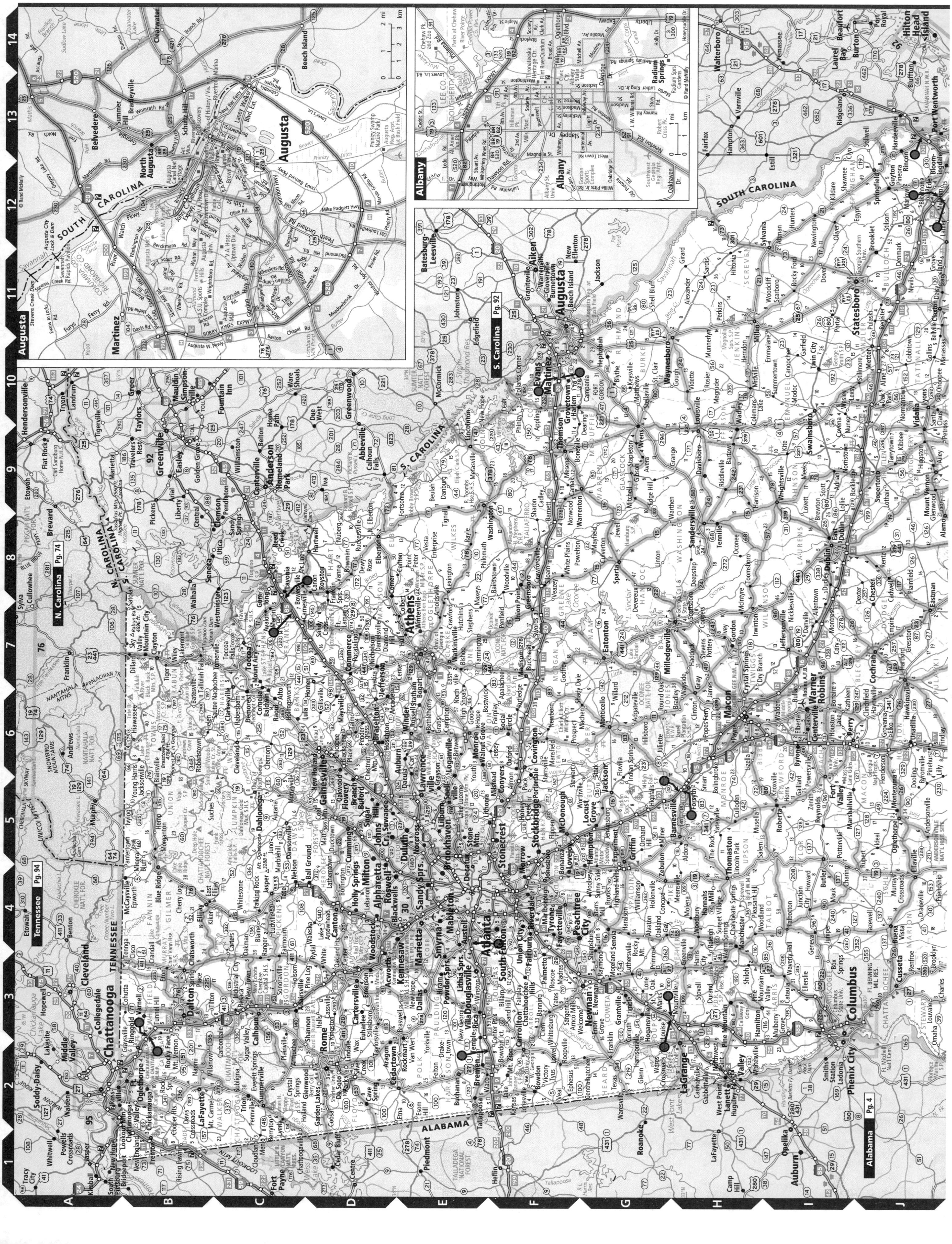

Mileage between cities	Albany	Americus	Athens	Atlanta	Augusta	Bainbridge	Brunswick	Chattanooga, TN	Columbus	Gainesville	Greenville, SC	Jacksonville, FL	La Grange	Macon	Rome	Savannah	Toccoa	Valdosta	Vidalia	Warner Robins	Waycross
ATLANTA	166	131	69		149	234	307	117	107	55	146	346	67	82	74	247	97	228	172	100	241
AUGUSTA	226	193	100	149		272	201	270	251	141	117	262	211	135	227	142	134	234	112	153	186
CHATTANOOGA, TN	288	253	172	117	270	347	428		220	158	249	468	180	204	74	369	200	350	294	222	363
COLUMBUS	87	64	171	107	251	130	258	220		165	256	284	47	98	152	263	207	167	188	108	200
JACKSONVILLE, FL	198	237	310	346	262	205	69	468	284	396	388		328	270	425	138	375	123	169	260	78
MACON	116	76	91	82	135	163	225	204	98	132	193	270	112		161	165	174	152	90	18	159
SAVANNAH	239	206	235	247	142	251	77	369	263	297	262	138	277	165	326		255	167	96	161	105
VALDOSTA	80	119	243	228	234	84	120	350	167	278	370	123	210	152	307	167	321		122	142	62

Total mileage through Georgia

- I-20: 203 miles
- I-85: 180 miles
- I-75: 355 miles
- I-95: 112 miles

For more than 40,000 interstate mileages, see the Mileage Directory on page 137

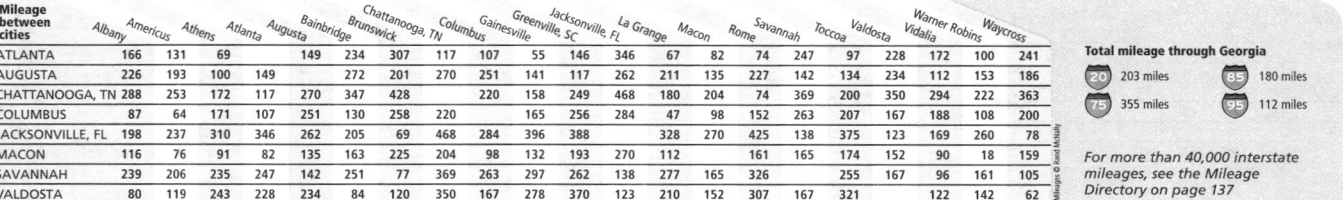

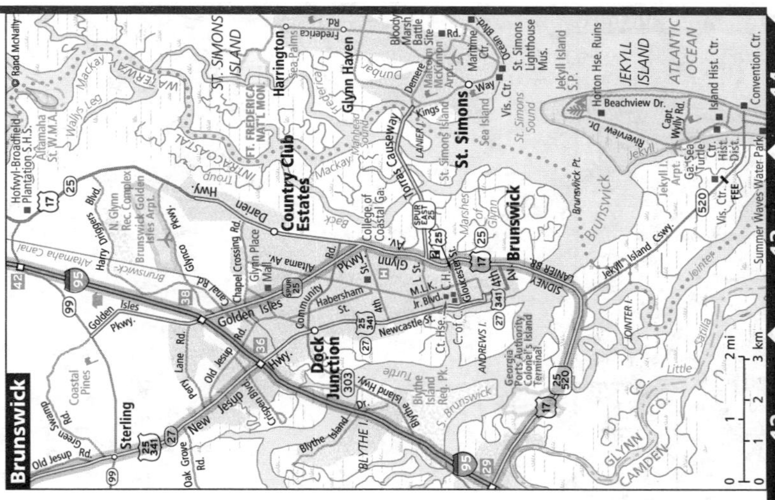

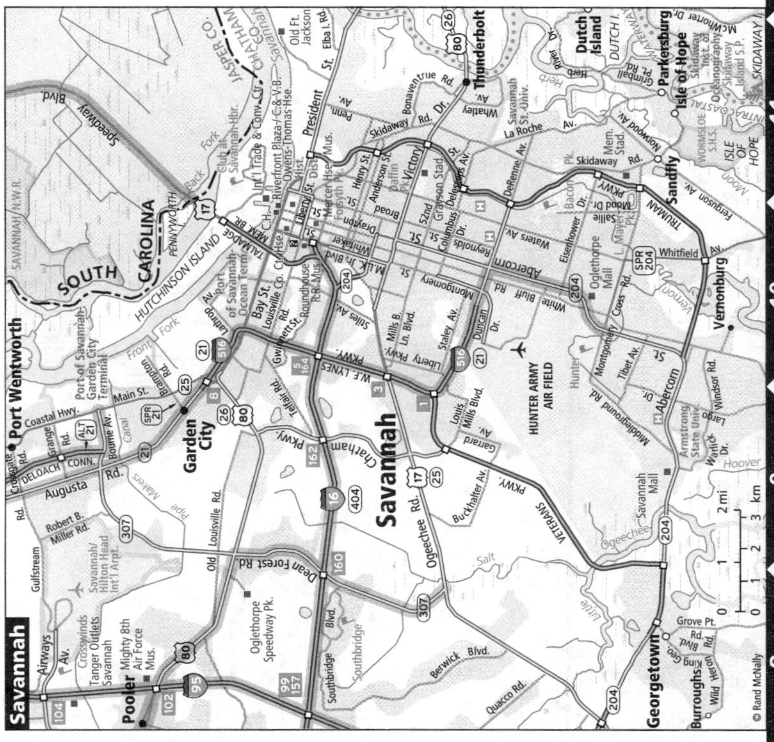

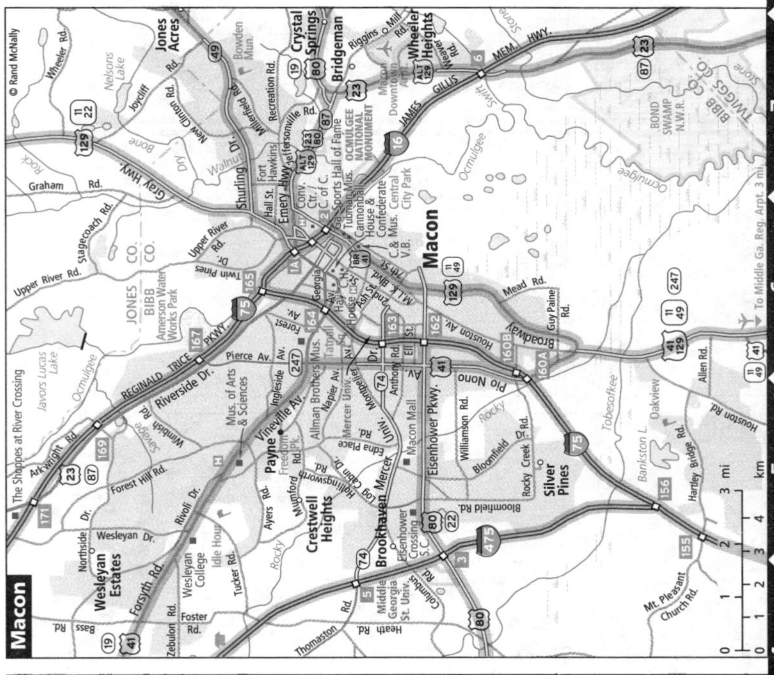

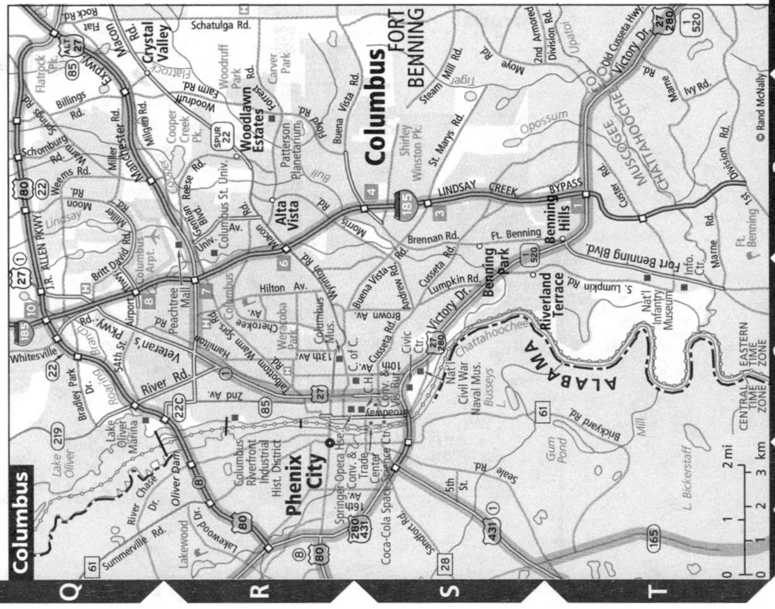

Nickname: The Aloha State
Capital: Honolulu, N-4
Land area: 6,423 sq. mi. (rank: 47th)
Population: 1,360,301 (rank: 40th)
Largest city: Honolulu, 337,256, N-4

Index of cities Pg. 130 | Map legend Pg. 1

Mileage between cities	Hilo	Honolulu	Kahului	Kailua	Kailua Kona	Kapa'a	Lahaina	Maunaloa	Wahiawā
HILO		225*	127*	86*	237	337*	149*	179*	236*
HONOLULU	225*		108*	177	11*	116*	130*	70*	20
KAHULUI	127*	108*		93*	119*	214*	22	57*	119*
KAILUA	86*	177	93*		188*	283*	116*	146*	188
KAILUA KONA	237	11*	119*	188*		128*	142*	81*	26*
KAPA'A	337*	116*	214*	283*	128*		236*	176*	128*
LAHAINA	149*	130*	22	116*	142*	236*		79*	141*
WAHIAWĀ	236*	20	119*	188	26*	128*	141*	81*	

*Via Air

Mileages © Rand McNally

Total mileage through Hawaii

H1 27 miles · H3 15 miles · H2 8 miles

For more than 40,000 interstate mileages, see the Mileage Directory on page 137

Route planning & on-the-road resources

Low clearances, weigh stations, & restricted routes: **Page A30**

Weigh station location

Designated route for vehicles with STAA-authorized dimensions

Road Conditions & Construction
(808) 587-2220; hidot.hawaii.gov

Toll Road Information
No tolls on state or federal highways

Route planning & on-the-road resources

Low clearances, weigh stations, & restricted routes: Page A30

- Weigh station location
- Designated route for vehicles with STAA-authorized dimensions

Road Conditions & Construction
511, (888) 432-7623
www.511.idaho.gov, www.itd.idaho.gov

Toll Road Information
No tolls on state or federal highways

Mileage between cities	Boise	Coeur d'Alene	Lewiston	Missoula, MT	Mountain Home	Pocatello	Salmon	Twin Falls
BOISE		455	357	484	45	236	343	130
COEUR D'ALENE	455		115	166	498	527	305	583
LEWISTON	357	115		280	399	590	419	484
MISSOULA, MT	484	166	280		440	361	141	477
MOUNTAIN HOME	45	498	399	440		191	299	86
POCATELLO	236	527	590	361	191		209	119
SALMON	343	305	419	141	299	209		261
TWIN FALLS	130	583	484	477	86	119	261	

Mileages © Rand McNally

Total mileage through Idaho

- 15: 196 miles
- 86: 63 miles
- 84: 276 miles
- 90: 74 miles

For more than 40,000 interstate mileages, see the Mileage Directory on page 137

Idaho

Nickname: The Gem State
Capital: Boise, K-2
Land area: 82,643 sq. mi. (rank: 11th)
Population: 1,567,582 (rank: 39th)
Largest city: Boise, 205,671, K-2

Index of cities Pg. 130
Map legend Pg. 1

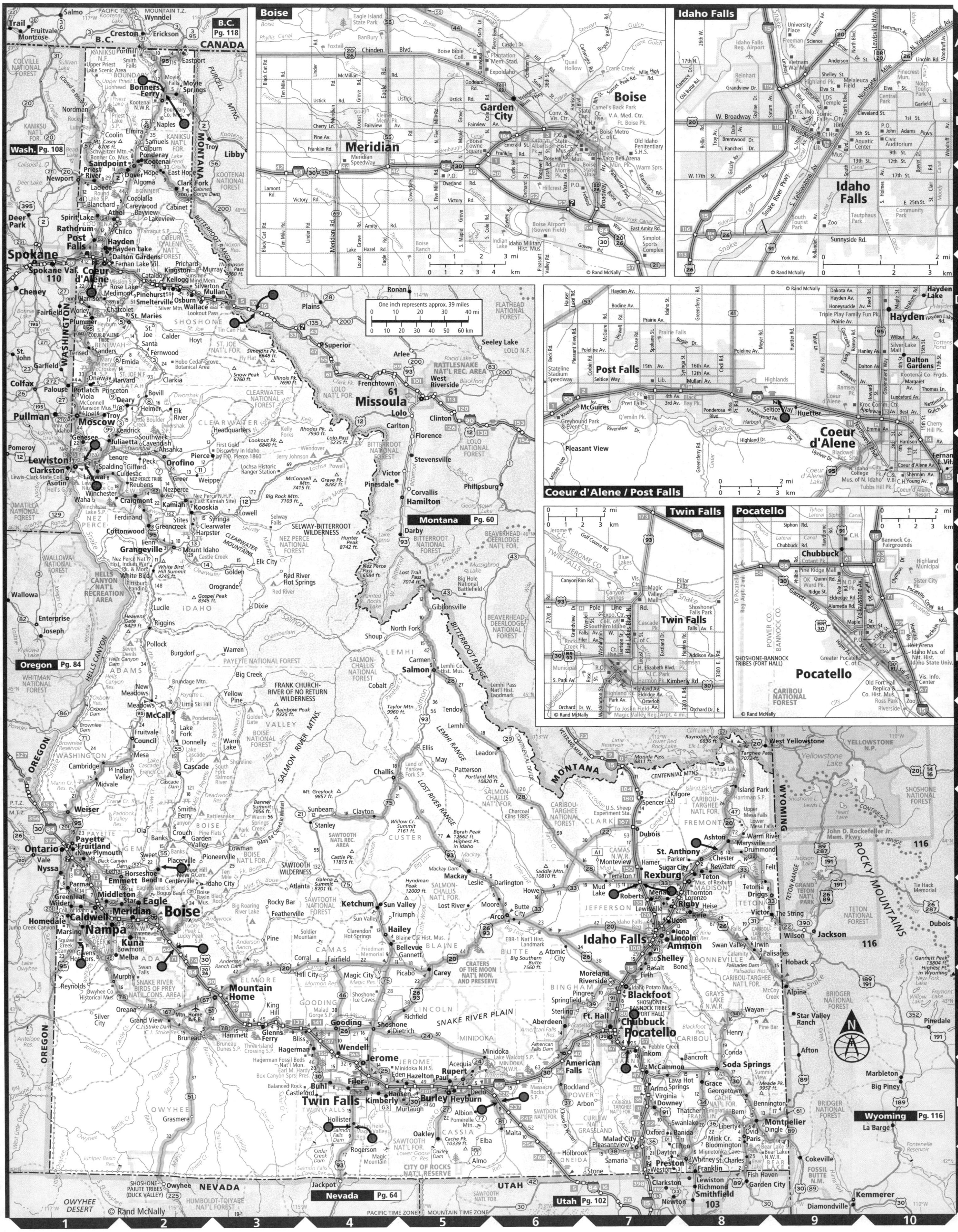

Illinois

Nickname: Land of Lincoln
Capital: Springfield, J-8
Land area: 55,519 sq. mi. (rank: 24th)
Population: 12,830,632 (rank: 5th)
Largest city: Chicago, 2,695,598, C-13

Index of cities Pg. 130 | Map legend Pg. 1

Route planning & on-the-road resources

Low clearances, weigh stations, & restricted routes: Page A31

Weigh station location

Designated route for vehicles with STAA-authorized dimensions

Road Conditions & Construction
(800) 452-4368; www.gettingaroundillinois.com, www.dot.il.gov

Toll Road/Bridge Information
Illinois Tollway (*I-Pass*): (800) 824-7277; www.illinoistollway.com
Skyway Concession Co. (Chicago Skyway) (*I-Pass*): (312) 552-7100; www.chicagoskyway.org

Determining Distances
(segments of one mile or less not shown)
Cumulative miles (red): the distance between red arrows
Intermediate miles (black): the distance between intersections & places

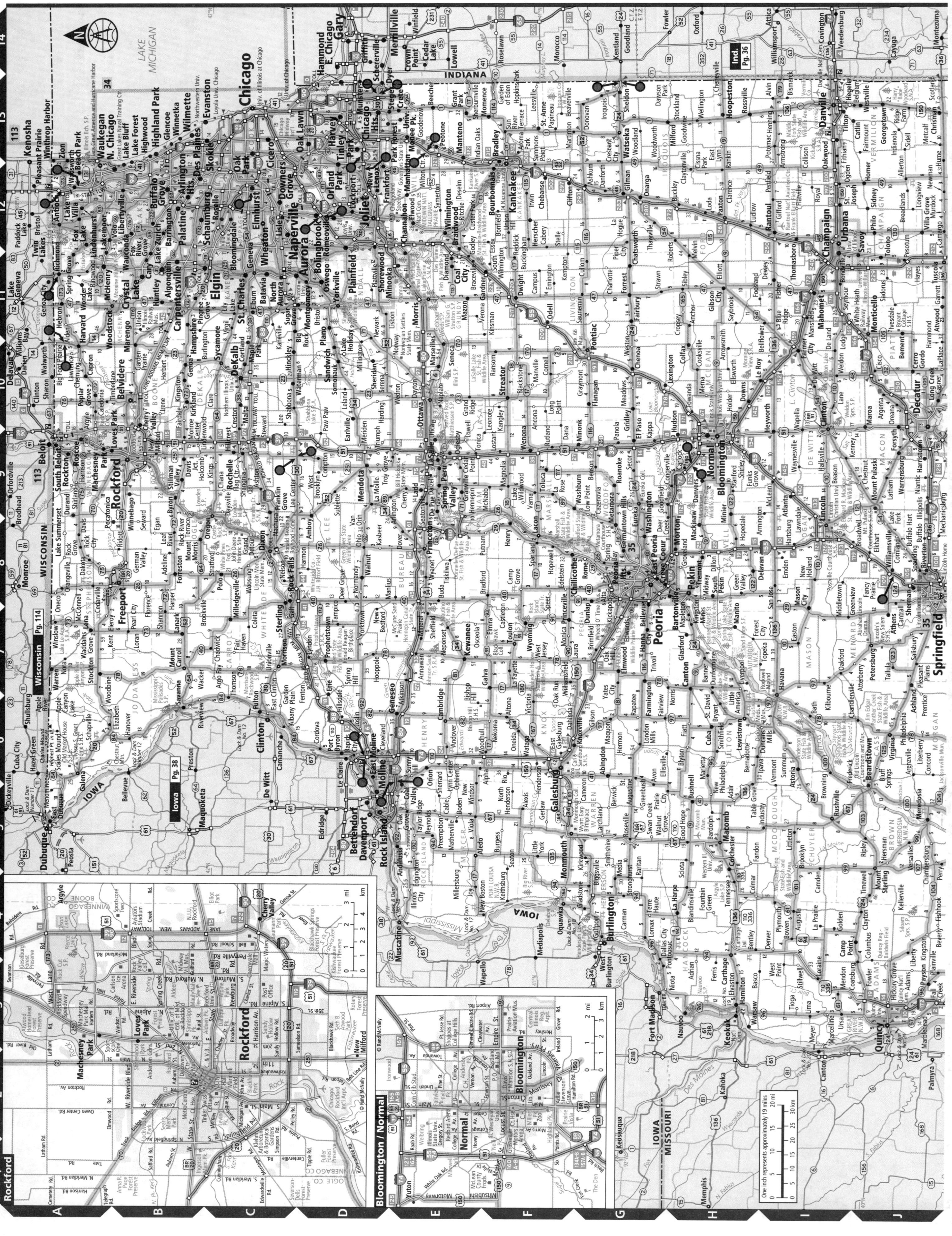

Mileage between cities	Bloomington	Cairo	Carbondale	Champaign	Chicago	De Kalb	Decatur	Dubuque, IA	Effingham	Elgin	Galesburg	Kankakee	Lawrenceville	Moline	Mt. Vernon	Peoria	Quincy	Rockford	St. Louis, MO	Springfield	Waukegan
CARBONDALE	249	54		196	332	365	184	406	124	368	293	275	146	335	57	240	240	380	104	174	374
CHAMPAIGN	54	237	196		137	170	60	256	76	173	143	80	126	185	143	90	197	185	175	88	180
CHICAGO	137	373	332	137		59	189	182	212	46	197	60	248	175	278	154	309	94	296	200	38
MOLINE	132	402	335	185	175	114	175	75	257	162	50	166	307		308	95	148	130	261	165	199
PEORIA	39	309	240	90	154	129	82	167	165	159	53	108	214	95	215		130	144	168	71	184
ROCKFORD	136	422	380	185	94	44	190	92	261	53	154	145	311	130	328	144	270		296	199	77
ST. LOUIS, MO	164	169	104	175	296	279	135	335	103	302	221	254	145	261	79	168	139	296		102	326
SPRINGFIELD	67	243	174	88	200	183	38	238	91	205	124	160	158	165	149	71	112	199	102		229

Total mileage through Illinois

- I-55: 313 miles
- I-80: 164 miles
- I-70: 156 miles
- I-90: 124 miles

For more than 40,000 interstate mileages, see the Mileage Directory on page 137

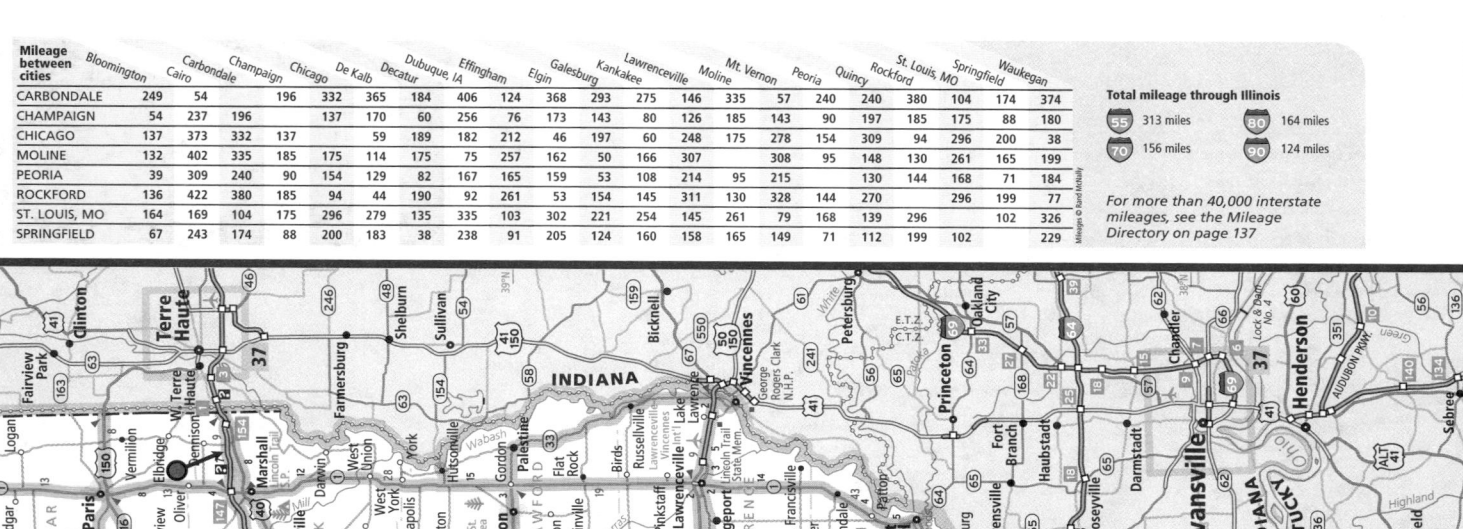

Sights to see

- Adler Planetarium G-15
- Art Institute of Chicago.............................. E-13
- Chicago Botanic Garden, Glencoe D-8
- Field Museum.. G-14
- Frank Lloyd Wright Home & Studio, Oak Park........H-8
- John G. Shedd Aquarium G-14
- Lincoln Park Zoo H-9
- Millennium Park.................................E-13
- Museum of Science & Industry J-10
- Navy Pier.. D-14
- Willis Tower E-12
- Wrigley Field G-9

Chicago Cultural Center

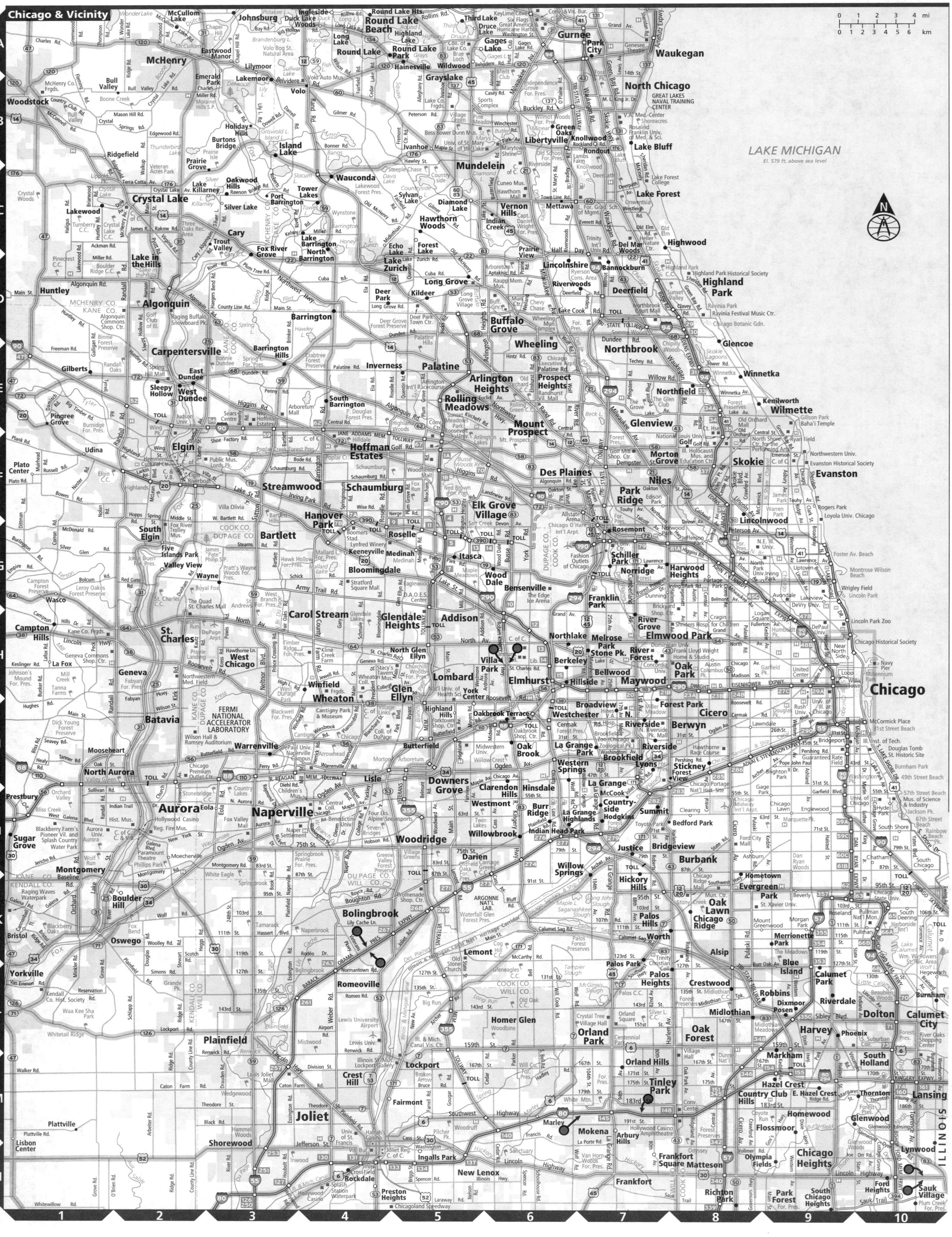

Children's Museum of Indianapolis

Sights to see

- Abraham Lincoln Presidential Library & Museum, Springfield.................................. M-16
- Buckingham Fountain, Chicago................... F-13
- Children's Museum of Indianapolis, Indianapolis.... D-18
- Fort Wayne Children's Zoo, Fort Wayne........... L-19
- Illinois State Capitol Complex, Springfield......... M-16
- Indiana State Capitol, Indianapolis.............. H-19
- Indiana State Museum, Indianapolis.............. H-19
- Indianapolis Motor Speedway and Hall of Fame Museum, Indianapolis.................................. D-16
- NCAA Hall of Champions, Indianapolis........... H-18
- President Benjamin Harrison Home, Indianapolis.... F-20

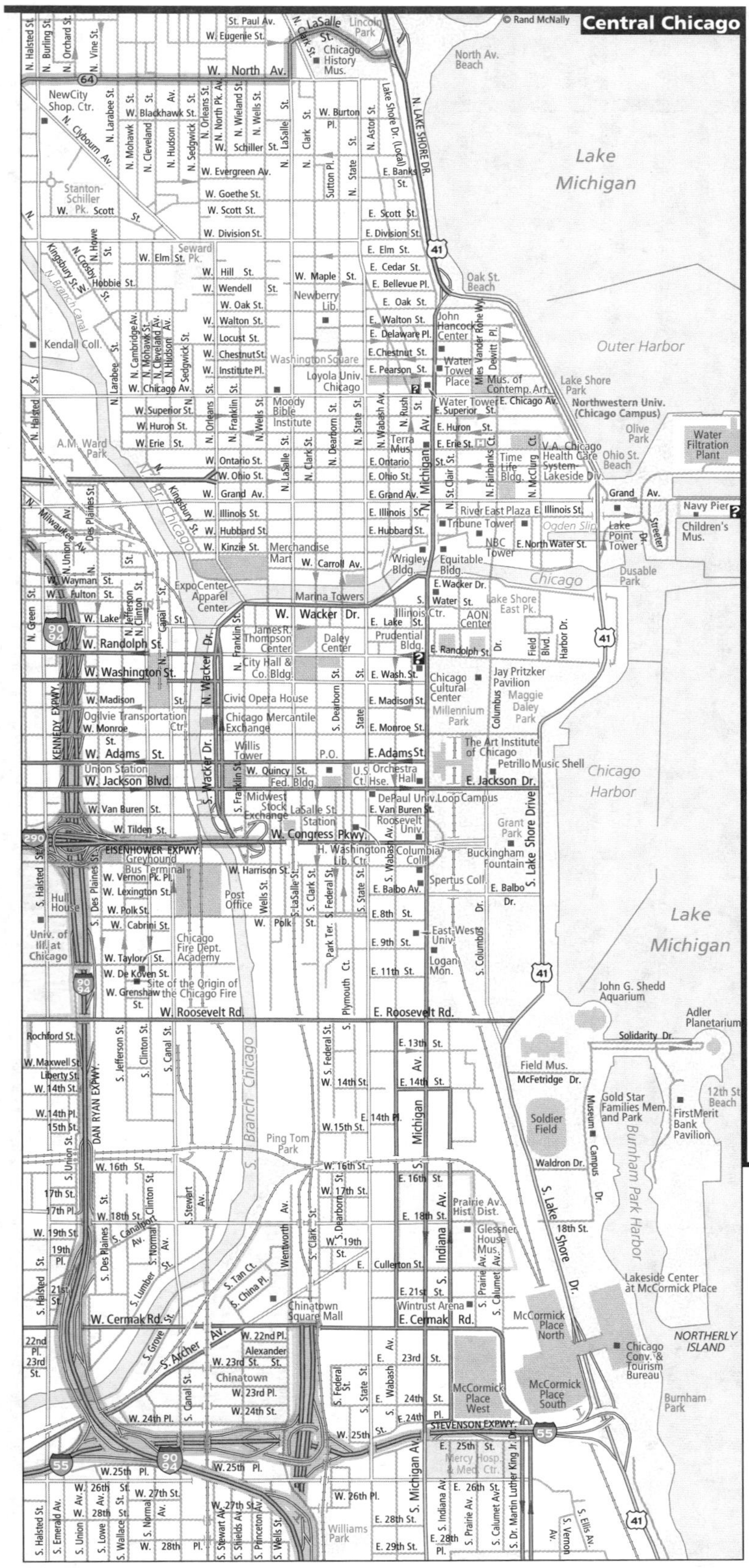

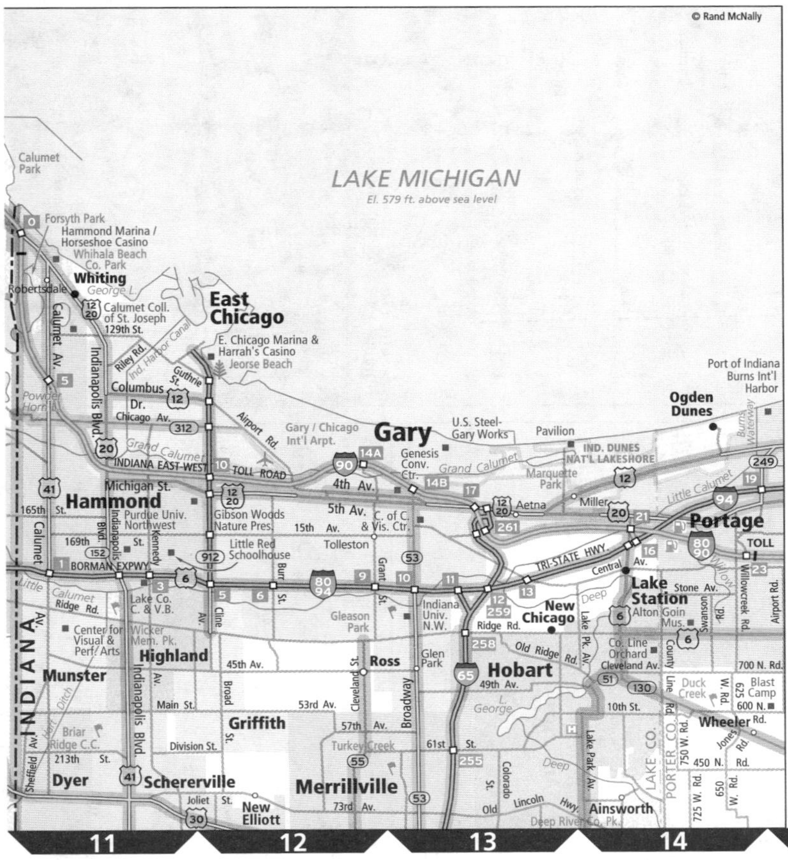

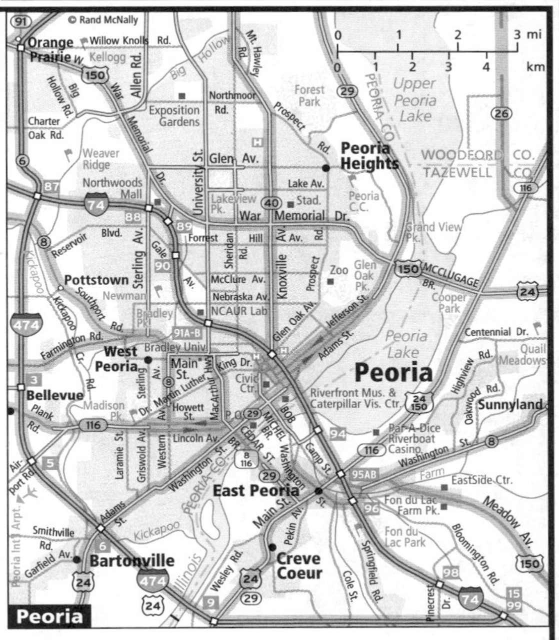

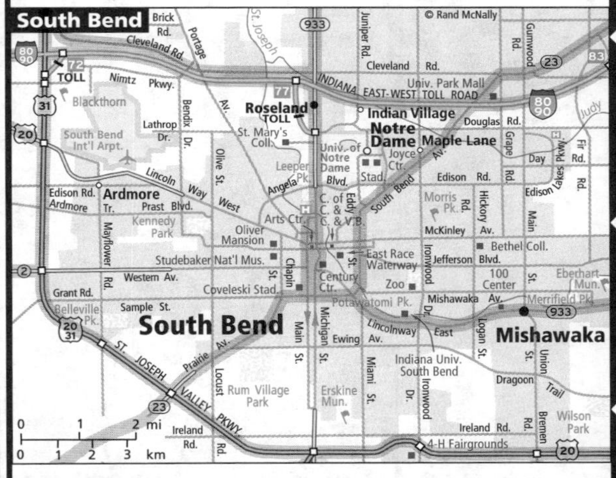

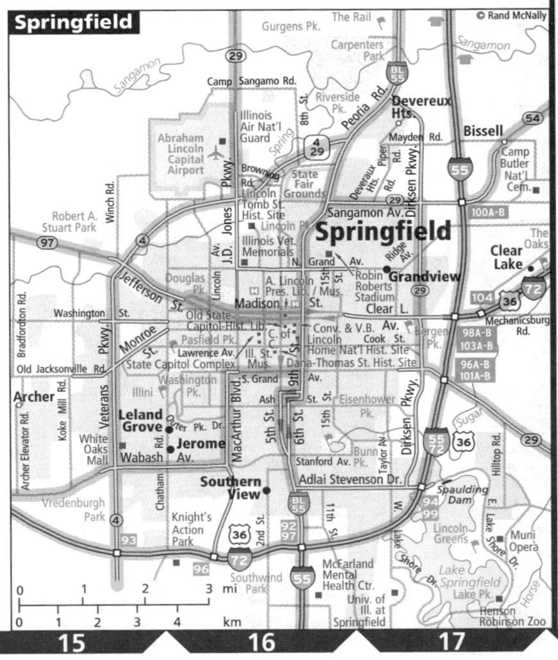

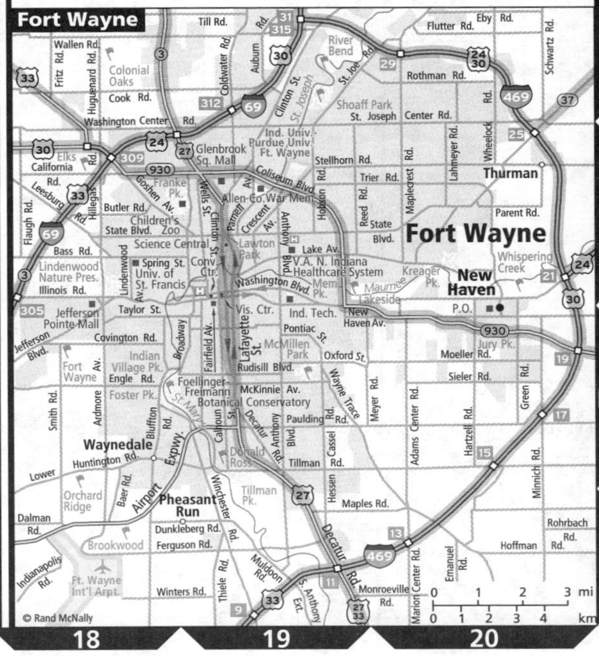

Indiana

Nickname: The Hoosier State
Capital: Indianapolis, J-9
Land area: 35,826 sq. mi. (rank: 38th)
Population: 6,483,802 (rank: 15th)
Largest city: Indianapolis, 820,445, J-9

Index of cities Pg. 130 | Map legend Pg. 1

Route planning & on-the-road resources

Low clearances, weigh stations, & restricted routes: Page A31

Weigh station location

Designated route for vehicles with STAA-authorized dimensions

Road Conditions & Construction
(800) 261-7623, (866) 849-1368; www.in.gov/dot, www.in.gov/indot/2420.htm

Toll Road Information
Indiana Toll Road Concession Co. (*E-ZPass*): www.indianatollroad.org
RiverLink (Louisville area toll bridges) (*RiverLink or E-ZPass*): (855) 748-5465; www.riverlink.com

Determining Distances
(segments of one mile or less not shown)
Cumulative miles (red): the distance between red arrows
Intermediate miles (black): the distance between intersections & places

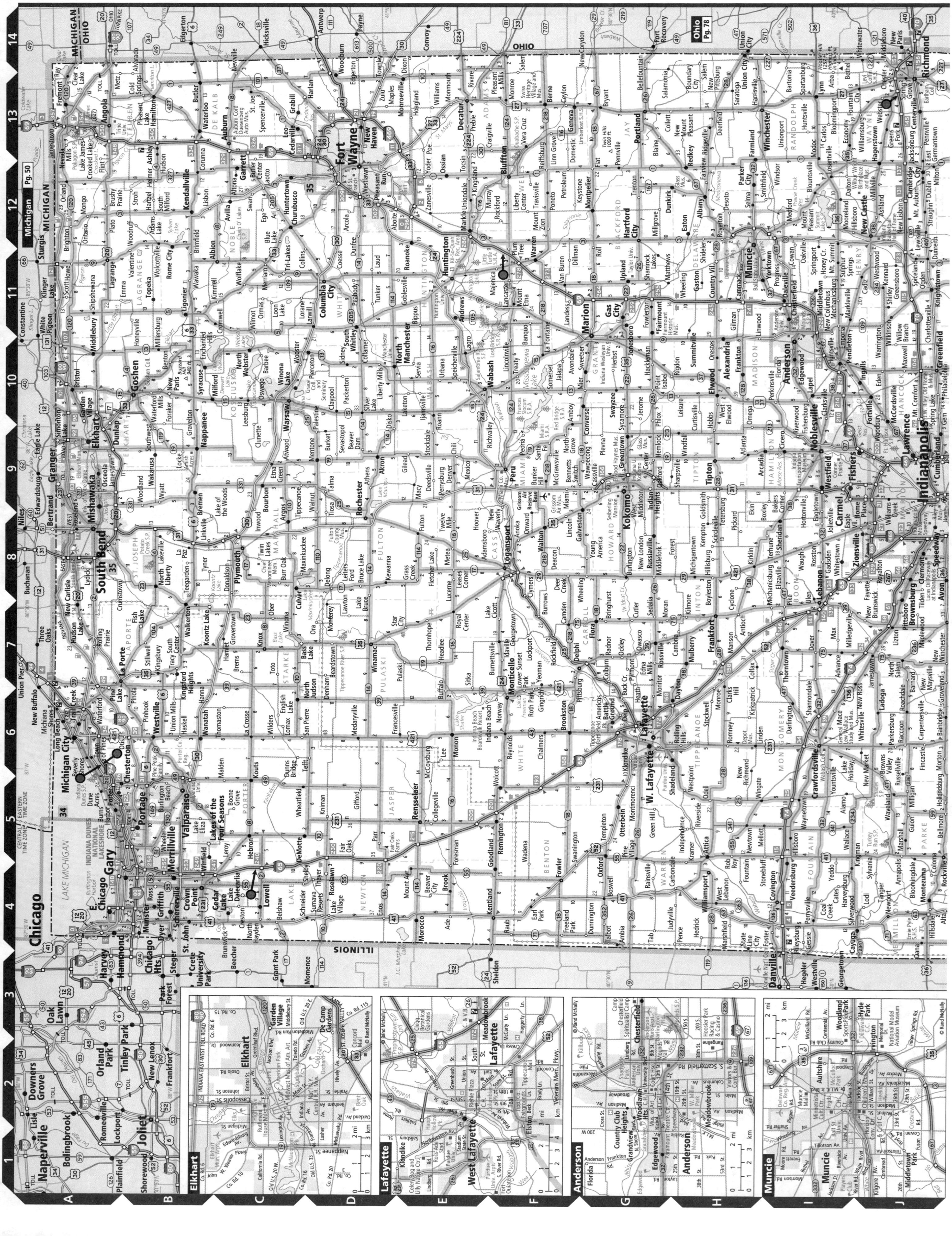

Mileage between cities	Anderson	Angola	Bloomington	Chicago, IL	Columbus	Crawfordsville	Danville, IL	Evansville	Fort Wayne	Gary	Greensburg	Indianapolis	Kokomo	Lafayette	Michigan City	Muncie	New Albany	Richmond	South Bend	Terre Haute	Vincennes
EVANSVILLE	226	349	121	289	181	178	167		313	273	202	180	235	198	294	244	112	256	323	109	54
FORT WAYNE	88	44	180	162	171	150	183	313		132	150	130	90	123	116	79	242	92	95	210	261
GARY	178	135	201	30	200	118	128	273	132		204	153	130	91	26	196	270	222	62	164	221
INDIANAPOLIS	43	166	53	183	44	53	95	180	130	153	50		60	66	174	61	114	73	148	76	129
NEW ALBANY	154	277	88	300	74	164	206	112	242	270	94	114	171	183	291	172		184	260	146	108
RICHMOND	61	140	123	252	114	129	170	256	92	222	70	73	116	136	243	44	184		205	152	204
SOUTH BEND	140	79	198	92	189	139	184	323	95	62	186	148	92	112	37	152	260	205		220	271
TERRE HAUTE	122	245	58	180	117	58	58	109	210	164	124	76	131	89	185	140	146	152	220		57

Total mileage through Indiana

- 65: 261 miles
- 70: 157 miles
- 74: 172 miles
- 90: 156 miles

For more than 40,000 interstate mileages, see the Mileage Directory on page 137

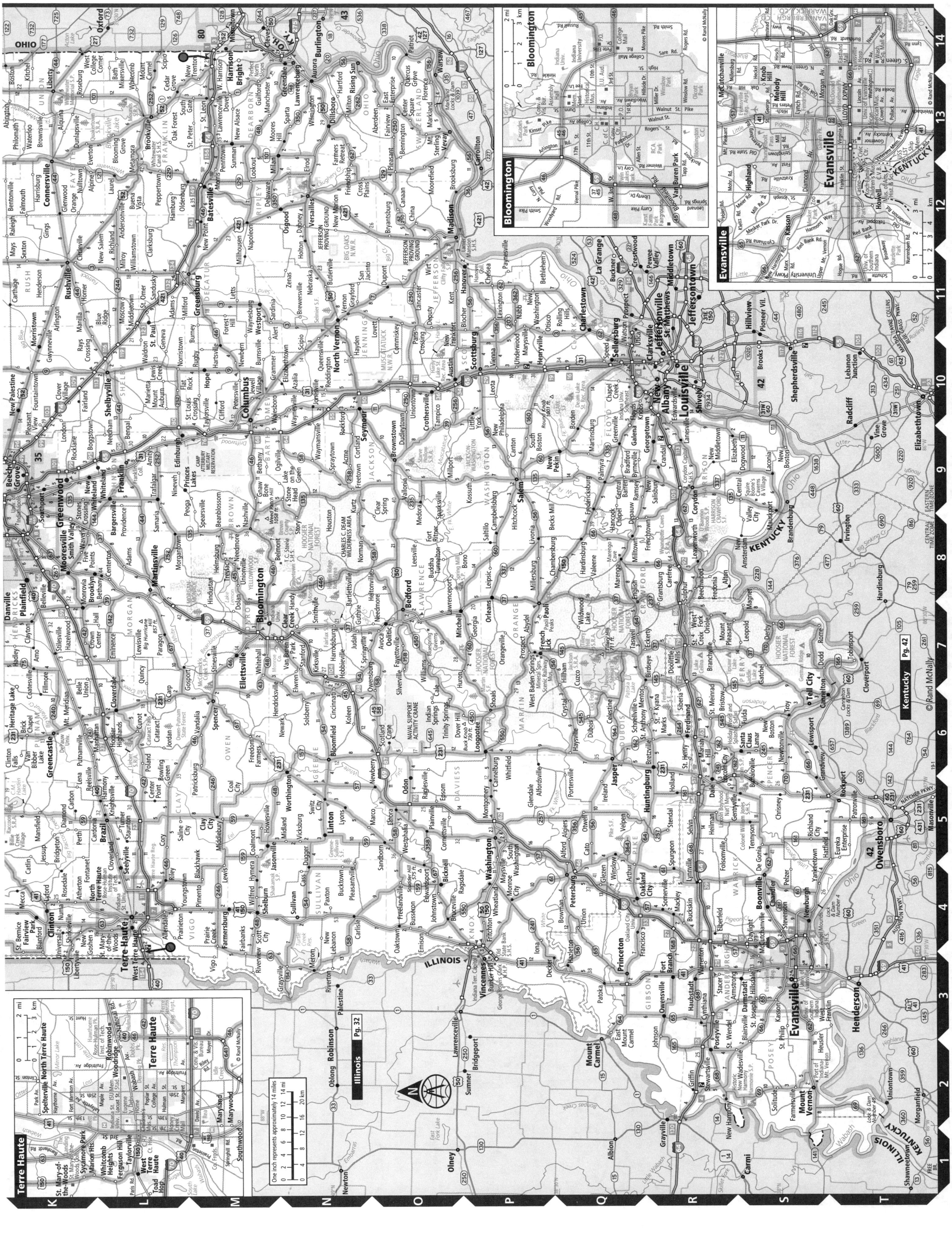

Nickname: The Hawkeye State
Capital: Des Moines, I-10
Land area: 55,857 sq. mi. (rank: 23rd)
Population: 3,046,355 (rank: 30th)
Largest city: Des Moines, 203,433, I-10

Index of cities Pg. 131 | Map legend Pg. 1

Route planning & on-the-road resources

Low clearances, weigh stations, & restricted routes: Page A31

Weigh station location

Designated route for vehicles with STAA-authorized dimensions

Road Conditions & Construction
511, (800) 288-1047; www.511ia.org, www.iowadot.gov

Toll Road Information
No tolls on state or federal highways

Determining Distances
(segments of one mile or less not shown)
Cumulative miles (red): the distance between red arrows
Intermediate miles (black): the distance between intersections & places

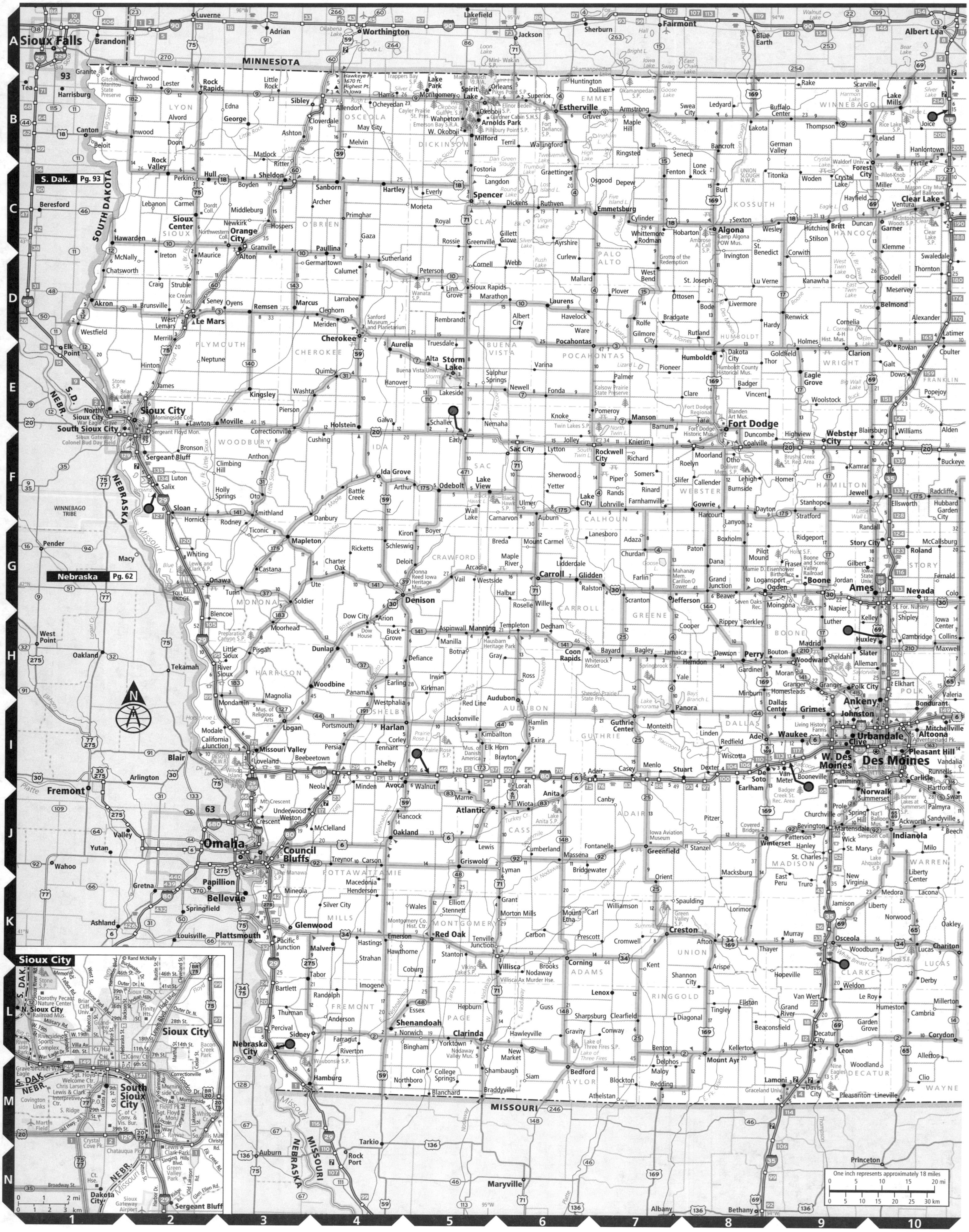

Mileage between cities	Ames	Burlington	Cedar Rapids	Council Bluffs	Davenport	Decorah	Des Moines	Dubuque	Fort Dodge	Iowa City	Keokuk	Mason City	Ottumwa	Sioux City	Sioux Falls, SD	Spirit Lake	Storm Lake	Waterloo
BURLINGTON	209		100	313	77	206	185	150	254	77	41	238	78	384	469	358	312	155
CEDAR RAPIDS	108	100		253	83	106	126	75	154	28	117	138	110	272	361	258	212	55
COUNCIL BLUFFS	160	313	253		296	329	127	327	180	241	330	246	213	95	180	180	126	253
DAVENPORT	192	77	83	296		175	168	77	237	59	118	221	134	367	452	341	295	138
DES MOINES	33	185	126	127	168	202		199	96	114	203	119	86	198	283	200	155	126
DUBUQUE	187	150	75	327	77	98	199		191	85	191	175	184	308	398	295	249	92
SIOUX CITY	232	384	272	95	367	304	198	308	128	312	401	213	285		85	109	78	220
WATERLOO	98	155	55	253	138	80	126	92	102	83	172	83	128	220	306	235	160	

Total mileage through Iowa

29	155 miles	80	303 miles
35	218 miles	218	257 miles

For more than 40,000 interstate mileages, see the Mileage Directory on page 137

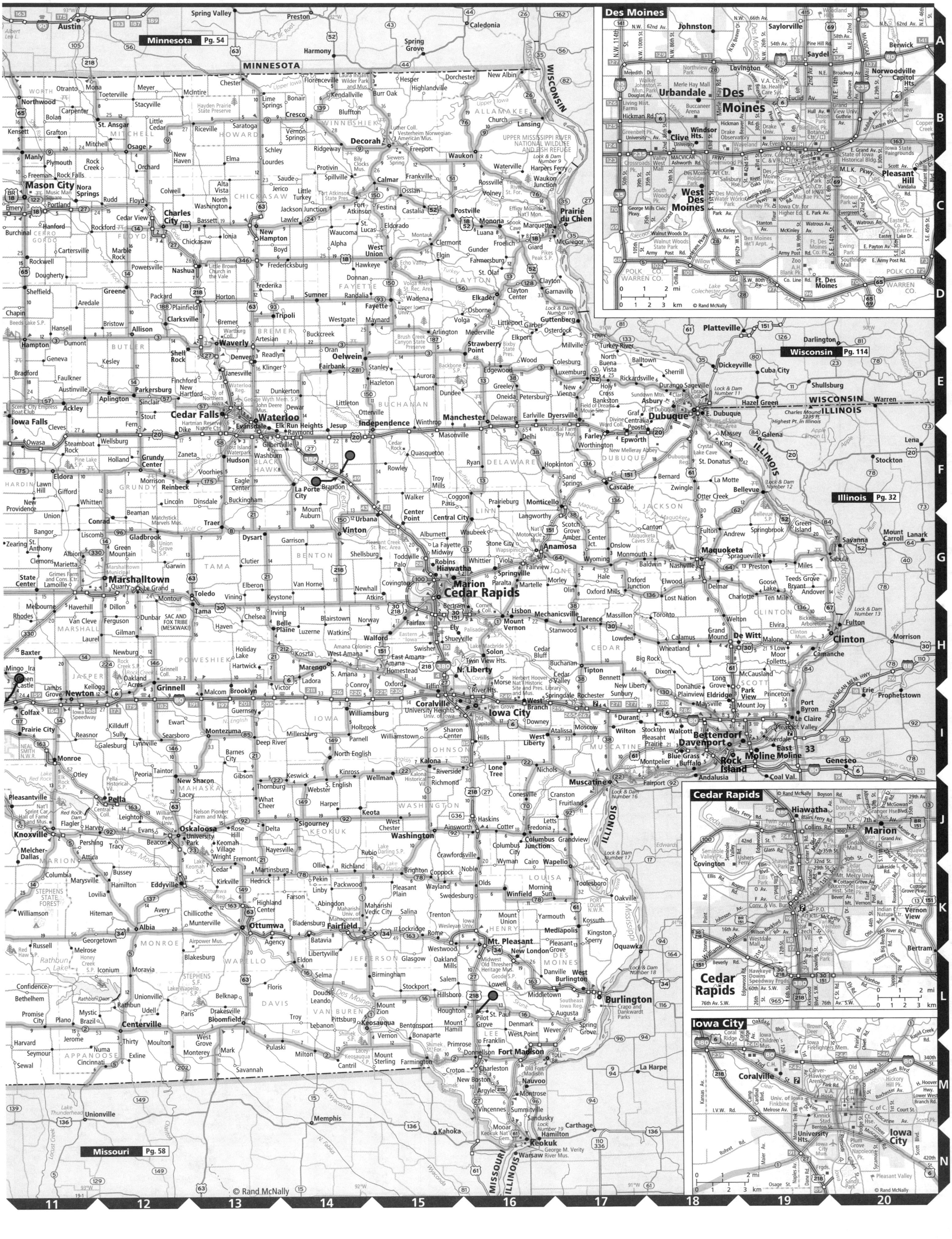

Kansas

Nickname: The Sunflower State
Capital: Topeka, D-16
Land area: 81,759 sq. mi. (rank: 13th)
Population: 2,853,118 (rank: 33rd)
Largest city: Wichita, 382,368, H-13

Index of cities Pg. 131
Map legend Pg. 1

Route planning & on-the-road resources

Low clearances, weigh stations, & restricted routes: Page A32

Weigh station location

Designated route for vehicles with STAA-authorized dimensions

Road Conditions & Construction
511, (800) 585-7623, (785) 296-3585
www.kandrive.org, www.ksdot.org

Toll Road Information
Kansas Turnpike Authority *(K-TAG)*:
(800) 873-5824, (316) 682-4537; www.ksturnpike.com

Determining Distances
(segments of one mile or less not shown)
Cumulative miles (red): the distance between red arrows
Intermediate miles (black): the distance between intersections & places

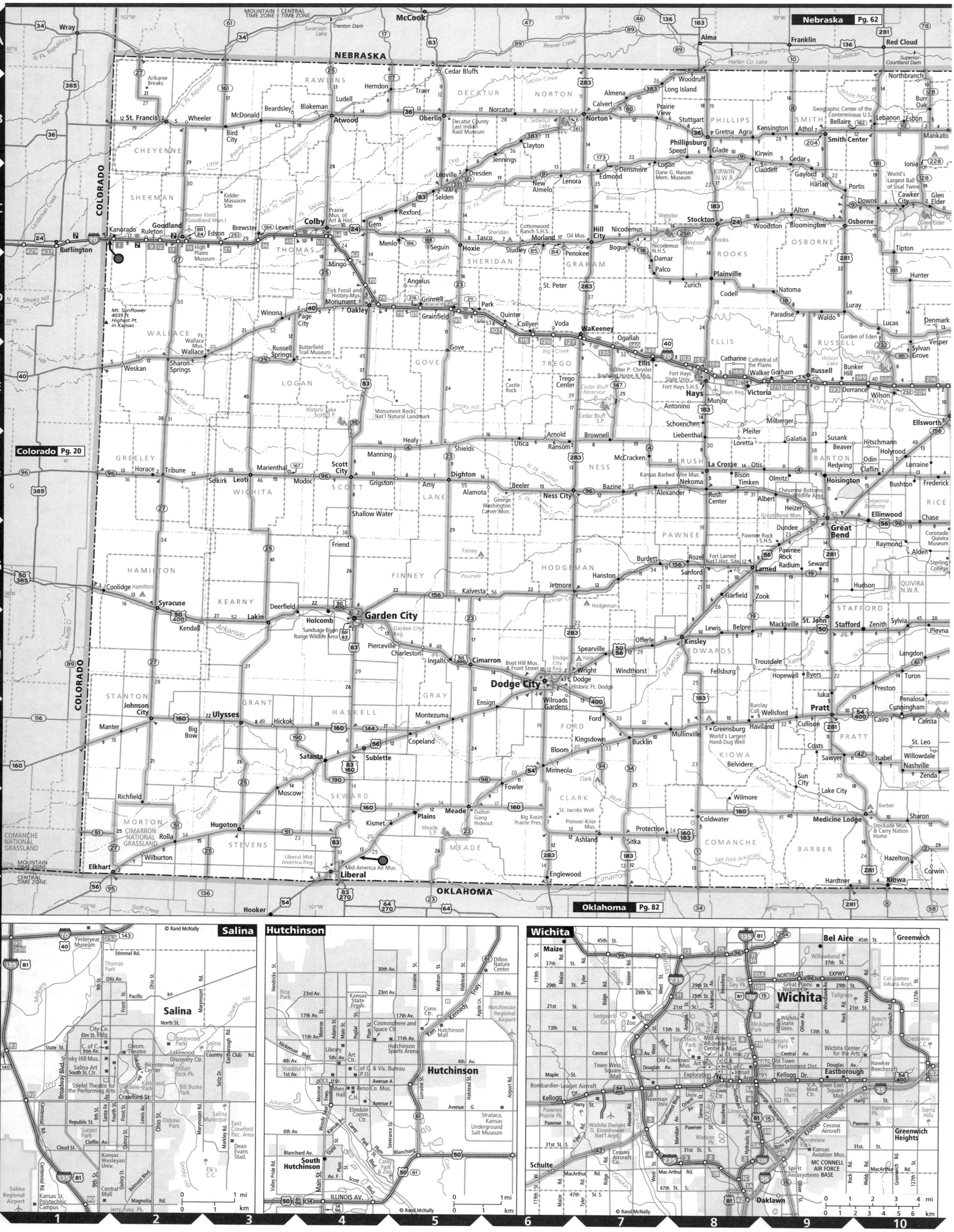

Mileage between cities	Arkansas City	Atchison	Coffeyville	Dodge City	Emporia	Fort Scott	Goodland	Great Bend	Hays	Hutchinson	Joplin, MO	Kansas City	Liberal	Manhattan	Oakley	Salina	Topeka	Wichita
DODGE CITY	212	324	289		240	304	192	85	104	122	338	332	86	229	134	164	273	155
GOODLAND	384	395	456	192	349	480		206	145	268	505	403	209	300	58	235	344	323
HUTCHINSON	111	234	184	122	112	194	268	62	129		233	217	189	138	212	74	182	51
JOPLIN, MO	162	196	78	338	177	61	505	300	366	233		151	395	252	449	274	196	183
KANSAS CITY	226	52	166	332	105	90	403	247	263	217	151		403	115	346	168	59	191
SALINA	152	160	225	164	117	244	235	79	96	74	274	168	246	65	179		109	92
TOPEKA	178	56	163	273	64	136	344	188	204	182	196	59	354	56	287	109		143
WICHITA	61	188	134	155	85	149	323	118	184	51	183	191	212	131	267	92	143	

Total mileage through Kansas

I-35: 235 miles
I-70: 424 miles
US 56: 464 miles
US 81: 220 miles

For more than 40,000 interstate mileages, see the Mileage Directory on page 137

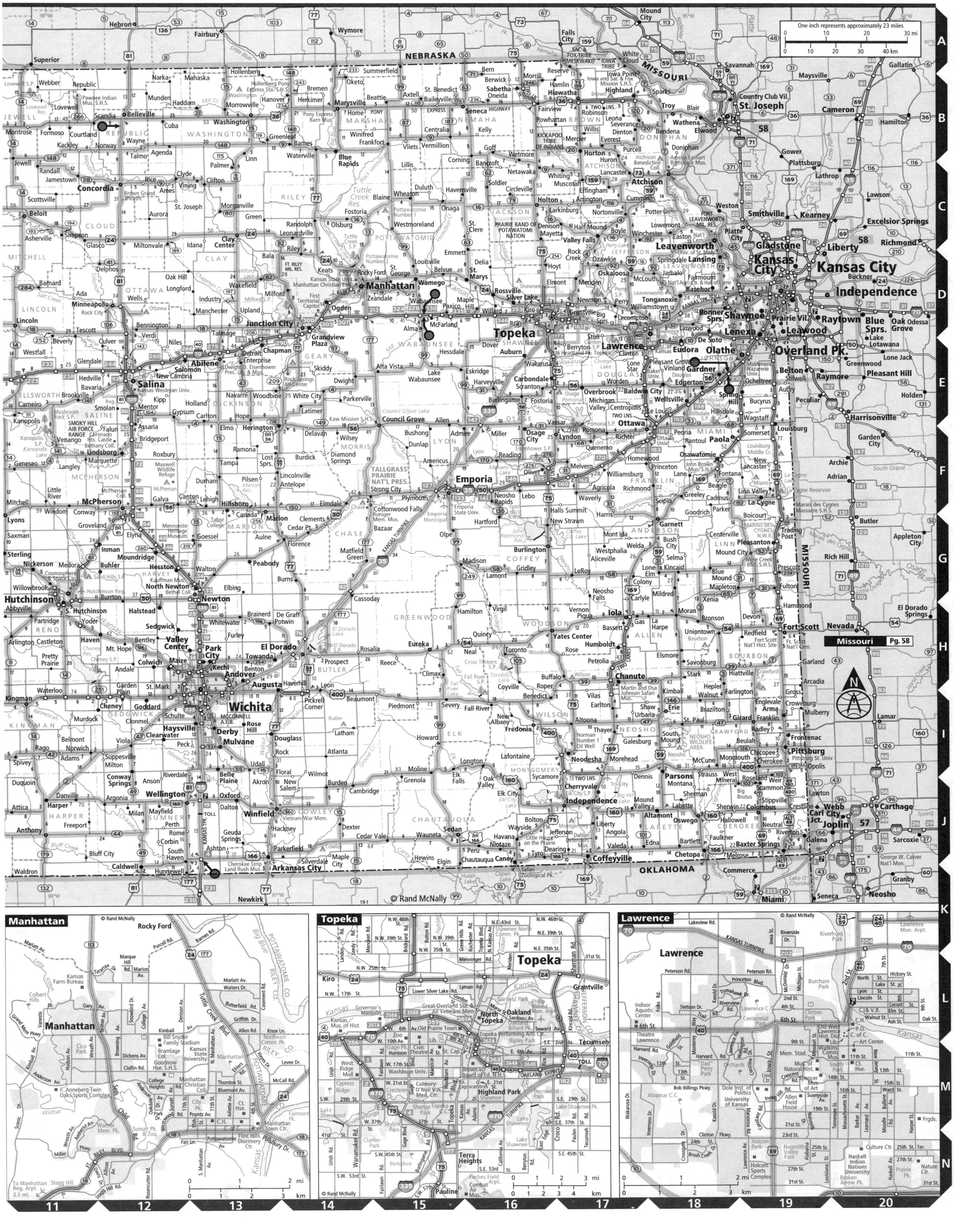

Kentucky

Nickname: The Bluegrass State
Capital: Frankfort, G-11
Land area: 39,486 sq. mi. (rank: 37th)
Population: 4,339,367 (rank: 26th)
Largest city: Louisville, 597,337, G-8

Index of cities Pg. 131 | Map legend Pg. 1

Route planning & on-the-road resources

Low clearances, weigh stations, & restricted routes: Page A32

Weigh station location

Designated route for vehicles with STAA-authorized dimensions

Road Conditions & Construction
511, (866) 737-3767
www.drive.ky.gov, transportation.ky.gov, www.goky.ky.gov

Toll Road Information
RiverLink (Louisville area toll bridges) (*RiverLink or E-ZPass*): (855) 748-5465; www.riverlink.com

Determining Distances
(segments of one mile or less not shown)
Cumulative miles (red): the distance between red arrows
Intermediate miles (black): the distance between intersections & places

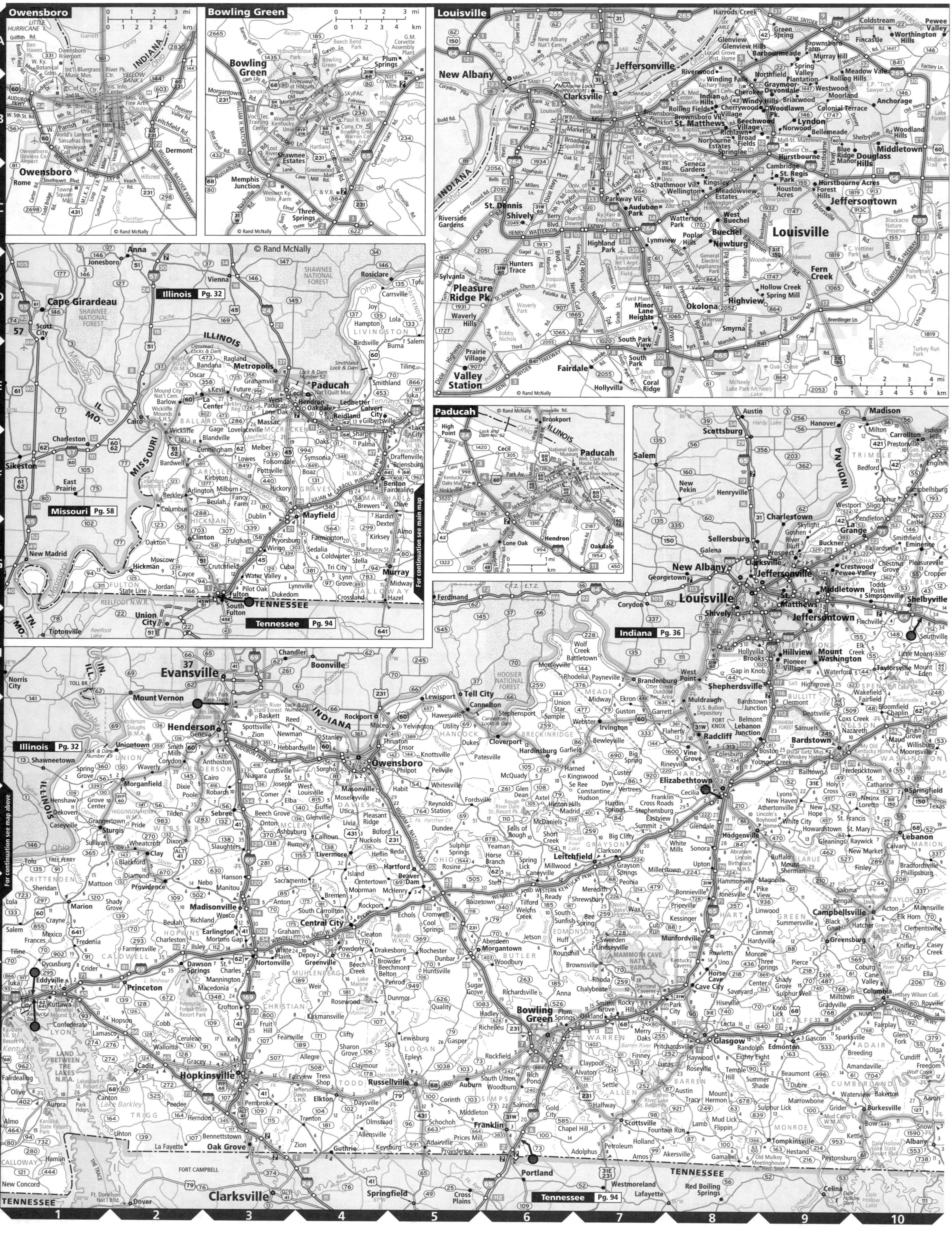

Mileage between cities	Ashland	Bardstown	Bowling Green	Cave City	Covington	Elizabethtown	Frankfort	Hopkinsville	Huntington, WV	Lexington	London	Louisville	Mayfield	Maysville	Owensboro	Paducah	Pikeville	Somerset
ASHLAND		179	271	244	140	204	142	327	18	120	173	189	385	85	298	376	96	177
BOWLING GREEN	271	97		31	210	70	147	66	276	151	144	115	160	217	72	151	266	109
COVINGTON	140	139	210	183		141	96	266	145	82	154	97	324	59	210	315	218	158
HOPKINSVILLE	327	153	66	101	266	124	202		332	207	214	171	84	272	96	75	349	179
LEXINGTON	120	59	151	124	82	84	25	207	125		76	72	265	65	178	256	142	80
LOUISVILLE	189	47	115	88	97	46	51	171	194	72	148		229	135	115	220	211	126
OWENSBORO	298	122	72	109	210	94	172	96	302	178	222	115	154	242		145	319	187
PADUCAH	376	202	151	188	315	174	252	75	381	256	301	220	24	322	145		398	267

Mileages © Rand McNally

Total mileage through Kentucky

64: 185 miles
65: 137 miles
71: 97 miles
75: 192 miles

For more than 40,000 interstate mileages, see the Mileage Directory on page 137

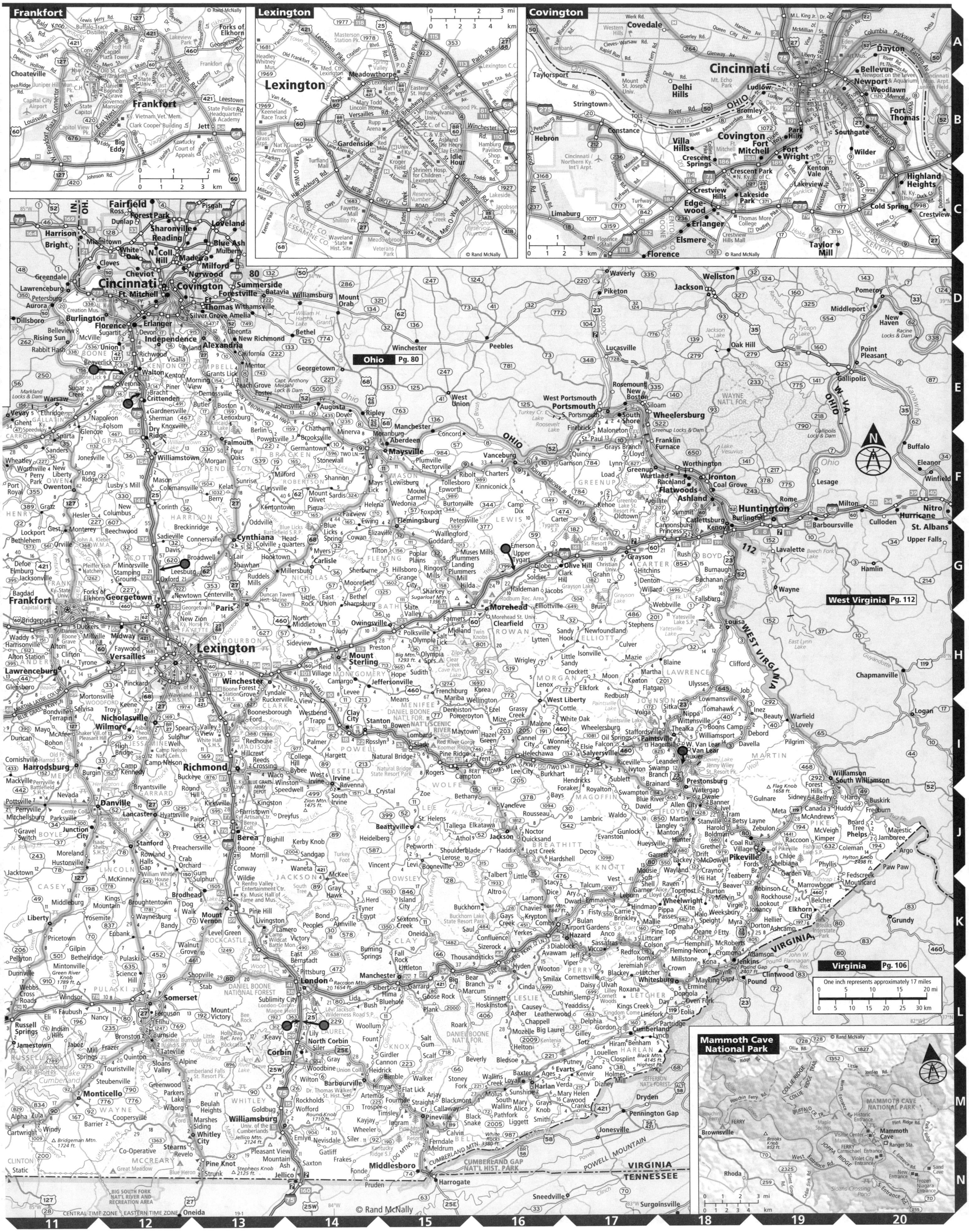

Louisiana

Nickname: The Pelican State
Capital: Baton Rouge, G-7
Land area: 43,204 sq. mi. (rank: 33rd)
Population: 4,533,372 (rank: 25th)
Largest city: New Orleans, 343,829, H-9

Index of cities Pg. 131 | Map legend Pg. 1

Mileage between cities	Baton Rouge	Beaumont, TX	Bogalusa	De Ridder	El Dorado, AR	Ferriday	Houma	Natchitoches	New Orleans	Shreveport	Vicksburg, MS
ALEXANDRIA	139	149	269	132	147	63	192	57	218	123	144
BATON ROUGE		183	131	249	284	101	88	196	79	261	159
GULFPORT, MS	135	318	69	383	359	227	131	330	78	375	203
LAFAYETTE	55	133	185	199	235	150	103	146	134	211	213
LAKE CHARLES	124	60	254	125	252	168	177	164	203	229	282
NEW ORLEANS	79	262	75	328	363	189	56	275		340	207
SHREVEPORT	261	206	342	149	91	185	315	74	340		171
VICKSBURG, MS	159	342	170	268	156	81	234	185	207	171	

Total mileage through Louisiana

- I-10: 274 miles
- I-49: 208 miles
- I-20: 190 miles
- I-55: 66 miles

For more than 40,000 interstate mileages, see the Mileage Directory on page 137

Route planning & on-the-road resources

Low clearances, weigh stations, & restricted routes: Page A32

- Weigh station location
- Designated route for vehicles with STAA-authorized dimensions

Road Conditions & Construction
511, (877) 452-3683
www.511la.org, www.dotd.la.gov

Toll Bridges
Louisiana Dept. of Trans. & Dev. (Hwy. 1 Bridge) (*GeauxPass*): (866) 662-8987; www.geauxpass.com
Lake Ponchartrain Causeway (*TollTag*): (504) 835-3118; www.thecauseway.us

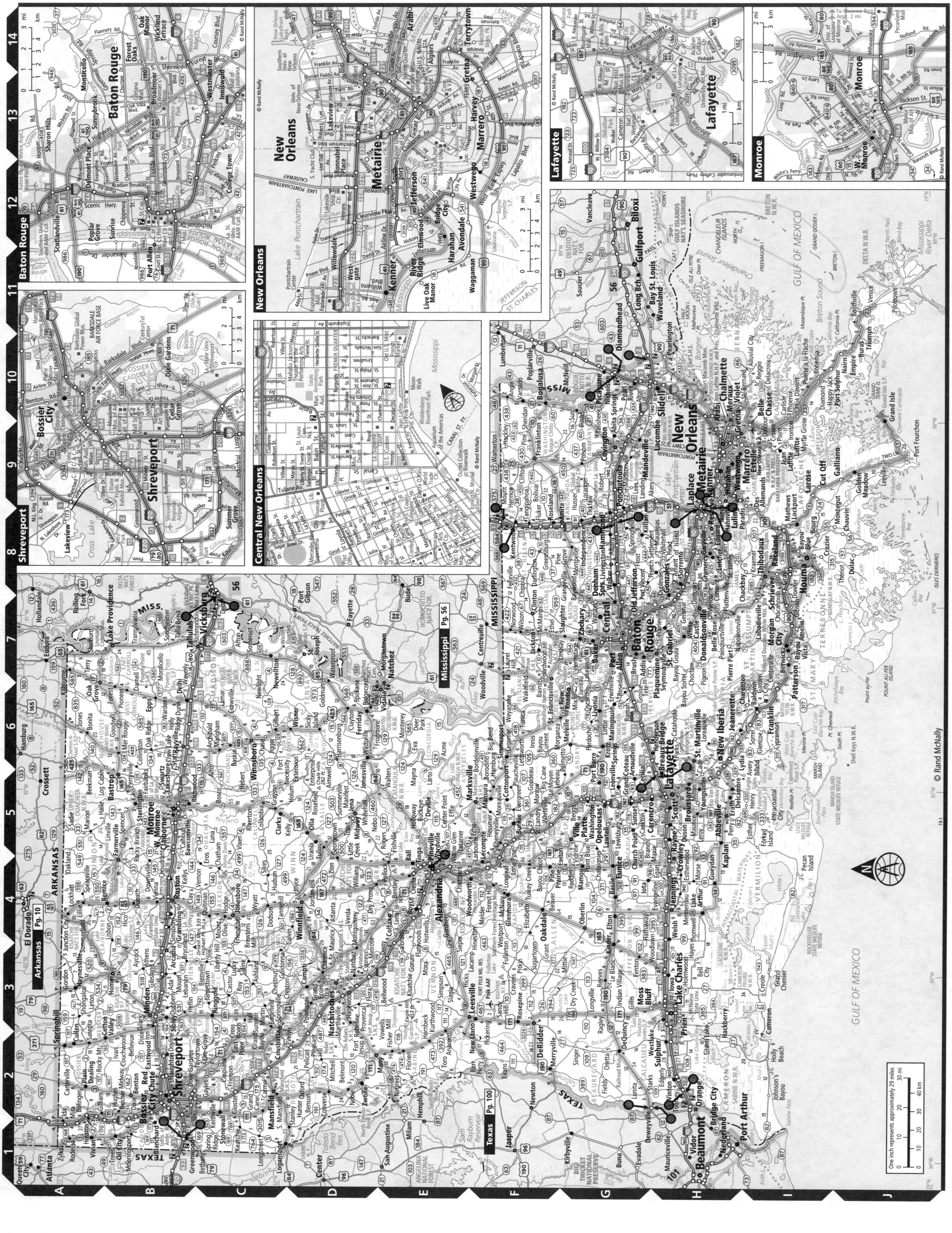

Route planning & on-the-road resources

Low clearances, weigh stations, & restricted routes: **Page A33**

Weigh station location

Designated route for vehicles with STAA-authorized dimensions

Road Conditions & Construction

511
(207) 624-3000, (800) 675-7453;
www.maine.gov/mdot

Toll Road Information

Maine Turnpike Authority ***(E-ZPass)***:
(877) 682-9433, (207) 871-7771
www.maineturnpike.com

Mileage between cities	Bangor	East Millinocket	Eastport	Houlton	Portland	Portsmouth, NH	Rangeley	Waterville
BANGOR		63	122	118	129	180	120	56
EAST MILLINOCKET	63		120	61	192	242	183	118
EASTPORT	122	120		118	253	304	244	180
HOULTON	118	61	118		247	298	238	174
PORTLAND	129	192	253	247		51	118	75
PORTSMOUTH, NH	180	242	304	298	51		165	125
RANGELEY	120	183	244	238	118	165		77
WATERVILLE	56	118	180	174	75	125	77	

Total mileage through Maine

95: 299 miles
2: 273 miles
1: 527 miles
201: 164 miles

For more than 40,000 interstate mileages, see the Mileage Directory on page 137

Maine

Nickname: The Pine Tree State
Capital: Augusta, F-4
Land area: 30,843 sq. mi. (rank: 39th)
Population: 1,328,361 (rank: 41st)
Largest city: Portland, 66,194, H-3

Index of cities Pg. 131
Map legend Pg. 1

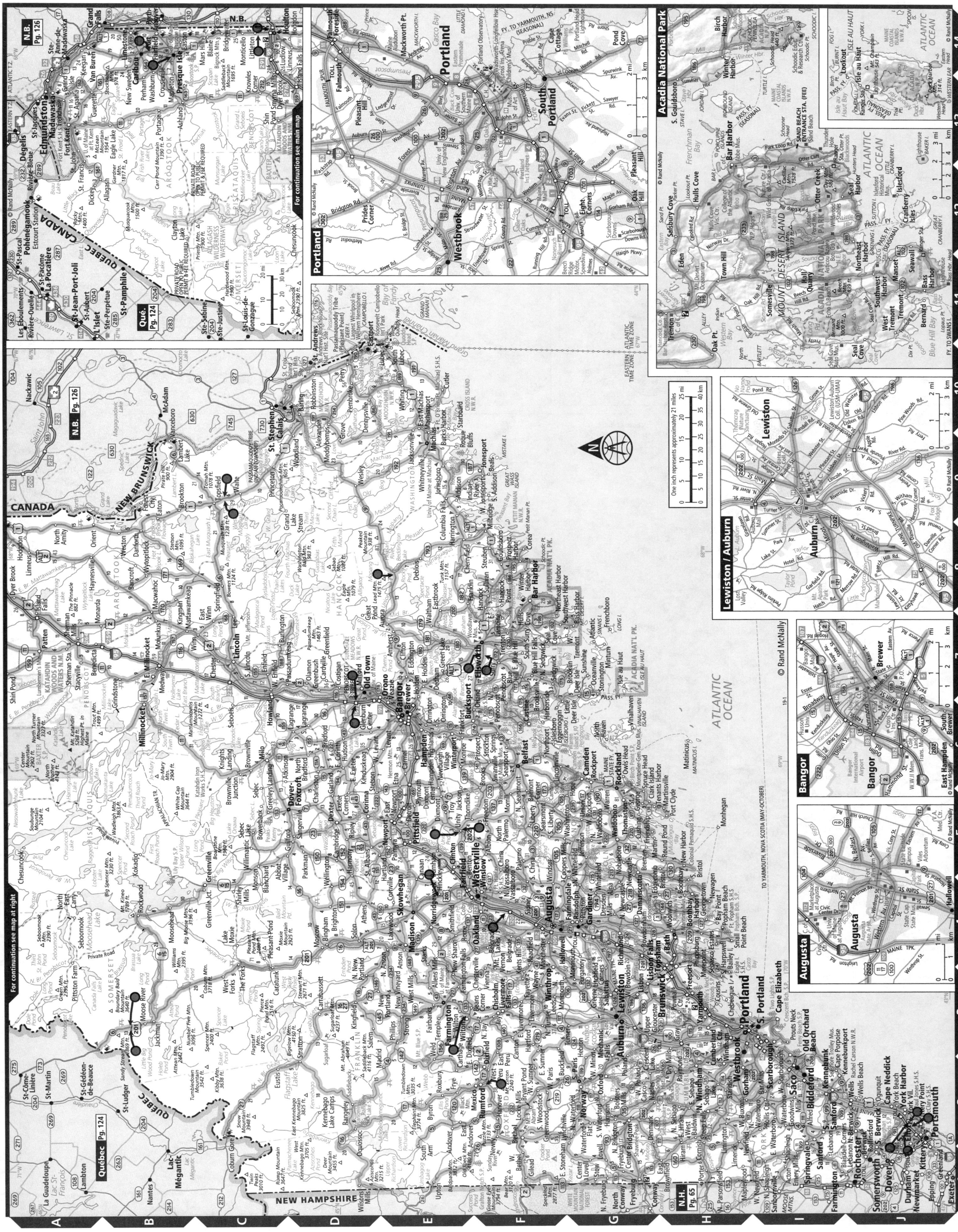

Maryland

Nickname: The Old Line State
Capital: Annapolis, E-14
Land area: 9,707 sq. mi. (rank: 42nd)
Population: 5,773,552 (rank: 19th)
Largest city: Baltimore, 620,961, C-13

Index of cities Pg. 131 | Map legend Pg. 1

Route planning & on-the-road resources

Low clearances, weigh stations, & restricted routes: Page A33

Weigh station location

Designated route for vehicles with STAA-authorized dimensions

Road Conditions & Construction
511, (855) 466-3511, (410) 582-5650, (800) 543-2515
www.md511.org, www.roads.maryland.gov

Toll Road Information
Maryland Transportation Authority (*E-ZPass*):
(866) 713-1596, In Maryland: (410) 537-1000; www.mdta.maryland.gov

Determining Distances
(segments of one mile or less not shown)
Cumulative miles (red): the distance between red arrows
Intermediate miles (black): the distance between intersections & places

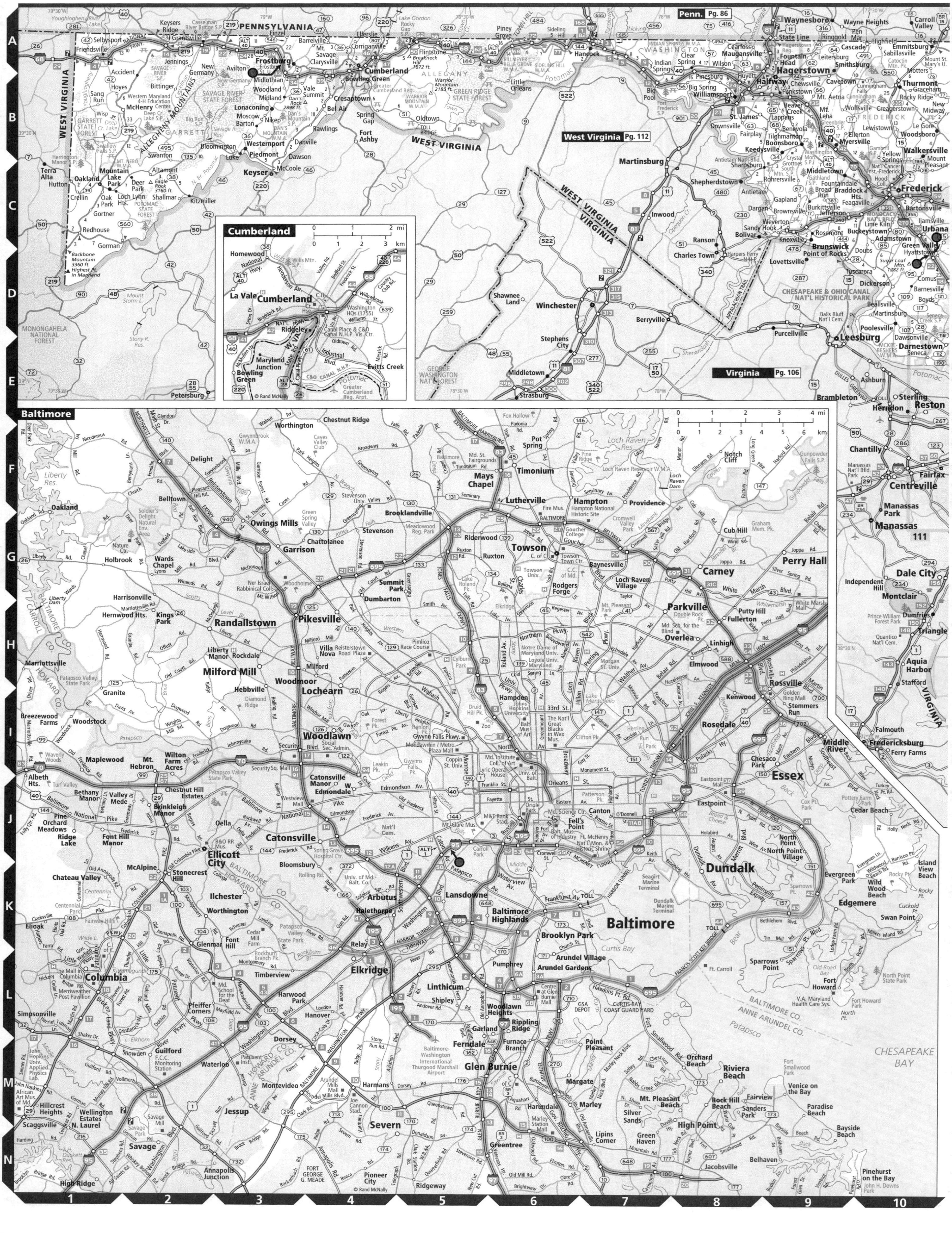

Mileage between cities	Aberdeen	Annapolis	Baltimore	Cambridge	Chestertown	Cumberland	Edgewood	Frederick	Hagerstown	Harrisburg, PA	Lexington Park	Ocean City	Pocomoke City	Rockville	St. Charles	Salisbury	Washington, DC	Wilmington, DE
ABERDEEN		61	33	117	65	172	10	83	108	85	125	146	162	74	95	132	72	43
ANNAPOLIS	61		30	58	49	159	53	70	95	115	73	118	122	42	41	89	33	100
BALTIMORE	33	30		85	76	136	25	47	72	83	91	145	149	42	63	116	40	72
CUMBERLAND	172	159	136	214	205		164	90	68	139	205	274	278	117	174	245	142	211
HAGERSTOWN	108	95	72	150	141	68	100	25		75	142	210	214	53	110	181	79	147
LEXINGTON PARK	125	73	91	129	120	205	113	118	142	174		189	192	89	38	160	80	160
SALISBURY	132	89	116	32	91	245	141	156	181	206	160	29	27	128	128		120	106
WASHINGTON, DC	72	33	40	90	81	142	65	57	79	125	80	150	154	28	48	120		112

Total mileage through Maryland

68 81 miles
81 12 miles
70 94 miles
95 110 miles

For more than 40,000 interstate mileages, see the Mileage Directory on page 137

For more than 40,000 interstate mileages, see the Mileage Directory on page 137

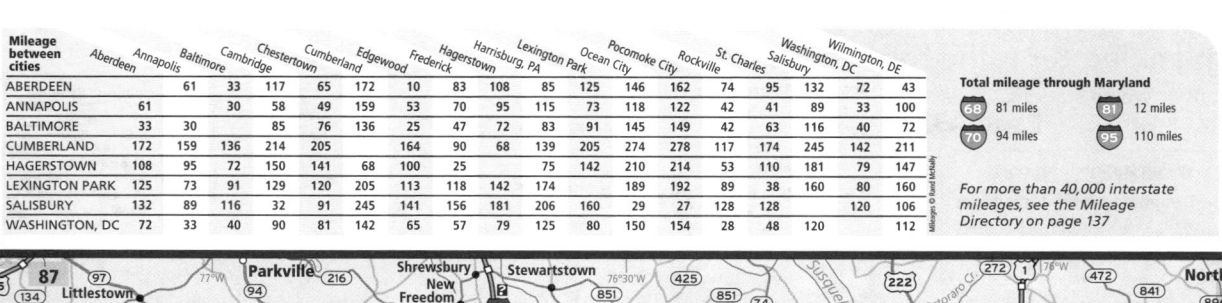

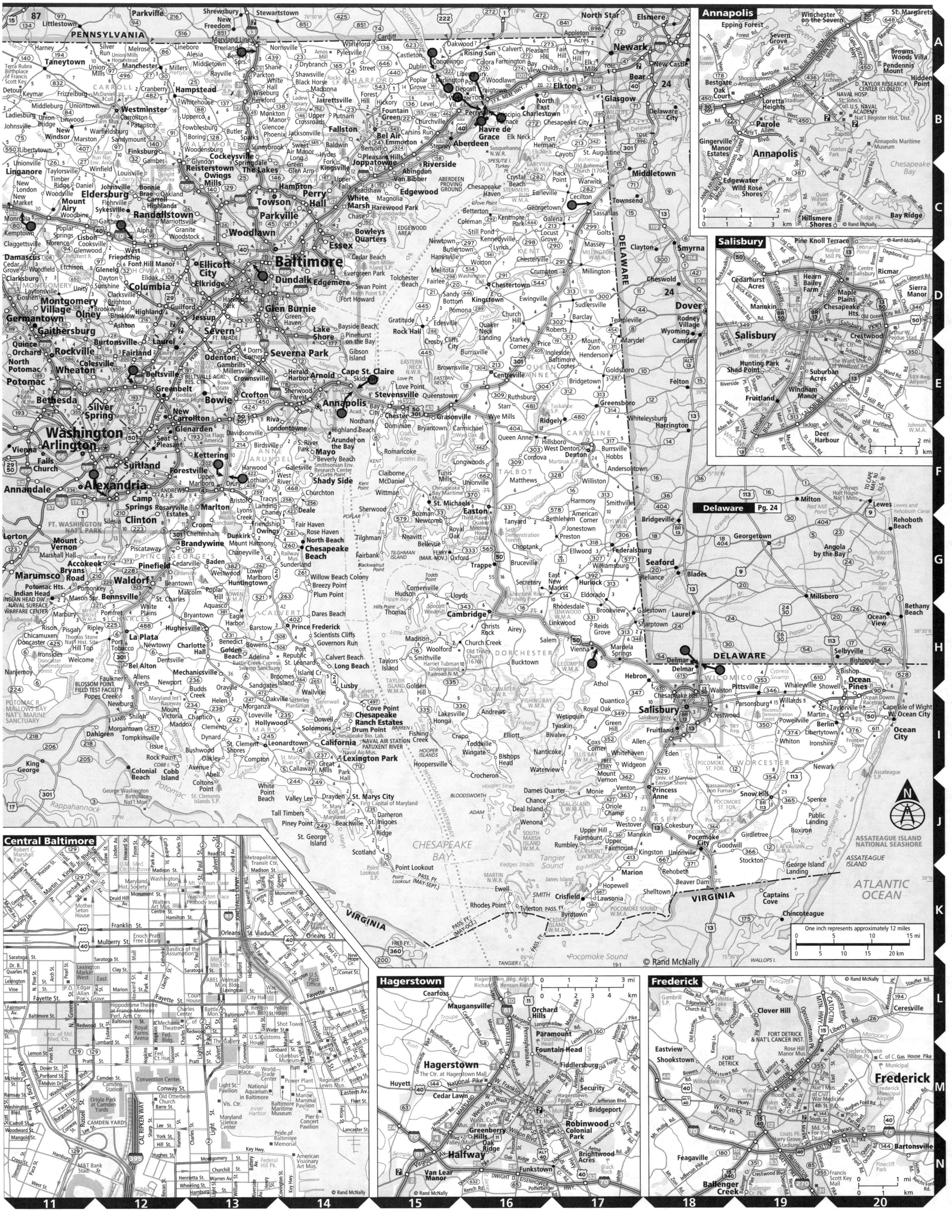

Massachusetts

Nickname: The Bay State
Capital: Boston, E-14
Land area: 7,800 sq. mi. (rank: 45th)
Population: 6,547,629 (rank: 14th)
Largest city: Boston, 617,594, E-14

Index of cities Pg. 131 | Map legend Pg. 1

Route planning & on-the-road resources

Low clearances, weigh stations, & restricted routes: Page A33

Weigh station location

Designated route for vehicles with STAA-authorized dimensions

Road Conditions & Construction

511, Metro Boston: (617) 986-5511
Central: (508) 499-5511, Western: (413) 754-5511
www.mass511.com

Toll Road Information

Massachusetts Department of Transportation (*E-ZPass):*
(877) 623-6846, (857) 368-4636; www.massdot.state.ma.us/highway

Determining Distances

(segments of one mile or less not shown)
Cumulative miles (red): the distance between red arrows
Intermediate miles (black): the distance between intersections & places

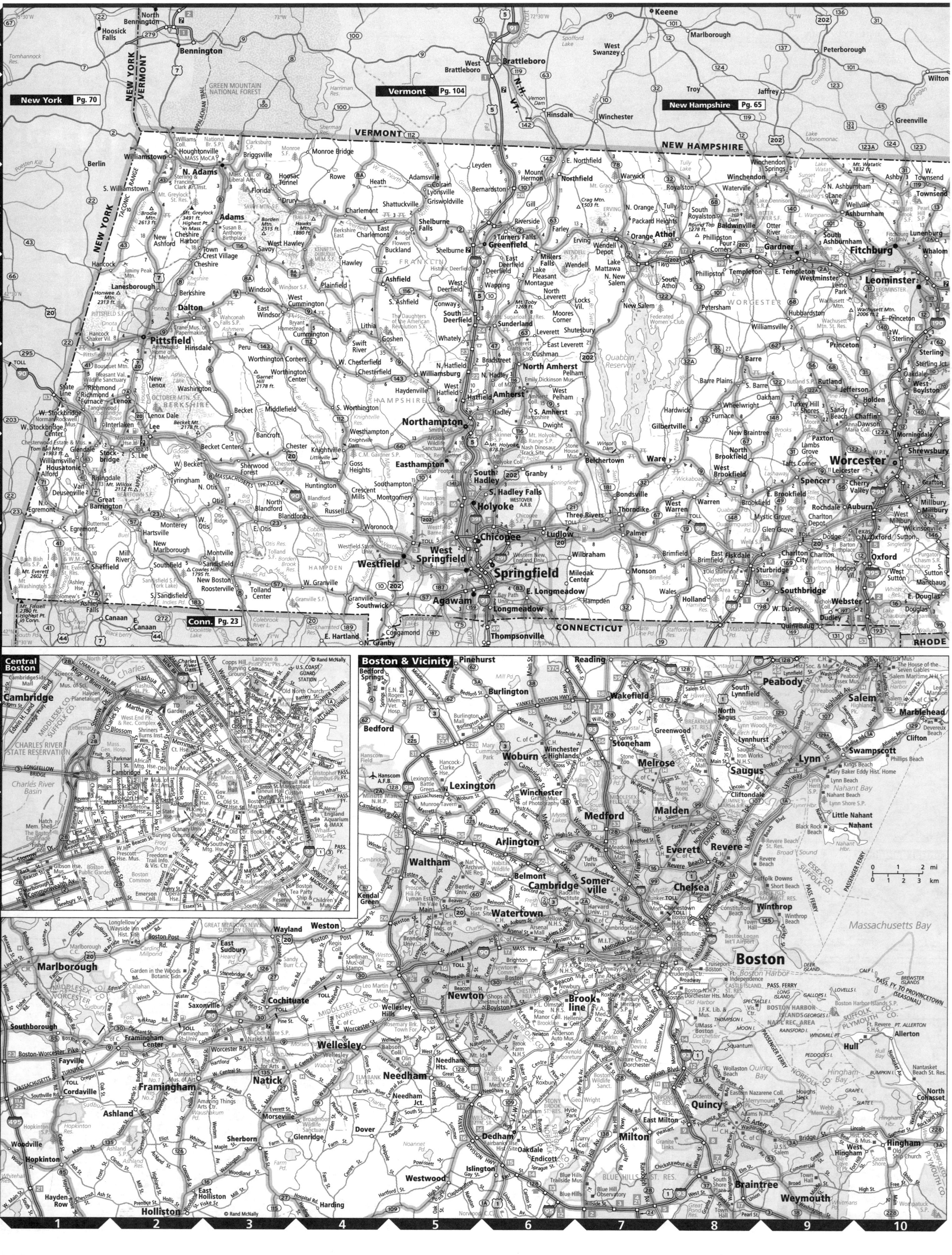

Mileage between cities	Albany, NY	Boston	Brockton	Falmouth	Fitchburg	Gloucester	Greenfield	Hartford, CT	Lowell	New Bedford	North Adams	Northampton	Pittsfield	Plymouth	Providence, RI	Provincetown	Springfield	Worcester
BOSTON	166		25	76	56	39	102	101	29	59	158	104	137	40	50	116	90	43
GLOUCESTER	199	39	63	115	74		120	133	47	98	191	136	169	78	90	154	122	75
LOWELL	170	29	52	103	34	47	80	104		86	162	107	140	69	71	144	93	42
NEW BEDFORD	202	59	38	40	94	98	140	136	86		194	139	172	37	31	91	126	79
PITTSFIELD	35	137	150	189	124	169	79	77	140	172	22	59		167	150	240	51	98
PLYMOUTH	197	40	33	33	89	78	135	131	69	37	189	134	167		53	77	121	74
SPRINGFIELD	81	90	103	143	77	122	38	26	93	126	73	18	51	121	104	194		51
WORCESTER	127	43	56	96	26	75	72	62	42	79	120	64	98	74	57	146	51	

Total mileage through Massachusetts

90	136 miles	93	47 miles
91	55 miles	95	92 miles

For more than 40,000 interstate mileages, see the Mileage Directory on page 137

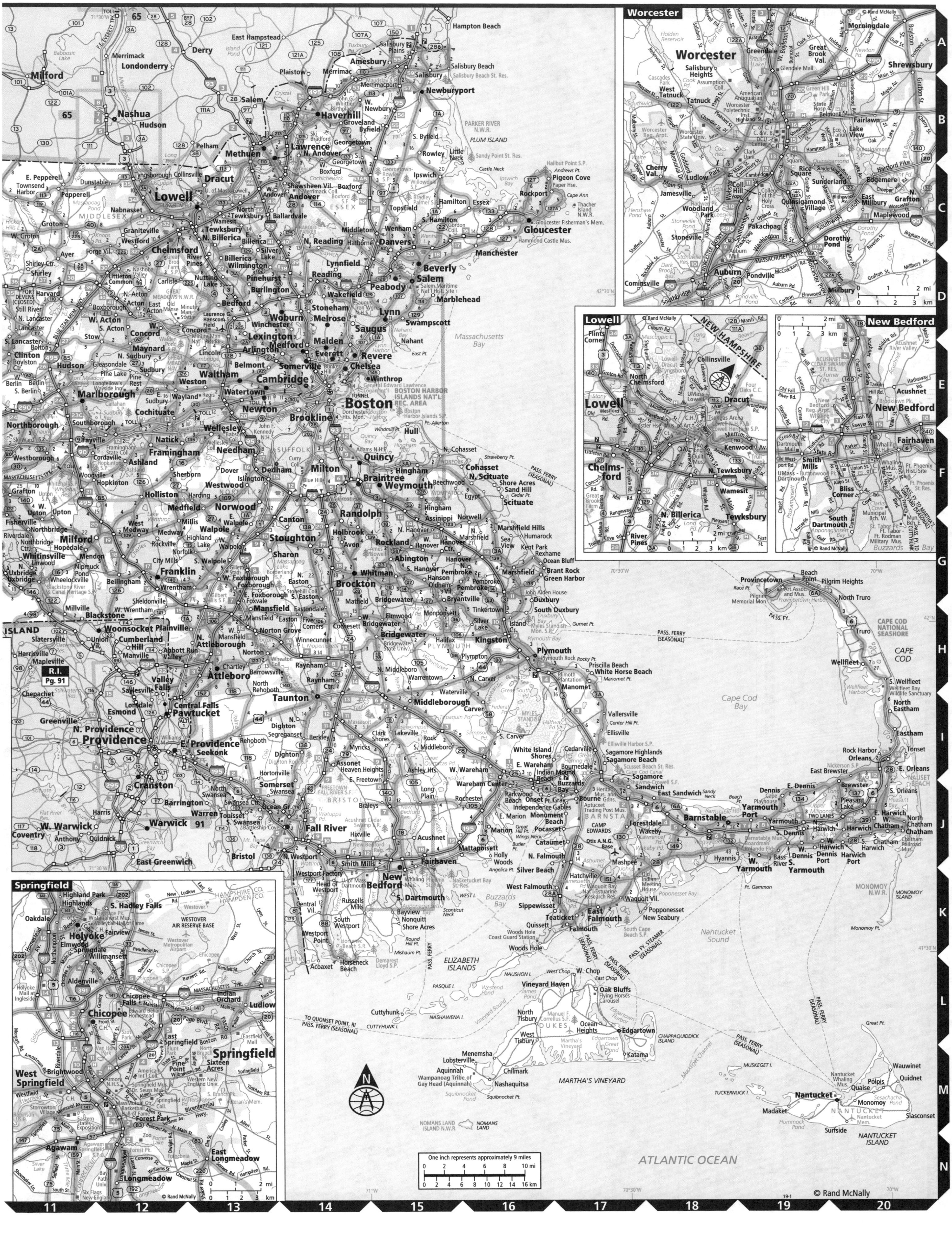

Michigan

Nickname: The Great Lake State
Capital: Lansing, Q-9
Land area: 56,539 sq. mi. (rank: 22nd)
Population: 9,883,640 (rank: 8th)
Largest city: Detroit, 713,777, R-12

Index of cities Pg. 131 | Map legend Pg. 1

Route planning & on-the-road resources

Low clearances, weigh stations, & restricted routes: Page A34

Weigh station location

Designated route for vehicles with STAA-authorized dimensions

Road Conditions & Construction
(800) 381-8477, (517) 373-2090; www.michigan.gov/drive

Toll Bridge/Tunnel Information
Mackinac Bridge Authority *(Mac Pass)*: (906) 643-7600; www.mackinacbridge.org

International Toll Bridge/Tunnel Information
Michigan Department of Transportation: Blue Water Bridge (Port Huron): (810) 984-3131; www.michigan.gov/mdot
Ambassador Bridge (Detroit): (800) 462-7434; www.ambassadorbridge.com
Detroit-Windsor Tunnel *(NEXPRESS)*: (313) 567-4422 ext. 200, (519) 258-7424 ext. 200; www.dwtunnel.com
International Bridge Administration (Sault Ste. Marie): (906) 635-5255, (705) 942-4345; www.saultbridge.com

Mileage between cities	Alpena	Ann Arbor	Benton Harbor	Chicago, IL	Detroit	Flint	Grand Rapids	Houghton	Ironwood	Jackson	Kalamazoo	Lansing	Mackinaw City	Menominee	Muskegon	Pontiac	Port Huron	Saginaw	Sault Ste. Marie	Toledo, OH	Traverse City
ANN ARBOR	227		144	240	43	54	132	538	648	36	98	64	272	509	172	49	102	86	329	55	242
CHICAGO, IL	428	240	98		283	272	177	421	408	207	146	217	413	260	185	284	338	304	469	242	322
DETROIT	244	43	188	283		69	158	555	600	79	142	90	290	491	197	32	64	104	346	59	259
FLINT	178	54	176	272	69		114	489	534	89	131	55	224	425	153	41	66	38	280	110	193
GRAND RAPIDS	251	132	81	177	158	114		502	586	106	52	68	236	446	41	138	180	146	292	188	145
KALAMAZOO	303	98	51	146	142	131	52	576	555	66		75	288	416	93	142	196	163	344	152	196
LANSING	228	64	122	217	90	55	68	493	539	38	775		228	430	108	70	122	88	284	120	183
MACKINAW CITY	94	272	317	413	290	224	236	266	311	262	288	228		202	251	262	290	188	56	328	102

Mileages © Rand McNally

Total mileage through Michigan

69	199 miles
94	275 miles
75	396 miles
96	192 miles

For more than 40,000 interstate mileages, see the Mileage Directory on page 137

Sights to see

- Cranbrook Art Museum, Bloomfield Hills D-5
- Detroit Zoo, Royal Oak E-6
- Edsel & Eleanor Ford House, Grosse Pointe Shores E-9
- Frederik Meijer Gardens, Grand Rapids. L-6
- Gerald R. Ford Museum, Grand Rapids L-5
- Gerald R. Ford Presidential Library, Ann Arbor M-10
- GM Renaissance Center, Detroit. K-10
- Henry Ford Mus. of American Innovation, Dearborn . . .H-5
- Motown Historical Museum, Detroit G-6
- New Detroit Science Center, Detroit G-7
- Sloan Museum, Flint L-2
- University of Michigan, Ann Arbor M-9

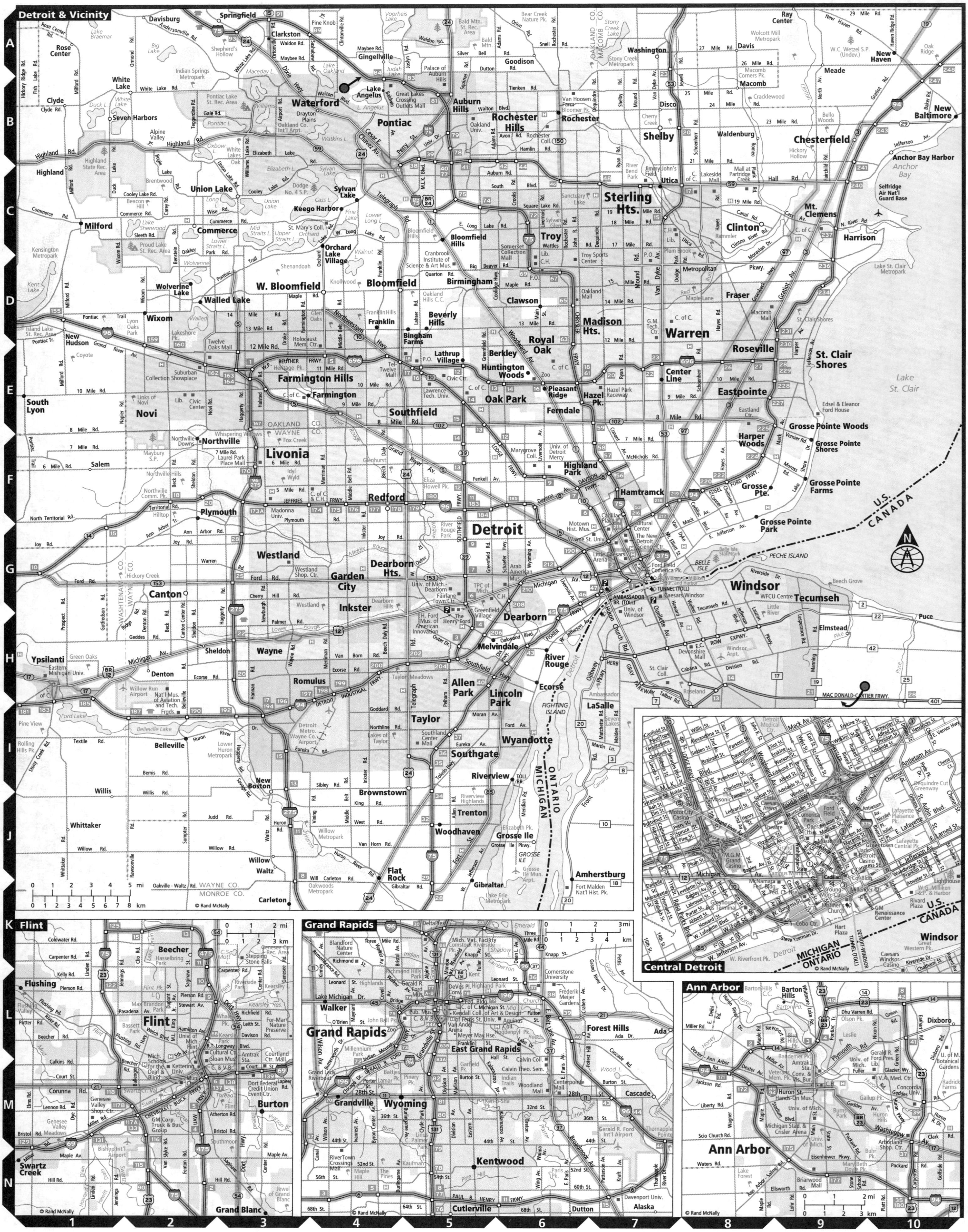

Walker Art Center, Minneapolis

Sights to see

- Bell Museum of Natural History, Minneapolis F-6
- Cathedral of St. Paul, St. Paul. M-7
- Frederick R. Weisman Art Museum, Minneapolis. M-4
- Mall of America, Bloomington. I-5
- Mill City Museum, Minneapolis L-3
- Minneapolis Institute of the Arts, Minneapolis N-2
- Minneapolis Sculpture Garden, Minneapolis M-1
- Minnesota History Center, Minneapolis M-7
- Minnesota State Capitol, St. Paul. L-7
- Ordway Center for the Performing Arts, St. Paul. M-7
- Science Museum of Minnesota, St. Paul M-7
- Walker Art Center, Minneapolis. M-1

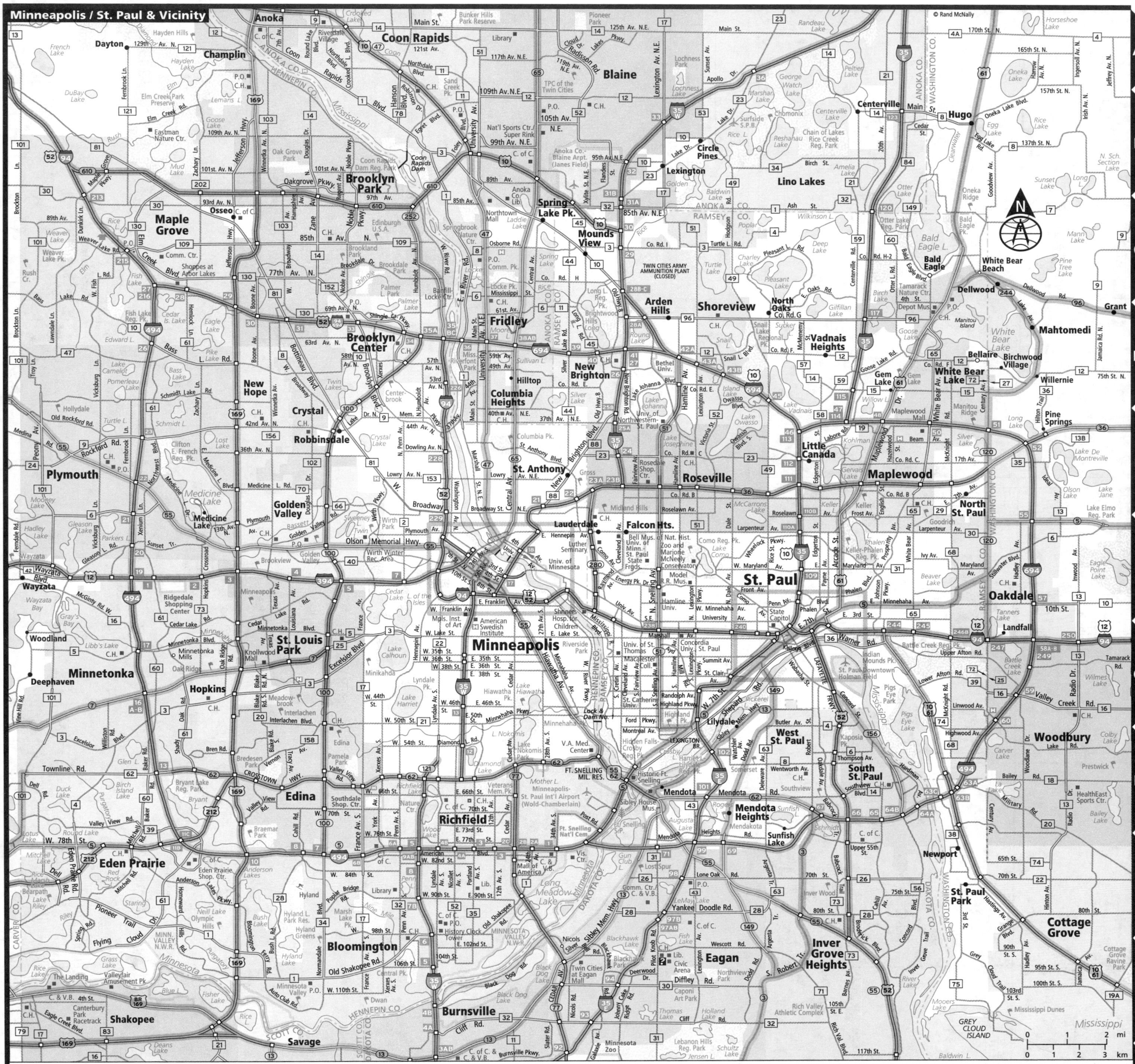

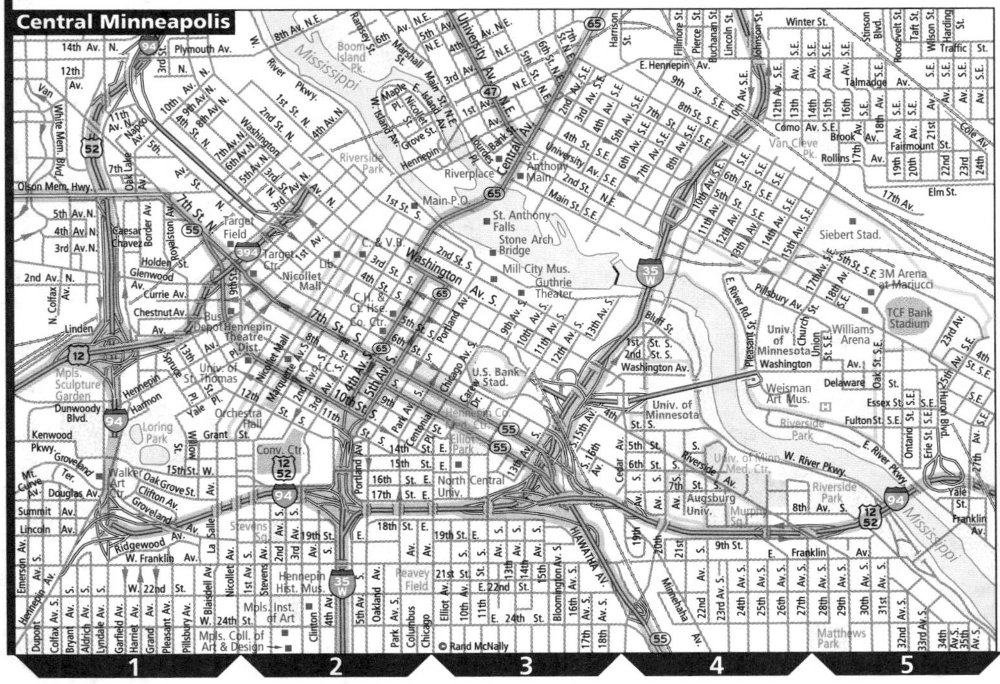

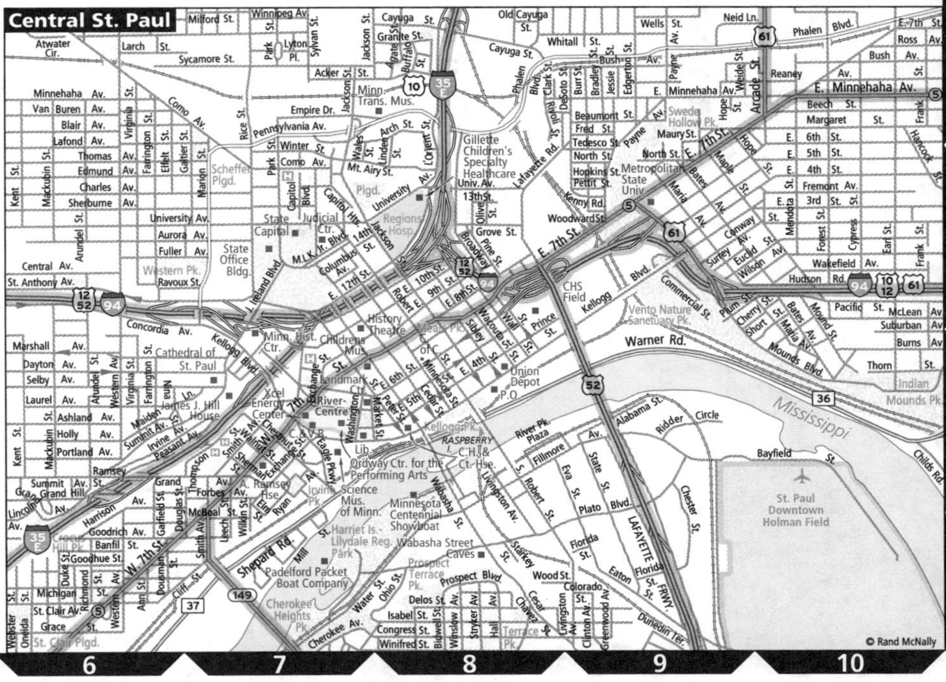

Nickname: The North Star State
Capital: St. Paul, O-10
Land area: 79,627 sq. mi. (rank: 14th)
Population: 5,303,925 (rank: 21st)
Largest city: Minneapolis, 382,578, O-9

Index of cities Pg. 132 | Map legend Pg. 1

Route planning & on-the-road resources

Low clearances, weigh stations, & restricted routes: Page A34

Weigh station location

Designated route for vehicles with STAA-authorized dimensions

Road Conditions & Construction
511, (651) 296-3000, In MN: (800) 657-3774
www.511mn.org, www.dot.state.mn.us

Toll Road Information
Boise Inc./Resolute Forest Products (International Falls Bridge):
www.fortfranceschamber.com/tourism-info/customs-info

Determining Distances
(segments of one mile or less not shown)
Cumulative miles (red): the distance between red arrows
Intermediate miles (black): the distance between intersections & places

Mileage between cities	Albert Lea	Austin	Bemidji	Brainerd	Duluth	Fairmont	Fergus Falls	Grand Forks, ND	Hibbing	International Falls	La Crosse, WI	Mankato	Marshall	Minneapolis	Moorhead	Red Wing	Rochester	St. Cloud	St. Paul	Sioux Falls, SD	Willmar
BEMIDJI	316	333		98	151	292	137	115	105	116	379	291	258	222	135	277	308	151	231	380	189
DULUTH	249	266	151	113		305	209	266	76	163	240	233	273	153	250	195	226	141	149	423	204
MINNEAPOLIS	96	112	222	134	153	152	180	317	208	295	158	80	153		235	57	88	70	9	270	94
MOORHEAD	329	345	135	136	250	357	58	82	212	249	391	303	219	235		290	321	175	244	245	173
ROCHESTER	62	38	308	220	226	118	266	402	281	368	71	86	236	88	321	48		155	79	236	182
ST. CLOUD	164	180	151	63	141	144	119	256	173	251	226	138	132	70	175	124	155		78	222	63
ST. PAUL	102	119	231	143	149	158	188	325	204	290	149	88	161	9	244	48	79	78		276	102
SIOUX FALLS, SD	177	198	380	334	423	122	237	320	478	495	298	156	93	270	245	278	236	222	276		162

Total mileage through Minnesota

35	260 miles	94	260 miles
90	276 miles	2	255 miles

For more than 40,000 interstate mileages, see the Mileage Directory on page 137

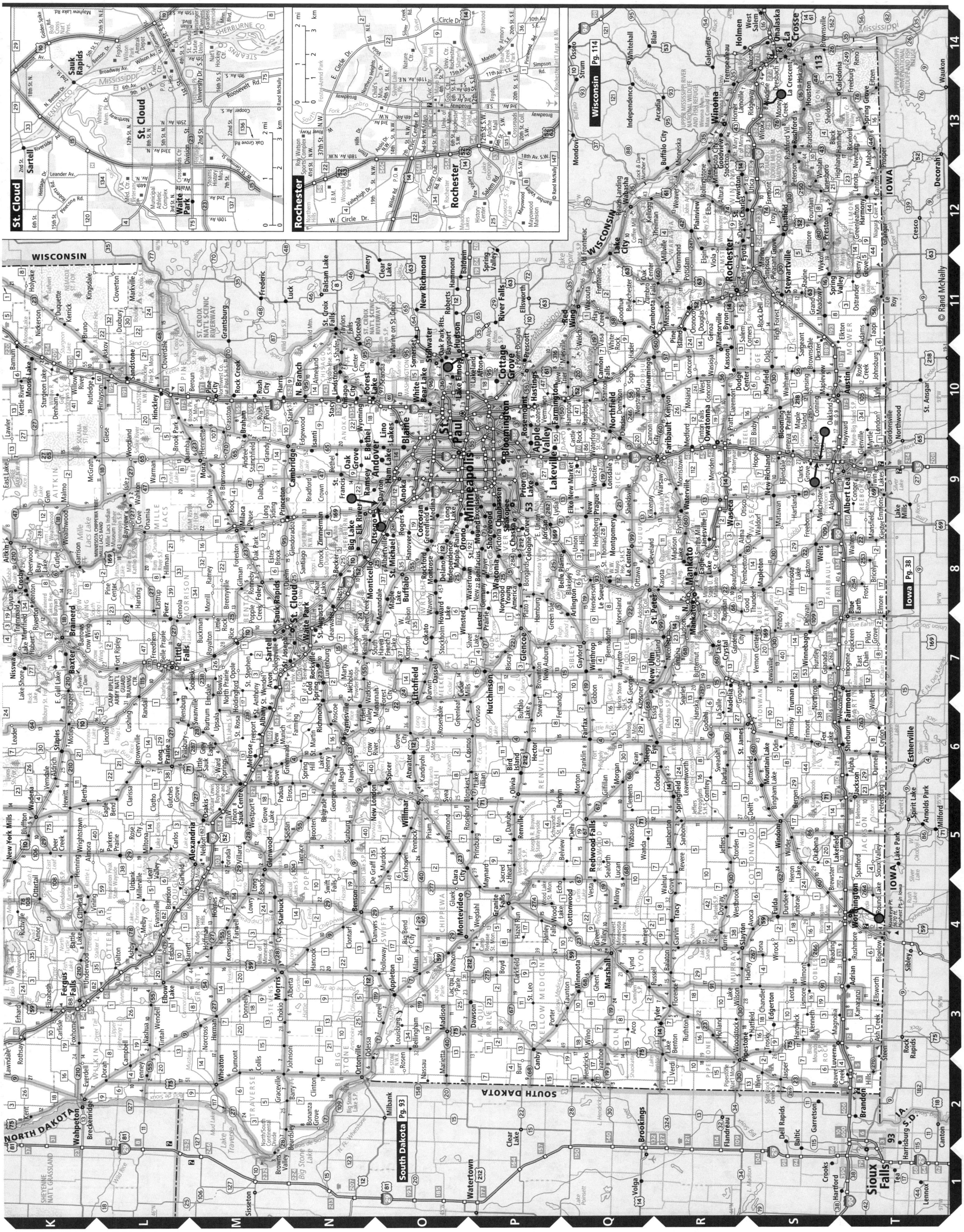

Mississippi

Nickname: The Magnolia State
Capital: Jackson, H-6
Land area: 46,923 sq. mi. (rank: 31st)
Population: 2,967,297 (rank: 31st)
Largest city: Jackson, 173,514, H-6

Index of cities Pg. 132 | Map legend Pg. 1

Mileage between cities	Biloxi	Greenville	Jackson	Memphis, TN	Meridian	Natchez	New Orleans, LA	Tupelo	Vicksburg
BILOXI		293	172	379	172	228	90	316	215
GREENVILLE	293		121	152	212	152	304	183	96
JACKSON	172	121		211	91	103	183	195	44
MEMPHIS, TN	379	152	211		234	314	394	105	251
MERIDIAN	172	212	91	234		194	198	144	135
NEW ORLEANS, LA	90	304	183	394	198	178		342	207
TUPELO	316	183	195	105	144	298	342		238
VICKSBURG	215	96	44	251	135	72	207	238	

Mileages © Rand McNally

Total mileage through Mississippi

10: 77 miles
55: 290 miles
20: 169 miles
59: 172 miles

For more than 40,000 interstate mileages, see the Mileage Directory on page 137

Route planning & on-the-road resources

Low clearances, weigh stations, & restricted routes: Page A34

Weigh station location

Designated route for vehicles with STAA-authorized dimensions

Road Conditions & Construction
511, (601) 359-7001
www.mdot.ms.gov, www.mdottraffic.com

Toll Road Information
No tolls on state or federal highways

Gateway Arch, St. Louis

Sights to see

- Andy Williams Moon River Theatre, Branson M-8
- Anheuser-Busch Brewery, St. Louis . . . I-7
- Dolly Parton's Dixie Stampede, Branson M-9

- Gateway Arch, St. Louis L-4
- Laumeier Sculpture Park, St. Louis . . J-4
- Magic House, Kirkwood I-4
- Missouri Botanical Garden, St. Louis . . I-6

- Shoji Tabuchi Theatre, Branson L-7
- St. Louis Art Museum, St. Louis H-6
- St. Louis Science Center, St. Louis ... H-6
- St. Louis Zoo, St. Louis H-6

- Shepherd of the Hills, Branson K-6
- White Water, Branson M-7
- Wonders of Wildlife Nat'l Museum & Aquarium, Springfield C-3

Springfield

Joplin

Cape Girardeau

St. Louis & Vicinity

Central St. Louis

Branson

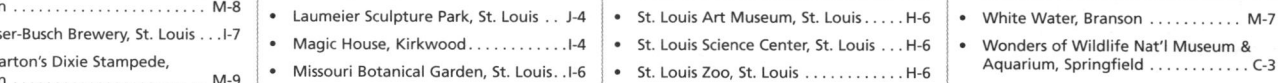

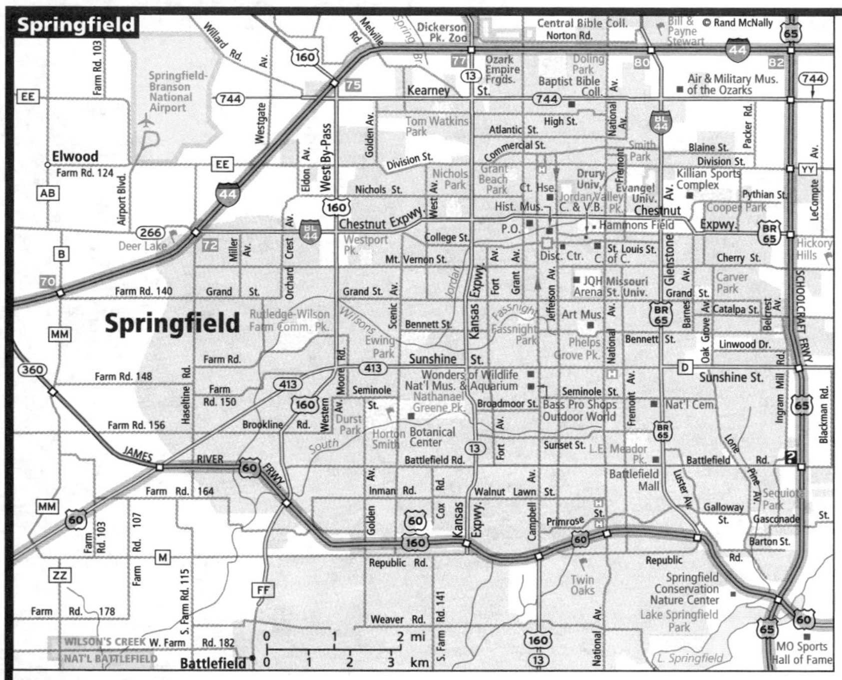

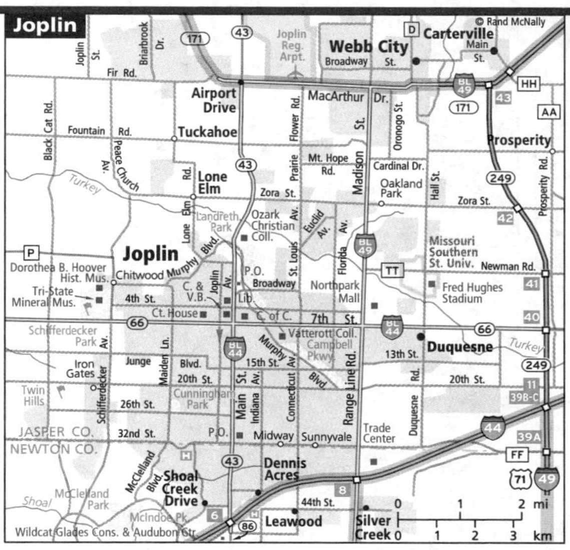

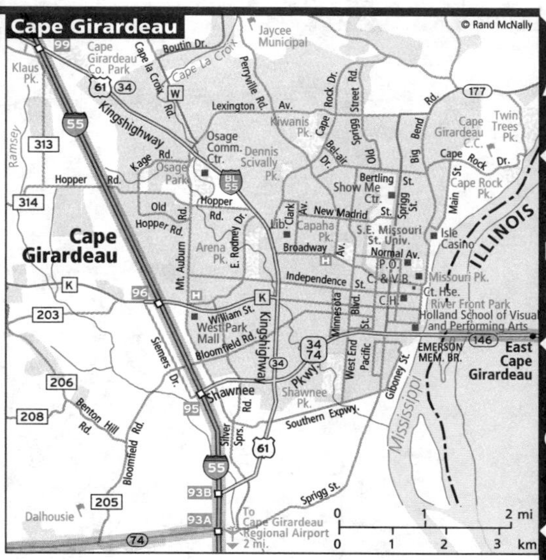

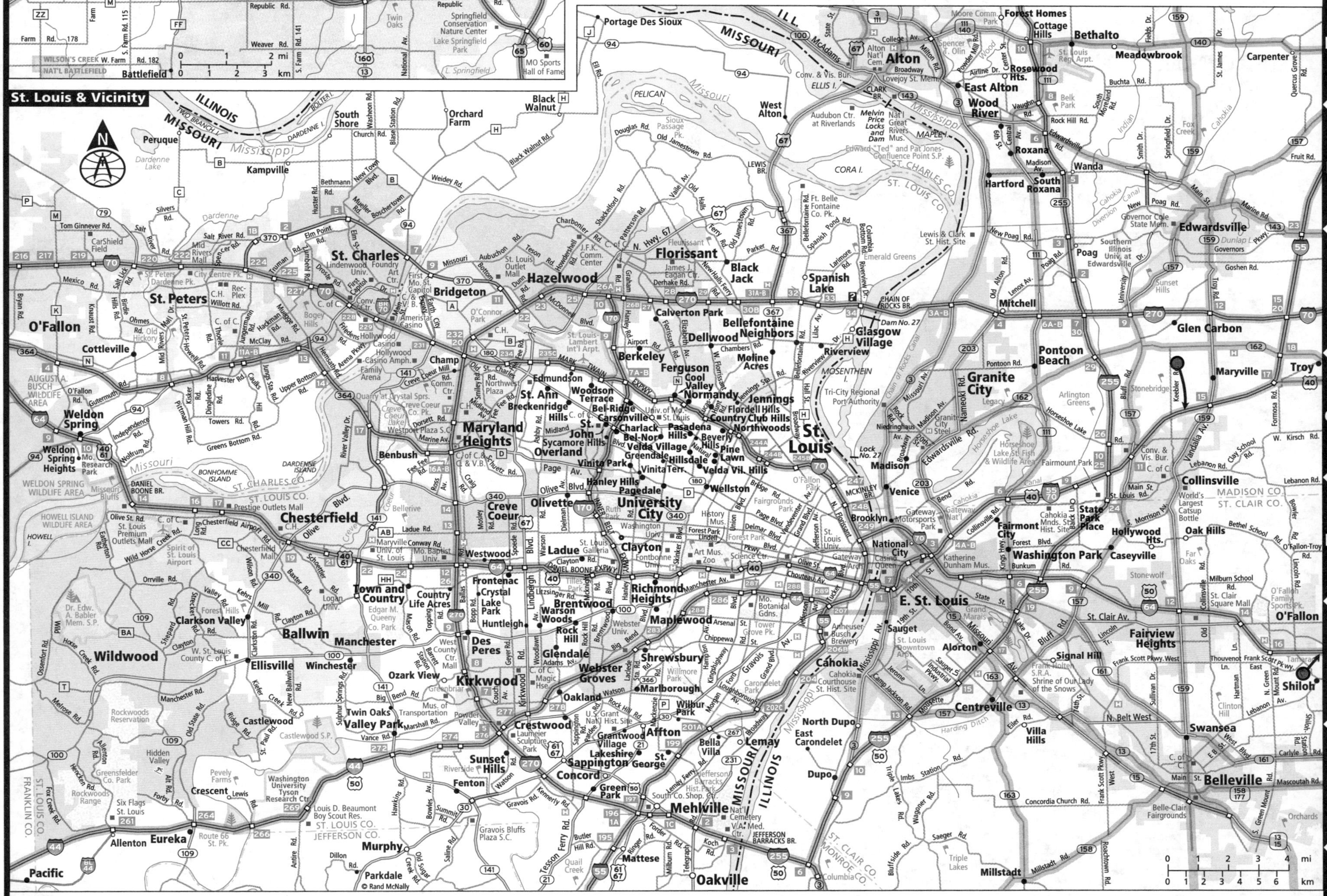

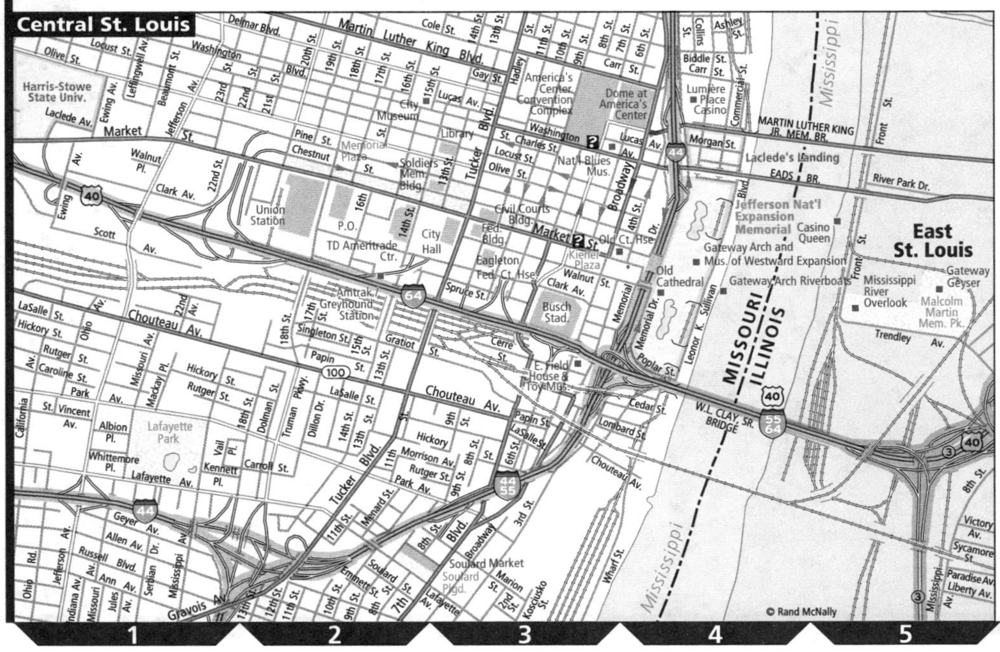

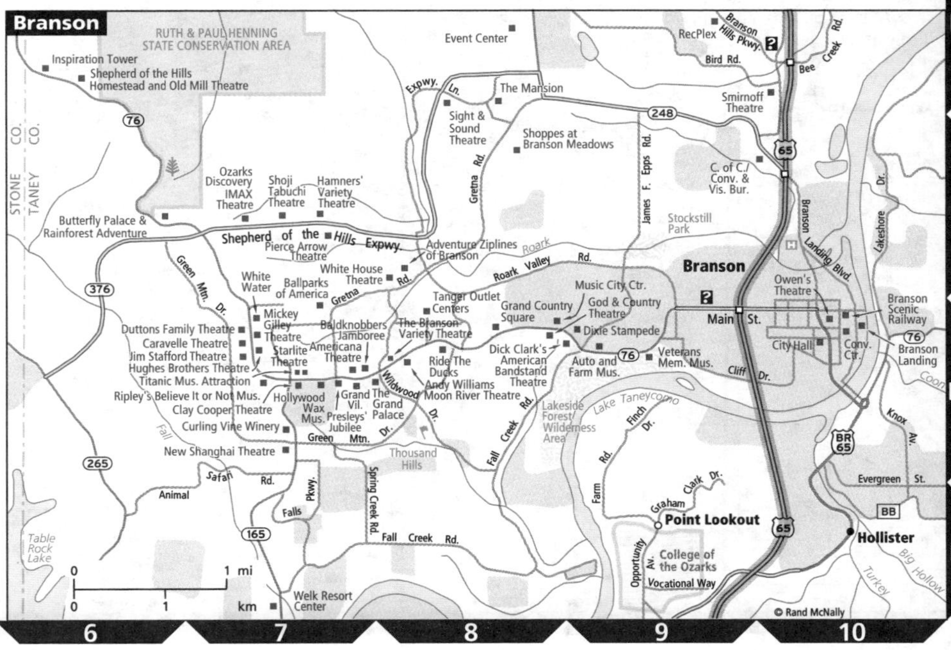

Nickname: The Show Me State
Capital: Jefferson City, G-14
Land area: 68,741 sq. mi. (rank: 18th)
Population: 5,988,927 (rank: 18th)
Largest city: Kansas City, 459,787, F-9

Index of cities Pg. 132 | Map legend Pg. 1

Route planning & on-the-road resources

Low clearances, weigh stations, & restricted routes: Page A35

Weigh station location

Designated route for vehicles with STAA-authorized dimensions

Road Conditions & Construction
(888) 275-6636, (573) 751-2551; www.modot.org

Toll Road Information
No tolls on state or federal highways

Determining Distances
(segments of one mile or less not shown)
Cumulative miles (red): the distance between red arrows
Intermediate miles (black): the distance between intersections & places

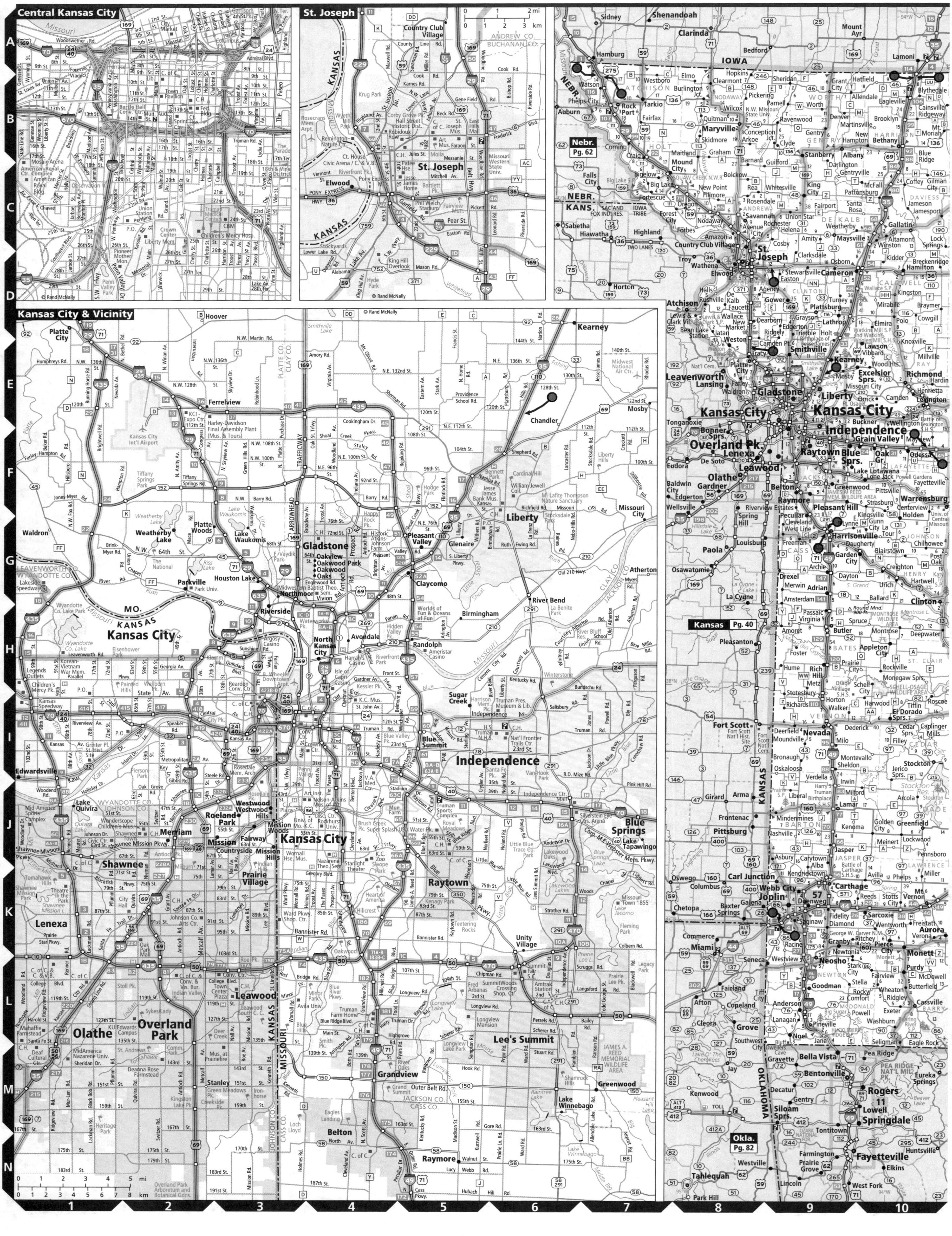

Mileage between cities	Branson	Brookfield	Cape Girardeau	Columbia	Hannibal	Hayti	Jefferson City	Joplin	Kansas City	Kirksville	Maryville	Osage Beach	Poplar Bluff	Rolla	St. Joseph	St. Louis	Springfield	West Plains
CAPE GIRARDEAU	296	315		225	219	80	234	349	349	316	447	279	86	200	407	114	270	182
COLUMBIA	206	95	225		97	302	32	242	124	96	222	77	261	95	182	126	168	194
JOPLIN	121	269	349	242	315	367	210		160	312	244	165	269	182	204	286	75	187
KANSAS CITY	213	114	349	124	209	426	156	160		157	95	201	385	219	55	250	170	279
POPLAR BLUFF	217	352	86	261	255	104	231	269	385	352	483	277		170	443	151	190	102
ST. JOSEPH	271	98	407	182	193	484	214	204	55	141	44	259	443	277		308	228	337
ST. LOUIS	250	216	114	126	120	192	134	286	250	217	347	179	151	104	308		213	204
SPRINGFIELD	42	221	270	168	242	288	136	75	170	259	268	91	190	108	228	213		108

Total mileage through Missouri

- I-35: 115 miles
- I-44: 290 miles
- I-55: 210 miles
- I-70: 252 miles

For more than 40,000 interstate mileages, see the Mileage Directory on page 137

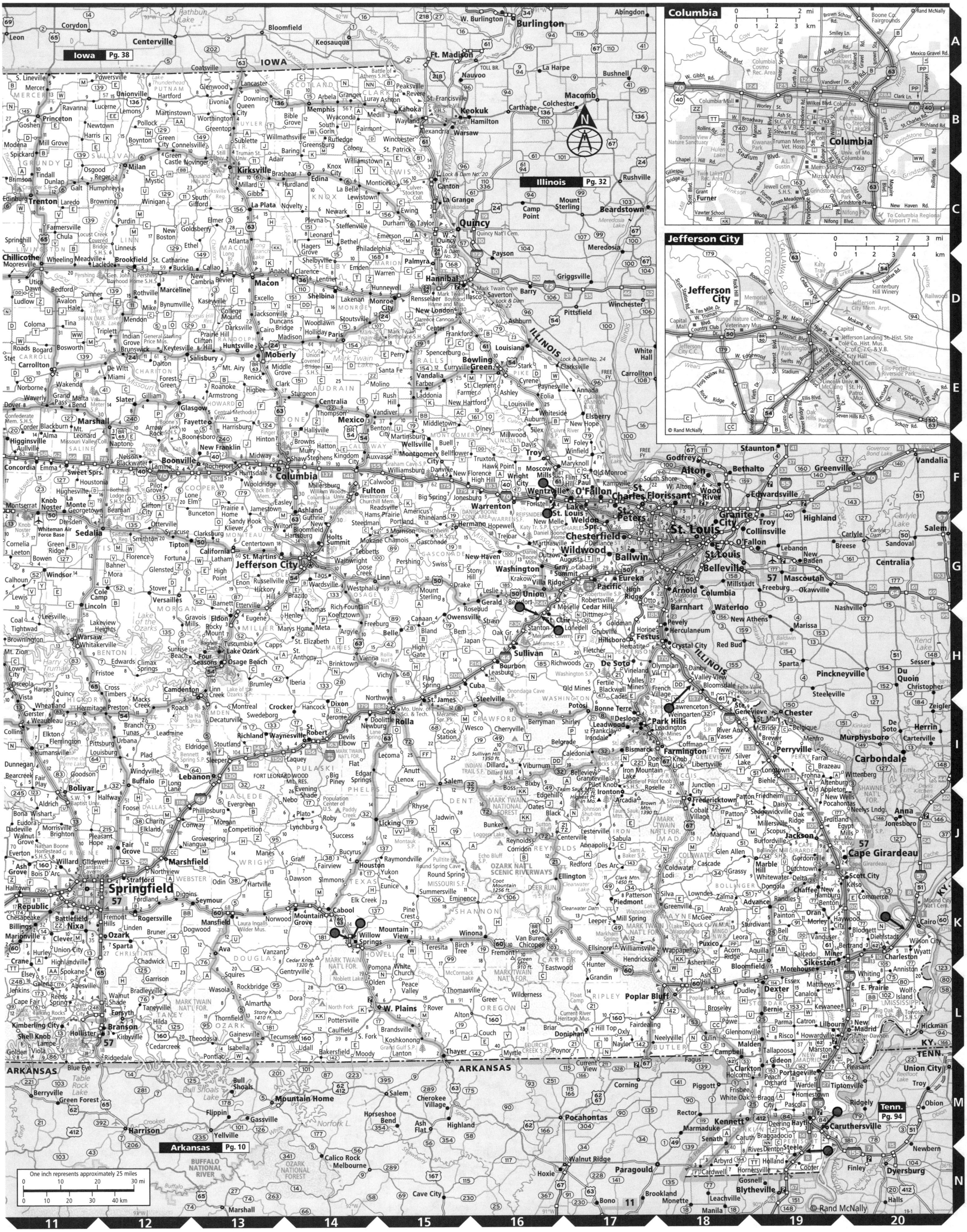

Montana

Nickname: The Treasure State
Capital: Helena, G-7
Land area: 145,546 sq. mi. (rank: 4th)
Population: 989,415 (rank: 44th)
Largest city: Billings, 104,170, I-13

Index of cities Pg. 132 | Map legend Pg. 1

Route planning & on-the-road resources

Low clearances, weigh stations, & restricted routes: Page A35

- Weigh station location
- Designated route for vehicles with STAA-authorized dimensions

Road Conditions & Construction
511, (800) 226-7623, (406) 444-6200
www.mdt511.com, www.mdt.mt.gov

Toll Road Information
No tolls on state or federal highways

Determining Distances
(segments of one mile or less not shown)
Cumulative miles (red): the distance between red arrows
Intermediate miles (black): the distance between intersections & places

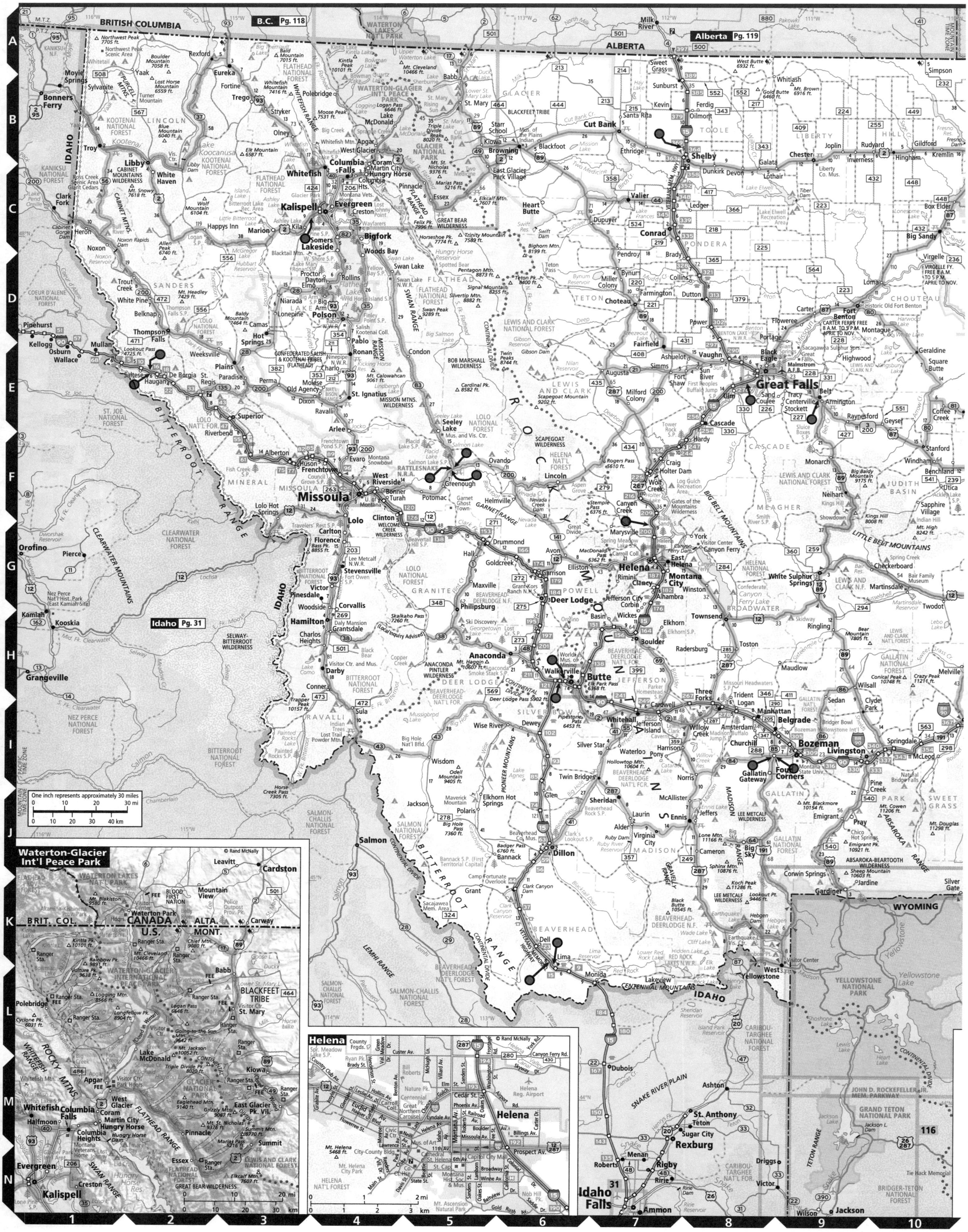

Mileage between cities	Billings	Bozeman	Butte	Dillon	Glasgow	Great Falls	Havre	Helena	Kalispell	Lewistown	Libby	Miles City	Missoula	St. Mary	Shelby	Sheridan, WY	Sidney	West Yellowstone
BILLINGS		141	223	257	277	218	248	238	464	125	534	147	343	377	304	130	271	231
BOZEMAN	141		85	119	366	190	302	100	326	163	396	288	205	304	270	271	412	89
BUTTE	223	85		66	425	155	267	66	241	244	311	370	120	269	235	352	494	149
GREAT FALLS	218	190	155	222	271		113	92	230	107	320	319	168	163	90	350	378	267
HELENA	238	100	66	132	362	92	204		193	195	281	385	113	206	172	368	509	177
KALISPELL	464	326	241	293	420	230	262	193		334	88	545	121	131	159	593	560	390
MILES CITY	147	288	370	403	196	319	334	385	545	211	680		490	476	403	203	127	377
MISSOULA	343	205	120	172	439	168	281	113	121	272	191	490		252	227	472	614	269

Mileages © Rand McNally

Total mileage through Montana

15: 396 miles
90: 552 miles
94: 249 miles

For more than 40,000 interstate mileages, see the Mileage Directory on page 137

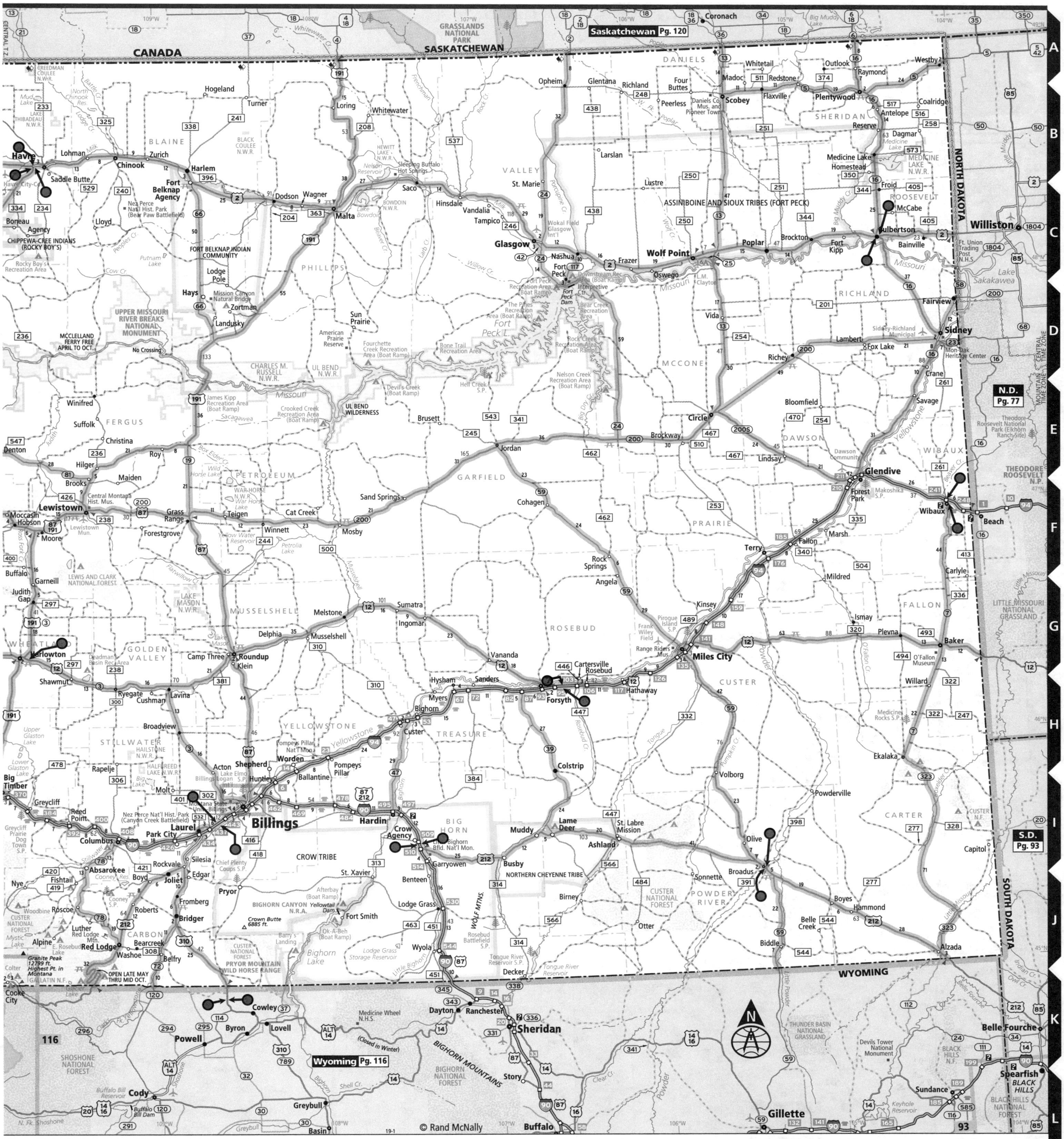

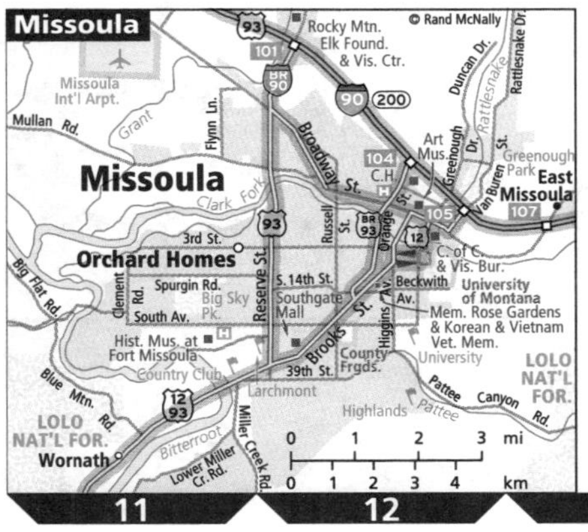

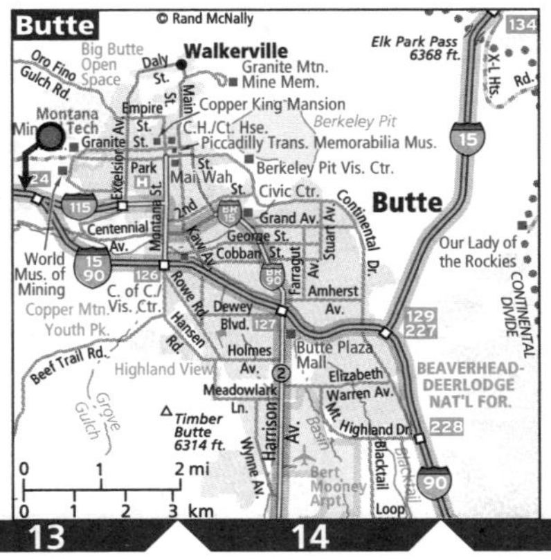

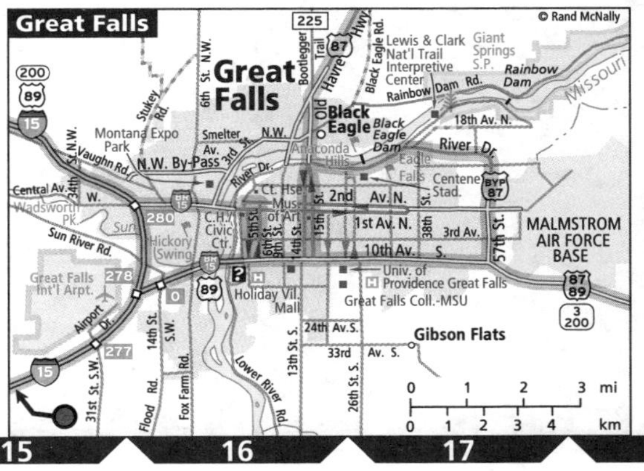

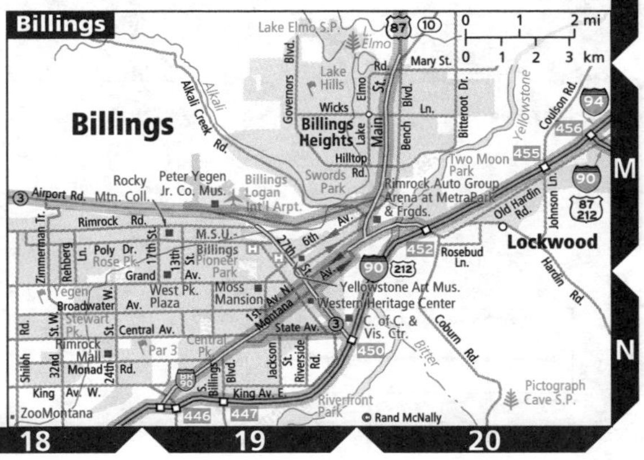

Nebraska

Nickname: The Cornhusker State
Capital: Lincoln, K-17
Land area: 76,824 sq. mi. (rank: 15th)
Population: 1,826,341 (rank: 38th)
Largest city: Omaha, 408,958, J-19

Index of cities Pg. 132 | Map legend Pg. 1

Route planning & on-the-road resources

Low clearances, weigh stations, & restricted routes: **Page A36**

Weigh station location

Designated route for vehicles with STAA-authorized dimensions

Road Conditions & Construction
511, (800) 906-9069, (402) 471-4567
www.511.nebraska.gov, www.dot.nebraska.gov

Toll Road Information
No tolls on state or federal highways

Determining Distances
(segments of one mile or less not shown)
Cumulative miles (red): the distance between red arrows
Intermediate miles (black): the distance between intersections & places

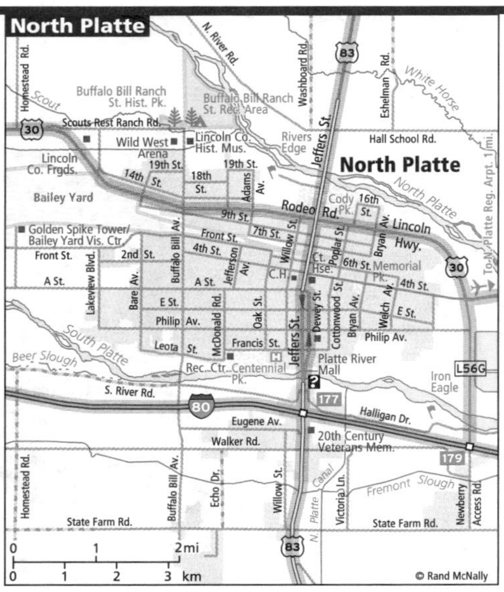

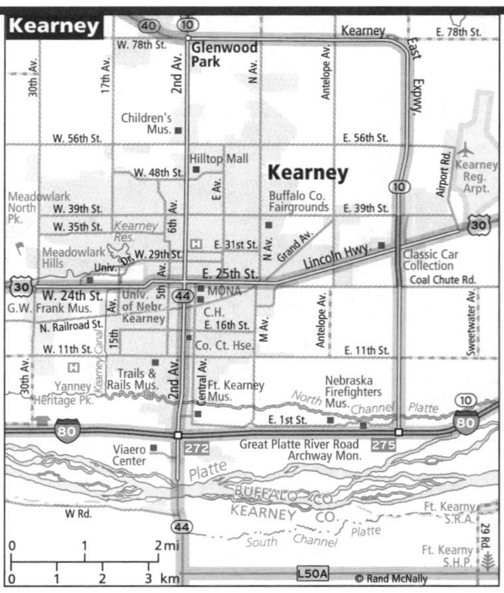

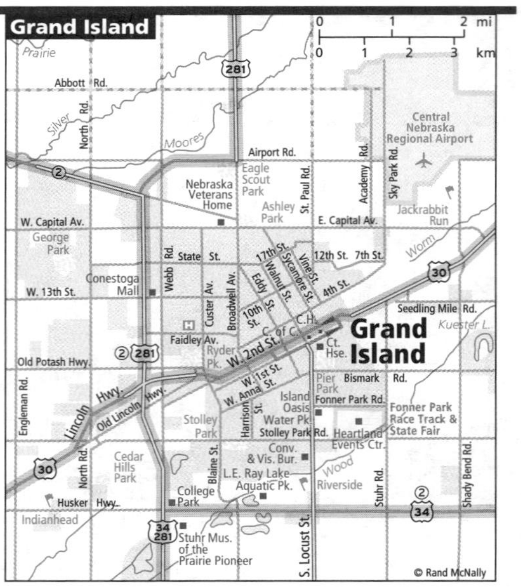

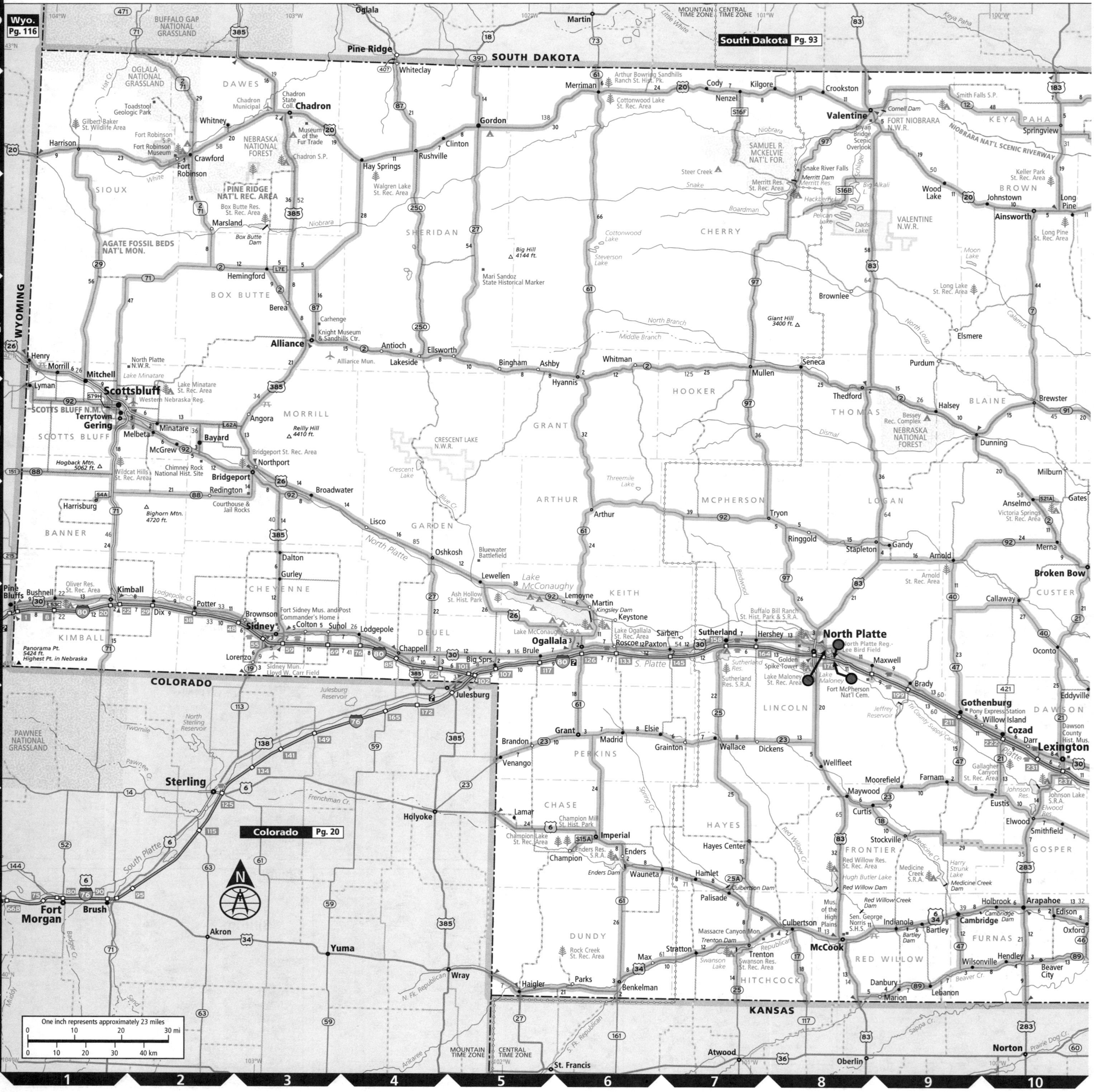

Mileage between cities	Alliance	Beatrice	Chadron	Cheyenne, WY	Columbus	Grand Island	Kearney	Lincoln	McCook	Nebraska City	Norfolk	North Platte	Ogallala	Omaha	O'Neill	Scottsbluff	Sioux City, IA	Valentine
GRAND ISLAND	318	135	370	361	64		50	101	154	146	110	145	194	152	115	323	184	212
LINCOLN	402	48	454	445	77	101	134		238	53	122	229	278	58	212	407	151	309
NORFOLK	328	162	323	471	45	110	160	122	263	179		255	304	113	104	432	82	186
NORTH PLATTE	176	262	229	220	209	145	99	229	67	273	255		53	280	206	182	373	129
OGALLALA	124	312	176	168	259	194	149	278	117	323	304	53		329	259	129	422	182
OMAHA	453	99	505	496	85	152	185	58	288	44	113	280	329		208	458	97	298
SCOTTSBLUFF	55	440	99	108	387	323	277	407	245	451	432	182	129	458	332		551	218
VALENTINE	163	343	137	349	230	212	196	309	197	354	186	129	182	298	111	218	236	

Total mileage through Nebraska

80	455 miles	83	226 miles
81	219 miles	20	436 miles

For more than 40,000 interstate mileages, see the Mileage Directory on page 137

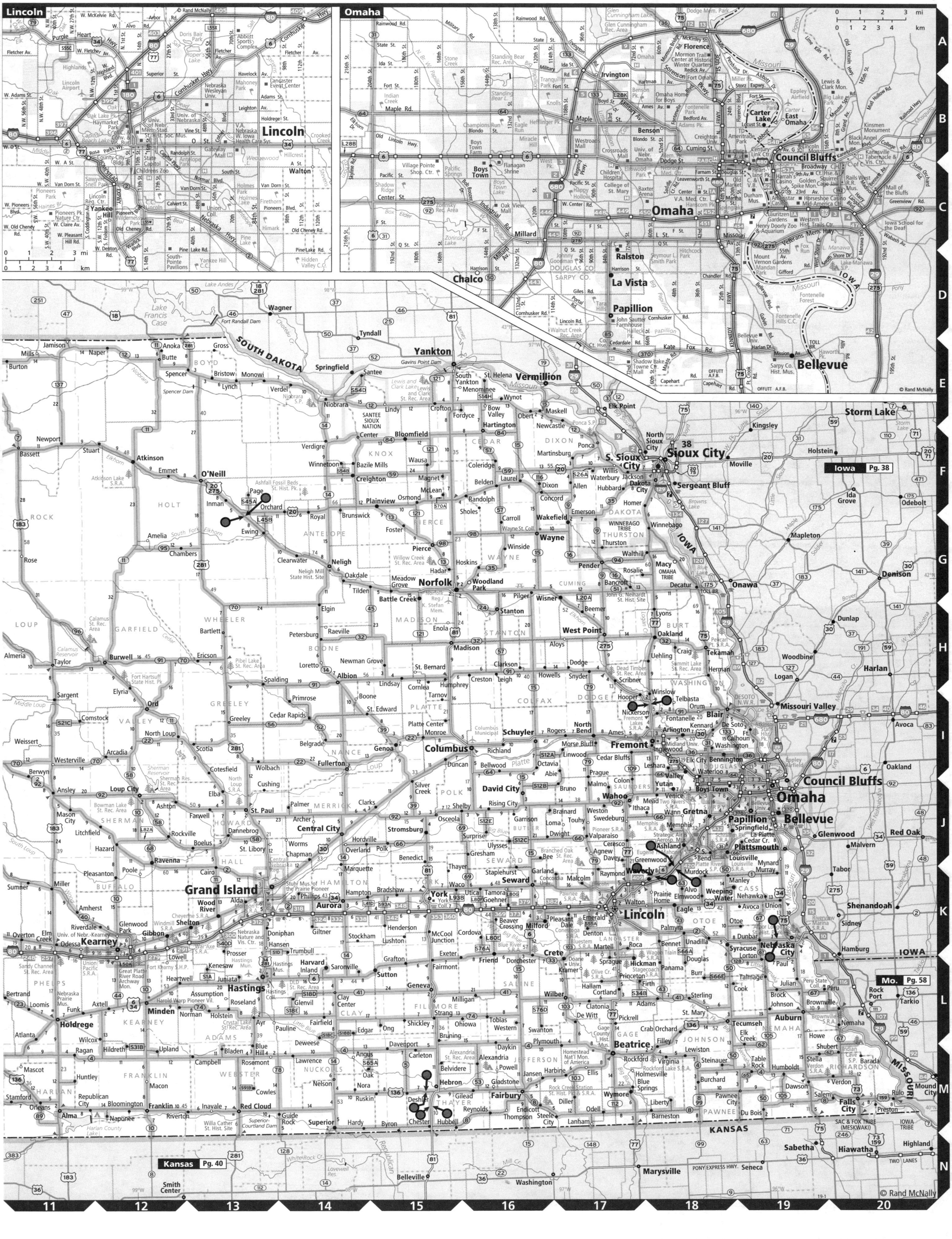

Nevada

Nickname: The Silver State
Capital: Carson City, F-2
Land area: 109,781 sq. mi. (rank: 7th)
Population: 2,700,551 (rank: 35th)
Largest city: Las Vegas, 583,756, L-8

Index of cities Pg. 132
Map legend Pg. 1

Mileage between cities	Austin	Beatty	Carson City	Elko	Ely	Hawthorne	Jackpot	Las Vegas	McDermitt	Panaca	Reno	Tonopah	Winnemucca
ELKO	158	369	304		190	323	118	436	200	308	288	276	125
ELY	147	260	319	190		271	206	245	347	121	319	167	271
LAS VEGAS	328	117	435	436	245	314	451		547	165	447	210	472
RENO	172	330	32	288	319	133	406	447	239	442		237	163
S. LAKE TAHOE, CA	200	346	28	332	347	149	451	464	283	459	60	253	208
TONOPAH	118	93	225	276	167	104	373	210	337	206	237		261
WENDOVER, UT	269	381	414	110	121	392	126	366	310	239	398	289	235
WINNEMUCCA	144	354	179	125	271	198	243	472	75	392	163	261	

Total mileage through Nevada
I-15: 124 miles
US 6: 307 miles
I-80: 411 miles
US 95: 652 miles

For more than 40,000 interstate mileages, see the Mileage Directory on page 137

Route planning & on-the-road resources

Low clearances, weigh stations, & restricted routes: **Page A36**

Weigh station location
Designated route for vehicles with STAA-authorized dimensions

Road Conditions & Construction
511
(877) 687-6237, (775) 888-7000
www.nevadadot.com
www.nvroads.com

Toll Road Information
No tolls on state or federal hwys.

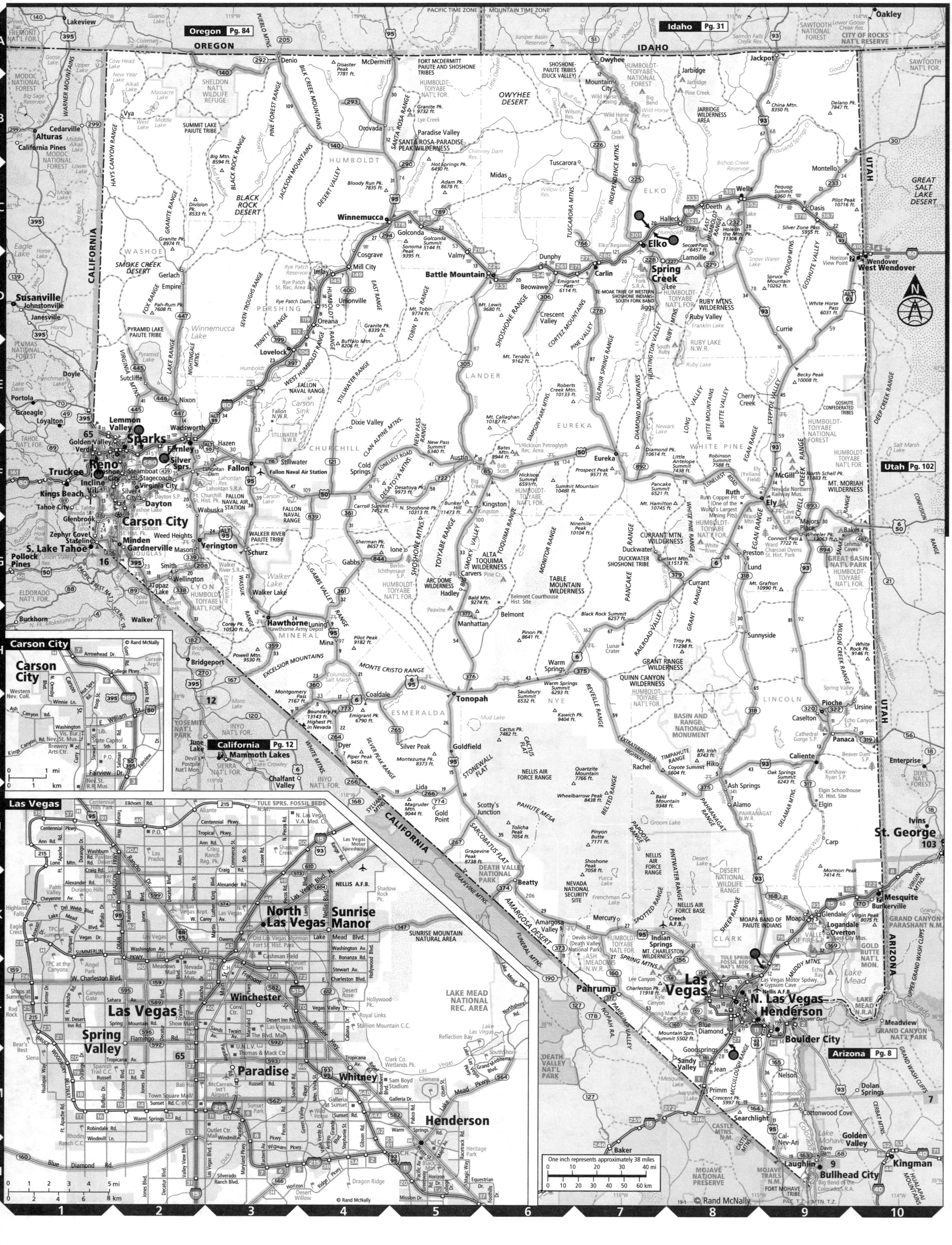

Route planning & on-the-road resources

Low clearances, weigh stations, & restricted routes: **Page A36**

Weigh station location

Designated route for vehicles with STAA-authorized dimensions

Road Conditions & Construction
511, (603) 271-3734
www.nhtmc.com, www.nh.gov/dot

Toll Road Information
Bureau of Turnpikes (*E-ZPass*):
(603) 485-3806
www.nh.gov/dot/org/operations/turnpikes

Mileage between cities	Berlin	Boston, MA	Concord	Keene	Lebanon	Littleton	Manchester	Nashua	Portsmouth
BERLIN		182	115	168	123	42	133	151	117
CONCORD	115	67		54	60	87	18	36	44
KEENE	168	90	54		60	140	55	50	99
LEBANON	123	121	60	60		84	72	90	111
LITTLETON	42	154	87	140	84		105	123	130
MANCHESTER	133	53	18	55	72	105		18	48
NASHUA	151	43	36	50	90	123	18		54
PORTSMOUTH	117	60	44	99	111	130	48	54	

Mileages © Rand McNally

Total mileage through New Hampshire
89: 61 miles
95: 16 miles
93: 132 miles
2: 36 miles

For more than 40,000 interstate mileages, see the Mileage Directory on page 137

New Hampshire

Nickname: The Granite State
Capital: Concord, K-7
Land area: 8,953 sq. mi. (rank: 44th)
Population: 1,316,470 (rank: 42nd)
Largest city: Manchester, 109,565, L-7

Index of cities Pg. 132
Map legend Pg. 1

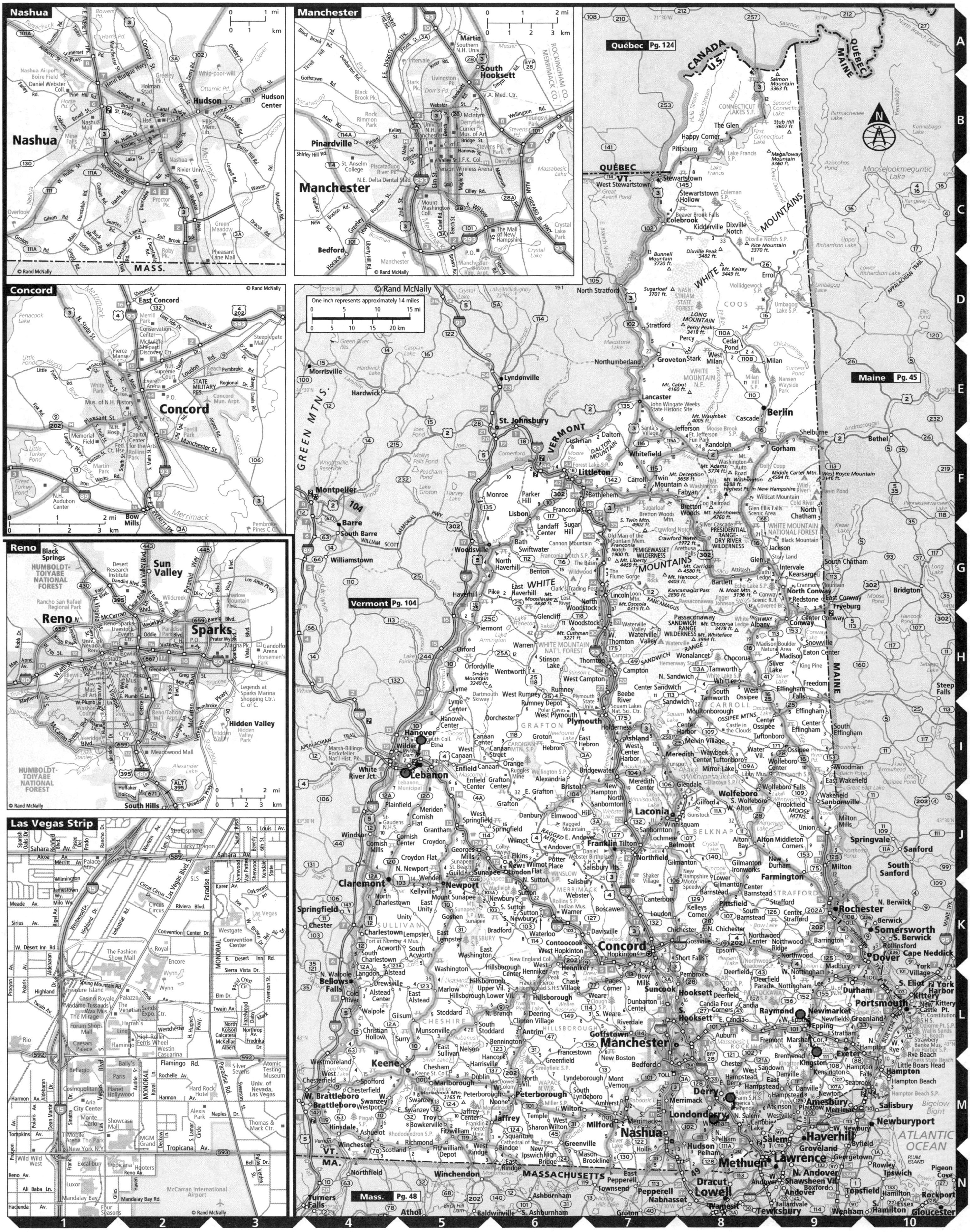

New Jersey

Nickname: The Garden State
Capital: Trenton, J-8
Land area: 7,354 sq. mi. (rank: 46th)
Population: 8,791,894 (rank: 11th)
Largest city: Newark, 277,140, F-12

Index of cities Pg. 132 | Map legend Pg. 1

Route planning & on-the-road resources

Low clearances, weigh stations, & restricted routes: Page A36

Weigh station location
Designated route for vehicles with STAA-authorized dimensions

Road Conditions & Construction
511,
(866) 511-6538
www.511nj.org
www.state.nj.us/transportation

Toll Road/Bridge/Tunnel Information *(all use E-ZPass)*
N.J. Turnpike Authority (N.J. Turnpike, Gdn. St. Pkwy.): (732) 750-5300; www.state.nj.us/turnpike
South Jersey Transportation Authority (Atlantic City Expressway): (609) 965-6060; www.sjta.com
Burlington County Bridge Commission: (856) 829-1900, (609) 387-1480; www.bcbridges.org
Del. River & Bay Auth. (Del. Mem. Br., Cape May/Lewes Fy.): (302) 571-6300; www.drba.net
Del. River Port Auth. (Philadelphia area bridges): (877) 567-3772, (856) 968-2000; www.drpa.org
Del. River Joint Toll Br. Commission (other Del. River bridges): (800) 363-0049; www.drjtbc.org
Port Auth. of N.Y. & N.J. (NYC area inter-state bridges & tunnels): (800) 221-9903; www.panynj.gov

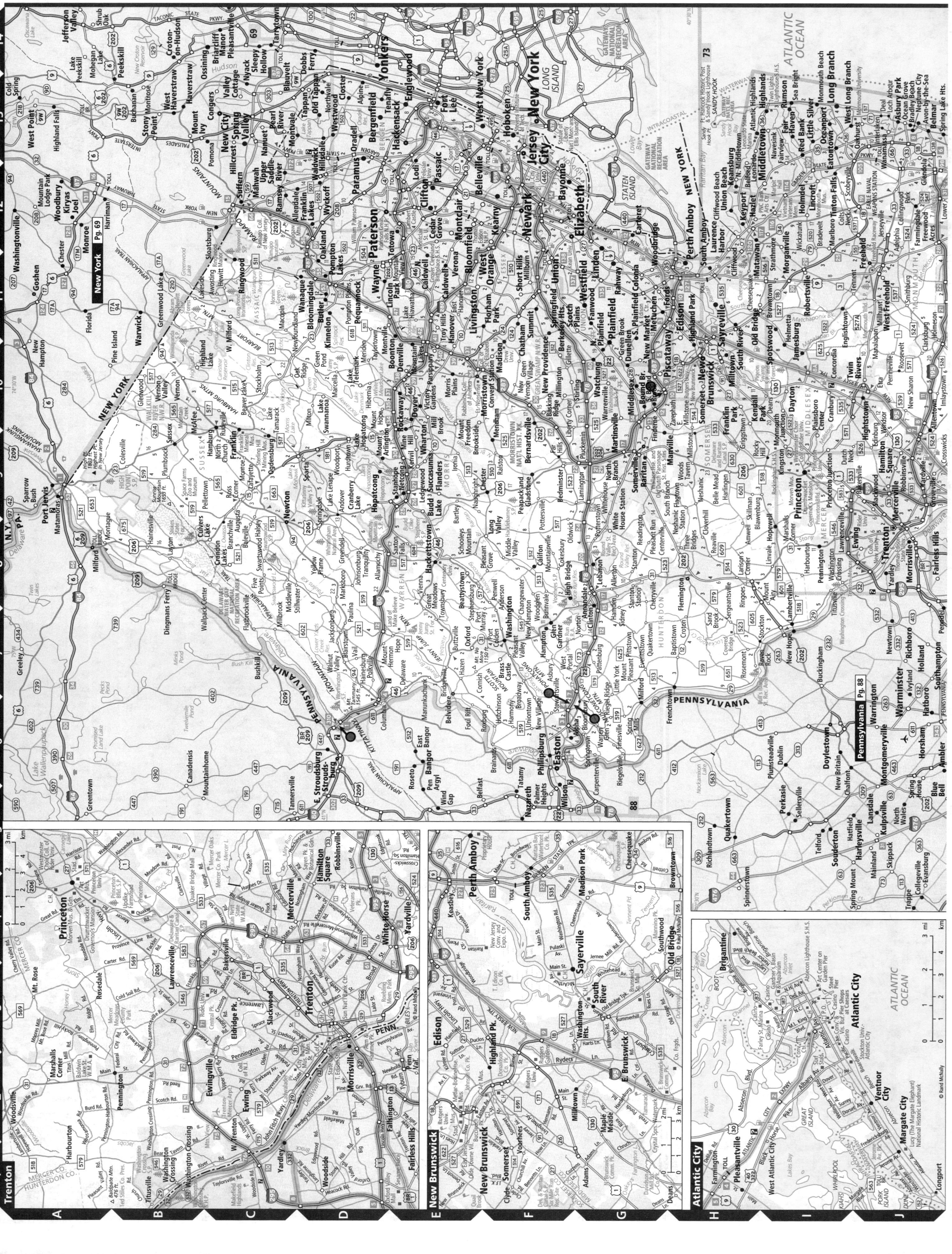

Mileage between cities	Atlantic City	Camden	Cape May	Cherry Hill	Elizabeth	Jersey City	Long Branch	Newark	New Brunswick	New York, NY	Paterson	Phillipsburg	Point Pleasant	Port Jervis, NY	Princeton	Somerville	Toms River	Trenton	Vineland	Willingboro	Wilmington, DE
ATLANTIC CITY		58	47	62	135	145	86	137	118	154	161	139	66	252	101	120	54	89	37	69	82
CAMDEN	58		90	10	88	98	87	90	71	107	114	88	81	204	51	69	60	39	36	18	32
NEWARK	137	90	169	78	6	8	45		25	28	24	60	64	113	50	33	80	55	115	67	115
NEW BRUNSWICK	118	71	150	59	23	33	41	25		42	49	55	43	133	16	19	43	26	96	48	96
PATERSON	161	114	193	102	30	17	69	24	49	26		67	88	104	58	41	104	79	139	91	139
PHILLIPSBURG	139	88	171	92	58	68	81	60	55	87	67		101	142	54	38	116	91	117	94	95
TRENTON	89	39	121	31	53	63	53	55	26	72	79	91	46	170	11	30	46		67	20	61
WILMINGTON, DE	82	32	100	36	114	124	113	115	96	133	139	95	107	230	73	91	86	61	49	46	

Total mileage through New Jersey

78: 68 miles
95: 78 miles
80: 68 miles

For more than 40,000 interstate mileages, see the Mileage Directory on page 137

New Mexico

Nickname: Land of Enchantment
Capital: Santa Fe, D-6
Land area: 121,298 sq. mi. (rank: 5th)
Population: 2,059,179 (rank: 36th)
Largest city: Albuquerque, 545,852, E-4

Index of cities Pg. 133 | Map legend Pg. 1

Mileage between cities	Alamogordo	Albuquerque	Carlsbad	Clovis	El Paso, TX	Hobbs	Las Cruces	Las Vegas	Lordsburg	Raton	Santa Fe	Socorro	Taos	Tucumcari
ALBUQUERQUE	235		280	220	267	349	224	120	343	227	58	78	129	173
CARLSBAD	292	280		192	217	70	264	282	377	389	273	358	344	273
CLOVIS	256	220	192		345	129	323	221	442	281	213	298	284	166
GALLUP	373	139	419	359	406	488	362	259	481	366	197	216	268	312
LAS CRUCES	67	224	264	323	49	368		343	119	450	282	149	353	303
ROSWELL	234	199	76	110	294	117	302	201	421	308	191	276	263	192
SANTA FE	227	58	273	213	325	342	282	65	401	172		136	71	166
TUCUMCARI	236	173	273	166	326	297	303	124	423	231	166	251	202	

Mileages © Rand McNally

Total mileage through New Mexico
- I-10: 164 miles
- I-25: 462 miles
- I-40: 374 miles

For more than 40,000 interstate mileages, see the Mileage Directory on page 137

Route planning & on-the-road resources

Low clearances, weigh stations, & restricted routes: Page A37

- Weigh station location
- Designated route for vehicles with STAA-authorized dimensions

Road Conditions & Construction
511
(800) 432-4269, (505) 827-5100
www.nmroads.com
www.dot.state.nm.us

Toll Road Information
No tolls on state or federal hwys.

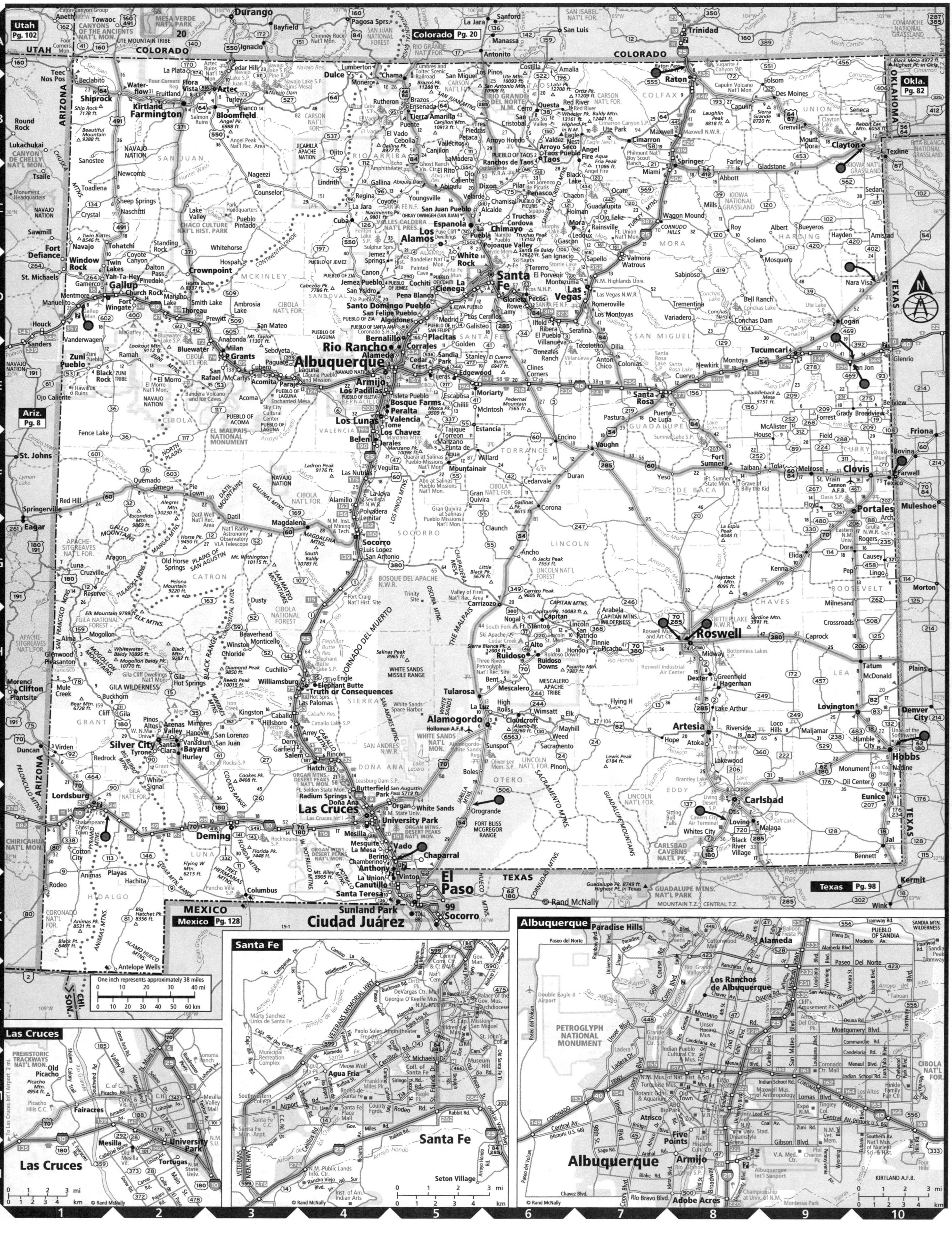

Route planning & on-the-road resources

Low clearances, weigh stations, & restricted routes: Page A37

Weigh station location

Designated route for vehicles with STAA-authorized dimensions

Road Conditions & Construction
511, (888) 465-1169
www.511ny.org, www.dot.ny.gov
Thruway: (800) 847-8929
www.thruway.ny.gov

Toll Road Information
see next page for listings

Mileage between cities	Albany	Buffalo	Hempstead	Kingston	New York	Newburgh	Poughkeepsie	Syracuse
ALBANY		291	191	55	161	87	78	145
BUFFALO	291		442	341	411	360	365	150
HEMPSTEAD	191	442		140	47	110	119	292
KINGSTON	55	341	140		110	36	28	195
NEW YORK	161	411	47	110		80	98	261
NEWBURGH	87	360	110	36	80		26	210
POUGHKEEPSIE	78	365	119	28	98	26		219
SYRACUSE	145	150	292	195	261	210	219	

Total mileage through New York

84: 72 miles
95: 24 miles
87: 334 miles
495: 66 miles

For more than 40,000 interstate mileages, see the Mileage Directory on page 137

New York/Southern

Nickname: The Empire State
Capital: Albany, NK-19
Land area: 47,126 sq. mi. (rank: 30th)
Population: 19,378,102 (rank: 3rd)
Largest city: New York, 8,175,133, SF-6

Index of cities Pg. 133 Map legend Pg. 1

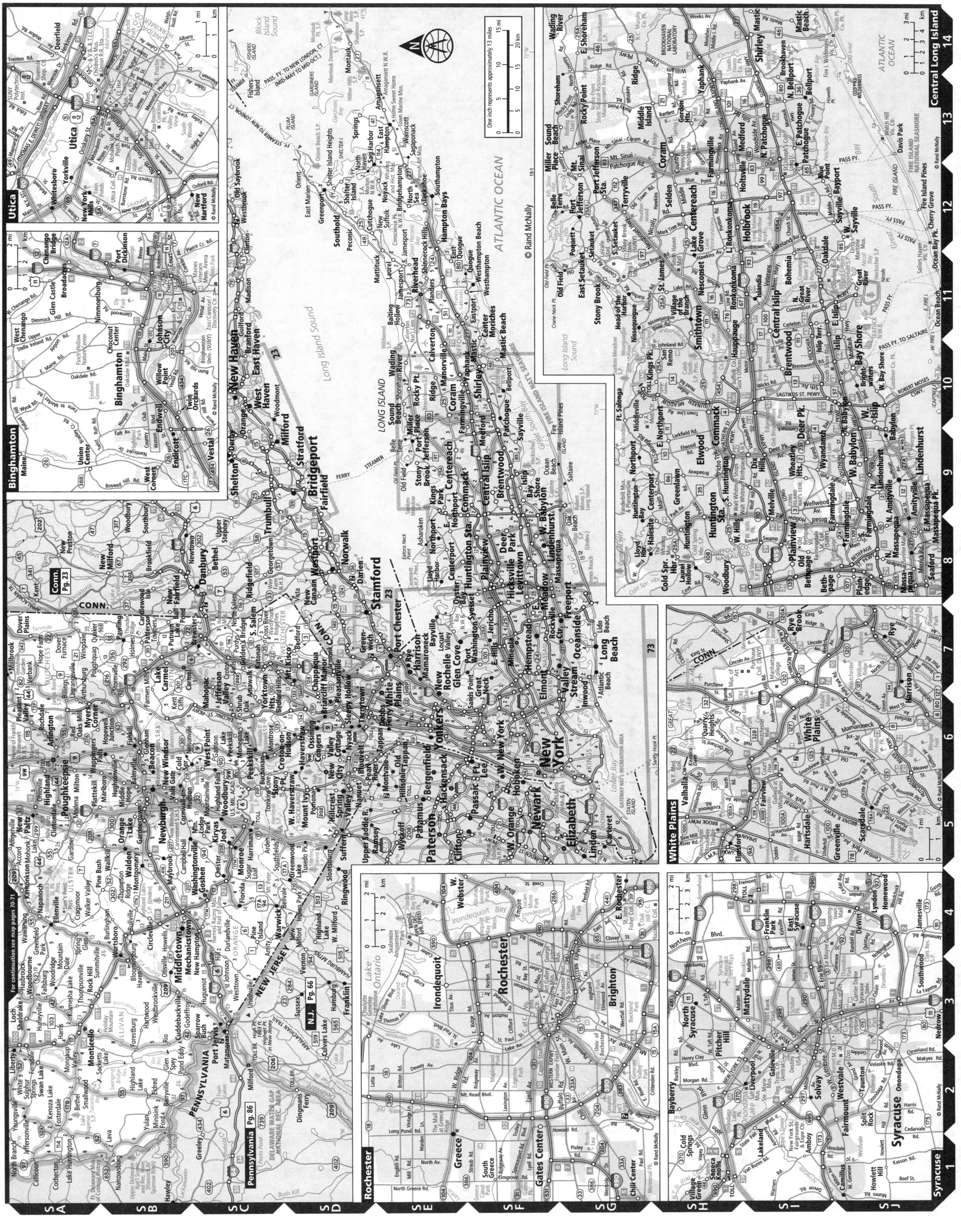

Nickname: The Empire State
Capital: Albany, NK-19
Land area: 47,126 sq. mi. (rank: 30th)
Population: 19,378,102 (rank: 3rd)
Largest city: New York, 8,175,133, SF-6

Index of cities Pg. 133 | Map legend Pg. 1

Route planning & on-the-road resources

Low clearances, weigh stations, & restricted routes: Page A37

Weigh station location

Designated route for vehicles with STAA-authorized dimensions

Road Conditions & Construction 511
511, (888) 465-1169
www.511ny.org
www.dot.ny.gov
Thruway: (800) 847-8929
www.thruway.ny.gov

Toll Road Information: *(all use E-ZPass)*
N.Y. State Thruway Authority: (518) 436-2805; www.thruway.ny.gov
MTA (N.Y. City in-state bridges & tunnels): (877) 690-5116, N.Y.C. only: 511 and say "bridges & tunnels"; www.mta.info/bandt
N.Y. State Bridge Auth. (Hudson R. bridges): (845) 691-7245; www.nysba.state.ny.us

International Toll Bridge Information:
Buffalo & Ft. Erie Public Br. Auth. (Peace Br.) *(E-ZPass)*: (716) 884-6744; www.peacebridge.com
Niagara Falls Bridge Comm. *(E-ZPass or ExpressPass)*: (716) 285-6322; www.niagarafallsbridges.com
Ogdensburg Bridge & Port Auth.: (315) 393-4080; www.ogdensport.com
Seaway Int'l Bridge Corp. *(Seaway Transit Card)*: (613) 932-6601; www.sibc.ca
Thousand Islands Br. Auth. (Alexandria Bay): (315) 482-2501; www.tibridge.com

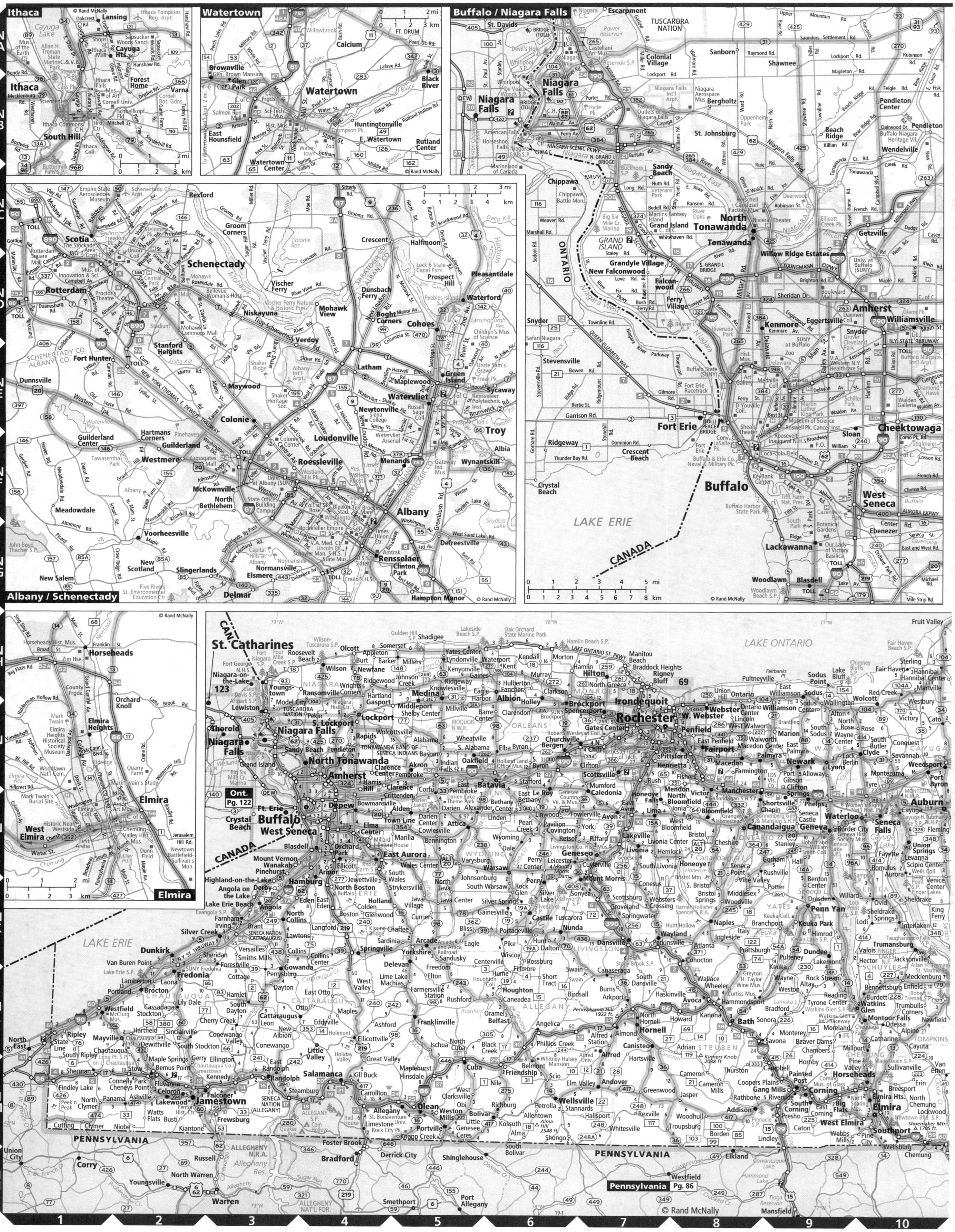

Mileage between cities	Albany	Auburn	Binghamton	Buffalo	Elmira	Glens Falls	Ithaca	Jamestown	Kingston	Lake Placid	Massena	New York	Niagara Falls	Olean	Oneonta	Oswego	Plattsburgh	Rochester	Syracuse	Utica	Watertown
ALBANY		172	140	291	195	52	182	357	55	139	217	161	302	306	81	175	164	226	145	94	175
BINGHAMTON	140	86		224	58	180	49	220	170	267	235	190	235	170	60	114	292	159	73	126	144
BUFFALO	291	127	224		150	308	172	79	341	344	306	411	21	80	277	157	390	75	150	199	214
JAMESTOWN	357	196	220	79	165	396	187		388	413	375	408	100	52	277	225	508	144	219	268	283
PLATTSBURGH	164	272	292	390	347	118	334	508	219	63	86	325	402	458	232	225		326	244	191	168
ROCHESTER	226	62	159	75	125	244	101	144	277	279	242	347	87	120	212	77	326		86	135	150
SYRACUSE	145	28	73	150	90	162	58	219	195	199	162	261	162	188	127	40	244	86		53	70
UTICA	94	81	126	199	142	112	110	268	145	166	183	251	211	237	69	84	191	135	53		80

Total mileage through New York

- I-81: 184 miles
- I-86: 176 miles
- I-87: 334 miles
- I-90: 385 miles

For more than 40,000 interstate mileages, see the Mileage Directory on page 137

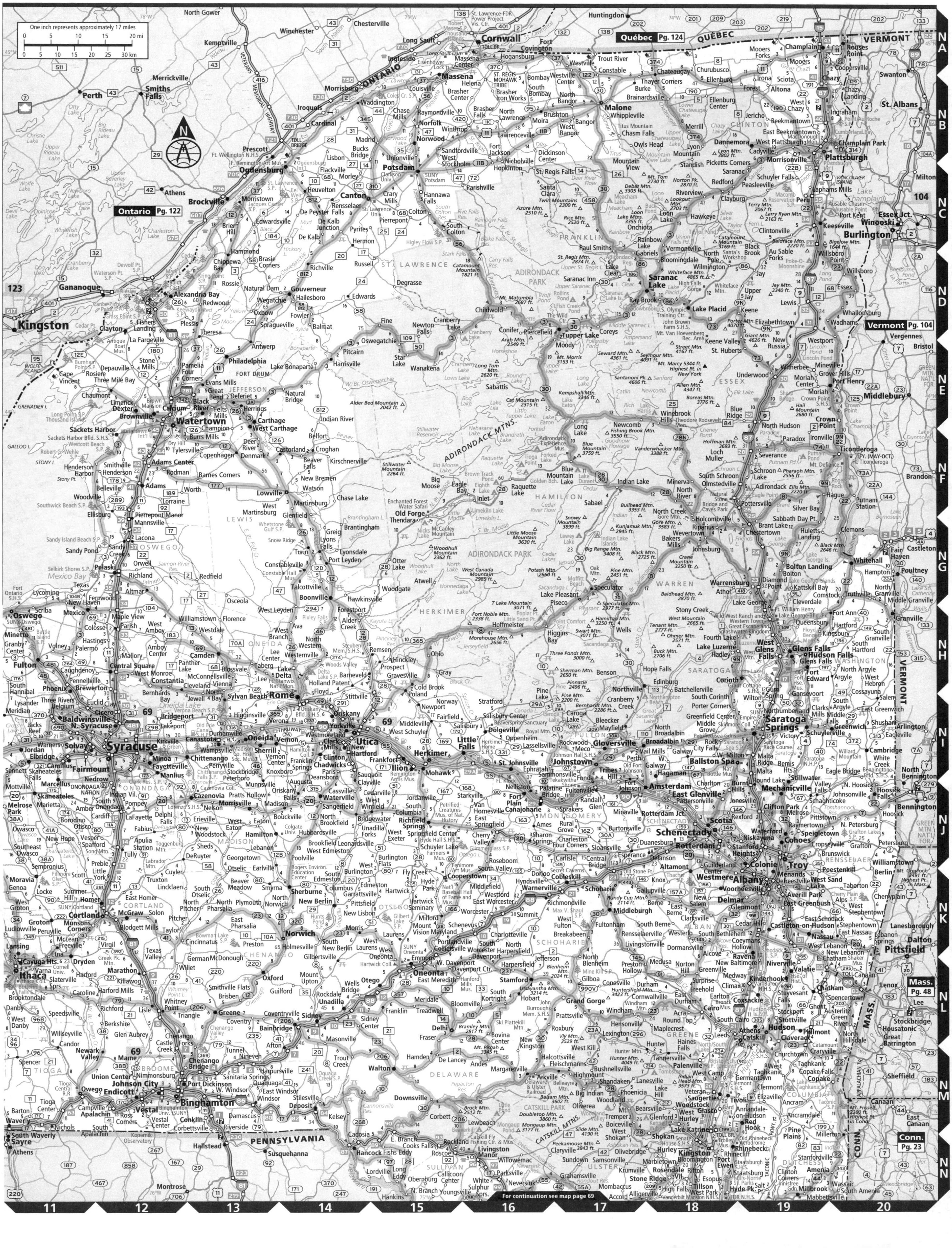

Sights to see

- American Museum of Natural History A-4
- Battery Park I-1
- Bronx Zoo E-12
- Brooklyn Bridge H-2
- Carnegie Hall C-4
- Central Park B-4
- Chrysler Building D-4
- Coney Island L-10
- Ellis Island I-9
- Empire State Building D-3
- Greenwich Village H-10
- Grand Central Terminal D-4

Ellis Island Museum

Brooklyn Bridge, New York City

Sights to see

- Guggenheim Museum A-5
- Intrepid Sea-Air Space Museum C-2
- Lincoln Center B-3
- Madison Square Garden D-2
- Metropolitan Museum of Art B-5
- National September 11 Memorial H-1
- New York Stock Exchange and Wall Street H-1
- Rockefeller Center C-4
- Staten Island Ferry .... I-2 and J-8
- Statue of Liberty I-9
- Times Square D-3
- Yankee Stadium E-11

North Carolina

Nickname: The Tar Heel State
Capital: Raleigh, E-12
Land area: 48,618 sq. mi. (rank: 29th)
Population: 9,535,483 (rank: 10th)
Largest city: Charlotte, 731,424, F-5

Index of cities Pg. 133 | Map legend Pg. 1

Route planning & on-the-road resources

Low clearances, weigh stations, & restricted routes: Page A38

Weigh station location

Designated route for vehicles with STAA-authorized dimensions

Road Conditions & Construction
511, (877) 511-4662; www.ncdot.gov/travel/511, www.ncdot.gov

Toll Road Information
North Carolina Turnpike Authority (*NC Quick Pass*): (877) 769-7277; www.ncdot.gov/turnpike

Determining Distances
(segments of one mile or less not shown)
Cumulative miles (red): the distance between red arrows
Intermediate miles (black): the distance between intersections & places

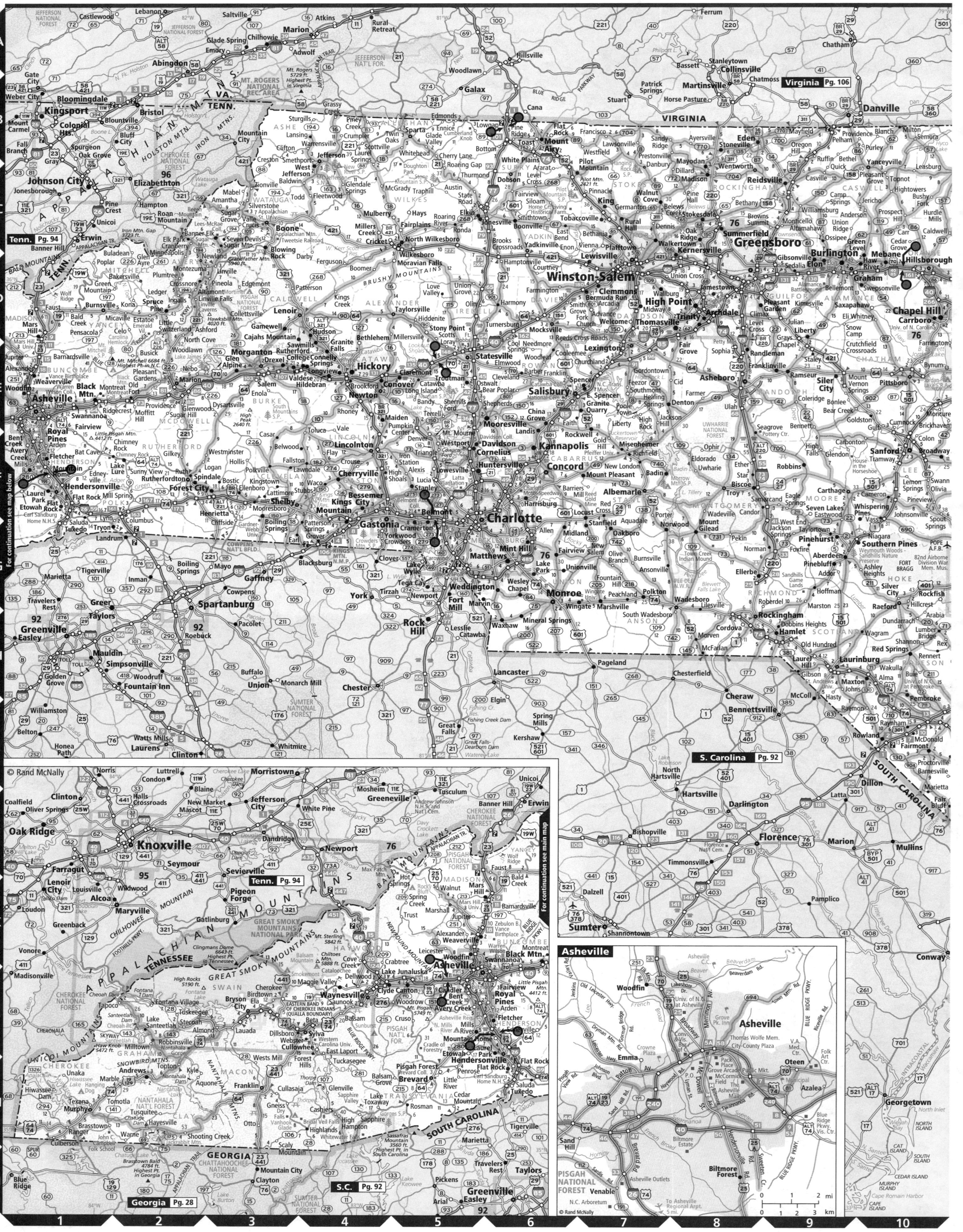

Mileage between cities	Asheville	Boone	Charlotte	Durham	Elizabeth City	Fayetteville	Greensboro	Greenville	Hickory	Knoxville, TN	Nags Head	New Bern	Raleigh	Roanoke Rapids	Rockingham	Rocky Mt.	Wilmington	Winston-Salem
ASHEVILLE		84	123	229	417	267	172	340	78	114	447	365	254	314	200	309	327	147
CHARLOTTE	123	117		147	334	139	95	258	57	228	364	282	172	231	73	226	199	77
FAYETTEVILLE	267	223	139	89	207		142	115	200	372	237	133	67	130	70	99	135	139
GREENSBORO	172	113	95	54	241	142		164	101	284	271	189	78	138	85	133	208	29
GREENVILLE	340	282	258	108	108	115	164		269	452	130	59	88	105	183	58	145	198
RALEIGH	254	197	172	24	167	67	78	88	185	368	197	114		90	98	59	133	112
WILMINGTON	327	325	199	154	216	135	208	145	260	432	238	97	133	196	130	165		241
WINSTON-SALEM	147	88	77	87	275	139	29	198	76	259	305	223	112	171	106	167	241	

Mileages © Rand McNally

Total mileage through North Carolina

40	419 miles	85	233 miles
77	102 miles	95	182 miles

For more than 40,000 interstate mileages, see the Mileage Directory on page 137

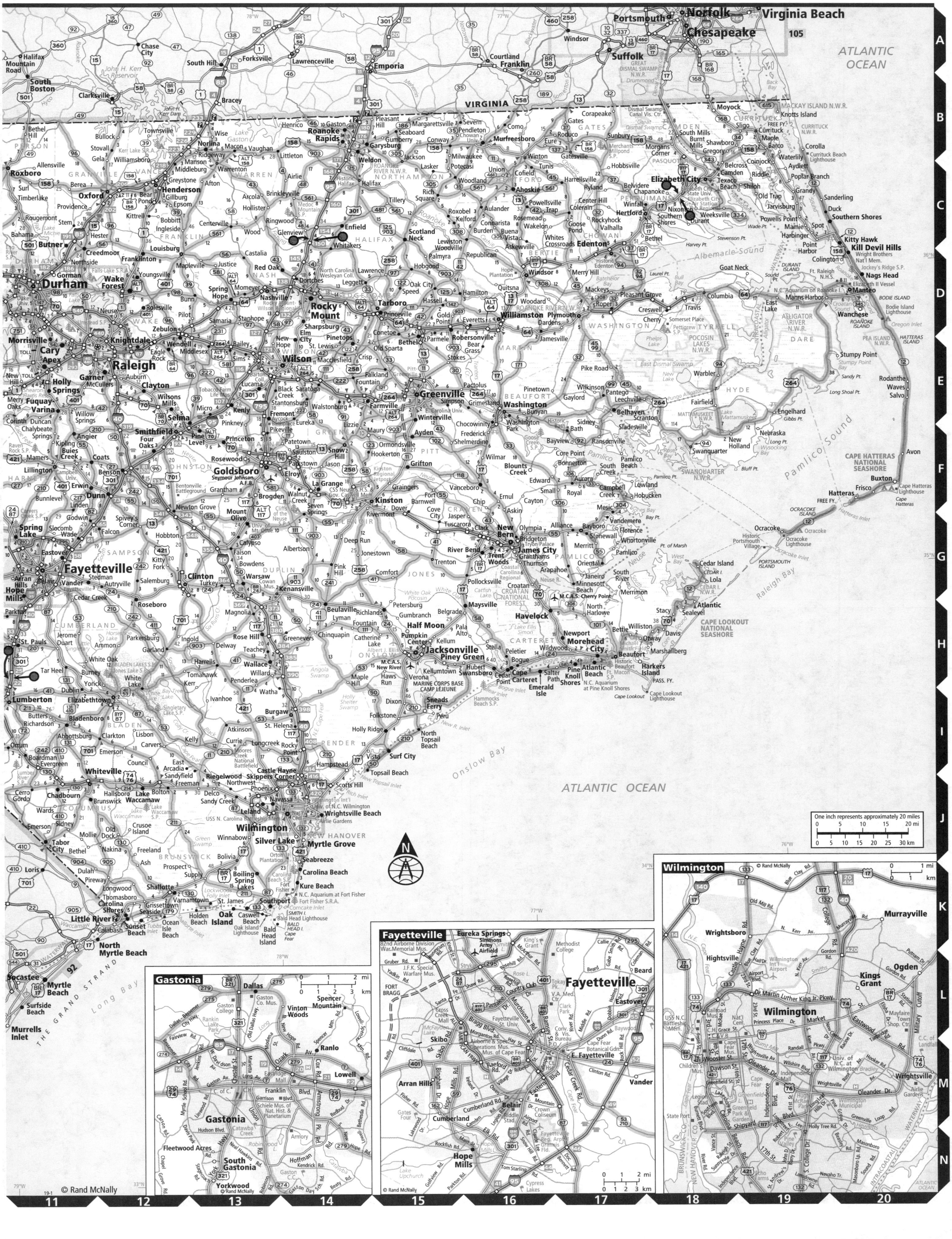

Sights to see

- Discovery Place, Charlotte H-4
- Duke Homestead State Historic Site & Tobacco Museum, Durham F-9
- Historic Bethabara Park, Winston-Salem A-1
- Mint Museum of Art, Charlotte H-5
- Morehead Planetarium & Science Center, Chapel Hill . . H-8
- North Carolina Museum of History, Raleigh I-12
- North Carolina Museum of Life & Science, Durham . . F-10
- North Carolina State Capitol, Raleigh I-13
- North Carolina State University, Raleigh I-13
- Old Salem, Winston-Salem B-2
- Reynolda House, Winston-Salem B-1

Old Salem, Winston-Salem

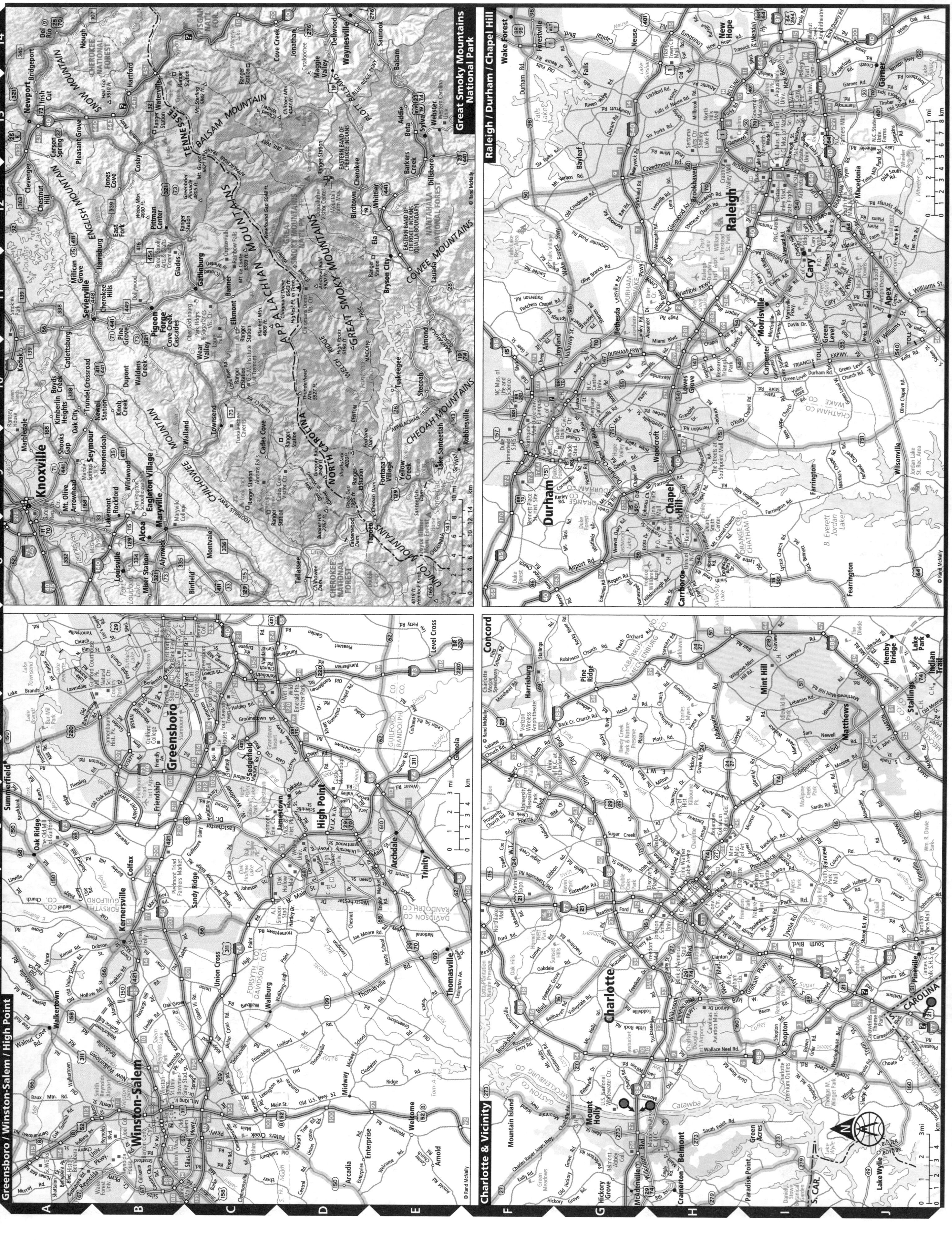

Route planning & on-the-road resources

Low clearances, weigh stations, & restricted routes: **Page A39**

Weigh station location

Designated route for vehicles with STAA-authorized dimensions

Road Conditions & Construction
511, (855) 637-6237
www.dot.nd.gov
www.dot.nd.gov/travel-info-v2

Toll Road Information
No tolls on state or federal highways

Mileage between cities	Bismarck	Devils Lake	Dickinson	Fargo	Garrison	Grand Forks	Minot	Williston
BISMARCK		180	99	195	76	272	110	230
DEVILS LAKE	180		277	166	167	89	122	248
DICKINSON	99	277		292	149	369	184	132
FARGO	195	166	292		266	81	301	422
GARRISON	76	167	149	266		256	47	144
GRAND FORKS	272	89	369	81	256		210	336
MINOT	110	122	184	301	47	210		125
WILLISTON	230	248	132	422	144	336	125	

Total mileage through North Dakota

- I-29: 218 miles
- I-94: 352 miles
- US 2: 359 miles
- US 83: 265 miles

For more than 40,000 interstate mileages, see the Mileage Directory on page 137

North Dakota

Nickname: The Peace Garden State
Capital: Bismarck, H-7
Land area: 69,000 sq. mi. (rank: 17th)
Population: 672,591 (rank: 48th)
Largest city: Fargo, 105,549, H-13

Index of cities Pg. 133
Map legend Pg. 1

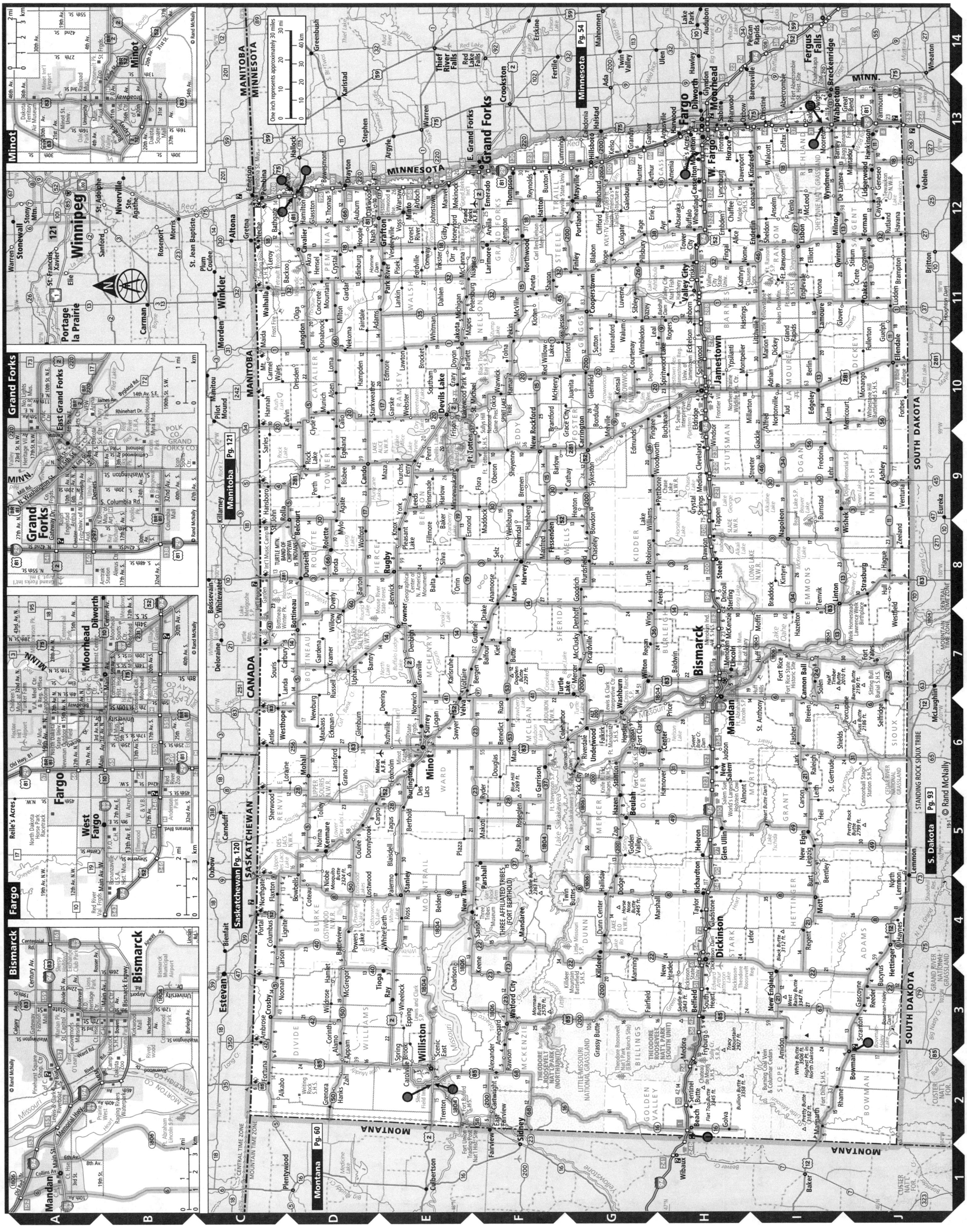

Nickname: The Buckeye State
Capital: Columbus, SB-9
Land area: 40,861 sq. mi. (rank: 35th)
Population: 11,536,504 (rank: 7th)
Largest city: Columbus, 787,033, SB-9

Index of cities Pg. 133 | Map legend Pg. 1

Route planning & on-the-road resources

Low clearances, weigh stations, & restricted routes: Page A39

Weigh station location

Designated route for vehicles with STAA-authorized dimensions

Road Conditions & Construction
(614) 466-7170; www.dot.state.oh.us, www.buckeyetraffic.org
Cincinnati metro area: 511; www.ohgo.com/dashboard/cincinnati
Ohio Turnpike: (440) 234-2030, (440) 234-2081; www.ohioturnpike.org

Toll Road Information
Ohio Turnpike and Infrastructure Commission *(E-ZPass)*:
(888) 876-7453, (440) 234-2081; www.ohioturnpike.org

Determining Distances
(segments of one mile or less not shown)
Cumulative miles (red): the distance between red arrows
Intermediate miles (black): the distance between intersections & places

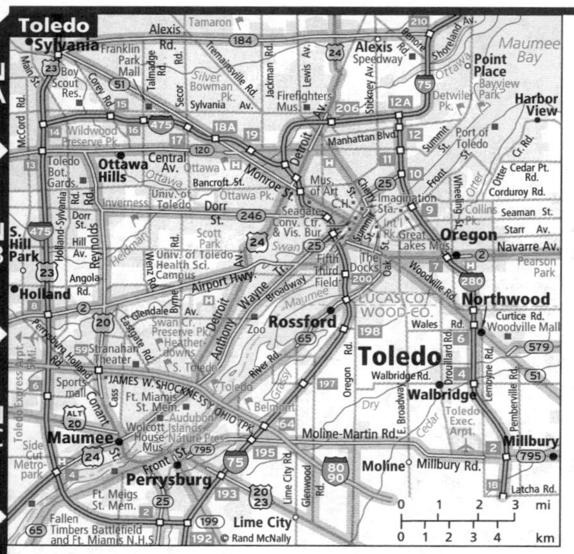

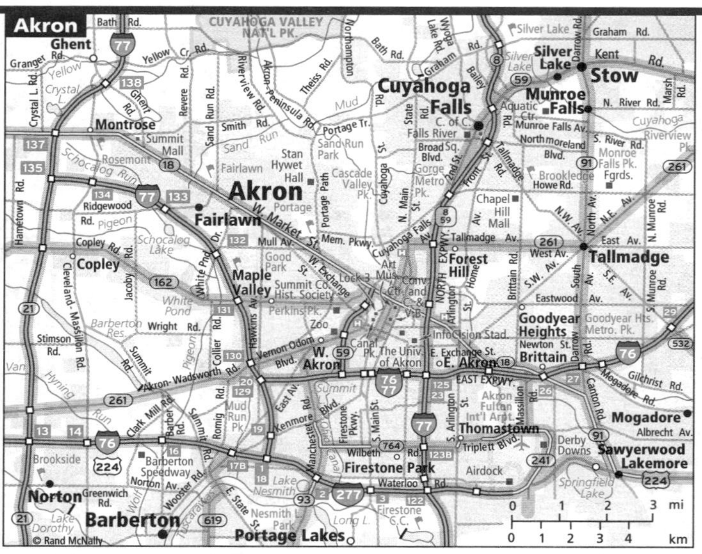

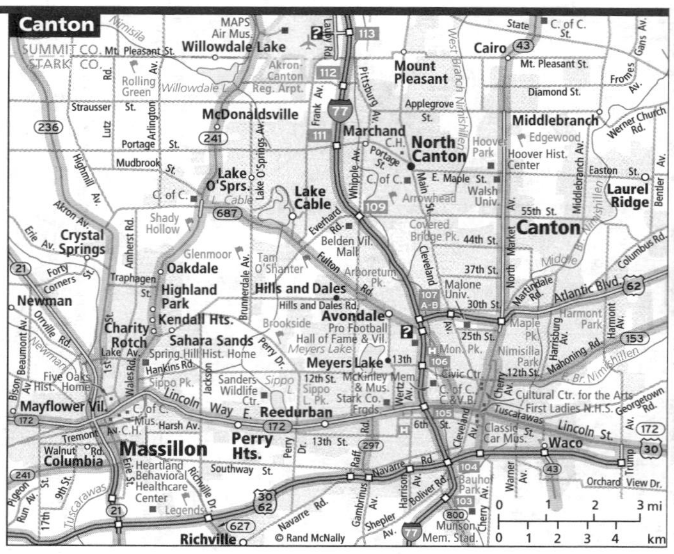

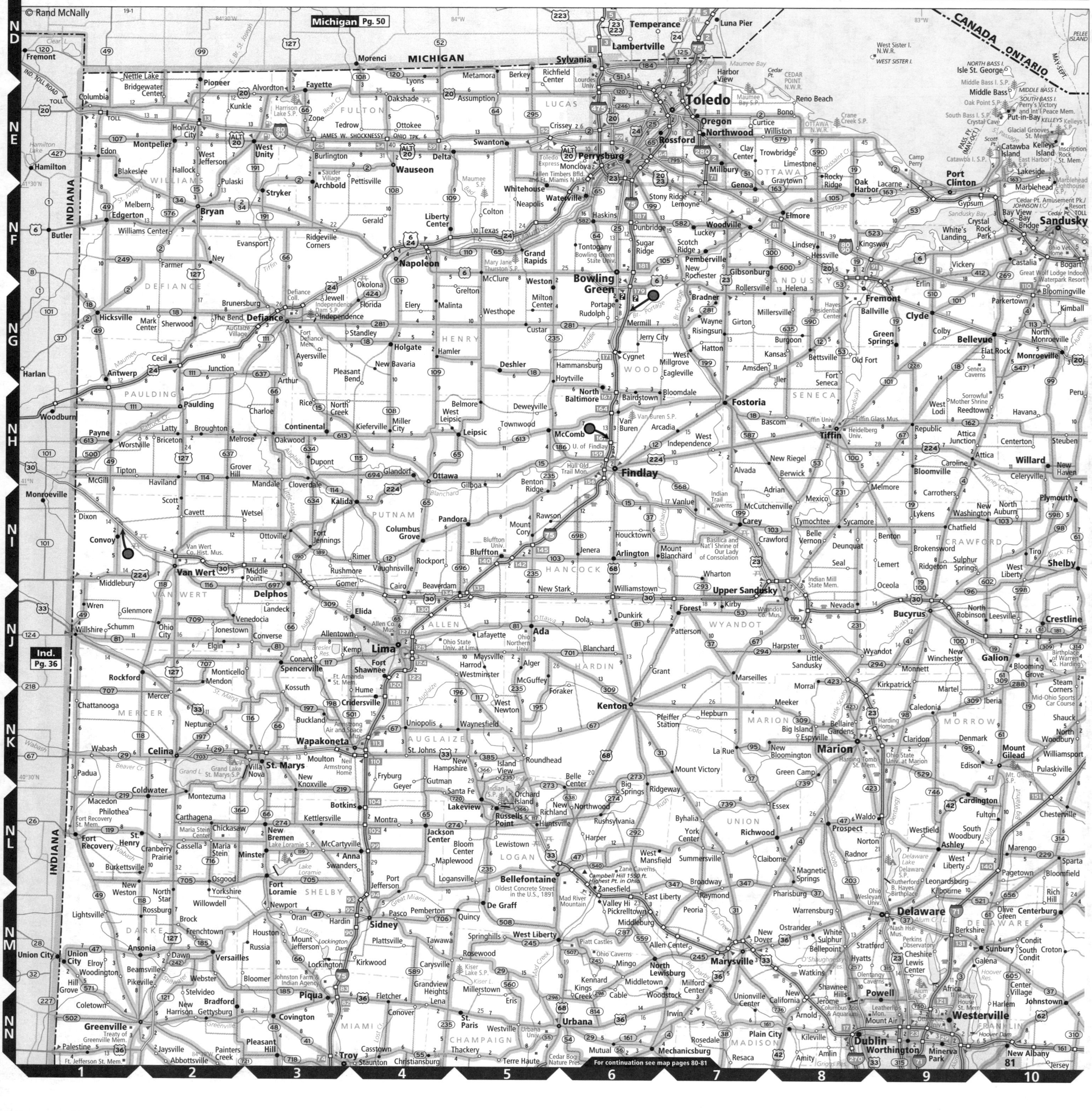

Mileage between cities	Akron	Ashtabula	Canton	Cincinnati	Cleveland	Columbus	Defiance	Findlay	Lima	Mansfield	Marion	New Philadelphia	Pittsburgh, PA	Sandusky	Steubenville	Toledo	Wheeling, WV	Youngstown
AKRON		83	20	232	40	124	181	132	154	62	100	47	107	85	82	133	102	48
CLEVELAND	40	61	60	250		142	159	121	156	80	118	86	132	62	125	111	141	73
COLUMBUS	124	197	126	108	142		135	96	91	66	50	118	184	112	150	142	126	172
FINDLAY	132	181	134	159	121	96	51		35	72	49	139	239	62	194	44	194	180
LIMA	154	216	156	125	156	91	44	35		94	54	162	261	96	217	77	217	202
MANSFIELD	62	135	64	174	80	66	123	72	94		40	70	169	53	125	99	125	111
TOLEDO	133	171	152	201	111	142	57	44	77	99	94	179	228	58	221		234	169
YOUNGSTOWN	48	57	57	280	73	172	218	180	202	111	148	84	68	122	66	169	91	

Total mileage through Ohio

71: 248 miles
75: 211 miles
80: 237 miles
90: 245 miles

For more than 40,000 interstate mileages, see the Mileage Directory on page 137

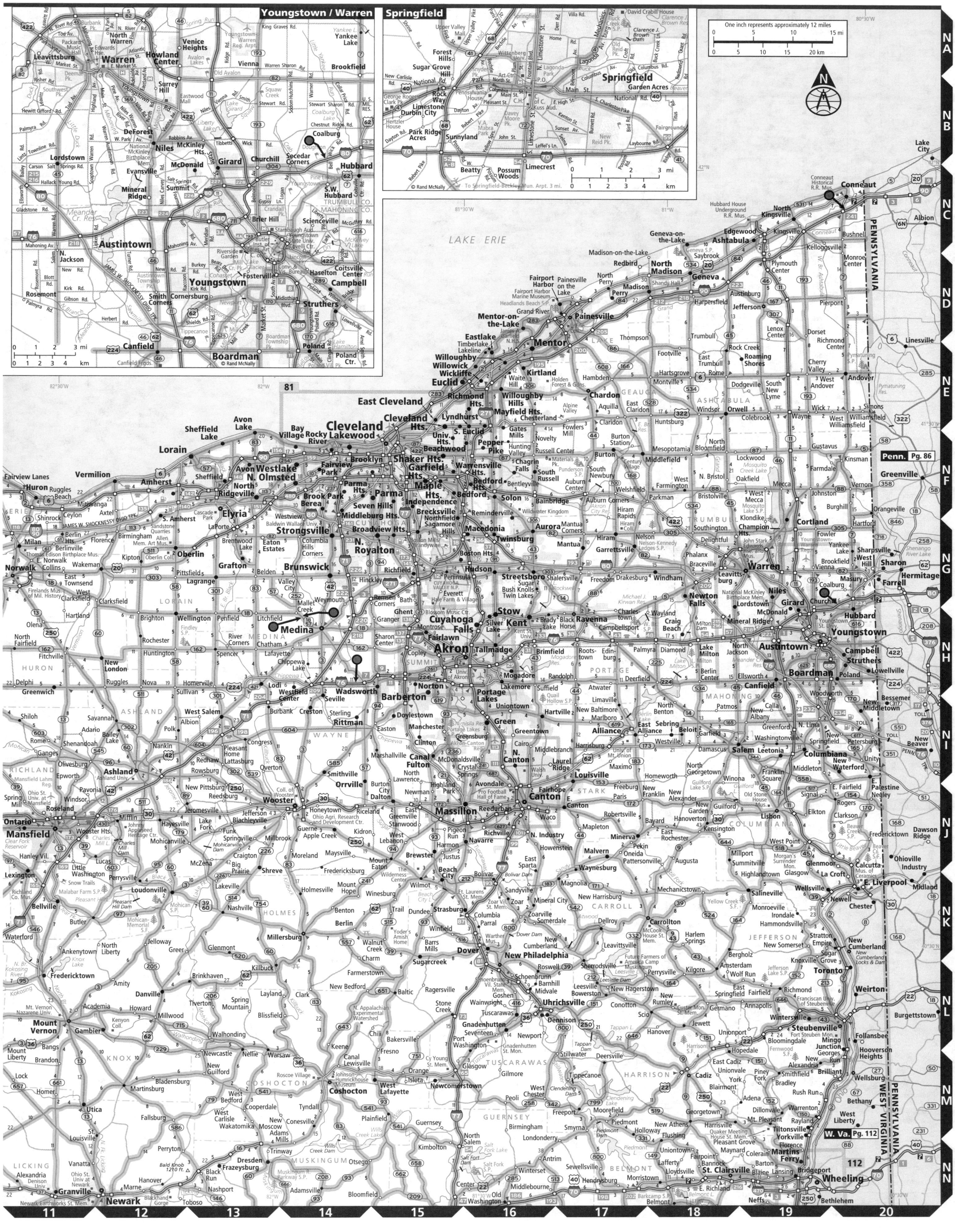

Nickname: The Buckeye State
Capital: Columbus, SB-9
Land area: 40,861 sq. mi. (rank: 35th)
Population: 11,536,504 (rank: 7th)
Largest city: Columbus, 787,033, SB-9

Index of cities Pg. 133 | Map legend Pg. 1

Route planning & on-the-road resources

Low clearances, weigh stations, & restricted routes: Page A39

Weigh station location

Designated route for vehicles with STAA-authorized dimensions

Road Conditions & Construction

(614) 466-7170; www.dot.state.oh.us, www.buckeyetraffic.org
Cincinnati metro area: 511; www.ohgo.com/dashboard/cincinnati
Ohio Turnpike: (440) 234-2030, (440) 234-2081; www.ohioturnpike.org

Toll Road Information

Ohio Turnpike and Infrastructure Commission *(E-ZPass)*:
(888) 876-7453, (440) 234-2081; www.ohioturnpike.org

Determining Distances

(segments of one mile or less not shown)
Cumulative miles (red): the distance between red arrows
Intermediate miles (black): the distance between intersections & places

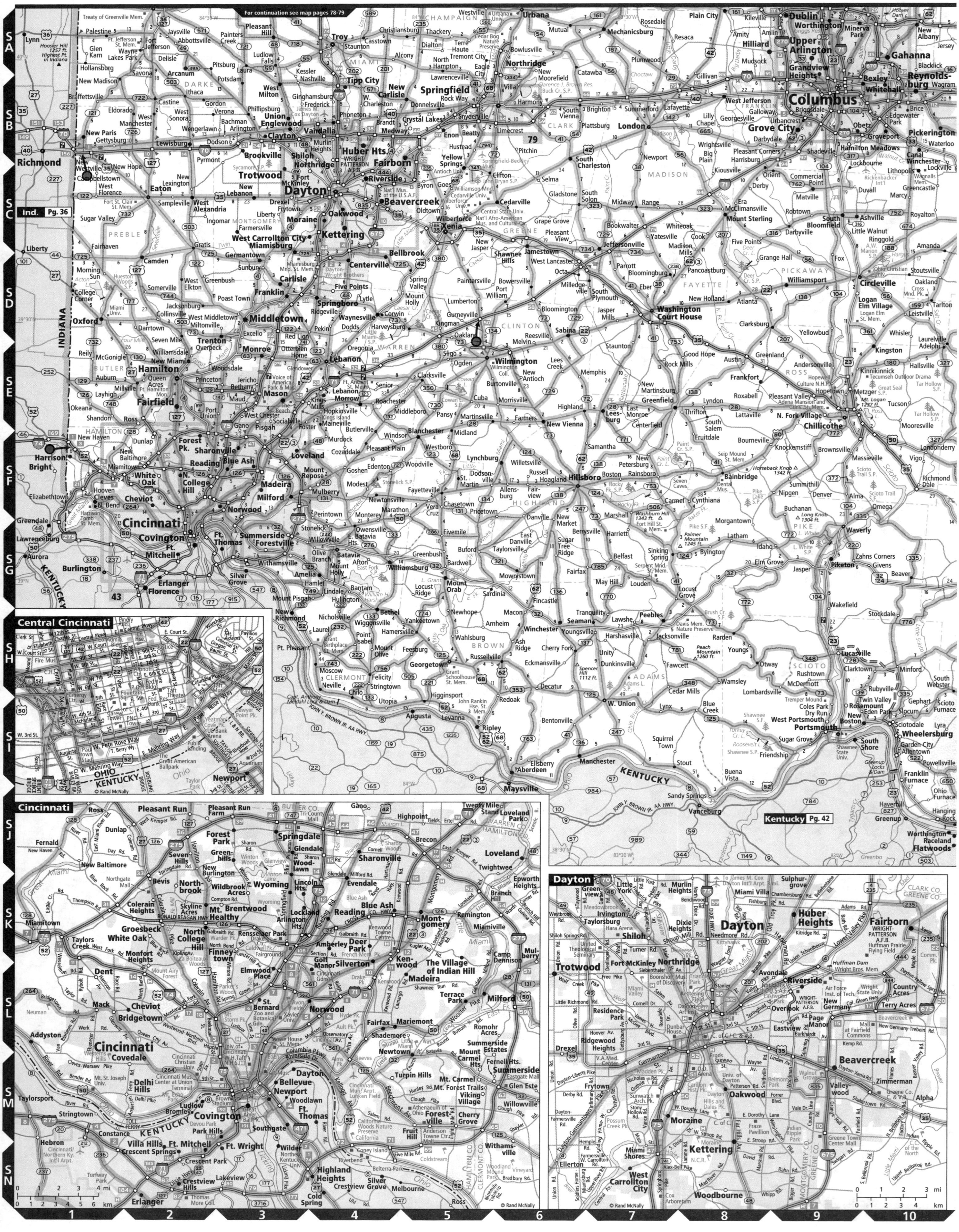

Mileage between cities	Athens	Cambridge	Chillicothe	Cincinnati	Cleveland	Columbus	Dayton	Gallipolis	Huntington, WV	Jackson	Lancaster	Marietta	Portsmouth	Springfield	Washington C.H.	Wheeling, WV	Wilmington	Zanesville
CINCINNATI	164	183	106		250	108	54	166	147	135	133	210	116	80	76	231	52	160
COLUMBUS	74	79	48	108	142		71	106	137	76	30	124	91	45	41	126	63	55
DAYTON	136	149	78	54	212	71		138	168	107	101	195	122	27	48	197	34	126
GALLIPOLIS	42	120	60	166	238	106	138		46	32	86	66	77	129	91	163	112	105
MARIETTA	46	48	104	210	165	124	195	66	140	86	90		131	168	135	90	156	69
PORTSMOUTH	85	162	44	116	233	91	122	77	45	47	83	131		114	76	210	96	139
SPRINGFIELD	118	123	69	80	186	45	27	129	159	98	74	168	114		39	171	39	100
ZANESVILLE	63	24	96	160	146	55	126	105	207	86	47	69	139	100	92	72	115	

Total mileage through Ohio

- 70: 226 miles
- 75: 211 miles
- 71: 248 miles
- 77: 160 miles

For more than 40,000 interstate mileages, see the Mileage Directory on page 137

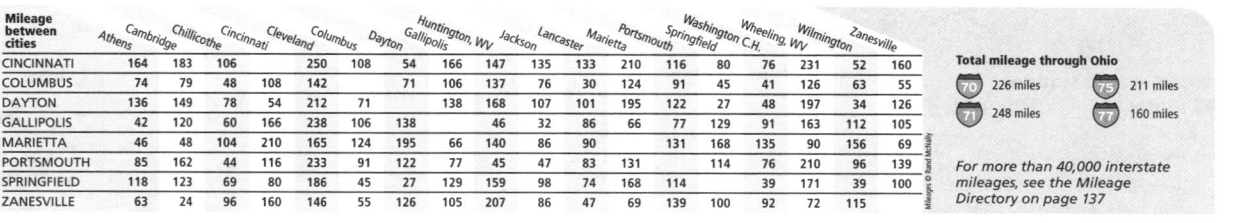

Nickname: The Sooner State
Capital: Oklahoma City, F-13
Land area: 68,595 sq. mi. (rank: 19th)
Population: 3,751,351 (rank: 28th)
Largest city: Oklahoma City, 579,999, F-13

Index of cities Pg. 134 | Map legend Pg. 1

Route planning & on-the-road resources

Low clearances, weigh stations, & restricted routes: Page A39

Weigh station location

Designated route for vehicles with STAA-authorized dimensions

Road Conditions & Construction
(844) 465-4997, (405) 522-2800; www.okroads.org, www.okladot.state.ok.us

Toll Road Information
Oklahoma Turnpike Authority *(PIKEPASS)*: (405) 425-3600; www.pikepass.com

Determining Distances
(segments of one mile or less not shown)
Cumulative miles (red): the distance between red arrows
Intermediate miles (black): the distance between intersections & places

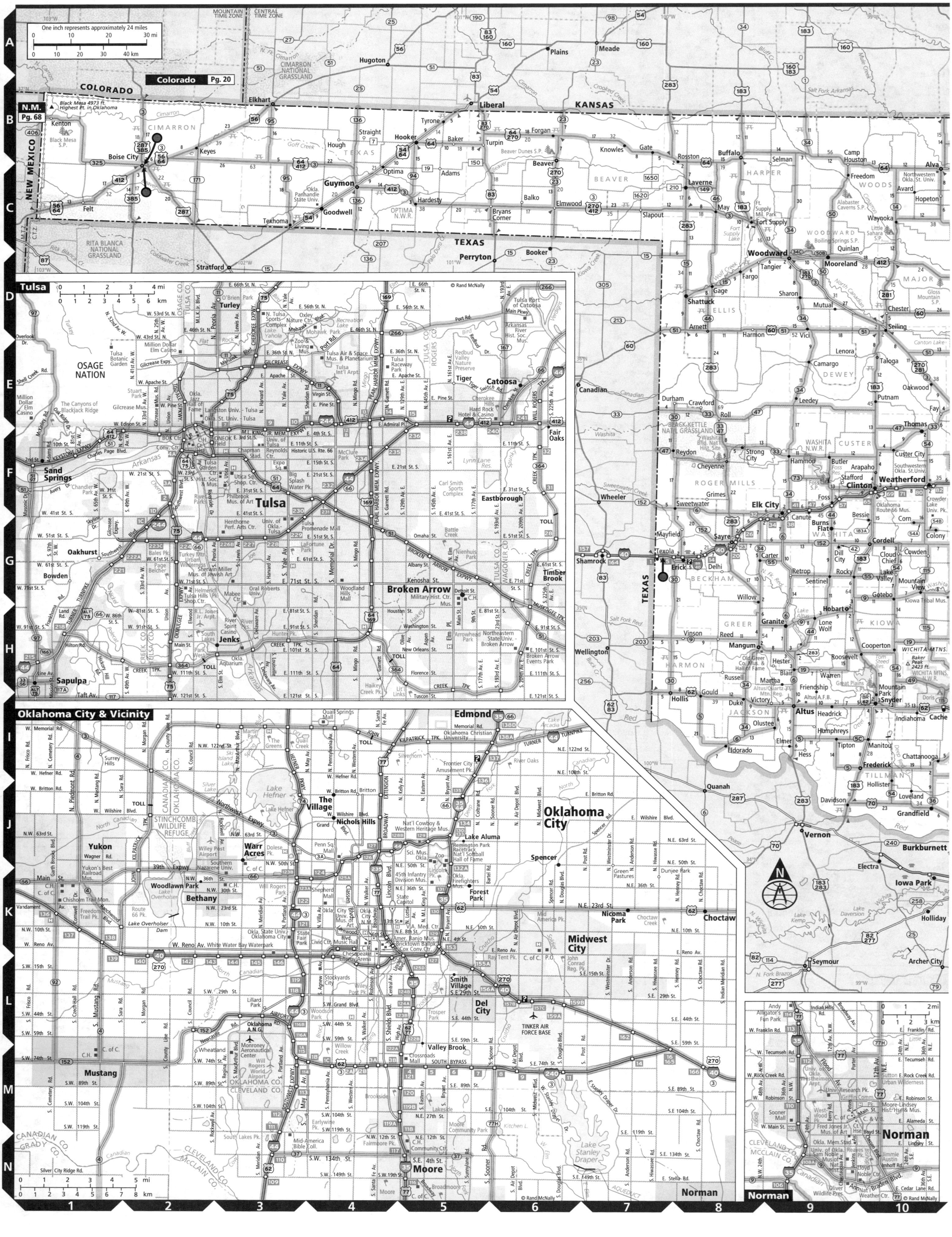

Mileage between cities	Altus	Ardmore	Bartlesville	Dallas, TX	Elk City	Enid	Ft. Smith, AR	Guymon	Joplin, MO	Lawton	McAlester	Muskogee	Oklahoma City	Ponca City	Stillwater	Tulsa	Wichita Falls, TX	Woodward
ARDMORE	156		246	109	209	196	234	362	312	101	121	192	97	202	161	201	120	238
ELK CITY	58	209	263	316		148	292	184	330	110	241	250	113	220	179	219	143	77
ENID	192	196	159	302	148		232	213	228	142	224	166	99	68	64	114	196	89
LAWTON	57	101	235	193	110	142	261	296	302		209	218	87	192	151	191	53	172
MUSKOGEE	270	192	91	236	250	166	72	378	117	218	66		137	142	120	50	272	254
OKLAHOMA CITY	139	97	149	204	113	99	180	266	216	87	128	137		105	64	104	140	142
TULSA	243	201	45	267	219	114	118	327	114	191	100	50	104	91	69		244	203
WICHITA FALLS, TX	86	120	289	139	143	196	314	317	356	53	218	272	140	245	204	244		225

Mileages © Rand McNally

Total mileage through Oklahoma

- I-35: 236 miles
- I-40: 331 miles
- I-44: 329 miles
- US 75: 227 miles

For more than 40,000 interstate mileages, see the Mileage Directory on page 137

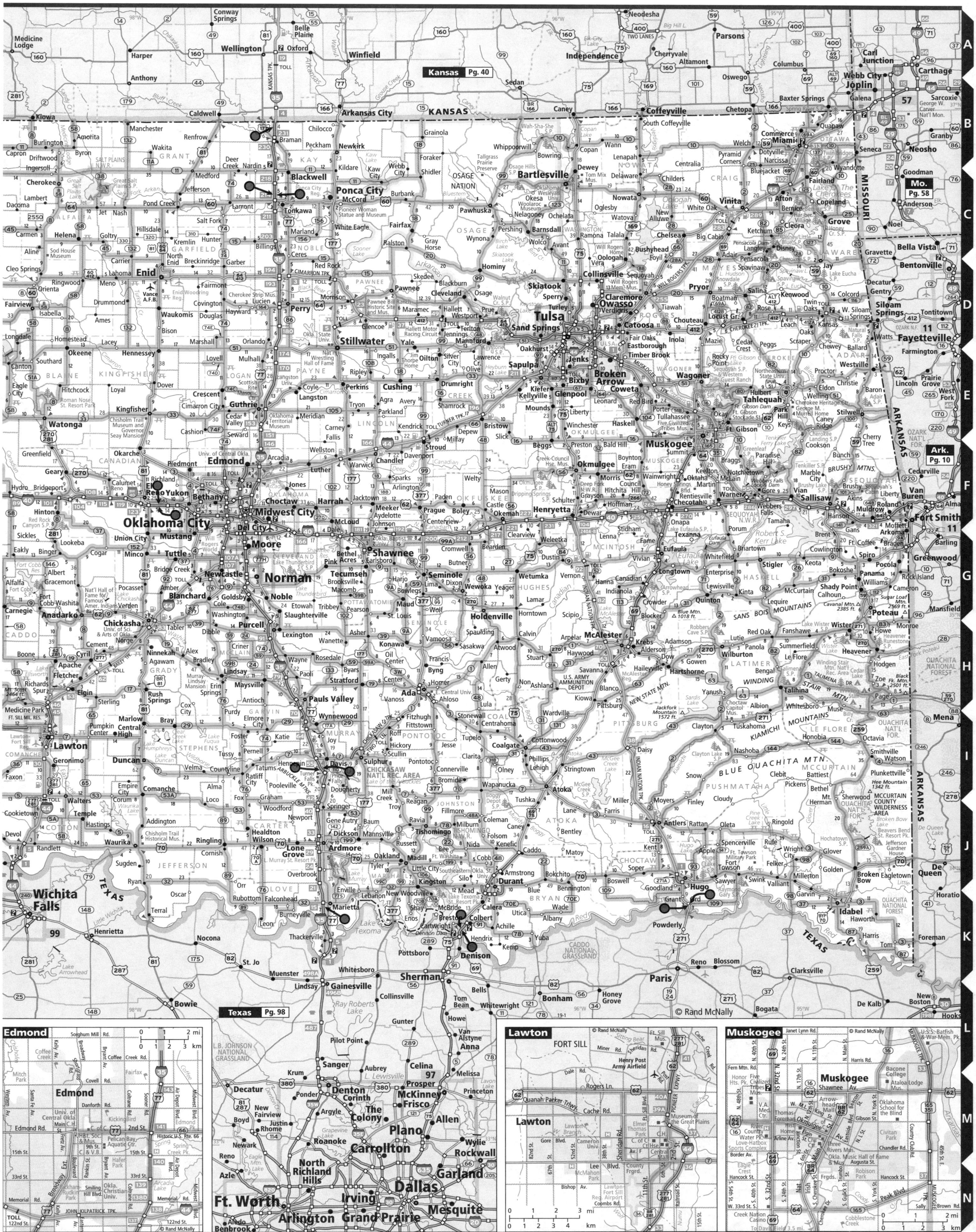

Nickname: The Beaver State
Capital: Salem, E-4
Land area: 95,988 sq. mi. (rank: 10th)
Population: 3,831,074 (rank: 27th)
Largest city: Portland, 583,776, C-5

Index of cities Pg. 134 | Map legend Pg. 1

Route planning & on-the-road resources

Low clearances, weigh stations, & restricted routes: Page A40

Weigh station location

Designated route for vehicles with STAA-authorized dimensions

Road Conditions & Construction
511
(800) 977-6368
(888) 275-6368
(503) 588-2941
www.oregon.gov/odot
www.tripcheck.com

Toll Bridge Information
Bridge of the Gods (Cascade Locks):
(541) 374-8619
portofcascadelocks.org/bridge-of-the-gods
Hood River Bridge (*BreezeBy*):
(541) 386-1645
www.portofhoodriver.com/bridge

Determining Distances
(segments of one mile or less not shown)
Cumulative miles (red): the distance between red arrows
Intermediate miles (black): the distance between intersections & places

Mileage between cities	Astoria	Bend	Brookings	Burns	Coos Bay	Corvallis	Crater Lake NP	Eugene	Grants Pass	John Day	Klamath Falls	Lakeview	Medford	Ontario	Pendleton	Portland	Salem	The Dalles
BEND	255		348	130	241	152	107	128	201	200	137	175	175	260	242	160	131	156
BURNS	384	130	478		371	281	237	258	331	70	266	139	305	130	246	290	260	285
CORVALLIS	169	152	249	281	142		187	48	183	371	217	305	211	456	290	82	37	165
EUGENE	198	128	217	258	109	48	142		138	328	172	260	166	388	319	110	66	194
MEDFORD	361	175	268	305	173	211	74	166	29	372	78	227		432	482	273	228	357
ONTARIO	466	260	701	130	594	456	367	388	461	131	397	269	432		167	374	425	291
PENDLETON	301	242	535	246	428	290	349	319	454	176	379	385	482	167		208	259	125
PORTLAND	99	160	327	290	220	82	250	110	246	383	280	335	273	374	208		51	83

Total mileage through Oregon

- 5: 308 miles
- 82: 11 miles
- 84: 375 miles
- 101: 348 miles

For more than 40,000 interstate mileages, see the Mileage Directory on page 137

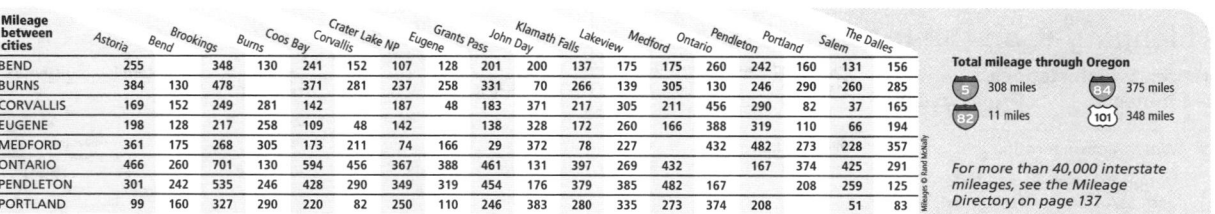

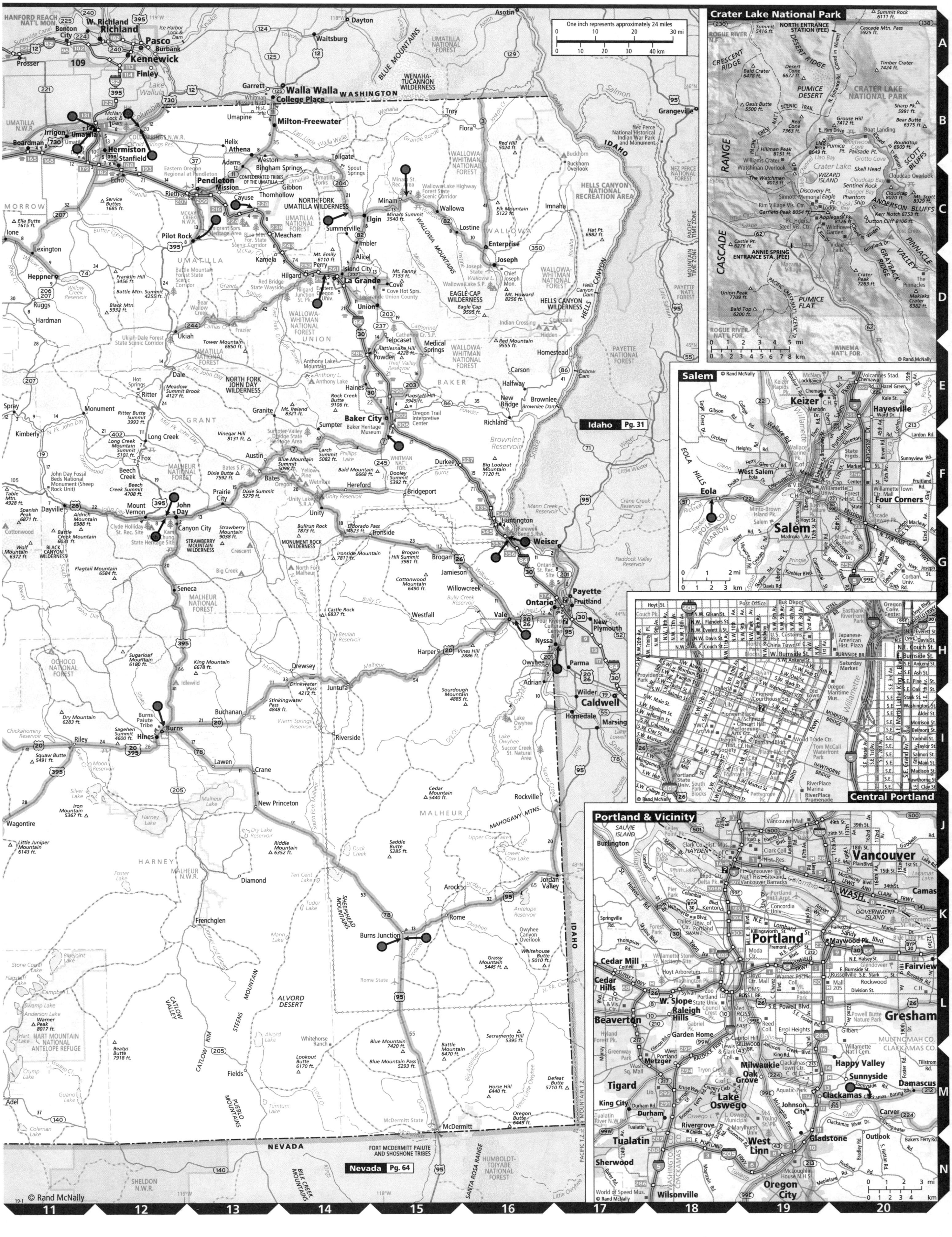

Nickname: The Keystone State
Capital: Harrisburg, EN-4
Land area: 44,743 sq. mi. (rank: 32nd)
Population: 12,702,379 (rank: 6th)
Largest city: Philadelphia, 1,526,006, EP-12

Index of cities Pg. 134 | Map legend Pg. 1

Route planning & on-the-road resources

Low clearances, weigh stations, & restricted routes: Page A40

Weigh station location

Designated route for vehicles with STAA-authorized dimensions

Road Conditions & Construction
511, (888) 783-6783, (800) 349-7623, (717) 787-2838
www.511pa.com; www.penndot.gov

Toll Road Information
Pennsylvania Turnpike Commission (*E-ZPass*): (800) 331-3414; www.paturnpike.com

Determining Distances
(segments of one mile or less not shown)
Cumulative miles (red): the distance between red arrows
Intermediate miles (black): the distance between intersections & places

Mileage between cities	Altoona	Beaver Falls	Bedford	Chambersburg	Du Bois	Erie	Greensburg	Harrisburg	Indiana	Johnstown	Kittanning	Meadville	New Castle	Philadelphia	Pittsburgh	State College	Uniontown	Warren	Washington	Williamsport	Youngstown, OH
ALTOONA		135	36	98	72	202	73	134	55	46	80	167	143	234	96	41	112	130	126	102	158
ERIE	202	118	228	290	148		155	308	150	190	124	41	100	419	127	208	184	64	150	260	101
HARRISBURG	134	243	102	54	160	308	177		179	138	204	272	250	109	205	87	185	218	211	83	265
JOHNSTOWN	46	106	40	102	85	190	45	138	38		61	154	114	238	68	85	80	154	106	146	129
NEW CASTLE	143	30	152	214	111	100	80	250	76	114	50	65		350	52	171	108	143	74	223	18
PITTSBURGH	96	39	107	169	102	127	34	205	60	68	42	92	52	305		136	51	171	29	196	68
STATE COLLEGE	41	175	76	138	61	208	113	87	95	85	120	173	171	193	136		152	119	166	67	172
WILLIAMSPORT	102	242	137	135	113	260	174	83	156	146	172	225	223	176	196	67	213	171	226		224

Total mileage through Pennsylvania

- 70: 168 miles
- 79: 183 miles
- 80: 311 miles
- 90: 46 miles

For more than 40,000 interstate mileages, see the Mileage Directory on page 137

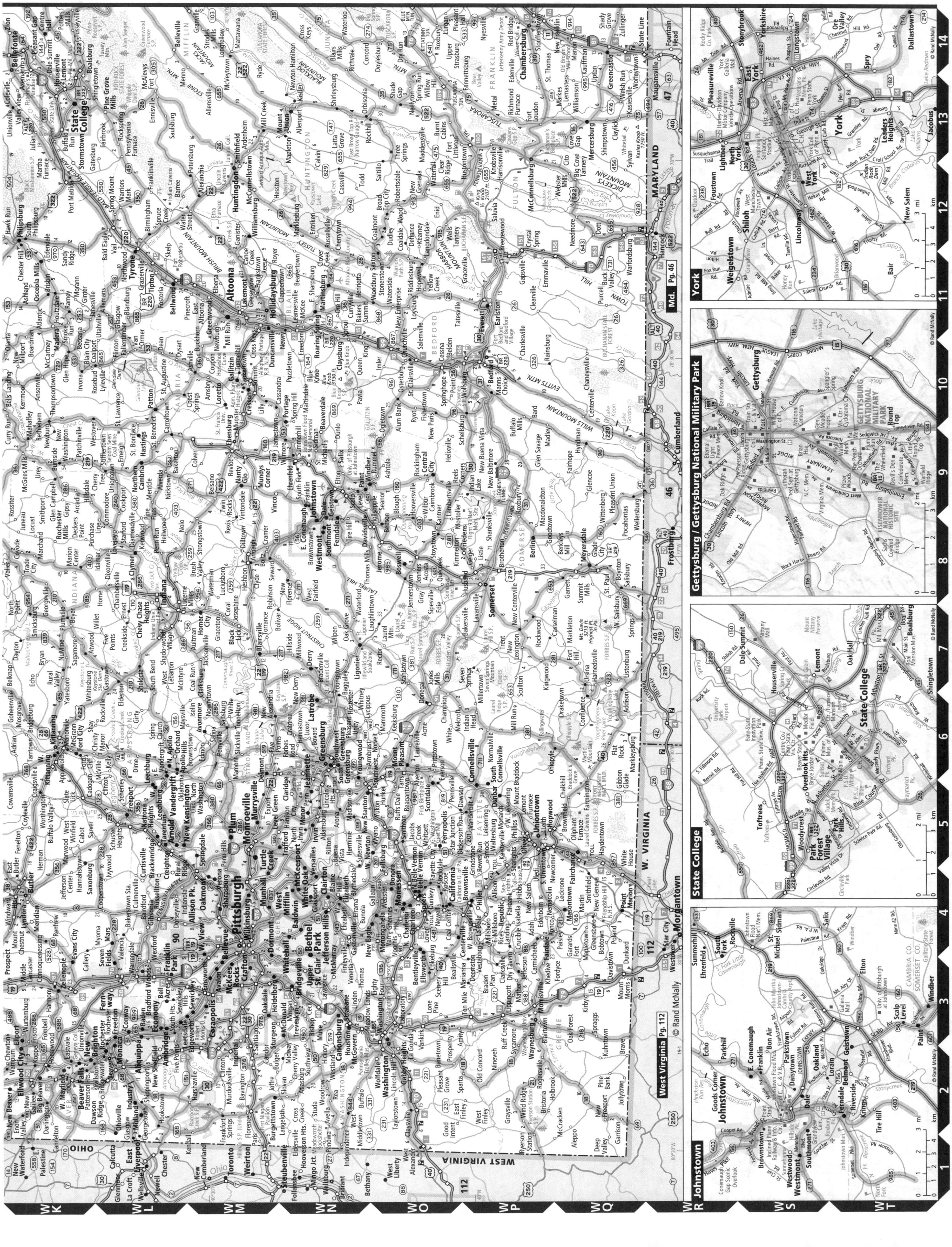

Nickname: The Keystone State
Capital: Harrisburg, EN-4
Land area: 44,743 sq. mi. (rank: 32nd)
Population: 12,702,379 (rank: 6th)
Largest city: Philadelphia, 1,526,006, EP-12

Index of cities Pg. 134 | Map legend Pg. 1

Route planning & on-the-road resources

Low clearances, weigh stations, & restricted routes: Page A40

Weigh station location

Designated route for vehicles with STAA-authorized dimensions

Road Conditions & Construction
511, (888) 783-6783, (800) 349-7623, (717) 787-2838
www.511pa.com; www.penndot.gov

Toll Road Information
Pennsylvania Turnpike Commission (*E-ZPass*): (800) 331-3414; www.paturnpike.com

Determining Distances
(segments of one mile or less not shown)
Cumulative miles (red): the distance between red arrows
Intermediate miles (black): the distance between intersections & places

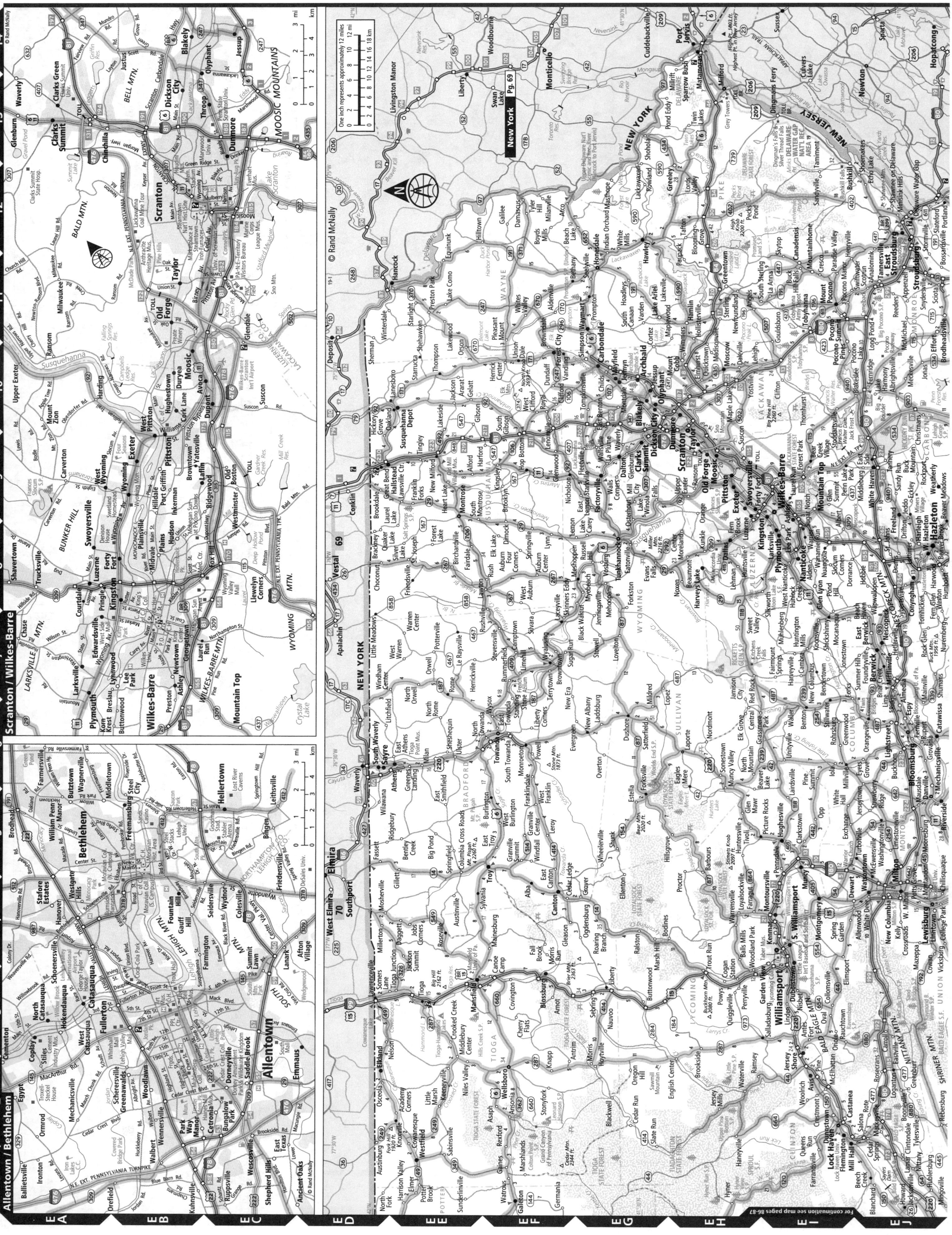

Mileage between cities	Allentown	Altoona	Baltimore, MD	Binghamton, NY	Chambersburg	Easton	Gettysburg	Harrisburg	Hazleton	Lancaster	Mansfield	Philadelphia	Pittsburgh	Port Jervis, NY	Reading	Scranton	State College	Trenton, NJ	Wilkes Barre	Williamsport	York
ALLENTOWN		213	150	133	136	18	123	82	48	72	177	63	284	144	38	75	176	76	71	127	100
CHAMBERSBURG	136	98	100	232		148	25	54	132	92	185	157	169	276	115	171	138	177	157	135	77
HARRISBURG	82	134	83	181	54	97	39		80	43	133	109	205	225	66	120	87	129	105	83	33
PHILADELPHIA	63	234	100	182	157	77	138	109	97	78	226		305	197	62	124	193	32	120	176	105
READING	38	192	111	159	115	55	96	66	54	34	175	62	262	195		100	151	82	79	125	61
SCRANTON	75	185	200	59	171	70	160	120	46	132	103	124	280	107	100		150	137	16	101	150
STATE COLLEGE	176	41	172	211	138	188	126	87	126	127	112	193	136	255	151	150		213	135	67	122
WILLIAMSPORT	127	102	169	125	135	139	122	83	77	123	50	176	196	206	125	101	67	189	86		119

Total mileage through Pennsylvania

76 350 miles

81 232 miles

80 311 miles

95 51 miles

For more than 40,000 interstate mileages, see the Mileage Directory on page 137

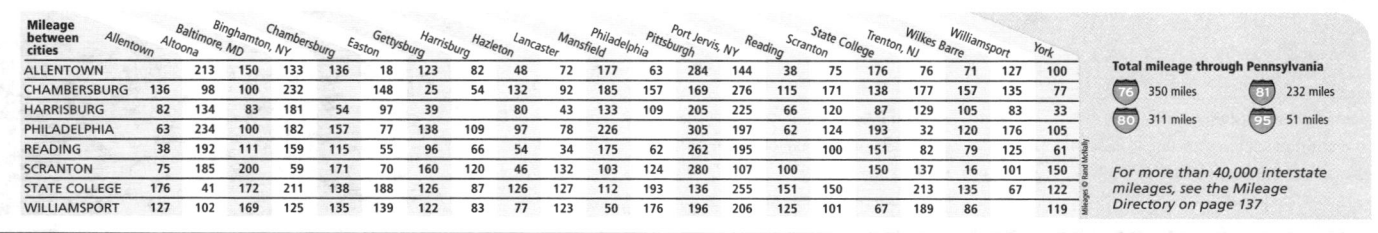

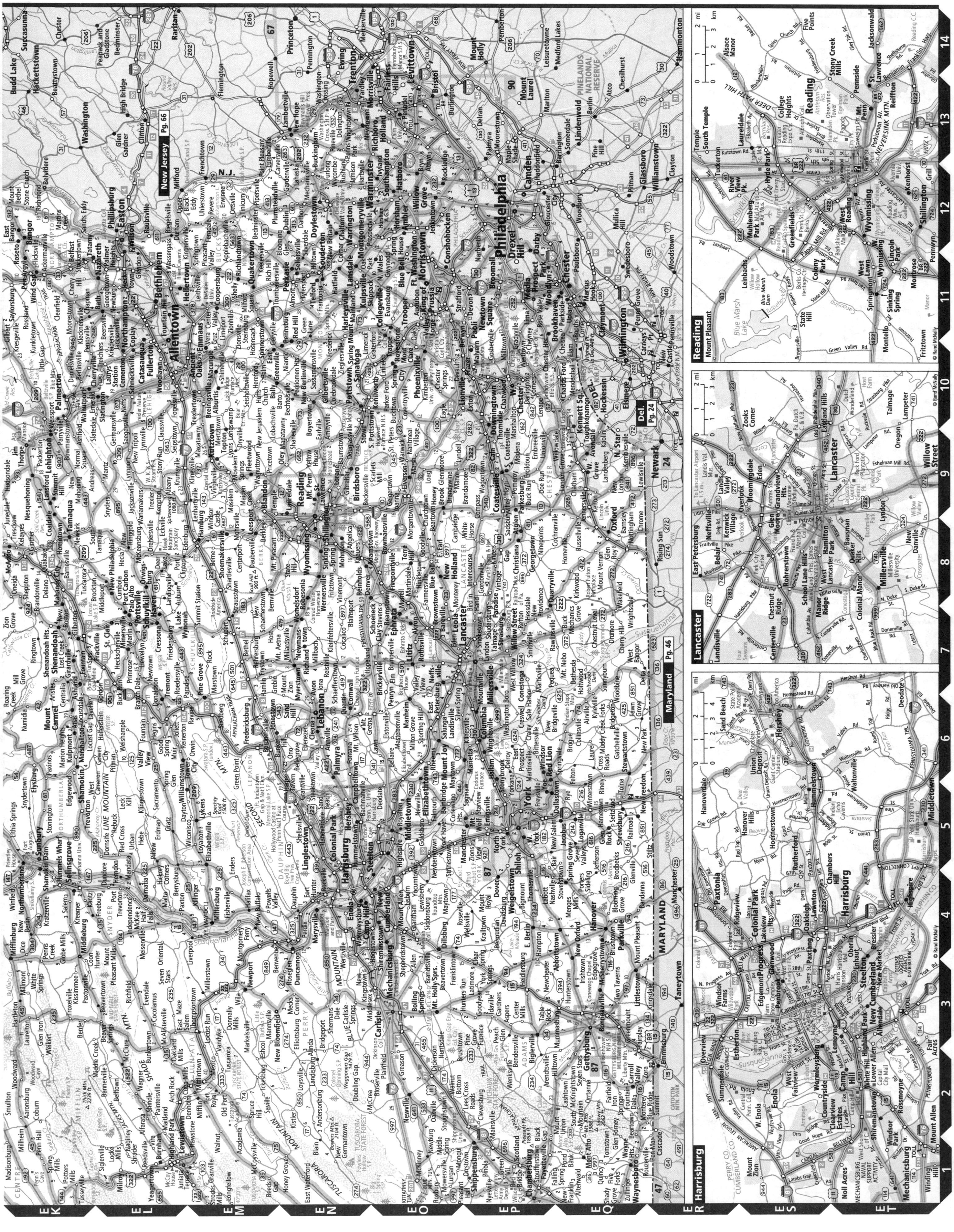

Sights to see

- Adventure Aquarium, Camden E-5
- The Andy Warhol Museum, Pittsburgh L-2
- Betsy Ross House, Philadelphia F-10
- Carnegie Science Center, Pittsburgh L-1
- Duquesne Incline, Pittsburgh M-1
- Franklin Institute Science Museum, Philadelphia F-6
- Independence Hall, Philadelphia G-9
- Liberty Bell, Philadelphia G-9
- National Constitution Center, Philadelphia F-9
- Philadelphia Museum of Art, Philadelphia E-4
- Point State Park, Pittsburgh M-1
- The Strip District, Pittsburgh L-3

Route planning & on-the-road resources

Low clearances, weigh stations, & restricted routes: Page A41

Weigh station location

Designated route for vehicles with STAA-authorized dimensions

Road Conditions & Construction
511
(888) 401-4511, (401) 222-2450
www.dot.ri.gov/travel

Toll Bridge Information
Rhode Island Turnpike & Bridge Authority
(E-ZPass): (401) 423-0800; www.ritba.org

Mileage between cities	Chepachet	Fall River, MA	Kingston	Newport	Providence	Warwick	Westerly	Woonsocket	Worcester, MA
FALL RIVER, MA	39		35	21	16	25	58	31	71
KINGSTON	41	35		16	29	24	23	43	86
NEWPORT	45	21	16		33	28	39	47	92
PROVIDENCE	23	16	29	33		10	42	14	57
WARWICK	26	25	24	28	10		37	24	67
WESTERLY	54	58	23	39	42	37		56	97
WOONSOCKET	14	31	43	47	14	24	56		29
WORCESTER, MA	38	71	86	92	57	67	97	29	

Total mileage through Rhode Island
I-95: 42 miles
US 1: 60 miles
US 6: 31 miles

For more than 40,000 interstate mileages, see the Mileage Directory on page 137

Rhode Island

Nickname: The Ocean State
Capital: Providence, D-6
Land area: 1,034 sq. mi. (rank: 50th)
Population: 1,052,567 (rank: 43rd)
Largest city: Providence, 178,042, D-6

Index of cities Pg. 134
Map legend Pg. 1

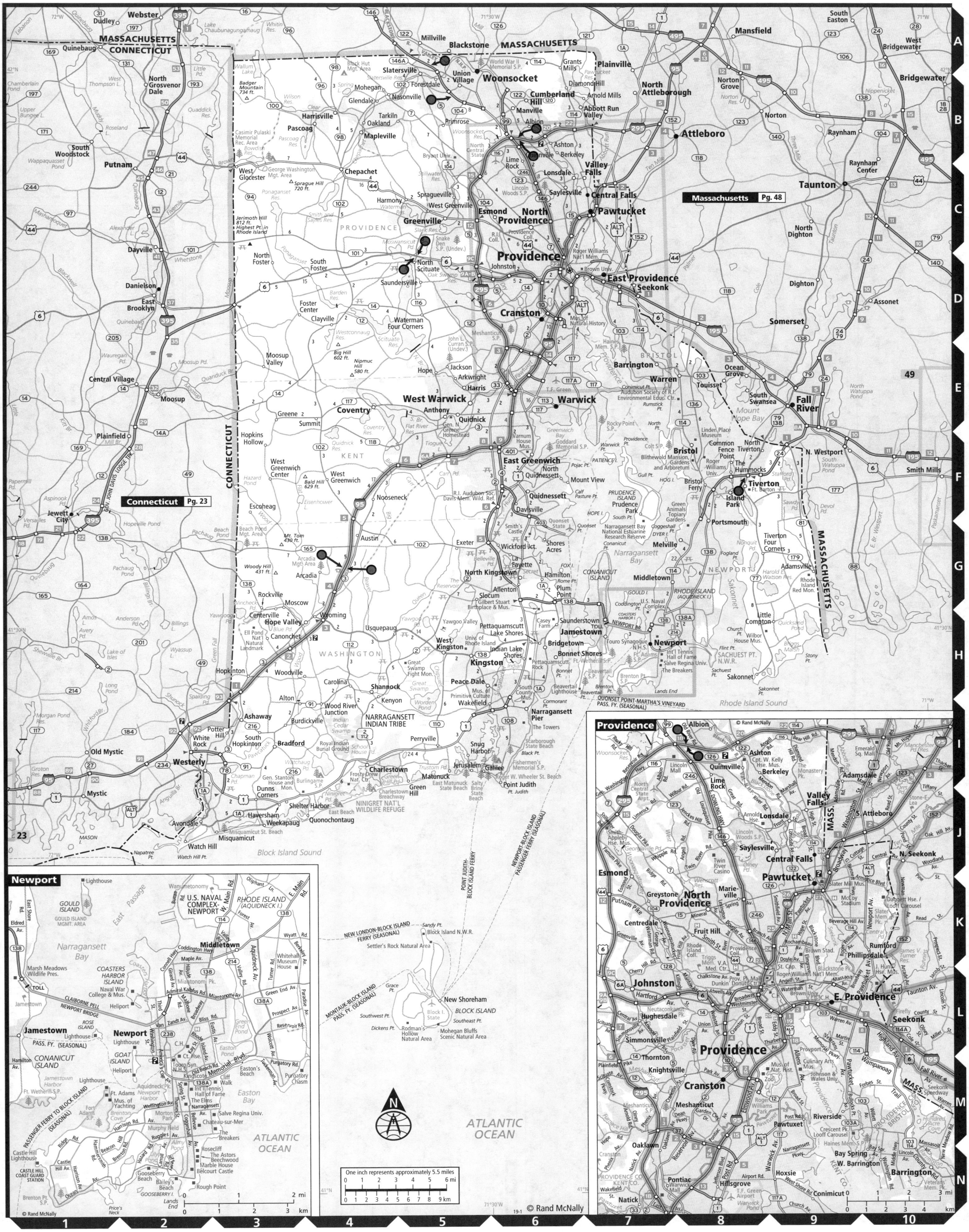

South Carolina

Nickname: The Palmetto State
Capital: Columbia, D-7
Land area: 30,061 sq. mi. (rank: 40th)
Population: 4,625,364 (rank: 24th)
Largest city: Columbia, 129,272, D-7

Index of cities Pg. 134 | Map legend Pg. 1

Mileage between cities	Anderson	Augusta, GA	Beaufort	Charleston	Charlotte, NC	Columbia	Georgetown	Greenwood	Myrtle Beach	Orangeburg	Savannah, GA	Spartanburg	Sumter
AUGUSTA, GA	103		117	175	160	72	208	60	216	71	142	120	116
CHARLESTON	238	175	68		207	112	59	179	96	75	111	201	104
CHARLOTTE, NC	131	160	231	207		93	179	139	176	138	257	73	132
COLUMBIA	129	72	135	112	93		127	89	149	42	161	93	45
FLORENCE	206	148	154	131	104	81	75	166	68	91	180	169	44
MYRTLE BEACH	273	216	164	96	176	149	37	233		141	207	237	95
SAVANNAH, GA	287	142	53	111	257	161	170	204	207	124		251	154
SPARTANBURG	60	120	225	201	73	93	235	63	237	132	251		137

Total mileage through South Carolina
20: 142 miles; 85: 106 miles
26: 221 miles; 95: 199 miles

For more than 40,000 interstate mileages, see the Mileage Directory on page 137

Route planning & on-the-road resources

Low clearances, weigh stations, & restricted routes: Page A41

Weigh station location

Designated route for vehicles with STAA-authorized dimensions

Road Conditions & Construction
511, (877) 511-4672, (855) 467-2368
www.511sc.org, www.dot.state.sc.us

Toll Road Info *(all use Palmetto Pass)*
Cross Island Pkwy. (Hilton Head I.): (843) 342-6718; www.crossislandparkway.org
Southern Connector (Greenville Co.): (864) 527-2150; www.southernconnector.com

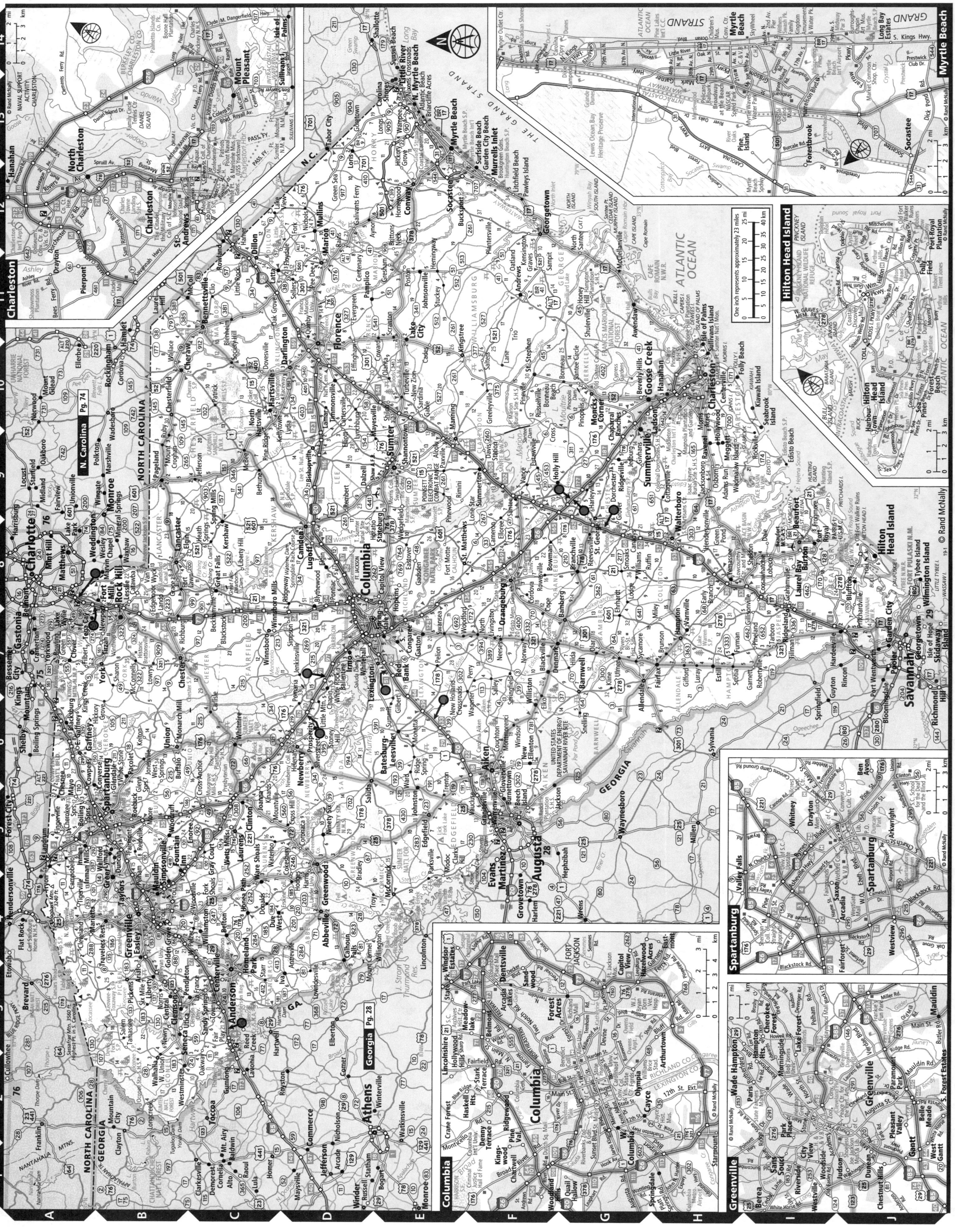

Low clearances, weigh stations, & restricted routes: Page A42

Weigh station location

Designated route for vehicles with STAA-authorized dimensions

Road Conditions & Construction

511, (866) 697-3511
www.sddot.com
www.safetravelusa.com/sd

Toll Road Information

No tolls on state or federal highways

Mileage between cities	Aberdeen	Belle Fourche	Mobridge	Pierre	Rapid City	Sioux City, IA	Sioux Falls	Watertown
ABERDEEN		312	100	162	353	285	204	96
BELLE FOURCHE	312		213	206	60	484	404	362
MOBRIDGE	100	213		110	243	384	304	196
PIERRE	162	206	110		191	305	225	189
RAPID CITY	353	60	243	191		428	348	406
SIOUX CITY, IA	285	484	384	305	428		85	184
SIOUX FALLS	204	404	304	225	348	85		104
WATERTOWN	96	362	196	189	406	184	104	

Total mileage through South Dakota

- I-29: 253 miles
- I-90: 413 miles
- US 12: 317 miles
- US 83: 242 miles

For more than 40,000 interstate mileages, see the Mileage Directory on page 137

South Dakota

Nickname: The Mount Rushmore State
Capital: Pierre, D-7
Land area: 75,811 sq. mi. (rank: 16th)
Population: 814,180 (rank: 46th)
Largest city: Sioux Falls, 153,888, F-13

Index of cities Pg. 134 | Map legend Pg. 1

Tennessee

Nickname: The Volunteer State
Capital: Nashville, C-11
Land area: 41,235 sq. mi. (rank: 34th)
Population: 6,346,105 (rank: 17th)
Largest city: Memphis, 646,889, G-2

Index of cities Pg. 134 | Map legend Pg. 1

Route planning & on-the-road resources

Low clearances, weigh stations, & restricted routes: Page A42

Weigh station location

Designated route for vehicles with STAA-authorized dimensions

Road Conditions & Construction
511, (877) 244-0065; www.tn511.com, www.tn.gov/tdot

Toll Road Information
No tolls on state or federal highways

Determining Distances
(segments of one mile or less not shown)
Cumulative miles (red): the distance between red arrows
Intermediate miles (black): the distance between intersections & places

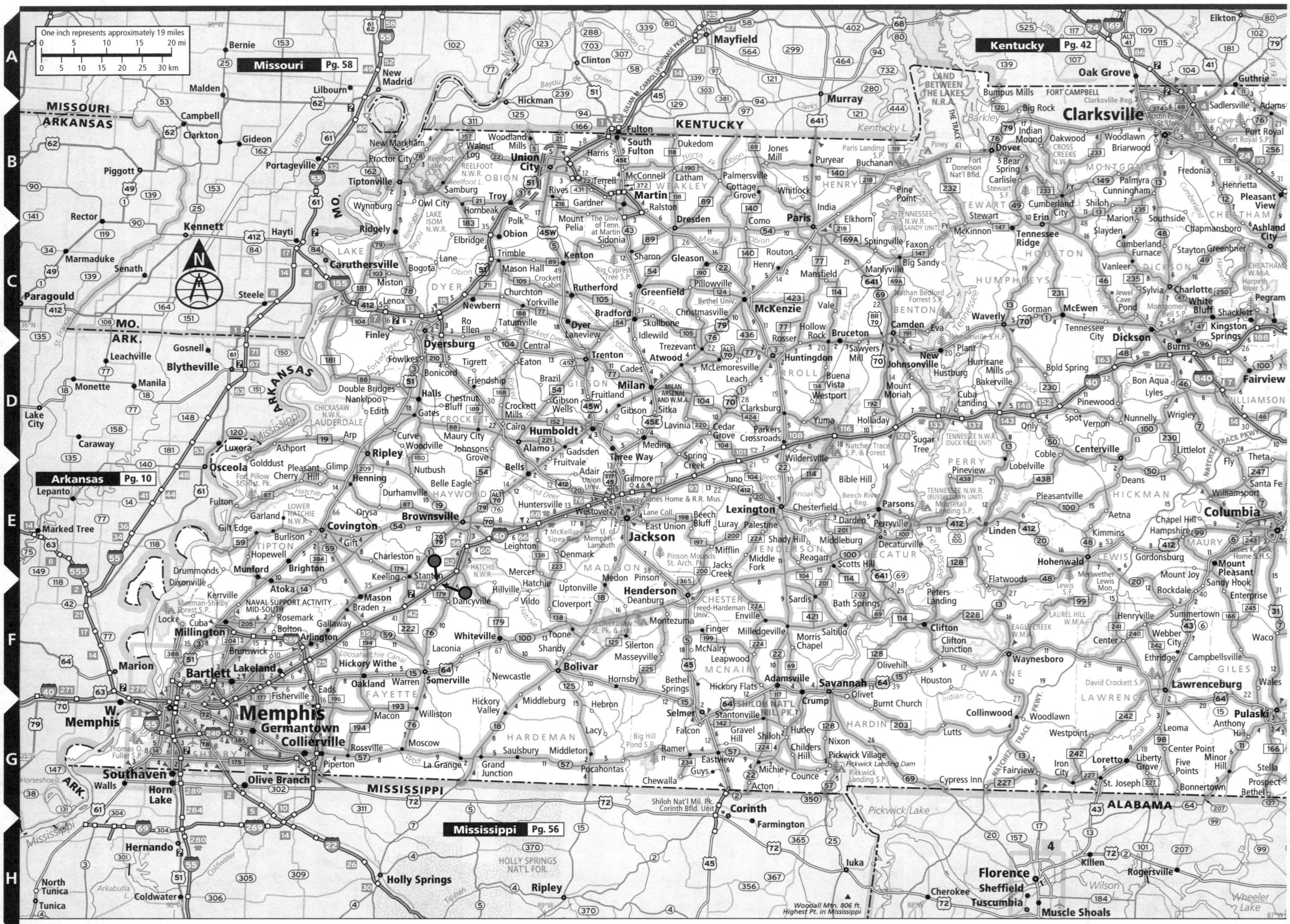

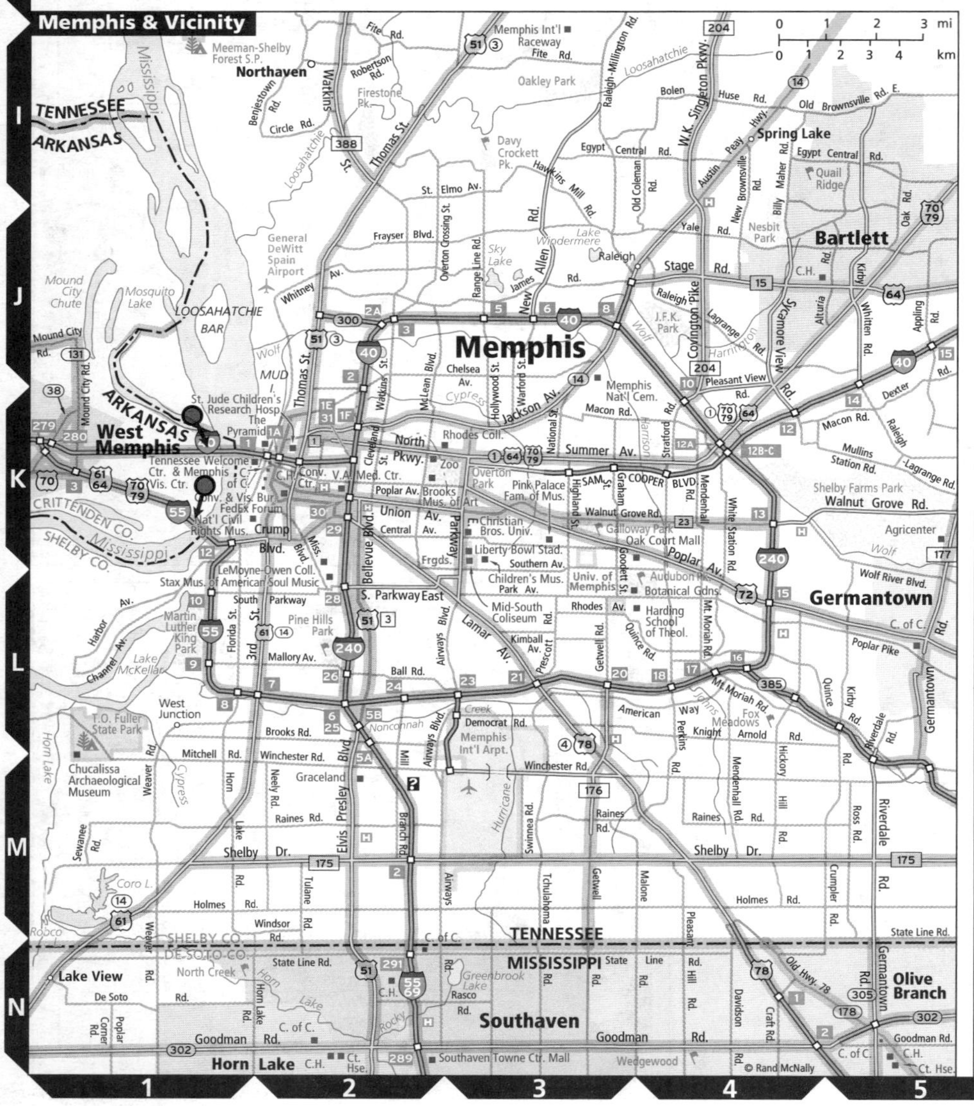

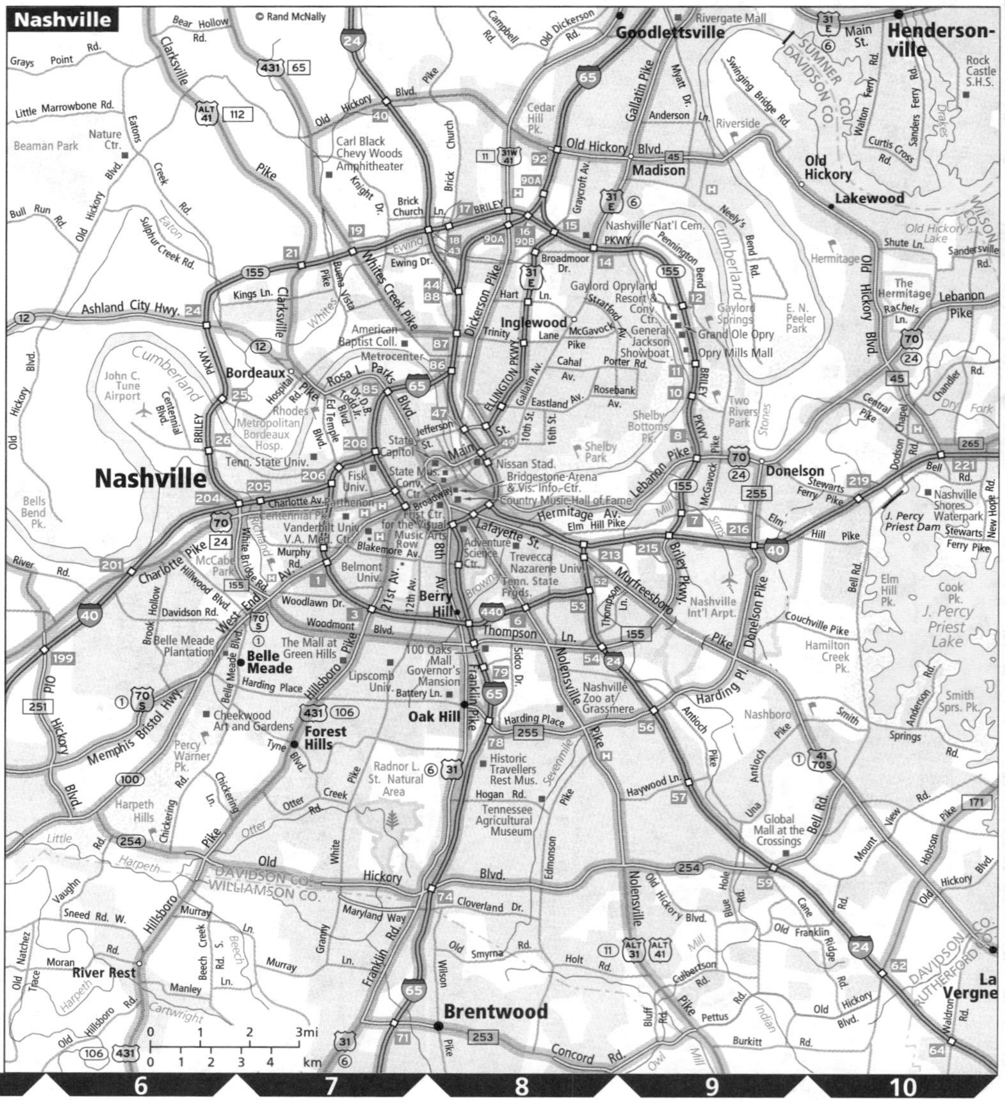

Mileage between cities	Atlanta, GA	Bristol	Chattanooga	Clarksville	Cookeville	Dyersburg	Fayetteville	Gatlinburg	Jackson	Johnson City	Kingsport	Knoxville	La Follette	Memphis	Morristown	Nashville	Oak Ridge	Union City
CHATTANOOGA	117	223		177	100	306	127	152	263	215	210	110	146	314	160	132	111	313
CLARKSVILLE	294	338	177		128	173	137	266	130	330	324	225	261	211	275	49	208	139
DYERSBURG	423	468	306	173	258		232	396	51	459	454	355	391	79	404	176	338	34
FAYETTEVILLE	214	346	127	137	136	232		274	188	337	332	233	269	243	282	90	216	224
JOHNSON CITY	268	24	215	330	206	459	337	107	415		24	104	142	496	67	283	128	464
KNOXVILLE	213	113	110	225	102	355	233	41	310	104	99		38	391	50	179	24	360
MEMPHIS	379	504	314	211	294	79	243	432	88	496	491	391	427		441	212	374	114
NASHVILLE	248	292	132	49	82	176	90	220	132	283	278	179	215	212	228		162	168

Mileages © Rand McNally

Total mileage through Tennessee

- 40: 455 miles
- 65: 121 miles
- 75: 161 miles
- 81: 76 miles

For more than 40,000 interstate mileages, see the Mileage Directory on page 137

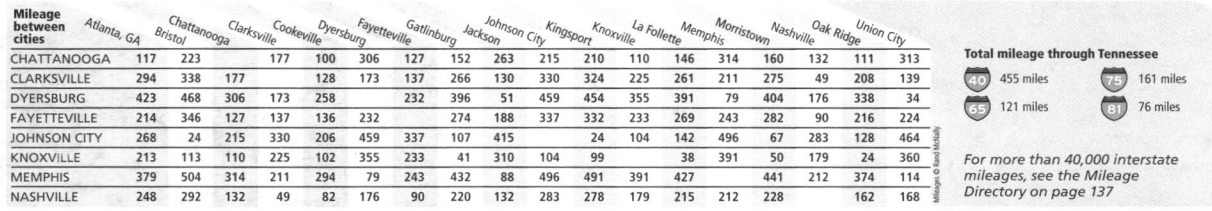

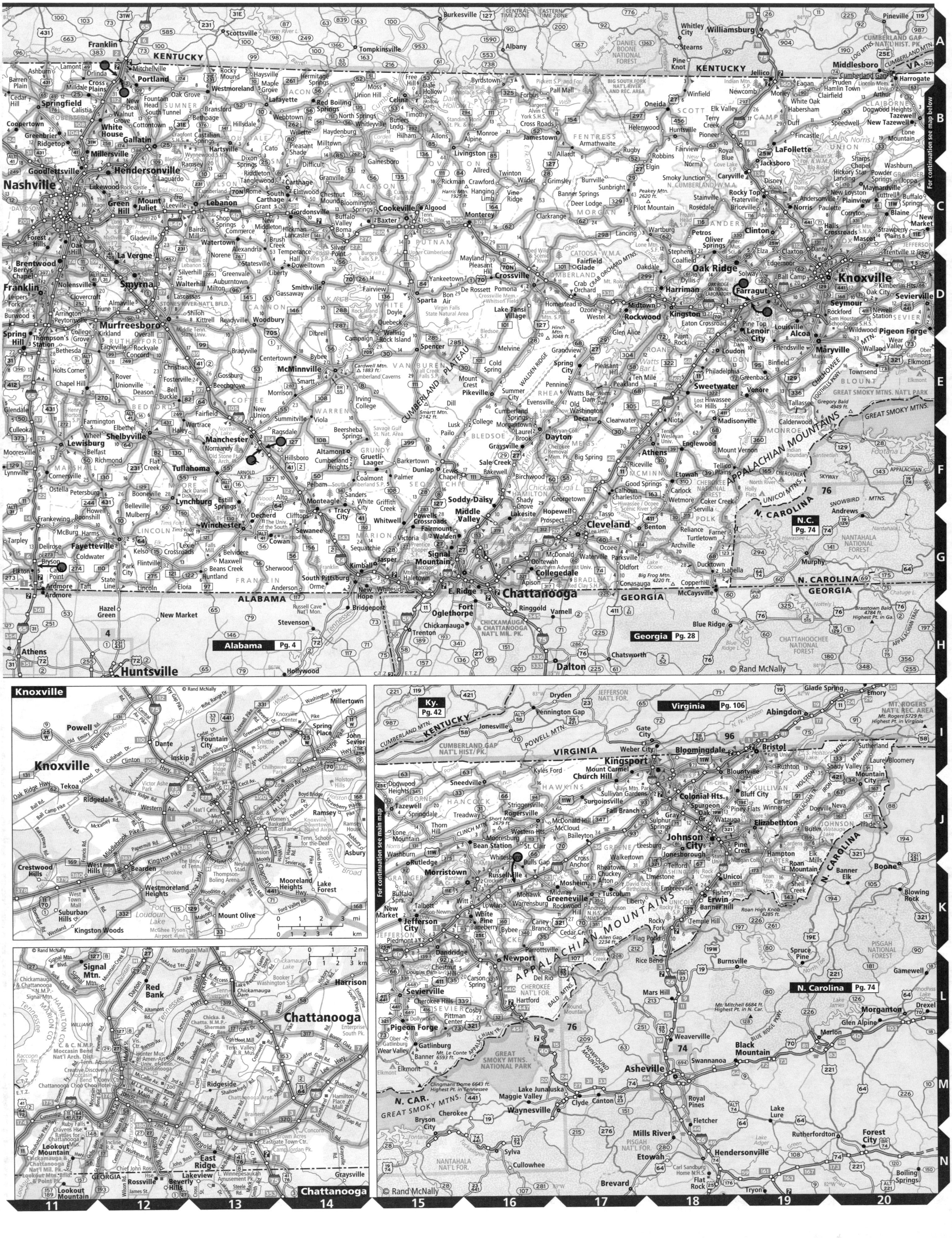

Sights to see

- Appalachian Caverns, Blountville . . . K-3
- Battleship USS Texas, La Porte . . . D-9
- Bayou Place, Houston . . . K-8
- Bristol Caverns, Bristol . . . J-6
- Bristol Motor Speedway, Bristol . . . K-4
- Contemporary Arts Museum, Houston . . . E-5
- Houston Fire Museum, Houston . . . E-5
- Houston Zoo, Houston . . . E-5
- Museum of Natural Science, Houston . . . E-5
- Rocky Mount Museum, Piney Flats . . . L-3
- Space Center Houston, Houston . . . G-8
- Wortham Theatre Center, Houston . . . K-8

Church Circle, Kingsport

Space Center Houston

Sights to see

- Dallas Museum of Art, Dallas B-2
- Dallas Zoo, Dallas H-10
- Fair Park, Dallas G-11
- Fort Worth Zoo, Fort Worth H-4
- Louis Tussaud's Palace of Wax & Ripley's Believe It or Not!, Grand Prairie G-8
- Old City Park, Dallas C-3
- Six Flags over Texas, Arlington H-7
- The Sixth Floor Museum at Dealey Plaza, Dallas B-1
- Stockyards Historic District, Fort Worth G-4
- Sundance Square, Fort Worth E-1
- Texas Civil War Museum, Fort Worth G-2

Nickname: The Lone Star State
Capital: Austin, EK-5
Land area: 261,231 sq. mi. (rank: 2nd)
Population: 25,145,561 (rank: 2nd)
Largest city: Houston, 2,099,451, EL-10

Index of cities Pg. 135 | Map legend Pg. 1

Route planning & on-the-road resources

Low clearances, weigh stations, & restricted routes: Page A42

Weigh station location

Designated route for vehicles with STAA-authorized dimensions

Road Conditions & Construction
(800) 452-9292
(512) 463-8588
www.txdot.gov
www.drivetexas.org

Toll Road Information *(all use TxTag)*
Texas Dept. of Transportation: (888) 468-9824; www.txtag.org
Cameron County Reg. Mobility Authority (TX 550): (956) 621-5571; www.ccrma.org
Harris County Toll Road Authority (Houston area) *(also EZTAG)*: (281) 875-3279; www.hctra.org
North Texas Tollway Authority (Dallas Metroplex) *(also TollTag)*: (972) 818-6882; www.ntta.org

(list continued on p. 100)

Toll Bridge Information
El Paso–Int'l Bridges: (912) 212-7500
www.elpasotexas.gov/international-bridges
Eagle Pass–Int'l Br. System: (830) 773-2622
www.eaglepasstx.us

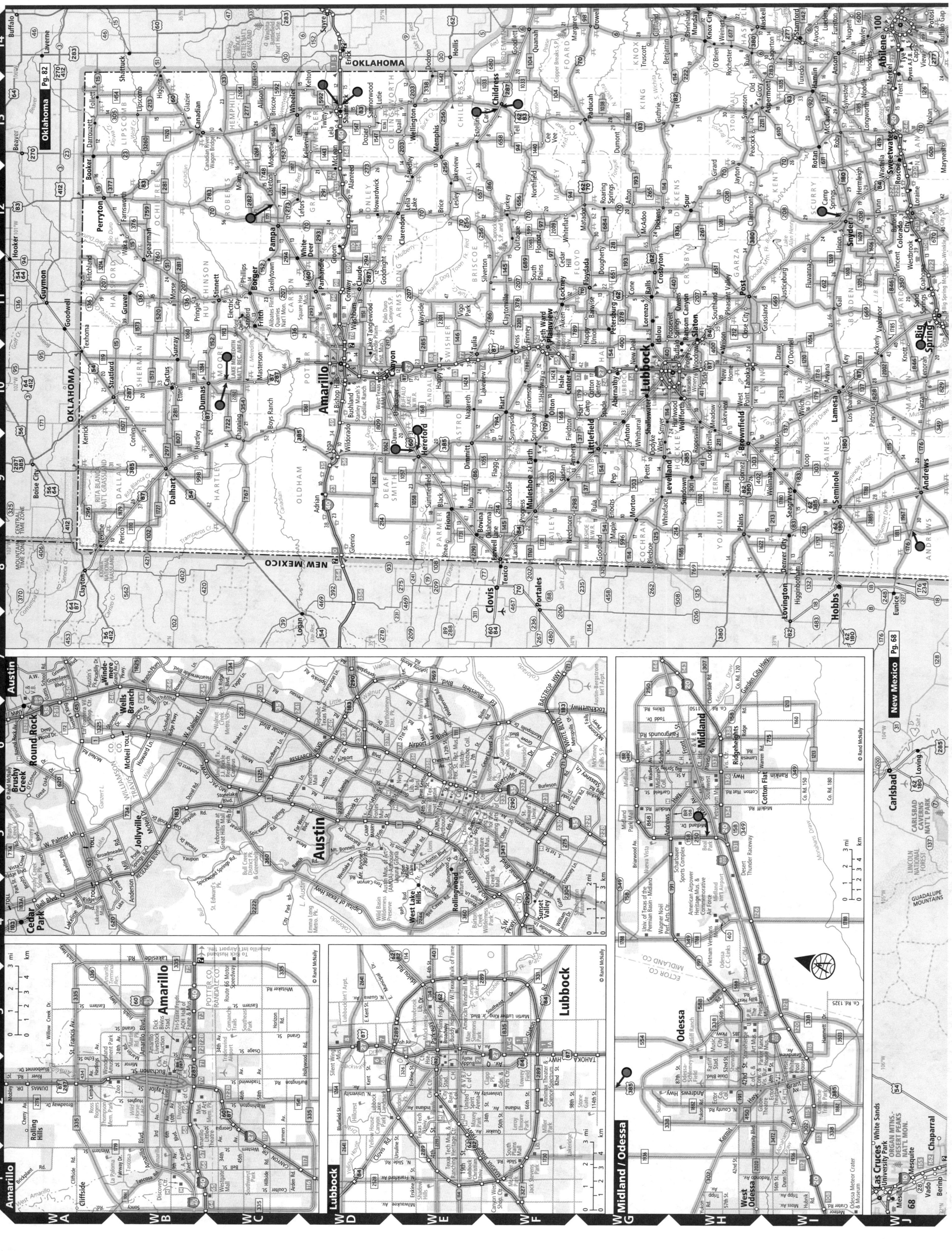

Mileage between cities	Abilene	Amarillo	Big Bend NP	Big Spring	Carlsbad, NM	Childress	Clovis, NM	Dallas	Del Rio	Eagle Pass	El Paso	Fort Stockton	Houston	Lubbock	Midland	Odessa	Pecos	Perryton	San Angelo	San Antonio	Van Horn
ABILENE		268	380	109	291	155	267	179	249	311	454	255	410	164	149	171	246	306	92	261	333
AMARILLO	268		470	226	300	116	104	363	454	510	436	344	600	120	237	258	335	120	318	511	423
DALLAS	179	363	561	290	472	248	448		426	420	635	436	242	345	330	352	427	402	269	276	514
EL PASO	454	436	325	346	217	570	345	635	427	483		240	753	423	305	284	210	545	404	554	121
LUBBOCK	164	120	349	106	182	144	103	345	333	390	423	224	576		117	138	215	240	197	390	302
ODESSA	171	258	211	63	162	286	204	352	258	314	284	85	550	138	22		76	378	132	351	164
SAN ANGELO	92	318	290	86	270	242	300	269	157	213	404	165	368	197	112	132	207	393		214	283
SAN ANTONIO	261	511	441	300	453	417	493	276	151	145	554	315	198	390	328	351	367	568	214		434

Total mileage through Texas

- I-10: 881 miles
- I-40: 177 miles
- I-20: 636 miles

For more than 40,000 interstate mileages, see the Mileage Directory on page 137

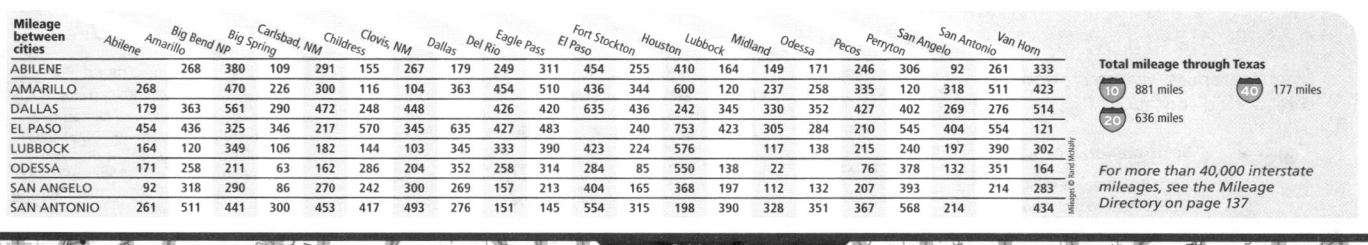

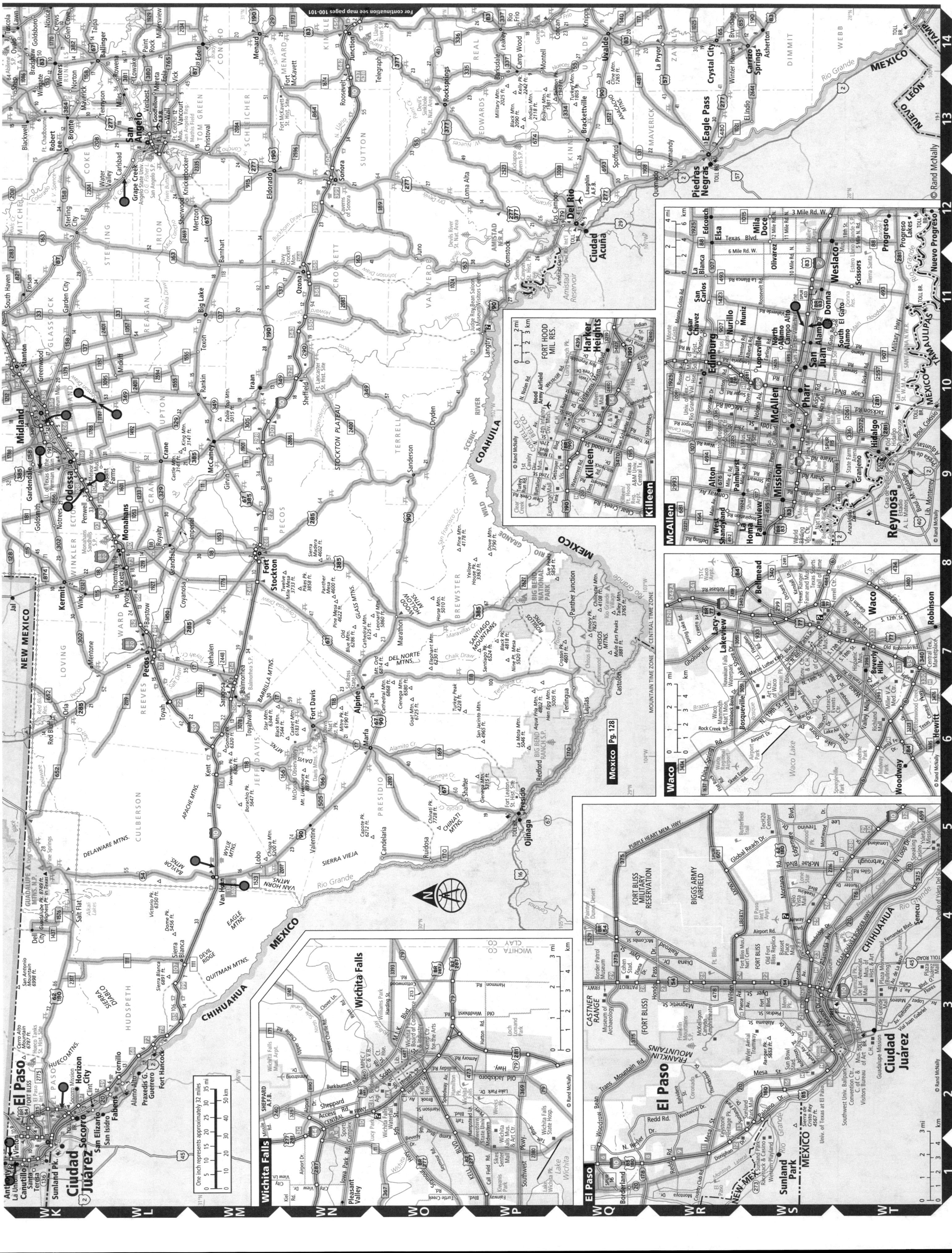

Nickname: The Lone Star State
Capital: Austin, EK-5
Land area: 261,231 sq. mi. (rank: 2nd)
Population: 25,145,561 (rank: 2nd)
Largest city: Houston, 2,099,451, EL-10

Index of cities Pg. 135 | Map legend Pg. 1

Route planning & on-the-road resources

Low clearances, weigh stations, & restricted routes: Page A42

Weigh station location

Designated route for vehicles with STAA-authorized dimensions

Road Conditions & Construction
(800) 452-9292
(512) 463-8588
www.txdot.gov
www.drivetexas.org

Toll Road Information (cont. from p. 98) *(all use TxTag)*
Central Texas Regional Mobility Authority (Austin area): (512) 996-9778; www.mobilityauthority.com
Ft. Bend Co. Toll Road Auth. (Houston area) *(also EZTAG)*: (855) 999-2024, (832) 735-7385; www.fbctra.com
North East Reg. Mobility Auth. (TX 49): (903) 630-7447; www.netrma.org
SH 130 Concession Co. (TX 130): (512) 371-4800; mysh130.com

Toll Bridge Info. (cont. from p. 98)
Cameron County–Int'l Br. System: (956) 574-8771; www.co.cameron.tx.us
Laredo–Int'l Br. System: (956) 791-2200 www.cityoflaredo.com/bridgesys
McAllen–Bridge Dept: (956) 681-1800 www.mcallen.net/departments/bridge

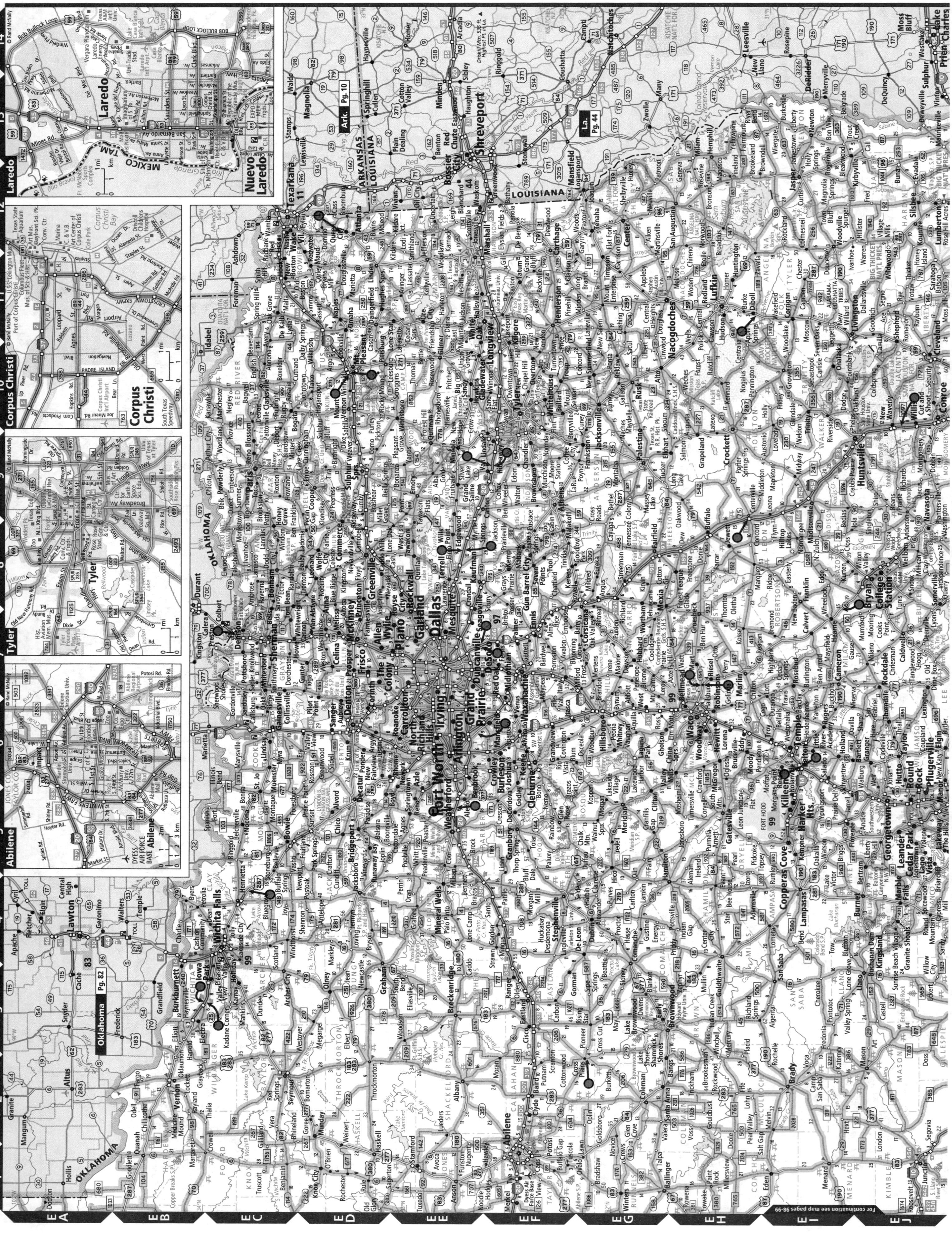

Mileage between cities	Abilene	Austin	Beaumont	Brownsville	Corpus Christi	Dallas	Fort Worth	Galveston	Houston	Laredo	Lufkin	McAllen	Paris	San Angelo	San Antonio	Shreveport, LA	Texarkana	Tyler	Victoria	Waco	Wichita Falls
ABILENE		221	457	538	403	179	149	458	410	413	363	499	285	92	261	368	358	280	347	183	151
AUSTIN	221		245	352	216	194	188	213	164	240	224	313	300	209	81	325	373	229	125	99	302
BROWNSVILLE	538	352	439		160	546	540	396	354	204	474	60	652	492	278	596	650	530	232	451	654
CORPUS CHRISTI	403	216	292	160		411	404	228	207	144	328	153	516	356	142	449	504	404	96	315	518
DALLAS	179	194	289	546	411		30	291	242	434	183	507	106	269	276	187	179	100	316	96	139
HOUSTON	410	164	85	354	207	242	262	49		354	120	347	308	369	198	242	296	199	124	186	376
SAN ANTONIO	261	81	280	278	142	276	269	247	198	160	314	238	381	214		406	455	310	114	180	383
SHREVEPORT, LA	368	325	206	596	449	187	217	291	242	565	120	589	154	458	406		72	98	366	226	324

Total mileage through Texas

- I-10: 881 miles
- I-20: 636 miles
- I-30: 223 miles
- I-35: 504 miles

For more than 40,000 interstate mileages, see the Mileage Directory on page 137

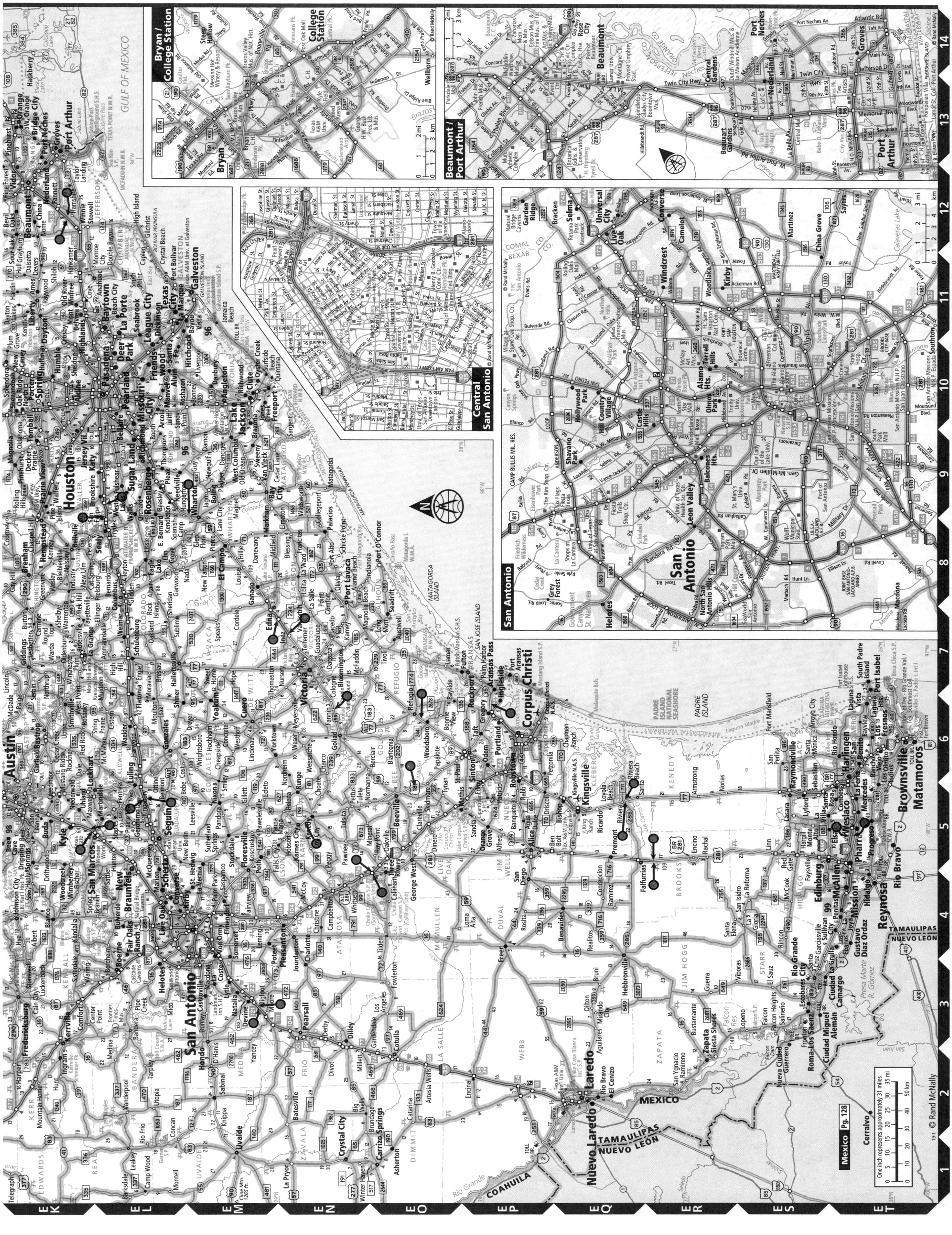

Nickname: The Beehive State
Capital: Salt Lake City, D-8
Land area: 82,169 sq. mi. (rank: 12th)
Population: 2,763,885 (rank: 34th)
Largest city: Salt Lake City, 186,440, D-8

Index of cities Pg. 135 | Map legend Pg. 1

Route planning & on-the-road resources

Low clearances, weigh stations, & restricted routes: Page A44

Weigh station location

Designated route for vehicles with STAA-authorized dimensions

Road Conditions & Construction
511, (866) 511-8824, (801) 887-3700, (801) 965-4000
www.udot.utah.gov, www.utahcommuterlink.com

Toll Road Information
Adams Avenue Parkway, Inc. (Washington Terrace) *(ExpressCard)*:
(801) 475-1909; www.adamsavenueparkway.com

Determining Distances
(segments of one mile or less not shown)
Cumulative miles (red): the distance between red arrows
Intermediate miles (black): the distance between intersections & places

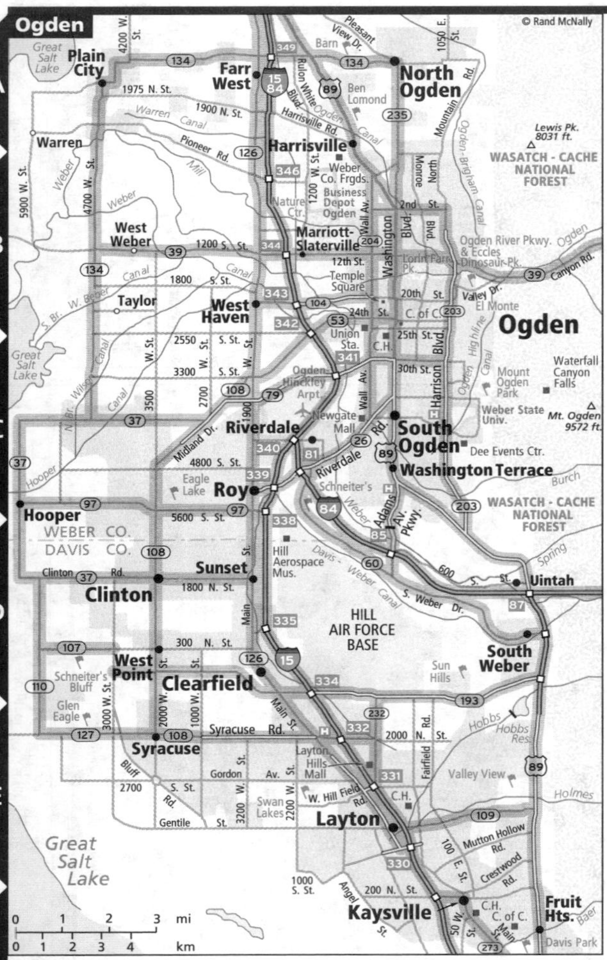

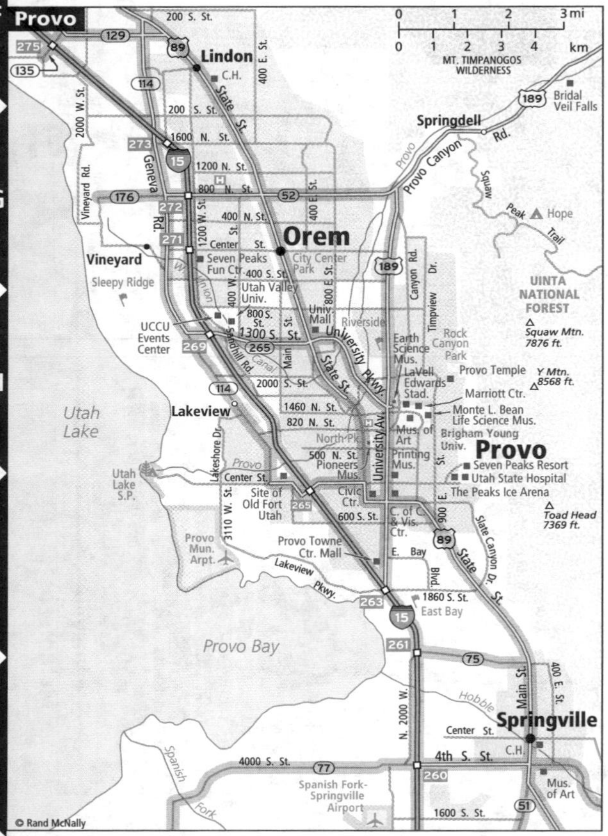

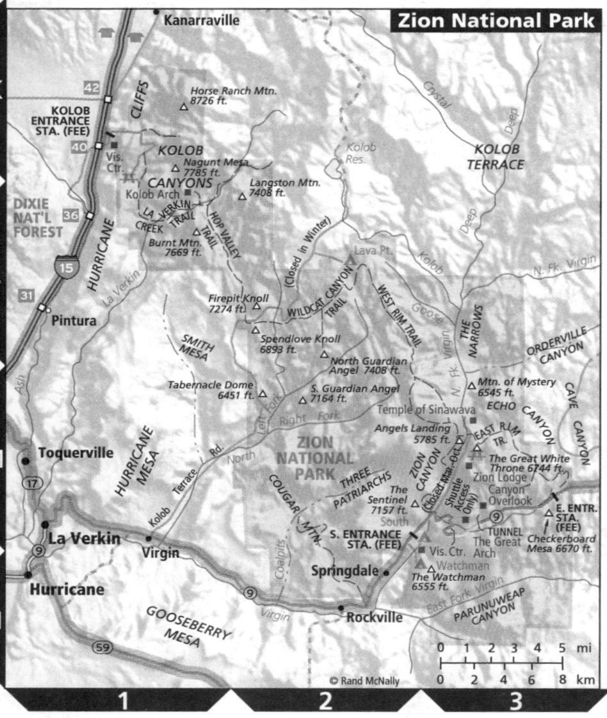

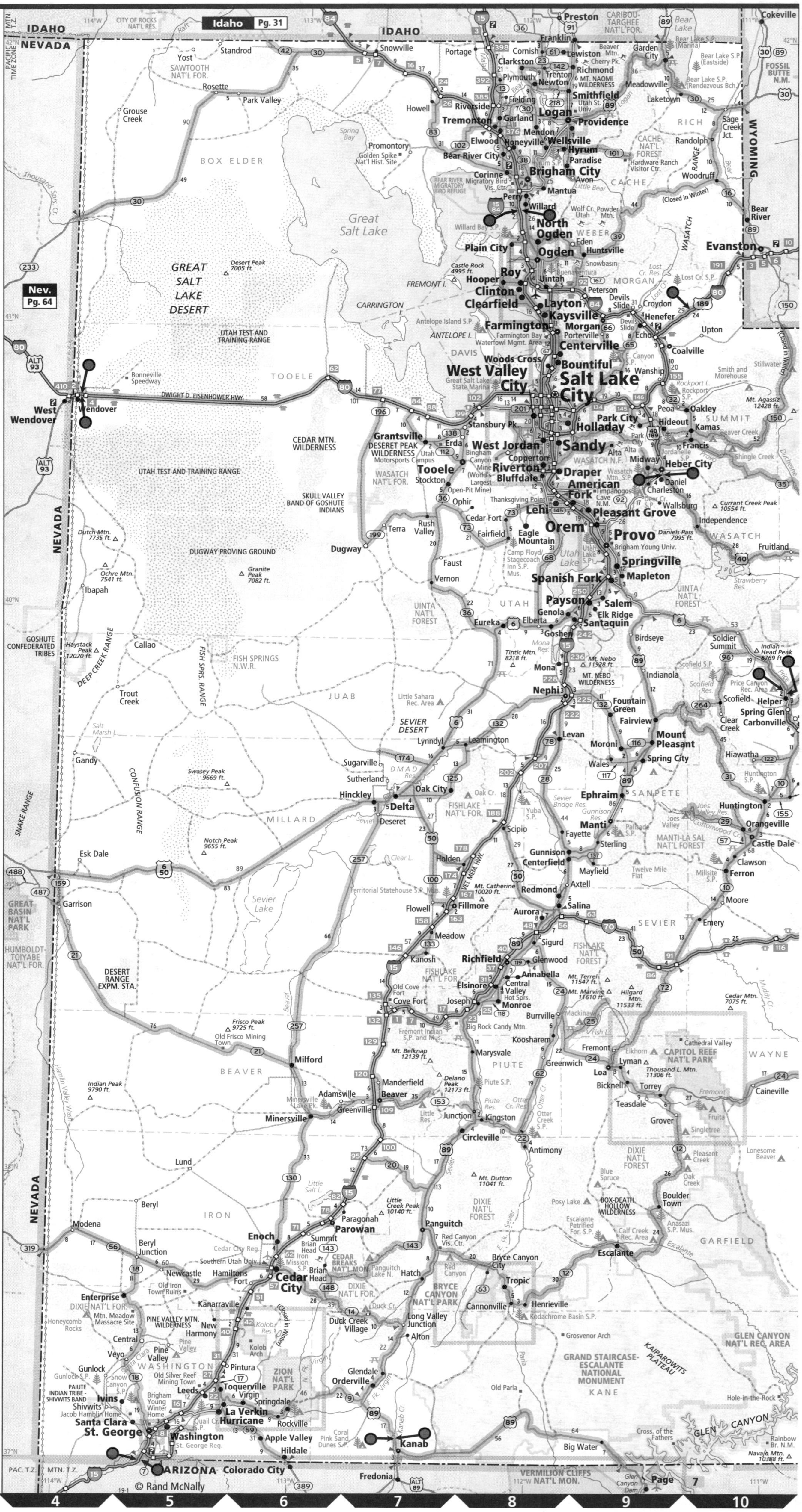

Mileage between cities	Bicknell	Blanding	Cedar City	Evanston, WY	Grand Jct., CO	Las Vegas, NV	Logan	Moab	Ogden	Page, AZ	Park City	Price	Provo	Richfield	St. George	Salt Lake City	Vernal	Wendover
GRAND JCT., CO	217	187	336	358		506	363	112	320	440	307	164	240	224	389	283	140	401
LOGAN	290	390	331	122	363	502		316	46	466	116	200	124	247	385	82	254	199
MOAB	169	74	288	310	112	458	316		272	319	259	116	192	176	341	235	220	353
OGDEN	246	346	288	75	320	458	46	272		422	69	156	80	204	341	39	207	156
PROVO	166	266	208	118	240	378	124	192	80	342	67	76		124	261	43	167	161
ST. GEORGE	223	415	55	379	389	121	385	341	341	260	328	287	261	169		304	412	333
SALT LAKE CITY	209	309	250	81	283	421	82	235	39	385	30	119	43	167	304		172	121
VERNAL	275	294	359	151	140	529	254	220	207	450	147	112	167	234	412	172		292

Total mileage through Utah

15 401 miles
80 196 miles
70 232 miles
84 119 miles

For more than 40,000 interstate mileages, see the Mileage Directory on page 137

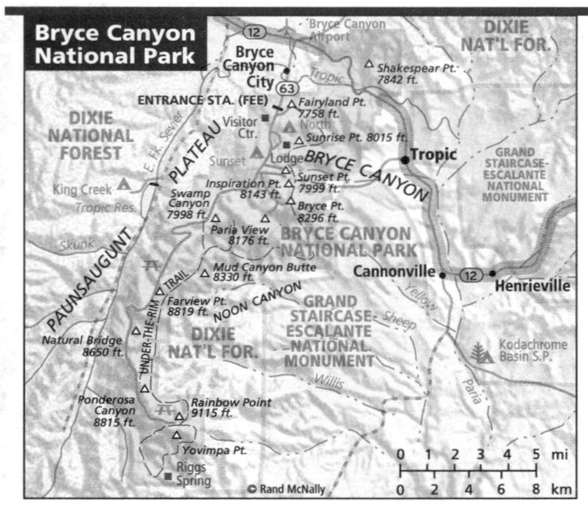

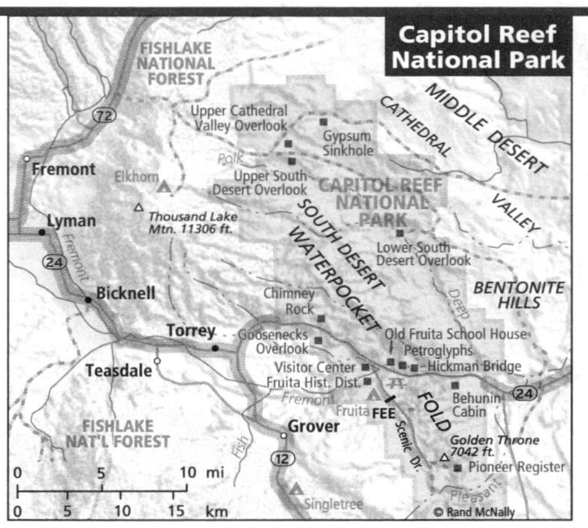

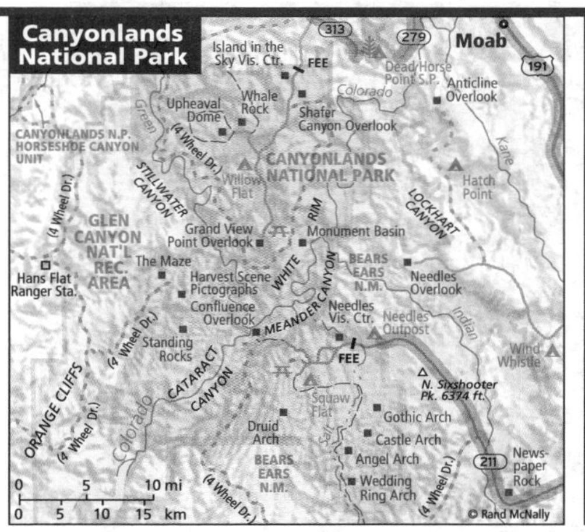

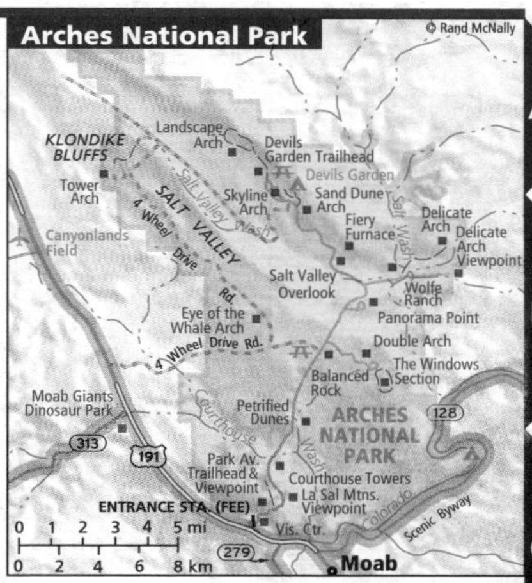

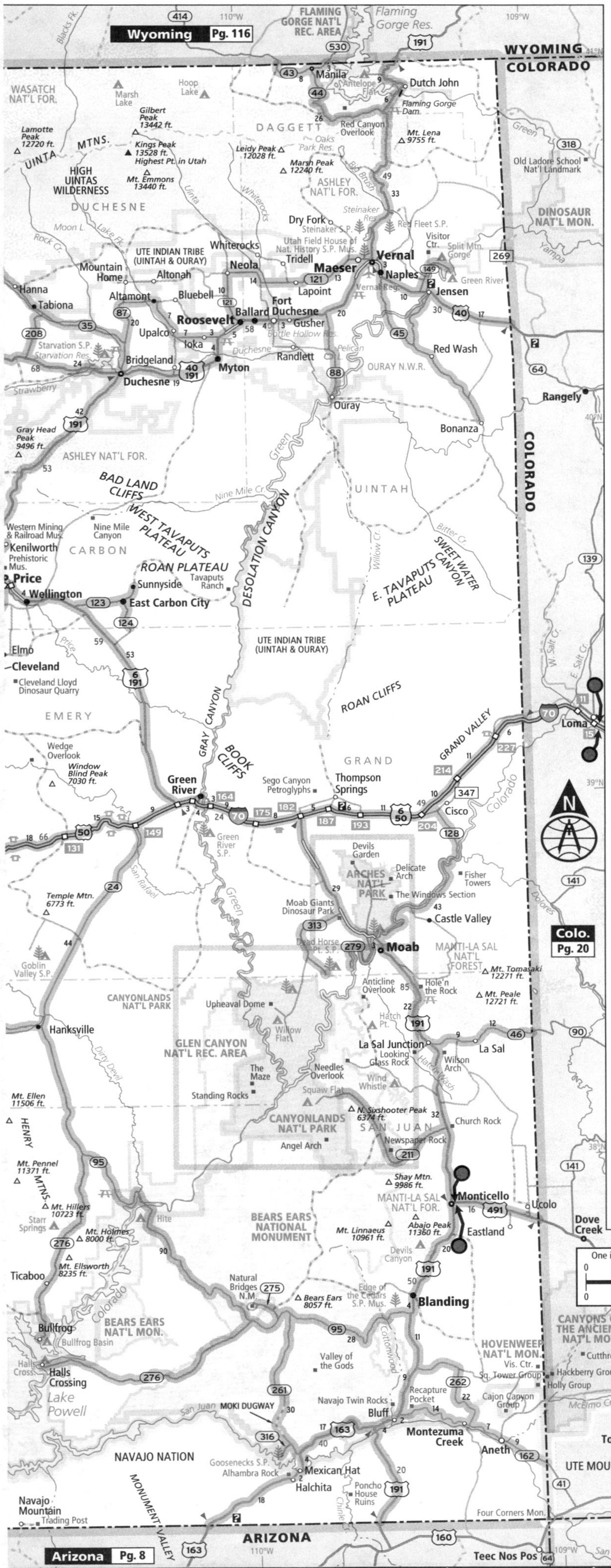

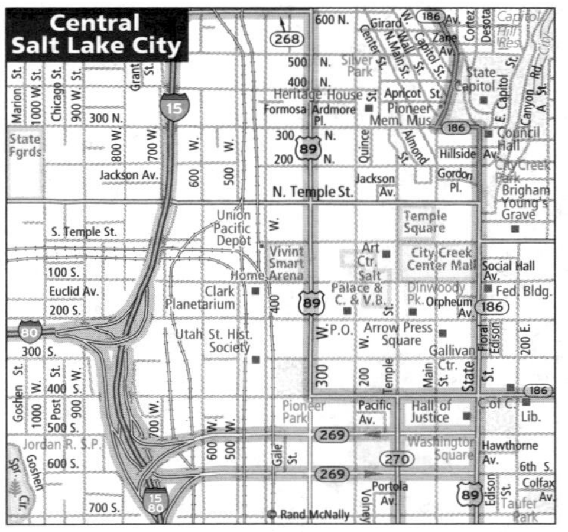

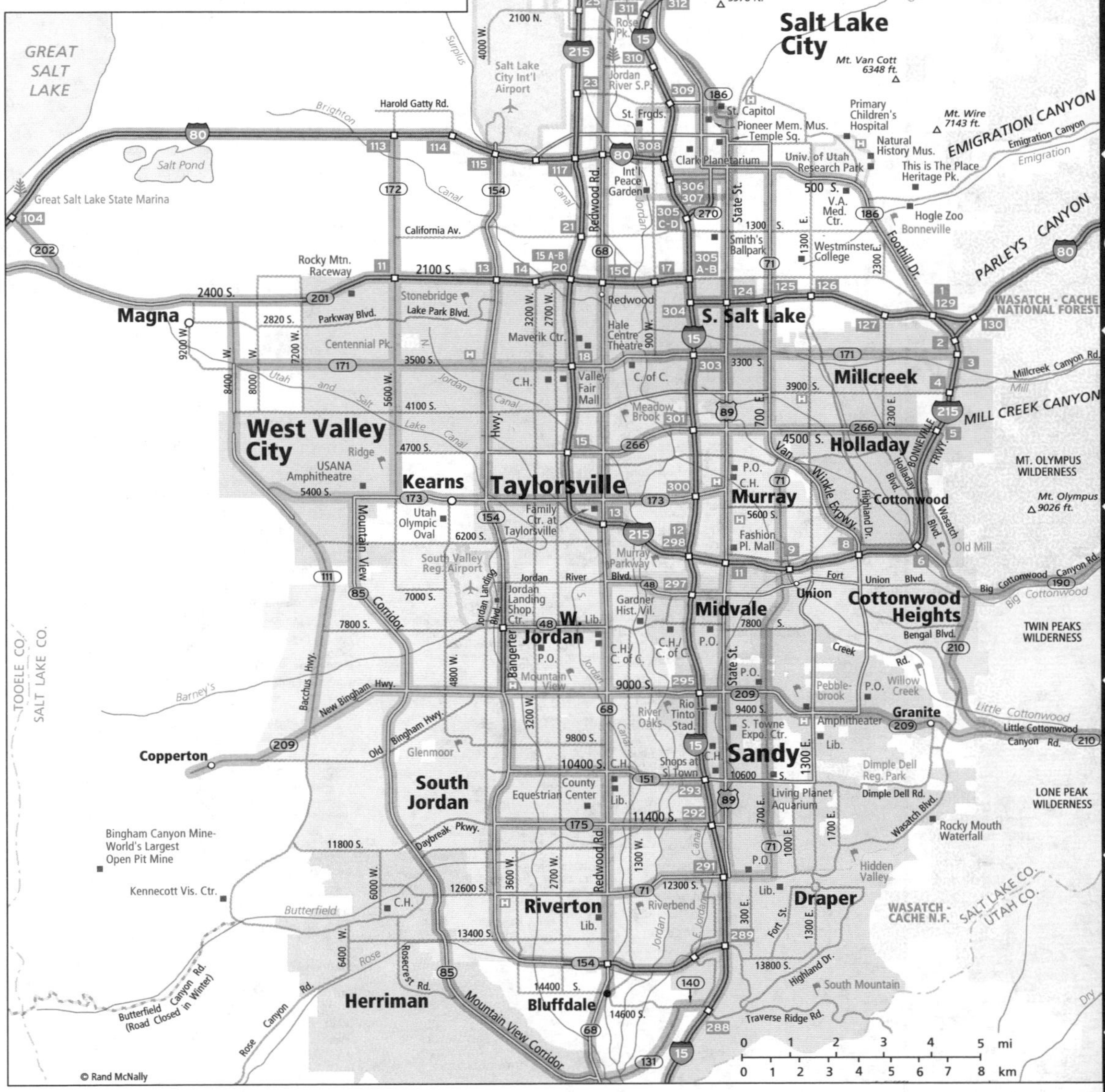

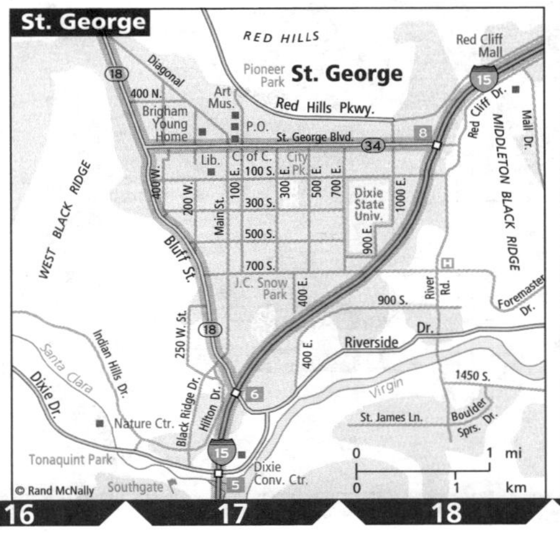

Vermont

Nickname: The Green Mountain State
Capital: Montpelier, E-5
Land area: 9,217 sq. mi. (rank: 43rd)
Population: 625,741 (rank: 49th)
Largest city: Burlington, 42,417, D-2

Index of cities Pg. 135 | Map legend Pg. 1

Mileage between cities	Albany, NY	Brattleboro	Burlington	Montpelier	Newport	Rutland	St. Johnsbury	White River Jct.
ALBANY, NY		78	146	193	246	90	200	141
BRATTLEBORO	78		151	115	168	73	122	63
BURLINGTON	146	151		38	94	67	77	91
MONTPELIER	193	115	38		82	102	39	56
NEWPORT	246	168	94	82		187	47	105
RUTLAND	90	73	67	102	187		142	45
ST. JOHNSBURY	200	122	77	39	47	142		60
WHITE RIVER JCT.	141	63	91	56	105	45	60	

Total mileage through Vermont

89: 130 miles
93: 11 miles
91: 177 miles
4: 64 miles

For more than 40,000 interstate mileages, see the Mileage Directory on page 137

Route planning & on-the-road resources

Low clearances, weigh stations, & restricted routes: Page A44

Weigh station location

Designated route for vehicles with STAA-authorized dimensions

Road Conditions & Construction
511
www.vtrans.vermont.gov

Toll Road Information
No tolls on state or federal highways

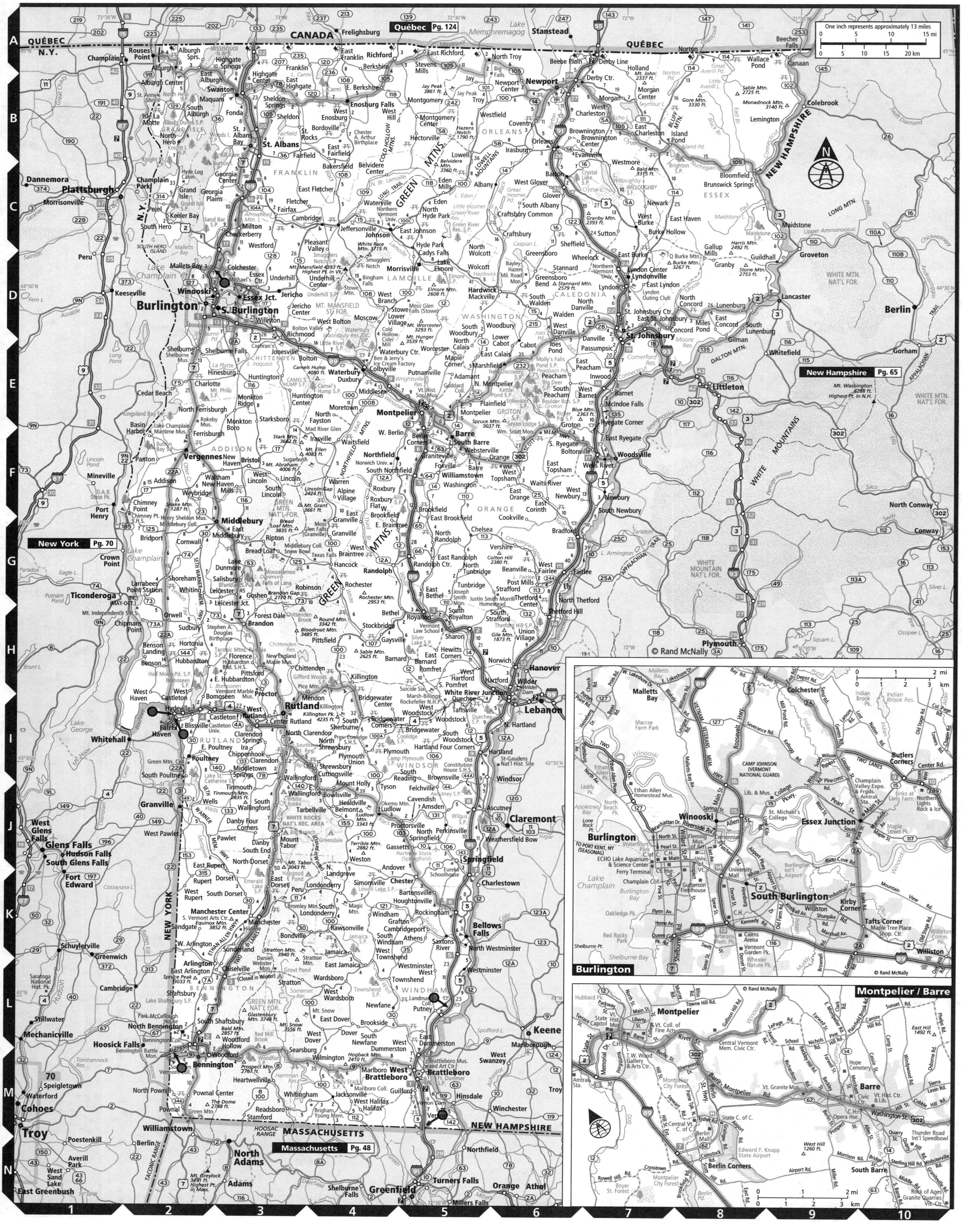

Historic Downtown Mall, Charlottesville

Sights to see

- Agecroft Hall and Gardens, Richmond C-7
- Children's Museum of Virginia, Portsmouth M-6
- Chrysler Museum of Art, Norfolk L-6
- Colonial Williamsburg, Williamsburg F-2
- Edgar Allan Poe Museum, Richmond C-8
- First Landing State Park, Virginia Beach L-9
- Hermitage Foundation Museum, Norfolk L-6
- Historic Jamestowne, Williamsburg G-1
- Nauticus, Norfolk L-6
- Ocean Breeze Waterpark, Virginia Beach M-10
- Old Cape Henry Lighthouse, Virginia Beach K-9
- Three Lakes Nature Center & Aquarium, Richmond ... B-8

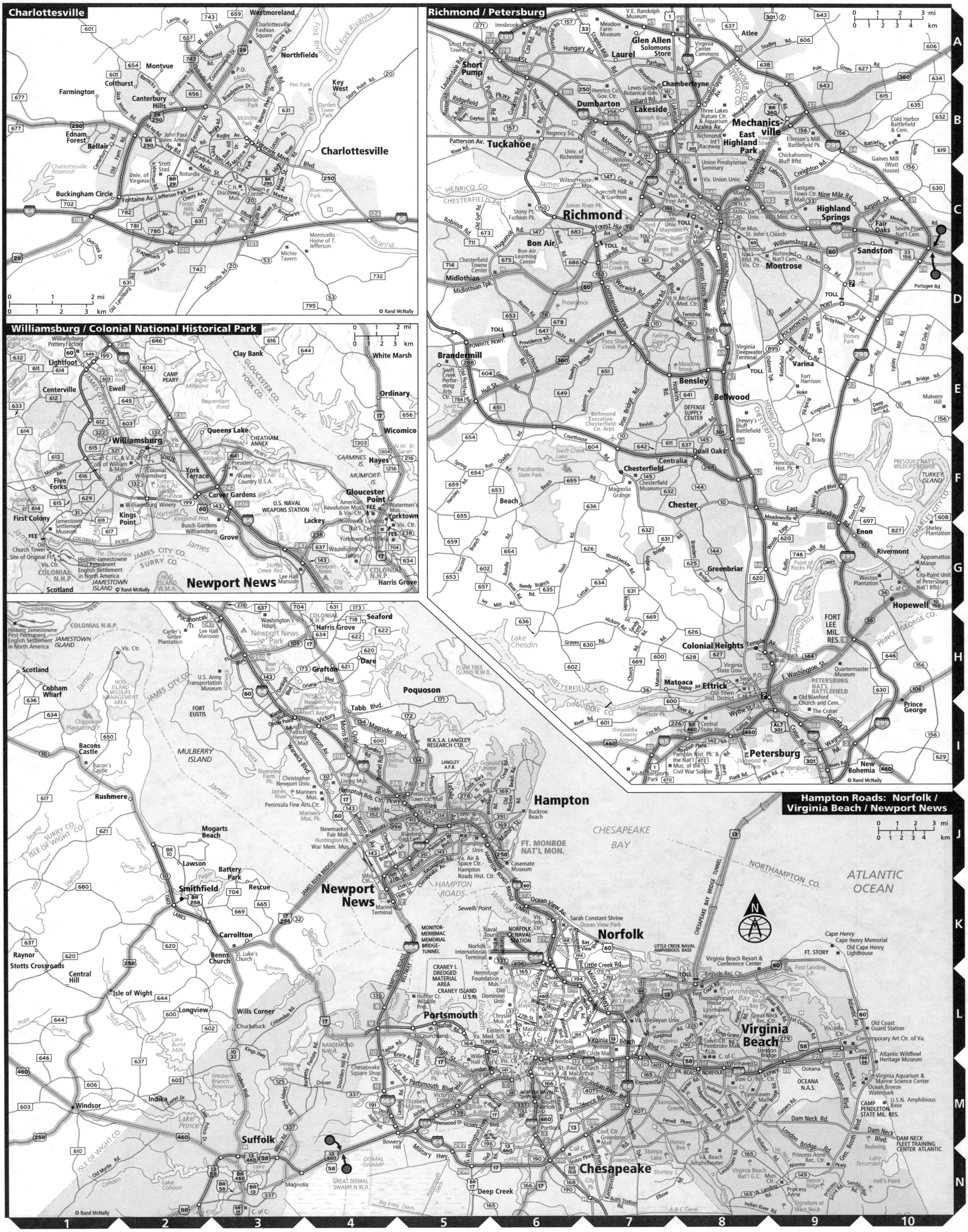

Virginia

Nickname: Old Dominion
Capital: Richmond, J-14
Land area: 39,490 sq. mi. (rank: 36th)
Population: 8,001,024 (rank: 12th)
Largest city: Virginia Beach, 437,994, L-18

Index of cities Pg. 135 | Map legend Pg. 1

Route planning & on-the-road resources

Low clearances, weigh stations, & restricted routes: Page A44

Weigh station location

Designated route for vehicles with STAA-authorized dimensions

Road Conditions & Construction
511
(866) 695-1182
(800) 367-7623;
www.511virginia.org
www.virginiadot.org/travel

Toll Road Information *(all use E-ZPass)*
Virginia Dept. of Transportation (all others): www.virginiadot.org/travel/faq-toll.asp
Chesapeake Expwy. (VA 168): (757) 204-0010; www.chesapeakeexpressway.com
Dulles Greenway: (703) 707-8870; www.dullesgreenway.com
Metro. Wash. Airports Authority (Dulles Toll Rd.): (877) 762-7824; www.dullestollroad.com
Pocahontas Pkwy. (Richmond): (866) 428-6339; www.pocahontas895.com
Richmond Metro. Trans. Auth. (toll rds. within Richmond): (804) 523-3300; www.rmaonline.org

Toll Bridge/Tunnel Info. *(all use E-ZPass)*
Chesapeake Bay Bridge-Tunnel: (757) 331-2960; www.cbbt.com
Elizabeth River Tunnels (Hampton Rds.): (855) 378-7623; www.driveert.com
South Norfolk Jordan Bridge: (855) 690-7652; www.snjb.net

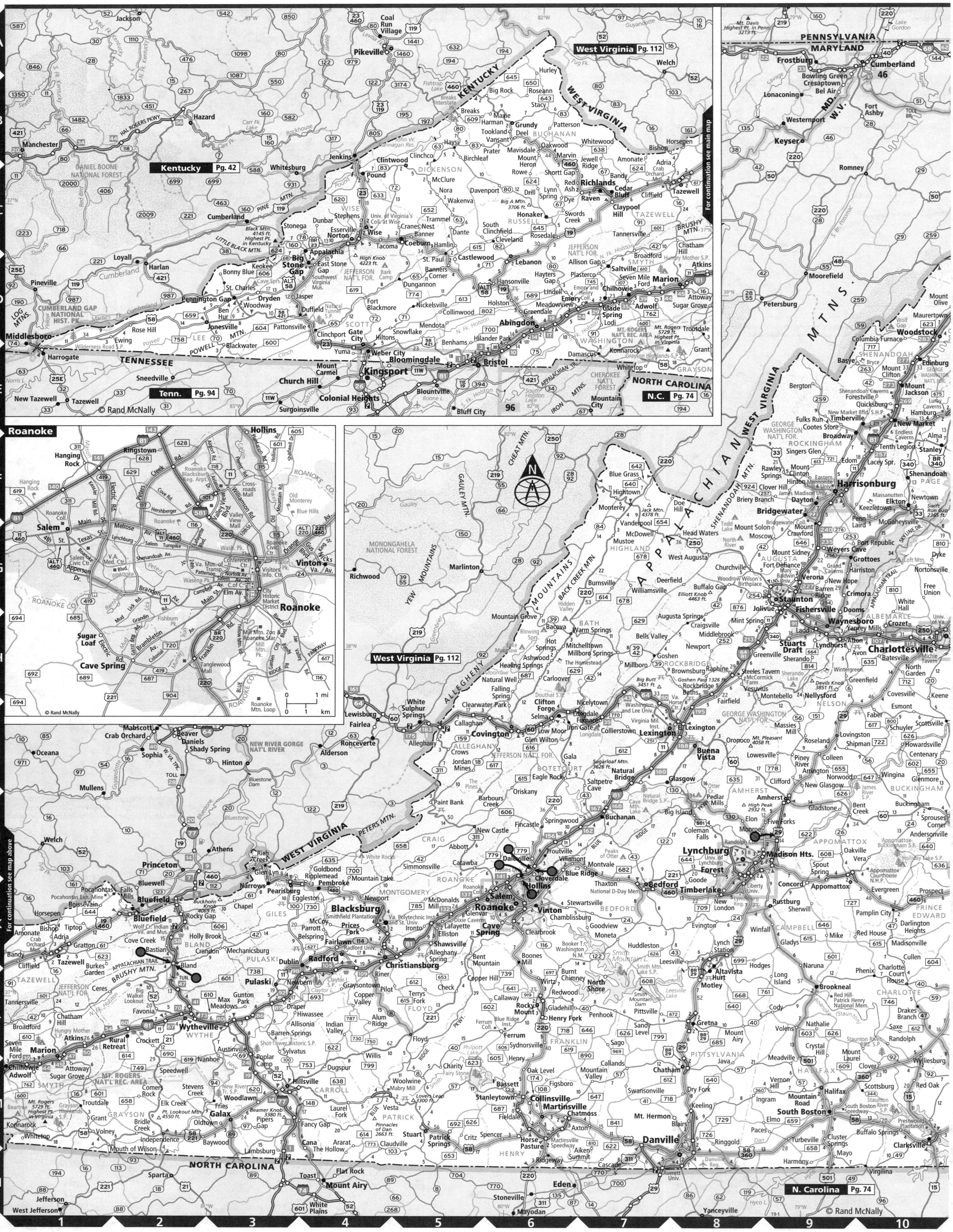

Mileage between cities	Bristol	Charlottesville	Chincoteague	Danville	Emporia	Fredericksburg	Hagerstown, MD	Harrisonburg	Lynchburg	Manassas	Norfolk	Richmond	Roanoke	Virginia Beach	Washington, DC	Williamsburg	Winchester	Wytheville
CHARLOTTESVILLE	254		264	132	138	78	171	62	66	90	165	72	118	178	118	124	128	184
EMPORIA	351	138	187	115		122	236	196	125	160	78	66	176	98	174	105	208	281
NORFOLK	415	165	106	191	78	143	257	223	189	181		92	279	16	195	44	229	345
RICHMOND	323	72	190	144	66	56	170	131	114	94	92		187	105	109	50	142	253
ROANOKE	147	118	378	89	176	195	220	111	53	214	279	187		293	244	238	178	77
WASHINGTON, DC	378	118	174	249	174	56	79	133	183	34	195	109	244	208		153	76	308
WINCHESTER	314	128	248	254	208	91	44	69	188	62	229	142	178	243	76	188		244
WYTHEVILLE	70	184	444	169	281	261	286	177	130	281	345	253	77	359	308	304	244	

Total mileage through Virginia

- 64: 298 miles
- 81: 325 miles
- 85: 69 miles
- 95: 179 miles

For more than 40,000 interstate mileages, see the Mileage Directory on page 137

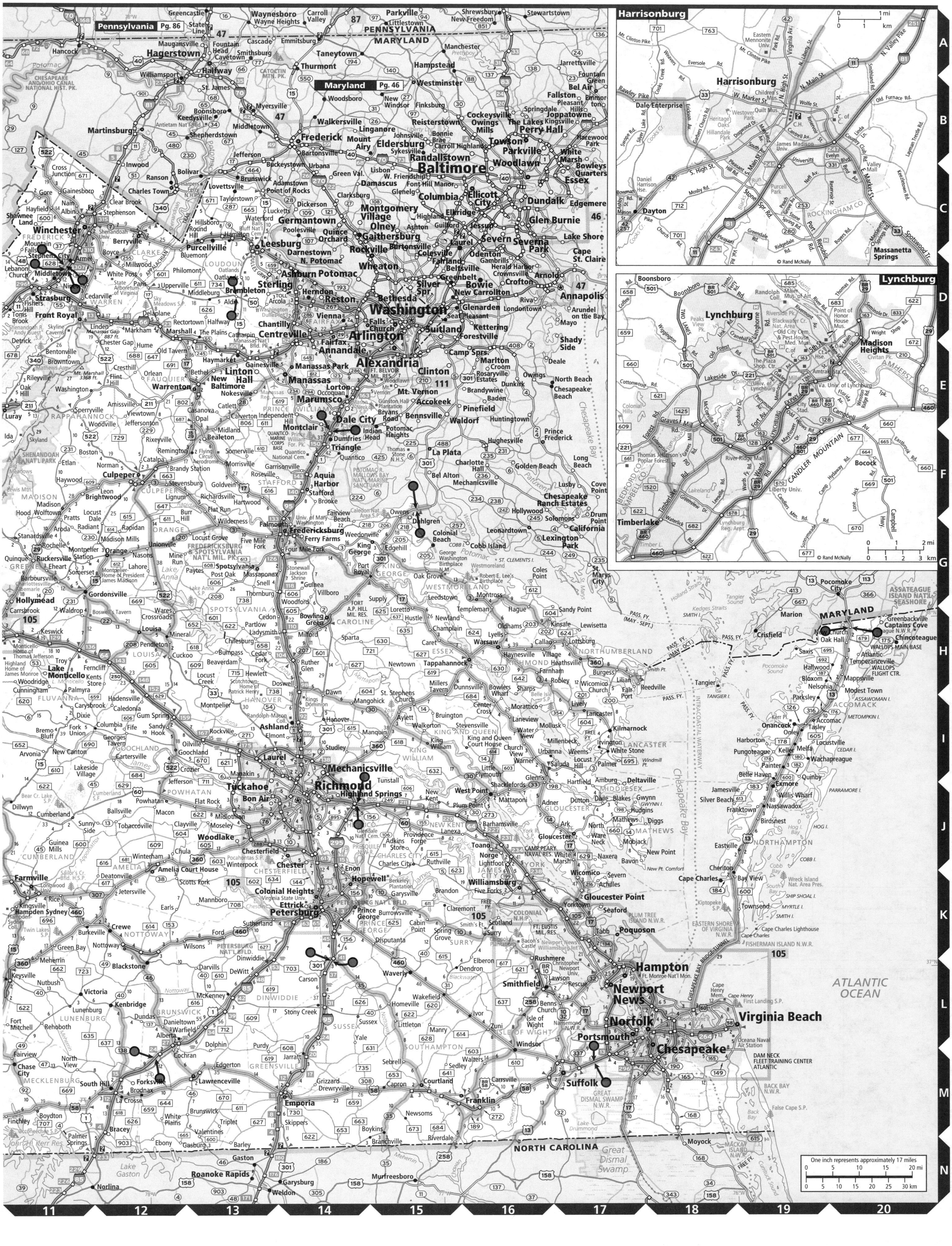

Washington

Nickname: The Evergreen State
Capital: Olympia, H-6
Land area: 66,455 sq. mi. (rank: 20th)
Population: 6,724,540 (rank: 13th)
Largest city: Seattle, 608,660, F-7

Index of cities Pg. 135 | Map legend Pg. 1

Route planning & on-the-road resources

Low clearances, weigh stations, & restricted routes: Page A45

Weigh station location

Designated route for vehicles with STAA-authorized dimensions

Road Conditions & Construction
511, (800) 695-7623; www.wsdot.wa.gov/traffic

Toll Bridge Information
Washington State Dept. of Transportation *(Good to Go!)*:
(360) 705-7000, (360) 705-7438; www.wsdot.wa.gov/tolling

Determining Distances
(segments of one mile or less not shown)
Cumulative miles (red): the distance between red arrows
Intermediate miles (black): the distance between intersections & places

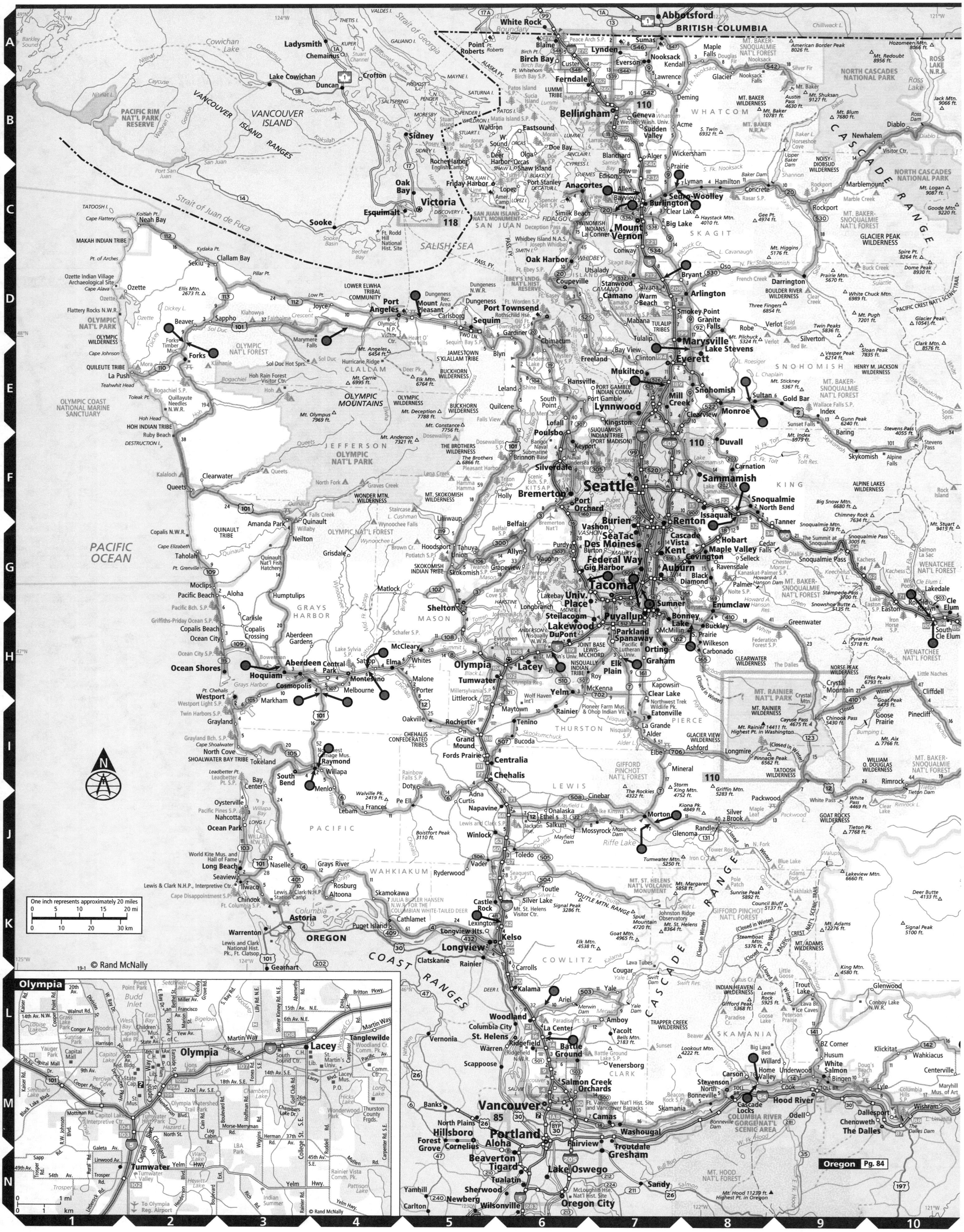

Mileage between cities	Aberdeen	Bellingham	Bremerton	Colville	Kennewick	Lewiston, ID	Longview	Olympia	Omak	Port Angeles	Portland, OR	Seattle	Spokane	Tacoma	The Dalles, OR	Vancouver, BC	Wenatchee	Yakima
BELLINGHAM	198		154*	433	306	396	217	149	271	124*	262	89	362	121	326	54	183	224
KENNEWICK	311	306	268*	209		133	256	262	189	340	214	223	138	235	131	359	138	82
PORTLAND, OR	141	262	171	424	214	348	49	113	377	228		172	353	141	83	315	301	185
SEATTLE	109	89	65*	351	223	313	128	60	236	83*	172		279	32	249	143	149	141
SPOKANE	368	362	324*	71	138	102	387	319	139	397*	353	279		291	269	416	169	201
TACOMA	77	121	33	362	235	325	96	28	248	106*	141	32	291		217	175	160	153
THE DALLES, OR	218	326	247	340	131	264	125	189	294	305	83	249	269	217		380	207	102
YAKIMA	230	224	186*	272	82	213	166	181	192	258*	185	141	201	153	102	278	105	

*Via Ferry

Total mileage through Washington

5: 277 miles	90: 297 miles
82: 133 miles	101: 373 miles

For more than 40,000 interstate mileages, see the Mileage Directory on page 137

Elliott Bay, Seattle

Sights to see

- Frye Art Museum, Seattle J-3
- Klondike Gold Rush National Historical Park, Seattle . . K-2
- Museum of Glass, Tacoma L-6
- Museum of Pop Culture, Seattle H-1
- Nordic Heritage Museum, Seattle C-7
- Pacific Science Center, Seattle H-1
- Pike Place Market, Seattle J-2
- Point Defiance Zoo & Aquarium, Tacoma K-5
- Seattle Aquarium, Seattle J-1
- Space Needle, Seattle H-1
- Washington State History Museum, Tacoma L-6
- Woodland Park Zoo, Seattle C-7

Low clearances, weigh stations, & restricted routes: Page A29

Weigh station location

Designated route for vehicles with STAA-authorized dimensions

Road Conditions & Construction
311, (202) 737-4404
(202) 673-6813
ddot.dc.gov

Toll Road Info
No toll roads; see MD and VA pages

Washington, D.C.

Land area: 61 sq. mi. | **Population:** 601,723

Sights to see

- Arlington National Cemetery, Arlington, VA N-1
- Frederick Douglass National Historic Site . . G-7
- John F. Kennedy Center for the Performing Arts L-3
- Martin Luther King Jr. Memorial M-4
- National African American Museum . . L-6
- National Arboretum F-7
- National Mall M-7
- National Zoological Park F-6
- The Pentagon, Arlington, VA G-6
- The Supreme Court of the United States M-9
- United States Botanic Garden M-8
- The White House K-5
- Wolf Trap National Park for the Performing Arts, Vienna, VA E-2

Washington, D.C. & Vicinity

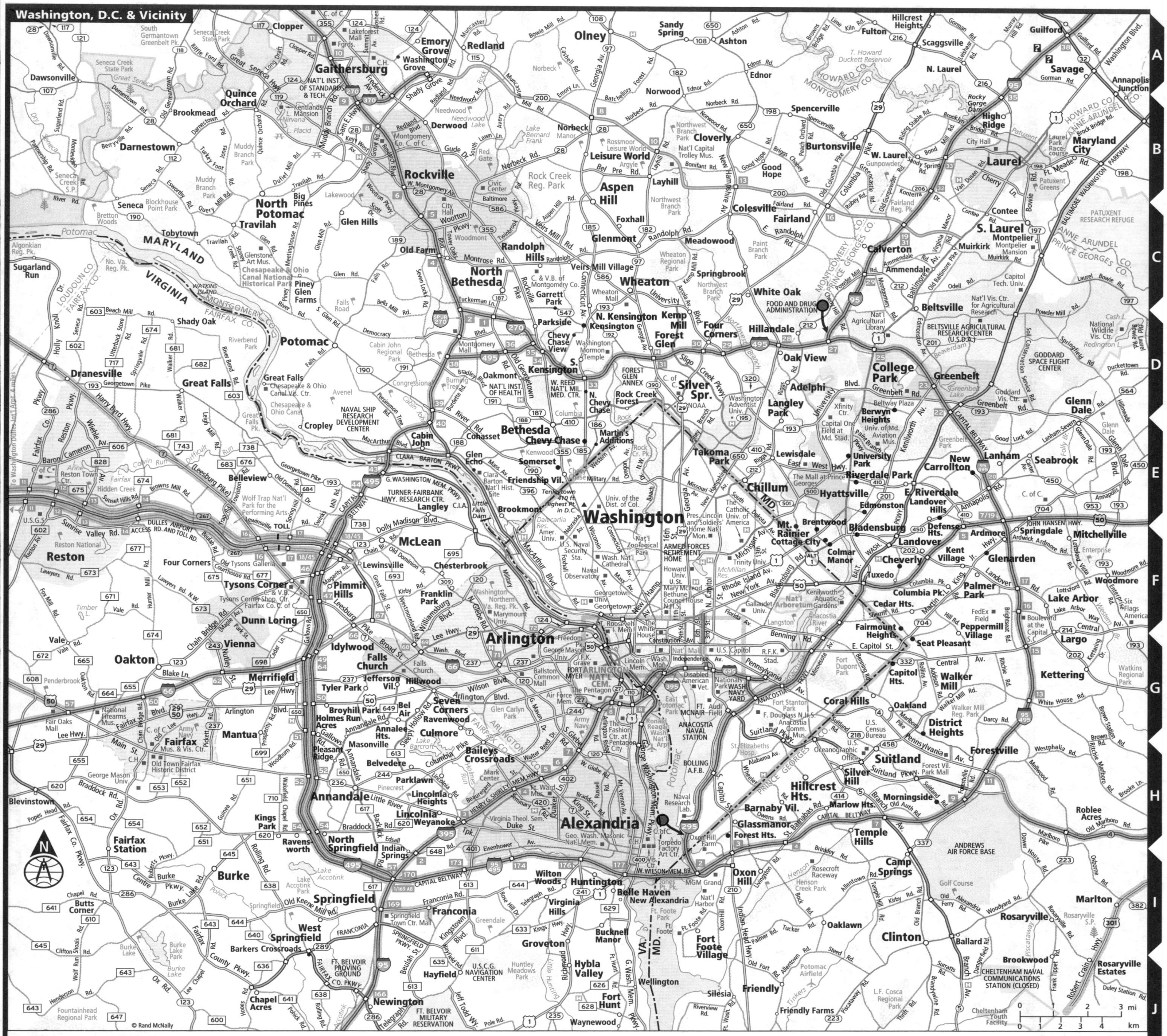

Central Washington, D.C.

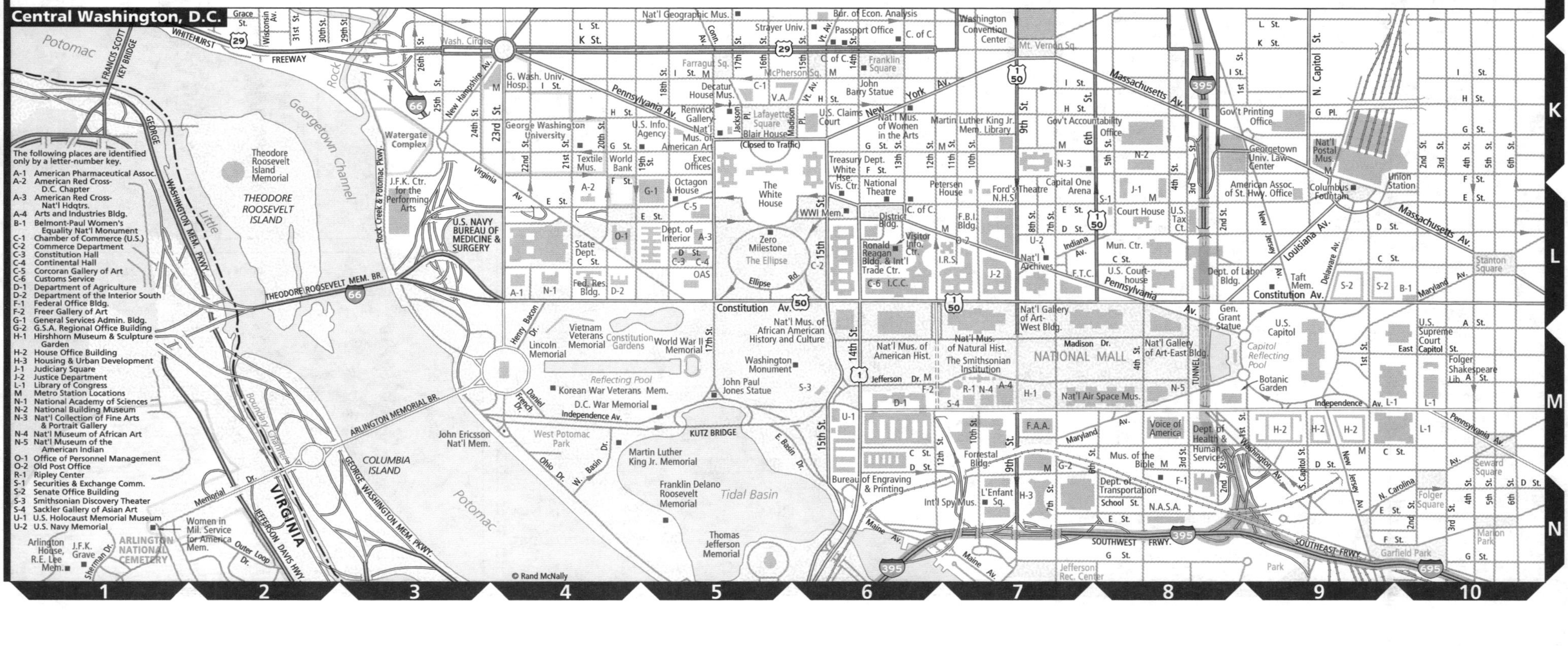

West Virginia

Nickname: The Mountain State
Capital: Charleston, J-3
Land area: 24,038 sq. mi. (rank: 41st)
Population: 1,852,994 (rank: 37th)
Largest city: Charleston, 51,400, J-3

Index of cities Pg. 135 | Map legend Pg. 1

Mileage between cities	Beckley	Charleston	Cumberland, MD	Huntington	Morgantown	Parkersburg	Wheeling	White Sulphur Sprs.
BECKLEY		59	241	109	170	135	236	62
CHARLESTON	59		225	50	154	76	177	124
CUMBERLAND, MD	241	225		275	73	182	155	265
HUNTINGTON	109	50	275		205	126	227	175
MORGANTOWN	170	154	73	205		111	78	201
PARKERSBURG	135	76	182	126	111		106	200
WHEELING	236	177	155	227	78	106		276
WH. SULPHUR SPRS.	62	124	265	175	201	200	276	

Mileages © Rand McNally

Total mileage through West Virginia

64	189 miles	77	187 miles
70	14 miles	79	161 miles

For more than 40,000 interstate mileages, see the Mileage Directory on page 137

Route planning & on-the-road resources

Low clearances, weigh stations, & restricted routes: **Page A45**

Weigh station location

Designated route for vehicles with STAA-authorized dimensions

Road Conditions & Construction
511, (877) 982-7623
www.wv511.org
www.transportation.wv.gov

Toll Road Information
W.V. Parkways Authority *(E-ZPass)*:
(304) 926-1900
www.transportation.wv.gov/turnpike

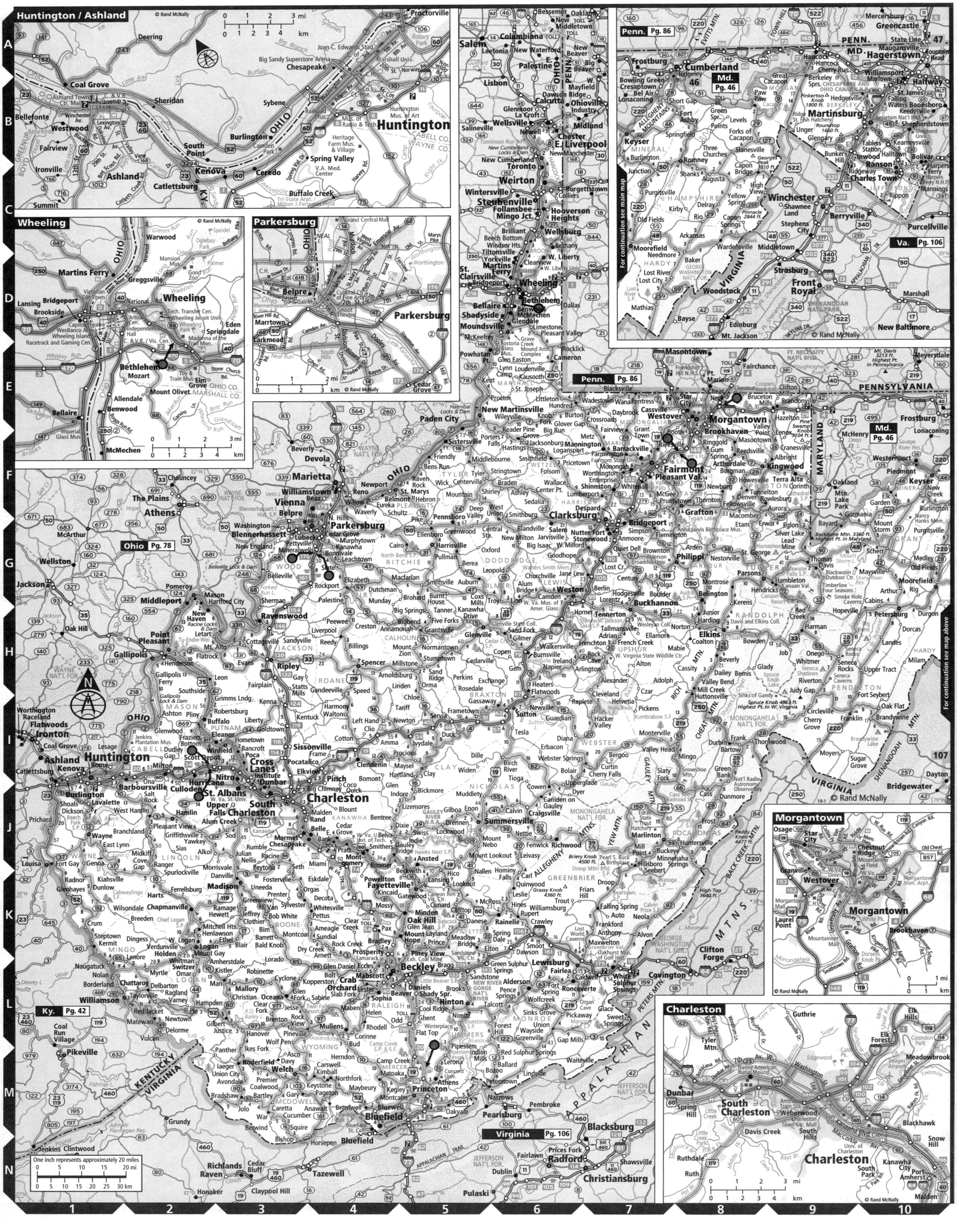

HarborPark promenade, Kenosha

Sights to see

- Angel Museum, Beloit...........................N-6
- Betty Brinn Children's Museum, Milwaukee........L-3
- Golden Rondelle Theatre, Racine.................J-10
- Harley Davidson Museum, Milwaukee..............M-2
- Henry Maier Festival Park, Milwaukee.............M-4
- J.M. Kohler Arts Center, Sheboygan.............F-10
- Kenosha History Center, Kenosha...............L-10
- Miller Brewery, Milwaukee.......................E-5
- Milwaukee Art Museum & War Mem., Milwaukee....L-4
- Milwaukee Public Museum, Milwaukee.............L-2
- Mitchell Park Horticultural Conservatory, Milwaukee...F-6
- Petit National Ice Center, Milwaukee..............F-4

La Crosse

Sheboygan

Milwaukee & Vicinity / Central Milwaukee

Janesville / Beloit

Kenosha / Racine

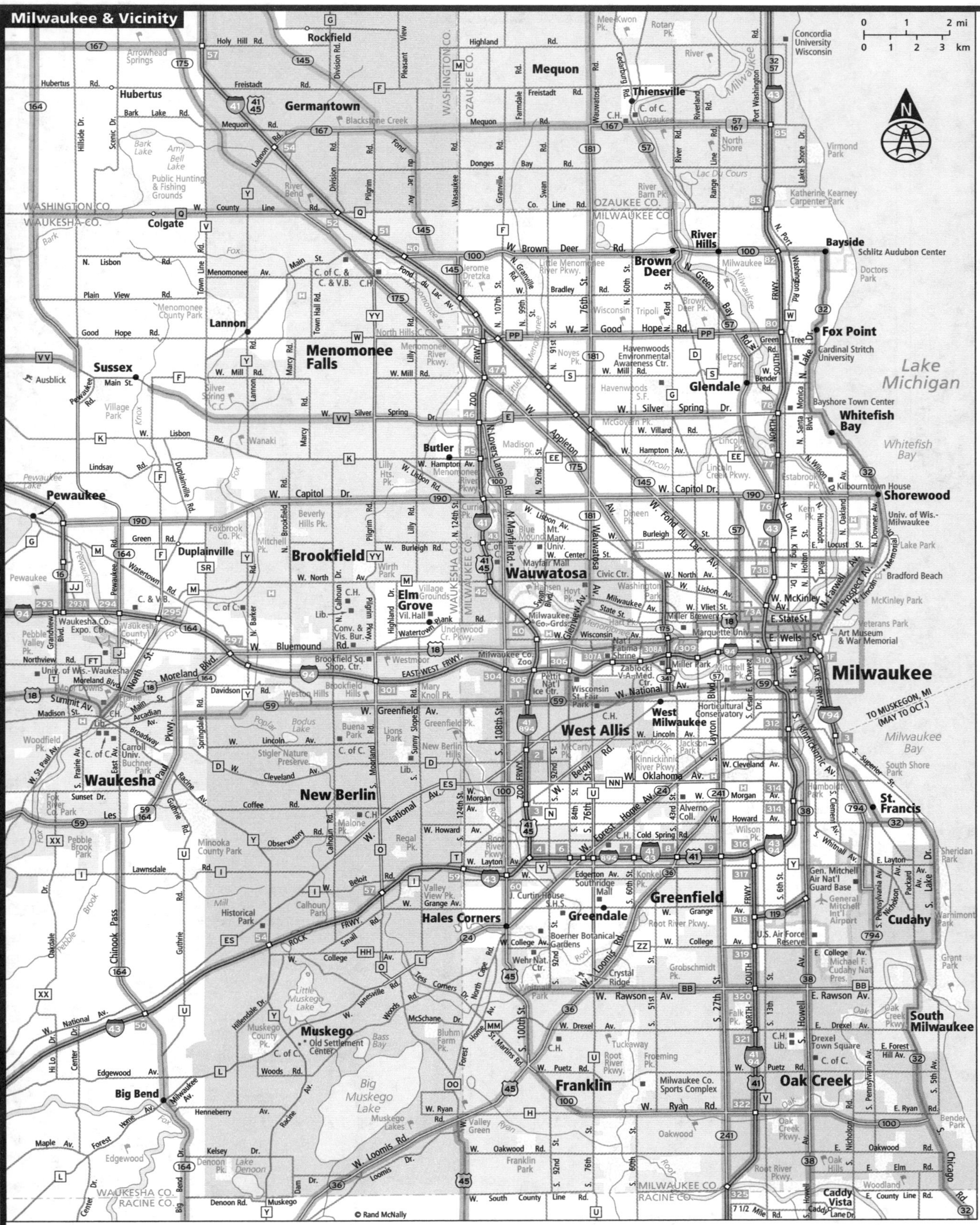

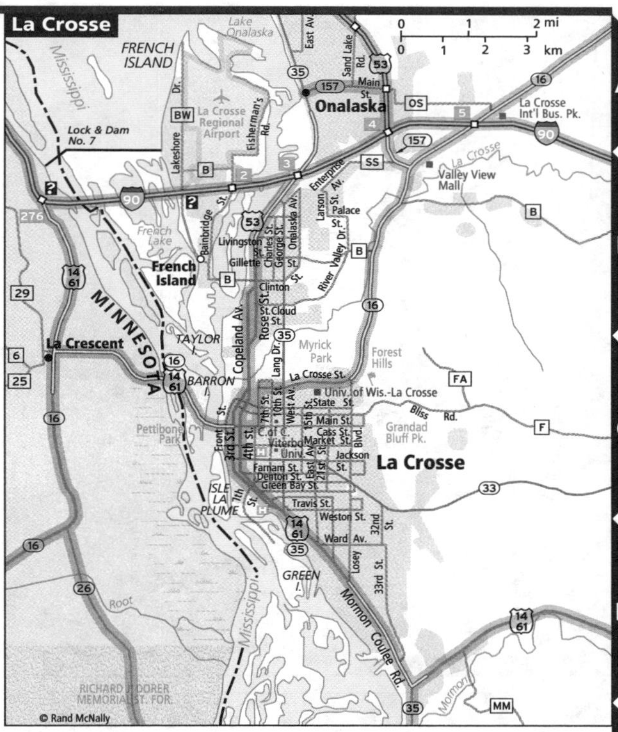

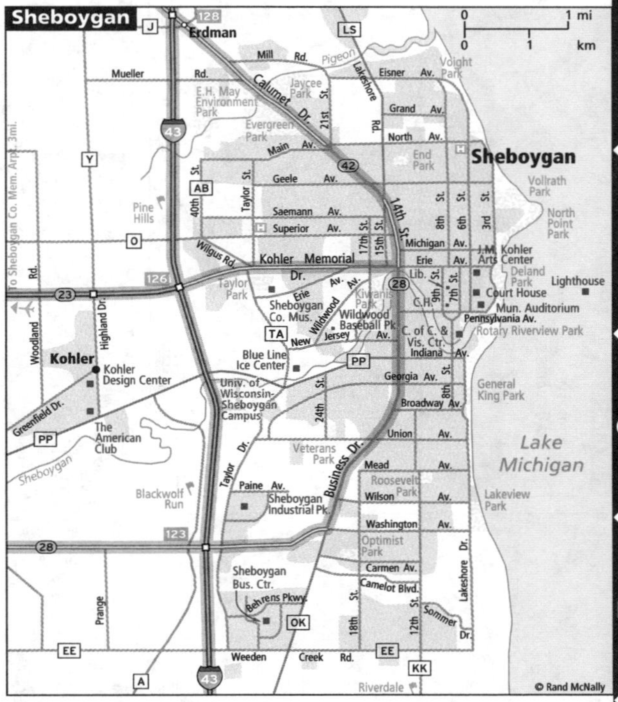

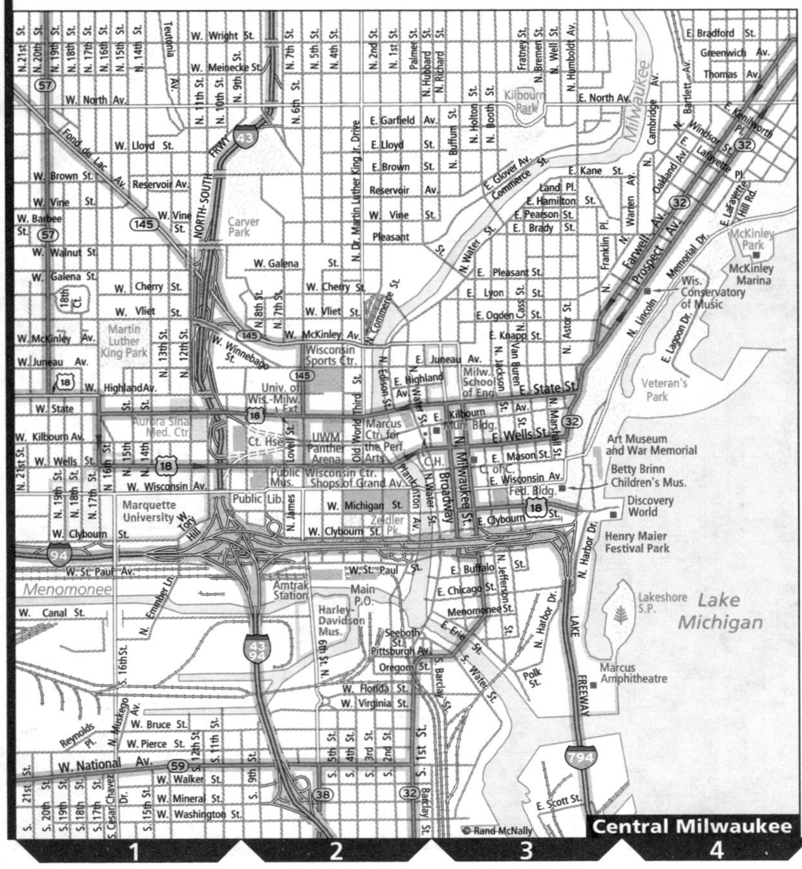

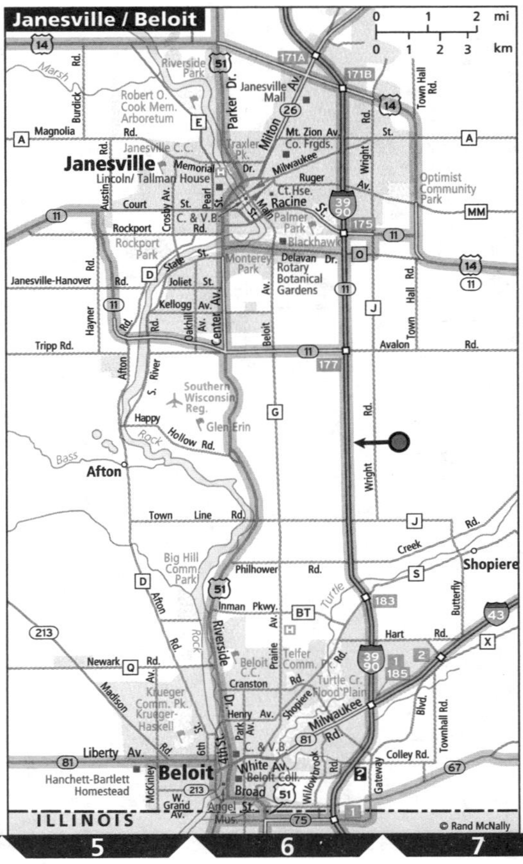

Wisconsin

Nickname: The Badger State
Capital: Madison, N-9
Land area: 54,158 sq. mi. (rank: 25th)
Population: 5,686,986 (rank: 20th)
Largest city: Milwaukee, 594,833, N-13

Index of cities Pg. 136 | Map legend Pg. 1

Route planning & on-the-road resources

Low clearances, weigh stations, & restricted routes: Page A46

Weigh station location

Designated route for vehicles with STAA-authorized dimensions

Road Conditions & Construction
511, (866) 511-9472; www.511wi.gov

Toll Road Information
No tolls on state or federal highways

Determining Distances
(segments of one mile or less not shown)
Cumulative miles (red): the distance between red arrows
Intermediate miles (black): the distance between intersections & places

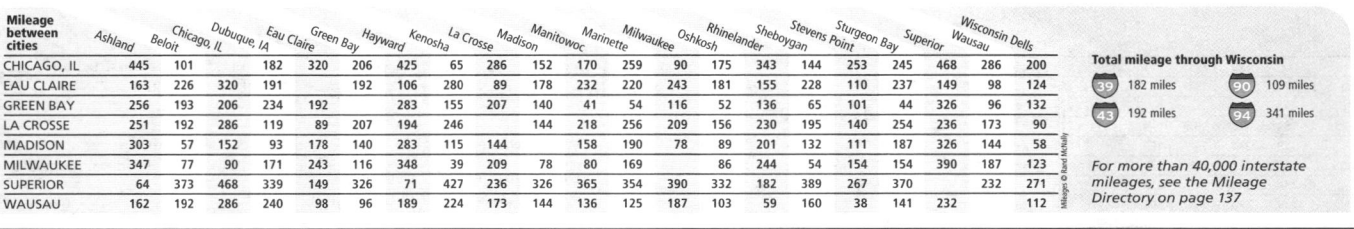

Mileage between cities	Ashland	Beloit	Chicago, IL	Dubuque, IA	Eau Claire	Green Bay	Hayward	Kenosha	La Crosse	Madison	Manitowoc	Marinette	Milwaukee	Oshkosh	Rhinelander	Sheboygan	Stevens Point	Sturgeon Bay	Superior	Wausau	Wisconsin Dells
CHICAGO, IL	445	101		182	320	206	425	65	286	152	170	259	90	175	343	144	253	245	468	286	200
EAU CLAIRE	163	226	320	191		192	106	280	89	178	232	220	243	181	155	228	110	237	149	98	124
GREEN BAY	256	193	206	234	192		283	155	207	140	41	54	116	52	136	65	101	44	326	96	132
LA CROSSE	251	192	286	119	89	207	194	246		144	218	256	209	156	230	195	140	254	236	173	90
MADISON	303	57	152	93	178	140	283	115	144		158	190	78	89	201	132	111	187	326	144	58
MILWAUKEE	347	77	90	171	243	116	348	39	209	78	80	169		86	244	54	154	154	390	187	123
SUPERIOR	64	373	468	339	149	326	71	427	236	326	365	354	390	332	182	389	267	370		232	271
WAUSAU	162	192	286	240	98	96	189	224	173	144	136	125	187	103	59	160	38	141	232		112

Mileages © Rand McNally

Total mileage through Wisconsin

39: 182 miles	90: 109 miles
43: 192 miles	94: 341 miles

For more than 40,000 interstate mileages, see the Mileage Directory on page 137

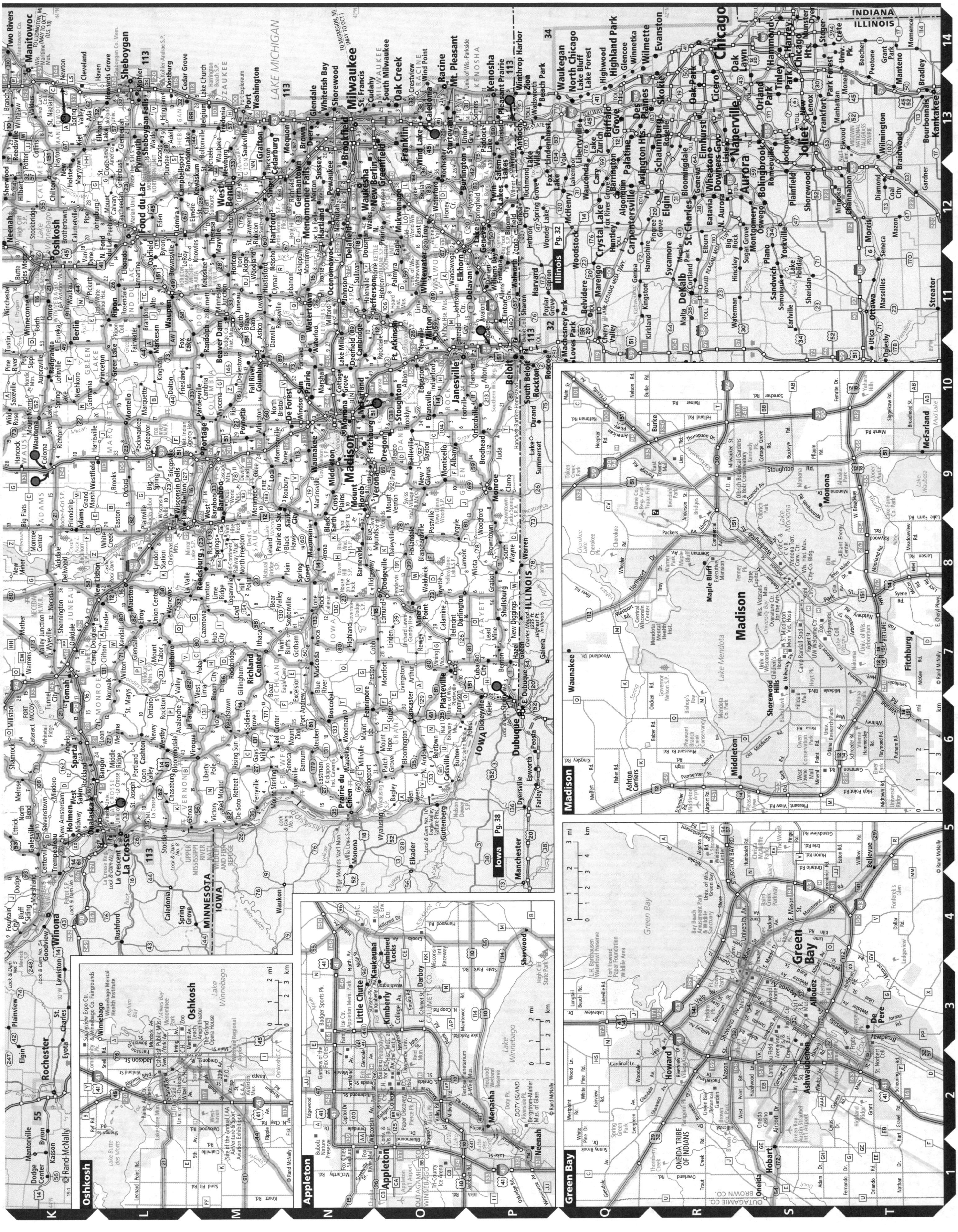

Wyoming

Nicknames: The Equality State
Capital: Cheyenne, M-9
Land area: 97,093 sq. mi. (rank: 9th)
Population: 563,626 (rank: 50th)
Largest city: Cheyenne, 59,466, M-9

Index of cities Pg. 136 | Map legend Pg. 1

Mileage between cities	Casper	Cheyenne	Cody	Jackson	Riverton	Rock Springs	Sheridan	Spearfish, SD
CASPER		179	213	283	119	225	148	219
CHEYENNE	179		392	432	273	257	326	290
CODY	213	392		301	138	278	148	344
JACKSON	283	432	301		163	175	378	504
RIVERTON	119	273	138	163		140	215	341
ROCK SPRINGS	225	257	278	175	140		373	444
SHERIDAN	148	326	148	378	215	373		197
SPEARFISH, SD	219	290	344	504	341	444	197	

Total mileage through Wyoming

I-25: 301 miles
I-90: 209 miles
I-80: 403 miles
US 20: 505 miles

For more than 40,000 interstate mileages, see the Mileage Directory on page 137

Route planning & on-the-road resources

Low clearances, weigh stations, & restricted routes: Page A46

Weigh station location

Designated route for vehicles with STAA-authorized dimensions

Road Conditions & Construction
511, (888) 996-7623
www.wyoroad.info

Toll Road Information
No tolls on state or federal highways

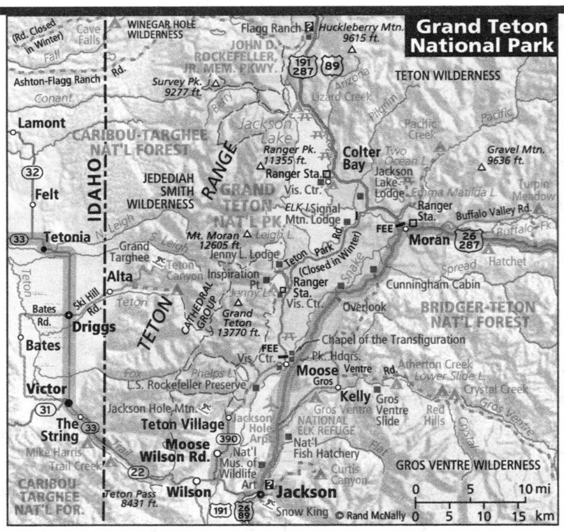

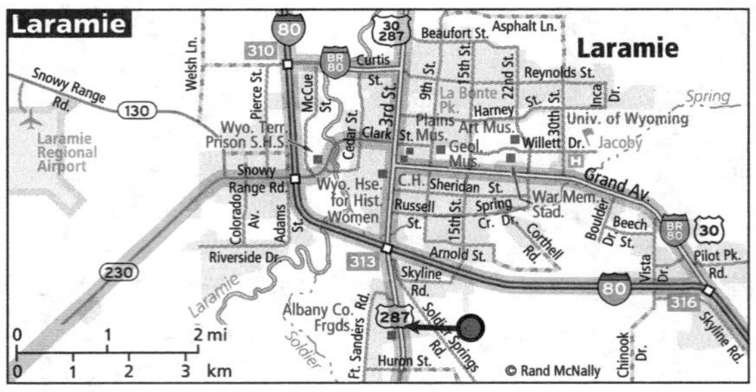

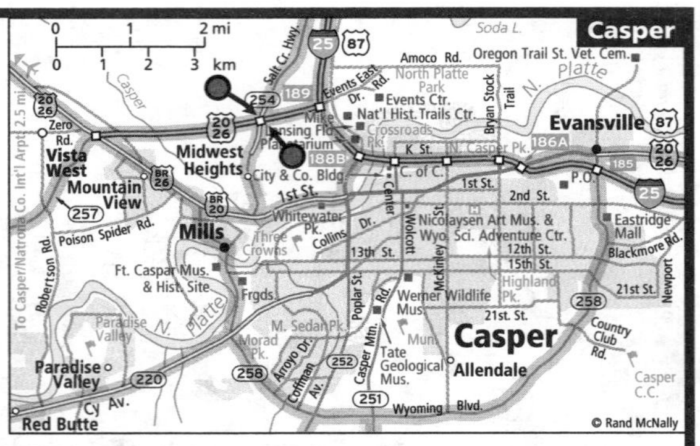

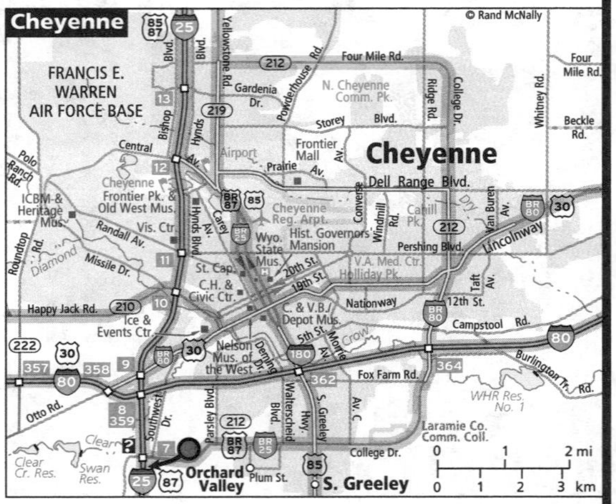

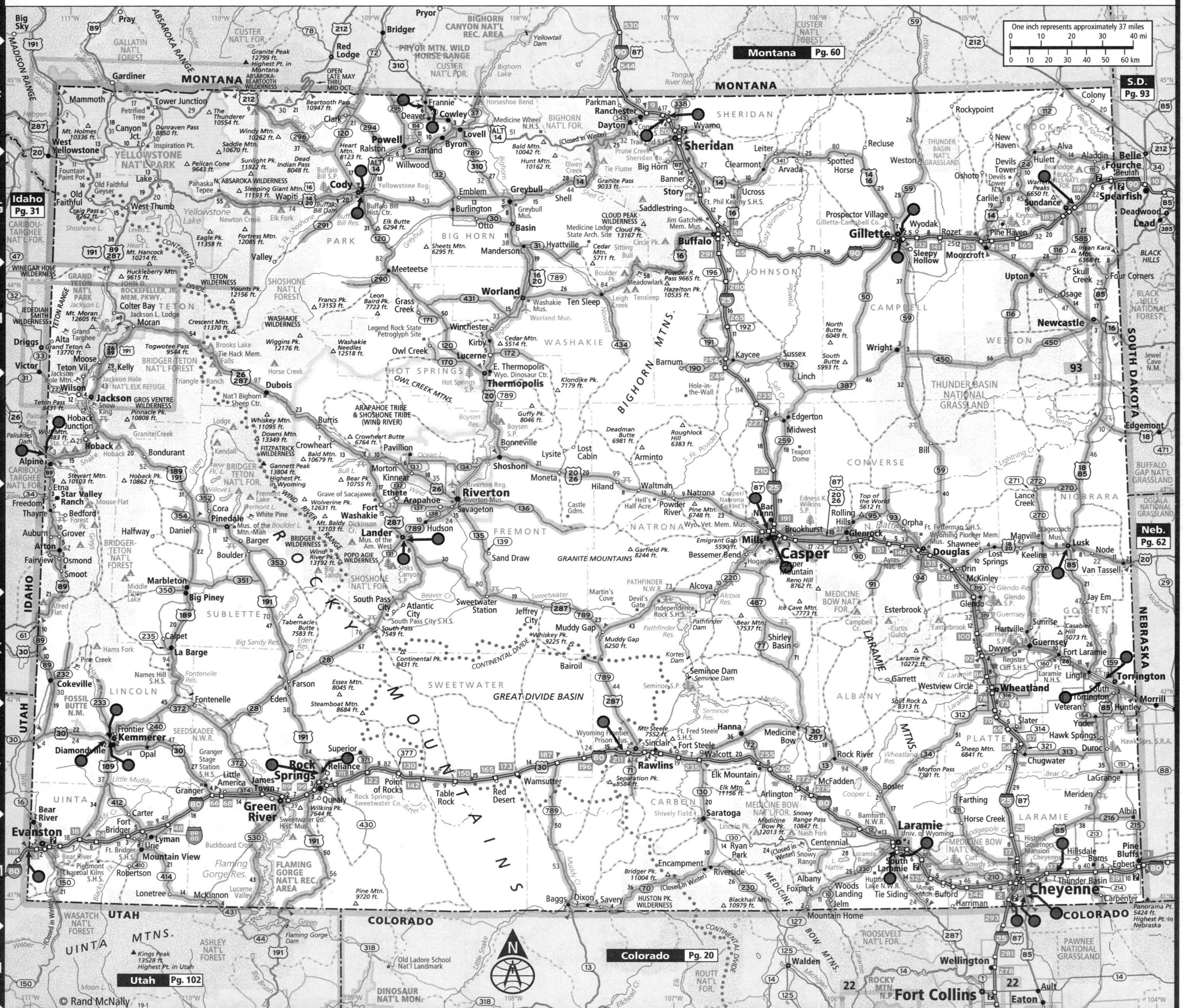

Capital: Ottawa, I-10
Land area: 3,511,023 sq. mi.
Population: 33,476,688
Largest city: Toronto, 2,615,060, I-10

Index of cities Pg. 136 | Map legend Pg. 1

Selected National Park locations

- Banff National Park G-3
- Cape Breton Highlands Nat'l Park. . G-13
- Fundy National Park H-12
- Glacier National Park G-3
- Gros Morne National Park F-13
- Jasper National Park. F-3
- Kejimkujik National Park H-12
- Kluane National Park & Reserve C-2
- Kootenay National Park. G-3
- Mount Revelstoke National Park. . . . G-3
- Parc National de la Maurice. H-11
- Prince Albert National Park F-5
- Prince Edward Island Nat'l Park. . . . H-12
- Pukaskwa National Park. H-8
- Riding Mountain National Park. H-6
- St. Lawrence Islands National Park . . I-10

Glossary of French terms

Áeroport . . . . Airport
Arrondissement. . . . . District
Baie . . . . Bay
Barrage . . . . Dam
Basilique. . . . . Basilica
Bibliothèque . . . . Library
Bois. . . . . Woods
Cap. . . . . Cape
Centre de recherches . . . Research centre (or center)
Centre des congrès. . . . . . . Convention centre (or center)
Chemin. . . . . Road
Chenal . . . . Channel
Chutes . . . . Falls
Débarquement . . . . Landing
Détroit . . . . Strait
Fleuve. . . . . Major river (that flows to the sea)
Hippodrome . . . . Race track
Hôtel de Ville. . . . . City or town hall
Hôtel du Parlement. . . . . Parliament building
Île . . . . Island
Jardin botanique. . . . . . . Botanical garden
Jardins . . . . Gardens
Jardin zoologique . . . . . . Zoological garden (or Zoo)
Lac . . . . Lake
Lieu historique . . . . Historic site
Lieu historique national . National historic site
Lieu natal. . . . . Birthplace
Mont . . . . Mountain
Musée. . . . . Museum
Oratoire . . . . Oratory
Parc. . . . . Park
Parc marin . . . . Marine park
Parc national . . . . National park (or provincial park in Québec)
Pont . . . . Bridge
Promenade . . . . Boulevard
Réserve faunique . . . . . . Wildlife reserve
Réserve indienne. . . . . . . Indian reserve (or reservation)
Rivière . . . . River
Rue. . . . . Street
Stade . . . . Stadium
Tribunal . . . . Court house
Université. . . . . University

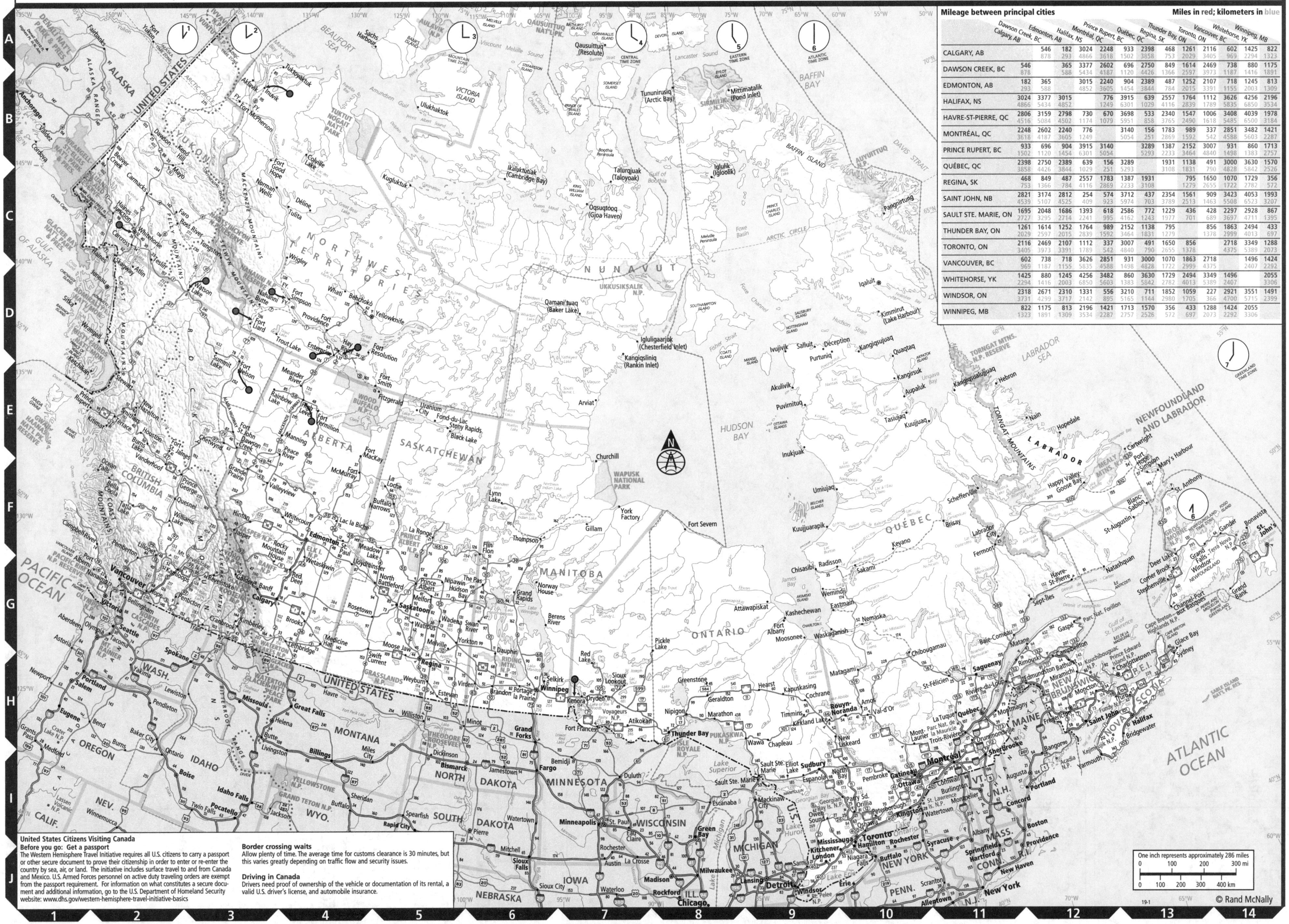

Mileage between principal cities

Miles in red; kilometers in blue (each cell: miles / kilometers)

	Calgary, AB	Dawson Creek, BC	Edmonton, AB	Halifax, NS	Montréal, QC	Prince Rupert, BC	Québec, QC	Regina, SK	Thunder Bay, ON	Toronto, ON	Vancouver, BC	Whitehorse, YK	Winnipeg, MB
CALGARY, AB		546 / 878	182 / 293	3024 / 4866	2248 / 3618	933 / 1502	2398 / 3858	468 / 753	1261 / 2029	2116 / 3405	602 / 969	1425 / 2294	822 / 1323
DAWSON CREEK, BC	546 / 878		365 / 588	3377 / 5434	2602 / 4187	696 / 1120	2750 / 4426	849 / 1366	1614 / 2597	2469 / 3973	738 / 1187	880 / 1416	1175 / 1891
EDMONTON, AB	182 / 293	365 / 588		3015 / 4852	2240 / 3605	904 / 1454	2389 / 3844	487 / 784	1252 / 2015	2107 / 3391	718 / 1155	1245 / 2003	813 / 1309
HALIFAX, NS	3024 / 4866	3377 / 5434	3015 / 4852		776 / 1249	3915 / 6301	639 / 1029	2557 / 4116	1764 / 2839	1112 / 1789	3626 / 5835	4256 / 6850	2196 / 3534
HAVRE-ST-PIERRE, QC	2806 / 4516	3159 / 5084	2798 / 4502	730 / 1174	670 / 1079	3698 / 5951	533 / 858	2340 / 3765	1547 / 2490	1006 / 1618	3408 / 5485	4039 / 6500	1978 / 3184
MONTRÉAL, QC	2248 / 3618	2602 / 4187	2240 / 3605	776 / 1249		3140 / 5054	156 / 251	1783 / 2869	989 / 1592	337 / 542	2851 / 4588	3482 / 5603	1421 / 2287
PRINCE RUPERT, BC	933 / 1502	696 / 1120	904 / 1454	3915 / 6301	3140 / 5054		3289 / 5293	1387 / 2233	2152 / 3464	3007 / 4840	931 / 1498	860 / 1383	1713 / 2757
QUÉBEC, QC	2398 / 3858	2750 / 4426	2389 / 3844	639 / 1029	156 / 251	3289 / 5293		1931 / 3108	1138 / 1831	491 / 790	3000 / 4828	3630 / 5842	1570 / 2526
REGINA, SK	468 / 753	849 / 1366	487 / 784	2557 / 4116	1783 / 2869	1387 / 2233	1931 / 3108		795 / 1279	1650 / 2655	1070 / 1722	1729 / 2782	356 / 572
SAINT JOHN, NB	2821 / 4539	3174 / 5107	2812 / 4525	254 / 409	574 / 923	3712 / 5974	437 / 703	2354 / 3789	1561 / 2513	909 / 1463	3423 / 5508	4053 / 6523	1993 / 3207
SAULT STE. MARIE, ON	1695 / 2727	2048 / 3295	1686 / 2714	1393 / 2241	618 / 995	2586 / 4162	772 / 1243	1229 / 1977	436 / 701	428 / 689	2297 / 3697	2928 / 4711	867 / 1395
THUNDER BAY, ON	1261 / 2029	1614 / 2597	1252 / 2015	1764 / 2839	989 / 1592	2152 / 3464	1138 / 1831	795 / 1279		856 / 1378	1863 / 2999	2494 / 4013	433 / 697
TORONTO, ON	2116 / 3405	2469 / 3973	2107 / 3391	1112 / 1789	337 / 542	3007 / 4840	491 / 790	1650 / 2655	856 / 1378		2718 / 4375	3349 / 5389	1288 / 2073
VANCOUVER, BC	602 / 969	738 / 1187	718 / 1155	3626 / 5835	2851 / 4588	931 / 1498	3000 / 4828	1070 / 1722	1863 / 2999	2718 / 4375		1496 / 2407	1424 / 2292
WHITEHORSE, YK	1425 / 2294	880 / 1416	1245 / 2003	4256 / 6850	3482 / 5603	860 / 1383	3630 / 5842	1729 / 2782	2494 / 4013	3349 / 5389	1496 / 2407		2055 / 3306
WINDSOR, ON	2318 / 3731	2671 / 4299	2310 / 3717	1331 / 2142	556 / 895	3210 / 5165	711 / 1144	1852 / 2980	1059 / 1705	227 / 366	2921 / 4700	3551 / 5715	1491 / 2399
WINNIPEG, MB	822 / 1323	1175 / 1891	813 / 1309	2196 / 3534	1421 / 2287	1713 / 2757	1570 / 2526	356 / 572	433 / 697	1288 / 2073	1424 / 2292	2055 / 3306	

United States Citizens Visiting Canada

Before you go: Get a passport
The Western Hemisphere Travel Initiative requires all U.S. citizens to carry a passport or other secure document to prove their citizenship in order to enter or re-enter the country by sea, air, or land. The initiative includes surface travel to and from Canada and Mexico. U.S. Armed Forces personnel on active duty traveling orders are exempt from the passport requirement. For information on what constitutes a secure document and additional information, go to the U.S. Department of Homeland Security website: www.dhs.gov/western-hemisphere-travel-initiative-basics

Border crossing waits
Allow plenty of time. The average time for customs clearance is 30 minutes, but this varies greatly depending on traffic flow and security issues.

Driving in Canada
Drivers need proof of ownership of the vehicle or documentation of its rental, a valid U.S. driver's license, and automobile insurance.

British Columbia
Capital: Victoria, M-7
Land area: 357,216 sq. mi. (rank: 4th)
Population: 4,400,057 (rank: 3rd)
Largest city: Vancouver, 603,502, L-7

Index of cities Pg. 136 | Map legend Pg. 1

Mileage between cities	Banff, AB	Cranbrook	Dawson Creek	Hope	Jasper, AB	Nanaimo	Port Alberni	Port Hardy	Revelstoke	Vancouver	Victoria	Whitehorse, YK	Williams Lake
BANFF, AB		173	571	430	423	569*	620*	808*	176	524	578*	1451	483
CRANBROOK	173		744	428	596	566*	617*	806*	246	521	575*	1623	553
DAWSON CREEK	571	744		644	326	782*	833*	1022*	706	738	791*	880	399
KAMLOOPS	307	377	576	124	275	262*	313*	502*	131	217	271*	1334	177
KELOWNA	299	327	671	148	376	286*	337*	526*	123	242	295*	1429	272
PRINCE GEORGE	633	702	250	394	231	533*	584*	772*	456	488	542*	1011	149
PRINCE RUPERT	1076	1145	696	837	677	976*	1027*	1215*	899	931	985*	859	592
VANCOUVER	524	521	738	94	492	46*	97*	285*	348		72*	1496	339

*Via Ferry

Total mileage through British Columbia
1: 538 miles in BC– N. Vancouver to AB line
16: 658 miles in BC– Prince Rupert to AB line

For more than 40,000 interstate mileages, see the Mileage Directory on page 137

Route planning & on-the-road resources

Low clearances, weigh stations, & restricted routes: Page A47

Weigh station location
Designated route for vehicles with STAA-authorized dimensions

Road Conditions & Construction
(800) 550-4997; www.drivebc.ca

Toll Road Information
No tolls on provincial or federal highways

Route planning & on-the-road resources

Low clearances, weigh stations, & restricted routes: Page A47

Weigh station location

Designated route for vehicles with STAA-authorized dimensions

Road Conditions & Construction
511, (877) 262-4997
(888) 799-1522, (855) 391-9743
www.ama.ab.ca, 511.alberta.ca

Toll Road Information
No tolls on provincial or federal highways

Mileage between cities	Calgary	Crowsnest Pass	Dawson Creek, BC	Drayton Valley	Drumheller	Edmonton	Fort McMurray	High Level	Jasper	Lethbridge	Red Deer	Slave Lake	Whitecourt
BANFF	78	202	571	234	163	260	544	689	423	217	167	419	317
CALGARY		138	546	192	85	182	465	663	407	139	89	340	292
DAWSON CR., BC	546	684		337	549	365	511	305	326	684	458	242	254
EDMONTON	182	320	365	89	172		281	483	226	321	95	156	111
LETHBRIDGE	139	90	684	331	175	321	604	802	546		227	479	431
MEDICINE HAT	178	192	724	370	153	360	575	841	585	102	267	518	470
PEACE RIVER	480	618	146	272	483	299	421	184	354	618	392	151	188
VERMILION	310	445	481	204	223	120	337	599	342	338	222	269	227

Total mileage through Alberta
1: 332 miles in AB
16: 397 miles in AB

For more than 40,000 interstate mileages, see the Mileage Directory on page 137

Alberta
Capital: Edmonton, E-16
Land area: 248,000 sq. mi. (rank: 6th)
Population: 3,645,257 (rank: 4th)
Largest city: Calgary, 1,096,833, I-16

Index of cities Pg. 136 | Map legend Pg. 1

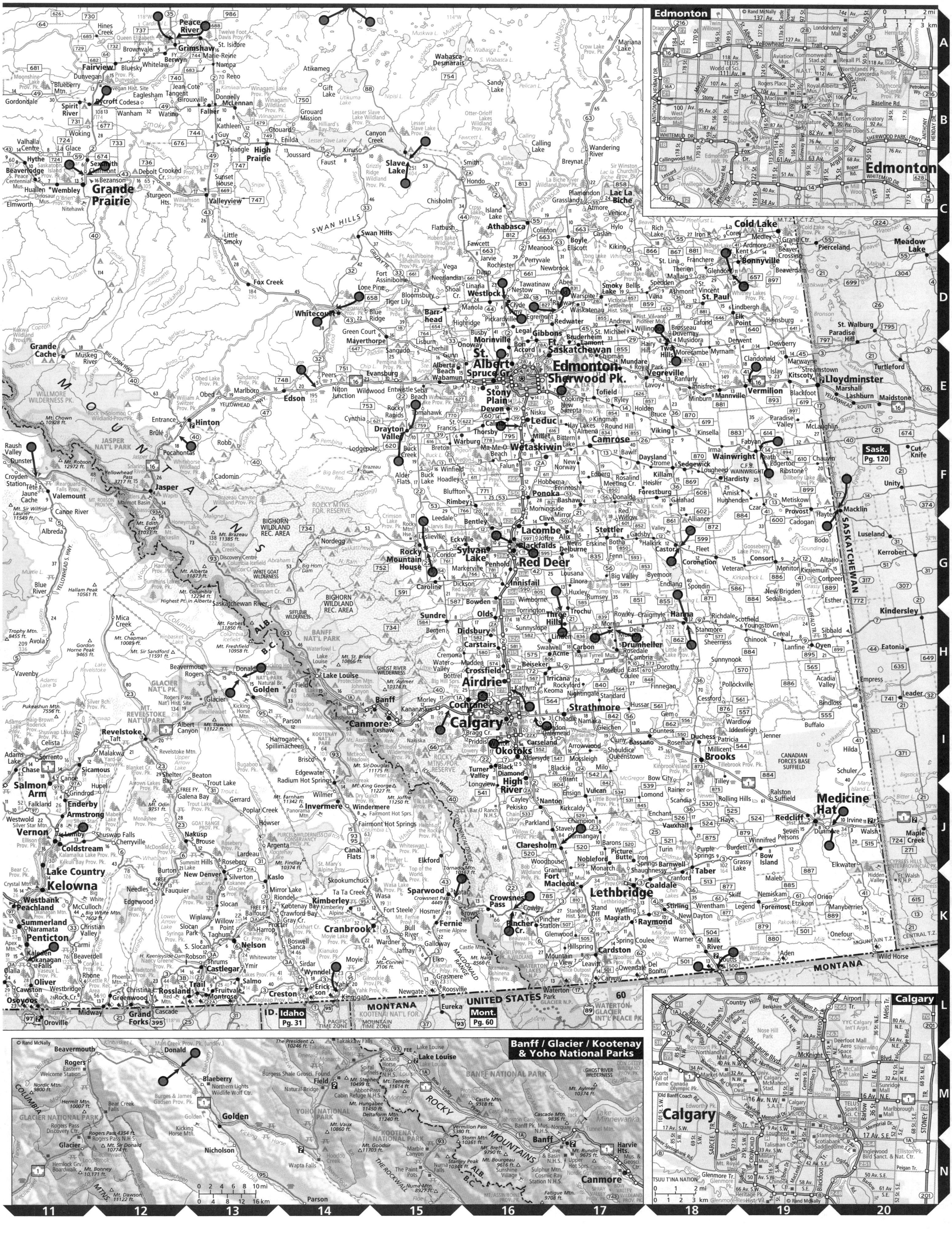

Saskatchewan
Capital: Regina, K-8
Land area: 228,445 sq. mi. (rank: 7th)
Population: 1,033,381 (rank: 6th)
Largest city: Saskatoon, 222,189, G-6

Index of cities Pg. 136 | Map legend Pg. 1

Mileage between cities	Flin Flon, MB	Hudson Bay	Kindersley	La Loche	La Ronge	Medicine Hat, AB	Melfort	Melville	North Battleford	Prince Albert	Regina	Saskatoon	Yorkton
ESTEVAN	527	312	367	664	505	391	298	179	371	357	125	285	184
LLOYDMINSTER	468	371	148	331	360	299	279	390	85	214	331	171	375
MEADOW LAKE	416	317	220	217	309	426	221	402	98	162	343	183	388
PRINCE ALBERT	255	155	211	318	148	393	59	248	129		232	88	233
REGINA	442	240	242	539	380	289	173	92	246	232		160	116
SASKATOON	342	204	124	379	236	306	111	219	86	88	160		205
SWIFT CURRENT	509	371	147	505	403	139	278	241	190	255	151	167	266
YORKTON	345	130	328	551	382	405	175	25	290	233	116	205	

Total mileage through Saskatchewan
1: 413 miles in SK
16: 437 miles in SK

For more than 40,000 interstate mileages, see the Mileage Directory on page 137

Route planning & on-the-road resources

Low clearances, weigh stations, & restricted routes: Page A50

Weigh station location

Designated route for vehicles with STAA-authorized dimensions

Road Conditions & Construction
(888) 335-7623
Saskatoon area: (306) 933-8333
Regina area: (306) 787-7623
www.saskatchewan.ca/residents/transportation/highways/highway-hotline

Toll Road Information:
No tolls on provincial or federal highways

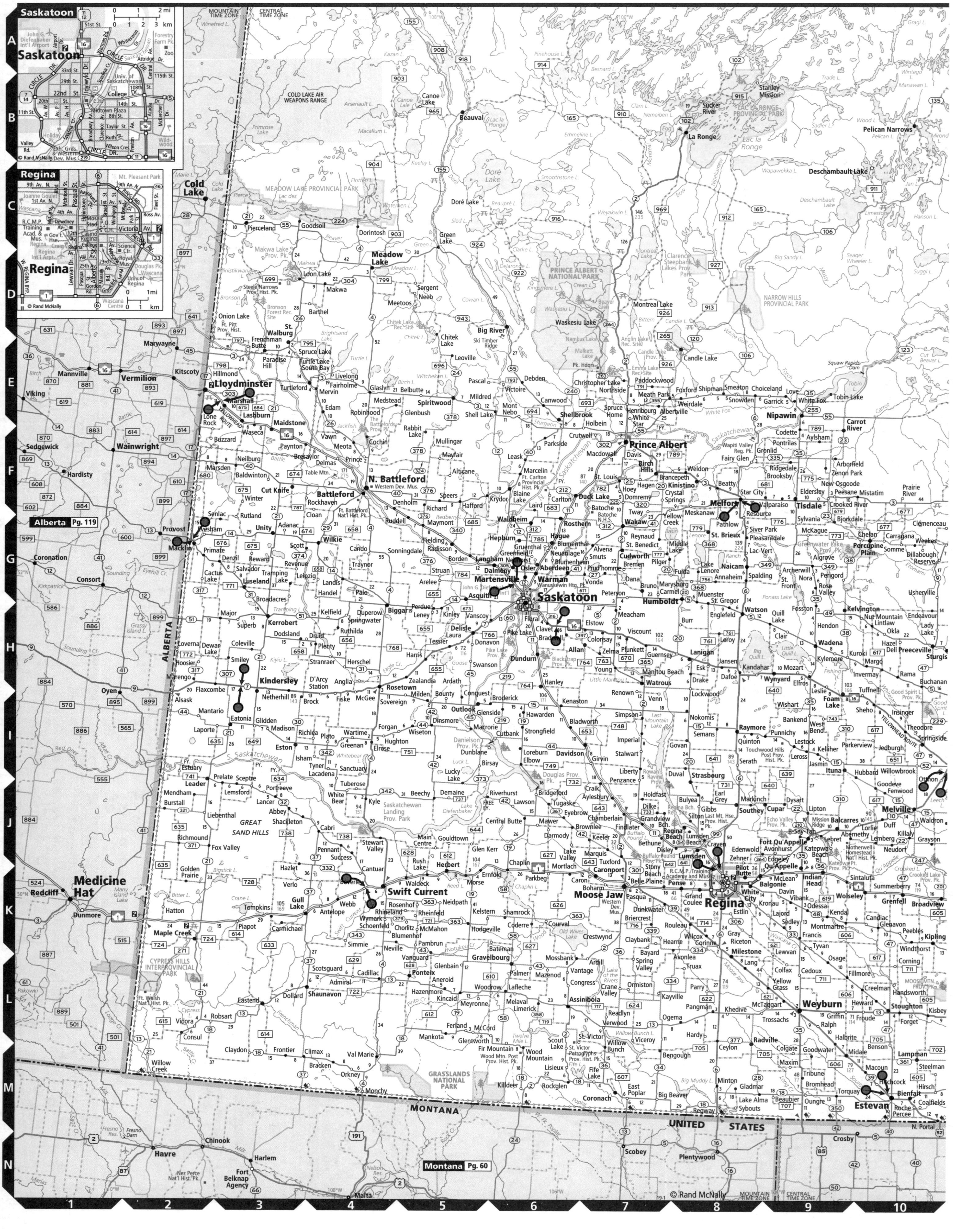

Route planning & on-the-road resources

Low clearances, weigh stations, & restricted routes: Page A47

Weigh station location

Designated route for vehicles with STAA-authorized dimensions

Road Conditions & Construction
511, (877) 627-6237, (204) 945-3704
www.manitoba.ca/roadinfo

Toll Road Information
No tolls on provincial or federal highways

Mileage between cities	Ashern	Brandon	Dauphin	Grand Rapids	Killarney	Minnedosa	Pine Falls	Portage la Prairie	Riverton	Russell	The Pas	Thompson	Winnipeg
BRANDON	204		134	358	62	33	215	80	213	114	364	562	134
DAUPHIN	127	134		282	183	105	268	149	172	92	247	485	203
FLIN FLON	368	459	342	255	520	429	547	509	451	345	95	244	483
MORDEN	188	132	221	342	86	152	167	71	167	236	462	546	87
PORTAGE LA PRAIRIE	153	80	149	307	118	80	134		132	164	414	511	53
SWAN RIVER	233	223	106	211	284	193	374	273	278	109	141	385	327
VIRDEN	248	53	166	393	104	77	259	124	258	74	324	568	178
WINNIPEG	114	134	203	269	152	134	81	53	80	218	388	472	

Total mileage through Manitoba
1: 306 miles in MB
16: 166 miles in MB

For more than 40,000 interstate mileages, see the Mileage Directory on page 137

Saskatchewan / Manitoba

Manitoba
Capital: Winnipeg, L-17
Land area: 213,729 sq. mi. (rank: 8th)
Population: 1,208,268 (rank: 5th)
Largest city: Winnipeg, 663,617, L-17

Index of cities Pg. 136 | Map legend Pg. 1

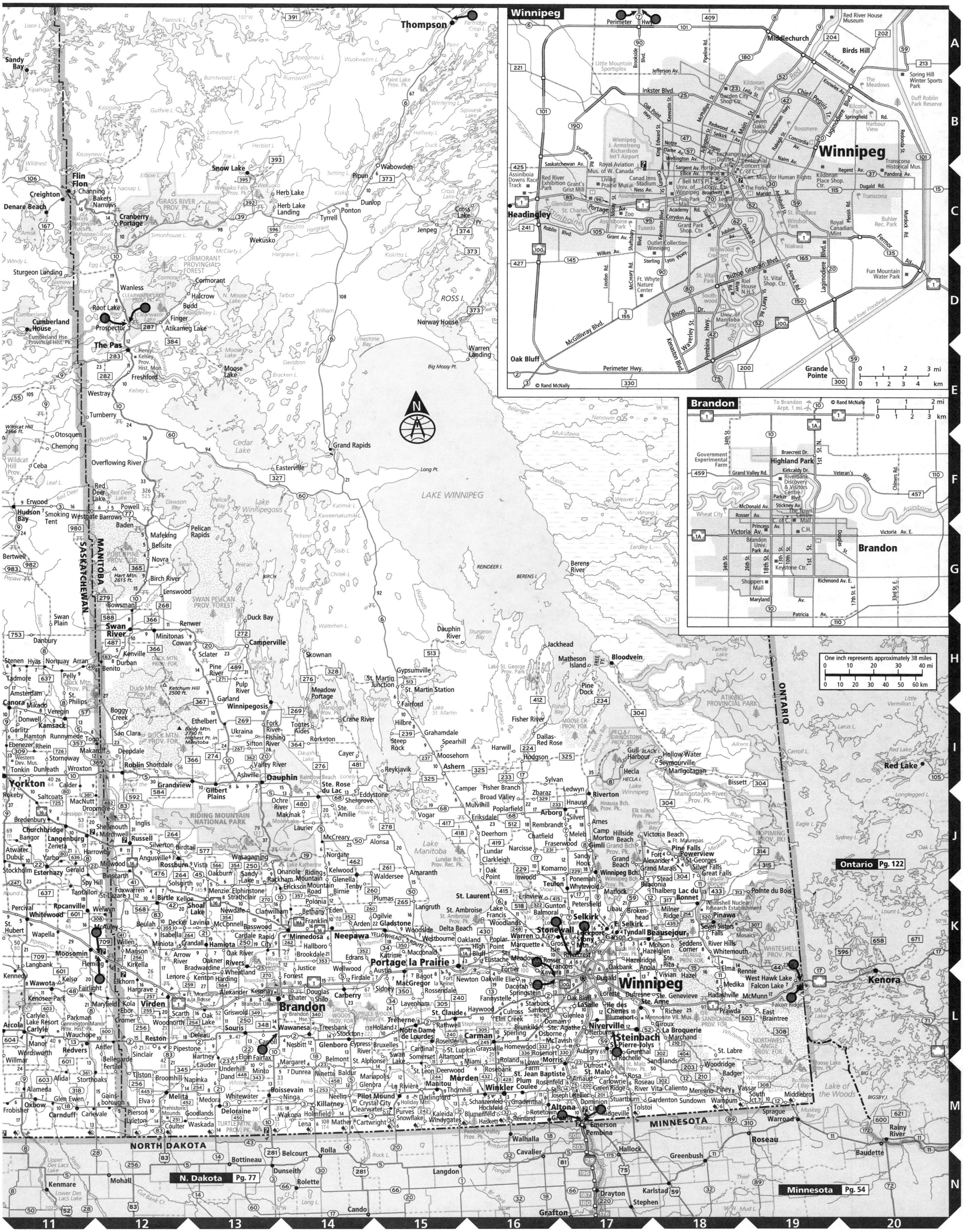

Capital: Toronto, I-10
Land area: 354,342 sq. mi. (rank: 5th)
Population: 12,851,821 (rank: 1st)
Largest city: Toronto, 2,615,060, I-10

Glossary of common French terms found on these maps: pg. 117

Index of cities Pg. 136 | Map legend Pg. 1

Route planning & on-the-road resources

Low clearances, weigh stations, & restricted routes: Page A49

Weigh station location

Designated route for vehicles with STAA-authorized dimensions

Road Conditions & Construction
511, (800) 268-4686
Toronto area: (416) 235-4686
www.mto.gov.on.ca/english/traveller

Toll Road Information
407 ETR (Toronto):
(888) 407-0407; www.407etr.com

Ontario–Michigan Toll Bridge/Tunnel Information
Ambassador Bridge (Windsor) *(A-Pass)*:
(800) 462-7434; www.ambassadorbridge.com
Federal Bridge Corp. (Blue Water Bridge, Sarnia):
(866) 422-6346; www.bluewaterbridge.ca
Detroit-Windsor Tunnel *(NEXPRESS)*: (313) 567-4422 ext. 200,
(519) 258-7424 ext. 200; www.dwtunnel.com
International Bridge Administration (Sault Ste. Marie):
(705) 942-4345, (906) 635-5255; www.saultbridge.com

Ontario–New York Toll Bridge Info.
Buffalo & Ft. Erie Public Br. Authority (Peace Bridge) *(E-ZPass)*:
(716) 884-6744; www.peacebridge.com
Niagara Falls Bridge Commission *(E-ZPass or ExpressPass)*: (716) 285-6322
www.niagarafallsbridges.com
For St. Lawrence River crossings, see New York, p. 70

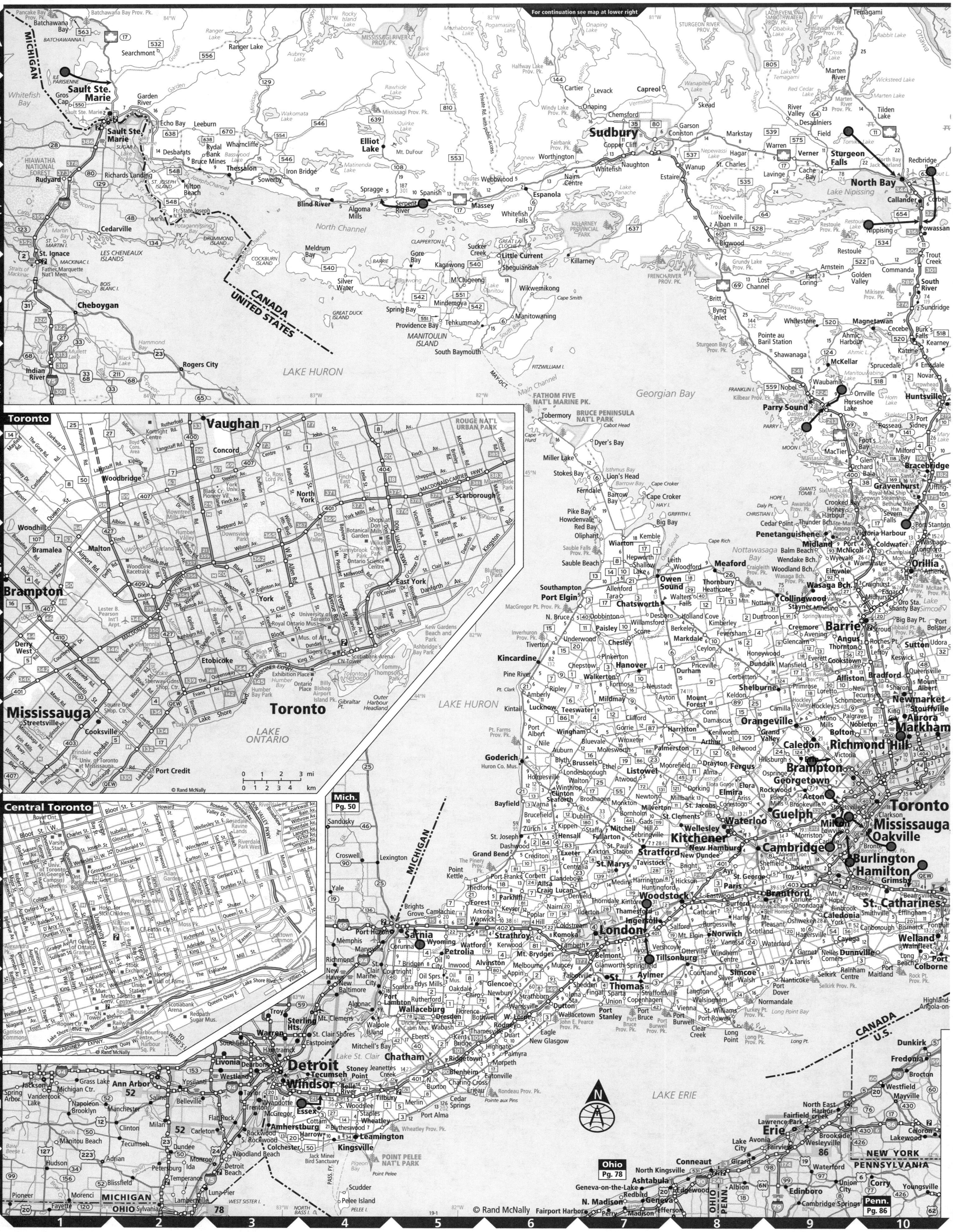

Mileage between cities	Barrie	Hamilton	Kenora	Kingston	London	Montréal, QC	Niagara Falls	Ottawa	Owen Sound	Pembroke	Peterborough	Sarnia	Sault Ste. Marie	Sudbury	Thunder Bay	Timmins	Toronto	Windsor
KINGSTON	211	204	1285		282	186	243	126	269	154	124	335	555	369	983	509	162	381
LONDON	165	88	1263	282		458	135	368	143	367	204	68	533	348	962	543	129	116
NIAGARA FALLS	129	47	1227	243	135	419		329	163	328	165	188	497	311	925	507	83	233
OTTAWA	270	290	1207	126	368	124	329		341	91	169	421	494	300	905	445	248	467
SUDBURY	182	272	925	369	348	424	311	300	238	209	247	401	195		623	182	242	445
THUNDER BAY	796	886	303	983	962	989	925	905	852	814	861	1015	436	623		501	856	1059
TORONTO	61	44	1158	162	129	338	83	248	118	247	84	182	428	242	856	438		227
WINDSOR	264	187	1361	381	116	556	233	467	259	466	302	96	631	445	1059	641	227	

Total mileage through Ontario

417 17 1358 miles

400 69 235 miles

401 513 miles

For more than 40,000 interstate mileages, see the Mileage Directory on page 137

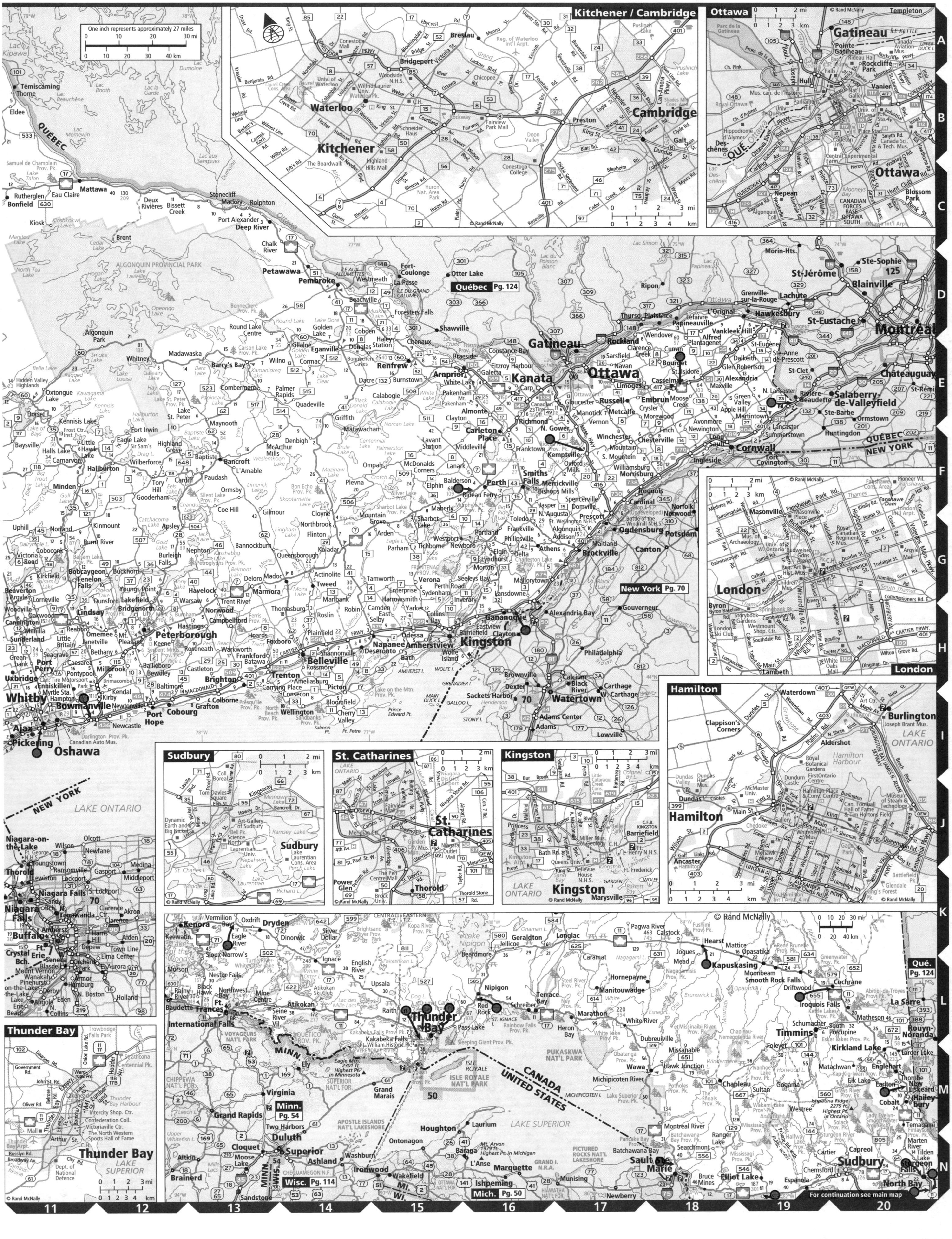

Capital: Québec, J-11
Land area: 527,079 sq. mi. (rank: 2nd)
Population: 7,903,001 (rank: 2nd)
Largest city: Montréal, 1,649,519, M-8

Glossary of common French terms found on these maps: pg. 117
Index of cities Pg. 136
Map legend Pg. 1

Route planning & on-the-road resources

Low clearances, weigh stations, & restricted routes: Page A49

Weigh station location

Designated route for vehicles with STAA-authorized dimensions

Road Conditions & Construction
511, (888) 355-0511; www.quebec511.gouv.qc.ca/en

Toll Bridge Information
Concession A25 (Pont Olivier-Charbonneau, Montréal) *(A25 Smart Link)*: (855) 766-8225, (514) 766-8225; www.a25.com
A30Express (near Montréal) *(A30 Express)*: (855) 783-3030, (514) 782-0800; www.a30express.com

Determining Distances
(segments of one mile or less not shown)
Cumulative miles (red), km (blue): the distance between red arrows
Intermediate miles (black): the distance between intersections & places

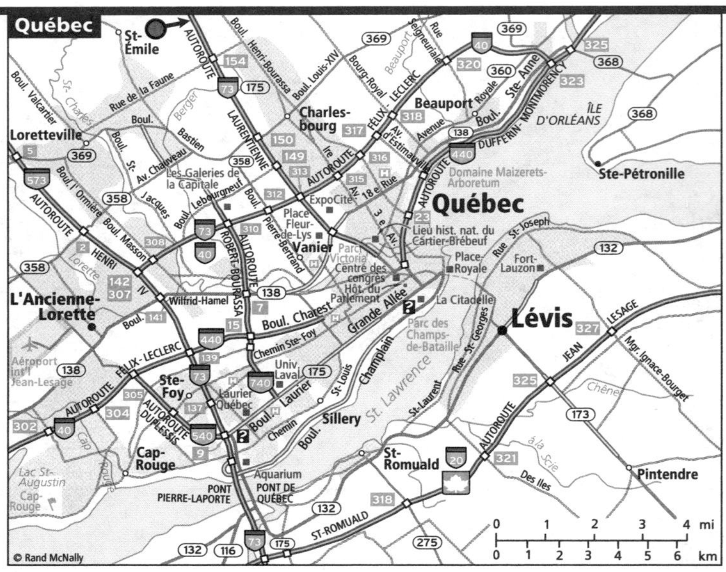

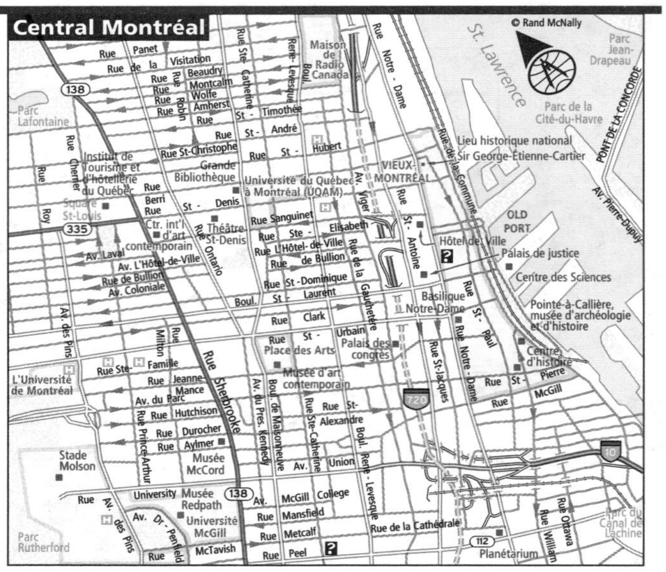

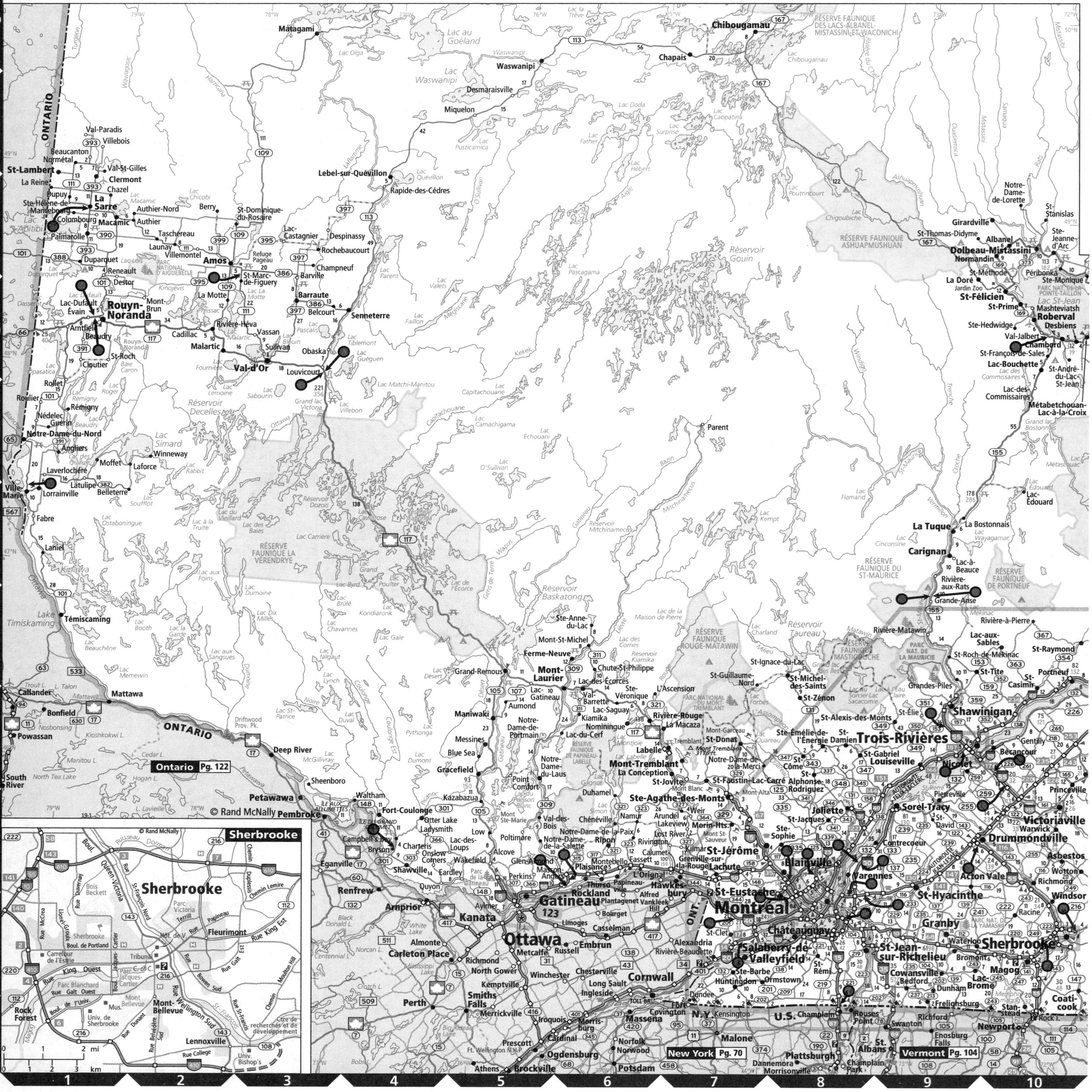

Mileage between cities	Baie-Comeau	Burlington, VT	Gaspé	Mont-Laurier	Montmagny	Montréal	North Bay, ON	Ottawa, ON	Québec	Rimouski	Rivière-du-Loup	Rouyn-Noranda	Saguenay	Salaberry-de-Valleyfield	Sept-Îles	Sherbrooke	Thetford Mines	Trois-Rivières
MONTRÉAL	411	97	566	145	188		346	124	159	333	266	389	289	44	534	95	143	89
OTTAWA, ON	533	217	687	123	310	124	222		282	455	387	324	411	99	657	214	266	205
QUÉBEC	253	222*	432	297	54	159	504	282		199	133	541	135	202	400	149	75	82
ROUYN-NORANDA	720*	485	953	243	575	389	186	324	541	720	653		531	418	921	482	530	461
SAGUENAY	196	352*	406	427	184	289	634	411	135	172*	108	531		331	339	279	205	211
SEPT-ÎLES	143	597*	319	678	349	534	879	657	400	206	268	921	339	577		523	450	465
SHERBROOKE	400	122	556	239	177	95	436	214	149	323	256	482	279	134	523		65	94
TROIS-RIVIÈRES	333	182	497	217	119	89	427	205	82	264	297	461	211	125*	465	94	88	

*Via Ferry

Total mileage through Québec

- 20 / 132 / Trans-Canada: 937 miles
- 15 / 117 / Trans-Canada: 412 miles
- 40 / 138: 765 miles

For more than 40,000 interstate mileages, see the Mileage Directory on page 137

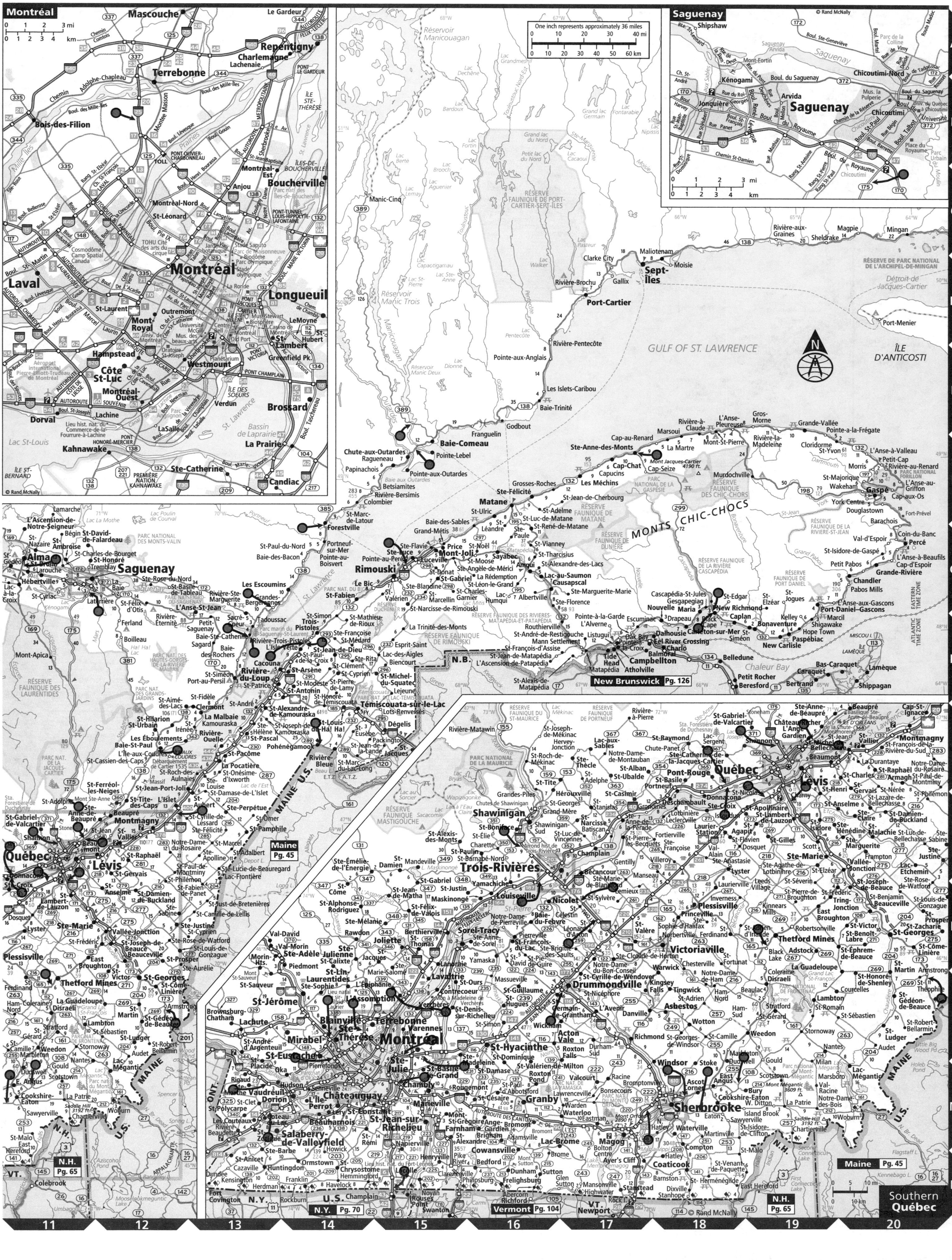

New Brunswick
Capital: Fredericton, H-4
Land area: 27,587 sq. mi. (rank: 11th)
Population: 751,171 (rank: 8th)
Largest city: Saint John, 70,063, J-5

Nova Scotia
Capital: Halifax, K-9
Land area: 20,594 sq. mi. (rank: 12th)
Population: 921,727 (rank: 7th)
Largest city: Halifax, 390,096, K-9

Index of cities Pg. 136 | Map legend Pg. 1

Route planning & on-the-road resources

Low clearances, weigh stations, & restricted routes: Pages A48-A49

Weigh station location

Designated route for vehicles with STAA-authorized dimensions

Road Conditions & Construction

New Brunswick:
511, (800) 561-4063, (506) 453-3939, (888) 747-7006; www.gnb.ca/roads

Nova Scotia:
511, (902) 424-3933, In Canada: (888) 780-4440; 511.gov.ns.ca

Prince Edward Island:
511, (902) 368-4770, In Canada: (855) 241-2680; www.gov.pe.ca/roadconditions

Newfoundland & Labrador:
Avalon: (709) 729-2382, Eastern: (709) 466-4120, Central: (709) 292-4300
Western: (709) 635-4217, Labrador: (709) 896-7840; www.roads.gov.nl.ca

Toll Road Information

Strait Crossing Bridge Ltd: (Confederation Bridge) *(StraitPass)*: (888) 437-6565 www.confederationbridge.com

Atlantic Hwy. Management Corp. Ltd. (Cobequid Pass, N.S. (Hwy 104)) *(E-Pass)*: (877) 727-7104, (902) 668-2211 www.cobequidpass.com

Halifax Harbor Bridges: *(MACPASS)*: (902) 463-2800; www.hdbc.ca

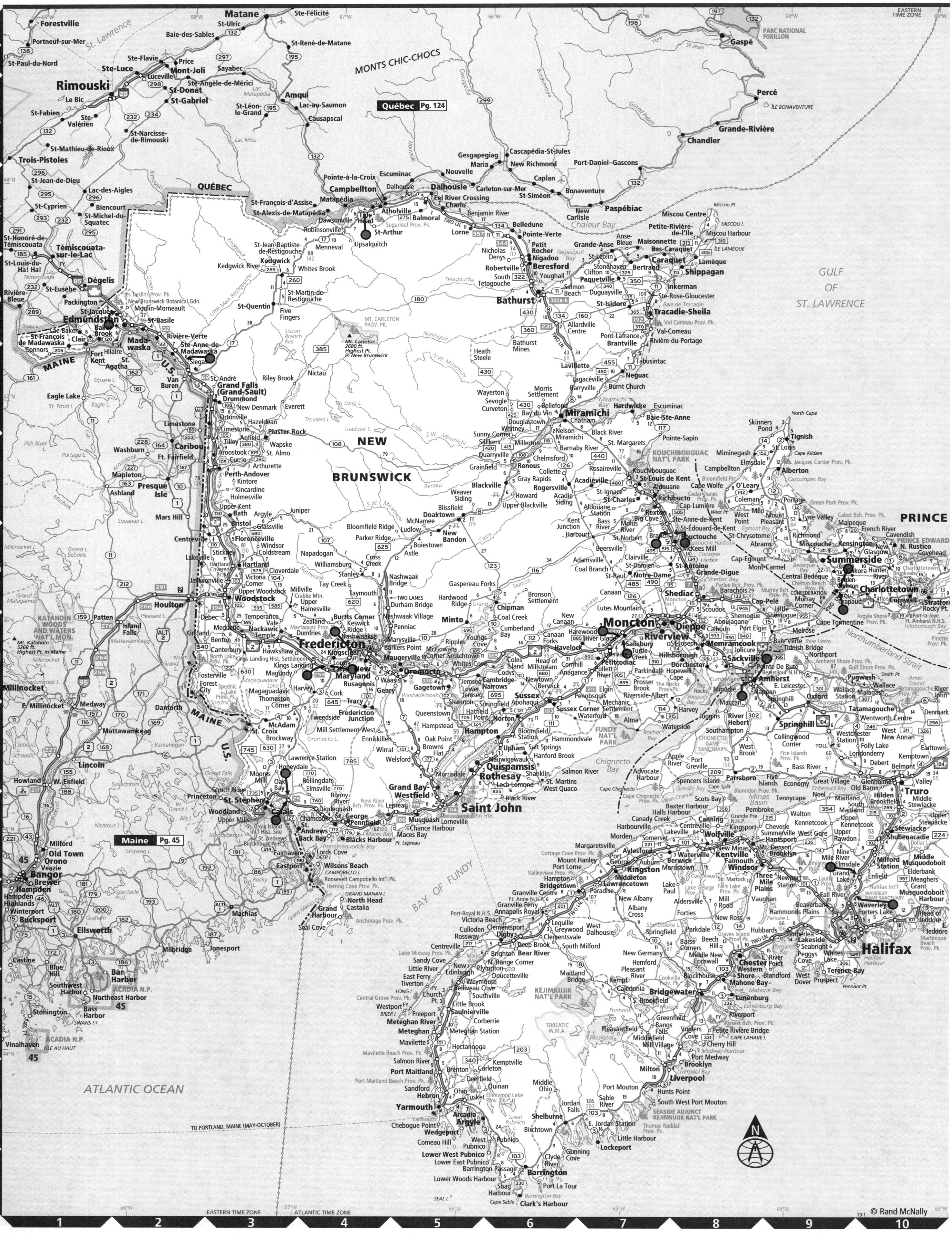

Mileage between cities	Amherst, NS	Bathurst, NB	Campbellton, NB	Charlottetown, PE	Corner Brook, NL	Edmundston, NB	Fredericton, NB	Gander, NL	Grand Falls, NB	Halifax, NS	Moncton, NB	New Glasgow, NS	Saint John, NB	St. John's, NL	St. Stephen, NB	Sydney, NS	Truro, NS	Yarmouth, NS
CHARLOTTETOWN, PE	82	214	281		580*	392	222	800*	354	207	112	182	204	1011*	274	334	148	389
EDMUNDSTON, NB	319	160	125	392*	817*		176	1037*	39	444	283	419	239	1247*	296	571	385	353
FREDERICTON, NB	149	178	249	222*	647	176		867	138	274	113	249	69	1078*	126	401	215	183
HALIFAX, NS	124	288	356	207*	498*	444	274	718*	405		164	100	256	928*	325	251	62	188
MONCTON, NB	39	137	204	112	537*	283	113	757*	244	164		139	95	968*	164	291	105	346
SAINT JOHN, NB	131	229	296	204	629*	239	69	849*	201	256	95	231		1060*	69	383	197	114
ST. JOHN'S, NL	928*	1092*	1159*	1011*	436	1247*	1078*	211	1209	928*	968*	829*	1060*		1129*	691*	869*	1111*
SYDNEY, NS	252	415	483	334	261*	571	401	481*	532	251	291	152	383	691*	452		193	434

*Via Ferry

Mileages © Rand McNally

Total mileage through Atlantic Provinces

2: 308 miles (NB) — 2: 565 miles (NL)

1: 101 miles (PE) — 104 105: 287 miles (NS)

For more than 40,000 interstate mileages, see the Mileage Directory on page 137

Prince Edward Island
Capital: Charlottetown, G-10
Land area: 2,185 sq. mi. (rank: 13th)
Population: 140,204 (rank: 10th)
Largest city: Charlottetown, 34,562, G-10

Newfoundland & Labrador
Capital: St. John's, F-20
Land area: 144,353 sq. mi. (rank: 10th)
Population: 514,536 (rank: 9th)
Largest city: St. John's, 106,172, F-20

Glossary of common French terms found on these maps: pg. 117

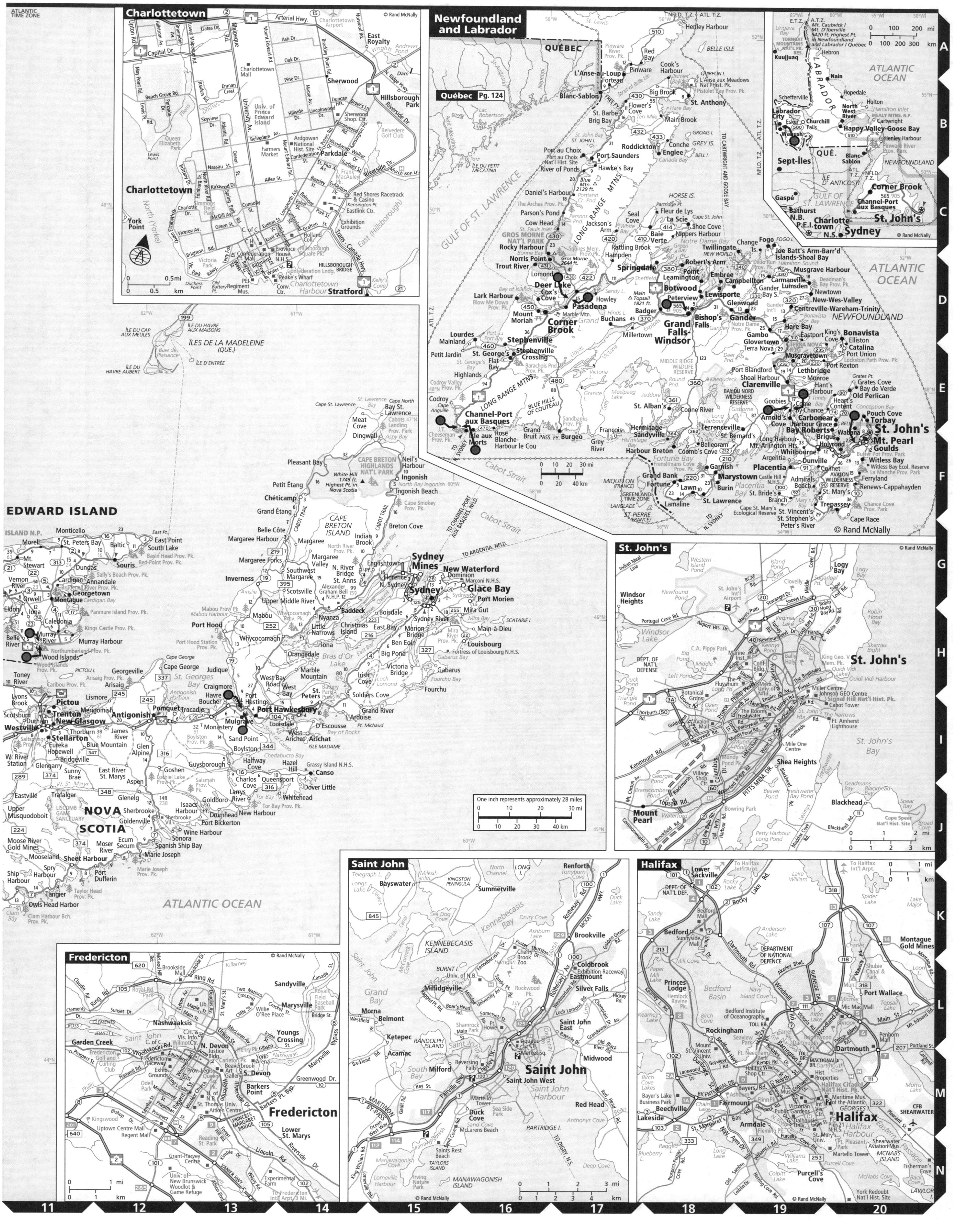

Mexico / Puerto Rico

Mexico
Capital: Mexico City, G-8
Land area: 758,450 sq. mi.
Population: 112,336,538
Largest city: Mexico City, 8,851,080, G-8

Puerto Rico (U.S.)
Capital: San Juan, A-13
Land area: 3,425 sq. mi.
Population: 3,725,789
Largest city: San Juan, 381,931, A-13

Index of cities Mexico: Pg. 136; P.R.: Pg. 134
Map legend Pg. 1

Sights to see

Mexico
- Chichen Itza Ruinas G-13
- Barranca del Cobre C-4
- Grutas de Cacahuamilpa H-8
- Parque Ecológico de Xochimilco I-3
- Parque Internacional del Río Bravo C-7
- Plaza de la Constitucion G-2
- Teotihuacán Ruinas G-8
- Tulum Ruinas G-14

Puerto Rico
- Bahía Fosforescente B-10
- Castillo del Morró A-13
- Museo de Arte de Ponce B-11
- Submarine Gardens A-13

On-the-road resources

Mexico Toll Information, Road Conditions, & Construction
www.gob.mx/carreteras (in Spanish)

Puerto Rico Toll Information, Road Conditions, & Construction
(800) 981-3021, (787) 977-2200; www.dtop.gov.pr

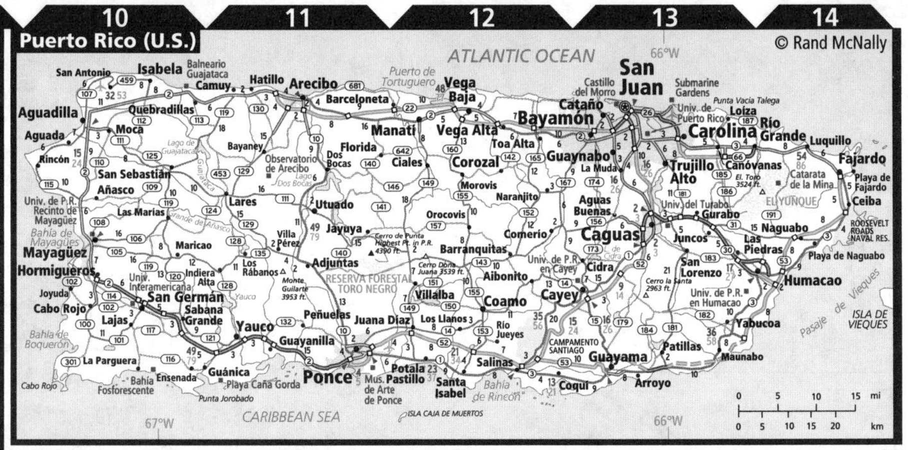

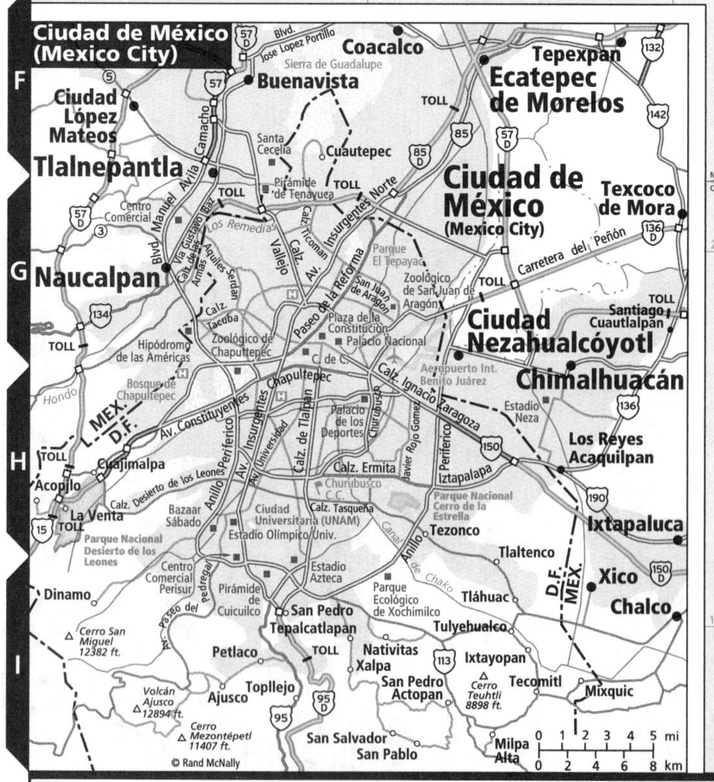

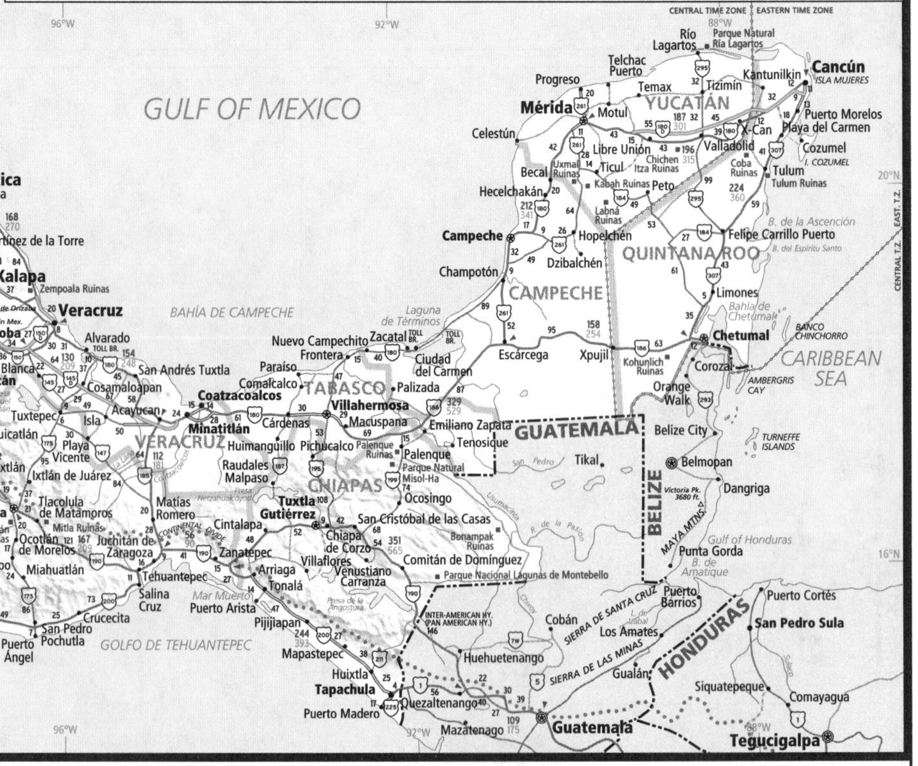

United States Citizens Visiting Mexico

Before you go: Get a passport
The Western Hemisphere Travel Initiative requires all U.S. citizens to carry a passport or other secure document to prove their citizenship in order to enter or re-enter the country by sea, air, or land. The initiative includes surface travel to and from Canada and Mexico. U.S. Armed Forces personnel on active duty traveling orders are exempt from the passport requirement. For information on what constitutes a secure document and additional information, go to the U.S. Department of Homeland Security website: www.dhs.gov/western-hemisphere-travel-initiative-basics

Border crossing waits
Allow plenty of time. The average time for customs clearance is 30 minutes, but this varies greatly depending on traffic flow and security issues.

Driving in Mexico
According to the U.S. Department of State, tourists traveling beyond the border zone must obtain a temporary import permit or risk having their car confiscated by Mexican customs officials. To acquire a permit, submit evidence of citizenship, title for the car, a car registration certificate, driver's license, and a processing fee to either a Banjercito (Mexican Army Bank) branch located at a Mexican Customs office at the port of entry, or at one of the Mexican consulates in the U.S. Mexican law also requires posting a bond at a Banjercito office to guarantee departure of the car from Mexico within a period determined at the time of application. Carry proof of car ownership (the current registration card or a letter of authorization from the finance or leasing company). Auto insurance policies, other than Mexican, are not valid in Mexico. A short-term liability policy is obtainable at the border.

Tourist cards
Tourist cards are valid up to six months, require a fee, and are required for all persons, regardless of age, to visit the interior of Mexico. Cards may be obtained from Mexican border authorities, Consuls of Mexico, or Federal Delegates in major cities. Cards are also distributed to passengers en route to Mexico by air.

Mileage between principal cities

Miles in red; kilometers in blue

	Acapulco, GR	Chihuahua, CH	Cuidad Juárez, CH	Guadalajara, JA	Hermosillo, SO	La Paz, BS	Matamoros, TM	Mazatlan, SI	Mérida, YU	Mexico City, DF
CUIDAD JUÁREZ, CH	1323 / 2129	233 / 375		910 / 1465	468 / 753	988 / 1590	933 / 1502	807 / 1299	1943 / 3127	1121 / 1804
GUADALAJARA, JA	509 / 819	678 / 1090	910 / 1465		864 / 1391	587 / 945	612 / 985	301 / 484	1140 / 1834	318 / 511
MÉRIDA, YU	1027 / 1652	1710 / 2752	1943 / 3127	1140 / 1834	2004 / 3225	1727 / 2779	1255 / 2020	1440 / 2318		822 / 1323
MEXICO CITY, DF	217 / 349	888 / 1429	1121 / 1804	318 / 511	1182 / 1902	905 / 1457	568 / 914	618 / 995	822 / 1323	
MONTERREY, NL	768 / 1236	506 / 814	739 / 1188	457 / 735	882 / 1419	813 / 1308	195 / 314	526 / 846	1270 / 2044	551 / 887
TIJUANA, BC	1872 / 3013	882 / 1419	782 / 1259	1392 / 2240	528 / 850	891 / 1434	1582 / 2546	1092 / 1757	2529 / 4070	1710 / 2752
TUXTLAS GUTIERREZ, CS	560 / 901	1467 / 2360	1700 / 2735	896 / 1442	1760 / 2833	1484 / 2388	1012 / 1628	1197 / 1926	486 / 782	579 / 931

	Monterrey, NL	Nogales, SO	Nuevo Laredo, TM	Oaxaca, OA	San Luis Potosí, SL	Tampico, TM	Tijuana, BC	Torreón, CO	Tuxtlas Gutierrez, CS	Veracruz, VE
CUIDAD JUÁREZ, CH	739 / 1188	374 / 602	874 / 1406	1394 / 2243	855 / 1375	1058 / 1703	782 / 1259	518 / 834	1700 / 2735	1357 / 2183
GUADALAJARA, JA	457 / 735	1034 / 1664	592 / 952	590 / 950	207 / 333	429 / 691	1392 / 2240	409 / 658	896 / 1442	553 / 891
MÉRIDA, YU	1270 / 2044	2174 / 3499	1409 / 2268	691 / 1111	1088 / 1751	947 / 1525	2529 / 4070	1442 / 2320	486 / 782	649 / 1045
MEXICO CITY, DF	551 / 887	1352 / 2176	678 / 1091	273 / 439	266 / 429	260 / 419	1710 / 2752	620 / 997	579 / 931	236 / 379
MONTERREY, NL		979 / 1576	135 / 218	790 / 1272	336 / 541	323 / 520	1387 / 2232	220 / 355	1027 / 1653	621 / 1000
TIJUANA, BC	1387 / 2232	484 / 779	1522 / 2449	1981 / 3188	1503 / 2419	1726 / 2778		1167 / 1878	2284 / 3676	1943 / 3127
TUXTLAS GUTIERREZ, CS	1027 / 1653	1931 / 3107	1166 / 1876	303 / 487	845 / 1360	704 / 1133	2284 / 3676	1198 / 1928		406 / 653

Glossary of Spanish terms

Spanish	English
Avenida (Av.)	Avenue
Bahía (B.)	Bay
Barranca	Canyon
Cabo (C.)	Cape
Calzada (Calz.)	Highway
Canal	Canal, strait
Carretera	Highway
Castillo	Fort
Centro Comercial	Shopping center
Cerro	Mountain
Ciudad	City
Deportes	Sports
Estadio	Stadium
Golfo	Gulf
Grutas	Caves
Hipódromo	Race track
Isla (I.)	Island
Lago (L.)	Lake
Parque Nacional (Nac.)	National park
Parque Natural	Wildlife park
Paseo	Drive
Playa	Beach
Presa	Reservoir
Punta (Pta.)	Point, headland
Sierra	Mountain
Via	Road

Index

United States Counties, cities, towns & places

Populations are from the 2010 U.S. Census or Rand McNally estimates

Index to Canada and Mexico cities and towns, page 136

Alabama

Map pp. 4 – 5

Georgia

Map pp. 28 – 29

* City keyed to p. 30
† City keyed to p. 95

Hawaii

Map p. 30

Idaho

Map p. 31

Illinois

Map pp. 32 – 33

* City keyed to pp. 34 – 35
† City keyed to p. 57

Indiana

Map pp. 36 – 37

* City keyed to p. 35

*, †, ‡, § See explanation under state title in this index. County and parish names are listed in capital letters and in boldface type. Independent cities (not in any county) are shown in italics.

Iowa

Map pp. 38 – 39

† City keyed to p. 63

Kansas

Map pp. 40 – 41

* City keyed to p. 58

Kentucky

Map pp. 42 – 43

* City keyed to p. 112

Louisiana

Map p. 44

Maine

Map p. 45

Maryland

Map pp. 46 – 47

* City keyed to p. 111

Massachusetts

Map pp. 48 – 49

Michigan

Map pp. 50 – 51

* City keyed to p. 52

*, †, ‡, § See explanation under state title in this index. County and parish names are listed in capital letters and in boldface type. Independent cities (not in any county) are shown in italics.

*, †, ‡, § See explanation under state title in this index. County and parish names are listed in capital letters and in boldface type. Independent cities (not in any county) are shown in italics.

New Mexico

Map p. 68

New York

Map pp. 69 – 71

Map keys	Atlas pages
NA – NN	70 – 71
SA – SJ	69

* City keyed to pp. 72 – 73

North Carolina

Map pp. 74 – 75

* City keyed to p. 76

North Dakota

Map p. 77

Ohio

Map pp. 78 – 81

Map keys	Atlas pages
NA – NN	78 – 79
SA – SN	80 – 81

* City keyed to p. 112

*, †, ‡, § See explanation under state title in this index. County and parish names are listed in capital letters and in boldface type. Independent cities (not in any county) are shown in italics.

*, †, ‡, § See explanation under state title in this index. County and parish names are listed in capital letters and in boldface type. Independent cities (not in any county) are shown in italics.

Texas

Map pp. 98 – 101

Map keys Atlas pages
EA – ET 100 – 101
WA – WT 98 – 99

* City keyed to p. 96
† City keyed to p. 97

Utah

Map pp. 102 – 103

Vermont

Map p. 104

Virginia

Map pp. 106 – 107

† City keyed to p. 105
‡ City keyed to p. 111

Washington

Map pp. 108 – 109

* City keyed to p. 110

West Virginia

Map p. 112

* City keyed to p. 46

*, †, ‡, § See explanation under state title in this index. County and parish names are listed in capital letters and in boldface type. Independent cities (not in any county) are shown in italics.

Belmont, 903 F-4
Benwood, 1420 D-6
BERKELEY CO., 104169 B-9
Berkeley Sprs., 624 B-9
Bethany, 1036 C-6
Bethlehem, 2499 D-6
Beverly, 702 H-8
Blennerhassett, 3089 G-3
Bluefield, 10447 M-4
Bluewell, 2184 M-4
Boaz, 1297 F-4
Bolivar, 1045 C-10
BOONE CO., 24629 K-3
Bradley, 2040 K-4
BRAXTON CO., 14523 H-5
Bridgeport, 8149 G-7
BROOKE CO., 24069 C-6
Brookhaven, 5171 K-10
Buckhannon, 5639 H-7
Buffalo, 1236 I-2
Buffalo Creek, 900 C-4
Bunker Hill, 700 B-9
CABELL CO., 96319 I-2
CALHOUN CO., 7627 H-4
Cameron, 946 E-6
Cassville, 701 E-7
Cedar Grv., 997 J-4
Ceredo, 1450 C-3
Chapmanville, 1256 K-2
Charles Town, 5259 C-10
Charleston, 51400 J-3
Chattaroy, 756 L-2
Chesapeake, 1554 J-4
Chester, 2585 B-6
Chestnut Ridge, 800 J-10
Clarksburg, 16578 G-7
Clay, 491 I-5
CLAY CO., 9386 I-5
Clendenin, 1227 I-4
Coalwood, 700 M-3
Crab Orchard, 2678 L-4
Craigsville, 2213 J-6
Cross Lanes, 9995 I-3
Culloden, 3061 I-2
Daniels, 1881 L-5
Danville, 691 K-3
Davis, 660 G-9
Despard, 1004 G-7
DODDRIDGE CO., 8202 G-6
Dunbar, 7907 J-3
E. Bank, 959 J-4
Eleanor, 1518 I-3
Elizabeth, 823 G-4
Elkins, 7094 H-8
Elkview, 1222 I-4
Enterprise, 961 F-7
Evans, 700 H-3
Fairlea, 1747 L-6
Fairmont, 18704 F-7
Falling Waters, 876 B-10
FAYETTE CO., 46039 K-5
Fayetteville, 2892 K-5
Follansbee, 2986 C-6
Ft. Ashby, 1380 B-8
Ft. Gay, 705 J-1
Franklin, 721 I-9
Gary, 968 M-3
Gassaway, 908 I-6
GILMER CO., 8693 G-5
Glendale, 1526 D-6
Glenville, 1537 H-5
Grafton, 5164 F-8
GRANT CO., 11937 G-10
Grantsville, 561 H-5
Granville, 781 J-9
GREENBRIER CO., 35480 K-6
Hamlin, 1142 J-2
HAMPSHIRE CO., 23964 C-8
HANCOCK CO., 30676 C-6
HARDY CO., 14025 D-7
HARRISON CO., 69099 F-6
Harrisville, 1876 G-5
Harts, 656 K-2
Hinton, 2676 L-5
Holden, 876 K-2
Hometown, 668 I-3
Hooverson Hts., 2590 C-6
Huntington, 49138 I-1
Hurricane, 6284 I-2
Institute, 1800 J-3
Inwood, 2954 B-9
JACKSON CO., 29211 H-3
JEFFERSON CO., 53498 C-10
KANAWHA CO., 193063 J-4
Kenova, 3216 I-1
Keyser, 5439 B-7
Kingwood, 2939 F-8
Lavalette, 1073 J-1
Lesage, 1358 I-2
LEWIS CO., 16372 G-6
Lewisburg, 3830 L-6
LINCOLN CO., 21720 J-2
Logan, 1779 K-2
LOGAN CO., 36743 L-2
Lubeck, 1311 G-3
Lumberport, 876 F-7
Mabscott, 1408 L-4
Madison, 3076 K-3
Malden, 850 J-3
Mallory, 1654 L-3
Man, 759 L-3
Mannington, 2063 F-7
MARION CO., 56418 F-7
Marlinton, 1054 J-7
Marlowe, 700 B-10
Marmet, 1503 J-3
MARSHALL CO., 33107 E-6
Martinsburg, 17227 B-10
Maryland Jct., 977 *E-3
Mason, 968 G-2
MASON CO., 27324 I-2
MCDOWELL CO., 22113 M-3
McMechen, 1926 D-6
MERCER CO., 62264 M-4
Middlebourne, 815 F-5
Mill Creek, 724 H-8
Milton, 2423 I-2
MINERAL CO., 28212 B-7
MINGO CO., 26839 K-1
Monongah, 1044 F-7
MONONGALIA CO., 96189 E-7
MONROE CO., 13502 L-6
Montcalm, 726 M-4
Montgomery, 1638 J-4
Moorefield, 2544 C-7
MORGAN CO., 17541 B-9
Morgantown, 29660 E-8
Moundsville, 9318 D-6
Mt. Gay, 700 K-2
Mt. Hope, 1414 K-5
Mullens, 1559 L-4
New Cumberland, 1103 B-6
New Haven, 1560 H-2
New Manchester, 700 B-6
New Martinsville, 5366 E-5
Newell, 1376 B-6
NICHOLAS CO., 26233 J-5
Nitro, 7178 I-3
N. Hills, 832 F-4
Nutter Fort, 1593 G-7
Oak Hill, 7730 K-5
Oceana, 1394 L-3
OHIO CO., 44443 D-6
Paden City, 2633 E-5
Parkersburg, 31492 G-4
Parsons, 1485 G-8
PENDLETON CO., 7695 H-9
Pennsboro, 1171 G-5
Petersburg, 2467 H-10
Peterstown, 653 M-5
Philippi, 2966 G-8
Piedmont, 876 F-10
Pinch, 3262 I-4
Pineville, 668 L-3
Piney View, 989 K-5
Pleasant Valley, 3149 F-7
PLEASANTS CO., 7605 F-5
Poca, 974 I-3
POCAHONTAS CO., 8719 J-8
Pocatalico, 1500 I-3
Pt. Pleasant, 4350 H-2
PRESTON CO., 33520 F-8
Princeton, 6432 M-5
Prosperity, 1498 K-4
PUTNAM CO., 55486 I-3
Rainelle, 1505 K-6
RALEIGH CO., 78859 L-4
Rand, 1631 J-3
RANDOLPH CO., 29405 H-8
Ranson, 4440 C-10
Ravenswood, 3876 H-3
Richwood, 2051 J-6
Ridgeley, 675 B-7
Ripley, 3252 H-3
RITCHIE CO., 10449 G-4
Rivesville, 934 F-7
ROANE CO., 14926 H-4
Robinette, 663 L-3
Romney, 1848 B-8
Ronceverte, 1765 L-6
Rupert, 942 K-6
St. Albans, 11044 J-3
St. Marys, 1860 F-4
Salem, 1586 G-6
Scott Depot, 1500 I-3
Seth, 750 K-3
Shady Spr., 2998 L-5
Shepherdstown, 1734 B-10
Shinnston, 2201 F-7
Sissonville, 4028 I-3
Sistersville, 1396 F-5
Smithers, 813 J-4
Sophia, 1344 L-4
S. Charleston, 13450 J-3
Spencer, 2322 H-4
Spring Valley, 900 B-3
Star City, 1825 E-8
Stonewood, 1806 G-7
SUMMERS CO., 13927 L-5
Summersville, 3572 J-5
Sutton, 994 I-6
TAYLOR CO., 16895 F-8
Tennerton, 1800 H-7
Terra Alta, 1477 F-9
TUCKER CO., 7141 G-8
TYLER CO., 9208 F-5
Union, 565 L-6
Upper Falls, 3701 J-3
UPSHUR CO., 24254 H-7
Verdunville, 687 K-2
Vienna, 10749 F-4
War, 862 M-3
Washington, 1175 G-3
Wayne, 1413 J-1
WAYNE CO., 42481 J-1
WEBSTER CO., 9154 I-7
Webster Sprs., 776 I-7
Weirton, 19746 C-6
Welch, 2406 M-3
Wellsburg, 2805 C-6
W. Hamlin, 774 J-2
W. Liberty, 1542 D-6
W. Union, 825 G-6
Weston, 4110 G-6
Westover, 3983 E-8
WETZEL CO., 16583 F-6
Wheeling, 28486 D-6
White Sulphur Sprs., 2444 L-7
Williamson, 3191 L-2
Williamstown, 2908 F-4
Winfield, 2301 I-3
WIRT CO., 5717 G-4
WOOD CO., 86956 G-3
WYOMING CO., 23796 L-4

Wisconsin

Map pp. 114 – 115

† City keyed to p. 113

Abbotsford, 2310 H-7
Adams, 1967 K-8
ADAMS CO., 20875 K-9
Albany, 1018 O-9
Algoma, 3167 D-12
Allenton, 823 M-12
Allouez, 13975 S-3
Alma, 781 J-3
Altoona, 6706 H-5
Amery, 2902 G-2
Amherst, 1035 J-10
Antigo, 8234 G-10
Appleton, 72623 J-12
Arcadia, 2925 J-4
Arena, 834 N-8
Argyle, 857 O-8
Arlington, 819 M-9
Ashland, 8216 C-6
ASHLAND CO., 16157 D-6
Ashwaubenon, 16963 S-3
Athens, 1105 H-8
Augusta, 1550 I-5
Baldwin, 3957 H-2
Balsam Lake, 1009 F-2
Bangor, 1459 K-6
Baraboo, 12048 M-9
Barneveld, 1231 N-8
Barron, 3423 F-4
BARRON CO., 45870 F-3
BAYFIELD CO., 15014 B-5
Bayside, 4389 †C-6
Beaver Dam, 16214 M-11
Belgium, 2245 M-13
Belleville, 2385 O-9
Bellevue, 14570 J-13
Belmont, 986 O-7
Beloit, 36966 P-10
Benton, 973 P-7
Berlin, 5524 K-10
Big Bend, 1290 †I-1
Birnamwood, 818 H-10
Biron, 839 J-8
Black Creek, 1316 J-12
Black Earth, 1338 N-9
Black River Falls, 3622 J-6
Blair, 1366 J-5
Blanchardville, 825 O-8
Bloomer, 3539 G-4
Bloomfield, 3722 P-12
Blue Mounds, 855 N-8
Bonduel, 1478 I-12
Boscobel, 3231 N-6
Boyceville, 1086 H-3
Brandon, 879 L-11
Brillion, 3148 K-13
Bristol, 2584 P-13
Brodhead, 3293 P-9
Brookfield, 37920 N-12
Brooklyn, 1401 O-9
BROWN CO., 248007 J-13
Brown Deer, 11999 N-13
Buffalo City, 1023 J-4
BUFFALO CO., 13587 I-4
Burlington, 10464 O-12
BURNETT CO., 15457 E-2
Butler, 1841 †D-3
Butte des Morts, 962 K-11
Caddy Vista, 900 †J-6
Cadott, 1437 H-5
Caledonia, 24705 O-13
CALUMET CO., 48971 K-12
Cambridge, 1457 N-10
Cameron, 1783 F-4
Campbellsport, 2016 L-12
Cashton, 1102 L-6
Cassville, 947 O-6
Cedar Grv., 2113 M-13
Cedarburg, 11412 M-13
Centuria, 948 F-2
Chetek, 2221 G-4
Chilton, 3933 K-12
CHIPPEWA CO., 62415 G-5
Chippewa Falls, 13661 H-5
CLARK CO., 34690 I-6
Clear Lake, 1070 G-3
Cleveland, 1485 K-13
Clinton, 2154 P-11
Clintonville, 4559 I-11
Colby, 1852 H-7
Colfax, 1158 H-4
COLUMBIA CO., 56833 M-10
Columbus, 4991 M-10
Combined Locks, 3328 O-4
Cornell, 1467 G-5
Cottage Grv., 6192 N-10
Crandon, 1920 F-11
CRAWFORD CO., 16644 N-6
Crestview, 3500 O-13
Crivitz, 984 A-11
Cross Plains, 3538 N-9
Cuba City, 2086 P-7
Cudahy, 18267 O-13
Cumberland, 2170 F-3
Dane, 995 N-9
DANE CO., 488073 O-9
Darien, 1580 P-11
Darlington, 2451 P-8
De Forest, 8936 N-10
De Pere, 23800 J-13
Deerfield, 2319 N-10
Delafield, 7085 N-12
Delavan, 8463 P-11
Denmark, 2123 J-13
Dickeyville, 1061 P-6
DODGE CO., 88759 M-11
Dodgeville, 4693 O-8
DOOR CO., 27785 C-12
Dorchester, 876 H-7
DOUGLAS CO., 44159 C-3
Dousman, 2302 N-12
Dresser, 895 G-2
DUNN CO., 43857 G-4
Durand, 1931 I-3
Eagle, 1950 O-12
Eagle River, 1398 E-10
E. Troy, 4281 O-12
Eau Claire, 65883 H-4
EAU CLAIRE CO., 98736 H-5
Eden, 875 L-12
Edgar, 1479 H-8
Edgerton, 5461 O-10
Elk Mound, 878 H-4
Elkhart Lake, 967 L-13
Elkhorn, 10084 P-12
Ellsworth, 3284 I-2
Elm Grv., 5934 †E-3
Elmwood, 817 I-3
Elroy, 1442 L-7
Evansville, 5012 O-10
Fall Creek, 1315 I-5
Fall River, 1712 M-10
Fennimore, 2497 O-6
Fitchburg, 25260 N-9
Florence, 592 E-12
FLORENCE CO., 4423 E-11
Fond du Lac, 43021 L-12
FOND DU LAC CO., 101633 L-11
Fontana, 1672 P-11
Footville, 808 P-10
FOREST CO., 9304 F-11
Ft. Atkinson, 12368 O-11
Fountain City, 859 K-4
Fox Lake, 1519 M-11
Fox Pt., 6701 †C-6
Franklin, 35451 O-13
Franksville, 1789 †I-8
Frederic, 1137 F-2
Fredonia, 2160 M-13
French Island, 4410 †B-8
Friendship, 725 K-8
Galesville, 1481 K-5
Genoa City, 3042 P-12
Germantown, 19749 N-13
Gillett, 1386 H-12
Glendale, 12872 N-13
Glenwood City, 1242 H-3
Grafton, 11459 M-13
GRANT CO., 51208 O-6
Grantsburg, 1341 E-2
Green Bay, 104057 D-11
GREEN CO., 36842 O-9
Green Lake, 960 L-10
GREEN LAKE CO., 19051 K-10
Greendale, 14046 †G-5
Greenfield, 36720 O-13
Greenwood, 1026 I-7
Hales Cors., 7692 †G-4
Hammond, 1922 H-2
Hartford, 14223 M-12
Hartland, 9110 N-12
Hayward, 2318 D-5
Hazel Green, 1256 P-7
Hewitt, 828 I-8
Highland, 842 N-7
Hilbert, 1132 K-12
Hillsboro, 1417 L-7
Hingham, 886 L-13
Hobart, 6182 S-1
Holmen, 9005 K-5
Horicon, 3655 M-11
Hortonville, 2711 J-11
Howard, 17399 D-11
Howards Grv., 3188 L-13
Hudson, 12719 H-1
Hurley, 1547 C-8
Hustisford, 1123 M-11
Independence, 1336 J-5
Iola, 1301 I-10
IOWA CO., 23687 N-7
IRON CO., 5916 D-7
Iron Ridge, 929 M-11
Ixonia, 1624 N-11
Jackson, 6753 M-12
JACKSON CO., 20449 J-7
Janesville, 63575 P-10
Jefferson, 7973 N-11
JEFFERSON CO., 83686 N-11
Johnson Creek, 2738 N-11
Juneau, 2814 M-11
JUNEAU CO., 26664 K-7
Kaukauna, 15462 J-12
Kenosha, 99218 P-13
KENOSHA CO., 166426 P-13
Keshena, 1262 H-11
Kewaskum, 4004 M-12
Kewaunee, 2952 J-14
KEWAUNEE CO., 20574 C-12
Kiel, 3738 K-13
Kimberly, 6468 J-12
King, 1750 J-10
Kohler, 2120 L-13
Kronenwetter, 7210 H-9
La Crosse, 51320 L-5
LA CROSSE CO., 114638 L-5
Lac du Flambeau, 1969 E-8
Ladysmith, 3414 F-5
LAFAYETTE CO., 16836 P-7
L. Delton, 2914 L-8
L. Geneva, 7651 P-12
L. Mills, 5708 N-11
L. Nebagamon, 1069 C-4
L. Wissota, 2738 H-5
Lancaster, 3868 O-6
LANGLADE CO., 19977 G-10
Lannon, 1107 †C-2
LINCOLN CO., 28743 G-8
Little Chute, 10449 J-12
Lodi, 3050 M-9
Lomira, 2430 L-12
Lone Rock, 888 N-7
Loyal, 1261 I-7
Luck, 1119 F-2
Luxemburg, 2515 D-12
Madison, 233209 N-9
Manawa, 1371 J-11
Manitowoc, 33736 K-14
MANITOWOC CO., 81442 K-13
Maple Bluff, 1313 R-8
Marathon, 1524 H-8
MARATHON CO., 134063 H-9
Marinette, 10968 B-12
MARINETTE CO., 41749 A-11
Marion, 1260 I-11
Markesan, 1476 L-10
MARQUETTE CO., 15404 L-9
Marshall, 3862 N-10
Marshfield, 19118 I-8
Mauston, 4423 L-8
Mayville, 5154 M-11
Mazomanie, 1652 N-8
McFarland, 7808 N-10
Medford, 4326 G-7
Menasha, 17353 J-12
MENOMINEE CO., 4232 H-11
Menomonee Falls, 35626 N-13
Menomonie, 16264 H-3
Mequon, 23132 N-13
Merrill, 9661 G-9
Merton, 3346 N-12
Middleton, 17442 N-9
Milltown, 917 F-2
Milton, 5546 O-11
Milwaukee, 594833 N-13
MILWAUKEE CO., 947735 O-13
Mineral Pt., 2487 O-8
Mishicot, 1442 J-14
Mondovi, 2777 I-4
Monona, 7533 N-10
Monroe, 10827 P-9
MONROE CO., 44673 L-6
Montello, 1495 L-10
Monticello, 1217 O-9
Montreal, 807 C-7
Mosinee, 3988 I-9
Mt. Horeb, 7009 N-9
Mt. Pleasant, 26197 O-13
Mukwonago, 7355 O-12
Muscoda, 1299 N-7
Muskego, 24135 †H-2
Nashotah, 1395 N-12
Necedah, 916 K-8
Neenah, 25501 K-12
Neillsville, 2463 I-7
Nekoosa, 2580 J-8
New Berlin, 39584 N-13
New Glarus, 2172 O-9
New Holstein, 3236 K-13
New Lisbon, 2554 L-8
New London, 7295 J-11
New Richmond, 8375 G-2
Newburg, 1254 M-13
Niagara, 1624 E-13
N. Fond du Lac, 5014 L-12
N. Hudson, 3768 H-1
N. Prairie, 2141 O-12
Oak Creek, 34451 O-13
Oakfield, 1075 L-11
Oconomowoc, 15759 N-12
Oconto, 4513 C-11
OCONTO CO., 37660 B-11
Oconto Falls, 2891 H-12
Omro, 3517 K-11
Onalaska, 17736 L-5
Oneida, 1000 I-12
ONEIDA CO., 35998 E-9
Oostburg, 2887 L-13
Oregon, 9231 O-9
Orfordville, 1442 P-10
Osceola, 2568 G-2
Oshkosh, 66083 K-11
Osseo, 1701 I-5
OUTAGAMIE CO., 176695 J-11
Owen, 940 H-7
OZAUKEE CO., 86395 M-13
Paddock Lake, 2992 P-13
Palmyra, 1781 O-11
Pardeeville, 2115 M-10
Park Falls, 2462 E-7
Pepin, 837 J-3
PEPIN CO., 7469 I-4
Peshtigo, 3502 B-11
Pewaukee, 13195 N-12
Pewaukee, 8166 †D-1
Phelps, 900 D-10
Phillips, 1478 F-7
PIERCE CO., 41019 I-2
Pittsville, 874 J-8
Platteville, 11224 O-7
Pleasant Prairie, 19719 P-13
Plover, 12123 J-9
Plymouth, 8445 L-13
POLK CO., 44205 F-3
Port Edwards, 1818 J-8
Port Washington, 11250 M-13
Portage, 10324 M-9
PORTAGE CO., 70019 J-9
Poynette, 2528 M-9
Prairie du Chien, 5911 N-5
Prairie du Sac, 3972 N-9
Prescott, 4258 I-1
PRICE CO., 14159 F-7
Princeton, 1214 L-10
Pulaski, 3539 I-12
Racine, 78860 O-13
RACINE CO., 195408 O-13
Randolph, 1811 M-10
Random Lake, 1594 M-13
Redgranite, 2149 K-10
Reedsburg, 9200 M-8
Reedsville, 1206 K-13
Rhinelander, 7798 F-9
Rib Lake, 910 G-7
Rice Lake, 8438 F-4
Richfield, 11300 N-12
Richland Ctr., 5184 M-7
RICHLAND CO., 18021 M-7
Rio, 1059 M-10
Ripon, 7733 L-11
River Falls, 15000 H-2
River Hills, 1597 †C-5
Roberts, 1651 H-2
Rochester, 3682 O-12
ROCK CO., 160331 O-10
Rosendale, 1063 L-11
Rothschild, 5269 H-9
RUSK CO., 14755 F-5
ST. CROIX CO., 84345 H-2
St. Croix Falls, 2133 F-2
St. Francis, 9365 N-13
Salem Lakes, 14500 P-13
Sauk City, 3410 N-9
SAUK CO., 61976 M-8
Saukville, 4451 M-13
SAWYER CO., 16557 E-6
Schofield, 2169 H-9
Seymour, 3451 I-12
Sharon, 1605 P-11
Shawano, 9305 I-11
SHAWANO CO., 41949 H-10
Sheboygan, 49288 L-13
SHEBOYGAN CO., 115507 L-13
Sheboygan Falls, 7775 L-13
Shell Lake, 1347 E-3
Sherwood, 2713 K-12
Shiocton, 921 J-11
Shorewood, 13162 N-13
Shorewood Hills, 1565 S-7
Shullsburg, 1226 P-7
Silver Lake P-12
Siren, 806 E-2
Sister Bay, 876 A-13
Slinger, 5068 M-12
Somerset, 2635 G-2
S. Milwaukee, 21156 O-13
Sparta, 9522 K-6
Spencer, 1925 I-7
Spooner, 2682 E-4
Spring Green, 1628 N-8
Spring Valley, 1352 H-3
Stanley, 3608 H-6
Stevens Pt., 26717 I-9
Stoughton, 12611 O-10
Stratford, 1578 H-8
Strum, 1114 I-5
Sturgeon Bay, 9144 C-13
Sturtevant, 6970 O-13
Suamico, 11346 D-11
Sun Prairie, 29364 N-10
Superior, 27244 B-3
Sussex, 10518 N-12
TAYLOR CO., 20689 G-7
Theresa, 1262 M-12
Thiensville, 3235 †A-5
Thorp, 1621 H-6
Tomah, 9093 K-7
Tomahawk, 3397 F-9
Trempealeau, 1529 K-5
TREMPEALEAU CO., 28816 J-5
Turtle Lake, 1050 F-3
Twin Lakes, 5989 P-12
Two Rivers, 11712 K-14
Union Grv., 4915 O-13
Valders, 962 K-13
VERNON CO., 29773 L-5
Verona, 10619 N-9
VILAS CO., 21430 D-9
Viroqua, 4362 M-6
Wales, 2549 N-12
Walworth, 2816 P-11
WALWORTH CO., 102228 O-11
Washburn, 2117 B-6
WASHBURN CO., 15911 E-4
WASHINGTON CO., 131887 M-12
Waterford, 5368 O-12
Waterloo, 3333 N-10
Watertown, 23861 N-11
Waukesha, 70718 N-12
WAUKESHA CO., 389891 O-12
Waunakee, 12097 N-9
Waupaca, 6069 J-10
WAUPACA CO., 52410 I-10
Waupun, 11340 L-11
Wausau, 39106 H-9
WAUSHARA CO., 24496 K-9
Wautoma, 2218 K-10
Wauwatosa, 46396 †E-4
W. Allis, 60411 †F-4
W. Baraboo, 1414 M-9
W. Bend, 31078 M-12
W. Milwaukee, 4206 †F-5
W. Salem, 4799 K-5
Westby, 2200 L-6
Westfield, 1254 L-9
Weston, 14868 H-9
Weyauwega, 1900 J-10
Whitefish Bay, 14110 N-13
Whitehall, 1558 J-5
Whitewater, 14390 O-11
Whiting, 1724 J-9
Williams Bay, 2564 P-12
Wind Lake, 5342 O-12
Wind Pt., 1723 O-13
Windsor, 3573 N-10
WINNEBAGO CO., 166994 K-11
Winneconne, 2383 K-11
Wisconsin Dells, 2678 L-9
Wisconsin Rapids, 18367 J-8
Wittenberg, 1081 H-10
Wonewoc, 816 L-7
WOOD CO., 74749 J-8
Woodruff, 966 E-9
Woodville, 1344 H-3
Wrightstown, 2827 J-12

Wyoming

Map p. 116

Afton, 1911 J-1
ALBANY CO., 36299 K-8
Alpine, 828 I-1
Arapahoe, 1656 J-4
Bar Nunn, 2213 J-7
Basin, 1285 G-5
BIG HORN CO., 11668 G-4
Buffalo, 4585 G-6
CAMPBELL CO., 46133 H-8
CARBON CO., 15885 L-6
Casper, 55316 J-7
Cheyenne, 59466 M-9
Cody, 9520 G-3
CONVERSE CO., 13833 I-8
CROOK CO., 7083 F-9
Douglas, 6120 J-8
Dubois, 971 I-3
Ethete, 1553 J-4
Evanston, 12359 M-1
Evansville, 2544 A-10
Ft. Washakie, 1759 J-4
FREMONT CO., 40123 J-5
Gillette, 29087 G-8
Glenrock, 2576 J-8
GOSHEN CO., 13249 K-10
Green River, 12515 L-3
Greybull, 1847 G-5
Guernsey, 1147 K-9
Hanna, 841 L-7
Hoback, 1176 I-1
HOT SPRINGS CO., 4812 H-4
Jackson, 9577 I-1
JOHNSON CO., 8569 H-7
Kemmerer, 2656 L-1
Lander, 7487 J-4
Laramie, 30816 M-8
LARAMIE CO., 91738 M-9
LINCOLN CO., 18106 K-1
Lovell, 2360 F-4
Lusk, 1567 J-10
Lyman, 2115 M-2
Marbleton, 1094 J-2
Mills, 3461 J-7
Moorcroft, 1009 G-9
Moose Wilson Road, 1821 C-6
NATRONA CO., 75450 J-6
Newcastle, 3532 H-10
NIOBRARA CO., 2484 J-10
Orchard Valley, 800 E-9
PARK CO., 28205 G-3
Pine Bluffs, 1129 M-10
Pinedale, 2030 J-2
PLATTE CO., 8667 L-9
Powell, 6314 F-4
Ranchester, 855 F-6
Rawlins, 9259 L-6
Riverton, 10615 J-4
Rock Sprs., 23036 L-3
Saratoga, 1690 M-6
Sheridan, 17444 F-6
SHERIDAN CO., 29116 F-7
Sleepy Hollow, 1308 G-8
S. Greeley, 4217 E-9
S. Laramie, 1560 M-8
Star Valley Ranch, 1503 J-1
Story, 828 G-6
SUBLETTE CO., 10247 K-2
Sundance, 1182 G-10
SWEETWATER CO., 43806 K-4
TETON CO., 21294 H-2
Thermopolis, 3009 H-4
Torrington, 6501 K-10
UINTA CO., 21118 L-1
Upton, 1100 H-9
Vista West, 951 A-8
WASHAKIE CO., 8533 H-5
WESTON CO., 7208 H-9
Wheatland, 3627 K-9
Wilson, 1482 I-1
Worland, 5487 H-5
Wright, 1807 H-8

Canada Cities and Towns

Populations are from latest available census or are Rand McNally estimates

Alberta

Map pp. 118 – 119

* City keyed to p. 117

Acme, 653 H-16
Airdrie, 42564 H-16
Alberta Bch., 865 E-15
Alix, 830 G-17
Athabasca, 2990 C-16
Banff, 7584 I-15
Barnwell, 771 K-18
Barrhead, 4432 D-15
Bashaw, 873 F-17
Bassano, 1282 I-18
Beaverlodge, 2365 C-11
Beiseker, 785 H-16
Bentley, 1073 G-16
Black Diamond, 2373 I-16
Blackfalds, 6300 G-16
Bon Accord, 1488 E-16
Bonnyville, 6216 D-19
Bow Island, 2025 J-19
Bowden, 1241 G-16
Boyle, 916 C-17
Bragg Creek, 595 I-16
Brooks, 13676 I-18
Bruderheim, 1155 E-17
Calgary, 1096833 I-16
Calmar, 1970 E-16
Camrose, 17286 F-17
Canmore, 12288 I-15
Carbon, 592 H-17
Cardston, 3580 K-17
Caroline, 501 G-15
Carseland, 568 I-17
Carstairs, 3442 H-16
Castor, 932 G-18
Claresholm, 3758 J-17
Clive, 675 G-16
Clyde, 503 D-16
Coaldale, 7493 K-18
Cochrane, 17580 I-16
Cold Lake, 13839 C-19
Consort, 689 G-19
Coronation, 947 G-18
Crossfield, 2853 H-16
Crowsnest Pass, 5565 K-16
Daysland, 807 F-17
Delburne, 830 G-17
Devon, 6510 E-16
Didsbury, 4957 H-16
Drayton Valley, 7049 F-15
Drumheller, 8029 H-17
Duchess, 992 I-18
Dunmore, 502 J-19
Eckville, 1125 G-16
Edmonton, 812201 E-16
Edson, 8475 E-14
Elk Pt., 1412 D-18
Evansburg, 880 E-15
Falher, 1075 B-13
Foremost, 526 K-19
Forestburg, 831 F-18
Ft. Macleod, 3117 K-17
Ft. McMurray, 61374 *E-4
Ft. Saskatchewan, 19051 E-16
Ft. Vermillion, 727 *E-4
Fox Creek, 1969 D-13
Gibbons, 3030 E-16
Gift Lake, 662 B-14
Grande Cache, 4319 E-11
Grande Prairie, 55032 C-11
Grassy Lake, 649 J-18
Hanna, 2673 H-18
Hardisty, 639 F-18
High Level, 3641 *E-4
High Prairie, 2600 B-13
High River, 12920 I-16
Hinton, 9640 E-13
Hythe, 820 C-11
Innisfail, 7876 G-16
Irricana, 1162 H-16
Jasper, 4051 F-12
Kikino, 959 C-17
Killam, 981 F-18
Kitscoty, 846 E-19
Lac La Biche, 2544 C-17
Lacombe, 11707 G-16
L. Louise, 500 H-14
Lamont, 1753 E-17
Leduc, 24279 E-16
Legal, 1225 D-16
Lethbridge, 83517 K-17
Linden, 725 H-16
Lloydminster, 18032 E-19
Magrath, 2217 K-17
Manning, 1164 *E-4
Mannville, 803 E-18
Marwayne, 612 E-19
Mayerthorpe, 1398 D-15
McLennan, 809 B-13
Medicine Hat, 60005 J-19
Milk River, 811 K-18
Millet, 2092 F-16
Morinville, 8569 E-16
Mundare, 855 E-17
Nanton, 2132 J-16
Nobleford, 1000 J-17
Okotoks, 24511 I-16
Olds, 8235 H-16
Onoway, 1039 E-16
Oyen, 973 H-19
Penhold, 2375 G-16
Picture Butte, 1650 J-17
Pincher Creek, 3685 K-16
Ponoka, 6773 F-16
Provost, 2041 F-19
Rainbow Lake, 870 *D-4
Raymond, 3743 K-18
Red Deer, 90564 G-16
Redcliff, 5588 J-19
Redwater, 1915 D-16
Rimbey, 2378 F-16
Rocky Mountain House, 6933 G-15
Rycroft, 628 B-11
St. Albert, 61466 E-16
St. Paul, 5400 D-18
Sedgewick, 857 F-18
Sexsmith, 2418 B-11
Sherwood Pk., 61660 E-16
Slave Lake, 6782 B-15
Smoky Lake, 1022 D-17
Spirit River, 1025 B-11
Spruce Grove, 26171 E-16
Stavely, 505 J-16
Stettler, 5748 G-17
Stirling, 1090 K-18
Stony Plain, 15051 E-16
Strathmore, 12305 I-17
Sundre, 2610 H-15
Swan Hills, 1465 C-14
Sylvan Lake, 12327 G-16
Taber, 8104 J-18
Thorsby, 797 E-16
Three Hills, 3198 H-17
Tofield, 2182 E-17
Trochu, 1072 H-17
Turner Valley, 2167 I-16
Two Hills, 1379 E-18
Valleyview, 1761 C-13
Vauxhall, 1288 J-18
Vegreville, 5717 E-18
Vermilion, 3930 E-19
Viking, 1041 E-18
Vulcan, 1836 J-17
Wabamun, 661 E-15
Wabasca-Desmarais, 1569 A-16
Wainwright, 5925 F-19
Warburg, 789 F-16
Wembley, 1383 C-11
Westlock, 4823 D-16
Wetaskiwin, 12525 F-16
Whitecourt, 9605 D-14

British Columbia

Map pp. 118 – 119

* City keyed to p. 117

100 Mile House, 1886 H-9
150 Mile House, 1172 G-9
Abbotsford, 133497 L-8
Armstrong, 4815 J-11
Ashcroft, 1628 I-9
Barriere, 1773 I-10
Bella Bella, 1095 G-3
Black Creek, 1900 K-5
Bowser, 1613 K-6
Burnaby, 223218 L-3
Burns Lake, 2029 D-5
Cache Creek, 1040 I-9
Campbell River, 31186 J-5
Canal Flats, 685 J-14
Cassidy, 971 L-7
Castlegar, 7816 L-13
Cawston, 1015 L-11
Chase, 2495 I-11
Chemainus, 3035 L-7
Cherryville, 614 J-12
Chetwynd, 2635 B-9
Chilliwack, 77936 L-8
Christina Lake, 1168 L-12
Clearwater, 2331 H-10
Clinton, 636 I-9
Cobble Hill, 637 L-7
Coldstream, 10314 J-11
Comox, 13627 K-5
Coombs, 1547 K-6
Coquitlam, 126456 L-4
Courtenay, 24099 K-5
Cranbrook, 19319 K-15
Creston, 5306 L-14
Crofton, 1092 L-7
Cumberland, 3398 K-6
Dawson Creek, 11583 B-10
Delta, 99863 M-2
Duncan, 4932 L-7
Elkford, 2523 J-15
Enderby, 2932 J-11
Erickson, 520 L-14
Esquimalt, 16209 M-7
Falkland, 805 J-11
Fanny Bay, 815 K-6
Fernie, 4448 K-15
Ft. Nelson, 3902 *D-3
Ft. St. James, 1691 D-7
Fraser Lake, 1167 D-6
Fruitvale, 2016 L-13
Gibsons, 4437 K-7
Gold River, 1267 K-4
Golden, 3701 I-13
Grand Forks, 3985 L-12
Greenwood, 708 L-12
Grindrod, 1453 J-11
Hagensborg, 600 G-4
Harrison Hot Sprs., 1468 L-9
Heriot Bay, 527 J-5
Hope, 5969 K-9
Houston, 3147 D-4
Hudson's Hope, 970 A-9
Invermere, 2955 J-14
Kaleden, 1224 K-11
Kamloops, 85678 J-10
Kaslo, 1026 K-13
Kelowna, 117312 K-11
Keremeos, 1330 L-11
Kimberley, 6652 K-14
Kitimat, 8335 D-3
Ladysmith, 7921 L-7
L. Country, 11708 J-11
L. Cowichan, 2974 L-6
Langley, 25081 L-8
Lantzville, 764 L-6
Lillooet, 2322 I-8
Lions Bay, 1318 K-7
Logan Lake, 2073 J-10
Lower Nicola, 1068 J-10
Lumby, 1731 J-11
Mackenzie, 3507 B-8
Malakwa, 596 I-12
McBride, 586 F-10
Merritt, 7113 J-10
Midway, 674 L-12
Mission, 36426 L-8
Montrose, 1030 L-13
Mount Currie, 1306 J-8
Nakusp, 1569 J-12
Nanaimo, 83810 L-6
Naramata, 1647 K-11
Nelson, 10230 K-13
New Denver, 504 K-13
New Hazelton, 666 B-4
New Westminster, 65976 M-3
N. Vancouver, 48196 L-7
Oak Bay, 18015 M-7
Okanagan Falls, 1100 L-11
Oliver, 4824 L-11
Osoyoos, 4845 L-11
Parksville, 11977 K-6
Peachland, 5200 K-11
Pemberton, 2369 J-8
Penticton, 32877 K-11
Pitt Meadows, 17736 M-5
Port Alberni, 17743 L-6
Port Alice, 805 J-3
Port Coquitlam, 56342 L-4
Port Edward, 544 D-1
Port Hardy, 4008 I-3
Port McNeill, 2505 I-4
Port Moody, 32975 L-3
Pouce Coupe, 738 B-10
Powell River, 13165 K-6
Prince George, 71974 E-8
Prince Rupert, 12508 C-1
Princeton, 2724 K-10
Qualicum Bch., 8687 K-6
Quesnel, 10007 F-8
Radium Hot Sprs., 777 I-14
Revelstoke, 7139 I-12
Richmond, 190473 L-7
Rossland, 3556 L-13
Royston, 1562 K-6
Saanich, 109752 A-1
Salmo, 1139 L-13
Salmon Arm, 17464 J-11
Savona, 540 I-10
Sechelt, 9291 K-7
Sicamous, 2441 I-11
Sidney, 11178 L-7
Smithers, 5404 C-4
Sointula, 576 I-4
Sooke, 11435 M-7
Sorrento, 1255 I-11
Sparwood, 3667 K-15
Squamish, 17158 K-7
Summerland, 11280 K-11
Surrey, 468251 L-8
Telkwa, 1350 C-4
Terrace, 11486 C-3
Tofino, 1876 L-5
Trail, 7681 L-13
Tumbler Ridge, 2710 C-10
Ucluelet, 1627 L-5
Union Bay, 1156 K-6
Valemount, 1020 F-11
Vancouver, 603502 L-7
Vanderhoof, 4480 D-7
Vernon, 38150 J-11
Victoria, 80017 M-7
W. Vancouver, 42694 K-1
Westbank, 3359 K-11
Whistler, 9824 J-8
White Rock, 19339 L-8
Williams Lake, 10832 G-8
Windermere, 1019 J-14
Wynndel, 870 L-14
Youbou, 966 L-6

Manitoba

Map p. 121

* City keyed to p. 117

Altona, 4088 M-16
Arborg, 1152 J-17
Beausejour, 3126 K-17
Boissevain, 1572 M-13
Brandon, 46061 L-13
Carberry, 1669 L-14
Carman, 3027 L-16
Dauphin, 8251 I-13
Deloraine, 977 M-13
Flin Flon, 5363 C-11
Gilbert Plains, 811 I-13
Gillam, 1281 *F-7
Gimli, 1890 J-17
Gladstone, 879 K-15
Grandview, 859 I-13
Hamiota, 868 K-13
Headingley, 3215 C-16
Ile des Chenes, 1253 L-17
Killarney, 2197 M-14
La Broquerie, 1073 L-18
Lac du Bonnet, 1328 K-18
LaSalle, 1957 L-17
Lockport, 790 K-17
MacGregor, 963 L-15
Manitou, 808 M-15
Melita, 1069 M-12
Minnedosa, 2587 K-14
Morden, 7812 M-16
Morris, 1797 M-17
Neepawa, 3629 K-14
Niverville, 3540 L-17
Pinawa, 1444 K-18
Plum Coulee, 843 M-16
Portage la Prairie, 12996 K-15
Rivers, 1189 K-13
Roblin, 1774 I-12
Russell, 1669 J-12
St. Laurent, 1450 K-16
St. Malo, 1148 M-17
St-Pierre-Jolys, 1099 L-17
Ste. Anne, 1626 L-17
Ste. Rose du Lac, 1023 J-14
Sanford, 852 L-16
Selkirk, 9834 K-17
Snow Lake, 723 C-13
Souris, 1837 L-13
Steinbach, 13524 L-17
Stonewall, 4536 K-16
Stony Mountain, 1696 K-17
Swan River, 3907 H-12
Teulon, 1124 K-17
The Pas, 5513 E-12
Thompson, 12829 A-15
Tyndall, 830 K-17
Virden, 3114 L-12
Warren, 798 K-16
Winkler, 10670 M-16
Winnipeg, 663617 L-17
Winnipeg Bch., 1011 J-17

New Brunswick

Map pp. 126 – 127

Aldouane, 868 F-7
Atholville, 1237 C-4
Baie-Ste-Anne, 1387 E-7
Balmoral, 1719 C-5
Bas-Caraquet, 1380 D-7
Bathurst, 12275 D-6
Belledune, 1548 C-6
Beresford, 4351 D-6
Bertrand, 1137 D-7
Blacks Hbr., 982 J-4
Blackville, 990 F-6
Bouctouche, 2423 G-8
Brantville, 966 E-7
Burtts Corner, 910 H-4
Campbellton, 7385 C-4
Cap-Pelé, 2256 G-8
Caraquet, 4169 D-7
Charlo, 1324 C-5
Chipman, 1236 G-6
Clair, 857 E-1
Dalhousie, 3512 C-5
Dieppe, 23310 H-8
Doaktown, 793 F-5
Dorchester, 1167 H-8
Drummond, 775 E-3
Edmundston, 16032 D-2
Eel River Crossing, 1209 C-5
Florenceville, 860 G-3
Fredericton, 56224 H-4
Fredericton Jct., 752 I-4
Geary, 1080 H-5
Grand Bay-Westfield, 5117 I-5
Grand Falls (Grand-Sault), 5706 E-3
Grande-Digue, 2182 G-8
Hampton, 4292 I-6
Hardwicke, 2329 E-7
Hartland, 947 G-3
Havelock, 1158 H-7
Hillsborough, 1350 H-8
Kedgwick, 993 D-3
Keswick Ridge, 1526 H-4
Kingsclear, 7391 H-4
Lamèque, 1432 D-8
Lepreau, 752 J-4
Maugerville, 1776 H-5
McAdam, 1284 I-3
Memramcook, 4831 H-8
Minto, 2505 H-5
Miramichi, 17811 E-6
Moncton, 69074 H-7
Musquash, 1200 J-5
Nackawic, 1049 H-3
Nauwigewauk, 1539 I-6
Neguac, 1678 E-7
New Bandon, 1195 G-5
New Maryland, 4232 H-4
Nicholas Denys, 873 D-6
Nigadoo, 952 D-6
Norton, 1301 I-6
Notre-Dame, 790 G-8
Oromocto, 8932 H-5
Pennfield, 2218 J-4
Perth-Andover, 1778 F-3
Petit Rocher, 1908 D-6
Petitcodiac, 1429 H-7
Plaster Rock, 1135 F-3
Pointe-Verte, 976 C-6
Quispamsis, 17886 I-5
Rexton, 818 F-7
Richibucto, 1286 F-7
Riverview, 19128 H-7
Robertville, 895 D-6
Rogersville, 1170 F-6
Rothesay, 11947 I-5
Rusagonis, 990 H-4
Sackville, 5558 H-8
St. Andrews, 1889 J-4
St. George, 1543 J-4
Saint John, 70063 J-5
St. Stephen, 4817 J-3
St-Antoine, 1770 G-7
St-Charles, 1982 F-7
St-Jacques, 1599 D-2
St-Joseph, 2171 H-8
St-Louis de Kent, 930 F-7
St-Paul, 866 G-7
St-Quentin, 2095 D-3
Ste-Anne-de-Madawaska, 1002 E-2
Salisbury, 2208 H-7
Scoudoc, 996 H-8
Shediac, 6053 G-8
Shippagan, 5032 D-8
Springfield, 1652 I-6
Sussex, 4312 H-6
Sussex Corner, 1495 I-6
Tabusintac, 833 E-7
Tide Head, 1036 C-4
Tracadie-Sheila, 4933 D-7
Upham, 1306 I-6
Val-Comeau, 800 D-7
Wilsons Bch., 930 J-4
Woodstock, 5254 G-3

Newfoundland & Labrador

Map p. 127

Arnold's Cove, 990 E-19
Badger, 793 D-18
Baie Verte, 1370 C-18
Bay Roberts, 5818 E-20
Bishop's Falls, 3341 D-18
Bonavista, 3589 D-20
Botwood, 3008 D-18
Brigus, 750 F-20
Burgeo, 1464 F-17
Burin, 2424 F-18
Carbonear, 4739 E-20
Carmanville, 737 D-19
Catalina, 990 E-20
Centreville-Wareham-Trinity, 1161 D-19
Channel-Port aux Basques, 4170 F-16
Clarenville, 6036 E-19
Corner Brook, 19886 D-16
Deer Lake, 4995 D-17
Dunville, 2853 F-19
Fortune, 1442 F-18
Gambo, 1984 D-19
Gander, 11054 D-19
Glenwood, 791 D-18
Glovertown, 2122 D-19
Goulds, 4525 F-20
Grand Bank, 2415 F-18
Grand Falls-Windsor, 13725 D-18
Harbour Breton, 1711 F-18
Harbour Grace, 3131 E-20
Hare Bay, 1031 D-19
Holyrood, 1995 F-20
La Scie, 899 C-18
Lewisporte, 3483 D-18
Marystown, 5506 F-18
Mount Moriah, 785 D-16
Mount Pearl, 24284 F-20
Musgrave Hbr., 969 D-19
New-Wes-Valley, 2265 D-19
Pasadena, 3352 D-17
Peterview, 809 D-18
Placentia, 3643 F-19
Port au Choix, 839 B-17
Pouch Cove, 1866 E-20
Robert's Arm, 807 D-18
Rocky Hbr., 979 D-16
Roddickton, 910 B-18
St. Alban's, 1233 E-18
St. Anthony, 2418 B-18
St. George's, 1207 E-16
St. John's, 106172 F-20
St. Lawrence, 1244 F-18
Springdale, 2907 D-18
Stephenville, 6719 E-16
Stephenville Crossing, 1875 E-16
Torbay, 7397 E-20
Twillingate, 2269 C-19
Wabana, 2346 E-20
Whitbourne, 916 F-19
Witless Bay, 1179 F-20

Northwest Territories

Map p. 117

Ft. MacPherson, 792 B-3
Ft. Simpson, 1238 D-4
Ft. Smith, 2093 D-5
Hay River, 3606 D-4
Inuvik, 3463 A-3
Yellowknife, 19234 D-5

Nova Scotia

Map pp. 126 – 127

Amherst, 9717 H-8
Antigonish, 4524 I-12
Arcadia, 770 M-5
Argyle, 8252 M-5
Arichat, 890 I-14
Aylesford, 892 J-7
Baddeck, 769 H-14
Barrington, 6994 N-6
Bear River, 880 K-6
Berwick, 2454 J-7
Bridgetown, 949 K-7
Bridgewater, 8241 L-8
Brookfield, 529 J-10
Brooklyn, 970 M-8
Brooklyn, 970 J-9
Canning, 761 J-8
Canso, 806 I-14
Centreville, 1073 J-8
Chester, 10599 K-8
Chéticamp, 980 F-14
Clark's Harbour, 820 N-6
Digby, 2152 K-6
Donkin, 573 G-16
Fall River, 1887 K-9
Falmouth, 1213 J-8
Glace Bay, 19076 G-16
Halifax, 390096 K-9
Hantsport, 1159 J-8
Hebron, 720 M-5
Hilden, 1720 J-10
Ingonish, 610 F-15
Inverness, 1387 G-13
Kentville, 6094 J-8
Kingston-Greenwood, 6595 J-7
Lakeside, 520 K-9
Lawrencetown, 625 K-7
Liverpool, 2653 M-7
Lockeport, 588 M-7
Louisbourg, 946 H-16
Lower W. Pubnico, 850 N-6
Lunenburg, 2313 L-8
Mahone Bay, 943 L-8
Meteghan, 980 L-5
Meteghan River, 550 L-5
Middle Musquodoboit, 720 J-10
Middleton, 1749 J-7
Milford Sta., 510 J-10
Milton, 1091 M-7
Mulgrave, 794 I-13
Musquodoboit Hbr., 890 K-10
New Glasgow, 9562 I-11
New Waterford, 8942 G-15
Oxford, 1151 I-9
Parrsboro, 1305 I-8
Pictou, 3437 I-11
Pomquet, 510 I-12
Port Hawkesbury, 3366 I-13
Port Hood, 840 H-13
Port Maitland, 500 M-5
Port Morien, 580 G-16
Pugwash, 744 H-9
River Hebert, 545 I-8
St. Peters, 730 I-14
Saulnierville, 540 L-5
Sheet Hbr., 830 J-11
Shelburne, 1686 M-6
Shubenacadie, 780 J-10
Springhill, 3868 I-9
Stellarton, 4485 I-11
Stewiacke, 1438 J-10
Sydney, 97398 G-15
Sydney Mines, 14135 G-15
Tatamagouche, 752 I-10
Terence Bay, 780 L-9
Three Mile Plains, 1300 J-9
Trenton, 2616 I-11
Truro, 12059 I-10
Waterville, 931 J-8
Waverley, 806 K-9
Wedgeport, 1180 M-5
Western Shore, 890 K-8
Westville, 3798 I-11
Windsor, 3785 J-8
Wolfville, 4269 J-8
Yarmouth, 6761 M-5

Nunavut

Map p. 117

Arviat, 2318 E-7
Ikaluktutiak (Cambridge Bay), 1608 B-6
Iqaluit, 6699 C-10
Kangiqsiniq (Rankin Inlet), 2266 D-7
Mittimatalik (Pond Inlet), 1549 B-8
Qamani-tuaq (Baker Lake), 1872 D-7

Ontario

Map pp. 122 – 123

Ailsa Craig, 1070 K-6
Ajax, 109600 I-11
Alban, 919 C-8
Alexandria, 3209 E-19
Alfred, 1530 D-18
Alliston, 15379 H-9
Almonte, 4752 E-16
Alvinston, 1040 K-6
Amherstburg, 21556 M-3
Amherstview, 6100 H-15
Angus, 8603 H-9
Arkona, 579 K-6
Arnprior, 8114 E-16
Arthur, 2421 I-8
Athens, 3118 G-16
Atikokan, 2787 L-14
Atwood, 880 I-7
Aurora, 53203 I-10
Avonmore, 560 E-18
Aylmer, 7151 L-7
Ayr, 4380 J-8
Ayton, 600 H-7
Bancroft, 3880 F-13
Barrie, 135711 H-10
Barry's Bay, 1262 E-13
Bath, 1040 H-15
Bayfield, 1023 J-6
Beachville, 880 D-15
Beaverton, 2915 G-11
Belle River, 4890 M-4
Belleville, 49454 H-14
Belmont, 1849 K-7
Bethany, 600 H-12
Bewdley, 830 H-12
Blenheim, 4563 M-5
Blind River, 3549 C-4
Bloomfield, 597 I-14
Blyth, 1005 I-6
Bobcaygeon, 3533 G-12
Bolton, 25954 I-9
Bonfield, 2016 C-11
Bothwell, 912 L-6
Bourget, 1060 E-18
Bowmanville, 43555 I-11
Bracebridge, 15409 F-10
Bradford, 22378 H-10
Brampton, 523911 I-9
Brantford, 93650 K-9
Breslau, 2415 A-16
Bridgenorth, 2167 H-12
Brighton, 10928 H-13
Brockville, 21870 G-17
Bruce Mines, 566 C-2
Brussels, 1157 I-7
Burford, 1952 K-8
Burk's Falls, 967 D-10
Burlington, 175779 J-9
Cache Bay, 643 C-9
Caesarea, 785 H-11
Caledon, 59460 I-9
Caledonia, 9999 K-9
Callander, 3864 C-10
Cambridge, 126748 J-8
Campbellford, 3493 H-13
Cannington, 1916 H-11
Capreol, 3276 B-7
Cardinal, 1690 F-17
Carleton Place, 9809 F-16
Casselman, 3626 E-18
Cayuga, 1622 K-9
Chalk River, 954 C-14
Chapleau, 2116 M-18
Chatham, 44074 M-5
Chatsworth, 6437 G-7
Chesley, 2015 H-7
Chesterville, 1514 F-18
Clifford, 790 I-7
Clinton, 3114 I-6
Cobalt, 1133 M-20
Cobden, 990 D-15
Cobourg, 18519 I-12
Cochrane, 5340 L-20
Colborne, 2068 I-13
Colchester, 2145 N-4
Coldwater, 1250 G-10
Collingwood, 19241 G-9
Conestogo, 1316 J-8
Cookstown, 1328 H-10
Cornwall, 46340 F-18
Cottam, 720 M-4
Courtland, 920 K-8
Creemore, 1222 H-9
Crysler, 560 E-18
Crystal Bch., 7421 K-11
Deep River, 4193 C-13
Deseronto, 1835 H-14
Drayton, 1880 I-8
Dresden, 2446 L-5
Dryden, 7617 K-13
Dundalk, 1988 H-8
Dunnville, 5789 K-10
Durham, 2823 H-8
Dutton, 1442 L-6
Eganville, 1226 E-14
Elliot Lake, 11348 B-4
Elmira, 9931 J-8
Elmvale, 2369 G-9
Elora, 3800 I-8
Embrun, 6380 E-17
Emo, 1252 L-13
Englehart, 1519 M-20
Enniskillen, 2930 H-11
Erin, 10770 I-9
Espanola, 5364 C-6
Essex, 19600 M-4
Everett, 870 H-9
Exeter, 4785 J-6
Fenelon Falls, 2040 G-11
Fergus, 19126 I-8
Forest, 2876 K-5
Ft. Erie, 29960 K-11
Ft. Frances, 7952 L-13
Foxboro, 1150 H-14
Frankford, 2507 H-13
Fullarton, 1660 J-7
Gananoque, 5194 H-16
Georgetown, 40150 I-9
Geraldton, 1893 K-16
Glencoe, 2086 L-6
Goderich, 7521 I-6
Gooderham, 500 F-12
Gore Bay, 850 D-5
Grafton, 1130 I-13
Grand Bend, 2102 J-6
Grand Valley, 1481 I-8
Gravenhurst, 11640 F-10
Green-bank, 567 H-11
Grimsby, 25325 K-10
Guelph, 121688 J-9
Haileybury, 9988 M-20
Haliburton, 1430 F-12
Hamilton, 519949 J-9
Hampton, 763 I-11
Hanover, 7490 H-7
Harley, 539 K-8
Harriston, 1981 I-7
Harrow, 2713 M-4
Harrowsmith, 700 G-15
Hastings, 1139 H-13
Havelock, 1265 G-13
Hawkesbury, 10551 D-19
Hearst, 5090 K-18
Hensall, 1173 J-6
Hepworth, 530 G-7
Hillsburgh, 1065 I-9
Hornepayne, 1050 L-18
Huntsville, 19056 E-10
Ignace, 1202 L-14
Ilderton, 680 K-6
Ingersoll, 12146 K-7
Ingleside, 1890 F-18
Iron Bridge, 632 C-3
Iroquois, 1139 F-17
Iroquois Falls, 4595 L-20
Kanata, 101760 E-16
Kapuskasing, 8196 L-19
Kearney, 841 E-10
Keene, 550 H-12
Kemptville, 3532 F-17
Kenora, 15348 K-12
Killaloe, 629 E-14
Killarney, 505 D-6
Kincardine, 11174 H-6
Kingston, 123363 H-15
Kingsville, 21362 M-4
Kirkland Lake, 8133 M-20
Kitchener, 219153 J-8
Komoka, 1532 K-6
L'Orignal, 2068 D-18
Lakefield, 2758 G-12
Lanark, 696 F-16
Lancaster, 730 E-19
Lappe, 1360 L-15
Larder Lake, 684 M-20
Leamington, 28403 M-4
Limoges, 1240 E-18
Lindsay, 20354 H-11
Lion's Head, 514 F-7
Listowel, 6867 I-7
Little Current, 1523 D-6
London, 366151 K-7
Long Sault, 1230 F-18
Longlac, 1388 K-17
Lucan, 2076 K-6
Lucknow, 1105 I-6
MacTier, 630 F-9
Madoc, 2197 G-14
Magnetawan, 1454 D-10
Mallorytown, 510 G-16
Manitouwadge, 2105 L-17
Marathon, 3353 L-17
Markdale, 1325 H-8
Markham, 301709 I-10
Marmora, 1483 G-13
Martintown, 530 E-18
Massey, 1040 C-5
Matheson, 980 L-20
Mattawa, 2023 C-11
Mattice, 690 K-18
Maxville, 811 E-18
McKellar, 1144 E-9
Meaford, 11100 G-8
Merlin, 720 M-5
Merrickville, 1030 F-17
Metcalfe, 1763 E-17
Midland, 16572 G-9
Mildmay, 1183 H-7
Millbrook, 1632 H-12
Milton, 84362 J-9
Milverton, 1519 J-7
Minden, 1110 F-11
Mississauga, 713443 J-10
Mitchell, 4448 J-7
Monkton, 540 J-7
Moonbeam, 1101 L-19
Moose Creek, 890 E-18
Morrisburg, 2756 F-18
Mount Albert, 3915 H-10
Mount Brydges, 2332 K-6
Mount Forest, 4757 I-8
Napanee, 15511 H-15
Navan, 760 E-17
Neustadt, 533 H-7
New Dundee, 1219 J-8
New Hamburg, 11953 J-8
New Liskeard, 4910 M-20
Newmarket, 79978 H-10
Newtonville, 549 I-12
Niagara Falls, 82997 K-11
Niagara-on-the-Lake, 15400 J-11
Nipigon, 1631 L-16
Nobleton, 3582 I-10
N. Bay, 53651 C-10
N. Gower, 1250 F-17
Norwich, 10721 K-8
Norwood, 1254 H-13
Nottawa, 530 G-9
Oakville, 182520 J-10
Oakwood, 740 H-11
Odessa, 1160 H-15
Oil Sprs., 704 L-5
Omemee, 1247 H-12
Orangeville, 27975 I-9
Orillia, 30586 G-10
Oshawa, 149607 I-11
Ottawa, 883391 E-17
Otterville, 820 K-8
Owen Sound, 21688 G-7
Paisley, 1003 H-7
Palmerston, 2599 I-7
Paris, 11763 K-8
Parkhill, 1885 K-6
Parry Sound, 6191 E-9
Pembroke, 14360 D-14
Penetanguishene, 9111 G-9
Perth, 5840 F-16
Petawawa, 15988 D-14
Peterborough, 78698 H-12
Petrolia, 5528 K-5
Pickering, 88721 I-11
Picton, 4487 H-14
Plantagenet, 1055 D-18
Port Burwell, 860 L-8
Port Colborne, 18424 K-10
Port Elgin, 7555 G-7
Port Hope, 16214 I-12
Port Lambton, 1350 L-4
Port McNicoll, 1790 G-9
Port Perry, 8981 H-11
Port Rowan, 850 L-8
Port Stanley, 2229 L-7
Powassan, 3378 C-10
Prescott, 4284 G-17
Queensville, 640 H-10
Rainy River, 842 L-12
Red Rock, 942 L-16
Renfrew, 8218 E-15
Richmond, 3797 E-16
Richmond Hill, 185541 I-10
Ridgetown, 3117 L-5
Ripley, 640 H-6
Rockland, 11099 E-17
Rockwood, 3869 J-9
Rodney, 1023 L-6
Russell, 15247 E-17
St. Catharines, 131400 K-10
St. Clements, 1261 J-8
St. George, 3124 J-9
St. Isidore, 752 E-18
St. Jacobs, 1891 J-8
St. Joseph, 1201 J-6
St. Marys, 6655 J-7
St. Thomas, 37905 L-7
Sarnia, 72366 K-5
Sault Ste. Marie, 75141 B-1
Schomberg, 590 I-10
Schreiber, 1126 L-16
Scotland, 600 K-8
Seaforth, 2627 J-6
Sebringville, 690 J-7
Seeleys Bay, 550 G-16
Sharbot Lake, 530 G-15
Shelburne, 5846 H-9
Simcoe, 14777 K-8
Smiths Falls, 8978 F-16
Smooth Rock Falls, 1376 L-19
Sombra, 710 L-4
S. River, 1049 D-10
Southampton, 3440 G-7
Spanish, 696 C-5
Spencerville, 550 F-17
Springfield, 763 K-7
Stayner, 4126 G-9
Stoney Pt., 1424 M-4
Stouffville, 24886 I-10
Straffordville, 910 L-8
Stratford, 30886 J-7
Strathroy, 14221 K-6
Sturgeon Falls, 6672 C-9
Sudbury, 160274 B-7
Sunderland, 1110 H-11
Sundridge, 985 D-10
Sutton, 5938 H-10
Sydenham, 900 G-15
Tamworth, 730 G-14
Tara, 1037 G-7
Tavistock, 2784 J-7
Tecumseh, 23610 M-4
Teeswater, 1011 I-7
Temagami, 820 M-20
Terrace Bay, 1471 L-16
Thamesford, 1990 K-7
Thamesville, 928 L-5
Thedford, 804 K-6
Thessalon, 1279 C-3
Thornbury, 2253 G-8
Thornton, 1001 H-10
Thorold, 17931 K-11
Thunder Bay, 108359 L-15
Tilbury, 4700 M-4
Tillsonburg, 15301 K-8
Timmins, 43165 L-19
Tiverton, 705 H-6
Toronto, 2615060 I-10
Trenton, 19370 H-13
Trout Creek, 552 D-10
Tweed, 6057 G-14
Uxbridge, 20623 H-11
Vankleek Hill, 1833 D-19
Vaughan, 288301 E-2
Vermilion Bay, 560 K-13
Verner, 1080 B-9
Verona, 1120 G-15
Victoria Hbr., 1550 G-9
Vienna, 733 L-8
Virginiatown, 780 M-20
Wainfleet, 6356 K-10
Walkerton, 4967 H-7
Wallaceburg, 10163 L-5
Warkworth, 640 H-13
Warwick, 3717 K-5
Wasaga Bch., 17537 G-9
Waterloo, 98780 J-8
Watford, 1592 K-6
Wawa, 2975 M-18
Welland, 50631 K-10
Wellesley, 10713 J-8
Wellington, 1860 I-14
W. Lorne, 1415 L-6
Westport, 628 G-16
Wheatley, 2925 M-4
Whitby, 122022 I-11
White River, 607 L-17
Whitestone, 918 D-9
Whitney, 770 E-12
Wiarton, 2291 G-7
Williamsburg, 550 F-18
Winchester, 2482 F-17
Windsor, 210891 M-3
Wingham, 2875 I-7
Woodstock, 37754 K-8
Woodville, 857 H-11
Wyoming, 2333 K-5
Yarker, 580 H-15
Zurich, 865 J-6

Prince Edward Island

Map pp. 126 – 127

Alberton, 1135 F-9
Borden-Carleton, 750 G-9
Charlottetown, 34562 G-10
Cornwall, 5162 G-10
Georgetown, 675 G-11
Kensington, 1496 G-9
Miscouche, 869 G-9
Montague, 1895 G-11
N. Rustico, 583 G-10
O'Leary, 812 F-8
Souris, 1173 G-12
Stratford, 8574 G-10
Summerside, 14751 G-9
Tignish, 779 F-9

Québec

Map pp. 124 – 125

* City keyed to p. 117

Acton Vale, 7664 L-9
Albanel, 2293 F-10
Alma, 30904 G-11
Amos, 12671 F-2
Amqui, 6322 G-16
Arundel, 604 L-7
Asbestos, 7096 L-10
Audet, 724 L-12
Aumond, 725 K-5
Baie-Comeau, 22113 F-15
Baie-des-Sables, 609 G-16
Baie-St-Paul, 7332 I-12
Barraute, 1980 G-3
Beauceville, 6354 K-12
Beaumont, 2420 J-12
Beaupré, 3439 J-12
Bécancour, 12438 K-10
Bedford, 2684 M-9
Bégin, 868 G-11
Berry, 625 F-2
Blainville, 53510 L-8
Blue Sea, 674 K-5
Bois-des-Filion, 9485 B-11
Bonaventure, 2775 H-19
Boucherville, 40753 C-14
Bromont, 7649 M-9
Brossard, 79273 E-14
Bryson, 647 L-4
Cacouna, 1939 H-13
Calumet, 551 L-7
Campbell's Bay, 775 L-4
Candiac, 19876 F-13
Cap-Chat, 2623 F-17
Caplan, 2039 H-18
Carignan, 7966 I-9
Carleton-sur-Mer, 3991 H-18
Cascapédia-St-Jules, 741 G-18
Causapscal, 2458 G-16
Chambord, 1773 G-10
Chandler, 7703 G-20
Chapais, 1610 D-7
Charlemagne, 5853 A-14
Chénéville, 792 L-6
Chibougamau, 7541 D-7
Chisasibi, 2659 *F-9
Chute-aux-Outardes, 1644 F-15
Chute-St-Philippe, 892 J-6
Châteauguay, 45904 M-8
Clermont, 3118 F-1
Cloridorme, 743 F-19
Coaticook, 9255 M-10
Colombier, 747 F-14
Contrecoeur, 6252 L-9
Cookshire-Eaton, 5171 M-11
Cowansville, 12489 M-9
Dégelis, 3051 I-15
Desbiens, 1053 G-10
Disraeli, 2502 L-11
Dolbeau-Mistassini, 14384 F-10
Donnacona, 6283 J-11
Dorval, 18208 E-11
Dosquet, 887 K-11
Drummondville, 71852 L-10
Dudswell, 1771 M-11
Dunham, 3471 M-9
Duparquet, 657 F-1
Dupuy, 930 F-1
E. Angus, 3741 M-11
E. Broughton, 2229 K-11
Escuminac, 588 H-17
Ferme-Neuve, 2822 J-6
Fermont, 2874 *F-11
Forestville, 3270 F-14
Fort-Coulonge, 1377 L-4
Frelighsburg, 1094 N-9
Gaspé, 15163 F-20
Gatineau, 265349 M-5
Gesgapegiag, 688 G-18
Girardville, 1100 F-10
Gracefield, 2355 K-5
Granby, 63433 M-9
Grand-Remous, 1168 J-5
Grande-Rivière, 3456 G-20
Grande-Vallée, 1137 E-19
Grenville-sur-la-Rouge, 2746 L-7
Ham-Nord, 832 L-11
Hampstead, 7153 E-12
Havre-St-Pierre, 3418 *F-12
Hébertville, 2441 G-11
Huntingdon, 2457 M-7
Joliette, 19621 L-8
Kamouraska, 589 I-13
Kazabazua, 847 L-5
Kiamika, 772 K-6
L'Ancienne-Lorette, 16745 B-4
L'Anse-St-Jean, 1208 G-13
L'Ascension, 844 K-6
L'Ascension-de-Notre-Seigneur, 1983 G-11
L'Isle-Verte, 1469 H-14
L'Islet, 3999 J-12
La Conception, 1287 K-7
La Doré, 1453 G-9
La Guadeloupe, 1787 L-12
La Macaza, 1053 K-7
La Malbaie, 8862 I-13
La Patrie, 749 M-11
La Pocatière, 4266 I-13
La Prairie, 23357 F-14
La Sarre, 7719 F-1
La Tuque, 11227 I-9
Labelle, 2445 K-7
Lac-au-Saumon, 1453 G-16
Lac-aux-Sables, 1373 J-10
Lac-Bouchette, 1174 G-10
Lac-Brome, 5609 M-9
Lac-des-Écorces, 2713 K-6
Lac-des-Aigles, 551 H-15
Lac-Mégantic, 5932 M-12
Lachute, 12551 L-7
Lamarche, 557 F-11
Lambton, 1584 L-11
Larouche, 1277 G-11
Laval, 401553 D-11
Le Bic, 1286 G-14
Lebel-sur-Quévillon, 2159 F-4
Les Éboulements, 1328 I-12
Les Escoumins, 2000 G-14
Les Méchins, 1107 F-17
Lévis, 138769 J-11
Longueuil, 231409 D-14
Lorrainville, 1272 I-1
Louiseville, 7517 K-9
Low, 920 L-5
Luceville, 1362 G-15
Lyster, 1628 K-11
Macamic, 2734 F-1
Magog, 25358 M-10
Malartic, 3449 G-2
Maliotenam, 1316 D-18
Maniwaki, 3930 K-5
Maria, 2536 G-18
Mascouche, 42491 A-12
Matagami, 1526 D-3
Matane, 14462 F-16
Matapédia, 664 H-17
Messines, 1608 K-5
Métabetchouan-Lac-à-la-Croix, 4097 G-10
Moisie, 930 D-18
Mont-Joli, 6665 G-15
Mont-Laurier, 13779 K-6
Mont-Royal, 19503 D-12
Mont-St-Michel, 633 J-6
Mont-Tremblant, 9494 K-7
Montebello, 978 L-6
Montmagny, 11491 J-12
Montréal, 1649519 M-8
Montréal-Ouest, 5085 E-12
Morin-Heights, 3925 L-7
Murdochville, 764 F-19
Namur, 596 L-6
Nantes, 1374 L-11
New Carlisle, 1358 H-19
New Richmond, 3810 G-18
Nicolet, 7828 K-9
Nominingue, 2019 K-6
Normandin, 3137 F-10
Normétal, 856 E-1
Notre-Dame-de-la-Merci, 978 K-7
Notre-Dame-de-la-Paix, 718 L-6
Notre-Dame-de-la-Salette, 757 L-5
Notre-Dame-du-Laus, 1518 K-5
Notre-Dame-du-Nord, 1075 H-1
Nouvelle, 1689 H-18
Ormstown, 3595 M-7
Otter Lake, 1109 L-4
Packington, 595 I-14
Palmarolle, 1465 F-1
Papineauville, 2165 L-6
Paspébiac, 3198 H-19
Percé, 3312 G-20
Petit-Saguenay, 727 H-13
Pierreville, 2176 L-9
Plaisance, 1103 L-6
Plessisville, 6688 K-10
Pohénégamook, 2770 I-14
Pointe-aux-Outardes, 1330 F-15
Pointe-Lebel, 1973 F-15
Pointe-à-la-Croix, 1472 H-17
Port-Cartier, 6651 D-17
Port-Daniel-Gascons, 2453 G-19
Portneuf, 3107 J-10
Portneuf-sur-Mer, 761 G-14
Price, 1673 G-15
Princeville, 5693 K-10
Québec, 516622 J-11
Quyon, 790 L-4
Racine, 1252 M-10
Ragueneau, 1405 F-15
Repentigny, 82000 A-14
Richmond, 3275 L-10
Rimouski, 46860 G-15
Ripon, 1522 L-6
Rivière-Beaudette, 1885 M-7
Rivière-Bleue, 1299 I-14
Rivière-du-Loup, 19447 H-13
Rivière-Héva, 1433 G-2
Rivière-Ouelle, 1058 I-13
Rivière-Pentecôte, 620 D-16
Rivière-Rouge, 4645 K-6
Rivière-à-Pierre, 671 J-10
Roberval, 10227 G-10
Rock Island, 901 N-10
Rouyn-Noranda, 41012 G-1
Sacré-Coeur, 1881 H-13
Saguenay, 144746 G-11
St-Aimé-des-Lacs, 1073 I-12
St-Alexandre-de-Kamouraska, 2050 I-13
St-Alexis-de-Matapédia, 548 H-17
St-Alexis-des-Monts, 3046 K-9
St-Alphonse-Rodriguez, 3134 K-8
St-Ambroise, 3546 G-11
St-André, 651 I-13
St-Anselme, 3458 K-12
St-Antonin, 4027 H-14
St-Arsène, 1253 H-14
St-Aubert, 1409 J-13
St-Bruno, 2636 G-11
St-Côme, 2198 K-8
St-Côme-Linière, 3274 L-12
St-Camille-de-Lellis, 844 K-13
St-Casimir, 1500 J-10
St-Charles-de-Bourget, 690 G-11
St-Clet, 1738 M-7
St-Cyprien, 1163 H-14
St-Cyprien, 548 K-13
St-Cyrille-de-Lessard, 753 J-12
St-Damase-de-L'Islet, 591 I-13
St-Damien, 2020 K-8
St-Damien-de-Buckland, 2071 K-12
St-David, 832 L-9
St-David-de-Falardeau, 2657 G-11
St-Donat, 4130 K-7
St-Donat, 890 G-15
St-Eustache, 44154 M-8
St-Eusèbe, 614 I-14
St-Fabien, 1906 G-14
St-Fabien-de-Panet, 992 K-13
St-Faustin-Lac-Carré, 3467 K-7
St-Félicien, 10278 G-10
St-Félix-d'Otis, 801 G-12
St-Ferdinand, 2067 L-11
St-Ferréol-les-Neiges, 2964 J-12
St-Fidèle, 920 H-13
St-François-d'Assise, 706 H-17
St-François-de-Sales, 654 G-10
St-Frédéric, 1085 K-12
St-Gabriel, 2844 K-8
St-Gabriel, 1180 G-15
St-Gabriel-de-Valcartier, 2933 J-11
St-Gédéon, 2001 G-11
St-Gédéon-de-Beauce, 2277 L-12
St-Georges, 31173 L-12
St-Gervais, 2058 J-12
St-Hilarion, 1181 I-12
St-Honoré, 5257 G-11
St-Honoré-de-Témiscouata, 780 I-14
St-Hyacinthe, 53236 L-9
St-Irénée, 674 I-13
St-Jacques, 4021 L-8
St-Jean-de-Dieu, 1606 H-14
St-Jean-Port-Joli, 3304 I-13
St-Jean-sur-Richelieu, 92394 M-8
St-Jérôme, 68456 L-7
St-Joseph-de-Beauce, 4722 K-12
St-Jovite, 4869 K-7
St-Just-de-Bretenières, 709 K-13
St-Lambert, 21555 E-1
St-Lambert-de-Lauzon, 6177 K-11
St-Léon-le-Grand, 992 G-16
St-Louis-de-Gonzague, 1389 K-12
St-Louis-du-Ha! Ha!, 1318 I-14
St-Ludger, 1255 L-12
St-Marc-de-Figuery, 771 G-3
St-Martin, 2462 L-12
St-Mathieu-de-Rioux, 678 H-14
St-Michel-des-Saints, 2201 J-8
St-Michel-du-Squatec, 1171 H-15
St-Modeste, 1128 H-14
St-Narcisse-de-Rimouski, 1017 G-15
St-Nazaire, 2114 G-11
St-Onésime-d'Ixworth, 559 I-13
St-Pacôme, 1658 I-13
St-Pamphile, 2685 J-13
St-Pascal, 3490 I-13
St-Paul-de-Montminy, 824 J-12
St-Paul-du-Nord, 710 G-14
St-Philémon, 742 J-12
St-Prime, 2758 G-10
St-Prosper, 3605 K-12
St-Raphaël, 2463 J-12
St-Raymond, 9615 J-10
St-Rémi, 7265 M-8
St-René-de-Matane, 1089 G-16
St-Robert-Bellarmin, 676 L-12
St-Roch-des-Aulnaies, 967 I-13
St-Sébastien, 697 L-12
St-Siméon, 1300 H-19
St-Siméon, 1179 H-13
St-Thomas-Didyme, 677 F-9
St-Tite, 3880 J-9
St-Tite-des-Caps, 1506 J-12
St-Ulric, 1642 F-16
St-Urbain, 1474 I-12
St-Valérien, 893 G-15
St-Vallier, 1046 J-12
St-Victor, 2451 K-12
St-Zénon, 1115 K-8
Ste-Agathe-des-Monts, 10115 L-7
Ste-Angèle-de-Mérici, 999 G-15
Ste-Anne-de-Beaupré, 2854 J-12
Ste-Anne-des-Monts, 6933 F-17
Ste-Anne-du-Lac, 619 J-6
Ste-Aurélie, 910 K-12
Ste-Barbe, 1403 M-7
Ste-Catherine, 16762 F-13
Ste-Croix, 2352 K-11
Ste-Émélie-de-l'Énergie, 1644 K-8
Ste-Félicité, 1175 F-16
Ste-Flavie, 919 G-15
Ste-Hedwidge, 824 G-10
Ste-Hélène, 911 I-13
Ste-Jeanne-d'Arc, 1089 F-10
Ste-Justine, 1845 K-12
Ste-Louise, 704 I-13
Ste-Luce, 2851 G-15
Ste-Marie, 12889 K-11
Ste-Monique, 865 F-10
Ste-Perpétue, 1774 J-13
Ste-Pétronille, 1041 B-6
Ste-Rose-de-Watford, 787 K-12
Ste-Sabine, 1120 K-12
Ste-Sophie, 13375 L-8
Salaberry-de-Valleyfield, 40077 M-7
Sawyerville, 805 M-11
Sayabec, 1864 G-16
Senneterre, 2953 G-4
Sept-Îles, 25686 D-17
Shannon, 5086 J-11
Shawinigan, 50060 K-9
Shawville, 1664 L-4
Sherbrooke, 154601 M-10
Sorel-Tracy, 34600 L-9
Stanstead, 2857 N-10
Stornoway, 559 L-11
Stratford, 1062 L-11
Tadoussac, 813 H-13
Taschereau, 981 F-2
Témiscaming, 2385 J-1
Témiscouata-sur-le-Lac, 5096 I-14
Terrebonne, 106322 B-12
Thetford Mines, 25709 L-11
Thurso, 2455 L-6
Trois-Pistoles, 3456 H-14
Trois-Rivières, 131338 K-9
Val-Barrette, 588 K-6
Val-d'Or, 31862 G-3
Val-des-Bois, 938 L-5
Vallée-Jonction, 1940 K-12
Varennes, 20994 L-8
Victoriaville, 43462 L-10
Ville-Marie, 2595 I-1
Wakefield, 610 L-5
Warwick, 4766 L-10
Waskaganish, 1955 *G-10
Waswanipi, 1777 D-5
Waterloo, 4330 M-9
Weedon, 2683 L-11
Wemindji, 1378 *G-9
Westmount, 19931 E-12
Windsor, 5367 M-10
Wotton, 1453 L-10

Saskatchewan

Map pp. 120 – 121

* City keyed to p. 117

Assiniboia, 2418 L-6
Balgonie, 1625 K-8
Battleford, 4065 F-4
Beauval, 756 B-5
Bienfait, 780 M-10
Biggar, 2161 H-4
Birch Hills, 1064 F-7
Buffalo Narrows, 1153 *F-5
Candle Lake, 765 E-8
Canora, 2219 I-11
Carlyle, 1441 L-11
Carnduff, 1126 M-11
Caronport, 1068 K-7
Carrot River, 1000 F-9
Creighton, 1498 C-11
Cudworth, 770 G-7
Cumberland House, 772 D-11
Dalmeny, 1702 G-6
Davidson, 1025 I-7
Delisle, 975 H-5
Deschambault Lake, 900 C-10
Esterhazy, 2472 J-11
Estevan, 11054 M-10
Eston, 1031 I-3
Foam Lake, 1148 I-9
Ft. Qu'Appelle, 2034 J-9
Gravelbourg, 1116 L-6
Grenfell, 1049 K-10
Gull Lake, 989 K-3
Hague, 878 G-6
Herbert, 759 K-5
Hudson Bay, 1477 F-11
Humboldt, 5678 G-8
Indian Head, 1815 K-9
Kamsack, 1825 I-11
Kelvington, 864 H-9
Kerrobert, 1061 H-3
Kindersley, 4678 H-3
Kipling, 1051 K-10
La Loche, 2611 *F-5
La Ronge, 2304 B-8
Langenburg, 1148 J-11
Langham, 1290 G-6
Lanigan, 1390 H-8
Lashburn, 967 E-3
Leader, 821 I-2
Lloydminster, 9772 E-2
Lumsden, 1631 J-8
Macklin, 1415 G-2
Maidstone, 1156 F-3
Maple Creek, 2176 K-2
Martensville, 7716 G-6
Meadow Lake, 5045 D-4
Melfort, 5576 F-8
Melville, 4517 J-10
Moose Jaw, 33274 K-7
Moosomin, 2485 K-11
Nipawin, 4265 E-9
N. Battleford, 13888 F-4
Osler, 1088 G-6
Outlook, 2204 I-5
Oxbow, 1285 M-11
Pelican Narrows, 790 B-10
Pilot Butte, 1848 K-8
Porcupine Plain, 855 G-10
Preeceville, 1070 H-10
Prince Albert, 35129 F-7
Radville, 860 L-8
Redvers, 975 L-11
Regina, 193100 K-8
Regina Bch., 1081 J-8
Rocanville, 857 K-11
Rosetown, 2317 H-4
Rosthern, 1572 G-6
Sandy Bay, 1233 A-11
Saskatoon, 222189 G-6
Shaunavon, 1756 L-4
Shellbrook, 1433 E-6
Southey, 778 J-8
Spiritwood, 916 E-5
Swift Current, 15503 K-4
Tisdale, 3180 F-9
Unity, 2389 G-3
Wadena, 1306 H-9
Wakaw, 985 G-7
Waldheim, 1035 G-6
Warman, 7084 G-6
Watrous, 1857 H-7
Watson, 777 H-8
Weyburn, 10484 L-9
White City, 1894 K-8
Whitewood, 950 K-11
Wilkie, 1301 G-4
Wolseley, 864 K-10
Wynyard, 1767 H-9
Yorkton, 15669 I-11

Yukon

Map p. 117

Carmacks, 503 C-2
Dawson, 1319 B-2
Haines Jct., 593 C-2
Watson Lake, 802 C-3
Whitehorse, 23272 C-2

Mexico Cities and Towns (map p. 128)

Populations are from 2010 Mexican Census or are Rand McNally estimates

Aguascalientes

Aguascalientes, 722250 F-7
Rincón de Romos, 27988 F-7

Baja California

Ensenada, 279765 A-1
Lázaro Cárdenas, 16294 B-1
Mexicali, 689775 A-2
Rosarito, 65278 C-2
San Felipe, 16702 A-2
Tecate, 64764 A-1
Tijuana, 1300983 A-1

Baja California Sur

Cabo San Lucas, 68463 E-3
Guerrero Negro, 13054 C-2
La Paz, 215178 E-3
San Jose del Cabo, 69788 E-4

Campeche

Campeche, 220389 G-12
Champotón, 30881 G-12
Ciudad del Carmen, 169466 H-12
Escárcega, 29477 G-12

Chiapas

Chiapa de Corzo, 45077 H-11
Cintalapa, 42467 H-11
Comitán de Domínguez, 97537 I-12
Huixtla, 32033 I-11
Ocosingo, 41878 H-12
Palenque, 42947 H-12
San Cristóbal de las Casas, 158027 H-11
Tapachula, 202672 I-11
Tonalá, 35322 I-11
Villaflores, 39180 I-11
Tuxtla Gutiérrez, 537102 H-11

Chihuahua

Chihuahua, 809232 C-5
Ciudad Juárez, 1321004 A-5
Cuauhtémoc, 114007 C-5
Delicias, 118071 C-6
Hidalgo del Parral, 104836 D-5
Jiménez, 34281 D-6
Madera, 15447 C-4
Nuevo Casas Grandes, 55553 B-5
Ojinaga, 22744 B-6
Santa Rosalía de Camargo, 40221 C-6

Coahuila

Ciudad Acuña, 134233 C-7
Matamoros, 52233 D-6
Melchor Múzquiz, 35060 C-7
Monclova, 215271 D-7
Nueva Rosita, 38158 C-7
Piedras Negras, 150178 C-8
Sabinas, 54905 C-7
Saltillo, 709671 D-7
San Pedro, 48746 D-7
Torreón, 608836 D-6

Colima

Colima, 137383 G-6
Manzanillo, 130035 G-6
Tecomán, 85689 H-6
Villa de Álvarez, 117600 G-6

Distrito Federal

Ciudad de México (Mexico City), 8851080 G-8
Mexico City, 8851080 G-8

Durango

Ciudad Lerdo, 79669 D-6
Durango, 518709 E-6
El Salto, 24241 E-6
Gómez Palacio, 257352 D-6
Santiago Papasquiaro, 26121 E-6

Guanajuato

Acámbaro, 57972 G-8
Celaya, 340387 G-8
Dolores Hidalgo, 59240 F-7
Guanajuato, 72237 F-7
Irapuato, 380941 G-7
León, 1238962 F-7
Moroleón, 43200 G-7
Pénjamo, 40070 G-7
Salamanca, 160169 G-7
Salvatierra, 37203 G-7
San Felipe, 28452 F-7
Silao, 74242 G-7

Guerrero

Acapulco, 673479 H-8
Chilapa de Álvarez, 31157 H-8
Chilpancingo,187251 H-8
Ciudad Altamirano, 25168 H-8
Iguala, 118468 H-8
Ometepec, 24120 I-9
Petatlán, 21659 H-7
Taxco, 52217 H-8
Tlapa de Comonfort, 46975 H-9
Zihuatanejo, 67408 H-7

Hidalgo

Apan, 26642 G-9
Ixmiquilpan, 34814 G-8
Pachuca, 256584 G-8
Tulancingo, 102406 G-9
Zacualtipán, 23125 G-8

Jalisco

Ameca, 36150 G-6
Arandas, 52175 G-7
Autlán, 45382 G-6
Cihuatlán, 18164 G-6
Ciudad Guzmán, 97750 G-6
Guadalajara, 1495182 G-6
Lagos de Moreno, 98206 F-7
Ocotlán, 83769 G-7
Puerto Vallarta, 203342 G-6
Sayula, 26789 G-6
Tecalitlán, 12411 G-6
Teocaltiche, 23726 F-7
Tepatitlán, 91959 G-7
Tequila, 29203 G-6
Zapopan, 1142483 G-6

México

Amecameca, 31687 G-8
Buenavista, 206081 F-2
Chalco, 168720 I-4
Chimalhuacán, 612383 G-4
Ciudad López Mateos, 489160 F-1
Ciudad Nezahualcóyotl, 1024585 G-3
Coacalco, 277959 F-2
Ecatepec de Morelos, 1655015 F-3
Ixtapaluca, 322271 H-4
Los Reyes Acaquilpan, 85359 H-4
Naucalpan, 792211 G-1
Tepexpan, 102667 F-4
Texcoco, 105165 G-4
Tlalnepantla, 653410 F-2
Toluca, 489333 G-8
Xico, 356352 I-4

Michoacán

Apatzingán de la Constitución, 99010 G-7
Ciudad Hidalgo, 60542 G-8
Ciudad Lázaro Cárdenas, 79200 H-7
La Piedad de Cabadas, 83323 G-7
Los Reyes de Salgado, 39209 G-7
Morelia, 597511 G-7
Pátzcuaro, 52298 G-7
Sahuayo, 64431 G-7
Tacámbaro, 25665 G-7
Uruapan, 264439 G-7
Zacapu, 52806 G-7
Zamora, 141627 G-7
Zitácuaro, 84307 G-8

Morelos

Cuautla, 154358 H-8
Cuernavaca, 338650 G-8

Nayarit

Acaponeta, 19140 F-5
Compostela, 17573 F-6
Ixtlán del Río, 23303 F-6
Tepic, 332863 F-6
Tuxpan, 21709 F-5

Nuevo León

Allende, 26065 D-8
Anáhuac, 16628 D-8
Cadereyta Jiménez, 68111 D-8
Cerralvo, 7169 D-8
China, 8997 D-8
Guadalupe, 673616 D-8
Linares, 63104 E-8
Montemorelos, 45108 D-8
Monterrey, 1135512 D-8
Sabinas Hidalgo, 33068 D-8
Santiago, 36840 D-8

Oaxaca

Huajuapan de León, 53043 H-9
Juchitán de Zaragoza, 74825 I-10
Matías Romero, 18944 H-10
Miahuatlán de Porfirio Diaz, 23940 I-9
Oaxaca, 255029 H-9
Puerto Escondido, 25902 I-9
Salina Cruz, 76596 I-10
San Pedro Pochutla, 13685 I-10
Santiago Pinotepa Nacional, 29604 I-9
Santo Domingo Tehuantepec, 42082 I-10
Tlaxiaco, 17543 H-9
Tuxtepec, 101810 H-10

Puebla

Acatlán de Osorio, 16307 H-9
Atlixco, 86690 G-9
Cholula, 127861 G-9
Huauchinango, 56206 G-9
Izúcar de Matamoros, 43006 H-9
Puebla, 1434062 G-9
Tehuacán, 248716 H-9
Tepeaca, 27449 G-9
Teziutlán, 58699 G-9
Xicotepec, 39803 G-9

Querétaro

Jalpan, 11010 F-8
Querétaro, 626495 G-8
San Juan del Río, 138878 G-8
Tequisquiapan, 29799 G-8

Quintana Roo

Cancún, 628306 F-14
Chetumal, 151243 G-13
Cozumel, 77236 F-14
Felipe Carrillo Puerto, 25744 G-13
Playa del Carmen, 149923 F-14
Tulum, 18233 G-14

San Luis Potosí

Cárdenas, 15469 F-8
Cerritos, 14804 F-8
Ciudad Valles, 124644 F-8
Ébano, 24296 F-9
Matehuala, 77328 E-8
Rioverde, 53128 F-8
San Luis Potosí, 722772 F-7
Tamazunchale, 24562 F-8

Sinaloa

Culiacán, 675773 E-5
El Rosario, 16001 F-5
El Dorado, 13197 E-5
Escuinapa, 30790 F-5
Guamúchil, 63743 D-4
Guasave, 71196 D-4
Los Mochis, 256613 D-4
Mazatlán, 381583 E-5
Navolato, 29153 E-4

Sonora

Agua Prieta, 77254 A-4
Caborca, 59922 B-3
Cananea, 31560 B-4
Ciudad Obregón, 298625 C-4
Empalme, 42516 C-3
Guaymas, 113082 C-3
Hermosillo, 715061 B-3
Navojoa, 113836 C-4
Nogales, 212513 A-3
Puerto Peñasco, 56756 A-2
San Luis Río Colorado, 158089 A-2

Tabasco

Cárdenas, 91558 H-11
Comalcalco, 41458 H-11
Huimanguillo,27344 H-11
Macuspana, 32225 H-11
Paraíso, 25186 H-11
Tenosique, 32579 H-12
Villahermosa, 353577 H-11

Tamaulipas

Ciudad Madero, 197216 F-9
Ciudad Mante, 84787 F-8
Ciudad Victoria, 305155 E-8
Matamoros, 449815 D-9
Nuevo Laredo, 373725 C-8
Reynosa, 589466 D-9
Río Bravo, 95647 D-9
San Fernando, 29665 E-9
Tampico, 297284 F-9
Valle Hermoso, 48918 D-9

Tlaxcala

Tlaxcala, 14689 G-9

Veracruz

Acayucan, 50934 H-10
Alvarado, 23128 G-10
Coatzacoalcos, 235938 H-10
Córdoba, 140896 G-9
Cosamaloapan, 30577 H-10
Martínez de la Torre, 60074 G-9
Minatitlán, 112046 H-10
Orizaba, 120844 G-9
Papantla, 53546 G-9
Poza Rica, 1852242 G-9
San Andrés Tuxtla, 61769 H-10
Tuxpan, 84750 F-9
Veracruz, 428323 G-10
Xalapa, 424755 G-9

Yucatán

Mérida, 777615 F-12
Motul, 23240 F-12
Progreso, 37369 F-12
Ticul, 32796 G-13
Tizimín, 46971 F-13
Valladolid, 48973 F-13

Zacatecas

Fresnillo, 120944 E-7
Guadalupe, 124623 F-7
Jerez de García Salinas, 43064 F-7
Río Grande, 32944 E-7
Zacatecas, 129011 F-7

*, †, ‡, § See explanation under state title in this index. County and parish names are listed in capital letters and in boldface type. Independent cities (not in any county) are shown in italics.

Motor Carriers' Mileage Directory

More than 40,000 Mileages Between Selected Cities

Mileages in this directory are from the Rand McNally MileMaker® Practical Routing System (© Rand McNally). This software alculates mileages over national Interstate, U.S., and primary state highways, and Canadian provincial highways, via highways designated as uck-usable by the Household Goods Carriers' Bureau Committee. When the MileMaker® System calculates "practical" mileages, it may factor in ighway segments that are not included in the federally designated National Network. **These mileages are for general reference only and should ot be used for the purposes of tariff computation.** For tariff purposes, refer to the applicable official tariff.

Please note that the mileages in this directory may vary from the mileages listed at the top of each individual state's road map. Different routes nd methods were used to calculate the distances.

City List

lene, TX
on, OH
any, GA
any, NY
ert Lea, MN
uquerque, NM
xandria, LA
xandria, VA
ntown, PA
oona, PA
arillo, TX
lerson, IN
Arbor, MI
leton, WI
eville, NC
nta, GA
ntic City, NJ
gusta, GA
ora, IL
tin, TX

ersfield, CA
timore, MD
gor, ME
on Rouge, LA
City, MI
onne, NJ
umont, TX
ngs, MT
ghamton, NY
mingham, AL
marck, ND
omington, IN
se, ID
ston, MA
ulder, CO
wling Green, KY
dgeport, CT
ckton, MA
ownsville, TX
ffalo, NY
tte, MT

lgary, AB
mden, NJ
nton, OH
sper, WY
dar Rapids, IA
ampaign, IL
arleston, SC
arleston, WV
arlotte, NC
attanooga, TN
eyenne, WY
icago, IL
ncinnati, OH
arksville, TN
earwater, FL
eveland, OH
Coeur d'Alene, ID
Colorado Sprs., CO
Columbia, MO
Columbia, SC
Columbus, GA
Columbus, OH
Concord, NH
Corpus Christi, TX

D

Dallas, TX
Davenport, IA
Dayton, OH
Daytona Beach, FL
Decatur, AL
Decatur, IL
Denver, CO
Des Moines, IA
Detroit, MI
Dubuque, IA
Duluth, MN
Durham, NC

E

East Orange, NJ
Eau Claire, WI
Elgin, IL
Elizabeth, NJ
El Paso, TX
Elyria, OH
Enid, OK
Erie, PA
Escondido, CA
Eugene, OR
Evansville, IN
Everett, WA

F

Fairfield, CA
Fall River, MA
Fargo, ND
Fayetteville, NC
Flagstaff, AZ
Flint, MI
Florence, SC
Ft. Collins, CO
Ft. Dodge, IA
Ft. Lauderdale, FL
Ft. Smith, AR
Ft. Wayne, IN
Ft. Worth, TX
Fredericton, NB
Fresno, CA

G

Gainesville, FL
Galveston, TX
Gary, IN
Grand Island, NE
Grand Rapids, MI
Great Falls, MT
Greeley, CO
Green Bay, WI
Greensboro, NC
Greenville, SC

H

Halifax, NS
Hamilton, OH
Harrisburg, PA
Hartford, CT
High Point, NC
Houston, TX
Huntington, WV
Huntsville, AL

I

Indianapolis, IN
Iowa City, IA

J

Jackson, MS
Jacksonville, FL
Janesville, WI
Jefferson City, MO
Jersey City, NJ
Joliet, IL

K

Kalamazoo, MI
Kansas City, MO
Kenosha, WI
Kingston, ON
Knoxville, TN

L

Lafayette, LA
Lake Charles, LA
Lancaster, PA
Lansing, MI
Laredo, TX
Las Vegas, NV
Lawrence, KS
Lawrence, MA
Lawton, OK
Lexington, KY
Lincoln, NE
Little Rock, AR
London, ON
Long Beach, CA
Longview, TX
Lorain, OH
Los Angeles, CA
Louisville, KY
Lowell, MA
Lubbock, TX
Lynchburg, VA

M

Macon, GA
Madison, WI
Manchester, NH
Mansfield, OH
Marquette, MI
Memphis, TN
Miami, FL
Midland, TX
Milwaukee, WI
Minneapolis, MN
Mobile, AL
Modesto, CA
Monroe, LA
Montgomery, AL
Montréal, QC
Muncie, IN

N

Nashua, NH
Nashville, TN
Newark, NJ
New Bedford, MA
New Britain, CT
New Brunswick, NJ
New Haven, CT
New Orleans, LA
Newport News, VA
New York, NY
Niagara Falls, NY
Norfolk, VA
Norman, OK
North Platte, NE

O

Oakland, CA
Oceanside, CA
Odessa, TX
Ogden, UT
Oklahoma City, OK
Omaha, NE
Orlando, FL
Owensboro, KY

P

Paterson, NJ
Pendleton, OR
Pensacola, FL
Peoria, IL
Philadelphia, PA
Phoenix, AZ
Pine Bluff, AR
Pittsburgh, PA
Pittsfield, MA
Pomona, CA
Pontiac, MI
Port Arthur, TX
Portland, ME
Portland, OR
Providence, RI
Provo, UT
Pueblo, CO

Q

Québec, QC

R

Racine, WI
Raleigh, NC
Rapid City, SD
Reading, PA
Regina, SK
Reno, NV
Richmond, VA
Riverside, CA
Roanoke, VA
Rochester, MN
Rochester, NY
Rockford, IL

S

Sacramento, CA
Saginaw, MI
St. Johnsbury, VT
St. Joseph, MO
St. Louis, MO
St. Paul, MN
St. Petersburg, FL
Salem, OR
Salinas, CA
Salisbury, MD
Salt Lake City, UT
San Angelo, TX
San Antonio, TX
San Bernardino, CA
San Diego, CA
San Francisco, CA
San Jose, CA
San Mateo, CA
Santa Ana, CA
Santa Barbara, CA
Santa Rosa, CA
Savannah, GA
Schenectady, NY
Scranton, PA
Seattle, WA
Shreveport, LA
Sioux City, IA
Sioux Falls, SD
South Bend, IN
Spokane, WA
Springfield, IL
Springfield, MA
Springfield, MO
Springfield, OH
Stamford, CT
Stockton, CA
Syracuse, NY

T

Tacoma, WA
Tallahassee, FL
Tampa, FL
Terre Haute, IN
Toledo, OH
Topeka, KS
Toronto, ON
Torrington, CT
Trenton, NJ
Troy, NY
Tucson, AZ
Tulsa, OK
Tupelo, MS
Tuscaloosa, AL
Tyler, TX

U

Utica, NY

V

Vallejo, CA
Vancouver, BC
Ventura, CA
Victoria, TX
Virginia Beach, VA

W

Waco, TX
Walnut Creek, CA
Warren, OH
Washington, DC
Waterbury, CT
Waterloo, IA
Waukegan, IL
Wausau, WI
West Palm Beach, FL
Wheeling, WV
Wichita, KS
Wichita Falls, TX
Wilmington, DE
Winnipeg, MB
Winston-Salem, NC
Worcester, MA

Y

Yakima, WA
Youngstown, OH

Mileage Directory

More than 40,000 Mileages Between Selected Cities

	Abilene, TX	Akron, OH	Albany, GA	Albany, NY	Albert Lea, MN	Albuquerque, NM	Alexandria, LA	Alexandria, VA	Allentown, PA	Altoona, PA	Amarillo, TX	Anderson, IN	Ann Arbor, MI	Appleton, WI	Asheville, NC	Atlanta, GA	Atlantic City, NJ	Augusta, GA	Aurora, IL	Austin, TX	Bakersfield, CA	Baltimore, MD	Bangor, ME	Baton Rouge, LA	Bay City, MI	Bayonne, NJ	Beaumont, TX	Billings, MT	Binghamton, NY	Birmingham, AL	Bismarck, ND	Bloomington, IN	Boise, ID	Boston, MA	Boulder, CO	Bowling Green, KY	Bridgeport, CT	Brockton, MA	Brownsville, TX	Buffalo, NY	Butte, MT	Calgary, AB	Camden, NJ
Abilene, TX		1356	980	1858	984	487	484	1513	1644	1510	268	1074	1294	1242	1138	963	1697	1123	1061	221	1291	1548	2173	622	1369	1726	457	1237	1742	819	1133	1010	1514	1947	711	909	1791	1954	538	1561	1459	1778	1650
Akron, OH	1356		880	496	770	1584	1106	356	375	197	1300	287	187	569	496	714	466	639	407	1371	2384	346	864	1100	284	438	1284	1618	385	706	1205	348	2046	638	1366	453	490	652	1652	216	1840	1997	414
Albany, GA	980	880		1176	1192	1470	617	786	962	885	1186	745	899	1094	375	166	990	226	932	906	2274	840	1470	478	996	1023	661	2004	1060	228	1728	687	2350	1244	1577	486	1088	1251	1100	1064	2226	2545	942
Albany, NY	1858	496	1176		1222	2069	1503	398	213	362	1785	760	638	1020	810	1010	302	934	859	1873	2835	344	392	1490	735	169	1673	2070	140	1091	1656	834	2498	166	1818	938	163	179	2112	291	2292	2449	255
Albert Lea, MN	984	770	1192	1222		1130	1004	1115	1134	956	955	612	645	294	1040	1021	1225	1174	391	1041	1850	1104	1614	1117	719	1197	1063	835	1111	969	522	593	1454	1388	832	746	1249	1401	1393	941	1057	1315	1174
Albuquerque, NM	487	1584	1470	2069	1130		948	1888	1908	1742	284	1328	1549	1384	1512	1386	1990	1546	1316	706	804	1923	2448	1086	1624	1990	931	1006	1958	1241	1144	1264	960	2222	479	1284	2055	2235	991	1788	1039	1548	1938
Alexandria, LA	484	1106	617	1503	1004	948		1159	1289	1211	664	896	1130	1125	766	557	1342	716	912	379	1752	1193	1818	139	1200	1371	150	1726	1387	413	1461	794	2004	1592	1201	658	1436	1599	588	1310	1949	2268	1294
Alexandria, VA	1513	356	786	398	1115	1888	1159		206	186	1604	582	532	914	466	637	206	542	752	1528	2692	56	686	1145	628	238	1328	1963	318	747	1550	644	2391	460	1702	698	304	466	1768	394	2185	2342	157
Allentown, PA	1644	375	962	213	1134	1908	1289	206		214	1624	610	550	932	596	795	124	720	770	1658	2712	145	532	1276	647	86	1459	1982	133	877	1568	672	2410	306	1730	769	150	314	1898	355	2204	2360	73
Altoona, PA	1510	197	885	362	956	1742	1211	186	214		1458	445	373	755	518	718	295	643	593	1526	2547	175	701	1198	470	275	1381	1804	246	800	1390	507	2232	475	1552	607	327	488	1820	210	2026	2183	244
Amarillo, TX	268	1300	1186	1785	955	284	664	1604	1624	1458		1044	1265	1213	1228	1102	1706	1262	1032	526	1088	1638	2164	802	1340	1706	647	969	1674	957	943	980	1247	1938	444	1000	1771	1951	788	1504	1192	1511	1654
Anderson, IN	1074	287	745	760	612	1328	896	582	610	445	1044		236	410	485	573	692	660	249	1113	2132	572	1151	891	310	692	1030	1460	649	518	1046	93	1866	925	1151	264	758	938	1420	480	1682	1839	641
Ann Arbor, MI	1294	187	899	638	645	1549	1130	532	550	373	1265	236		443	630	728	642	778	282	1333	2258	521	1030	1124	96	614	1308	1493	527	730	1079	327	1921	804	1241	477	685	816	1685	358	1715	1872	590
Appleton, WI	1242	569	1094	1020	294	1384	1125	914	932	755	1213	410	443		858	922	1023	1032	217	1281	2104	903	1412	1120	464	995	1204	1126	909	867	712	433	1744	1186	1086	613	1048	1199	1633	740	1348	1505	972
Asheville, NC	1138	496	375	810	1040	1512	766	466	596	518	1228	485	630	858		208	650	184	696	1153	2316	500	1125	736	727	678	920	1876	694	356	1494	451	2223	899	1472	338	743	906	1359	679	2098	2286	601
Atlanta, GA	963	714	166	1010	1021	1386	557	637	795	718	1102	573	728	922	208		842	149	760	920	2190	692	1324	526	824	877	709	1832	894	147	1556	514	2178	1098	1426	314	942	1106	1148	896	2054	2373	793
Atlantic City, NJ	1697	466	990	302	1225	1990	1342	206	124	295	1706	692	642	1023	650	842		746	862	1712	2794	151	590	1329	738	142	1512	2073	244	931	1659	754	2501	364	1812	840	208	370	1952	465	2295	2452	58
Augusta, GA	1123	639	226	934	1174	1546	716	542	720	643	1262	660	778	1032	184	149	746		871	1080	2350	596	1226	670	875	779	853	1984	819	306	1710	626	2332	1000	1580	468	844	1007	1292	822	2207	2526	698
Aurora, IL	1061	407	932	859	391	1316	912	752	770	593	1032	249	282	217	696	760	862	871		1100	1999	742	1251	907	356	834	1022	1239	748	705	826	271	1662	1025	981	452	886	1038	1452	578	1462	1618	811
Austin, TX	221	1371	906	1873	1041	706	379	1528	1658	1526	526	1113	1333	1281	1153	920	1712	1080	1100		1495	1563	2188	428	1408	1740	245	1494	1757	777	1346	1049	1772	1962	969	924	1806	1968	352	1576	1717	2036	1664
Bakersfield, CA	1291	2384	2274	2835	1850	804	1752	2692	2712	2547	1088	2132	2258	2104	2316	2190	2794	2350	1999	1495		2727	3228	1890	2333	2810	1748	1257	2724	2045	1671	2068	802	3002	1055	2088	2863	3014	1746	2555	1124	1596	2742
Baltimore, MD	1548	346	840	344	1104	1923	1193	56	145	175	1638	572	521	903	500	692	151	596	742	1563	2727		631	1180	618	184	1363	1952	261	782	1539	634	2381	405	1692	686	249	412	1802	372	2175	2332	103
Bangor, ME	2173	864	1470	392	1614	2448	1818	686	532	701	2164	1151	1030	1412	1125	1324	590	1226	1251	2188	3228	631		1805	1127	458	1988	2462	532	1406	2048	1213	2890	240	2210	1298	382	264	2427	683	2684	2536	542
Baton Rouge, LA	622	1100	478	1490	1117	1086	139	1145	1276	1198	802	891	1124	1120	736	526	1329	670	907	428	1890	1180	1805		1194	1358	183	1865	1374	400	1599	789	2142	1579	1339	653	1423	1586	622	1305	2087	2406	1281
Bay City, MI	1369	284	996	735	719	1624	1200	628	647	470	1340	310	96	464	727	824	738	875	356	1408	2333	618	1127	1194		710	1334	1568	624	827	1154	402	1996	901	1316	574	762	914	1760	454	1790	1946	687
Bayonne, NJ	1726	438	1023	169	1197	1990	1371	238	86	275	1706	692	614	995	678	877	142	779	834	1740	2810	184	458	1358	710		1541	2045	178	959	1631	754	2473	232	1793	851	76	239	1980	399	2267	2424	95
Beaumont, TX	457	1284	661	1673	1063	931	150	1328	1459	1381	647	1030	1308	1204	920	709	1512	853	1022	245	1748	1363	1988	183	1334	1541		1714	1557	583	1494	966	1992	1762	1188	836	1606	1769	439	1488	1936	2256	1464
Billings, MT	1237	1618	2004	2070	835	1006	1726	1963	1982	1804	969	1460	1493	1126	1876	1832	2073	1984	1239	1494	1257	1952	2462	1865	1568	2045	1714		1959	1780	416	1482	620	2236	545	1556	2097	2249	1758	1789	224	542	2022
Binghamton, NY	1742	385	1060	140	1111	1958	1387	318	133	246	1674	649	527	909	694	894	244	819	748	1757	2724	261	532	1374	624	178	1557	1959		976	1545	722	2387	306	1707	827	211	319	1996	224	2181	2338	192
Birmingham, AL	819	706	228	1091	969	1241	413	747	877	800	957	518	730	867	356	147	931	306	705	777	2045	782	1406	400	827	959	583	1780	976		1502	460	2126	1180	1348	259	1024	1187	1022	911	2002	2321	883
Bismarck, ND	1133	1205	1728	1656	522	1144	1461	1550	1568	1390	943	1046	1079	712	1494	1556	1659	1710	826	1346	1671	1539	2048	1599	1154	1631	1494	416	1545	1502		1069	1035	1822	683	1249	1684	1835	1698	1376	638	796	1608
Bloomington, IN	1010	348	687	834	593	1264	794	644	672	507	980	93	327	433	451	514	754	626	271	1049	2068	634	1213	789	402	754	966	1482	722	460	1069		1838	987	1087	206	819	1000	1357	553	1705	1862	703
Boise, ID	1514	2046	2350	2498	1454	960	2004	2391	2410	2232	1247	1866	1921	1744	2223	2178	2501	2332	1662	1772	802	2381	2890	2142	1996	2473	1992	620	2387	2126	1035	1838		2664	822	1902	2526	2677	2035	2217	426	898	2450
Boston, MA	1947	638	1244	166	1388	2222	1592	460	306	475	1938	925	804	1186	899	1098	364	1000	1025	1962	3002	405	240	1579	901	232	1762	2236	306	1180	1822	987	2664		1984	1072	156	24	2201	457	2458	2615	316
Boulder, CO	711	1366	1577	1818	832	479	1201	1702	1730	1552	444	1151	1241	1086	1472	1426	1812	1580	981	969	1055	1692	2210	1339	1316	1793	1188	545	1707	1348	683	1087	822	1984		1151	1845	1997	1232	1537	767	1086	1761
Bowling Green, KY	909	453	486	938	746	1284	658	698	769	607	1000	264	477	613	338	314	840	468	452	924	2088	686	1298	653	574	851	836	1556	827	259	1249	206	1902	1072	1151		916	1079	1204	657	1778	2042	792
Bridgeport, CT	1791	490	1088	163	1249	2055	1436	304	150	327	1771	758	666	1048	743	942	208	844	886	1806	2863	249	382	1423	762	76	1606	2097	211	1024	1684	819	2526	156	1845	916		163	2045	433	2320	2476	160
Brockton, MA	1954	652	1251	179	1401	2235	1599	466	314	488	1951	938	818	1199	906	1106	370	1007	1038	1968	3014	412	264	1586	914	239	1769	2249	319	1187	1835	1000	2677	24	1997	1079	163		2208	470	2471	2628	323
Brownsville, TX	538	1652	1100	2112	1393	991	588	1768	1898	1820	788	1420	1685	1633	1359	1148	1952	1292	1452	352	1746	1802	2427	622	1760	1980	439	1758	1996	1022	1698	1357	2035	2201	1232	1204	2045	2208		1856	1980	2299	1904
Buffalo, NY	1561	216	1064	291	941	1788	1310	394	355	210	1504	480	358	740	679	896	465	822	578	1576	2555	372	683	1305	454	399	1488	1789	224	911	1376	553	2217	457	1537	657	433	470	1856		2012	2168	414
Butte, MT	1459	1840	2226	2292	1057	1039	1949	2185	2204	2026	1192	1682	1715	1348	2098	2054	2295	2207	1462	1717	1124	2175	2684	2087	1790	2267	1936	224	2181	2002	638	1705	426	2458	767	1778	2320	2471	1980	2012		472	2244
Calgary, AB	1778	1997	2545	2449	1315	1548	2268	2342	2360	2183	1511	1839	1872	1505	2286	2373	2452	2526	1618	2036	1596	2332	2536	2406	1946	2424	2256	542	2338	2321	796	1862	898	2615	1086	2042	2476	2628	2299	2168	472		2401
Camden, NJ	1650	414	942	255	1174	1938	1294	157	73	244	1654	641	590	972	601	793	58	698	811	1664	2742	103	542	1281	687	95	1464	2022	192	883	1608	703	2450	316	1761	792	160	323	1904	414	2244	2401	
Canton, OH	1358	20	860	516	790	1586	1108	352	384	194	1302	288	206	588	476	694	462	619	427	1373	2390	342	874	1102	303	447	1285	1638	405	708	1224	350	2066	648	1386	454	499	661	1654	236	1860	2017	411
Casper, WY	959	1446	1749	1897	765	729	1449	1791	1809	1632	692	1266	1320	1056	1622	1578	1900	1730	1061	1217	1106	1780	2290	1587	1395	1872	1437	278	1786	1525	520	1238	705	2064	268	1302	1925	2076	1480	1617	500	820	1849
Cedar Rapids, IA	962	596	1012	1047	181	1109	941	940	959	782	933	416	470	276	858	840	1050	994	210	1020	1828	930	1439	936	545	1022	1042	1019	936	788	702	412	1491	1213	811	564	1074	1226	1372	766	1241	1494	999
Champaign, IL	961	430	791	916	448	1216	783	726	754	589	932	153	343	331	596	619	836	772	130	1000	2020	715	1295	778	418	836	918	1299	804	564	938	150	1718	1069	1019	311	901	1082	1308	635	1521	1731	784
Charleston, SC	1290	686	339	922	1295	1714	884	526	730	696	1430	741	825	1114	266	317	730	175	952	1248	2518	580	1210	837	922	762	1020	2132	842	474	1750	707	2479	984	1728	594	828	990	1459	868	2355	2542	681
Charleston, WV	1229	212	669	658	894	1456	977	372	443	316	1262	300	351	693	284	502	514	427	532	1244	2351	361	973	964	448	525	1147	1742	542	566	1329	338	2129	747	1377	326	590	754	1525	438	1965	2122	466
Charlotte, NC	1208	476	404	772	1153	1626	802	397	558	480	1342	564	616	971	123	244	600	160	810	1166	2430	452	1087	772	712	640	956	1990	656	392	1607	524	2336	861	1585	452	705	868	1394	659	2212	2400	553
Chattanooga, TN	964	600	289	945	904	1320	558	600	730	653	1036	456	625	804	225	117	784	270	644	922	2124	635	1260	545	722	813	728	1714	829	146	1439	398	2060	1034	1310	196	878	1041	1167	814	1936	2256	736
Cheyenne, WY	782	1310	1613	1761	776	552	1272	1654	1673	1496	515	1130	1184	1030	1486	1442	1764	1594	925	1040	1131	1644	2153	1410	1259	1736	1260	456	1650	1389	594	1102	737	1927	90	1166	1788	1940	1303	1480	678	998	1713
Chicago, IL	1082	365	892	817	405	1336	919	710	728	551	1052	208	240	194	656	720	820	830	42	1121	2035	699	1209	914	314	792	1053	1253	706	663	839	231	1698	983	1018	411	844	996	1473	536	1475	1632	768
Cincinnati, OH	1114	232	632	718	680	1390	863	524	552	387	1106	122	250	496	364	461	634	538	335	1128	2194	513	1097	858	347	634	1041	1546	606	464	1132	133	1950	871	1213	210	699	884	1409	437	1768	1925	582
Clarksville, TN	843	533	467	1060	730	1218	592	715	875	688	934	345	557	592	340	294	899	448	457	858	2022	750	1374	588	654	927	770	1541	944	240	1266	227	1887	1149	1136	87	992	1156	1139	738	1763	2082	851
Clearwater, FL	1259	1080	330	1317	1504	1724	822	920	1124	1091	1440	1056	1211	1404	660	478	1124	481	1244	1112	2528	974	1604	684	1308	1157	867	2314	1236	545	2040	998	2662	1378	1910	798	1222	1385	1306	1263	2537	2856	1076
Cleveland, OH	1374	40	893	474	748	1602	1124	381	400	222	1318	287	165	528	534	745	491	678	386	1389	2362	370	866	1118	262	463	1301	1596	362	724	1183	366	2025	640	1345	470	515	653	1670	193	1819	1976	440
Coeur d'Alene, ID	1745	2127	2512	2578	1343	1312	2234	2472	2490	2312	1478	1968	2001	1634	2384	2340	2581	2493	1748	2002	1131	2460	2970	2372	2076	2553	2222	510	2466	2288	924	1990	456	2744	1053	2064	2606	2757	2266	2298	286	428	2530
Colorado Sprs., CO	633	1375	1545	1875	890	376	1030	1670	1698	1533	366	1119	1298	1143	1440	1394	1780	1548	1038	891	1102	1660	2267	1168	1373	1780	1012	630	1764	1316	768	1090	907	2041	102	1119	1845	2054	1154	1594	852	1171	1729
Columbia, MO	760	659	851	1144	389	906	706	954	982	817	731	403	596	544	724	678	1064	832	363	780	1761	944	1523	774	671	1064	775	1153	1033	627	917	339	1499	1297	748	403	1130	1310	1132	863	1375	1694	1013
Columbia, SC	1187	572	316	867	1187	1610	781	475	653	576	1326	632	711	1005	157	214	678	72	844	1145	2414	529	1159	734	808	712	917	2024	752	371	1641	598	2370	933	1619	486	777	940	1356	754	2246	2434	631
Columbus, GA	917	806	87	1120	1124	1385	510	748	905	828	1101	676	830	1024	318	107	952	251	862	882	2189	802	1435	454	927	987	638	1934	1004	144	1659	618	2280	1239	1512	473	1053	1216	1076	1006	2156	2476	903
Columbus, OH	1232	124	751	610	758	1461	982	419	447	282	1177	164	190	557	401	579	529	589	396	1247	2265	409	989	976	287	529	1160	1606	498	582	1193	225	2020	763	1284	328	594	776	1528	329	1829	1986	478
Concord, NH	1995	687	1292	150	1367	2214	1640	508	354	524	1930	906	784	1166	947	1147	412	1048	1004	2010	2981	453	224	1627	881	280	1810	2215	285	1228	1802	979	2644	67	1963	1120	204	92	2249	436	2439	2596	364
Corpus Christi, TX	403	1505	953	1965	1257	855	442	1620	1751	1673	653	1274	1550	1497	1212	1001	1804	1145	1316	216	1610	1655	2280	475	1624	1833	292	1622	1849	875	1563	1210	1900	2054	1096	1058	1898	2061	160	1709	1844	2164	1756
Dallas, TX	179	1177	800	1678	847	647	304	1334	1464	1331	363	918	1139	1087	958	782	1518	942	906	194	1452	1368	1994	442	1213	1546	289	1425	1562	639	1164	854	1703	1768	900	730	1611	1774	546	1382	1648	1967	1470
Davenport, IA	1005	516	960	967	264	1152	934	860	879	702	976	336	390	293	778	788	970	942	140	1062	1871	850	1359	929	465	942	1013	1115	856	734	785	332	1534	1133	853	493	994	1146	1414	686	1337	1578	919
Dayton, OH	1148	194	703	680	700	1402	934	490	518	353	1118	105	197	498	434	531	600	608	337	1199	2206	480	1059	928	294	600	1112	1548	568	534	1134	167	1962	833	1225	280	665	846	1480	399	1770	1927	548
Daytona Beach, FL	1268	955	287	1192	1461	1733	832	795	999	966	1448	1014	1094	1362	535	436	999	356	1200	1120	2537	850	1479	693	1192	1032	876	2272	1110	554	1996	956	2618	1253	1867	754	1097	1260	1315	1138	2494	2814	951
Decatur, AL	822	627	311	1070	870	1196	491	726	856	779	912	439	651	787	350	196	910	356	626	837	2001	760	1385	478	748	938	661	1680	954	82	1422	380	2026	1159	1275	180	1003	1166	1100	832	1902	2222	862
Decatur, IL	921	485	779	971	440	1175	771	781	809	644	891	208	395	350	651	606	891	760	169	960	1979	770	1350	766	469	891	882	1291	860	552	942	163	1647	1124	970	300	956	1137	1312	690	1514	1734	840
Denver, CO	692	1356	1558	1807	822	450	1182	1684	1719	1547	425	1132	1230	1076	1453	1408	1794	1562	971	950	1033	1673	2199	1320	1305	1782	1170	558	1696	1330	695	1069	835	1973	27	1132	1834	1986	1214	1526	780	1099	1742
Des Moines, IA	836	681	1098	1133	147	983	856	1026	1044	867	807	501	556	401	942	836	1126	1078	296	894	1702	1015	1525	1021	630	1108	916	946	1022	874	668	497	1365	1299	685	650	1160	1312	1246	852	1168	1461	1084
Detroit, MI	1319	190	912	642	688	1573	1142	535	553	376	1289	246	43	487	643	740	644	779	325	1358	2302	524	1034	1138	114	616	1320	1536	532	743	1123	338	1964	808	1284	490	669	820	1689	361	1759	1916	593
Dubuque, IA	1036	548	1030	999	218	1182	1004	918	911	734	1007	405	422	202	848	858	1002	1012	161	1093	1902	882	1391	998	497	974	1082	1056	888	803	739	402	1565	1165	885	563	1027	1178	1445	719	1278	1532	951
Duluth, MN	1232	836	1360	1288	249	1378	1252	1181	1200	1022	1202	678	711	335	1125	1188	1291	1341	457	1289	2098	1170	1680	1343	597	1263	1311	861	1176	1133	447	700	1479	1454	1080	881	1315	1467	1641	1007	1083	1164	1240
Durham, NC	1351	515	550	650	1198	1740	945	253	458	424	1456	602	654	996	229	387	457	306	834	1303	2544	308	938	916	751	490	1098	2046	569	535	1632	640	2450	712	1798	564	556	718	1538	633	2268	2424	409
East Orange, NJ	1728	424	1028	154	1182	1992	1373	243	88	260	1708	694	599	981	680	880	147	784	820	1742	2796	188	455	1360	696	16	1543	2030	163	961	1617	756	2458	229	1778	853	73	236	1982	385	2253	2410	100
Eau Claire, WI	1164	685	1209	1137	182	1310	1184	1030	1048	871	1135	527	560	198	974	1037	1140	1190	306	1221	2030	1019	1529	1192	634	1112	1243	935	1026	982	522	550	1555	1303	1012	729	1164	1316	1573	856	1157	1314	1088
Elgin, IL	1087	411	936	862	364	1303	956	756	774	597	1058	253	286	189	700	764	866	875	37	1126	2023	745	1254	919	360	837	1049	1212	751	709	798	275	1686	1029	1005	455	890	1042	1478	582	1434	1591	814
Elizabeth, NJ	1719	430	1016	161	1189	1983	1364	232	78	266	1699	686	606	987	671	871	135	772	826	1734	2787	176	458	1351	702	11	1534	2037	170	952	1623	747	2465	232	1785	844	76	239	1973	391	2259	2416	88
El Paso, TX	454	1736	1436	2313	1283	267	939	1969	2099	1895	436	1481	1701	1536	1593	1418	2153	1578	1488	581	914	2003	2628	1018	1776	2181	834	1274	2197	1274	1411	1417	1227	2402	746	1364	2246	2409	832	1941	1306	1815	2104
Elyria, OH	1355	49	874	502	722	1583	1104	394	412	235	1299	260	138	520	545	703	504	688	359	1370	2335	384	894	1100	235	476	1282	1570	390	706	1156	348	1998	668	1318	452	521	680	1651	221	1792	1949	453
Enid, OK	346	1052	980	1537	658	577	604	1398	1376	1210	293	796	1017	912	1022	896	1457	1056	783	485	1381	1337	1916	742	1091	1457	592	1128	1426	751	923	732	1406	1690	602	794	1523	1703	837	1256	1350	1669	1406
Erie, PA	1469	124	972	377	849	1697	1218	377	370	202	1413	388	256	637	587	805	480	730	486	1484	2393	366	769	1213	363	433	1396	1698	405	819	1284	461	2126	543	1456	566	475	556	1764	90	1906	2063	458
Escondido, CA	1199	2398	2181	2850	1865	818	1684	2707	2726	2561	1102	2147	2273	2118	2331	2163	2808	2323	2014	1326	215	2741	3242	1762	2348	2825	1580	1272	2738	2020	1686	2083	928	3016	1070	2102	2877	3029	1577	2570	1138	1611	2757
Eugene, OR	2049	2582	2885	3033	1837	1496	2540	2928	2946	2768	1782	2402	2456	2128	2758	2714	3036	2867	2198	2238	750	2916	3426	2678	2532	3008	2528	1004	2922	2662	1418	2374	539	3200	1358	2438	3062	3212	2489	2754	780	922	2986
Evansville, IN	938	457	568	943	636	1211	672	734	806	612	927	226	460	486	442	396	877	550	325	953	2015	723	1322	680	534	888	850	1447	832	342	1136	121	1793	1096	1042	139	928	1089	1234	662	1669	1928	836
Everett, WA	2035	2458	2844	2910	1675	1482	2526	2803	2822	2644	1768	2300	2333	1966	2716	2672	2913	2824	2079	2294	1059	2792	3302	2664	2408	2885	2514	842	2798	2620	1256	2322	525	3076	1344	2396	2937	3089	2556	2629	618	649	2862
Fairfield, CA	1648	2442	2559	2894	1908	1089	2038	2788	2806	2628	1373	2262	2317	2162	2619	2475	2897	2635	2058	1775	285	2776	3286	2176	2392	2869	2029	1134	2783	2330	1548	2234	600	3060	1218	2298	2922	3073	2026	2614	1001	1474	2846
Fall River, MA	1926	626	1223	195	1385	2190	1571	439	286	462	1906	893	801	1183	878	1078	343	980	1022	1941	2998	384	292	1558	898	212	1741	2233	334	1160	1819	954	2660	52	1981	1052	135	30	2180	485	2455	2612	296
Fargo, ND	1166	1012	1535	1463	330	1320	1272	1356	1375	1198	1002	854	886	519	1301	1364	1466	1516	632	1263	1864	1346	1855	1410	961	1438	1305	608	1352	1308	195	876	1227	1630	886	1056	1491	1642	1615	1182	831	988	1415
Fayetteville, NC	1349	567	478	710	1250	1772	943	313	516	484	1488	655	706	1048	267	376	517	234	887	1307	2576	368	996	900	803	550	1079	2133	629	533	1684	693	2480	772	1728	595	616	778	1518	693	2356	2477	469
Flagstaff, AZ	811	1908	1793	2393	1454	324	1272	2212	2231	2066	608	1652	1872	1708	1836	1710	2313	1870	1639	1030	480	2246	2772	1410	1947	2313	1254	1072	2282	1565	1468	1588	860	2546	803	1607	2378	2559	1404	2112	940	1412	2262
Flint, MI	1326	241	954	693	677	1581	1158	586	604	427	1297	268	54	476	685	782	696	833	314	1366	2291	576	1085	1152	48	668	1292	1525	582	785	1112	360	1953	859	1273	531	720	872	1717	412	1748	1904	645
Florence, SC	1264	579	392	795	1263	1687	858	398	602	569	1403	709	719	1082	234	290	602	148	920	1221	2491	452	1082	810	816	635	994	2100	714	448	1718	675	2447	856	1696	562	700	863	1432	762	2323	2510	554
Ft. Collins, CO	745	1354	1611	1806	821	515	1235	1700	1718	1540	478	1185	1229	1074	1506	1461	1809	1614	970	1003	1094	1689	2198	1373	1304	1781	1223	500	1695	1383	638	1121	752	1972	54	1185	1834	1985	1267	1526	722	1041	1758
Ft. Dodge, IA	908	750	1166	1201	124	1054	928	1094	1113	936	879	570	624	392	1012	994	1204	1148	364	965	1755	1084	1593	1090	699	1176	988	865	1090	942	644	566	1418	1367	738	718	1228	1380	1317	920	1087	1437	1153
Ft. Lauderdale, FL	1474	1192	492	1429	1666	1938	1037	1032	1236	1202	1654	1218	1332	1568	772	641	1236	592	1406	1326	2742	1086	1716	898	1428	1268	1081	2477	1348	759	2202	1160	2824	1490	2072	960	1334	1497	1520	1375	2700	3018	1188
Ft. Smith, AR	455	935	750	1512	631	722	375	1170	1300	1094	438	680	902	848	794	668	1354	828	667	473	1526	1203	1828	513	975	1382	441	1355	1398	523	1088	616	1632	1602	829	564	1446	1610	825	1140	1577	1896	1306

Rand McNally software packages offer more than standard mileages:

Truck-type, hazmat, and lowest-cost routing
HHG tariff mileage
Fuel network management

Visit trucking.randmcnally.com to learn more about what Rand McNally trucking applications can do for your bottom line.

Mileages in this Mileage Directory are from the Rand McNally *MileMaker Practical Routing System*, © Rand McNally. **These mileages are for general reference only and should not be used for the purposes of tariff computation.** For tariff purposes, refer to the applicable official tariff. Mileages between each of the 300 cities listed in this chart are computed over National Interstate, U.S. and primary state highways, and Canadian provincial highways via highways designated as truck-usable by the Household Goods Carriers' Bureau Committee. Practical routing may have highway segments not included in the federally designated National Network.

	Casper, WY	Cedar Rapids, IA	Champaign, IL	Charleston, SC	Charleston, WV	Charlotte, NC	Chattanooga, TN	Cheyenne, WY	Chicago, IL	Cincinnati, OH	Clarksville, TN	Clearwater, FL	Cleveland, OH	Coeur d'Alene, ID	Colorado Sprs., CO	Columbia, MO	Columbia, SC	Columbus, GA	Columbus, OH	Concord, NH
bilene, TX	959	962	961	1290	1229	1208	964	782	1082	1114	843	1259	1374	1745	633	760	1187	917	1232	1995
kron, OH	1446	596	430	686	212	476	600	1310	365	232	533	1080	40	2127	1375	659	572	806	124	687
lbany, GA	1749	1012	791	339	669	404	289	1613	892	632	467	330	893	2512	1545	851	316	87	751	1292
lbany, NY	1897	1047	916	922	658	772	945	1761	817	718	1060	1317	474	2578	1875	1144	867	1120	610	150
lbert Lea, MN	765	181	448	1295	894	1153	904	776	405	680	730	1504	748	1343	890	389	1187	1124	758	1367
lbuquerque, NM	729	1109	1216	1714	1546	1626	1320	552	1336	1390	1218	1724	1602	1312	376	906	1610	1385	1461	2214
lexandria, LA	1449	941	783	884	977	802	558	1272	919	863	592	822	1124	2234	1030	706	781	510	982	1640
lexandria, VA	1791	940	726	526	372	397	600	1654	710	524	715	920	381	2472	1670	954	475	748	419	508
llentown, PA	1809	959	754	730	443	558	730	1673	728	552	845	1124	400	2490	1698	982	653	905	447	354
ltoona, PA	1632	782	589	696	316	480	653	1496	551	387	688	1091	222	2312	1533	817	576	828	282	524
marillo, TX	692	933	932	1430	1262	1342	1036	515	1052	1106	934	1440	1318	1478	366	731	1326	1101	1177	1930
nderson, IN	1266	416	153	741	300	564	456	1130	208	122	345	1056	287	1968	1119	403	632	676	164	906
nn Arbor, MI	1320	470	343	825	351	616	625	1184	240	250	557	1211	165	2001	1298	596	711	830	190	784
ppleton, WI	1056	276	331	1114	693	971	804	1030	194	496	592	1404	547	1634	1143	544	1005	1024	557	1166
sheville, NC	1622	858	596	266	284	123	225	1486	656	364	340	660	536	2384	1440	724	157	318	401	947
tlanta, GA	1578	840	619	317	502	244	117	1442	720	461	294	478	721	2340	1394	678	214	107	579	1147
tlantic City, NJ	1900	1050	836	730	514	600	784	1764	820	634	899	1124	491	2581	1780	1064	678	952	529	412
ugusta, GA	1730	994	772	175	427	160	270	1594	830	538	448	481	678	2493	1548	832	72	251	589	1048
urora, IL	1061	210	130	952	532	810	644	925	42	335	457	1244	386	1748	1038	363	844	862	396	1004
ustin, TX	1217	1020	1000	1248	1244	1166	922	1040	1121	1128	858	1112	1389	2002	891	780	1145	882	1247	2010
akersfield, CA	1106	1828	2020	2518	2351	2430	2124	1131	2035	2194	2022	2528	2362	1131	1102	1761	2414	2189	2265	2981
altimore, MD	1780	930	715	580	361	452	635	1644	699	513	750	974	370	2460	1660	944	529	802	409	453
angor, ME	2290	1439	1295	1210	973	1087	1260	2153	1209	1097	1374	1604	866	2970	2267	1523	1159	1435	989	224
aton Rouge, LA	1587	936	778	837	964	772	545	1410	914	858	588	684	1118	2372	1168	774	734	454	976	1627
ay City, MI	1395	545	418	922	448	712	722	1259	314	347	654	1308	262	2076	1373	671	808	927	287	881
ayonne, NJ	1872	1022	836	762	525	640	813	1736	792	634	927	1157	463	2553	1780	1064	712	987	529	280
eaumont, TX	1437	1042	918	1020	1147	956	728	1260	1053	1041	770	867	1301	2222	1012	775	917	638	1160	1810
illings, MT	278	1019	1299	2132	1742	1990	1714	456	1253	1546	1541	2314	1596	510	630	1153	2024	1934	1606	2215
inghamton, NY	1786	936	804	842	542	656	829	1650	706	606	944	1236	362	2466	1764	1033	752	1004	498	285
irmingham, AL	1525	788	564	474	566	392	146	1389	665	464	240	545	724	2288	1316	627	371	144	582	1228
ismarck, ND	520	702	938	1750	1329	1607	1439	594	839	1132	1266	2040	1183	924	768	917	1641	1659	1193	1802
loomington, IN	1238	412	150	707	338	564	398	1102	231	133	227	998	366	1990	1055	339	598	618	225	979
oise, ID	705	1491	1718	2479	2129	2336	2060	737	1698	1950	1887	2662	2025	456	907	1499	2370	2280	2020	2644
oston, MA	2064	1213	1069	984	747	861	1034	1927	983	871	1149	1378	640	2744	2041	1297	933	1209	763	67
oulder, CO	268	811	1019	1728	1377	1585	1310	90	1018	1213	1136	1910	1345	1053	102	748	1619	1492	1284	1963
owling Green, KY	1302	564	311	594	326	452	196	1166	411	210	87	798	470	2064	1119	403	486	416	328	1120
ridgeport, CT	1925	1074	901	828	590	705	878	1788	844	699	992	1222	515	2606	1845	1130	777	1053	594	204
rockton, MA	2076	1226	1082	990	754	868	1041	1940	996	884	1156	1385	653	2757	2054	1310	940	1216	776	92
rownsville, TX	1480	1372	1308	1459	1525	1394	1167	1303	1473	1409	1139	1306	1670	2266	1154	1132	1356	1076	1528	2249
uffalo, NY	1617	766	635	868	438	659	814	1480	536	437	738	1263	193	2298	1594	863	754	1006	329	436
utte, MT	500	1241	1521	2355	1965	2212	1936	678	1475	1768	1763	2537	1819	286	852	1375	2246	2156	1829	2438
algary, AB	820	1494	1731	2542	2122	2400	2256	998	1632	1925	2082	2856	1976	428	1171	1694	2434	2476	1986	2496
amden, NJ	1849	999	784	681	466	553	736	1713	768	582	851	1076	440	2530	1729	1013	631	903	478	364
anton, OH	1466	615	432	666	192	456	611	1329	385	234	535	1060	60	2146	1376	660	552	804	126	696
asper, WY		890	1117	1878	1528	1736	1460	179	1097	1349	1287	2060	1424	786	353	899	1770	1680	1420	2043
edar Rapids, IA	890		267	1114	702	972	723	754	247	499	550	1324	574	1527	868	261	1006	943	570	1192
hampaign, IL	1117	267		852	440	710	502	981	137	237	328	1102	446	1807	987	290	744	722	307	1061
harleston, SC	1878	1114	852		474	207	438	1742	912	620	596	456	725	2640	1696	980	112	363	636	1032
harleston, WV	1528	702	440	474		264	419	1392	491	196	406	868	251	2250	1345	630	360	612	162	795
harlotte, NC	1736	972	710	207	264		338	1600	769	477	453	602	516	2498	1553	837	93	354	426	909
hattanooga, TN	1460	723	502	438	419	338		1324	602	358	178	600	618	2222	1278	562	334	220	476	1082
heyenne, WY	179	754	981	1742	1392	1600	1324		961	1213	1150	1924	1288	964	175	762	1634	1544	1284	1907
hicago, IL	1097	247	137	912	491	769	602	961		294	394	1202	343	1761	1075	384	803	822	355	962
incinnati, OH	1349	499	237	620	196	477	358	1213	294		291	944	250	2054	1181	465	511	564	108	863
larksville, TN	1287	550	328	596	406	453	178	1150	394	291		778	551	2049	1104	388	487	398	409	1197
learwater, FL	2060	1324	1102	456	868	602	600	1924	1202	944	778		1120	2823	1878	1162	506	417	1030	1426
leveland, OH	1424	574	446	725	251	516	618	1288	343	250	551	1120		2104	1402	676	611	824	142	619
oeur d'Alene, ID	786	1527	1807	2640	2250	2498	2222	964	1761	2054	2049	2823	2104		1138	1661	2532	2442	2114	2724
olorado Sprs., CO	353	868	987	1696	1345	1553	1278	175	1075	1181	1104	1878	1402	1138		716	1587	1460	1252	2020
olumbia, MO	899	261	290	980	630	837	562	762	384	465	388	1162	676	1661	716		871	782	536	1289
olumbia, SC	1770	1006	744	112	360	93	334	1634	803	511	487	506	611	2532	1587	871		315	522	981
olumbus, GA	1680	943	722	363	612	354	220	1544	822	564	398	417	824	2442	1460	782	315		682	1257
olumbus, OH	1420	570	307	636	162	426	476	1284	355	108	409	1030	142	2114	1252	536	522	682		755
oncord, NH	2043	1192	1061	1032	795	909	1082	1907	962	863	1197	1426	619	2724	2020	1289	981	1257	755	
orpus Christi, TX	1345	1236	1161	1312	1378	1248	1020	1168	1337	1262	992	1159	1522	2130	1019	997	1209	930	1380	2102
allas, TX	1148	825	806	1110	1050	1028	784	971	926	934	664	1079	1194	1934	729	586	1007	736	1053	1816
avenport, IA	933	83	187	1034	622	892	672	797	177	419	498	1272	494	1623	911	258	926	891	490	1113
ayton, OH	1361	511	249	690	194	458	428	1225	296	54	361	1014	212	2056	1193	477	553	634	71	825
aytona Beach, FL	2018	1280	1060	331	743	477	558	1882	1160	890	735	162	994	2780	1835	1120	381	374	905	1301
ecatur, AL	1426	689	485	524	500	442	126	1290	585	384	160	625	645	2188	1243	527	421	226	503	1208
ecatur, IL	1046	259	60	907	495	764	490	910	189	292	316	1090	498	1800	938	223	798	710	362	1116
enver, CO	280	800	1000	1709	1359	1566	1291	103	1007	1194	1117	1892	1334	1066	74	730	1600	1474	1265	1953
es Moines, IA	764	126	352	1200	788	1057	808	628	332	584	635	1409	659	1454	742	292	1091	1028	655	1278
etroit, MI	1364	514	386	826	352	616	638	1228	283	263	570	1224	168	2044	1342	648	712	843	191	787
ubuque, IA	964	75	256	1104	692	962	740	828	182	488	567	1341	526	1564	942	335	996	960	559	1145
uluth, MN	1011	429	570	1382	960	1239	1070	1024	471	764	897	1671	814	1368	1137	636	1273	1290	824	1433
urham, NC	1848	1006	743	302	303	146	452	1712	794	500	566	696	554	2554	1666	950	238	497	464	760
ast Orange, NJ	1858	1008	838	767	528	642	815	1722	777	636	929	1162	448	2538	1782	1066	716	990	531	277
au Claire, WI	944	261	419	1230	809	1088	920	956	320	612	746	1520	663	1442	1070	569	1122	1140	673	1282
lgin, IL	1085	234	173	956	535	814	647	949	46	338	434	1248	389	1720	1062	389	848	867	399	1008
lizabeth, NJ	1865	1014	829	756	519	633	806	1728	784	627	921	1150	455	2545	1774	1058	704	981	523	280
l Paso, TX	996	1261	1368	1745	1684	1663	1420	819	1489	1569	1298	1701	1754	1578	644	1059	1642	1372	1613	2450
lyria, OH	1398	547	420	734	261	525	600	1261	317	232	532	1129	28	2078	1375	658	620	805	123	647
nid, OK	851	636	684	1224	1014	1136	830	673	804	858	728	1294	1070	1636	552	434	1120	895	929	1682
rie, PA	1525	675	543	777	346	567	722	1389	444	345	646	1172	101	2206	1503	772	662	915	237	522
scondido, CA	1120	1843	2034	2490	2365	2408	2139	1146	2050	2209	2036	2446	2376	1411	1116	1776	2388	2117	2280	2996
ugene, OR	1240	2026	2254	3014	2664	2872	2597	1272	2234	2486	2423	3197	2560	494	1444	2036	2906	2816	2556	3180
vansville, IN	1192	455	202	698	362	555	280	1056	289	215	106	880	475	1955	1010	294	589	500	333	1088
verett, WA	1118	1859	2139	2972	2582	2830	2554	1258	2093	2386	2380	3155	2436	332	1430	1993	2864	2774	2446	3055
airfield, CA	1101	1887	2114	2803	2524	2732	2456	1133	2094	2346	2283	2813	2420	868	1303	1896	2700	2474	2416	3040
all River, MA	2060	1210	1036	963	726	840	1013	1924	979	834	1128	1358	668	2740	1981	1265	912	1188	730	119
argo, ND	712	509	745	1557	1136	1414	1246	787	646	939	1072	1846	990	1116	943	728	1448	1466	1000	1609
ayetteville, NC	1879	1057	795	217	355	139	496	1743	846	552	596	612	606	2642	1696	980	166	477	517	820
lagstaff, AZ	818	1432	1539	2037	1870	1950	1644	875	1660	1714	1542	2047	1925	1212	700	1230	1934	1708	1784	2538
lint, MI	1353	502	375	880	406	670	679	1216	272	304	612	1266	220	2034	1330	628	766	885	245	838
lorence, SC	1846	1082	820	130	368	104	411	1710	880	588	564	525	619	2608	1664	948	81	392	529	904
t. Collins, CO	223	799	1026	1762	1412	1619	1344	45	1006	1247	1170	1944	1333	1008	138	782	1654	1526	1318	1952
t. Dodge, IA	683	154	421	1268	856	1126	877	681	401	653	704	1478	728	1372	795	338	1160	1097	723	1346
t. Lauderdale, FL	2223	1486	1264	568	980	714	763	2086	1365	1106	940	269	1232	2985	2040	1324	618	579	1142	1538
t. Smith, AR	1078	610	567	993	884	906	602	900	688	770	498	1064	953	1863	797	349	892	665	814	1650

	Corpus Christi, TX	Dallas, TX	Davenport, IA	Dayton, OH	Daytona Beach, FL	Decatur, AL	Decatur, IL	Denver, CO	Des Moines, IA	Detroit, MI	Dubuque, IA	Duluth, MN	Durham, NC	East Orange, NJ	Eau Claire, WI	Elgin, IL	Elizabeth, NJ	El Paso, TX	Elyria, OH	Enid, OK	Erie, PA	Escondido, CA	Eugene, OR	Evansville, IN
bilene, TX	403	179	1005	1148	1268	822	921	692	836	1319	1036	1232	1351	1728	1164	1087	1719	454	1355	346	1469	1199	2049	938
kron, OH	1505	1177	516	194	955	627	485	1356	681	190	548	836	515	424	685	411	430	1736	49	1052	124	2398	2582	457
lbany, GA	953	800	960	703	287	311	779	1558	1098	912	1030	1360	550	1028	1209	936	1016	1436	874	980	972	2181	2885	568
lbany, NY	1965	1678	967	680	1192	1070	971	1807	1133	642	999	1288	650	154	1137	862	161	2313	502	1537	377	2850	3033	943
lbert Lea, MN	1257	847	264	700	1461	870	440	822	147	688	218	249	1198	1182	182	364	1189	1283	722	658	849	1865	1837	636
lbuquerque, NM	855	647	1152	1402	1733	1196	1175	450	983	1573	1182	1378	1740	1992	1310	1303	1983	267	1583	577	1697	818	1496	1211
lexandria, LA	442	304	934	934	832	491	771	1182	856	1142	1004	1252	945	1373	1184	956	1364	939	1104	604	1218	1684	2540	672
lexandria, VA	1620	1334	860	490	795	726	781	1684	1026	535	893	1181	253	243	1030	756	232	1969	394	1398	377	2707	2928	734
llentown, PA	1751	1464	879	518	999	856	809	1719	1044	553	911	1200	458	88	1048	774	78	2099	412	1376	370	2726	2946	806
ltoona, PA	1673	1331	702	353	966	779	644	1547	867	376	734	1022	424	260	871	597	266	1895	235	1210	202	2561	2768	612
marillo, TX	653	363	976	1118	1448	912	891	425	807	1289	1007	1202	1456	1708	1135	1058	1699	436	1299	293	1413	1102	1782	927
nderson, IN	1274	918	336	105	1014	439	208	1132	501	246	405	678	602	694	527	253	686	1481	260	796	388	2147	2402	226
nn Arbor, MI	1550	1139	390	197	1094	651	395	1230	556	43	422	711	654	599	560	286	606	1701	138	1017	266	2273	2456	460
ppleton, WI	1497	1087	293	498	1362	787	350	1076	401	487	202	335	996	981	198	189	987	1536	520	912	648	2118	2128	486
sheville, NC	1212	958	778	434	535	350	651	1453	944	643	848	1125	229	680	974	700	671	1593	545	1022	587	2331	2758	442
tlanta, GA	1001	782	788	531	436	196	606	1408	926	740	858	1188	387	880	1037	764	871	1418	703	896	805	2163	2714	396
tlantic City, NJ	1804	1518	970	600	999	910	891	1794	1136	644	1002	1291	457	147	1140	866	135	2153	504	1457	480	2808	3036	877
ugusta, GA	1145	942	942	608	356	356	760	1562	1078	779	1012	1341	306	784	1190	875	772	1578	688	1056	730	2323	2867	550
urora, IL	1316	906	140	337	1200	626	169	971	296	325	161	457	834	820	306	37	826	1468	359	783	486	2014	2198	325
ustin, TX	216	194	1062	1199	1120	837	960	950	894	1358	1093	1289	1308	1742	1221	1126	1734	581	1370	485	1484	1326	2238	953
akersfield, CA	1610	1452	1871	2206	2537	2001	1979	1033	1702	2302	1902	2098	2544	2796	2030	2023	2787	914	2335	1381	2463	215	750	2015
altimore, MD	1655	1368	850	480	850	760	770	1673	1015	524	882	1170	308	188	1019	745	176	2003	384	1337	366	2741	2916	723
angor, ME	2280	1994	1359	1059	1479	1385	1350	2199	1525	1034	1391	1680	938	455	1529	1254	458	2628	894	1916	769	3242	3426	1322
aton Rouge, LA	475	442	929	928	693	478	766	1320	1021	1138	998	1343	916	1360	1192	950	1351	1018	1100	742	1213	1762	2678	668
ay City, MI	1624	1213	465	294	1192	748	469	1305	630	114	497	597	751	696	634	360	702	1776	235	1091	363	2348	2532	534
ayonne, NJ	1833	1546	942	600	1032	938	891	1782	1108	616	974	1263	490	16	1112	837	11	2181	476	1457	433	2825	3008	888
eaumont, TX	292	289	1013	1112	876	661	882	1170	916	1320	1082	1311	1098	1543	1243	1049	1534	834	1282	592	1396	1580	2528	850
illings, MT	1622	1425	1115	1548	2272	1680	1291	558	946	1536	1056	861	2046	2030	935	1212	2037	1274	1570	1128	1698	1272	1004	1447
inghamton, NY	1849	1562	856	568	1110	954	860	1696	1022	530	888	1176	569	163	1026	751	170	2197	390	1426	266	2738	2922	832
irmingham, AL	875	639	734	534	554	82	552	1330	874	743	803	1133	535	961	982	709	952	1274	706	751	819	2020	2662	342
ismarck, ND	1563	1164	785	1134	1996	1422	942	695	668	1123	739	447	1632	1617	522	798	1623	1411	1156	923	1284	1686	1418	1136
loomington, IN	1210	854	332	167	956	380	163	1069	497	338	402	700	640	756	550	275	747	1417	348	732	461	2083	2374	121
oise, ID	1900	1703	1534	1962	2618	2026	1647	835	1365	1964	1565	1479	2450	2458	1555	1686	2465	1227	1998	1406	2126	928	539	1793
oston, MA	2054	1768	1133	833	1253	1159	1124	1973	1299	808	1165	1454	712	229	1303	1029	232	2402	668	1690	543	3016	3200	1096
oulder, CO	1096	900	854	1225	1867	1275	970	27	685	1284	885	1080	1698	1778	1012	1005	1785	746	1318	602	1446	1070	1358	1042
owling Green, KY	1058	730	493	280	754	180	300	1132	650	490	563	881	564	853	729	455	844	1364	452	794	566	2102	2438	109
ridgeport, CT	1898	1611	994	665	1097	1003	956	1834	1160	669	1027	1315	556	73	1164	890	76	2246	528	1523	475	2877	3062	953
rockton, MA	2061	1774	1146	846	1260	1166	1137	1986	1312	820	1178	1467	718	236	1316	1042	239	2409	680	1703	556	3029	3212	1116
rownsville, TX	160	546	1414	1480	1315	1100	1312	1214	1246	1689	1445	1641	1538	1982	1573	1478	1973	832	1651	837	1764	1577	2489	1234
uffalo, NY	1709	1382	686	399	1138	832	690	1526	852	361	719	1007	633	385	856	582	391	1941	221	1256	96	2570	2754	662
utte, MT	1844	1648	1337	1770	2494	1902	1514	780	1168	1759	1278	1083	2268	2253	1157	1434	2259	1306	1792	1350	1920	1138	780	1669
algary, AB	2164	1967	1578	1927	2814	2222	1734	1099	1461	1916	1532	1164	2424	2410	1314	1591	2416	1815	1949	1669	2076	1611	922	1928
amden, NJ	1756	1470	919	548	951	862	840	1742	1084	593	951	1240	409	100	1088	814	88	2104	453	1406	429	2757	2986	828
anton, OH	1506	1178	535	196	935	629	487	1375	701	209	567	856	494	432	704	430	439	1738	69	1054	144	2404	2602	459
asper, WY	1345	1148	933	1361	2018	1426	1046	280	764	1364	964	1011	1848	1858	944	1085	1865	996	1398	851	1525	1120	1240	1192
edar Rapids, IA	1236	825	83	511	1280	689	259	800	126	514	75	429	1006	1008	261	234	1014	1261	547	636	675	1843	2026	455
hampaign, IL	1161	806	187	249	1060	485	60	1000	352	386	256	570	743	838	419	173	829	1368	420	684	543	2034	2254	202
harleston, SC	1312	1110	1034	690	331	524	907	1709	1200	826	1104	1382	302	767	1230	956	756	1745	734	1224	777	2490	3014	698
harleston, WV	1378	1050	622	194	743	500	495	1359	788	352	692	960	303	528	809	535	519	1684	261	1014	346	2365	2664	362
harlotte, NC	1248	1028	892	458	477	442	764	1566	1057	616	962	1239	146	642	1088	814	633	1663	525	1136	567	2408	2872	555
hattanooga, TN	1020	784	672	428	558	126	490	1291	808	638	740	1070	452	815	920	647	806	1420	600	830	722	2139	2597	280
heyenne, WY	1168	971	797	1225	1882	1290	910	103	628	1228	828	1024	1712	1722	956	949	1728	819	1261	673	1389	1146	1272	1056
hicago, IL	1337	926	177	296	1160	585	189	1007	332	283	182	471	794	777	320	46	784	1489	317	804	444	2050	2234	289
incinnati, OH	1262	934	419	54	890	384	292	1194	584	263	488	764	500	636	612	338	627	1569	232	858	345	2209	2486	215
larksville, TN	992	664	498	361	735	160	316	1117	635	570	567	897	566	929	746	434	921	1298	532	728	646	2036	2423	106
learwater, FL	1159	1079	1272	1014	162	625	1090	1892	1409	1224	1341	1671	696	1162	1520	1248	1150	1701	1129	1294	1172	2446	3197	880
leveland, OH	1522	1194	494	212	994	645	498	1334	659	168	526	814	554	448	663	389	455	1754	28	1070	101	2376	2560	475
oeur d'Alene, ID	2130	1934	1623	2056	2780	2188	1800	1066	1454	2044	1564	1368	2554	2538	1442	1720	2545	1578	2078	1636	2206	1411	494	1955
olorado Sprs., CO	1019	729	911	1193	1835	1243	938	74	742	1342	942	1137	1666	1782	1070	1062	1774	644	1375	552	1503	1116	1444	1010
olumbia, MO	997	586	258	477	1120	527	223	730	292	648	335	636	950	1066	569	389	1058	1059	658	434	772	1776	2036	294
olumbia, SC	1209	1007	926	553	381	421	798	1600	1091	712	996	1273	238	716	1122	848	704	1642	620	1120	662	2388	2906	589
olumbus, GA	930	736	891	634	374	226	710	1474	1028	843	960	1290	497	990	1140	867	981	1372	805	895	915	2117	2816	500
olumbus, OH	1380	1053	490	71	905	503	362	1265	655	191	559	824	464	531	673	399	523	1613	123	929	237	2280	2556	333
oncord, NH	2102	1816	1113	825	1301	1208	1116	1953	1278	787	1145	1433	760	277	1282	1008	280	2450	647	1682	522	2996	3180	1088
orpus Christi, TX		411	1279	1332	1168	953	1176	1078	1110	1542	1310	1505	1390	1835	1438	1342	1826	696	1504	702	1618	1442	2354	1086
allas, TX	411		868	1004	1088	642	765	881	699	1163	899	1094	1171	1548	1027	932	1540	635	1176	302	1290	1380	2238	758
avenport, IA	1279	868		431	1229	654	179	843	168	434	77	420	926	928	268	164	934	1304	467	679	595	1886	2070	384
ayton, OH	1332	1004	431		960	455	304	1206	596	210	500	766	496	602	614	340	593	1555	194	870	307	2221	2498	285
aytona Beach, FL	1168	1088	1229	960		634	1048	1848	1366	1095	1298	1628	572	1036	1477	1204	1024	1710	1004	1303	1046	2456	3154	837
ecatur, AL	953	642	654	455	634		472	1257	774	664	724	1054	577	940	902	630	931	1277	626	707	740	2015	2562	262
ecatur, IL	1176	765	179	304	1048	472		951	345	438	249	573	798	893	422	196	884	1328	472	643	598	1994	2182	191
enver, CO	1078	881	843	1206	1848	1257	951		674	1274	874	1070	1680	1768	1002	995	1774	717	1307	584	1435	1048	1370	1023
es Moines, IA	1110	699	168	596	1366	774	345	674		599	199	395	1090	1093	327	320	1100	1135	633	510	760	1717	1900	541
etroit, MI	1542	1163	434	210	1095	664	438	1274	599		466	754	655	602	603	329	608	1726	142	1041	269	2316	2500	494
ubuque, IA	1310	899	77	500	1298	724	249	874	199	466		343	995	960	192	141	966	1335	499	710	627	1916	2058	454
uluth, MN	1505	1094	420	766	1628	1054	573	1070	395	754	343		1264	1248	152	430	1255	1530	788	906	916	2112	1862	767
urham, NC	1390	1171	926	496	572	577	798	1680	1090	655	995	1264		494	1112	838	483	1806	564	1250	606	2558	2985	668
ast Orange, NJ	1835	1548	928	602	1036	940	893	1768	1093	602	960	1248	494		1097	823	9	2183	462	1460	418	2810	2994	890
au Claire, WI	1438	1027	268	614	1477	902	422	1002	327	603	192	152	1112	1097		278	1104	1463	637	838	764	2044	1936	616
lgin, IL	1342	932	164	340	1204	630	196	995	320	329	141	430	838	823	278		830	1456	362	831	490	2038	2214	329
lizabeth, NJ	1826	1540	934	593	1024	931	884	1774	1100	608	966	1255	483	9	1104	830		2174	468	1451	425	2802	3001	881
l Paso, TX	696	635	1304	1555	1710	1277	1328	717	1135	1726	1335	1530	1806	2183	1463	1456	2174		1736	730	1849	745	1657	1393
lyria, OH	1504	1176	467	194	1004	626	472	1307	633	142	499	788	564	462	637	362	468	1736		1051	129	2350	2534	456
nid, OK	702	302	679	870	1303	707	643	584	510	1041	710	906	1250	1460	838	831	1451	730	1051		1165	1396	1942	679
rie, PA	1618	1290	595	307	1046	740	598	1435	760	269	627	916	606	418	764	490	425	1849	129	1165		2478	2662	570
scondido, CA	1442	1380	1886	2221	2456	2015	1994	1048	1717	2316	1916	2112	2558	2810	2044	2038	2802	745	2350	1396	2478		958	2030
ugene, OR	2354	2238	2070	2498	3154	2562	2182	1370	1900	2500	2058	1862	2985	2994	1936	2214	3001	1657	2534	1942	2662	958		2329
vansville, IN	1086	758	384	285	837	262	191	1023	541	494	454	767	668	890	616	329	881	1393	456	679	570	2030	2329	
verett, WA	2422	2224	1955	2388	3112	2520	2131	1356	1786	2376	1896	1700	2886	2870	1774	2052	2877	1750	2410	1928	2538	1266	311	2286
airfield, CA	1891	1737	1930	2358	2822	2286	2043	1231	1761	2360	1960	1993	2846	2854	2088	2082	2861	1194	2394	1666	2522	496	488	2189
all River, MA	2033	1747	1130	800	1232	1139	1092	1970	1296	804	1162	1450	690	208	1299	1025	212	2381	664	1658	571	3012	3196	1088
argo, ND	1479	1080	592	941	1804	1229	749	876	475	930	546	254	1439	1424	328	605	1430	1370	963	840	1091	1878	1610	943
ayetteville, NC	1371	1169	977	549	486	583	850	1710	1143	707	1047	1316	90	554	1164	890	543	1804	616	1282	676	2550	3016	698
lagstaff, AZ	1268	971	1475	1726	2056	1520	1499	675	1306	1897	1506	1702	2062	2315	1634	1627	2306	572	1907	901	2020	495	1231	1534
lint, MI	1582	1171	422	251	1149	706	427	1262	588	69	455	743	708	654	592	318	660	1734	193	1049	320	2306	2490	492
lorence, SC	1286	1083	1002	561	400	497	875	1677	1168	720	1072	1350	174	640	1198	924	628	1719	628	1197	670	2464	2982	666
t. Collins, CO	1131	934	842	1259	1902	1309	955	66	673	1272	873	1068	1732	1767	1001	994	1773	782	1306	637	1434	1108	1288	1076
t. Dodge, IA	1182	771	237	665	1434	843	413	727	96	668	191	371	1160	1162	304	330	1168	1207	701	582	829	1770	1866	609
t. Lauderdale, FL	1373	1293	1434	1177	242	839	1252	2054	1572	1332	1504	1834	808	1274	1682	1410	1262	1915	1241	1508	1283	2660	3360	1042
t. Smith, AR	689	278	654	754	1073	478	528	811	484	926	685	879	1020	1384	813	695	1374	911	936	232	1050	1540	2168	593

Mileage Directory, continued

	Everett, WA	Fairfield, CA	Fall River, MA	Fargo, ND	Fayetteville, NC	Flagstaff, AZ	Flint, MI	Florence, SC	Ft. Collins, CO	Ft. Dodge, IA	Ft. Lauderdale, FL	Ft. Smith, AR	Ft. Wayne, IN	Ft. Worth, TX	Fredericton, NB	Fresno, CA	Gainesville, FL	Galveston, TX	Gary, IN	Grand Island, NE	Grand Rapids, MI	Great Falls, MT	Greeley, CO	Green Bay, WI	Greensboro, NC	Greenville, SC	Halifax, NS	Hamilton, OH	Harrisburg, PA	Hartford, CT	High Point, NC	Houston, TX	Huntington, WV	Huntsville, AL	Indianapolis, IN	Iowa City, IA	Jackson, MS	Jacksonville, FL	Janesville, WI	Jefferson City, MO	Jersey City, NJ	Joliet, IL	Kalamazoo, MI	K[...] City, MO
Abilene, TX	2035	1648	1926	1166	1349	811	1326	1264	745	908	1474	455	1162	149	2369	1401	1163	458	1088	725	1231	1455	727	1281	1300	1110	2595	1152	1564	1848	1282	410	1179	846	1028	951	582	1179	1107	709	1729	1044	1200	6
Akron, OH	2458	2442	626	1012	567	1908	241	579	1354	750	1192	935	218	1207	1061	2494	931	1347	335	966	319	1747	1324	580	457	571	1287	232	304	538	447	1298	263	634	299	572	929	862	479	667	436	375	280	7
Albany, GA	2844	2559	1223	1535	478	1793	954	392	1611	1166	492	750	833	830	1666	2384	182	766	861	1269	962	2222	1593	1105	499	313	1892	669	883	1145	481	746	656	330	705	989	398	198	1002	859	1026	900	930	9
Albany, NY	2910	2894	195	1463	710	2393	693	795	1806	1201	1429	1512	686	1708	589	2945	1168	1778	787	1417	771	2199	1776	1032	701	867	814	718	297	106	709	1758	709	1046	784	1023	1326	1099	930	1153	165	827	731	12
Albert Lea, MN	1675	1908	1385	330	1250	1454	677	1263	821	124	1666	631	567	893	1764	1960	1356	1135	439	432	582	1065	791	326	1140	1092	2031	684	1063	1297	1129	1086	834	894	573	209	945	1372	297	416	1195	401	551	3
Albuquerque, NM	1482	1089	2190	1320	1772	324	1581	1687	515	1054	1938	722	1416	622	2645	914	1628	933	1343	852	1486	1225	515	1416	1682	1534	2870	1394	1828	2122	1671	884	1498	1220	1283	1097	1047	1643	1297	964	1992	1299	1455	7
Alexandria, LA	2526	2038	1571	1272	943	1272	1158	858	1235	928	1037	375	984	334	2014	1862	726	254	919	940	1062	1945	1217	1125	894	704	2240	901	1209	1493	876	234	930	511	851	918	176	742	990	674	1374	895	1032	6
Alexandria, VA	2803	2788	439	1356	313	2212	586	398	1700	1094	1032	1170	573	1364	882	2802	771	1434	680	1310	664	2093	1669	926	304	495	1108	524	139	360	322	1414	422	702	594	917	982	702	824	963	242	720	624	10
Allentown, PA	2822	2806	286	1375	518	2231	604	602	1718	1113	1236	1300	592	1494	729	2822	975	1564	698	1329	682	2111	1688	944	482	653	955	552	82	208	495	1544	494	832	622	935	1112	906	842	991	88	739	643	11
Altoona, PA	2644	2628	462	1198	484	2066	427	569	1540	936	1202	1094	414	1361	898	2656	942	1486	521	1152	505	1934	1510	766	405	575	1123	387	134	374	417	1466	366	755	457	758	1035	873	665	826	273	561	466	9
Amarillo, TX	1768	1373	1906	1002	1488	608	1297	1403	478	879	1654	438	1132	338	2361	1198	1344	649	1059	544	1202	1188	460	1252	1398	1250	2586	1110	1544	1838	1387	600	1214	936	999	921	763	1359	1078	680	1709	1015	1171	6
Anderson, IN	2300	2262	893	854	655	1652	268	709	1185	570	1218	680	88	946	1348	2242	908	1115	178	786	256	1590	1145	422	545	537	1573	103	531	824	534	1067	274	445	43	392	720	924	320	412	695	217	202	5
Ann Arbor, MI	2333	2317	801	886	706	1872	54	719	1229	624	1332	902	155	1166	1112	2368	1063	1344	210	840	132	1623	1199	455	597	682	1380	237	480	713	586	1296	328	658	278	446	953	1002	353	605	612	250	98	7
Appleton, WI	1966	2162	1183	519	1048	1708	476	1082	1074	392	1568	848	365	1114	1439	2214	1257	1289	224	685	380	1255	1044	32	938	910	1706	499	862	1095	928	1240	650	794	385	287	949	1272	140	553	994	226	350	5
Asheville, NC	2716	2619	878	1301	267	1836	685	234	1506	1012	772	794	526	988	1321	2426	511	1025	626	1142	720	2037	1488	870	172	62	1547	401	516	800	161	1005	280	326	470	834	590	442	768	732	680	664	681	8
Atlanta, GA	2672	2475	1078	1364	376	1710	782	290	1461	994	641	668	661	812	1521	2300	330	814	690	1097	790	2050	1443	934	336	146	1747	499	716	1000	318	794	485	188	534	817	380	346	830	688	880	728	759	8
Atlantic City, NJ	2913	2897	343	1466	517	2313	696	602	1809	1204	1236	1354	683	1548	786	2904	975	1618	790	1420	774	2203	1779	1035	508	698	1012	634	170	265	526	1598	566	886	704	1026	1166	906	933	1073	145	830	734	11
Augusta, GA	2824	2635	980	1516	234	1870	833	148	1614	1148	592	828	701	972	1422	2460	332	958	800	1250	895	2204	1596	1044	255	117	1648	576	641	901	236	938	478	342	644	970	540	262	984	840	782	839	856	9
Aurora, IL	2079	2058	1022	632	887	1639	314	920	970	364	1406	667	206	933	1401	2109	1096	1108	76	580	219	1369	940	229	777	748	1668	338	700	934	766	1059	488	632	224	187	736	1112	100	372	832	30	188	4
Austin, TX	2294	1775	1941	1263	1307	1030	1366	1221	1003	965	1326	473	1200	188	2384	1600	1015	213	1127	821	1270	1714	985	1320	1258	1068	2610	1166	1579	1863	1240	164	1194	860	1067	1008	540	1031	1146	748	1744	1083	1240	7
Bakersfield, CA	1059	285	2998	1864	2576	480	2291	2491	1094	1755	2742	1526	2182	1426	3377	110	2432	1716	2052	1435	2196	1279	1094	2136	2486	2338	3645	2198	2632	2910	2475	1666	2302	2024	2087	1816	1851	2447	2016	1793	2809	2008	2164	16
Baltimore, MD	2792	2776	384	1346	368	2246	576	452	1689	1084	1086	1203	562	1398	828	2837	826	1468	669	1300	654	2082	1659	915	358	549	1053	513	83	306	377	1448	412	737	584	906	1017	756	813	952	187	710	614	10
Bangor, ME	3302	3286	292	1855	998	2772	1085	1082	2198	1593	1716	1828	1079	2024	197	3337	1455	2093	1178	1809	1163	2592	2168	1424	988	1182	421	1097	612	327	1006	2073	1024	1362	1163	1416	1642	1386	1322	1532	449	1219	1123	16
Baton Rouge, LA	2664	2176	1558	1410	896	1410	1152	810	1373	1090	898	513	978	472	2001	2000	588	288	914	1078	1057	2084	1355	1120	864	674	2227	896	1196	1480	846	268	924	497	846	912	172	603	985	782	1360	890	1026	8
Bay City, MI	2408	2392	898	961	803	1947	48	816	1304	699	1428	975	229	1241	1134	2443	1160	1419	284	915	156	1697	1274	437	694	780	1402	334	577	810	683	1370	424	754	352	521	1022	1098	428	679	708	325	173	7
Bayonne, NJ	2885	2869	212	1438	550	2313	668	635	1781	1176	1268	1382	655	1576	655	2920	1008	1646	762	1392	746	2175	1751	1007	540	735	880	634	164	133	560	1626	576	914	704	998	1194	938	905	1073	7	802	706	11
Beaumont, TX	2514	2029	1741	1305	1079	1254	1292	994	1223	988	1081	441	1118	310	2184	1854	771	105	1053	928	1196	1933	1205	1243	1048	858	2410	1079	1379	1663	1030	85	1108	680	985	996	354	786	1069	743	1544	1006	1166	7
Billings, MT	842	1134	2233	608	2133	1072	1525	2100	500	865	2477	1355	1417	1307	2612	1253	2167	1716	1287	775	1430	219	524	1120	1988	1929	2880	1549	1912	2145	1978	1668	1700	1704	1435	1060	1756	2182	1145	1185	2043	1269	1400	10
Binghamton, NY	2798	2783	334	1352	629	2282	582	714	1695	1090	1348	1398	576	1592	728	2834	1086	1662	676	1306	660	2088	1665	921	581	751	954	606	181	233	593	1642	592	930	673	912	1211	1018	819	1042	176	716	620	11
Birmingham, AL	2620	2330	1160	1308	533	1565	785	448	1383	942	759	523	606	669	1603	2155	449	688	635	1045	735	1999	1365	879	484	294	1828	502	798	1081	466	668	530	102	479	765	237	464	776	635	962	674	704	7
Bismarck, ND	1256	1548	1819	195	1684	1468	1112	1718	638	644	2202	1088	1001	1158	2198	1667	1892	1454	873	529	1016	546	662	706	1574	1546	2466	1135	1498	1731	1564	1406	1286	1428	1021	730	1520	1908	731	949	1629	856	986	7
Bloomington, IN	2322	2234	954	876	693	1588	360	675	1121	566	1160	616	180	882	1409	2178	850	1052	201	758	309	1612	1103	445	583	503	1635	136	592	886	572	1003	288	387	53	388	617	866	343	348	757	240	278	4
Boise, ID	525	600	2660	1227	2480	860	1953	2447	752	1418	2824	1632	1843	1584	3040	719	2514	1994	1715	1098	1858	581	802	1738	2392	2275	3308	1953	2340	2573	2382	1945	2080	2050	1842	1479	2048	2529	1679	1531	2472	1671	1828	13
Boston, MA	3076	3060	52	1630	772	2546	859	856	1972	1367	1490	1602	853	1797	436	3112	1229	1867	953	1583	937	2366	1942	1198	762	956	662	871	386	101	780	1847	798	1136	937	1190	1416	1160	1096	1306	223	993	898	14
Boulder, CO	1344	1218	1981	886	1728	803	1273	1696	54	738	2072	829	1163	781	2360	1165	1762	1190	1035	418	1178	764	54	1118	1640	1524	2628	1216	1650	1893	1630	1142	1328	1299	1106	799	1245	1778	999	780	1791	991	1148	6
Bowling Green, KY	2396	2298	1052	1056	595	1607	531	562	1185	718	960	564	352	760	1495	2198	650	899	381	821	481	1775	1167	625	507	390	1720	248	689	973	496	850	276	186	225	541	482	665	523	412	854	420	450	5
Bridgeport, CT	2937	2922	135	1491	616	2378	720	700	1834	1228	1334	1446	707	1641	578	2973	1073	1711	814	1444	798	2227	1804	1060	606	800	804	699	230	57	624	1691	642	979	770	1051	1260	1004	958	1138	67	854	758	12
Brockton, MA	3089	3073	30	1642	778	2559	872	863	1985	1380	1497	1610	866	1804	460	3124	1236	1874	966	1596	950	2379	1955	1211	768	963	686	884	392	114	788	1854	804	1142	950	1202	1422	1167	1109	1319	230	1006	910	14
Brownsville, TX	2556	2026	2180	1615	1518	1404	1717	1432	1266	1317	1520	825	1508	540	2623	1852	1210	396	1479	1173	1622	1977	1248	1672	1486	1297	2849	1447	1818	2102	1468	354	1476	1120	1375	1360	793	1225	1498	1100	1983	1435	1592	10
Buffalo, NY	2629	2614	485	1182	693	2112	412	762	1526	920	1375	1140	406	1411	879	2665	1114	1551	506	1136	490	1919	1495	752	640	754	1105	437	287	397	630	1502	488	838	503	743	1134	1045	650	872	398	546	450	9
Butte, MT	618	1001	2455	831	2356	940	1748	2323	722	1087	2700	1577	1637	1529	2834	1120	2390	1938	1509	997	1652	155	746	1342	2210	2151	3102	1771	2134	2367	2200	1890	1922	1926	1657	1282	1978	2404	1367	1407	2266	1492	1622	12
Calgary, AB	649	1474	2612	988	2477	1412	1904	2510	1041	1437	3018	1896	1796	1848	2758	1592	2708	2258	1666	1316	1809	326	1066	1498	2367	2339	3026	1928	2290	2524	2356	2209	2079	2245	1814	1523	2297	2724	1524	1726	2422	1648	1778	15
Camden, NJ	2862	2846	296	1415	469	2262	645	554	1758	1153	1188	1306	632	1500	739	2852	927	1570	738	1369	722	2151	1728	984	460	650	964	582	119	217	478	1550	517	838	653	975	1118	858	882	1022	98	779	683	11
Canton, OH	2478	2462	634	1031	547	1909	261	559	1374	769	1172	937	219	1208	1070	2500	911	1348	354	985	339	1768	1344	600	437	551	1296	234	301	547	427	1300	242	635	300	592	931	842	498	669	445	395	299	7
Casper, WY	1118	1101	2060	712	1879	818	1353	1846	223	683	2223	1078	1244	1029	2439	1216	1912	1439	1114	498	1258	497	247	1088	1792	1674	2707	1352	1739	1972	1781	1390	1479	1450	1242	878	1494	1928	1058	931	1870	1070	1227	7
Cedar Rapids, IA	1859	1887	1210	509	1057	1432	502	1082	799	154	1486	610	394	871	1589	1938	1176	1113	264	410	407	1245	769	308	948	910	1857	502	889	1122	937	1064	654	712	392	28	764	1192	174	273	1020	220	376	3
Champaign, IL	2139	2114	1036	745	795	1539	375	820	1026	421	1264	567	217	833	1462	2130	954	1003	137	637	280	1482	996	343	686	648	1729	240	674	968	675	954	390	491	129	243	607	970	212	299	839	113	249	3
Charleston, SC	2972	2803	963	1557	217	2037	880	130	1762	1268	568	993	783	1140	1406	2628	307	1125	882	1398	958	2293	1744	1126	302	212	1632	658	663	884	284	1105	524	509	726	1091	708	238	1024	988	766	921	938	11
Charleston, WV	2582	2524	726	1136	355	1870	406	368	1412	856	980	884	322	1080	1169	2460	719	1219	461	1048	484	1872	1394	705	246	359	1395	222	364	648	235	1171	50	506	312	678	801	650	603	638	528	500	428	7
Charlotte, NC	2830	2732	840	1414	139	1950	670	104	1619	1126	714	906	588	1058	1284	2540	453	1060	739	1256	748	2150	1601	983	96	101	1509	486	478	762	77	1041	314	418	583	948	626	384	881	846	643	778	692	9
Chattanooga, TN	2554	2456	1013	1246	496	1644	679	411	1344	877	763	602	544	814	1456	2234	452	833	572	980	672	1934	1326	816	394	249	1682	396	651	935	384	813	382	102	416	700	382	468	714	570	816	612	642	6
Cheyenne, WY	1258	1133	1924	787	1743	875	1216	1710	45	681	2086	900	1108	852	2303	1241	1776	1262	978	361	1121	675	51	1062	1655	1538	2571	1216	1603	1836	1644	1213	1342	1314	1106	742	1316	1792	942	794	1734	934	1090	6
Chicago, IL	2093	2094	979	646	846	1660	272	880	1006	401	1365	688	162	954	1358	2145	1055	1138	30	617	177	1383	976	206	736	708	1626	297	658	892	726	1090	448	592	183	223	743	1070	114	392	790	45	146	5
Cincinnati, OH	2386	2346	834	939	552	1714	304	588	1247	653	1106	770	182	964	1293	2304	796	1104	264	869	355	1675	1229	508	442	416	1519	28	472	770	431	1055	148	391	110	475	687	796	406	474	637	303	300	5
Clarksville, TN	2380	2283	1128	1072	596	1542	612	564	1170	704	940	498	432	694	1571	2132	630	834	378	806	520	1760	1152	604	509	392	1797	328	766	1050	498	785	357	167	305	526	416	646	540	396	930	399	489	5
Clearwater, FL	3155	2813	1358	1846	612	2047	1266	525	1944	1478	269	1064	1144	1109	1800	2638	153	972	1172	1580	1272	2534	1926	1416	696	607	2026	982	1058	1280	678	952	920	644	1016	1300	677	221	1314	1170	1160	1212	1242	12
Cleveland, OH	2436	2420	668	990	606	1925	220	619	1333	728	1232	953	214	1224	1062	2472	970	1364	313	944	298	1726	1303	559	497	610	1288	250	329	563	486	1316	302	651	316	550	947	902	457	685	461	354	258	8
Coeur d'Alene, ID	332	868	2740	1116	2642	1212	2034	2608	1008	1372	2985	1863	1925	1814	3120	1021	2675	2224	1795	1283	1938	335	1032	1628	2496	2436	3388	2057	2420	2653	2486	2176	2208	2212	1943	1568	2264	2691	1653	1693	2551	1778	1908	15
Colorado Sprs., CO	1430	1303	1981	943	1696	700	1330	1664	138	795	2040	797	1207	703	2417	1212	1730	1014	1092	475	1235	849	139	1175	1609	1492	2685	1184	1619	1912	1598	965	1296	1267	1074	856	1128	1746	1056	748	1783	1048	1204	5
Columbia, MO	1993	1896	1265	728	980	1230	628	948	782	338	1324	349	490	613	1720	1871	1014	874	390	418	533	1372	764	583	893	776	1945	468	903	1196	882	825	580	551	358	238	603	1030	409	32	1067	346	502	1
Columbia, SC	2864	2700	912	1448	166	1934	766	81	1654	1160	618	892	674	1037	1356	2524	357	1022	773	1290	843	2185	1636	1017	188	103	1581	549	574	834	169	1002	410	406	617	982	605	288	916	880	714	812	787	9
Columbus, GA	2774	2474	1188	1466	477	1708	885	392	1526	1097	579	665	764	766	1631	2299	269	742	792	1200	892	2154	1508	1036	446	256	1857	602	826	1110	428	722	588	246	636	920	334	284	933	790	990	832	862	9
Columbus, OH	2446	2416	730	1000	517	1784	245	529	1318	723	1142	814	156	1082	1185	2375	881	1222	324	939	323	1736	1300	569	407	521	1411	108	368	662	397	1174	137	510	176	546	805	812	467	544	532	364	284	6
Concord, NH	3055	3040	119	1609	820	2538	838	904	1952	1346	1538	1650	832	1846	421	3091	1277	1915	932	1562	916	2345	1922	1178	810	1004	646	863	434	149	828	1895	846	1184	929	1169	1464	1208	1076	1298	271	972	876	14
Corpus Christi, TX	2422	1891	2033	1479	1371	1268	1582	1286	1131	1182	1373	689	1362	404	2476	1716	1063	228	1343	1038	1487	1841	1113	1536	1340	1150	2702	1300	1671	1955	1322	207	1328	972	1228	1224	646	1078	1363	964	1836	1300	1456	9
Dallas, TX	2224	1737	1747	1080	1169	971	1171	1083	934	771	1293	278	1006	30	2190	1561	983	291	933	639	1076	1644	916	1126	1120	930	2416	972	1385	1668	1102	242	1000	666	873	813	402	999	952	554	1549	889	1045	5
Davenport, IA	1955	1930	1130	592	977	1475	422	1002	842	237	1434	654	314	914	1509	1981	1124	1156	184	453	327	1328	812	332	868	830	1777	422	809	1042	857	1107	574	660	312	59	758	1140	158	266	940	140	296	3
Dayton, OH	2388	2358	800	941	549	1726	251	561	1259	665	1177	754	128	1034	1255	2316	867	1174	266	881	302	1678	1241	510	439	486	1481	41	438	732	428	1126	168	461	117	487	757	867	408	486	603	305	248	6
Daytona Beach, FL	3112	2822	1232	1804	486	2056	1149	400	1902	1434	242	1073	1052	1118	1676	2647	99	981	1130	1538	1230	2491	1884	1374	571	481	1901	927	933	1154	553	961	794	630	974	1258	686	92	1271	1128	1035	1169	1200	12
Decatur, AL	2520	2286	1139	1229	583	1520	706	497	1309	843	839	478	526	672	1582	2110	529	766	555	946	655	1899	1291	799	520	344	1808	422	776	1060	509	746	450	25	399	666	315	544	696	536	941	594	624	6
Decatur, IL	2131	2043	1092	749	850	1499	427	875	955	413	1252	528	272	793	1514	2089	942	967	188	566	332	1485	925	390	740	704	1781	295	729	1023	730	919	446	479	184	236	595	958	216	231	894	153	301	3
Denver, CO	1356	1231	1970	876	1710	675	1262	1677	66	727	2054	811	1154	762	2349	1143	1744	1172	1024	407	1167	776	66	1108	1622	1506	2617	1198	1632	1882	1612	1123	1310	1280	1087	788	1227	1760	988	762	1780	980	1136	6
Des Moines, IA	1786	1761	1296	475	1143	1306	588	1168	673	96	1572	484	478	745	1674	1812	1261	987	350	284	493	1165	643	433	1033	996	1942	588	974	1208	1022	938	738	798	477	114	850	1276	314	271	1106	306	462	1
Detroit, MI	2376	2360	804	930	707	1897	69	720	1272	668	1332	926	172	1191	1074	2412	1076	1384	253	884	158	1666	1242	498	597	696	1342	250	483	716	587	1335	328	670	288	490	966	1002	397	657	615	294	142	7
Dubuque, IA	1896	1960	1162	546	1047	1506	455	1072	873	191	1504	685	346	945	1541	2012	1194	1187	216	484	359	1282	843	234	937	900	1809	492	841	1074	927	1138	642	730	381	85	827	1209	99	347	972	210	328	3
Duluth, MN	1700	1993	1450	254	1316	1702	743	1350	1068	371	1834	879	635	1141	1542	2208	1523	1382	505	679	648	990	1038	329	1206	1178	1810	767	1129	1363	1195	1334	918	1060	653	457	1171	1539	363	664	1261	487	617	5
Durham, NC	2886	2846	690	1439	90	2062	708	174	1732	1160	808	1020	626	1200	1134	2654	548	1204	764	1368	786	2175	1714	1008	54	244	1360	525	391	612	72	1184	354	554	614	982	768	478	906	959	493	802	730	10
East Orange, NJ	2870	2854	208	1424	554	2315	654	640	1767	1162	1274	1384	640	1578	652	2906	1012	1648	747	1378	732	2160	1737	993	546	737	877	636	166	130	564	1628	578	916	706	984	1196	944	891	1075	14	788	692	11
Eau Claire, WI	1774	2088	1299	328	1164	1634	592	1198	1001	304	1682	813	482	1073	1678	2140	1372	1315	354	612	497	1064	971	192	1055	1026	1946	616	978	1212	1044	1266	766	909	502	290	1020	1388	212	596	1110	336	466	5
Elgin, IL	2052	2082	1025	605	890	1627	318	924	994	330	1410	695	208	959	1404	2133	1100	1134	79	604	223	1342	964	208	781	752	1672	342	704	937	770	1085	492	636	228	211	779	1114	72	398	836	62	192	5
Elizabeth, NJ	2877	2861	212	1430	543	2306	660	628	1773	1168	1262	1374	646	1570	655	2897	1000	1639	754	1384	738	2168	1743	999	534	728	880	627	158	133	552	1619	570	908	698	991	1188	932	897	1066	14	794	698	11
El Paso, TX	1750	1194	2381	1370	1804	572	1734	1719	782	1207	1915	911	1568	605	2824	1020	1605	801	1495	912	1638	1492	782	1568	1755	1566	3050	1607	2019	2303	1737	752	1636	1301	1436	1249	1038	1621	1449	1116	2184	1451	1608	9
Elyria, OH	2410	2394	664	963	616	1907	193	628	1306	701	1241	936	187	1206	1090	2445	980	1346	286	917	271	1700	1276	532	506	620	1316	231	342	576	496	1297	260	633	298	524	928	911	430	666	474	327	231	7
Enid, OK	1928	1666	1658	840	1282	901	1049	1197	637	582	1508	232	884	297	2113	1491	1198	593	811	398	954	1347	619	944	1192	1044	2338	862	1296	1590	1181	545	966	730	751	624	648	1213	824	432	1460	767	923	3
Erie, PA	2538	2522	571	1091	676	2020	320	670	1434	829	1283	1050	314	1320	965	2573	1022	1459	414	1045	398	1827	1404	660	548	662	1191	345	308	483	538	1410	396	746	412	651	1042	953	558	780	431	455	358	8
Escondido, CA	1266	496	3012	1878	2550	495	2306	2464	1108	1770	2660	1540	2197	1350	3392	321	2350	1546	2067	1450	2210	1294	1109	2150	2500	2310	3660	2212	2646	2925	2490	1498	2316	2039	2102	1831	1783	2366	2030	1808	2823	2023	2180	165
Eugene, OR	311	488	3196	1610	3016	1231	2490	2982	1288	1866	3360	2168	2378	2120	3575	640	3049	2530	2250	1634	2394	829	1338	2121	2928	2811	3843	2488	2876	3108	2918	2480	2616	2586	2378	2014	2584	3065	2146	2068	3007	2206	2363	190
Evansville, IN	2286	2189	1088	943	698	1534	492	666	1076	609	1042	593	314	788	1518	2125	732	928	273	712	414	1666	1058	498	610	494	1744	253	726	995	600	880	314	269	180	432	496	748	410	302	891	293	384	4
Everett, WA		796	3072	1448	2974	1382	2365	2940	1274	1704	3317	2154	2257	2106	3452	949	3007	2516	2126	1620	2270	667	1324	1960	2828	2768	3720	2389	2752	2984	2818	2466	2540	2544	2275	1900	2596	3022	1984	2025	2883	2109	2240	186
Fairfield, CA	796		3056	1741	2876	766	2350	2776	1148	1814	3027	1811	2239	1711	3436	175	2717	1996	2111	1494	2254	1156	1198	2194	2788	2671	3703	2349	2736	2969	2778	1947	2476	2310	2238	1875	2136	2732	2075	1928	2868	2067	2223	176
Fall River, MA	3072	3056		1626	750	2514	856	836	1969	1364	1469	1581	842	1777	488	3108	1208	1846	949	1580	934	2362	1939	1195	741	935	714	834	365	129	760	1826	776	1115	905	1186	1395	1140	1093	1274	202	990	894	138
Fargo, ND	1448	1741	1626		1491	1644	918	1525	830	452	2009	899	810	1075	2005	1860	1699	1371	680	467	824	738	844	513	1382	1353	2273	942	1305	1538	1371	1322	1094	1236	828	537	1330	1714	538	760	1436	662	792	60
Fayetteville, NC	2974	2876	750	1491		2096	761	90	1763	1211	723	1054	678	1199	1194	2686	462	1184	816	1399	839	2227	1745	1060	142	265	1420	577	451	672	124	1164	406	568	667	1034	766	394	958	989	553	855	782	110
Flagstaff, AZ	1382	766	2514	1644	2096		1905	2010	839	1378	2261	1046	1740	946	2968	590	1951	1256	1666	1175	1810	1095	839	1740	2005	1857	3194	1717	2152	2445	1995	1208	1821	1544	1607	1420	1370	1967	1620	1288	2316	1622	1778	110
Flint, MI	2365	2350	856	918	761	1905		773	1262	656	1386	934	187	1199	1087	2401	1118	1377	242	872	114	1655	1231	488	651	737	1354	292	534	768	641	1328	382	712	310	479	981	1056	386	637	666	282	130	75
Florence, SC	2940	2776	836	1525	90	2010	773		1730	1236	637	967	690	1113	1278	2601	376	1098	850	1366	851	2261	1712	1094	168	180	1504	626	536	757	174	1078	418	482	694	1059	681	307	992	956	638	888	795	1072
Ft. Collins, CO	1274	1148	1969	830	1763	839	1262	1730		726	2106	864	1151	815	2348	1204	1796	1225	1023	406	1166	719	33	1106	1675	1558	2616	1250	1648	1881	1664	1176	1362	1333	1140	787	1280	1812	987	814	1780	979	1136	65
Ft. Dodge, IA	1704	1814	1364	452	1211	1378	656	1236	726		1640	557	548	817	1743	1865	1330	1059	418	337	561	1084	696	424	1102	1064	2011	656	1043	1276	1091	1010	808	866	546	182	918	1346	290	365	1174	374	530	26
Ft. Lauderdale, FL	3317	3027	1469	2009	723	2261	1386	637	2106	1640		1278	1306	1323	1912	2852	315	1186	1335	1742	1435	2696	2088	1579	808	718	2138	1144	1170	1391	790	1166	1030	835	1179	1462	891	328	1476	1333	1272	1374	1405	1448
Ft. Smith, AR	2154	1811	1581	899	1054	1046	934	967	864	557	1278		768	306	2026	1636	968	566	694	568	839	1574	846	887	962	814	2250	747	1219	1504	953	518	836	502	636	598	420	985	715	317	1385	652	808	29

Mileages in this Mileage Directory are from the Rand McNally *MileMaker Practical Routing System*, © Rand McNally. **These mileages are for general reference only and should not be used for the purposes of tariff computation.** For tariff purposes, refer to the applicable official tariff. Mileages between each of the 300 cities listed in this chart are computed over National Interstate, U.S. and primary state highways, and Canadian provincial highways via highways designated as truck-usable by the Household Goods Carriers' Bureau Committee. Practical routing may have highway segments not included in the federally designated National Network.

	Kenosha, WI	Kingston, ON	Knoxville, TN	Lafayette, LA	Lake Charles, LA	Lancaster, PA	Lansing, MI	Laredo, TX	Las Vegas, NV	Lawrence, KS	Lawrence, MA	Lawton, OK	Lexington, KY	Lincoln, NE	Little Rock, AR	London, ON	Long Beach, CA	Longview, TX	Lorain, OH	Los Angeles, CA
Abilene, TX	1133	1702	1023	572	516	1601	1272	413	1128	604	1958	203	1055	726	499	1437	1261	310	1356	1256
Akron, OH	439	476	493	1156	1224	339	251	1611	2099	823	650	1126	325	872	860	308	2379	1090	57	2368
Albany, GA	964	1269	385	533	602	920	957	1097	2111	1016	1256	990	554	1175	598	1030	2243	674	875	2238
Albany, NY	891	252	834	1545	1613	278	703	2109	2551	1309	178	1611	832	1323	1361	437	2830	1603	504	2820
Albert Lea, MN	365	1079	926	1092	1105	1098	622	1281	1565	381	1399	781	754	338	721	812	1845	877	723	1834
Albuquerque, NM	1388	1956	1398	1036	990	1863	1526	785	641	750	2234	497	1374	812	878	1692	799	775	1588	788
Alexandria, LA	984	1526	668	89	107	1246	1102	586	1589	684	1604	493	804	942	335	1260	1746	178	1106	1742
Alexandria, VA	784	526	490	1200	1269	138	596	1765	2431	1119	471	1427	546	1216	1017	546	2687	1259	402	2676
Allentown, PA	802	341	620	1330	1399	70	615	1895	2462	1147	318	1450	618	1235	1147	501	2706	1389	420	2696
Altoona, PA	625	413	543	1253	1322	169	437	1765	2285	982	487	1285	490	1058	1014	362	2542	1244	243	2531
Amarillo, TX	1104	1672	1114	752	706	1579	1242	663	925	574	1950	213	1090	596	594	1408	1083	491	1304	1072
Anderson, IN	281	629	371	946	1014	566	213	1352	1880	568	937	870	202	692	628	364	2128	858	262	2116
Ann Arbor, MI	314	428	517	1180	1248	515	64	1573	1974	760	816	1091	348	746	858	162	2253	1088	140	2242
Appleton, WI	143	878	744	1175	1244	896	421	1521	1819	634	1198	1039	572	592	801	610	2098	1032	522	2088
Asheville, NC	728	902	114	792	860	554	695	1356	2154	888	910	1051	286	1050	641	762	2312	866	552	2301
Atlanta, GA	792	1102	213	580	649	753	784	1145	2027	844	1110	925	383	1005	515	859	2185	657	704	2174
Atlantic City, NJ	894	452	674	1384	1453	140	706	1949	2541	1229	375	1532	688	1326	1201	612	2788	1443	512	2778
Augusta, GA	903	1027	289	724	793	678	843	1289	2187	996	1012	1084	460	1158	674	897	2345	817	695	2334
Aurora, IL	88	716	583	962	1030	735	259	1340	1714	530	1036	858	411	487	620	449	1994	851	360	1983
Austin, TX	1172	1741	1038	378	304	1616	1311	240	1364	701	1973	355	1070	823	514	1476	1388	268	1371	1383
Bakersfield, CA	2071	2692	2202	1840	1808	2667	2236	1520	287	1600	3013	1301	2178	1519	1682	2426	135	1579	2337	112
Baltimore, MD	774	469	525	1235	1304	82	586	1800	2420	1108	416	1461	535	1206	1051	526	2722	1293	391	2711
Bangor, ME	1283	471	1150	1860	1928	598	1095	2424	2943	1688	218	1990	1147	1715	1676	743	3222	1918	896	3212
Baton Rouge, LA	979	1520	655	55	124	1234	1098	620	1727	822	1590	632	799	1080	361	1256	1825	316	1100	1820
Bay City, MI	388	450	614	1250	1318	612	98	1648	2048	834	913	1166	446	821	932	183	2328	1162	237	2317
Bayonne, NJ	866	386	702	1412	1481	151	678	1977	2526	1229	244	1532	700	1298	1229	546	2805	1471	484	2794
Beaumont, TX	1118	1704	838	133	60	1416	1237	436	1572	705	1774	476	982	930	404	1438	1642	191	1284	1637
Billings, MT	1213	1927	1762	1815	1761	1946	1470	1633	972	1048	2248	1182	1610	858	1511	1660	1252	1553	1572	1241
Binghamton, NY	780	210	718	1429	1498	191	592	1993	2440	1198	318	1500	716	1212	1245	370	2719	1487	392	2708
Birmingham, AL	737	1127	257	455	524	835	730	1020	1882	717	1192	780	405	953	370	862	2040	514	706	2030
Bismarck, ND	799	1513	1380	1549	1536	1532	1057	1586	1386	812	1834	1046	1208	663	1178	1246	1666	1307	1158	1655
Bloomington, IN	303	721	337	844	912	628	305	1288	1816	504	998	807	165	666	564	456	2064	795	353	2053
Boise, ID	1734	2355	2108	2092	2038	2374	1898	1910	629	1389	2676	1459	1956	1182	1789	2088	864	1830	2000	842
Boston, MA	1057	418	924	1634	1702	372	869	2198	2717	1462	28	1764	921	1489	1450	603	2996	1692	670	2986
Boulder, CO	1054	1675	1357	1289	1236	1686	1218	1107	770	586	1996	656	1205	502	986	1408	1050	1027	1320	1040
Bowling Green, KY	484	873	224	708	776	727	476	1164	1880	568	1084	822	152	730	412	608	2082	642	453	2072
Bridgeport, CT	918	419	767	1478	1546	216	730	2042	2578	1294	168	1597	765	1350	1294	579	2858	1536	536	2847
Brockton, MA	1070	431	930	1641	1709	379	882	2205	2730	1475	52	1778	928	1502	1457	616	3010	1699	682	2998
Brownsville, TX	1524	2072	1277	572	499	1856	1662	204	1616	1052	2212	707	1350	1175	794	1807	1640	562	1652	1635
Buffalo, NY	610	260	704	1360	1428	327	422	1815	2270	1028	468	1331	528	1043	1064	152	2550	1294	223	2539
Butte, MT	1435	2149	1984	2037	1984	2168	1693	1855	840	1270	2470	1404	1832	1081	1734	1882	1119	1775	1794	1108
Calgary, AB	1592	2242	2173	2356	2303	2325	1849	2174	1312	1590	2532	1723	2001	1400	2053	2221	1592	2094	1950	1580
Camden, NJ	842	400	626	1336	1405	88	655	1901	2490	1178	328	1480	640	1275	1152	560	2737	1394	460	2726
Canton, OH	459	496	501	1157	1226	336	271	1612	2119	825	659	1128	326	891	861	328	2384	1092	76	2374
Casper, WY	1127	1755	1508	1538	1484	1774	1298	1356	821	834	2075	905	1356	581	1234	1488	1100	1276	1399	1090
Cedar Rapids, IA	283	904	745	990	1059	924	448	1259	1544	359	1225	759	573	316	617	638	1823	856	549	1812
Champaign, IL	202	777	482	833	902	709	320	1240	1748	436	1080	758	310	543	516	510	2014	746	421	2004
Charleston, SC	984	1050	371	892	960	662	890	1456	2354	1144	995	1252	542	1306	842	944	2512	984	742	2502
Charleston, WV	564	698	309	1019	1088	401	416	1484	2106	794	758	1089	174	956	732	470	2346	962	268	2335
Charlotte, NC	842	864	228	828	896	516	680	1392	2267	1002	872	1164	399	1164	754	734	2425	902	532	2414
Chattanooga, TN	676	1037	110	600	668	688	668	1164	1961	726	1046	859	280	888	449	756	2119	658	600	2108
Cheyenne, WY	997	1618	1372	1360	1306	1638	1162	1178	846	657	1939	727	1220	445	1056	1352	1126	1098	1263	1115
Chicago, IL	65	674	542	969	1038	693	217	1360	1750	566	994	879	370	523	651	407	2030	882	318	2020
Cincinnati, OH	366	646	250	912	982	507	315	1368	1942	630	882	932	82	775	617	381	2189	847	232	2178
Clarksville, TN	463	953	225	642	711	803	557	1098	1865	553	1160	756	232	714	346	688	2017	577	533	2006
Clearwater, FL	1276	1444	696	739	807	1056	1268	1303	2365	1326	1390	1269	866	1488	912	1342	2509	954	1137	2504
Cleveland, OH	418	453	510	1173	1242	364	230	1628	2078	841	651	1144	342	850	877	286	2357	1108	30	2346
Coeur d'Alene, ID	1721	2436	2270	2323	2270	2454	1978	2140	1112	1556	2756	1690	2118	1366	2020	2168	1391	2061	2080	1380
Colorado Sprs., CO	1111	1732	1325	1118	1072	1654	1276	1029	817	554	2053	578	1173	559	954	1466	1096	856	1377	1086
Columbia, MO	435	1031	609	829	898	938	574	1020	1477	165	1309	557	457	326	379	766	1756	616	663	1746
Columbia, SC	876	960	262	789	858	611	776	1353	2252	1036	944	1149	433	1198	739	830	2410	881	628	2398
Columbus, GA	894	1212	316	509	578	864	888	1074	2026	946	1220	923	486	1108	513	962	2184	611	806	2173
Columbus, OH	427	589	368	1031	1100	402	255	1487	2012	700	774	1003	200	846	736	309	2260	966	124	2249
Concord, NH	1036	430	972	1682	1750	420	848	2246	2696	1454	42	1757	969	1469	1498	582	2976	1740	649	2965
Corpus Christi, TX	1389	1925	1130	425	352	1708	1527	144	1480	917	2066	571	1204	1040	647	1660	1504	416	1505	1499
Dallas, TX	978	1546	844	392	349	1422	1116	434	1288	518	1779	193	876	640	319	1282	1442	130	1177	1437
Davenport, IA	213	824	665	984	1052	844	368	1302	1586	402	1145	802	493	359	610	558	1866	841	469	1856
Dayton, OH	369	593	320	983	1052	473	262	1439	1954	642	844	944	152	787	687	328	2201	918	202	2190
Daytona Beach, FL	1232	1319	640	748	816	932	1159	1312	2374	1284	1264	1278	811	1446	921	1214	2518	962	1012	2513
Decatur, AL	658	1047	236	533	602	814	651	1076	1838	692	1171	735	326	854	325	782	1996	555	627	1985
Decatur, IL	242	829	538	821	890	764	372	1200	1698	386	1135	717	366	474	480	562	1974	711	473	1964
Denver, CO	1043	1664	1339	1271	1217	1667	1208	1088	748	568	1985	638	1186	491	967	1398	1028	1009	1309	1017
Des Moines, IA	368	990	830	945	958	1009	533	1133	1418	233	1310	633	658	190	574	723	1697	730	634	1686
Detroit, MI	357	390	530	1192	1260	518	90	1598	2017	803	819	1115	362	790	896	125	2297	1126	143	2286
Dubuque, IA	166	856	734	1054	1122	876	400	1333	1618	433	1177	833	562	390	680	590	1897	929	501	1886
Duluth, MN	431	971	1012	1340	1353	1164	688	1528	1813	628	1466	1029	840	586	969	878	2092	1125	789	2082
Durham, NC	866	777	342	970	1039	390	719	1535	2380	1115	722	1278	477	1276	868	774	2538	1046	572	2528
East Orange, NJ	852	372	704	1414	1483	153	664	1979	2512	1231	241	1534	702	1284	1231	532	2791	1473	469	2780
Eau Claire, WI	280	994	860	1246	1315	1013	537	1461	1745	561	1314	961	688	518	873	727	2025	1057	638	2014
Elgin, IL	66	720	586	1005	1074	739	263	1366	1738	554	1040	884	414	511	646	453	2018	877	364	2008
Elizabeth, NJ	858	378	696	1406	1474	150	670	1970	2518	1222	244	1525	693	1290	1222	538	2782	1464	476	2771
El Paso, TX	1540	2109	1478	968	894	2056	1679	606	784	902	2414	652	1510	964	954	1844	807	766	1741	803
Elyria, OH	391	481	492	1154	1223	378	203	1610	2051	822	679	1125	324	823	858	260	2330	1089	8	2320
Enid, OK	879	1424	908	692	638	1331	994	725	1218	278	1702	142	842	400	388	1160	1376	430	1056	1366
Erie, PA	518	356	612	1268	1336	348	331	1724	2178	936	554	1239	438	951	972	248	2458	1202	131	2447
Escondido, CA	2086	2707	2216	1713	1639	2682	2250	1352	301	1614	3028	1316	2193	1534	1697	2440	91	1511	2352	102
Eugene, OR	2214	2892	2644	2628	2574	2910	2434	2263	915	1924	3212	1996	2492	1718	2324	2624	878	2366	2536	856
Evansville, IN	357	878	327	722	791	764	437	1192	1771	459	1107	753	190	620	441	612	2010	671	457	1999
Everett, WA	2053	2767	2602	2614	2560	2786	2310	2432	1150	1888	3088	1982	2450	1704	2310	2500	1186	2352	2412	1164
Fairfield, CA	2130	2751	2504	2126	2088	2770	2294	1801	572	1785	3072	1586	2352	1578	1968	2484	415	1864	2396	393
Fall River, MA	1054	446	903	1613	1682	352	866	2178	2714	1430	80	1732	900	1486	1429	632	2993	1672	671	2982
Fargo, ND	606	1320	1187	1360	1347	1340	864	1502	1579	623	1641	963	1015	474	989	1054	1858	1118	965	1848
Fayetteville, NC	918	837	372	951	1020	450	771	1515	2414	1145	783	1311	529	1306	901	844	2572	1043	623	2560
Flagstaff, AZ	1712	2280	1722	1360	1314	2186	1850	1178	317	1074	2558	821	1698	1136	1202	2015	475	1098	1912	465
Flint, MI	346	402	571	1207	1276	570	55	1605	2006	792	870	1123	402	779	890	135	2286	1120	194	2275
Florence, SC	952	922	338	866	934	534	783	1430	2328	1112	868	1226	510	1274	816	838	2486	958	636	2475
Ft. Collins, CO	1042	1663	1391	1323	1270	1682	1207	1141	810	620	1984	690	1239	490	1020	1396	1089	1062	1308	1078
Ft. Dodge, IA	357	1058	899	1016	1030	1078	602	1205	1471	305	1379	705	727	243	646	792	1750	801	703	1740
Ft. Lauderdale, FL	1438	1556	859	953	1021	1168	1396	1517	2579	1489	1502	1483	1028	1650	1126	1450	2723	1168	1248	2718
Ft. Smith, AR	741	1308	680	464	472	1258	878	712	1363	326	1615	261	710	498	160	1043	1521	244	940	1510

	Louisville, KY	Lowell, MA	Lubbock, TX	Lynchburg, VA	Macon, GA	Madison, WI	Manchester, NH	Mansfield, OH	Marquette, MI	Memphis, TN	Miami, FL	Midland, TX	Milwaukee, WI	Minneapolis, MN	Mobile, AL	Modesto, CA	Monroe, LA	Montgomery, AL	Montréal, QC	Muncie, IN	Nashua, NH	Nashville, TN	Newark, NJ	New Bedford, MA
Abilene, TX	1018	1950	164	1335	1012	1129	1977	1298	1454	634	1494	149	1165	1079	776	1495	465	827	1878	1092	1962	844	1720	1940
Akron, OH	340	642	1420	444	767	517	668	62	625	724	1214	1507	464	778	962	2469	1043	794	603	250	653	516	432	640
Albany, GA	596	1247	1146	610	116	1040	1274	816	1279	463	513	1131	990	1302	278	2477	515	156	1385	756	1259	420	1017	1238
Albany, NY	825	170	1906	597	1063	968	196	548	1077	1226	1451	2008	916	1230	1341	2920	1444	1174	222	725	181	1013	164	202
Albert Lea, MN	683	1391	1075	1126	1108	263	1418	721	493	737	1687	1128	328	96	1135	1935	905	1057	1255	630	1403	776	1191	1399
Albuquerque, NM	1303	2226	323	1709	1469	1275	2252	1525	1586	1008	1958	429	1354	1225	1240	1008	930	1329	2132	1346	2237	1219	1984	2204
Alexandria, LA	768	1595	650	980	605	1028	1622	1047	1299	387	1057	634	1009	1098	339	1956	128	421	1711	914	1607	594	1365	1586
Alexandria, VA	616	463	1679	184	670	862	490	419	970	881	1054	1664	809	1123	969	2814	1100	802	620	565	474	669	232	453
Allentown, PA	687	310	1744	383	848	880	336	437	988	1012	1258	1794	828	1141	1127	2832	1230	960	434	593	322	799	80	300
Altoona, PA	494	478	1579	305	771	703	505	260	811	878	1225	1661	650	964	1050	2655	1152	882	529	428	490	670	269	477
Amarillo, TX	1019	1942	120	1425	1185	1100	1968	1241	1425	724	1674	237	1136	1049	956	1292	646	1045	1848	1062	1953	935	1700	1920
Anderson, IN	152	928	1165	531	660	359	955	228	596	511	1240	1218	306	620	773	2289	766	606	805	19	940	327	687	907
Ann Arbor, MI	364	808	1385	583	814	392	834	153	438	748	1354	1438	339	653	986	2344	1068	818	603	226	819	540	608	816
Appleton, WI	501	1190	1333	924	1008	108	1216	520	202	740	1588	1386	106	285	1122	2188	995	954	930	428	1201	676	990	1197
Asheville, NC	357	902	1304	286	255	806	929	466	1043	506	794	1288	754	1067	540	2520	707	372	1018	487	914	293	672	892
Atlanta, GA	424	1102	1128	447	82	868	1128	645	1108	380	661	1113	818	1130	329	2394	498	161	1218	584	1114	248	872	1092
Atlantic City, NJ	758	367	1826	368	874	972	394	528	1080	1065	1258	1848	919	1233	1173	2924	1283	1006	524	675	378	853	137	357
Augusta, GA	532	1004	1288	366	135	1022	1030	662	1217	540	615	1273	928	1282	472	2554	657	305	1143	662	1015	402	774	994
Aurora, IL	340	1028	1152	763	848	138	1055	358	403	527	1426	1205	113	399	926	2084	782	793	892	267	1040	514	828	1036
Austin, TX	1033	1965	383	1350	977	1184	1992	1312	1494	649	1346	320	1204	1136	628	1694	423	792	1916	1131	1976	860	1735	1955
Bakersfield, CA	2107	3005	1127	2514	2273	1995	3031	2330	2306	1812	2762	1220	2074	1944	2044	204	1734	2133	2868	2151	3016	2023	2805	3012
Baltimore, MD	604	408	1714	218	724	851	435	408	960	916	1108	1698	799	1112	1024	2803	1134	856	565	555	420	704	178	398
Bangor, ME	1204	226	2285	848	1354	1360	228	927	1469	1541	1738	2323	1308	1622	1656	3312	1759	1489	289	1115	234	1328	453	298
Baton Rouge, LA	762	1582	788	967	549	1023	1609	1042	1294	382	918	772	1004	1211	200	2094	206	364	1698	909	1594	588	1352	1572
Bay City, MI	460	905	1460	680	912	466	931	250	346	814	1451	1513	414	727	1082	2418	1070	915	625	301	916	636	705	912
Bayonne, NJ	769	236	1826	400	907	944	262	500	1052	1094	1291	1876	891	1205	1209	2896	1312	1042	391	675	247	881	6	226
Beaumont, TX	946	1765	622	1150	732	1107	1792	1225	1416	565	1102	608	1127	1158	383	1948	303	548	1881	1048	1777	772	1535	1756
Billings, MT	1539	2239	1090	1974	1918	1111	2266	1570	1110	1547	2498	1207	1176	842	1946	1160	1708	1867	2103	1478	2251	1586	2040	2247
Binghamton, NY	714	309	1794	481	947	857	336	436	966	1110	1370	1892	805	1118	1226	2809	1328	1058	326	614	321	897	172	342
Birmingham, AL	369	1184	985	568	230	814	1210	648	1052	234	780	970	763	1075	258	2249	354	90	1300	536	1195	193	954	1174
Bismarck, ND	1137	1826	1064	1560	1643	697	1852	1156	696	1311	2222	1180	762	428	1710	1574	1361	1589	1689	1064	1837	1310	1626	1833
Bloomington, IN	94	990	1101	569	602	381	1017	290	618	447	1181	1154	329	642	715	2261	702	547	897	111	1002	269	748	969
Boise, ID	1885	2668	1367	2360	2265	1658	2694	1998	1729	1893	2844	1484	1736	1461	2242	626	1985	2214	2531	1885	2679	1932	2468	2675
Boston, MA	978	29	2059	622	1128	1134	53	701	1243	1315	1512	2097	1082	1396	1430	3086	1533	1263	310	889	43	1102	227	59
Boulder, CO	1134	1987	564	1609	1514	978	2014	1348	1288	1116	2093	681	1056	927	1438	1245	1182	1436	1851	1169	1999	1181	1788	1995
Bowling Green, KY	115	1076	1075	535	401	561	1102	394	798	277	980	1059	509	822	514	2291	596	347	1045	283	1087	68	846	1066
Bridgeport, CT	834	159	1891	466	972	996	186	553	1104	1159	1356	1941	944	1257	1274	2948	1377	1107	385	740	171	946	71	150
Brockton, MA	997	52	2072	628	1135	1148	77	714	1256	1322	1519	2104	1095	1409	1437	3100	1540	1270	334	902	64	1109	234	38
Brownsville, TX	1314	2204	668	1589	1171	1536	2231	1593	1846	929	1540	606	1556	1488	822	1946	694	986	2320	1439	2216	1140	1974	2194
Buffalo, NY	544	460	1625	514	950	688	487	267	796	929	1398	1711	636	949	1166	2640	1248	998	397	444	472	720	394	492
Butte, MT	1761	2462	1312	2196	2140	1333	2488	1792	1332	1769	2720	1429	1398	1064	2168	1028	1930	2089	2325	1700	2473	1808	2262	2469
Calgary, AB	1930	2618	1631	2353	2460	1490	2508	1948	1414	2088	3040	1748	1555	1221	2487	1500	2249	2408	2248	1857	2526	2127	2418	2626
Camden, NJ	710	320	1774	320	826	920	346	477	1029	1018	1210	1800	868	1181	1125	2872	1236	958	476	624	331	804	90	310
Canton, OH	341	651	1422	424	747	536	678	64	645	726	1194	1508	484	798	963	2488	1045	796	623	252	662	517	442	649
Casper, WY	1285	2067	812	1760	1664	1025	2094	1397	1255	1292	2244	929	1090	858	1687	1128	1431	1613	1930	1284	2078	1332	1867	2074
Cedar Rapids, IA	502	1216	1054	934	927	168	1243	547	479	556	1506	1107	246	276	954	1914	810	876	1080	434	1228	594	1017	1224
Champaign, IL	239	1072	1052	672	706	250	1099	372	516	398	1285	1105	227	512	797	2140	653	652	953	172	1084	373	830	1051
Charleston, SC	613	987	1456	413	265	1062	1014	709	1264	707	590	1440	1010	1324	640	2721	825	472	1144	743	998	550	757	978
Charleston, WV	244	750	1383	232	555	641	776	235	790	597	1002	1380	589	902	818	2551	918	651	825	283	762	388	520	740
Charlotte, NC	470	864	1374	206	288	920	891	499	1054	619	736	1358	867	1180	576	2634	743	408	980	547	876	407	634	854
Chattanooga, TN	306	1037	1130	422	204	752	1064	542	990	314	783	1114	700	1012	399	2328	499	232	1153	474	1049	132	807	1028
Cheyenne, WY	1148	1931	635	1624	1528	921	1957	1261	1232	1156	2108	752	1000	870	1509	1159	1253	1477	1794	1148	1942	1195	1731	1938
Chicago, IL	299	986	1173	722	806	152	1013	316	380	534	1386	1226	90	413	920	2120	789	752	850	226	998	474	786	994
Cincinnati, OH	97	874	1227	428	548	444	901	174	688	482	1127	1264	392	705	719	2372	800	552	824	124	886	273	628	849
Clarksville, TN	196	1152	1009	536	382	578	1178	475	778	211	961	994	488	839	495	2225	530	328	1125	363	1163	49	922	1142
Clearwater, FL	906	1382	1425	807	402	1352	1408	1104	1590	777	282	1410	1300	1613	484	2731	794	455	1538	1068	1393	732	1152	1372
Cleveland, OH	357	643	1438	483	808	495	670	80	604	742	1254	1524	443	756	979	2447	1061	812	580	252	654	533	457	675
Coeur d'Alene, ID	2047	2748	1598	2482	2427	1620	2774	2078	1618	2055	3006	1714	1684	1350	2454	928	2216	2375	2610	1986	2759	2094	2548	2755
Colorado Sprs., CO	1102	2044	486	1577	1482	1035	2071	1316	1346	1084	2061	603	1114	984	1321	1330	1011	1404	1908	1137	2056	1149	1775	1995
Columbia, MO	386	1300	851	861	766	447	1327	600	756	394	1345	904	467	483	793	1922	562	714	1207	421	1312	433	1059	1279
Columbia, SC	505	936	1353	298	200	954	963	594	1150	604	640	1337	901	1214	537	2618	722	370	1076	634	948	441	706	926
Columbus, GA	526	1212	1082	557	98	972	1239	748	1210	378	600	1067	920	1232	257	2392	451	90	1328	687	1224	352	982	1202
Columbus, OH	216	766	1297	393	666	505	793	66	629	600	1164	1382	453	766	837	2442	919	670	716	146	778	391	524	744
Concord, NH	970	51	2051	670	1176	1114	18	693	1222	1363	1560	2145	1062	1375	1478	3066	1581	1311	249	870	36	1150	275	126
Corpus Christi, TX	1167	2057	532	1442	1024	1401	2084	1446	1710	782	1394	470	1420	1352	675	1810	547	840	2173	1292	2069	993	1827	2048
Dallas, TX	839	1771	345	1155	831	990	1797	1118	1299	454	1314	330	1010	941	595	1655	285	646	1722	936	1782	665	1541	1761
Davenport, IA	422	1137	1096	854	876	170	1163	467	505	549	1454	1150	216	358	948	1956	804	821	1000	354	1148	542	937	1144
Dayton, OH	167	836	1239	425	618	446	863	136	635	552	1198	1292	394	708	789	2384	871	622	769	88	848	343	594	815
Daytona Beach, FL	864	1256	1434	682	360	1309	1283	978	1548	786	264	1419	1258	1570	493	2740	803	464	1414	1013	1268	689	1026	1246
Decatur, AL	289	1163	988	547	280	734	1189	568	973	190	860	972	683	996	338	2204	432	170	1219	457	1174	113	932	1153
Decatur, IL	294	1127	1012	727	694	254	1154	427	563	386	1273	1065	274	515	785	2070	641	640	1004	227	1139	361	885	1106
Denver, CO	1116	1977	546	1590	1495	967	2003	1330	1278	1097	2074	662	1046	916	1420	1257	1164	1418	1840	1151	1988	1162	1777	1984
Des Moines, IA	587	1302	928	1019	1012	292	1329	632	603	641	1592	981	371	242	1040	1788	757	961	1166	519	1314	680	1102	1310
Detroit, MI	376	811	1410	584	828	435	838	156	455	761	1354	1463	383	696	998	2387	1080	831	565	235	822	552	611	818
Dubuque, IA	491	1169	1127	924	945	93	1195	499	404	618	1524	1180	171	312	1017	1987	874	891	1032	424	1180	612	969	1176
Duluth, MN	769	1457	1323	1192	1275	329	1484	787	251	963	1854	1376	394	153	1361	2019	1152	1220	1033	696	1469	942	1257	1465
Durham, NC	546	714	1517	166	434	944	742	538	1092	732	831	1502	892	1206	718	2746	886	551	872	586	726	520	484	705
East Orange, NJ	771	232	1828	405	912	929	259	486	1038	1096	1296	1878	877	1190	1211	2881	1314	1044	376	674	244	883	10	223
Eau Claire, WI	618	1307	1256	1042	1124	179	1334	637	320	812	1704	1310	244	96	1211	2116	1067	1070	1170	546	1319	792	1107	1315
Elgin, IL	343	1032	1178	767	850	111	1058	362	381	571	1430	1230	92	372	964	2108	826	796	895	271	1043	518	832	1040
Elizabeth, NJ	762	236	1819	393	900	936	262	492	1044	1087	1284	1869	883	1197	1202	2888	1305	1035	383	668	247	874	6	226
El Paso, TX	1474	2405	423	1790	1466	1428	2432	1678	1739	1089	1936	305	1507	1377	1217	1114	920	1282	2284	1499	2417	1300	2175	2396
Elyria, OH	339	671	1419	492	790	468	698	62	577	724	1263	1506	416	730	960	2420	1042	793	608	225	682	514	470	678
Enid, OK	771	1694	414	1220	979	803	1720	993	1114	518	1528	490	882	752	841	1585	585	839	1600	814	1705	729	1452	1672
Erie, PA	452	546	1533	497	858	596	573	175	704	837	1306	1620	544	857	1074	2548	1156	907	483	352	558	628	428	578
Escondido, CA	2122	3020	1168	2528	2212	2010	3046	2344	2320	1827	2681	1050	2088	1959	1962	414	1666	2027	2882	2165	3031	2038	2820	3027
Eugene, OR	2422	3204	1902	2896	2800	2113	3230	2534	2112	2429	3380	1962	2178	1844	2778	548	2522	2750	3066	2420	3214	2468	3004	3211
Evansville, IN	119	1099	1047	594	484	448	1126	399	672	288	1062	1088	382	709	597	2216	610	429	1049	244	1111	151	882	1103
Everett, WA	2379	3080	1888	2814	2758	1951	3106	2410	1950	2387	3338	2006	2016	1682	2786	856	2508	2707	2942	2318	3090	2426	2880	3087
Fairfield, CA	2282	3064	1412	2756	2558	2054	3090	2394	2242	2098	3048	1500	2132	2003	2329	83	2019	2418	2927	2280	3075	2328	2864	3071
Fall River, MA	970	79	2026	601	1108	1131	104	688	1240	1294	1492	2076	1079	1392	1410	3084	1512	1242	362	876	91	1082	206	14
Fargo, ND	944	1633	1122	1368	1450	504	1659	963	503	1122	2030	1310	570	236	1520	1767	1172	1396	1496	872	1644	1118	1433	1640
Fayetteville, NC	599	774	1515	255	362	996	802	590	1145	766	746	1499	944	1257	699	2780	884	532	932	638	786	550	544	765
Flagstaff, AZ	1627	2549	646	2033	1793	1599	2576	1849	1910	1332	2282	752	1678	1548	1563	684	1253	1652	2456	1670	2561	1543	2308	2528
Flint, MI	418	862	1418	637	869	424	889	208	389	772	1408	1471	372	685	1040	2376	1027	872	578	258	874	594	662	870
Florence, SC	581	860	1429	279	276	1030	886	602	1157	680	659	1414	978	1292	614	2694	798	446	1016	650	871	518	630	850
Ft. Collins, CO	1168	1976	598	1643	1548	966	2002	1306	1277	1150	2127	715	1045	915	1472	1174	1216	1470	1839	1203	1987	1215	1776	1983
Ft. Dodge, IA	656	1370	999	1088	1081	284	1397	701	595	709	1660	1052	362	218	1108	1840	829	1030	1234	588	1382	748	1171	1378
Ft. Lauderdale, FL	1069	1493	1639	919	564	1514	1520	1215	1752	991	26	1624	1463	1775	698	2945	1008	669	1650	1230	1504	894	1263	1484
Ft. Smith, AR	675	1605	558	990	751	753	1632	878	1062	290	1300	606	771	726	613	1730	342	609	1485	698	1618	501	1375	1597

Mileage Directory, continued

	New Britain, CT	New Brunswick, NJ	New Haven, CT	New Orleans, LA	Newport News, VA	New York, NY	Niagara Falls, NY	Norfolk, VA	Norman, OK	North Platte, NE	Oakland, CA	Oceanside, CA	Odessa, TX	Ogden, UT	Oklahoma City, OK	Omaha, NE	Orlando, FL	Owensboro, KY	Paterson, NJ	Pendleton, OR	Pensacola, FL	Peoria, IL	Philadelphia, PA	Phoenix, AZ	Pine Bluff, AR	Pittsburgh, PA	Pittsfield, MA	Pomona, CA	Pontiac, MI	Port Arthur, TX	Portland, ME	Portland, OR	Providence, RI	Provo, UT	Pueblo, CO	Québec, QC	Racine, WI	Raleigh, NC	Rapid City, SD	Reading, PA	Regina, SK	Reno, NV	Richmond, VA
Abilene, TX	1861	1716	1809	701	1537	1754	1582	1532	283	660	1628	1210	171	1209	290	743	1272	953	1727	1732	833	954	1647	887	508	1413	1889	1228	1338	505	2044	1939	1910	1065	591	2035	1146	1376	1004	1624	1481	1576	1457
Akron, OH	528	448	509	1046	518	453	237	530	1059	1094	2474	2408	1528	1741	1040	818	1004	447	423	2265	957	492	404	2046	876	107	531	2343	217	1281	735	2471	610	1784	1410	761	452	540	1282	362	1553	2265	444
Albany, GA	1139	998	1106	422	703	1042	1084	698	936	1397	2549	2192	1152	2045	927	1164	290	552	1046	2568	232	863	939	1869	614	851	1208	2209	939	658	1341	2775	1207	2039	1489	1547	977	540	1684	943	2077	2569	684
Albany, NY	118	184	145	1434	525	163	302	509	1544	1545	2926	2859	2030	2193	1525	1270	1241	933	154	2716	1336	943	248	2532	1377	456	35	2795	669	1670	263	2923	180	2236	1918	372	903	654	1734	246	2005	2717	499
Albert Lea, MN	1287	1207	1268	1128	1277	1212	962	1289	714	560	1940	1874	1150	1207	695	285	1464	676	1182	1579	1193	358	1164	1593	764	866	1257	1809	689	1084	1484	1726	1369	1250	932	1412	354	1223	515	1121	871	1731	1203
Albuquerque, NM	2112	1980	2073	1166	1912	2018	1810	1924	561	710	1079	828	424	658	542	863	1736	1250	1991	1178	1297	1208	1928	462	920	1645	2104	764	1592	979	2319	1386	2174	578	334	2290	1400	1765	851	1886	1290	1088	1832
Alexandria, LA	1506	1361	1454	218	1132	1399	1332	1126	490	1068	2027	1695	656	1698	505	858	836	688	1373	2222	396	837	1292	1372	238	1160	1534	1713	1170	164	1688	2430	1555	1526	987	1874	996	971	1362	1270	1809	2036	1093
Alexandria, VA	354	214	322	1089	177	257	416	189	1354	1438	2819	2716	1686	2086	1346	1163	844	724	257	2610	964	811	154	2350	1033	256	430	2652	562	1326	556	2816	423	2129	1706	770	797	258	1627	167	1898	2610	102
Allentown, PA	209	76	169	1220	336	114	367	320	1383	1457	2838	2736	1816	2104	1363	1182	1048	795	88	2628	1122	839	63	2370	1163	284	244	2671	580	1456	404	2835	270	2148	1733	584	815	463	1646	38	1916	2628	307
Altoona, PA	365	286	345	1142	348	289	232	360	1218	1279	2660	2570	1682	1927	1198	1004	1015	602	260	2450	1045	674	234	2205	1030	96	394	2506	402	1378	572	2658	446	1970	1568	687	638	429	1468	192	1739	2452	273
Amarillo, TX	1828	1696	1789	881	1628	1734	1526	1640	277	470	1363	1112	258	942	258	580	1452	966	1707	1466	1013	924	1644	746	636	1361	1820	1048	1308	695	2035	1672	1890	862	324	2006	1116	1480	718	1602	1253	1372	1548
Anderson, IN	815	682	776	858	696	721	501	708	804	914	2294	2156	1240	1561	784	639	1017	251	694	2086	768	238	631	1791	644	348	795	2092	280	1071	1022	2292	877	1604	1154	963	294	628	1124	588	1395	2086	616
Ann Arbor, MI	704	624	684	1070	694	628	379	706	1024	968	2349	2282	1460	1616	1005	693	1144	471	599	2140	981	366	580	2012	874	282	674	2218	48	1305	901	2346	785	1659	1341	761	326	680	1157	538	1428	2140	619
Appleton, WI	1086	1005	1066	1132	1075	1010	760	1088	972	813	2194	2128	1408	1461	952	538	1366	526	980	1869	1117	306	962	1846	844	664	1055	2063	486	1213	1283	2017	1167	1504	1186	1088	132	1022	806	920	1060	1985	1001
Asheville, NC	813	668	761	680	415	706	700	410	979	1270	2592	2340	1310	1918	970	1037	584	406	680	2442	535	681	598	1976	657	466	842	2276	670	917	996	2648	862	1934	1475	1181	741	254	1557	576	1842	2442	377
Atlanta, GA	1013	850	961	470	573	906	918	568	852	1225	2465	2174	1135	1872	844	992	440	382	879	2396	324	691	790	1848	531	684	1041	2150	768	706	1195	2603	1062	1889	1430	1381	804	412	1512	776	1904	2396	535
Atlantic City, NJ	259	118	226	1273	332	161	478	316	1465	1548	2929	2818	1870	2196	1445	1273	1048	866	161	2720	1168	921	61	2452	1217	366	334	2753	672	1510	460	2926	327	2239	1815	673	906	462	1737	124	2008	2720	306
Augusta, GA	896	754	862	614	458	798	843	453	1012	1378	2625	2334	1295	2026	1004	1146	405	535	804	2550	468	844	695	2008	691	609	966	2310	806	850	1097	2756	964	2042	1583	1306	916	296	1665	701	2058	2550	440
Aurora, IL	924	844	905	919	914	848	600	926	791	708	2089	2022	1227	1356	771	433	1204	364	819	1880	956	128	800	1778	662	503	894	1958	326	1087	1122	2086	1006	1399	1081	1050	100	860	903	758	1174	1880	840
Austin, TX	1876	1730	1824	507	1495	1769	1596	1490	371	949	1755	1336	340	1467	386	840	1124	968	1742	1990	685	993	1662	1014	523	1428	1904	1354	1376	259	2058	2198	1925	1284	849	2074	1185	1334	1243	1639	1695	1781	1472
Bakersfield, CA	2901	2784	2881	1970	2716	2825	2576	2728	1365	1294	275	196	1198	743	1346	1570	2540	2054	2796	972	2101	1966	2732	481	1724	2449	2870	140	2302	1763	3098	858	2982	663	1138	3026	2073	2570	1362	2690	1728	406	2636
Baltimore, MD	300	159	268	1124	231	202	392	244	1389	1428	2808	2750	1720	2076	1380	1153	898	713	202	2600	1018	800	100	2386	1067	246	375	2686	552	1360	502	2806	368	2118	1695	714	786	313	1616	111	1887	2600	157
Bangor, ME	338	478	364	1749	812	437	694	796	1924	1937	3318	3251	2345	2585	1904	1662	1528	1324	449	3108	1652	1335	535	2911	1692	796	363	3186	1060	1985	129	3316	291	2628	2274	233	1295	942	2126	566	2070	3109	786
Baton Rouge, LA	1493	1348	1441	79	1102	1386	1326	1097	628	1206	2165	1774	794	1837	643	996	696	682	1359	2360	257	832	1278	1450	315	1146	1521	1791	1164	180	1675	2568	1542	1664	1125	1861	991	941	1500	1256	1947	2174	1064
Bay City, MI	801	720	781	1167	790	725	476	803	1099	1043	2424	2357	1535	1690	1079	768	1241	560	696	2214	1077	441	677	2086	948	379	770	2292	84	1375	998	2421	882	1734	1415	783	401	777	1232	634	1502	2214	716
Bayonne, NJ	127	30	95	1302	365	31	412	349	1465	1520	2901	2834	1898	2168	1445	1245	1081	877	30	2692	1204	918	88	2452	1245	366	201	2770	644	1538	329	2898	196	2211	1815	540	878	495	1709	119	1980	2692	340
Beaumont, TX	1676	1531	1624	262	1285	1569	1510	1280	477	1056	2009	1590	632	1686	493	891	880	866	1542	2210	440	915	1462	1267	414	1330	1704	1608	1348	21	1858	2417	1725	1509	970	2044	1131	1124	1350	1440	1842	2019	1247
Billings, MT	2136	2055	2116	1944	2125	2060	1810	2138	1241	633	1166	1280	1228	517	1222	845	2276	1486	2030	745	2003	1209	2012	1211	1554	1714	2105	1216	1536	1762	2333	893	2217	594	672	2260	1202	2072	323	1969	473	957	2051
Binghamton, NY	224	183	230	1318	492	192	236	439	1433	1434	2815	2748	1914	2082	1414	1159	1160	821	163	2606	1220	832	182	2421	1261	340	175	2684	558	1554	402	2812	320	2125	1806	484	792	574	1622	159	1894	2606	418
Birmingham, AL	1095	949	1043	344	721	988	932	716	708	1173	2320	2030	992	1821	699	940	558	327	961	2344	253	636	880	1704	386	748	1123	2004	770	580	1277	2552	1144	1811	1260	1462	750	560	1460	858	1850	2345	683
Bismarck, ND	1722	1641	1702	1702	1711	1646	1396	1724	979	473	1580	1695	1202	931	960	609	2000	1175	1616	1160	1767	879	1598	1607	1220	1300	1691	1630	1122	1501	1919	1307	1803	1038	810	1847	788	1658	339	1556	352	1371	1637
Bloomington, IN	877	744	838	800	733	782	574	746	740	885	2266	2092	1176	1533	720	653	959	124	756	2056	710	235	693	1727	581	409	869	2028	370	969	1084	2264	939	1550	1090	1054	316	666	1124	650	1417	2058	653
Boise, ID	2564	2483	2544	2221	2524	2488	2238	2537	1518	956	632	937	1384	305	1499	1233	2622	1832	2458	222	2299	1628	2440	1000	1831	2142	2533	872	1964	2040	2761	428	2645	382	950	2689	1735	2476	942	2398	1092	423	2444
Boston, MA	113	252	138	1523	586	211	469	571	1698	1711	3092	3026	2119	2359	1678	1436	1302	1098	223	2882	1426	1109	309	2685	1466	570	137	2960	834	1759	110	3090	50	2402	2048	400	1070	716	1900	340	2090	2883	560
Boulder, CO	1884	1803	1864	1418	1773	1808	1558	1786	715	276	1250	1079	702	517	696	553	1871	1081	1778	1041	1496	948	1751	942	1028	1462	1853	1014	1284	1237	2081	1248	1965	504	145	2009	1055	1724	389	1708	829	1042	1693
Bowling Green, KY	986	841	935	599	721	879	678	734	750	949	2330	2112	1081	1597	741	717	758	72	853	2120	509	396	792	1746	428	509	973	2047	516	834	1169	2328	1036	1613	1154	1202	496	590	1236	750	1598	2121	641
Bridgeport, CT	51	96	18	1367	430	55	444	414	1530	1572	2954	2886	1963	2220	1511	1298	1146	942	67	2744	1270	970	153	2518	1310	431	134	2822	696	1603	253	2950	119	2263	1880	488	931	560	1761	184	2032	2744	404
Brockton, MA	126	258	144	1530	593	218	482	578	1711	1724	3105	3038	2126	2372	1691	1449	1309	1106	230	2896	1432	1122	316	2698	1473	583	150	2974	848	1766	135	3102	44	2415	2061	424	1082	723	1913	347	2184	2896	568
Brownsville, TX	2115	1970	2063	701	1724	2008	1878	1719	723	1199	2006	1588	629	1730	738	1192	1318	1248	1982	2254	879	1345	1900	1265	804	1708	2144	1606	1728	453	2298	2460	2164	1569	1112	2483	1537	1564	1595	1878	2047	2033	1686
Buffalo, NY	408	404	435	1250	556	414	21	569	1264	1264	2645	2578	1733	1912	1244	989	1187	652	385	2436	1161	662	404	2251	1080	219	326	2514	388	1486	553	2642	470	1955	1637	555	623	638	1453	329	1724	2436	482
Butte, MT	2358	2277	2338	2166	2347	2282	2032	2360	1463	856	1033	1148	1450	384	1444	1067	2498	1708	2252	522	2225	1432	2234	1078	1776	1936	2327	1084	1758	1985	2555	669	2439	461	895	2483	1425	2294	546	2192	653	824	2273
Calgary, AB	2514	2434	2495	2485	2504	2438	2190	2516	1782	1174	1505	1620	1769	856	1763	1386	2817	1968	2409	663	2544	1672	2390	1551	2095	2093	2484	1556	1916	2304	2525	811	2596	934	1214	2400	1581	2450	865	2348	468	1296	2430
Camden, NJ	211	71	179	1225	287	114	426	272	1413	1497	2878	2766	1822	2144	1394	1222	1000	818	114	2668	1120	869	10	2401	1168	315	286	2702	620	1462	413	2876	280	2188	1764	626	855	414	1686	72	1956	2668	258
Canton, OH	538	457	518	1048	514	462	257	527	1061	1113	2494	2414	1530	1761	1041	838	984	449	432	2284	958	517	401	2048	877	98	552	2362	236	1282	744	2492	618	1804	1411	781	471	520	1302	358	1575	2284	436
Casper, WY	1963	1882	1943	1666	1924	1887	1638	1936	964	356	1133	1130	950	400	944	632	2022	1232	1858	924	1744	1028	1839	957	1276	1542	1932	1065	1364	1485	2160	1130	2044	443	395	2088	1116	1874	257	1796	618	924	1844
Cedar Rapids, IA	1113	1032	1093	947	1098	1037	788	1110	692	538	1918	1852	1128	1186	673	263	1284	495	1008	1710	1012	177	989	1572	659	691	1082	1788	514	1063	1310	1916	1194	1229	910	1238	284	1031	699	946	1050	1710	1030
Champaign, IL	958	826	920	790	836	864	656	848	691	765	2146	2044	1127	1412	671	490	1063	241	838	1936	814	90	774	1678	532	491	950	1979	386	958	1165	2143	1020	1456	1022	1110	214	768	979	732	1287	1936	756
Charleston, SC	878	738	846	781	442	782	890	437	1180	1526	2792	2501	1462	2174	1171	1294	380	662	781	2698	592	937	679	2176	858	656	954	2477	852	1018	1080	2904	947	2190	1731	1294	997	278	1813	691	2098	2698	423
Charleston, WV	651	515	609	908	396	554	459	408	1022	1176	2556	2374	1401	1824	1002	943	792	352	527	2448	748	525	466	2010	748	225	689	2310	378	1145	843	2554	718	1840	1380	983	576	328	1462	424	1677	2348	316
Charlotte, NC	775	610	724	716	333	652	680	328	1092	1384	2705	2419	1380	2031	1084	1151	526	519	642	2555	571	794	550	2088	771	446	804	2390	644	953	958	2762	824	2048	1588	1143	854	172	1670	538	1956	2555	295
Chattanooga, TN	948	803	896	489	624	841	845	637	787	1108	2399	2148	1136	1756	778	876	562	264	814	2280	394	574	734	1783	465	602	976	2084	664	726	1130	2486	997	1772	1312	1316	688	478	1394	712	1788	2280	544
Cheyenne, WY	1827	1746	1807	1489	1788	1751	1502	1800	786	220	1164	1154	773	432	767	496	1885	1096	1722	956	1567	891	1703	1014	1099	1405	1796	1090	1228	1308	2024	1162	1908	474	218	1952	998	1738	300	1660	740	956	1708
Chicago, IL	882	802	862	926	872	806	557	884	812	745	2126	2059	1248	1392	792	470	1164	328	777	1916	915	154	758	1799	668	461	852	1994	284	1094	1079	2124	964	1436	1117	1007	78	820	917	716	1188	1916	798
Cincinnati, OH	761	624	718	804	592	662	458	605	866	997	2378	2218	1286	1644	846	722	906	205	636	2168	714	322	572	1853	633	289	753	2124	290	1038	968	2375	818	1688	1216	982	379	526	1211	530	1480	2168	512
Clarksville, TN	1063	917	1011	580	739	956	759	751	684	934	2315	2046	1015	1582	676	702	739	120	929	2106	490	400	848	1680	362	590	1091	1981	598	768	1245	2312	1112	1598	1139	1283	475	592	1221	826	1614	2106	659
Clearwater, FL	1274	1132	1240	628	836	1176	1284	831	1250	1708	2803	2457	1432	2356	1241	1476	108	865	1176	2880	438	1174	1073	2134	892	1051	1348	2475	1250	864	1475	3086	1342	2372	1803	1688	1288	674	1995	1086	2388	2880	818
Cleveland, OH	553	473	534	1064	543	478	214	555	1077	1072	2452	2386	1549	1720	1057	797	1044	465	448	2244	974	470	429	2064	893	132	509	2322	196	1298	736	2450	653	1762	1444	738	430	580	1260	387	1531	2244	472
Coeur d'Alene, ID	2644	2563	2624	2452	2633	2568	2318	2646	1749	1142	900	1420	1736	656	1730	1353	2784	1994	2538	235	2511	1718	2520	1350	2062	2222	2613	1356	2044	2270	2840	383	2724	734	1180	2768	1710	2579	832	2477	760	826	2559
Colorado Sprs., CO	1903	1770	1864	1247	1741	1809	1616	1754	623	334	1335	1126	526	594	538	606	1839	1049	1782	1104	1378	1005	1719	840	996	1435	1910	1061	1342	1060	2138	1332	1965	551	42	2066	1112	1692	474	1676	914	1126	1661
Columbia, MO	1187	1054	1148	786	1025	1093	884	1038	410	546	1927	1785	926	1194	471	314	1123	333	1066	1718	850	256	1003	1370	421	720	1179	1720	640	784	1394	1924	1249	1210	751	1365	448	976	833	960	1265	1718	945
Columbia, SC	828	688	796	678	391	730	776	386	1077	1418	2689	2398	1359	2065	1068	1185	430	553	737	2589	532	828	628	2073	755	542	899	2374	738	914	1030	2796	896	2082	1622	1238	888	228	1704	634	1990	2589	372
Columbus, GA	1123	960	1071	398	683	1016	1028	678	851	1328	2464	2128	1089	1976	842	1096	378	484	989	2499	252	794	900	1805	530	794	1151	2148	870	635	1305	2706	1172	1954	1404	1490	916	522	1614	886	2008	2500	645
Columbus, OH	653	519	613	922	558	558	350	570	936	1067	2448	2289	1404	1715	917	792	954	323	531	2238	832	392	468	1924	752	184	645	2224	218	1156	859	2446	714	1758	1287	874	440	490	1270	426	1541	2239	478
Concord, NH	161	300	186	1571	634	259	449	619	1690	1690	3071	3004	2167	2338	1670	1415	1350	1147	271	2862	1474	1089	357	2678	1514	618	185	2940	814	1807	95	3068	118	2381	2063	333	1059	764	1879	388	2030	2862	608
Corpus Christi, TX	1968	1823	1916	554	1577	1861	1730	1572	587	1064	1871	1452	494	1594	603	1056	1171	1101	1834	2118	732	1209	1754	1129	657	1562	1996	1470	1594	306	2150	2324	2017	1433	976	2336	1401	1416	1460	1732	1911	1897	1539
Dallas, TX	1682	1536	1630	521	1358	1575	1402	1352	188	766	1726	1390	352	1398	204	657	1092	774	1548	1922	652	798	1467	1068	329	1234	1710	1408	1182	337	1864	2128	1731	1225	686	1880	990	1196	1061	1445	1512	1736	1278
Davenport, IA	1033	952	1013	940	1018	957	708	1031	735	581	1962	1895	1171	1228	716	306	1232	424	928	1752	1005	97	909	1614	652	611	1002	1830	434	1022	1230	1960	1114	1272	953	1158	214	951	795	866	1133	1752	938
Dayton, OH	723	590	684	874	589	628	420	602	878	1009	2390	2230	1314	1656	858	734	975	275	602	2180	784	334	538	1865	704	255	715	2166	236	1108	929	2387	784	1700	1228	926	381	522	1212	496	1483	2180	509
Daytona Beach, FL	1148	1008	1116	637	711	1050	1159	706	1259	1666	2812	2466	1440	2314	1250	1433	54	822	1050	2837	447	1132	948	2143	901	926	1224	2484	1122	873	1350	3044	1216	2330	1812	1562	1246	548	1952	960	2346	2838	692
Decatur, AL	1074	928	1022	422	750	966	852	762	653	1073	2276	2024	994	1721	654	841	637	248	940	2244	333	557	859	1659	341	684	1102	1960	691	659	1256	2452	1123	1738	1216	1377	670	602	1360	837	1770	2246	670
Decatur, IL	1014	881	975	778	891	919	711	903	650	694	2075	2003	1086	1342	631	462	1050	230	893	1866	802	82	830	1638	522	546	1006	1938	438	946	1220	2072	1076	1385	973	1162	254	824	972	787	1290	1866	811
Denver, CO	1873	1792	1853	1400	1755	1797	1548	1767	697	266	1262	1057	684	530	678	542	1852	1062	1768	1054	1477	937	1732	814	1009	1449	1842	992	1274	1218	2070	1260	1954	482	116	1998	1044	1706	402	1690	841	1054	1675
Des Moines, IA	1198	1118	1178	1033	1184	1122	874	1196	560	467	1792	1726	1002	1060	547	137	1370	580	1093	1584	1097	263	1074	1446	616	777	1168	1662	600	937	1395	1790	1280	1103	784	1323	370	1116	626	1032	1016	1584	1104
Detroit, MI	707	626	687	1083	696	631	382	709	1048	1012	2392	2326	1484	1659	1029	736	1144	484	602	2184	994	410	583	2036	912	286	676	2261	32	1318	904	2390	788	1702	1384	723	370	680	1200	541	1471	2184	622
Dubuque, IA	1065	984	1045	1010	1054	989	740	1067	766	612	1992	1926	1202	1260	747	337	1302	493	960	1784	1074	167	941	1645	722	643	1034	1862	466	1091	1262	1947	1146	1302	984	1190	198	1020	736	898	1087	1784	980
Duluth, MN	1353	1273	1334	1354	1343	1278	1028	1355	962	807	2025	2122	1398	1455	942	532	1632	806	1248	1604	1383	529	1230	1840	1011	932	1323	2057	754	1332	1550	1752	1434	1498	1180	1191	420	1290	761	1187	720	1816	1269
Durham, NC	606	466	574	860	189	509	654	184	1206	1496	2818	2567	1524	2144	1196	1264	621	632	508	2668	714	828	406	2202	884	486	682	2502	682	1096	808	2875	674	2160	1702	1021	864	24	1784	419	1980	2668	151
East Orange, NJ	124	35	92	1304	370	36	397	354	1467	1506	2886	2820	1900	2154	1448	1231	1086	880	24	2678	1206	904	93	2454	1247	368	186	2755	629	1540	326	2884	192	2196	1818	526	864	500	1694	121	1965	2678	344
Eau Claire, WI	1203	1122	1184	1204	1193	1127	878	1205	894	741	2122	2055	1331	1388	876	466	1482	656	1098	1680	1233	379	1079	1774	916	782	1173	1990	604	1266	1400	1827	1284	1432	1113	1328	270	1137	695	1037	871	1913	1118
Elgin, IL	928	848	908	962	918	852	603	930	816	733	2114	2047	1252	1380	797	458	1208	368	823	1904	959	158	804	1766	688	506	898	1982	330	1132	1125	2104	1009	1424	1106	1053	79	864	876	762	1148	1904	843
Elizabeth, NJ	127	23	95	1295	358	34	404	342	1458	1512	2893	2811	1891	2160	1439	1237	1074	871	30	2684	1198	912	81	2446	1238	360	193	2746	635	1531	329	2891	196	2203	1809	532	870	488	1701	112	1972	2684	332
El Paso, TX	2316	2171	2264	1097	1992	2209	1962	1988	732	977	1174	756	284	925	695	1015	1714	1408	2183	1446	1275	1361	2102	433	964	1797	2345	774	1744	849	2498	1652	2365	845	601	2442	1553	1832	1118	2080	1557	1201	1912
Elyria, OH	566	486	547	1045	556	490	242	568	1058	1045	2426	2359	1528	1693	1039	770	1053	446	461	2216	956	443	443	2046	875	145	536	2294	168	1280	764	2424	648	1736	1418	766	403	590	1240	402	1505	2217	482
Enid, OK	1580	1448	1541	821	1422	1486	1278	1434	118	454	1656	1405	512	1100	99	417	1306	718	1459	1624	848	676	1396	1040	431	1113	1572	1340	1060	640	1787	1830	1642	1065	509	1758	880	1276	820	1354	1272	1624	1342
Erie, PA	488	443	493	1159	539	448	118	551	1172	1173	2554	2487	1641	1820	1153	898	1096	560	418	2344	1070	571	419	2160	988	127	412	2422	296	1394	639	2551	556	1864	1545	641	531	620	1361	372	1632	2344	465
Escondido, CA	2916	2798	2896	1842	2730	2840	2590	2743	1380	1308	475	20	1030	758	1361	1584	2458	2069	2810	1070	2020	1980	2747	371	1739	2464	2885	86	2316	1594	3112	1066	2996	678	1153	3040	2087	2584	1377	2704	1742	528	2650
Eugene, OR	3100	3018	3080	2757	3060	3024	2774	3072	2054	1492	520	940	1941	840	2034	1768	3158	2368	2994	319	2834	2164	2976	1224	2366	2678	3068	962	2500	2576	3296	110	3180	918	1486	3224	2204	3011	1325	2933	1254	470	2980
Evansville, IN	986	878	971	681	758	916	683	771	686	840	2221	2039	1110	1488	667	608	840	39	890	2012	592	287	829	1673	457	514	978	1974	504	848	1192	2218	1072	1504	1045	1207	370	694	1127	786	1484	2012	678
Everett, WA	2976	2895	2956	2743	2965	2900	2650	2978	2040	1478	828	1248	2028	926	2020	1685	3115	2326	2870	305	2843	2049	2852	1521	2352	2554	2945	1191	2376	2562	3172	201	3056	904	1472	3100	2042	2911	1164	2809	1117	779	2890
Fairfield, CA	2960	2879	2940	2255	2920	2884	2635	2933	1650	1352	38	477	1479	731	1632	1629	2825	2228	2854	693	2386	2024	2836	762	2010	2538	2929	420	2360	2044	3156	596	3040	736	1346	3084	2131	2872	1358	2794	1605	177	2840
Fall River, MA	122	231	117	1502	565	190	498	550	1665	1708	3088	3022	2098	2356	1646	1433	1282	1078	202	2880	1405	1106	288	2652	1446	567	165	2957	831	1738	162	3086	16	2398	2016	452	1066	696	1896	320	2168	2880	540
Fargo, ND	1529	1448	1509	1514	1518	1453	1204	1531	896	610	1772	1888	1332	1124	877	420	1807	982	1424	1352	1578	686	1405	1782	1031	1107	1498	1823	930	1326	1726	1500	1610	1201	986	1654	596	1464	550	1362	543	1564	1444
Fayetteville, NC	666	526	634	840	230	569	714	224	1239	1527	2851	2560	1521	2174	1230	1294	536	663	568	2698	694	880	466	2235	917	555	742	2536	734	1076	868	2905	734	2191	1732	1081	931	66	1814	479	2032	2698	211
Flagstaff, AZ	2436	2303	2397	1489	2235	2342	2134	2248	885	1034	756	504	748	558	866	1186	2060	1574	2315	1079	1621	1532	2252	140	1244	1968	2428	440	1916	1302	2643	1286	2498	478	658	2614	1724	2088	1174	2209	1543	765	2155
Flint, MI	758	678	739	1124	748	682	434	760	1056	1000	2381	2314	1492	1648	1037	725	1198	518	653	2173	1035	398	635	2044	906	337	727	2250	35	1333	956	2378	840	1691	1373	775	359	734	1189	592	1460	2172	674
Florence, SC	752	610	718	754	314	654	784	309	1154	1494	2766	2474	1436	2142	1144	1262	449	630	654	2666	609	905	551	2150	832	550	826	2450	746	991	953	2872	820	2158	1699	1166	965	152	1781	564	2066	2666	296
Ft. Collins, CO	1872	1791	1852	1452	1808	1796	1546	1820	750	265	1180	1118	736	447	730	541	1905	1116	1766	970	1530	936	1748	978	1062	1450	1841	1054	1272	1271	2069	1178	1953	490	181	1997	1043	1758	344	1706	784	971	1727
Ft. Dodge, IA	1267	1186	1247	1101	1252	1191	942	1264	638	465	1846	1779	1074	1112	619	190	1438	648	1162	1636	1166	331	1143	1517	688	845	1236	1714	668	1009	1464	1756	1348	1156	837	1392	438	1185	545	1100	993	1637	1172
Ft. Lauderdale, FL	1385	1244	1352	842	948	1288	1396	943	1464	1870	3017	2671	1646	2518	1455	1638	211	1026	1288	3042	652	1336	1185	2348	1106	1162	1460	2689	1359	1078	1586	3249	1453	2534	2017	1800	1450	785	2158	1197	2550	3042	929
Ft. Smith, AR	1516	1372	1466	582	1192	1409	1161	1206	188	696	1801	1550	628	1327	180	485	1078	608	1384	1851	670	560	1302	1184	202	998	1546	1486	946	450	1700	2058	1565	1292	742	1643	752	1044	1006	1281	1438	1852	147

Mileages in this Mileage Directory are from the Rand McNally *MileMaker Practical Routing System,* © Rand McNally. **These mileages are for general reference only and should not be used for the purposes of tariff computation.** For tariff purposes, refer to the applicable official tariff. Mileages between each of the 300 cities listed in this chart are computed over National Interstate, U.S. and primary state highways, and Canadian provincial highways via highways designated as truck-usable by the Household Goods Carriers' Bureau Committee. Practical routing may have highway segments not included in the federally designated National Network.

	Roanoke, VA	Rochester, MN	Rochester, NY	Rockford, IL	Sacramento, CA	Saginaw, MI	St. Johnsbury, VT	St. Joseph, MO	St. Louis, MO	St. Paul, MN	St. Petersburg, FL	Salem, OR	Salinas, CA	Salisbury, MD	Salt Lake City, UT	San Angelo, TX	San Antonio, TX	San Bernardino, CA	San Diego, CA	San Francisco, CA	San Jose, CA	San Mateo, CA	Santa Ana, CA	Santa Barbara, CA	Santa Rosa, CA	Savannah, GA	Schenectady, NY	Scranton, PA	Seattle, WA	Shreveport, LA	Sioux City, IA	Sioux Falls, SD	South Bend, IN	Spokane, WA	Springfield, IL	Springfield, MA	Springfield, MO	Springfield, OH	Stamford, CT	Stockton, CA	Syracuse, NY	Tacoma, WA	Tallahassee, FL	Tampa, FL
bilene, TX	1281	1045	1626	1080	1566	1359	2053	656	786	1085	1279	1987	1556	1629	1108	92	261	1203	1179	1636	1595	1622	1242	1351	1683	1177	1869	1681	2013	368	843	928	1146	1775	888	1874	575	1162	1769	1524	1701	2025	1018	1288
kron, OH	390	716	281	459	2396	274	691	806	544	769	1081	2519	2570	454	1747	1446	1452	2323	2399	2482	2510	2502	2364	2457	2498	735	480	348	2436	1070	880	944	277	2157	513	563	756	168	469	2444	356	2448	962	1058
lbany, GA	600	1240	1129	975	2548	986	1350	1033	728	1293	330	2821	2477	832	2051	1070	941	2185	2160	2557	2516	2542	2224	2347	2603	239	1188	1000	2822	613	1256	1341	851	2542	797	1171	746	729	1066	2507	1132	2832	87	307
lbany, NY	587	1168	226	910	2848	726	200	1281	1029	1221	1318	2971	3022	374	2199	1948	1953	2774	2880	2934	2962	2953	2816	2908	2950	972	17	179	2888	1541	1331	1396	729	2609	989	80	1242	653	152	2895	145	2900	1260	1294
lbert Lea, MN	1073	62	1006	325	1862	710	1416	325	468	102	1504	1773	2036	1214	1213	1071	1122	1789	1895	1948	1976	1968	1830	1923	1964	1273	1206	1107	1653	881	209	177	497	1374	430	1302	506	714	1228	1910	1081	1665	1270	1481
lbuquerque, NM	1656	1191	1854	1270	1079	1614	2264	802	1040	1231	1743	1434	1007	2004	621	520	713	743	815	1087	1046	1073	784	877	1134	1634	2053	1932	1460	832	956	999	1402	1342	1142	2147	830	1416	2033	1037	1929	1472	1482	1752
lexandria, LA	926	1064	1375	964	2027	1190	1698	726	668	1104	842	2478	1955	1261	1704	574	430	1689	1664	2035	1994	2021	1727	1836	2082	770	1515	1326	2504	123	949	1034	978	2265	771	1519	542	960	1414	1985	1458	2516	581	852
lexandria, VA	243	1061	404	804	2742	619	566	1102	878	1114	920	2864	2895	126	2092	1603	1609	2631	2703	2827	2855	2846	2672	2765	2844	575	412	256	2781	1197	1225	1289	623	2502	809	386	1091	464	282	2788	388	2793	863	897
llentown, PA	373	1080	290	822	2760	637	412	1129	867	1133	1125	2884	2934	185	2110	1734	1739	2650	2722	2846	2874	2866	2692	2784	2862	779	226	75	2800	1327	1243	1307	641	2520	837	234	1080	491	129	2808	204	2812	1044	1102
ltoona, PA	296	902	276	646	2582	460	580	964	702	955	1091	2706	2756	284	1933	1600	1606	2485	2558	2668	2696	2688	2526	2620	2684	746	374	185	2622	1250	1066	1130	464	2342	672	400	915	326	305	2630	276	2634	966	1068
marillo, TX	1372	1015	1570	1052	1363	1330	1980	627	756	1055	1459	1720	1291	1720	948	318	510	1027	1099	1371	1330	1357	1068	1161	1418	1350	1769	1648	1746	548	740	784	1118	1508	858	1863	545	1132	1749	1321	1645	1758	1198	1468
nderson, IN	478	558	545	300	2216	300	955	529	288	611	1056	2340	2336	681	1567	1160	1194	2071	2143	2302	2330	2322	2112	2205	2318	790	744	635	2278	839	700	785	140	1998	236	841	501	119	736	2264	620	2290	819	1034
nn Arbor, MI	530	591	423	334	2272	86	833	704	509	644	1211	2394	2446	630	1622	1381	1414	2197	2304	2357	2385	2376	2238	2331	2374	875	622	524	2311	1068	754	818	177	2032	412	719	721	174	644	2318	498	2323	1004	1188
ppleton, WI	871	240	805	170	2116	508	1215	579	456	277	1406	2063	2290	1012	1467	1329	1362	2042	2148	2202	2230	2222	2084	2176	2218	1164	1004	906	1944	1012	499	467	296	1664	360	1100	669	512	1026	2164	880	1956	1167	1382
sheville, NC	233	1005	744	748	2573	718	1005	906	600	1058	661	2697	2520	545	1924	1228	1200	2255	2328	2600	2558	2586	2297	2390	2675	316	822	633	2694	805	1128	1214	610	2415	670	826	764	460	721	2550	765	2706	475	638
tlanta, GA	433	1068	962	804	2465	815	1204	860	556	1121	479	2650	2393	703	1878	1053	989	2129	2142	2473	2432	2459	2170	2263	2520	247	1021	833	2650	595	1084	1168	679	2370	625	1025	662	558	921	2423	965	2662	272	456
tlantic City, NJ	427	1171	401	914	2852	728	470	1211	949	1224	1124	2974	3026	181	2202	1787	1793	2732	2804	2937	2965	2956	2774	2866	2953	779	316	185	2891	1381	1334	1398	733	2612	919	290	1162	573	186	2898	315	2903	1066	1102
ugusta, GA	358	1221	886	957	2682	865	1106	1014	708	1274	481	2805	2553	588	2032	1213	1133	2289	2302	2633	2592	2619	2330	2423	2680	142	946	758	2802	755	1236	1322	784	2524	778	927	822	612	822	2583	890	2814	293	458
urora, IL	710	337	643	72	2012	347	1054	474	275	390	1244	2134	2186	850	1362	1148	1181	1938	2044	2098	2125	2117	1979	2072	2114	1002	843	744	2057	831	495	565	134	1778	179	939	488	351	864	2059	718	2069	1006	1220
ustin, TX	1296	1102	1641	1120	1766	1398	2068	737	824	1142	1131	2246	1683	1644	1327	208	81	1330	1306	1763	1722	1749	1368	1478	1810	1142	1884	1696	2272	325	940	1025	1186	2033	927	1888	614	1226	1784	1718	1716	2284	870	1140
akersfield, CA	2460	1910	2620	1990	275	2323	3030	1647	1844	1950	2547	814	203	2808	706	1318	1468	167	233	283	242	269	144	149	330	2438	2820	2721	1030	1636	1663	1684	2112	1100	1946	2916	1634	2220	2841	233	2695	999	2286	2557
altimore, MD	278	1050	348	794	2731	608	511	1091	829	1104	975	2854	2905	116	2082	1638	1643	2666	2738	2816	2844	2836	2707	2800	2833	630	357	200	2770	1232	1214	1278	612	2491	798	332	1042	453	227	2778	332	2782	917	952
angor, ME	902	1560	618	1302	3240	1118	207	1670	1408	1613	1604	3364	3414	662	2591	2263	2268	3166	3272	3326	3354	3346	3208	3300	3342	1259	409	518	3280	1856	1723	1788	1122	3000	1378	316	1621	1032	404	3288	537	3292	1547	1582
aton Rouge, LA	913	1104	1370	958	2165	1185	1685	864	664	1217	703	2616	2093	1232	1843	634	463	1767	1742	2173	2132	2159	1806	1914	2220	714	1501	1313	2642	261	1087	1172	972	2403	766	1506	574	954	1401	2124	1445	2654	442	713
ay City, MI	626	666	520	408	2346	15	930	779	583	719	1308	2470	2520	727	1696	1455	1489	2272	2378	2432	2460	2451	2313	2406	2448	972	719	621	2386	1142	829	893	251	2106	486	816	796	270	741	2393	595	2398	1101	1285
ayonne, NJ	455	1143	335	886	2824	700	338	1211	949	1196	1158	2946	2998	214	2174	1816	1821	2749	2804	2909	2937	2928	2790	2883	2926	812	182	122	2863	1409	1306	1370	705	2584	919	159	1162	573	55	2870	249	2875	1100	1134
eaumont, TX	1096	1124	1553	1042	2020	1324	1868	759	747	1164	886	2466	1937	1415	1692	450	280	1584	1559	2017	1976	2003	1622	1731	2064	897	1685	1496	2492	206	982	1067	1112	2253	849	1689	611	1138	1584	1972	1628	2504	625	896
illings, MT	1921	894	1854	1175	1088	1558	2265	975	1278	850	2316	942	1262	2062	553	1287	1480	1196	1302	1174	1202	1193	1237	1330	1190	2084	2054	1955	820	1610	748	668	1346	540	1265	2150	1199	1562	2076	1135	1930	832	2080	2292
inghamton, NY	472	1056	159	800	2737	614	334	1170	918	1110	1236	2861	2911	304	2088	1832	1837	2663	2769	2823	2851	2842	2704	2797	2839	891	130	59	2776	1426	1220	1284	618	2498	878	220	1130	542	190	2784	73	2788	1142	1213
irmingham, AL	515	957	976	748	2320	818	1286	809	501	1066	564	2600	2248	851	1826	909	864	1984	1999	2328	2287	2314	2026	2118	2375	395	1103	914	2598	452	1048	1116	624	2318	570	1107	517	561	1003	2278	1047	2610	303	574
ismarck, ND	1507	514	1440	761	1502	1144	1851	739	1042	437	2040	1354	1676	1648	967	1219	1428	1610	1716	1588	1616	1608	1651	1744	1604	1808	1640	1542	1234	1338	512	431	932	954	951	1736	963	1148	1662	1550	1516	1246	1802	2016
loomington, IN	516	580	618	324	2188	392	1028	521	224	634	998	2312	2272	743	1539	1096	1130	2007	2080	2274	2302	2294	2048	2142	2290	756	818	696	2300	775	696	781	198	2021	201	912	437	181	798	2236	693	2312	760	976
oise, ID	2307	1513	2282	1652	554	1986	2693	1321	1625	1469	2662	476	728	2490	341	1564	1757	852	958	640	668	660	894	988	656	2430	2482	2383	504	1888	1326	1286	1774	426	1611	2578	1534	1976	2504	602	2358	514	2426	2638
oston, MA	676	1334	392	1076	3014	892	172	1444	1182	1387	1378	3138	3188	436	2365	2037	2042	2940	3046	3100	3128	3120	2982	3074	3116	1034	184	292	3054	1630	1497	1562	896	2774	1152	90	1395	806	178	3062	311	3066	1321	1356
oulder, CO	1556	893	1602	972	1172	1306	2013	641	874	933	1910	1296	1258	1801	523	761	954	994	1100	1258	1286	1278	1035	1128	1274	1678	1802	1703	1322	1084	646	667	1094	1084	934	1898	782	1239	1824	1220	1678	1334	1649	1887
owling Green, KY	482	761	722	492	2252	564	1133	585	280	814	798	2376	2291	796	1603	999	1005	2026	2098	2338	2330	2358	2068	2160	2354	566	922	806	2374	622	808	893	370	2094	349	999	492	307	894	2300	798	2386	560	774
ridgeport, CT	520	1195	368	938	2876	753	262	1276	1015	1248	1222	3000	3050	280	2226	1881	1886	2802	2870	2962	2989	2980	2843	2936	2978	877	180	169	2915	1474	1359	1423	757	2636	984	83	1227	639	22	2922	282	2927	1165	1200
rockton, MA	683	1347	405	1090	3027	904	196	1457	1195	1400	1386	3150	3202	442	2378	2044	2049	2953	3060	3113	3141	3132	2994	3087	3129	1040	196	305	3067	1638	1510	1574	908	2788	1165	103	1408	819	186	3074	324	3079	1328	1362
rownsville, TX	1535	1454	1921	1472	2017	1750	2307	1089	1176	1494	1325	2508	1934	1854	1612	492	278	1582	1556	2014	1974	2000	1620	1729	2061	1336	2124	1935	2534	596	1292	1377	1538	2296	1278	2128	966	1506	2023	1970	2067	2546	1064	1335
uffalo, NY	504	887	75	630	2568	445	485	1001	748	940	1264	2690	2742	526	1918	1651	1657	2494	2600	2654	2681	2673	2535	2628	2670	918	275	281	2607	1274	1051	1115	449	2328	708	371	961	372	411	2615	150	2619	1146	1240
utte, MT	2143	1116	2076	1397	955	1780	2487	1197	1501	1073	2538	716	1129	2284	420	1509	1702	1063	1169	1041	1069	1061	1104	1197	1057	2306	2276	2178	596	1832	970	890	1568	316	1487	2372	1421	1784	2298	1003	2152	608	2302	2514
algary, AB	2300	1307	2233	1554	1428	1937	2396	1516	1820	1230	2856	858	1602	2441	892	1828	2021	1535	1642	1513	1541	1533	1576	1669	1530	2625	2433	2334	678	2152	1289	1209	1724	458	1744	2529	1740	1941	2454	1475	2308	709	2622	2834
amden, NJ	379	1120	349	862	2800	677	422	1160	898	1173	1076	2924	2974	136	2150	1740	1744	2681	2753	2886	2914	2905	2722	2815	2902	731	268	134	2840	1333	1283	1347	681	2560	868	243	1110	522	139	2847	264	2852	1019	1053
anton, OH	370	736	301	478	2416	293	711	807	545	789	1061	2540	2590	451	1767	1448	1454	2328	2400	2502	2530	2522	2370	2462	2518	715	501	357	2456	1072	899	964	298	2176	515	572	758	170	478	2464	376	2468	942	1038
asper, WY	1706	824	1682	1052	1055	1385	2092	721	1024	864	2061	1178	1229	1889	406	1010	1203	1044	1150	1141	1169	1160	1086	1178	1157	1830	1882	1783	1096	1333	559	598	1174	816	1010	1978	945	1375	1903	1102	1757	1108	1826	2038
edar Rapids, IA	880	169	832	202	1841	535	1242	304	287	282	1324	1965	2015	1039	1192	1049	1101	1767	1873	1927	1954	1946	1808	1901	1943	1092	1031	932	1837	828	272	361	324	1558	249	1127	409	526	1053	1888	907	1849	1089	1300
hampaign, IL	618	450	700	186	2068	408	1110	380	175	503	1102	2192	2242	824	1418	1048	1081	1958	2030	2154	2182	2173	2000	2092	2170	871	900	778	2117	726	551	636	166	1838	88	994	388	262	880	2115	775	2129	865	1080
harleston, SC	405	1262	934	1004	2829	912	1090	1162	856	1314	456	2953	2720	572	2180	1380	1300	2456	2470	2800	2760	2786	2498	2590	2847	111	936	780	2950	922	1385	1470	866	2672	926	910	990	659	806	2751	912	2962	399	493
harleston, WV	178	840	503	584	2479	438	853	811	506	894	869	2602	2554	470	1830	1319	1325	2290	2362	2564	2592	2584	2331	2424	2581	524	669	481	2560	942	1034	1119	408	2281	523	673	719	185	569	2526	578	2572	750	846
harlotte, NC	196	1119	724	862	2686	702	967	1019	714	1172	602	2810	2633	463	2037	1298	1236	2368	2388	2713	2672	2699	2410	2503	2788	257	784	595	2808	841	1242	1327	672	2528	783	788	877	449	683	2663	728	2820	484	579
hattanooga, TN	368	951	879	686	2411	712	1140	744	438	1004	601	2533	2328	716	1762	1054	1008	2063	2144	2407	2366	2393	2104	2197	2454	369	956	768	2532	597	966	1052	562	2253	508	960	602	455	856	2358	900	2544	394	578
heyenne, WY	1570	836	1546	916	1087	1249	1956	585	888	876	1925	1210	1261	1753	438	832	1068	1126	1232	1191	1200	1192	1111	1204	1189	1694	1745	1647	1236	1156	589	610	1038	994	874	1842	809	1239	1767	1134	1621	1248	1690	1902
hicago, IL	669	351	601	94	2048	304	1011	510	296	404	1204	2172	2222	808	1398	1168	1202	1974	2080	2134	2162	2154	2015	2108	2150	962	801	702	2071	862	531	578	93	1792	200	897	509	310	822	2096	676	2083	965	1180
incinnati, OH	375	644	502	386	2300	337	912	612	350	697	944	2424	2397	622	1650	1204	1210	2133	2205	2386	2414	2405	2174	2267	2402	670	702	580	2364	827	783	868	246	2084	320	796	563	80	677	2347	577	2376	738	922
larksville, TN	483	777	803	512	2238	644	1254	570	265	830	778	2360	2225	831	1588	933	939	1960	2033	2323	2264	2342	2002	2095	2340	546	1002	883	2358	557	793	878	428	2080	334	1075	428	388	971	2284	878	2370	540	755
learwater, FL	800	1551	1328	1287	2802	1298	1484	1344	1039	1604	22	3133	2731	966	2362	1318	1147	2451	2426	2811	2770	2797	2489	2598	2857	356	1330	1175	3133	892	1567	1652	1162	2853	1108	1305	1060	1041	1200	2761	1308	3144	238	23
leveland, OH	430	694	258	438	2375	252	668	808	561	748	1120	2498	2549	479	1726	1464	1470	2301	2407	2460	2488	2480	2342	2435	2477	775	458	373	2414	1088	858	922	256	2135	516	554	774	186	494	2422	333	2426	998	1097
oeur d'Alene, ID	2429	1402	2362	1682	856	2066	2772	1483	1786	1358	2823	430	996	2570	692	1795	1988	1335	1441	908	936	928	1376	1226	924	2592	2562	2464	310	2118	1256	1176	1854	30	1772	2658	1707	2070	2584	902	2438	322	2588	2800
olorado Sprs., CO	1524	950	1660	1030	1258	1363	2070	602	842	990	1878	1380	1305	1769	608	684	877	1040	1146	1343	1371	1362	1082	1174	1360	1646	1859	1723	1408	913	703	724	1152	1168	902	1955	750	1207	1824	1304	1735	1419	1617	1855
olumbia, MO	808	449	928	382	1850	661	1339	182	126	489	1162	1972	1964	1053	1200	847	862	1700	1722	1935	1963	1954	1742	1834	1952	930	1128	1007	1971	584	405	490	450	1692	186	1222	168	491	1108	1896	1004	1983	927	1139
olumbia, SC	291	1153	820	896	2720	798	1039	1053	748	1206	507	2844	2618	521	2071	1277	1197	2353	2367	2698	2656	2683	2394	2487	2744	161	879	690	2842	819	1276	1361	757	2562	818	860	886	544	756	2648	823	2854	395	483
olumbus, GA	543	1170	1072	906	2464	917	1315	964	658	1224	417	2753	2392	813	1982	1006	918	2121	2096	2472	2431	2458	2160	2262	2518	263	1131	943	2752	549	1186	1272	782	2473	728	1135	661	660	1031	2422	1075	2764	172	394
olumbus, OH	340	704	394	448	2370	277	804	683	420	758	1031	2494	2468	518	1721	1322	1328	2204	2276	2456	2484	2476	2245	2338	2472	685	594	472	2424	946	854	938	252	2145	390	688	633	45	573	2418	469	2436	856	1008
oncord, NH	724	1313	372	1056	2994	871	105	1427	1174	1366	1426	3116	3168	484	2344	2085	2090	2920	3026	3080	3107	3099	2961	3054	3096	1082	157	340	3033	1678	1477	1541	875	2754	1134	138	1387	798	226	3041	290	3045	1369	1404
orpus Christi, TX	1388	1318	1774	1336	1882	1614	2160	953	1041	1358	1178	2374	1799	1707	1476	356	142	1446	1421	1879	1838	1865	1484	1593	1926	1189	1977	1788	2400	449	1156	1241	1402	2160	1143	1981	830	1359	1876	1834	1920	2412	917	1188
allas, TX	1102	907	1446	926	1726	1204	1873	542	630	947	1098	2176	1654	1450	1404	269	276	1384	1359	1734	1693	1720	1422	1531	1781	996	1690	1502	2202	187	757	842	992	1964	732	1694	419	1006	1590	1684	1522	2214	837	1108
avenport, IA	800	252	752	132	1884	455	1162	346	265	365	1272	2008	2058	959	1234	1092	1144	1810	1916	1970	1998	1989	1851	1944	1986	1040	951	852	1933	821	367	452	244	1654	169	1048	402	445	973	1931	827	1945	1034	1248
ayton, OH	372	646	464	388	2312	284	874	624	362	699	1015	2436	2410	588	1662	1234	1240	2145	2217	2398	2426	2417	2186	2279	2414	740	664	542	2366	898	795	880	228	2086	332	758	575	27	644	2359	539	2378	808	992
aytona Beach, FL	674	1508	1203	1244	2812	1182	1359	1301	996	1562	161	3092	2740	841	2320	1326	1156	2460	2435	2820	2778	2806	2498	2607	2866	231	1205	1050	3090	901	1524	1609	1119	2811	1066	1180	1069	928	1076	2770	1182	3102	253	138
ecatur, AL	494	934	897	670	2275	738	1265	709	421	987	644	2500	2204	842	1727	912	918	1940	2012	2284	2242	2270	1980	2074	2330	445	1082	894	2498	530	932	1017	544	2218	491	1086	473	481	982	2234	972	2510	383	654
ecatur, IL	673	453	755	189	1997	460	1165	331	135	506	1090	2120	2172	880	1348	1007	1041	1918	1990	2083	2111	2102	1960	2052	2099	859	955	834	2109	691	543	628	248	1830	38	1049	348	318	934	2044	830	2121	852	1068
enver, CO	1537	882	1592	962	1185	1295	2002	616	855	922	1892	1309	1236	1782	536	743	936	972	1078	1270	1298	1290	1013	1106	1287	1660	1791	1693	1334	1066	635	656	1084	1096	915	1888	764	1220	1813	1232	1667	1346	1630	1868
es Moines, IA	966	208	917	286	1715	620	1327	178	373	248	1410	1838	1889	1124	1066	923	975	1641	1747	1801	1828	1820	1682	1775	1817	1178	1117	1018	1764	733	198	283	409	1484	334	1213	359	610	1136	1762	992	1776	1174	1386
etroit, MI	530	634	426	378	2314	104	836	748	533	688	1224	2438	2488	633	1665	1405	1439	2240	2346	2400	2428	2420	2282	2374	2416	876	626	527	2354	1106	798	862	213	2075	455	722	746	187	647	2362	501	2366	1017	1201
ubuque, IA	870	191	784	93	1915	487	1194	377	335	270	1342	1994	2089	991	1266	1123	1174	1841	1947	2000	2028	2020	1882	1975	2017	1110	983	885	1874	891	308	398	276	1594	238	1080	483	514	1005	1962	859	1886	1104	1318
uluth, MN	1139	226	1072	392	1947	605	1482	573	679	149	1672	1800	2121	1280	1461	1318	1370	2036	2142	2033	2061	2052	2078	2170	2049	1440	1272	1173	1678	1129	455	423	564	1399	582	1368	754	780	1294	1994	1148	1690	1434	1648
urham, NC	156	1144	660	886	2800	742	818	1132	828	1196	696	2924	2746	319	2150	1461	1400	2532	2552	2826	2786	2812	2524	2616	2902	352	664	508	2864	984	1356	1440	711	2584	826	638	990	488	534	2776	640	2876	640	674
ast Orange, NJ	457	1128	320	872	2808	686	335	1214	952	1182	1162	2932	2982	219	2160	1818	1823	2735	2806	2894	2922	2914	2776	2869	2910	816	168	108	2848	1411	1292	1356	690	2569	921	156	1164	576	52	2856	235	2860	1104	1139
au Claire, WI	989	94	922	242	2044	625	1332	506	529	87	1520	1872	2218	1129	1395	1252	1303	1970	2076	2130	2158	2149	2011	2104	2146	1290	1122	1023	1754	1062	388	356	412	1474	432	1218	687	630	1143	2091	997	1766	1283	1498
lgin, IL	713	310	647	53	2036	350	1057	498	301	364	1248	2150	2210	854	1386	1173	1206	1962	2068	2122	2150	2142	2004	2096	2138	1006	847	748	2030	856	520	538	138	1751	204	943	514	354	868	2084	722	2042	1010	1224
lizabeth, NJ	448	1135	327	878	2816	692	338	1205	943	1188	1150	2938	2990	207	2166	1809	1814	2726	2798	2901	2929	2921	2767	2860	2917	805	174	114	2855	1402	1298	1362	698	2575	912	159	1155	567	55	2863	241	2867	1092	1127
l Paso, TX	1736	1343	2006	1422	1185	1766	2508	955	1193	1383	1720	1700	1102	2084	888	404	554	750	724	1182	1141	1168	798	897	1229	1632	2325	2136	1728	823	1108	1152	1554	1609	1295	2329	982	1569	2224	1138	2081	1739	1460	1730
lyria, OH	439	668	286	410	2348	226	696	781	543	721	1130	2472	2522	493	1699	1446	1452	2274	2380	2434	2462	2454	2316	2408	2450	784	486	386	2388	1069	831	896	230	2108	489	582	756	167	506	2396	361	2400	979	1106
nid, OK	1166	718	1322	798	1656	1082	1732	330	498	761	1235	1978	1584	1466	1106	432	566	1320	1392	1664	1623	1650	1362	1454	1711	1144	1521	1400	1906	487	517	602	870	1666	510	1615	297	884	1510	1615	1397	1918	1052	1215
rie, PA	487	796	161	538	2476	353	571	909	657	849	1172	2600	2650	476	1826	1559	1565	2402	2508	2562	2590	2581	2443	2536	2578	826	361	323	2516	1182	959	1023	357	2236	616	457	869	281	453	2523	236	2528	1054	1148
scondido, CA	2474	1925	2634	2004	486	2338	3044	1662	1859	1965	2466	1021	403	2823	720	1149	1300	76	30	483	442	469	71	196	530	2377	2834	2736	1238	1568	1678	1698	2126	1441	1961	2930	1648	2235	2856	439	2710	1206	2204	2476
ugene, OR	2842	1896	2818	2176	474	2522	3228	1858	2160	1852	3198	66	616	3026	877	2060	2211	910	976	528	556	547	887	846	544	2966	3018	2920	283	2424	1750	1669	2310	463	2146	3114	2082	2512	3040	520	2894	251	2962	3174
vansville, IN	540	647	727	382	2144	525	1137	476	171	700	880	2266	2218	832	1494	1028	1034	1954	2026	2229	2257	2248	1995	2088	2246	648	927	806	2265	652	699	784	324	1985	240	1021	383	312	931	2190	802	2276	642	857
verett, WA	2760	1734	2694	2014	784	2398	3104	1815	2118	1690	3155	247	924	2902	863	2058	2280	1218	1284	836	864	856	1196	1154	852	2924	2894	2796	28	2410	1588	1508	2186	362	2104	2990	2039	2402	2916	829	2770	60	2920	3132
airfield, CA	2703	1969	2678	2048	47	2382	3089	1718	2021	2009	2832	550	134	2886	696	1598	1749	447	514	46	74	65	425	364	62	2724	2878	2780	768	1921	1722	1699	2170	838	2007	2974	1942	2372	2900	52	2754	736	2571	2842
all River, MA	656	1330	421	1074	3011	888	224	1412	1150	1384	1358	3134	3185	415	2362	2016	2022	2937	3005	3096	3124	3116	2978	3071	3112	1012	212	300	3050	1610	1494	1558	892	2771	1119	118	1362	774	157	3058	339	3062	1300	1334
argo, ND	1314	321	1248	568	1695	951	1658	550	854	244	1847	1548	1869	1455	1160	1253	1344	1802	1908	1781	1808	1800	1844	1936	1797	1616	1447	1348	1426	1149	323	242	740	1147	758	1544	774	955	1469	1742	1323	1438	1609	1823
ayetteville, NC	245	1196	720	938	2830	793	878	1162	858	1249	612	2954	2780	360	2180	1439	1359	2515	2529	2860	2818	2845	2556	2649	2906	266	724	568	2952	981	1386	1470	764	2672	878	698	1021	540	594	2810	700	2963	554	589
lagstaff, AZ	1980	1514	2177	1594	755	1937	2588	1126	1364	1554	2066	1294	684	2328	521	844	1126	419	492	764	722	749	460	553	810	1958	2377	2256	1360	1156	1280	1323	1726	1242	1466	2471	1153	1740	2357	714	2252	1872	1805	2076
lint, MI	584	623	477	366	2304	38	888	737	541	676	1266	2426	2478	685	1654	1413	1447	2230	2336	2389	2417	2409	2271	2364	2406	929	677	578	2343	1100	787	851	209	2064	444	773	754	228	699	2351	552	2355	1058	1242
lorence, SC	269	1230	804	972	2797	806	962	1130	824	1282	526	2921	2694	444	2148	1354	1274	2430	2444	2774	2733	2760	2471	2564	2820	180	808	653	2918	896	1353	1438	834	2640	894	783	963	552	678	2724	785	2930	468	502
t. Collins, CO	1590	881	1590	960	1102	1294	2001	630	908	921	1944	1226	1276	1798	452	795	988	1033	1139	1188	1216	1208	1074	1167	1204	1713	1790	1692	1252	1119	634	655	1082	1038	919	1886	817	1273	1812	1150	1666	1264	1683	1922
t. Dodge, IA	1034	184	986	282	1768	689	1396	249	441	224	1478	1804	1942	1193	1118	995	1046	1694	1800	1854	1882	1874	1736	1828	1870	1246	1185	1086	1682	805	128	213	478	1403	403	1281	430	679	1207	1816	1061	1694	1243	1454
t. Lauderdale, FL	912	1714	1440	1449	3016	1418	1596	1506	1201	1766	250	3295	2945	1078	2524	1524	1361	2665	2640	3025	2984	3011	2703	2812	3071	468	1442	1286	3295	1106	1730	1814	1324	3016	1270	1416	1274	1165	1312	2975	1419	3307	458	242
t. Smith, AR	938	692	1205	688	1801	965	1708	355	391	732	1083	2106	1729	1286	1333	545	554	1465	1537	1809	1768	1795	1506	1599	1856	916	1406	1336	2132	252	578	661	756	1894	494	1530	180	767	1424	1759	1282	2144	822	1093

Mileage Directory, continued

	Terre Haute, IN	Toledo, OH	Topeka, KS	Toronto, ON	Torrington, CT	Trenton, NJ	Troy, NY	Tucson, AZ	Tulsa, OK	Tupelo, MS	Tuscaloosa, AL	Tyler, TX	Utica, NY	Vallejo, CA	Vancouver, BC	Ventura, CA	Victoria, TX	Virginia Beach, VA	Waco, TX	Walnut Creek, CA	Warren, OH	Washington, DC	Waterbury, CT	Waterloo, IA	Waukegan, IL	Wausau, WI	West Palm Beach, FL	Wheeling, WV	Wichita, KS	Wichita Falls, TX	Wilmington, DE	Winnipeg, MB	Winston-Salem, NC	Worcester, MA	Yakima, WA	Youngstown, OH	
Abilene, TX	957	1258	587	1549	1860	1686	1865	771	394	737	767	280	1750	1640	2150	1324	347	1552	183	1618	1401	1514	1840	962	1112	1255	1432	1355	447	151	1619	1386	1282	1908	1872	1404	Abilene, TX
Akron, OH	377	133	848	316	528	424	500	1989	937	732	760	1133	405	2454	2573	2430	1421	544	1272	2467	40	352	507	651	417	651	1149	102	975	1180	397	1235	428	600	2358	48	Akron, OH
Albany, GA	677	850	1040	1142	1138	971	1183	1753	865	362	260	711	1184	2560	2958	2320	870	717	839	2538	912	792	1118	1067	942	1175	450	846	1038	936	911	1759	480	1205	2708	912	Albany, GA
Albany, NY	863	584	1333	386	84	220	7	2474	1423	1194	1148	1640	94	2906	3025	2882	1882	512	1774	2918	465	383	137	1102	869	1103	1386	516	1460	1665	280	1687	724	127	2810	474	Albany, NY
Albert Lea, MN	536	647	405	926	1287	1183	1226	1535	610	840	970	875	1130	1920	1790	1896	1163	1303	942	1933	793	1111	1266	126	378	272	1624	872	540	835	1156	553	1111	1349	1575	807	Albert Lea, MN
Albuquerque, NM	1212	1513	734	1803	2112	1948	2073	498	648	1112	1242	744	1978	1090	1596	850	828	1938	711	1069	1629	1888	2091	1109	1366	1401	1896	1587	591	508	1921	1540	1657	2183	1319	1632	Albuquerque, NM
Alexandria, LA	779	1081	690	1372	1506	1332	1510	1256	462	371	361	215	1511	2039	2640	1809	358	1146	343	2017	1150	1158	1485	982	962	1163	995	1104	662	440	1264	1491	876	1553	2362	1154	Alexandria, LA
Alexandria, VA	673	478	1143	494	354	186	405	2286	1284	850	803	1295	441	2799	2918	2738	1537	203	1429	2812	336	8	334	996	762	996	989	293	1270	1480	126	1580	337	420	2702	317	Alexandria, VA
Allentown, PA	701	496	1171	450	208	76	220	2416	1261	980	933	1426	257	2818	2936	2758	1667	322	1560	2830	340	191	188	1014	780	1015	1193	321	1298	1503	80	1598	510	268	2721	334	Allentown, PA
Altoona, PA	536	319	1006	310	364	254	369	2147	1096	903	856	1287	328	2640	2759	2593	1590	374	1426	2653	177	182	344	837	603	837	1160	156	1133	1338	227	1421	432	436	2544	158	Altoona, PA
Amarillo, TX	928	1229	558	1519	1828	1664	1789	689	364	828	958	460	1694	1375	1884	1134	625	1654	427	1353	1345	1604	1807	933	1082	1226	1612	1303	418	224	1637	1222	1373	1899	1606	1348	Amarillo, TX
Anderson, IN	122	185	592	476	814	651	764	1733	682	543	572	902	669	2274	2414	2179	1190	722	1014	2287	332	579	794	471	259	493	1176	290	719	924	624	1077	516	886	2200	335	Anderson, IN
Ann Arbor, MI	356	55	784	274	703	600	642	1954	902	756	784	1131	547	2329	2448	2305	1420	720	1234	2342	209	528	683	525	292	526	1288	288	919	1145	573	1110	568	766	2232	224	Ann Arbor, MI
Appleton, WI	378	445	659	724	1085	982	1024	1789	850	843	920	1075	929	2174	2080	2150	1403	1102	1182	2187	591	910	1065	294	156	102	1526	670	794	1092	954	743	909	1147	1866	605	Appleton, WI
Asheville, NC	543	582	912	779	812	638	817	1910	908	474	411	903	818	2630	2831	2363	1128	430	1054	2581	528	466	792	913	706	940	729	461	1040	1105	570	1524	147	860	2582	527	Asheville, NC
Atlanta, GA	506	679	868	970	1012	822	1016	1735	782	279	201	693	1017	2476	2786	2236	918	588	822	2455	746	643	992	896	770	1003	599	679	955	919	762	1587	317	1060	2537	745	Atlanta, GA
Atlantic City, NJ	783	587	1253	560	258	89	309	2470	1343	1034	987	1479	367	2909	3028	2840	1721	319	1614	2922	450	190	238	1105	872	1106	1192	403	1380	1585	82	1690	541	325	2812	427	Atlantic City, NJ
Augusta, GA	658	730	1020	922	894	727	942	1895	942	439	361	853	942	2636	2940	2396	1061	473	982	2615	670	548	874	1048	881	1156	549	604	1115	1079	667	1740	236	961	2690	670	Augusta, GA
Aurora, IL	216	284	554	563	924	820	863	1720	669	584	759	894	768	2069	2194	2045	1222	940	1001	2082	430	749	903	266	66	272	1364	509	689	911	793	856	748	986	1978	444	Aurora, IL
Austin, TX	996	1297	684	1588	1875	1702	1880	898	462	752	725	229	1765	1766	2408	1451	127	1510	99	1745	1416	1528	1855	1020	1150	1312	1284	1370	544	302	1634	1482	1239	1923	2130	1419	Austin, TX
Bakersfield, CA	2016	2260	1572	2539	2900	2752	2839	597	1453	1916	2046	1548	2744	286	1174	122	1583	2742	1515	265	2406	2692	2880	1828	2059	2121	2700	2391	1395	1312	2725	2004	2461	2962	933	2421	Bakersfield, CA
Baltimore, MD	662	467	1133	474	300	132	350	2320	1222	885	838	1330	385	2788	2907	2773	1572	258	1464	2802	326	41	279	985	752	986	1043	282	1260	1515	72	1570	392	366	2692	306	Baltimore, MD
Bangor, ME	1242	976	1712	622	378	508	399	2853	1802	1510	1462	1954	486	3298	3140	3274	2197	799	2089	3310	830	670	357	1494	1261	1495	1673	856	1839	2044	568	1709	1022	265	3202	824	Bangor, ME
Baton Rouge, LA	774	1076	828	1368	1492	1318	1497	1335	600	366	348	353	1498	2177	2778	1888	392	1116	450	2155	1146	1146	1472	990	957	1158	856	1099	801	578	1250	1630	846	1540	2500	1148	Baton Rouge, LA
Bay City, MI	431	152	859	296	800	697	739	2028	977	852	881	1205	644	2404	2522	2379	1494	817	1309	2416	306	625	780	600	366	508	1385	385	994	1219	670	1106	664	862	2308	320	Bay City, MI
Bayonne, NJ	783	559	1253	494	127	60	176	2498	1343	1062	1015	1508	260	2881	3000	2857	1749	352	1642	2894	404	224	106	1077	844	1078	1226	403	1380	1585	121	1662	574	193	2784	397	Bayonne, NJ
Beaumont, TX	914	1259	790	1550	1676	1502	1680	1152	484	549	531	189	1681	2020	2628	1704	209	1300	267	1998	1328	1328	1655	1042	1096	1242	1039	1282	650	423	1434	1524	1029	1723	2350	1332	Beaumont, TX
Billings, MT	1387	1495	1008	1774	2135	2032	2074	1327	1237	1650	1780	1523	1979	1146	956	1303	1594	2151	1396	1158	1641	1960	2114	964	1226	1026	2436	1720	1064	1193	2004	748	1959	2197	742	1655	Billings, MT
Binghamton, NY	752	473	1222	318	223	195	144	2363	1312	1078	1032	1524	126	2795	2914	2770	1766	442	1658	2808	354	302	203	991	758	992	1304	400	1349	1554	200	1576	608	267	2698	362	Binghamton, NY
Birmingham, AL	450	682	741	973	1094	920	1098	1592	637	134	58	550	1099	2332	2734	2092	792	736	678	2310	752	747	1074	843	716	948	717	705	810	776	852	1532	466	1141	2484	754	Birmingham, AL
Bismarck, ND	1027	1081	772	1360	1721	1618	1660	1642	993	1414	1544	1306	1565	1560	1370	1717	1468	1738	1247	1573	1227	1546	1700	647	813	612	2160	1306	802	1100	1590	414	1545	1783	1156	1241	Bismarck, ND
Bloomington, IN	58	277	528	568	876	712	838	1669	618	485	513	838	746	2246	2437	2115	1126	760	950	2259	393	641	856	467	282	516	1118	351	655	860	685	1100	554	948	2198	396	Bloomington, IN
Boise, ID	1786	1923	1362	2202	2563	2460	2502	1116	1515	1996	2126	1800	2407	612	640	872	1872	2551	1673	625	2069	2388	2542	1491	1722	1644	2782	2146	1342	1470	2432	1367	2345	2625	362	2083	Boise, ID
Boston, MA	1016	750	1486	552	152	282	173	2627	1576	1284	1236	1729	260	3072	3190	3048	1971	573	1863	3085	604	444	131	1268	1035	1269	1447	630	1613	1818	342	1730	796	43	2976	598	Boston, MA
Boulder, CO	1034	1243	559	1522	1883	1770	1822	977	712	1219	1349	997	1727	1230	1459	1102	1069	1800	870	1243	1389	1699	1862	811	1042	1103	2030	1409	538	667	1743	1106	1594	1945	1182	1403	Boulder, CO
Bowling Green, KY	218	428	592	720	986	812	942	1681	679	284	312	685	847	2310	2510	2134	974	748	825	2323	498	698	966	620	462	696	918	451	719	876	761	1280	482	1033	2262	501	Bowling Green, KY
Bridgeport, CT	848	612	1318	528	50	126	170	2563	1408	1128	1080	1572	258	2934	3052	2909	1815	417	1707	2946	456	288	30	1130	896	1130	1291	468	1446	1651	186	1714	640	117	2837	449	Bridgeport, CT
Brockton, MA	1029	763	1499	564	165	288	186	2726	1589	1290	1244	1736	274	3085	3204	3060	1978	580	1870	3098	617	452	144	1281	1048	1282	1454	643	1626	1831	349	1754	802	56	2988	611	Brockton, MA
Brownsville, TX	1304	1627	1036	1919	2114	1941	2119	1149	814	988	970	530	2120	2018	2672	1702	232	1739	451	1996	1697	1768	2094	1371	1502	1664	1478	1650	896	654	1872	1834	1468	2162	2394	1700	Brownsville, TX
Buffalo, NY	582	304	1052	100	374	417	294	2194	1142	936	964	1337	199	2625	2744	2601	1626	582	1477	2638	185	391	424	822	588	822	1332	270	1179	1384	422	1406	611	458	2528	193	Buffalo, NY
Butte, MT	1610	1717	1231	1996	2357	2254	2296	1194	1460	1872	2002	1745	2201	1013	732	1170	1817	2374	1618	1026	1863	2182	2336	1186	1449	1248	2658	1942	1286	1415	2226	971	2181	2419	518	1877	Butte, MT
Calgary, AB	1820	1874	1550	2116	2514	2410	2453	1666	1779	2191	2322	2064	2358	1485	602	1642	2136	2530	1937	1498	2020	2339	2493	1440	1606	1404	2976	2099	1606	1734	2383	822	2338	2576	659	2034	Calgary, AB
Camden, NJ	732	536	1202	509	211	39	262	2422	1292	986	939	1431	316	2858	2976	2788	1673	274	1566	2870	399	142	190	1054	821	1055	1145	352	1329	1534	32	1639	493	277	2762	375	Camden, NJ
Canton, OH	379	152	849	336	537	421	520	1990	939	733	762	1134	425	2474	2592	2436	1423	541	1274	2486	52	349	516	670	437	671	1129	82	976	1181	394	1255	408	609	2378	57	Canton, OH
Casper, WY	1185	1322	807	1601	1962	1859	1902	1227	960	1396	1526	1245	1806	1113	1233	1152	1317	1950	1118	1126	1468	1788	1942	890	1140	1034	2182	1546	787	916	1832	932	1744	2024	1018	1483	Casper, WY
Cedar Rapids, IA	355	472	383	751	1112	1009	1051	1514	588	659	789	854	956	1898	1974	1874	1141	1124	920	1912	618	937	1092	55	271	314	1444	695	515	813	982	733	919	1174	1758	632	Cedar Rapids, IA
Champaign, IL	93	345	460	624	958	794	920	1620	569	456	618	789	824	2126	2254	2066	1078	862	901	2138	475	723	938	322	180	385	1222	433	595	811	767	969	656	1030	2038	478	Champaign, IL
Charleston, SC	800	776	1169	969	878	710	930	2063	1109	606	528	1021	965	2804	3088	2564	1229	456	1149	2782	718	531	858	1170	962	1196	525	651	1282	1246	650	1780	283	944	2838	717	Charleston, SC
Charleston, WV	387	302	818	538	660	486	664	2002	900	604	622	1006	627	2536	2698	2397	1294	422	1145	2550	244	372	640	757	542	776	937	177	945	1142	436	1360	216	708	2488	249	Charleston, WV
Charlotte, NC	656	567	1026	759	774	582	779	1981	1022	524	447	939	780	2744	2944	2476	1164	348	1067	2695	508	402	754	1027	820	1054	670	441	1153	1164	522	1638	77	822	2695	507	Charlotte, NC
Chattanooga, TN	388	576	750	868	948	774	952	1737	716	250	203	695	953	2468	2669	2170	937	650	823	2389	646	600	927	778	654	886	721	596	878	913	706	1470	370	995	2420	649	Chattanooga, TN
Cheyenne, WY	1049	1186	630	1465	1826	1723	1765	1050	783	1260	1390	1068	1670	1144	1374	1177	1140	1814	941	1158	1332	1652	1806	754	985	1047	2045	1409	609	738	1696	1006	1608	1888	1096	1346	Cheyenne, WY
Chicago, IL	180	242	590	520	882	778	820	1742	690	591	718	925	725	2106	2208	2082	1214	898	1022	2118	387	706	861	302	38	286	1324	468	725	932	751	870	707	944	1992	402	Chicago, IL
Cincinnati, OH	184	201	654	493	760	592	722	1795	744	489	517	890	626	2358	2500	2240	1179	619	1030	2370	277	521	740	554	345	579	1065	231	781	986	565	1163	413	832	2286	280	Cincinnati, OH
Clarksville, TN	214	508	577	800	1062	888	1066	1616	614	219	293	620	929	2295	2496	2068	908	765	759	2308	578	715	1042	604	441	712	898	532	704	810	820	1296	484	1110	2246	581	Clarksville, TN
Clearwater, FL	988	1162	1351	1364	1272	1105	1324	2018	1179	676	558	990	1360	2814	3270	2572	1076	851	1118	2792	1112	926	1252	1378	1254	1486	226	1046	1352	1216	1045	2070	678	1340	3020	1112	Clearwater, FL
Cleveland, OH	395	111	865	293	553	449	478	2006	955	749	778	1150	382	2432	2552	2408	1439	569	1290	2446	57	378	532	629	396	630	1188	141	992	1197	422	1214	468	601	2336	73	Cleveland, OH
Coeur d'Alene, ID	1896	2003	1516	2282	2642	2540	2582	1466	1746	2158	2288	2030	2486	880	446	1442	2102	2660	1904	892	2148	2468	2622	1472	1734	1534	2943	2228	1572	1701	2512	1114	2467	2705	232	2164	Coeur d'Alene, ID
Colorado Sprs., CO	1002	1300	527	1579	1902	1739	1879	875	680	1187	1317	826	1784	1315	1544	1148	991	1768	792	1328	1446	1667	1882	868	1099	1160	1998	1377	506	590	1711	1163	1562	2002	1266	1423	Colorado Sprs., CO
Columbia, MO	286	587	189	878	1186	1023	1148	1312	349	497	627	615	1053	1907	2108	1808	902	1052	681	1920	704	951	1166	316	413	582	1282	662	306	611	995	948	846	1258	1858	707	Columbia, MO
Columbia, SC	690	662	1060	854	828	660	874	1960	1006	503	426	918	875	2701	2978	2460	1126	406	1046	2679	603	480	807	1061	854	1088	575	536	1179	1143	600	1672	169	894	2730	602	Columbia, SC
Columbus, GA	608	782	970	1073	1122	932	1126	1689	780	278	194	647	1128	2475	2889	2235	846	698	776	2454	851	752	1102	998	872	1106	537	789	954	873	872	1690	428	1170	2640	855	Columbus, GA
Columbus, OH	254	142	724	429	652	448	613	1866	814	608	636	1008	518	2428	2561	2311	1297	584	1148	2441	169	416	632	624	406	640	1099	126	852	1057	460	1224	378	724	2346	172	Columbus, OH
Concord, NH	1008	730	1478	582	200	330	143	2620	1568	1332	1285	1777	240	3051	3170	3027	2019	621	1911	3064	652	492	179	1248	1014	1248	1495	678	1605	1810	390	1668	844	87	2954	646	Concord, NH
Corpus Christi, TX	1157	1480	900	1772	1968	1794	1972	1014	678	841	823	404	1973	1882	2536	1567	96	1592	315	1860	1550	1620	1947	1236	1367	1528	1331	1504	760	518	1726	1699	1321	2015	2258	1553	Corpus Christi, TX
Dallas, TX	802	1103	501	1393	1681	1507	1685	952	267	558	587	100	1571	1738	2340	1505	316	1372	96	1716	1222	1334	1661	825	956	1118	1252	1176	361	139	1439	1300	1103	1728	2062	1225	Dallas, TX
Davenport, IA	275	392	426	671	1032	929	971	1556	632	652	782	897	876	1942	2070	1918	1184	1044	964	1954	538	857	1012	138	201	330	1392	615	561	856	902	816	839	1094	1854	552	Davenport, IA
Dayton, OH	196	148	666	440	722	558	684	1807	756	560	588	960	588	2370	2508	2252	1249	616	1100	2382	239	487	702	566	347	581	1135	197	793	998	531	1165	410	794	2288	242	Dayton, OH
Daytona Beach, FL	946	1046	1308	1238	1148	980	1198	2028	1188	685	568	999	1234	2823	3227	2580	1085	726	1127	2801	987	800	1127	1336	1210	1444	199	920	1361	1224	920	2028	553	1214	2978	986	Daytona Beach, FL
Decatur, AL	371	602	716	894	1073	899	1077	1594	592	123	136	598	1021	2287	2634	2047	870	776	738	2265	672	726	1052	744	636	869	797	626	765	789	831	1453	495	1120	2386	675	Decatur, AL
Decatur, IL	107	397	411	676	1013	849	974	1580	529	443	606	754	879	2055	2246	2026	1081	917	861	2068	530	778	992	314	220	388	1210	488	545	771	822	972	712	1085	2006	533	Decatur, IL
Denver, CO	1016	1232	540	1511	1872	1752	1811	948	693	1200	1330	978	1716	1242	1472	1080	1050	1781	852	1256	1378	1680	1852	800	1031	1092	2012	1391	520	649	1725	1095	1575	1934	1194	1392	Denver, CO
Des Moines, IA	441	558	257	836	1198	1094	1137	1388	463	744	874	728	1041	1773	1901	1748	1015	1210	795	1786	703	1023	1177	126	356	418	1530	781	392	687	1067	699	1004	1260	1686	718	Des Moines, IA
Detroit, MI	367	59	828	236	706	603	646	1978	927	768	797	1170	550	2372	2491	2348	1458	723	1259	2385	212	532	686	569	335	570	1289	291	964	1169	576	1153	568	768	2276	227	Detroit, MI
Dubuque, IA	345	424	457	703	1064	961	1003	1587	662	722	852	928	908	1972	2010	1948	1215	1081	994	1986	570	890	1044	92	176	240	1462	685	592	887	934	770	908	1126	1796	584	Dubuque, IA
Duluth, MN	658	713	653	844	1353	1249	1292	1783	858	1066	1186	1123	1196	2005	1816	2144	1411	1369	1190	2018	859	1178	1332	374	444	235	1792	938	788	1082	1222	381	1177	1415	1600	873	Duluth, MN
Durham, NC	690	606	1140	733	606	438	656	2124	1135	668	590	1082	692	2858	3000	2590	1307	204	1210	2808	546	258	586	1060	844	1078	766	480	1266	1332	378	1662	86	672	2808	546	Durham, NC
East Orange, NJ	785	545	1255	480	124	65	162	2500	1345	1064	1018	1510	245	2866	2985	2842	1752	356	1644	2879	389	228	103	1063	830	1064	1230	405	1382	1588	126	1648	594	190	2770	382	East Orange, NJ
Eau Claire, WI	508	563	586	842	1202	1099	1142	1716	791	916	1036	1056	1046	2102	1890	2078	1343	1219	1123	2114	708	1026	1182	207	294	99	1640	787	721	1016	1072	553	1027	1265	1676	723	Eau Claire, WI
Elgin, IL	220	288	578	566	927	824	866	1708	694	628	762	920	771	2094	2167	2070	1248	944	1026	2106	433	752	907	232	46	246	1368	512	714	937	797	830	752	990	1952	448	Elgin, IL
Elizabeth, NJ	776	551	1247	486	131	53	168	2491	1336	1056	1009	1501	252	2873	2991	2833	1743	345	1635	2886	396	218	106	1069	836	1070	1218	396	1374	1579	114	1654	567	193	2776	389	Elizabeth, NJ
El Paso, TX	1364	1665	886	1956	2316	2142	2320	317	801	1192	1222	735	2130	1186	1864	870	669	2008	650	1164	1781	1968	2295	1261	1518	1554	1874	1739	743	600	2074	1590	1737	2363	1586	1784	El Paso, TX
Elyria, OH	376	84	847	321	566	462	505	1988	937	731	759	1132	410	2406	2524	2382	1421	582	1272	2418	72	391	545	602	369	603	1198	151	974	1179	435	1187	477	628	2310	86	Elyria, OH
Enid, OK	680	981	261	1271	1580	1416	1541	982	114	622	752	400	1446	1668	2042	1428	607	1448	386	1646	1097	1398	1559	636	834	928	1466	1055	121	196	1389	1059	1167	1651	1764	1100	Enid, OK
Erie, PA	490	212	960	196	487	432	381	2102	1050	844	873	1246	285	2534	2652	2509	1534	565	1385	2546	93	374	466	730	496	731	1240	179	1088	1293	406	1314	520	504	2437	101	Erie, PA
Escondido, CA	2030	2275	1587	2554	2914	2766	2854	428	1467	1930	1968	1480	2758	487	1381	170	1414	2757	1396	465	2420	2706	2894	1843	2074	2136	2618	2406	1409	1327	2740	2018	2476	2977	1140	2435	Escondido, CA
Eugene, OR	2322	2458	1898	2738	3098	2996	3038	1340	2050	2532	2662	2336	2942	500	426	865	2325	3086	2208	512	2604	2924	3078	1966	2228	2027	3318	2682	1878	2006	2968	1608	2880	3160	296	2620	Eugene, OR
Evansville, IN	109	433	483	724	985	849	946	1616	564	336	395	714	851	2201	2402	2061	1003	784	854	2214	502	734	964	510	335	582	1000	456	610	807	798	1166	586	1057	2152	505	Evansville, IN
Everett, WA	2227	2335	1884	2614	2974	2872	2914	1637	2036	2490	2620	2322	2818	808	115	1174	2393	2992	2194	821	2480	2800	2954	1804	2066	1866	3255	2560	1864	1992	2844	1471	2799	3037	163	2495	Everett, WA
Fairfield, CA	2182	2319	1758	2598	2959	2856	2898	877	1738	2201	2331	1834	2802	18	911	391	1863	2947	1800	31	2465	2784	2938	1887	2118	2180	2985	2542	1738	1598	2828	1881	2741	3021	670	2480	Fairfield, CA
Fall River, MA	984	747	1454	580	159	261	201	2698	1544	1263	1216	1708	289	3068	3187	3044	1950	552	1842	3082	591	424	139	1265	1032	1266	1426	604	1581	1786	321	1780	774	72	2972	585	Fall River, MA
Fargo, ND	834	888	584	1167	1528	1425	1467	1622	804	1225	1355	1117	1372	1752	1563	1910	1385	1545	1164	1765	1034	1353	1508	454	620	419	1967	1113	685	1017	1398	224	1352	1590	1348	1048	Fargo, ND
Fayetteville, NC	742	658	1170	793	666	498	717	2122	1168	665	588	1080	752	2863	3088	2622	1288	244	1208	2841	635	319	646	1112	897	1131	680	532	1296	1305	438	1715	139	732	2838	615	Fayetteville, NC
Flagstaff, AZ	1535	1836	1057	2127	2435	2272	2397	255	972	1435	1565	1068	2302	767	1498	527	1240	2262	1034	745	1952	2212	2415	1432	1690	1725	2220	1910	914	832	2244	1863	1981	2507	1220	1956	Flagstaff, AZ
Flint, MI	388	110	816	249	758	654	697	1986	935	810	838	1163	602	2361	2480	2337	1452	774	1267	2374	264	583	737	558	324	558	1343	343	951	1177	627	1142	622	820	2264	278	Flint, MI
Florence, SC	767	670	1137	862	750	583	802	2036	1083	580	502	994	838	2778	3056	2538	1202	329	1122	2756	611	404	730	1138	930	1164	594	544	1256	1220	523	1748	176	817	2806	610	Florence, SC
Ft. Collins, CO	1069	1231	593	1510	1871	1768	1810	1013	746	1253	1383	1031	1715	1160	1388	1140	1103	1834	904	1172	1377	1696	1851	799	1030	1092	2064	1444	573	702	1740	1050	1628	1933	1110	1391	Ft. Collins, CO
Ft. Dodge, IA	509	626	329	905	1266	1163	1205	1460	534	813	943	800	1110	1826	1820	1802	1087	1278	866	1838	772	1091	1246	102	367	394	1598	849	464	759	1135	675	1072	1328	1604	786	Ft. Dodge, IA
Ft. Lauderdale, FL	1151	1283	1514	1475	1384	1216	1436	2232	1393	890	772	1204	1471	3028	3432	2786	1290	963	1332	3006	1224	1038	1364	1541	1416	1648	46	1157	1566	1430	1157	2232	790	1451	3182	1223	Ft. Lauderdale, FL
Ft. Smith, AR	563	864	350	1156	1517	1343	1519	1127	118	392	522	275	1331	1812	2269	1572	595	1220	374	1791	982	1170	1495	610	719	902	1236	940	291	314	1275	1120	939	1563	1992	985	Ft. Smith, AR

Mileages in this Mileage Directory are from the Rand McNally *MileMaker Practical Routing System*, © Rand McNally. **These mileages are for general reference only and should not be used for the purposes of tariff computation.** For tariff purposes, refer to the applicable official tariff. Mileages between each of the 300 cities listed in this chart are computed over National Interstate, U.S. and primary state highways, and Canadian provincial highways via highways designated as truck-usable by the Household Goods Carriers' Bureau Committee. Practical routing may have highway segments not included in the federally designated National Network.

	Abilene, TX	Akron, OH	Albany, GA	Albany, NY	Albert Lea, MN	Albuquerque, NM	Alexandria, LA	Alexandria, VA	Allentown, PA	Altoona, PA	Amarillo, TX	Anderson, IN	Ann Arbor, MI	Appleton, WI	Asheville, NC	Atlanta, GA	Atlantic City, NJ	Augusta, GA	Aurora, IL	Austin, TX	Bakersfield, CA	Baltimore, MD	Bangor, ME	Baton Rouge, LA	Bay City, MI	Bayonne, NJ	Beaumont, TX	Billings, MT	Binghamton, NY	Birmingham, AL	Bismarck, ND	Bloomington, IN	Boise, ID	Boston, MA	Boulder, CO	Bowling Green, KY	Bridgeport, CT	Brockton, MA	Brownsville, TX	Buffalo, NY	Butte, MT	Calgary, AB	Camden, NJ	Canton, OH
t. Wayne, IN	1162	218	833	686	567	1416	984	573	592	414	1132	88	155	365	526	661	683	701	206	1200	2182	562	1079	978	229	655	1118	1417	576	606	1001	180	1843	853	1163	352	707	866	1508	406	1637	1796	632	219
t. Worth, TX	149	1207	830	1708	893	622	334	1364	1494	1361	338	946	1166	1114	988	812	1548	972	933	188	1426	1398	2024	472	1241	1576	310	1307	1592	669	1158	882	1584	1797	781	760	1641	1804	540	1411	1529	1848	1500	1208
redericton, NB	2369	1061	1666	589	1764	2645	2014	882	729	898	2361	1348	1112	1439	1321	1521	786	1422	1401	2384	3377	828	197	2001	1134	655	2184	2612	728	1603	2198	1409	3040	436	2360	1495	578	460	2623	879	2834	2758	739	1070
resno, CA	1401	2494	2384	2945	1960	914	1862	2802	2822	2656	1198	2242	2368	2214	2426	2300	2904	2460	2109	1600	110	2837	3337	2000	2443	2920	1854	1253	2834	2155	1667	2178	719	3112	1165	2198	2973	3124	1852	2665	1120	1592	2852	2500
ainesville, FL	1163	931	182	1168	1356	1628	726	771	975	942	1344	908	1063	1257	511	330	975	332	1096	1015	2432	826	1455	588	1160	1008	771	2167	1086	449	1892	850	2514	1229	1762	650	1073	1236	1210	1114	2390	2708	927	911
alveston, TX	458	1347	766	1778	1135	933	254	1434	1564	1486	649	1115	1344	1289	1025	814	1618	958	1108	213	1716	1468	2093	288	1419	1646	105	1716	1662	688	1454	1052	1994	1867	1190	899	1711	1874	396	1551	1938	2258	1570	1348
ary, IN	1088	335	861	787	439	1343	919	680	698	521	1059	178	210	224	626	690	790	800	76	1127	2052	669	1178	914	284	762	1053	1287	676	635	873	201	1715	953	1035	381	814	966	1479	506	1509	1666	738	354
rand Island, NE	725	966	1269	1417	432	852	940	1310	1329	1152	544	786	840	685	1142	1097	1420	1250	580	821	1435	1300	1809	1078	915	1392	928	775	1306	1045	529	758	1098	1583	418	821	1444	1596	1173	1136	997	1316	1369	985
rand Rapids, MI	1231	319	962	771	582	1486	1062	664	682	505	1202	256	132	380	720	790	774	895	219	1270	2196	654	1163	1057	156	746	1196	1430	660	735	1016	309	1858	937	1178	481	798	950	1622	490	1652	1809	722	339
reat Falls, MT	1455	1747	2222	2199	1065	1225	1945	2093	2111	1934	1188	1590	1623	1255	2037	2050	2203	2204	1369	1714	1279	2082	2592	2084	1697	2175	1933	219	2088	1999	546	1612	581	2366	764	1775	2227	2379	1977	1919	155	326	2151	1768
reeley, CO	727	1324	1593	1776	791	515	1217	1669	1688	1510	460	1145	1199	1044	1488	1443	1779	1596	940	985	1094	1659	2168	1355	1274	1751	1205	524	1665	1365	662	1103	802	1942	54	1167	1804	1955	1248	1495	746	1066	1728	1344
reen Bay, WI	1281	580	1105	1032	326	1416	1125	926	944	766	1252	422	455	32	870	934	1035	1044	229	1320	2136	915	1424	1120	437	1007	1243	1120	921	879	706	445	1738	1198	1118	625	1060	1211	1672	752	1342	1498	984	600
reensboro, NC	1300	457	499	701	1140	1682	894	304	482	405	1398	545	597	938	172	336	508	255	777	1258	2486	358	988	864	694	540	1048	1988	581	484	1574	583	2392	762	1640	507	606	768	1486	640	2210	2367	460	437
reenville, SC	1110	571	313	867	1092	1534	704	495	653	575	1250	537	682	910	62	146	698	117	748	1068	2338	549	1182	674	780	735	858	1929	751	294	1546	503	2275	956	1524	390	800	963	1297	754	2151	2339	650	551
alifax, NS	2595	1287	1892	814	2031	2870	2240	1108	955	1123	2586	1573	1380	1706	1547	1747	1012	1648	1668	2610	3645	1053	421	2227	1402	880	2410	2880	954	1828	2466	1635	3308	662	2628	1720	804	686	2849	1105	3102	3026	964	1296
amilton, OH	1152	232	669	718	684	1394	901	524	552	387	1110	103	237	499	401	499	634	576	338	1166	2198	513	1097	896	334	634	1079	1549	606	502	1135	136	1953	871	1216	248	699	884	1447	437	1771	1928	582	234
arrisburg, PA	1564	304	883	297	1063	1828	1209	139	82	134	1544	531	480	862	516	716	170	641	700	1579	2632	83	612	1196	577	164	1379	1912	181	798	1498	592	2340	386	1650	689	230	392	1818	287	2134	2290	119	301
artford, CT	1848	538	1145	106	1297	2122	1493	360	208	374	1838	824	713	1095	800	1000	265	901	934	1863	2910	306	327	1480	810	133	1663	2145	233	1081	1731	886	2573	101	1893	973	57	114	2102	397	2367	2524	217	547
igh Point, NC	1282	447	481	709	1129	1671	876	322	495	417	1387	534	586	928	161	318	526	236	766	1240	2475	377	1006	846	683	560	1030	1978	593	466	1564	572	2382	780	1630	496	624	788	1468	630	2200	2356	478	427
ouston, TX	410	1298	746	1758	1086	884	234	1414	1544	1466	600	1067	1296	1240	1005	794	1598	938	1059	164	1666	1448	2073	268	1370	1626	85	1668	1642	668	1406	1003	1945	1847	1142	850	1691	1854	354	1502	1890	2209	1550	1300
untington, WV	1179	263	656	709	834	1498	930	422	494	366	1214	274	328	650	280	485	566	478	488	1194	2302	412	1024	924	424	576	1108	1700	592	530	1286	288	2080	798	1328	276	642	804	1476	488	1922	2079	517	242
untsville, AL	846	634	330	1046	894	1220	511	702	832	755	936	445	658	794	326	188	886	342	632	860	2024	737	1362	497	754	914	680	1704	930	102	1428	387	2050	1136	1299	186	979	1142	1120	838	1926	2245	838	635
dianapolis, IN	1028	299	705	784	573	1283	851	594	622	457	999	43	278	385	470	534	704	644	224	1067	2087	584	1163	846	352	704	985	1435	673	479	1021	53	1842	937	1106	225	770	950	1375	503	1657	1814	653	300
wa City, IA	951	572	989	1023	209	1097	918	917	935	758	921	392	446	287	834	817	1026	970	187	1008	1816	906	1416	912	521	998	996	1060	912	765	730	388	1479	1190	799	541	1051	1202	1360	743	1282	1523	975	592
ackson, MS	582	929	398	1326	945	1047	176	982	1112	1035	763	720	953	949	590	380	1166	540	736	540	1851	1017	1642	172	1022	1194	354	1756	1211	237	1520	617	2048	1416	1245	482	1260	1422	793	1134	1978	2297	1118	931
acksonville, FL	1179	862	198	1099	1372	1643	742	702	906	873	1359	924	1002	1272	442	346	906	262	1112	1031	2447	756	1386	603	1098	938	786	2182	1018	464	1908	866	2529	1160	1778	665	1004	1167	1225	1045	2404	2724	858	842
anesville, WI	1107	479	1002	930	297	1297	990	824	842	665	1078	320	353	140	768	830	933	984	100	1146	2016	813	1322	985	428	905	1069	1145	819	776	731	343	1679	1096	999	523	958	1109	1498	650	1367	1524	882	498
efferson City, MO	709	667	859	1153	416	964	674	963	991	826	680	412	605	553	732	688	1073	840	372	748	1793	952	1532	782	679	1073	743	1185	1042	635	949	348	1531	1306	780	412	1138	1319	1100	872	1407	1726	1022	669
ersey City, NJ	1729	436	1026	165	1195	1992	1374	242	88	273	1709	695	612	994	680	880	145	782	832	1744	2809	187	449	1360	708	7	1544	2043	176	962	1629	757	2472	223	1791	854	67	230	1983	398	2266	2422	98	445
oliet, IL	1044	375	900	827	401	1299	895	720	739	561	1015	217	250	226	664	728	830	839	30	1083	2008	710	1219	890	325	802	1006	1269	716	674	856	240	1671	993	991	420	854	1006	1435	546	1492	1648	779	395
alamazoo, MI	1200	280	930	731	551	1455	1032	624	643	466	1171	202	98	350	681	759	734	856	188	1240	2164	614	1123	1026	173	706	1166	1400	620	704	986	278	1828	898	1148	450	758	910	1592	450	1622	1778	683	299
ansas City, MO	638	783	975	1268	341	784	668	1078	1106	941	608	527	720	595	848	803	1188	956	490	705	1637	1068	1647	806	795	1188	727	1026	1157	751	788	465	1372	1421	624	527	1253	1434	1057	987	1248	1567	1137	784
enosha, WI	1133	439	964	891	365	1388	984	784	802	625	1104	281	314	143	728	792	894	903	88	1172	2071	774	1283	979	388	866	1118	1213	780	737	799	303	1734	1057	1054	484	918	1070	1524	610	1435	1592	842	459
ingston, ON	1702	476	1269	252	1079	1956	1526	526	341	413	1672	629	428	878	902	1102	452	1027	716	1741	2692	469	471	1520	450	386	1704	1927	210	1127	1513	721	2355	418	1675	873	419	431	2072	260	2149	2242	400	496
noxville, TN	1023	493	385	834	926	1398	668	490	620	543	1114	371	517	744	114	213	674	289	583	1038	2202	525	1150	655	614	702	838	1762	718	257	1380	337	2108	924	1357	224	767	930	1277	704	1984	2173	626	501
afayette, LA	572	1156	533	1545	1092	1036	89	1200	1330	1253	752	946	1180	1175	792	580	1384	724	962	378	1840	1235	1860	55	1250	1412	133	1815	1429	455	1549	844	2092	1634	1289	708	1478	1641	572	1360	2037	2356	1336	1157
ake Charles, LA	516	1224	602	1613	1105	990	107	1269	1399	1322	706	1014	1248	1244	860	649	1453	793	1030	304	1808	1304	1928	124	1318	1481	60	1761	1498	524	1536	912	2038	1702	1236	776	1546	1709	499	1428	1984	2303	1405	1226
ancaster, PA	1601	339	920	278	1098	1863	1246	138	70	169	1579	566	515	896	554	753	140	678	735	1616	2667	82	598	1234	612	151	1416	1946	191	835	1532	628	2374	372	1686	727	216	379	1856	327	2168	2325	88	336
ansing, MI	1272	251	957	703	622	1526	1102	596	615	437	1242	213	64	421	695	784	706	843	259	1311	2236	586	1095	1098	98	678	1237	1470	592	730	1057	305	1898	869	1218	476	730	882	1662	422	1693	1849	655	271
aredo, TX	413	1611	1097	2109	1281	785	586	1765	1895	1765	663	1352	1573	1521	1356	1145	1949	1289	1340	240	1520	1800	2424	620	1648	1977	436	1633	1993	1020	1586	1288	1910	2198	1107	1164	2042	2205	204	1815	1855	2174	1901	1612
as Vegas, NV	1128	2099	2111	2551	1565	641	1589	2431	2462	2285	925	1880	1974	1819	2154	2027	2541	2187	1714	1364	287	2420	2943	1727	2048	2526	1572	972	2440	1882	1386	1816	629	2717	770	1880	2578	2730	1616	2270	840	1312	2490	2119
awrence, KS	604	823	1016	1309	381	750	684	1119	1147	982	574	568	760	634	888	844	1229	996	530	701	1600	1108	1688	822	834	1229	705	1048	1198	717	812	504	1389	1462	586	568	1294	1475	1052	1028	1270	1590	1178	825
awrence, MA	1958	650	1256	178	1399	2234	1604	471	318	487	1950	937	816	1198	910	1110	375	1012	1036	1973	3013	416	218	1590	913	244	1774	2248	318	1192	1834	998	2676	28	1996	1084	168	52	2212	468	2470	2532	328	659
awton, OK	203	1126	990	1611	781	497	493	1427	1450	1285	213	870	1091	1039	1051	925	1532	1084	858	355	1301	1461	1990	632	1166	1532	476	1182	1500	780	1046	807	1459	1764	656	822	1597	1778	707	1331	1404	1723	1480	1128
exington, KY	1055	325	554	832	754	1374	804	546	618	490	1090	202	348	572	286	383	688	460	411	1070	2178	535	1147	799	446	700	982	1610	716	405	1208	165	1956	921	1205	152	765	928	1350	528	1832	2001	640	326
incoln, NE	726	872	1175	1323	338	812	942	1216	1235	1058	596	692	746	592	1050	1005	1326	1158	487	823	1519	1206	1715	1080	821	1298	930	858	1212	953	663	666	1182	1489	502	730	1350	1502	1175	1043	1081	1400	1275	891
ttle Rock, AR	499	860	598	1361	721	878	335	1017	1147	1014	594	628	858	801	641	515	1201	674	620	514	1682	1051	1676	361	932	1229	404	1511	1245	370	1178	564	1789	1450	986	412	1294	1457	794	1064	1734	2053	1152	861
ondon, ON	1437	308	1030	437	812	1692	1260	546	501	362	1408	364	162	610	762	859	612	897	449	1476	2426	526	743	1256	183	546	1438	1660	370	862	1246	456	2088	603	1408	608	579	616	1807	152	1882	2221	560	328
ong Beach, CA	1261	2379	2243	2830	1845	799	1746	2687	2706	2542	1083	2128	2253	2098	2312	2185	2788	2345	1994	1388	135	2722	3222	1825	2328	2805	1642	1252	2719	2040	1666	2064	864	2996	1050	2082	2858	3010	1640	2550	1119	1592	2737	2384
ongview, TX	310	1090	674	1603	877	775	178	1259	1389	1244	491	858	1088	1032	866	657	1443	817	851	268	1579	1293	1918	316	1162	1471	191	1553	1487	514	1307	795	1830	1692	1027	642	1536	1699	562	1294	1775	2094	1394	1092
orain, OH	1356	57	875	504	723	1588	1106	402	420	243	1304	262	140	522	552	704	512	695	360	1371	2337	391	896	1100	237	484	1284	1572	392	706	1158	353	2000	670	1320	453	536	682	1652	223	1794	1950	460	76
os Angeles, CA	1256	2368	2238	2820	1834	788	1742	2676	2696	2531	1072	2116	2242	2088	2301	2174	2778	2334	1983	1383	112	2711	3212	1820	2317	2794	1637	1241	2708	2030	1655	2053	842	2986	1040	2072	2847	2998	1635	2539	1108	1580	2726	2374
ouisville, KY	1018	340	596	825	683	1303	768	616	687	494	1019	152	364	501	357	424	758	532	340	1033	2107	604	1204	762	460	769	946	1539	714	369	1137	94	1885	978	1134	115	834	997	1314	544	1761	1930	710	341
owell, MA	1950	642	1247	170	1391	2226	1595	463	310	478	1942	928	808	1190	902	1102	367	1004	1028	1965	3005	408	226	1582	905	236	1765	2239	309	1184	1826	990	2668	29	1987	1076	159	52	2204	460	2462	2618	320	651
ubbock, TX	164	1420	1146	1906	1075	323	650	1679	1744	1579	120	1165	1385	1333	1304	1128	1826	1288	1152	383	1127	1714	2285	788	1460	1826	622	1090	1794	985	1064	1101	1367	2059	564	1075	1891	2072	668	1625	1312	1631	1774	1422
ynchburg, VA	1335	444	610	597	1126	1709	980	184	383	305	1425	531	583	924	286	447	368	366	763	1350	2514	218	848	967	680	400	1150	1974	481	568	1560	569	2360	622	1609	535	466	628	1589	514	2196	2353	320	424
acon, GA	1012	767	116	1063	1108	1469	605	670	848	771	1185	660	814	1008	255	82	874	135	848	977	2273	724	1354	549	912	907	732	1918	947	230	1643	602	2265	1128	1514	401	972	1135	1171	950	2140	2460	826	747
adison, WI	1129	517	1040	968	263	1275	1028	862	880	703	1100	359	392	108	806	868	972	1022	138	1184	1995	851	1360	1023	466	944	1107	1111	857	814	697	381	1658	1134	978	561	996	1148	1536	688	1333	1490	920	536
anchester, NH	1977	668	1274	196	1418	2252	1622	490	336	505	1968	955	834	1216	929	1128	394	1030	1055	1992	3031	435	228	1609	931	262	1792	2266	336	1210	1852	1017	2694	53	2014	1102	186	77	2231	487	2488	2508	346	678
ansfield, OH	1298	62	816	548	721	1525	1047	419	437	260	1241	228	153	520	466	645	528	662	358	1312	2330	408	927	1042	250	500	1225	1570	436	648	1156	290	1998	701	1348	394	553	714	1593	267	1792	1948	477	64
arquette, MI	1454	625	1279	1077	493	1586	1299	970	988	811	1425	596	438	202	1043	1108	1080	1217	403	1494	2306	960	1469	1294	346	1052	1416	1110	966	1052	696	618	1729	1243	1288	798	1104	1256	1846	796	1332	1414	1029	645
emphis, TN	634	724	463	1226	737	1008	387	881	1012	878	724	511	748	740	506	380	1065	540	527	649	1812	916	1541	382	814	1094	565	1547	1110	234	1311	447	1893	1315	1116	277	1159	1322	929	929	1769	2088	1018	726
iami, FL	1494	1214	513	1451	1687	1958	1057	1054	1258	1225	1674	1240	1354	1588	794	661	1258	615	1426	1346	2762	1108	1738	918	1451	1291	1102	2498	1370	780	2222	1181	2844	1512	2093	980	1356	1519	1540	1398	2720	3040	1210	1194
idland, TX	149	1507	1131	2008	1128	429	634	1664	1794	1661	237	1218	1438	1386	1288	1113	1848	1273	1205	320	1220	1698	2323	772	1513	1876	608	1207	1892	970	1180	1154	1484	2097	681	1059	1941	2104	606	1711	1429	1748	1800	1508
ilwaukee, WI	1165	464	990	916	328	1354	1009	809	828	650	1136	306	339	106	754	818	919	928	113	1204	2074	799	1308	1004	414	891	1127	1176	805	763	762	329	1736	1082	1056	509	944	1095	1556	636	1398	1555	868	484
inneapolis, MN	1079	778	1302	1230	96	1225	1098	1123	1141	964	1049	620	653	285	1067	1130	1233	1282	399	1136	1944	1112	1622	1211	727	1205	1158	842	1118	1075	428	642	1461	1396	927	822	1257	1409	1488	949	1064	1221	1181	798
obile, AL	776	962	278	1341	1135	1240	339	969	1127	1050	956	773	986	1122	540	329	1173	472	926	628	2044	1024	1656	200	1082	1209	383	1946	1226	258	1710	715	2242	1430	1438	514	1274	1437	822	1166	2168	2487	1125	963
odesto, CA	1495	2469	2477	2920	1935	1008	1956	2814	2832	2655	1292	2289	2344	2188	2520	2394	2924	2554	2084	1694	204	2803	3312	2094	2418	2896	1948	1160	2809	2249	1574	2261	626	3086	1245	2291	2948	3100	1946	2640	1028	1500	2872	2488
onroe, LA	465	1043	515	1444	905	930	128	1100	1230	1152	646	766	1068	995	707	498	1283	657	782	423	1734	1134	1759	206	1070	1312	303	1708	1328	354	1361	702	1985	1533	1182	596	1377	1540	694	1248	1930	2249	1236	1045
ontgomery, AL	827	794	156	1174	1057	1329	421	802	960	882	1045	606	818	954	372	161	1006	305	793	792	2133	856	1489	364	915	1042	548	1867	1058	90	1589	547	2214	1263	1436	347	1107	1270	986	998	2089	2408	958	796
ontréal, QC	1878	603	1385	222	1255	2132	1711	620	434	529	1848	805	603	930	1018	1218	524	1143	892	1916	2868	565	289	1698	625	391	1881	2103	326	1300	1689	897	2531	310	1851	1045	385	334	2320	397	2325	2248	476	623
uncie, IN	1092	250	756	725	630	1346	914	565	593	428	1062	19	226	428	487	584	675	662	267	1131	2151	555	1115	909	301	675	1048	1478	614	536	1064	111	1885	889	1169	283	740	902	1439	444	1700	1857	624	252
ashua, NH	1962	653	1259	181	1403	2237	1607	474	322	490	1953	940	819	1201	914	1114	378	1015	1040	1976	3016	420	234	1594	916	247	1777	2251	321	1195	1837	1002	2679	43	1999	1087	171	64	2216	472	2473	2526	331	662
ashville, TN	844	516	420	1013	776	1219	594	669	799	670	935	327	540	676	293	248	853	402	514	860	2023	704	1328	588	636	881	772	1586	897	193	1310	269	1932	1102	1181	68	946	1109	1140	720	1808	2127	804	517
ewark, NJ	1720	432	1017	164	1191	1984	1365	232	80	269	1700	687	608	990	672	872	137	774	828	1735	2805	178	453	1352	705	6	1535	2040	172	954	1626	748	2468	227	1788	846	71	234	1974	394	2262	2418	90	442
New Bedford, MA	1940	640	1238	202	1399	2204	1586	453	300	477	1920	907	816	1197	892	1092	357	994	1036	1955	3012	398	298	1572	912	226	1756	2247	342	1174	1833	969	2675	59	1995	1066	150	38	2194	492	2469	2626	310	649
New Britain, CT	1861	528	1139	118	1287	2112	1506	354	209	365	1828	815	704	1086	813	1013	259	896	924	1876	2901	300	338	1493	801	127	1676	2136	224	1095	1722	877	2564	113	1884	986	51	126	2115	408	2358	2514	211	538
New Brunswick, NJ	1716	448	998	184	1207	1980	1361	214	76	286	1696	682	624	1005	668	850	118	754	844	1730	2784	159	478	1348	720	30	1531	2055	183	949	1641	744	2483	252	1803	841	96	258	1970	404	2277	2434	71	457
New Haven, CT	1809	509	1106	145	1268	2073	1454	322	169	345	1789	776	684	1066	761	961	226	862	905	1824	2881	268	364	1441	781	95	1624	2116	230	1043	1702	838	2544	138	1864	935	18	144	2063	435	2338	2495	179	518
New Orleans, LA	701	1046	422	1434	1128	1166	218	1089	1220	1142	881	858	1070	1132	680	470	1273	614	919	507	1970	1124	1749	79	1167	1302	262	1944	1318	344	1702	800	2221	1523	1418	599	1367	1530	701	1250	2166	2485	1225	1048
Newport News, VA	1537	518	703	525	1277	1912	1132	177	336	348	1628	696	694	1075	415	573	332	458	914	1495	2716	231	812	1102	790	365	1285	2125	492	721	1711	733	2524	586	1773	721	430	593	1724	556	2347	2504	287	514
New York, NY	1754	453	1042	163	1212	2018	1399	257	114	289	1734	721	628	1010	706	906	161	798	848	1769	2825	202	437	1386	725	31	1569	2060	192	988	1646	782	2488	211	1808	879	55	218	2008	414	2282	2438	114	462
Niagara Falls, NY	1582	237	1084	302	962	1810	1332	416	367	232	1526	501	379	760	700	918	478	843	600	1596	2576	392	694	1326	476	412	1510	1810	236	932	1396	574	2238	469	1558	678	444	482	1878	21	2032	2190	426	257
Norfolk, VA	1532	530	698	509	1289	1924	1126	189	320	360	1640	708	706	1088	410	568	316	453	926	1490	2728	244	796	1097	803	349	1280	2138	439	716	1724	746	2537	571	1786	734	414	578	1719	569	2360	2516	272	527
Norman, OK	283	1059	936	1544	714	561	490	1354	1383	1218	277	804	1024	972	979	852	1465	1012	791	371	1365	1389	1924	628	1099	1465	477	1241	1433	708	979	740	1518	1698	715	750	1530	1711	723	1264	1463	1782	1413	1061
North Platte, NE	660	1094	1397	1545	560	710	1068	1438	1457	1279	470	914	968	813	1270	1225	1548	1378	708	949	1294	1428	1937	1206	1043	1520	1056	633	1434	1173	473	885	956	1711	276	949	1572	1724	1199	1264	856	1174	1497	1113
Oakland, CA	1628	2474	2549	2926	1940	1079	2027	2819	2838	2660	1363	2294	2349	2194	2592	2465	2929	2625	2089	1755	275	2808	3318	2165	2424	2901	2009	1166	2815	2320	1580	2266	632	3092	1250	2330	2954	3105	2006	2645	1033	1505	2878	2494
Oceanside, CA	1210	2408	2192	2859	1874	828	1695	2716	2736	2570	1112	2156	2282	2128	2340	2174	2818	2334	2022	1336	196	2750	3251	1774	2357	2834	1590	1280	2748	2030	1695	2092	937	3026	1079	2112	2886	3038	1588	2578	1148	1620	2766	2414
Odessa, TX	171	1528	1152	2030	1150	424	656	1686	1816	1682	258	1240	1460	1408	1310	1135	1870	1295	1227	340	1198	1720	2345	794	1535	1898	632	1228	1914	992	1202	1176	1384	2119	702	1081	1963	2126	629	1733	1450	1769	1822	1530
Ogden, UT	1209	1741	2045	2193	1207	658	1698	2086	2104	1927	942	1561	1616	1461	1918	1872	2196	2026	1356	1467	743	2076	2585	1837	1690	2168	1686	517	2082	1821	931	1533	305	2359	517	1597	2220	2372	1730	1912	384	856	2144	1761
Oklahoma City, OK	290	1040	927	1525	695	542	505	1346	1363	1198	258	784	1005	952	970	844	1445	1004	771	386	1346	1380	1904	643	1079	1445	493	1222	1414	699	960	720	1499	1678	696	741	1511	1691	738	1244	1444	1763	1394	1041
Omaha, NE	743	818	1164	1270	285	863	858	1163	1182	1004	647	639	693	538	1037	992	1273	1146	433	840	1570	1153	1662	996	768	1245	891	845	1159	940	609	653	1233	1436	553	717	1298	1449	1192	989	1067	1386	1222	838
Orlando, FL	1272	1004	290	1241	1464	1736	836	844	1048	1015	1452	1017	1144	1366	584	440	1048	405	1204	1124	2540	898	1528	696	1241	1081	880	2276	1160	558	2000	959	2622	1302	1871	758	1146	1309	1318	1187	2498	2817	1000	984
Owensboro, KY	953	447	552	933	676	1250	688	724	795	602	966	251	471	526	406	382	866	535	364	968	2054	713	1324	682	560	877	866	1486	821	327	1175	124	1832	1098	1081	72	942	1106	1248	652	1708	1968	818	449
Paterson, NJ	1727	423	1046	154	1182	1991	1373	257	88	260	1707	694	599	980	680	879	161	804	819	1742	2796	202	449	1359	696	30	1542	2030	163	961	1616	756	2458	223	1778	853	67	230	1982	385	2252	2409	114	432
Pendleton, OR	1732	2265	2568	2716	1579	1178	2222	2610	2628	2450	1466	2086	2140	1869	2442	2396	2720	2550	1880	1990	972	2600	3108	2360	2214	2692	2210	745	2606	2344	1160	2056	222	2882	1041	2120	2744	2896	2254	2436	522	663	2668	2284
Pensacola, FL	833	957	232	1336	1193	1297	396	964	1122	1045	1013	768	981	1117	535	324	1168	468	956	685	2101	1018	1652	257	1077	1204	440	2003	1220	253	1767	710	2299	1426	1496	509	1270	1432	879	1161	2225	2544	1120	958
Peoria, IL	954	492	863	943	358	1208	837	811	839	674	924	238	366	306	681	691	921	844	128	993	1966	800	1335	832	441	918	915	1209	832	636	879	235	1628	1109	948	396	970	1122	1345	662	1432	1672	869	517
Philadelphia, PA	1647	404	939	248	1164	1928	1292	154	63	234	1644	631	580	962	598	790	61	695	800	1662	2732	100	535	1278	677	88	1462	2012	182	880	1598	693	2440	309	1751	792	153	316	1900	404	2234	2390	10	401
Phoenix, AZ	887	2046	1869	2532	1593	462	1372	2350	2370	2205	746	1791	2012	1846	1976	1848	2452	2008	1778	1014	481	2386	2911	1450	2086	2452	1267	1211	2421	1704	1607	1727	1000	2685	942	1746	2518	2698	1265	2251	1078	1551	2401	2048

Mileage Directory, continued

	Casper, WY	Cedar Rapids, IA	Champaign, IL	Charleston, SC	Charleston, WV	Charlotte, NC	Chattanooga, TN	Cheyenne, WY	Chicago, IL	Cincinnati, OH	Clarksville, TN	Clearwater, FL	Cleveland, OH	Coeur d'Alene, ID	Colorado Sprs., CO	Columbia, MO	Columbia, SC	Columbus, GA	Columbus, OH	Concord, NH	Corpus Christi, TX	Dallas, TX	Davenport, IA	Dayton, OH	Daytona Beach, FL	Decatur, AL	Decatur, IL	Denver, CO	Des Moines, IA	Detroit, MI	Dubuque, IA	Duluth, MN	Durham, NC	East Orange, NJ	Eau Claire, WI	Elgin, IL	Elizabeth, NJ	El Paso, TX	Elyria, OH	Enid, OK	Erie, PA	Escondido, CA	Eugene, OR
Ft. Wayne, IN	1244	394	217	783	322	588	544	1108	162	182	432	1144	214	1925	1207	490	674	764	156	832	1362	1006	314	128	1052	526	272	1154	478	172	346	635	626	640	482	208	646	1568	187	884	314	2197	2378
Ft. Worth, TX	1029	871	833	1140	1080	1058	814	852	954	964	694	1109	1224	1814	703	613	1037	766	1082	1846	404	30	914	1034	1118	672	793	762	745	1191	945	1141	1200	1578	1073	959	1570	605	1206	297	1320	1350	2120
Fredericton, NB	2439	1589	1462	1406	1169	1284	1456	2303	1358	1293	1571	1800	1062	3120	2417	1720	1356	1631	1185	421	2476	2190	1509	1255	1676	1582	1514	2349	1674	1074	1541	1542	1134	652	1678	1404	655	2824	1090	2113	965	3392	3575
Fresno, CA	1216	1938	2130	2628	2460	2540	2234	1241	2145	2304	2132	2638	2472	1021	1212	1871	2524	2299	2375	3091	1716	1561	1981	2316	2647	2110	2089	1143	1812	2412	2012	2208	2654	2906	2140	2133	2897	1020	2445	1491	2573	321	640
Gainesville, FL	1912	1176	954	307	719	453	452	1776	1055	796	630	153	970	2675	1730	1014	357	269	881	1277	1063	983	1124	867	99	529	942	1744	1261	1076	1194	1523	548	1012	1372	1100	1000	1605	980	1198	1022	2350	3049
Galveston, TX	1439	1113	1003	1125	1219	1060	833	1262	1138	1104	834	972	1364	2224	1014	874	1022	742	1222	1915	228	291	1156	1174	981	766	967	1172	987	1384	1187	1382	1204	1648	1315	1134	1639	801	1346	593	1459	1546	2530
Gary, IN	1114	264	137	882	461	739	572	978	30	264	378	1172	313	1795	1092	390	773	792	324	932	1343	933	184	266	1130	555	188	1024	350	253	216	505	764	747	354	79	754	1495	286	811	414	2067	2250
Grand Island, NE	498	410	637	1398	1048	1256	980	361	617	869	806	1580	944	1283	475	418	1290	1200	939	1562	1038	639	453	881	1538	946	566	407	284	884	484	679	1368	1378	612	604	1384	912	917	398	1045	1450	1634
Grand Rapids, MI	1258	407	280	958	484	748	672	1121	177	355	520	1272	298	1938	1235	533	843	892	323	916	1487	1076	327	302	1230	655	332	1167	493	158	359	648	786	732	497	223	738	1638	271	954	398	2210	2394
Great Falls, MT	497	1245	1482	2293	1872	2150	1934	675	1383	1675	1760	2534	1726	335	849	1372	2185	2154	1736	2345	1841	1644	1328	1678	2491	1899	1485	776	1165	1666	1282	990	2175	2160	1064	1342	2168	1492	1700	1347	1827	1294	829
Greeley, CO	247	769	996	1744	1394	1601	1326	51	976	1229	1152	1926	1303	1032	139	764	1636	1508	1300	1922	1113	916	812	1241	1884	1291	925	66	643	1242	843	1038	1714	1737	971	964	1743	782	1276	619	1404	1109	1338
Green Bay, WI	1088	308	343	1126	705	983	816	1062	206	508	604	1416	559	1628	1175	583	1017	1036	569	1178	1536	1126	332	510	1374	799	390	1108	433	498	234	329	1008	993	192	208	999	1568	532	944	660	2150	2121
Greensboro, NC	1792	948	686	302	246	96	394	1655	736	442	509	696	497	2496	1609	893	188	446	407	810	1340	1120	868	439	571	520	740	1622	1033	597	937	1206	54	546	1055	781	534	1755	506	1192	548	2500	2928
Greenville, SC	1674	910	648	212	359	101	249	1538	708	416	392	607	610	2436	1492	776	103	256	521	1004	1150	930	830	486	481	344	704	1506	996	696	900	1178	244	737	1026	752	728	1566	620	1044	662	2310	2811
Halifax, NS	2707	1857	1729	1632	1395	1509	1682	2571	1626	1519	1797	2026	1288	3388	2685	1945	1581	1857	1411	646	2702	2416	1777	1481	1901	1808	1781	2617	1942	1342	1809	1810	1360	877	1946	1672	880	3050	1316	2338	1191	3660	3843
Hamilton, OH	1352	502	240	658	222	486	396	1216	297	28	328	982	250	2057	1184	468	549	602	108	863	1300	972	422	41	927	422	295	1198	588	250	492	767	525	636	616	342	627	1607	231	862	345	2212	2488
Harrisburg, PA	1739	889	674	663	364	478	651	1603	658	472	766	1058	329	2420	1619	903	574	826	368	434	1671	1385	809	438	933	776	729	1632	974	483	841	1129	391	166	978	704	158	2019	342	1296	308	2646	2876
Hartford, CT	1972	1122	968	884	648	762	935	1836	892	770	1050	1280	563	2653	1912	1196	834	1110	662	149	1955	1668	1042	732	1154	1060	1023	1882	1208	716	1074	1363	612	130	1212	937	133	2303	576	1590	483	2925	3108
High Point, NC	1781	937	675	284	235	77	384	1644	726	431	498	678	486	2486	1598	882	169	428	397	828	1322	1102	857	428	553	509	730	1612	1022	587	927	1195	72	564	1044	770	552	1737	496	1181	538	2490	2918
Houston, TX	1390	1064	954	1105	1171	1041	813	1213	1090	1055	785	952	1316	2176	965	825	1002	722	1174	1895	207	242	1107	1126	961	746	919	1123	938	1335	1138	1334	1184	1628	1266	1085	1619	752	1297	545	1410	1498	2480
Huntington, WV	1479	654	390	524	50	314	382	1342	448	148	357	920	302	2208	1296	580	410	588	137	846	1328	1000	574	168	794	450	446	1310	738	328	642	918	354	578	766	492	570	1636	260	966	396	2316	2616
Huntsville, AL	1450	712	491	509	506	418	102	1314	592	391	167	644	651	2212	1267	551	406	246	510	1184	972	666	660	461	630	25	479	1280	798	670	730	1060	554	916	909	636	908	1301	633	730	746	2039	2586
Indianapolis, IN	1242	392	129	726	312	583	416	1106	183	110	305	1016	316	1943	1074	358	617	636	176	929	1228	873	312	117	974	399	184	1087	477	288	381	653	614	706	502	228	698	1436	298	751	412	2102	2378
Iowa City, IA	878	28	243	1091	678	948	700	742	223	475	526	1300	550	1568	856	238	982	920	546	1169	1224	813	59	487	1258	666	236	788	114	490	85	457	982	984	290	211	991	1249	524	624	651	1831	2014
Jackson, MS	1494	764	607	708	801	626	382	1316	743	687	416	677	947	2264	1128	603	605	334	805	1464	646	402	758	757	686	315	595	1227	850	966	827	1171	768	1196	1020	779	1188	1038	928	648	1042	1783	2584
Jacksonville, FL	1928	1192	970	238	650	384	468	1792	1070	796	646	221	902	2691	1746	1030	288	284	812	1208	1078	999	1140	867	92	544	958	1760	1276	1002	1209	1539	478	944	1388	1114	932	1621	911	1213	953	2366	3065
Janesville, WI	1058	174	212	1024	603	881	714	942	114	406	540	1314	457	1653	1056	409	916	933	467	1076	1363	952	158	408	1271	696	216	988	314	397	99	363	906	891	212	72	897	1449	430	824	558	2030	2146
Jefferson City, MO	931	273	299	988	638	846	570	794	392	474	396	1170	685	1693	748	32	880	790	544	1298	964	554	266	486	1128	536	231	762	271	657	347	664	959	1075	596	398	1066	1116	666	432	780	1808	2068
Jersey City, NJ	1870	1020	839	766	528	643	816	1734	790	637	930	1160	461	2551	1783	1067	714	990	532	271	1836	1549	940	603	1035	941	894	1780	1106	615	972	1261	493	14	1110	836	14	2184	474	1460	431	2823	3007
Joliet, IL	1070	220	113	921	500	778	612	934	45	303	399	1212	354	1778	1048	346	812	832	364	972	1300	889	140	305	1169	594	153	980	306	294	210	487	802	788	336	62	794	1451	327	767	455	2023	2206
Kalamazoo, MI	1227	376	249	938	428	692	642	1090	146	300	489	1242	258	1908	1204	502	787	862	284	876	1456	1045	296	248	1200	624	301	1136	462	142	328	617	730	692	466	192	698	1608	231	923	358	2180	2363
Kansas City, MO	772	320	396	1104	753	961	686	636	526	589	512	1287	800	1534	592	124	995	906	660	1413	922	511	362	601	1243	651	347	606	194	764	393	589	1074	1190	521	514	1182	936	782	311	896	1652	1908
Kenosha, WI	1127	283	202	984	564	842	676	997	65	366	463	1276	418	1721	1111	435	876	894	427	1036	1389	978	213	369	1232	658	242	1043	368	357	166	431	866	852	280	66	858	1540	391	879	518	2086	2214
Kingston, ON	1755	904	777	1050	698	864	1037	1618	674	646	953	1444	453	2436	1732	1031	960	1212	589	430	1925	1546	824	593	1319	1047	829	1664	990	390	856	971	777	372	994	720	378	2109	481	1424	356	2707	2892
Knoxville, TN	1508	745	482	371	309	228	110	1372	542	250	225	696	510	2270	1325	609	262	316	368	972	1130	844	665	320	640	236	538	1339	830	530	734	1012	342	704	860	586	696	1478	492	908	612	2216	2644
Lafayette, LA	1538	990	833	892	1019	828	600	1360	969	912	642	739	1173	2323	1118	829	789	509	1031	1682	425	392	984	983	748	533	821	1271	945	1192	1054	1340	970	1414	1246	1005	1406	968	1154	692	1268	1713	2628
Lake Charles, LA	1484	1059	902	960	1088	896	668	1306	1038	982	711	807	1242	2270	1072	898	858	578	1100	1750	352	349	1052	1052	816	602	890	1217	958	1260	1122	1353	1039	1483	1315	1074	1474	894	1223	638	1336	1639	2574
Lancaster, PA	1774	924	709	662	401	516	688	1638	693	507	803	1056	364	2454	1654	938	611	864	402	420	1708	1422	844	473	932	814	764	1667	1009	518	876	1164	390	153	1013	739	150	2056	378	1331	348	2682	2910
Lansing, MI	1298	448	320	890	416	680	668	1162	217	315	557	1268	230	1978	1276	574	776	888	255	848	1527	1116	368	262	1159	651	372	1208	533	90	400	688	719	664	537	263	670	1679	203	994	331	2250	2434
Laredo, TX	1356	1259	1240	1456	1484	1392	1164	1178	1360	1368	1098	1303	1628	2140	1029	1020	1353	1074	1487	2246	144	434	1302	1439	1312	1076	1200	1088	1133	1598	1333	1528	1535	1979	1461	1366	1970	606	1610	725	1724	1352	2263
Las Vegas, NV	821	1544	1748	2354	2106	2267	1961	846	1750	1942	1865	2365	2078	1112	817	1477	2252	2026	2012	2696	1480	1288	1586	1954	2374	1838	1698	748	1418	2017	1618	1813	2380	2512	1745	1738	2518	784	2051	1218	2178	301	915
Lawrence, KS	834	359	436	1144	794	1002	726	657	566	630	553	1326	841	1556	554	165	1036	946	700	1454	917	518	402	642	1284	692	386	568	233	803	433	628	1115	1231	561	554	1222	902	822	278	936	1614	1924
Lawrence, MA	2075	1225	1080	995	758	872	1046	1939	994	882	1160	1390	651	2756	2053	1309	944	1220	774	42	2066	1779	1145	844	1264	1171	1135	1985	1310	819	1177	1466	722	241	1314	1040	244	2414	679	1702	554	3028	3212
Lawton, OK	905	759	758	1252	1089	1164	859	727	879	932	756	1269	1144	1690	578	557	1149	923	1003	1757	571	193	802	944	1278	735	717	638	633	1115	833	1029	1278	1534	961	884	1525	652	1125	142	1239	1316	1996
Lexington, KY	1356	573	310	542	174	399	280	1220	370	82	232	866	342	2118	1173	457	433	486	200	969	1204	876	493	152	811	326	366	1186	658	362	562	840	477	702	688	414	693	1510	324	842	438	2193	2492
Lincoln, NE	581	316	543	1306	956	1164	888	445	523	775	714	1488	850	1366	559	326	1198	1108	846	1469	1040	640	359	787	1446	854	474	491	190	790	390	586	1276	1284	518	511	1290	964	823	400	951	1534	1718
Little Rock, AR	1234	617	516	842	732	754	449	1056	651	617	346	912	877	2020	954	379	739	513	736	1498	647	319	610	687	921	325	480	967	574	896	680	969	868	1231	873	646	1222	954	858	388	972	1697	2324
London, ON	1488	638	510	944	470	734	756	1352	407	381	688	1342	286	2168	1466	766	830	962	309	582	1660	1282	558	328	1214	782	562	1398	723	125	590	878	774	532	727	453	538	1844	260	1160	248	2440	2624
Long Beach, CA	1100	1823	2014	2512	2346	2425	2119	1126	2030	2189	2017	2509	2357	1391	1096	1756	2410	2184	2260	2976	1504	1442	1866	2201	2518	1996	1974	1028	1697	2297	1897	2092	2538	2791	2025	2018	2782	807	2330	1376	2458	91	878
Longview, TX	1276	856	746	984	962	902	658	1098	882	847	577	954	1108	2061	856	616	881	611	966	1740	416	130	841	918	962	555	711	1009	730	1126	929	1125	1046	1473	1057	877	1464	766	1089	430	1202	1511	2366
Lorain, OH	1399	549	421	742	268	532	600	1263	318	232	533	1137	30	2080	1377	663	628	806	124	649	1505	1177	469	202	1012	627	473	1309	634	143	501	789	572	469	638	364	476	1741	8	1056	131	2352	2536
Los Angeles, CA	1090	1812	2004	2502	2335	2414	2108	1115	2020	2178	2006	2504	2346	1380	1086	1746	2398	2173	2249	2965	1499	1437	1856	2190	2513	1985	1964	1017	1686	2286	1886	2082	2528	2780	2014	2008	2771	803	2320	1366	2447	102	856
Louisville, KY	1285	502	239	613	244	470	306	1148	299	97	196	906	357	2047	1102	386	505	526	216	970	1167	839	422	167	864	289	294	1116	587	376	491	769	546	771	618	343	762	1474	339	771	452	2122	2422
Lowell, MA	2067	1216	1072	987	750	864	1037	1931	986	874	1152	1382	643	2748	2044	1300	936	1212	766	51	2057	1771	1137	836	1256	1163	1127	1977	1302	811	1169	1457	714	232	1307	1032	236	2405	671	1694	546	3020	3204
Lubbock, TX	812	1054	1052	1456	1383	1374	1130	635	1173	1227	1009	1425	1438	1598	486	851	1353	1082	1297	2051	532	345	1096	1239	1434	988	1012	546	928	1410	1127	1323	1517	1828	1256	1178	1819	423	1419	414	1533	1168	1902
Lynchburg, VA	1760	934	672	413	232	206	422	1624	722	428	536	807	483	2482	1577	861	298	557	393	670	1442	1155	854	425	682	547	727	1590	1019	584	924	1192	166	405	1042	767	393	1790	492	1220	497	2528	2896
Macon, GA	1664	927	706	265	555	288	204	1528	806	548	382	402	808	2427	1482	766	200	98	666	1176	1024	831	876	618	360	280	694	1495	1012	828	945	1275	434	912	1124	850	900	1466	790	979	858	2212	2800
Madison, WI	1025	168	250	1062	641	920	752	921	152	444	578	1352	495	1620	1035	447	954	972	505	1114	1401	990	170	446	1309	734	254	967	292	435	93	329	944	929	179	111	936	1428	468	803	596	2010	2113
Manchester, NH	2094	1243	1099	1014	776	891	1064	1957	1013	901	1178	1408	670	2774	2071	1327	963	1239	793	18	2084	1797	1163	863	1283	1189	1154	2003	1329	838	1195	1484	742	259	1334	1058	262	2432	698	1720	573	3046	3230
Mansfield, OH	1397	547	372	709	235	499	542	1261	316	174	475	1104	80	2078	1316	600	594	748	66	693	1446	1118	467	136	978	568	427	1330	632	156	499	787	538	486	637	362	492	1678	62	993	175	2344	2534
Marquette, MI	1255	479	516	1264	790	1054	990	1232	380	688	778	1590	604	1618	1346	756	1150	1210	629	1222	1710	1299	505	635	1548	973	563	1278	603	455	404	251	1092	1038	320	381	1044	1739	577	1114	704	2320	2112
Memphis, TN	1292	556	398	707	597	619	314	1156	534	482	211	777	742	2055	1084	394	604	378	600	1363	782	454	549	552	786	190	386	1097	641	761	618	963	732	1096	812	571	1087	1089	724	518	837	1827	2429
Miami, FL	2244	1506	1285	590	1002	736	783	2108	1386	1127	961	282	1254	3006	2061	1345	640	600	1164	1560	1394	1314	1454	1198	264	860	1273	2074	1592	1354	1524	1854	831	1296	1704	1430	1284	1936	1263	1528	1306	2681	3380
Midland, TX	929	1107	1105	1440	1380	1358	1114	752	1226	1264	994	1410	1524	1714	603	904	1337	1067	1382	2145	470	330	1150	1292	1419	972	1065	662	981	1463	1180	1376	1502	1878	1310	1230	1869	305	1506	490	1620	1050	1962
Milwaukee, WI	1090	246	227	1010	589	867	700	1000	90	392	488	1300	443	1684	1114	467	901	920	453	1062	1420	1010	216	394	1258	683	274	1046	371	383	171	394	892	877	244	92	883	1507	416	882	544	2088	2178
Minneapolis, MN	858	276	512	1324	902	1180	1012	870	413	705	839	1613	756	1350	984	483	1214	1232	766	1375	1352	941	358	708	1570	996	515	916	242	696	312	153	1206	1190	96	372	1197	1377	730	752	857	1959	1844
Mobile, AL	1687	954	797	640	818	576	399	1509	920	719	495	484	979	2454	1321	793	537	257	837	1478	675	595	948	789	493	338	785	1420	1040	998	1017	1361	718	1211	1211	964	1202	1217	960	841	1074	1962	2778
Modesto, CA	1128	1914	2140	2721	2551	2634	2328	1159	2120	2372	2225	2731	2447	928	1330	1922	2618	2392	2442	3066	1810	1655	1956	2384	2740	2204	2070	1257	1788	2387	1987	2019	2746	2881	2116	2108	2888	1114	2420	1585	2548	414	548
Monroe, LA	1431	810	653	825	918	743	499	1253	789	800	530	794	1061	2216	1011	562	722	451	919	1581	547	285	804	871	803	432	641	1164	757	1080	874	1152	886	1314	1067	826	1305	920	1042	585	1156	1666	2522
Montgomery, AL	1613	876	652	472	651	408	232	1477	752	552	328	455	812	2375	1404	714	370	90	670	1311	840	646	821	622	464	170	640	1418	961	831	891	1220	551	1044	1070	796	1035	1282	793	839	907	2027	2750
Montréal, QC	1930	1080	953	1144	825	980	1153	1794	850	824	1125	1538	580	2610	1908	1207	1076	1328	716	249	2173	1722	1000	769	1414	1219	1004	1840	1166	565	1032	1033	872	376	1170	895	383	2284	608	1600	483	2882	3066
Muncie, IN	1284	434	172	743	283	547	474	1148	226	124	363	1068	252	1986	1137	421	634	687	146	870	1292	936	354	88	1013	457	227	1151	519	235	424	696	586	674	546	271	668	1499	225	814	352	2165	2420
Nashua, NH	2078	1228	1084	998	762	876	1049	1942	998	886	1163	1393	654	2759	2056	1312	948	1224	778	36	2069	1782	1148	848	1268	1174	1139	1988	1314	822	1180	1469	726	244	1319	1043	247	2417	682	1705	558	3031	3214
Nashville, TN	1332	594	373	550	388	407	132	1195	474	273	49	732	533	2094	1149	433	441	352	391	1150	993	665	542	343	689	113	361	1162	680	552	612	942	520	883	792	518	874	1300	514	729	628	2038	2468
Newark, NJ	1867	1017	830	757	520	634	807	1731	786	628	922	1152	457	2548	1775	1059	706	982	524	275	1827	1541	937	594	1026	932	885	1777	1102	611	969	1257	484	10	1107	832	6	2175	470	1452	428	2820	3004
New Bedford, MA	2074	1224	1051	978	740	854	1028	1938	994	849	1142	1372	675	2755	1995	1279	926	1202	744	126	2048	1761	1144	815	1246	1153	1106	1984	1310	818	1176	1465	705	223	1315	1040	226	2396	678	1672	578	3027	3211
New Britain, CT	1963	1113	958	878	661	775	948	1827	882	761	1063	1274	553	2644	1903	1187	828	1123	653	161	1968	1682	1033	723	1148	1074	1014	1873	1198	707	1065	1353	606	124	1203	928	127	2316	566	1580	488	2916	3100
New Brunswick, NJ	1882	1032	826	738	515	610	803	1746	802	624	917	1132	473	2563	1770	1054	688	960	519	300	1823	1536	952	590	1008	928	881	1792	1118	626	984	1273	466	35	1122	848	23	2171	486	1448	443	2798	3018
New Haven, CT	1943	1093	920	846	609	724	896	1807	862	718	1011	1240	534	2624	1864	1148	796	1071	613	186	1916	1630	1013	684	1116	1022	975	1853	1178	687	1045	1334	574	92	1184	908	95	2264	547	1541	493	2896	3080
New Orleans, LA	1666	947	790	781	908	716	489	1489	926	804	580	628	1064	2452	1247	786	678	398	922	1571	554	521	940	874	637	422	778	1400	1033	1083	1010	1354	860	1304	1204	962	1295	1097	1045	821	1159	1842	2757
Newport News, VA	1924	1098	836	442	396	333	624	1788	872	592	739	836	543	2633	1741	1025	391	683	558	634	1577	1358	1018	589	711	750	891	1755	1184	696	1054	1343	189	370	1193	918	358	1992	556	1422	539	2730	3060
New York, NY	1887	1037	864	782	554	652	841	1751	806	662	956	1176	478	2568	1809	1093	730	1016	558	259	1861	1575	957	628	1050	966	919	1797	1122	631	989	1278	509	36	1127	852	34	2209	490	1486	448	2840	3024
Niagara Falls, NY	1638	788	656	890	459	680	835	1502	557	458	759	1284	214	2318	1616	884	776	1028	350	448	1730	1402	708	420	1159	852	711	1548	874	382	740	1028	654	397	878	603	404	1962	242	1278	118	2590	2774
Norfolk, VA	1936	1110	848	437	408	328	637	1800	884	605	751	831	555	2646	1754	1038	386	678	570	619	1572	1352	1031	602	706	762	903	1767	1196	709	1067	1355	184	354	1205	930	342	1988	568	1434	551	2743	3072
Norman, OK	964	692	691	1180	1022	1092	787	786	812	866	684	1250	1077	1749	623	490	1077	851	936	1690	587	188	735	878	1259	663	650	697	566	1048	766	962	1206	1467	894	816	1458	732	1058	118	1172	1380	2054
North Platte, NE	356	538	765	1526	1176	1384	1108	220	745	997	934	1708	1072	1142	334	546	1418	1328	1067	1690	1064	766	581	1009	1666	1073	694	266	412	1012	612	807	1496	1506	741	733	1512	977	1045	454	1173	1308	1492
Oakland, CA	1133	1918	2146	2792	2556	2705	2399	1164	2126	2378	2315	2803	2452	900	1335	1927	2689	2464	2448	3071	1871	1726	1962	2390	2812	2276	2075	1262	1792	2392	1992	2025	2818	2886	2122	2114	2893	1174	2426	1656	2554	475	520
Oceanside, CA	1130	1852	2044	2501	2374	2419	2148	1154	2059	2218	2046	2457	2386	1420	1126	1785	2398	2128	2289	3004	1452	1390	1895	2230	2466	2024	2003	1057	1726	2326	1926	2122	2567	2820	2055	2047	2811	756	2359	1405	2487	20	940
Odessa, TX	950	1128	1127	1462	1401	1380	1136	773	1248	1286	1015	1432	1546	1736	595	926	1359	1089	1404	2167	494	352	1171	1314	1440	994	1086	684	1002	1484	1202	1398	1524	1900	1331	1252	1891	284	1528	512	1641	1030	1941
Ogden, UT	400	1186	1412	2174	1824	2031	1756	432	1392	1644	1582	2356	1720	656	602	1194	2065	1976	1715	2338	1594	1398	1228	1656	2314	1721	1342	530	1060	1659	1260	1455	2144	2154	1388	1380	2160	925	1693	1100	1820	758	840
Oklahoma City, OK	944	673	671	1171	1002	1084	778	767	792	846	676	1241	1057	1730	604	471	1068	842	917	1670	603	204	716	858	1250	654	631	678	547	1029	747	942	1196	1448	876	797	1439	695	1039	99	1153	1361	2034
Omaha, NE	632	263	490	1294	943	1151	876	496	470	722	702	1476	797	1353	610	314	1185	1096	792	1415	1056	657	306	734	1433	841	462	542	137	736	337	532	1264	1231	466	458	1237	1015	770	417	898	1584	1768
Orlando, FL	2022	1284	1063	380	792	526	562	1885	1164	906	739	108	1044	2784	1839	1123	430	378	954	1350	1171	1092	1232	975	54	637	1050	1852	1370	1144	1302	1632	621	1086	1482	1208	1074	1714	1053	1306	1096	2458	3158
Owensboro, KY	1232	495	241	662	352	519	264	1096	328	205	120	865	465	1994	1049	333	553	484	323	1147	1101	774	424	275	822	248	230	1062	580	484	493	806	632	880	656	368	871	1408	446	718	560	2069	2368
Paterson, NJ	1858	1008	838	781	527	642	814	1722	777	636	929	1176	448	2538	1782	1066	737	989	531	271	1834	1548	928	602	1050	940	893	1768	1093	602	960	1248	508	24	1098	823	30	2183	461	1459	418	2810	2994
Pendleton, OR	924	1710	1936	2698	2348	2555	2280	956	1916	2168	2106	2880	2244	235	1126	1718	2589	2499	2238	2862	2118	1922	1752	2180	2837	2244	1866	1054	1584	2184	1784	1604	2668	2678	1680	1904	2684	1446	2216	1624	2344	1070	319
Pensacola, FL	1744	1012	814	592	814	571	394	1567	915	714	490	438	974	2511	1378	850	532	252	832	1474	732	652	1005	784	447	333	802	1477	1097	994	1074	1383	714	1206	1233	959	1198	1275	956	898	1070	2020	2834
Peoria, IL	1028	177	90	937	525	794	574	891	154	322	400	1174	470	1718	1005	256	828	794	392	1089	1209	798	97	334	1132	557	82	937	263	410	167	529	828	904	379	158	912	1361	443	676	571	1980	2164
Philadelphia, PA	1839	989	774	679	466	550	734	1703	758	572	848	1073	429	2520	1719	1003	628	900	468	357	1754	1467	909	538	948	859	830	1732	1074	583	941	1230	406	93	1079	804	81	2102	443	1396	419	2747	2976
Phoenix, AZ	957	1572	1678	2176	2010	2088	1783	1014	1799	1853	1680	2134	2064	1350	840	1370	2073	1805	1924	2678	1129	1068	1614	1865	2143	1659	1638	814	1446	2036	1645	1840	2202	2454	1774	1766	2446	433	2046	1040	2160	371	1224

Mileages in this Mileage Directory are from the Rand McNally *MileMaker Practical Routing System*, © Rand McNally. **These mileages are for general reference only and should not be used for the purposes of tariff computation.** For tariff purposes, refer to the applicable official tariff. Mileages between each of the 300 cities listed in this chart are computed over National Interstate, U.S. and primary state highways, and Canadian provincial highways via highways designated as truck-usable by the Household Goods Carriers' Bureau Committee. Practical routing may have highway segments not included in the federally designated National Network.

	Everett, WA	Fairfield, CA	Fall River, MA	Fargo, ND	Fayetteville, NC	Flagstaff, AZ	Flint, MI	Florence, SC	Ft. Collins, CO	Ft. Dodge, IA	Ft. Lauderdale, FL	Ft. Smith, AR	Ft. Wayne, IN	Ft. Worth, TX	Fredericton, NB	Fresno, CA	Gainesville, FL	Galveston, TX	Gary, IN	Grand Island, NE	Grand Rapids, MI	Great Falls, MT	Greeley, CO	Green Bay, WI	Greensboro, NC	Greenville, SC	Halifax, NS	Hamilton, OH	Harrisburg, PA	Hartford, CT	High Point, NC	Houston, TX	Huntington, WV	Huntsville, AL	Indianapolis, IN	Iowa City, IA	Jackson, MS	Jacksonville, FL	Janesville, WI	Jefferson City, MO	Jersey City, NJ	Joliet, IL	Kalamazoo, MI	Kansas City, MO
Ft. Wayne, IN	2257	2239	842	810	678	1740	187	690	1151	548	1306	768		1034	1240	2292	996	1203	132	764	176	1544	1121	377	568	579	1508	134	521	755	558	1154	298	533	130	370	808	959	275	500	653	174	122	614
Ft. Worth, TX	2106	1711	1777	1075	1199	946	1199	1113	815	817	1323	306	1034		2220	1536	1013	311	960	633	1103	1526	797	1153	1150	960	2446	1002	1414	1698	1132	262	1030	696	900	860	432	1028	979	581	1579	916	1072	546
Fredericton, NB	3452	3436	488	2005	1194	2968	1087	1278	2348	1743	1912	2026	1240	2220		3487	1652	2289	1328	1959	1200	2742	2318	1412	1184	1378	274	1293	808	523	1203	2269	1220	1558	1360	1565	1838	1582	1472	1728	646	1369	1217	1844
Fresno, CA	949	175	3108	1860	2686	590	2401	2601	1204	1865	2852	1636	2292	1536	3487		2542	1821	2162	1545	2305	1275	1204	2246	2596	2448	3755	2308	2742	3020	2585	1772	2412	2134	2197	1926	1961	2557	2126	1903	2918	2118	2274	1747
Gainesville, FL	3007	2717	1208	1699	462	1951	1118	376	1796	1330	315	968	996	1013	1652	2542		876	1024	1432	1125	2386	1778	1268	547	457	1877	834	908	1130	529	856	770	525	868	1152	581	72	1166	1023	1010	1064	1094	1138
Galveston, TX	2516	1996	1846	1371	1184	1256	1377	1098	1225	1059	1186	566	1203	311	2289	1821	876		1138	929	1282	1935	1207	1328	1152	963	2515	1142	1484	1768	1134	49	1170	786	1070	1102	459	891	1154	842	1649	1091	1250	799
Gary, IN	2126	2111	949	680	816	1666	242	850	1023	418	1335	694	132	960	1328	2162	1024	1138		634	147	1417	993	236	706	678	1596	267	628	861	696	1090	418	562	153	240	742	1040	147	399	760	44	116	514
Grand Island, NE	1620	1494	1580	467	1399	1175	872	1366	406	337	1742	568	764	633	1959	1545	1432	929	634		777	994	376	717	1311	1194	2227	872	1259	1492	1300	881	998	969	762	398	1021	1448	598	450	1390	590	746	291
Grand Rapids, MI	2270	2254	934	824	839	1810	114	851	1166	561	1435	839	176	1103	1200	2305	1125	1282	147	777		1560	1136	392	729	772	1468	312	612	846	718	1233	460	662	260	384	886	1140	290	542	744	187	52	658
Great Falls, MT	667	1156	2362	738	2227	1095	1655	2261	719	1084	2696	1574	1544	1526	2742	1275	2386	1935	1417	994	1560		743	1249	2118	2090	3009	1677	2041	2274	2107	1886	1830	1923	1565	1274	1975	2402	1275	1404	2173	1399	1529	1245
Greeley, CO	1324	1198	1939	844	1745	839	1231	1712	33	696	2088	846	1121	797	2318	1204	1778	1207	993	376	1136	743		1076	1657	1540	2586	1232	1618	1851	1646	1158	1344	1315	1122	757	1262	1794	957	796	1749	949	1106	640
Green Bay, WI	1960	2194	1195	513	1060	1740	488	1094	1106	424	1579	887	377	1153	1412	2246	1268	1328	236	717	392	1249	1076		950	922	1679	511	874	1107	940	1279	662	806	397	318	949	1284	172	592	1006	238	362	627
Greensboro, NC	2828	2788	741	1382	142	2005	651	168	1675	1102	808	962	568	1150	1184	2596	547	1152	706	1311	729	2118	1657	950		193	1410	468	403	663	21	1132	296	496	557	924	718	478	848	902	544	745	673	1017
Greenville, SC	2768	2671	935	1353	265	1857	737	180	1558	1064	718	814	579	960	1378	2448	457	963	678	1194	772	2090	1540	922	193		1604	454	573	857	175	943	340	320	522	887	528	388	820	784	738	717	734	900
Halifax, NS	3720	3703	714	2273	1420	3194	1354	1504	2616	2011	2138	2250	1508	2446	274	3755	1877	2515	1596	2227	1468	3009	2586	1679	1410	1604		1519	1034	749	1428	2495	1446	1784	1585	1833	2064	1808	1740	1954	871	1636	1484	2069
Hamilton, OH	2389	2349	834	942	577	1717	292	626	1250	656	1144	747	134	1002	1293	2308	834	1142	267	872	312	1677	1232	511	468	454	1519		472	770	457	1093	174	429	114	478	724	834	409	477	637	306	258	592
Harrisburg, PA	2752	2736	365	1305	451	2152	534	536	1648	1043	1170	1219	521	1414	808	2742	908	1484	628	1259	612	2041	1618	874	403	573	1034	472		287	415	1464	414	753	543	865	1033	840	772	911	167	669	572	1027
Hartford, CT	2984	2969	129	1538	672	2445	768	757	1881	1276	1391	1504	755	1698	523	3020	1130	1768	861	1492	846	2274	1851	1107	663	857	749	770	287		682	1748	698	1036	836	1098	1316	1062	1005	1205	124	902	806	1320
High Point, NC	2818	2778	760	1371	124	1995	641	174	1664	1091	790	953	558	1132	1203	2585	529	1134	696	1300	718	2107	1646	940	21	175	1428	457	415	682		1114	286	485	546	913	700	460	838	891	562	734	662	1006
Houston, TX	2466	1947	1826	1322	1164	1208	1328	1078	1176	1010	1166	518	1154	262	2269	1772	856	49	1090	881	1233	1886	1158	1279	1132	943	2495	1093	1464	1748	1114		1122	766	1021	1053	439	871	1105	793	1629	1042	1202	750
Huntington, WV	2540	2476	776	1094	406	1821	382	418	1362	808	1030	836	298	1030	1220	2412	770	1170	418	998	460	1830	1344	662	296	340	1446	174	414	698	286	1122		458	264	630	753	701	560	589	579	458	402	704
Huntsville, AL	2544	2310	1115	1236	568	1544	712	482	1333	866	835	502	533	696	1558	2134	525	786	562	969	662	1923	1315	806	496	320	1784	429	753	1036	485	766	458		406	690	334	540	703	560	917	601	631	675
Indianapolis, IN	2275	2238	905	828	667	1607	310	694	1140	546	1179	636	130	900	1360	2197	868	1070	153	762	260	1565	1122	397	557	522	1585	114	543	836	546	1021	264	406		368	674	884	295	366	707	192	228	482
Iowa City, IA	1900	1875	1186	537	1034	1420	479	1059	787	182	1462	598	370	860	1565	1926	1152	1102	240	398	384	1274	757	318	924	887	1833	478	865	1098	913	1053	630	690	368		741	1168	204	250	997	196	352	308
Jackson, MS	2596	2136	1395	1330	766	1370	981	681	1280	918	891	420	808	432	1838	1961	581	459	742	1021	886	1975	1262	949	718	528	2064	724	1033	1316	700	439	753	334	674	741		596	814	611	1197	719	855	726
Jacksonville, FL	3022	2732	1140	1714	394	1967	1056	307	1812	1346	328	985	959	1028	1582	2557	72	891	1040	1448	1140	2402	1794	1284	478	388	1808	834	840	1062	460	871	701	540	884	1168	596		1182	1038	942	1080	1110	1154
Janesville, WI	1984	2075	1093	538	958	1620	386	992	987	290	1476	715	275	979	1472	2126	1166	1154	147	598	290	1275	957	172	848	820	1740	409	772	1005	838	1105	560	703	295	204	814	1182		418	904	130	260	508
Jefferson City, MO	2025	1928	1274	760	989	1288	637	956	814	365	1333	317	500	581	1728	1903	1023	842	399	450	542	1404	796	592	902	784	1954	477	911	1205	891	793	589	560	366	250	611	1038	418		1076	355	511	156
Jersey City, NJ	2883	2868	202	1436	553	2316	666	638	1780	1174	1272	1385	653	1579	646	2918	1010	1649	760	1390	744	2173	1749	1006	544	738	871	637	167	124	562	1629	579	917	707	997	1197	942	904	1076		800	704	1191
Joliet, IL	2109	2067	990	662	855	1622	282	888	979	374	1374	652	174	916	1369	2118	1064	1091	44	590	187	1399	949	238	745	717	1636	306	669	902	734	1042	458	601	192	196	719	1080	130	355	800		156	470
Kalamazoo, MI	2240	2223	894	792	782	1778	130	795	1136	530	1405	808	122	1072	1217	2274	1094	1250	116	746	52	1529	1106	362	673	734	1484	258	572	806	662	1202	402	631	228	352	855	1110	260	511	704	156		626
Kansas City, MO	1866	1768	1389	601	1104	1108	753	1072	658	265	1448	297	614	546	1844	1747	1138	799	514	291	658	1245	640	627	1017	900	2069	592	1027	1320	1006	750	704	675	482	308	726	1154	508	156	1191	470	626	
Kenosha, WI	2053	2130	1054	606	918	1712	346	952	1042	357	1438	741	236	1006	1433	2181	1128	1203	95	653	251	1343	1012	154	809	780	1700	370	732	966	798	1155	520	664	256	259	808	1144	81	444	864	96	220	562
Kingston, ON	2767	2751	446	1320	837	2280	402	922	1663	1058	1556	1308	556	1574	695	2802	1295	1766	644	1274	515	2057	1633	889	789	959	962	633	389	358	801	1718	748	1054	671	881	1350	1226	788	1040	384	684	532	1154
Knoxville, TN	2602	2504	903	1187	372	1722	571	338	1391	899	859	680	413	874	1346	2312	549	944	512	1027	607	1924	1373	756	284	167	1572	288	541	824	273	924	274	212	356	721	492	547	654	618	705	551	568	733
Lafayette, LA	2614	2126	1613	1360	951	1360	1207	866	1323	1016	953	464	1034	422	2056	1950	642	238	969	1028	1112	2034	1305	1175	919	730	2282	950	1251	1535	901	218	979	552	900	967	226	658	1040	763	1416	945	1082	756
Lake Charles, LA	2560	2088	1682	1347	1020	1314	1276	934	1270	1030	1021	472	1102	369	2125	1914	711	165	1037	974	1180	1980	1252	1244	988	798	2350	1019	1320	1603	970	145	1048	621	969	1036	296	727	1109	774	1484	1014	1150	769
Lancaster, PA	2786	2770	352	1340	450	2186	570	534	1682	1078	1168	1258	556	1452	794	2777	908	1522	663	1294	647	2076	1652	908	440	611	1020	507	43	273	459	1502	452	790	578	900	1070	838	807	946	154	704	608	1062
Lansing, MI	2310	2294	866	864	771	1850	55	783	1207	602	1396	878	134	1144	1142	2346	1120	1322	187	818	68	1600	1177	432	661	747	1410	302	545	778	651	1273	392	657	255	424	926	1066	331	582	676	228	76	698
Laredo, TX	2432	1801	2178	1502	1515	1178	1605	1430	1141	1205	1517	712	1440	428	2621	1626	1207	403	1367	1061	1510	1852	1123	1560	1484	1294	2846	1406	1816	2099	1466	354	1434	1117	1307	1248	791	1223	1386	988	1980	1323	1479	945
Las Vegas, NV	1150	572	2714	1579	2414	317	2006	2328	810	1471	2579	1363	1896	1263	3093	396	2268	1574	1768	1151	1911	994	810	1851	2323	2174	3360	1945	2380	2626	2312	1525	2057	1861	1834	1532	1688	2284	1732	1509	2524	1724	1880	1353
Lawrence, KS	1888	1785	1430	623	1145	1074	792	1112	620	305	1489	326	656	513	1884	1709	1179	809	554	314	697	1267	602	666	1058	940	2110	633	1067	1361	1047	760	745	716	522	347	693	1194	547	197	1232	510	666	41
Lawrence, MA	3088	3072	80	1641	783	2558	870	868	1984	1379	1502	1615	864	1809	414	3123	1240	1878	964	1595	948	2377	1954	1210	774	968	640	882	397	112	792	1858	808	1147	949	1201	1427	1172	1108	1317	235	1005	908	1433
Lawton, OK	1982	1586	1732	963	1311	821	1123	1226	690	705	1483	261	958	167	2187	1411	1173	478	885	521	1028	1401	672	1078	1220	1072	2413	936	1370	1664	1210	429	1040	759	825	748	592	1188	904	506	1535	841	998	434
Lexington, KY	2450	2352	900	1015	529	1698	402	510	1239	727	1028	710	244	906	1343	2288	718	1045	340	876	438	1752	1221	584	420	338	1569	120	538	822	409	996	126	332	184	549	628	718	482	466	702	379	399	581
Lincoln, NE	1704	1578	1486	474	1306	1136	779	1274	490	243	1650	498	670	635	1865	1629	1340	931	540	101	684	1077	460	624	1219	1102	2133	778	1165	1398	1208	882	907	878	668	304	929	1356	504	358	1296	496	652	200
Little Rock, AR	2310	1968	1429	989	901	1202	890	816	1020	646	1126	160	716	349	1872	1792	816	489	651	724	795	1730	1002	840	810	662	2098	655	1067	1351	800	440	684	349	583	594	261	832	666	347	1232	603	764	385
London, ON	2500	2484	632	1054	844	2015	135	838	1396	792	1450	1043	290	1309	967	2536	1194	1502	377	1008	248	1790	1366	622	716	814	1234	368	440	543	705	1453	446	789	406	614	1084	1120	521	775	544	417	266	888
Long Beach, CA	1186	415	2993	1858	2572	475	2286	2486	1089	1750	2723	1521	2176	1412	3372	241	2412	1608	2047	1430	2190	1274	1089	2130	2481	2332	3640	2193	2627	2905	2470	1560	2296	2019	2082	1812	1845	2428	2011	1788	2804	2003	2160	1632
Longview, TX	2352	1864	1672	1118	1043	1098	1120	958	1062	801	1168	244	946	160	2114	1689	857	257	882	766	1025	1772	1044	1071	994	804	2340	885	1309	1593	976	208	914	611	813	844	276	873	897	584	1474	834	994	541
Lorain, OH	2412	2396	671	965	623	1912	194	636	1308	703	1248	940	188	1207	1092	2447	988	1346	288	919	272	1701	1278	534	514	628	1318	232	350	583	503	1298	262	634	303	525	929	918	432	672	482	329	232	787
Los Angeles, CA	1164	393	2982	1848	2560	465	2275	2475	1078	1740	2718	1510	2165	1407	3362	218	2408	1604	2036	1420	2180	1263	1078	2120	2470	2322	3629	2182	2616	2894	2459	1555	2286	2008	2072	1800	1840	2424	2000	1778	2793	1992	2148	1622
Louisville, KY	2379	2282	970	944	599	1627	418	581	1168	656	1069	675	240	869	1400	2217	759	1009	269	804	369	1680	1150	513	489	409	1626	135	608	877	478	960	194	296	113	478	591	774	411	395	772	308	338	510
Lowell, MA	3080	3064	79	1633	774	2549	862	860	1976	1370	1493	1605	856	1801	423	3115	1232	1870	956	1586	940	2369	1946	1202	766	959	648	874	389	104	784	1850	800	1139	940	1193	1419	1164	1100	1309	226	996	900	1426
Lubbock, TX	1888	1412	2026	1122	1515	646	1418	1429	598	999	1639	558	1252	315	2481	1237	1329	624	1179	665	1322	1309	580	1372	1466	1276	2707	1230	1664	1958	1448	576	1334	1011	1119	1042	748	1345	1198	800	1829	1135	1292	730
Lynchburg, VA	2814	2756	601	1368	255	2033	637	279	1643	1088	919	990	554	1185	1044	2624	658	1255	692	1279	715	2104	1625	936	119	304	1270	454	303	523	132	1235	282	523	543	910	804	589	835	870	404	731	659	987
Macon, GA	2758	2558	1108	1450	362	1793	869	276	1548	1081	564	751	748	861	1551	2383	254	837	776	1184	876	2138	1530	1020	383	193	1776	586	769	1030	365	817	572	276	620	904	429	270	918	774	910	816	846	889
Madison, WI	1951	2054	1131	504	996	1599	424	1030	966	284	1514	753	314	1018	1510	2105	1204	1192	185	577	329	1241	936	140	887	858	1778	448	810	1043	876	1144	598	741	334	178	852	1220	43	456	942	168	298	486
Manchester, NH	3106	3090	104	1659	802	2576	889	886	2002	1397	1520	1632	882	1827	424	3141	1259	1897	982	1613	967	2396	1972	1228	792	986	650	901	416	131	810	1877	828	1165	967	1220	1446	1190	1126	1336	253	1023	927	1453
Mansfield, OH	2410	2394	688	963	590	1849	208	602	1306	701	1215	878	157	1148	1124	2439	954	1288	286	917	286	1699	1276	532	480	594	1349	174	367	600	470	1239	202	575	240	523	870	885	430	609	498	327	246	726
Marquette, MI	1950	2242	1240	503	1145	1910	389	1157	1277	595	1752	1062	525	1327	1291	2416	1442	1501	410	888	402	1240	1247	175	1035	1096	1559	676	918	1152	1025	1453	766	980	571	489	1122	1458	342	765	1050	411	453	796
Memphis, TN	2387	2098	1294	1122	766	1332	772	680	1150	709	991	290	598	484	1737	1922	681	624	534	812	677	1766	1132	740	675	527	1963	519	932	1216	664	575	548	214	466	532	210	696	605	403	1096	510	646	518
Miami, FL	3338	3048	1492	2030	746	2282	1408	659	2127	1660	26	1300	1327	1344	1935	2872	336	1206	1356	1764	1456	2716	2109	1600	830	741	2160	1165	1192	1414	812	1186	1054	856	1200	1484	912	351	1496	1354	1294	1394	1425	1470
Midland, TX	2006	1500	2076	1310	1499	752	1471	1414	715	1052	1624	606	1306	300	2520	1325	1314	575	1232	782	1376	1426	697	1425	1450	1260	2745	1302	1714	1998	1432	526	1330	996	1173	1095	733	1329	1252	853	1879	1188	1344	782
Milwaukee, WI	2016	2132	1079	570	944	1678	372	978	1045	362	1463	771	261	1037	1458	2184	1153	1212	120	656	276	1306	1015	116	834	806	1726	395	758	991	824	1163	546	690	281	262	833	1168	84	476	890	122	246	564
Minneapolis, MN	1682	2003	1392	236	1257	1548	685	1292	915	218	1775	726	575	988	1772	2054	1465	1229	446	526	590	972	885	279	1148	1120	2039	709	1071	1304	1137	1180	860	1002	595	304	1040	1480	304	510	1203	429	559	434
Mobile, AL	2786	2329	1410	1520	699	1563	1040	614	1472	1108	698	613	861	625	1853	2154	388	488	890	1211	990	2165	1454	1134	668	478	2078	757	1048	1331	650	468	781	357	734	931	193	404	1004	801	1212	909	959	918
Modesto, CA	856	83	3084	1767	2780	684	2376	2694	1174	1840	2945	1730	2265	1629	3462	94	2635	1914	2138	1520	2280	1183	1224	2220	2689	2541	3730	2376	2762	2996	2678	1866	2502	2228	2265	1902	2054	2650	2102	1954	2894	2094	2250	1796
Monroe, LA	2508	2019	1512	1172	884	1253	1027	798	1216	829	1008	342	854	315	1955	1844	698	388	789	921	932	1927	1198	995	835	645	2181	838	1150	1434	817	340	867	452	720	787	117	714	860	530	1314	765	901	570
Montgomery, AL	2707	2418	1242	1396	532	1652	872	446	1470	1030	669	609	694	676	1686	2243	359	652	722	1132	822	2086	1452	966	500	310	1911	589	880	1164	482	632	614	189	566	853	244	374	863	723	1045	761	791	840
Montréal, QC	2942	2927	362	1496	932	2456	578	1016	1839	1234	1650	1485	732	1750	510	2978	1390	1986	819	1450	691	2232	1809	902	905	1075	778	809	505	328	918	1966	876	1255	847	1056	1535	1320	963	1216	387	860	708	1330
Muncie, IN	2318	2280	876	872	638	1670	258	650	1203	588	1230	698	80	964	1311	2260	920	1134	196	804	247	1608	1163	440	528	540	1537	86	514	788	517	1085	258	464	61	410	738	920	339	430	678	235	193	547
Nashua, NH	3090	3075	91	1644	786	2561	874	871	1987	1382	1504	1618	868	1812	430	3126	1244	1882	968	1598	952	2381	1957	1213	776	971	656	886	400	116	796	1862	812	1150	952	1204	1430	1174	1111	1321	238	1008	912	1436
Nashville, TN	2426	2328	1082	1118	550	1543	594	518	1215	748	894	501	415	695	1525	2133	584	835	444	851	544	1805	1197	688	462	346	1750	311	719	1003	452	786	340	120	288	571	418	600	584	442	884	482	513	558
Newark, NJ	2880	2864	206	1433	544	2308	662	630	1776	1171	1263	1375	650	1570	649	2915	1002	1640	756	1387	740	2169	1746	1002	535	729	875	628	159	128	554	1620	570	909	699	993	1189	934	900	1067	8	796	700	1184
New Bedford, MA	3087	3071	14	1640	765	2528	870	850	1983	1378	1484	1597	857	1791	495	3122	1222	1860	964	1594	948	2377	1953	1209	756	950	721	849	379	136	774	1840	791	1129	919	1200	1409	1154	1108	1288	217	1004	908	1405
New Britain, CT	2976	2960	122	1529	666	2436	758	752	1872	1267	1385	1516	745	1712	535	3011	1124	1781	852	1483	836	2265	1842	1098	657	870	761	761	300	12	676	1761	712	1050	827	1089	1330	1056	996	1196	118	892	796	1311
New Brunswick, NJ	2895	2879	231	1448	526	2303	678	610	1791	1186	1244	1372	665	1566	674	2894	984	1636	772	1402	756	2185	1761	1017	516	707	900	624	154	153	535	1616	566	904	694	1008	1184	914	915	1063	33	812	716	1180
New Haven, CT	2956	2940	117	1509	634	2397	739	718	1852	1247	1352	1466	726	1660	560	2991	1092	1729	832	1463	817	2245	1822	1078	624	818	786	717	248	38	643	1709	660	998	788	1069	1278	1022	976	1157	86	873	777	1272
New Orleans, LA	2743	2255	1502	1514	840	1489	1124	754	1452	1101	842	582	946	551	1945	2080	532	367	926	1157	1069	2163	1434	1132	808	618	2171	841	1140	1424	790	347	870	441	818	924	183	547	997	794	1304	902	1038	910
Newport News, VA	2965	2920	565	1518	230	2235	748	314	1808	1252	948	1192	718	1388	1008	2826	687	1390	842	1444	826	2255	1790	1087	240	431	1234	618	314	487	258	1370	446	726	708	1074	955	618	985	1034	368	882	786	1151
New York, NY	2900	2884	190	1453	569	2342	682	654	1796	1191	1288	1409	670	1604	633	2935	1026	1674	776	1407	760	2189	1766	1022	560	763	859	662	193	112	578	1654	604	943	733	1013	1223	958	920	1101	29	817	721	1218
Niagara Falls, NY	2650	2635	498	1204	714	2134	434	784	1546	942	1396	1161	428	1432	892	2686	1135	1572	527	1158	512	1940	1516	772	662	775	1117	458	306	408	651	1524	510	860	524	764	1154	1066	671	893	410	568	472	1010
Norfolk, VA	2978	2933	550	1531	224	2248	760	309	1820	1264	943	1206	732	1382	993	2838	682	1385	854	1456	838	2267	1802	1100	234	426	1219	630	327	472	253	1365	459	738	720	1087	950	613	998	1046	352	895	798	1162
Norman, OK	2040	1650	1665	896	1239	885	1056	1154	750	638	1464	188	892	183	2120	1475	1154	479	818	454	961	1460	732	1011	1148	1000	2346	869	1303	1597	1138	430	972	687	758	680	588	1170	837	439	1468	774	930	368
North Platte, NE	1478	1352	1708	610	1527	1034	1000	1494	265	465	1870	696	892	761	2087	1404	1560	1057	762	145	905	852	235	845	1439	1322	2354	1000	1387	1620	1428	1009	1126	1097	890	526	1149	1576	726	578	1518	718	874	418
Oakland, CA	828	38	3088	1772	2851	756	2381	2766	1180	1846	3017	1801	2271	1701	3468	176	2706	1976	2142	1526	2286	1188	1230	2226	2760	2612	3735	2381	2768	3000	2750	1927	2508	2299	2270	1907	2126	2722	2106	1959	2899	2099	2255	1801
Oceanside, CA	1248	477	3022	1888	2560	504	2314	2474	1118	1779	2671	1550	2206	1360	3401	302	2361	1557	2076	1459	2220	1303	1118	2160	2510	2321	3669	2222	2656	2934	2499	1508	2326	2048	2111	1840	1794	2376	2040	1817	2832	2032	2188	1662
Odessa, TX	1906	1479	2098	1332	1521	748	1492	1436	736	1074	1646	628	1328	322	2541	1304	1336	598	1254	803	1397	1447	718	1447	1472	1282	2767	1324	1736	2020	1454	550	1352	1018	1194	1117	755	1351	1273	875	1901	1210	1366	804
Ogden, UT	826	731	2356	1124	2174	558	1648	2142	447	1112	2518	1327	1538	1279	2735	850	2208	1688	1410	793	1553	539	496	1493	2086	1970	3002	1648	2034	2268	2076	1640	1774	1745	1537	1174	1743	2224	1374	1226	2166	1366	1522	1066
Oklahoma City, OK	2020	1632	1646	877	1230	866	1037	1144	730	619	1455	180	872	198	2101	1456	1145	494	798	435	942	1441	712	992	1139	991	2326	849	1284	1577	1128	446	954	678	739	661	603	1160	818	420	1448	755	911	350
Omaha, NE	1685	1629	1433	420	1294	1186	725	1262	541	190	1638	485	615	652	1812	1680	1328	948	487	152	630	1064	511	570	1206	1090	2080	725	1112	1345	1196	899	894	865	614	251	916	1344	451	346	1243	443	600	185
Orlando, FL	3115	2825	1282	1807	536	2060	1198	449	1905	1438	211	1078	1105	1121	1724	2650	113	984	1134	1541	1234	2494	1886	1378	620	531	1950	942	982	1204	602	964	844	633	978	1261	689	141	1274	1131	1084	1172	1204	1248
Owensboro, KY	2326	2228	1078	982	663	1574	518	630	1116	648	1026	608	339	803	1521	2164	717	943	312	752	454	1705	1098	538	575	458	1746	244	716	1000	564	894	303	254	212	472	511	732	449	342	880	332	422	458
Paterson, NJ	2870	2854	202	1424	568	2315	653	654	1766	1162	1288	1384	640	1578	646	2906	1026	1648	747	1378	731	2160	1736	992	560	736	871	636	166	124	578	1628	578	916	706	984	1196	958	891	1075	17	787	692	1192
Pendleton, OR	305	693	2880	1352	2698	1079	2172	2666	970	1636	3042	1851	2061	1802	3258	889	2732	2212	1934	1316	2076	570	1020	1863	2610	2494	3526	2172	2558	2792	2600	2164	2298	2268	2061	1698	2267	2748	1888	1750	2690	1890	2046	1589
Pensacola, FL	2843	2386	1405	1578	694	1621	1035	609	1530	1166	652	670	856	682	1848	2211	342	545	885	1268	985	2222	1512	1129	662	473	2074	752	1043	1326	644	525	776	352	729	988	250	358	1026	859	1207	924	954	976
Peoria, IL	2049	2024	1106	686	880	1532	398	905	936	331	1336	560	258	826	1485	2075	1026	1000	160	547	303	1423	906	345	770	734	1753	325	759	1018	760	952	476	563	214	154	660	1042	171	264	916	116	272	350
Philadelphia, PA	2852	2836	288	1405	466	2252	635	551	1748	1143	1185	1302	622	1497	732	2842	924	1567	728	1359	712	2141	1718	974	457	648	957	572	109	210	476	1547	518	835	643	965	1116	855	872	1012	91	769	673	1128
Phoenix, AZ	1521	762	2652	1782	2235	140	2044	2150	978	1517	2348	1184	1878	1038	3108	587	2038	1234	1806	1314	1948	1234	978	1878	2144	1996	3334	1856	2290	2584	2134	1186	1960	1683	1746	1560	1471	2054	1760	1426	2456	1762	1918	1248

Mileage Directory, continued

	Kenosha, WI	Kingston, ON	Knoxville, TN	Lafayette, LA	Lake Charles, LA	Lancaster, PA	Lansing, MI	Laredo, TX	Las Vegas, NV	Lawrence, KS	Lawrence, MA	Lawton, OK	Lexington, KY	Lincoln, NE	Little Rock, AR	London, ON	Long Beach, CA	Longview, TX	Lorain, OH	Los Angeles, CA	Louisville, KY	Lowell, MA	Lubbock, TX	Lynchburg, VA	Macon, GA	Madison, WI	Manchester, NH	Mansfield, OH	Marquette, MI	Memphis, TN	Miami, FL	Midland, TX	Milwaukee, WI	Minneapolis, MN	Mobile, AL	Modesto, CA	Monroe, LA	Montgomery, AL	Montréal, QC	Muncie, IN	Nashua, NH	Nashville, TN	Newark, NJ	New Bedford, MA
Ft. Wayne, IN	236	556	413	1034	1102	556	134	1440	1896	656	864	958	244	670	716	290	2176	946	188	2165	240	856	1252	554	748	314	882	157	525	598	1327	1306	261	575	861	2265	854	694	732	80	868	415	650	8
Ft. Worth, TX	1006	1574	874	422	369	1452	1144	428	1263	513	1809	167	906	635	349	1309	1412	160	1207	1407	869	1801	315	1185	861	1018	1827	1148	1327	484	1344	300	1037	988	625	1629	315	676	1750	964	1812	695	1570	17
Fredericton, NB	1433	695	1346	2056	2125	794	1142	2621	3093	1884	414	2187	1343	1865	1872	967	3372	2114	1092	3362	1400	423	2481	1044	1551	1510	424	1124	1291	1737	1935	2520	1458	1772	1853	3462	1955	1686	510	1311	430	1525	649	4
Fresno, CA	2181	2802	2312	1950	1914	2777	2346	1626	396	1709	3123	1411	2288	1629	1792	2536	241	1689	2447	218	2217	3115	1237	2624	2383	2105	3141	2439	2416	1922	2872	1325	2184	2054	2154	94	1844	2243	2978	2260	3126	2133	2915	31
Gainesville, FL	1128	1295	549	642	711	908	1120	1207	2268	1179	1240	1173	718	1340	816	1194	2412	857	988	2408	759	1232	1329	658	254	1204	1259	954	1442	681	336	1314	1153	1465	388	2635	698	359	1390	920	1244	584	1002	12
Galveston, TX	1203	1766	944	238	165	1522	1322	403	1574	809	1878	478	1045	931	489	1502	1608	257	1346	1604	1009	1870	624	1255	837	1192	1897	1288	1501	624	1206	575	1212	1229	488	1914	388	652	1986	1134	1882	835	1640	18
Gary, IN	95	644	512	969	1037	663	187	1367	1768	554	964	885	340	540	651	377	2047	882	288	2036	269	956	1179	692	776	185	982	286	410	534	1356	1232	120	446	890	2138	789	722	819	196	968	444	756	9
Grand Island, NE	653	1274	1027	1028	974	1294	818	1061	1151	314	1595	521	876	101	724	1008	1430	766	919	1420	804	1586	665	1279	1184	577	1613	917	888	812	1764	782	656	526	1211	1520	921	1132	1450	804	1598	851	1387	15
Grand Rapids, MI	251	515	607	1112	1180	647	68	1510	1911	697	948	1028	438	684	795	248	2190	1025	272	2180	369	940	1322	715	876	329	967	286	402	677	1456	1376	276	590	990	2280	932	822	691	247	952	544	740	9
Great Falls, MT	1343	2057	1924	2034	1980	2076	1600	1852	994	1267	2377	1401	1752	1077	1730	1790	1274	1772	1701	1263	1680	2369	1309	2104	2138	1241	2396	1699	1240	1766	2716	1426	1306	972	2165	1183	1927	2086	2232	1608	2381	1805	2169	23
Greeley, CO	1012	1633	1373	1305	1252	1652	1177	1123	810	602	1954	672	1221	460	1002	1366	1089	1044	1278	1078	1150	1946	580	1625	1530	936	1972	1276	1247	1132	2109	697	1015	885	1454	1224	1198	1452	1809	1163	1957	1197	1746	19
Green Bay, WI	154	889	756	1175	1244	908	432	1560	1851	666	1210	1078	584	624	840	622	2130	1071	534	2120	513	1202	1372	936	1020	140	1228	532	175	740	1600	1425	116	279	1134	2220	995	966	902	440	1213	688	1002	12
Greensboro, NC	809	789	284	919	988	440	661	1484	2323	1058	774	1220	420	1219	810	716	2481	994	514	2470	489	766	1466	119	383	887	792	480	1035	675	830	1450	834	1148	668	2689	835	500	905	528	776	462	535	7
Greenville, SC	780	959	167	730	798	611	747	1294	2174	940	968	1072	338	1102	662	814	2332	804	628	2322	409	959	1276	304	193	858	986	594	1096	527	741	1260	806	1120	478	2541	645	310	1075	540	971	346	729	9
Halifax, NS	1700	962	1572	2282	2350	1020	1410	2846	3360	2110	640	2413	1569	2133	2098	1234	3640	2340	1318	3629	1626	648	2707	1270	1776	1778	650	1349	1559	1963	2160	2745	1726	2039	2078	3730	2181	1911	778	1537	656	1750	875	7
Hamilton, OH	370	633	288	950	1019	507	302	1406	1945	633	882	936	120	778	655	368	2193	885	232	2182	135	874	1230	454	586	448	901	174	676	519	1165	1302	395	709	757	2376	838	589	809	86	886	311	628	8
Harrisburg, PA	732	389	541	1251	1320	43	545	1816	2380	1067	397	1370	538	1165	1067	440	2627	1309	350	2616	608	389	1664	303	769	810	416	367	918	932	1192	1714	758	1071	1048	2762	1150	880	505	514	400	719	159	3
Hartford, CT	966	358	824	1535	1603	273	778	2099	2626	1361	112	1664	822	1398	1351	543	2905	1593	583	2894	877	104	1958	523	1030	1043	131	600	1152	1216	1414	1998	991	1304	1331	2996	1434	1164	328	788	116	1003	128	1
High Point, NC	798	801	273	901	970	459	651	1466	2312	1047	792	1210	409	1208	800	705	2470	976	503	2459	478	784	1448	132	365	876	810	470	1025	664	812	1432	824	1137	650	2678	817	482	918	517	796	452	554	7
Houston, TX	1155	1718	924	218	145	1502	1273	354	1525	760	1858	429	996	882	440	1453	1560	208	1298	1555	960	1850	576	1235	817	1144	1877	1239	1453	575	1186	526	1163	1180	468	1866	340	632	1966	1085	1862	786	1620	18
Huntington, WV	520	748	274	979	1048	452	392	1434	2057	745	808	1040	126	907	684	446	2296	914	262	2286	194	800	1334	282	572	598	828	202	766	548	1054	1330	546	860	781	2502	867	614	876	258	812	340	570	7
Huntsville, AL	664	1054	212	552	621	790	657	1117	1861	716	1147	759	332	878	349	789	2019	611	634	2008	296	1139	1011	523	276	741	1165	575	980	214	856	996	690	1002	357	2228	452	189	1255	464	1150	120	909	11
Indianapolis, IN	256	671	356	900	969	578	255	1307	1834	522	949	825	184	668	583	406	2082	813	303	2072	113	940	1119	543	620	334	967	240	571	466	1200	1173	281	595	734	2265	720	566	847	61	952	288	699	9
Iowa City, IA	259	881	721	967	1036	900	424	1248	1532	347	1201	748	549	304	594	614	1812	844	525	1800	478	1193	1042	910	904	178	1220	523	489	532	1484	1095	262	304	931	1902	787	853	1056	410	1204	571	993	12
Jackson, MS	808	1350	492	226	296	1070	926	791	1688	693	1427	592	628	929	261	1084	1845	276	929	1840	591	1419	748	804	429	852	1446	870	1122	210	912	733	833	1040	193	2054	117	244	1535	738	1430	418	1189	14
Jacksonville, FL	1144	1226	547	658	727	838	1066	1223	2284	1194	1172	1188	718	1356	832	1120	2428	873	918	2424	774	1164	1345	589	270	1220	1190	885	1458	696	351	1329	1168	1480	404	2650	714	374	1320	920	1174	600	934	11
Janesville, WI	81	788	654	1040	1109	807	331	1386	1732	547	1108	904	482	504	666	521	2011	897	432	2000	411	1100	1198	835	918	43	1126	430	342	605	1496	1252	84	304	1004	2102	860	863	963	339	1111	584	900	11
Jefferson City, MO	444	1040	618	763	774	946	582	988	1509	197	1317	506	466	358	347	775	1788	584	672	1778	395	1309	800	870	774	456	1336	609	765	403	1354	853	476	510	801	1954	530	723	1216	430	1321	442	1067	12
Jersey City, NJ	864	384	705	1416	1484	154	676	1980	2524	1232	235	1535	702	1296	1232	544	2804	1474	482	2793	772	226	1829	404	910	942	253	498	1050	1096	1294	1879	890	1203	1212	2894	1314	1045	387	678	238	884	8	2
Joliet, IL	96	684	551	945	1014	704	228	1323	1724	510	1005	841	379	496	603	417	2003	834	329	1992	308	996	1135	731	816	168	1023	327	411	510	1394	1188	122	429	909	2094	765	761	860	235	1008	482	796	10
Kalamazoo, MI	220	532	568	1082	1150	608	76	1479	1880	666	908	998	399	652	764	266	2160	994	232	2148	338	900	1292	659	846	298	927	246	453	646	1425	1344	246	559	959	2250	901	791	708	193	912	513	700	9
Kansas City, MO	562	1154	733	756	769	1062	698	945	1353	41	1433	434	581	200	385	888	1632	541	787	1622	510	1426	730	987	889	486	1453	726	796	518	1470	782	564	434	918	1796	570	840	1330	547	1436	558	1184	14
Kenosha, WI		748	615	1034	1102	767	291	1412	1786	602	1068	930	443	559	716	481	2066	946	392	2055	372	1060	1224	795	879	115	1087	390	328	599	1458	1278	39	373	992	2156	854	825	924	299	1072	546	860	10
Kingston, ON	748		927	1576	1644	399	457	1980	2408	1194	429	1499	744	1180	1280	282	2688	1510	483	2676	760	421	1793	689	1155	826	442	527	720	1144	1578	1846	773	1087	1382	2778	1464	1214	186	618	433	936	380	4
Knoxville, TN	615	927		710	779	578	581	1275	2039	774	935	937	172	936	527	648	2197	769	492	2186	244	927	1189	311	300	692	953	434	930	391	880	1174	640	954	510	2406	609	342	1043	374	938	179	697	9
Lafayette, LA	1034	1576	710		74	1288	1152	570	1678	772	1645	582	854	1030	423	1310	1775	266	1156	1770	818	1637	738	1022	604	1078	1664	1096	1348	437	973	723	1059	1187	255	2044	215	419	1753	964	1648	643	1407	16
Lake Charles, LA	1102	1644	779	74		1357	1221	496	1632	747	1714	536	922	976	435	1379	1702	228	1224	1697	886	1706	682	1090	673	1147	1732	1166	1417	505	1042	668	1128	1200	323	2008	233	488	1822	1032	1717	712	1476	16
Lancaster, PA	767	399	578	1288	1357		580	1853	2414	1102	384	1405	576	1200	1105	480	2662	1347	385	2652	645	376	1699	300	806	845	402	402	953	970	1190	1752	792	1106	1085	2797	1188	918	500	548	387	757	146	3
Lansing, MI	291	457	581	1152	1221	580		1550	1951	737	881	1068	413	724	835	190	2230	1065	204	2220	364	872	1363	648	872	369	899	218	394	717	1418	1416	317	630	985	2321	972	818	633	204	884	539	672	8
Laredo, TX	1412	1980	1275	570	496	1853	1550		1390	940	2210	595	1310	1063	753	1716	1414	508	1611	1409	1273	2202	543	1586	1168	1424	2228	1552	1733	888	1538	414	1444	1375	819	1720	663	984	2156	1370	2213	1099	1972	21
Las Vegas, NV	1786	2408	2039	1678	1632	2414	1951	1390		1315	2728	1138	1934	1234	1519	2141	282	1416	2052	271	1863	2720	964	2350	2110	1710	2747	2077	2021	1649	2599	1089	1789	1660	1881	490	1570	1970	2584	1898	2732	1860	2520	27
Lawrence, KS	602	1194	774	772	747	1102	737	940	1315		1473	401	622	222	415	927	1594	519	828	1584	551	1465	695	1026	930	526	1492	765	837	484	1510	748	605	475	883	1812	598	804	1370	586	1477	598	1224	14
Lawrence, MA	1068	429	935	1645	1714	384	881	2210	2728	1473		1776	932	1501	1462	615	3008	1704	681	2997	990	12	2070	633	1140	1146	28	713	1254	1326	1524	2109	1094	1407	1442	3098	1544	1274	285	900	21	1114	238	
Lawton, OK	930	1499	937	582	536	1405	1068	595	1138	401	1776		916	523	417	1234	1296	320	1130	1286	845	1768	260	1248	1008	926	1794	1068	1251	547	1504	347	962	875	785	1504	475	836	1674	889	1779	758	1526	17
Lexington, KY	443	744	172	854	922	576	413	1310	1934	622	932	916		784	558	480	2173	788	324	2162	72	924	1210	406	470	520	951	266	758	423	1049	1205	468	782	660	2378	742	493	916	206	936	214	694	9
Lincoln, NE	559	1180	936	1030	976	1200	724	1063	1234	222	1501	523	784		588	914	1514	768	825	1504	712	1493	716	1188	1092	483	1519	823	794	720	1671	870	562	432	1119	1604	771	1040	1356	710	1504	760	1293	15
Little Rock, AR	716	1280	527	423	435	1105	835	753	1519	415	1462	417	558	588		1015	1677	232	860	1666	522	1453	664	838	598	705	1480	801	1014	137	1147	649	724	816	454	1886	185	457	1452	646	1465	348	1223	14
London, ON	481	282	648	1310	1379	480	190	1716	2141	927	615	1234	480	914	1015		2420	1245	261	2410	495	606	1528	666	946	559	633	274	524	880	1473	1581	506	820	1117	2511	1198	949	458	353	618	671	540	6
Long Beach, CA	2066	2688	2197	1775	1702	2662	2230	1414	282	1594	3008	1296	2173	1514	1677	2420		1573	2332	23	2102	3000	1122	2508	2268	1990	3026	2324	2301	1808	2743	1113	2069	1939	2025	334	1728	2089	2863	2146	3011	2018	2800	30
Longview, TX	946	1510	769	266	228	1347	1065	508	1416	519	1704	320	788	768	232	1245	1573		1090	1568	752	1696	476	1080	706	935	1722	1031	1244	367	1188	461	955	972	470	1782	159	521	1682	877	1707	578	1465	16
Lorain, OH	392	483	492	1156	1224	385	204	1611	2052	828	681	1130	324	825	860	261	2332	1090		2321	340	673	1425	500	790	470	700	62	578	724	1271	1478	418	731	962	2422	1043	794	610	226	684	516	478	6
Los Angeles, CA	2055	2676	2186	1770	1697	2652	2220	1409	271	1584	2997	1286	2162	1504	1666	2410	23	1568	2321		2092	2989	1111	2498	2258	1979	3016	2314	2290	1797	2739	1108	2058	1928	2020	312	1723	2117	2852	2135	3000	2008	2789	29
Louisville, KY	372	760	244	818	886	645	364	1273	1863	551	990	845	72	712	522	495	2102	752	340	2092		981	1140	476	510	449	1008	281	686	386	1090	1169	397	710	624	2308	706	456	932	171	993	178	764	9
Lowell, MA	1060	421	927	1637	1706	376	872	2202	2720	1465	12	1768	924	1493	1453	606	3000	1696	673	2989	981		2062	625	1132	1138	37	704	1246	1318	1516	2100	1086	1399	1434	3090	1536	1266	294	892	21	1106	230	
Lubbock, TX	1224	1793	1189	738	682	1699	1363	543	964	695	2070	260	1210	716	664	1528	1122	476	1425	1111	1140	2062		1500	1177	1220	2089	1362	1546	800	1660	117	1256	1170	941	1330	631	992	1968	1183	2074	1010	1820	20
Lynchburg, VA	795	689	311	1022	1090	300	648	1586	2350	1026	633	1248	406	1188	838	666	2508	1080	500	2498	476	625	1500		494	873	652	467	1022	703	941	1485	820	1134	778	2717	921	611	806	514	636	490	395	6
Macon, GA	879	1155	300	604	673	806	872	1168	2110	930	1140	1008	470	1092	598	946	2268	706	790	2258	510	1132	1177	494		956	1158	732	1194	462	585	1162	904	1216	352	2477	546	185	1271	672	1143	336	902	11
Madison, WI	115	826	692	1078	1147	845	369	1424	1710	526	1146	926	520	483	705	559	1990	935	470	1979	449	1138	1220	873	956		1164	468	311	643	1534	1274	78	271	1042	2080	898	901	1001	377	1149	623	938	11
Manchester, NH	1087	442	953	1664	1732	402	899	2228	2747	1492	28	1794	951	1519	1480	633	3026	1722	700	3016	1008	37	2089	652	1158	1164		731	1273	1345	1542	2127	1112	1426	1460	3116	1563	1293	261	919	18	1132	257	1
Mansfield, OH	390	527	434	1096	1166	402	218	1552	2077	765	713	1068	266	823	801	274	2324	1031	62	2314	281	704	1362	467	732	468	731		592	666	1238	1448	416	729	903	2420	984	735	654	190	716	457	495	7
Marquette, MI	328	720	930	1348	1417	953	394	1733	2021	837	1254	1251	758	794	1014	524	2301	1244	578	2290	686	1246	1546	1022	1194	311	1273	592		914	1774	1599	290	406	1307	2269	1169	1140	782	596	1258	861	1046	12
Memphis, TN	599	1144	391	437	505	970	717	888	1649	484	1326	547	423	720	137	880	1808	367	724	1797	386	1318	800	703	462	643	1345	666	914		1012	784	624	831	400	2016	325	322	1316	529	1330	212	1088	13
Miami, FL	1458	1578	880	973	1042	1190	1418	1538	2599	1510	1524	1504	1049	1671	1147	1473	2743	1188	1271	2739	1090	1516	1660	941	585	1534	1542	1238	1774	1012		1644	1484	1796	719	2966	1029	690	1672	1250	1527	914	1286	15
Midland, TX	1278	1846	1174	723	668	1752	1416	414	1089	748	2109	347	1205	870	649	1581	1113	461	1478	1108	1169	2100	117	1485	1162	1274	2127	1448	1599	784	1644		1309	1223	926	1418	616	977	2022	1236	2112	995	1870	20
Milwaukee, WI	39	773	640	1059	1128	792	317	1444	1789	605	1094	962	468	562	724	506	2069	955	418	2058	397	1086	1256	820	904	78	1112	416	290	624	1484	1309		336	1018	2159	879	850	949	324	1097	572	886	10
Minneapolis, MN	373	1087	954	1187	1200	1106	630	1375	1660	475	1407	875	782	432	816	820	1939	972	731	1928	710	1399	1170	1134	1216	271	1426	729	406	831	1796	1223	336		1230	2030	999	1162	1262	638	1410	884	1199	14
Mobile, AL	992	1382	510	255	323	1085	985	819	1881	883	1442	785	660	1119	454	1117	2025	470	962	2020	624	1434	941	778	352	1042	1460	903	1307	400	719	926	1018	1230		2247	310	168	1550	791	1445	448	1204	14
Modesto, CA	2156	2778	2406	2044	2008	2797	2321	1720	490	1812	3098	1504	2378	1604	1886	2511	334	1782	2422	312	2308	3090	1330	2717	2477	2080	3116	2420	2269	2016	2966	1418	2159	2030	2247		1937	2336	2953	2307	3102	2227	2890	30
Monroe, LA	854	1464	609	215	233	1188	972	663	1570	598	1544	475	742	771	185	1198	1728	159	1043	1723	706	1536	631	921	546	898	1563	984	1169	325	1029	616	879	999	310	1937		362	1652	784	1548	532	1306	15
Montgomery, AL	825	1214	342	419	488	918	818	984	1970	804	1274	836	493	1040	457	949	2089	521	794	2117	456	1266	992	611	185	901	1293	735	1140	322	690	977	850	1162	168	2336	362		1382	624	1278	280	1036	12
Montréal, QC	924	186	1043	1753	1822	500	633	2156	2584	1370	285	1674	916	1356	1452	458	2863	1682	610	2852	932	294	1968	806	1271	1001	261	654	782	1316	1672	2022	949	1262	1550	2953	1652	1382		794	279	1107	385	3
Muncie, IN	299	618	374	964	1032	548	204	1370	1898	586	900	889	206	710	646	353	2146	877	226	2135	171	892	1183	514	672	377	919	190	596	529	1250	1236	324	638	791	2307	784	624	794		904	345	670	8
Nashua, NH	1072	433	938	1648	1717	387	884	2213	2732	1477	21	1779	936	1504	1465	618	3011	1707	684	3000	993	21	2074	636	1143	1149	18	716	1258	1330	1527	2112	1097	1410	1445	3102	1548	1278	279	904		1117	242	9
Nashville, TN	546	936	179	643	712	757	539	1099	1860	598	1114	758	214	760	348	671	2018	578	516	2008	178	1106	1010	490	336	623	1132	457	861	212	914	995	572	884	448	2227	532	280	1107	345	1117		876	10
Newark, NJ	860	380	697	1407	1476	146	672	1972	2520	1224	238	1526	694	1293	1223	540	2800	1465	478	2789	764	230	1820	395	902	938	257	495	1046	1088	1286	1870	886	1199	1204	2890	1306	1036	385	670	242	876		2
New Bedford, MA	1068	454	917	1627	1696	366	880	2192	2728	1444	86	1747	914	1500	1444	639	3007	1686	686	2997	984	86	2041	615	1122	1146	112	702	1254	1308	1506	2091	1093	1407	1424	3098	1526	1256	368	890	98	1096	220	
New Britain, CT	956	370	838	1548	1616	274	768	2113	2616	1352	124	1654	835	1389	1364	555	2896	1606	574	2885	868	116	1948	517	1024	1034	142	591	1142	1229	1408	2012	982	1295	1345	2986	1447	1177	340	779	127	1016	122	1
New Brunswick, NJ	876	391	692	1402	1471	132	688	1967	2536	1219	263	1522	690	1308	1219	551	2778	1461	494	2768	759	255	1816	376	882	954	282	510	1062	1084	1266	1866	901	1214	1182	2906	1302	1014	406	665	266	871	25	2
New Haven, CT	937	396	786	1496	1565	235	749	2061	2596	1313	149	1615	783	1369	1312	582	2876	1554	554	2866	853	141	1910	484	990	1014	168	571	1123	1177	1374	1960	962	1276	1293	2966	1395	1125	366	759	152	965	89	13
New Orleans, LA	990	1466	599	134	203	1178	1070	699	1806	876	1534	711	745	1112	425	1201	1904	395	1046	1900	708	1526	867	911	493	1035	1553	987	1306	394	862	852	1016	1223	144	2173	281	308	1642	876	1538	532	1296	151
Newport News, VA	946	700	514	1157	1226	314	758	1721	2502	1190	598	1450	570	1352	1040	708	2711	1232	564	2700	640	589	1703	191	586	1024	616	580	1132	905	970	1688	971	1285	905	2919	1072	738	746	678	601	692	359	58
New York, NY	880	400	731	1441	1510	176	693	2006	2540	1258	222	1560	728	1313	1257	560	2820	1499	498	2809	798	214	1854	419	926	958	241	515	1066	1122	1310	1904	906	1219	1238	2910	1340	1070	384	703	226	910	33	20
Niagara Falls, NY	632	251	725	1381	1450	346	444	1836	2292	1049	480	1352	550	1064	1086	142	2570	1316	244	2560	566	472	1646	536	971	709	498	288	818	950	1418	1732	656	970	1188	2661	1270	1020	410	466	484	742	406	50
Norfolk, VA	958	647	526	1152	1220	326	771	1716	2514	1202	582	1463	582	1364	1053	720	2723	1226	576	2712	652	574	1698	189	582	1036	600	593	1144	918	966	1683	984	1297	900	2932	1067	732	731	691	585	705	344	56
Norman, OK	863	1432	864	578	524	1338	1002	611	1202	334	1709	80	850	456	345	1167	1360	316	1064	1350	778	1701	340	1176	936	859	1728	1000	1184	475	1485	427	895	808	781	1569	471	795	1607	822	1712	686	1459	168
North Platte, NE	781	1402	1155	1156	1102	1422	946	1074	1009	442	1723	556	1004	229	852	1136	1289	894	1047	1278	932	1714	591	1407	1312	705	1741	1045	1016	940	1891	708	784	654	1339	1379	1049	1260	1578	932	1726	979	1514	172
Oakland, CA	2162	2783	2477	2116	2068	2802	2326	1780	562	1817	3104	1576	2384	1610	1957	2516	395	1854	2428	373	2313	3095	1402	2788	2548	2086	3122	2426	2274	2087	3037	1480	2164	2035	2319	84	2008	2408	2958	2312	3107	2298	2896	310
Oceanside, CA	2095	2716	2226	1724	1650	2690	2260	1362	310	1624	3037	1325	2202	1543	1706	2450	73	1522	2360	84	2131	3028	1178	2537	2222	2019	3055	2353	2330	1836	2692	1061	2098	1968	1973	396	1676	2038	2892	2174	3040	2047	2829	303
Odessa, TX	1299	1868	1196	744	691	1774	1438	438	1068	770	2130	369	1227	892	671	1603	1092	482	1500	1087	1190	2122	138	1507	1184	1295	2149	1470	1620	806	1666	22	1331	1244	948	1398	637	999	2043	1258	2134	1017	1892	211
Ogden, UT	1428	2050	1803	1787	1733	2069	1593	1605	458	1084	2370	1154	1651	876	1483	1783	738	1525	1694	727	1580	2362	1062	2055	1960	1352	2389	1692	1663	1588	2539	1179	1431	1302	1936	757	1680	1908	2226	1580	2374	1627	2162	237
Oklahoma City, OK	844	1412	856	593	540	1318	982	626	1184	314	1690	87	830	437	336	1147	1342	331	1044	1330	759	1682	379	1167	927	840	1708	981	1165	466	1476	434	876	789	796	1550	486	786	1588	802	1693	677	1440	166
Omaha, NE	506	1127	923	946	932	1146	670	1080	1286	209	1448	540	771	58	575	860	1565	704	772	1554	700	1440	768	1175	1080	430	1466	770	741	708	1658	887	509	379	1106	1655	758	1028	1303	657	1451	747	1240	144
Orlando, FL	1236	1368	657	751	820	980	1228	1316	2377	1288	1314	1281	826	1449	924	1263	2521	966	1061	2516	868	1306	1438	731	363	1312	1332	1028	1550	789	234	1422	1262	1574	496	2744	806	467	1462	1028	1317	692	1076	129
Owensboro, KY	396	868	292	737	806	753	463	1208	1810	498	1110	792	178	660	456	603	2049	686	447	2038	109	1102	1086	584	468	487	1128	389	711	303	1048	1103	422	748	582	2254	626	414	1039	270	1114	136	872	109
Paterson, NJ	851	371	704	1414	1483	153	664	1979	2511	1231	235	1534	701	1284	1231	531	2790	1473	469	2780	771	226	1828	419	932	929	253	486	1037	1095	1310	1878	876	1190	1211	2880	1314	1044	376	674	238	883	24	21
Pendleton, OR	1956	2574	2326	2310	2258	2593	2118	2128	848	1608	2894	1678	2175	1400	2008	2307	1034	2049	2218	1012	2104	2886	1586	2578	2484	1854	2912	2216	1854	2112	3062	1702	1920	1586	2460	796	2204	2432	2750	2104	2898	2150	2686	2894
Pensacola, FL	988	1377	505	312	381	1080	980	877	1938	940	1437	842	656	1176	511	1112	2082	527	956	2078	619	1429	999	774	347	1064	1456	898	1302	458	673	983	1013	1287	57	2304	368	163	1545	786	1440	443	1199	141
Peoria, IL	205	800	567	886	955	794	344	1232	1681	392	1121	750	396	453	513	534	1960	744	445	1950	324	1113	1045	757	778	210	1139	457	518	452	1358	1098	229	453	850	2050	706	724	976	257	1124	445	913	112
Philadelphia, PA	832	390	623	1334	1402	78	645	1898	2480	1168	321	1470	641	1265	1150	550	2727	1392	450	2716	710	312	1764	316	823	910	339	467	1019	1014	1207	1797	858	1171	1122	2862	1232	955	469	614	324	802	82	30
Phoenix, AZ	1850	2419	1860	1401	1327	2326	1989	1039	351	1212	2696	960	1837	1274	1341	2154	374	1198	2051	370	1766	2688	786	2172	1932	1738	2715	1988	2049	1471	2369	738	1817	1688	1650	680	1353	1715	2595	1809	2700	1682	2446	2667

Mileage Directory/Ft. Wayne, IN—Phoenix, AZ

Mileages in this Mileage Directory are from the Rand McNally *MileMaker Practical Routing System*, © Rand McNally. **These mileages are for general reference only and should not be used for the purposes of tariff computation.** For tariff purposes, refer to the applicable official tariff. Mileages between each of the 300 cities listed in this chart are computed over National Interstate, U.S. and primary state highways, and Canadian provincial highways via highways designated as truck-usable by the Household Goods Carriers' Bureau Committee. Practical routing may have highway segments not included in the federally designated National Network.

	New Britain, CT	New Brunswick, NJ	New Haven, CT	New Orleans, LA	Newport News, VA	New York, NY	Niagara Falls, NY	Norfolk, VA	Norman, OK	North Platte, NE	Oakland, CA	Oceanside, CA	Odessa, TX	Ogden, UT	Oklahoma City, OK	Omaha, NE	Orlando, FL	Owensboro, KY	Paterson, NJ	Pendleton, OR	Pensacola, FL	Peoria, IL	Philadelphia, PA	Phoenix, AZ	Pine Bluff, AR	Pittsburgh, PA	Pittsfield, MA	Pomona, CA	Pontiac, MI	Port Arthur, TX	Portland, ME	Portland, OR	Providence, RI	Provo, UT	Pueblo, CO	Québec, QC	Racine, WI	Raleigh, NC	Rapid City, SD	Reading, PA	Regina, SK	Reno, NV	Richmond, VA	Riverside, CA
Wayne, IN	745	665	726	946	718	670	428	732	892	892	2271	2206	1328	1538	872	615	1105	339	640	2061	856	258	622	1878	732	324	722	2140	200	1159	950	2270	826	1581	1242	889	250	652	1079	579	1350	2062	639	2129
Worth, TX	1712	1566	1660	551	1388	1604	1432	1382	183	761	1701	1360	322	1279	198	652	1121	803	1578	1802	682	826	1497	1038	359	1264	1740	1378	1210	358	1894	2010	1761	1200	661	1907	1018	1226	1056	1475	1507	1710	1308	1353
edericton, NB	535	674	560	1945	1008	633	892	993	2120	2087	3468	3401	2541	2735	2101	1812	1724	1521	646	3258	1848	1485	732	3108	1888	992	559	3336	1079	2182	326	3466	488	2778	2460	377	1445	1139	2276	762	2292	3259	983	3326
esno, CA	3011	2894	2991	2080	2826	2935	2686	2838	1475	1404	176	302	1304	850	1456	1680	2650	2164	2906	889	2211	2075	2842	587	1834	2559	2980	246	2412	1868	3208	748	3092	773	1248	3136	2182	2679	1472	2800	1724	296	2746	271
inesville, FL	1124	984	1092	532	687	1026	1135	682	1154	1560	2706	2361	1336	2208	1145	1328	113	717	1026	2732	342	1026	924	2038	796	902	1200	2379	1103	768	1326	2938	1192	2224	1666	1538	1140	524	1848	936	2240	2732	668	2353
lveston, TX	1781	1636	1729	367	1390	1674	1572	1385	479	1057	1976	1557	598	1688	494	948	984	943	1648	2212	545	1000	1567	1234	499	1435	1810	1575	1388	119	1964	2418	1830	1510	972	2149	1216	1230	1352	1544	1803	2021	1352	1549
ry, IN	852	772	832	926	842	776	527	854	818	762	2142	2076	1254	1410	798	487	1134	312	747	1934	885	160	728	1806	667	431	822	2012	254	1094	1049	2140	933	1453	1134	977	108	790	951	686	1222	1934	767	2000
and Island, NE	1483	1402	1463	1157	1444	1407	1158	1456	454	145	1526	1459	803	793	435	152	1541	752	1378	1316	1268	547	1359	1314	767	1061	1452	1394	884	976	1680	1524	1564	836	518	1608	654	1394	426	1316	878	1317	1364	1384
and Rapids, MI	836	756	817	1069	826	760	512	838	961	905	2286	2220	1397	1553	942	630	1234	454	731	2076	985	303	712	1948	811	415	806	2155	138	1238	1034	2284	918	1596	1278	849	264	812	1094	670	1365	2077	752	2144
eat Falls, MT	2265	2185	2245	2163	2255	2189	1940	2267	1460	852	1188	1303	1447	539	1441	1064	2494	1705	2160	570	2222	1423	2141	1234	1772	1844	2235	1238	1666	1981	2462	718	2346	616	891	2390	1332	2201	542	2099	500	979	2180	1227
eeley, CO	1842	1761	1822	1434	1790	1766	1516	1802	732	235	1230	1118	718	496	712	511	1886	1098	1736	1020	1512	906	1718	978	1044	1420	1811	1054	1242	1253	2039	1226	1923	540	181	1967	1013	1740	368	1676	808	1020	1709	1042
een Bay, WI	1098	1017	1078	1132	1087	1022	772	1100	1011	845	2226	2160	1447	1493	992	570	1378	538	992	1863	1129	345	974	1878	874	676	1067	2095	498	1300	1295	2010	1179	1536	1218	1060	144	1034	838	932	1054	2017	1013	2084
eensboro, NC	657	516	624	808	240	560	662	234	1148	1439	2760	2510	1472	2086	1139	1206	620	575	560	2610	662	770	457	2144	826	428	732	2445	624	1045	858	2818	726	2103	1644	1072	822	79	1726	469	1923	2611	201	2434
eenville, SC	870	707	818	618	431	763	775	426	1000	1322	2612	2321	1282	1970	991	1090	531	458	736	2494	473	734	648	1996	678	542	898	2297	722	855	1052	2700	919	1986	1527	1238	793	270	1609	634	1894	2494	392	2286
lifax, NS	761	900	786	2171	1234	859	1117	1219	2346	2354	3735	3669	2767	3002	2326	2080	1950	1746	871	3526	2074	1753	957	3334	2114	1218	785	3604	1347	2408	551	3732	713	3046	2727	645	1713	1364	2543	988	2559	3526	1208	3593
milton, OH	761	624	717	841	618	662	458	630	869	1000	2381	2222	1324	1648	849	725	942	244	636	2172	752	325	572	1856	671	289	752	2157	278	1076	967	2378	818	1691	1219	967	382	550	1214	530	1484	2172	538	2146
rrisburg, PA	300	154	248	1140	314	193	306	327	1303	1387	2768	2656	1736	2034	1284	1112	982	716	166	2558	1043	759	109	2290	1083	205	328	2592	510	1376	482	2764	349	2078	1654	668	745	396	1575	66	1846	2558	240	2580
rtford, CT	12	153	38	1424	487	112	408	472	1597	1620	3000	2934	2020	2268	1577	1345	1204	1000	124	2792	1326	1018	210	2584	1367	469	77	2870	744	1660	197	2998	114	2311	1947	431	978	617	1808	241	2080	2792	462	2858
gh Point, NC	676	535	643	790	258	578	651	253	1138	1428	2750	2499	1454	2076	1128	1196	602	564	578	2600	644	760	476	2134	816	417	741	2434	614	1027	877	2806	744	2092	1633	1080	811	98	1715	488	1912	2600	220	2423
uston, TX	1761	1616	1709	347	1370	1654	1524	1365	430	1009	1927	1508	550	1640	446	899	964	894	1628	2164	525	952	1547	1186	450	1354	1790	1526	1340	99	1944	2370	1810	1462	923	2129	1167	1210	1303	1524	1754	1972	1332	1500
ntington, WV	712	566	660	870	446	604	510	459	972	1126	2508	2326	1352	1774	954	894	844	303	578	2298	776	476	518	1960	700	276	740	2260	355	1104	894	2505	760	1790	1332	1034	534	379	1414	474	1634	2298	366	2250
ntsville, AL	1050	904	998	441	726	943	860	738	687	1097	2299	2048	1018	1745	678	865	633	254	916	2268	352	563	835	1683	365	690	1078	1984	698	678	1232	2476	1099	1762	1240	1418	677	579	1384	813	1777	2269	646	1972
dianapolis, IN	827	694	788	818	708	733	524	720	758	890	2270	2111	1194	1537	739	614	978	212	706	2061	729	214	643	1746	599	359	819	2046	322	1026	1034	2268	889	1580	1109	1005	268	640	1104	600	1370	2062	627	2035
wa City, IA	1089	1008	1069	924	1074	1013	764	1087	680	526	1907	1840	1117	1174	661	251	1261	472	984	1698	988	154	965	1560	636	668	1058	1776	490	1005	1286	1904	1170	1217	899	1214	261	1008	740	922	1079	1698	994	1764
ckson, MS	1330	1184	1278	183	955	1223	1154	950	588	1149	2126	1794	755	1743	603	916	689	511	1196	2267	250	660	1116	1471	215	983	1358	1811	993	352	1512	2474	1379	1708	1086	1698	820	794	1436	1093	1868	2135	917	1786
cksonville, FL	1056	914	1022	547	618	958	1066	613	1170	1576	2722	2376	1351	2224	1160	1344	141	732	958	2748	358	1042	855	2054	812	833	1130	2394	1030	784	1256	2954	1124	2240	1722	1470	1156	456	1863	868	2256	2748	600	2369
nesville, WI	996	915	976	997	985	920	671	998	837	726	2106	2040	1273	1374	818	451	1274	449	891	1888	1026	171	872	1760	709	574	965	1976	396	1078	1193	2036	1077	1416	1098	1121	82	932	809	830	1080	1898	911	1964
fferson City, MO	1196	1063	1157	794	1034	1101	893	1046	439	578	1959	1817	875	1226	420	346	1131	342	1075	1750	859	264	1012	1426	389	728	1188	1752	648	752	1402	1956	1258	1242	783	1373	456	984	865	969	1297	1750	954	1742
rsey City, NJ	118	33	86	1304	368	29	410	352	1468	1518	2899	2832	1901	2166	1448	1243	1084	880	17	2690	1207	916	91	2456	1248	369	197	2768	642	1541	320	2896	186	2209	1818	536	876	498	1707	122	1978	2690	342	2756
liet, IL	892	812	873	902	882	817	568	895	774	718	2099	2032	1210	1366	755	443	1172	332	787	1890	924	116	769	1762	646	471	862	1968	294	1070	1090	2096	974	1409	1090	1018	109	828	932	726	1204	1890	808	1956
lamazoo, MI	796	716	777	1038	786	721	472	798	930	874	2255	2188	1366	1522	911	600	1204	422	692	2046	954	272	673	1918	780	375	766	2124	142	1206	994	2252	878	1565	1247	866	232	756	1063	630	1334	2046	712	2112
nsas City, MO	1311	1180	1272	910	1151	1218	1010	1162	368	418	1801	1662	804	1066	350	185	1248	458	1192	1589	976	350	1128	1248	429	845	1303	1598	762	750	1518	1796	1373	1087	628	1486	562	1099	706	1086	1138	1592	1071	1586
nosha, WI	956	876	937	990	946	880	632	958	863	781	2162	2095	1299	1428	844	506	1236	396	851	1956	988	205	832	1850	732	535	926	2030	358	1159	1154	2104	1038	1472	1153	1082	11	892	877	790	1148	1952	872	2019
ngston, ON	370	391	396	1466	700	400	251	647	1432	1402	2783	2716	1868	2050	1412	1127	1368	868	371	2574	1377	800	390	2419	1296	479	287	2652	394	1701	459	2780	432	2093	1775	344	760	782	1591	367	1776	2574	626	2640
oxville, TN	838	692	786	599	514	731	725	526	864	1155	2477	2226	1196	1803	856	923	657	292	704	2326	505	567	623	1860	543	491	866	2161	556	836	1020	2534	887	1820	1360	1206	627	367	1442	601	1729	2327	434	2150
fayette, LA	1548	1402	1496	134	1157	1441	1381	1152	578	1156	2116	1724	744	1787	593	946	751	737	1414	2310	312	886	1334	1401	325	1201	1576	1742	1219	131	1730	2518	1597	1614	1075	1916	1046	996	1450	1311	1898	2125	1118	1716
ke Charles, LA	1616	1471	1565	203	1226	1510	1450	1220	524	1102	2068	1650	691	1733	540	932	820	806	1483	2258	381	955	1402	1327	343	1270	1645	1668	1288	57	1799	2464	1666	1568	1029	1984	1115	1065	1396	1380	1884	2079	1187	1642
ncaster, PA	274	132	235	1178	314	176	346	326	1338	1422	2802	2690	1774	2069	1318	1146	980	753	153	2593	1080	794	78	2326	1121	240	310	2626	544	1414	469	2800	336	2112	1688	649	780	395	1610	34	1881	2593	239	2615
nsing, MI	768	688	749	1070	758	693	444	771	1002	946	2326	2260	1438	1593	982	670	1228	463	664	2118	980	344	645	1989	851	347	738	2195	70	1278	966	2324	850	1636	1318	791	304	744	1134	602	1405	2118	684	2184
redo, TX	2113	1967	2061	699	1721	2006	1836	1716	611	1074	1780	1362	438	1605	626	1080	1316	1208	1979	2128	877	1232	1898	1039	763	1668	2141	1380	1616	451	2295	2336	2162	1363	987	2314	1425	1561	1483	1876	1934	1807	1683	1354
s Vegas, NV	2616	2536	2596	1806	2502	2540	2292	2514	1202	1009	562	310	1068	458	1184	1286	2377	1810	2511	848	1938	1681	2480	351	1562	2196	2586	246	2018	1620	2814	1022	2698	378	860	2741	1788	2406	1078	2437	1443	447	2422	234
wrence, KS	1352	1219	1313	876	1190	1258	1049	1202	334	442	1817	1624	770	1084	314	209	1288	498	1231	1608	940	392	1168	1212	457	884	1344	1558	804	726	1558	1814	1414	1048	589	1528	603	1140	729	1125	1161	1608	1110	1548
wrence, MA	124	263	149	1534	598	222	480	582	1709	1723	3104	3037	2130	2370	1690	1448	1314	1110	235	2894	1437	1121	321	2696	1478	582	148	2972	846	1771	88	3100	79	2414	2060	375	1081	728	1912	352	2066	2894	572	2961
wton, OK	1654	1522	1615	711	1450	1560	1352	1463	80	556	1576	1325	369	1154	87	540	1281	792	1534	1678	842	750	1470	960	459	1187	1646	1260	1134	524	1861	1884	1716	1075	536	1832	943	1304	944	1428	1395	1585	1370	1249
xington, KY	835	690	783	745	570	728	550	582	850	1004	2384	2202	1227	1651	830	771	826	178	701	2175	656	396	641	1837	574	400	863	2138	388	980	1017	2382	884	1668	1208	1074	455	503	1290	598	1557	2176	490	2126
ncoln, NE	1389	1308	1369	1112	1352	1313	1064	1364	456	229	1610	1543	892	876	437	58	1449	660	1284	1400	1176	453	1265	1274	630	967	1358	1478	790	978	1586	1608	1470	920	601	1514	560	1302	579	1222	1012	1400	1272	1467
tle Rock, AR	1364	1219	1312	425	1040	1257	1086	1053	345	852	1957	1706	671	1483	336	575	924	456	1231	2008	511	513	1150	1341	44	916	1393	1642	902	413	1547	2214	1414	1448	898	1609	729	894	1094	1128	1526	2008	960	1630
ndon, ON	555	551	582	1201	708	560	142	720	1167	1136	2516	2450	1603	1783	1147	860	1263	603	531	2307	1112	534	550	2154	1031	371	472	2385	128	1436	700	2514	617	1826	1508	616	494	799	1324	482	1754	2307	634	2374
ng Beach, CA	2896	2778	2876	1904	2711	2820	2570	2723	1360	1289	395	73	1092	738	1342	1565	2521	2049	2790	1034	2082	1960	2727	374	1720	2444	2866	39	2297	1656	3093	986	2977	658	1133	3021	2068	2564	1358	2685	1723	492	2630	59
ngview, TX	1606	1461	1554	395	1232	1499	1316	1226	316	894	1854	1522	482	1525	331	704	966	686	1473	2049	527	744	1392	1198	242	1146	1635	1539	1132	206	1789	2256	1656	1352	814	1840	959	1071	1188	1370	1656	1863	1193	1514
rain, OH	574	494	554	1046	564	498	244	576	1064	1047	2428	2360	1500	1694	1044	772	1061	447	469	2218	956	445	450	2051	876	152	538	2296	170	1280	766	2424	655	1738	1419	768	405	597	1235	408	1506	2218	489	2285
s Angeles, CA	2885	2768	2866	1900	2700	2809	2560	2712	1350	1278	373	84	1087	727	1330	1554	2516	2038	2780	1012	2078	1950	2716	370	1709	2433	2854	28	2286	1652	3082	963	2966	647	1122	3010	2057	2554	1347	2674	1712	470	2620	54
uisville, KY	868	759	853	708	640	798	566	652	778	932	2313	2131	1190	1580	759	700	868	109	771	2104	619	324	710	1766	538	396	860	2066	404	943	1074	2310	954	1596	1137	1089	384	572	1219	668	1486	2104	560	2055
well, MA	116	255	141	1526	589	214	472	574	1701	1714	3095	3028	2122	2362	1682	1440	1306	1102	226	2886	1429	1113	312	2688	1470	573	140	2964	838	1763	97	3092	71	2405	2052	384	1073	720	1903	344	2074	2886	564	2952
bbock, TX	1948	1816	1910	867	1703	1854	1646	1698	340	591	1402	1178	138	1062	379	768	1438	1086	1828	1586	999	1045	1764	786	674	1481	1940	1086	1428	670	2155	1792	2010	901	444	2126	1237	1542	838	1722	1373	1411	1623	1075
nchburg, VA	517	376	484	911	191	419	536	189	1176	1407	2788	2537	1507	2055	1167	1175	731	584	419	2578	774	757	316	2172	854	376	629	2473	610	1147	718	2786	585	2072	1612	968	808	192	1694	329	1909	2579	114	2462
acon, GA	1024	882	990	493	586	926	971	582	936	1312	2548	2222	1184	1960	927	1080	363	468	932	2484	347	778	823	1932	614	738	1094	2232	854	730	1225	2690	1092	1976	1516	1434	892	424	1598	830	1992	2484	568	2221
adison, WI	1034	954	1014	1035	1024	958	709	1036	859	705	2086	2019	1295	1352	840	430	1312	487	929	1854	1064	210	910	1738	747	612	1004	1954	436	1116	1231	2002	1115	1396	1077	1159	104	970	775	868	1046	1876	949	1943
anchester, NH	142	282	168	1553	616	241	498	600	1728	1741	3122	3055	2149	2389	1708	1466	1332	1128	253	2912	1456	1139	339	2715	1496	600	167	2990	864	1789	98	3120	98	2432	2078	351	1099	746	1930	370	2042	2913	590	2980
ansfield, OH	591	510	571	987	580	515	288	593	1000	1045	2426	2353	1470	1692	981	770	1028	389	486	2216	898	457	467	1988	817	170	583	2288	184	1222	798	2422	672	1736	1351	812	403	564	1233	424	1504	2216	506	2278
arquette, MI	1142	1062	1123	1306	1132	1066	818	1144	1184	1016	2274	2330	1620	1663	1165	741	1550	711	1037	1854	1302	518	1019	2049	1047	721	1112	2265	424	1474	1340	2001	1224	1706	1388	940	318	1118	1005	976	969	2065	1058	2254
emphis, TN	1229	1084	1177	394	905	1122	950	918	475	940	2087	1836	806	1588	466	708	789	303	1095	2112	458	452	1014	1471	153	781	1257	1772	788	562	1412	2318	1278	1578	1028	1474	611	758	1227	992	1659	2112	825	1760
iami, FL	1408	1266	1374	862	970	1310	1418	966	1485	1891	3037	2692	1666	2539	1476	1658	234	1048	1310	3062	673	1358	1207	2369	1127	1185	1482	2710	1382	1099	1609	3270	1476	2556	2038	1822	1471	808	2178	1220	2571	3064	952	2684
dland, TX	2012	1866	1960	852	1688	1904	1732	1683	427	708	1480	1061	22	1179	434	887	1422	1103	1878	1702	983	1098	1797	738	659	1563	2040	1079	1482	623	2194	1910	2060	1007	561	2180	1290	1528	955	1774	1490	1506	1607	1053
lwaukee, WI	982	901	962	1016	971	906	656	984	895	784	2164	2098	1331	1431	876	509	1262	422	876	1920	1013	229	858	1817	758	560	951	2033	382	1184	1179	2068	1063	1474	1156	1107	28	918	840	816	1111	1956	897	2022
inneapolis, MN	1295	1214	1276	1223	1285	1219	970	1297	808	654	2035	1968	1244	1302	789	379	1574	748	1190	1586	1287	453	1171	1688	858	874	1265	1904	696	1179	1492	1734	1376	1345	1027	1420	362	1231	608	1129	777	1826	1210	1892
obile, AL	1345	1182	1293	144	905	1238	1188	900	781	1339	2319	1973	948	1936	796	1106	496	582	1211	2460	57	850	1122	1650	408	1001	1373	1991	1026	380	1527	2666	1394	1901	1279	1712	1005	744	1626	1108	2058	2328	867	1965
odesto, CA	2986	2906	2966	2173	2919	2910	2661	2932	1569	1379	84	396	1398	757	1550	1655	2744	2254	2880	796	2304	2050	2862	680	1928	2564	2956	339	2387	1962	3183	656	3068	763	1372	3111	2158	2772	1384	2820	1632	204	2839	364
onroe, LA	1447	1302	1395	281	1072	1340	1270	1067	471	1049	2008	1676	637	1680	486	758	806	626	1314	2204	368	706	1232	1353	142	1100	1475	1694	1107	312	1630	2410	1496	1507	968	1815	866	912	1278	1210	1710	2018	1034	1668
ontgomery, AL	1177	1014	1125	308	738	1070	1020	732	795	1260	2408	2038	999	1908	786	1028	467	414	1044	2432	163	724	955	1715	427	833	1206	2056	858	545	1360	2638	1226	1898	1348	1545	837	577	1547	940	1938	2432	699	2030
ontréal, QC	340	406	366	1642	746	384	410	731	1607	1578	2958	2892	2043	2226	1588	1303	1462	1039	376	2750	1545	976	469	2595	1468	606	257	2828	570	1879	278	2956	361	2269	1950	159	936	876	1766	468	1782	2750	720	2816
uncie, IN	779	665	759	876	678	703	466	691	822	932	2312	2174	1258	1580	802	657	1028	270	674	2104	786	257	614	1809	663	330	760	2110	270	1090	986	2310	860	1622	1172	951	312	612	1142	571	1413	2104	598	2098
ashua, NH	127	266	152	1538	601	226	484	585	1712	1726	3107	3040	2134	2374	1693	1451	1317	1114	238	2898	1440	1124	324	2700	1481	585	152	2976	850	1774	105	3104	83	2417	2063	369	1084	731	1915	355	2060	2898	576	2964
ashville, TN	1016	871	965	532	692	910	742	705	686	979	2298	2047	1017	1627	677	747	692	136	883	2150	443	445	802	1682	364	572	1045	1982	580	769	1199	2358	1066	1644	1184	1265	559	546	1266	780	1659	2151	612	1972
ewark, NJ	122	25	89	1296	359	33	406	344	1459	1514	2896	2829	1892	2162	1440	1240	1076	872	24	2686	1199	913	82	2446	1239	361	195	2764	638	1532	323	2892	190	2206	1810	534	873	490	1703	113	1974	2686	334	2753
ew Bedford, MA	136	245	131	1516	580	204	504	564	1680	1722	3103	3036	2112	2370	1660	1447	1296	1092	217	2894	1419	1120	303	2667	1460	581	172	2972	846	1753	169	3100	31	2413	2030	459	1080	710	1911	334	2182	2894	554	2960
ew Britain, CT		147	34	1437	481	106	420	466	1588	1611	2992	2924	2033	2258	1568	1336	1198	1013	118	2782	1340	1009	204	2575	1380	460	88	2860	734	1674	209	2988	106	2302	1938	443	969	612	1799	242	2070	2782	456	2849
ew Brunswick, NJ	147		114	1292	340	49	417	325	1455	1530	2910	2808	1888	2178	1436	1255	1056	868	49	2702	1176	911	63	2442	1235	356	216	2743	654	1528	348	2908	215	2221	1805	555	888	471	1719	116	1990	2702	314	2732
ew Haven, CT	34	114		1385	448	73	448	433	1548	1591	2972	2905	1981	2238	1529	1316	1164	961	86	2762	1288	989	172	2536	1329	450	115	2840	714	1622	234	2970	101	2282	1899	469	949	579	1780	203	2050	2762	423	2829
ew Orleans, LA	1437	1292	1385		1046	1330	1272	1041	707	1285	2244	1852	873	1916	722	1100	640	666	1303	2440	201	844	1222	1530	379	1090	1465	1870	1110	260	1619	2646	1486	1743	1204	1805	1003	885	1619	1200	2051	2254	1008	1845
ewport News, VA	481	340	448	1046		384	578	19	1378	1572	2952	2740	1709	2219	1369	1339	760	748	384	2744	900	921	284	2374	1056	418	556	2675	724	1282	683	2950	550	2236	1776	896	958	188	1789	342	2060	2744	79	2664
ew York, NY	106	49	73	1330	384		426	368	1493	1535	2916	2849	1926	2182	1474	1260	1100	906	29	2706	1233	933	107	2480	1273	395	194	2784	658	1566	307	2913	174	2226	1844	534	893	514	1724	147	1994	2706	358	2773
iagara Falls, NY	420	417	448	1272	578	426		590	1285	1286	2666	2600	1754	1934	1266	1010	1208	673	397	2457	1182	684	416	2272	1102	240	338	2536	409	1506	566	2664	482	1976	1658	567	644	659	1474	348	1746	2458	503	2524
orfolk, VA	466	325	433	1041	19	368	590		1391	1584	2964	2752	1704	2232	1382	1351	756	760	368	2756	895	933	268	2387	1069	431	541	2688	736	1277	667	2962	534	2248	1789	880	971	184	1801	294	2072	2756	92	2676
orman, OK	1588	1455	1548	707	1378	1493	1285	1391		582	1640	1389	449	1213	19	473	1262	726	1467	1738	838	684	1403	1024	387	1120	1579	1324	1068	525	1794	1944	1649	1178	581	1765	876	1232	876	1361	1328	1650	1298	1314
orth Platte, NE	1611	1530	1591	1285	1572	1535	1286	1584	582		1384	1318	729	651	563	280	1669	880	1505	1176	1396	675	1487	1172	895	1189	1580	1253	1012	1104	1808	1382	1692	694	376	1736	782	1522	344	1444	821	1176	1491	1242
akland, CA	2992	2910	2972	2244	2952	2916	2666	2964	1640	1384		457	1458	763	1621	1660	2815	2260	2886	725	2376	2056	2868	742	2000	2570	2961	400	2392	2023	3188	627	3072	768	1378	3116	2163	2844	1390	2825	1637	209	2872	426
ceanside, CA	2924	2808	2905	1852	2740	2849	2600	2752	1389	1318	457		1040	767	1370	1594	2470	2078	2820	1079	2030	1989	2756	391	1748	2472	2894	77	2326	1604	3122	1047	3006	686	1162	3050	2096	2593	1386	2714	1752	536	2660	83
dessa, TX	2033	1888	1981	873	1709	1926	1754	1704	449	729	1458	1040		1082	456	909	1444	1125	1900	1603	1005	1120	1818	717	680	1585	2062	1058	1504	646	2216	1810	2082	1002	552	2201	1312	1549	976	1796	1511	1485	1629	1032
gden, UT	2258	2178	2238	1916	2219	2182	1934	2232	1213	651	763	767	1082		1194	928	2316	1527	2153	524	1994	1323	2134	698	1526	1837	2228	702	1660	1734	2456	730	2340	80	644	2383	1430	2170	657	2092	988	554	2139	691
klahoma City, OK	1568	1436	1529	722	1369	1474	1266	1382	19	563	1621	1370	456	1194		454	1254	706	1447	1718	854	664	1384	1005	378	1100	1560	1306	1048	541	1775	1924	1630	1159	562	1746	856	1222	857	1342	1309	1631	1289	1294
maha, NE	1336	1255	1316	1100	1339	1260	1010	1351	473	280	1660	1594	909	928	454		1436	647	1230	1452	1164	400	1212	1326	617	914	1305	1530	736	912	1533	1658	1417	970	652	1461	507	1290	525	1169	958	1452	1259	1518
rlando, FL	1198	1056	1164	640	760	1100	1208	756	1262	1669	2815	2470	1444	2316	1254	1436		826	1100	2840	450	1135	997	2146	905	975	1272	2487	1172	876	1399	3047	1266	2333	1815	1612	1248	598	1956	1010	2348	2840	742	2462
wensboro, KY	1013	868	961	666	748	906	673	760	726	880	2260	2078	1125	1527	706	647	826		879	2051	577	326	818	1713	472	504	968	2014	512	863	1195	2258	1062	1544	1084	1197	409	658	1166	776	1523	2052	668	2002
aterson, NJ	118	49	86	1303	384	29	397	368	1467	1505	2886	2820	1900	2153	1447	1230	1100	879		2676	1206	904	106	2454	1247	368	186	2755	628	1540	320	2884	186	2196	1817	525	864	514	1694	121	1965	2678	358	2744
endleton, OR	2782	2702	2762	2440	2744	2706	2457	2756	1738	1176	725	1079	1603	524	1718	1452	2840	2051	2676		2518	1846	2658	1218	2050	2360	2752	1014	2183	2258	2980	208	2864	601	1168	2908	1946	2694	1067	2616	996	592	2662	1004
ensacola, FL	1340	1176	1288	201	900	1233	1182	895	838	1396	2376	2030	1005	1994	854	1164	450	577	1206	2518		908	1118	1708	466	996	1368	2048	1020	438	1522	2724	1389	1958	1336	1708	1000	740	1683	1103	2115	2385	862	2022
eoria, IL	1009	911	989	844	921	933	684	933	684	675	2056	1989	1120	1323	664	400	1135	326	904	1846	908		859	1671	555	576	978	1924	410	924	1206	2054	1090	1366	1048	1134	218	854	890	817	1228	1847	841	1914
hiladelphia, PA	204	63	172	1222	284	107	416	268	1403	1487	2868	2756	1818	2134	1384	1212	997	818	106	2658	1118	859		2390	1166	305	279	2692	610	1459	406	2865	272	2178	1754	619	845	411	1676	62	1946	2658	256	2680
hoenix, AZ	2575	2442	2536	1530	2374	2480	2272	2387	1024	1172	742	391	717	698	1005	1326	2146	1713	2454	1218	1708	1671	2390		1383	2108	2567	341	2055	1282	2782	1332	2636	618	796	2752	1864	2228	1314	2348	1682	768	2294	315

Mileage Directory, continued

	Roanoke, VA	Rochester, MN	Rochester, NY	Rockford, IL	Sacramento, CA	Saginaw, MI	St. Johnsbury, VT	St. Joseph, MO	St. Louis, MO	St. Paul, MN	St. Petersburg, FL	Salem, OR
Ft. Wayne, IN	502	515	471	256	2193	220	882	593	376	568	1144	2320
Ft. Worth, TX	1132	954	1476	952	1701	1231	1903	565	658	994	1128	2058
Fredericton, NB	1099	1710	815	1452	3390	1124	403	1823	1605	1763	1801	3512
Fresno, CA	2570	2020	2730	2100	165	2433	3140	1757	1954	2060	2657	704
Gainesville, FL	650	1403	1179	1139	2706	1150	1335	1196	891	1456	153	2985
Galveston, TX	1202	1195	1616	1128	1986	1409	1973	830	832	1236	991	2468
Gary, IN	639	385	571	128	2065	274	981	498	302	438	1173	2188
Grand Island, NE	1226	492	1202	572	1448	905	1612	240	544	532	1580	1572
Grand Rapids, MI	662	528	555	270	2208	146	966	642	446	581	1274	2332
Great Falls, MT	2051	1058	1984	1304	1110	1687	2394	1194	1497	980	2534	764
Greeley, CO	1572	851	1560	930	1152	1264	1971	599	890	891	1926	1276
Green Bay, WI	883	272	816	208	2148	445	1227	611	495	270	1418	2057
Greensboro, NC	109	1086	662	828	2742	684	868	1075	770	1139	697	2866
Greenville, SC	290	1058	819	800	2625	770	1062	958	653	1111	607	2748
Halifax, NS	1324	1978	1040	1720	3658	1392	629	2091	1830	2030	2027	3780
Hamilton, OH	400	647	502	390	2303	324	912	615	353	700	982	2428
Harrisburg, PA	294	1010	262	752	2690	567	492	1050	788	1063	1058	2814
Hartford, CT	577	1243	332	986	2923	800	205	1343	1081	1296	1280	3047
High Point, NC	122	1076	694	818	2732	673	886	1064	759	1128	679	2854
Houston, TX	1182	1147	1568	1078	1938	1360	1953	782	784	1187	971	2419
Huntington, WV	229	798	554	541	2430	414	904	762	458	852	920	2552
Huntsville, AL	470	940	903	676	2299	744	1242	733	428	993	673	2524
Indianapolis, IN	490	533	568	276	2192	342	979	505	243	586	1017	2316
Iowa City, IA	857	197	808	178	1830	511	1218	292	264	310	1301	1952
Jackson, MS	750	933	1198	788	2126	1014	1522	785	492	1046	696	2522
Jacksonville, FL	582	1419	1110	1154	2722	1088	1266	1212	906	1472	222	3001
Janesville, WI	781	243	715	34	2029	418	1125	492	322	296	1314	2084
Jefferson City, MO	816	442	937	392	1882	670	1347	214	134	517	1171	2004
Jersey City, NJ	458	1141	333	884	2822	699	329	1214	952	1194	1160	2944
Joliet, IL	678	367	611	108	2021	315	1022	454	259	420	1212	2144
Kalamazoo, MI	606	498	516	240	2178	163	926	610	415	550	1243	2300
Kansas City, MO	932	400	1054	479	1724	784	1464	54	250	440	1286	1845
Kenosha, WI	742	311	675	90	2084	379	1086	546	348	364	1276	2152
Kingston, ON	680	1025	217	768	2706	440	330	1138	916	1078	1444	2828
Knoxville, TN	258	892	768	634	2458	604	1030	791	486	945	697	2582
Lafayette, LA	968	1153	1425	1014	2115	1240	1740	814	718	1193	758	2566
Lake Charles, LA	1037	1166	1494	1082	2079	1308	1808	801	787	1206	826	2512
Lancaster, PA	331	1044	302	788	2725	602	478	1084	822	1098	1057	2848
Lansing, MI	594	568	487	312	2248	88	898	682	486	622	1268	2372
Laredo, TX	1533	1342	1880	1360	1791	1638	2304	976	1064	1382	1322	2384
Las Vegas, NV	2297	1626	2335	1704	578	2038	2746	1363	1602	1666	2384	978
Lawrence, KS	972	441	1093	520	1740	825	1503	78	290	481	1327	1862
Lawrence, MA	688	1346	404	1088	3026	903	147	1456	1194	1399	1390	3150
Lawton, OK	1195	842	1396	878	1576	1156	1806	453	582	882	1288	1932
Lexington, KY	352	720	594	462	2306	436	1027	639	334	773	866	2430
Lincoln, NE	1134	398	1108	478	1532	811	1518	148	452	438	1488	1656
Little Rock, AR	785	782	1129	640	1957	922	1556	443	345	822	931	2262
London, ON	648	758	222	502	2438	173	602	872	651	811	1342	2562
Long Beach, CA	2455	1906	2614	1984	406	2318	3025	1642	1839	1946	2528	940
Longview, TX	1027	938	1359	870	1854	1152	1798	573	576	978	973	2304
Lorain, OH	446	670	288	412	2350	227	698	783	548	722	1137	2474
Los Angeles, CA	2444	1894	2604	1974	383	2308	3014	1632	1828	1934	2523	918
Louisville, KY	422	649	609	392	2236	450	1020	568	263	702	907	2358
Lowell, MA	680	1337	396	1080	3018	895	156	1448	1186	1390	1382	3140
Lubbock, TX	1447	1136	1690	1172	1402	1450	2100	747	876	1176	1444	1840
Lynchburg, VA	53	1072	563	816	2710	670	728	1043	738	1125	808	2834
Macon, GA	486	1155	1015	890	2548	902	1234	948	642	1208	403	2737
Madison, WI	819	209	753	73	2008	456	1163	470	360	262	1352	2049
Manchester, NH	706	1364	422	1106	3044	921	123	1474	1212	1417	1408	3168
Mansfield, OH	413	668	332	410	2348	240	742	747	485	720	1104	2472
Marquette, MI	968	442	861	382	2196	354	1272	781	669	397	1590	2048
Memphis, TN	649	724	994	578	2087	805	1421	576	283	837	796	2366
Miami, FL	934	1734	1462	1470	3037	1441	1618	1527	1222	1788	262	3318
Midland, TX	1432	1189	1776	1224	1490	1503	2203	800	930	1229	1429	1958
Milwaukee, WI	767	274	701	93	2086	404	1111	549	380	327	1302	2114
Minneapolis, MN	1080	88	1014	334	1957	718	1424	420	563	9	1614	1780
Mobile, AL	765	1123	1231	978	2318	1072	1536	975	682	1236	503	2714
Modesto, CA	2664	1996	2705	2074	72	2408	3115	1744	2048	2036	2750	611
Monroe, LA	867	965	1313	834	2008	1060	1639	627	538	1005	813	2458
Montgomery, AL	598	1045	1064	836	2408	905	1369	896	588	1154	474	2688
Montréal, QC	796	1200	333	944	2881	615	148	1314	1092	1254	1539	3005
Muncie, IN	461	576	509	320	2235	291	920	547	306	629	1068	2358
Nashua, NH	691	1349	407	1092	3029	906	141	1459	1197	1402	1394	3152
Nashville, TN	437	822	785	558	2282	626	1208	615	310	875	732	2406
Newark, NJ	450	1137	330	880	2818	695	333	1206	944	1190	1152	2942
New Bedford, MA	670	1345	428	1088	3026	902	231	1426	1164	1398	1372	3148
New Britain, CT	591	1234	344	976	2914	791	217	1334	1072	1286	1274	3038
New Brunswick, NJ	445	1153	340	896	2833	710	358	1202	940	1206	1133	2956
New Haven, CT	539	1214	371	956	2894	771	244	1295	1033	1267	1241	3018
New Orleans, LA	857	1116	1316	970	2244	1157	1629	968	675	1229	647	2694
Newport News, VA	267	1223	583	966	2874	780	692	1207	902	1276	837	2998
New York, NY	484	1158	350	900	2838	715	317	1240	978	1211	1176	2962
Niagara Falls, NY	526	908	87	652	2589	466	498	1022	770	962	1285	2711
Norfolk, VA	279	1236	596	978	2887	793	676	1220	915	1289	832	3010
Norman, OK	1122	774	1329	810	1640	1089	1739	386	515	814	1269	1992
North Platte, NE	1354	620	1330	700	1306	1033	1740	368	672	660	1708	1430
Oakland, CA	2734	2001	2710	2080	79	2414	3120	1749	2053	2041	2822	582
Oceanside, CA	2484	1934	2644	2014	467	2347	3054	1671	1868	1974	2476	1002
Odessa, TX	1454	1210	1798	1246	1469	1525	2225	822	952	1251	1451	1858
Ogden, UT	2002	1268	1977	1346	685	1680	2388	1016	1320	1308	2356	778
Oklahoma City, OK	1114	755	1309	792	1621	1070	1720	367	496	795	1260	1972
Omaha, NE	1121	345	1054	424	1583	758	1465	136	439	385	1476	1706
Orlando, FL	724	1512	1252	1248	2815	1231	1408	1304	1000	1565	107	3096
Owensboro, KY	530	686	717	422	2182	550	1127	515	210	740	866	2306
Paterson, NJ	457	1128	320	872	2808	686	329	1213	951	1181	1176	2932
Pendleton, OR	2526	1638	2501	1871	724	2204	2912	1540	1844	1594	2880	257
Pensacola, FL	760	1180	1226	999	2376	1068	1532	1032	740	1293	458	2772
Peoria, IL	703	346	728	144	1978	431	1138	336	168	462	1174	2102
Philadelphia, PA	376	1110	339	852	2790	667	415	1150	888	1163	1074	2914
Phoenix, AZ	2118	1654	2316	1732	752	2076	2726	1266	1503	1694	2154	1287

	Salinas, CA	Salisbury, MD	Salt Lake City, UT	San Angelo, TX	San Antonio, TX	San Bernardino, CA	San Diego, CA	San Francisco, CA	San Jose, CA	San Mateo, CA	Santa Ana, CA	Santa Barbara, CA
Ft. Wayne, IN	2367	672	1544	1248	1282	2121	2226	2279	2307	2300	2161	2254
Ft. Worth, TX	1629	1480	1285	240	269	1354	1329	1709	1668	1695	1392	1501
Fredericton, NB	3564	858	2741	2459	2464	3316	3422	3476	3504	3496	3358	3450
Fresno, CA	140	2918	816	1424	1574	272	339	184	149	180	250	254
Gainesville, FL	2634	817	2214	1220	1051	2355	2330	2715	2673	2700	2393	2502
Galveston, TX	1904	1520	1694	417	247	1551	1526	1984	1942	1970	1589	1698
Gary, IN	2239	778	1416	1175	1208	1991	2097	2151	2178	2170	2032	2125
Grand Island, NE	1622	1409	799	811	902	1374	1480	1534	1562	1554	1416	1508
Grand Rapids, MI	2382	762	1559	1318	1352	2134	2240	2294	2322	2314	2176	2268
Great Falls, MT	1284	2191	575	1506	1699	1218	1324	1196	1224	1216	1259	1352
Greeley, CO	1326	1768	502	777	970	1033	1139	1238	1266	1257	1074	1167
Green Bay, WI	2322	1024	1499	1368	1401	2074	2180	2234	2262	2254	2116	2208
Greensboro, NC	2689	370	2092	1390	1328	2424	2480	2769	2728	2754	2466	2558
Greenville, SC	2541	560	1976	1200	1138	2276	2290	2621	2579	2606	2318	2410
Halifax, NS	3832	1084	3008	2685	2690	3584	3690	3743	3771	3763	3625	3718
Hamilton, OH	2401	622	1654	1241	1248	2136	2208	2389	2417	2408	2178	2271
Harrisburg, PA	2864	206	2040	1654	1659	2571	2643	2776	2804	2795	2612	2705
Hartford, CT	3097	336	2274	1938	1943	2849	2936	3009	3036	3028	2890	2983
High Point, NC	2678	388	2082	1372	1310	2414	2462	2758	2717	2744	2455	2548
Houston, TX	1855	1500	1646	368	198	1502	1477	1935	1894	1921	1540	1649
Huntington, WV	2504	520	1780	1270	1276	2240	2312	2516	2544	2535	2282	2374
Huntsville, AL	2227	818	1751	936	942	1963	2035	2307	2266	2293	2004	2097
Indianapolis, IN	2290	693	1543	1115	1149	2026	2098	2278	2306	2298	2067	2160
Iowa City, IA	2004	1015	1180	1037	1089	1755	1862	1915	1943	1934	1796	1889
Jackson, MS	2054	1085	1749	672	635	1787	1762	2134	2093	2120	1826	1934
Jacksonville, FL	2650	748	2230	1236	1066	2370	2346	2730	2689	2716	2409	2518
Janesville, WI	2203	922	1380	1194	1228	1955	2061	2114	2142	2134	1996	2089
Jefferson City, MO	1996	1062	1232	796	829	1732	1779	1967	1995	1986	1774	1866
Jersey City, NJ	2996	217	2172	1818	1824	2748	2808	2908	2935	2926	2789	2882
Joliet, IL	2195	819	1372	1131	1164	1947	2053	2107	2135	2126	1988	2081
Kalamazoo, MI	2352	723	1528	1287	1320	2104	2210	2263	2291	2283	2144	2238
Kansas City, MO	1841	1178	1072	726	788	1577	1683	1809	1837	1828	1618	1711
Kenosha, WI	2258	882	1434	1220	1254	2010	2116	2170	2198	2189	2051	2144
Kingston, ON	2880	512	2056	1788	1822	2632	2738	2791	2819	2810	2672	2766
Knoxville, TN	2405	606	1809	1113	1119	2141	2213	2485	2444	2471	2182	2275
Lafayette, LA	2044	1287	1793	584	414	1717	1692	2124	2082	2109	1756	1864
Lake Charles, LA	1996	1355	1740	510	340	1644	1618	2076	2036	2062	1682	1791
Lancaster, PA	2899	163	2075	1692	1697	2606	2678	2810	2838	2830	2647	2740
Lansing, MI	2422	695	1599	1358	1392	2174	2280	2334	2362	2354	2216	2308
Laredo, TX	1708	1851	1406	366	160	1356	1331	1788	1748	1774	1394	1503
Las Vegas, NV	490	2530	421	1161	1338	226	332	570	528	556	266	360
Lawrence, KS	1802	1218	1090	690	782	1538	1644	1825	1853	1844	1580	1672
Lawrence, MA	3200	447	2376	2048	2054	2952	3058	3112	3140	3131	2993	3086
Lawton, OK	1504	1543	1160	290	436	1240	1312	1584	1543	1570	1281	1374
Lexington, KY	2382	644	1657	1145	1151	2117	2189	2392	2420	2412	2158	2251
Lincoln, NE	1706	1315	882	813	904	1458	1564	1618	1646	1637	1499	1592
Little Rock, AR	1885	1133	1490	589	595	1621	1678	1965	1924	1951	1662	1755
London, ON	2612	672	1789	1524	1557	2364	2470	2524	2552	2544	2406	2498
Long Beach, CA	323	2803	700	1211	1362	69	110	403	362	389	24	113
Longview, TX	1782	1362	1531	400	349	1515	1490	1862	1820	1848	1553	1662
Lorain, OH	2524	500	1700	1446	1452	2276	2382	2436	2464	2455	2317	2410
Los Angeles, CA	301	2792	690	1206	1357	60	120	381	340	367	31	94
Louisville, KY	2310	714	1586	1108	1114	2046	2118	2322	2349	2340	2087	2180
Lowell, MA	3192	439	2368	2040	2046	2944	3050	3104	3131	3123	2985	3078
Lubbock, TX	1330	1795	944	197	390	1066	1148	1410	1369	1396	1107	1200
Lynchburg, VA	2716	299	2061	1425	1430	2452	2524	2796	2755	2782	2494	2586
Macon, GA	2476	716	1966	1102	1012	2212	2191	2556	2515	2542	2254	2346
Madison, WI	2182	960	1358	1216	1266	1934	2040	2094	2122	2113	1975	2068
Manchester, NH	3218	466	2395	2067	2072	2970	3076	3130	3158	3150	3012	3104
Mansfield, OH	2522	517	1698	1388	1394	2268	2340	2434	2462	2453	2310	2402
Marquette, MI	2370	1069	1669	1541	1575	2244	2350	2282	2310	2302	2286	2379
Memphis, TN	2016	997	1594	724	730	1751	1824	2096	2054	2081	1792	1885
Miami, FL	2966	1100	2544	1552	1382	2686	2660	3045	3004	3031	2724	2833
Midland, TX	1408	1780	1050	112	328	1055	1030	1488	1446	1474	1093	1202
Milwaukee, WI	2260	908	1438	1252	1285	2012	2118	2172	2200	2192	2054	2147
Minneapolis, MN	2131	1221	1308	1165	1217	1883	1989	2043	2071	2062	1924	2017
Mobile, AL	2247	1035	1942	834	663	1967	1942	2327	2286	2313	2005	2114
Modesto, CA	117	2912	722	1517	1668	366	432	92	84	87	344	324
Monroe, LA	1937	1202	1686	555	504	1670	1645	2017	1975	2002	1708	1817
Montgomery, AL	2336	868	1914	917	828	2032	2006	2416	2374	2402	2070	2206
Montréal, QC	3055	596	2232	1964	1998	2807	2913	2967	2994	2986	2848	2941
Muncie, IN	2354	664	1586	1178	1212	2089	2162	2320	2348	2340	2130	2224
Nashua, NH	3203	450	2380	2052	2057	2955	3061	3115	3143	3134	2996	3089
Nashville, TN	2226	785	1633	934	941	1962	2034	2306	2265	2292	2004	2096
Newark, NJ	2992	209	2168	1810	1815	2744	2799	2904	2932	2923	2785	2878
New Bedford, MA	3200	429	2376	2030	2036	2951	3020	3111	3139	3130	2992	3085
New Britain, CT	3088	331	2264	1951	1956	2840	2927	3000	3028	3019	2881	2974
New Brunswick, NJ	3008	190	2184	1806	1811	2722	2794	2919	2946	2938	2764	2856
New Haven, CT	3068	298	2244	1899	1905	2820	2888	2980	3008	3000	2861	2954
New Orleans, LA	2172	1176	1922	712	542	1846	1822	2252	2211	2238	1884	1994
Newport News, VA	2919	147	2225	1627	1565	2654	2726	2960	2958	2980	2696	2789
New York, NY	3012	233	2188	1844	1849	2764	2833	2924	2952	2944	2805	2898
Niagara Falls, NY	2763	538	1939	1672	1678	2514	2620	2674	2702	2694	2556	2648
Norfolk, VA	2931	132	2238	1622	1560	2667	2739	2973	2970	2992	2708	2801
Norman, OK	1568	1470	1219	370	452	1304	1376	1648	1607	1634	1346	1438
North Platte, NE	1480	1537	657	747	922	1232	1338	1392	1420	1412	1274	1367
Oakland, CA	102	2918	728	1578	1728	427	494	8	41	28	404	332
Oceanside, CA	385	2832	730	1160	1310	92	38	465	424	451	52	178
Odessa, TX	1387	1802	1045	132	351	1034	1009	1466	1426	1452	1072	1181
Ogden, UT	859	2184	39	1259	1452	682	788	771	799	790	723	816
Oklahoma City, OK	1550	1462	1200	377	468	1285	1358	1630	1588	1615	1326	1419
Omaha, NE	1757	1262	934	830	921	1509	1615	1668	1696	1688	1550	1643
Orlando, FL	2743	890	2322	1330	1159	2463	2438	2823	2782	2809	2502	2610
Owensboro, KY	2258	822	1533	1043	1049	1993	2065	2268	2296	2288	2034	2127
Paterson, NJ	2982	233	2159	1817	1823	2734	2806	2894	2922	2914	2776	2868
Pendleton, OR	822	2708	560	1782	1976	994	1100	733	761	752	1036	1068
Pensacola, FL	2304	1030	2000	890	720	2024	2000	2384	2343	2370	2062	2172
Peoria, IL	2152	909	1329	1040	1074	1904	2010	2064	2092	2084	1946	2038
Philadelphia, PA	2964	134	2140	1736	1742	2671	2743	2876	2904	2895	2712	2805
Phoenix, AZ	670	2466	660	836	987	317	352	750	708	736	355	464

	Santa Rosa, CA	Savannah, GA	Schenectady, NY	Scranton, PA	Seattle, WA	Shreveport, LA	Sioux City, IA	Sioux Falls, SD
Ft. Wayne, IN	2295	832	671	565	2235	926	678	741
Ft. Worth, TX	1755	1026	1720	1532	2084	217	752	837
Fredericton, NB	3492	1456	606	715	3430	2053	1873	1938
Fresno, CA	231	2548	2929	2831	920	1746	1773	1794
Gainesville, FL	2761	207	1181	1026	2985	796	1419	1504
Galveston, TX	2030	1002	1790	1601	2494	291	1048	1133
Gary, IN	2167	932	771	672	2105	862	548	612
Grand Island, NE	1550	1349	1401	1302	1598	823	184	249
Grand Rapids, MI	2310	1007	755	656	2248	1005	691	756
Great Falls, MT	1212	2302	2184	2085	645	1829	967	886
Greeley, CO	1254	1695	1760	1662	1302	1101	604	625
Green Bay, WI	2250	1176	1016	918	1938	1051	531	499
Greensboro, NC	2844	351	708	520	2806	932	1298	1382
Greenville, SC	2667	262	879	690	2746	743	1181	1266
Halifax, NS	3760	1682	832	940	3698	2278	2141	2205
Hamilton, OH	2405	707	702	580	2367	865	786	871
Harrisburg, PA	2792	713	308	120	2730	1248	1173	1237
Hartford, CT	3025	934	123	192	2962	1532	1406	1470
High Point, NC	2834	333	721	532	2796	914	1287	1372
Houston, TX	1982	982	1770	1581	2444	242	999	1084
Huntington, WV	2532	574	720	532	2518	894	986	1070
Huntsville, AL	2354	442	1058	870	2522	549	956	1041
Indianapolis, IN	2294	776	768	647	2253	793	676	760
Iowa City, IA	1932	1070	1008	909	1878	805	312	397
Jackson, MS	2180	594	1338	1150	2574	215	1008	1092
Jacksonville, FL	2777	138	1112	956	3000	811	1434	1520
Janesville, WI	2131	1082	914	816	1962	877	408	470
Jefferson City, MO	1984	940	1137	1016	2003	552	437	522
Jersey City, NJ	2924	815	178	121	2861	1412	1304	1369
Joliet, IL	2123	970	811	712	2087	814	504	589
Kalamazoo, MI	2280	986	716	616	2218	974	660	724
Kansas City, MO	1826	1056	1254	1132	1842	546	276	362
Kenosha, WI	2186	1034	875	776	2031	926	474	538
Kingston, ON	2808	1099	236	268	2745	1490	1188	1252
Knoxville, TN	2560	420	846	658	2580	707	1014	1099
Lafayette, LA	2170	769	1556	1368	2592	211	1037	1122
Lake Charles, LA	2123	838	1625	1436	2538	229	1024	1109
Lancaster, PA	2826	712	292	132	2764	1285	1208	1272
Lansing, MI	2350	939	687	588	2288	1045	732	796
Laredo, TX	1835	1334	2121	1932	2410	565	1180	1264
Las Vegas, NV	616	2275	2535	2436	1128	1473	1379	1400
Lawrence, KS	1841	1096	1293	1172	1866	574	300	385
Lawrence, MA	3128	1044	195	304	3066	1642	1509	1573
Lawton, OK	1631	1173	1595	1474	1960	377	640	725
Lexington, KY	2408	591	794	655	2428	768	862	947
Lincoln, NE	1634	1257	1308	1209	1682	748	151	236
Little Rock, AR	2012	763	1373	1184	2288	212	666	751
London, ON	2540	994	421	428	2478	1225	922	986
Long Beach, CA	450	2433	2814	2716	1158	1630	1658	1679
Longview, TX	1908	870	1615	1426	2330	62	796	880
Lorain, OH	2452	792	488	394	2390	1070	833	897
Los Angeles, CA	427	2422	2804	2705	1136	1626	1648	1668
Louisville, KY	2338	663	809	688	2357	732	791	876
Lowell, MA	3120	1036	187	296	3058	1634	1501	1565
Lubbock, TX	1456	1342	1890	1768	1866	533	861	904
Lynchburg, VA	2812	462	609	420	2792	1018	1266	1351
Macon, GA	2603	165	1074	886	2736	644	1170	1256
Madison, WI	2110	1120	953	854	1929	916	401	436
Manchester, NH	3146	1063	213	322	3084	1660	1527	1592
Mansfield, OH	2450	758	532	411	2388	1011	831	895
Marquette, MI	2298	1313	1061	962	1928	1224	698	666
Memphis, TN	2142	628	1237	1049	2365	347	799	884
Miami, FL	3092	490	1464	1309	3316	1126	1750	1834
Midland, TX	1534	1327	2020	1831	1984	518	988	1072
Milwaukee, WI	2188	1060	900	802	1994	935	480	502
Minneapolis, MN	2059	1382	1214	1115	1660	976	301	270
Mobile, AL	2373	538	1353	1164	2764	408	1198	1282
Modesto, CA	138	2642	2904	2806	828	1839	1748	1725
Monroe, LA	2063	711	1456	1267	2486	98	850	934
Montgomery, AL	2462	350	1186	997	2685	459	1119	1204
Montréal, QC	2983	1194	222	384	2920	1662	1364	1428
Muncie, IN	2337	793	709	598	2296	857	718	804
Nashua, NH	3131	1048	198	307	3069	1646	1512	1576
Nashville, TN	2353	500	1025	836	2404	558	838	923
Newark, NJ	2920	806	177	117	2858	1404	1301	1365
New Bedford, MA	3128	1027	219	314	3065	1624	1508	1572
New Britain, CT	3016	928	135	182	2954	1545	1397	1461
New Brunswick, NJ	2935	788	198	127	2873	1399	1316	1380
New Haven, CT	2996	896	162	188	2934	1493	1377	1441
New Orleans, LA	2299	658	1445	1257	2721	340	1191	1276
Newport News, VA	2976	492	538	432	2943	1170	1430	1450
New York, NY	2940	831	176	137	2878	1438	1321	1385
Niagara Falls, NY	2691	939	287	293	2628	1296	1072	1136
Norfolk, VA	2989	486	523	381	2956	1165	1443	1463
Norman, OK	1695	1101	1528	1407	2018	373	573	658
North Platte, NE	1408	1477	1529	1430	1456	951	373	408
Oakland, CA	55	2713	2910	2811	800	1911	1754	1730
Oceanside, CA	511	2387	2844	2744	1220	1578	1687	1708
Odessa, TX	1513	1348	2042	1853	1884	540	1009	1094
Ogden, UT	787	2124	2177	2078	804	1582	1021	998
Oklahoma City, OK	1676	1092	1509	1388	1999	388	554	638
Omaha, NE	1685	1244	1254	1156	1663	735	97	182
Orlando, FL	2870	280	1254	1099	3093	904	1528	1612
Owensboro, KY	2284	634	917	833	2304	666	738	823
Paterson, NJ	2910	830	168	108	2848	1411	1292	1356
Pendleton, OR	749	2648	2700	2602	283	2106	1492	1411
Pensacola, FL	2431	492	1348	1160	2821	465	1255	1340
Peoria, IL	2080	943	927	828	2027	724	461	546
Philadelphia, PA	2892	728	261	124	2830	1330	1273	1337
Phoenix, AZ	796	2097	2516	2395	1500	1256	1418	1462

	South Bend, IN	Spokane, WA	Springfield, IL	Springfield, MA	Springfield, MO	Springfield, OH	Stamford, CT	Stockton, CA	Syracuse, NY	Tacoma, WA	Tallahassee, FL
Ft. Wayne, IN	96	1954	300	767	588	142	686	2242	546	2247	906
Ft. Worth, TX	1020	1845	760	1724	447	1034	1620	1659	1552	2096	867
Fredericton, NB	1281	3150	1531	512	1817	1229	600	3438	733	3442	1744
Fresno, CA	2222	990	2056	3026	1744	2330	2951	123	2805	889	2396
Gainesville, FL	1014	2706	960	1156	964	893	1052	2665	1158	2997	148
Galveston, TX	1198	2254	934	1794	708	1201	1689	1939	1733	2506	730
Gary, IN	62	1826	206	867	515	280	792	2112	646	2116	935
Grand Island, NE	694	1314	530	1497	464	895	1423	1496	1277	1610	1346
Grand Rapids, MI	116	1968	349	851	658	315	776	2256	630	2260	1035
Great Falls, MT	1474	366	1494	2280	1418	1692	2205	1158	2059	657	2299
Greeley, CO	1052	1062	889	1856	799	1255	1782	1199	1636	1314	1665
Green Bay, WI	308	1658	399	1112	708	524	1038	2196	892	1949	1179
Greensboro, NC	654	2526	768	688	933	430	584	2719	652	2818	578
Greenville, SC	662	2468	722	883	816	513	778	2571	822	2758	413
Halifax, NS	1548	3418	1798	738	2043	1454	826	3705	959	3710	1969
Hamilton, OH	250	2088	323	796	566	68	677	2350	577	2379	776
Harrisburg, PA	571	2450	757	312	1000	412	208	2737	252	2742	964
Hartford, CT	804	2684	1051	26	1294	706	79	2970	251	2974	1222
High Point, NC	642	2516	758	708	922	420	603	2708	664	2808	560
Houston, TX	1148	2206	886	1774	659	1152	1669	1890	1713	2456	710
Huntington, WV	401	2238	474	724	670	160	620	2477	628	2530	762
Huntsville, AL	551	2242	497	1062	496	488	958	2258	1002	2534	402
Indianapolis, IN	148	1974	212	862	455	131	748	2240	644	2265	779
Iowa City, IA	300	1598	225	1104	386	501	1029	1876	883	1890	1066
Jackson, MS	802	2294	594	1342	493	784	1238	2084	1282	2586	435
Jacksonville, FL	1030	2721	976	1086	979	835	982	2680	1090	3012	164
Janesville, WI	206	1684	225	1010	534	422	936	2076	790	1974	1076
Jefferson City, MO	458	1724	195	1231	136	500	1116	1928	1012	2015	936
Jersey City, NJ	703	2582	922	150	1165	576	45	2868	247	2873	1102
Joliet, IL	104	1808	162	907	471	319	833	2068	687	2099	974
Kalamazoo, MI	86	1938	318	812	628	262	737	2225	590	2230	1004
Kansas City, MO	572	1564	309	1348	172	615	1232	1770	1128	1854	1052
Kenosha, WI	166	1752	251	971	560	383	896	2131	750	2042	1038
Kingston, ON	596	2466	846	332	1129	570	398	2752	137	2757	1350
Knoxville, TN	496	2300	555	850	649	347	746	2435	790	2592	490
Lafayette, LA	1028	2354	820	1560	631	1010	1456	2074	1500	2604	497
Lake Charles, LA	1096	2300	889	1629	642	1078	1525	2032	1569	2550	565
Lancaster, PA	606	2484	792	299	1035	446	194	2772	262	2776	1000
Lansing, MI	154	2009	389	783	699	238	709	2296	563	2300	1030
Laredo, TX	1426	2172	1166	2125	854	1465	2021	1744	1956	2422	1061
Las Vegas, NV	1826	1142	1662	2631	1470	1968	2556	520	2410	1140	2123
Lawrence, KS	612	1587	350	1387	200	656	1273	1786	1168	1878	1018
Lawrence, MA	907	2786	1163	102	1406	818	189	3073	322	3078	1332
Lawton, OK	944	1720	684	1690	372	958	1575	1534	1471	1971	1027
Lexington, KY	328	2148	393	848	546	178	743	2354	670	2440	659
Lincoln, NE	600	1397	438	1404	372	801	1329	1579	1183	1694	1254
Little Rock, AR	710	2050	447	1377	215	714	1272	1916	1204	2300	670
London, ON	344	2198	579	518	864	305	558	2486	297	2490	1136
Long Beach, CA	2106	1238	1941	2910	1628	2215	2836	358	2690	1126	2267
Longview, TX	941	2092	678	1619	450	944	1514	1812	1434	2342	712
Lorain, OH	231	2110	490	584	761	168	514	2397	363	2402	980
Los Angeles, CA	2096	1216	1930	2900	1618	2204	2825	336	2679	1104	2262
Louisville, KY	258	2078	322	903	476	194	813	2282	684	2369	669
Lowell, MA	899	2778	1155	93	1398	810	181	3065	314	3069	1324
Lubbock, TX	1238	1628	979	1984	666	1252	1870	1360	1765	1878	1183
Lynchburg, VA	640	2512	755	548	961	416	444	2746	553	2804	689
Macon, GA	766	2457	712	1055	745	645	950	2506	1018	2748	196
Madison, WI	244	1650	263	1049	572	460	974	2055	828	1941	1114
Manchester, NH	926	2804	1182	120	1425	836	208	3092	341	3096	1351
Mansfield, OH	244	2108	455	626	698	109	531	2395	407	2400	922
Marquette, MI	482	1648	572	1157	882	612	1082	2244	936	1940	1353
Memphis, TN	592	2086	386	1242	284	578	1137	2046	1069	2376	535
Miami, FL	1345	3036	1291	1439	1294	1188	1334	2996	1442	3328	479
Midland, TX	1292	1745	1032	2024	719	1306	1920	1443	1852	1996	1168
Milwaukee, WI	192	1714	283	996	592	408	922	2134	776	2006	1063
Minneapolis, MN	506	1380	524	1310	601	722	1235	2004	1089	1672	1376
Mobile, AL	878	2484	784	1357	683	816	1253	2277	1297	2776	242
Modesto, CA	2196	898	2034	3000	1837	2398	2926	31	2780	796	2489
Monroe, LA	848	2246	640	1460	398	898	1355	1967	1399	2497	552
Montgomery, AL	712	2406	658	1190	605	648	1085	2366	1129	2697	213
Montréal, QC	772	2642	1022	302	1305	760	374	2928	253	2932	1482
Muncie, IN	152	2016	254	814	519	102	719	2282	584	2308	837
Nashua, NH	910	2790	1166	105	1410	821	192	3076	326	3080	1336
Nashville, TN	433	2124	379	1029	473	370	924	2256	860	2416	493
Newark, NJ	699	2578	913	154	1156	568	49	2865	244	2869	1094
New Bedford, MA	907	2786	1134	126	1377	788	171	3072	346	3077	1314
New Britain, CT	795	2674	1042	38	1285	696	73	2961	262	2966	1216
New Brunswick, NJ	715	2594	909	178	1152	564	74	2880	254	2885	1076
New Haven, CT	775	2654	1002	64	1246	657	40	2942	289	2946	1184
New Orleans, LA	964	2482	777	1449	676	900	1345	2203	1389	2732	386
Newport News, VA	785	2664	919	513	1115	581	408	2922	564	2955	779
New York, NY	719	2598	947	138	1190	602	33	2886	264	2890	1118
Niagara Falls, NY	470	2349	730	383	982	394	423	2636	162	2640	1166
Norfolk, VA	797	2676	931	497	1127	593	393	2934	510	2968	774
Norman, OK	876	1780	618	1622	305	891	1508	1598	1404	2030	1008
North Platte, NE	822	1172	658	1625	592	1023	1551	1354	1405	1468	1474
Oakland, CA	2202	869	2039	3006	1908	2404	2932	74	2786	768	2561
Oceanside, CA	2136	1450	1970	2940	1658	2244	2865	420	2719	1188	2215
Odessa, TX	1314	1766	1054	2046	741	1328	1941	1422	1873	1896	1190
Ogden, UT	1468	686	1306	2273	1240	1670	2198	732	2052	816	2121
Oklahoma City, OK	858	1760	598	1603	285	872	1489	1580	1385	2010	999
Omaha, NE	546	1384	425	1350	360	748	1276	1630	1130	1675	1241
Orlando, FL	1123	2814	1069	1229	1072	1002	1124	2773	1232	3105	257
Owensboro, KY	357	2024	280	1025	422	302	921	2230	792	2316	628
Paterson, NJ	690	2568	921	150	1164	575	45	2856	234	2860	1118
Pendleton, OR	1993	205	1830	2796	1764	2194	2722	772	2576	295	2646
Pensacola, FL	874	2542	842	1352	741	811	1248	2334	1292	2833	196
Peoria, IL	220	1748	71	1024	381	348	949	2026	803	2039	937
Philadelphia, PA	671	2550	858	236	1100	512	131	2837	254	2842	1016
Phoenix, AZ	1865	1382	1605	2610	1292	1879	2496	705	2392	1511	1892

Rand McNally software packages offer more than standard mileages:

- **Truck-type, hazmat, and lowest-cost routing**
- **HHG tariff mileage**
- **Fuel network management**

Visit trucking.randmcnally.com to learn more about what Rand McNally trucking applications can do for your bottom line.

Mileages in this Mileage Directory are from the Rand McNally *MileMaker Practical Routing System,* © Rand McNally. **These mileages are for general reference only and should not be used for the purposes of tariff computation.** For tariff purposes, refer to the applicable official tariff. Mileages between each of the 300 cities listed in this chart are computed over National Interstate, U.S. and primary state highways, and Canadian provincial highways via highways designated as truck-usable by the Household Goods Carriers' Bureau Committee. Practical routing may have highway segments not included in the federally designated National Network.

	Terre Haute, IN	Toledo, OH	Topeka, KS	Toronto, ON	Torrington, CT	Trenton, NJ	Troy, NY	Tucson, AZ	Tulsa, OK	Tupelo, MS	Tuscaloosa, AL	Tyler, TX	Utica, NY	Vallejo, CA	Vancouver, BC	Ventura, CA
Ft. Wayne, IN	210	112	680	402	745	641	691	1821	770	631	660	990	596	2251	2370	2227
Ft. Worth, TX	829	1130	496	1421	1711	1537	1715	922	303	587	617	130	1601	1712	2220	1475
Fredericton, NB	1438	1127	1908	847	574	704	595	3050	1998	1706	1659	2151	683	3448	3360	3424
Fresno, CA	2126	2370	1682	2649	3010	2862	2949	702	1562	2026	2156	1658	2854	188	1064	228
Gainesville, FL	840	1014	1203	1214	1124	956	1174	1922	1083	580	462	894	1210	2718	3122	2475
Galveston, TX	999	1322	792	1614	1780	1607	1785	1118	555	654	636	248	1786	1987	2630	1671
Gary, IN	164	212	578	490	851	748	790	1748	696	591	688	924	695	2123	2242	2098
Grand Island, NE	705	842	262	1121	1482	1379	1421	1165	450	916	1046	736	1326	1506	1734	1482
Grand Rapids, MI	305	188	721	362	836	732	775	1891	839	734	788	1068	680	2266	2384	2242
Great Falls, MT	1570	1625	1227	1904	2264	2161	2204	1350	1456	1869	1999	1742	2108	1168	782	1325
Greeley, CO	1051	1201	575	1480	1841	1738	1780	1013	728	1235	1365	1013	1685	1210	1438	1140
Green Bay, WI	390	457	691	736	1097	994	1036	1821	889	798	932	1114	941	2206	2074	2182
Greensboro, NC	632	548	1082	740	656	488	708	2072	1078	616	538	1031	704	2800	2942	2532
Greenville, SC	596	634	965	854	870	679	874	1883	929	426	349	841	875	2624	2884	2384
Halifax, NS	1664	1395	2134	1114	800	930	821	3275	2224	1932	1884	2377	909	3715	3627	3691
Hamilton, OH	187	189	657	480	760	592	722	1799	747	527	555	928	626	2361	2504	2244
Harrisburg, PA	621	426	1092	388	299	129	304	2336	1182	901	854	1346	304	2748	2866	2678
Hartford, CT	915	659	1385	491	51	183	113	2526	1475	1184	1138	1630	200	2981	3100	2956
High Point, NC	622	537	1071	730	675	507	716	2054	1067	598	520	1013	717	2789	2932	2521
Houston, TX	950	1273	743	1565	1760	1587	1765	1070	506	634	616	199	1766	1938	2582	1623
Huntington, WV	338	278	770	588	710	537	716	1952	850	556	584	956	678	2488	2654	2348
Huntsville, AL	378	609	740	900	1049	875	1053	1618	616	150	155	647	1054	2311	2658	2070
Indianapolis, IN	76	227	547	518	826	663	788	1688	636	504	532	856	693	2250	2390	2134
Iowa City, IA	332	448	372	727	1088	985	1028	1502	577	636	766	842	932	1887	2015	1863
Jackson, MS	603	904	717	1196	1329	1155	1334	1355	534	195	185	313	1334	2137	2710	1908
Jacksonville, FL	856	953	1218	1145	1054	886	1106	1938	1099	596	478	910	1142	2734	3137	2491
Janesville, WI	301	355	571	634	995	892	934	1702	715	708	829	940	839	2086	2100	2062
Jefferson City, MO	295	596	221	887	1195	1031	1156	1369	317	506	636	582	1061	1939	2140	1840
Jersey City, NJ	786	558	1256	492	118	63	172	2501	1346	1065	1018	1510	256	2879	2998	2855
Joliet, IL	184	252	534	531	892	788	831	1704	652	568	727	877	736	2079	2224	2054
Kalamazoo, MI	274	152	690	379	796	692	735	1860	808	704	757	1037	640	2235	2354	2210
Kansas City, MO	412	713	66	1000	1312	1148	1272	1190	276	622	752	541	1178	1781	1980	1685
Kenosha, WI	248	316	626	595	956	852	895	1793	742	656	791	990	800	2142	2168	2118
Kingston, ON	750	442	1218	162	336	403	256	2362	1310	1152	1180	1553	157	2763	2844	2739
Knoxville, TN	430	468	798	760	837	663	842	1796	794	360	313	805	842	2516	2716	2248
Lafayette, LA	829	1130	778	1422	1547	1374	1552	1285	551	421	403	303	1552	2127	2728	1838
Lake Charles, LA	898	1200	753	1490	1616	1442	1620	1211	526	490	471	239	1621	2080	2676	1764
Lancaster, PA	656	460	1126	429	274	98	285	2374	1216	938	891	1383	314	2782	2901	2714
Lansing, MI	334	120	762	304	768	664	707	1931	880	755	783	1108	612	2306	2425	2282
Laredo, TX	1236	1537	924	1828	2112	1938	2116	924	701	992	967	469	2005	1792	2546	1476
Las Vegas, NV	1763	1976	1288	2255	2616	2499	2555	466	1290	1752	1882	1385	2460	573	1266	333
Lawrence, KS	451	752	27	1041	1351	1187	1312	1155	219	588	718	517	1217	1797	2003	1646
Lawrence, MA	1027	762	1498	563	163	293	184	2639	1587	1295	1248	1740	272	3084	3202	3059
Lawton, OK	754	1055	384	1345	1654	1490	1615	902	191	650	780	289	1520	1588	2096	1348
Lexington, KY	258	300	646	592	834	660	839	1828	728	430	458	832	718	2364	2565	2224
Lincoln, NE	612	748	170	1027	1388	1285	1327	1217	452	824	954	738	1232	1590	1818	1566
Little Rock, AR	512	835	439	1126	1364	1190	1368	1271	274	240	370	275	1254	1969	2426	1728
London, ON	485	178	952	129	521	563	441	2096	1045	887	915	1288	346	2496	2823	2472
Long Beach, CA	2010	2256	1568	2534	2895	2747	2834	490	1448	1910	2030	1542	2739	407	1301	86
Longview, TX	742	1065	525	1356	1606	1432	1610	1083	298	470	461	41	1484	1865	2466	1636
Lorain, OH	382	86	852	323	573	470	508	1993	942	732	760	1132	412	2408	2526	2383
Los Angeles, CA	2000	2244	1556	2524	2884	2736	2824	485	1437	1900	2030	1538	2728	384	1278	68
Louisville, KY	186	315	575	606	867	730	829	1708	656	394	422	795	734	2293	2494	2154
Lowell, MA	1019	754	1489	555	155	285	176	2630	1579	1287	1240	1732	264	3075	3194	3051
Lubbock, TX	1048	1349	678	1640	1948	1784	1910	740	485	903	933	446	1814	1414	2004	1173
Lynchburg, VA	619	534	1050	614	516	348	604	2107	1105	671	624	1116	605	2768	2929	2560
Macon, GA	592	766	954	1050	1022	855	1070	1784	865	362	284	742	1070	2560	2873	2320
Madison, WI	339	394	550	672	1033	930	972	1680	754	746	867	978	877	2066	2066	2041
Manchester, NH	1046	780	1516	582	182	312	144	2657	1606	1314	1266	1758	290	3102	3220	3078
Mansfield, OH	319	99	789	367	590	487	552	1930	879	673	701	1074	456	2406	2524	2376
Marquette, MI	563	494	861	593	1142	1038	1081	1991	1063	971	1106	1288	986	2254	2065	2352
Memphis, TN	394	700	508	991	1228	1054	1233	1406	404	105	235	410	1118	2099	2502	1859
Miami, FL	1172	1305	1534	1498	1406	1239	1458	2253	1414	911	793	1225	1494	3049	3452	2806
Midland, TX	1101	1402	732	1693	2011	1837	2015	622	538	887	918	430	1900	1491	2120	1176
Milwaukee, WI	274	341	629	620	981	878	920	1759	773	682	816	998	825	2144	2130	2120
Minneapolis, MN	600	655	499	934	1294	1191	1234	1630	705	934	1064	970	1138	2015	1797	1990
Mobile, AL	706	937	907	1228	1344	1154	1348	1534	727	278	204	506	1349	2330	2900	2088
Modesto, CA	2208	2346	1784	2624	2986	2882	2924	796	1656	2119	2249	1752	2829	95	971	322
Monroe, LA	649	1018	622	1310	1446	1272	1451	1238	451	312	302	196	1452	2020	2622	1791
Montgomery, AL	538	769	828	1061	1176	986	1181	1599	724	222	104	557	1182	2419	2822	2179
Montréal, QC	926	618	1394	338	306	442	216	2537	1486	1324	1356	1724	274	2938	2850	2914
Muncie, IN	140	173	610	465	778	634	729	1751	700	562	590	920	634	2292	2433	2197
Nashua, NH	1031	765	1501	566	166	296	188	2642	1591	1298	1252	1744	275	3087	3206	3062
Nashville, TN	260	491	622	782	1016	842	1020	1617	615	220	246	621	910	2340	2540	2070
Newark, NJ	778	554	1248	489	121	55	170	2492	1338	1057	1010	1502	254	2876	2994	2851
New Bedford, MA	998	761	1468	587	174	275	208	2713	1558	1277	1230	1722	296	3083	3202	3059
New Britain, CT	906	650	1376	503	42	177	124	2517	1466	1198	1151	1643	212	2972	3090	2947
New Brunswick, NJ	773	569	1243	499	146	26	191	2488	1333	1052	1005	1498	275	2890	3010	2830
New Haven, CT	867	630	1337	530	57	144	151	2582	1427	1146	1099	1591	239	2952	3070	2928
New Orleans, LA	786	1021	900	1313	1436	1262	1440	1414	680	342	292	432	1442	2256	2858	1967
Newport News, VA	783	639	1214	656	480	316	532	2310	1308	854	776	1268	616	2932	3080	2762
New York, NY	811	574	1282	509	105	79	170	2526	1372	1091	1044	1536	253	2896	3014	2871
Niagara Falls, NY	603	324	1074	90	386	429	306	2214	1164	958	986	1358	212	2646	2766	2622
Norfolk, VA	795	652	1227	669	465	300	516	2305	1320	849	771	1263	563	2944	3092	2774
Norman, OK	687	988	317	1278	1587	1423	1548	966	124	578	708	286	1453	1652	2156	1412
North Platte, NE	833	970	390	1249	1610	1507	1549	1208	578	1043	1174	864	1454	1364	1594	1340
Oakland, CA	2214	2351	1790	2630	2990	2888	2930	857	1728	2190	2321	1823	2834	22	942	359
Oceanside, CA	2040	2284	1596	2563	2924	2776	2863	438	1476	1940	1978	1491	2768	468	1362	151
Odessa, TX	1123	1424	753	1714	2032	1859	2037	602	560	909	939	452	1922	1470	2021	1154
Ogden, UT	1480	1618	1057	1897	2258	2154	2197	814	1210	1691	1821	1495	2102	743	942	790
Oklahoma City, OK	668	968	298	1259	1567	1404	1529	947	104	569	699	301	1434	1633	2136	1393
Omaha, NE	600	695	160	974	1335	1232	1274	1268	381	811	941	703	1179	1640	1800	1616
Orlando, FL	949	1095	1312	1288	1196	1029	1248	2031	1192	689	571	1002	1284	2826	3230	2584
Owensboro, KY	148	423	522	714	1012	838	936	1655	604	352	380	729	841	2240	2441	2101
Paterson, NJ	785	544	1255	480	118	79	161	2500	1345	1064	1017	1509	245	2866	2985	2842
Pendleton, OR	2004	2142	1580	2420	2782	2678	2720	1334	1734	2214	2345	2018	2626	705	420	1042
Pensacola, FL	701	932	964	1224	1339	1149	1344	1592	784	334	242	564	1344	2388	2958	2145
Peoria, IL	178	368	416	647	1008	879	947	1613	562	555	685	787	852	2036	2164	2012
Philadelphia, PA	722	526	1192	499	204	32	255	2419	1282	984	936	1428	306	2848	2966	2778
Phoenix, AZ	1674	1976	1196	2266	2574	2410	2536	116	1111	1574	1655	1168	2440	753	1636	437

	Victoria, TX	Virginia Beach, VA	Waco, TX	Walnut Creek, CA	Warren, OH	Washington, DC	Waterbury, CT	Waterloo, IA	Waukegan, IL	Wausau, WI	West Palm Beach, FL	Wheeling, WV	Wichita, KS	Wichita Falls, TX	Wilmington, DE	Winnipeg, MB	Winston-Salem, NC	Worcester, MA	Yakima, WA	Youngstown, OH
Ft. Wayne, IN	1278	744	1102	2264	258	570	724	447	216	450	1264	282	806	1012	614	1034	540	814	2155	265
Ft. Worth, TX	310	1402	89	1690	1252	1364	1690	871	984	1164	1281	1206	356	114	1469	1294	1133	1758	1942	1255
Fredericton, NB	2393	996	2285	3461	1026	867	554	1644	1411	1482	1870	1052	2036	2241	764	1930	1218	462	3352	1020
Fresno, CA	1688	2852	1625	166	2516	2802	2990	1938	2169	2231	2810	2501	1505	1422	2835	2000	2571	3072	823	2530
Gainesville, FL	980	702	1022	2696	963	776	1103	1230	1106	1338	273	896	1256	1119	896	1922	529	1190	2872	962
Galveston, TX	166	1405	234	1965	1392	1434	1760	1113	1181	1327	1144	1345	652	424	1538	1590	1134	1828	2352	1394
Gary, IN	1213	868	1028	2136	357	676	831	319	68	320	1294	436	713	938	721	904	677	914	2026	372
Grand Island, NE	943	1470	722	1518	988	1307	1462	410	641	702	1701	1065	277	575	1351	687	1264	1544	1456	1002
Grand Rapids, MI	1357	852	1171	2279	342	661	815	462	229	463	1394	421	856	1082	705	1047	700	898	2170	356
Great Falls, MT	1812	2281	1615	1181	1770	2090	2244	1190	1356	1155	2654	1849	1283	1412	2134	810	2089	2327	566	1785
Greeley, CO	1085	1816	886	1222	1347	1666	1820	769	1000	1061	2046	1426	555	684	1710	1064	1610	1903	1160	1361
Green Bay, WI	1442	1114	1221	2219	603	922	1076	326	168	96	1538	682	826	1132	966	736	921	1159	1859	617
Greensboro, NC	1256	254	1159	2750	489	310	636	1003	787	1021	765	422	1209	1274	429	1605	29	723	2750	488
Greenville, SC	1066	445	969	2602	603	500	849	966	759	993	675	536	1102	1066	620	1577	175	917	2634	602
Halifax, NS	2619	1221	2511	3728	1252	1092	779	1912	1678	1750	2095	1278	2261	2466	990	2198	1444	687	3619	1246
Hamilton, OH	1216	644	1067	2374	277	520	740	557	348	582	1102	231	784	989	565	1166	438	832	2288	280
Harrisburg, PA	1588	341	1480	2760	285	124	279	944	710	944	1126	242	1219	1424	102	1528	430	347	2651	265
Hartford, CT	1872	474	1764	2994	503	346	30	1177	944	1178	1348	529	1512	1717	243	1762	696	62	2884	497
High Point, NC	1238	273	1141	2740	478	328	654	992	776	1010	747	412	1198	1263	447	1594	18	742	2740	478
Houston, TX	124	1385	186	1916	1343	1414	1740	1064	1133	1278	1124	1296	603	376	1518	1542	1114	1808	2304	1346
Huntington, WV	1245	472	1096	2500	294	422	690	708	498	734	988	228	896	1094	486	1316	267	758	2438	300
Huntsville, AL	889	752	762	2289	678	702	1029	768	642	875	793	632	789	812	807	1459	471	1096	2409	682
Indianapolis, IN	1145	734	968	2263	344	591	806	447	234	468	1138	301	674	879	635	1052	528	898	2174	347
Iowa City, IA	1129	1101	909	1900	594	914	1068	83	247	324	1421	672	506	801	958	761	895	1150	1800	609
Jackson, MS	563	970	441	2116	974	982	1309	819	786	986	849	928	707	538	1087	1550	699	1376	2408	977
Jacksonville, FL	995	633	1038	2712	894	708	1034	1246	1122	1354	286	827	1272	1135	827	1938	460	1122	2888	893
Janesville, WI	1268	1012	1047	2100	501	820	975	191	92	178	1434	580	706	958	865	762	819	1057	1884	516
Jefferson City, MO	870	1060	649	1952	712	960	1174	328	422	591	1291	670	325	560	1004	980	854	1267	1890	715
Jersey City, NJ	1752	355	1644	2892	402	226	97	1076	842	1076	1228	406	1383	1588	124	1660	577	184	2782	395
Joliet, IL	1205	908	984	2092	398	717	872	275	74	302	1332	477	669	895	761	886	716	954	2008	412
Kalamazoo, MI	1326	812	1140	2248	302	621	776	432	198	432	1363	381	826	1051	666	1016	644	858	2138	316
Kansas City, MO	827	1176	608	1794	828	1074	1290	318	550	610	1406	787	195	490	1121	820	970	1384	1730	832
Kenosha, WI	1294	972	1074	2154	462	781	935	258	27	224	1396	541	761	984	825	830	780	1018	1952	476
Kingston, ON	1842	650	1642	2776	445	510	388	960	726	960	1512	531	1353	1552	408	1414	816	379	2666	453
Knoxville, TN	1047	540	939	2467	538	490	817	800	593	827	817	486	925	990	595	1411	259	884	2468	541
Lafayette, LA	342	1172	401	2105	1200	1200	1527	1046	1012	1213	911	1154	751	528	1305	1580	901	1595	2451	1204
Lake Charles, LA	268	1240	327	2058	1268	1268	1596	1114	1080	1281	980	1222	697	482	1374	1566	970	1663	2398	1272
Lancaster, PA	1625	340	1518	2795	320	124	254	978	746	980	1126	276	1254	1458	59	1564	468	334	2686	300
Lansing, MI	1397	784	1212	2319	274	593	748	503	269	503	1353	353	896	1122	637	1087	632	830	2210	288
Laredo, TX	186	1736	338	1770	1656	1765	2092	1259	1390	1552	1476	1610	784	541	1870	1722	1466	2159	2269	1659
Las Vegas, NV	1452	2528	1352	551	2122	2428	2595	1544	1775	1836	2537	2138	1267	1149	2472	1719	2298	2678	988	2136
Lawrence, KS	822	1216	602	1810	868	1116	1331	359	590	652	1447	826	160	454	1160	843	1010	1423	1748	871
Lawrence, MA	1982	584	1874	3096	616	456	143	1280	1046	1281	1458	641	1625	1830	354	1704	807	51	2988	609
Lawton, OK	477	1477	256	1566	1171	1426	1633	759	908	1052	1441	1129	244	53	1532	1182	1196	1726	1818	1174
Lexington, KY	1120	596	971	2377	370	546	814	628	421	655	986	323	773	970	610	1239	390	882	2316	372
Lincoln, NE	945	1378	724	1602	894	1214	1368	316	547	609	1609	972	279	577	1258	694	1172	1450	1540	908
Little Rock, AR	564	1067	415	1947	904	1016	1343	672	694	839	1084	858	447	430	1122	1209	786	1411	2148	908
London, ON	1577	734	1377	2509	336	543	571	692	459	693	1408	422	1086	1287	568	1393	687	564	2400	345
Long Beach, CA	1476	2737	1458	385	2401	2687	2874	1823	2054	2116	2681	2386	1390	1307	2720	1998	2456	2958	1060	2416
Longview, TX	332	1246	169	1843	1134	1258	1585	855	925	1070	1126	1088	489	266	1364	1338	976	1653	2190	1138
Lorain, OH	1421	590	1272	2420	79	398	553	604	370	604	1206	158	979	1184	443	1188	485	630	2311	94
Los Angeles, CA	1471	2726	1453	362	2390	2676	2864	1812	2044	2105	2676	2375	1379	1296	2709	1988	2445	2946	1038	2405
Louisville, KY	1084	666	934	2306	384	616	847	557	350	584	1028	338	702	899	680	1168	460	939	2244	388
Lowell, MA	1974	576	1866	3088	607	448	134	1272	1038	1272	1450	633	1616	1822	345	1714	798	42	2978	601
Lubbock, TX	505	1718	349	1392	1465	1679	1928	1054	1202	1346	1598	1423	538	208	1784	1342	1448	2020	1726	1468
Lynchburg, VA	1359	209	1251	2778	456	184	496	989	773	1007	876	348	1177	1302	288	1591	144	583	2720	437
Macon, GA	941	601	870	2538	798	676	1002	982	858	1090	523	732	1038	968	795	1674	364	1090	2624	798
Madison, WI	1306	1050	1086	2078	539	858	1013	185	129	144	1472	618	685	980	903	728	858	1096	1850	554
Manchester, NH	2001	603	1893	3114	634	474	161	1298	1065	1299	1477	660	1643	1848	372	1680	826	69	3006	628
Mansfield, OH	1363	607	1214	2418	108	416	570	602	368	602	1172	125	916	1121	460	1186	451	662	2309	111
Marquette, MI	1615	1158	1395	2267	648	967	1121	496	342	223	1710	727	996	1305	1011	631	1006	1204	1850	662
Memphis, TN	699	931	550	2077	769	882	1208	610	577	778	949	723	577	601	986	1341	650	1276	2252	772
Miami, FL	1310	985	1353	3027	1246	1060	1386	1562	1436	1670	68	1180	1587	1450	1179	2253	812	1474	3203	1246
Midland, TX	442	1702	334	1469	1552	1664	1990	1107	1256	1399	1582	1505	591	295	1769	1530	1432	2058	1842	1554
Milwaukee, WI	1326	998	1105	2157	487	806	961	263	52	187	1422	566	764	1016	850	793	805	1043	1916	501
Minneapolis, MN	1257	1311	1037	2028	800	1120	1274	220	386	185	1734	880	634	929	1164	459	1119	1357	1582	815
Mobile, AL	592	920	634	2308	1006	974	1324	1009	970	1176	656	960	900	732	1094	1740	649	1391	2600	1010
Modesto, CA	1782	2946	1718	73	2491	2810	2965	1914	2144	2206	2904	2568	1598	1516	2854	1907	2664	3048	730	2506
Monroe, LA	464	1087	324	1998	1088	1100	1426	866	832	1033	966	1042	644	421	1204	1392	816	1494	2344	1092
Montgomery, AL	756	752	686	2397	839	808	1156	931	803	1036	627	793	898	783	926	1620	482	1224	2572	842
Montréal, QC	2090	733	1818	2952	572	604	358	1135	902	973	1607	658	1529	1728	502	1420	932	330	2842	580
Muncie, IN	1208	705	1032	2306	295	562	758	489	277	511	1188	272	737	942	606	1095	499	850	2218	298
Nashua, NH	1986	588	1878	3100	619	460	146	1283	1050	1284	1462	644	1628	1833	357	1698	810	54	2990	612
Nashville, TN	910	719	761	2288	560	668	995	650	524	757	852	514	749	812	774	1341	438	1063	2291	564
Newark, NJ	1744	346	1636	2888	398	218	101	1072	838	1072	1220	398	1375	1580	115	1656	568	188	2779	392
New Bedford, MA	1964	567	1856	3096	606	438	153	1279	1046	1280	1440	618	1595	1800	336	1788	789	78	2986	599
New Britain, CT	1885	468	1777	2984	494	340	21	1168	934	1168	1342	520	1503	1708	237	1752	690	74	2875	488
New Brunswick, NJ	1740	327	1632	2904	414	198	126	1087	854	1088	1201	393	1370	1576	96	1672	550	213	2794	407
New Haven, CT	1833	435	1725	2964	474	308	37	1148	915	1149	1310	487	1464	1669	204	1733	658	99	2856	468
New Orleans, LA	471	1060	530	2234	1091	1090	1416	1002	969	1170	800	1044	880	657	1194	1733	790	1484	2580	1094
Newport News, VA	1494	36	1396	2945	498	182	460	1153	924	1158	905	455	1341	1504	256	1742	273	547	2884	479
New York, NY	1778	371	1670	2908	418	242	85	1092	859	1093	1244	432	1409	1614	140	1677	593	172	2800	412
Niagara Falls, NY	1647	604	1498	2659	206	412	436	842	610	844	1353	292	1200	1406	434	1364	632	430	2550	214
Norfolk, VA	1489	16	1391	2958	511	194	445	1166	936	1171	900	468	1354	1516	240	1754	268	532	2896	491
Norman, OK	493	1404	272	1630	1104	1354	1566	692	841	985	1422	1062	177	134	1460	1116	1124	1659	1878	1107
North Platte, NE	1071	1598	850	1377	1116	1435	1590	538	769	830	1829	1193	405	616	1479	829	1392	1672	1316	1130
Oakland, CA	1843	2978	1790	15	2496	2816	2970	1918	2150	2211	2975	2574	1770	1587	2860	1912	2736	3053	702	2511
Oceanside, CA	1424	2766	1406	446	2430	2716	2904	1852	2083	2144	2629	2414	1418	1336	2748	2028	2485	2986	1122	2444
Odessa, TX	466	1724	355	1448	1573	1686	2012	1128	1277	1421	1604	1527	613	317	1790	1552	1454	2080	1744	1576
Ogden, UT	1566	2246	1368	756	1764	2082	2237	1186	1416	1478	2476	1841	1036	1165	2127	1264	2040	2320	664	1778
Oklahoma City, OK	508	1396	287	1611	1085	1346	1547	673	822	965	1413	1043	158	140	1376	1096	1115	1639	1858	1088
Omaha, NE	962	1365	741	1654	841	1160	1314	263	494	555	1596	918	299	594	1204	640	1160	1397	1592	855
Orlando, FL	1089	775	1130	2805	1036	850	1176	1339	1214	1447	171	970	1365	1228	969	2031	602	1264	2980	1036
Owensboro, KY	1018	774	869	2253	492	724	992	550	374	622	986	446	649	846	788	1206	550	1060	2192	495
Paterson, NJ	1751	370	1643	2879	389	242	97	1062	829	1063	1244	405	1382	1587	139	1647	594	184	2770	382
Pendleton, OR	2090	2770	1892	718	2288	2606	2762	1710	1970	1769	3000	2364	1560	1689	2650	1350	2564	2844	142	2302
Pensacola, FL	649	915	692	2366	1002	970	1319	1067	966	1198	610	955	957	789	1089	1798	644	1386	2658	1005
Peoria, IL	1114	947	894	2048	514	808	988	232	184	344	1295	518	551	804	852	910	741	1070	1948	528
Philadelphia, PA	1670	271	1562	2860	389	140	183	1044	811	1045	1142	342	1319	1524	29	1629	490	270	2752	365
Phoenix, AZ	1102	2400	1083	731	2092	2351	2554	1572	1828	1864	2306	2050	1054	971	2384	2002	2120	2646	1358	2094

Mileage Directory, continued

	Abilene, TX	Akron, OH	Albany, GA	Albany, NY	Albert Lea, MN	Albuquerque, NM	Alexandria, LA	Alexandria, VA	Allentown, PA	Altoona, PA	Amarillo, TX	Anderson, IN	Ann Arbor, MI	Appleton, WI	Asheville, NC	Atlanta, GA	Atlantic City, NJ	Augusta, GA	Aurora, IL	Austin, TX	Bakersfield, CA	Baltimore, MD	Bangor, ME	Baton Rouge, LA	Bay City, MI	Bayonne, NJ	Beaumont, TX	Billings, MT	Binghamton, NY	Birmingham, AL	Bismarck, ND	Bloomington, IN	Boise, ID	Boston, MA	Boulder, CO	Bowling Green, KY	Bridgeport, CT	Brockton, MA	Brownsville, TX	Buffalo, NY	Butte, MT	Calgary, AB	Camden, NJ
Pine Bluff, AR	508	876	614	1377	764	920	238	1033	1163	1030	636	644	874	844	657	531	1217	691	662	523	1724	1067	1692	315	948	1245	414	1554	1261	386	1220	581	1831	1466	1028	428	1310	1473	804	1080	1776	2095	1168
Pittsburgh, PA	1413	107	851	456	866	1645	1160	256	284	96	1361	348	282	664	466	684	366	609	503	1428	2449	246	796	1146	379	366	1330	1714	340	748	1300	409	2142	570	1462	509	431	583	1708	219	1936	2093	315
Pittsfield, MA	1889	531	1208	35	1257	2104	1534	430	244	394	1820	795	674	1055	842	1041	334	966	894	1904	2870	375	363	1521	770	201	1704	2105	175	1123	1691	869	2533	137	1853	973	134	150	2144	326	2327	2484	286
Pomona, CA	1228	2343	2209	2795	1809	764	1713	2652	2671	2506	1048	2092	2218	2063	2276	2150	2753	2310	1958	1354	140	2686	3186	1791	2292	2770	1608	1216	2684	2004	1630	2028	872	2960	1014	2047	2822	2974	1606	2514	1084	1556	2702
Pontiac, MI	1338	217	939	669	689	1592	1170	562	580	402	1308	280	48	486	670	768	672	806	326	1376	2302	552	1060	1164	84	644	1348	1536	558	770	1122	370	1964	834	1284	516	696	848	1728	388	1758	1916	620
Port Arthur, TX	505	1281	658	1670	1084	979	164	1326	1456	1378	695	1071	1305	1213	917	706	1510	850	1087	259	1763	1360	1985	180	1375	1538	21	1762	1554	580	1501	969	2040	1759	1237	834	1603	1766	453	1486	1985	2304	1462
Portland, ME	2044	735	1341	263	1484	2319	1688	556	404	572	2035	1022	901	1283	996	1195	460	1097	1122	2058	3098	502	129	1675	998	329	1858	2333	402	1277	1919	1084	2761	110	2081	1169	253	135	2298	553	2555	2525	413
Portland, OR	1939	2471	2775	2923	1726	1386	2430	2816	2835	2658	1672	2292	2346	2017	2648	2603	2926	2756	2086	2198	858	2806	3316	2568	2421	2898	2417	893	2812	2552	1307	2264	428	3090	1248	2328	2950	3102	2460	2642	669	811	2876
Providence, RI	1910	610	1207	180	1369	2174	1555	423	270	446	1890	877	785	1167	862	1062	327	964	1006	1925	2982	368	291	1542	882	196	1725	2217	320	1144	1803	939	2645	50	1965	1036	119	44	2164	470	2439	2596	280
Provo, UT	1065	1784	2039	2236	1250	578	1526	2129	2148	1970	862	1604	1659	1504	1934	1889	2239	2042	1399	1284	663	2118	2628	1664	1734	2211	1509	594	2125	1811	1008	1550	382	2402	504	1613	2263	2415	1569	1955	461	934	2188
Pueblo, CO	591	1410	1489	1918	932	334	987	1706	1733	1568	324	1154	1341	1186	1475	1430	1815	1583	1081	849	1138	1695	2274	1125	1415	1815	970	672	1806	1260	810	1090	950	2048	145	1154	1880	2061	1112	1637	895	1214	1764
Québec, QC	2035	761	1547	372	1412	2290	1874	770	584	687	2006	963	761	1088	1181	1381	673	1306	1050	2074	3026	714	233	1861	783	540	2044	2260	484	1462	1847	1054	2689	400	2009	1202	488	424	2483	555	2483	2400	626
Racine, WI	1146	452	977	903	354	1400	996	797	815	638	1116	294	326	132	741	804	906	916	100	1185	2073	786	1295	991	401	878	1131	1202	792	750	788	316	1735	1070	1055	496	931	1082	1537	623	1425	1581	855
Raleigh, NC	1376	540	540	654	1223	1765	971	258	463	429	1480	628	680	1022	254	412	462	296	860	1334	2570	313	942	941	777	495	1124	2072	574	560	1658	666	2476	716	1724	590	560	723	1564	638	2294	2450	414
Rapid City, SD	1004	1282	1684	1734	515	851	1362	1627	1646	1468	718	1124	1157	806	1557	1512	1737	1665	903	1243	1362	1616	2126	1500	1232	1709	1350	323	1622	1460	339	1124	942	1900	389	1236	1761	1913	1595	1453	546	865	1686
Reading, PA	1624	362	943	246	1121	1886	1270	167	38	192	1602	588	538	920	576	776	124	701	758	1639	2690	111	566	1256	634	119	1440	1969	159	858	1556	650	2398	340	1708	750	184	347	1878	329	2192	2348	72
Regina, SK	1481	1553	2077	2005	871	1290	1809	1898	1916	1739	1253	1395	1428	1060	1842	1904	2008	2058	1174	1695	1728	1887	2070	1947	1502	1980	1842	473	1894	1850	352	1417	1092	2090	829	1598	2032	2184	2047	1724	653	468	1956
Reno, NV	1576	2265	2569	2717	1731	1088	2036	2610	2628	2452	1372	2086	2140	1985	2442	2396	2720	2550	1880	1781	406	2600	3109	2174	2214	2692	2019	957	2606	2345	1371	2058	423	2883	1042	2121	2744	2896	2033	2436	824	1296	2668
Richmond, VA	1457	444	684	499	1203	1832	1093	102	307	273	1548	616	619	1001	377	535	306	440	840	1472	2636	157	786	1064	716	340	1247	2051	418	683	1637	653	2444	560	1693	641	404	568	1686	482	2273	2430	258
Riverside, CA	1202	2332	2184	2784	1798	752	1687	2640	2660	2494	1036	2080	2206	2052	2265	2138	2742	2298	1946	1328	166	2675	3176	1766	2281	2758	1582	1205	2672	1993	1619	2016	862	2950	1003	2036	2811	2962	1580	2502	1072	1544	2690
Roanoke, VA	1281	390	600	587	1073	1656	926	243	373	296	1372	478	530	871	233	433	427	358	710	1296	2460	278	902	913	626	455	1096	1921	472	515	1507	516	2307	676	1556	482	520	683	1535	504	2143	2300	379
Rochester, MN	1045	716	1240	1168	62	1191	1064	1061	1080	902	1015	558	591	240	1005	1068	1171	1221	337	1102	1910	1050	1560	1104	666	1143	1124	894	1056	957	514	580	1513	1334	893	761	1195	1347	1454	887	1116	1307	1120
Rochester, NY	1626	281	1129	226	1006	1854	1375	404	290	276	1570	545	423	805	744	962	401	886	643	1641	2620	348	618	1370	520	335	1553	1854	159	976	1440	618	2282	392	1602	722	368	405	1921	75	2076	2233	349
Rockford, IL	1080	459	975	910	325	1270	964	804	822	646	1052	300	334	170	748	804	914	957	72	1120	1990	794	1302	958	408	886	1042	1175	800	748	761	324	1652	1076	972	492	938	1090	1472	630	1397	1554	862
Sacramento, CA	1566	2396	2548	2848	1862	1079	2027	2742	2760	2582	1363	2216	2272	2116	2573	2465	2852	2682	2012	1766	275	2731	3240	2165	2346	2824	2020	1088	2737	2320	1502	2188	554	3014	1172	2252	2876	3027	2017	2568	955	1428	2800
Saginaw, MI	1359	274	986	726	710	1614	1190	619	637	460	1330	300	86	508	718	815	728	865	347	1398	2323	608	1118	1185	15	700	1324	1558	614	818	1144	392	1986	892	1306	564	753	904	1750	445	1780	1937	677
St. Johnsbury, VT	2053	691	1350	200	1416	2264	1698	566	412	580	1980	955	833	1215	1005	1204	470	1106	1054	2068	3030	511	207	1685	930	338	1868	2265	334	1286	1851	1028	2693	172	2013	1133	262	196	2307	485	2487	2396	422
St. Joseph, MO	656	806	1033	1281	325	802	726	1102	1129	964	627	529	704	579	906	860	1211	1014	474	737	1647	1091	1670	864	779	1211	759	975	1170	809	739	521	1321	1444	641	585	1276	1457	1089	1001	1197	1516	1160
St. Louis, MO	786	544	728	1029	468	1040	668	878	867	702	756	288	509	456	600	556	949	708	275	824	1844	829	1408	664	583	949	747	1278	918	501	1042	224	1625	1182	874	280	1015	1195	1176	748	1501	1820	898
St. Paul, MN	1085	769	1293	1221	102	1231	1104	1114	1133	955	1055	611	644	277	1058	1121	1224	1274	390	1142	1950	1104	1613	1217	719	1196	1164	850	1110	1066	437	634	1469	1387	933	814	1248	1400	1494	940	1073	1230	1173
St. Petersburg, FL	1279	1081	330	1318	1504	1743	842	920	1125	1091	1459	1056	1211	1406	661	479	1124	481	1244	1131	2547	975	1604	703	1308	1158	886	2316	1236	564	2040	998	2662	1378	1910	798	1222	1386	1325	1264	2538	2856	1076
Salem, OR	1987	2519	2821	2971	1773	1434	2478	2864	2884	2706	1720	2340	2394	2063	2697	2650	2974	2805	2134	2246	814	2854	3364	2616	2470	2946	2466	942	2861	2600	1354	2312	476	3138	1296	2376	3000	3150	2508	2690	716	858	2924
Salinas, CA	1556	2570	2477	3022	2036	1007	1955	2895	2934	2756	1291	2336	2446	2290	2520	2393	3026	2553	2186	1683	203	2905	3414	2093	2520	2998	1937	1262	2911	2248	1676	2272	728	3188	1258	2291	3050	3202	1934	2742	1129	1602	2974
Salisbury, MD	1629	454	832	374	1214	2004	1261	126	185	284	1720	681	630	1012	545	703	181	588	850	1644	2808	116	662	1232	727	214	1415	2062	304	851	1648	743	2490	436	1801	796	280	442	1854	526	2284	2441	136
Salt Lake City, UT	1108	1747	2051	2199	1213	621	1704	2092	2110	1933	948	1567	1622	1467	1924	1878	2202	2032	1362	1327	706	2082	2591	1843	1696	2174	1692	553	2088	1826	967	1539	341	2365	523	1603	2226	2378	1612	1918	420	892	2150
San Angelo, TX	92	1446	1070	1948	1071	520	574	1603	1734	1600	318	1160	1381	1329	1228	1053	1787	1213	1148	208	1318	1638	2263	634	1455	1816	450	1287	1832	909	1219	1096	1564	2037	761	999	1881	2044	492	1651	1509	1828	1740
San Antonio, TX	261	1452	941	1953	1122	713	430	1609	1739	1606	510	1194	1414	1362	1200	989	1793	1133	1181	81	1468	1643	2268	463	1489	1821	280	1480	1837	864	1428	1130	1757	2042	954	1005	1886	2049	278	1657	1702	2021	1744
San Bernardino, CA	1203	2323	2185	2774	1789	743	1689	2631	2650	2485	1027	2071	2197	2042	2255	2129	2732	2289	1938	1330	167	2666	3166	1767	2272	2749	1584	1196	2663	1984	1610	2007	852	2940	994	2026	2802	2953	1582	2494	1063	1535	2681
San Diego, CA	1179	2399	2160	2880	1895	815	1664	2703	2722	2558	1099	2143	2304	2148	2328	2142	2804	2302	2044	1306	233	2738	3272	1742	2378	2804	1559	1302	2769	1999	1716	2080	958	3046	1100	2098	2870	3060	1556	2600	1169	1642	2753
San Francisco, CA	1636	2482	2557	2934	1948	1087	2035	2827	2846	2668	1371	2302	2357	2202	2600	2473	2937	2633	2098	1763	283	2816	3326	2173	2432	2909	2017	1174	2823	2328	1588	2274	640	3100	1258	2338	2962	3113	2014	2654	1041	1513	2886
San Jose, CA	1595	2510	2516	2962	1976	1046	1994	2855	2874	2696	1330	2330	2385	2230	2558	2432	2965	2592	2125	1722	242	2844	3354	2132	2460	2937	1976	1202	2851	2287	1616	2302	668	3128	1286	2330	2989	3141	1974	2681	1069	1541	2914
San Mateo, CA	1622	2502	2542	2953	1968	1073	2021	2846	2866	2688	1357	2322	2376	2222	2586	2459	2956	2619	2117	1749	269	2836	3346	2159	2451	2928	2003	1193	2842	2314	1608	2294	660	3120	1278	2358	2980	3132	2000	2673	1061	1533	2905
Santa Ana, CA	1242	2364	2224	2816	1830	784	1727	2672	2692	2526	1068	2112	2238	2084	2297	2170	2774	2330	1979	1368	144	2707	3208	1806	2313	2790	1622	1237	2704	2026	1651	2048	894	2982	1035	2068	2843	2994	1620	2535	1104	1576	2722
Santa Barbara, CA	1351	2457	2347	2908	1923	877	1836	2765	2784	2620	1161	2205	2331	2176	2390	2263	2866	2423	2072	1478	149	2800	3300	1914	2406	2883	1731	1330	2797	2118	1744	2142	898	3074	1128	2160	2936	3087	1729	2628	1197	1669	2815
Santa Rosa, CA	1683	2498	2603	2950	1964	1134	2082	2844	2862	2684	1418	2318	2374	2218	2675	2520	2953	2680	2114	1810	330	2833	3342	2220	2448	2926	2064	1190	2839	2375	1604	2290	656	3116	1274	2354	2978	3129	2061	2670	1057	1530	2902
Savannah, GA	1177	735	239	972	1273	1634	770	575	779	746	1350	790	875	1164	316	247	779	142	1002	1142	2438	630	1259	714	972	812	897	2084	891	395	1808	756	2430	1034	1678	566	877	1040	1336	918	2306	2625	731
Schenectady, NY	1869	480	1188	17	1206	2053	1515	412	226	374	1769	744	622	1004	822	1021	316	946	843	1884	2820	357	409	1501	719	182	1685	2054	130	1103	1640	818	2482	184	1802	922	180	196	2124	275	2276	2433	268
Scranton, PA	1681	348	1000	179	1107	1932	1326	256	75	185	1648	635	524	906	633	833	185	758	744	1696	2721	200	518	1313	621	122	1496	1955	59	914	1542	696	2383	292	1703	806	169	305	1935	281	2178	2334	134
Seattle, WA	2013	2436	2822	2888	1653	1460	2504	2781	2800	2622	1746	2278	2311	1944	2694	2650	2891	2802	2057	2272	1030	2770	3280	2642	2386	2863	2492	820	2776	2598	1234	2300	504	3054	1322	2374	2915	3067	2534	2607	596	678	2840
Shreveport, LA	368	1070	613	1541	881	832	123	1197	1327	1250	548	839	1068	1012	805	595	1381	755	831	325	1636	1232	1856	261	1142	1409	206	1610	1426	452	1338	775	1888	1630	1084	622	1474	1638	596	1274	1832	2152	1333
Sioux City, IA	843	880	1256	1331	209	956	949	1225	1243	1066	740	700	754	499	1128	1084	1334	1236	495	940	1663	1214	1723	1087	829	1306	982	748	1220	1032	512	696	1326	1497	646	808	1359	1510	1292	1051	970	1289	1283
Sioux Falls, SD	928	944	1341	1396	177	999	1034	1289	1307	1130	784	785	818	467	1214	1168	1398	1322	565	1025	1684	1278	1788	1172	893	1370	1067	668	1284	1116	431	781	1286	1562	667	893	1423	1574	1377	1115	890	1209	1347
South Bend, IN	1146	277	851	729	497	1402	978	623	641	464	1118	140	177	296	610	679	733	784	134	1186	2112	612	1122	972	251	705	1112	1346	618	624	932	198	1774	896	1094	370	757	908	1538	449	1568	1724	681
Spokane, WA	1775	2157	2542	2609	1374	1342	2265	2502	2520	2342	1508	1998	2032	1664	2415	2370	2612	2524	1778	2033	1100	2491	3000	2403	2106	2584	2253	540	2498	2318	954	2021	426	2774	1084	2094	2636	2788	2296	2328	316	458	2560
Springfield, IL	888	513	797	989	430	1142	771	809	837	672	858	236	412	360	670	625	919	778	179	927	1946	798	1378	766	486	919	849	1265	878	570	951	201	1611	1152	934	349	984	1165	1278	708	1487	1744	868
Springfield, MA	1874	563	1171	80	1302	2147	1519	386	234	400	1863	841	719	1100	826	1025	290	927	939	1888	2916	332	316	1506	816	159	1689	2150	220	1107	1736	912	2578	90	1898	999	83	103	2128	371	2372	2529	243
Springfield, MO	575	756	746	1242	506	830	542	1091	1080	915	545	501	721	669	764	662	1162	822	488	614	1634	1042	1621	574	796	1162	611	1199	1130	517	963	437	1546	1395	782	492	1227	1408	966	961	1421	1740	1110
Springfield, OH	1162	168	729	653	714	1416	960	464	491	326	1132	119	174	512	460	558	573	612	351	1226	2220	453	1032	954	270	573	1138	1562	542	561	1148	181	1976	806	1239	307	639	819	1506	372	1784	1941	522
Stamford, CT	1769	469	1066	152	1228	2033	1414	282	129	305	1749	736	644	1026	721	921	186	822	864	1784	2841	227	404	1401	741	55	1584	2076	190	1003	1662	798	2504	178	1824	894	22	184	2023	411	2298	2454	139
Stockton, CA	1524	2444	2507	2895	1910	1037	1985	2788	2808	2630	1321	2264	2318	2164	2550	2423	2898	2583	2059	1718	233	2778	3288	2124	2393	2870	1972	1135	2784	2278	1550	2236	602	3062	1220	2300	2922	3074	1970	2615	1003	1475	2847
Syracuse, NY	1701	356	1132	145	1081	1929	1458	388	204	276	1645	620	498	880	765	965	315	890	718	1716	2695	332	537	1445	595	249	1628	1930	73	1047	1516	693	2358	311	1678	798	282	324	2067	150	2152	2308	264
Tacoma, WA	2025	2448	2832	2900	1665	1472	2516	2793	2812	2634	1758	2290	2323	1956	2706	2662	2903	2814	2069	2284	999	2782	3292	2654	2398	2875	2504	832	2788	2610	1246	2312	514	3066	1334	2386	2927	3079	2546	2619	608	709	2852
Tallahassee, FL	1018	962	87	1260	1270	1482	581	863	1044	966	1198	819	1004	1167	475	272	1066	293	1006	870	2286	917	1547	442	1101	1100	625	2080	1142	303	1802	760	2426	1321	1649	560	1165	1328	1064	1146	2302	2622	1019
Tampa, FL	1288	1058	307	1294	1481	1752	852	897	1102	1068	1468	1034	1188	1382	638	456	1102	458	1220	1140	2557	952	1582	713	1285	1134	896	2292	1213	574	2016	976	2638	1356	1887	774	1200	1362	1335	1240	2514	2834	1053
Terre Haute, IN	957	377	677	863	536	1212	779	673	701	536	928	122	356	378	543	506	783	658	216	996	2016	662	1242	774	431	783	914	1387	752	450	1027	58	1786	1016	1034	218	848	1029	1304	582	1610	1820	732
Toledo, OH	1258	133	850	584	647	1513	1081	478	496	319	1229	185	55	445	582	679	587	730	284	1297	2260	467	976	1076	152	559	1259	1495	473	682	1081	277	1923	750	1243	428	612	763	1627	304	1717	1874	536
Topeka, KS	587	848	1040	1333	405	734	690	1143	1171	1006	558	592	784	659	912	868	1253	1020	554	684	1572	1133	1712	828	859	1253	790	1008	1222	741	772	528	1362	1486	559	592	1318	1499	1036	1052	1231	1550	1202
Toronto, ON	1549	316	1142	386	926	1803	1372	494	450	310	1519	476	274	724	779	970	560	922	563	1588	2539	474	622	1368	296	494	1550	1774	318	973	1360	568	2202	552	1522	720	528	564	1919	100	1996	2116	509
Torrington, CT	1860	528	1138	84	1287	2112	1506	354	208	364	1828	814	703	1085	812	1012	258	894	924	1875	2900	300	378	1492	800	127	1676	2135	223	1094	1721	876	2563	152	1883	986	50	165	2114	374	2357	2514	211
Trenton, NJ	1686	424	971	220	1183	1948	1332	186	76	254	1664	651	600	982	638	822	89	727	820	1702	2752	132	508	1318	697	60	1502	2032	195	920	1618	712	2460	282	1770	812	126	288	1941	417	2254	2410	39
Troy, NY	1865	500	1183	7	1226	2073	1510	405	220	369	1789	764	642	1024	817	1016	309	942	863	1880	2839	350	399	1497	739	176	1680	2074	144	1098	1660	838	2502	173	1822	942	170	186	2119	294	2296	2453	262
Tucson, AZ	771	1989	1753	2474	1535	498	1256	2286	2416	2147	689	1733	1954	1789	1910	1735	2470	1895	1720	898	597	2320	2853	1335	2028	2498	1152	1327	2363	1592	1642	1669	1116	2627	977	1681	2563	2726	1149	2194	1194	1666	2422
Tulsa, OK	394	937	865	1423	610	648	462	1284	1261	1096	364	682	902	850	908	782	1343	942	669	462	1453	1222	1802	600	977	1343	484	1237	1312	637	993	618	1515	1576	712	679	1408	1589	814	1142	1460	1779	1292
Tupelo, MS	737	732	362	1194	840	1112	371	850	980	903	828	543	756	843	474	279	1034	439	584	752	1916	885	1510	366	852	1062	549	1650	1078	134	1414	485	1996	1284	1219	284	1128	1290	988	936	1872	2191	986
Tuscaloosa, AL	767	760	260	1148	970	1242	361	803	933	856	958	572	784	920	411	201	987	361	759	725	2046	838	1462	348	881	1015	531	1780	1032	58	1544	513	2126	1236	1349	312	1080	1244	970	964	2002	2322	939
Tyler, TX	280	1133	711	1640	875	744	215	1295	1426	1287	460	902	1131	1075	903	693	1479	853	894	229	1548	1330	1954	353	1205	1508	189	1523	1524	550	1306	838	1800	1729	997	685	1572	1736	530	1337	1745	2064	1431
Utica, NY	1750	405	1184	94	1130	1978	1511	441	257	328	1694	669	547	929	818	1017	367	942	768	1765	2744	385	486	1498	644	260	1681	1979	126	1099	1565	742	2407	260	1727	847	258	274	2120	199	2201	2358	316
Vallejo, CA	1640	2454	2560	2906	1920	1090	2039	2799	2818	2640	1375	2274	2329	2174	2630	2476	2909	2636	2069	1766	286	2788	3298	2177	2404	2881	2020	1146	2795	2332	1560	2246	612	3072	1230	2310	2934	3085	2018	2625	1013	1485	2858
Vancouver, BC	2150	2573	2958	3025	1790	1596	2640	2918	2936	2759	1884	2414	2448	2080	2831	2786	3028	2940	2194	2408	1174	2907	3140	2778	2522	3000	2628	956	2914	2734	1370	2437	640	3190	1459	2510	3052	3204	2672	2744	732	602	2976
Ventura, CA	1324	2430	2320	2882	1896	850	1809	2738	2758	2593	1134	2179	2305	2150	2363	2236	2840	2396	2045	1451	122	2773	3274	1888	2379	2857	1704	1303	2770	2092	1717	2115	872	3048	1102	2134	2909	3060	1702	2601	1170	1642	2788
Victoria, TX	347	1421	870	1882	1163	828	358	1537	1667	1590	625	1190	1420	1403	1128	918	1721	1061	1222	127	1583	1572	2197	392	1494	1749	209	1594	1766	792	1468	1126	1872	1971	1069	974	1815	1978	232	1626	1817	2136	1673
Virginia Beach, VA	1552	544	717	512	1303	1938	1146	203	322	374	1654	722	720	1102	430	588	319	473	940	1510	2742	258	799	1116	817	352	1300	2151	442	736	1738	760	2551	573	1800	748	417	580	1739	582	2374	2530	274
Waco, TX	183	1272	839	1774	942	711	343	1429	1560	1426	427	1014	1234	1182	1054	822	1614	982	1001	99	1515	1464	2089	450	1309	1642	267	1396	1658	678	1247	950	1673	1863	870	825	1707	1870	451	1477	1618	1937	1566
Walnut Creek, CA	1618	2467	2538	2918	1933	1069	2017	2812	2830	2653	1353	2287	2342	2187	2581	2455	2922	2615	2082	1745	265	2802	3310	2155	2416	2894	1998	1158	2808	2310	1573	2259	625	3085	1243	2323	2946	3098	1996	2638	1026	1498	2870
Warren, OH	1401	40	912	465	793	1629	1150	336	340	177	1345	332	209	591	528	746	450	670	430	1416	2406	326	830	1146	306	404	1328	1641	354	752	1227	393	2069	604	1389	498	456	617	1697	185	1863	2020	399
Washington, DC	1514	352	792	383	1111	1888	1158	8	191	182	1604	579	528	910	466	643	190	548	749	1528	2692	41	670	1146	625	224	1328	1960	302	747	1546	641	2388	444	1699	698	288	452	1768	391	2182	2339	142
Waterbury, CT	1840	507	1118	137	1266	2091	1485	334	188	344	1807	794	683	1065	792	992	238	874	903	1855	2880	279	357	1472	780	106	1655	2114	203	1074	1700	856	2542	131	1862	966	30	144	2094	424	2336	2493	190
Waterloo, IA	962	651	1067	1102	126	1109	982	996	1014	837	933	471	525	294	913	896	1105	1048	266	1020	1828	985	1494	990	600	1077	1042	964	991	843	647	467	1491	1268	811	620	1130	1281	1371	822	1186	1440	1054
Waukegan, IL	1112	417	942	869	378	1366	962	762	780	603	1082	259	292	156	706	770	872	881	66	1150	2059	752	1261	957	366	844	1096	1226	758	716	813	282	1722	1035	1042	462	896	1048	1502	588	1449	1606	821
Wausau, WI	1255	651	1175	1103	272	1401	1163	996	1015	837	1226	493	526	102	940	1003	1106	1156	272	1312	2121	986	1495	1158	508	1078	1242	1026	992	948	612	516	1644	1269	1103	696	1130	1282	1664	822	1248	1404	1055
West Palm Beach, FL	1432	1149	450	1386	1624	1896	995	989	1193	1160	1612	1176	1288	1526	729	599	1192	549	1364	1284	2700	1043	1673	856	1385	1226	1039	2436	1304	717	2160	1118	2782	1447	2030	918	1291	1454	1478	1332	2658	2976	1145
Wheeling, WV	1355	102	846	516	872	1587	1104	293	321	156	1303	290	288	670	461	679	403	604	509	1370	2391	282	856	1099	385	403	1282	1720	400	705	1306	351	2146	630	1409	451	468	631	1650	270	1942	2099	352
Wichita, KS	447	975	1038	1460	540	591	662	1270	1298	1133	418	719	919	794	1040	955	1380	1115	689	544	1395	1260	1839	801	994	1380	650	1064	1349	810	802	655	1342	1613	538	719	1446	1626	896	1179	1286	1606	1329
Wichita Falls, TX	151	1180	936	1665	835	508	440	1480	1503	1338	224	924	1145	1092	1105	919	1585	1079	911	302	1312	1515	2044	578	1219	1585	423	1193	1554	776	1100	860	1470	1818	667	876	1651	1831	654	1384	1415	1734	1534
Wilmington, DE	1619	397	911	280	1156	1921	1264	126	80	227	1637	624	573	954	570	762	82	667	793	1634	2725	72	568	1250	670	121	1434	2004	200	852	1590	685	2432	342	1743	761	186	349	1872	422	2226	2383	32
Winnipeg, MB	1386	1235	1759	1687	553	1540	1491	1580	1598	1421	1222	1077	1110	743	1524	1587	1690	1740	856	1482	2004	1570	1709	1630	1106	1662	1524	748	1576	1532	414	1100	1367	1730	1106	1280	1714	1754	1834	1406	971	822	1639
Winston-Salem, NC	1282	428	480	724	1111	1657	876	337	510	432	1373	516	568	909	147	317	541	236	748	1239	2461	392	1022	846	664	574	1029	1959	608	466	1545	554	2345	796	1594	482	640	802	1468	611	2181	2338	493
Worcester, MA	1908	600	1205	127	1349	2183	1553	420	268	436	1899	886	766	1147	860	1060	325	961	986	1923	2962	366	265	1540	862	193	1723	2197	267	1141	1783	948	2625	43	1945	1033	117	56	2162	418	2419	2576	277
Yakima, WA	1872	2358	2708	2810	1575	1319	2362	2702	2721	2544	1606	2200	2232	1866	2582	2537	2812	2690	1978	2130	933	2692	3202	2500	2308	2784	2350	742	2698	2484	1156	2198	362	2976	1182	2262	2837	2988	2394	2528	518	659	2762
Youngstown, OH	1404	48	912	474	807	1632	1154	317	334	158	1348	335	224	605	527	745	427	670	444	1419	2421	306	824	1148	320	397	1332	1655	362	754	1241	396	2083	598	1403	501	449	611	1700	193	1877	2034	375

Mileages in this Mileage Directory are from the Rand McNally *MileMaker Practical Routing System*, © Rand McNally. **These mileages are for general reference only and should not be used for the purposes of tariff computation.** For tariff purposes, refer to the applicable official tariff. Mileages between each of the 300 cities listed in this chart are computed over National Interstate, U.S. and primary state highways, and Canadian provincial highways via highways designated as truck-usable by the Household Goods Carriers' Bureau Committee. Practical routing may have highway segments not included in the federally designated National Network.

	Casper, WY	Cedar Rapids, IA	Champaign, IL	Charleston, SC	Charleston, WV	Charlotte, NC	Chattanooga, TN	Cheyenne, WY	Chicago, IL	Cincinnati, OH	Clarksville, TN	Clearwater, FL	Cleveland, OH	Coeur d'Alene, ID	Colorado Sprs., CO	Columbia, MO	Columbia, SC	Columbus, GA	Columbus, OH	Concord, NH	Corpus Christi, TX	Dallas, TX	Davenport, IA	Dayton, OH	Daytona Beach, FL	Decatur, AL	Decatur, IL	Denver, CO	Des Moines, IA	Detroit, MI	Dubuque, IA	Duluth, MN	Durham, NC	East Orange, NJ	Eau Claire, WI	Elgin, IL	Elizabeth, NJ	El Paso, TX	Elyria, OH	Enid, OK	Erie, PA	Escondido, CA	Eugene, OR	Evansville, IN
ine Bluff, AR	1276	659	532	858	748	771	465	1099	668	633	362	892	893	2062	996	421	755	530	752	1514	657	329	652	704	901	341	522	1009	616	912	722	1011	884	1247	916	688	1238	964	875	431	988	1739	2366	457
ittsburgh, PA	1542	691	491	656	225	446	602	1405	461	289	590	1051	132	2222	1435	720	542	794	184	618	1562	1234	611	255	926	684	546	1449	777	286	643	932	486	368	782	506	360	1797	145	1113	127	2464	2678	514
ittsfield, MA	1932	1082	950	954	689	804	976	1796	852	753	1091	1348	509	2613	1910	1179	899	1151	645	185	1996	1710	1002	715	1224	1102	1006	1842	1168	676	1034	1323	682	186	1173	898	193	2345	536	1572	412	2885	3068	978
omona, CA	1065	1788	1979	2477	2310	2390	2084	1090	1994	2154	1981	2475	2322	1356	1061	1720	2374	2148	2224	2940	1470	1408	1830	2166	2484	1960	1938	992	1662	2261	1862	2057	2502	2755	1990	1982	2746	774	2294	1340	2422	86	882	1974
ontiac, MI	1364	514	386	852	378	644	664	1228	284	290	598	1250	196	2044	1342	640	738	870	218	814	1594	1182	434	236	1122	691	438	1274	600	32	466	754	682	629	604	330	635	1744	168	1060	296	2316	2500	504
ort Arthur, TX	1485	1063	958	1018	1145	953	726	1308	1094	1038	768	864	1298	2270	1060	784	914	635	1156	1807	306	337	1022	1108	873	659	946	1218	937	1318	1091	1332	1096	1540	1266	1132	1531	849	1280	640	1394	1594	2576	848
ortland, ME	2160	1310	1165	1080	843	958	1130	2024	1079	968	1245	1475	736	2840	2138	1394	1030	1305	859	95	2150	1864	1230	929	1350	1256	1220	2070	1395	904	1262	1550	808	326	1400	1125	329	2498	764	1787	639	3112	3296	1192
ortland, OR	1130	1916	2143	2904	2554	2762	2486	1162	2124	2375	2312	3086	2450	383	1332	1924	2796	2706	2446	3068	2324	2128	1960	2387	3044	2452	2072	1260	1790	2390	1947	1752	2875	2884	1827	2104	2891	1652	2424	1830	2551	1066	110	2218
rovidence, RI	2044	1194	1020	947	710	824	997	1908	964	818	1112	1342	653	2724	1965	1249	896	1172	714	118	2017	1731	1114	784	1216	1123	1076	1954	1280	788	1146	1434	674	192	1284	1009	196	2365	648	1642	556	2996	3180	1072
rovo, UT	443	1229	1456	2190	1840	2048	1772	474	1436	1688	1598	2372	1762	734	551	1210	2082	1954	1758	2381	1433	1225	1272	1700	2330	1738	1385	482	1103	1702	1302	1498	2160	2196	1432	1424	2203	845	1736	1065	1864	678	918	1504
ueblo, CO	395	910	1022	1731	1380	1588	1312	218	1117	1216	1139	1803	1444	1180	42	751	1622	1404	1287	2063	976	686	953	1228	1812	1216	973	116	784	1384	984	1180	1702	1818	1113	1106	1809	601	1418	509	1545	1153	1486	1045
uébec, QC	2088	1238	1110	1294	983	1143	1316	1952	1007	982	1283	1688	738	2768	2066	1365	1238	1490	874	333	2336	1880	1158	926	1562	1377	1162	1998	1323	723	1190	1191	1021	526	1328	1053	532	2442	766	1758	641	3040	3224	1207
acine, WI	1116	284	214	997	576	854	688	998	78	379	475	1288	430	1710	1112	448	888	908	440	1049	1401	990	214	381	1246	670	254	1044	370	370	198	420	879	864	270	79	870	1553	403	880	531	2087	2204	370
aleigh, NC	1874	1031	768	278	328	172	478	1738	820	526	592	674	580	2579	1692	976	228	522	490	764	1416	1196	951	522	548	602	824	1706	1116	680	1020	1290	24	500	1137	864	488	1832	590	1276	620	2584	3011	694
apid City, SD	257	699	979	1813	1462	1670	1394	300	917	1211	1221	1995	1260	832	474	833	1704	1614	1270	1879	1460	1061	795	1212	1952	1360	972	402	626	1200	736	761	1784	1694	695	876	1701	1118	1234	820	1361	1377	1325	1127
eading, PA	1796	946	732	691	424	538	712	1660	716	530	826	1086	387	2477	1676	960	634	886	426	388	1732	1445	866	496	960	837	787	1690	1032	541	898	1187	419	121	1037	762	112	2080	400	1354	372	2704	2933	786
egina, SK	618	1050	1287	2098	1677	1956	1788	740	1188	1480	1614	2388	1531	760	914	1265	1990	2008	1541	2030	1911	1512	1133	1483	2346	1770	1290	841	1016	1471	1087	720	1980	1965	871	1148	1972	1557	1505	1272	1632	1742	1254	1484
eno, NV	924	1710	1936	2698	2348	2555	2280	956	1916	2168	2106	2880	2244	826	1126	1718	2589	2500	2239	2862	1897	1736	1752	2180	2838	2246	1866	1054	1584	2184	1784	1816	2668	2678	1913	1904	2684	1201	2217	1624	2344	528	470	2012
chmond, VA	1844	1018	756	423	316	295	544	1708	798	512	659	818	469	2559	1661	945	372	645	478	608	1539	1278	938	509	692	670	811	1675	1104	622	980	1269	151	344	1118	843	332	1912	482	1342	465	2650	2980	678
verside, CA	1054	1776	1968	2466	2298	2378	2072	1079	1983	2142	1970	2449	2310	1344	1050	1710	2362	2120	2213	2928	1444	1382	1819	2154	2458	1948	1928	981	1650	2250	1850	2046	2492	2744	1979	1971	2735	748	2284	1330	2411	67	908	1963
oanoke, VA	1706	880	618	405	178	196	368	1570	669	375	483	800	430	2429	1524	808	291	543	340	724	1388	1102	800	372	674	494	673	1537	966	530	870	1139	156	457	989	713	448	1736	439	1166	487	2474	2842	540
ochester, MN	824	169	450	1262	840	1119	951	836	351	644	777	1551	694	1402	950	449	1153	1170	704	1313	1318	907	252	646	1508	934	453	882	208	634	191	226	1144	1128	94	310	1135	1343	668	718	796	1925	1896	647
ochester, NY	1682	832	700	934	503	724	879	1546	601	502	803	1328	258	2362	1660	928	820	1072	394	372	1774	1446	752	464	1203	897	755	1592	917	426	784	1072	660	320	922	647	327	2006	286	1322	161	2634	2818	727
ockford, IL	1052	202	186	1004	584	862	686	916	94	386	512	1287	438	1682	1030	382	896	906	448	1056	1336	926	132	388	1244	670	189	962	286	378	93	392	886	872	242	53	878	1422	410	798	538	2004	2176	382
acramento, CA	1055	1841	2068	2829	2479	2686	2411	1087	2048	2300	2238	2802	2375	856	1258	1850	2720	2464	2370	2994	1882	1726	1884	2312	2812	2275	1997	1185	1715	2314	1915	1947	2800	2808	2044	2036	2816	1185	2348	1656	2476	486	476	2144
aginaw, MI	1385	535	408	912	438	702	712	1249	304	337	644	1298	252	2066	1363	661	798	917	277	871	1614	1204	455	284	1182	738	460	1295	620	104	487	605	742	686	625	350	692	1766	226	1082	353	2338	2522	525
. Johnsbury, VT	2092	1242	1110	1090	853	967	1140	1956	1011	912	1254	1484	668	2772	2070	1339	1039	1315	804	105	2160	1873	1162	874	1359	1265	1165	2002	1327	836	1194	1482	818	335	1332	1057	338	2508	696	1732	571	3044	3228	1137
. Joseph, MO	721	304	380	1162	811	1019	744	585	510	612	570	1344	808	1483	602	182	1053	964	683	1427	953	542	346	624	1301	709	331	616	178	748	377	573	1132	1214	506	498	1205	955	781	330	909	1662	1858	476
. Louis, MO	1024	287	175	856	506	714	438	888	296	350	265	1039	561	1786	842	126	748	658	421	1174	1041	630	265	362	996	421	135	855	373	533	335	679	828	952	529	301	943	1193	543	508	657	1859	2160	171
. Paul, MN	864	282	503	1314	894	1172	1004	876	404	697	830	1604	748	1358	990	489	1206	1224	758	1366	1358	947	365	699	1562	987	506	922	248	688	270	149	1196	1182	87	364	1188	1383	721	758	849	1965	1852	700
. Petersburg, FL	2061	1324	1102	456	869	602	601	1925	1204	944	778	22	1120	2823	1878	1162	507	417	1031	1426	1178	1098	1272	1015	161	644	1090	1892	1410	1224	1342	1672	696	1162	1520	1248	1150	1720	1130	1313	1172	2466	3198	880
alem, OR	1178	1965	2192	2953	2602	2810	2533	1210	2172	2424	2360	3133	2498	430	1380	1972	2844	2753	2494	3116	2374	2176	2008	2436	3092	2500	2120	1309	1838	2438	1994	1800	2924	2932	1872	2150	2938	1700	2472	1878	2600	1021	66	2266
alinas, CA	1229	2015	2242	2720	2554	2633	2328	1261	2222	2397	2225	2731	2549	996	1305	1964	2618	2392	2468	3168	1799	1654	2058	2410	2740	2204	2172	1236	1889	2488	2089	2121	2746	2982	2218	2210	2990	1102	2522	1584	2650	403	616	2218
alisbury, MD	1889	1039	824	572	470	463	716	1753	808	622	831	966	479	2570	1769	1053	521	813	518	484	1707	1450	959	588	841	842	880	1782	1124	633	991	1280	319	219	1129	854	207	2084	493	1446	476	2823	3026	832
alt Lake City, UT	406	1192	1418	2180	1830	2037	1762	438	1398	1650	1588	2362	1726	692	608	1200	2071	1982	1721	2344	1476	1404	1234	1662	2320	1727	1348	536	1066	1665	1266	1461	2150	2160	1395	1386	2166	888	1699	1106	1826	720	877	1494
an Angelo, TX	1010	1049	1048	1380	1319	1298	1054	832	1168	1204	933	1318	1464	1795	684	847	1277	1006	1322	2085	356	269	1092	1234	1326	912	1007	743	923	1405	1123	1318	1441	1818	1252	1173	1809	404	1446	432	1559	1149	2060	1028
an Antonio, TX	1203	1101	1081	1300	1325	1236	1008	1025	1202	1210	939	1147	1470	1988	877	862	1197	918	1328	2090	142	276	1144	1280	1156	918	1041	936	975	1439	1174	1370	1379	1823	1303	1206	1814	554	1452	566	1565	1300	2211	1034
an Bernardino, CA	1044	1767	1958	2456	2290	2368	2063	1070	1974	2133	1960	2451	2301	1335	1040	1700	2353	2121	2204	2920	1446	1384	1810	2145	2460	1940	1918	972	1641	2240	1841	2036	2482	2735	1970	1962	2726	750	2274	1320	2402	76	910	1954
an Diego, CA	1150	1873	2030	2470	2362	2388	2144	1176	2080	2205	2033	2426	2407	1441	1146	1722	2367	2096	2276	3026	1421	1359	1916	2217	2435	2012	1990	1078	1747	2346	1947	2142	2531	2806	2076	2068	2798	724	2380	1392	2508	30	976	2026
an Francisco, CA	1141	1927	2154	2800	2564	2713	2407	1172	2134	2386	2323	2811	2460	908	1343	1935	2698	2472	2456	3080	1879	1734	1970	2398	2820	2284	2083	1270	1801	2400	2000	2033	2826	2894	2130	2122	2901	1182	2434	1664	2562	483	528	2229
an Jose, CA	1169	1954	2182	2760	2592	2672	2366	1200	2162	2414	2264	2770	2488	936	1371	1963	2656	2431	2484	3107	1838	1693	1998	2426	2778	2242	2111	1298	1828	2428	2028	2061	2786	2922	2158	2150	2929	1141	2462	1623	2590	442	556	2257
an Mateo, CA	1160	1946	2173	2786	2584	2699	2393	1192	2154	2405	2342	2797	2480	928	1362	1954	2683	2458	2476	3099	1865	1720	1989	2417	2806	2270	2102	1290	1820	2420	2020	2052	2812	2914	2149	2142	2921	1168	2454	1650	2581	469	547	2248
anta Ana, CA	1086	1808	2000	2498	2331	2410	2104	1111	2015	2174	2002	2489	2342	1376	1082	1742	2394	2160	2245	2961	1484	1422	1851	2186	2498	1980	1960	1013	1682	2282	1882	2078	2524	2776	2011	2004	2767	788	2316	1362	2443	71	887	1995
anta Barbara, CA	1178	1901	2092	2590	2424	2503	2197	1204	2108	2267	2095	2598	2435	1226	1174	1834	2487	2262	2338	3054	1593	1531	1944	2279	2607	2074	2052	1106	1775	2374	1975	2170	2616	2869	2104	2096	2860	897	2408	1454	2536	196	846	2088
anta Rosa, CA	1157	1943	2170	2847	2581	2788	2454	1189	2150	2402	2340	2857	2477	924	1360	1952	2744	2518	2472	3096	1926	1781	1986	2414	2866	2330	2099	1287	1817	2416	2017	2049	2902	2910	2146	2138	2917	1229	2450	1711	2578	530	544	2246
avannah, GA	1830	1092	871	111	524	257	369	1694	962	670	546	356	775	2592	1646	930	161	263	685	1082	1189	996	1040	740	231	445	859	1660	1178	876	1110	1440	352	816	1290	1006	805	1632	784	1144	826	2377	2966	648
chenectady, NY	1882	1031	900	936	669	784	956	1745	801	702	1002	1330	458	2562	1859	1128	879	1131	594	157	1977	1690	951	664	1205	1082	955	1791	1117	626	983	1272	664	168	1122	847	174	2325	486	1521	361	2834	3018	927
cranton, PA	1783	932	778	780	481	595	768	1647	702	580	883	1175	373	2464	1723	1007	690	943	472	340	1788	1502	852	542	1050	894	834	1693	1018	527	885	1173	508	108	1023	748	114	2136	386	1400	323	2736	2920	806
eattle, WA	1096	1837	2117	2950	2560	2808	2532	1236	2071	2364	2358	3133	2414	310	1408	1971	2842	2752	2424	3033	2400	2202	1933	2366	3090	2498	2109	1334	1764	2354	1874	1678	2864	2848	1754	2030	2855	1728	2388	1906	2516	1238	283	2265
hreveport, LA	1333	828	726	922	942	841	597	1156	862	827	557	892	1088	2118	913	584	819	549	946	1678	449	187	821	898	901	530	691	1066	733	1106	891	1129	984	1411	1062	856	1402	823	1069	487	1182	1568	2424	652
oux City, IA	559	272	551	1385	1034	1242	966	589	531	783	793	1567	858	1256	703	405	1276	1186	854	1477	1156	757	367	795	1524	932	543	635	198	798	308	455	1356	1292	388	520	1298	1108	831	517	959	1678	1750	699
oux Falls, SD	598	361	636	1470	1119	1327	1052	610	578	868	878	1652	922	1176	724	490	1361	1272	938	1541	1241	842	452	880	1609	1017	628	656	283	862	398	423	1440	1356	356	538	1362	1152	896	602	1023	1698	1669	784
outh Bend, IN	1174	324	196	866	408	672	562	1038	93	246	428	1162	256	1854	1152	450	757	782	252	875	1402	992	244	228	1119	544	248	1084	409	213	276	564	711	690	412	138	698	1554	230	870	357	2126	2310	324
pokane, WA	816	1558	1838	2672	2281	2528	2253	994	1792	2084	2080	2853	2135	30	1168	1692	2562	2473	2145	2754	2160	1964	1654	2086	2811	2218	1830	1096	1484	2075	1594	1399	2584	2569	1474	1751	2575	1609	2108	1666	2236	1441	463	1985
pringfield, IL	1010	249	88	926	523	783	508	874	200	320	334	1108	516	1772	902	186	818	728	390	1134	1143	732	169	332	1066	491	38	915	334	455	238	582	826	921	432	204	912	1295	489	610	616	1961	2146	240
pringfield, MA	1978	1127	994	910	673	788	960	1842	897	796	1075	1305	554	2658	1955	1222	860	1135	688	138	1981	1694	1048	758	1180	1086	1049	1888	1213	722	1080	1368	638	156	1218	943	159	2329	582	1615	457	2930	3114	1021
pringfield, MO	945	409	388	990	719	877	602	809	509	563	428	1060	774	1707	750	168	886	661	633	1387	830	419	402	575	1069	473	348	764	359	746	483	754	990	1164	687	514	1155	982	756	297	869	1648	2082	383
pringfield, OH	1375	525	262	659	185	449	455	1239	310	80	388	1041	186	2070	1207	491	544	660	45	798	1359	1006	445	27	928	481	318	1220	610	187	514	780	488	576	630	354	567	1569	167	884	281	2235	2512	312
tamford, CT	1903	1053	880	806	569	683	856	1767	822	677	971	1200	494	2584	1824	1108	756	1031	573	226	1876	1590	973	644	1076	982	934	1813	1138	647	1005	1294	534	52	1143	868	55	2224	506	1501	453	2856	3040	931
tockton, CA	1102	1888	2115	2751	2526	2663	2358	1134	2096	2347	2284	2761	2422	901	1304	1896	2648	2422	2418	3041	1834	1684	1931	2359	2770	2234	2044	1232	1762	2362	1962	1994	2776	2856	2091	2084	2863	1138	2396	1614	2523	439	520	2190
yracuse, NY	1757	907	775	912	578	728	900	1621	676	577	878	1308	333	2438	1735	1004	823	1075	469	290	1920	1522	827	539	1182	972	830	1667	992	501	859	1148	640	235	997	722	241	2081	361	1397	236	2710	2894	802
acoma, WA	1108	1849	2129	2962	2572	2820	2544	1248	2083	2376	2370	3144	2426	322	1419	1983	2854	2764	2436	3045	2412	2214	1945	2378	3102	2510	2121	1346	1776	2366	1886	1690	2876	2860	1766	2042	2867	1739	2400	1918	2528	1206	251	2276
allahassee, FL	1826	1089	865	399	750	484	394	1690	965	738	540	238	998	2588	1617	927	395	172	856	1369	917	837	1034	808	253	383	852	1630	1174	1017	1104	1434	640	1104	1283	1010	1092	1460	979	1052	1054	2204	2962	642
ampa, FL	2038	1300	1080	433	846	579	578	1902	1180	922	755	23	1097	2800	1855	1139	483	394	1008	1404	1188	1108	1248	992	138	654	1068	1868	1386	1201	1318	1648	674	1139	1498	1224	1127	1730	1106	1323	1148	2476	3174	857
erre Haute, IN	1185	355	93	800	387	656	388	1049	180	184	214	988	395	1896	1002	286	690	608	254	1008	1157	802	275	196	946	371	107	1016	441	367	345	658	690	785	508	220	776	1364	376	680	490	2030	2322	109
oledo, OH	1322	472	345	776	302	567	576	1186	242	201	508	1162	111	2003	1300	587	662	782	142	730	1480	1103	392	148	1046	602	397	1232	558	59	424	713	606	545	563	288	551	1665	84	981	212	2275	2458	433
opeka, KS	807	383	460	1169	818	1026	750	630	590	654	577	1351	865	1516	527	189	1060	970	724	1478	900	501	426	666	1308	716	411	540	257	828	457	653	1140	1255	586	578	1247	886	847	261	960	1587	1898	483
oronto, ON	1601	751	624	969	538	759	868	1465	520	493	800	1364	293	2282	1579	878	854	1073	429	582	1772	1393	671	440	1238	894	676	1511	836	236	703	844	733	480	842	566	486	1956	321	1271	196	2554	2738	724
orrington, CT	1962	1112	958	878	660	774	948	1826	882	760	1062	1272	553	2642	1902	1186	828	1122	652	200	1968	1681	1032	722	1148	1073	1013	1872	1198	706	1064	1353	606	124	1202	927	127	2316	566	1580	487	2914	3098	985
renton, NJ	1859	1009	794	710	486	582	774	1723	778	592	888	1105	449	2540	1739	1023	660	932	488	330	1794	1507	929	558	980	899	849	1752	1094	603	961	1249	438	65	1099	824	53	2142	462	1416	432	2766	2996	849
roy, NY	1902	1051	920	930	664	779	952	1765	820	722	1066	1324	478	2582	1879	1148	874	1126	614	143	1972	1685	971	684	1198	1077	974	1811	1137	646	1003	1292	656	162	1142	866	168	2320	505	1541	381	2854	3038	946
ucson, AZ	1227	1514	1620	2063	2002	1981	1737	1050	1742	1795	1616	2018	2006	1466	875	1312	1960	1689	1866	2620	1014	952	1556	1807	2028	1594	1580	948	1388	1978	1587	1783	2124	2500	1716	1708	2491	317	1988	982	2102	428	1340	1616
ulsa, OK	960	588	569	1109	900	1022	716	783	690	744	614	1179	955	1746	680	349	1006	780	814	1568	678	267	632	756	1188	592	529	693	463	927	662	858	1135	1345	791	694	1336	801	937	114	1050	1467	2050	564
upelo, MS	1396	659	456	606	604	524	250	1260	591	489	219	676	749	2158	1187	497	503	278	608	1332	841	558	652	560	685	123	443	1200	744	768	722	1066	668	1064	916	628	1056	1192	731	622	844	1930	2532	336
uscaloosa, AL	1526	789	618	528	622	447	203	1390	718	517	293	558	778	2288	1317	627	426	194	636	1285	823	587	782	588	568	136	606	1330	874	797	852	1186	590	1018	1036	762	1009	1222	759	752	873	1968	2662	395
yler, TX	1245	854	789	1021	1006	939	695	1068	925	890	620	990	1150	2030	826	615	918	647	1008	1777	404	100	897	960	999	598	754	978	728	1170	928	1123	1082	1510	1056	920	1501	735	1132	400	1246	1480	2336	714
tica, NY	1806	956	824	965	627	780	953	1670	725	626	927	1360	382	2486	1784	1053	875	1128	518	240	1973	1571	876	588	1234	1021	879	1716	1041	550	908	1196	692	245	1046	771	252	2130	410	1446	285	2758	2942	851
allejo, CA	1113	1898	2126	2804	2536	2744	2468	1144	2106	2358	2295	2814	2432	880	1315	1907	2701	2475	2428	3051	1882	1738	1942	2370	2823	2287	2055	1242	1773	2372	1972	2005	2858	2866	2102	2094	2873	1186	2406	1668	2534	487	500	2201
ancouver, BC	1233	1974	2254	3088	2698	2944	2669	1374	2208	2500	2496	3270	2552	446	1544	2108	2978	2889	2561	3170	2536	2340	2070	2502	3227	2634	2246	1472	1901	2491	2010	1816	3000	2985	1890	2167	2991	1864	2524	2042	2652	1381	426	2402
entura, CA	1152	1874	2066	2564	2397	2476	2170	1177	2082	2240	2068	2572	2408	1442	1148	1808	2460	2235	2311	3027	1567	1505	1918	2252	2580	2047	2026	1080	1748	2348	1948	2144	2590	2842	2078	2070	2833	870	2382	1428	2509	170	865	2061
ictoria, TX	1317	1141	1078	1229	1294	1164	937	1140	1214	1179	908	1076	1439	2102	991	902	1126	846	1297	2019	96	316	1184	1249	1085	870	1081	1050	1015	1458	1215	1411	1307	1752	1343	1248	1743	669	1421	607	1534	1414	2325	1003
irginia Beach, VA	1950	1124	862	456	422	348	650	1814	898	619	765	851	569	2660	1768	1052	406	698	584	621	1592	1372	1044	616	726	776	917	1781	1210	723	1081	1369	204	356	1219	944	345	2008	582	1448	565	2757	3086	784
aco, TX	1118	920	901	1149	1145	1067	823	941	1022	1030	759	1118	1290	1904	792	681	1046	776	1148	1911	315	96	964	1100	1127	738	861	852	795	1259	994	1190	1210	1644	1123	1026	1635	650	1272	386	1385	1396	2208	854
alnut Creek, CA	1126	1912	2138	2782	2550	2695	2389	1158	2118	2370	2308	2792	2446	892	1328	1920	2679	2454	2441	3064	1860	1716	1954	2382	2801	2265	2068	1256	1786	2385	1986	2018	2808	2880	2114	2106	2886	1164	2418	1646	2546	465	512	2214
arren, OH	1468	618	475	718	244	508	646	1332	387	277	578	1112	57	2148	1446	704	603	851	169	652	1550	1222	538	239	987	672	530	1378	703	212	570	859	546	389	708	433	396	1781	72	1097	93	2420	2604	502
Washington, DC	1788	937	723	531	372	402	600	1652	706	521	715	926	378	2468	1667	951	480	752	416	492	1620	1334	857	487	800	726	778	1680	1023	532	890	1178	258	228	1026	752	216	1968	391	1398	374	2706	2924	734
Waterbury, CT	1942	1092	938	858	640	754	927	1806	861	740	1042	1252	532	2622	1882	1166	807	1102	632	179	1947	1661	1012	702	1127	1052	992	1852	1177	686	1044	1332	586	103	1182	907	106	2295	545	1559	466	2894	3078	964
Waterloo, IA	890	55	322	1170	757	1027	778	754	302	554	604	1378	629	1472	868	316	1061	998	624	1248	1236	825	138	566	1336	744	314	800	126	569	92	374	1060	1063	207	232	1069	1261	602	636	730	1843	1966	510
Waukegan, IL	1140	271	180	962	542	820	654	985	38	345	441	1254	396	1734	1099	413	854	872	406	1014	1367	956	201	347	1210	636	220	1031	356	335	176	444	844	830	294	46	836	1518	369	834	496	2074	2228	335
Wausau, WI	1034	314	385	1196	776	1054	886	1047	286	579	712	1486	630	1534	1160	582	1088	1106	640	1248	1528	1118	330	581	1444	869	388	1092	418	570	240	235	1078	1064	99	246	1070	1554	603	928	731	2136	2027	582
West Palm Beach, FL	2182	1444	1222	525	937	670	721	2045	1324	1065	898	226	1188	2943	1998	1282	575	537	1099	1495	1331	1252	1392	1135	199	797	1210	2012	1530	1289	1462	1792	766	1230	1640	1368	1218	1874	1198	1466	1240	2618	3318	1000
Wheeling, WV	1546	695	433	651	177	441	596	1409	466	231	532	1046	141	2228	1377	662	536	789	126	678	1504	1176	615	197	920	626	488	1391	781	291	685	938	480	405	787	512	396	1739	151	1055	179	2406	2682	456
Wichita, KS	787	518	595	1282	945	1153	878	609	725	781	704	1352	992	1572	506	316	1179	954	852	1605	760	361	561	793	1361	765	545	520	392	964	592	788	1266	1382	721	714	1374	743	974	121	1088	1409	1878	610
Wichita Falls, TX	916	813	811	1246	1142	1164	913	738	932	986	810	1216	1197	1701	590	611	1143	873	1057	1810	518	139	856	998	1224	789	771	649	687	1169	887	1082	1332	1588	1016	937	1579	600	1179	196	1293	1327	2006	807
Wilmington, DE	1832	982	767	650	436	522	706	1696	751	565	820	1045	422	2512	1711	995	600	872	460	390	1726	1439	902	531	920	831	822	1725	1067	576	934	1222	378	126	1072	797	114	2074	435	1389	406	2740	2968	798
Winnipeg, MB	932	733	969	1780	1360	1638	1470	1006	870	1163	1296	2070	1214	1114	1163	948	1672	1690	1224	1668	1699	1300	816	1165	2028	1453	972	1095	699	1153	770	381	1662	1648	553	830	1654	1590	1187	1059	1314	2018	1608	1166
Winston-Salem, NC	1744	919	656	283	216	77	370	1608	707	413	484	678	468	2467	1562	846	169	428	378	844	1321	1103	839	410	553	495	712	1575	1004	568	908	1177	86	594	1027	752	567	1737	477	1167	520	2476	2880	586
Worcester, MA	2024	1174	1030	944	708	822	995	1888	944	832	1110	1340	601	2705	2002	1258	894	1170	724	87	2015	1728	1094	794	1214	1120	1085	1934	1260	768	1126	1415	672	190	1265	990	193	2363	628	1651	504	2977	3160	1057
Yakima, WA	1018	1758	2038	2838	2488	2695	2420	1096	1992	2286	2246	3020	2336	232	1266	1858	2730	2640	2346	2954	2258	2062	1854	2288	2978	2386	2006	1194	1686	2276	1796	1600	2808	2770	1676	1952	2776	1586	2310	1764	2437	1140	296	2152
Youngstown, OH	1483	632	478	717	249	507	649	1346	402	280	581	1112	73	2164	1423	707	602	855	172	646	1553	1225	552	242	986	675	533	1392	718	227	584	873	546	382	723	448	389	1784	86	1100	101	2435	2620	505

Mileage Directory, continued

	Everett, WA	Fairfield, CA	Fall River, MA	Fargo, ND	Fayetteville, NC	Flagstaff, AZ	Flint, MI	Florence, SC	Ft. Collins, CO	Ft. Dodge, IA	Ft. Lauderdale, FL	Ft. Smith, AR
Pine Bluff, AR	2352	2010	1446	1031	917	1244	906	832	1062	688	1106	202
Pittsburgh, PA	2554	2538	567	1107	555	1968	337	550	1450	845	1162	998
Pittsfield, MA	2945	2929	165	1498	742	2428	728	826	1841	1236	1460	1546
Pomona, CA	1191	420	2957	1823	2536	440	2250	2450	1054	1714	2689	1486
Pontiac, MI	2376	2360	831	930	734	1916	39	746	1272	668	1359	946
Port Arthur, TX	2562	2044	1738	1326	1076	1302	1333	991	1271	1009	1078	450
Portland, ME	3172	3156	162	1726	868	2643	956	953	2069	1464	1586	1700
Portland, OR	201	596	3086	1500	2905	1286	2378	2872	1178	1756	3249	2058
Providence, RI	3056	3040	16	1610	734	2498	840	820	1953	1348	1453	1565
Provo, UT	904	736	2398	1201	2191	478	1691	2158	490	1156	2534	1292
Pueblo, CO	1472	1346	2016	986	1732	658	1373	1699	181	837	2017	742
Québec, QC	3100	3084	452	1654	1081	2614	735	1166	1997	1392	1800	1643
Racine, WI	2042	2131	1066	596	931	1724	359	965	1043	388	1450	752
Raleigh, NC	2911	2872	696	1464	66	2088	734	152	1758	1185	785	1044
Rapid City, SD	1164	1358	1896	550	1814	1174	1189	1781	344	545	2158	1006
Reading, PA	2809	2794	320	1362	479	2209	592	564	1706	1100	1197	1281
Regina, SK	1117	1605	2168	543	2032	1543	1460	2066	784	993	2550	1438
Reno, NV	779	177	2880	1564	2698	765	2172	2666	971	1637	3042	1852
Richmond, VA	2890	2840	540	1444	211	2155	674	296	1727	1172	929	1112
Riverside, CA	1216	446	2946	1812	2524	428	2238	2439	1042	1703	2663	1474
Roanoke, VA	2760	2703	656	1314	245	1980	584	269	1590	1034	912	938
Rochester, MN	1734	1969	1330	321	1196	1514	623	1230	881	184	1714	692
Rochester, NY	2694	2678	421	1248	720	2177	477	804	1590	986	1440	1205
Rockford, IL	2014	2048	1074	568	938	1594	366	972	960	282	1449	688
Sacramento, CA	784	47	3011	1695	2830	755	2304	2797	1102	1768	3016	1801
Saginaw, MI	2398	2382	888	951	793	1937	38	806	1294	689	1418	965
St. Johnsbury, VT	3104	3089	224	1658	878	2588	888	962	2001	1396	1596	1708
St. Joseph, MO	1815	1718	1412	550	1162	1126	737	1130	630	249	1506	355
St. Louis, MO	2118	2021	1150	854	858	1364	541	824	908	441	1201	391
St. Paul, MN	1690	2009	1384	244	1249	1554	676	1282	921	224	1766	732
St. Petersburg, FL	3155	2832	1358	1847	612	2066	1266	526	1944	1478	250	1083
Salem, OR	247	550	3134	1548	2954	1294	2426	2921	1226	1804	3295	2106
Salinas, CA	924	134	3185	1869	2780	684	2478	2694	1276	1942	2945	1729
Salisbury, MD	2902	2886	415	1455	360	2328	685	444	1798	1193	1078	1286
Salt Lake City, UT	863	696	2362	1160	2180	521	1654	2148	452	1118	2524	1333
San Angelo, TX	2086	1598	2016	1253	1439	844	1413	1354	795	995	1532	545
San Antonio, TX	2280	1749	2022	1344	1359	1126	1447	1274	988	1046	1361	554
San Bernardino, CA	1218	447	2937	1802	2515	419	2230	2430	1033	1694	2665	1465
San Diego, CA	1284	514	3005	1908	2529	492	2336	2444	1139	1800	2640	1537
San Francisco, CA	836	46	3096	1781	2860	764	2389	2774	1188	1854	3025	1809
San Jose, CA	864	74	3124	1808	2818	722	2417	2733	1216	1882	2984	1768
San Mateo, CA	856	65	3116	1800	2845	749	2409	2760	1208	1874	3011	1795
Santa Ana, CA	1196	425	2978	1844	2556	460	2271	2471	1074	1736	2703	1506
Santa Barbara, CA	1154	364	3071	1936	2649	553	2364	2564	1167	1828	2812	1599
Santa Rosa, CA	852	62	3112	1797	2906	810	2406	2820	1204	1870	3071	1856
Savannah, GA	2924	2724	1012	1616	266	1958	929	180	1713	1246	468	916
Schenectady, NY	2894	2878	212	1447	724	2377	677	808	1790	1185	1442	1406
Scranton, PA	2796	2780	300	1348	568	2256	578	653	1692	1086	1286	1336
Seattle, WA	28	768	3050	1426	2952	1360	2343	2918	1252	1682	3295	2132
Shreveport, LA	2410	1921	1610	1149	981	1156	1100	896	1119	805	1106	252
Sioux City, IA	1588	1722	1494	323	1386	1280	787	1353	634	128	1730	578
Sioux Falls, SD	1508	1699	1558	242	1470	1323	851	1438	655	213	1814	661
South Bend, IN	2186	2170	892	740	764	1726	209	834	1082	478	1324	756
Spokane, WA	302	838	2771	1147	2672	1242	2064	2640	1038	1403	3016	1894
Springfield, IL	2104	2007	1119	758	878	1466	444	894	919	403	1270	494
Springfield, MA	2990	2974	118	1544	698	2471	773	783	1886	1281	1416	1530
Springfield, MO	2039	1942	1362	774	1021	1153	754	963	817	430	1274	180
Springfield, OH	2402	2372	774	955	540	1740	228	552	1273	679	1165	767
Stamford, CT	2916	2900	157	1469	594	2357	699	678	1812	1207	1312	1424
Stockton, CA	829	52	3058	1742	2810	714	2351	2724	1150	1816	2975	1759
Syracuse, NY	2770	2754	339	1323	700	2252	552	785	1666	1061	1419	1282
Tacoma, WA	60	736	3062	1438	2963	1372	2355	2930	1264	1694	3307	2144
Tallahassee, FL	2920	2571	1300	1609	554	1805	1058	468	1683	1243	458	822
Tampa, FL	3132	2842	1334	1824	589	2076	1242	502	1922	1454	242	1093
Terre Haute, IN	2227	2182	984	834	742	1535	388	767	1069	509	1151	563
Toledo, OH	2335	2319	747	888	658	1836	110	670	1231	626	1283	864
Topeka, KS	1884	1758	1454	584	1170	1057	816	1137	593	329	1514	350
Toronto, ON	2614	2598	580	1167	793	2127	249	862	1510	905	1475	1156
Torrington, CT	2974	2959	159	1528	666	2435	758	750	1871	1266	1384	1517
Trenton, NJ	2872	2856	261	1425	498	2272	654	583	1768	1163	1216	1343
Troy, NY	2914	2898	201	1467	717	2397	697	802	1810	1205	1436	1519
Tucson, AZ	1637	877	2698	1622	2122	255	1986	2036	1013	1460	2232	1127
Tulsa, OK	2036	1738	1544	804	1168	972	935	1083	746	534	1393	118
Tupelo, MS	2490	2201	1263	1225	665	1435	810	580	1253	813	890	392
Tuscaloosa, AL	2620	2331	1216	1355	588	1565	838	502	1383	943	772	522
Tyler, TX	2322	1834	1708	1117	1080	1068	1163	994	1031	800	1204	275
Utica, NY	2818	2802	289	1372	752	2302	602	838	1715	1110	1471	1331
Vallejo, CA	808	18	3068	1752	2863	767	2361	2778	1160	1826	3028	1812
Vancouver, BC	115	911	3187	1563	3088	1498	2480	3056	1388	1820	3432	2269
Ventura, CA	1174	391	3044	1910	2622	527	2337	2538	1140	1802	2786	1572
Victoria, TX	2393	1863	1950	1385	1288	1240	1452	1202	1103	1087	1290	595
Virginia Beach, VA	2992	2947	552	1545	244	2262	774	329	1834	1278	963	1220
Waco, TX	2194	1800	1842	1164	1208	1034	1267	1122	904	866	1332	374
Walnut Creek, CA	821	31	3082	1765	2841	745	2374	2756	1172	1838	3006	1791
Warren, OH	2480	2465	591	1034	635	1952	264	611	1377	772	1224	982
Washington, DC	2800	2784	424	1353	319	2212	583	404	1696	1091	1038	1170
Waterbury, CT	2954	2938	139	1508	646	2415	737	730	1851	1246	1364	1495
Waterloo, IA	1804	1887	1265	454	1112	1432	558	1138	799	102	1541	610
Waukegan, IL	2066	2118	1032	620	897	1690	324	930	1030	367	1416	719
Wausau, WI	1866	2180	1266	419	1131	1725	558	1164	1092	394	1648	902
West Palm Beach, FL	3275	2985	1426	1967	680	2220	1343	594	2064	1598	46	1236
Wheeling, WV	2560	2542	604	1113	532	1910	343	544	1444	849	1157	940
Wichita, KS	1864	1738	1581	685	1296	914	951	1256	573	464	1566	291
Wichita Falls, TX	1992	1598	1786	1017	1305	832	1177	1220	702	759	1430	314
Wilmington, DE	2844	2828	321	1398	438	2244	627	523	1740	1135	1157	1275
Winnipeg, MB	1471	1881	1780	224	1715	1863	1142	1748	1050	675	2232	1120
Winston-Salem, NC	2799	2741	774	1352	139	1981	622	176	1628	1072	790	939
Worcester, MA	3037	3021	72	1590	732	2507	820	817	1933	1328	1451	1563
Yakima, WA	163	670	2972	1348	2838	1220	2264	2806	1110	1604	3182	1992
Youngstown, OH	2495	2480	585	1048	615	1956	278	610	1391	786	1223	985

	Ft. Wayne, IN	Ft. Worth, TX	Fredericton, NB	Fresno, CA	Gainesville, FL	Galveston, TX	Gary, IN	Grand Island, NE	Grand Rapids, MI	Great Falls, MT	Greeley, CO	Green Bay, WI	Greensboro, NC	Greenville, SC	Halifax, NS	Hamilton, OH
Pine Bluff, AR	732	359	1888	1834	796	499	667	767	811	1772	1044	874	826	678	2114	671
Pittsburgh, PA	324	1264	992	2559	902	1435	431	1061	415	1844	1420	676	428	542	1218	289
Pittsfield, MA	722	1740	559	2980	1200	1810	822	1452	806	2235	1811	1067	732	898	785	752
Pomona, CA	2140	1378	3336	246	2379	1575	2012	1394	2155	1238	1054	2095	2445	2297	3604	2157
Pontiac, MI	200	1210	1079	2412	1103	1388	254	884	138	1666	1242	498	624	722	1347	278
Port Arthur, TX	1159	358	2182	1868	768	119	1094	976	1238	1981	1253	1300	1045	855	2408	1076
Portland, ME	950	1894	326	3208	1326	1964	1049	1680	1034	2462	2039	1295	858	1052	551	967
Portland, OR	2270	2010	3466	748	2938	2418	2140	1524	2284	718	1226	2010	2818	2700	3732	2378
Providence, RI	826	1761	488	3092	1192	1830	933	1564	918	2346	1923	1179	726	919	713	818
Provo, UT	1581	1200	2778	773	2224	1510	1453	836	1596	616	540	1536	2103	1986	3046	1691
Pueblo, CO	1242	661	2460	1248	1666	972	1134	518	1278	891	181	1218	1644	1527	2727	1219
Québec, QC	889	1907	377	3136	1538	2149	977	1608	849	2390	1967	1060	1072	1238	645	967
Racine, WI	250	1018	1445	2182	1140	1216	108	654	264	1332	1013	144	822	793	1713	382
Raleigh, NC	652	1226	1139	2679	524	1230	790	1394	812	2201	1740	1034	79	270	1364	550
Rapid City, SD	1079	1056	2276	1472	1848	1352	951	426	1094	542	368	838	1726	1609	2543	1214
Reading, PA	579	1475	762	2800	936	1544	686	1316	670	2099	1676	932	469	634	988	530
Regina, SK	1350	1507	2292	1724	2240	1803	1222	878	1365	500	808	1054	1923	1894	2559	1484
Reno, NV	2062	1710	3259	296	2732	2021	1934	1317	2077	979	1020	2017	2611	2494	3526	2172
Richmond, VA	639	1308	983	2746	668	1352	767	1364	752	2180	1709	1013	201	392	1208	538
Riverside, CA	2129	1353	3326	271	2353	1549	2000	1384	2144	1227	1042	2084	2434	2286	3593	2146
Roanoke, VA	502	1132	1099	2570	650	1202	639	1226	662	2051	1572	883	109	290	1324	400
Rochester, MN	515	954	1710	2020	1403	1195	385	492	528	1058	851	272	1086	1058	1978	647
Rochester, NY	471	1476	815	2730	1179	1616	571	1202	555	1984	1560	816	662	819	1040	502
Rockford, IL	256	952	1452	2100	1139	1128	128	572	270	1304	930	208	828	800	1720	390
Sacramento, CA	2193	1701	3390	165	2706	1986	2065	1448	2208	1110	1152	2148	2742	2625	3658	2303
Saginaw, MI	220	1231	1124	2433	1150	1409	274	905	146	1687	1264	445	684	770	1392	324
St. Johnsbury, VT	882	1903	403	3140	1335	1973	981	1612	966	2394	1971	1227	868	1062	629	912
St. Joseph, MO	593	565	1823	1757	1196	830	498	240	642	1194	599	611	1075	958	2091	615
St. Louis, MO	376	658	1605	1954	891	832	302	544	446	1497	890	495	770	653	1830	353
St. Paul, MN	568	994	1763	2060	1456	1236	438	532	581	980	891	270	1139	1111	2030	700
St. Petersburg, FL	1144	1128	1801	2657	153	991	1173	1580	1274	2534	1926	1418	697	607	2027	982
Salem, OR	2320	2058	3512	704	2985	2468	2188	1572	2332	764	1276	2057	2866	2748	3780	2428
Salinas, CA	2367	1629	3564	140	2634	1904	2239	1622	2382	1284	1326	2322	2689	2541	3832	2401
Salisbury, MD	672	1480	858	2918	817	1520	778	1409	762	2191	1768	1024	370	560	1084	622
Salt Lake City, UT	1544	1285	2741	816	2214	1694	1416	799	1559	575	502	1499	2092	1976	3008	1654
San Angelo, TX	1248	240	2459	1424	1220	417	1175	811	1318	1506	777	1368	1390	1200	2685	1241
San Antonio, TX	1282	269	2464	1574	1051	247	1208	902	1352	1699	970	1401	1328	1138	2690	1248
San Bernardino, CA	2121	1354	3316	272	2355	1551	1991	1374	2134	1218	1033	2074	2424	2276	3584	2136
San Diego, CA	2226	1329	3422	339	2330	1526	2097	1480	2240	1324	1139	2180	2480	2290	3690	2208
San Francisco, CA	2279	1709	3476	184	2715	1984	2151	1534	2294	1196	1238	2234	2769	2621	3743	2389
San Jose, CA	2307	1668	3504	149	2673	1942	2178	1562	2322	1224	1266	2262	2728	2579	3771	2417
San Mateo, CA	2300	1695	3496	180	2700	1970	2170	1554	2314	1216	1257	2254	2754	2606	3763	2408
Santa Ana, CA	2161	1392	3358	250	2393	1589	2032	1416	2176	1259	1074	2116	2466	2318	3625	2178
Santa Barbara, CA	2254	1501	3450	254	2502	1698	2125	1508	2268	1352	1167	2208	2558	2410	3718	2271
Santa Rosa, CA	2295	1755	3492	231	2761	2030	2167	1550	2310	1212	1254	2250	2844	2667	3760	2405
Savannah, GA	832	1026	1456	2548	207	1002	932	1349	1007	2302	1695	1176	351	262	1682	707
Schenectady, NY	671	1720	606	2929	1181	1790	771	1401	755	2184	1760	1016	708	879	832	702
Scranton, PA	565	1532	715	2831	1026	1601	672	1302	656	2085	1662	918	520	690	940	580
Seattle, WA	2235	2084	3430	920	2985	2494	2105	1598	2248	645	1302	1938	2806	2746	3698	2367
Shreveport, LA	926	217	2053	1746	796	291	862	823	1005	1829	1101	1051	932	743	2278	865
Sioux City, IA	678	752	1873	1773	1419	1048	548	184	691	967	604	531	1298	1181	2141	786
Sioux Falls, SD	741	837	1938	1794	1504	1133	612	249	756	886	625	499	1382	1266	2205	871
South Bend, IN	96	1020	1281	2222	1014	1198	62	694	116	1474	1052	308	654	662	1548	250
Spokane, WA	1954	1845	3150	990	2706	2254	1826	1314	1968	366	1062	1658	2526	2468	3418	2088
Springfield, IL	300	760	1531	2056	960	934	206	530	349	1494	889	399	768	722	1798	323
Springfield, MA	767	1724	512	3026	1156	1794	867	1497	851	2280	1856	1112	688	883	738	796
Springfield, MO	588	447	1817	1744	964	708	515	464	658	1418	799	708	933	816	2043	566
Springfield, OH	142	1034	1229	2330	893	1201	280	895	315	1692	1255	524	430	513	1454	68
Stamford, CT	686	1620	600	2951	1052	1689	792	1423	776	2205	1782	1038	584	778	826	677
Stockton, CA	2242	1659	3438	123	2665	1939	2112	1496	2256	1158	1199	2196	2719	2571	3705	2350
Syracuse, NY	546	1552	733	2805	1158	1733	646	1277	630	2059	1636	892	652	822	959	577
Tacoma, WA	2247	2096	3442	889	2997	2506	2116	1610	2260	657	1314	1949	2818	2758	3710	2379
Tallahassee, FL	906	867	1744	2396	148	730	935	1346	1035	2299	1665	1179	578	413	1969	776
Tampa, FL	1121	1138	1778	2666	130	1001	1150	1558	1250	2511	1904	1394	674	584	2004	959
Terre Haute, IN	210	829	1438	2126	840	999	164	705	305	1570	1051	390	632	596	1664	187
Toledo, OH	112	1130	1127	2370	1014	1322	212	842	188	1625	1201	457	548	634	1395	189
Topeka, KS	680	496	1908	1682	1203	792	578	262	721	1227	575	691	1082	965	2134	657
Toronto, ON	402	1421	847	2649	1214	1614	490	1121	362	1904	1480	736	740	854	1114	480
Torrington, CT	745	1711	574	3010	1124	1780	851	1482	836	2264	1841	1097	656	870	800	760
Trenton, NJ	641	1537	704	2862	956	1607	748	1379	732	2161	1738	994	488	679	930	592
Troy, NY	691	1715	595	2949	1174	1785	790	1421	775	2204	1780	1036	708	874	821	722
Tucson, AZ	1821	922	3050	702	1922	1118	1748	1165	1891	1350	1013	1821	2072	1883	3275	1799
Tulsa, OK	770	303	1998	1562	1083	555	696	450	839	1456	728	889	1078	929	2224	747
Tupelo, MS	631	587	1706	2026	580	654	591	916	734	1869	1235	798	616	426	1932	527
Tuscaloosa, AL	660	617	1659	2156	462	636	688	1046	788	1999	1365	932	538	349	1884	555
Tyler, TX	990	130	2151	1658	894	248	924	736	1068	1742	1013	1114	1031	841	2377	928
Utica, NY	596	1601	683	2854	1210	1786	695	1326	680	2108	1685	941	704	875	909	626
Vallejo, CA	2251	1712	3448	188	2718	1987	2123	1506	2266	1168	1210	2206	2800	2624	3715	2361
Vancouver, BC	2370	2220	3360	1064	3122	2630	2242	1734	2384	782	1438	2074	2942	2884	3627	2504
Ventura, CA	2227	1475	3424	228	2475	1671	2098	1482	2242	1325	1140	2182	2532	2384	3691	2244
Victoria, TX	1278	310	2393	1688	980	166	1213	943	1357	1812	1085	1442	1256	1066	2619	1216
Virginia Beach, VA	744	1402	996	2852	702	1405	868	1470	852	2281	1816	1114	254	445	1221	644
Waco, TX	1102	89	2285	1625	1022	234	1028	722	1171	1615	886	1221	1159	969	2511	1067
Walnut Creek, CA	2264	1690	3461	166	2696	1965	2136	1518	2279	1181	1222	2219	2750	2602	3728	2374
Warren, OH	258	1252	1026	2516	963	1392	357	988	342	1770	1347	603	489	603	1252	277
Washington, DC	570	1364	867	2802	776	1434	676	1307	661	2090	1666	922	310	500	1092	520
Waterbury, CT	724	1690	554	2990	1103	1760	831	1462	815	2244	1820	1076	636	849	779	740
Waterloo, IA	447	871	1644	1938	1230	1113	319	410	462	1190	769	326	1003	966	1912	557
Waukegan, IL	216	984	1411	2169	1106	1181	68	641	229	1356	1000	168	787	759	1678	348
Wausau, WI	450	1164	1482	2231	1338	1327	320	702	463	1155	1061	96	1021	993	1750	582
West Palm Beach, FL	1264	1281	1870	2810	273	1144	1294	1701	1394	2654	2046	1538	765	675	2095	1102
Wheeling, WV	282	1206	1052	2501	896	1345	436	1065	421	1849	1426	682	422	536	1278	231
Wichita, KS	806	356	2036	1505	1256	652	713	277	856	1283	555	826	1209	1102	2261	784
Wichita Falls, TX	1012	114	2241	1422	1119	424	938	575	1082	1412	684	1132	1274	1066	2466	989
Wilmington, DE	614	1469	764	2835	896	1538	721	1351	705	2134	1710	966	429	620	990	565
Winnipeg, MB	1034	1294	1930	2000	1922	1590	904	687	1047	810	1064	736	1605	1577	2198	1166
Winston-Salem, NC	540	1133	1218	2571	529	1134	677	1264	700	2089	1610	921	29	175	1444	438
Worcester, MA	814	1758	462	3072	1190	1828	914	1544	898	2327	1903	1159	723	917	687	832
Yakima, WA	2155	1942	3352	823	2872	2352	2026	1456	2170	566	1160	1859	2750	2634	3619	2288
Youngstown, OH	265	1255	1020	2530	962	1394	372	1002	356	1785	1361	617	488	602	1246	280

	Harrisburg, PA	Hartford, CT	High Point, NC	Houston, TX	Huntington, WV	Huntsville, AL	Indianapolis, IN	Iowa City, IA	Jackson, MS	Jacksonville, FL	Janesville, WI	Jefferson City, MO	Jersey City, NJ	Joliet, IL	Kalamazoo, MI
Pine Bluff, AR	1083	1367	816	450	700	365	599	636	215	812	709	389	1248	646	780
Pittsburgh, PA	205	469	417	1354	276	690	359	668	983	833	574	728	369	471	375
Pittsfield, MA	328	77	741	1790	740	1078	819	1058	1358	1130	965	1188	197	862	766
Pomona, CA	2592	2870	2434	1526	2260	1984	2046	1776	1811	2394	1976	1752	2768	1968	2124
Pontiac, MI	510	744	614	1340	355	698	322	490	993	1030	396	648	642	294	142
Port Arthur, TX	1376	1660	1027	99	1104	678	1026	1005	352	784	1078	752	1541	1070	1206
Portland, ME	482	197	877	1944	894	1232	1034	1286	1512	1256	1193	1402	320	1090	994
Portland, OR	2764	2998	2806	2370	2505	2476	2268	1904	2474	2954	2036	1956	2896	2096	2252
Providence, RI	349	114	744	1810	760	1099	889	1170	1379	1124	1077	1258	186	974	878
Provo, UT	2078	2311	2092	1462	1790	1762	1580	1217	1708	2240	1416	1242	2209	1409	1565
Pueblo, CO	1654	1947	1633	923	1332	1240	1109	899	1086	1722	1098	783	1818	1090	1247
Québec, QC	668	431	1080	2129	1034	1418	1005	1214	1698	1470	1121	1373	536	1018	866
Racine, WI	745	978	811	1167	534	677	268	261	820	1156	82	456	876	109	232
Raleigh, NC	396	617	98	1210	379	579	640	1008	794	456	932	984	498	828	756
Rapid City, SD	1575	1808	1715	1303	1414	1384	1104	740	1436	1863	809	865	1707	932	1063
Reading, PA	66	241	488	1524	474	813	600	922	1093	868	830	969	122	726	630
Regina, SK	1846	2080	1912	1754	1634	1777	1370	1079	1868	2256	1080	1297	1978	1204	1334
Reno, NV	2558	2792	2600	1972	2298	2269	2062	1698	2135	2748	1898	1750	2690	1890	2046
Richmond, VA	240	462	220	1332	366	646	627	994	917	600	911	954	342	808	712
Riverside, CA	2580	2858	2423	1500	2250	1972	2035	1764	1786	2369	1964	1742	2756	1956	2112
Roanoke, VA	294	577	122	1182	229	470	490	857	750	582	781	816	458	678	606
Rochester, MN	1010	1243	1076	1147	798	940	533	197	933	1419	243	442	1141	367	498
Rochester, NY	262	332	694	1568	554	903	568	808	1198	1110	715	937	333	611	516
Rockford, IL	752	986	818	1078	541	676	276	178	788	1154	34	392	884	108	240
Sacramento, CA	2690	2923	2732	1938	2430	2299	2192	1830	2126	2722	2029	1882	2822	2021	2178
Saginaw, MI	567	800	673	1360	414	744	342	511	1014	1088	418	670	699	315	163
St. Johnsbury, VT	492	205	886	1953	904	1242	979	1218	1522	1266	1125	1347	329	1022	926
St. Joseph, MO	1050	1343	1064	782	762	733	505	292	785	1212	492	214	1214	454	610
St. Louis, MO	788	1081	759	784	458	428	243	264	492	906	322	134	952	259	415
St. Paul, MN	1063	1296	1128	1187	852	993	586	310	1046	1472	296	517	1194	420	550
St. Petersburg, FL	1058	1280	679	971	920	673	1017	1301	696	222	1314	1171	1160	1212	1243
Salem, OR	2814	3047	2854	2419	2552	2524	2316	1952	2522	3001	2084	2004	2944	2144	2300
Salinas, CA	2864	3097	2678	1855	2504	2227	2290	2004	2054	2650	2203	1996	2996	2195	2352
Salisbury, MD	206	336	388	1500	520	818	693	1015	1085	748	922	1062	217	819	723
Salt Lake City, UT	2040	2274	2082	1646	1780	1751	1543	1180	1749	2230	1380	1232	2172	1372	1528
San Angelo, TX	1654	1938	1372	368	1270	936	1115	1037	672	1236	1194	796	1818	1131	1287
San Antonio, TX	1659	1943	1310	198	1276	942	1149	1089	635	1066	1228	829	1824	1164	1320
San Bernardino, CA	2571	2849	2414	1502	2240	1963	2026	1755	1787	2370	1955	1732	2748	1947	2104
San Diego, CA	2643	2936	2462	1477	2312	2035	2098	1862	1762	2346	2061	1779	2808	2053	2210
San Francisco, CA	2776	3009	2758	1935	2516	2307	2278	1915	2134	2730	2114	1967	2908	2107	2263
San Jose, CA	2804	3036	2717	1894	2544	2266	2306	1943	2093	2689	2142	1995	2935	2135	2291
San Mateo, CA	2795	3028	2744	1921	2535	2293	2298	1934	2120	2716	2134	1986	2926	2126	2283
Santa Ana, CA	2612	2890	2455	1540	2282	2004	2067	1796	1826	2409	1996	1774	2789	1988	2144
Santa Barbara, CA	2705	2983	2548	1649	2374	2097	2160	1889	1934	2518	2089	1866	2882	2081	2238
Santa Rosa, CA	2792	3025	2834	1982	2532	2354	2294	1932	2180	2777	2131	1984	2924	2123	2280
Savannah, GA	713	934	333	982	574	442	776	1070	594	138	1082	940	815	970	986
Schenectady, NY	308	123	721	1770	720	1058	768	1008	1338	1112	914	1137	178	811	716
Scranton, PA	120	192	532	1581	532	870	647	909	1150	956	816	1016	121	712	616
Seattle, WA	2730	2962	2796	2444	2518	2522	2253	1878	2574	3000	1962	2003	2861	2087	2218
Shreveport, LA	1248	1532	914	242	894	549	793	805	215	811	877	552	1412	814	974
Sioux City, IA	1173	1406	1287	999	986	956	676	312	1008	1434	408	437	1304	504	660
Sioux Falls, SD	1237	1470	1372	1084	1070	1041	760	397	1092	1520	470	522	1369	589	724
South Bend, IN	571	804	642	1148	401	551	148	300	802	1030	206	458	703	104	86
Spokane, WA	2450	2684	2516	2206	2238	2242	1974	1598	2294	2721	1684	1724	2582	1808	1938
Springfield, IL	757	1051	758	886	474	497	212	225	594	976	225	195	922	162	318
Springfield, MA	312	26	708	1774	724	1062	862	1104	1342	1086	1010	1231	150	907	812
Springfield, MO	1000	1294	922	659	670	496	455	386	493	979	534	136	1165	471	628
Springfield, OH	412	706	420	1152	160	488	131	501	784	835	422	500	576	319	262
Stamford, CT	208	79	603	1669	620	958	748	1029	1238	982	936	1116	45	833	737
Stockton, CA	2737	2970	2708	1890	2477	2258	2240	1876	2084	2680	2076	1928	2868	2068	2225
Syracuse, NY	252	251	664	1713	628	1002	644	883	1282	1090	790	1012	247	687	590
Tacoma, WA	2742	2974	2808	2456	2530	2534	2265	1890	2586	3012	1974	2015	2873	2099	2230
Tallahassee, FL	964	1222	560	710	762	402	779	1066	435	164	1076	936	1102	974	1004
Tampa, FL	1035	1256	656	981	896	650	994	1278	706	198	1291	1148	1138	1188	1220
Terre Haute, IN	621	915	622	950	338	378	76	332	603	856	301	295	786	184	274
Toledo, OH	426	659	537	1273	278	609	227	448	904	953	355	596	558	252	152
Topeka, KS	1092	1385	1071	743	770	740	547	372	717	1218	571	221	1256	534	690
Toronto, ON	388	491	730	1565	588	900	518	727	1196	1145	634	887	492	531	379
Torrington, CT	299	51	675	1760	710	1049	826	1088	1329	1054	995	1195	118	892	796
Trenton, NJ	129	183	507	1587	537	875	663	985	1155	886	892	1031	63	788	692
Troy, NY	304	113	716	1765	716	1053	788	1028	1334	1106	934	1156	172	831	735
Tucson, AZ	2336	2526	2054	1070	1952	1618	1688	1502	1355	1938	1702	1369	2501	1704	1860
Tulsa, OK	1182	1475	1067	506	850	616	636	577	534	1099	715	317	1346	652	808
Tupelo, MS	901	1184	598	634	556	150	504	636	195	596	708	506	1065	568	704
Tuscaloosa, AL	854	1138	520	616	584	155	532	766	185	478	829	636	1018	727	757
Tyler, TX	1346	1630	1013	199	956	647	856	842	313	910	940	582	1510	877	1037
Utica, NY	304	200	717	1766	678	1054	693	932	1334	1142	839	1061	256	736	640
Vallejo, CA	2748	2981	2789	1938	2488	2311	2250	1887	2137	2734	2086	1939	2879	2079	2235
Vancouver, BC	2866	3100	2932	2582	2654	2658	2390	2015	2710	3137	2100	2140	2998	2224	2354
Ventura, CA	2678	2956	2521	1623	2348	2070	2134	1863	1908	2491	2062	1840	2855	2054	2210
Victoria, TX	1588	1872	1238	124	1245	889	1145	1129	563	995	1268	870	1752	1205	1326
Virginia Beach, VA	341	474	273	1385	472	752	734	1101	970	633	1012	1060	355	908	812
Waco, TX	1480	1764	1141	186	1096	762	968	909	441	1038	1047	649	1644	984	1140
Walnut Creek, CA	2760	2994	2740	1916	2500	2289	2263	1900	2116	2712	2100	1952	2892	2092	2248
Warren, OH	285	503	478	1343	294	678	344	594	974	894	501	712	402	398	302
Washington, DC	124	346	328	1414	422	702	591	914	982	708	820	960	226	717	621
Waterbury, CT	279	30	654	1740	690	1029	806	1068	1309	1034	975	1174	97	872	776
Waterloo, IA	944	1177	992	1064	708	768	447	83	819	1246	191	328	1076	275	432
Waukegan, IL	710	944	776	1133	498	642	234	247	786	1122	92	422	842	74	198
Wausau, WI	944	1178	1010	1278	734	875	468	324	986	1354	178	591	1076	302	432
West Palm Beach, FL	1126	1348	747	1124	988	793	1138	1421	849	286	1434	1291	1228	1332	1363
Wheeling, WV	242	529	412	1296	228	632	301	672	928	827	580	670	406	477	381
Wichita, KS	1219	1512	1198	603	896	789	674	506	707	1272	706	325	1383	669	826
Wichita Falls, TX	1424	1717	1263	376	1094	812	879	801	538	1135	958	560	1588	895	1051
Wilmington, DE	102	243	447	1518	486	807	635	958	1087	827	865	1004	124	761	666
Winnipeg, MB	1528	1762	1594	1542	1316	1459	1052	761	1550	1938	762	980	1660	886	1016
Winston-Salem, NC	430	696	18	1114	267	471	528	895	699	460	819	854	577	716	644
Worcester, MA	347	62	742	1808	758	1096	898	1150	1376	1122	1057	1267	184	954	858
Yakima, WA	2651	2884	2740	2304	2438	2409	2174	1800	2408	2888	1884	1890	2782	2008	2138
Youngstown, OH	265	497	478	1346	300	682	347	609	977	893	516	715	395	412	316

Mileage Directory/Pine Bluff, AR—Youngstown, OH

and McNally software packages offer more than standard ileages:

- **Truck-type, hazmat, and lowest-cost routing**
- **HHG tariff mileage**
- **Fuel network management**

isit trucking.randmcnally.com to learn more about what Rand cNally trucking applications can do for your bottom line.

Mileages in this Mileage Directory are from the Rand McNally *MileMaker Practical Routing System*, © Rand McNally. **These mileages are for general reference only and should not be used for the purposes of tariff computation.** For tariff purposes, refer to the applicable official tariff. Mileages between each of the 300 cities listed in this chart are computed over National Interstate, U.S. and primary state highways, and Canadian provincial highways via highways designated as truck-usable by the Household Goods Carriers' Bureau Committee. Practical routing may have highway segments not included in the federally designated National Network.

	Kenosha, WI	Kingston, ON	Knoxville, TN	Lafayette, LA	Lake Charles, LA	Lancaster, PA	Lansing, MI	Laredo, TX	Las Vegas, NV	Lawrence, KS	Lawrence, MA	Lawton, OK	Lexington, KY	Lincoln, NE	Little Rock, AR	London, ON	Long Beach, CA	Longview, TX	Lorain, OH	Los Angeles, CA	Louisville, KY	Lowell, MA	Lubbock, TX	Lynchburg, VA	Macon, GA	Madison, WI	Manchester, NH	Mansfield, OH	Marquette, MI	Memphis, TN	Miami, FL	Midland, TX	Milwaukee, WI	Minneapolis, MN	Mobile, AL	Modesto, CA	Monroe, LA	Montgomery, AL	Montréal, QC	Muncie, IN	Nashua, NH	Nashville, TN	Newark, NJ	New Bedford, MA
e Bluff, AR	732	1296	543	325	343	1121	851	763	1562	457	1478	459	574	630	44	1031	1720	242	876	1709	538	1470	674	854	614	747	1496	817	1047	153	1127	659	758	858	408	1928	142	427	1468	663	1481	364	1239	1460
sburgh, PA	535	479	491	1201	1270	240	347	1668	2196	884	582	1187	400	967	916	371	2444	1146	152	2433	396	573	1481	376	738	612	600	170	721	781	1185	1563	560	874	1001	2564	1100	833	606	330	585	572	361	581
sfield, MA	926	287	866	1576	1645	310	738	2141	2586	1344	148	1646	863	1358	1393	472	2866	1635	538	2854	860	140	1940	629	1094	1004	167	583	1112	1257	1482	2040	951	1265	1373	2956	1475	1206	257	760	152	1045	195	172
nona, CA	2030	2652	2161	1742	1668	2626	2195	1380	246	1558	2972	1260	2138	1478	1642	2385	39	1539	2296	28	2066	2964	1086	2473	2232	1954	2990	2288	2265	1772	2710	1079	2033	1904	1991	339	1694	2056	2828	2110	2976	1982	2764	2972
ntiac, MI	358	394	556	1219	1288	544	70	1616	2018	804	846	1134	388	790	902	128	2297	1132	170	2286	404	838	1428	610	854	436	864	184	424	788	1382	1482	382	696	1026	2387	1107	858	570	270	850	580	638	846
t Arthur, TX	1159	1701	836	131	57	1414	1278	451	1620	726	1771	524	980	978	413	1436	1656	206	1280	1652	943	1763	670	1147	730	1116	1789	1222	1474	562	1099	623	1184	1179	380	1962	312	545	1879	1090	1774	769	1532	1753
tland, ME	1154	459	1020	1730	1799	469	966	2295	2814	1558	88	1861	1017	1586	1547	700	3093	1789	766	3082	1074	97	2155	718	1225	1231	98	798	1340	1412	1609	2194	1179	1492	1527	3183	1630	1360	278	986	105	1199	323	169
tland, OR	2104	2780	2534	2518	2464	2800	2324	2336	1022	1814	3100	1884	2382	1608	2214	2514	986	2256	2424	963	2310	3092	1792	2786	2690	2002	3120	2422	2001	2318	3270	1910	2068	1734	2666	656	2410	2638	2956	2310	3104	2358	2892	3100
vidence, RI	1038	432	887	1597	1666	336	850	2162	2698	1414	79	1716	884	1470	1414	617	2977	1656	655	2966	954	71	2010	585	1092	1115	98	672	1224	1278	1476	2060	1063	1376	1394	3068	1496	1226	361	860	83	1066	190	31
vo, UT	1472	2093	1820	1614	1568	2112	1636	1363	378	1048	2414	1075	1668	920	1448	1826	658	1352	1738	647	1596	2405	901	2072	1976	1396	2432	1736	1706	1578	2556	1007	1474	1345	1901	763	1507	1898	2269	1622	2417	1644	2206	2413
eblo, CO	1153	1775	1360	1075	1029	1688	1318	987	860	589	2060	536	1208	601	898	1508	1133	814	1419	1122	1137	2052	444	1612	1516	1077	2078	1351	1388	1028	2038	561	1156	1027	1279	1372	968	1348	1950	1172	2063	1184	1810	2030
ébec, QC	1082	344	1206	1916	1984	649	791	2314	2741	1528	375	1832	1074	1514	1609	616	3021	1840	768	3010	1089	384	2126	968	1434	1159	351	812	940	1474	1822	2180	1107	1420	1712	3111	1815	1545	159	951	369	1265	534	459
cine, WI	11	760	627	1046	1115	780	304	1425	1788	603	1081	943	455	560	729	494	2068	959	405	2057	384	1073	1237	808	892	104	1099	403	318	611	1471	1290	28	362	1005	2158	866	837	936	312	1084	559	873	1080
eigh, NC	892	782	367	996	1065	395	744	1561	2406	1140	728	1304	503	1302	894	799	2564	1071	597	2554	572	720	1542	192	424	970	746	564	1118	758	808	1528	918	1231	744	2772	912	577	876	612	731	546	490	710
pid City, SD	877	1591	1442	1450	1396	1610	1134	1483	1078	729	1912	944	1290	579	1094	1324	1358	1188	1235	1347	1219	1903	838	1694	1598	775	1930	1233	1005	1227	2178	955	840	608	1626	1384	1278	1547	1766	1142	1915	1266	1703	1911
ading, PA	790	367	601	1311	1380	34	602	1876	2437	1125	352	1428	598	1222	1128	482	2685	1370	408	2674	668	344	1722	329	830	868	370	424	976	992	1220	1774	816	1129	1108	2820	1210	940	468	571	355	780	113	334
gina, SK	1148	1776	1729	1898	1884	1881	1405	1934	1443	1161	2066	1395	1557	1012	1526	1754	1723	1656	1506	1712	1486	2074	1373	1909	1992	1046	2042	1504	969	1659	2571	1490	1111	777	2058	1632	1710	1938	1782	1413	2060	1659	1974	2182
no, NV	1952	2574	2327	2125	2079	2593	2118	1807	447	1608	2894	1585	2176	1400	2008	2307	492	1863	2218	470	2104	2886	1411	2579	2484	1876	2913	2216	2065	2112	3064	1506	1956	1826	2328	204	2018	2432	2750	2104	2898	2151	2686	2894
hmond, VA	872	626	434	1118	1187	239	684	1683	2422	1110	572	1370	490	1272	960	634	2630	1193	489	2620	560	564	1623	114	568	949	590	506	1058	825	952	1607	897	1210	867	2839	1034	699	720	598	576	612	334	554
erside, CA	2019	2640	2150	1716	1642	2615	2184	1354	234	1548	2961	1249	2126	1467	1630	2374	59	1514	2285	54	2055	2952	1075	2462	2221	1943	2980	2278	2254	1760	2684	1053	2022	1892	1965	364	1668	2030	2816	2098	2964	1972	2753	2960
anoke, VA	742	680	258	968	1037	331	594	1533	2297	972	688	1195	352	1134	785	648	2455	1027	446	2444	422	680	1447	53	486	819	706	413	968	649	934	1432	767	1080	765	2664	867	598	796	461	691	437	450	670
chester, MN	311	1025	892	1153	1166	1044	568	1342	1626	441	1346	842	720	398	782	758	1906	938	670	1894	649	1337	1136	1072	1155	209	1364	668	442	724	1734	1189	274	88	1123	1996	965	1045	1200	576	1349	822	1137	1345
chester, NY	675	217	768	1425	1494	302	487	1880	2335	1093	404	1396	594	1108	1129	222	2614	1359	288	2604	609	396	1690	563	1015	753	422	332	861	994	1462	1776	701	1014	1231	2705	1313	1064	333	509	407	785	330	428
ckford, IL	90	768	634	1014	1082	788	312	1360	1704	520	1088	878	462	478	640	502	1984	870	412	1974	392	1080	1172	816	890	73	1106	410	382	578	1470	1224	93	334	978	2074	834	836	944	320	1092	558	880	1088
cramento, CA	2084	2706	2458	2115	2079	2725	2248	1791	578	1740	3026	1576	2306	1532	1957	2438	406	1854	2350	383	2236	3018	1402	2710	2548	2008	3044	2348	2196	2087	3037	1490	2086	1957	2318	72	2008	2408	2881	2235	3029	2282	2818	3026
ginaw, MI	379	440	604	1240	1308	602	88	1638	2038	825	903	1156	436	811	922	173	2318	1152	227	2308	450	895	1450	670	902	456	921	240	354	805	1441	1503	404	718	1072	2408	1060	905	615	291	906	626	695	902
Johnsbury, VT	1086	330	1030	1740	1808	478	898	2304	2746	1503	147	1806	1027	1518	1556	602	3025	1798	698	3014	1020	156	2100	728	1234	1163	123	742	1272	1421	1618	2203	1111	1424	1536	3115	1639	1369	148	920	141	1208	333	231
Joseph, MO	546	1138	791	814	801	1084	682	976	1363	78	1456	453	639	148	443	872	1642	573	783	1632	568	1448	747	1043	948	470	1474	747	781	576	1527	800	549	420	975	1744	627	896	1314	547	1459	615	1206	1426
Louis, MO	348	916	486	718	787	822	486	1064	1602	290	1194	582	334	452	345	651	1839	576	548	1828	263	1186	876	738	642	360	1212	485	669	283	1222	930	380	563	682	2048	538	588	1092	306	1197	310	944	1164
Paul, MN	364	1078	945	1193	1206	1098	622	1382	1666	481	1399	882	773	438	822	811	1946	978	722	1934	702	1390	1176	1125	1208	262	1417	720	397	837	1788	1229	327	9	1236	2036	1005	1154	1254	629	1402	875	1190	1398
Petersburg, FL	1276	1444	697	758	826	1057	1268	1322	2384	1327	1390	1288	866	1488	931	1342	2528	973	1137	2523	907	1382	1444	808	403	1352	1408	1104	1590	796	262	1429	1302	1614	503	2750	813	474	1539	1068	1394	732	1152	1372
em, OR	2152	2828	2582	2566	2512	2848	2372	2384	978	1862	3150	1932	2430	1656	2262	2562	940	2304	2474	918	2358	3140	1840	2834	2737	2049	3168	2472	2048	2366	3318	1958	2114	1780	2714	611	2458	2688	3005	2358	3152	2406	2942	3148
inas, CA	2258	2880	2405	2044	1996	2899	2422	1708	490	1802	3200	1504	2382	1706	1885	2612	323	1782	2524	301	2310	3192	1330	2716	2476	2182	3218	2522	2370	2016	2966	1408	2260	2131	2247	117	1937	2336	3055	2354	3203	2226	2992	3200
isbury, MD	882	512	606	1287	1355	163	695	1851	2530	1218	447	1543	644	1315	1133	672	2803	1362	500	2792	714	439	1795	299	716	960	466	517	1069	997	1100	1780	908	1221	1035	2912	1202	868	596	664	450	785	209	429
t Lake City, UT	1434	2056	1809	1793	1740	2075	1599	1406	421	1090	2376	1160	1657	882	1490	1789	700	1531	1700	690	1586	2368	944	2061	1966	1358	2395	1698	1669	1594	2544	1050	1438	1308	1942	722	1686	1914	2232	1586	2380	1633	2168	2376
n Angelo, TX	1220	1788	1113	584	510	1692	1358	366	1161	690	2048	290	1145	813	589	1524	1211	400	1446	1206	1108	2040	197	1425	1102	1216	2067	1388	1541	724	1552	112	1252	1165	834	1517	555	917	1964	1178	2052	934	1810	2030
n Antonio, TX	1254	1822	1119	414	340	1697	1392	160	1338	782	2054	436	1151	904	595	1557	1362	349	1452	1357	1114	2046	390	1430	1012	1266	2072	1394	1575	730	1382	328	1285	1217	663	1668	504	828	1998	1212	2057	941	1815	2036
n Bernardino, CA	2010	2632	2141	1717	1644	2606	2174	1356	226	1538	2952	1240	2117	1458	1621	2364	69	1515	2276	60	2046	2944	1066	2452	2212	1934	2970	2268	2244	1751	2686	1055	2012	1883	1967	366	1670	2032	2807	2089	2955	1962	2744	2951
n Diego, CA	2116	2738	2213	1692	1618	2678	2280	1331	332	1644	3058	1312	2189	1564	1678	2470	110	1490	2382	120	2118	3050	1148	2524	2191	2040	3076	2340	2350	1824	2660	1030	2118	1989	1942	432	1645	2006	2913	2162	3061	2034	2799	3020
n Francisco, CA	2170	2791	2485	2124	2076	2810	2334	1788	570	1825	3112	1584	2392	1618	1965	2524	403	1862	2436	381	2322	3104	1410	2796	2556	2094	3130	2434	2282	2096	3045	1488	2172	2043	2327	92	2017	2416	2967	2320	3115	2306	2904	3111
n Jose, CA	2198	2819	2444	2082	2036	2838	2362	1748	528	1853	3140	1543	2420	1646	1924	2552	362	1820	2464	340	2349	3131	1369	2755	2515	2122	3158	2462	2310	2054	3004	1446	2200	2071	2286	84	1975	2374	2994	2348	3143	2265	2932	3139
n Mateo, CA	2189	2810	2471	2109	2062	2830	2354	1774	556	1844	3131	1570	2412	1637	1951	2544	389	1848	2455	367	2340	3123	1396	2782	2542	2113	3150	2453	2302	2081	3031	1474	2192	2062	2313	87	2002	2402	2986	2340	3134	2292	2923	3130
nta Ana, CA	2051	2672	2182	1756	1682	2647	2216	1394	266	1580	2993	1281	2158	1499	1662	2406	24	1553	2317	31	2087	2985	1107	2494	2254	1975	3012	2310	2286	1792	2724	1093	2054	1924	2005	344	1708	2070	2848	2130	2996	2004	2785	2992
nta Barbara, CA	2144	2766	2275	1864	1791	2740	2308	1503	360	1672	3086	1374	2251	1592	1755	2498	113	1662	2410	94	2180	3078	1200	2586	2346	2068	3104	2402	2379	1885	2833	1202	2147	2017	2114	324	1817	2206	2941	2224	3089	2096	2878	3085
nta Rosa, CA	2186	2808	2560	2170	2123	2826	2350	1835	616	1841	3128	1631	2408	1634	2012	2540	450	1908	2452	427	2338	3120	1456	2812	2603	2110	3146	2450	2298	2142	3092	1534	2188	2059	2373	138	2063	2462	2983	2337	3131	2353	2920	3128
vannah, GA	1034	1099	420	769	838	712	939	1334	2275	1096	1044	1173	591	1257	763	994	2433	870	792	2422	663	1036	1342	462	165	1120	1063	758	1313	628	490	1327	1060	1382	538	2642	711	350	1194	793	1048	500	806	1027
henectady, NY	875	236	846	1556	1625	292	687	2121	2535	1293	195	1595	794	1308	1373	421	2814	1615	488	2804	809	187	1890	609	1074	953	213	532	1061	1237	1464	2020	900	1214	1353	2904	1456	1186	222	709	198	1025	177	219
ranton, PA	776	268	658	1368	1436	132	588	1932	2436	1172	304	1474	655	1209	1184	428	2716	1426	394	2705	688	296	1768	420	886	854	322	411	962	1049	1309	1831	802	1115	1164	2806	1267	997	384	598	307	836	117	314
attle, WA	2031	2745	2580	2592	2538	2764	2288	2410	1128	1866	3066	1960	2428	1682	2288	2478	1158	2330	2390	1136	2357	3058	1866	2792	2736	1929	3084	2388	1928	2365	3316	1984	1994	1660	2764	828	2486	2685	2920	2296	3069	2404	2858	3065
reveport, LA	926	1490	707	211	229	1285	1045	565	1473	574	1642	377	768	748	212	1225	1630	62	1070	1626	732	1634	533	1018	644	916	1660	1011	1224	347	1126	518	935	976	408	1839	98	459	1662	857	1646	558	1404	1624
ux City, IA	474	1188	1014	1037	1024	1208	732	1180	1379	300	1509	640	862	151	666	922	1658	796	833	1648	791	1501	861	1266	1170	401	1527	831	698	799	1750	988	480	301	1198	1748	850	1119	1364	718	1512	838	1301	1508
ux Falls, SD	538	1252	1099	1122	1109	1272	796	1264	1400	385	1573	725	947	236	751	986	1679	880	897	1668	876	1565	904	1351	1256	436	1592	895	666	884	1834	1072	502	270	1282	1725	934	1204	1428	804	1576	923	1365	1572
uth Bend, IN	166	596	496	1028	1096	606	154	1426	1826	612	907	944	328	600	710	344	2106	941	231	2096	258	899	1238	640	766	244	926	244	482	592	1345	1292	192	506	878	2196	848	712	772	152	910	433	699	907
okane, WA	1752	2466	2300	2354	2300	2484	2009	2172	1142	1587	2786	1720	2148	1397	2050	2198	1238	2092	2110	1216	2078	2778	1628	2512	2457	1650	2804	2108	1648	2086	3036	1745	1714	1380	2484	898	2246	2406	2642	2016	2790	2124	2578	2786
ringfield, IL	251	846	555	820	889	792	389	1166	1662	350	1163	684	393	438	447	579	1941	678	490	1930	322	1155	979	755	712	263	1182	455	572	386	1291	1032	283	524	784	2034	640	658	1022	254	1166	379	913	1134
ringfield, MA	971	332	850	1560	1629	299	783	2125	2631	1387	102	1690	848	1404	1377	518	2910	1619	584	2900	903	93	1984	548	1055	1049	120	626	1157	1242	1439	2024	996	1310	1357	3000	1460	1190	302	814	105	1029	154	126
ringfield, MO	560	1129	649	631	642	1035	699	854	1470	200	1406	372	546	372	215	864	1628	450	761	1618	476	1398	666	961	745	572	1425	698	882	284	1294	719	592	601	683	1837	398	605	1305	519	1410	473	1156	1377
ringfield, OH	383	570	347	1010	1078	446	238	1465	1968	656	818	958	178	801	714	305	2215	944	168	2204	194	810	1252	416	645	460	836	109	612	578	1188	1306	408	722	816	2398	898	648	760	102	821	370	568	788
amford, CT	896	398	746	1456	1525	194	709	2021	2556	1273	189	1575	743	1329	1272	558	2836	1514	514	2825	813	181	1870	444	950	974	208	531	1082	1137	1334	1920	922	1235	1253	2926	1355	1085	374	719	192	924	49	171
ockton, CA	2131	2752	2435	2074	2032	2772	2296	1744	520	1786	3073	1534	2354	1579	1916	2486	358	1812	2397	336	2282	3065	1360	2746	2506	2055	3092	2395	2244	2046	2996	1443	2134	2004	2277	31	1967	2366	2928	2282	3076	2256	2865	3072
racuse, NY	750	137	790	1500	1569	262	563	1956	2410	1168	322	1471	670	1183	1204	297	2690	1434	363	2679	684	314	1765	553	1018	828	341	407	936	1069	1442	1852	776	1089	1297	2780	1399	1129	253	584	326	860	244	346
coma, WA	2042	2757	2592	2604	2550	2776	2300	2422	1140	1878	3078	1971	2440	1694	2300	2490	1126	2342	2402	1104	2369	3069	1878	2804	2748	1941	3096	2400	1940	2376	3328	1996	2006	1672	2776	796	2497	2697	2932	2308	3080	2416	2869	3077
llahassee, FL	1038	1350	490	497	565	1000	1030	1061	2123	1018	1332	1027	659	1254	670	1136	2267	712	980	2262	669	1324	1183	689	196	1114	1351	922	1353	535	479	1168	1063	1376	242	2489	552	213	1482	837	1336	493	1094	1314
mpa, FL	1252	1422	674	768	836	1034	1246	1332	2394	1304	1367	1298	843	1466	941	1319	2538	982	1114	2533	884	1358	1454	785	380	1329	1386	1081	1568	806	255	1439	1278	1590	513	2760	823	484	1516	1045	1370	709	1128	1349
re Haute, IN	248	750	430	829	898	656	334	1236	1763	451	1027	754	258	612	512	485	2010	742	382	2000	186	1019	1048	619	592	339	1046	319	563	394	1172	1101	274	600	706	2208	649	538	926	140	1031	260	778	998
edo, OH	316	442	468	1130	1200	460	120	1537	1976	752	762	1055	300	748	835	178	2256	1065	86	2244	315	754	1349	534	766	394	780	99	494	700	1305	1402	341	655	937	2346	1018	769	618	173	765	491	554	761
peka, KS	626	1218	798	778	753	1126	762	924	1288	27	1498	384	646	170	439	952	1568	525	852	1556	575	1489	678	1050	954	550	1516	789	861	508	1534	732	629	499	907	1784	622	828	1394	610	1501	622	1248	1468
ronto, ON	595	162	760	1422	1490	429	304	1828	2255	1041	563	1345	592	1027	1126	129	2534	1356	323	2524	606	555	1640	614	1050	672	582	367	593	991	1498	1693	620	934	1228	2624	1310	1061	338	465	566	782	489	587
rrington, CT	956	336	837	1547	1616	274	768	2112	2616	1351	163	1654	834	1388	1364	521	2895	1606	573	2884	867	155	1948	516	1022	1033	182	590	1142	1228	1406	2011	981	1294	1344	2986	1446	1176	306	778	166	1016	121	174
enton, NJ	852	403	663	1374	1442	98	664	1938	2499	1187	293	1490	660	1285	1190	563	2747	1432	470	2736	730	285	1784	348	855	930	312	487	1038	1054	1239	1837	878	1191	1154	2882	1272	986	442	634	296	842	55	275
oy, NY	895	256	842	1552	1620	285	707	2116	2555	1312	184	1615	839	1327	1368	441	2834	1610	508	2824	829	176	1910	604	1070	972	144	552	1081	1233	1458	2015	920	1234	1348	2924	1451	1181	216	729	188	1020	170	208
cson, AZ	1793	2362	1796	1285	1211	2374	1931	924	466	1155	2639	902	1828	1217	1271	2096	490	1083	1993	485	1708	2630	740	2107	1784	1680	2657	1930	1991	1406	2253	622	1759	1630	1534	796	1238	1599	2537	1751	2642	1617	2492	2713
lsa, OK	742	1310	794	551	526	1216	880	701	1290	219	1587	191	728	452	274	1045	1448	298	942	1437	656	1579	485	1105	865	754	1606	879	1063	404	1414	538	773	705	727	1656	451	724	1486	700	1591	615	1338	1558
pelo, MS	656	1152	360	421	490	938	755	992	1752	588	1295	650	430	824	240	887	1910	470	732	1900	394	1287	903	671	362	746	1314	673	971	105	911	887	682	934	278	2119	312	222	1324	562	1298	220	1057	1277
scaloosa, AL	791	1180	313	403	471	891	783	967	1882	718	1248	780	458	954	370	915	2030	461	760	2030	422	1240	933	624	284	867	1266	701	1106	235	793	918	816	1064	204	2249	302	104	1356	590	1252	246	1010	1230
er, TX	990	1553	805	303	239	1383	1108	469	1385	517	1740	289	832	738	275	1288	1542	41	1132	1538	795	1732	446	1116	742	978	1758	1074	1288	410	1225	430	998	970	506	1752	196	557	1724	920	1744	621	1502	1722
ca, NY	800	157	842	1552	1621	314	612	2005	2460	1217	272	1520	718	1232	1254	346	2739	1484	412	2728	734	264	1814	605	1070	877	290	456	986	1118	1494	1900	825	1138	1349	2829	1452	1182	274	634	275	910	254	296
llejo, CA	2142	2763	2516	2127	2080	2782	2306	1792	573	1797	3084	1588	2364	1590	1969	2496	407	1865	2408	384	2293	3075	1414	2768	2560	2066	3102	2406	2254	2099	3049	1491	2144	2015	2330	95	2020	2419	2938	2292	3087	2340	2876	3083
ncouver, BC	2168	2844	2716	2728	2676	2901	2425	2546	1266	2003	3202	2096	2565	1818	2426	2823	1301	2466	2526	1278	2494	3194	2004	2929	2873	2066	3220	2524	2065	2502	3452	2120	2130	1797	2900	971	2622	2822	2850	2433	3206	2540	2994	3202
ntura, CA	2118	2739	2248	1838	1764	2714	2282	1476	333	1646	3059	1348	2224	1566	1728	2472	86	1636	2383	68	2154	3051	1173	2560	2320	2041	3078	2376	2352	1859	2806	1176	2120	1990	2088	322	1791	2179	2914	2197	3062	2070	2851	3059
ctoria, TX	1294	1842	1047	342	268	1625	1397	186	1452	822	1982	477	1120	945	564	1577	1476	332	1421	1471	1084	1974	505	1359	941	1306	2001	1363	1615	699	1310	442	1326	1257	592	1782	464	756	2090	1208	1986	910	1744	1964
ginia Beach, VA	972	650	540	1172	1240	340	784	1736	2528	1216	584	1477	596	1378	1067	734	2737	1246	590	2726	666	576	1718	209	601	1050	603	607	1158	931	985	1702	998	1311	920	2946	1087	752	733	705	588	719	346	567
aco, TX	1074	1642	939	401	327	1518	1212	338	1352	602	1874	256	971	724	415	1377	1458	169	1272	1453	934	1866	349	1251	870	1086	1893	1214	1395	550	1353	334	1105	1037	634	1718	324	686	1818	1032	1878	761	1636	1856
alnut Creek, CA	2154	2776	2467	2105	2058	2795	2319	1770	551	1810	3096	1566	2377	1602	1947	2509	385	1843	2420	362	2306	3088	1392	2778	2538	2078	3114	2418	2267	2077	3027	1469	2157	2028	2308	73	1998	2397	2952	2306	3100	2288	2888	3096
arren, OH	462	445	538	1200	1268	320	274	1656	2122	868	616	1171	370	894	904	336	2401	1134	79	2390	384	607	1465	456	798	539	634	108	648	769	1246	1552	487	800	1006	2491	1088	839	572	295	619	560	398	606
ashington, DC	781	510	490	1200	1268	124	593	1765	2428	1116	456	1426	546	1214	1016	543	2687	1258	398	2676	616	448	1679	184	676	858	474	416	967	882	1060	1664	806	1120	974	2810	1100	808	604	562	460	668	218	438
aterbury, CT	935	388	817	1527	1596	254	748	2092	2595	1331	143	1633	814	1368	1343	571	2874	1585	553	2864	847	134	1928	496	1002	1013	161	570	1121	1208	1386	1990	961	1274	1324	2965	1426	1156	358	758	146	995	101	153
aterloo, IA	258	960	800	1046	1114	978	503	1259	1544	359	1280	759	628	316	672	692	1823	855	604	1812	557	1272	1054	989	982	185	1298	602	496	610	1562	1107	263	220	1009	1914	866	931	1135	489	1283	650	1072	1279
aukegan, IL	27	726	593	1012	1080	746	269	1390	1775	590	1046	908	421	547	694	459	2054	925	370	2044	350	1038	1202	773	858	129	1065	368	342	577	1436	1256	52	386	970	2144	832	803	902	277	1050	524	838	1046
ausau, WI	224	960	827	1213	1281	980	503	1552	1836	652	1281	1052	655	609	839	693	2116	1070	604	2105	584	1272	1346	1007	1090	144	1299	602	223	778	1670	1399	187	185	1176	2206	1033	1036	973	511	1284	757	1072	1280
est Palm Beach, FL	1396	1512	817	911	980	1126	1353	1476	2537	1447	1458	1441	986	1609	1084	1408	2681	1126	1206	2676	1028	1450	1598	876	523	1472	1477	1172	1710	949	68	1582	1422	1734	656	2904	966	627	1607	1188	1462	852	1220	1440
heeling, WV	541	531	486	1154	1222	276	353	1610	2138	826	641	1129	323	972	858	422	2386	1088	158	2375	338	633	1423	348	732	618	660	125	727	723	1180	1505	566	880	960	2568	1042	793	658	272	644	514	398	618
chita, KS	761	1353	925	751	697	1254	896	784	1267	160	1625	244	773	279	447	1086	1390	489	979	1379	702	1616	538	1177	1038	685	1643	916	996	577	1587	591	764	634	900	1598	644	898	1529	737	1628	749	1375	1595
chita Falls, TX	984	1552	990	528	482	1458	1122	541	1149	454	1830	53	970	577	430	1287	1307	266	1184	1296	899	1822	208	1302	968	980	1848	1121	1305	601	1450	295	1016	929	732	1516	421	783	1728	942	1833	812	1580	1800
lmington, DE	825	408	595	1305	1374	59	637	1870	2472	1160	354	1532	610	1258	1122	568	2720	1364	443	2709	680	345	1784	288	795	903	372	460	1011	986	1179	1769	850	1164	1094	2854	1204	926	502	606	357	774	115	336
nnipeg, MB	830	1414	1411	1580	1566	1564	1087	1722	1719	843	1704	1182	1239	694	1209	1393	1998	1338	1188	1988	1168	1714	1342	1591	1674	728	1680	1186	631	1341	2253	1530	793	459	1740	1907	1392	1620	1420	1095	1698	1341	1656	1788
nston-Salem, NC	780	816	259	901	970	468	632	1466	2298	1010	807	1196	390	1172	786	687	2456	976	485	2445	460	798	1448	144	364	858	826	451	1006	650	812	1432	805	1119	649	2664	816	482	932	499	810	438	568	789
orcester, MA	1018	379	884	1595	1663	334	830	2159	2678	1423	51	1726	882	1450	1411	564	2958	1653	630	2946	939	42	2020	583	1090	1096	69	662	1204	1276	1474	2058	1043	1357	1391	3048	1494	1224	330	850	54	1063	188	78
kima, WA	1952	2666	2468	2451	2398	2686	2210	2269	988	1748	2988	1818	2316	1540	2148	2400	1060	2190	2311	1038	2244	2978	1726	2720	2624	1850	3006	2309	1850	2252	3203	1842	1916	1582	2600	730	2344	2572	2842	2218	2990	2291	2779	2986
ungstown, OH	476	453	541	1204	1272	300	288	1659	2136	871	609	1174	372	908	908	345	2416	1138	94	2405	388	601	1468	437	798	554	628	111	662	772	1246	1554	501	815	1010	2506	1092	842	580	298	612	564	392	599

Mileage Directory/Pine Bluff, AR—Youngstown, OH

Mileage Directory, continued

	New Britain, CT	New Brunswick, NJ	New Haven, CT	New Orleans, LA	Newport News, VA	New York, NY	Niagara Falls, NY	Norfolk, VA	Norman, OK	North Platte, NE	Oakland, CA	Oceanside, CA	Odessa, TX	Ogden, UT	Oklahoma City, OK	Omaha, NE	Orlando, FL	Owensboro, KY	Paterson, NJ	Pendleton, OR	Pensacola, FL	Peoria, IL	Philadelphia, PA	Phoenix, AZ	Pine Bluff, AR	Pittsburgh, PA	Pittsfield, MA	Pomona, CA	Pontiac, MI	Port Arthur, TX	Portland, ME	Portland, OR	Providence, RI	Provo, UT	Pueblo, CO	Québec, QC	Racine, WI	Raleigh, NC	Rapid City, SD	Reading, PA	Regina, SK	Reno, NV	Richmond, VA
Pine Bluff, AR	1380	1235	1329	379	1056	1273	1102	1069	387	895	2000	1748	680	1526	378	617	905	472	1247	2050	466	555	1166	1383		932	1409	1684	918	422	1563	2256	1430	1490	940	1625	745	910	1137	1144	1569	2050	976
Pittsburgh, PA	460	356	450	1090	418	395	240	431	1120	1189	2570	2472	1585	1837	1100	914	975	504	368	2360	996	576	305	2108	932		488	2408	312	1327	666	2568	551	1880	1470	764	548	500	1378	262	1649	2361	344
Pittsfield, MA	88	216	115	1465	556	194	338	541	1579	1580	2961	2894	2062	2228	1560	1305	1272	968	186	2752	1368	978	279	2567	1409	488		2830	704	1702	233	2958	150	2271	1953	406	938	686	1769	278	2040	2752	530
Pomona, CA	2860	2743	2840	1870	2675	2784	2536	2688	1324	1253	400	77	1058	702	1306	1530	2487	2014	2755	1014	2048	1924	2692	341	1684	2408	2830		2262	1622	3057	990	2941	622	1098	2986	2032	2528	1322	2649	1687	472	2595
Pontiac, MI	734	654	714	1110	724	658	409	736	1068	1012	2392	2326	1504	1660	1048	736	1172	512	628	2183	1020	410	610	2055	918	312	704	2262		1345	932	2390	816	1702	1384	728	370	708	1200	568	1472	2184	650
Port Arthur, TX	1674	1528	1622	260	1282	1566	1506	1277	525	1104	2023	1604	646	1734	541	912	876	863	1540	2258	438	924	1459	1282	422	1327	1702	1622	1345		1856	2466	1723	1557	1018	2041	1172	1122	1398	1437	1849	2067	1244
Portland, ME	209	348	234	1619	683	307	566	667	1794	1808	3188	3122	2216	2456	1775	1533	1399	1195	320	2980	1522	1206	406	2782	1563	666	233	3057	932	1856		3186	162	2498	2145	278	1166	813	1996	437	2058	2980	657
Portland, OR	2988	2908	2970	2646	2950	2913	2664	2962	1944	1382	627	1047	1810	730	1924	1658	3047	2258	2884	208	2724	2054	2865	1332	2256	2568	2958	990	2390	2466	3186		3070	808	1376	3114	2094	2900	1214	2822	1143	578	2870
Providence, RI	106	215	101	1486	550	174	482	534	1649	1692	3072	3006	2082	2340	1630	1417	1266	1062	186	2864	1389	1090	272	2636	1430	551	150	2941	816	1723	162	3070		2382	2000	451	1050	680	1880	304	2152	2864	524
Provo, UT	2302	2221	2282	1743	2236	2226	1976	2248	1178	694	768	686	1002	80	1159	970	2333	1544	2196	601	1958	1366	2178	618	1490	1880	2271	622	1702	1557	2498	808	2382		593	2426	1473	2186	700	2135	1065	559	2156
Pueblo, CO	1938	1805	1899	1204	1776	1844	1658	1789	581	376	1378	1162	552	644	562	652	1815	1084	1817	1168	1336	1048	1754	796	940	1470	1953	1098	1384	1018	2145	1376	2000	593		2108	1155	1728	517	1712	956	1168	1696
Québec, QC	443	555	469	1805	896	534	567	880	1765	1736	3116	3050	2201	2383	1746	1461	1612	1197	525	2908	1708	1134	619	2752	1625	764	406	2986	728	2041	278	3114	451	2426	2108		1094	1026	1924	617	1934	2908	870
Racine, WI	969	888	949	1003	958	893	644	971	876	782	2163	2096	1312	1430	856	507	1248	409	864	1946	1000	218	845	1864	745	548	938	2032	370	1172	1166	2094	1050	1473	1155	1094		904	866	802	1137	1954	884
Raleigh, NC	612	471	579	885	188	514	659	184	1232	1522	2844	2593	1549	2170	1222	1290	598	658	514	2694	740	854	411	2228	910	500	686	2528	708	1122	813	2900	680	2186	1728	1026	904		1810	424	2006	2694	156
Rapid City, SD	1799	1719	1780	1619	1789	1724	1474	1801	876	344	1390	1386	976	657	857	525	1956	1166	1694	1067	1683	890	1676	1314	1137	1378	1769	1322	1200	1398	1996	1214	1880	700	517	1924	866	1810		1633	534	1181	1714
Reading, PA	242	116	203	1200	342	147	348	294	1361	1444	2825	2714	1796	2092	1342	1169	1010	776	121	2616	1103	817	62	2348	1144	262	278	2649	568	1437	437	2822	304	2135	1712	617	802	424	1633		1904	2616	268
Regina, SK	2070	1990	2050	2051	2060	1994	1746	2072	1328	821	1637	1752	1511	988	1309	958	2348	1523	1965	996	2115	1228	1946	1682	1569	1649	2040	1687	1472	1849	2058	1143	2152	1065	956	1934	1137	2006	534	1904		1428	1986
Reno, NV	2782	2702	2762	2254	2744	2706	2458	2756	1650	1176	209	536	1485	554	1631	1452	2840	2052	2678	592	2385	1847	2658	768	2050	2361	2752	472	2184	2067	2980	578	2864	559	1168	2908	1954	2694	1181	2616	1428		2664
Richmond, VA	456	314	423	1008	79	358	503	92	1298	1491	2872	2660	1629	2139	1289	1259	742	668	358	2662	862	841	256	2294	976	344	530	2595	650	1244	657	2870	524	2156	1696	870	884	156	1714	268	1986	2664	
Riverside, CA	2849	2732	2829	1845	2664	2773	2524	2676	1314	1242	426	83	1032	691	1294	1518	2462	2002	2744	1004	2022	1914	2680	315	1672	2397	2818	26	2250	1597	3046	1016	2930	610	1086	2974	2020	2517	1310	2638	1676	461	2584
Roanoke, VA	591	445	539	857	267	484	526	279	1122	1354	2734	2484	1454	2002	1114	1121	724	530	457	2526	760	703	376	2118	801	366	619	2419	558	1094	773	2732	640	2018	1559	958	754	182	1641	354	1856	2526	187
Rochester, MN	1234	1153	1214	1116	1223	1158	908	1236	774	620	2001	1934	1210	1268	755	345	1512	686	1128	1638	1180	346	1110	1654	824	812	1203	1870	634	1145	1430	1785	1315	1311	993	1358	300	1170	574	1067	863	1792	1149
Rochester, NY	344	340	371	1316	583	350	87	596	1329	1330	2710	2644	1798	1977	1309	1054	1252	717	320	2501	1226	728	339	2316	1145	284	261	2579	452	1550	489	2708	406	2020	1702	491	688	665	1518	316	1789	2502	509
Rockford, IL	976	896	956	970	966	900	652	978	810	700	2080	2014	1246	1346	792	424	1248	422	872	1871	999	144	852	1732	682	554	946	1948	378	1052	1174	2066	1058	1390	1072	1102	91	912	838	810	1109	1871	892
Sacramento, CA	2914	2833	2894	2244	2874	2838	2589	2887	1640	1306	79	467	1469	685	1621	1583	2815	2182	2808	724	2376	1978	2790	752	1999	2492	2884	410	2315	2034	3111	584	2995	690	1300	3039	2086	2826	1312	2748	1559	131	2794
Saginaw, MI	791	710	771	1157	780	715	466	793	1089	1033	2414	2347	1525	1680	1070	758	1231	550	686	2204	1068	431	667	2076	938	370	760	2282	74	1365	988	2412	872	1724	1405	773	391	767	1222	624	1492	2204	706
St. Johnsbury, VT	217	358	244	1629	692	317	498	676	1739	1740	3120	3054	2225	2388	1720	1465	1408	1127	329	2912	1532	1138	415	2726	1572	674	221	2990	864	1865	128	3118	223	2430	2112	227	1098	822	1928	446	1930	2912	666
St. Joseph, MO	1334	1202	1295	968	1207	1240	1022	1220	386	368	1749	1671	822	1016	367	136	1304	515	1213	1540	1032	336	1150	1266	486	866	1316	1606	748	780	1541	1746	1396	1059	637	1472	548	1158	655	1108	1087	1540	1127
St. Louis, MO	1072	940	1033	675	902	978	770	915	515	672	2053	1868	952	1320	496	439	1000	210	951	1844	740	168	888	1503	387	604	1064	1804	552	756	1279	2050	1134	1336	877	1250	360	853	959	846	1391	1844	822
St. Paul, MN	1286	1206	1267	1229	1276	1211	962	1289	814	660	2041	1974	1251	1308	795	385	1565	740	1181	1594	1293	462	1163	1694	864	865	1256	1910	688	1185	1484	1742	1368	1351	1033	1412	354	1222	614	1120	785	1832	1202
St. Petersburg, FL	1274	1133	1241	647	837	1176	1285	832	1269	1708	2822	2476	1451	2356	1260	1476	107	866	1176	2880	458	1174	1074	2154	912	1051	1349	2494	1252	884	1476	3087	1342	2373	1822	1688	1288	674	1996	1086	2388	2880	818
Salem, OR	3038	2956	3018	2694	2998	2962	2711	3010	1992	1430	582	1002	1858	778	1972	1706	3096	2306	2932	257	2772	2102	2914	1287	2305	2616	3006	946	2439	2514	3234	47	3118	856	1424	3162	2142	2947	1261	2870	1192	533	2918
Salinas, CA	3088	3008	3068	2172	2919	3012	2763	2931	1568	1480	102	385	1387	859	1550	1757	2743	2258	2982	822	2304	2152	2964	670	1928	2666	3058	328	2489	1951	3285	724	3169	865	1341	3213	2260	2772	1486	2922	1733	305	2839
Salisbury, MD	331	190	298	1176	147	233	538	132	1470	1537	2918	2832	1802	2184	1462	1262	890	822	233	2708	1030	909	134	2466	1149	355	406	2768	660	1412	532	2916	399	2228	1804	745	895	318	1726	159	1996	2708	216
Salt Lake City, UT	2264	2184	2244	1922	2225	2188	1939	2238	1219	657	728	730	1045	39	1200	934	2322	1533	2159	560	2000	1329	2140	660	1532	1843	2234	665	1666	1740	2462	766	2346	43	650	2390	1436	2176	663	2098	1024	520	2145
San Angelo, TX	1951	1806	1899	712	1627	1844	1672	1622	370	747	1578	1160	132	1259	377	830	1330	1043	1817	1782	890	1040	1736	836	598	1503	1979	1177	1424	464	2134	1990	2000	1098	641	2122	1232	1467	1036	1714	1570	1608	1547
San Antonio, TX	1956	1811	1905	542	1565	1849	1678	1560	452	922	1728	1310	351	1452	468	921	1159	1049	1823	1976	720	1074	1742	987	604	1509	1985	1328	1458	295	2139	2182	2006	1291	834	2156	1266	1404	1324	1720	1776	1755	1527
San Bernardino, CA	2840	2722	2820	1846	2654	2764	2514	2667	1304	1232	427	92	1034	682	1285	1509	2463	1993	2734	994	2024	1904	2671	317	1663	2388	2809	35	2240	1598	3037	1018	2921	602	1077	2964	2011	2508	1301	2628	1666	452	2574
San Diego, CA	2927	2794	2888	1822	2726	2833	2620	2739	1376	1338	494	38	1009	788	1358	1615	2438	2065	2806	1100	2000	2010	2743	352	1688	2460	2916	116	2347	1574	3143	1084	2989	708	1149	3071	2118	2557	1408	2700	1773	558	2646
San Francisco, CA	3000	2919	2980	2252	2960	2924	2674	2973	1648	1392	8	465	1466	771	1630	1668	2823	2268	2894	733	2384	2064	2876	750	2008	2578	2969	408	2400	2031	3196	636	3080	776	1386	3124	2171	2852	1398	2834	1645	217	2880
San Jose, CA	3028	2946	3008	2211	2958	2952	2702	2970	1607	1420	41	424	1426	799	1588	1696	2782	2296	2922	761	2343	2092	2904	708	1966	2606	2997	367	2428	1990	3224	663	3108	804	1414	3152	2199	2810	1426	2861	1673	245	2878
San Mateo, CA	3019	2938	3000	2238	2980	2944	2694	2992	1634	1412	28	451	1452	790	1615	1688	2809	2288	2914	752	2370	2084	2895	736	1993	2598	2988	394	2420	2017	3216	655	3100	796	1405	3144	2190	2838	1418	2852	1664	236	2900
Santa Ana, CA	2881	2764	2861	1884	2696	2805	2556	2708	1346	1274	404	52	1072	723	1326	1550	2502	2034	2776	1036	2062	1946	2712	355	1704	2429	2850	24	2282	1636	3078	995	2962	643	1118	3006	2052	2549	1343	2670	1708	493	2616
Santa Barbara, CA	2974	2856	2954	1994	2789	2898	2648	2801	1438	1367	332	178	1181	816	1419	1643	2610	2127	2868	1068	2172	2038	2805	464	1797	2522	2943	122	2375	1746	3171	954	3055	736	1211	3099	2146	2642	1435	2763	1801	532	2708
Santa Rosa, CA	3016	2935	2996	2299	2976	2940	2691	2989	1695	1408	55	511	1513	787	1676	1685	2870	2284	2910	749	2431	2080	2892	796	2054	2594	2985	454	2417	2078	3213	652	3097	792	1402	3141	2188	2928	1414	2850	1661	233	2896
Savannah, GA	928	788	896	658	492	831	939	486	1101	1477	2713	2387	1348	2124	1092	1244	280	634	830	2648	492	943	728	2097	779	706	1004	2398	902	895	1130	2856	996	2141	1682	1343	1046	328	1764	740	2157	2648	473
Schenectady, NY	135	198	162	1445	538	176	287	523	1528	1529	2910	2844	2042	2177	1509	1254	1254	917	168	2700	1348	927	261	2516	1389	484	52	2779	652	1682	280	2908	197	2220	1902	371	888	668	1718	260	1989	2701	512
Scranton, PA	182	127	188	1257	432	137	293	381	1407	1430	2811	2744	1853	2078	1388	1156	1099	833	108	2602	1160	828	124	2395	1200	280	210	2680	554	1494	389	2808	284	2121	1758	542	789	513	1619	100	1890	2602	358
Seattle, WA	2954	2873	2934	2721	2943	2878	2628	2956	2018	1456	800	1220	1884	804	1999	1663	3093	2304	2848	283	2821	2027	2830	1500	2330	2532	2923	1162	2354	2540	3150	172	3034	882	1450	3078	2020	2889	1142	2787	1070	750	2868
Shreveport, LA	1545	1399	1493	340	1170	1438	1296	1165	373	951	1911	1578	540	1582	388	735	904	666	1411	2106	465	724	1330	1256	182	1126	1573	1596	1112	215	1727	2312	1594	1410	871	1820	939	1010	1246	1308	1686	1920	1132
Sioux City, IA	1397	1316	1377	1191	1430	1321	1072	1443	573	373	1754	1687	1009	1021	554	97	1528	738	1292	1492	1255	461	1273	1418	708	975	1366	1622	798	1003	1594	1639	1478	1064	746	1522	506	1381	428	1230	860	1545	1350
Sioux Falls, SD	1461	1380	1441	1276	1450	1385	1136	1463	658	408	1730	1708	1094	998	638	182	1612	823	1356	1411	1340	546	1337	1462	793	1040	1430	1644	862	1088	1658	1558	1542	1040	766	1586	528	1466	348	1295	780	1522	1376
South Bend, IN	795	715	775	964	785	719	470	797	876	822	2202	2136	1314	1468	858	546	1123	357	690	1993	874	220	671	1865	727	374	765	2071	220	1154	992	2198	876	1512	1194	930	180	737	1010	629	1281	1992	710
Spokane, WA	2674	2594	2654	2482	2664	2598	2349	2676	1780	1172	869	1450	1766	686	1760	1384	2814	2024	2568	205	2542	1748	2550	1382	2092	2252	2644	1386	2075	2301	2871	353	2755	764	1211	2799	1741	2610	862	2508	790	796	2590
Springfield, IL	1042	909	1002	777	919	947	730	931	618	658	2039	1970	1054	1306	598	425	1069	280	921	1830	842	71	858	1605	489	574	1024	1906	456	858	1248	2036	1104	1349	937	1180	264	852	945	815	1299	1830	839
Springfield, MA	38	178	64	1449	513	138	383	497	1622	1625	3006	2940	2046	2273	1603	1350	1229	1025	150	2796	1352	1024	236	2610	1393	495	51	2875	748	1686	187	3004	104	2316	1998	405	984	643	1814	267	2085	2797	488
Springfield, MO	1285	1152	1246	676	1115	1190	982	1127	305	592	1908	1658	741	1240	285	360	1072	422	1164	1764	741	381	1100	1292	257	817	1277	1593	764	620	1491	1970	1346	1245	786	1462	573	1016	879	1058	1312	1764	1035
Springfield, OH	696	564	657	900	581	602	394	593	891	1023	2404	2244	1328	1670	872	748	1002	302	575	2194	811	348	512	1879	730	229	688	2180	214	1135	903	2400	758	1714	1242	918	395	514	1226	470	1497	2194	501
Stamford, CT	73	74	40	1345	408	33	423	393	1508	1551	2932	2865	1941	2198	1489	1276	1124	921	45	2722	1248	949	131	2496	1288	410	155	2800	674	1582	274	2929	141	2242	1859	510	909	539	1740	162	2010	2722	383
Stockton, CA	2961	2880	2942	2203	2922	2886	2636	2934	1598	1354	74	420	1422	732	1580	1630	2773	2230	2856	772	2334	2026	2837	705	1958	2540	2930	363	2362	1986	3158	628	3042	738	1347	3086	2132	2802	1360	2794	1606	178	2842
Syracuse, NY	262	254	289	1389	564	264	162	510	1404	1405	2786	2719	1873	2052	1385	1130	1232	792	234	2576	1292	803	254	2392	1220	359	180	2654	528	1626	407	2783	324	2096	1777	411	763	645	1593	230	1864	2576	490
Tacoma, WA	2966	2885	2946	2732	2955	2890	2640	2968	2030	1468	768	1188	1896	816	2010	1675	3105	2316	2860	295	2833	2039	2842	1511	2342	2544	2935	1131	2366	2552	3162	141	3046	894	1462	3090	2032	2901	1153	2799	1082	719	2880
Tallahassee, FL	1216	1076	1184	386	779	1118	1166	774	1008	1474	2561	2215	1190	2121	999	1241	257	628	1118	2646	196	937	1016	1892	650	933	1291	2233	1044	622	1418	2852	1284	2112	1521	1630	1050	616	1760	1028	2150	2646	760
Tampa, FL	1250	1110	1218	657	814	1153	1262	808	1279	1686	2832	2486	1460	2334	1270	1453	84	842	1152	2857	467	1152	1050	2163	921	1028	1326	2504	1228	893	1452	3064	1318	2350	1832	1666	1266	650	1972	1063	2365	2858	795
Terre Haute, IN	906	773	867	786	783	811	603	795	687	833	2214	2040	1123	1480	668	600	949	148	785	2004	701	178	722	1674	528	438	898	1975	400	955	1112	2210	968	1497	1038	1083	261	716	1068	679	1375	2004	703
Toledo, OH	650	569	630	1021	639	574	324	652	988	970	2351	2284	1424	1618	968	695	1095	423	544	2142	932	368	526	1976	851	228	619	2220	86	1256	847	2348	731	1661	1343	776	328	632	1159	484	1430	2142	565
Topeka, KS	1376	1243	1337	900	1214	1282	1074	1227	317	390	1790	1596	753	1057	298	160	1312	522	1255	1580	964	416	1192	1196	481	908	1368	1532	828	838	1583	1788	1438	1022	562	1552	628	1165	689	1150	1121	1581	1134
Toronto, ON	503	499	530	1313	656	509	90	669	1278	1249	2630	2563	1714	1897	1259	974	1288	714	480	2420	1224	647	499	2266	1142	319	420	2498	241	1548	648	2628	565	1940	1622	495	607	738	1438	430	1650	2421	582
Torrington, CT	42	146	57	1436	480	105	386	465	1587	1610	2990	2924	2032	2258	1567	1335	1196	1012	118	2782	1339	1008	204	2574	1380	459	62	2860	734	1673	248	2988	143	2300	1937	482	968	611	1798	242	2070	2782	455
Trenton, NJ	177	26	144	1262	316	79	429	300	1423	1507	2888	2776	1859	2154	1404	1232	1029	838	79	2678	1149	879	32	2410	1206	324	252	2711	630	1499	378	2884	245	2198	1774	591	865	443	1695	82	1966	2678	287
Troy, NY	124	191	151	1440	532	170	306	516	1548	1549	2930	2863	2037	2197	1529	1274	1248	936	161	2720	1344	947	255	2536	1384	464	42	2798	672	1677	269	2928	186	2240	1922	366	907	662	1738	253	2009	2721	506
Tucson, AZ	2517	2488	2582	1414	2310	2526	2214	2305	966	1208	857	438	602	814	947	1268	2031	1655	2500	1334	1592	1613	2419	116	1281	2050	2509	456	1998	1166	2724	1448	2682	732	832	2695	1806	2150	1349	2397	1788	884	2229
Tulsa, OK	1466	1333	1427	680	1308	1372	1164	1320	124	578	1728	1476	560	1210	104	381	1192	604	1345	1734	784	562	1282	1111	316	998	1458	1412	946	505	1672	1940	1528	1174	624	1643	754	1160	873	1239	1342	1734	1227
Tupelo, MS	1198	1052	1146	342	854	1091	958	849	578	1043	2190	1940	909	1691	569	811	689	352	1064	2214	334	555	984	1574	256	788	1226	1875	796	547	1380	2422	1247	1681	1131	1481	669	693	1330	961	1762	2215	794
Tuscaloosa, AL	1151	1005	1099	292	776	1044	986	771	708	1174	2321	1978	939	1821	699	941	571	380	1017	2345	242	685	936	1655	328	804	1179	2005	824	528	1333	2552	1200	1812	1261	1518	803	616	1460	914	1892	2346	738
Tyler, TX	1643	1498	1591	432	1268	1536	1358	1263	286	864	1823	1491	452	1495	301	703	1002	729	1509	2018	564	787	1428	1168	285	1189	1671	1509	1174	210	1826	2226	1692	1322	783	1882	1002	1108	1158	1406	1654	1832	1230
Utica, NY	212	275	239	1442	616	253	212	563	1453	1454	2834	2768	1922	2102	1434	1179	1284	841	245	2626	1344	852	306	2440	1270	408	130	2704	578	1678	357	2832	274	2144	1826	399	812	698	1642	282	1913	2626	542
Vallejo, CA	2972	2890	2952	2256	2932	2896	2646	2944	1652	1364	22	468	1470	743	1633	1640	2826	2240	2866	705	2388	2036	2848	753	2011	2550	2941	411	2372	2034	3168	607	3052	748	1358	3096	2143	2884	1370	2806	1617	189	2852
Vancouver, BC	3090	3010	3070	2858	3080	3014	2766	3092	2156	1594	942	1362	2021	942	2136	1800	3230	2441	2985	420	2958	2164	2966	1636	2468	2668	3060	1306	2491	2676	3287	315	3171	1018	1586	3002	2157	3026	1278	2924	1070	894	3006
Ventura, CA	2947	2830	2928	1967	2762	2871	2622	2774	1412	1340	359	151	1154	790	1393	1616	2584	2101	2842	1042	2145	2012	2778	437	1771	2495	2916	96	2348	1719	3144	973	3028	709	1184	3072	2119	2616	1409	2736	1774	527	2682
Victoria, TX	1885	1740	1833	471	1494	1778	1647	1489	493	1071	1843	1424	466	1566	508	962	1089	1018	1751	2090	649	1114	1670	1102	574	1478	1913	1442	1463	223	2067	2297	1934	1405	948	2253	1307	1332	1365	1648	1817	1869	1455
Virginia Beach, VA	468	327	435	1060	36	371	604	16	1404	1598	2978	2766	1724	2246	1396	1365	775	774	370	2770	915	947	271	2400	1083	444	543	2702	750	1297	670	2976	536	2262	1803	883	985	204	1815	296	2086	2770	105
Waco, TX	1777	1632	1725	530	1396	1670	1498	1391	272	850	1790	1406	355	1368	287	741	1130	869	1643	1892	692	894	1562	1083	424	1329	1805	1424	1278	282	1960	2098	1826	1289	750	1975	1086	1236	1144	1540	1596	1799	1373
Walnut Creek, CA	2984	2904	2964	2234	2945	2908	2659	2958	1630	1377	15	446	1448	756	1611	1654	2805	2253	2879	718	2366	2048	2860	731	1989	2563	2954	390	2386	2013	3182	620	3066	761	1370	3110	2156	2834	1382	2818	1630	202	2865
Warren, OH	494	414	474	1091	498	418	206	511	1104	1116	2496	2430	1573	1764	1085	841	1036	492	389	2288	1002	514	389	2092	920	87	500	2366	240	1326	701	2494	575	1806	1455	730	474	572	1304	342	1576	2288	424
Washington, DC	340	198	308	1090	182	242	412	194	1354	1435	2816	2716	1686	2082	1346	1160	850	724	242	2606	970	808	140	2351	1032	253	414	2652	558	1326	542	2814	408	2126	1702	754	794	264	1624	152	1895	2607	108
Waterbury, CT	21	126	37	1416	460	85	436	445	1566	1590	2970	2904	2012	2237	1547	1314	1176	992	97	2762	1319	988	183	2554	1359	438	107	2839	712	1652	228	2968	123	2280	1917	461	948	590	1778	222	2049	2762	434
Waterloo, IA	1168	1087	1148	1002	1153	1092	842	1166	692	538	1918	1852	1128	1186	673	263	1339	550	1062	1710	1067	232	1044	1572	714	746	1137	1788	568	1063	1365	1855	1249	1228	910	1293	290	1086	644	1002	995	1710	1073
Waukegan, IL	934	854	915	969	924	859	610	936	841	769	2150	2083	1277	1416	822	494	1214	374	829	1970	966	184	811	1828	710	513	904	2018	336	1138	1132	2118	1016	1460	1142	1060	40	870	890	768	1161	1941	850
Wausau, WI	1168	1088	1149	1170	1158	1093	844	1171	985	830	2211	2144	1421	1478	965	555	1447	622	1063	1769	1198	344	1045	1864	881	747	1138	2080	570	1251	1366	1916	1250	1521	1203	1131	214	1104	784	1002	960	2002	1084
West Palm Beach, FL	1342	1201	1310	800	905	1244	1353	900	1422	1829	2975	2629	1604	2476	1413	1596	171	986	1244	3000	610	1295	1142	2306	1064	1120	1417	2647	1316	1036	1544	3207	1410	2493	1975	1756	1408	742	2116	1154	2508	3000	886
Wheeling, WV	520	393	487	1044	455	432	292	468	1062	1193	2574	2414	1527	1841	1043	918	970	446	405	2364	955	518	342	2050	874	58	548	2350	318	1280	726	2572	588	1884	1412	816	553	506	1384	299	1654	2365	381
Wichita, KS	1503	1370	1464	880	1341	1409	1200	1354	177	405	1770	1418	613	1036	158	299	1365	649	1382	1560	957	551	1319	1054	489	1036	1495	1354	962	698	1710	1766	1565	1001	427	1686	762	1292	700	1276	1151	1560	1261
Wichita Falls, TX	1708	1576	1669	657	1504	1614	1406	1516	134	616	1587	1336	317	1165	140	594	1228	846	1587	1689	789	804	1524	971	440	1240	1700	1272	1188	471	1915	1896	1770	1086	547	1886	996	1358	997	1482	1449	1596	1424
Wilmington, DE	237	96	204	1194	256	140	434	240	1460	1479	2860	2748	1790	2127	1376	1204	969	788	139	2650	1089	852	29	2384	1138	297	312	2684	602	1431	438	2858	305	2170	1746	652	838	383	1668	54	1939	2652	227
Winnipeg, MB	1752	1672	1733	1733	1742	1677	1364	1754	1116	829	1912	2028	1552	1264	1096	640	2031	1206	1647	1350	1798	910	1629	2002	1251	1331	1722	1963	1154	1546	1697	1498	1834	1341	1206	1572	819	1688	769	1586	356	1704	1668
Winston-Salem, NC	690	550	658	790	273	593	632	268	1124	1392	2736	2485	1454	2040	1115	1160	602	550	594	2564	644	741	490	2120	802	399	756	2420	596	1026	892	2770	758	2056	1597	1095	792	112	1679	490	1894	2564	235
Worcester, MA	74	213	99	1484	547	172	430	532	1659	1672	3053	2986	2080	2320	1639	1397	1264	1060	184	2844	1386	1070	270	2646	1427	531	98	2922	796	1720	136	3050	57	2363	2009	420	1030	677	1861	301	2132	2844	522
Yakima, WA	2875	2794	2856	2580	2884	2800	2550	2896	1878	1316	702	1122	1744	664	1858	1592	2980	2192	2770	142	2658	1948	2752	1358	2190	2454	2844	1065	2276	2398	3072	185	2956	742	1308	3000	1942	2834	1063	2708	992	733	2804
Youngstown, OH	488	407	468	1094	479	412	214	491	1107	1130	2511	2444	1576	1778	1088	855	1036	495	382	2302	1005	528	365	2094	924	68	509	2380	254	1329	694	2508	569	1821	1458	738	489	560	1319	323	1590	2302	404

Mileages in this Mileage Directory are from the Rand McNally *MileMaker Practical Routing System*, © Rand McNally. **These mileages are for general reference only and should not be used for the purposes of tariff computation.** For tariff purposes, refer to the applicable official tariff. Mileages between each of the 300 cities listed in this chart are computed over National Interstate, U.S. and primary state highways, and Canadian provincial highways via highways designated as truck-usable by the Household Goods Carriers' Bureau Committee. Practical routing may have highway segments not included in the federally designated National Network.

	Roanoke, VA	Rochester, MN	Rochester, NY	Rockford, IL	Sacramento, CA	Saginaw, MI	St. Johnsbury, VT	St. Joseph, MO	St. Louis, MO	St. Paul, MN	St. Petersburg, FL	Salem, OR	Salinas, CA	Salisbury, MD	Salt Lake City, UT	San Angelo, TX	San Antonio, TX	San Bernardino, CA	San Diego, CA	San Francisco, CA	San Jose, CA	San Mateo, CA	Santa Ana, CA	Santa Barbara, CA	Santa Rosa, CA	Savannah, GA	Schenectady, NY	Scranton, PA	Seattle, WA	Shreveport, LA	Sioux City, IA	Sioux Falls, SD	South Bend, IN	Spokane, WA	Springfield, IL	Springfield, MA	Springfield, MO	Springfield, OH	Stamford, CT	Stockton, CA	Syracuse, NY	Tacoma, WA	Tallahassee, FL	Tampa, FL
ine Bluff, AR	801	824	1145	682	1999	938	1572	486	387	864	912	2305	1928	1149	1532	598	604	1663	1688	2008	1966	1993	1704	1797	2054	779	1389	1200	2330	182	708	793	727	2092	489	1393	257	730	1288	1958	1220	2342	650	921
ttsburgh, PA	366	812	284	554	2492	370	674	866	604	865	1051	2616	2666	355	1843	1503	1509	2388	2460	2578	2606	2598	2429	2522	2594	706	484	280	2532	1126	975	1040	374	2252	574	495	817	229	410	2540	359	2544	933	1028
ttsfield, MA	619	1203	261	946	2884	760	221	1316	1064	1256	1349	3006	3058	406	2234	1979	1985	2809	2916	2969	2997	2988	2850	2943	2985	1004	52	210	2923	1573	1366	1430	765	2644	1024	51	1277	688	155	2930	180	2935	1291	1326
omona, CA	2419	1870	2579	1948	410	2282	2990	1606	1804	1910	2494	946	328	2768	665	1177	1328	35	116	408	367	394	24	122	454	2398	2779	2680	1162	1596	1622	1644	2071	1386	1906	2875	1593	2180	2800	363	2654	1131	2233	2504
ontiac, MI	558	634	452	378	2315	74	864	748	552	688	1252	2439	2489	660	1666	1424	1458	2240	2347	2400	2428	2420	2282	2375	2417	902	652	554	2354	1112	798	862	220	2075	456	748	764	214	674	2362	528	2366	1044	1228
ort Arthur, TX	1094	1145	1550	1052	2034	1365	1865	780	756	1185	884	2514	1951	1412	1740	464	295	1598	1574	2031	1990	2017	1636	1746	2078	895	1682	1494	2540	215	1003	1088	1154	2301	858	1686	620	1135	1582	1986	1626	2552	622	893
ortland, ME	773	1430	489	1174	3111	988	128	1541	1279	1484	1476	3234	3285	532	2462	2134	2139	3037	3143	3196	3224	3216	3078	3171	3213	1130	280	389	3150	1727	1594	1658	992	2871	1248	187	1491	903	274	3158	407	3162	1418	1452
ortland, OR	2732	1785	2708	2066	584	2412	3118	1746	2050	1742	3087	47	724	2916	766	1990	2182	1018	1084	636	663	655	995	954	652	2856	2908	2808	172	2312	1639	1558	2198	353	2036	3004	1970	2400	2929	628	2783	141	2852	3064
ovidence, RI	640	1315	406	1058	2995	872	223	1396	1134	1368	1342	3118	3169	399	2346	2000	2006	2921	2989	3080	3108	3100	2962	3055	3097	996	197	284	3034	1594	1478	1542	876	2755	1104	104	1346	758	141	3042	324	3046	1284	1318
ovo, UT	2018	1311	2020	1390	690	1724	2430	1059	1336	1351	2373	856	865	2228	43	1098	1291	602	708	776	804	796	643	736	792	2141	2220	2121	882	1410	1064	1040	1512	764	1349	2316	1245	1714	2242	738	2096	894	2112	2350
ueblo, CO	1559	993	1702	1072	1300	1405	2112	637	877	1033	1822	1424	1341	1804	650	641	834	1077	1149	1386	1414	1405	1118	1211	1402	1682	1902	1758	1450	871	746	766	1194	1211	937	1998	786	1242	1859	1347	1777	1462	1521	1832
uébec, QC	958	1358	491	1102	3039	773	227	1472	1250	1412	1688	3162	3213	745	2390	2122	2156	2964	3071	3124	3152	3144	3006	3099	3141	1343	371	542	3078	1820	1522	1586	930	2799	1180	405	1462	918	510	3086	411	3090	1630	1666
acine, WI	754	300	688	91	2086	391	1098	548	360	354	1288	2142	2260	895	1436	1232	1266	2011	2118	2171	2199	2190	2052	2146	2188	1046	888	789	2020	939	506	528	180	1741	264	984	573	395	909	2132	763	2032	1050	1266
aleigh, NC	182	1170	665	912	2826	767	822	1158	853	1222	674	2947	2772	318	2176	1467	1404	2508	2557	2852	2810	2838	2549	2642	2928	328	668	513	2889	1010	1381	1466	737	2610	852	643	1016	514	539	2802	645	2901	616	650
apid City, SD	1641	574	1518	838	1312	1222	1928	655	959	614	1996	1261	1486	1726	663	1036	1324	1301	1408	1398	1426	1418	1343	1435	1414	1764	1718	1619	1142	1246	428	348	1010	862	945	1814	879	1226	1740	1360	1593	1153	1760	1972
eading, PA	354	1067	316	810	2748	624	446	1108	846	1120	1086	2870	2922	159	2098	1714	1720	2628	2700	2834	2861	2852	2670	2763	2850	740	260	100	2787	1308	1230	1295	629	2508	815	267	1058	470	162	2794	230	2799	1028	1063
egina, SK	1856	863	1789	1109	1559	1492	1930	1087	1391	785	2388	1192	1733	1996	1024	1570	1776	1666	1773	1645	1673	1664	1708	1801	1661	2157	1989	1890	1070	1686	860	780	1281	790	1299	2085	1312	1497	2010	1606	1864	1082	2150	2365
eno, NV	2526	1792	2502	1871	131	2204	2912	1540	1844	1832	2880	533	305	2708	520	1608	1755	452	558	217	245	236	493	532	233	2648	2701	2602	750	1920	1545	1522	1992	796	1830	2797	1764	2194	2722	178	2576	719	2646	2858
chmond, VA	187	1149	509	892	2794	706	666	1127	822	1202	818	2918	2839	216	2145	1547	1527	2574	2646	2880	2878	2900	2616	2708	2896	473	512	358	2868	1132	1350	1376	710	2590	839	488	1035	501	383	2842	490	2880	760	795
verside, CA	2408	1858	2568	1938	436	2271	2978	1596	1792	1898	2468	971	354	2756	654	1152	1302	9	97	434	392	420	40	148	480	2386	2768	2668	1188	1571	1612	1632	2060	1375	1894	2864	1582	2168	2789	389	2643	1156	2207	2478
oanoke, VA		1019	553	762	2657	616	782	990	684	1072	800	2780	2663	359	2008	1371	1377	2399	2471	2743	2702	2729	2440	2533	2759	455	599	410	2739	965	1213	1298	586	2460	701	603	907	363	499	2693	543	2750	682	777
ochester, MN	1019		952	272	1924	656	1362	386	456	79	1552	1832	2098	1160	1274	1131	1183	1849	1956	2009	2037	2028	1890	1983	2025	1320	1152	1053	1712	942	267	236	444	1432	418	1248	567	660	1174	1970	1028	1724	1258	1528
ochester, NY	553	952		696	2632	510	421	1066	813	1005	1328	2756	2806	461	1983	1716	1722	2558	2664	2718	2746	2738	2600	2692	2734	984	210	217	2672	1340	1116	1180	514	2392	773	306	1026	437	347	2680	86	2684	1210	1306
ockford, IL	762	272	696		2002	398	1106	464	295	326	1288	2111	2176	902	1352	1168	1200	1928	2034	2088	2116	2108	1970	2062	2104	1056	894	796	1992	850	399	500	187	1713	198	992	508	402	916	2050	770	2004	1050	1264
acramento, CA	2657	1924	2632	2002		2336	3043	1672	1975	1964	2822	538	175	2840	650	1589	1739	438	504	87	115	107	415	399	103	2713	2832	2734	756	1911	1676	1653	2124	826	1961	2928	1896	2326	2854	47	2708	724	2560	2832
aginaw, MI	616	656	510	398	2336		920	769	574	709	1298	2460	2510	717	1686	1446	1479	2262	2368	2422	2450	2442	2304	2396	2438	962	710	611	2376	1132	819	883	242	2096	477	806	786	261	731	2384	585	2388	1091	1275
Johnsbury, VT	782	1362	421	1106	3043	920		1476	1224	1416	1484	3166	3217	542	2394	2143	2148	2969	3075	3128	3156	3148	3010	3103	3145	1140	206	397	3082	1736	1526	1590	924	2803	1184	179	1436	848	284	3090	339	3094	1427	1462
Joseph, MO	990	386	1066	464	1672	769	1476		308	426	1344	1794	1846	1200	1022	743	818	1586	1692	1757	1785	1777	1628	1720	1774	1112	1266	1154	1793	603	227	312	558	1514	295	1362	228	638	1255	1719	1141	1805	1109	1321
Louis, MO	684	456	813	295	1975	574	1224	308		569	1040	2098	2047	938	1326	872	906	1783	1855	2061	2089	2080	1824	1917	2077	808	1013	892	2096	556	531	616	362	1817	102	1107	213	376	993	2022	889	2108	801	1016
Paul, MN	1072	79	1005	326	1964	709	1416	426	569		1604	1790	2138	1213	1314	1171	1223	1889	1996	2049	2077	2068	1930	2024	2066	1373	1205	1106	1668	982	308	276	498	1389	516	1301	607	713	1227	2010	1081	1680	1367	1582
Petersburg, FL	800	1552	1328	1288	2822	1298	1484	1344	1040	1604		3134	2750	967	2362	1336	1166	2470	2445	2830	2789	2816	2508	2617	2876	356	1330	1176	3133	911	1568	1652	1162	2854	1108	1306	1079	1042	1201	2780	1308	3145	257	23
lem, OR	2780	1832	2756	2111	538	2460	3166	1794	2098	1790	3134		678	2964	814	2038	2230	972	1039	590	618	610	950	909	606	2902	2956	2856	221	2362	1686	1605	2248	399	2084	3052	2020	2450	2978	583	2832	187	2900	3112
linas, CA	2663	2098	2806	2176	175	2510	3217	1846	2047	2138	2750	678		3011	824	1506	1657	355	422	106	61	88	332	230	157	2641	3006	2908	896	1839	1850	1827	2298	966	2135	3102	1836	2423	3028	135	2882	864	2489	2760
lisbury, MD	359	1160	461	902	2840	717	542	1200	938	1213	967	2964	3011		2190	1719	1695	2747	2819	2926	2954	2945	2788	2881	2942	621	388	246	2880	1300	1323	1387	721	2600	908	362	1150	562	258	2887	376	2892	909	944
lt Lake City, UT	2008	1274	1983	1352	650	1686	2394	1022	1326	1314	2362	814	824	2190		1141	1334	644	750	736	764	756	686	778	752	2130	2183	2084	841	1588	1027	1004	1474	722	1312	2279	1246	1676	2204	698	2058	852	2127	2340
n Angelo, TX	1371	1131	1716	1168	1589	1446	2143	743	872	1171	1336	2038	1506	1719	1141		214	1153	1128	1586	1545	1572	1192	1300	1632	1266	1960	1771	2064	458	930	1015	1234	1826	974	1964	661	1248	1859	1541	1791	2076	1076	1346
n Antonio, TX	1377	1183	1722	1200	1739	1479	2148	818	906	1223	1166	2230	1657	1695	1334	214		1304	1279	1736	1696	1722	1342	1451	1783	1178	1965	1776	2258	406	1021	1106	1268	2018	1008	1969	695	1306	1864	1692	1797	2270	905	1176
n Bernardino, CA	2399	1849	2558	1928	438	2262	2969	1586	1783	1889	2470	972	355	2747	644	1153	1304		106	435	394	421	49	150	482	2377	2758	2660	1190	1572	1602	1623	2050	1366	1885	2854	1572	2159	2780	390	2634	1158	2209	2480
n Diego, CA	2471	1956	2664	2034	504	2368	3075	1692	1855	1996	2445	1039	422	2819	750	1128	1279	106		502	460	488	89	214	548	2356	2864	2747	1256	1548	1708	1729	2156	1472	1957	2960	1644	2231	2848	457	2740	1224	2184	2455
n Francisco, CA	2743	2009	2718	2088	87	2422	3128	1757	2061	2049	2830	590	106	2926	736	1586	1736	435	502		45	20	412	336	63	2721	2918	2820	808	1919	1762	1738	2210	878	2047	3014	1916	2412	2940	82	2794	776	2569	2840
n Jose, CA	2702	2037	2746	2116	115	2450	3156	1785	2089	2077	2789	618	61	2954	764	1545	1696	394	460	45		27	371	291	96	2680	2946	2847	836	1878	1790	1766	2238	905	2075	3042	1875	2440	2968	74	2822	804	2528	2798
n Mateo, CA	2729	2028	2738	2108	107	2442	3148	1777	2080	2068	2816	610	88	2945	756	1572	1722	421	488	20	27		398	318	82	2707	2938	2839	827	1905	1782	1758	2230	897	2066	3034	1902	2431	2960	78	2813	796	2555	2826
nta Ana, CA	2440	1890	2600	1970	415	2304	3010	1628	1824	1930	2508	950	332	2788	686	1192	1342	49	89	412	371	398		125	459	2418	2800	2701	1167	1611	1644	1664	2092	1407	1926	2896	1614	2200	2821	368	2675	1136	2247	2518
nta Barbara, CA	2533	1983	2692	2062	399	2396	3103	1720	1917	2024	2617	909	230	2881	778	1300	1451	150	214	336	291	318	125		387	2511	2892	2794	1126	1720	1736	1757	2184	1196	2019	2988	1706	2293	2914	351	2768	1094	2356	2627
nta Rosa, CA	2759	2025	2734	2104	103	2438	3145	1774	2077	2066	2876	606	157	2942	752	1632	1783	482	548	63	96	82	459	387		2768	2934	2836	824	1965	1778	1755	2226	894	2063	3030	1963	2428	2956	129	2810	792	2615	2886
vannah, GA	455	1320	984	1056	2713	962	1140	1112	808	1373	356	2902	2641	621	2130	1266	1178	2377	2356	2721	2680	2707	2418	2511	2768		986	830	2902	809	1336	1420	916	2622	877	960	910	708	856	2671	962	2914	299	333
henectady, NY	599	1152	210	894	2832	710	206	1266	1013	1205	1330	2956	3006	388	2183	1960	1965	2758	2864	2918	2946	2938	2800	2892	2934	986		187	2872	1553	1315	1380	714	2592	973	98	1226	637	166	2880	129	2884	1273	1308
ranton, PA	410	1053	217	796	2734	611	397	1154	892	1106	1176	2856	2908	246	2084	1771	1776	2660	2747	2820	2847	2839	2701	2794	2836	830	187		2774	1365	1217	1281	615	2494	862	217	1104	516	148	2781	131	2785	1082	1152
attle, WA	2739	1712	2672	1992	756	2376	3082	1793	2096	1668	3133	221	896	2880	841	2064	2258	1190	1256	808	836	827	1167	1126	824	2902	2872	2774		2388	1566	1486	2164	280	2082	2968	2017	2380	2894	800	2748	32	2898	3110
reveport, LA	965	942	1340	850	1911	1132	1736	603	556	982	911	2362	1839	1300	1588	458	406	1572	1548	1919	1878	1905	1611	1720	1965	809	1553	1365	2388		826	911	921	2148	658	1557	419	924	1453	1869	1414	2400	650	921
oux City, IA	1213	267	1116	399	1676	819	1526	227	531	308	1568	1686	1850	1323	1027	930	1021	1602	1708	1762	1790	1782	1644	1736	1778	1336	1315	1217	1566	826		85	608	1286	517	1412	451	809	1337	1724	1191	1578	1332	1544
oux Falls, SD	1298	236	1180	500	1653	883	1590	312	616	276	1652	1605	1827	1387	1004	1015	1106	1623	1729	1738	1766	1758	1664	1757	1755	1420	1380	1281	1486	911	85		672	1206	602	1476	536	894	1401	1700	1255	1498	1417	1629
uth Bend, IN	586	444	514	187	2124	242	924	558	362	498	1162	2248	2298	721	1474	1234	1268	2050	2156	2210	2238	2230	2092	2184	2226	916	714	615	2164	921	608	672		1885	264	810	574	242	735	2172	589	2176	924	1139
okane, WA	2460	1432	2392	1713	826	2096	2803	1514	1817	1389	2854	399	966	2600	722	1826	2018	1366	1472	878	905	897	1407	1196	894	2622	2592	2494	280	2148	1286	1206	1885		1803	2688	1738	2100	2614	870	2468	291	2618	2830
ringfield, IL	701	418	773	198	1961	477	1184	295	102	516	1108	2084	2135	908	1312	974	1008	1885	1957	2047	2075	2066	1926	2019	2063	877	973	862	2082	658	517	602	264	1803		1069	315	346	962	2008	848	2094	871	1086
ringfield, MA	603	1248	306	992	2928	806	179	1362	1107	1301	1306	3052	3102	362	2279	1964	1969	2854	2960	3014	3042	3034	2896	2988	3030	960	98	217	2968	1557	1412	1476	810	2688	1069		1320	731	104	2976	225	2980	1248	1282
ringfield, MO	907	567	1026	508	1896	786	1436	228	213	607	1079	2020	1836	1150	1246	661	695	1572	1644	1916	1875	1902	1614	1706	1963	910	1226	1104	2017	419	451	536	574	1738	315	1320		589	1206	1867	1101	2029	818	1088
ringfield, OH	363	660	437	402	2326	261	848	638	376	713	1042	2450	2423	562	1676	1248	1306	2159	2231	2412	2440	2431	2200	2293	2428	708	637	516	2380	924	809	894	242	2100	346	731	589		617	2373	513	2392	834	1018
amford, CT	499	1174	347	916	2854	731	284	1255	993	1227	1201	2978	3028	258	2204	1859	1864	2780	2848	2940	2968	2960	2821	2914	2956	856	166	148	2894	1453	1337	1401	735	2614	962	104	1206	617		2902	261	2906	1144	1178
ockton, CA	2693	1970	2680	2050	47	2384	3090	1719	2022	2010	2780	583	135	2887	698	1541	1692	390	457	82	74	78	368	351	129	2671	2880	2781	800	1869	1724	1700	2172	870	2008	2976	1867	2373	2902		2755	769	2519	2790
racuse, NY	543	1028	86	770	2708	585	339	1141	889	1081	1308	2832	2882	376	2058	1791	1797	2634	2740	2794	2822	2813	2675	2768	2810	962	129	131	2748	1414	1191	1255	589	2468	848	225	1101	513	261	2755		2760	1214	1284
coma, WA	2750	1724	2684	2004	724	2388	3094	1805	2108	1680	3145	187	864	2892	852	2076	2270	1158	1224	776	804	796	1136	1094	792	2914	2884	2785	32	2400	1578	1498	2176	291	2094	2980	2029	2392	2906	769	2760		2910	3122
llahassee, FL	682	1258	1210	1050	2560	1091	1427	1109	801	1367	257	2900	2489	909	2127	1076	905	2209	2184	2569	2528	2555	2247	2356	2615	299	1273	1082	2898	650	1332	1417	924	2618	871	1248	818	834	1144	2519	1214	2910		273
mpa, FL	777	1528	1306	1264	2832	1275	1462	1321	1016	1582	23	3112	2760	944	2340	1346	1176	2480	2455	2840	2798	2826	2518	2627	2886	333	1308	1152	3110	921	1544	1629	1139	2830	1086	1282	1088	1018	1178	2790	1284	3122	273	
rre Haute, IN	565	538	647	274	2136	421	1057	468	172	592	989	2260	2219	772	1486	1044	1077	1954	2026	2222	2250	2241	1996	2088	2238	758	847	726	2205	722	639	724	220	1926	145	941	384	210	826	2183	722	2217	751	966
ledo, OH	481	593	369	336	2273	142	779	706	472	646	1162	2396	2448	576	1624	1344	1378	2199	2306	2359	2387	2378	2240	2333	2375	826	568	470	2313	1045	756	820	155	2034	414	664	685	125	590	2320	444	2325	956	1140
peka, KS	997	466	1117	544	1712	849	1528	79	315	506	1352	1836	1775	1242	1063	674	765	1511	1618	1798	1826	1818	1552	1645	1814	1120	1317	1196	1862	582	261	346	638	1547	374	1411	224	680	1297	1760	1192	1874	1042	1328
ronto, ON	605	872	170	614	2552	286	481	985	763	925	1364	2676	2726	620	1903	1635	1669	2478	2584	2638	2666	2658	2520	2612	2654	1018	370	376	2592	1336	1035	1100	443	2312	693	466	976	417	506	2600	245	2604	1247	1340
rrington, CT	590	1233	310	976	2913	790	256	1333	1071	1286	1273	3037	3087	330	2264	1950	1956	2839	2926	2999	3026	3018	2880	2973	3015	928	101	182	2952	1544	1396	1460	794	2674	1041	77	1284	695	72	2960	228	2964	1216	1250
renton, NJ	416	1130	352	872	2810	687	388	1170	908	1182	1105	2934	2984	165	2160	1776	1782	2691	2763	2896	2924	2915	2732	2825	2912	760	234	137	2850	1370	1293	1357	691	2570	877	208	1120	532	104	2857	266	2862	1048	1082
roy, NY	594	1172	230	914	2852	730	193	1285	1033	1225	1324	2976	3026	381	2202	1955	1960	2778	2884	2938	2966	2958	2820	2912	2954	978	16	186	2892	1548	1335	1400	733	2612	993	87	1246	657	159	2900	149	2904	1266	1301
ucson, AZ	2054	1596	2258	1674	868	2018	2669	1207	1445	1636	2038	1402	785	2402	776	721	872	432	408	865	824	851	470	580	912	1949	2458	2337	1615	1140	1361	1404	1807	1497	1547	2552	1234	1821	2542	820	2334	1627	1777	2048
ulsa, OK	1052	671	1207	688	1727	967	1617	306	394	711	1198	1988	1656	1332	1216	480	543	1391	1464	1736	1694	1722	1432	1526	1782	1030	1407	1286	2014	355	482	566	756	1776	496	1501	183	770	1387	1686	1282	2026	937	1208
upelo, MS	618	828	1001	682	2190	842	1390	679	386	940	696	2470	2119	966	1697	827	833	1854	1926	2199	2157	2184	1896	1988	2245	527	1206	1018	2468	410	902	987	649	2188	489	1210	388	586	1106	2149	1076	2480	434	705
uscaloosa, AL	571	958	1029	802	2320	871	1342	809	517	1070	578	2600	2249	906	1827	857	811	1972	1947	2329	2288	2315	2010	2118	2375	449	1159	971	2598	400	1032	1117	678	2318	619	1163	518	614	1059	2279	1103	2610	317	588
yler, TX	1063	936	1402	914	1823	1196	1835	571	618	976	1009	2274	1751	1398	1500	370	310	1485	1460	1831	1790	1817	1523	1632	1878	907	1651	1463	2300	98	794	879	984	2061	721	1656	448	987	1551	1781	1478	2312	748	1019
tica, NY	595	1076	135	820	2757	634	289	1190	938	1130	1360	2880	2931	428	2108	1840	1846	2683	2789	2842	2870	2862	2724	2817	2859	1014	78	183	2796	1464	1240	1304	638	2517	898	175	1150	562	243	2804	53	2808	1266	1337
allejo, CA	2714	1981	2690	2060	59	2394	3100	1729	2033	2021	2833	562	125	2898	708	1590	1740	438	505	30	64	50	416	355	50	2725	2890	2791	780	1922	1734	1710	2182	850	2019	2986	1954	2384	2912	76	2766	748	2572	2843
ancouver, BC	2876	1848	2809	2129	899	2512	2998	1930	2233	1805	3270	364	1039	3016	978	2200	2394	1333	1399	951	978	970	1310	1269	967	3038	3008	2910	143	2524	1702	1622	2301	416	2219	3105	2154	2516	3030	944	2884	175	3035	3247
entura, CA	2506	1957	2666	2036	393	2370	3076	1694	1890	1997	2591	928	257	2854	752	1274	1424	124	188	362	318	345	99	27	414	2484	2866	2767	1145	1693	1710	1730	2158	1244	1992	2962	1680	2266	2887	346	2741	1114	2330	2600
ictoria, TX	1305	1223	1691	1241	1854	1484	2077	858	946	1263	1095	2344	1771	1624	1448	327	114	1418	1393	1851	1810	1837	1456	1565	1897	1106	1893	1705	2371	366	1062	1147	1271	2133	1048	1897	736	1276	1793	1806	1837	2383	834	1105
irginia Beach, VA	293	1249	610	992	2901	807	679	1234	928	1302	852	3024	2945	134	2252	1642	1580	2681	2753	2986	2984	3006	2722	2815	3003	506	525	383	2970	1185	1456	1477	811	2690	945	500	1141	607	395	2948	513	2981	794	828
aco, TX	1197	1003	1542	1020	1790	1299	1969	638	726	1043	1138	2146	1718	1545	1374	216	180	1400	1375	1798	1757	1784	1438	1547	1844	1035	1786	1597	2172	226	841	926	1088	1934	828	1790	515	1126	1685	1748	1617	2184	876	1147
alnut Creek, CA	2725	1994	2703	2072	72	2406	3114	1742	2046	2034	2812	575	104	2910	721	1568	1718	417	483	23	43	42	394	334	69	2703	2903	2804	792	1900	1746	1724	2195	862	2032	2999	1898	2396	2924	64	2778	760	2550	2821
arren, OH	422	738	250	482	2419	296	660	851	589	792	1112	2542	2593	435	1770	1491	1497	2345	2451	2504	2532	2524	2386	2479	2521	767	449	314	2458	1114	902	966	300	2180	558	529	801	213	434	2466	325	2470	994	1089
ashington, DC	243	1058	388	800	2738	616	550	1098	878	1111	926	2860	2895	120	2088	1604	1608	2630	2703	2824	2852	2844	2672	2765	2840	580	396	242	2778	1197	1222	1285	620	2498	806	372	1091	460	266	2786	374	2790	868	903
aterbury, CT	570	1212	360	956	2892	770	236	1313	1051	1266	1252	3016	3066	310	2243	1930	1935	2818	2906	2978	3006	2998	2860	2952	2994	908	154	161	2932	1524	1376	1440	774	2653	1020	56	1264	675	52	2940	274	2944	1195	1230
aterloo, IA	936	114	887	183	1841	590	1297	304	342	227	1379	1902	2015	1094	1192	1049	1101	1767	1873	1926	1954	1946	1808	1901	1943	1148	1086	988	1782	859	220	306	378	1502	304	1182	484	580	1108	1888	962	1794	1144	1356
aukegan, IL	720	324	653	77	2072	357	1064	534	326	378	1254	2166	2246	861	1422	1198	1232	1998	2104	2158	2186	2178	2040	2132	2174	1012	853	754	2044	905	555	552	144	1765	229	949	538	361	875	2120	728	2056	1016	1230
ausau, WI	954	193	887	208	2134	591	1298	596	494	177	1486	1963	2308	1095	1484	1342	1393	2060	2166	2219	2247	2239	2100	2194	2236	1255	1087	988	1844	1050	478	446	378	1564	398	1183	707	595	1109	2181	963	1856	1249	1464
est Palm Beach, FL	868	1672	1397	1408	2975	1376	1553	1464	1160	1725	227	3254	2903	1035	2482	1490	1319	2623	2598	2983	2942	2969	2661	2770	3030	425	1399	1244	3253	1064	1688	1772	1283	2974	1228	1374	1232	1122	1269	2933	1376	3265	417	203
heeling, WV	355	818	336	560	2496	375	734	808	546	871	1046	2620	2594	392	1847	1445	1451	2330	2402	2582	2610	2602	2371	2464	2598	700	536	339	2538	1068	979	1045	379	2258	516	555	759	171	446	2544	411	2550	928	1023
ichita, KS	1124	600	1244	680	1692	984	1654	212	442	640	1372	1816	1598	1369	1042	534	625	1334	1406	1778	1636	1797	1375	1468	1794	1203	1444	1323	1842	546	399	484	772	1602	509	1538	258	807	1424	1739	1320	1854	1110	1381
ichita Falls, TX	1248	895	1449	932	1587	1210	1860	507	636	935	1235	1944	1515	1596	1171	237	383	1251	1323	1595	1554	1581	1292	1385	1642	1132	1649	1528	1970	324	694	778	998	1732	738	1743	425	1012	1629	1545	1525	1982	974	1244
ilmington, DE	348	1102	357	846	2782	660	448	1142	880	1155	1046	2906	2956	106	2133	1708	1714	2664	2736	2868	2896	2888	2705	2798	2884	700	294	142	2822	1302	1266	1330	664	2542	850	269	1093	505	164	2830	271	2834	988	1022
innipeg, MB	1538	545	1471	791	1835	1114	1568	770	1073	468	2070	1546	2009	1679	1300	1472	1564	1942	2048	1921	1948	1940	1984	2076	1937	1839	1671	1572	1424	1368	542	462	962	1145	982	1767	994	1179	1693	1882	1546	1436	1832	2048
inston-Salem, NC	108	1057	676	800	2695	655	902	1028	723	1110	678	2818	2664	403	2046	1372	1310	2400	2472	2744	2703	2730	2441	2534	2797	333	736	547	2777	914	1251	1336	624	2498	739	722	908	401	618	2694	680	2789	560	655
orcester, MA	638	1295	353	1038	2976	852	192	1405	1143	1348	1340	3098	3150	397	2326	1998	2003	2901	3008	3061	3089	3080	2942	3035	3077	994	144	253	3015	1592	1458	1522	857	2736	1113	51	1356	767	139	3022	272	3027	1282	1316
akima, WA	2666	1634	2594	1914	658	2298	3004	1680	1984	1590	3020	232	798	2802	700	1924	2116	1134	1158	710	738	730	1070	1028	726	2789	2794	2694	141	2246	1488	1407	2086	201	1970	2890	1904	2302	2816	703	2669	153	2786	2998
oungstown, OH	427	753	258	496	2434	311	668	854	592	806	1112	2556	2608	415	1784	1494	1500	2360	2447	2519	2547	2538	2400	2494	2536	766	458	307	2473	1118	916	980	315	2194	561	523	804	216	428	2480	333	2485	994	1089

Mileage Directory, continued

	Terre Haute, IN	Toledo, OH	Topeka, KS	Toronto, ON	Torrington, CT	Trenton, NJ	Troy, NY	Tucson, AZ	Tulsa, OK	Tupelo, MS	Tuscaloosa, AL	Tyler, TX	Utica, NY	Vallejo, CA	Vancouver, BC	Ventura, CA	Victoria, TX	Virginia Beach, VA	Waco, TX
Pine Bluff, AR	528	851	481	1142	1380	1206	1384	1281	316	256	328	285	1270	2011	2468	1771	574	1083	424
Pittsburgh, PA	438	228	908	319	459	324	464	2050	998	788	804	1189	408	2550	2668	2495	1478	444	1329
Pittsfield, MA	898	619	1368	420	62	252	42	2509	1458	1226	1179	1671	130	2941	3060	2916	1913	543	1805
Pomona, CA	1975	2220	1532	2498	2860	2711	2798	456	1412	1875	2005	1509	2704	411	1306	96	1442	2702	1424
Pontiac, MI	400	86	828	241	734	630	672	1998	946	796	824	1174	578	2372	2491	2348	1463	750	1278
Port Arthur, TX	955	1256	838	1548	1673	1499	1677	1166	505	547	528	210	1678	2034	2676	1719	223	1297	282
Portland, ME	1112	847	1583	648	248	378	269	2724	1672	1380	1333	1826	357	3168	3287	3144	2067	670	1960
Portland, OR	2210	2348	1788	2628	2988	2884	2928	1448	1940	2422	2552	2226	2832	607	315	973	2297	2976	2098
Providence, RI	968	731	1438	565	143	245	186	2682	1528	1247	1200	1692	274	3052	3171	3028	1934	536	1826
Provo, UT	1497	1661	1022	1940	2300	2198	2240	732	1174	1681	1812	1322	2144	748	1018	709	1405	2262	1289
Pueblo, CO	1038	1343	562	1622	1937	1774	1922	832	624	1131	1261	783	1826	1358	1586	1184	948	1803	750
Québec, QC	1083	776	1552	495	482	591	366	2695	1643	1481	1518	1882	399	3096	3002	3072	2253	883	1975
Racine, WI	261	328	628	607	968	865	907	1806	754	669	803	1002	812	2143	2157	2119	1307	985	1086
Raleigh, NC	716	632	1165	738	611	443	662	2150	1160	693	616	1108	698	2884	3026	2616	1332	204	1236
Rapid City, SD	1068	1159	689	1438	1798	1695	1738	1349	873	1330	1460	1158	1642	1370	1278	1409	1365	1815	1144
Reading, PA	679	484	1150	430	242	82	253	2397	1239	961	914	1406	282	2806	2924	2736	1648	296	1540
Regina, SK	1375	1430	1121	1650	2070	1966	2009	1788	1342	1762	1892	1654	1913	1617	1070	1774	1817	2086	1596
Reno, NV	2004	2142	1581	2421	2782	2678	2721	884	1734	2215	2346	1832	2626	189	894	527	1869	2770	1799
Richmond, VA	703	565	1134	582	455	287	506	2229	1227	794	738	1230	542	2852	3006	2682	1455	105	1373
Riverside, CA	1964	2208	1520	2488	2848	2700	2787	431	1400	1864	1970	1483	2692	437	1332	121	1416	2690	1398
Roanoke, VA	565	481	997	605	590	416	594	2054	1052	618	571	1063	595	2714	2876	2506	1305	293	1197
Rochester, MN	538	593	466	872	1233	1130	1172	1596	671	828	958	936	1076	1981	1848	1957	1223	1249	1003
Rochester, NY	647	369	1117	170	310	352	230	2258	1207	1001	1029	1402	135	2690	2809	2666	1691	610	1542
Rockford, IL	274	336	544	614	976	872	914	1674	688	682	802	914	820	2060	2129	2036	1241	992	1020
Sacramento, CA	2136	2273	1712	2552	2913	2810	2852	868	1727	2190	2320	1823	2757	59	899	393	1854	2901	1790
Saginaw, MI	421	142	849	286	790	687	730	2018	967	842	871	1196	634	2394	2512	2370	1484	807	1299
St. Johnsbury, VT	1057	779	1528	481	256	388	193	2669	1617	1390	1342	1835	289	3100	2998	3076	2077	679	1969
St. Joseph, MO	468	706	79	985	1333	1170	1285	1207	306	679	809	571	1190	1729	1930	1694	858	1234	638
St. Louis, MO	172	472	315	763	1071	908	1033	1445	394	386	517	618	938	2033	2233	1890	946	928	726
St. Paul, MN	592	646	506	925	1286	1182	1225	1636	711	940	1070	976	1130	2021	1805	1997	1263	1302	1043
St. Petersburg, FL	989	1162	1352	1364	1273	1105	1324	2038	1198	696	578	1009	1360	2833	3270	2591	1095	852	1138
Salem, OR	2260	2396	1836	2676	3037	2934	2976	1402	1988	2470	2600	2274	2880	562	364	928	2344	3024	2146
Salinas, CA	2219	2448	1775	2726	3087	2984	3026	785	1656	2119	2249	1751	2931	125	1039	257	1771	2945	1718
Salisbury, MD	772	576	1242	620	330	165	381	2402	1332	966	906	1398	428	2898	3016	2854	1624	134	1545
Salt Lake City, UT	1486	1624	1063	1903	2264	2160	2202	776	1216	1697	1827	1500	2108	708	978	752	1448	2252	1374
San Angelo, TX	1044	1344	674	1635	1950	1776	1955	721	480	827	857	370	1840	1590	2200	1274	327	1642	216
San Antonio, TX	1077	1378	765	1669	1956	1782	1960	872	543	833	811	310	1846	1740	2394	1424	114	1580	180
San Bernardino, CA	1954	2199	1511	2478	2839	2691	2778	432	1391	1854	1972	1485	2683	438	1333	124	1418	2681	1400
San Diego, CA	2026	2306	1618	2584	2926	2763	2884	408	1464	1926	1947	1460	2789	505	1399	188	1393	2753	1375
San Francisco, CA	2222	2359	1798	2638	2999	2896	2938	865	1736	2199	2329	1831	2842	30	951	362	1851	2986	1798
San Jose, CA	2250	2387	1826	2666	3026	2924	2966	824	1694	2157	2288	1790	2870	64	978	318	1810	2984	1757
San Mateo, CA	2241	2378	1818	2658	3018	2915	2958	851	1722	2184	2315	1817	2862	50	970	345	1837	3006	1784
Santa Ana, CA	1996	2240	1552	2520	2880	2732	2820	470	1432	1896	2010	1523	2724	416	1310	99	1456	2722	1438
Santa Barbara, CA	2088	2333	1645	2612	2973	2825	2912	580	1526	1988	2118	1632	2817	355	1269	27	1565	2815	1547
Santa Rosa, CA	2238	2375	1814	2654	3015	2912	2954	912	1782	2245	2375	1878	2859	50	967	414	1897	3003	1844
Savannah, GA	758	826	1120	1018	928	760	978	1949	1030	527	449	907	1014	2725	3038	2484	1106	506	1035
Schenectady, NY	847	568	1317	370	101	234	16	2458	1407	1206	1159	1651	78	2890	3008	2866	1893	525	1786
Scranton, PA	726	470	1196	376	182	137	186	2337	1286	1018	971	1463	183	2791	2910	2767	1705	383	1597
Seattle, WA	2205	2313	1862	2592	2952	2850	2892	1615	2014	2468	2598	2300	2796	780	143	1145	2371	2970	2172
Shreveport, LA	722	1045	582	1336	1544	1370	1548	1140	355	410	400	98	1464	1922	2524	1693	366	1185	226
Sioux City, IA	639	756	261	1035	1396	1293	1335	1361	482	902	1032	794	1240	1734	1702	1710	1062	1456	841
Sioux Falls, SD	724	820	346	1100	1460	1357	1400	1404	566	987	1117	879	1304	1710	1622	1730	1147	1477	926
South Bend, IN	220	155	638	443	794	691	733	1807	756	649	678	984	638	2182	2301	2158	1271	811	1088
Spokane, WA	1926	2034	1547	2312	2674	2570	2612	1497	1776	2188	2318	2061	2517	850	416	1244	2133	2690	1934
Springfield, IL	145	414	374	693	1041	877	993	1547	496	489	619	721	898	2019	2219	1992	1048	945	828
Springfield, MA	941	664	1411	466	77	208	87	2552	1501	1210	1163	1656	175	2986	3105	2962	1897	500	1790
Springfield, MO	384	685	224	976	1284	1120	1246	1234	183	388	518	448	1150	1954	2154	1680	736	1141	515
Springfield, OH	210	125	680	417	695	532	657	1821	770	586	614	987	562	2384	2516	2266	1276	607	1126
Stamford, CT	826	590	1297	506	72	104	159	2542	1387	1106	1059	1551	243	2912	3030	2887	1793	395	1685
Stockton, CA	2183	2320	1760	2600	2960	2857	2900	820	1686	2149	2279	1781	2804	76	944	346	1806	2948	1748
Syracuse, NY	722	444	1192	245	228	266	149	2334	1282	1076	1103	1478	53	2766	2884	2741	1837	513	1617
Tacoma, WA	2217	2325	1874	2604	2964	2862	2904	1627	2026	2480	2610	2312	2808	748	175	1114	2383	2981	2184
Tallahassee, FL	751	956	1042	1247	1216	1048	1266	1777	937	434	317	748	1266	2572	3035	2330	834	794	876
Tampa, FL	966	1140	1328	1340	1250	1082	1301	2048	1208	705	588	1019	1337	2843	3247	2600	1105	828	1147
Terre Haute, IN		306	475	597	905	741	866	1616	565	445	504	785	771	2194	2342	2062	1074	809	897
Toledo, OH	306		776	289	649	546	588	1918	866	707	735	1108	493	2331	2450	2306	1397	666	1198
Topeka, KS	475	776		1065	1375	1212	1337	1138	227	612	742	598	1242	1770	1998	1618	805	1240	585
Toronto, ON	597	289	1065		469	512	389	2208	1157	998	1027	1400	294	2610	2718	2586	1688	683	1489
Torrington, CT	905	649	1375	469		176	90	2516	1465	1197	1150	1642	178	2970	3090	2946	1884	467	1776
Trenton, NJ	741	546	1212	512	176		227	2459	1301	1023	976	1468	311	2868	2986	2798	1710	302	1602
Troy, NY	866	588	1337	389	90	227		2478	1427	1202	1154	1647	98	2910	3028	2886	1888	518	1781
Tucson, AZ	1616	1918	1138	2208	2516	2459	2478		1053	1509	1540	1052	2383	868	1752	553	986	2325	968
Tulsa, OK	565	866	227	1157	1465	1301	1427	1053		507	637	296	1331	1739	2152	1499	583	1334	363
Tupelo, MS	445	707	612	998	1197	1023	1202	1509	507		127	508	1126	2202	2604	1962	758	868	653
Tuscaloosa, AL	504	735	742	1027	1150	976	1154	1540	637	127		498	1155	2332	2735	2092	740	791	626
Tyler, TX	785	1108	598	1400	1642	1468	1647	1052	296	508	498		1526	1835	2436	1605	297	1283	130
Utica, NY	771	493	1242	294	178	311	98	2383	1331	1126	1155	1526		2814	2934	2790	1889	565	1666
Vallejo, CA	2194	2331	1770	2610	2970	2868	2910	868	1739	2202	2332	1835	2814		922	382	1854	2958	1801
Vancouver, BC	2342	2450	1998	2718	3090	2986	3028	1752	2152	2604	2735	2436	2934	922		1288	2508	3106	2310
Ventura, CA	2062	2306	1618	2586	2946	2798	2886	553	1499	1962	2092	1605	2790	382	1288		1539	2788	1520
Victoria, TX	1074	1397	805	1688	1884	1710	1888	986	583	758	740	297	1889	1854	2508	1539		1508	221
Virginia Beach, VA	809	666	1240	683	467	302	518	2325	1334	868	791	1283	565	2958	3106	2788	1508		1411
Waco, TX	897	1198	585	1489	1776	1602	1781	968	363	653	626	130	1666	1801	2310	1520	221	1411	
Walnut Creek, CA	2206	2344	1782	2622	2984	2880	2922	847	1717	2180	2310	1813	2828	22	936	360	1833	2972	1780
Warren, OH	422	155	893	285	493	402	469	2034	982	776	805	1178	374	2476	2596	2452	1466	524	1317
Washington, DC	670	474	1140	491	339	171	390	2286	1284	850	803	1295	426	2796	2915	2738	1537	208	1430
Waterbury, CT	885	629	1355	519	20	156	143	2496	1445	1177	1130	1622	231	2950	3069	2926	1864	447	1756
Waterloo, IA	410	527	383	806	1167	1064	1106	1514	588	714	844	854	1011	1898	1918	1874	1141	1179	920
Waukegan, IL	226	294	614	573	934	830	873	1771	720	634	769	968	778	2130	2182	2106	1272	950	1052
Wausau, WI	474	528	676	807	1168	1064	1107	1806	881	881	1002	1113	1012	2191	1980	2167	1434	1184	1213
West Palm Beach, FL	1109	1240	1472	1432	1342	1173	1392	2191	1352	849	731	1162	1428	2986	3390	2744	1248	920	1290
Wheeling, WV	380	234	850	370	519	362	523	1992	940	730	758	1131	460	2554	2674	2437	1420	481	1271
Wichita, KS	602	903	143	1200	1502	1339	1464	996	173	680	810	458	1368	1750	1978	1441	666	1368	445
Wichita Falls, TX	808	1108	438	1399	1707	1544	1669	917	244	704	723	236	1574	1599	2106	1358	423	1530	203
Wilmington, DE	714	518	1184	516	236	61	288	2391	1274	955	908	1400	324	2840	2959	2771	1642	243	1534
Winnipeg, MB	1057	1112	803	1288	1752	1648	1691	1842	1024	1444	1575	1336	1596	1893	1424	2050	1604	1768	1384
Winston-Salem, NC	604	519	1035	711	689	522	731	2054	1053	598	520	1012	732	2753	2914	2508	1238	288	1140
Worcester, MA	977	711	1447	512	113	243	134	2588	1537	1244	1198	1690	222	3033	3152	3008	1932	534	1824
Yakima, WA	2144	2234	1720	2514	2874	2771	2814	1474	1874	2356	2486	2158	2718	682	278	1048	2230	2910	2032
Youngstown, OH	425	169	896	293	487	385	478	2037	985	780	808	1181	382	2491	2610	2467	1470	505	1320

	Walnut Creek, CA	Warren, OH	Washington, DC	Waterbury, CT	Waterloo, IA	Waukegan, IL	Wausau, WI	West Palm Beach, FL	Wheeling, WV	Wichita, KS	Wichita Falls, TX	Wilmington, DE	Winnipeg, MB	Winston-Salem, NC	Worcester, MA	Yakima, WA	Youngstown, OH
Pine Bluff, AR	1989	920	1032	1359	714	710	881	1064	874	489	440	1138	1251	802	1427	2190	924
Pittsburgh, PA	2563	87	253	438	746	513	747	1120	58	1036	1240	297	1331	399	531	2454	68
Pittsfield, MA	2954	500	414	107	1137	904	1138	1417	548	1495	1700	312	1722	756	98	2844	509
Pomona, CA	390	2366	2652	2839	1788	2018	2080	2647	2350	1354	1272	2684	1963	2420	2922	1065	2380
Pontiac, MI	2386	240	558	712	568	336	570	1316	318	962	1188	602	1154	596	796	2276	254
Port Arthur, TX	2013	1326	1326	1652	1063	1138	1251	1036	1280	698	471	1431	1546	1026	1720	2398	1329
Portland, ME	3182	701	542	228	1365	1132	1366	1544	726	1710	1915	438	1697	892	136	3072	694
Portland, OR	620	2494	2814	2968	1855	2118	1916	3207	2572	1766	1896	2858	1498	2770	3050	185	2508
Providence, RI	3066	575	408	123	1249	1016	1250	1410	588	1565	1770	305	1834	758	57	2956	569
Provo, UT	761	1806	2126	2280	1228	1460	1521	2493	1884	1001	1086	2170	1341	2056	2363	742	1821
Pueblo, CO	1370	1455	1702	1917	910	1142	1203	1975	1412	427	547	1746	1206	1597	2009	1308	1458
Québec, QC	3110	730	754	461	1293	1060	1131	1756	816	1686	1886	652	1572	1095	420	3000	738
Racine, WI	2156	474	794	948	290	40	214	1408	553	762	996	838	819	792	1030	1942	489
Raleigh, NC	2834	572	264	590	1086	870	1104	742	506	1292	1358	383	1688	112	677	2834	560
Rapid City, SD	1382	1304	1624	1778	644	890	784	2116	1384	700	997	1668	769	1679	1861	1063	1319
Reading, PA	2818	342	152	222	1002	768	1002	1154	299	1276	1482	54	1586	490	301	2708	323
Regina, SK	1630	1576	1895	2049	995	1161	960	2508	1654	1151	1449	1939	356	1894	2132	992	1590
Reno, NV	202	2288	2607	2762	1710	1941	2002	3000	2365	1560	1596	2652	1704	2564	2844	733	2302
Richmond, VA	2865	424	108	434	1073	850	1084	886	381	1261	1424	227	1668	235	522	2804	404
Riverside, CA	415	2354	2640	2828	1776	2007	2068	2622	2339	1342	1260	2673	1952	2409	2910	1144	2368
Roanoke, VA	2725	422	243	570	936	720	954	868	355	1124	1248	348	1538	108	638	2666	427
Rochester, MN	1994	738	1058	1212	114	324	193	1672	818	600	895	1102	545	1057	1295	1634	753
Rochester, NY	2703	250	388	360	887	653	887	1397	336	1244	1449	357	1471	676	353	2594	258
Rockford, IL	2072	482	800	956	183	77	208	1408	560	680	932	846	791	800	1038	1914	496
Sacramento, CA	72	2419	2738	2892	1841	2072	2134	2975	2496	1692	1587	2782	1835	2695	2976	658	2434
Saginaw, MI	2406	296	616	770	590	357	591	1376	375	984	1210	660	1114	655	852	2298	311
St. Johnsbury, VT	3114	660	550	236	1297	1064	1298	1553	734	1654	1860	448	1568	902	192	3004	668
St. Joseph, MO	1742	851	1098	1313	304	534	596	1464	808	212	507	1142	770	1028	1405	1680	854
St. Louis, MO	2046	589	878	1051	342	326	494	1160	546	442	636	880	1073	723	1143	1984	592
St. Paul, MN	2034	792	1111	1266	227	378	177	1725	871	640	935	1155	468	1110	1348	1590	806
St. Petersburg, FL	2812	1112	926	1252	1379	1254	1486	227	1046	1372	1235	1046	2070	678	1340	3020	1112
Salem, OR	575	2542	2860	3016	1902	2166	1963	3254	2620	1816	1944	2906	1546	2818	3098	232	2556
Salinas, CA	104	2593	2895	3066	2015	2246	2308	2903	2594	1598	1515	2956	2009	2664	3150	798	2608
Salisbury, MD	2910	435	120	310	1094	861	1095	1035	392	1369	1596	106	1679	403	397	2802	415
Salt Lake City, UT	721	1770	2088	2243	1192	1422	1484	2482	1847	1042	1171	2133	1300	2046	2326	700	1784
San Angelo, TX	1568	1491	1604	1930	1049	1198	1342	1490	1445	534	237	1708	1472	1372	1998	1924	1494
San Antonio, TX	1718	1497	1608	1935	1101	1232	1393	1319	1451	625	383	1714	1564	1310	2003	2116	1500
San Bernardino, CA	417	2345	2630	2818	1767	1998	2060	2623	2330	1334	1251	2664	1942	2400	2901	1134	2360
San Diego, CA	483	2451	2703	2906	1873	2104	2166	2598	2402	1406	1323	2736	2048	2472	3008	1158	2447
San Francisco, CA	23	2504	2824	2978	1926	2158	2219	2983	2582	1778	1595	2868	1921	2744	3061	710	2519
San Jose, CA	43	2532	2852	3006	1954	2186	2247	2942	2610	1636	1554	2896	1948	2703	3089	738	2547
San Mateo, CA	42	2524	2844	2998	1946	2178	2239	2969	2602	1797	1581	2888	1940	2730	3080	730	2538
Santa Ana, CA	394	2386	2672	2860	1808	2040	2100	2661	2371	1375	1292	2705	1984	2441	2942	1070	2400
Santa Barbara, CA	334	2479	2765	2952	1901	2132	2194	2770	2464	1468	1385	2798	2076	2534	3035	1028	2494
Santa Rosa, CA	69	2521	2840	2994	1943	2174	2236	3030	2598	1794	1642	2884	1937	2797	3077	726	2536
Savannah, GA	2703	767	580	908	1148	1012	1255	425	700	1203	1132	700	1839	333	994	2789	766
Schenectady, NY	2903	449	396	154	1086	853	1087	1399	536	1444	1649	294	1671	736	144	2794	458
Scranton, PA	2804	314	242	161	988	754	988	1244	339	1323	1528	142	1572	547	253	2694	307
Seattle, WA	792	2458	2778	2932	1782	2044	1844	3253	2538	1842	1970	2822	1424	2777	3015	141	2473
Shreveport, LA	1900	1114	1197	1524	859	905	1050	1064	1068	546	324	1302	1368	914	1592	2246	1118
Sioux City, IA	1746	902	1222	1376	220	555	478	1688	979	399	694	1266	542	1251	1458	1488	916
Sioux Falls, SD	1724	966	1285	1440	306	552	446	1772	1045	484	778	1330	462	1336	1522	1407	980
South Bend, IN	2195	300	620	774	378	144	378	1283	379	772	998	664	962	624	857	2086	315
Spokane, WA	862	2180	2498	2653	1502	1765	1564	2974	2258	1602	1732	2542	1145	2498	2736	201	2194
Springfield, IL	2032	558	806	1020	304	229	398	1228	516	509	738	850	982	739	1113	1970	561
Springfield, MA	2999	529	372	56	1182	949	1183	1374	555	1538	1743	269	1767	722	51	2890	523
Springfield, MO	1898	801	1091	1264	484	538	707	1232	759	258	425	1093	994	908	1356	1904	804
Springfield, OH	2396	213	460	675	580	361	595	1122	171	807	1012	505	1179	401	767	2302	216
Stamford, CT	2924	434	266	52	1108	875	1109	1269	446	1424	1629	164	1693	618	139	2816	428
Stockton, CA	64	2466	2786	2940	1888	2120	2181	2933	2544	1739	1545	2830	1882	2694	3022	703	2480
Syracuse, NY	2778	325	374	274	962	728	963	1376	411	1320	1525	271	1546	680	272	2669	333
Tacoma, WA	760	2470	2790	2944	1794	2056	1856	3265	2550	1854	1982	2834	1436	2789	3027	153	2485
Tallahassee, FL	2550	994	868	1195	1144	1016	1249	417	928	1110	974	988	1832	560	1282	2786	994
Tampa, FL	2821	1089	903	1230	1356	1230	1464	203	1023	1381	1244	1022	2048	655	1316	2998	1089
Terre Haute, IN	2206	422	670	885	410	226	474	1109	380	602	808	714	1057	604	977	2144	425
Toledo, OH	2344	155	474	629	527	294	528	1240	234	903	1108	518	1112	519	711	2234	169
Topeka, KS	1782	893	1140	1355	383	614	676	1472	850	143	438	1184	803	1035	1447	1720	896
Toronto, ON	2622	285	491	519	806	573	807	1432	370	1200	1399	516	1288	711	512	2514	293
Torrington, CT	2984	493	339	20	1167	934	1168	1342	519	1502	1707	236	1752	689	113	2874	487
Trenton, NJ	2880	402	171	156	1064	830	1064	1173	362	1339	1544	61	1648	522	243	2771	385
Troy, NY	2922	469	390	143	1106	873	1107	1392	523	1464	1669	288	1691	731	134	2814	478
Tucson, AZ	847	2034	2286	2496	1514	1771	1806	2191	1992	996	917	2391	1842	2054	2588	1474	2037
Tulsa, OK	1717	982	1284	1445	588	720	881	1352	940	173	244	1274	1024	1053	1537	1874	985
Tupelo, MS	2180	776	850	1177	714	634	881	849	730	680	704	955	1444	598	1244	2356	780
Tuscaloosa, AL	2310	805	803	1130	844	769	1002	731	758	810	723	908	1575	520	1198	2486	808
Tyler, TX	1813	1178	1295	1622	854	968	1113	1162	1131	458	236	1400	1336	1012	1690	2158	1181
Utica, NY	2828	374	426	231	1011	778	1012	1428	460	1368	1574	324	1596	732	222	2718	382
Vallejo, CA	22	2476	2796	2950	1898	2130	2191	2986	2554	1750	1599	2840	1893	2753	3033	682	2491
Vancouver, BC	936	2596	2915	3069	1918	2182	1980	3390	2674	1978	2106	2959	1424	2914	3152	278	2610
Ventura, CA	360	2452	2738	2926	1874	2106	2167	2744	2437	1441	1358	2771	2050	2508	3008	1048	2467
Victoria, TX	1833	1466	1537	1864	1141	1272	1434	1248	1420	666	423	1642	1604	1238	1932	2230	1470
Virginia Beach, VA	2972	524	208	447	1179	950	1184	920	481	1368	1530	243	1768	288	534	2910	505
Waco, TX	1780	1317	1430	1756	920	1052	1213	1290	1271	445	203	1534	1384	1140	1824	2032	1320
Walnut Creek, CA		2490	2808	2963	1912	2142	2204	2964	2567	1762	1577	2853	1905	2726	3046	694	2504
Warren, OH	2490		333	473	673	440	674	1181	94	1020	1225	377	1258	460	565	2380	16
Washington, DC	2808	333		318	992	759	993	994	290	1267	1480	112	1577	342	406	2700	314
Waterbury, CT	2963	473	318		1147	913	1147	1321	498	1482	1687	216	1731	669	92	2854	466
Waterloo, IA	1912	673	992	1147		268	331	1499	750	518	813	1036	678	974	1229	1704	687
Waukegan, IL	2142	440	759	913	268		238	1374	519	749	962	803	844	758	996	1966	454
Wausau, WI	2204	674	993	1147	331	238		1607	753	810	1105	1037	642	992	1230	1765	688
West Palm Beach, FL	2964	1181	994	1321	1499	1374	1607		1114	1525	1388	1114	2190	746	1408	3140	1180
Wheeling, WV	2567	94	290	498	750	519	753	1114		978	1183	334	1337	393	591	2460	91
Wichita, KS	1762	1020	1267	1482	518	749	810	1525	978		298	1311	905	1162	1574	1700	1023
Wichita Falls, TX	1577	1225	1480	1687	813	962	1105	1388	1183	298		1586	1236	1250	1779	1830	1228
Wilmington, DE	2853	377	112	216	1036	803	1037	1114	334	1311	1586		1621	462	303	2744	358
Winnipeg, MB	1905	1258	1577	1731	678	844	642	2190	1337	905	1236	1621		1576	1814	1346	1272
Winston-Salem, NC	2726	460	342	669	974	758	992	746	393	1162	1250	462	1576		756	2704	459
Worcester, MA	3046	565	406	92	1229	996	1230	1408	591	1574	1779	303	1814	756		2936	559
Yakima, WA	694	2380	2700	2854	1704	1966	1765	3140	2460	1700	1830	2744	1346	2704	2936		2394
Youngstown, OH	2504	16	314	466	687	454	688	1180	91	1023	1228	358	1272	459	559	2394	